REMEDIES FOR TORTS, BREAC
AND EQUITABLE WRONGS

Remedies for Torts, Breach of Contract, and Equitable Wrongs

Fourth Edition

ANDREW BURROWS MA, DCL, LLM (HARVARD),
QC (HON), FBA

Barrister and Honorary Bencher of Middle Temple
Professor of the Law of England in the University of Oxford and a Fellow of All Souls College

He sits as a Deputy High Court Judge and is a Door Tenant of Fountain Court Chambers, London. He was President of the Society of Legal Scholars (2015–16) and a Law Commissioner for England and Wales (1994–1999). He has written extensively on the areas of contract, tort, and unjust enrichment and his other books include *The Law of Restitution, Understanding the Law of Obligations: Essays on Contract, Tort and Restitution, A Casebook on Contract, A Restatement of the English Law of Unjust Enrichment, A Restatement of the English Law of Contract*, and *Thinking about Statutes: Interpretation, Interaction, Improvement*. He is a joint author of *Anson's Law of Contract*, the general editor of *English Private Law*, and an editor of *Chitty on Contracts* and *Clerk & Lindsell on Torts*.

Great Clarendon Street, Oxford, OX2 6DP,
United Kingdom

Oxford University Press is a department of the University of Oxford.
It furthers the University's objective of excellence in research, scholarship,
and education by publishing worldwide. Oxford is a registered trade mark of
Oxford University Press in the UK and in certain other countries

© Andrew Burrows 2019

The moral rights of the author have been asserted

Third Edition published in 2004
Fourth Edition published in 2019

Impression: 5

All rights reserved. No part of this publication may be reproduced, stored in
a retrieval system, or transmitted, in any form or by any means, without the
prior permission in writing of Oxford University Press, or as expressly permitted
by law, by licence or under terms agreed with the appropriate reprographics
rights organization. Enquiries concerning reproduction outside the scope of the
above should be sent to the Rights Department, Oxford University Press, at the
address above

You must not circulate this work in any other form
and you must impose this same condition on any acquirer

Crown copyright material is reproduced under Class Licence
Number C01P0000148 with the permission of OPSI
and the Queen's Printer for Scotland

Published in the United States of America by Oxford University Press
198 Madison Avenue, New York, NY 10016, United States of America

British Library Cataloguing in Publication Data
Data available

Library of Congress Control Number: 2018967076

ISBN 978–0–19–870594–9 (pbk.)
ISBN 978–0–19–870593–2 (hbk.)

Printed and bound by
CPI Group (UK) Ltd, Croydon, CR0 4YY

Links to third party websites are provided by Oxford in good faith and
for information only. Oxford disclaims any responsibility for the materials
contained in any third party website referenced in this work.

For Rachel

Preface to the fourth edition

The central objective of the book remains, as ever, to provide a clear and succinct analysis and critique of the principles governing judicial remedies. It is hoped that it will be a stimulating guide not only to students but also to practitioners.

This edition, 15 years on from the last, has required extensive rewriting. Huge swathes of new material have been incorporated, especially new cases (the most important of which are listed below) and new academic analysis (eg on corrective justice, civil recourse, damages valuing the right infringed, a non-compensatory cost of cure, and contributory negligence). There has also been rewriting to reflect developments in my own thinking (eg on methodology, proof of loss, and the award of interest). The structure of the book remains essentially unchanged with two main exceptions. First, the law on the impact of the Human Rights Act 1998, which was previously a section of the first chapter, has been expanded to form a separate chapter (chapter 2) albeit that the vertical cause of action created by the 1998 Act is a statutory wrong that is not a tort and, therefore, strictly speaking lies outside the scope of this book. Secondly, in line with the Supreme Court's reasoning in *Morris-Garner v One Step (Support) Ltd* [2018] UKSC 20, [2018] 2 WLR 1353, a new chapter on negotiating damages (chapter 18) has been inserted at the end of Part Two on Compensation: in previous editions, much of that material was to be found in the chapter on restitutionary remedies (which is now chapter 19).

In the last edition, reflecting their increased importance in practice, and the considerable modern academic attention devoted to them, there was a new final part and chapter on remedies for equitable wrongs, such as breach of fiduciary duty and breach of confidence. That has now been reflected in the change to the title of the book. Most importantly, that last chapter (chapter 26) reveals that there is a coherence of remedial function between remedies for common law and equitable wrongs. One might argue that the better title for the book would now be 'Remedies for Civil Wrongs'. But apart from a concern that the term 'civil wrong' is unfamiliar to some (and indeed it has been suggested to me that some practitioners may think that the reference is to civil law, as in France and Germany) the book does not cover remedies for all civil wrongs: in particular, some statutory wrongs that are not torts are not covered (an obvious example being unfair dismissal).

There have been many important new cases that are covered in this new edition. They include in the order in which they appear in the text: *Vidal-Hall v Google Inc* (the tort of privacy); *Alseran v Ministry of Defence* (damages under the Human Rights Act 1998); *Barker v Corus (UK) Plc* and *Gregg v Scott* (factual causation and loss of a chance); *Flame SA v Glory Wealth Shipping PTE Ltd, The Glory Wealth* (proof of loss); *Omak Maritime Ltd v Mamola Challenger Shipping Co, The Mamola Challenger* (contractual reliance damages); *Wellesley Partners LLP v Withers LLP* (remoteness in tort where concurrent contractual liability); *The Achilleas* and *Supershield Ltd v Siemens Building Technologies FE Ltd* (remoteness in contract); *BPE Solicitors v Hughes-Holland* (the *SAAMCO* principle); *Pritchard v Co-operative Group Ltd* (contributory negligence not a defence to trespass to the person); *Fulton Shipping Inc of Panama v Globalia Business Travel SAU of Spain, The New Flamenco* and *Swynson Ltd v Lowick Rose LLP* (compensating advantages); *Golden Strait Corp v Nippon Yusen Kubishika Kaisha, The Golden Victory* and *Bunge SA v Nidera BV* (date for assessment); *Network Rail Infrastructure Ltd v Conarken Group Ltd* (pecuniary loss consequent on property damage); *Coles v Hetherton, Bee v Jensen, Stevens v Equity Syndicate Management Ltd, Beechwood Birmingham Ltd v Hover Group UK Ltd*, and *West*

Midlands Travel Ltd v Aviva Insurance UK Ltd (damage to vehicles); *4 Eng Ltd v Harper* and *Parabola Investments Ltd v Browallia Cal Ltd* (damages for the tort of deceit); *ARB v IVF Hammersmith* (contract claim for wrongful birth); *Knauer v Ministry of Justice* (multiplier in claims for death); *Rabone v Pennine Care NHS Foundation Trust* and *Smith v Lancashire Teaching Hospitals NHS Foundation Trust* (bereavement damages and the Human Rights Act 1998); *Rowlands v Chief Constable of Merseyside Police* (aggravated and punitive damages); *Gulati v MGN Ltd* and *Milner v Carnival Plc* (assessing damages for mental distress); *Sempra Metals Ltd v IRC* (interest as damages); *P & O Nedlloyd BV v Arab Metals Co* (no limitation period for specific performance); *Morris-Garner v One Step (Support) Ltd* (equitable damages and negotiating damages); *Forsyth-Grant v Allen* and *Devenish Nutrition Ltd v Sanofi-Aventis SA* (no restitution for the torts of nuisance or breach of statutory duty); *Muuse v Secretary of State for the Home Department*, *AXA Insurance UK Plc v Financial Claims Solutions Ltd*, and *Borders (UK) Ltd v Commissioner of Police of the Metropolis* (punitive damages); *R (on the application of Lumba) v Secretary of State for the Home Department* (no vindicatory damages in tort); *Isabella Shipowner SA v Shagang Shipping Co Ltd*, *MSC Mediterranean Shipping Co SA v Cottones Anstalt*, and *Reichman v Beveridge* (the *White and Carter* principle); *Cavendish Square Holding BV v Talal El Makdessi* and *ParkingEye Ltd v Beavis* (penalties); *Ashworth v Royal National Theatre* (specific performance); *PJS v News Group Newspapers*, *OPO v Rhodes*, and *Araci v Fallon* (interim injunctions); *Coventry v Lawrence* (damages in substitution for an injunction for private nuisance); *Lauritzencool AB v Lady Navigation Inc* (indirect specific performance); *AIB Group (UK) Ltd v Mark Redler & Co*, *Main v Giambrone & Law*, and *Interactive Technology Corp Ltd v Ferster* (equitable compensation for breach of fiduciary duty); *Vercoe v Rutland Fund Management Ltd* and *MVF 3 APS v Bestnet Europe Ltd* (compensatory damages for breach of confidence); *Murad v Al-Saraj* (account of profits for breach of fiduciary duty); *FHR European Ventures LLP v Cedar Properties LLC* (constructive trust of bribe acquired in breach of fiduciary duty); *Novoship (UK) Ltd v Mikhaylyuk* (account of profits for dishonest assistance); *Williams v Central Bank of Nigeria* (limitation period for dishonest assistance).

New statutory material includes (again in the order in which it is dealt with) the Courts Act 2003, ss 100–101 and the Damages (Variation of Periodical Payments) Order 2005 (reviewable periodic payments); the Damages (Personal Injury) Order 2012 and the Civil Liability Act 2018 (setting the discount rate); the Damages for Bereavement (Variation of Sum)(England and Wales) Order 2013 (raising the sum for bereavement damages); the Defamation Act 2013, s 11 (removing the right to a jury trial in defamation cases); the Crime and Courts Act 2013, ss 34–39 (punitive damages); and the Consumer Rights Act 2015, s 58 (specific performance).

I would like to thank my excellent research assistant, Eleni Katsampouka, and the team at OUP for its help and efficiency.

The law is stated as at 1 December 2018.

Andrew Burrows

1 March 2019
Oxford

Contents

Table of Cases	xv
Table of Legislation	liii

PART ONE INTRODUCTION

1. General — 3
  1. Judicial remedies — 3
  2. Procedure — 4
  3. Enforcement — 5
  4. Orders made to assist the claimant in collecting evidence to establish its case — 5
  5. Torts and breach of contract — 5
  6. Concurrent liability between the tort of negligence and breach of contract — 6
  7. Should one continue to distinguish torts and breach of contract? — 8
  8. The primary functions of judicial remedies for torts and breach of contract — 9
  9. Legal and equitable remedies — 10
  10. Equitable wrongs — 11
  11. Combining remedies — 13
  12. Breach of European Union law — 15
  13. Economic analysis, bargaining around non-monetary remedies, and the consumer surplus — 16
  14. Corrective justice, civil recourse, and rights — 18
  15. Approach and methodology — 20
  16. The layout of the book — 21

2. The impact of the Human Rights Act 1998 — 22
  1. Introduction — 22
  2. A non-tortious public wrong — 23
  3. The assessment of damages for the HRA cause of action — 26

PART TWO COMPENSATION

Section One General Principles in Assessing Compensatory Damages

3. Introduction to compensatory damages — 35
  1. Compensation, compensatory damages, and types of loss — 35
  2. The compensatory aims — 38
  3. Theoretical underpinnings of compensation — 39
  4. Damages valuing the right infringed? — 46
  5. A non-compensatory cost of cure? — 48

4. Factual causation — 51
  1. Introduction — 51
  2. The 'but for' test — 52

3. Additional sufficient events	52
4. Material increase of risk	55

5. Proof of loss and loss of a chance — 58

1. Introduction — 58
2. Uncertainty about past fact: balance of probabilities — 58
3. Future or hypothetical events: assessment proportionate to the chances? — 60
4. Miscellaneous points — 73

6. Contractual reliance damages — 75

1. Introduction — 75
2. Protection of the reliance interest where direct protection of the expectation interest is barred — 76
3. Protection of the reliance interest even when direct protection of the expectation interest is not barred — 77
4. No escape from a known bad bargain — 78
5. Pre-contractual expenses — 81

7. Principles limiting compensatory damages — 83

1. Introduction — 83
2. Remoteness — 86
3. Intervening cause — 107
4. The *SAAMCO* principle — 117
5. The duty to mitigate — 127
6. Contributory negligence — 132
7. The demise of impecuniosity as a limitation — 144

8. Compensating advantages — 147

1. Introduction — 147
2. Indirect compensating advantages are not deducted — 148
3. Some compensating advantages provided by third parties are not deducted — 152

9. Form of compensatory damages, date for assessment, taxation — 163

1. The form of compensatory damages — 163
2. The date for the assessment of compensatory damages — 169
3. Taxation — 182

Section Two Damages for the Different Types of Loss

10. Pecuniary loss (except consequent on personal injury, death, or loss of reputation) — 187

1. Breach of contract—basic pecuniary loss — 187
2. Breach of contract—additional pecuniary loss — 205
3. Torts—damage to property, including destruction — 206
4. Torts—wrongful interference with goods or land, other than causing property damage — 219
5. Torts—pure economic loss — 222

11. Personal injury losses — 234
1. Claims by the injured person — 234
2. Claims by the deceased's estate — 253

12. Losses on death — 256
1. Dependants — 256
2. Actionability by injured person — 257
3. The three heads of recoverable loss — 258
4. Fatal Accidents Act 1976, section 4 — 265
5. The relationship between actions under the Law Reform (Miscellaneous Provisions) Act 1934 and the Fatal Accidents Act 1976 where the wrong has caused death — 267

13. Loss of reputation — 268
1. When are damages awarded for loss of reputation? — 268
2. Assessing damages for loss of reputation — 273

14. Mental distress or physical inconvenience (except consequent on personal injury or death) — 276
1. When are damages awarded for mental distress or physical inconvenience? — 277
2. Assessing damages for mental distress or physical inconvenience — 288

SECTION THREE MISCELLANEOUS ISSUES RELEVANT TO COMPENSATORY DAMAGES

15. Interest as damages and interest on damages — 295
1. Introduction — 295
2. Interest as damages — 296
3. Interest on damages: statutory interest under section 35A Senior Courts Act 1981 — 301

16. Limitation periods — 309
1. Introduction — 309
2. The normal time limits — 310
3. The main exceptions to the normal time limits — 311

17. Equitable (compensatory) damages — 315
1. When may equitable damages be awarded? — 315
2. When are equitable damages more advantageous than common law damages? — 317
3. Non-compensatory equitable damages? — 319

18. Negotiating damages — 321
1. Introduction — 321
2. *Morris-Garner v One Step (Support) Ltd* — 323
3. The purpose of negotiating damages — 324
4. The availability of negotiating damages — 328

PART THREE RESTITUTION AND PUNISHMENT

19. Restitutionary remedies (for torts and breach of contract) — 335
   1. Introduction — 335
   2. Restitution for torts — 338
   3. Restitution for breach of contract — 352

20. Punitive damages — 360
   1. Are punitive damages awarded for breach of contract? — 360
   2. When are punitive damages awarded for torts? — 361
   3. The quantum of punitive damages — 372
   4. Should the law on punitive damages be reformed? — 374

PART FOUR COMPELLING PERFORMANCE OR PREVENTING (OR COMPELLING THE UNDOING OF) A WRONG

21. The award of an agreed sum — 381
   1. General points — 382
   2. Award of an agreed price — 383
   3. Award of an agreed sum payable on breach—liquidated damages — 388
   4. Award of an agreed sum (other than an agreed price) payable on an event other than breach — 397

22. Specific performance — 401
   1. Introduction — 401
   2. The bars to specific performance — 402
   3. Other issues — 436

23. Injunctions — 440
   1. Introduction — 440
   2. Final prohibitory injunctions — 443
   3. Final mandatory injunctions — 462
   4. Final *quia timet* injunctions — 467
   5. Interim injunctions — 469
   6. The claimant's conduct as a bar to an injunction — 486
   7. Appointment of a receiver — 491

24. Delivery up — 493
   1. Delivery up of goods — 493
   2. Delivery up for destruction or destruction on oath — 497

PART FIVE DECLARING RIGHTS

25. Nominal and contemptuous damages and declarations — 503
   1. Nominal damages — 503
   2. Contemptuous damages — 503
   3. Declarations — 504

PART SIX REMEDIES FOR EQUITABLE WRONGS

26. Remedies for equitable wrongs   509
    1. Introduction   509
    2. Compensation for equitable wrongs   511
    3. Restitution and punishment for equitable wrongs   525
    4. Compelling performance or preventing (or compelling the undoing of) an equitable wrong   538
    5. Declaring rights   541
    6. Miscellaneous issues on remedies for equitable wrongs   542
    7. Conclusion   544

Index   547

Table of Cases

For the benefit of digital users, indexed terms that span two pages (e.g., 52–53) may, on occasion, appear on only one of those pages.

4 Eng Ltd v Harper [2008] EWHC 9, [2009] Ch 91 . . . . vii–viii, 64, 67–68, 227–28
32Red Plc v WHG (International) Ltd [2013] EWHC 815 (Ch) 321–22

A v Bottrill [2002] UKPC 44, [2003] 1 AC 449 377
AB v Ministry of Defence [2012] UKSC 9, [2013] 1 AC 78. . . . . .309, 313
AB v CD [2014] EWCA Civ 229, [2015] 1 WLR 771 455
AB v South West Water Services Ltd [1993] QB 507. . . . . 287–88, 362, 368–69
AB Consolidated Ltd v Europe Strength Food Co Pty Ltd [1978] 2 NZLR 515 533
AB Corpn v CD Co, The Sine Nomine [2002] 1 Lloyd's Rep 805 359
Abbahall Ltd v Smee [2002] EWCA Civ 1831, [2003] 1 WLR 1472. 207
ABC v Telegraph Media Group Ltd [2018] EWCA Civ 2329. 540
Abrahams v Herbert Reiach Ltd [1922] 1 KB 477. 71
Abrahams v Performing Right Society [1995] ICR 1028 383
Absolute Lofts South West London Ltd v Artisan Home Improvements Ltd [2015]
    EWHC 2608 (IPEC), [2017] ECDR 6. . . . . 284–85, 367–68
ACB v Thomson Medical Pte Ltd [2017] SGCA 20, [2017] 1 SLR 918. 375
Achilleas, The See Transfield Shipping Inc v Mercator Shipping Inc, The Achilleas
Ackroyds (London) Ltd v Islington Plastics Ltd [1962] RPC 97 521
Adams v Bracknell Forest Borough Council [2004] UKHL 29, [2005] 1AC 76 285–86
Adan v Securicor Custodial Services Ltd [2004] EWHC 394 (QB), [2005] PIQR P6 53
Adderley v Dixon (1824) 1 Sim & St 607 . . . . .407–8, 409
Addis v Gramophone Co Ltd [1909] AC 488. . . . . 268, 269, 270–71, 276, 277, 281, 282, 360, 361
Admiral Management Services Ltd v Para-Protect Europe Ltd [2002] EWHC 233 (Ch),
    [2002] 1 WLR 2722. 230
Admiralty Comrs v SS Chekiang [1926] AC 637. 216
Admiralty Comrs v SS Susquehanna [1926] AC 655 216
Adventure Film Productions SA v Tully [1993] EMLR 376. 496
Aerial Advertising Co v Batchelors Peas Ltd (Manchester) [1938] 2 All ER 788 . . . . .269, 273
Aerospace Publishing Ltd v Thames Water Utilities [2007] EWCA Civ 3, [2007] NPC 5. . . . . . . 210, 214
Ageas (UK) Ltd v Kwik-Fit (GB) Ltd [2014] EWHC 2178 (QB). 174
Agenor, The See President of India v Taygetos Shipping Co SA, The Agenor
Agius v Great Western Colliery Co [1899] 1 QB 413 205–6
Agricultural Land Management Ltd v Jackson (No 2) [2014] WASC 102 . . . . .515, 517–18
Agricultural Supplies (Ipswich) Ltd v Rushmere [1967] 3 KIR 55 487
AIB Group (UK) Ltd v Mark Redler & Co [2014] UKSC 58, [2015] AC 1503 . . . . vii–viii, 511–12, 515,
                                                                                                                                      517–19, 520, 540
AKAS Jamal v Moolla Dawood Sons & Co [1916] 1 AC 175. 195–96
Alaskan Trader, The See Clea Shipping Corpn v Bulk Oil International Ltd, The Alaskan Trader
Albacruz (Cargo Owners) v Albazero (Owners), The Albazero [1977] AC 774. . . . . 201, 202, 203, 204
Albert (L) & Son v Armstrong Rubber Co 178 F 2d 182 (1949) 78
Alcoa Minerals of Jamaica Inc v Broderick [2002] 1 AC 371. . . . . .145, 175
Alcock v Chief Constable of South Yorkshire Police [1992] 1 AC 310, [1991] 3 WLR 1057. . . . .234, 285–86
Alder v Moore [1961] 2 QB 57. 398
Alecos M, The See Sealace Shipping Co Ltd v Oceanvoice Ltd, The Alecos M
Alexander & Co v Henry & Co, Mitchell Henry and Waller & Co (1895) 12 RPC 360. 229
Alexander v Cambridge Credit Corpn Ltd (1987) 9 NSWLR 310, CA. 115
Alexander v Home Office [1988] 2 All ER 118 284–85
Alexander v Rolls Royce Motor Cars Ltd [1996] RTR 95, CA. 216–17
Alexander v Standard Telephones and Cables plc [1990] ICR 291 422–23
Al-Fayed v Observer Ltd (1986) Times, 14 July. 479
Alfred McAlpine Construction Ltd v Panatown Ltd [2001] 1 AC 518. . . . . 190, 197, 198–99, 202, 203
Algeiba v Australind (1921) 8 Ll L Rep 210 212

Table of Cases

Algemene Transport-en Expeditie Onderneming van Gend en Loos NV v Nederlandse
    Belastingadministratie: 26/62 [1963] ECR 1, [1963] CMLR 105, ECJ 15
Ali Reza-Delta Transport Co Ltd v United Arab Shipping Co [2003] EWCA Civ 864, [2003]
    2 Lloyd's Rep 450.. 210
Allen v Bloomsbury Health Authority [1993] 1 All ER 651... 249–50
Allen v Greenwood [1980] Ch 119 462
Allen v Gulf Oil Refining Ltd [1981] AC 1001, HL [1980] QB 156 CA 452
Alley v Deschamps (1806) 13 Ves 225.. 410–11
Alliance and Leicester Building Society v Edgestop Ltd [1994] 2 All ER 38, [1993] 1 WLR 1462 136–37
Allied London Investments Ltd v Hambro Life Assurance Ltd [1985] 1 EGLR 45.................... 304–5
Allied Maples Group Ltd v Simmons & Simmons (a firm) [1995] 1 WLR 1602................. 65, 67–68
Alperton Rubber Co v Manning (1917) 86 LJ Ch 377 541
Alseran v Ministry of Defence [2017] EWHC 3289 (QB), [2018] 3 WLR 95 .... vii–viii, 24, 28,
    180, 283–85, 290
Amalgamated Metal Trading Ltd v City of London Police Financial Investigation Unit
    [2003] EWHC 703 (Comm), [2003] 1 WLR 2711 506
Amble Assets LLP v Longbenton Foods Ltd [2011] EWHC 3774 (Ch), [2012]
    1 All ER (Comm) 764... 394–95
Amec Developments Ltd v Jury's Hotel Management (UK) Ltd (2000) 82 P & CR 286 321–22
American Braided Wire Co v Thomson (1890) 44 Ch D 274 228–29
American Cyanamid Co v Ethicon Ltd [1975] AC 396, [1974] FSR 312 .... 469–70, 471–73, 474–75,
    476–77, 478–81, 482–83, 485–86, 491, 538–40
AMEV-UDC Finance Ltd v Austin (1986) 162 CLR 170 398–99
Amministrazione delle Finanze dello Stato SpA San Georgio, Case 199/82, [1983] ECR 3595 ..... 16, 298
Amstrad plc v Seagate Technology Inc (1998) 86 BLR 34 183
Anchor Brewhouse Developments Ltd v Berkley House (Docklands Developments) Ltd
    [1987] 2 EGLR 173 446
Ancient Order of Foresters in Victoria Friendly Society Ltd v Lifeplan Australia Friendly
    Society Ltd [2018] HCA 43, (2018) 360 ALR 1 .... 344, 536
Anders Utkilens Rederi A/S v O/Y Lovisa Stevedoring Co A/B, The Golfstraum [1985]
    2 All ER 669 .... 408–9, 411
Anderson v Davis and Anderson [1992] PIQR Q87... 243
Anderson v Hoen, The Flying Fish (1865) 3 Moo PCCNS 77 128–29
André & Cie SA v Ets Michel Blanc & Fils [1977] 2 Lloyd's Rep 166 225–26
Andreae v Selfridge & Co Ltd [1938] Ch 1.. 221
Andrews v Freeborough [1967] 1 QB 1, [1966] 3 WLR 342 .... 237, 253
Andrews v Schooling [1991] 1 WLR 783 167–68
Andrews and New Zealand Banking Group Ltd (2012) 247 CLR 20 398
Andros Springs (Owners) v Owners of World Beauty, The World Beauty [1970] P 144................ 215
Aneco Reinsurance Underwriting Ltd (in liquidation) v Johnson & Higgins Ltd [2001]
    UKHL 51, [2001] 2 All ER (Comm) 929... 125–26
Anglia Television Ltd v Reed [1972] 1 QB 60... 77, 81
Anglo-African Shipping Co of New York Inc v J Mortner Ltd [1962] 1 Lloyd's Rep 81 384
Anglo-Continental Holidays Ltd v Typaldos (London) Ltd [1967] 2 Lloyd's Rep 61................ 269–70
Anglo-Cyprian Trade Agencies Ltd v Paphos Wine Industries Ltd [1951] 1 All ER 873................ 503
Anns v Merton London Borough Council [1978] AC 728... 314
Ansell Rubber Co Pty Ltd v Allied Rubber Industries Pty Ltd [1972] RPC 811 .... 521, 533, 541
Anton Piller KG v Manufacturing Processes Ltd [1976] Ch 55... 485–86
Anufrijeva v Southwark London Borough Council [2003] EWCA Civ 1406, [2004] 2 WLR 603 .... 24, 370
Appleton v Garrett [1996] PIQR P1... 284–85, 287–88
Aquaculture Corpn v New Zealand Green Mussel Co Ltd [1990] 3 NZLR 299 .... 521, 537
Aquafaith, The See Isabella Shipowner SA v Shagang Shipping Co Ltd, The Aquafaith
Arab Bank plc v John D Wood (Commercial) Ltd [2000] 1 WLR 857................................ 154
Araci v Fallon [2011] EWCA Civ 668 .... vii–viii, 455
ARB v IVF Hammersmith [2018] EWCA Civ 2803, [2017] EWHC 2438 (QB), [2018]
    2 WLR 1223 .... vii–viii, 252
Archer v Brown [1985] QB 401, [1984] 2 All ER 267 .... 145, 226–27, 284–85, 291–92, 368–69, 371
Argentino, The See Gracie (Owners) v Argentino (Owners), The Argentino
Argyll (Duchess of) v Duke of Argyll [1967] Ch 302... 487, 538–39
Armitage, Marsden and HM Prison Service v Johnson [1997] ICR 275 .... 284–85, 289–90
Armstrong v Sheppard & Short Ltd [1959] 2 QB 384.. 445–46

Table of Cases

Arnup v White Ltd [2008] EWCA Civ 447, [2008] ICR 1064 266
Aronson v Mologa Holzindustrie A/G Leningrad (1927) 32 Com Cas 276 176
Arpad, The [1934] P 189 .... 88–89, 219–21
Ashgar v Ahmed (1985) 17 HLR 25, CA 284–85, 365
Ashworth v Royal National Theatre [2014] EWHC 1176 (QB), [2014] 4 All ER 238 .... viii, 423
Aspect Contracts (Asbestos) Ltd v Higgins Construction plc [2015] UKSC 38, [2015] 1 WLR 2961 505
Associated British Ports v Transport and General Workers' Union [1989] 3 All ER 822 472
Associated Distributors Ltd v Hall [1938] 2 KB 83 398
Associated Portland Cement Manufacturers Ltd v Teigland Shipping A/S, The Oakworth
 [1975] 1 Lloyd's Rep 581 408–9
Astley v Austrust Ltd (1999) 197 CLR 1 140
Astro Exito Navegacion SA v Southland Enterprise Co Ltd, The Messiniaki Tolmi [1982] QB 1248 482
AT v Gavril Dulghieru [2009] EWHC 225 (QB) 367, 371
Athletes Foot Marketing Associates Inc v Cobra Sports Ltd [1980] RPC 343 480
Atlas Tiles v Briers 144 CLR 202 183
Attica Sea Carriers Corpn v Ferrostaal Poseidon Bulk Reederei GmbH, The Puerto Buitrago
 [1976] 1 Lloyd's Rep 250, CA 384–85, 386, 387
Attorney-General v Barker [1990] 3 All ER 257, CA 455, 480
Attorney-General v Birmingham Borough Council (1858) 4 K & J 528 446–47
Attorney-General v Blake [2001] 1 AC 268, [2000] 3 WLR 625 .... 326, 329–30, 343–44, 345, 350,
 351–52, 353–54, 356, 357–58, 359, 361, 392, 530
Attorney-General v Colchester Corpn [1955] 2 QB 207 .... 418, 465
Attorney-General v Geothermal Produce NZ Ltd [1987] 2 NZLR 348 145
Attorney-General v Guardian Newspapers Ltd [1987] 1 WLR 1248 539
Attorney-General v Guardian Newspapers Ltd (No 2) [1990] 1 AC 109 .... 512, 521, 522, 533
Attorney-General v Kingston-on-Thames Corpn (1865) 34 LJ Ch 481 467–68
Attorney-General v Manchester Corpn [1893] 2 Ch 87 467–68
Attorney-General v Nottingham Corpn [1904] 1 Ch 673 467–68
Attorney-General v Observer Newspapers Ltd [1986] NLJ Rep 799 .... 473, 539
Attorney-General v PYA Quarries Ltd [1957] 2 QB 169 445
Attorney-General v Punch Ltd [2002] UKHL 50, [2003] 1 AC 1046 .... 441, 538–39
Attorney-General v Staffordshire County Council [1905] 1 Ch 336 464–65
Attorney-General v Times Newspapers Ltd [1992] 1 AC 191 .... 441, 538–39
Attorney-General for Dominion of Canada v Ritchie Contracting and Supply Co [1919] AC 999 467
Attorney-General for Hong Kong v Reid [1994] 1 AC 324, [1993] 3 WLR 1143 .... 530, 531–32
Attorney-General of the Republic of Ghana v Texaco Overseas Tankships Ltd, The Texaco
 Melbourne [1994] 1 Lloyd's Rep 473 .... 178, 181
Attorney-General of Trinidad and Tobago v Ramanoop [2005] UKPC 15, [2006] 1 AC 328 363–64
Attorney-General's Reference (No 1 of 1985) [1986] QB 491 530–31
Austin Rover Group Ltd v Amalgamated Union of Engineering Workers [1985] IRLR 162 482
Australian Coarse Grain Pty Ltd v Barley Marketing Board of Queensland (1982) 57 ALJR 425 475
Australian Hardwoods Pty Ltd v Railways Comr [1961] 1 WLR 425 432
Auty v National Coal Board [1985] 1 All ER 930 .... 158, 239, 244, 245, 258–59, 261
Avon County Council v Millard (1985) 274 Estates Gazette 1025 455
Avon Insurance plc v Swire Fraser [2000] 1 All ER (Comm) 573 122–23
AXA Insurance UK Plc v Financial Claims Solutions Ltd [2018] EWCA Civ 1330 ..... vii–viii, 365, 367, 371

B v D [2014] EWCA Civ 229, [2015] 1 WLR 771 472
BBMB Finance (Hong Kong) Ltd v Eda Holdings Ltd [1990] 1 WLR 409 172
BHP Petroleum Ltd v British Steel plc and Dalmine SpA [1999] 2 All ER (Comm) 544 93
BP Exploration Co (Libya) Ltd v Hunt (No 2) [1983] 2 AC 352, [1982] 1 All ER 925 ...... 302, 304–5, 542
Bacon v Cooper (Metals) Ltd [1982] 1 All ER 397 .... 130, 205, 217–18
Bailey v Bullock [1950] 2 All ER 1167 .... 269, 277, 279
Bailey v Ministry of Defence [2008] EWCA Civ 883, [2009] 1 WLR 1052 52
Bailey v Namol Pty Ltd (1994) 12 ALR 228 537
Bain v Fothergill (1874) LR 7 HL 158 .... 76, 77, 317
Baird Textiles Holdings Ltd v Marks & Spencer plc [2001] EWCA Civ 274, [2002]
 1 All ER (Comm) 737 71
Bairstow v Queens Moat Houses plc [2001] EWCA Civ 712, [2001] 2 BCLC 531 515
Baker v Baker (1993) 25 HLR 408 .... 511–12, 525–26
Baker v Willoughby [1970] AC 467 .... 51–52, 53–54, 55

Balfour Beatty Construction (Scotland) Ltd v Scottish Power plc 1994 SLT 807 96
Ball v Coggs (1710) 1 Bro Parl Cas 140. 409
Ballami, The *See* Veflings (George) Rederi A/S v President of India, The Ballami
Ballantine v Newalls Insulation Co Ltd [2001] ICR 25. 156
Ballard v Metropolitan Police Comr (1983) 133 NLJ 1133 284–85
Banbury v Bank of Montreal [1918] AC 626 168
Banca Nazional del Lavoro SpA v Playboy Club London Ltd [2018] UKSC 43, [2018] 1 WLR 4041 222
Banco de Portugal v Waterlow & Sons Ltd [1932] AC 452. . . . . .130, 131
Bank Mellat v Nikpour [1982] Com LR 158. 485–86
Bank of America (Canada) v Mutual Trust Co [2002] SCC 43, (2002) 211 DLR (4th) 385 . . . . .297, 358
Bank of Credit and Commerce International (Overseas) v Price Waterhouse (No 3)
    (1998) Times, 2 April 115
Bank of Credit and Commerce International SA (in liquidation) v Ali (No 2) [2002] 3 All ER 750. 67
Bank of New Zealand v New Zealand Guardian Trust Co Ltd [1999] 1 NZLR 664. 514
Bank of Scotland v A Ltd [2001] EWCA Civ 52, [2001] 1 WLR 751 506
Barbara v Home Office (1984) 134 NLJ 888. 284–85
Barber v Somerset County Council [2004] UKHL 13, [2004] 1 WLR 1089 . . . . .234, 276
Barclays Bank International Ltd v Levin Bros (Bradford) Ltd [1977] QB 270. 181
Barclays Bank plc v Fairclough Building Ltd [1995] QB 214. . . . . .138, 141
Barclays Bank plc v Fairclough Building Ltd (No 2) (1995) 44 Con LR 35 141
Barisic v Devenport [1978] 2 NSWLR 111, NSWCA 135
Barker v Corus (UK) plc [2005] UKHL 20, [2006] 2 AC 572 . . . . vii–viii, 57, 58, 62–63
Barnett v Chelsea and Kensington Hospital Management Committee [1969] 1 QB 428 . . . . 52, 61
Barnett v Cohen [1921] 2 KB 461 259–60
Bartlett v Barclays Bank Trust Co Ltd (No 2) [1980] Ch 515. 511–12
Barton v County Natwest Bank Ltd (1999) Lloyd's Rep Banking 408. 51
Basham, Re [1986] 1 WLR 1498. 538
Baskcomb v Beckwith (1869) LR 8 Eq 100. 438
Bass v Clivley (1829) Taml 80. 401
Bates v Lord Hailsham of St Marylebone [1972] 1 WLR 1373 484–85
Battishill v Reed (1856) 18 CB 163
Baxter v Four Oaks Properties Ltd [1965] Ch 816. 455–56
BB v United Kingdom (2004) 39 EHRR 635 24
BDA v Quirino [2015] EWHC 2974 (QB) 290
Beach v Reed Corrugated Cases Ltd [1956] 1 WLR 807. . . . . .69, 182
Beaverbrook Newspapers Ltd v Keys [1978] ICR 582. 472–73
Bee v Jensen [2007] EWCA Civ 923, [2007] 4 All ER 791 . . . . vii–viii, 215
Beecham Group Ltd v Bristol Laboratories Pty Ltd (1968) 118 CLR 618 475
Beechwood Birmingham Ltd v Hoyer Group UK Ltd [2010] EWCA Civ 647, [2011] QB 357. . . . . . vii–viii, 215
Beese v Woodhouse [1970] 1 WLR 586 484–85
Beesley v New Century Group Ltd [2008] EWHC 3033 (QB). 258–59
Behnke v Bede Shipping Co Ltd [1927] 1 KB 649. . . . . .404, 405
Behrens v Bertram Mills Circus Ltd [1957] 2 QB 1. 285–86
Behrens v Richards [1905] 2 Ch 614. 445–46
Bell v Midland Rly Co (1861) 10 CBNS 287. 366
Bell v Peter Browne & Co [1990] 2 QB 495 123
Bellingham v Dhillon [1973] QB 304 148–49
Bell's Indenture, Re [1980] 1 WLR 1217. 511–12
Beloff v Pressdram Ltd [1973] 1 All ER 241. 367–68
Benarr v Kettering Health Authority [1988] NLJR 179 249–50
Bence Graphics International Ltd v Fasson UK Ltd [1998] QB 87. 194
Benham v Gambling [1941] AC 157. 171
Benson v Biggs Wall & Co Ltd [1982] 3 All ER 300 248–49
Benson v Frederick (1766) 3 Burr 1845 362
Beoco Ltd v Alfa Laval Co Ltd [1995] QB 137. . . . . .114, 142–43
Berriello v Felixstowe Dock and Rly Co [1989] 1 WLR 695 154–55
Berry v British Transport Commission [1962] 1 QB 306. . . . . .83, 187
Berry v Humm & Co [1915] 1 KB 627 258–59
Berryman v London Borough of Hounslow [1997] PIQR P83 . . . . .105–6, 234
Bestobell Paints Ltd v Bigg [1975] FSR 421 479
Beswick v Beswick [1968] AC 58. . . . . 201, 382–83, 409, 410–11, 416–17, 436

Betts v Neilson (1868) 3 Ch App 429. 317
BICC plc v Burndy Corp [1985] Ch 232. 394–95
Bigg v Howard Son & Gooch [1990] 1 EGLR 173. 279–80
Biggins v Minton [1977] 1 WLR 701. 315–16
Billett v Ministry of Defence [2015] EWCA Civ 773, [2016] PIQR Q1 239
Birkett v Hayes [1982] 2 All ER 710, [1982] 1 WLR 816 307
Birmingham Corpn v Sowsbery [1970] RTR 84 215–16
Bishop v Cunard White Star Co Ltd, The Queen Mary [1950] P 240. 171
Bishop v Metropolitan Police Comr [1990] 1 LS Gaz R 30, CA 371
Blackett v Bates (1865) 1 Ch App 117. 416
Blackshaw v Lord [1984] QB 1. 274
Blamire v South Cumbria HA [1993] PIQR Q1. 249
Bliss v South East Thames Regional Health Authority [1985] IRLR 308 ....281, 282–83
Bloomsbury Publishing Group Ltd v News Group Newspapers Ltd [2003] EWHC 1205 (Ch),
    [2003] 1 WLR 1633. 441
Bloxham v Robinson (1996) 7 TCLR 122, NZCA. 282–83
Blue Circle Industries plc v Ministry of Defence [1999] Ch 289. 122–23
Blue Town Investments Ltd v Higgs and Hill plc [1990] 1 WLR 696 486
Boardman v Phipps [1967] 2 AC 46 ....526, 527, 528
Bodlewell, The [1907] P 286. ....215, 216
Bold v Brough, Nicholson and Hall Ltd [1964] 1 WLR 201. ....70–71, 182–83
Bone v Seale [1975] 1 WLR 797. ....283–85, 291
Bonnard v Perryman [1891] 2 Ch 269 ....443–44, 479
Bonnington Castings v Wardlaw [1956] AC 613. 52
Booker v Bell [1989] 1 Lloyd's Rep 516. 504
Boomer v Muir 24 P 2d 570 (1933) 352–53
Borag, The See Compania Financiera Soleada SA v Hamoor Tanker Corpn Inc, The Borag
Borders (UK) Ltd v Commissioner of Police of the Metropolis [2005] EWCA Civ 197 .... vii–viii,
    365, 367, 370, 371
Borealis AB v Geogas Trading SA [2010] EWHC 2789 (Comm),
    [2011] 1 Lloyd's Rep 482 ....84–85, 113–14, 130
Boston Deep Sea Fishing and Ice Co v Ansell (1888) 39 Ch D 339 ....526, 529
Bostridge v Oxleas NHS Foundation Trust [2015] EWCA Civ 79, [2015] Med LR 113 364
Bourgoin SA v Ministry of Agriculture, Fisheries and Food [1986] QB 716, [1985] 3 All ER 585 15
Bower v Bantam Investments Ltd [1972] 1 WLR 1120. 456
Bowlay Logging Ltd v Dolmar Ltd (1978) 4 WWR 105 78
Box v Midland Bank Ltd [1979] 2 Lloyd's Rep 391 225
Boyo v Lambeth London Borough Council [1995] IRLR 50. 419
BPE Solicitors v Hughes-Holland [2017] UKSC 21, [2018] AC 599. ....vii–viii, 85–86, 117,
    122–23, 125, 126–27
Brace v Calder [1895] 2 QB 253. 127–28
Brace v Wehnert (1858) 25 Beav 348. 428
Bracewell v Appleby [1975] Ch 408. ....221–22, 318, 321–22, 324–25, 449, 490
Bradburn v Great Western Rly Co (1872) LR 10 Exch 1 ....153, 158, 215
Bradford v Robinson Rentals Ltd [1967] 1 WLR 337 88
Bradford City Metropolitan Council v Arora [1991] 2 QB 507, [1991] 3 All ER 545. ...362, 368–69
Bradford City Metropolitan Council v Brown (1986) 19 HLR 16, CA. 480
Branchett v Beaney [1992] 3 All ER 910. 281
Brand v Berki [2014] EWHC 2979 (QB) 443–44
Brasserie du Pecheur SA v Germany, R v Secretary of State for Transport, ex p Factortame
    Ltd: C-46 & 48/93 [1996] QB 404, [1998] 1 All ER 736. 15
Brett v East India and London Shipping Co Ltd (1864) 2 Hem & M 404 419
Brice v Brown [1984] 1 All ER 997 ....88, 234
Bridge v Campbell Discount Co Ltd [1962] AC 600. ....389, 398
Briody v St Helen's and Knowsley Area Health Authority [2001] EWCA Civ 1010,
    [2002] QB 856. 239–40
Bristol Airport plc v Powdrill [1990] Ch 744. 404
Bristol and West Building Society v Fancy and Jackson (a firm) [1997] 4 All ER 582 122–23
Bristol and West Building Society v May May & Merrimans (No 2) [1998] 1 WLR 336. 154
Bristol and West Building Society v Mothew [1998] Ch 1, [1996] 4 All ER 698. ....122–23, 511–12, 514, 515
British and Commonwealth Holdings plc v Quadrex Holdings Inc [1989] QB 842. 167

British Columbia and Vancouvers Island Spar, Lumber and Saw-Mill Co Ltd v Nettleship
  (1868) LR 3 CP 499...98, 99
British Guiana Credit v Da Silva [1965] 1 WLR 248.................................69
British Motor Trade Association v Gilbert [1951] 2 All ER 641 357–58
British Motor Trade Association v Salvadori [1949] Ch 556..........................230
British Racing Drivers' Club Ltd v Hextall Erskine & Co [1996] 3 All ER 667....113–14
British Sugar plc v NEI Power Projects Ltd (1997) 87 BLR 42........................93
British Telecommunications plc v One in a Million Ltd [1999] 1 WLR 903......443–44
British Transport Commission v Gourley [1956] AC 185 .... 38, 182–84, 238, 261
British Westinghouse Electric and Manufacturing Co Ltd v Underground Electric
  Rlys Co of London Ltd [1912] AC 673.......................... 38, 46–47, 127, 148–49
Broome v Cassell [1972] AC 1027 360
Brown v KMR Services Ltd [1995] 4 All ER 598 .... 96, 98, 101, 105–6
Brown v Ministry of Defence [2006] EWCA Civ 546, [2006] PIQR Q5 ....66, 239
Browne v Associated Newspapers Ltd [2007] EWCA Civ 295, [2008] QB 103...........540
Browning v War Office [1963] 1 QB 750..154–55
Brunsden v Humphrey (1884) 14 QBD 141 163
BSkyB Ltd v HP Enterprise Services UK Ltd [2010] EWHC 862 (TCC), (2010) 131 Con LR 42........183
Buckland v Palmer [1984] 1 WLR 1109 163
Buckley v Lane Herdman & Co [1977] CLY 3143...................................279–80
Budget Rent a Car International Inc v Mamos Slough Ltd (1977) 121 Sol Jo 374 473
Bulmer Ltd and Showerings Ltd v J Bollinger SA [1977] 2 CMLR 625 ....487–88, 489
Bunge SA v Nidera NV [2015] UKSC 43, [2015] Bus LR 987....................vii–viii, 6, 174
Burdett-Coutts v Hertfordshire County Council [1984] IRLR 91......................506
Burdis v Livsey [2002] EWCA Civ 510, [2003] QB 36 .... 130, 212–13, 214–15
Burgess v Florence Nightingale Hospital For Gentlewomen [1955] 1 QB 349, [1955] 2 WLR 533......259
Burke v Tower Hamlets Health Authority (1989) Times, 10 August 163
Burnden Holdings (UK) Ltd v Fielding [2018] UKSC 14, [2018] 2 WLR 885 543
Burns v Edman [1970] 2 QB 541 ....83, 259
Burns v MAN Automotive (Aust) Pty Ltd (1986) 161 CLR 653 145
Burrows v Rhodes [1899] 1 QB 816..227–28
Burton v Pinkerton (1867) LR 2 Exch 340 279
Buxton v Lister (1746) 3 Atk 383..405, 407–8
Bwllfa and Merthyr Dare Steam Collieries (1891) Ltd v Pontypridd Waterworks Co [1903] AC 426......169

C & P Haulage (a firm) v Middleton [1983] 1 WLR 1461 ....78, 503
CBS (UK) Ltd v Lambert [1983] Ch 37...485
CCC Films (London) Ltd v Impact Quadrant Films Ltd [1985] QB 16...............77, 78
CMS Dolphin Ltd v Simonet [2001] 2 BCLC 704................................357–58, 526
CN Marine Inc v Stena Line A/B and Regie Voor Maritiem Transport, The Stena Nautica
  (No 2) [1982] 2 Lloyd's Rep 336 ....404, 408, 411
Cable (Lord), Re, Garratt v Waters [1977] 1 WLR 7................................472
Cachia v Faluyi [2001] EWCA Civ 998, [2001] 1 WLR 1966..........................257
Cadbury Schweppes Inc v FBI Foods Ltd (1999) 167 DLR (4th) 577............511–12, 533
Cain v Francis [2008] EWCA Civ 1451, [2009] QB 754...........................312–13
Cairns v Modi [2012] EWCA Civ 1382, [2013] 1 WLR 1015 ....273, 274, 290
Calabar Properties Ltd v Stitcher [1984] 1 WLR 287............................279–80
Caledonia North Sea Ltd v British Telecommunications plc [2002] UKHL 4, [2002] 1 Lloyd's
  Rep 553..93
Calliope, The [1970] P 172 ....85, 116–17, 134
Caltex Oil (Australia) Pty Ltd v Dredge 'Willemstad' (1976) 136 CLR 529...........231–32
Calveley v Chief Constable of the Merseyside Police [1989] AC 1228..........272, 285–86
Cambridge Nutrition Ltd v BBC [1990] 3 All ER 523..........................476–77, 479
Cambridge Water Co Ltd v Eastern Counties Leather plc [1994] 2 AC 264 89
Camden London Borough Council v Alpenoak Ltd [1985] NLJ Rep 1209.................440
Cameron v Vinters Defence Systems Ltd [2007] EWHC 2267 (QB), [2008] PIQR P5 245
Camilla M, The *See* Star Sea Transport Corpn of Monrovia v Slater, The Camilla M
Campbell v MGN Ltd [2004] UKHL 22, [2004] 2 AC 457, [2004] 2 All ER 995............. 13, 22,
  195–96, 521, 522, 525
Campbell Mostyn (Provisions) Ltd v Barnett Trading Co [1954] 1 Lloyd's Rep 65 148
Canadian Aero Services v O'Malley (1974) 40 DLR (3d) 371 526

Canadian Pacific Rly v Gaud [1949] 2 KB 239...481–82
Candlewood Navigation Corpn Ltd v Mitsui OSK Lines Ltd, The Mineral Transporter,
    The Ibaraki Maru [1986] AC 1, [1985] 2 All ER 935...................................6–7, 231
Cannon v Hartley [1949] Ch 213...429
Canson Enterprises Ltd v Broughton & Co (1991) 85 DLR (4th) 129........................513, 514
Caparo Industries plc v Dickman [1990] 2 AC 605, [1990] 1 All ER 568..................6–7, 222
Capps v Miller [1989] 1 WLR 839...135
Carlos Federspiel & Co SA v Charles Twigg & Co Ltd [1957] 1 Lloyd's Rep 240.....................441
Carlos Sevilleja Garcia v Marex Financial Ltd [2018] EWCA Civ 1468, [2019] QB 173..............187
Carlslogie Steamship Co Ltd v Royal Norwegian Government [1952] AC 292................107–8
Carmarthenshire County Council v Lewis [1955] AC 549..45
Carpenters Estates Ltd v Davies [1940] Ch 160..416
Carr-Saunders v Dick McNeil Associates Ltd [1986] 1 WLR 922, [1986] 2 All ER 888............221–22,
    284–85, 321–22
Carson v John Fairfax & Sons Ltd (1993) 178 CLR 44...274
Cartledge v Jopling [1963] AC 758...234
Cassell & Co Ltd v Broome [1972] AC 1027, [1972] 2 WLR 645...................274, 351–52, 361–62,
    364–65, 367–69, 370, 373, 375, 376
Castle v Wilkinson (1870) 5 Ch App 534..430–31
Caterpillar (NI) Ltd v John Holt & Co (Liverpool) Ltd [2013] EWCA Civ 1232, [2014] 1 WLR 2365.....382
Catnic Components Ltd v Hill & Smith Ltd [1983] FSR 512.......................228–29, 305, 368–69
Cattanach v Melchior (2003) 77 ALJR 1312...250
Cattley v Pollard [2006] EWHC 3130 (Ch), [2007] Ch 353..................................490, 544
Cavendish Square Holding BV v Talal El Makdessi ('Makdessi') [2015] UKSC 67,
    [2016] AC 1172...vii–viii, 390, 391, 392, 393–96, 398, 400
Caxton Publishing Co Ltd v Sutherland Publishing Co [1939] AC 178..........................219
Cayne v Global Natural Resources plc [1984] 1 All ER 225....................473, 476–77, 478–79, 538
Cedar Holdings Ltd v Green [1981] Ch 129...437
Celanese International Corpn v BP Chemicals Ltd [1999] RPC 203........................343–44, 529
Celestial Aviation Trading 71 Ltd v Paramount Airways Private Ltd [2010] EWHC 185,
    [2011] 1 Lloyd's Rep 9..394–95
Cellulose Acetate Silk Co Ltd v Widnes Foundry (1925) Ltd [1933] AC 20....................393, 394
Cemp Properties (UK) Ltd v Dentsply Research and Development Corpn
    (Denton Hall & Burgin, third party) [1991] 2 EGLR 197..................................225–26
Cerberus Software Ltd v Rowley [2001] EWCA Civ 78, [2001] ICR 376, [2001] IRLR 160.....148–49, 383
Challender v Royle (1887) 36 Ch D 425..469–70
Chan v Hackney London Borough Council [1997] ICR 1014, EAT..............................157
Chaplin v Hicks [1911] 2 KB 786...63–64, 65, 73
Chapman v Michaelson [1908] 2 Ch 612; aff'd [1909] 1 Ch 238.................................504
Chappell v Times Newspapers Ltd [1975] 1 WLR 482...433
Chappell & Co Ltd v Columbia Graphophone Co [1914] 2 Ch 745.........................498–99
Charrington v Simons & Co Ltd [1971] 1 WLR 598..466
Charter v Sullivan [1957] 2 QB 117...196
Charterhouse Credit Co Ltd v Tolly [1963] 2 QB 683..70
Cheetham & Co Ltd v Thornham Spinning Co Ltd [1964] 2 Lloyd's Rep 17...................495
Chekiang, The See Admiralty Comrs v SS Chekiang
Chesneau v Interhome Ltd [1983] CLY 988..225–26
Chester v Afshar [2004] UKHL 41, [2005] 1 AC 345..108–9
Chesworth v Farrar [1967] 1 QB 407...339, 340
Chewings v Williams [2009] EWHC 2490 (QB), [2010] PIQR Q1..............................165
Chicago Coliseum Club v Dempsey 256 Ill App 542 (1932).......................................82
Chief Constable of the North Wales Police v Evans [1982] 3 All ER 141........................426
Childs v Lewis (1924) 40 TLR 870..272
Chinn v Hochstrasser (Inspector of Taxes) [1979] Ch 447.......................................407
Chitty v Bray (1883) 48 LT 860..486
Chubb Cash Ltd v John Crilley & Son [1983] 1 WLR 599.................................172, 219
Church of Scientology of California v Miller (1987) Times, 23 October.....................490, 544
Cia de Seguros Imperio (a body corporate) v Heath (REBX) Ltd [2001] 1 WLR 112.............544
City of New Orleans v Fireman's Charitable Association...354
Clark v BET plc [1997] IRLR 348..71
Clark v Chief Constable of Cleveland Constabulary [1999] 21 LS Gaz R 38................272, 289

Table of Cases

Clark v Macourt [2013] HCA 56, (2013) 88 ALJR 190...151
Clark v Marsiglia 1 Denio 317 (NY, 1845) 384
Clark v Nomura Ltd [2000] IRLR 766..71
Clark v Urquhart [1930] AC 28 ....224, 226–27
Clarke v Price (1819) 2 Wils Ch 157 419
Clay v Pooler [1982] 3 All ER 570 ....248–49, 258–59
Clay v TUI UK Ltd [2018] EWCA Civ 1177, [2018] 4 All ER 672 114
Clea Shipping Corpn v Bulk Oil International Ltd, The Alaskan Trader [1984] 1 All ER 129 ......385, 386
Cleaver v Mutual Reserve Fund Life Association [1892] 1 QB 147 382–83
Clef Aquitaine SARL v Laporte Materials (Barrow) Ltd (sued as Sovereign Chemicals
    Industries Ltd) [2001] QB 488..227–28
Clegg v Hands (1890) 44 Ch D 503 460–61
Clenshaw v Tanner [2002] EWCA Civ 1848 156
Clifton Securities Ltd v Huntley [1948] 2 All ER 283 221
Clippens Oil Co Ltd v Edinburgh and District Water Trustees [1907] AC 291 145
Clough v First Choice Holidays and Flights Ltd [2006] EWCA Civ 15, [2006] PIQR P22 56
Cluett Peabody & Co Inc v McIntyre Hogg Marsh & Co Ltd [1958] RPC 335................489
Clunis v Camden and Islington HA [1998] QB 978 235–36
Clyde Navigation Trustees v Bowring SS (1929) 34 Ll L Rep 319, Ct of Sess 209–10
Clyde, The (1856) Sw 23, 5 LT 121..209–10
Coastal (Bermuda) Petroleum Ltd v VTT Vulcan Petroleum SA (No 2), The Marine Star
    [1994] 2 Lloyd's Rep 629 ....191, 192
Cockburn v Alexander (1848) 6 CB 791...69
Codex Corpn v Racal-Milgo Ltd [1984] FSR 87 345–46
Coflexip SA v Stolt Comex Seaway MS Ltd [2001] 1 All ER 952 443–44
Cohen v Roche [1927] 1 KB 169 ....403–5, 493–94, 495
Colbeam Palmer Ltd v Stock Affiliates Pty Ltd 122 CLR 25...................339–41, 342, 343, 345–46
Coles v Hetherton [2013] EWCA Civ 1704, [2015] 1 WLR 160..........................vii–viii, 214
Collard v Saunders [1971] CLY 11161 279
Colledge v Bass Mitchells & Butlers Ltd [1988] 1 All ER 536 160
Colliery v Brown (1788) 1 Cox Eq Cas 428 430
Collins Stewart Ltd v The Financial Times Ltd [2005] EWHC 262 (QB), [2006] EMLR 5 288
Colls v Home and Colonial Stores Ltd [1904] AC 179 ....463, 464
Commissioner for Customs & Excise v Barclays Bank [2006] UKHL 28, [2007] 1 AC 181 ....6–7, 231
Commissioner of Police of the Metropolis v Shaw [2012] ICR 464 287–88
Commonwealth of Australia v Amann Aviation Pty Ltd (1991) 66 ALJR 123 ....60, 70–71, 73, 80, 81
Compania Financiera Soleada SA v Hamoor Tanker Corpn Inc, The Borag [1981] 1 WLR 274,
    [1981] 1 All ER 856..84–85, 96, 131
Compania Naviera Maropan SA v Bowaters Lloyd Pulp and Paper Mills Ltd
    [1955] 2 QB 68..84–85, 115–16
Connolly v Camden and Islington Area Health Authority [1981] 3 All ER 250......................248
Connor v Chief Constable of Cambridgeshire (1984) Times, 11 April 362–63
Cooden Engineering Co Ltd v Stanford [1953] 1 QB 86 398
Cook v Deeks [1916] 1 AC 554 526
Cook v Evatt (No 2) [1992] 1 NZLR 676 537
Cook v JL Kier & Co Ltd [1970] 1 WLR 774 235–36
Cook v Lewis [1951] SCR 830 56
Cooke v United Bristol Health Care [2003] EWCA Civ 1370, [2004] PIQR Q2...............246–47
Cookson v Knowles [1979] AC 556, HL [1977] QB 913..........................171, 234–35, 245, 260,
                                                                          261–62, 304, 305, 306, 307
Cooper v Firth Brown Ltd [1963] 1 WLR 418...238
Co-operative Insurance Society Ltd v Argyll Stores (Holdings) Ltd [1998] AC 1,
    [1997] 2 WLR 898..402, 415, 416, 417, 418, 428–29, 436, 465
Copley v Lawn [2009] EWCA Civ 580, [2009] PIQR P21 215
Cork v Kirby Maclean Ltd [1952] 2 All ER 402 142
Corporacion Nacional del Cobre de Chile v Sogemin Metals Ltd [1997] 1 WLR 1396........136–37, 514
Corr v IBC Vehicles Ltd [2008] UKHL 13, [2008] 1 AC 884...................................257–58
Cory v Thames Ironworks Co (1868) LR 3 QB 181..97, 131
Cosemar SA v Marimarna Shipping Co Ltd, The Mathew [1990] 2 Lloyd's Rep 323.........154–55
Cottingham v Attey Bower & Jones [2000] PNLR 557 122–23
Couch v Attorney General (No 2) [2010] NZSC 27, [2010] NZLR 149..........................377

Coulls v Bagot's Executor and Trustee Co Ltd [1967] ALR 385. . . . . 201, 382–83, 410–11
Coulson (William) & Sons v James Coulson & Co (1887) 3 TLR 846 479
County Ltd v Girozentrale Securities [1996] 3 All ER 834. 115–16
County Sound plc v Ocean Sound Ltd [1991] FSR 367 476
Courage v Crehan, Case C-453/99, [2001] ECR I-6297 15
Coventry v Lawrence [2014] UKSC 13, [2014] AC 822 . . . . vii–viii, 444–45, 447, 449–50, 451, 453
Cowley (Lord) v Byas (1877) 5 Ch D 944. 468
Cowper v Laidler [1903] 2 Ch 337. 445
Cox v Ergo Versicherung AG [2014] UKSC 22, [2014] AC 1379 180
Cox v Hockenhull [2000] 1 WLR 750. 258–59
Cox v Philips Industries Ltd [1976] 1 WLR 638 282–83
Coyne v Citizen Finance Ltd (1991) 172 CLR 211 273
Crabb v Arun District Council [1976] Ch 179. . . . . 487–88, 538
Crabtree v Wilson [1993] PIQR Q24, CA. 261
Cream Holdings Ltd v Banerjee [2003] EWCA Civ 103, [2003] Ch 650 . . . . 472, 480, 539–40
Credit Suisse Asset Management Ltd v Armstrong [1996] ICR 882. 459–60
Cresswell v Eaton [1991] 1 WLR 1113 258–59
Crofton v NHS Litigation Authority [2007] EWCA Civ 71, [2007] 1 WLR 923. 239–40
Croke (a minor) v Wiseman [1982] 1 WLR 71 . . . . 247, 248
Cronin v Redbridge London Borough Council (1987) Times, 20 May 165
Crosley v Derby Gas Light Co (1838) 3 My & Cr 428. 344–45
Cross v David Martin and Mortimer [1989] 1 EGLR 154 279–80
Crossley & Sons Ltd v Lightowler (1867) 2 Ch App 478. 53
Croudace Construction Ltd v Cawoods Concrete Products Ltd [1978] 2 Lloyd's Rep 55 93
CTB v News Group Newspapers Ltd [2011] EWHC 1232 (QB). 441
Cud v Rutter (1720) 1 P Wms 570 407
Cullen v Chief Constable of the Royal Ulster Constabulary [2003] UKHL 39, [2003] 1 WLR 1763. 503
Cullen v Trappell (1980) 146 CLR 1 183
Cullinane v British Rema Manufacturing Co Ltd [1954] 1 QB 292 . . . . 77, 192, 194, 205–6
Cunningham v Harrison [1973] QB 942. . . . . 168–69, 239–41, 242
Cunningham v Wheeler (1994) 113 DLR (4th) 1, Can SC. 183
Curwen v James [1963] 1 WLR 748. 170

Daiches v Bluelake Investments Ltd (1985) 275 Estates Gazette 462 491–92
Daish v Wauton [1972] 2 QB 262. 239–40
Daly v General Steam Navigation Co Ltd, The Dragon [1981] 1 WLR 120. 242
Damon Cia Naviera SA v Hapag-Lloyd International SA, The Blankenstein, The Bartenstein,
   The Birkenstein [1985] 1 All ER 475 382
Dance v Goldingham (1873) 8 Ch App 902 538
Daniel v Ferguson [1891] 2 Ch 27 . . . . 464, 482
Daniels v Thompson [1998] 3 NZLR 22, NZCA 371
Daraydan Holdings Ltd v Solland International Ltd [2004] EWHC 622 (Ch) 531–32
Darbishire v Warran [1963] 1 WLR 1067. . . . . 212, 214
Darley Main Colliery Co v Mitchell (1886) 11 App Cas 127 163
Darlington Borough Council v Wiltshier Northern Ltd [1995] 1 WLR 68 201
Davies v Davies [2016] EWCA Civ 463 525–26
Davies v Gas Light and Coke Co [1909] 1 Ch 708. 463
Davies v Powell Duffryn Associated Collieries Ltd [1942] AC 601, [1942] 1 All ER 657. . . . . 263, 265–66, 267
Davies v Swan Motor Co (Swansea) Ltd [1949] 2 KB 291 134
Davies v Taylor [1974] AC 207, [1972] 3 WLR 801. . . . . 60, 67, 259–60
Davis v Foreman [1894] 3 Ch 654 456
Davis & Co (Wines) Ltd v Afa-Minerva (EMI) Ltd [1974] 2 Lloyd's Rep 27. 225–26
Dawson, Re [1966] 2 NSWLR 211. 511–12
Day v Mead [1987] 2 NZLR 443. 514
Dean v Ainley [1987] 1 WLR 1729 197
Deane v Ealing London Borough Council [1993] ICR 329. 284–85
Decro-Wall International SA v Practitioners in Marketing Ltd [1971] 2 All ER 216. . . . . 408, 461
Deeny v Gooda Walker Ltd (in liquidation) [1995] 4 All ER 289. 163
Deeny v Gooda Walker Ltd (in liquidation) (No 2) [1996] 1 WLR 426. 182–83
Deepak Fertilisers and Petrochemicals Corpn v Davy McKee (London) Ltd
   [1999] 1 All ER (Comm) 69. 93

Table of Cases

De Beers UK Ltd v Atos Origin IT Services UK Ltd [2010] EWHC 3276 198–99
De Falco v Crawley Borough Council [1980] QB 460 483
De Francesco v Barnum (1890) 45 Ch D 430..419, 420
De Sales v Ingrilli (2002) 212 CLR 338 263
Defrenne v Sabena, Case 43/75 [1976] ECR 455 [1981] 1 All ER 122 15
De La Bere v Pearson Ltd [1908] 1 KB 280..109–10
Delaware Mansions Ltd v Westminster City Council [2001] UKHL 55...................................207
Delfe v Delamotte (1857) 3 K & J 581..341–42
Denkavit Internationaal BV, VITIC Amsterdam BV and Voormeer BV v Bundesamt für
  Finanzen: C-283, 291, 292/94 [1996] ECR I-5063, [1996] STC 1445 15
Denne v Light (1857) 8 De GM & G 774 431
Dennis v London Passenger Transport Board [1948] 1 All ER 779 ....154–55, 168–69
Dennis v Ministry of Defence [2003] EWHC 793 (QB), [2003] NLJR 634 .... 23–24, 291–92, 447, 449
Derby Resources AG v Blue Corinth Marine Co Ltd, The Athenian Harmony [1998] 2 Lloyd's Rep 410 211
Dering v Uris [1964] 2 QB 669..503–4
Design 5 v Keniston Housing Association Ltd (1986) 34 BLR 92....................................154–55
Design Progression Ltd v Thurloe Properties Ltd [2004] EWHC 324 (Ch), [2005] 1 WLR 1 366
Despina R, The See Elefterotria (Owners) v Despina R (Owners), The Despina R
Deutsche Rückversicherung AG v Walbrook Insurance Co Ltd [1995] 1 WLR 1017 475
De Vitre v Betts (1873) LR 6 HL 319..345–46
Devenish Nutrition Ltd v Sanofi-Aventis SA [2008] EWCA Civ 1086, [2009] 3 WLR 198,
  [2007] EWHC 2394 (Ch)... vii–viii, 350, 371, 373–74
Devonshire and Smith v Jenkins [1979] LAG Bulletin 114, CA 365, 371
Dews v National Coal Board [1988] AC 1 ....238, 239
Dexter v Courtaulds Ltd [1984] 1 WLR 372...306
Dicker v Popham Radford & Co (1890) 63 LT 379...467
Dickinson v Jones Alexander & Co [1990] Fam Law 137...278
Diesen v Samson 1971 SLT 49 278
Diestal v Stevenson [1906] 2 KB 345..393
Dietman v Brent London Borough Council [1987] ICR 737: aff'd [1988] ICR 842.....................419
Di Fernando v Simon, Smits & Co [1920] 3 KB 409...177
Dillenkofer v Germany: C-178-9/94, 188–190/94 ECR I-4845, [1996] All ER (EC) 917 15
Dillwyn v Llewellyn (1862) 4 De GF & J 517...538
Dimbleby & Sons Ltd v National Union of Journalists [1984] 1 WLR 427 .... 476–77, 478–79
Dimond v Lovell [2002] 1 AC 384, [2000] 2 WLR 1121..................146, 148–49, 212–13, 214–15
Distributori Automatici Italia SpA v Holford General Trading Co Ltd [1985] 3 All ER 750 443
Dixon v Clement Jones Solicitors (a firm) [2004] EWCA Civ 1005, [2005] PNLR 6..................65
Dixon v Smith (1860) 5 H & N 450..272
Dobson v Thames Water Utilities Ltd [2009] EWCA Civ 28, [2009] 3 All ER 319......... 25, 283–84, 291
Dodd Properties (Kent) Ltd v Canterbury City Council [1980] 1 WLR 433, [1980 1 All ER 928 .... 38, 145,
  170, 171, 175, 207, 208, 209
Dodsworth v Dodsworth (1973) 228 Estates Gazette 1115 ....511–12, 525–26
Doherty v Allman (or Allen) (1878) 3 App Cas 709..455, 466
Dolbey v Goodwin [1955] 2 All ER 166 262
Doloret v Rothschild (1824) 1 Sim & St 590...408–9
Dominator, The See Dreyfus (Louis) et Cie v Parnaso Cia Naviera SA, The Dominator
Dominion Coal Co Ltd v Dominion Iron and Steel Co Ltd and National Trust Co Ltd
  [1909] AC 293..416
Dominion Mosaics and Tile Co Ltd v Trafalgar Trucking Co Ltd [1990] 2 All ER 246......... 206, 207–8,
  209–10, 217–18
Donald v Ntuli [2010] EWCA Civ 1276, [2011] 1 WLR 294.......................................441, 540
Donnell v Bennett (1883) 22 Ch D 835..461
Donnelly v Joyce [1974] QB 454 ....214–15, 240–41
Dougan v Ley (1946) 71 CLR 142 405
Doughty v Turner Manufacturing Co Ltd [1964] 1 QB 518...87
Douglas v Hello! Ltd (No 6) [2007] UKHL 21, [2008] 1 AC 1, HL: [2005] EWCA Civ 595,
  [2006] QB 125...524, 525
Douglas v Hello! Ltd (No 6) [2003] EWHC 786, [2003] 3 All ER 996 537
Dowling v Betjemann (1862) 2 John & H 544..404–5
Downs v Chappell [1996] 3 All ER 344..122–23
Dowson & Mason Ltd v Potter [1986] 1 WLR 1419, [1986] 2 All ER 418.........................522, 523

Table of Cases

Dowty Boulton Paul Ltd v Wolverhampton Corpn [1971] 1 WLR 204 416
Doyle v Olby (Ironmongers) Ltd [1969] 2 QB 158 .... 38, 90, 223–24, 225–26, 227
Doyle v Wallace [1998] PIQR Q146 .... 66, 238
Drake v Foster Wheeler Ltd [2010] EWHC 2004 (QB), [2011] 1 All ER 63 241
Dragon, The See Daly v General Steam Navigation Co Ltd, The Dragon
Drane v Evangelou [1978] 1 WLR 455 .... 284–85, 360–61, 365, 366
Draper v British Optical Association [1938] 1 All ER 115.. 468
Draper v Trist [1939] 3 All ER 513 228–29
Dreyfus (Louis) et Cie v Parnaso Cia Naviera SA, The Dominator [1959] 1 QB 498; rvsd
  [1960] 2 QB 49.. 506
Dryden v Johnson Matthey plc [2018] UKSC 18, [2018] 2 WLR 1109 234
DSD v Metropolitan Police Commissioner [2018] UKSC 11, [2018] 2 WLR 895 25–26
DSD v Metropolitan Police Commissioner [2014] EWHC 2493 (QB), [2015] 1 WLR 1833 26
Dubai Aluminium Co Ltd v Salaam (Livingstone, third parties) [2002] UKHL 48,
  [2003] 2 AC 366 511–12
Duce v Rourke [1951] 1 WWR 305.. 112
Duce v Worcestershire Acute Hospitals NHS Trust [2018] EWCA Civ 1307, [2018] PIQR P18 108–9
Duncuft v Albrecht (1841) 12 Sim 189 407
Dunford and Elliott Ltd v Johnson and Firth Brown Ltd [1977] 1 Lloyd's Rep 505 475
Dunhill (Alfred) v Sunoptic SA and C Dunhill [1979] FSR 337 .... 473, 480
Dunlop Pneumatic Tyre Co Ltd v New Garage and Motor Co Ltd [1915] AC 79 388
Dunnachie v Kingston-Upon-Hull City Council [2004] UKHL 36, [2005] 1 AC 226 282
Dunton v Dover District Council (1977) 76 LGR 87 .... 284–85, 448
Duport Steels Ltd v Sirs [1980] ICR 161 .... 472–73, 478
Durell v Pritchard (1865) 1 Ch App 244.. 463
Dudarec v Andrews [2006] EWCA Civ 256, [2006] 1 WLR 3002................................... 65
Durham v BAI (Run Off) Ltd [2012] UKSC 14, [2012] 1 WLR 867............................... 57
Durham Tees Valley Airport Ltd v Bmibaby [2010] EWCA Civ 485, [2011] 1 Lloyd's Rep 68......... 72
Dynamic, The See Ocean Marine Navigation Ltd v Koch Carbon Inc, The Dynamic
Dyster v Randall & Sons [1926] Ch 932 432

E Worlsey & Co Ltd v Cooper [1939] 1 All ER 290... 272
Eagle v Chambers [2003] EWCA Civ 1107, [2004] RTR 115...................... 134, 238, 239–40, 247
Earle v Charalambous [2006] EWCA Civ 1092, [2007] HLR 8.................................. 291
East v Maurer [1991] 2 All ER 733, [1991] 1 WLR 461, CA 223, 227–28
Eastern Counties Rly Co v Hawkes (1855) 5 HL Cas 331 403
Eastwood v Lever (1863) 4 De GJ & Sm 114 317
Eastwood v Magnox Electric plc [2004] UKHL 35, [2005] 1 AC 503, [2004] 3 WLR 322 .....270–71, 282
Eaton Mansions (Westminster) Ltd v Stinger Compania de Inversion SA [2013] EWCA Civ 1308,
  [2014] HLR 4...288, 321–22
Edelsten v Edelsten (1863) 1 De GJ & Sm 185..341–42
Edgington v Fitzmaurice (1885) 29 Ch D 459 .... 51, 137
Edison, The See Liesbosch, Dredger (Owners) v SS Edison (Owners)
Edwards v Chesterfield Royal Hospital NHS Foundation Trust [2011] UKSC 58,
  [2012] 2 AC 22... 270–71, 282
Edwards v Lee's Administrators 96 SW 2d 1028 (1920) 339–40
Eeles v Cobham Hire Services Ltd [2009] EWCA Civ 204, [2010] 1 WLR 409 167–68
Egan v Egan [1975] Ch 218..443–44
Ehmler v Hall [1993] 1 EGLR 137... 209
Ehrman v Bartholomew [1898] 1 Ch 671.. 419
Elbinger AG v Armstrong (1874) LR 9 QB 473 194–95
Electrolux Ltd v Electrix Ltd (1953) 71 RPC 23...487–88
Eleftherotria (Owners) v Despina R (Owners), The Despina R [1979] AC 685 .... 178, 179, 181
Ellis v Duke of Bedford [1899] 1 Ch 494 504
Elliott v Pierson [1948] 1 All ER 939...406–7
Elmore v Pirrie (1887) 57 LT 333.. 435
Elsley v J G Collins Insurance Agencies Ltd [1978] 2 SCR 916, 83 DLR (3d) 1 .... 394, 462, 522
Emanuel v Emanuel [1982] 1 WLR 669 485–86
Emeh v Kensington and Chelsea and Westminster Area Health Authority
  [1985] QB 1012 .... 84–85, 249–51
Emerald Construction Co v Lowthian [1966] 1 All ER 1013 443–44

Empresa Exportadora de Azucar v Industria Azucarera Nacional SA, The Playa Larga
  [1983] 2 Lloyd's Rep 171 175–76
Endeavour, The (1890) 6 Asp MC 511..208
EnergySolutions EU Ltd v Nuclear Decommissioning Authority [2017] UKSC 34,
  [2017] 1 WLR 1373...15
English v Dedham Vale Properties Ltd [1978] 1 WLR 93 526
English Churches Housing Group v Shine [2004] EWCA Civ 434, [2004] HLR 42..................291
Equitas Ltd v Walsham Brothers & Co Ltd [2013] EWHC 3264 (Comm), [2014] PNLR 8 299–300
Erie County Natural Gas and Fuel Co Ltd v Carroll [1911] AC 105..............................148–49
Erinford Properties Ltd v Cheshire County Council [1974] Ch 261 469–70
Erven Warnink BV v J Townend & Sons (Hull) Ltd [1979] AC 731.............................443–44
Essa v Laing Ltd [2004] EWCA Civ 02, [2004] ICR 746..90–91
Esso Petroleum Co Ltd v Kingswood Motors (Addlestone) Ltd [1974] QB 142..............464, 482–83
Esso Petroleum Co Ltd v Mardon [1976] QB 801, [1976] 2 WLR 583..........................131, 225
Esso Petroleum Co Ltd v Niad Ltd [2001] All ER (D) 324 (Nov)...............................358, 359
ETK v News Group Newspapers Ltd [2011] EWCA Civ 439, [2011] 1 WLR 1827 441
Euro London Appointments Ltd v Claessens Int Ltd [2006] EWCA Civ 385, [2006] 2 Lloyd's Rep 436......399
Euroption Strategic Fund Ltd v Skandinaviska Enskilda Banken AB [2012] EWHC 584 (Comm),
  [2013] 1 BCLC 125..7
Evans v Clayhope Properties Ltd [1988] 1 WLR 358 492
Evans Marshall & Co v Bertola SA [1973] 1 WLR 349.............................408–9, 411, 440, 461
Evening Standard Co Ltd v Henderson [1987] IRLR 64...459–60
Exchange Telegraph Co Ltd v Gregory & Co [1896] 1 QB 147 73
Eximenco Handels AG v Partrederiet Oro Chief and Levantes Maritime Corpn, The Oro Chief
  [1983] 2 Lloyd's Rep 509 ....404, 408–9
Experience Hendrix LLC v PPX Enterprises Inc [2003] EWCA Civ 323,
  [2003] 1 All ER (Comm) 830 ....321–22, 326, 330
Export Credits Guarantee Department v Universal Oil Products Co [1983] 2 All ER 205........399, 400
Express Newspapers plc v Mitchell [1982] IRLR 465 ....467, 482
Exxon Shipping Co v Baker 554 US 471 (2008)..375

F v Wirral Metropolitan Borough Council [1991] Fam 69 285–86
F & B Entertainments Ltd v Leisure Enterprises Ltd (1976) 240 Estates Gazette 455 225–26
Faber v Gosworth UDC (1903) 88 LT 549 504
Fairchild v Glenhaven Funeral Services Ltd (1978) Ltd [2002] UKHL 22, [2003] 1 AC 32......55, 56–57, 62–63
Falcke v Gray (1859) 4 Drew 651...404–5
Farley v Skinner [2001] UKHL 49, [2002] 2 AC 732..........251, 277, 278, 279, 280–81, 282–83, 291–92
Farmer Giles Ltd v Wessex Water Authority [1988] 2 EGLR 189 208
Farraj v King's Healthcare NHS Trust [2006] EWHC 1228, [2006] PIQR P29 251–52
Farwell v Walbridge (1851) 2 Gr 332...494
Fawcett and Holmes' Contract, Re (1889) 42 Ch D 150..438
Federal Commerce and Navigation Co Ltd v Tradax Export SA, The Maratha Envoy [1977] QB 324.....181
Federal Sugar Refining Co v US Sugar Equalisation Bd 286 F 575 (1920)......................339–40
Fellowes & Son v Fisher [1976] QB 122 ....470–71, 473, 475, 476, 480
Fells v Read (1796) 3 Ves 70 494
Femis-Bank (Anguilla) Ltd v Lazar [1991] Ch 391 479
Ferdinand Retzlaff, The [1972] 2 Lloyd's Rep 120 55
Ferguson v Wilson (1866) 2 Ch App 77 ....315–16, 430–31
FHR European Ventures LLP v Cedar Properties LLC [2014] UKSC 45,
  [2015] AC 250 ....vii–viii, 529, 531–32
Fidler v Sun Life Assurance Co of Canada (2006) 271 DLR (4th) 1............................377–78
Field Common Ltd v Elmbridge BC [2008] EWHC 2079 (Ch), [2009] 1 P & CR 1..............321–22
Fielding v Variety Inc [1967] 2 QB 841, [1967] 3 WLR 415...67
Films Rover International Ltd v Cannon Film Sales Ltd [1986] 3 All ER 772......................483
Financial Services Authority v Rourke (2001) Times November 12...............................504
Financial Services Authority v Sinaloa Gold Plc [2013] UKSC 11, [2013] 2 AC 28...............469–70
Financings v Baldock [1963] 2 QB 104...70
Finelli v Dee (1968) 76 DLR (2d) 393 (Ont CA)...384
Fiona Trust and Holding Corp v Privalov [2011] EWHC 664 (Comm) 305
Fire and All Risks Insurance Co Ltd v Callinan (1978) 140 CLR 427..........................234–35
First Interstate Bank of California v Cohen Arnold & Co [1996] PNLR 17 65

First National Commercial Bank plc v Humberts [1995] 2 All ER 673 123
First Subsea Ltd v Balltec Ltd [2017] EWCA Civ 186, [2018] Ch 25 543
Fish v Wilcox and Gwent Health Authority (1993) 13 BMLR 134, CA 249–50
Fisher v Brooker [2009] UKHL 41, [2009] 1 WLR 1764 . . . . 489, 504, 505
Fisher v Jackson [1891] 2 Ch 84. 423
Fitter v Veal 12 Mod Rep 542 163
Fitzgerald v Lane [1989] AC 328 135
Flame SA v Glory Wealth Shipping PTE Ltd, The Glory Wealth [2013] EWHC 3153 (Comm),
    [2014] QB 1080 . . . . vii–viii, 67
Fletcher v Autocar and Transporters Ltd [1968] 2 QB 322 . . . . 36, 37
Fletcher v Bealey (1885) 28 Ch D 688. 468
Fletcher v Fletcher (1844) 4 Hare 67 538
Flight v Bolland 1828) 4 Russ 298 426–27
Flight v Booth (1834) 1 Bing NC 370 438
Flora v Wakom (Heathrow) Ltd [2006] EWCA Civ 1103, [2007] 1 WLR 482 166–67
Flying Fish, The See Anderson v Hoen, The Flying Fish
Foaminol Laboratories Ltd v British Artid Plastics Ltd [1941] 2 All ER 393. 269–70
Foley v Burnell (1783) 1 Bro CC 274. 538
Folias, The See Services Europe Atlantique Sud (SEAS) v Stockholms Rederiaktiebolag
    SVEA, The Folias
Forbes v Wandsworth HA [1997] QB 402 313
Force India Formula One Team Ltd v 1 Malaysia Racing Team Sdh Bhd [2013] EWCA Civ 780,
    [2013] RPC 36; [2012] EWHC 616 (Ch), [2012] RPC 29 . . . . 321–22, 512, 524
Forsikringsaktieselskapet Vesta v Butcher, Bain Dawles Ltd and Aquacultural Insurance
    Services Ltd [1989] AC 852, [1988] 3 WLR 565. . . . . 137–38, 139, 140–41
Forster v Outred & Co [1982] 1 WLR 86 . . . . .123, 232, 311
Forster v Silvermere Golf and Equestrian Centre Ltd (1981) 42 P & CR 255 175
Forsyth-Grant v Allen [2008] EWCA Civ 505, [2008] Env LR 41. . . . . vii–viii, 350
Fortescue v Lostwithiel and Fowey Rly Co [1894] 3 Ch 621 416
Fortunity, The, Motor Cruiser Four of Hearts (Owners) v Fortunity (Owners)
    [1961] 1 WLR 351. . . . . .209, 210–11
Forum Craftsman, The See Islamic Republic of Iran Shipping Lines v Ierax Shipping Co
    of Panama, The Forum Craftsman
Fosesco International v Fordath [1975] FSR 507. 472
Foster v Tyne and Wear CC [1986] 1 All ER 567. 239
Fothergill v Rowland (1873) LR 17 Eq 132. . . . . 407–8, 456, 461
Fox v Fox (1870) LR 11 Eq 142. 538
France v Gaudet (1871) LR 6 QB 199 219–20
Francis v Brown (1998) 30 HLR 143 373
Francis v Cowcliffe Ltd (1976) 33 P & CR 368. 431
Francome v Mirror Group Newspapers Ltd [1984] 1 WLR 892 . . . . .473, 538–39
Francovich and Bonifaci v Italy: C-6&9/90 [1991] ECR 1–5357, [1993] 2 CMLR 66 15
Franklin v Giddins [1978] Qd R 72 541
Franklin v South Eastern Rly Co (1858) 3 H & N 211 . . . . 259–60, 263
Fraser v Evans [1969] 1 QB 349 . . . . .479, 539
Frawley v Neill (1999) Times, 5 April 433
Freeman v Lockett [2006] EWHC 102 (QB), [2006] Lloyd's Rep Med 151 239–40
Fritz v Hobson (1880) 14 Ch D 542. 221
Froom v Butcher [1976] QB 286 . . . . .133, 134
Frost v Chief Constable of South Yorkshire Police [1998] QB 254, [1997] 3 WLR 1194. 234
Fry v Fry (1859) 27 Beav 144 511–12
Fullwood v Fullwood (1878) 9 Ch D 176 489
Fulwell v Bragg (1983) 127 Sol Jo 171 476
Fulton Shipping Inc of Panama v Globalia Business Travel SAU of Spain, The New Flamenco
    [2017] UKSC 43, [2017] 1 WLR 2581 . . . . .vii–viii, 151–52
Fyffes Group Ltd v Templeman [2000] 2 Lloyd's Rep 643 . . . . 509–10, 529, 535

Gaca v Pirelli General plc [2004] EWCA Civ 373, [2004] 1 WLR 2683. 159–60
Gafford v Graham [1999] 3 EGLR 75 . . . . .466, 488
Galbraith v Mitchenall Estates Ltd [1965] 2 QB 473. 394–95
Gale v Abbott (1862) 6 LT 852 481–82

Table of Cases

Galoo Ltd (in liquidation) v Bright Grahame Murray [1994] 1 WLR 1360 .... 107, 109, 113–14, 115
Gammell v Wilson [1982] AC 27, [1980] 3 WLR 591 .... 254, 264
Garden City, The *See* Polish Steamship Co v Atlantic Maritime Co, The Garden City
Garden Cottage Foods Ltd v Milk Marketing Board [1984] AC 130, [1983] 2 All ER 770 .... 15, 473
Gardner v Dyson [1967] 1 WLR 1497 37
Gardner v Marsh and Parsons [1997] 1 WLR 489 .... 150, 188
Garnac Grain Co Inc v Faure and Fairclough Ltd [1968] AC 1130n 85–86
Gator Shipping Corpn v Trans-Asiatic Oil Ltd SA and Occidental Shipping Establishment,
   The Odenfeld [1978] 2 Lloyd's Rep 357 .... 385, 386
Gazelle, The (1844) 2 Wm Rob 279 217–18
Gbaja-Biamila v DHL International (UK) Ltd [2000] ICR 730, EAT 287–88
Gebrüder Metalmann GmbH & Co KG v NBR (London) Ltd [1984] 1 Lloyd's Rep 614 .... 131, 132
Geest plc v Lansiquot [2002] UKPC 48, [2002] 1 WLR 3111 .... 85–86, 128
General Accident Assurance Corpn v Noel [1902] 1 KB 377 462
General and Finance Facilities Ltd v Cooks Cars (Romford) Ltd [1963] 1 WLR 644 172
General Billposting Co Ltd v Atkinson [1909] AC 118 .... 459–60, 486
General Tire and Rubber Co v Firestone Tyre and Rubber Co Ltd [1975]
   1 WLR 819 .... 229, 321–22, 524–25
George v Metropolitan Police Comr (1984) Times, 31 March 284–85, 362–63
George v Pinnock [1973] 1 WLR 118 242
Gerber Garment Technology Inc v Lectra Systems Ltd [1997] RPC 443, CA 228–29
Gerula v Flores [1995] CCL 8583, Ont CA 537
Giambrone v JMC Holidays Ltd (Sunworld Holidays Ltd) (No 2) [2004] EWCA Civ 158,
   [2004] 2 All ER 891 .... 234, 240–41
Gilbert-Ash (Northern) Ltd v Modern Engineering (Bristol) Ltd [1974] AC 689 391
Giles v Thompson [1994] 1 AC 142 .... 214, 304
Giles & Co Ltd v Morris [1972] 1 WLR 307 .... 416–17, 419, 420
Gillett v Holt [2001] Ch 210 .... 511–12, 525–26, 538
Gillette UK Ltd v Edenwest Ltd [1994] RPC 279 .... 228, 342
GKN Centrax Gears Ltd v Matbro Ltd [1976] 2 Lloyd's Rep 555 .... 99, 269–70
GKN (Cwmbran) Ltd v Lloyd [1972] ICR 214 421
GKN Distributors Ltd v Tyne Tees Fabrication Ltd (1985) 50 P & CR 403 439
Glasbrook v Richardson (1874) 23 WR 51 433
Godbold v Mahmood [2005] EWHC 1002, [2006] PIQR Q5 166–67
Goddard v Midland Rly Co (1891) 8 TLR 126 486
Gold v Haringey Health Authority [1988] QB 481, [1987] 3 WLR 649 249–50
Golden Strait Corpn v Nippon Yusen Kubishika Kaisha, The Golden Victory [2007] UKHL 12,
   [2007] 2 AC 353 .... vii–viii, 38, 47, 174
Goldman v Hargrave [1967] 1 AC 645 45
Goldsoll v Goldman [1914] 2 Ch 603 .... 73, 230
Golfstraum, The *See* Anders Utkilens Rederi A/S v O/Y Lovisa Stevedoring Co A/B, The Golfstraum
Gondall v Dillon Newsagents Ltd [2001] RLR 221 325
Goodhart v Hyett (1883) 25 Ch D 182 467
Gorham v British Telecommunications plc [2000] 1 WLR 2129 233
Gorris v Scott (1874) LR 9 Exch 125 122–23
Gosling v Anderson (1972) 223 Estates Gazette 1743 225–26
Gough v Thorne [1966] 1 WLR 1387 133
Gouriet v Union of Post Office Workers [1978] AC 435 505
Govia Thameslink Railway Ltd v ASLEF [2016] EWHC 985 (QB) 478–79
Gracie (Owners) v Argentino (Owners), The Argentino (1889) 14 App Cas 519 .... 88–89, 215
Graham v Delderfield [1992] FSR 313 473
Graham v Dodds [1983] 1 WLR 808 .... 260, 261
Gran Gelato Ltd v Richcliff (Group) Ltd [1992] Ch 560 .... 137–38, 225–26
Grant v Dawkins [1973] 1 WLR 1406 437–38
Gravesham Borough Council v British Railways Board [1978] Ch 379 .... 416, 418, 431, 464, 465
Gray v Motor Accident Commission (1999) 73 ALJR 45 371
Gray v Thames Trains [2009] UKHL 33, [2009] 1 AC 1339 235–36
Greater Nottingham Co-operative Society Ltd v Cementation Piling and Foundations Ltd
   [1989] QB 71, [1988] 2 All ER 971 7
Green v Turner [1999] PNLR 28 .... 122–23, 124
Greene v Associated Newspapers Ltd [2004] EWCA Civ 1462, [2005] QB 972 479–80

Table of Cases

Greene v West Cheshire Rly Co (1871) LR 13 Eq 44. 416
Greenhill v Isle of Wight (Newport Junction) Rly Co (1871) 23 LT 885 .... 415, 428
Greenwich Healthcare NHS Trust v London and Quadrant Housing Trust [1998] 3 All ER 437 505
Greer v Alstons Engineering Sales and Services Ltd [2003] UKPC 46, (2003) 147 SJLB 783 503
Gregg v Scott [2005] UKHL 2, [2005] 2 AC 176 .... vii–viii, 52, 59–60, 61, 62–63
Gregg v Scott [2002] EWCA Civ 1471, [2003] Lloyd's Rep Med 105 67–68
Gregory v Kelly [1978] RTR 426 133
Grein v Imperial Airways Ltd [1937] 1 KB 50 256
Greta Holme, The *See* No 7 Steam Sand Pump Dredger (Owners) v Greta Holme (Owners), The Greta Holme
Grieves v FT Everard & Sons [2007] UKHL 39, [2008] 1 AC 281. 234
Griffith v Clay & Sons Ltd [1912] 2 Ch 291 221–22
Griffith v Spratley (1787) 1 Cox Eq Cas 383. 430
Griffiths v Williams (1995) Times, 24 November, CA 234, 284–85
Grobbelaar v News Group Newspapers Ltd [2002] UKHL 40, [2002] 1 WLR 3024 .... 443–44, 487, 503–4
Groom v Crocker [1939] 1 KB 194 .... 269, 277
Groom v Selby [2001] EWCA Civ 1522, [2002] PIQR P201 250–51
Grosvenor Hotel Co v Hamilton [1894] 2 QB 836 209
Grupo Torras SA v Al-Sabah (No 5) [2001] Lloyd's Rep Bank 36. 509–10
Guaranty Trust Co of New York v Hannay & Co [1915] 2 KB 536. 504
Guinness plc v Saunders [1990] 2 AC 663 .... 526, 527
Gulf Oil (GB) Ltd v Page [1987] Ch 327. 479
Gulati v MGN Ltd [2015] EWCA Civ 1291, [2017] QB 149 .... vii–viii, 284–85, 290–91, 525
Gull v Saunders (1913) 17 CLR 82. 194
Gunton v Richmond-upon-Thames London Borough Council [1981] Ch 448 419
Guppys (Bridport) Ltd v Brookling (1983) 269 Estates Gazette 846. 366
Guppys (Bridport) Ltd v James (1984) 269 Estates Gazette 846 .... 284–85, 360–61
Gurtner v Circuit [1968] 2 QB 587 .... 410–11, 429
GUS Property Management Ltd v Littlewoods Mail Order Stores Ltd 1982 SLT 533 203–4
Gwembe Valley Development Co Ltd v Koshy [2003] EWCA Civ 1048, [2004] 1 BCLC 131. ..... 512, 543, 544
GWK Ltd v Dunlop Rubber Co Ltd (1926) 42 TLR 376. .... 73, 272

H v Ministry of Defence [1991] 2 QB 103 274–75
H v S [2002] EWCA Civ 792, [2002] 3 WLR 1179 266–67
HOK Sport Ltd v Aintree Racecourse Co Ltd [2002] EWHC 3094 (TCC), [2003] Lloyd's Rep PN 148 122–23
Habib Bank Ltd v Habib Bank AG Zurich [1981] 1 WLR 1265. 487–88
Habton Farms v Nimmo [2003] EWCA Civ 68, [2004] QB. 173, 188
Hackney London Borough v Adams [2003] IRLR 402 289–90
Hadley v Baxendale (1854) 9 Exch 341 .... 91, 92, 93–95, 97, 98, 99, 100, 101, 102–3, 104, 296–97
Hadlow v Peterborough CC [2011] EWCA Civ 1329. 87
Hadmor Productions Ltd v Hamilton [1982] ICR 114. 478
Hale v London Underground Ltd [1993] PIQR Q30. 235–36
Halifax Building Society v Thomas [1996] Ch 217 349
Hall v Meyrick [1957] 2 QB 455. 65
Hall (J and E) Ltd v Barclay [1937] 3 All ER 620, CA 220
Hall (R and H) Ltd and W H Pim Junior & Co's Arbitration, Re (1928) 139 LT 50 .... 192, 205–6
Hall & Co Ltd v Pearlberg [1956] 1 WLR 244 .... 182, 221
Hall Ltd v Barclay [1937] 3 All ER 620 192
Halsey v Esso Petroleum Co Ltd [1961] 1 WLR 683. 447–48
Halsey v Milton Keynes General NHS Trust [2004] EWCA Civ 576, [2004] 1 WLR 3002. 53
Halvanon Insurance Co v Central Reinsurance Corpn [1984] 2 Lloyd's Rep 420 167–68
Hamilton v Open Window Bakery Ltd (2004) 235 DLR (4th) 193. 69–70
Hamilton Jones v David & Snape [2003] EWHC 3147 (Ch), [2004] 1 WLR 924 .... 279, 286–87
Hammond & Co v Bussey (1887) 20 QBD 79 205–6
Hampstead and Suburban Properties Ltd v Diomedous [1969] 1 Ch 248. 456
Hanson v Radcliffe UDC [1922] 2 Ch 490 504
Harakas v Baltic Mercantile and Shipping Exchange Ltd [1982] 2 All ER 701 479
Harbutt's Plasticine Ltd v Wayne Tank and Pump Co Ltd [1970] 1 QB 447 .... 205, 207–8, 217–18
Harding v Wealands [2006] UKHL 32, [2007] 2 AC 1. 180
Hardman v Amin (2000) 59 BMLR 58, [2000] Lloyd's Med Rep 448. 250–51

Hardwick v Hudson [1999] 1 WLR 1770 241
Harland & Wolff plc v McIntyre [2006] EWCA Civ 287, [2006] 1 WLR 2577 266
Harris v Digital Pulse Pty Ltd (2003) 197 ALR 626, NSWCA 537
Harris v Empress Motors Ltd [1984] 1 WLR 212 261
Harris v Empress Motors Ltd [1983] 1 WLR 65. 248–49
Harris (infant) v Harris [1973] 1 Lloyd's Rep 445 247
Harrison v Duke of Rutland [1893] 1 QB 142 506
Harrison v Good (1871) LR 11 Eq 338 456
Harrow London Borough Council v Donohue [1995] 1 EGLR 257 463
Hart v EP Dutton & Co Inc 93 NYS 2d 871 (1949). 339–40
Hart v Emelkirk Ltd [1983] 1 WLR 1289 491–92
Hartle v Laceys [1999] Lloyd's Rep PN 315 296–97
Hartog v Colin and Shields [1939] 3 All ER 566 430
Harvela Investments Ltd v Royal Trust Co of Canada (CI) Ltd [1986] AC 207,
  [1985] 2 All ER 966. .... 407, 438–39
Hasham v Zenab [1960] AC 316 .... 317, 401
Hassall v Secretary of State for Social Security [1995] 1 WLR 812 157
Hatton v Sutherland [2002] EWCA Civ 76, [2002] 2 All ER 1 .... 234, 276
Haugesund Kommune v Depfa ACS Bank (No 2) [2011] EWCA Civ 33, [2011] 3 All ER 655 122–23
Haviland v Long [1952] 2 QB 80 199
Haward v Fawcetts [2006] UKHL 9, [2006] 1 WLR 682. 314
Hawkins v McGee 84 NH 114, 146A 641 (1929). 39
Haxton v Philips Electronics UK Ltd [2014] EWCA Civ 4, [2014] 1 WLR 2721 243
Hay v Hughes [1975] QB 790, [1975] 2 WLR 34. .... 258–59, 265–66
Hayden v Hayden [1992] 1 WLR 986 266
Hayes v James & Charles Dodd (a firm) [1990] 2 All ER 815 .... 281, 282–83
Hayward v Zurich Insurance Co Ltd [2016] UKSC 48, [2017] AC 142 51
Heath v Keys (1984) Times, 28 May 207
Hebridean Coast, The *See* Lord Citrine, The (Owners) v Hebridean Coast (Owners),
  The Hebridean Coast
Hedley Byrne & Co Ltd v Heller & Partners Ltd [1964] AC 465, [1963] 2 All ER 575,
  [1963] 3 WLR 101 .... 6–7, 222, 225
Heil v Rankin [2001] QB 272 .... 36, 37, 171, 235–36
Heil v Rankin (No 2) [2001] PIQR Q16, CA 53
Henderson v All Around the World Recordings Limited [2014] EWHC 3087 (IEPC) 284–85
Henderson v Merrett Syndicates [1995] 2 AC 145, [1994] 3 WLR 761 .... 6–7, 105–6,
                                                                      141–42, 144, 232, 233, 311
Henry v Henry [2010] UKPC 3, [2010] 1 All ER 988. 525–26
Heranger, SS (Owners) v SS Diamond (Owners) [1939] AC 94 85–86
Herbage v Pressdram Ltd [1984] 1 WLR 1160. 479
Herbert Clayton v Oliver [1930] AC 209 269
Hercy v Birch (1804) 9 Ves 357 409
Heron II, The *See* Koufos v C Czarnikow Ltd, The Heron II
Herring v Ministry of Defence [2003] EWCA Civ 528, [2004] 1 All ER 44. 244
Herrmann v Withers LLP [2012] EWHC 1492 (Ch), [2012] PNLR 28 131–32
Hewison v Meridian Shipping PTE [2002] EWCA Civ 1821, [2003] PIQR P252. .... 83, 238
Hewitt's Contract, Re [1963] 1 WLR 1298 438–39
Heywood v Wellers [1976] QB 446 .... 278, 282–83
Hicks v Chief Constable of the South Yorkshire Police [1992] 1 All ER 690. .... 254, 285–86
Hill v CA Parsons & Co Ltd [1972] Ch 305 .... 420, 421–22, 426, 456
Hill v Debenham Tewson & Chinnock (1958) 171 Estates Gazette 835. 279
Hill Samuel & Co Ltd v Littaur [1985] NLJ Rep 57. 443
Hillesden Securities Ltd v Ryjak Ltd [1983] 1 WLR 959. 220
Hinz v Berry [1970] 2 QB 40 .... 234, 285–86
Hipkiss v Gaydon [1961] CLY 9042. 279
Hobbs v London and South Western Rly Co (1875) LR 10 QB 111 .... 277, 279, 282–83
Hodge v Clifford Cowling & Co [1990] 2 EGLR 89 149
Hodgson v Duce (1856) 28 LTOS 155. 408–9
Hodgson v Trapp [1989] AC 807 .... 156, 157, 158, 184, 239–40, 245
Hoenig v Isaacs [1952] 2 All ER 176 382
Hoffberger v Ascot International Bloodstock Bureau Ltd (1976) 120 Sol Jo 130 131

Table of Cases

Hoffman v Sofaer [1982] 1 WLR 1350 .... 181, 242
Hoffmann-La Roche & Co AG v Secretary of State for Trade and Industry [1975] AC 295......... 469–70
Hogan v Bentinck West Hartley Collieries (Owners) Ltd [1949] 1 All ER 588.................... 107–8
Hohler v Aston [1920] 2 Ch 420 410
Holden v Chief Constable of Lancashire [1987] QB 380 362–63
Holden Ltd v Bostock & Co Ltd (1902) 18 TLR 317 130
Hollebone v Midhurst and Fernhurst Builders Ltd and Eastman and White of Midhurst Ltd
  [1968] 1 Lloyd's Rep 38 .... 207, 217–18
Holley v Smyth [1998] QB 726.. 479
Hollister Inc v Medik Ostomy Supplies Ltd [2012] EWCA Civ 1419,
  [2013] Bus LR 428... 228, 341–42, 344, 345–46
Holtham v Metropolitan Police Comr (1987) The Times, 28 November........................... 304
Home Office v Dorset Yacht Co Ltd [1970] AC 1004 .... 45, 110, 112, 113
Hooper v Bromet (1904) 90 LT 234, CA.. 486
Hooper v Oates [2013] EWCA Civ 91, [2014] Ch 287 173
Hooper v Rogers [1975] Ch 43.. 318, 467–68
Hope v Walter [1900] 1 Ch 257 431
Hopkins v Norcros plc [1994] ICR 11.. 158–59
Horkulak v Cantor Fitzgerald International [2004] EWCA Civ 1287, [2005] ICR 402 71
Horne v Midland Rly Co (1873) LR 8 CP 131 .... 98, 99
Horsfall v Haywards (a firm) [1999] 1 FLR 1182... 129
Horsler v Zorro [1975] Ch 302... 316, 439
Horton v Caplin Contracts Ltd [2002] EWCA Civ 1604, [2003] PIQR P180 112
Hospital Products Ltd v United States Surgical Corpn (1985) 156 CLR 41...................... 355, 526
Hotel Services Ltd v Hilton International Hotels (UK) Ltd [2000] 1 All ER (Comm) 750 93
Hotson v East Berkshire Area Health Authority [1987] AC 750...................... 52, 61, 62–63
Hounslow London Borough Council v Twickenham Garden Developments Ltd
  [1971] Ch 233 .... 384, 481–83
Housecroft v Burnett [1986] 1 All ER 332, CA 171, 240–41, 247, 249
Howard v Hopkyns (1742) 2 Atk 371 436–37
Howard Perry Ltd v British Railways Board [1980] 1 WLR 1375 .... 405, 406, 494–95, 496
Howitt v Heads [1973] QB 64.. 261–62
Howlett, Re, [1949] Ch 767.. 487–88
Hubbard v Pitt [1976] QB 142.. 474, 475
Hubbard v Vosper [1972] 2 QB 84... 469–70, 487, 539
Huckle v Money (1763) 2 Wils 205 362
Hughes v Lord Advocate [1963] AC 837... 87
Hughes v McKeown [1985] 1 WLR 963 .... 235–36, 247
Hughes v Southwark London Borough Council [1988] IRLR 55 422
Hungerfords v Walker (1989) 171 CLR 125 297
Hunt v Hourmont [1983] CLY 983 278
Hunt v Severs [1994] 2 AC 350 .... 158, 168–69, 170, 212–13, 214–15, 240–43, 266–67
Hunter v Butler [1996] RTR 396 .... 83, 259
Hunter v Canary Wharf Ltd [1997] AC 655, [1997] 2 WLR 684..................... 283–86, 291
Hurditch v Sheffield Health Authority [1989] QB 562 165
Hussain v Hussain [1986] Fam 134 440
Hussain v New Taplow Paper Mills Ltd [1988] AC 514 .... 158, 159–60
Hussey v Eels [1990] 2 QB 227... 149–50, 151–52
Hutcheson v Popdog Ltd (News Group Newspapers Ltd, third party) [2011] EWCA Civ 1580,
  [2012] 1 WLR 782... 441
Huxham v Llewellyn (1873) 28 LT 577 433
Hydraulic Engineering Co Ltd v McHaffie, Goslett & Co (1878) 4 QBD 670 205–6
Hyundai Heavy Industries Co Ltd v Papadopoulos [1980] 1 WLR 1129.......................... 382

IBL Ltd v Coussens [1991] 2 All ER 133, CA... 175–76
Ibeneweka v Egbuna [1964] 1 WLR 219.. 504
ICE Architects Ltd v Empowering People Inspiring Communities [2018] EWHC 281 (QB)........... 382
Ichard v Frangoulis [1977] 2 All ER 461... 235–36
IM Properties plc v Cape and Dalgleish (a firm) [1999] QB 297 301
Imerman v Tchenguiz [2010] EWCA Civ 908, [2011] WLR 592 538–39
Imperial Gas Light and Coke Co v Broadbent (1859) 7 HL Cas 600 445

India (Republic) v India Steamship Co Ltd, The Indian Endurance, The Indian Grace [1993] AC 410 163
Industrial Development Consultants Ltd v Cooley [1972] 1 WLR 443, 116 526
Industrial Furnaces Ltd v Reaves [1970] RPC 605 .... 498, 541
Inniss v Attorney-General for St Christopher and Nevis [2008] UKPC 42 363–64
Instil Group Inc v Zahoor [2003] EWHC 165 (Ch), [2003] 2 All ER 252 538–39
Inter Export LLC v Lasytsya [2018] EWCA Civ 2068 224
Interactive Technology Corporation Ltd v Ferster [2018] EWCA Civ 1594 .... vii–viii, 520
Interfirm Comparison (Australia) Pty Ltd v Law Society of New South Wales [1977] RPC 137 521
International Energy Group Ltd v Zurich Insurance plc UK Branch [2015] UKSC 33, [2016] AC 509 57
International General Electric Co of New York Ltd v Customs and Excise Comrs [1962] Ch 784 506
International Military Services Ltd v Capital and Counties plc [1982] 1 WLR 575 305
International Minerals and Chemical Corpn v Karl O Helm AG [1986] 1 Lloyd's Rep 81 ...... 93, 179, 296–97
Invercargill City Council v Hamlin [1996] AC 624 313
Inverugie Investments Ltd v Hackett [1995] 1 WLR 713 .... 325, 327–28
Inwards v Baker [1965] 2 QB 29 538
Ionic Bay, The See Mills v Hassall
Iqbal v Whipps Cross University Hospital NHS Trust [2007] EWCA Civ 1190, [2008] PIQR P9 248
Irani v Southampton and South West Hampshire Health Authority
 [1985] ICR 590 .... 421, 422–23, 425, 426
IRC v Hambrook [1956] 2 QB 641 154–55
Iron Trades Mutual Insurance Co Ltd v JK Buckenham Ltd [1990] 1 All ER 808,
 [1989] 2 Lloyd's Rep 85 .... 8, 313–14
Irvine v Talksport Ltd [2003] EWCA Civ 423, [2003] 2 All ER (Comm) 141 229
Isabella Shipowner SA v Shagang Shipping Co Ltd, The Aquafaith [2012] EWHC 1077
 (Comm), [2012] 2 Lloyd's Rep 61 .... vii–viii, 386
Isenberg v East India House Estate Co Ltd (1863) 3 De GJ & Sm 263 463
Islamic Republic of Iran Shipping Lines v Denby [1987] 1 Lloyd's Rep 367 .... 529, 530–31
Islamic Republic of Iran Shipping Lines v Ierax Shipping Co of Panama, The Forum Craftsman
 [1991] 1 Lloyd's Rep 81 98
Island Records Ltd v Tring International plc [1996] 1 WLR 1256 345–46
Islander Trucking Ltd & Hogg Robinson v Gardner Mountain (Marine) Ltd [1990] 1 All ER 826 8
Italian State Rlys v Minnehaha (1921) 6 Ll L Rep 12 212

J (A Minor), Re, [1993] Fam 15 475
JEB Fasteners Ltd v Marks, Bloom & Co [1983] 1 All ER 583 52
Jackson v Horizon Holidays Ltd [1975] 1 WLR 1468 .... 201, 278
Jackson v Murray [2015] UKSC 5, [2015] 2 All ER 805 .... 134, 135
Jackson v Normanby Brick Co [1899] 1 Ch 438 442
Jackson v Royal Bank of Scotland plc [2005] UKHL 3, [2005] 1 WLR 377 .... 64, 96, 105
Jaggard v Sawyer [1995] 1 WLR 269 .... 221–22, 315–16, 317, 318, 321–22, 327, 446, 456
Jakeman v South West Thames RHA [1990] IRLR 62 .... 481–82, 483
Jameel v Wall Street Journal Europe SPRL [2003] EWHC 2945 (QB), [2004] 2 All ER 92 73
James Finlay & Co Ltd v NV Kwik Hoo Tong [1929] 1 KB 400 129
Jameson v Central Electricity Generating Board (Babcock Energy, third party) [2000] 1 AC 455,
 [1999] 2 WLR 141 257–58
Janciuk v Winerite Ltd [1998] IRLR 63, EAT 69–70
Jaques v Millar (1877) 6 Ch D 153 437
Jarvis v Swans Tours Ltd [1973] QB 233 .... 277, 278, 279–80
Jaura v Ahmed [2002] EWCA Civ 210 305
Jayes v IMI (Kynoch) Ltd [1985] ICR 155 113–14
Jefford v Gee [1970] 2 QB 130 .... 234–35, 260, 302, 304–5, 306
Jenkins v Richard Thomas and Baldwins Ltd [1966] 1 WLR 476 170
Jennings v Rice [2002] EWCA Civ 159, [2003] 1 P & CR 8 .... 511–12, 525–26
Jeune v Queens Cross Properties Ltd [1974] Ch 97 416
JIH v News Group Newspapers Ltd [2011] EWCA Civ 42, [2011] 1 WLR 1645 441
Jobling v Associated Dairies Ltd [1982] AC 794 .... 54, 55, 254
Jobson v Johnson [1989] 1 WLR 1026 .... 391, 394
Jockey Club v Buffham [2002] EWHC 1866 (QB), [2003] QB 462 .... 441, 538–39
John v MGN Ltd [1997] QB 586, [1996] 3 WLR 593 .... 274, 288–89, 364–65, 372
John D Wood & Co Ltd v Knatchbull [2002] EWHC 2822 (QB), [2003] 08 EG 131 65
John Grimes Partnership Ltd v Gubbins [2013] EWCA Civ 37, [2013] PNLR 17 103

Table of Cases

John Trenberth Ltd v National Westminster Bank Ltd (1980) 39 P & CR 104 .... 447–48, 481–82
Johnson v Agnew [1980] AC 367, [1979] 1 All ER 883. ... 14, 47, 173, 174–75, 317, 319, 403, 434, 437, 439
Johnson v Gore Wood & Co (a firm) [2002] 2 AC 1 .... 187, 281, 282–83, 286–87
Johnson v Shrewsbury and Birmingham Rly Co (1853) 3 De GM & G 914 419
Johnson v Unisys Ltd [2001] UKHL 13, [2003] 1 AC 518 .... 270–71, 282
Johnson v Wyatt (1863) 2 De GJ & Sm 18 488
Johnstone v Bloomsbury Health Authority [1992] QB 333, [1991] 2 All ER 293 7
Jolley v Sutton London Borough Council [2000] 1 WLR 1082 87
Jones v Gooday (1841) 8 M & W 146 208
Jones v Griffith [1969] 1 WLR 795 66
Jones v Gwent County Council [1992] IRLR 521 422
Jones v Heavens (1877) 4 Ch D 636 462
Jones v Jones [1985] QB 704, [1984] 3 WLR 862 243
Jones v Lee and Guilding [1980] ICR 310 421
Jones v Livox Quarries Ltd [1952] 2 QB 608 .... 133, 134
Jones v Port of London Authority [1954] 1 Lloyd's Rep 489 209–10
Jones v Ruth [2011] EWCA Civ 804, [2012] 1 All ER 490 66
Jones v Stones [1999] 1 WLR 1739 487–88
Jones v Stroud District Council [1986] 1 WLR 1141 .... 208, 212–14
Joseph v National Magazine Co Ltd [1959] Ch 14 .... 269, 428
Joyce v Yeomans [1981] 1 WLR 549 .... 248, 249
Joyner v Weeks [1891] 2 QB 31 199
JSC BTA Bank v Ablyazov [2013] EWHC 867 (Comm) 300
JXL v Britton [2014] EWHC 2571 (QB) 234, 284–85

Kaines (UK) Ltd v Osterreichische Warrenhandelsgesellschaft Austrowaren Gesellschaft
  mbH (formerly CGL Handelsgesellschaft mbH) [1993] 2 Lloyd's Rep 1 132
Kandalla v British Airways Board [1981] QB 158, [1980] 2 WLR 730 259–60
Karagozlu v Commissioner of Police of the Metropolis [2006] EWCA Civ 1691,
  [2007] 1 WLR 1881 283–84
Kars v Kars (1996) 71 ALJR 107 240–41
Kasapis v Laimos Bros [1959] 2 Lloyd's Rep 378 45
Kaye v Robertson [1991] FSR 62 479
Kaye Steam Navigation Co Ltd v W & R Barnett Ltd (1932) 48 TLR 440 69
Keays v Honda Canada Inc (2008) 294 DLR (4th) 577 377–78
Keech v Sandford (1726) Sel Cas Ch 61 .... 526, 531
Keenan v Handley (1864) 2 De GJ & Sm 283 410
Kelk v Pearson (1871) 6 Ch App 809 464
Kelly v Dawes (1990) Times, 27 September 166
Kelly v Sherlock (1866) LR 1 QB 686 503–4
Kelsen v Imperial Tobacco Co (of Great Britain and Ireland) Ltd [1957] 2 QB 334 .... 462, 463
Kemp v Intasun Holidays Ltd [1987] 2 FTLR 234 96
Kendall (Henry) & Sons (a firm) v William Lillico & Sons Ltd [1969] 2 AC 31 205–6
Kennard v Cory Bros & Co Ltd [1922] 2 Ch 1 .... 463, 464–65
Kennaway v Thompson [1981] QB 88 .... 445, 447, 448
Kennedy v Bryan (1984) Times, 3 May 238
Kenny v Good Pty Ltd v MGICA (1992) Ltd (1999) 163 ALR 611 122
Kenny v Preen [1963] 1 QB 499 360–61
Kerby v Redbridge Health Authority [1993] 4 Med LR 178, [1994] PIQR Q1 .... 252–53, 285–86
Kerry v England [1898] AC 742 55
Ketley v Gooden (1997) 73 P & CR 305 .... 463, 489
Khakshouri v Jiminez [2017] EWHC 3392 (QB) 175
Khashoggi v IPC Magazines Ltd [1986] 3 All ER 577 479
Khodaparast v Shad [2000] 1 All ER 545 284–85
Kiam v MGN Ltd [2002] EWCA Civ 43, [2003] QB 281 274
Kingston-upon-Hull City Council v Dunnachie (No 3) [2003] IRLR 843, EAT 244
Kirchner & Co v Gruban [1909] 1 Ch 413 458
Kirklees Metropolitan Borough Council v Wickes Building Supplies Ltd [1993] AC 227 469–70
Kitchen v Royal Air Forces Association [1958] 1 WLR 563 64
Kitetechnology BV v Unicor GmbH Plastmaschinen [1995] FSR 765 13
Knauer v Ministry of Justice [2016] UKSC 9, [2016] AC 908 .... vii–viii, 38, 261

Knightley v Johns [1982] 1 WLR 349 111–12
Knutson v Farr (1984) 12 DLR (4th) 658, BCCA273 237
Köbler v Austria: C-224/01 [2004] QB 848, [2004] 2 WLR 976, ECJ 15
Kotke v Saffarini [2005] EWCA Civ 221, [2005] PIQR P26..................................... 256–57
Koufos v C Czarnikow Ltd, The Heron II [1969] 1 AC 350 .... 38, 89, 92, 94–95, 98, 99, 101–2, 105, 191, 194–95
Kpohraror v Woolwich Building Society [1996] 4 All ER 119................................... 93, 269
Kralj v McGrath [1986] 1 All ER 54... 234, 252–53, 287–88
Kuddus v Chief Constable of Leicestershire Constabulary [2001] UKHL 29, [2002] 2 AC 122 .... 24, 361, 362, 366, 367–70, 373, 376, 377, 536, 537
Kurt A Becher GmbH v Roplak Enterprises, The World Navigator [1991] 2 Lloyd's Rep 23, CA 69
Kuwait Airways Corpn v Iraqi Airways Co (Nos 4 & 5) [2002] UKHL 19, [2002] 2 AC 883 ..... 55, 90, 220–21
Kuwait Airways Corpn v Kuwait Insurance Co SAK (No 2) [2000] 1 All ER (Comm) 972 304–5
Kuwait Oil Tanker Co SAK v Al Bader [2000] 2 All ER (Comm) 271 542

LAC Minerals Ltd v International Corona Resources Ltd (1989) 61 DLR (4th) 14 .... 533, 534
L E Jones (Insurance Brokers) Ltd v Portsmouth City Council [2002] EWCA Civ 1723, [2003] 1 WLR 427.. 130
Ladd v Marshall [1954] 1 WLR 1489... 169
Lagden v O'Connor [2003] UKHL 64, [2004] 1 AC 1067 .... 84, 145–46, 214, 296
Lake v Bayliss [1974] 1 WLR 1073.. 355, 357–58
Lamare v Dixon (1873) LR 6 HL 414.. 432
Lamb v Camden London Borough Council [1981] QB 625 .... 107, 113
Lambert v Lewis [1982] AC 225... 114–15
Lamine v Dorrell (1705) 2 Ld Raym 1216 340
Lamkins v International Harvester Co 182 SW 2d 203 (1994) 97
Lancashire County Council v Municipal Mutual Insurance Ltd [1997] QB 897, [1996] 3 WLR 493 373
Land Hessen v Gray and Gerrish (31 July 1998, unreported) 155
Land Rover Group Ltd v UPF (UK) Ltd (in receivership) [2002] EWHC 3183 (QB), [2003] 2 BCLC 222 482
Lane v O'Brien Homes Ltd [2004] EWHC 303 (QB) 321–22, 357–58
Landfast (Anglia) Ltd v Cameron Taylor One Ltd [2008] EWHC 343 (TCC) 203–4
Langen and Wind Ltd v Bell [1972] Ch 685.. 407, 438
Langford v Hebran [2001] EWCA Civ 361, [2001] PIQR Q13 66
Lansing Linde Ltd v Kerr [1991] 1 WLR 251 476
Lash Atlantico, The [1987] 2 Lloyd's Rep 114, CA... 181
Lauritzencool AB v Lady Navigation In c[2005] EWCA Civ 579, [2005] 1 WLR 3686 .... vii–viii, 459
Lavarack v Woods of Colchester Ltd [1967] 1 QB 278 .... 69, 70–71, 72, 149, 151
Lawrence v Chief Constable of Staffordshire [2000] PIQR Q349 307
Lawrence v Horton (1890) 59 LJ Ch 440.. 462
Lawrence David Ltd v Ashton [1991] 1 All ER 385.. 476, 480
Law Society v Sephton & Co [2006] UKHL 22, [2006] 2 AC 543................................. 311
Laws v Florinplace Ltd [1981] 1 All ER 659 472
Lazard Bros & Co Ltd v Fairfield Properties Co (Mayfair) Ltd (1977) 121 Sol Jo 793 433–34
Lazenby Garages Ltd v Wright [1976] 1 WLR 459 196
LE Jones (Insurance Brokers) Ltd v Portsmouth City Council [2002] EWCA Civ 1723, [2003] 1 WLR 427... 85–86
League Against Cruel Sports Ltd v Scott [1986] QB 240, [1985] 2 All ER 489 445–46
Leakey v National Trust for Places of Historic Interest or Natural Beauty [1980] QB 485 45
Lee v Taunton and Somerset NHS Trust [2001] 1 FLR 419 250–51
Leeds Industrial Co-operative Society Ltd v Slack [1924] AC 851 318
Legends Live Ltd v Harrison [2016] EWHC 1938 (QB).. 489
Legg v Inner London Education Authority [1972] 1 WLR 1245.................................. 490
Leidig v Intervention Board for Agricultural Produce [2000] Lloyd's Rep PN 144, CA 122–23
Leigh and Sillavan Ltd v Aliakmon Shipping Co Ltd, The Aliakmon [1986] AC 785, [1986] 2 All ER 145, [1986] 2 WLR 902... 6–7, 231
Leisure Data v Bell [1988] FSR 367 .... 481–82, 483
Lejonvarn v Burgess [2017] EWCA Civ 254, [2017] PNLR 25 6–7
Lemos v Kennedy Leigh Development Co Ltd (1961) 105 Sol Jo 178 468
Leney & Sons Ltd v Callingham and Thompson [1908] 1 KB 79 491–92
Lever v Goodwin (1887) 36 Ch D 1...341–42, 343

Levi v Bates [2015] EWCA Civ 206, [2016] QB 91 284–85
Levi v Gordon, 12 November 1992 (unreported CA)...287–88
Ley v Hamilton (1935) 153 LT 384, HL... 73
Libertarian Investments Ltd v Hall [2013] HKCFA 93, [2014] 1 HKC 368 517–18
Liesbosch, The *See* Owners of the Dredger Liesbosch v Owners of SS Edison
Liffen v Watson [1940] 1 KB 556.. 159
Lillywhite v Trimmer (1867) 36 LJ Ch 525..445–46
Lim Poh Choo v Camden and Islington Area Health Authority [1980] AC 174 ....38, 163–64, 170,
235, 237, 239–40, 245
Linden Gardens Trust Ltd v Lenesta Sludge Disposals Ltd [1994] 1 AC 85....................201, 202–3
Lindsay Petroleum Co v Hurd (1874) LR 5 PC 221 ....433, 489
Lingen v Simpson (1824) 1 Sim & St 600 404
Lion Laboratories Ltd v Evans [1985] QB 526.. 539
Lion Nathan Ltd v C-C Bottlers Ltd [1996] 1 WLR 1438.......................................71–72
Lister v Hodgson (1867) LR 4 Eq 30 429
Lister & Co v Stubbs (1890) 45 Ch D 1 530–32
Litvinoff v Kent (1918) 34 TLR 298... 486
Livingstone v Rawyards Coal Co (1880) 5 App Cas 25... 38
Llandudno UDC v Woods [1899] 2 Ch 705..445–46, 506
Llanover, The [1947] P 80 210–11
Lloyd v Stanbury [1971] 1 WLR 535..77, 81
Lloyds and Scottish Finance Ltd v Modern Cars and Caravans (Kingston) Ltd [1966] 1 QB 764 131
Lloyd's Bank plc v Crosse and Crosse [2001] PNLR 34 122–23
LNS v Persons Unknown [2010] EWHC 119 (QB), [2010] EMLR 16 479–80
Locabail International Finance Ltd v Agroexport, The Sea Hawk [1986] 1 WLR 657,
[1986] 1 All ER 901..481–82, 483
Lodder v Slowey [1904] AC 442..352–53
Loftus, Re [2006] EWCA Civ 1124, [2007] 1 WLR 1124 ....490, 544
Logicrose Ltd v Southend United Football Club Ltd [1988] 1 WLR 1256...................... 529
Lombard North Central plc v Butterworth [1987] QB 527 ....70, 398
London and South of England Building Society v Stone [1983] 1 WLR 1242..................129, 130
London, Chatham and Dover Rly Co v South Eastern Rly Co [1893] AC 429 .... 179–80, 296–99
London Corpn, The [1935] P 70 212
London Joint Stock Bank v Macmillan and Arthur [1918] AC 777 109–10
Long v Bowring (1864) 33 Beav 585 436–37
Longden v British Coal Corpn [1998] AC 653..158, 239
Lonrho plc v Fayed (No 5) [1993] 1 WLR 1489...272, 285–86
Loomis v Rohan (1974) 46 DLR (3d) 423, BCSC 371
Lord v Pacific Steam Navigation Co Ltd, The Oropesa [1943] P 32 112
Lord Citrine, The (Owners) v Hebridean Coast (Owners), The Hebridean Coast [1961] AC 545......209, 216
Lordsvale Finance plc v Bank of Zambia [1996] QB 752.. 391
Lowe v Guise [2002] EWCA Civ 197, [2002] QB 1369.. 242
Lowther v Lord Lowther (1806) 13 Ves 95 494
LSREF III Wight Ltd v Gateley LLP [2016] EWCA Civ 359, [2016] PNLR 21 ....122–23, 130
Lubren v London Borough of Lambeth (1987) 20 HLR 165 279–80
Luganda v Service Hotels Ltd [1969] 2 Ch 209 ....416–17, 482
Lumley v Wagner (1852) 21 LJ Ch 898.. 457, 458, 459–60
Lunn Poly Ltd v Liverpool and Lancashire Properties Ltd [2006] EWCA Civ 430,
[2006] 2 EGLR 29..321–22
Lytton v Great Northern Rly Co (1856) 2 K & J 394.. 435

M v Home Office [1994] 1 AC 377 440–41
M (H) v M (K) (1992) 96 DLR (4th) 289 512
McAll v Brooks [1984] RTR 99, CA 214–15
McAuley v London Transport Executive [1957] 2 Lloyd's Rep 500 128
McCall v Abelesz [1976] QB 585..279–80
McCallion v Dodd [1966] NZLR 710... 45
McCamley v Cammell Laird Shipbuilders Ltd [1990] 1 WLR 963..............................159–60
McCann v Sheppard [1973] 2 All ER 881... 248
McCarey v Associated Newspapers Ltd (No 2) [1965] 2 QB 86, [1965] 2 WLR 45 .... 272, 273, 284–85
McClaren v Home Office [1990] ICR 824...424–25

McClaren v News Group Newspapers Ltd [2012] EWHC 2466, [2012] EMLR 33 479
Macclesfield (Earl) v Davies (1814) 3 Ves & B 16 494
McConnel v Wright [1903] 1 Ch 546 . . . . .224, 226–27
McConnell v Police Authority for Northern Ireland [1997] IRLR 625. 287–88
Mcdonald Estate v Martin [1995] CCL 1142 (Man CA) 537
McFarlane v Tayside Health Board [2000] 2 AC 59, [1999] 3 WLR 1301 . . . . .250–51, 252
McGhee v National Coal Board [1973] 1 WLR 1 . . . . .56, 57, 62–63
McKenzie v McDonald [1927] VLR 134. 511–12
McKew v Holland and Hannen and Cubitts (Scotland) Ltd [1969] 3 All ER 1621. . . . . .114, 117
McLeish v Amoo-Gottfried & Co (1993) 137 Sol Jo LB 204 278
McLoughlin v O'Brian [1983] 1 AC 410. . . . . .234, 285–86
McManus v Beckham [2002] EWCA Civ 939, [2002] 1 WLR 2982 112
McMillan v Singh (1984) 17 HLR 120. . . . . 284–85, 361, 365
McNally v Welltrade International Ltd [1978] IRLR 497 225–26
McRae v Commonwealth Disposals Commission (1950) 84 CLR 377 76–77
Maersk Colombo, The See Southampton Container Terminals Ltd v Schiffahrts-Gesellschaft
    Hansa Australia MBH & Co, The Maersk Colombo
Mafo v Adams [1970] 1 QB 548. . . . . 283–84, 368–69
Magrane v Archbold (1813) 1 Dow 107 436–37
Maharaj v A-G of Trinidad and Tobago (No 2) [1979] AC 385. 22–23
Mahesan S/O Thambiah v Malaysia Government Officers' Co-operative Housing Society Ltd
    [1979] AC 374 . . . . .345–46, 529
Mahoney v Purnell [1996] 3 All ER 61, [1997] 1 FLR 612. 12
Main v Giamborne & Law [2017] EWCA Civ 1193, [2018] PNLR 2 . . . . vii–viii, 122–23, 519
Maira, The See National Bank of Greece SA v Pinios Shipping Co, The Maira
Maira, The (No 3) See National Bank of Greece SA v Pinios Shipping Co and George Dionysios
    Tsitsilianis, The Maira (No 3)
Makanjuola v Metropolitan Police Comr (1989) Times, 8 August 362–63
Malhotra v Choudhury [1980] Ch 52 . . . . 176, 315–16, 317
Malik v BCCI SA (in liquidation) [1998] AC 20 270–71
Malins v Freeman (1836) 2 Keen 25 430
Mallett v McMonagle [1970] AC 166 59
Malloch v Aberdeen Corpn [1971] 1 WLR 1578. 423
Malone v Rowan [1984] 3 All ER 402 261
Malyon v Lawrence Messer & Co [1968] 2 Lloyd's Rep 539. 234
Malyon v Plummer [1964] 1 QB 330, [1963] 2 WLR 1213 259
Manners v Pearson & Son [1898] 1 Ch 581 177
Manson v Associated Newspapers Ltd [1965] 1 WLR 1038. 364–65
Manus, Akt v R J Fullwood and Bland Ltd (1954) 71 RPC 243. 228–29
Maratha Envoy, The See Federal Commerce and Navigation Co Ltd v Tradax Export SA,
    The Maratha Envoy
Marathon Asset Management LLP v Seddon [2017] EWHC 300 (Comm),
    [2017] ICR 791 . . . . 321–22, 326, 329–30, 524
Marbé v George Edwardes (Daly's Theatre) Ltd [1928] 1 KB 269. . . . . .269, 273
Marcic v Thames Water Utilities Ltd [2003] UKHL 66, [2004] 2 AC 42 318–19
Marcic v Thames Water Utilities Ltd (No 2) [2002] QB 1003, [2002] 2 WLR 1000 318–19
Marco Productions Ltd v Pagola [1945] KB 111 . . . . .457, 459–60
Marcus v Myers and Davis (1895) 11 TLR 327 269
Maredelanto Cia Naviera SA v Bergbau-Handel GmbH, The Mihalis Angelos [1971] 1 QB 164 73
Mareva Cia Naviera SA v International Bulkcarriers SA, The Mareva [1975] 2 Lloyd's Rep 509 485
Marine Star, The See Coastal (Bermuda) Petroleum Ltd v VTT Vulcan Petroleum SA (No 2),
    The Marine Star
Marpessa, The, See Mersey Docks and Harbour Board v Marpessa (Owners)
Marsh v National Autistic Society [1993] ICR 453 . . . . .419, 422–23
Martin v Benson [1927] 1 KB 771 503–4
Martins v Choudhary [2007] EWCA Civ 1379, [2008] 1 WLR 617 287–88
Maskell v Ivory [1970] Ch 502 403
Mason v Clarke [1954] 1 QB 460. 432
Mathew, The See Cosemar SA v Marimarna Shipping Co Ltd, The Mathew
Matthews v Kuwait Bechtel Corpn [1959] 2 QB 57. 234
Mattocks v Mann [1993] RTR 13. . . . . .130, 145

Table of Cases

Meade v London Borough of Haringey [1979] 1 WLR 637 ... 483
Meadows Indemnity Co Ltd v Insurance Corpn of Ireland Ltd [1989] 2 Lloyd's Rep 298 ... 505
Meah v McCreamer [1985] 1 All ER 367 ... 235–36
Meah v McCreamer (No 2) [1986] 1 All ER 943 ... 235–36
Measures Bros Ltd v Measures [1910] 2 Ch 248 ... 487
Mediana, The [1900] AC 113 ... 36, 74, 216–17
Mehmet v Perry [1977] 2 All ER 529 ... 258–59
Melachrino v Nickoll and Knight [1920] 1 KB 693 ... 132
Mellstrom v Garner [1970] 1 WLR 603 ... 505
Meng Leong Development Pte Ltd v Jip Hong Trading Co Pte Ltd [1985] AC 511 ... 434–35
Mercers Co v New Hampshire Insurance Co [1991] 1 WLR 1173 ... 168
Merchants' Trading Co v Banner (1871) LR 12 Eq 18 ... 435
Mercury Communications Ltd v Scott-Garner [1984] Ch 37 ... 476–77, 478–79
Merest v Harvey (1814) 5 Taunt 442 ... 284–85
Mergenthaler Linotype Co v Intertype Co Ltd (1926) 43 RPC 381 ... 497–98
Meredith v Wilson (1893) 69 LT 336 ... 486
Merrett v Babb [2001] EWCA Civ 214, [2001] QB 1174 ... 6–7
Mersey Docks and Harbour Board v Marpessa (Owners) [1907] AC 241 ... 216
Merson v Cartwright [2005] UKPC 38 ... 363–64
Mertens v Home Freeholds Co [1921] 2 KB 526 ... 197–98
Messenger Newspapers Group Ltd v National Graphical Association [1984] IRLR 397 ... 52, 287–88, 367
Messier-Dowty Ltd v Sabena SA (No 2) [2000] 1 WLR 2040 ... 505
Messiniaki Tolmi, The *See* Astro Exito Navegacion SA v Southland Enterprise Co Ltd (No 2)
    The Messiniaki Tolmi
Metaalhandel J A Magnus BV v Ardfields Transport Ltd and Eastfell Ltd (t/a Jones Transport)
    [1988] 1 Lloyd's Rep 197 ... 181
Metal Box Ltd v Currys Ltd [1988] 1 WLR 175 ... 304, 305
Metall & Rohstoff AG v ACLI Metals (London) Ltd [1984] 1 Lloyd's Rep 598 ... 368–69
Metallgesellschaft Ltd v IRC: Hoescht AG v IRC, Cases C-397–410/98 [2001] Ch 620,
    [2001] 2 WLR 1497, [2001] ECR I-1727 ... 16
Meters Ltd v Metropolitan Gas Meters Ltd (1911) 28 RPC 157 ... 229, 321–22
Metropolitan Bank v Heiron (1880) 5 Ex D 319 ... 529
Metropolitan Electric Supply Co Ltd v Ginder [1901] 2 Ch 799 ... 460–61
Metropolitan Police Commissioner v Gerald, The Times, 26 June 1998 ... 284–85
Metropolitan Police District Receiver v Croydon Corpn [1957] 2 QB 154 ... 155
Michael v Chief Constable of South Wales [2015] UKSC 2, [2015] AC 1732 ... 25–26
Microsoft Corpn v Plato Technology Ltd (1999) Times, 17 August ... 443–44
Middleton v Dodswell (1806) 13 Ves 266 ... 538
Middleton v Elliott Turbomachinery Ltd (1990) Times, 29 October, CA ... 254
Midland Bank Trust Co Ltd v Hett, Stubbs & Kemp (a firm) [1979] Ch 384,
    [1978] 3 All ER 571, [1978] 3 WLR 167 ... 6–7, 8, 45, 232, 311
Mihalis Angelos, The *See* Maredelanto Cia Naviera SA v Bergbau-Handel GmbH,
    The Mihalis Angelos
Milan Nigeria Ltd v Angeliki B Maritime Co [2011] EWHC 892 (Comm) ... 178
Miliangos v George Frank (Textiles) Ltd [1976] AC 443 ... 177–78, 179, 180, 181, 307
Miliangos v George Frank (Textiles) Ltd (No 2) [1977] QB 489, [1976] 2 Lloyd's Rep 434 ... 307–8
Miller v Jackson [1977] QB 966 ... 315–16, 449
Millington v Duffy (1984) 17 HLR 232 ... 283–85, 365
Mills v Hassall, The Ionic Bay [1983] ICR 330 ... 160
Milner v Carnival plc [2010] EWCA Civ 389, [2011] 1 Lloyd's Rep 374 ... vii–viii, 280–81, 291
Milward v Earl of Thanet (1801) 5 Ves 720n ... 433–34
Ministry of Defence v Ashman (1993) 66 P & CR 195 ... 325–26
Ministry of Defence v Thompson [1993] 2 EGLR 107 ... 325
Ministry of Defence v Wheeler [1998] 1 WLR 637 ... 64
Ministry of Sound (Ireland) Ltd v World Online Ltd [2003] EWHC 2178 (Ch),
    [2003] 2 All ER (Comm) 823 ... 381, 384
Minscombe Properties Ltd v Sir Alfred McAlpine & Son Ltd (1986) 279 Estates Gazette 759, CA ... 197–98
Mitchell v Liverpool Area Health Authority (1985) Times, 17 June, CA ... 239
Mitchell v Mulholland (No 2) [1972] 1 QB 65 ... 171
Mobil North Sea Ltd v PJ Pipe & Valve Co [2001] EWCA Civ 741, [2001] 2 All ER (Comm) 289 ... 149
Moeliker v Reyrolle & Co Ltd [1977] 1 WLR 132 ... 235–36, 239

Mohidin v Commmissioner of Police for the Metropolis [2015] EWHC 2740....................290
Monarch Steamship Co Ltd v A/B Karlshamns Oljefabriker [1949] AC 196 ....38, 93, 108, 145
Moore v DER Ltd [1971] 3 All ER 517 211
Moore v Zerfahs [1999] Lloyd's Rep PN 144, CA 115
Moorjani v Durban Estates Ltd [2015] EWCA Civ 1252, [2016] 1 WLR 2265......................291
Moran v University College Salford (No 2) [1994] ELR 187 481–82
Morecambe and Heysham Borough v Mecca Ltd [1962] RPC 145..................................490
Morgan v Fry [1968] 1 QB 521 rev'd [1968] 2 QB 710 230–31
Moriarty v McCarthy [1978] 1 WLR 155 ....242, 247
Morning Star Co-operative Society v Express Newspapers [1979] FSR 113 472
Morris v Richards [2003] EWCA Civ 232, [2004] PIQR Q3 84–85
Morris v Tarrant [1971] 2 QB 143 221
Morris-Garner v One Step (Support) Ltd [2018] UKSC 20, [2018] 2 WLR 1353.......vii, 38, 48, 200, 216,
            220, 221–22, 230, 314, 315–16, 317, 319, 321, 322, 323, 324, 326–27, 328,
            329–31, 336, 337–38, 343–44, 348–49, 353–54, 356–58, 523–24, 532–33
Mortimer v Bailey [2004] EWCA Civ 1514, [2005] 2 P & CR 9 ....466, 486
Mortimer v Beckett [1920] 1 Ch 571...457, 458
Mortlock v Buller (1804) 10 Ves 292..437–38
Morton-Norwich Products Inc v Intercen Ltd (No 2) [1981] FSR 337............................368–69
Mosley v News Group Newspapers Ltd [2008] EWHC 1777 (QB), [2008] EMLR 20 ....369, 525, 537
Moss v Christchurch RDC [1925] 2 KB 750...208
Moss v Heckingbottom (1958) 172 Estates Gazette 207...279
Mountford v Scott [1975] Ch 258..429, 431
MSC Mediterranean Shipping Co SA v Cottonex Anstalt [2016] EWCA Civ 789,
       [2016] 2 Lloyd's Rep 494 ....vii–viii, 386–87
Muhammad Issa el Sheikh Ahmad v Ali [1947] AC 414 145
Muirhead v Industrial Tank Specialities Ltd [1986] QB 507, [1985] 3 All ER 705 ....6–7, 88, 231
Mulholland v McCrea [1961] NI 135, CA 257–58
Mulholland v Mitchell [1971] AC 666..169–70
Mullard v Ben Line Steamers Ltd [1970] 1 WLR 1414 142
Mulvaine v Joseph (1968) 112 Sol Jo 927 ....66, 272
Munnelly v Calcon Ltd, John Sisk & Sons (Dublin) Ltd and Doyle [1978] IR 387....................208
Murad v Al-Saraj [2005] EWCA 959, [2005] WTLR 1573, CA [2004] EWHC 1235........vii–viii, 349, 528
Murphy v Brentwood District Council [1991] 1 AC 398, [1990] 2 All ER 908........ 6–7, 202, 231, 314
Murphy v Culhane [1977] QB 94...137
Murphy v Lush (1986) 60 ALJR 523 475
Murphy v Stone Wallwork (Charlton) Ltd [1969] 1 WLR 1023 169–70
Murray v Shuter [1976] QB 972, [1975] 3 WLR 597..253, 267
Murrell v Healy [2001] EWCA Civ 486, [2001] 4 All ER 345 53
Mutual Reserve Fund Life Association v New York Life Insurance Co (1896) 75 LT 528..............457
Muuse v Secretary of State for the Home Department [2010] EWCA Civ 453...............vii–viii, 363
MVF 3 APS v Bestnet Europe Ltd [2016] EWCA Civ 541, [2017] FSR 5.......... vii–viii, 321–22, 524–25
My Kinda Town (t/a Chicago Pizza Pie Factory) v Soll [1982] FSR 147, rev'd
       [1983] RPC 407... 341–42, 343, 345

Napier, ex p (1852) 18 QB 692, 21 LJQB 332, 17 Jur 380 3–4
National Bank of Greece SA v Pinios Shipping Co, The Maira [1989] 3 WLR 185 7
National Commercial Bank Jamaica Ltd v Olint Corp Ltd [2009] UKPC 16, [2009] 1 WLR 1405 ...... 483, 484
National Provincial Bank of England v Marshall (1888) 40 Ch D 112................................462
National Provincial Plate Glass Insurance Co v Prudential Assurance Co (1877) 6 Ch D 757..........464
National Westminster Bank plc v Rabobank Nederland (No 3) [2007] EWHC 1742 (Comm),
       [2008] 1 All ER (Comm) 243 83
Naughton v O'Callaghan [1990] 3 All ER 191 .... 174–75, 225–27
Nawala, The See NWL Ltd v Woods, The Nawala
Neal v Bingle [1998] QB 466..157
Needler Financial Services v Taber [2002] 3 All ER 501..149–50
Neilson v Betts (1871) LR 5 HL 1...345–46
Network Rail Infrastructure Ltd v Conarken Group Ltd [2011] EWCA Civ 644,
       [2012] 1 All ER (Comm) 692 .... vii–viii, 88–89, 209
Newport Association Football Club Ltd v Football Association of Wales Ltd [1995] 2 All ER 87.......506

Table of Cases

Newport (Essex) Engineering Co Ltd v Press and Shear Machinery Co Ltd
  (1984) 24 BLR 71, CA. 167–68
Newsweek Inc v BBC [1979] RPC 441 . . . . 475, 476
Nichols Advanced Vehicle Systems Inc v Rees and Oliver [1979] RPC 127 . . . . 284–85, 367–68
Nichrotherm Electrical Co Ltd, Cox, Drew and Francis v J R Percy and G A Harvey &
  Co (London) Ltd [1956] RPC 272 521–22
No 7 Steam Sand Pump Dredger (Owners) v Greta Holme (Owners), The Greta Holme [1897] AC 596. 216
Noble v Owens [2010] EWCA Civ 224, [2010] 1 WLR 2491. 169
Nocton v Lord Ashburton [1914] AC 932 511–12
Norberg v Wynrib (1992) 92 DLR (4th) 440 537
Normans Bay Ltd v Coudert Brothers [2003] EWCA Civ 215 107
North v Great Northern Rly Co (1860) 2 Giff 64. . . . . 405, 406, 494
North Australian Territory Co, Re, Archer's Case [1892] 1 Ch 322 526
North Island Wholesale Groceries Ltd v Hewin [1982] 2 NZLR 176, NZCA. 183
North Sea Energy Holdings NV v Petroleum Authority of Thailand [1999] 1 All ER (Comm) 173 67
Norton Tool Co Ltd v Tewson [1972] ICR 501 282
Nottingham Building Society v Eurodynamics Systems plc [1993] FSR 468. . . . . 483, 484, 496
Nottingham University v Fishel [2000] ICR 1462 . . . . 526, 527
Nottinghamshire Healthcare NHS Trust v News Group Newspapers Ltd [2002] EWHC 409,
  [2002] RPC 49. 367–68
Novoship (UK) Ltd v Mikhaylyuk [2014] EWCA Civ 908, [2015] QB 499. . . . . vii–viii, 535–36
Nurse v Barns (1664) T Raym 77 77
NV Algemene Transporten Expeditie Onderneming van Gend en Loos v Nederlandse
  Administratie der Belastingen Case 26/62, [1963] ECR 1. 15
NWL Ltd v Woods, The Nawala [1979] 1 WLR 1294. . . . . 472–73, 476, 478–79
Nykredit Mortgage Bank plc v Edward Erdman Group Ltd (No 2)
  [1997] 1 WLR 1627. . . . . 119, 120, 122–23, 232

Oakacre Ltd v Claire Cleaners (Holdings) Ltd [1982] Ch 197. 317
Oakley v Walker (1977) 121 Sol Jo 619 243
Oakworth, The See Associated Portland Cement Manufacturers Ltd v Teigland Shipping A/S,
  The Oakworth
Obagi v Stanborough (Developments) Ltd (1993) 69 P & CR 573,
  (upheld 7 April 1999, unreported), CA 67
OBG Ltd v Allan [2007] UKHL 21, [2008] 1 AC 1 13
O'Brien v Independent Assessor [2007] UKHL 10, [2007] 2 AC 312. 239–40
Ocean Marine Navigation Ltd v Koch Carbon Inc, The Dynamic [2003] EWHC 1936 (Comm),
  [2003] 2 Lloyd's Rep 693 386
O'Connell v Jackson [1972] 1 QB 270 133
O'Connor v Hewitson [1979] Crim LR 46, CA 371
Odenfeld, The See Gator Shipping Corpn v Trans-Asiatic Oil Ltd SA and Occidental Shipping
  Establishment, The Odenfeld
Odessa Tramways Co v Mendel (1878) 8 Ch D 235 407
Offer-Hoar v Larkstore Ltd [2006] EWCA Civ 1079, [2006] 1 WLR 2926 203–4
Office Overload Ltd v Gunn [1977] FSR 39 . . . . 476, 480
Official Custodian for Charities v Mackey [1985] Ch 168 480
Ogden v Fossick (1862) 4 De GF & J 426 . . . . 426–27, 435
O'Grady v Westminster Scaffolding Ltd [1962] 2 Lloyd's Rep 238 . . . . 211–12, 214
Ogwo v Taylor [1988] AC 431 88
O'Laoire v Jackel International Ltd (No 2) [1991] ICR 718 281
Oliver v Ashman [1962] 2 QB 210, [1961] 3 WLR 669. 248
Olwell v Nye and Nissen Co 26 Wash 2d 282 (1946) 339–40
Omak Maritime Ltd v Mamola Challenger Shipping Co, The Mamola Challenger
  [2010] EWHC 2026 (Comm), [2011] 1 Lloyd's Rep 47. . . . . vii–viii, 78–79
On Demand Information plc v Michael Gerson (Finance) plc [2002] UKHL 13, [2003] 1 AC 368. 394–95
OOO Abbott v Design and Display Ltd [2017] EWHC 932 (IPEC), [2017] FSR 43 344
OPO v Rhodes [2015] UKSC 32, [2016] AC 219. . . . . vii–viii, 285–86, 444
Orion Property Trust Ltd v Du Cane Court Ltd [1962] 1 WLR 1085. 469–70
Oro Chief, The See Eximenco Handels AG v Partrederiet Oro Chief and Levantes Maritime
  Corpn, The Oro Chief

Oropesa, The *See* Lord v Pacific Steam Navigation Co Ltd, The Oropesa
Orwell Steel Ltd v Asphalt and Tarmac (UK) Ltd [1984] 1 WLR 1097 443
Osman v United Kingdom (1998) 5 BHRC 293, (1998) 29 EHRR 245, ECtHR 22
O'Sullivan v Williams [1992] 3 All ER 385 163
Ottercroft Ltd v Scandia Care Ltd [2016] EWCA Civ 867 464
Oughton v Seppings (1830) 1 B & Ad 241 340–41
Overseas Tankship (UK) Ltd v Miller Steamship Co Pty, The Wagon Mound (No 2)
 [1967] 1 AC 617 89
Overseas Tankship (UK) Ltd v Morts Dock and Engineering Co Ltd, The Wagon Mound
 [1961] AC 388 .... 86–87, 88–89, 90, 94–95, 106, 220–21
Overstone Ltd v Shipway [1962] 1 WLR 117 70
Owen v Martin [1992] PIQR Q151, CA 262–63
Owen and Smith (t/a Nuagin Car Service) v Reo Motors (Britain) Ltd (1934) 151 LT 274 284–85
Owens v Brimmell [1977] QB 859, [1977] 2 WLR 943 133
Owners of the Dredger Liesbosch v Owners of SS Edison [1933] AC 449 .... 84, 88–89, 144,
 145–46, 206, 209–10, 211, 296
Oxy Electric Ltd v Zainuddin [1991] 1 WLR 115 486
Ozalid Group (Export) Ltd v African Continental Bank Ltd [1979] 2 Lloyd's Rep 231 179

P & O Nedlloyd BV v Arab Metals Co [2006] EWCA Civ 1717, [2007] 1 WLR 2288, ... vii–viii, 314,
 433, 490, 544
P & O Nedlloyd BV v Arab Metals Co [2005] EWHC 1276 (Comm),
 [2005] 1 WLR 3733 .... vii–viii, 504, 505
P Perl (Exporters) Ltd v Camden London Borough Council [1984] QB 342, [1983] 3 All ER 161 110
Pacific Colocotronis, The *See* Shell Tankers (UK) Ltd v Astro Comino Armadora SA,
 The Pacific Colocotronis
Page v Plymouth Hospitals NHS Trust [2004] EWHC 1154 (QB), [2004] 3 All ER 367 247
Page v Sheerness Steel Co plc [1999] 1 AC 345 160
Page v Smith [1996] AC 155, [1995] 2 WLR 644 .... 234, 285–86
Page One Records Ltd v Britton [1968] 1 WLR 157 .... 419, 458, 459, 461
Paludina, The *See* Singleton Abbey (SS) (Owners) v SS Paludina (Owners), The Paludina
Parabola Investments Ltd v Browallia Cal Ltd [2010] EWCA Civ 486, [2011] QB 477 ...... vii–viii, 227–28
Paragon Finance plc v Thakerar & Co [1999] 1 All ER 400 .... 490, 543, 544
Paragon Properties Ltd v Magna Envestments Ltd (1972) 24 DLR 156 375
Parana, The (1877) 2 PD 118 101–2
Parker v Camden London Borough Council [1986] Ch 162, [1985] 2 All ER 141 .... 482, 492
Parker v Chief Constable of Essex [2018] EWCA Civ 788 363
Parker v McKenna (1874) 10 Ch App 96 526
ParkingEye Ltd v Beavis ('ParkingEye') [2015] UKSC 67, [2016] AC 1172 .... vii–viii, 390, 391, 392
Parkinson v St James and Seacroft University Hospital NHS Trust [2003] UKHL 52,
 [2004] 1 AC 309 251–52
Parkinson v St James and Seacroft University Hospital NHS Trust [2001] EWCA Civ 530,
 [2002] QB 266 250–51
Parry v Cleaver [1970] AC 1 .... 153, 154, 155, 158–60, 161, 162
Parry v North West Surrey Health Authority (2000) Times, 5 January 168
Parsons v BNM Laboratories Ltd [1964] 1 QB 95 .... 153, 157, 182–83
Parsons (H) (Livestock) Ltd v Uttley Ingham & Co Ltd [1978] QB 791 .... 89, 92, 94–95, 96, 98, 105
Pascoe v Turner [1979] 1 WLR 431 538
Patel v Ali [1984] Ch 283 431–32
Patel v Hooper & Jackson [1999] 1 WLR 1792 .... 168, 188, 280, 283–84
Patel v WH Smith (Eziot) Ltd [1987] 1 WLR 853 446
Paton Calvert & Co Ltd v Rosedale Associated Manufacturers Ltd [1966] RPC 61 497–98
Pattisson v Gilford (1874) LR 18 Eq 259 467–68
Paula Lee Ltd v Robert Zehil & Co Ltd [1983] 2 All ER 390 71–72
Pauling's Settlement Trusts, Re, [1962] 1 WLR 86 .... 490, 544
Payzu Ltd v Saunders [1919] 2 KB 581 .... 128, 131
Peacock v Amusement Equipment Co Ltd [1954] 2 QB 347 265–66
Peacock v Penson (1848) 11 Beav 355 435
Pearson v Sanders Witherspoon [2000] PNLR 110, CA 230
Peel v Peel (1869) 17 WR 586 410
Peevyhouse v Garland Coal Mining Co 382 P 2d 109 (1962) 199

Table of Cases

Pegase, The *See* Satef-Huttenes Albertus SpA v Paloma Tercera Shipping Co SA, The Pegase
Pell Frischmann Engineering Co Ltd v Bow Valley Iran Ltd [2009] UKPC 45,
    [2011] 1 WLR 2370, [2010] BLR 73 .... 314, 315–16, 321–22, 327–28, 329, 330–31
Penarth Dock Engineering Co Ltd v Pounds [1963] 1 Lloyd's Rep 359 .... 321–22, 324–25
Peninsular Maritime Ltd v Padseal Ltd (1981) 259 Estates Gazette 860 .... 482, 483
Pennington v Brinsop Hall Coal Co (1877) 5 Ch D 769 .... 446, 447
Perera v Vandiyar [1953] 1 WLR 672 .... 279, 360–61
Performance Cars Ltd v Abraham [1962] 1 QB 33 .... 47, 53–54
Performing Right Society Ltd v Mitchell and Booker Ltd [1924] 1 KB 762 443–44
Perry v Raleys Solicitors [2019] UKSC 5 67–68
Perry v Sidney Phillips & Son (a firm) [1982] 1 WLR 1297, [1982] 1 All ER 1005 .... 145, 170, 188,
    232, 279–80, 283–84, 286–87, 291–92, 307
Peter Pan Manufacturing Corpn v Corsets Silhouette Ltd [1964] 1 WLR 96,
    [1964] RPC 45 .... 521, 533, 535, 538–39, 541
Peters v East Midlands SHA [2009] EWCA Civ 145, [2010] QB 48 239–40
Peterson v Personal Representatives of Cyril Rivlin [2002] EWCA Civ 194,
    [2002] Lloyd's Rep PN 386 122–23
Petrotrade Inc v Smith [2000] 1 Lloyd's Rep 486 529
Philadelphia, The [1917] P 101 210–11
Philco Radio and Television Corpn of Great Britain Ltd v J Spurling Ltd [1949] 2 KB 33 85–86
Philip Bernstein (Successors) Ltd v Lydiate Textiles Ltd [1962] CA Transcript 238 400
Philips v Ward [1956] 1 WLR 471 .... 170, 188
Philips Hong Kong Ltd v A-G of Hong Kong (1993) 61 BLR 41 389
Phillips v Homfray [1892] 1 Ch 465 348
Phillips v Homfray (1883) 24 Ch D 439 .... 339, 343–44, 347, 348
Phillips v Homfray (1871) 6 Ch App 770 .... 347, 348
Phillips v Lamdin [1949] 2 KB 33 404
Phipps v Jackson (1887) 56 LJ Ch 550 416
Phoebus D Kyprianou Co v Wm H Pim Jnr & Co [1977] 2 Lloyd's Rep 570 69
Phonographic Performance Ltd v Department of Trade and Industry [2004] EWHC 1795 (Ch),
    [2004] 1 WLR 2893 15
Phonographic Performance Ltd v Maitra [1998] 1 WLR 870 .... 443–44, 451–52
Pickett v British Rail Engineering Ltd [1980] AC 136, [1978] 3 WLR 955 .... 248, 306–7
Pidduck v Eastern Scottish Omnibuses Ltd [1990] 1 WLR 993 266
Pilkington v Wood [1953] Ch 770 129
Pilmer v Duke Group Ltd (in liquidation) (2001) 75 ALJR 1067 513–14
Piper v Darling (1940) 67 Ll L Rep 419 284–85
Piper v Daybell Court-Cooper & Co (1969) 210 Estates Gazette 1047 279
Pirelli General Cable Works Ltd v Oscar Faber & Partners [1983] 2 AC 1 .... 232, 313–14
PJS v News Group Newspapers [2016] UKSC 26, [2016] AC 1081 .... vii–viii, 441, 480, 540
Platform Home Loans Ltd v Oyston Shipways Ltd [2000] 2 AC 190 .... 122–23, 124, 135
Playa Larga, The *See* Empresa Exportadora de Azucar v Industria Azucarera Nacional SA,
    The Playa Larga
Polemis and Furness Withy & Co, Re [1921] 3 KB 560 .... 86–87, 90
Polini v Gray (1879) 11 Ch D 741 469–70
Polish Steamship Co v Atlantic Maritime Co, The Garden City [1985] QB 41 305
Pollard v Clayton (1855) 1 K & J 462 .... 405, 416, 433
Polly Peck International plc v Nadir (No 2) [1992] 4 All ER 769 486
Porter v National Union of Journalists [1980] IRLR 404 476
Portman Building Society v Bevan Ashford [2000] 1 EGLR 81 122–23
Posner v Scott-Lewis [1987] Ch 25 .... 417, 435
Potton Ltd v Yorkclose Ltd [1990] FSR 11 .... 341–42, 343, 345
Pounder v London Underground Ltd [1995] PIQR P217 256–57
Powell v Benney [2007] EWCA Civ 1283 525–26
Powell v Brent London Borough Council [1988] ICR 176 .... 422–23, 425, 426
Powell v Rees (1837) 7 Ad & El 426 341
Powell Duffryn Steam Coal Co v Taff Vale Rly Co (1874) 9 Ch App 331 464–65
Pratt v British Medical Association [1919] 1 KB 244 272
President of India v La Pintada Cia Navigacion SA [1985] AC 104 .... 93, 296–97, 298, 303, 542
President of India v Lips Maritime Corpn [1985] 2 Lloyd's Rep 180 181
President of India v Taygetos Shipping Co SA, The Agenor [1985] 1 Lloyd's Rep 155 181

Preston v Luck (1884) 27 Ch D 497 438
Price v Strange [1978] Ch 337 . . . . 315, 420, 427–28, 438
Price's Patent Candle Co Ltd v Bauwen's Patent Candle Co Ltd (1858) 4 K & J 727. . . . . .342, 344–45
Pride of Derby and Derbyshire Angling Association Ltd v British Celanese Ltd
    [1953] Ch 149 . . . . 445, 446, 447–48, 463–64
Priestley v Maclean (1860) 2 F & F 288. 67
Primary Group (UK) Ltd v Royal Bank of Scotland [2014] EWHC 1082,
    [2014] 2 All ER (Comm) 1121 321–22
Primavera v Allied Dunbar Assurance plc [2002] EWCA Civ 1327, [2003] PNLR 12. 149–50
Prince Albert v Strange (1849) 2 De G & Sm 704 541
Prison Officers Association v Iqbal [2009] EWCA Civ 1312, [2010] QB 732 . . . . .283–85, 289
Pritchard v Co-operative Group Ltd [2011] EWCA Civ 329, [2012] QB 320 . . . . .vii–viii, 136–37
Pritchard v JH Cobden Ltd [1988] Fam 22, [1987] 2 WLR 627. 243
Prichet v Boevey (1833) 1 Cr & M 775 187
Proctor v Bayley (1889) 42 Ch D 390 . . . . .315–16, 467
Provident Financial Group plc v Hayward [1989] 3 All ER 298 459–60
Prudential Assurance v Newman Industries (No 2) [1982] 1 Ch 204 187
Prudential Assurance Co Ltd v HMRC [2018] UKSC 39, [2018] 3 WLR 652. . . . 295, 297, 298, 336, 542–43
PST Energy 7 Shipping LLC v OW Bunker Malta Ltd, The Res Cogitans [2016] UKSC 23,
    [2016] AC 1034. 382
Puerto Buitrago, The See Attica Sea Carriers Corpn v Ferrostaal Poseidon Bulk Reederei GmbH,
    The Puerto Buitrago
Pugh v Howells (1984) 48 P & CR 298 464
Pusey v Pusey (1684) 1 Vern 273. 494
Pyx Granite Co Ltd v Ministry of Housing and Local Government [1958] 1 QB 554. 505

Quadrant Visual Communications Ltd v Hutchison Telephone (UK) Ltd [1993] BCLC 442. . . . . . .432, 436
Queen Mary, The See Bishop v Cunard White Star Co Ltd, The Queen Mary
Queensland Mines Ltd v Hudson (1978) 18 ALR 1, 52 ALJR 399 526
Quinn v Burch Bros (Builders) Ltd [1966] 2 QB 370 114
Quorum A/S v Schramm (No 2) [2002] 2 All ER (Comm) 179 304–5

R v A-G for England and Wales [2003] UKPC 22, [2003] EMLR 24 392
R v BBC, ex p Lavelle [1983] 1 WLR 23 424–25
R v Civil Service Appeal Board, ex p Bruce [1989] ICR 171 425
R v Criminal Injuries Compensation Board, ex p K (minors) [1999] QB 1131, [1999] 2 WLR 948 266
R v Derbyshire County Council, ex p Noble [1990] ICR 808 424–25
R v East Berkshire Health Authority, ex p Walsh [1985] QB 152 424–25
R v Governor of Brockhill Prison, ex p Evans (No 2) [1999] QB 1043. 289
R v HM Treasury, ex p British Telecommunications plc: C-392/93 [1996] QB 615,
    [1996] 3 WLR 203, [1996] ECR I-1631 15
R v Home Secretary, ex p Broom [1986] QB 198. 424–25
R v IRC, ex p Rossminster Ltd [1980] AC 952. 506
R v Jennings (1966) 57 DLR (2d) 644, Can SC. 183
R v Kensington and Chelsea Royal London Borough Council, ex p Hammell [1989] QB 518. 483
R v Kensington Income Tax General Comrs [1917] 1 KB 486. 484–85
R v Ministry of Agriculture, Fisheries and Food, ex p Monsanto plc [1999] QB 1161 472–73
R v Secretary of State for Health, ex p Imperial Tobacco Ltd [2001] 1 WLR 127 472–73
R v Secretary of State for Transport, ex p Factortame Ltd (No 2) [1991] 1 AC 603. . . . . . . 440–41, 472–73, 480
R v Secretary of State for Transport, ex p Factortame Ltd (No 5) [2000] 1 AC 524 (HL),
    [1997] Eu LR 475. . . . . .15, 369–70
R v Secretary of State for Transport, ex p Factortame Ltd (No 6) [2001] 1 WLR 942 15
R (Bernard) v Enfield London Borough Council [2002] EWHC 2282 (Admin),
    [2003] HLR 4. . . . . 24, 284–85, 289
R (Faulkner) v Secretary of State for Justice [2013] UKSC 23, [2013] 2 WLR 1157. 28
R (Greenfield) v Secretary of State for the Home Department [2005] UKHL 14,
    [2005] 1 WLR 673. . . . . 22–23, 24, 25, 26–27, 28, 29
R (KB) v Mental Health Review Tribunal [2003] EWHC 193 (Admin), [2004] QB 936,
    [2003] HRLR 4 . . . . .24, 60–61, 284–85, 289, 370
R (Lumba) v Secretary of State for the Home Department [2011] UKSC 12,
    [2012] 1 AC 245 . . . . vii–viii, 363, 364, 373–74, 503

Table of Cases xliii

Rabone v Pennine Care NHS Foundation Trust [2012] UKSC 2, [2012] 2 AC 72......vii–viii, 24, 256–57, 264
Race Relations Board v Applin [1973] QB 815...467, 506
Radford v de Froberville [1977] 1 WLR 1262 (Ch).........................38, 47, 172–73, 197–98, 199
Rae v Yorkshire Bank plc [1988] BTLC 35..281
Raflatac Ltd v Eade [1999] 1 Lloyd's Rep 506...141–42
Rahman v Arearose Ltd [2001] QB 351...54
Rainbow Estates Ltd v Tokenhold Ltd [1999] Ch 64...........................411, 417–18, 427, 435–36
Rajbenback v Mamon [1955] 1 QB 283..506
Ramdath v Daley and Daley [1993] 1 EGLR 82..365
Ramwade Ltd v W J Emson & Co Ltd [1987] RTR 72...145
Ramzan v Brookwide Ltd [2011] EWCA Civ 985, [2012] 1 All ER 903.....................325, 365, 370
Rand v East Dorset Health Authority (2000) 50 BMLR 39...250–51
Rank Film Distributors Ltd v Video Information Centre (a firm) [1982] AC 380..................486
Rantzen v Mirror Group Newspapers (1986) Ltd [1994] QB 670..274
Ratcliffe v Evans [1892] 2 QB 524..66, 73
Raven Red Ash Coal Co v Ball 39 SE 2d 213 (1946)..339–40
Reader v Molesworth Bright Clegg [2007] EWCA Civ 169, [2007] 1 WLR 1082..............257–58
Reading v A-G [1951] AC 507..355, 529–30
Redgrave v Hurd (1881) 20 Ch D 1..137–38
Redland Bricks Ltd v Morris [1970] AC 652, [1969] 2 WLR 1437......319, 442–43, 445, 447, 463–64, 467–68
Redler Grain Silos Ltd v BICC Ltd [1982] 1 Lloyd's Rep 435..486
Redpath v Belfast and County Down Rly [1947] NI 167...154, 159
Redrow Homes Ltd v Bett Bros plc [1999] 1 AC 197...367–68
Redwood Music Ltd v Chappell & Co Ltd [1982] RPC 109...344
Reed v Madon [1989] Ch 408, [1989] 2 All ER 431..278, 284–85
Rees v Darlington Memorial Hospital NHS Trust [2003] UKHL 52, [204] 1 AC 309,
  [2003] 4 All ER 987...38, 237, 251, 252, 285–86
Reeves v Metropolitan Police Comr [2000] 1 AC 360..113–14, 136
Regal (Hastings) Ltd v Gulliver [1967] 2 AC 134...526–27
Regan v Paul Properties Ltd [2006] EWCA Civ 1391, [2007] Ch 135.............................445, 450
Regan v Williamson [1976] 1 WLR 305..258–59
Regent International Hotels (UK) Ltd v Pageguide Ltd (1985) Times, 13 May..........417, 421, 429
Reichman v Beveridge [2006] EWCA Civ 1659, [2007] 1 P & CR 20....................vii–viii, 387
Reid v Rush & Tompkins Group plc [1989] 3 All ER 228, [1990] 1 WLR 212............................7
Reid-Newfoundland Co v Anglo-American Telegraph Ltd [1912] AC 555................355, 357–58
Reilly v Merseyside Health Authority [1995] 6 Med LR 246...285–86
Rely-a-Bell Burglar and Fire Alarm Co Ltd v Eisler [1926] Ch 609.......................................458
Rewe-Zentralfinanz GmbH v Landwirtschaftskammer fur Saarland: 33/76 [1976] ECR 1989,
  [1977] 1 CMLR 533..16
Reynolds v Strutt and Parker LLP [2011] EWHC 2263 (QB)..135
Rialas v Mitchell (1984) 128 Sol Jo 704...239–40
Richardson v Howie [2004] EWCA Civ 1127, [2005] PIQR Q3..287–88
Richardson v Silvester (1873) LR 9 QB 34..226
Riches v News Group Newspapers [1986] QB 256..373–74
Riches v Owen (1868) 3 Ch App 820...491–92
Rigby v Chief Constable of Northamptonshire [1985] 1 WLR 1242..52
Rigby v Connol (1880) 14 Ch D 482..419
Rigby v Ferodo Ltd [1988] ICR 29..69
Rijn, The *See* Santa Martha Baay Scheepvaart and Handelsmaatschappij NV v Scanbulk A/S, The Rijn
Rileys v Halifax Corpn (1907) 97 LT 278..464
Rio Claro, The *See* Transworld Oil Ltd v North Bay Shipping Corpn, The Rio Claro
Riverside Mental Health NHS Trust v Fox [1994] 1 FLR 614..506
Robb v Hammersmith and Fulham London Borough Council [1991] ICR 514...........422, 426
Roberts v J Hampson & Co [1990] 1 WLR 94..283–84
Roberts v Johnstone [1989] QB 878, [1988] 3 WLR 1247..242
Robertson v Lestrange [1985] 1 All ER 950..262
Robinson v Harman (1848) 18 LJ Ex 202, 1 Exch 850..38, 78–79
Robinson v PE Jones (Contractors) Ltd [2011] EWCA Civ 9, [2012] QB 44..............................7
Robinson v St Helens Metropolitan Borough Council [2002] EWCA Civ 1099,
  [2003] PIQR P128...285–86
Robophone Facilities Ltd v Blank [1966] 1 WLR 1428...92, 394

Rock Refrigeration Ltd v Jones [1997] ICR 938. 459–60
Rodocanachi v Milburn (1886) 18 QBD 67 . . . . 191–92, 219–20
Rolin v Steward (1854) 14 CB 595. . . . . 73, 269
Ronan v Sainsbury's Supermarkets Ltd [2006] EWCA Civ 1074. 239
Ronex Properties Ltd v John Laing Construction Ltd [1983] QB 398 309
Rookes v Barnard [1964] AC 1129, [1964] 1 All ER 367 . . . . 24, 153, 283, 287–88, 319–20, 346, 361,
    362, 365–66, 367–69, 370, 371, 373–74, 376, 377
Roper v Johnson (1873) LR 8 CP 167 85–86
Rose v Ford [1937] AC 826. . . . . .235–36, 253
Rosedale Associated Manufacturers Ltd v Airfix Products Ltd [1956] RPC 360 497–98
Ross v Caunters [1980] Ch 297, [1979] 3 WLR 605 233
Rothwell v Chemical and Insulating Co Ltd *See* Grieves v FT Everard & Sons
Rourke v Barton (1982) Times, 23 June 235–36
Rouse v Squires [1973] QB 889 111
Roussel-Uclaf v GD Searle & Co [1977] FSR 125; aff'd [1978] 1 Lloyd's Rep 225. . . . . .472–73, 491
Rowe v Turner, Hopkins & Partners [1980] 2 NZLR 550; rev'd [1982] 1 NZLR 178, NZCA 139, 140
Rowlands v Chief Constable of Merseyside Police [2006] EWCA Civ 1773,
    [2007] 1 WLR 1065. . . . . vii–viii, 287–88, 373
Rowley v London and North Western Rly Co (1873) LR 8 Exch 221. 37
Royal Bank of Canada v W Got & Associates Electric Ltd (2000) 178 DLR (4th) 385. 377–78
Royal Brunei Airlines Sdn Bhd v Tan [1995] 2 AC 378 . . . . 509–10, 511–12
Royal Devon and Exeter NHS Foundation Trust v ATOS IT Services UK Ltd
    [2017] EWCA Civ 2196, [2018] 2 All ER (Comm) 535. 506
Royscot Trust Ltd v Rogerson [1991] 2 QB 297. . . . . 90, 137–38, 225–26
Rubber Improvement Ltd v Daily Telegraph Ltd [1964] AC 234 182
Rudd v Lascelles [1900] 1 Ch 815 437–38
Rumsey v Owen, White v Catlin (1978) 245 Estates Gazette 225 96
Rushton v Turner Bros Asbestos Co Ltd [1960] 1 WLR 96 113–14
Rust v Victoria Graving Dock Co and London and St Katharine Dock Co (1887) 36 Ch D 113. 209
Ruxley Electronics and Construction Ltd v Forsyth [1996] AC 344. . . . . 197, 198, 199, 210, 278, 291–92
Ryan v Mutual Tontine Westminster Chambers Association [1893] 1 Ch 116 . . . . . . 415–16, 417, 435, 464–65
Rylands v Fletcher (1868) LR 3 HL 330. 89

S, Re [1995] 3 All ER 290 505
SS Celia (Owners) v SS Volturno (Owners) [1921] 2 AC 544 177
Sachs v Miklos [1948] 2 KB 23. 175–76
Sainsbury's Supermarkets Ltd v Mastercard Incorporated [2016] CAT 11 299
St Albans City and District Council v International Computers Ltd [1996] 4 All ER 481 201
Saleslease Ltd v Davis [1999] 1 WLR 1664. 220–21
Salih v Enfield Health Authority [1991] 3 All ER 400. 249–50
Salt v Stratstone Specialist Ltd [2015] EWCA Civ 745, [2016] RTR 285 .225–26
Saltman Engineering Co Ltd v Campbell Engineering Ltd [1948] 65 RPC 203 . . . . 521, 522
Sandeman Coprimar SA v Transitos y Transportes Integrates SL [2003] EWCA Civ 113,
    [2003] QB 1270. 90
Sanders v Ernest A Neale Ltd [1974] ICR 565 421
Santa Martha Baay Scheepvaart and Handelsmaatschappij NV v Scanbulk A/S, The Rijn
    [1981] 2 Lloyd's Rep 267 69
Santos Gomes v Higher Level Care Ltd [2018] EWCA Civ 418, [2018] 2 All ER 740 241
Satef-Huttenes Albertus SpA v Paloma Tercera Shipping Co SA, The Pegase
    [1981] 1 Lloyd's Rep 175 . . . . 92, 96, 99, 191, 195
Saunders v Edwards [1987] 1 WLR 1116. . . . . .283–85, 304
Savile v Kilner (1872) 26 LT 277 489
Savile v Roberts (1698) 1 Ld Raym 374. . . . . 187, 272, 284–85
Saxby v Easterbrook and Hannaford (1878) 3 CPD 339. 443–44
Sayce v TNT (UK) Ltd [2011] EWCA Civ 1583, [2012] 1 WLR 1261 215
Sayers v Collyer (1884) 28 Ch D 103. 488
Sayers v Harlow UDC [1958] 1 WLR 623. 139
Sayers v Hunters [2012] EWCA Civ 1715, [2013] 1 WLR 1695 312
Scally v Southern Health and Social Services Board [1992] 1 AC 294, [1991] 4 All ER 563. 7
Scandinavian Trading Tanker Co AB v Flota Petrolera Ecuatoriana, The Scaptrade
    [1983] 2 AC 694 . . . . 394–95, 422–23, 459

Scaptrade, The *See* Scandinavian Trading Tanker Co AB v Flota Petrolera Ecuatoriana, The Scaptrade
Schering Agrochemicals Ltd v Resibel NV SA (26 November 1992, unreported), CA 84–85, 98, 142
Schering Chemicals Ltd v Falkman Ltd [1982] QB 1 539
Schneider v Eisovitch [1960] 2 QB 430 168–69
Schott Kem Ltd v Bentley [1991] 1 QB 61 167–68
Schwabacher, Re, (1907) 98 LT 127 407
Scott v Musial [1959] 2 QB 429, [1959] 3 All ER 193 37
Scovin-Bradford v Valpoint Properties Ltd [1971] Ch 1007 229
Sea Hawk, The *See* Locabail International Finance Ltd v Agroexport, The Sea Hawk
Seager v Copydex Ltd [1967] 1 WLR 923 .... 521, 533, 535
Seager v Copydex Ltd (No 2) [1969] 1 WLR 809, [1969] 2 All ER 718 .... 321–22, 523–24
Sealace Shipping Co Ltd v Oceanvoice Ltd, The Alecos M [1991] 1 Lloyd's Rep 120 192–93
Secretary of State for Defence v Guardian Newspapers Ltd [1985] AC 339 496
Secretary of State for Environment, Food and Rural Affairs v Meier [2009] UKSC 11,
    [2009] 1 WLR 2780 441
Secretary of State for the Home Department v Central Broadcasting Ltd [1993] EMLR 253 479
Selvanayagam v University of the West Indies [1983] 1 All ER 824 128
Semelhago v Paramadevan (1996) 136 DLR (4th) 1 403
Sempra Metals Ltd v IRC [2007] UKHL 34, [2008] 1 AC 561 ...... vii–viii, 295, 296, 297–300, 303, 542–43
Senior v Pawson (1866) LR 3 Eq 330 463
Serco Ltd v National Union of Rail, Maritime & Transport Workers [2011] EWCA Civ 226,
    [2011] ICR 848 478–79
Series 5 Software Ltd v Clarke [1996] 1 All ER 853 480–81
Service Corpn International plc v Channel Four Television Corpn [1999] EMLR 83 533
Services Europe Atlantique Sud (SEAS) v Stockholms Rederiaktiebolag SVEA,
    The Folias [1979] AC 685 .... 178, 181
Sevcon Ltd v Lucas CAV Ltd [1986] 2 All ER 104 311
Seven Seas Properties Ltd v Al-Essa [1988] 1 WLR 1272 437
Seven Seas Properties Ltd v Al-Essa (No 2) [1993] 3 All ER 577 96
Severn Trent Water Ltd v Barnes [2004] EWCA Civ 570 .... 221–22, 321–22, 327
Sharif v Garrett & Co (a firm) [2001] EWCA Civ 1269, [2002] 1 WLR 3118 65
Sharneyford Supplies Ltd v Edge (Barrington Black Austin & Co, third party) [1987] Ch 305 225–26
Sharp v Harrison [1922] 1 Ch 502 .... 464, 466
Sharp v Milligan (1856) 22 Beav 606 433
Shaw v Applegate [1977] 1 WLR 970 488
Shaw v Kovac [2017] EWCA Civ 1028, [2017] 1 WLR 4773 237
Shearman v Folland [1950] 2 KB 43 .... 38, 239–40
Shearson Lehman Bros Inc v Maclaine Watson & Co Ltd [1987] 1 WLR 480 167–68
Shearson Lehman Hutton Inc v Maclaine Watson & Co Ltd (No 2) [1990] 3 All ER 723 305
Sheffield Gas Consumers' Co v Harrison (1853) 17 Beav 294 409
Shelfer v City of London Electric Lighting Co [1895] 1 Ch 287 .... 444–46, 447, 448–50
Shell-Mex Ltd v Elton Cop Dyeing Co Ltd (1928) 34 Com Cas 39 406–7
Shell Tankers (UK) Ltd v Astro Comino Armadora SA, The Pacific Colocotronis
    [1981] 2 Lloyd's Rep 40 307–8
Shell UK Ltd v Lostock Garage Ltd [1976] 1 WLR 1187 487
Shepherd v Croft [1911] 1 Ch 521 438
Shepherd v The Post Office (1995) The Times, 15 June 257
Shepherd Homes Ltd v Sandham [1971] Ch 340 .... 466, 481–82, 490
Shiloh Spinners Ltd v Harding [1973] AC 691 .... 394–95, 417
Shindler v Northern Raincoat Co Ltd [1960] 1 WLR 1038 132
Shotton v Hammond (1976) 120 Sol Jo 780 481–82
Shove v Downs Surgical plc [1984] 1 All ER 7 182–83
Siddell v Vickers (1892) 9 RPC 152, CA 341–42, 343, 344–45
Sienkiewicz v Greif (UK) Ltd [2011] UKSC 10, [2011] 2 AC 229 57
Simmons v Castle [2012] EWCA Civ 1039, [2012] EWCA Civ 1288, [2013] 1 WLR 1239 .... 236, 273, 288
Simms, Re, ex p Trustee [1934] Ch 1 219
Simple Simon Catering Ltd v J E Binstock Miller & Co (1973) 117 Sol Jo 529 188
Simpson v London and North Western Rly Co (1876) 1 QBD 274 74
Sinclair v Bowden (1962) 183 Estates Gazette 95 279
Sindall (William) plc v Cambridgeshire County Council [1994] 1 WLR 1016 226
Sine Nomine, The *See* AB Corpn v CD Co, The Sine Nomine

Singh v Nazeer [1979] Ch 474 439
Sir Cliff Richard v BBC [2018] EWHC 1837 (Ch)........................ 272, 273, 284–85, 290–91, 525
Skelton v Collins (1966) 115 CLR 94... 237
Sky Petroleum Ltd v VIP Petroleum Ltd [1974] 1 WLR 576 .... 405, 406, 414–15, 416–17, 456, 482
Slater v Hoyle & Smith Ltd [1920] 2 KB 11 .... 148, 151–52, 192, 193, 194, 195
Slazenger & Sons v Feltham & Co (1889) 6 RPC 531 497–98
Slazenger & Sons v Spalding & Bros [1910] 1 Ch 257... 341–42
Slipper v BBC [1991] 1 QB 283 110
Smiley v Townshend [1950] 2 KB 311... 199
Smith v Eric Bush [1990] 1 AC 605... 6–7
Smith v Finch [2009] EWHC 53 (QB) 135
Smith v Grigg Ltd [1924] 1 KB 655.. 469–70
Smith v Inner London Education Authority [1978] 1 All ER 411................................. 472–73
Smith v Lancashire Teaching Hospitals NHS Foundation Trust [2017] EWCA Civ 1916,
 [2018] QB 804 .... vii–viii, 24, 264
Smith v Leech Brain & Co Ltd [1962] 2 QB 405 88
Smith v Littlewoods Organisation Ltd [1987] AC 241 .... 45, 110
Smith v London and South Western Rly Co (1854) Kay 408....................................... 342
Smith v Manchester City Council (or Manchester Corpn) (1974) 17 KIR 1..................... 239, 249
Smith v Peters (1875) LR 20 Eq 511... 482
Smith v Smith (1875) LR 20 Eq 500... 463
Smith Kline & French Laboratories Ltd v Long [1989] 1 WLR 1, CA 224
Smith New Court Securities Ltd v Scrimgeour Vickers (Asset Management) Ltd
 [1997] AC 254 .... 90, 122–23, 175, 224, 226–27
Smithkline Beecham Plc v Apotex Europe Ltd [2006] EWCA Civ 658, [2007] Ch 71.............. 469–70
Smoker v London Fire and Civil Defence Authority [1991] 2 AC 502......................... 158–59
Soames v Edge (1860) John 669... 435
Société Commerciale de Reassurance v ERAS (International) Ltd [1992] 2 All ER 82n........... 313–14
Société des Industries Métallurgiques SA v Bronx Engineering Co Ltd
 [1975] 1 Lloyd's Rep 465 .... 406, 408–9
Société Française Bunge SA v Belcan NV, The Federal Huron [1985] 3 All ER 378................. 181
Société Générale v Geys [2012] UKSC 63, [2013] 1 AC 523 386–87
Solholt, The *See* Sotiros Shipping Inc and Aeco Maritime SA v Sameiet Solholt, The Solholt
Solloway v McLaughlin [1938] AC 247... 176
Somerset (Duke) v Cookson (1735) 3 P Wms 390 494
Sotiros Shipping Inc v Sameiet Solholt, The Solholt [1983] 1 Lloyd's Rep 605 128
South Australia Asset Management Corpn (SAAMCO) v York Montague Ltd [1997] AC 191,
 [1995] QB 375 .... vii–viii, 83–84, 85–86, 109, 117, 118, 119–20, 122–23, 124–27,
 135, 174–75, 188, 223, 519–20
South Wales Rly Co v Wythes (1854) 5 De GM & G 880... 428
Southampton Container Terminals Ltd v Schiffahrts-Gesellschaft Hansa Australia MBH & Co,
 The Maersk Colombo [2001] EWCA Civ 717, [2001] 2 Lloyd's Rep 275 210
Sowden v Lodge [2004] EWCA Civ 1370, [2005] 1 WLR 2129................................... 239–40
Spalding (A G) & Bros v A W Gamage Ltd (1918) 35 RPC 101, CA 228, 272
Spalding (A G) & Bros v A W Gamage Ltd (1915) 84 LJ Ch 449 342
Sparham-Souter v Town and Country Developments (Essex) Ltd [1976] QB 858................... 313
Spartan Steel and Alloys Ltd v Martin & Co (Contractors) Ltd [1973] QB 27,
 [1972] 3 All ER 557.. 6–7, 231–32
Spencer v Wincanton Holdings Ltd [2009] EWCA Civ 1404, [2010] PIQR P8 114
Spiliada Maritime Corpn v Louis Dreyfus Corpn [1983] Com LR 268 69
Spiros C, The *See* Tradigrain SA v King Diamond Shipping SA, The Spiros C
Spittle v Bunney [1988] 1 WLR 847... 258–59
Sport International Bussum BV v Inter-Footwear Ltd [1984] 1 WLR 776, CA................... 394–95
Spring v Guardian Assurance plc [1995] 2 AC 296, [1994] 3 WLR 354........................ 65, 232
Spring Form Inc v Toy Brokers Ltd [2002] FSR 276 345–46
Spur Industries Inc v De E Webb Development Co 494 P 2d 700 (Ariz, 1972)................... 452–53
SS Singleton Abbey (Owners) v SS Paludina (Owners), The Paludina [1927] AC 16 85–86
Stadium Capital Holdings (No 2) Ltd v St Marylebone Property Co Plc [2010] EWCA Civ 952..... 321–22
Standard Chartered Bank v Pakistan National Shipping Corpn [2001] EWCA Civ 55,
 [2001] 1 All ER (Comm) 822 .... 84–86, 230

Table of Cases

Standard Chartered Bank v Pakistan National Shipping Corpn (No 2) [2002] UKHL 43,
  [2003] 1 AC 959 ....136–38, 139
Stanley v Saddique [1992] QB 1, [1991] 2 WLR 459................................. 258–59, 266–67
Stansbie v Troman [1948] 2 KB 48.. 110
Stapley v Gypsum Mines Ltd [1953] AC 663 134
Star Sea Transport Corpn of Monrovia v Slater, The Camilla M [1978] IRLR 507............472–73, 477
Steedman v Drinkle [1916] 1 AC 275 432
Stena Nautica (No 2), The See CN Marine Inc v Stena Line A/B and Regie Voor Maritiem
  Transport, The Stena Nautica (No 2)
Sterling Industrial Facilities Ltd v Lydiate Textiles Ltd (1962) 106 Sol Jo 669........................ 400
Stevens v Equity Management Ltd [2015] EWCA Civ 93, [2015] 4 All ER 458 ....vii–viii, 146, 215
Stevenson v United Road Transport Union [1977] ICR 893 423–25
Stewart v Glentaggart 1963 SLT 119 182–83
Stockloser v Johnson [1954] 1 QB 476 394–95
Stocznia Gdanska SA v Latvian Shipping Co and Latreefers Inc [1998] 1 WLR 574.................. 382
Stoke-on-Trent City Council v W & J Wass Ltd [1988] 1 WLR 1406................. 348, 349, 350, 351
Stokes v Moore 262 Ala 5977 (1955)...462
Stollmeyer v Petroleum Development Co Ltd [1918] AC 498n..................................447–48
Stollmeyer v Trinidad Lake Petroleum Co [1918] AC 485.....................................448, 506
Storer v Great Western Rly (1842) 2 Y & C Ch Cas 48... 416
Strand Electric and Engineering Co Ltd v Brisford Entertainments Ltd
  [1952] 2 QB 246.. 220, 321–22, 324–25
Stratford & Son Ltd v Lindley [1965] AC 269 469–70
Stretchline Intellectual Properties Ltd v H & M Hennes & Mauritz (UK) Ltd [2016] EWHC
  162 (Pat), [2016] RPC 15 359
Strutt v Whitnell [1975] 1 WLR 870 128
Sudbrook Trading Estate Ltd v Eggleton [1983] 1 AC 444....................................403, 429
Suggitt v Suggitt [2012] EWCA Civ 1140 525–26
Suisse Atlantique Société d'Armement Maritime SA v Rotterdamsche Kolen Centrale NV
  [1967] 1 AC 361 393
Suleman v Shahsavari [1988] 1 WLR 1181... 173
Summers v Salford Corpn [1943] AC 283 234
Supershield Ltd v Siemens Building Technologies FE Ltd [2010] EWCA Civ 7,
  [2010] 1 Lloyd's Rep 349 ....vii–viii, 102–3
Surrey County Council v Bredero Homes Ltd [1993] 1 WLR 1361 ....317, 327, 354, 357–58, 359
Sutcliffe v Pressdram Ltd [1991] 1 QB 153.. 274
Sutherland Publishing Co Ltd v Caxton Publishing Co Ltd [1936] Ch 323 228–29
Sutton v Sutton [1984] Ch 184..427–28
Swift v Secretary of State for Justice [2013] EWCA Civ 193, [2014] QB 373....................256–57
Swindle v Harrison [1997] 4 All ER 705..511–12
Swingcastle Ltd v Alastair Gibson (a firm) [1991] 2 AC 223 .... 38, 188
Swordheath Properties Ltd v Tabet [1979] 1 WLR 285.. 221
Swynson Ltd v Lowick Rose LLP [2017] UKSC 32, [2018] AC 313 ....vii–viii, 155, 160
Sykes v Sykes (1824) 3 B & C 541... 272
Sylvia Shipping Co Ltd v Progress Bulk Carriers Ltd [2010] EWHC 542 (Comm),
  [2010] 2 Lloyd's Rep 81 102

Tabcorp Holdings Ltd v Bowen Investments Pty Ltd [2009] HCA 8, (2009) 236 CLR 272............. 199
Tableland Peanuts v Peanut Marketing Board (1984) 58 ALJR 283 475
Taff Vale Rly Co v Jenkins [1913] AC 1..259–60
Tai Hing Cotton Mill Ltd v Liu Chong Hing Bank Ltd [1986] AC 80, [1985] 2 All ER 947 7
Takitota v Attorney-General [2009] UKPC 11, (2009) 26 BHRC 578 363–64
Talbot v Berkshire County Council [1994] QB 290, [1993] 4 All ER 9 163
Talbot v General Television Corpn Pty Ltd [1981] RPC 1, [1980] VR 224 ....521, 523
Tamares (Vincent Square) Ltd v Fairpoint [2007] EWHC 212, [2007] 1 WLR 2167 321–22
Tameside and Glossop Acute Services NHS Trust v Thompstone [2008] EWCA Civ 5,
  [2008] 1 WLR 2207..166–67
Tamplin v James (1879) 15 Ch D 215 430
Tang Min Sit (Personal Representatives) v Capacious Investments Ltd [1996] AC 514 345–46
Target Holdings Ltd v Redfern [1996] AC 421.................505, 512, 513, 515, 517–18, 519, 520, 540

Tate & Lyle Food and Distribution Ltd v Greater London Council [1983] 2 AC 509,
    [1982] 1 WLR 149, [1981] 2 All ER 256...52, 230, 302
Tate & Lyle Food and Distribution Ltd v Greater London Council [1981] 3 All ER 716............302, 305
Taylor v Beere [1982] 1 NZLR 81 375
Taylor v Neville (prior to 1746) (1746) 3 Atk 384..407–8
Taylor v NUM [1984] IRLR 445..482
Taylor v O'Connor [1971] AC 115...184, 262
Taylor and Foulstone v National Union of Mineworkers (Yorkshire Area) [1984] IRLR 445.........481–82
Taylor Fashions Ltd v Liverpool Victoria Trustees Co Ltd [1981] 1 All ER 897..................487–88
Taylor (CR) (Wholesale) Ltd v Hepworths Ltd [1977] 1 WLR 659......................................208
Teacher v Calder (1899) 1 F 39..353
Techno Land Improvements Ltd v British Leyland (UK) Ltd (1979) 252 Estates Gazette 805........148–49
Tehno-Impex v Gebr van Weelde Scheepvaartkantoor BV [1981] QB 648..................................297
Telegraph Despatch and Intelligence Co v McLean (1873) 8 Ch App 658................................486
Tennant Radiant Heat Ltd v Warrington Development Corpn [1988] 1 EGLR 41............................85
Test Claimants in the FII Group Litigation v HMRC [2012] UKSC 19, [2012] 2 AC 337...................16
Tetley v Chitty [1986] 1 All ER 663...448
Texaco Ltd v Mulberry Filling Station Ltd [1972] 1 WLR 814....................................460–61, 482
Texaco Melbourne, The *See* A-G of the Republic of Ghana v Texaco Overseas Tankships Ltd,
    The Texaco Melbourne
Thai Airways International Public Co Ltd v KI Holdings Co Ltd [2015] EWHC 1250 (Comm),
    [2016] 1 All ER (Comm) 675 ....130, 149
Thake v Maurice [1986] QB 644, [1986] 2 WLR 337...249–50
Thames Guaranty Ltd v Campbell [1985] QB 210...431
Thomas v Bunn [1991] 1 AC 362...301
Thomas v National Union of Mineworkers (South Wales Area) [1986] Ch 20..........................476–77
Thomas v Pearce [2000] FSR 718...509–10
Thomas v Wignall [1987] QB 1098...184
Thomas Borthwick v South Otago Freezing Co Ltd [1978] 1 NZLR 538................................482–83
Thomas Marshall Ltd v Guinle [1979] Ch 227...419, 491
Thomas (PA) & Co v Mould [1968] 2 QB 913...444, 445
Thompson v Arnold [2007] EWHC 1875 (QB), [2008] PIQR P1..257–58
Thompson v Metropolitan Police Comr [1998] QB 498, [1997] 3 WLR 403 ....284–85, 288–89,
                                                                                   363, 371, 372, 373
Thorn v Public Works Comrs (1863) 32 Beav 490...404–5
Thorne v Heard and Marsh [1894] 1 Ch 599...544
Thornett & Fehr and Yuills Ltd, Re [1921] 1 KB 219..69
Tipping v Eckersley (1855) 2 K & J 264...455
Tito v Waddell (No 2) [1977] Ch 106 ....38, 197–98, 200, 353, 354, 355, 359, 409, 416–17, 465, 504
Tiuta International Ltd v De Villiers Surveyors Ltd [2017] UKSC 77,
    [2017] 1 WLR 4627...38, 160–61, 232
Todd v Gee (1810) 17 Ves 273..315
Tollemache and Cobbold Breweries Ltd v Reynolds (1983) 268 Estates Gazette 52................463, 487
Tolnay v Criterion Film Productions Ltd [1936] 2 All ER 1625..269
Tomkinson v First Pennsylvania Banking and Trust Co [1961] AC 1007..................................177
Topfell Ltd v Galley Properties Ltd [1979] 1 WLR 446..437–38
Toropdar v D [2009] EWHC 567 (QB), [2010] Lloyd's R IR 358...505
Torquay Hotel Co Ltd v Cousins [1969] 2 Ch 106...467
Total Liban SA v Vitol Energy SA [2001] QB 643...205–6
Tradigrain SA v King Diamond Shipping SA, The Spiros C [2000] 2 Lloyd's Rep 319................382–83
Trafigura Beheer BV v Mediterranean Shipping Co SA [2007] EWCA Civ 794,
    [2008] 1 All ER (Comm) 385 175–76
Trans Trust SPRL v Danubian Trading Co Ltd [1952] 2 QB 297...145
Transfield Shipping Inc v Mercator Shipping Inc, The Achilleas [2008] UKHL 48,
    [2009] 1 AC 61................................vii–viii, 98, 99–100, 101–3, 104, 105, 117, 119–20
Transfield Shipping Inc v Mercator Shipping Inc, The Achilleas [2007] 2 Lloyd's Rep 555............104
Transoceanica Francesca and Nicos V, The [1987] 2 Lloyd's Rep 155..................................181
Transworld Oil Ltd v North Bay Shipping Corpn, The Rio Claro [1987] 2 Lloyd's Rep 173..............96
Trask v Clark & Sons [1980] CLY 2588...279
Treadaway v Chief Constable of West Midlands (1994) Times, 25 October...............................363
Tredegar Iron and Coal Co Ltd v Hawthorn Bros & Co (1902) 18 TLR 716...............................132

Table of Cases xlix

Tremain v Pike [1969] 1 WLR 1556. 88
Trevor (J) & Sons v Solomon (1978) 248 Estates Gazette 779 479
Tripp v Thomas (1824) 3 B & C 427 73
Tulk v Moxhay (1848) 18 LJ Ch 83 317
Turf Club Auto Emporium Pte Ltd v Yeo Boong Hua [2018] SGCA 44. 332
Turner v Clowes (1869) 20 LT 214. 409
Turner v Ministry of Defence (1969) 113 Sol Jo 585, CA. 160
Twinsectra Ltd v Yardley [2002] UKHL 12, [2002] 2 AC 164 509–10

UCB Bank plc v Hepherd Winstanley and Pugh [1999] Lloyd's Rep PN 963 . . . . .138, 140–41
UCB Corporate Services Ltd v Clyde & Co (a firm) [2000] 2 All ER (Comm) 257, CA 133
Underhill v Ministry of Food [1950] 1 All ER 591 506
Union Discount Co Ltd v Zoller (Union Cal Ltd, Pt 20 defendant) [2001] EWCA Civ 1755,
    [2002] 1 WLR 1517. 83
United Australia Ltd v Barclays Bank Ltd [1941] AC 1, [1940] 4 All ER 20 . . . . 14, 340, 345–46
United Horse-Shoe and Nail Co Ltd v Stewart (1888) 13 App Cas 401 . . . . .228–29, 343
United Pan-Europe Communications NV v Deutsche Bank AG [2000] 2 BCLC 461 533
United Scientific Holdings Ltd v Burnley Borough Council [1978] AC 904. 514
United States v Carroll 159 F 2d 169 (1947). 42–43
Universal City Studios Inc v Mukhtar & Sons Ltd [1976] 1 WLR 568 486
Universal Thermosensors Ltd v Hibben [1992] 1 WLR 840 523–24
Uren v John Fairfax & Sons Pty Ltd (1966) 117 CLR 118. 375
Uzinterimpex JSC v Standard Bank plc [2008] EWCA Civ 819, [2008] 2 Lloyd's Rep 456 . . . 46–47, 128–29

Vacwell Engineering Co Ltd v BDH Chemicals Ltd [1971] 1 QB 88 87
Van Colle v Chief Constable of the Hertfordshire Police [2008] UKHL 50, [2009] 1 AC 225 . . . . .23, 25–26
Van der Garde BV v Force India Formula One Team [2010] EWHC 2373 (QB) 198–99, 321–22
Vanderpant v Mayfair Hotel Co Ltd [1930] 1 Ch 138. 448
Veflings Rederi A/S v President of India, The Ballami [1979] 1 WLR 59. 181
Vento v Chief Constable of West Yorkshire Police (No 2) [2002] EWCA Civ 1871,
    [2003] IRLR 102 . . . . 284–85, 289–90
Verani Ltd v Manuel Revert y Cia SA [2003] EWCA Civ 1651, [2004] 2 Lloyd's Rep 14. 181
Vercoe v Rutland Fund Management Ltd [2010] EWHC 424 (Ch) . . . . vii–viii, 321–22, 524
Verderame v Commercial Union Assurance Co plc [1992] BCLC 793 286–87
Vernon v Bosley [1997] 1 All ER 577 234
Verrall v Great Yarmouth Borough Council [1981] QB 202 403
Vertex Data Science Ltd v Powergen Retail Ltd [2006] EWHC 1340 (Comm),
    [2006] 2 Lloyd's Rep 591 459
Vestergaard Frandsen A/S v Bestnet Europe Ltd [2013] UKSC 31, [2013] 1 WLR 1556. 509–10
Victoria Laundry (Windsor) Ltd v Newman Industries Ltd [1949] 2 KB 528. . . . . . 92, 94–95, 96, 97, 98, 124, 195
Vidal-Hall v Google Inc [2015] EWCA Civ 311, [2016] QB 1003 . . . . vii–viii, 12–13, 521, 525
Vine v National Dock Labour Board [1957] AC 488 423
Virgo Fidelis Senior School v Boyle [2004] IRLR 268. . . . . .289–90, 362
Vivasseur v Krupp (1878) 9 Ch D 351. 498–99
Voaden v Champion, The Baltic Surveyor and Timbuktu [2002] EWCA Civ 89,
    [2002] 1 Lloyd's Rep 623 218
Von Joel v Hornsey [1895] 2 Ch 774. . . . . .464, 482
Vorvis v Insurance Corp of British Columbia [1989] 1 SCR 1085 375

W v Meah [1986] 1 All ER 935. . . . . .234, 284–85
W v Veolia Environment Services (UK) plc [2011] EWHC 2020 (QB), [2012] 1 All ER (Comm) 667. 146
W v W [1999] 2 NZLR 1. 371
W L Thompson Ltd v Robinson (Gunmakers) Ltd [1955] Ch 177 . . . . .147, 196
Wadcock v London Borough of Brent [1990] IRLR 223. 422
Wadey v Surrey County Council [2000] 1 WLR 820 156–57
Wadham Stringer Finance Ltd v Meaney [1981] 1 WLR 39. 389
Wadsworth v Lydall [1981] 2 All ER 401, [1981] 1 WLR 598 . . . . 179–80, 296–97
Wagon Mound, The *See* Overseas Tankship (UK) Ltd v Morts Dock and Engineering Co Ltd,
    The Wagon Mound
Wagon Mound (No 2), The *See* Overseas Tankship (UK) Ltd v Miller Steamship Co Pty,
    The Wagon Mound (No 2)

Table of Cases

Wainwright v Home Office [2003] UKHL 53, [2003] 3 WLR 1137 ....285–86, 521
Wait, Re [1927] 1 Ch 606... 405, 406, 408–9, 495
Wait and James v Midland Bank (1926) 31 Com Cas 523 495
Wakeham v Wood (1981) 43 P & CR 40.. 466
Walker v Eastern Counties Rly Co (1848) 6 Hare 594 403
Walker v Geo H Medlicott & Son [1999] 1 All ER 685.. 129
Walker v John McLean & Sons Ltd [1979] 1 WLR 760.. 171
Walker v Mullen (1984) Times, 19 January 241–42
Walker v Northumberland County Council [1995] 1 All ER 737.................................... 234
Wall v Rederiaktiebolaget Luggude [1915] 3 KB 66 394
Wallace v Manchester City Council (1998) 30 HLR 1111 .... 279–80, 291
Waller v Waller [1967] 1 All ER 305 538
Wallersteiner v Moir (No 2) [1975] QB 373.. 511–12, 542
Walsh v Shanahan [2013] EWCA Civ 411 532–33
Walter v Alltools Ltd (1944) 61 TLR 39, CA.. 272, 284–85
Walters v Morgan (1861) 3 De GF & J 718.. 430
Walton v Calderdale Healthcare NHS Trust [2005] EWHC 1053 (QB), [2006] PIQR Q3 239–40
Wapshott v Davies Donovan (a firm) [1996] PNLR 361... 279–80
Ward v Allies & Morrison Architects [2012] EWCA Civ 1287, [2013] PIQR Q1..................... 249
Ward v Cannock Chase District Council [1986] Ch 546 .... 113, 206, 207, 283–84
Ward v James [1966] 1 QB 273.. 274–75
Ward v Newalls Insulation Co Ltd [1998] 1 WLR 1722 238
Warman International Ltd v Dwyer (1995) 182 CLR 544 .... 526, 528, 535
Warmington v Miller [1973] QB 877.. 431
Warner v Clark (1984) 134 NLJ 763, CA 361
Warner v Islip (1984) 134 NLJ 763, CA... 367
Warner Bros Pictures Inc v Nelson [1937] 1 KB 209........................... 457, 458, 459, 461, 462
Warren v Mendy [1989] 1 WLR 853 .... 459, 461
Warriner v Warriner [2002] EWCA Civ 81, [2002] 1 WLR 1703 246–47
Watford Electronics Ltd v Sanderson CFL Ltd [2001] EWCA Civ 317, [2001] 1 All ER (Comm) 696.... 93
Watkins v Secretary of State for the Home Department [2004] EWCA Civ 966 372
Watkins v Secretary of State for the Home Department [2006] UKHL 17, [2006] 2 AC 395......24, 25–26
Watson v Croft Promosport Ltd [2009] EWCA Civ 15, [2009] 3 All ER 249 .... 445, 447, 449–50
Watson v Willmott [1991] 1 QB 140, [1990] 3 WLR 1103.. 266
Watson, Laidlaw & Co Ltd v Pott, Cassels and Williamson (1914) 31 RPC 104, HL 229–30, 321–22
Watts v Morrow [1991] 1 WLR 1421...................... 188, 277, 280, 281, 282–84, 286–87, 291–92
Watts v Spence [1976] Ch 165 225–26
Watts, Watts & Co Ltd v Mitsui & Co Ltd [1917] AC 227 394
Wayling v Jones (1995) 69 P & CR 170... 511–12
Webster v Cecil (1861) 30 Beav 62.. 430
Weld-Blundell v Stephens [1920] AC 956... 110–11
Weller v Associated Newspapers Ltd [2015] EWCA Civ 1176, [2016] 1 WLR 1541 443–44
Wellesley Partners LLP v Withers LLP [2015] EWCA Civ 1146, [2016] Ch 529 ....vii–viii, 91, 106
Wells v Wells [1999] 1 AC 345 .... 83, 184, 242, 244–45, 246–47, 260, 262, 307
Wentworth v Wiltshire County Council [1993] QB 654, [1993] 2 All ER 256 302
Wertheim v Chicoutimi Pulp Co [1911] AC 301.. 38, 195
West v Ian Finlay [2014] EWCA Civ 316, [2014] BLR 324 305
West v Versil Ltd (1996) Times, 31 August.. 158
West & Son Ltd v Shephard [1964] AC 326 .... 36, 237
West Midlands Travel Ltd v Aviva Insurance UK Ltd [2013] EWCA Civ 887,
    [2014] RTR 10 ....vii–viii, 215–16
Westdeutsche Landesbank Girozentrale v Islington London Borough Council [1996] AC 669..... 303, 542
Western v MacDermott (1866) 2 Ch App 72 486
Western Trust & Savings Ltd v Clive Travers & Co [1997] PNLR 295, CA 129
Western Web Offset Printers Ltd v Independent Media Ltd [1995] 37 LS Gaz R 24 200
Westwood v Secretary of State for Employment [1985] AC 20.................................. 148, 157
Wham-O Manufacturing Co v Lincoln Industries Ltd [1982] RPC 281 497–98
Wheelwright v Walker (1883) 23 Ch D 752 538
White v Chief Constable of South Yorkshire Police [1999] 2 AC 455............................ 285–86
White v Jones [1995] 2 AC 207, [1995] 1 All ER 691, [1995] 2 WLR 187 .... 6–7, 8, 45, 201, 233
White v Metropolitan Police Comr (1982) Times, 24 April..................... 272, 284–85, 362–63

White and Carter (Councils) Ltd v McGregor [1962] AC 413 . . . . vii–viii, 132, 383–85, 386–87
White Arrow Express Ltd v Lamey's Distribution Ltd (1995) 15 Tr LR 69 191
Whitehead v Searle [2008] EWCA Civ 285, [2009] 1 WLR 549 . . . . 65, 170
Whiteley Ltd v Hilt [1918] 2 KB 808 494
Whiten v Pilot Insurance Co (2002) 209 DLR (4th) 257, [2003] SCC 18 . . . . 361, 377–78
Whitmore v Euroways Express Coaches Ltd (1984) Times, 4 May. 285–86
Whitwham v Westminster Brymbo Coal & Coke Co [1896] 1 Ch 894 . . . . 221, 321–22
Whitwood Chemical Co v Hardman [1891] 2 Ch 416 . . . . 457, 458
Wickham Holdings Ltd v Brooke House Motors Ltd [1967] 1 WLR 295, CA 219
Wieland v Cyril Lord Carpets Ltd [1969] 3 All ER 1006 116
Wilkinson v Clements (1872) 8 Ch App 96 435
Wilkinson v Downton [1897] 2 QB 57 . . . . 285–86, 444
Wilkinson v Lloyd (1845) 7 QB 27 352–53
Wilkes v Wood (1763) Lofft 1 362
William Bros v Agius Ltd [1920] 2 KB 11, [1914] AC 510 . . . . 151–52, 191–92, 193, 196, 219–20
William Robinson & Co Ltd v Heuer [1898] 2 Ch 451 457
Williams v Barton [1927] 2 Ch 9 526
Williams v BOC Gases Ltd [2000] PIQR Q253 159–60
Williams v Central Bank of Nigeria [2014] UKSC 10, [2014] AC 1189 . . . . vii–viii, 543, 544
Williams v Greatrex [1957] 1 WLR 31 433
Williams v Natural Life Health Foods Ltd [1998] 2 All ER 577, [1998] 1 WLR 830 6–7
Williams v Settle [1960] 1 WLR 1072 367–68
Williams v The Bermuda Hospitals Board [2016] UKPC 4, [2016] AC 888 52
Willis v Childe (1851) 13 Beav 117 423
Willmott v Barber (1880) 15 Ch D 96 487–88
Willson v Ministry of Defence [1991] 1 All ER 638 165
Wilsher v Essex Area Health Authority [1988] AC 1074 62–63
Wilson v Furness Rly Co (1869) LR 9 Eq 28 416
Wilson v National Coal Board (1981) 1981 SLT 67, HL 160
Wilson v United Counties Bank Ltd [1920] AC 102 . . . . 73, 269
Wise v Kaye [1962] 1 QB 638 . . . . 237, 248
Withers v General Theatre Corpn Ltd [1933] 2 KB 536 . . . . 69, 269
Wolstenholme v Leach's of Shudehill Ltd [2016] EWHC 588 (QB) 258–59
Wolverhampton and Walsall Rly Co v London and North Western Rly Co (1873) LR 16 Eq 433 . . . . 416, 457
Wolverhampton Corpn v Emmons [1901] 1 KB 515 . . . . 416, 417
Wong v Parkside Health NHS Trust [2001] EWCA Civ 1721, [2003] 3 All ER 932 285–86
Wood v Bentall Simplex Ltd [1992] PIQR P332 266
Wood v Conway Corpn [1914] 2 Ch 47 445
Wood v Law Society (1995) Times, 2 March 286–87
Woodar Investment Development Ltd v Wimpey Construction (UK) Ltd [1980] 1 WLR 277 201
Woodward v Hutchins [1977] 1 WLR 760 539
Wookey v Wookey [1991] Fam 121 441
Woollerton and Wilson Ltd v Richard Costain Ltd [1970] 1 WLR 411 . . . . 445–46, 447–48
Woolwich Equitable Building Society v IRC [1993] AC 70 298
Workers Trust & Merchant Bank Ltd v Dojap Investments Ltd [1993] AC 573 394–95
World Beauty The, *See* Andros Springs (Owners) v Owners of World Beauty,
    The World Beauty
Wright v British Railways Board [1983] 2 AC 773, [1983] 2 All ER 698 . . . . 36, 171, 234–36, 307
Wright v Lodge [1993] 4 All ER 299 111
Wroth v Tyler [1974] Ch 30 . . . . 95, 172–73, 317, 430–31
Wrotham Park Estate Co v Parkside Homes Ltd [1974] 1 WLR 798 . . . . 48–49, 317, 321–22, 323,
                    326, 327, 328, 329–30, 331, 332, 336, 350, 354, 355, 356–58, 466, 490
WWF-World Wide Fund for Nature v World Wide Wrestling Federation [2006] EWHC 184
    rev'd on appeal, [2007] EWCA Civ 286, [2008] 1 WLR 445 . . . . 321–22, 341

X v Y [1988] 2 All ER 648 538–39
Xena Systems Ltd v Cantideck [2013] EWPCC 1 299

Yachuk v Oliver Blais Co Ltd [1949] AC 386 133
Yam Seng Pte Limited v International Trade Corporation Limited [2013] EWHC 111 (QB),
    [2013] 1 Lloyd's Rep 526 79

Yates v Whyte (1838) 4 Bing NC 272. 153
Yearworth v North Bristol NHS Trust [2009] EWCA Civ 37, [2009] 2 All ER 986 .... 278, 284–85
Yeoman Credit Ltd v Waragowski [1961] 1 WLR 1124, [1961] 3 All ER 145 .... 70, 297–98
Yetton v Eastwoods Froy Ltd [1967] 1 WLR 104. 127–28
YM v Gloucester Hospitals NHS Foundation Trust [2006] EWHC 820, [2006] PIQR P27 166–67
Yorkshire Electricity Board v Naylor [1968] AC 529 171
Youell v Bland Welch & Co Ltd (Superhulls Cover Case) (No 2) [1990] 2 Lloyd's Rep 431 ...... 84–85, 126
Young v Purdy [1996] 2 FLR 795. 114
Yousif v Salama [1980] 1 WLR 1540 485–86
Youyang Pty Ltd v Minter Ellison Morris Fletcher (2003) 196 ALR 482 .... 513–14, 515

Z v United Kingdom (App No 29392/95) (2001) 34 EHRR 97, 10 BHRC 384, ECtHR. 22
Z Ltd v A-Z and AA-LL [1982] QB 558. 441
ZYX Music GmbH v King [1995] 3 All ER 1 367–68
Zinovieff v British Transport Commission (1954) Times, 1 April 182, 261
Zockoll Group Ltd v Mercury Communications Ltd [1998] FSR 354 483–84
Zucker v Tyndall Holdings plc [1992] 1 WLR 1127 401

DECISIONS OF THE EUROPEAN COURT OF JUSTICE

These are listed below numerically and are also included in the preceding alphabetical list

26/62: NV Algemene Transport-en Expeditie Onderneming van Gend en Loos
    NV v Nederlandse Belastingadministratie [1963] ECR 1, [1963] CMLR 105, ECJ. 15
43/75: Defrenne v Sabena [1976] ECR 455, [1981] 1 All ER 122 15
33/76: Rewe-Zentralfinanz GmbH v Landwirtschaftskammer für Saarland [1976] ECR 1989,
    [1977] 1 CMLR 533 16
Case 199/82: Amministrazione delle Finanze dello Stato SpA San Georgio, [1983] ECR 3595 ...... 16, 298
C-6&9/90: Francovich and Bonifaci v Italy [1991] ECR I-5357, [1993] 2 CMLR 66 15
C-46 & 48/93: Brasserie du Pecheur SA v Germany, R v Secretary of State for Transport,
    ex p Factortame Ltd: [1996] QB 404, [1996] 2 WLR 506, [1996] ECR I-1029. 15
C-392/93: R v HM Treasury, ex p British Telecommunications plc [1996] QB 615,
    [1996] 3 WLR 203, [1996] ECR I-1631 15
C-178–9/94, 188, 189–190/94: Dillenkofer v Germany[1996] ECR I-4845,
    [1996] All ER (EC) 917, [1996] 3 CMLR 469 15
C-283, 291, 292/94: Denkavit Internationaal BV, VITIC Amsterdam BV and
    Voormeer BV v Bundesamt für Finanzen [1996] ECR I-5063. 15
C-397–410/98: Metallgesellschaft Ltd v IRC: Hoescht v IRC [2001] Ch 620,
    [2001] 2 WLR 1497, [2001] ECR I-1727 16
C-453/99: Courage v Crehan [2001] ECR I-6297 15
C-224/01: Köbler v Austria [2004] QB 848, [2004] 2 WLR 976, ECJ. 15

Table of Legislation

UNITED KINGDOM

Statutes

Administration of Justice Act 1970
    s 44A 301, 307–8
Administration of Justice
    Act 1982 . . . . 262–63, 264, 265, 301
    s 1(1)(a) 237
    s 1(1)((b) 237
    s 2 258–59
    s 3 256
    s 4 256
    s 4(1) 253
    s 4(2) 254
    s 5 239–40
    Sch 1 301
Animals Act 1971 89
Arbitration Act 1996
    s 49 303–4
Banking Act 1979
    s 47 138
Carriage by Air Act 1961
    Sch 1, art 22 83
    Sch 1, art 29 311
Carriage of Passengers by Road Act 1974
    Sch 1, art 13(1) 83
Chancery Amendment Act 1858
    (Lord Cairn's Act) 314, 318, 319, 321,
                         437, 444, 511, 521, 522
    s 2 . . . . 315, 437–38
Civil Liability Act 2018 . . . . .viii, 245–46, 262
    Pt 1 238
    s 10 246–47
Civil Partnership Act 2004 263
Civil Procedure Act 1997
    s 7 485–86
Common Law Procedure Act 1854
    s 78 493
Compensation Act 2006 57
    s 3 . . . . .57, 62
Consumer Credit Act 1974
    s 100 400
    s 100(5) 495
Consumer Protection Act 1987
    Pt I (ss 1–9) 206, 311
    s 5 206
Consumer Rights Act 2015 . . . 393–94, 395–96, 412
    Pt 1 . . . . 402, 412, 416–17
    Pt 2 . . . . 390, 391, 395, 396, 399, 400
    s 19 412
    s 19(1)–(2) 412
    s 23 412
    s 23(3) 412
    ss 42–43 412
    s 42(1) 412

    s 43(3) 412
    ss 54–55 412
    s 54(2) 412
    s 55(3) 412
    s 58 . . . . viii, 412
    s 58(3) 412
    s 63 . . . . .396, 400
    Sch 2, para 6 . . . . .396, 400
Contracts (Rights of Third Parties)
    Act 1999 . . . . 201, 204, 317, 410
    s 1(5) 204
Copyright Act 1956
    s 17(3) 284–85, 367–68
    s 18 499
Copyright, Designs and Patents Act 1988
    ss 96–98 228
    s 96(2) 341–42
    s 97(1) 228, 342
    s 97(2) 284–85, 367–68
    s 99 499
    s 99(4) 499
    s 114 499
    s 191(2) 341–42
    s 191J(1) 228, 342
    s 191J(2) 367–68
    s 195 499
    s 204 499
    s 229(2) 341–42
    s 229(3) 367–68
    s 230 499
    s 230(7) 499
    s 231 499
    s 233(1) 228, 342
    s 233(2) 499
County Courts Act 1984
    s 38 . . . . 4, 440
    s 50 167–68
    s 66 . . . . .274, 372
    s 69 . . . . 301, 303–4
    Sch 1 497
Courts Act 2003 166
    ss 100–101 166–67
Courts and Legal Services Act 1990 497
    s 8 274
    s 8(2) 372
Criminal Justice Act 1988 371
Criminal Justice and Courts Act 2015
    s 57 83
Crime and Courts Act 2013
    ss 34–39 . . . . viii, 367–68, 377
    s 39 287–88
Crown Proceedings Act 1947
    s 21 440–41
    s 21(1)(a) 401, 440–41
    s 21(1)(b) 496

Table of Legislation

Damages Act 1996 166–67
  s 1..........................242, 245
  s 1(2) 262
  s 2(1) 166–67
  s 2(3) 166–67
  s 2(8) 166–67
  s 2(9) 166–67
  s 2B............................166–67
  s 3..........................254, 258
  s 3(4) 254
  s 4............................166–67
  s 6............................166–67
  s 7................................262
  s A1(2)..........................246–47
  Sch 1 245–46
Damages (Scotland) Act 1976 253
Damages (Scotland) Act 1993 253
Defamation Act 1996...............273, 311
Defamation Act 2013
  s 11................. viii, 37, 274, 372
Employment Rights Act 1996........ 270–71, 425
  s 47B...........................289–90
  s 112(4) 282
  ss 113–117.........................425
  s 117(3)(a).........................282
  ss 118–127.........................282
Equality Act 2010 284–85
  s 97(2) 284–85
  s 119...........................284–85
  s 124...........................284–85
European Communities Act 1972 369–70
  s 2(1) 15
European Union Withdrawal Act 2018
  Sch 1, para 4 15
Fatal Accidents Act 1846–1959 ....254, 256
Fatal Accidents Act 1976.....24, 37, 57, 64, 65–66,
     148, 156, 171–72, 182, 243, 248–49, 251,
     252–53, 254, 256–58, 261, 262–63, 264,
     265–67, 276, 285–86, 305, 312
  s 1(1) 257–58, 312
  s 1(2) 256
  s 1(2)(b)...........................264
  s 1(3) 256–57
  s 1(4)–(4A) 256–57
  s 1(5)(a)..........................256–57
  s 1(5)(b)(i)........................256–57
  s 1(5)(b)(ii).......................256–57
  s 1A 263
  s 1A(2)............................263
  s 1A(4)............................264
  s 1A(5)............................263
  s 2(1) 257
  s 2(2) 257
  s 2(3) 257
  s 3(3) 263, 265
  s 3(4) 262–63
  s 3(5) 264, 267
  s 4.................148, 261–62, 265–67
  s 4(1) 261, 265
  s 4(2) 254
  s 5 257–58

Health and Social Care (Community Health
    and Standards) Act 2003
  Pt III (ss 150–169)................156–57
Housing Act 1985
  s 21...............................492
Housing Act 1988..................375
  ss 27–28..........................373
Human Fertilisation and Embryology
    Act 2008
  s 43.............................256–57
Human Rights Act 1998 ....vii, 12–13, 21, 22,
     23–24, 25–26, 27, 28, 29, 256–57,
     264, 285, 289, 364, 370, 479–80
  s 3(1) 22, 257
  s 4................................264
  s 6..............................318–19
  s 6(1) 22–23, 257
  s 6(3) 22
  s 7(5) 311
  s 8.........................23, 28, 29
  s 8(1)–(4)..........................23
  s 8(1) 26
  s 8(3) 23–24, 26, 364, 370, 402
  s 8(4) 23–24, 26, 370
  s 12...............................423
  s 12(3) 22, 479–80, 539–40
Industrial Relations Act 1971 .... 420–22, 425
International Transport Conventions Act 1983 256
Judgments Act 1838..................303
  s 17.............................295–96
  s 17(1) 301
  s 17(2) 301
Judicature Acts 1873–1875 ....10, 317, 504, 505, 509
Landlord and Tenant Act 1927
  s 18...............................199
Landlord and Tenant Act 1985
  s 17....................... 416, 427–28
Landlord and Tenant Act 1988...............366
  s 1(3) 366
Late Payment of Commercial Debts
    (Interest) Act 1998 295–96
  s 3(2) 295–96
  s 4...............................295–96
  s 5...............................295–96
  ss 8–9............................295–96
  s 11..............................295–96
Latent Damage Act 1986................313–14
Law of Property (Miscellaneous Provisions)
    Act 1989
  s 3................................76
Law Reform (Contributory Negligence)
    Act 1945 ....116, 132–33, 134, 137,
     138, 140, 141, 257–58
  s 1(1) 134, 136
  s 4.................... 136–38, 139, 140, 143
Law Reform (Frustrated Contracts)
    Act 1943 .... 304–5, 352, 542
Law Reform (Miscellaneous Provisions)
    Act 1934 .....254, 256, 265, 267, 301, 311–12
  s 1(1) 132–33, 253
  s 1 (1A) 253

s 1(2) 254
s 1(2)(c)...................254–55, 264, 267
s 1(3) 339
s 3(1) 542
Law Reform (Personal Injuries) Act 1948
  s 2(1) 157
  s 2(4) 239–40
Legal Aid, Sentencing and Punishment
  of Offenders Act 2012..................236
Limitation Act 1939......................489
Limitation Act 1980.........15, 285–86, 309, 311,
                            313–14, 339, 544
  s 2................................311, 496
  s 3(1) 311
  s 4A 311
  s 5................................310, 544
  s 8(1) 310
  ss 11–14..............................311
  s 11...............................311, 312
  s 11(4) 311
  s 11(2) 311
  s 11(5) 311–12
  s 11A 311
  s 12...................................312
  s 12(1) 312
  s 12(2) 312
  s 14(1) 311–12
  s 14(3) 311
  s 14A 8, 314
  s 14A(4)(a) 313–14
  s 14A(4)(b) 313–14
  s 14A(5).............................313–14
  s 14A(10)............................313–14
  s 14B 313–14
  s 15(1) 497
  s 21...................................543
  s 21(1) 543, 544
  s 21(1)(a)............................543
  s 21(1)(b)............................543
  s 21(3) 544
  s 23................................339, 544
  s 28................................311, 505
  s 29(5) 382
  s 32...................................311
  s 32(1)(c)............................298
  s 32A 311
  s 33....................310, 311, 312, 313
  s 33(1) 312
  s 33(3) 312
  s 33(5) 312
  s 36(1) 314, 433, 489–90, 496, 544
  s 36(2) 433, 434, 489, 490, 544
Lord Cairns's Act See Chancery
  Amendment Act 1858
Marrriage (Same Sex Couples) Act 2013
  s 11................................256–57
  Sch 3 256–57
Mental Health Act 1983...................289
Merchant Shipping Act 1995
  s 185...................................83
  s 190..................................311

Misrepresentation Act 1967 338–39
  s 2(1) 90, 122–23, 137–38, 223, 225–26
  s 2(2) 226
Occupiers' Liability Act 1957 45
Official Secrets Act 1989 ....356, 357–58
Patents Act 1977
  s 61(1)(d)..........................341–42
  s 61(2) 345–46
  s 62(1) 228, 342
Pneumoconiosis etc (Workers'
  Compensation) Act 1979........156, 265–66
Proceedings Against Estates Act 1970.........339
Protection from Eviction Act 1977 375
Protection from Harassment Act 1997 91,
                              284–85, 443–44
  s 1(1) 284–85
  s 8(3) 284–85
Reserve and Auxiliary Forces (Protection
  of Civil Interests) Act 1951
  s 13(2) 367–68
Road Traffic Act 1988
  s 151...............................167–68
Sale of Goods Act 1893
  s 51...................................173
  s 52................................493–94
Sale of Goods Act 1979 ....172, 406–7
  s 8(2) 381
  s 14(3) 142
  s 49...................................382
  s 49(1) 382
  s 49(2) 382
  s 50(3) 195, 196
  s 51(3) 191, 192
  s 52........................403–4, 405, 406
  s 53(3) 193, 194
Senior Courts Act 1981 ....295–96, 302, 303
  s 32............................167–68, 382
  s 32A 165
  s 32A(1)..............................165
  s 32A(2)..............................165
  s 35A 296–97, 298–99, 300, 301,
                              302, 303–4, 542–43
  s 35A(1)..............................301
  s 35A(4)............................295–96
  s 37(1) 440, 491–92
  s 49...................................437
  s 50........315–16, 321–22, 437, 444, 454–55,
                              511, 512, 520, 521, 522
  s 69...............................274, 372
  s 69(1) 274
Social Security Contributions and Benefits
  Act 1992..............................156
Social Security (Recovery of Benefits)
  Act 1997.........153–54, 155, 156, 157, 265
  s 1(2)(a).............................156
  s 3......................153–54, 156, 157
  ss 4–5...............................157
  s 6...................................156
  s 8.....................153–54, 156–57
  s 17....................153–54, 157
  s 29...................................156

s 33 157
  Sch 2 . . . . 153–54, 156–57
  Sch 3 157
Supply of Goods and Services Act 1982
  s 15(1) 381
Supreme Court Act 1981
  s 32A 165, 254
  s 35A 123, 303–4, 542
  s 35A(2) 301
  s 37 492
  s 37(1) 538
  s 49 317
  s 50 323–24
Torts (Interference with Goods)
  Act 1977 . . . . 206, 493–94
  s 2 219
  s 2(2) 493
  s 3 . . . . 220, 493, 496
  s 3(7) 496
  s 4 . . . . 484, 494, 496, 497
  s 11 138
Trade Marks Act 1994
  s 14(2) 342
Trade Union and Labour Relations
  Act 1974
  s 17 477
Trade Union and Labour Relations
  (Consolidation) Act 1992
  s 146 289–90
  s 219 477
  s 220 477
  s 221(1) 485
  s 221(2) 476–77, 478–79
  s 236 420
  s 244 477

Statutory Instruments
Civil Procedure Rules 1998,
  SI 1998/3132 . . . . 4, 13, 166–67, 310
  r 3(4)(2)(b) 310
  PD 6B, para 3.1(9) 12–13
  r 16.4(e) 235
  PD 16, para 4.2 235
  Pt 24 443
  r 25.1(1)(b) 440–41
  r 25.1(c)(i) 496
  r 25(1)(e) 496
  r 25.1(1)(f) 485
  r 25.1(1)(h) 485–86
  r 25.1(c)(i) 486
  r 25.3 484
  rr 25.6–25.9 . . . . 167–68, 382
  r 25.8 168
  r 25.9 168
  PD 25, para 4 484
  r 31.12 5
  r 40.8 301
  r 40.20 504
  Pt 41 165
  r 41.2 165
  r 41.3 165
  rr 41.4–41.10 166–67
  r 47.8 301
  r 52.21 169
  Pt 54 . . . . 423, 424–25
  r 59.11 274
  Sch 1 . . . . 274, 418–19
Consumer Protection from Unfair Trading
  Regulations 2008, SI 2008/1277
  Pt 4A 12
Copyright and Related Rights Regulations
  1996, SI 1996/2967
  reg 17 228
Copyright and Rights in Databases
  Regulations 1997, SI 1997/3032 228
  reg 23 228
County Court Remedies Regulations 2014,
  SI 2014/982 . . . . 4, 440
Court Funds Rules 2011, SI 2011/1734 306
Damages for Bereavement (Variation of Sum)
  (England and Wales) Order 2013,
  SI 2013/510 . . . . viii, 171–72, 263
Damages (Personal Injury) Order 2001,
  SI 2001/2301 . . . . viii, 245
Damages (Personal Injury) Order 2017,
  SI 2017/206 245
Damages (Variation of Periodical Payments)
  Order 2005, SI 2005/841 . . . . . viii, 54, 166–67
Employment Rights (Increase of Limits)
  Order 2018, SI 2018/194 282
High Court and County Courts Jurisdiction
  Order 1991, SI 1991/724 4
Intellectual Property (Enforcement etc)
  Regulations 2006, SI 2006/1028
  reg 3 . . . . 228, 284–85, 325, 367–68
Judgment Debts (Rate of Interest) Order 1993,
  SI 1993/564 301
Late Payment of Commercial Debts
  (Amendment) Regulations 2015,
  SI 2015/1336 295–96
Late Payment of Commercial Debts
  Regulations 2013, SI 2013/395 295–96
Marriage (Same Sex Couples) Act 2013
  (Consequential and Contrary Provisions
  and Scotland) Order 2014, SI 2014/560 . . . 256–57
Motor Cycles (Protective Helmet) Regulations
  1980, SI 1980/1279 135
Rules of the Supreme Court 1883
  Ord 25, r 5 504
Rules of the Supreme Court
  Ord 45, r 8 418–19
  Ord 53 424–25
Social Security (Recovery of Benefits)
  Regulations 1997, SI 1997/2205 156
  reg 2(2)(a) 156
Unfair Terms in Consumer Contracts
  Regulations 1999, SI 1999/2083 . . . . . 390, 396
  Sch 2, para (e) 396
Working Time Regulations 1998,
  SI 1998/1833 282

NATIONAL LEGISLATION

France

Code Civil
  Art 1382 287

New Zealand

Injury Prevention, Rehabilitation and
  Compensation Act 2001
  s 319..................................371

Trinidad and Tobago

Constitution
  s 14..............................363–64

United States of America

Uniform Commercial Code
  s 2–610a.............................132
  s 2–708(2)...........................196
  s 2–709(1)(b) 384
  s 2–710...........................205–6
  s 2–715...........................205–6
  s 2–716(1)..........................405
  s 2–723(1)..........................132

EUROPEAN LEGISLATION

Conventions

EC Treaty
  Art 81..............................350
European Convention of Human Rights
  and Fundamental Freedoms
  Art 2......................... 256–57, 264
  Art 3................................28
  Art 5................................28
  Art 5(1)............................28
  Art 5(4)........................28, 289
  Art 6............................26–27
  Art 8............12–13, 22, 256–57, 264, 289

Art 10..............................423
Art 14..............................264
Art 41.............................. 23

Regulations

593/2008 Rome I Regulation 180
  Art 12(1)(a).........................180
  Art 12(2)...........................180
  Art 12(c) 180
864/2007 Rome II Regulation 180
  Art 15(c) 180
  Art 15(d)...........................180

Directives

2004/24/EC Intellectual Property Rights
  Enforcement Directive
  Art 13..........228, 284–85, 341–42, 367–68

INTERNATIONAL PRINCIPLES

Principles of European contract Law..........143
  Art 9:504............................143
UNIDROIT Principles of International commercial
  Contracts
  Art 7.4.7............................143

RESTATEMENTS (AMERICAN LAW INSTITUTE)

Second Restatement of Contracts 41, 459–60
  s 87..................................41
  s 90..................................41
  s 158(2) 41
  s 272(2) 41
  s 351(3) 41
  s 353................................283
Second Restatement of Torts
  para 908.............................375

PART ONE
INTRODUCTION

1

General

1. Judicial remedies	3
2. Procedure	4
3. Enforcement	5
4. Orders made to assist the claimant in collecting evidence to establish its case	5
5. Torts and breach of contract	5
6. Concurrent liability between the tort of negligence and breach of contract	6
7. Should one continue to distinguish torts and breach of contract?	8
8. The primary functions of judicial remedies for torts and breach of contract	9
9. Legal and equitable remedies	10
10. Equitable wrongs	11
11. Combining remedies	13
12. Breach of European Union law	15
13. Economic analysis, bargaining around non-monetary remedies, and the consumer surplus	16
14. Corrective justice, civil recourse, and rights	18
15. Approach and methodology	20
16. The layout of the book	21

1. Judicial remedies

The concept of a remedy has rarely been subjected to rigorous analysis.[1] Views may differ as to precisely what one is talking about. In this book, a remedy is used to denote the relief that a person can seek from a court.[2] The focus is therefore entirely on judicial remedies; and not on what are sometimes termed 'self-help' remedies, which are available without coming to court, such as out of court settlements, termination of a contract, and the ejection of trespassers.[3] Put another way, this book examines what a person can obtain from

---

[1] Notable exceptions are K Barker, 'Rescuing Remedialism in Unjust Enrichment Law: Why Remedies are Right' [1998] CLJ 301; P Birks, 'Rights, Wrongs, and Remedies' (2000) 20 OJLS 1; R Zakrzewski, *Remedies Reclassified* (OUP 2005); S Smith, 'Rights, Remedies and Causes of Action' in *Structure and Justification in Private Law* (eds C Rickett and R Grantham, Hart Publishing 2008) 405; S Smith'Duties, Liabilities and Damages' (2012) 125 Harvard LR 1727.

[2] Or from an equivalent body (where appeals can be made to the courts), such as an arbitrator or employment tribunal.

[3] For introductory examinations of some self-help remedies, see, eg, D Harris, D Campbell, and R Halson, *Remedies in Contract and Tort* (2nd edn, Butterworths 2002) chs 2, 3, and 21; FH Lawson, *Remedies of English Law* (2nd edn, Butterworths 1980) chs 1–2. Note also that this book does not discuss judicial remedies available in a claim for judicial review (a quashing order, a prohibiting order, and a mandatory order) even though, arguably, they can be awarded for a tort or breach of contract committed by a public authority: see, eg, *Ex p Napier* (1852) 18 QB 692, at 695. Such remedies are better considered in books on administrative law. See P Craig, *Administrative Law* (8th edn, Sweet & Maxwell 2016) ch 26.

a court to counter an infringement (or threatened infringement) of his or her rights by a tort or breach of contract (or, in chapter 26, by an equitable wrong); but it is not concerned with any other legally permissible options open to a person to counter such an infringement.

A judicial remedy may be either coercive or non-coercive:[4] that is, it may be either a court order to do or not to do something, backed up by enforcement procedures[5] or a court pronouncement indicating or altering what the parties' rights or duties are or were. Examples of the former are damages, specific performance, injunctions, and the award of an agreed sum, while the declaration is the most obvious example of the latter.

This book follows the conventional practice of treating damages as a remedy. In the context of torts and breach of contract, the law of (judicial) remedies looks at the (judicial) relief available for a tort or breach of contract, and damages is one such remedy. There is another view, advocated by Zakrzewski,[6] which defines the law of remedies in terms of the judgment awards and orders made by the courts,[7] and their enforcement, and which treats the law of damages as being essentially concerned with secondary rights which, alongside primary rights, belong outside the law of remedies. While it may be analytically possible to treat the law of damages in that way, it seems unhelpful to do so. On the contrary, this book is based on the view that it is illuminating and practically useful to analyse the relief that a party may seek from a court for a tort or breach of contract. To see the law of remedies as including the law on injunctions and specific performance but not the law on damages cuts across that useful and illuminating approach.

2. Procedure

Our concern will be with the substantive law governing judicial remedies and not with the adjectival law dictating the procedure by which those remedies are obtained. For that, reference should be made to the Civil Procedure Rules and accompanying Practice Directions. It will also be assumed throughout that a court in England or Wales has jurisdiction in respect of the claim[8] and that the claimant is proceeding within the appropriate civil court.[9]

---

[4] FH Lawson, *Remedies of English Law* (2nd edn, Butterworths 1980) 12–14.
[5] Damages and the award of an agreed sum take the form of an award by the court which constitutes a judgment debt owed by one party to the other. That is, a court gives judgment for the claimant for £1,000 rather than saying that 'the defendant shall pay the claimant £1,000'. Such awards can still be regarded, loosely, as 'court orders' and they are certainly coercive because they are backed up by enforcement procedures. Indeed the same enforcement procedures apply to an award of damages as to an award of costs where the standard wording is in the form of a direct order to pay ('The claimant shall pay the defendant its costs of £1,000'). Note that an undertaking given by a defendant to the court and accepted in place of an injunction is enforceable and hence coercive even though, plainly, it does not comprise a court order.
[6] R Zakrzewski, *Remedies Reclassified* (OUP 2005).
[7] For Zakrzewski there is a fundamental division of judgment awards and orders between what he terms 'replicative' and 'transformative' remedies. The former merely replicate the claimant's substantive rights, while the latter confer rights that are different from the claimant's substantive rights.
[8] AV Dicey, JHC Morris, and LA Collins, *Dicey, Morris and Collins on the Conflict of Laws* (15th edn, Sweet & Maxwell 2012) chs 11–12.
[9] Eg, a personal injury action worth less than £50,000 must be brought in a county court: see High Court and County Courts Jurisdiction Order 1991, SI 1991/724. All the remedies covered in this book can be awarded by both the High Court and the county courts: County Courts Act 1984, s 38. But note that by the County Court Remedies Regulations 2014 (SI 2014/982) the county court generally has no jurisdiction to grant a search (*Anton Piller*) order).

3. Enforcement

There is a distinction between the coercive remedies granted by the courts for a tort or breach of contract, and the enforcement or execution of those remedies which may require further court orders. This book is not concerned with the latter secondary realm of judicial involvement. Suffice it to say that for some non-monetary remedies, such as injunctions and specific performance, enforcement is by proceedings for contempt of court, with the ultimate sanction being imprisonment; whereas for monetary remedies, such as damages and the award of an agreed sum, there are several methods of enforcing payment, examples being a writ of *fieri facias* (or, in the county court, a warrant of execution), an attachment of earnings order, a third party debt order, or a charging order.

To give some general perspective to the role of the judicial remedies, two further points on enforcement are worth emphasising. First, enforcement of judicial remedies is at the claimant's discretion. This means that, even after it has been granted a judicial remedy, a claimant has the choice of settling for a different resolution of the dispute.[10] Secondly, even judicial methods may not succeed in enforcing the remedy. For example, a defendant who has insufficient assets cannot comply with a monetary remedy;[11] and imprisoning or fining a defendant for failing to carry out an order of specific performance does not guarantee performance.

4. Orders made to assist the claimant in collecting evidence to establish its case

Although the case that the claimant is trying to establish involves a tort or breach of contract, orders made to assist the claimant in collecting evidence, like specific disclosure and inspection,[12] cannot realistically be described as remedies for a tort or breach of contract; rather, in so far as it is at all sensible to describe such orders as remedies, they are remedies to help the claimant in its attempt to show that a tort or breach of contract has been committed. Or, to put it another way, on the assumption that a tort or breach of contract has been committed or is threatened, such orders are not the relief that the claimant seeks but rather are means towards obtaining that relief. They are therefore not considered in this book.

5. Torts and breach of contract

Tortious and contractual obligations are the two main types of obligations recognised in English law. A contractual obligation arises where one person makes an agreement with another under which one or both make(s) a promise to the other, provided generally that the agreement is supported by consideration or is made by deed, and is not invalidated on grounds such as mistake, misrepresentation, or frustration. The promisor is under an

---

[10] The possibility of bargaining round non-monetary remedies has attracted much academic interest—see below, pp 17–18.
[11] The Green Paper, *Towards Effective Enforcement: A Single Piece of Bailiff Law and a Regulatory Structure for Enforcement* (Cmnd 5096, Lord Chancellor's Department, 2001) para 1.31 stated that only 35% of all warrants of execution issued (which account for about 85% of all enforcement effort) are paid and that the estimated value of unpaid post-judgment debt is more than £600 million per year. See, generally, J Baldwin and R Cunnington, 'The Crisis of Enforcement of Civil Judgments in England and Wales' [2004] PL 305.
[12] CPR 31.12.

obligation to perform the promise she has made and, should she fail to do so, the promisee has a cause of action against her for breach of contract. A tortious obligation, on the other hand, is an obligation not to wrong another by conduct that the different torts specify to be wrongful. Should a person break such an obligation, the person wronged has a cause of action against her for the tort.[13]

This book will, generally, not be concerned with the claimant's establishing such causes of action, ie it will not in general be concerned with how the claimant establishes the defendant's tort or breach of contract. Rather it will focus on the judicial remedies available to a claimant assuming that it can establish a tort or breach of contract or, more rarely, a threatened tort or breach of contract.

There are two major qualifications to this. The first is that in relation to torts actionable only on proof of damage, like negligence, nuisance, and deceit (as opposed to breach of contract and torts actionable per se),[14] some of the principles that are concerned with establishing relevant damage, and hence generally[15] with establishing the tort, are principles of compensatory damages for an established liability in relation to torts actionable per se and breach of contract. Examples are factual causation, intervening cause, remoteness, and the restrictions on recovery for mental distress. So as to provide a rounded picture of such principles, this book includes cases dealing with them, even where they concern the establishment of a tort actionable only on proof of damage.

Secondly, for reasons there explained, liquidated damages and similar clauses are discussed in chapter 21 on the award of an agreed sum, even though the essential question is whether the clause is valid, and hence whether the defendant is contractually liable to pay the agreed sum.

6. Concurrent liability between the tort of negligence and breach of contract[16]

On the same facts and in relation to the same loss, the claimant may be able to show not only that the defendant has broken its contract but also that it has committed the tort of negligence. For example, where a carrier contracts to carry goods for the owner, it will usually be a term of the contract that the carrier takes reasonable care of the goods in transit. If the carrier then negligently damages the goods, it is not only in breach of contract but is also liable to the owner for the tort of negligence. The number of potential overlaps between breach of contract and the tort of negligence has increased in recent times. This is particularly so since the tort of negligence has been expanded to allow the recovery in

---

[13] P Birks, 'Rights, Wrongs and Remedies' (2000) 20 OJLS 1, 22, criticised this paragraph because it cuts across a taxonomy which distinguishes events from rights. But it is hard to see what is incorrect or unhelpful about lining up alongside each other (primary) rights engendered by a contract and (primary) rights protected by torts. Crucially the breach of those (primary) rights (which is the wrong constituting the cause of action) then triggers judicial remedies. Birks' approach appears to produce the odd consequence that a (*quia timet*) injunction to restrain an anticipated tort is not concerned with a 'tortious right' because a tortious right cannot be anterior to the tort.

[14] Most torts are actionable only on proof of damage. But libel and trespass to the person, land, or goods are torts actionable per se.

[15] Sometimes the damage and hence the tort is clearly established and the dispute concerns further damage. One is then concerned only with compensatory damages.

[16] See, eg, F Reynolds, 'Tort Actions in Contractual Situations' (1985) 11 NZULR 215; B Markesinis, 'An Expanding Tort Law – The Price of a Rigid Contract Law' (1987) 103 LQR 354; K Barker, 'Are we up to Expectations? Solicitors, Beneficiaries and the Tort/Contract Divide' (1994) 14 OJLS 137; P Cane, *Tort Law and Economic Interests* (2nd edn, Clarendon Press 1996) 129–149, 307–334; A Burrows, *Understanding the Law of Obligations* (Hart Publishing 1998) 16–44; *Chitty on Contracts* (33rd edn, Sweet & Maxwell 2018) paras 1-152–1-210.

some situations of pure economic loss (that is economic loss not consequent on physical damage).[17]

Clearly what the claimant cannot here do is to recover damages both for the breach of contract and for the tort of negligence, for this would be to recover double damages for the same loss. Moreover it would generally seem unacceptable, as being inconsistent with what the parties have themselves agreed, for the tort of negligence to impose a standard of liability that is more onerous than that laid down by the express or implied terms of the contract.[18] But provided it is consistent with the terms of the contract, there is in principle no objection to the claimant choosing to obtain judgment either for the breach of contract or for the tort of negligence, depending on which is more favourable to him. This was traditionally accepted where the defendant was exercising a 'common calling', for example if he were a carrier, innkeeper, bailee, or farrier; and, after a period of some uncertainty,[19] the House of Lords in *Henderson v Merrett Syndicates Ltd*[20] fully accepted concurrent consistent liability for breach of contract and the tort of negligence. The case dealt with the liability of Lloyd's underwriting agents to Names at Lloyd's. Giving the leading speech Lord Goff said the following:

'My own belief is that, in the present context, the common law is not antipathetic to concurrent liability, and that there is no sound basis for a rule which automatically restricts the claimant to either a tortious or a contractual remedy. The result may be untidy; but, given that the tortious duty is imposed by the general law, and the contractual duty is attributable to the will of the parties, I do not find it objectionable that the claimant may be entitled to take advantage of the remedy which is most advantageous to him, subject only to ascertaining whether the tortious duty is so inconsistent with the applicable contract that, in accordance with ordinary principle, the parties must be taken to have agreed that the tortious remedy is to be limited or excluded.'[21]

Why might a claimant, who can establish a breach of contract and tortious negligence (or, conceivably, a different tort), wish to frame its cause of action in tort rather than contract, or vice versa? Leaving aside matters of procedure and conflict of laws, the most significant reasons are twofold.

First, the claimant may be entitled to a higher quantum of damages in contract than in tort or vice versa.[22] This may be because the aim of the compensatory damages differs.

---

[17] See, eg, *Hedley Byrne & Co Ltd v Heller & Partners Ltd* [1964] AC 465; *Midland Bank Trust Co Ltd v Hett, Stubbs and Kemp* [1979] Ch 384; *Smith v Eric Bush* [1990] 1 AC 605; *Henderson v Merrett Syndicates Ltd* [1995] 2 AC 145; *White v Jones* [1995] 2 AC 207; *Merrett v Babb* [2001] EWCA Civ 214, [2001] QB 1174; *Lejonvarn v Burgess* [2017] EWCA Civ 254, [2017] PNLR 25. But the recovery of pure economic loss for tortious negligence is still very restricted: see, eg, *Spartan Steel & Alloys Ltd v Martin & Co (Contractors) Ltd* [1973] QB 27; *Candlewood Navigation Corpn Ltd v Mitsui OSK Lines Ltd* [1986] AC 1; *Muirhead v Industrial Tank Specialities Ltd* [1986] QB 507; *Leigh and Sillavan Ltd v Aliakmon Shipping Co Ltd* [1986] AC 785; *Caparo Industries Plc v Dickman* [1990] 2 AC 605; *Murphy v Brentwood District Council* [1991] 1 AC 398; *Williams v Natural Life Health Foods Ltd* [1998] 1 WLR 830; *Commissioner for Customs & Excise v Barclays Bank* [2006] UKHL 28, [2007] 1 AC 181.
[18] *Tai Hing Cotton Mill Ltd v Liu Chong Hing Bank Ltd* [1986] AC 80, at 107; *National Bank of Greece SA v Pinios Shipping Co No 1, The Maira* [1989] 3 WLR 185 (rvsd on a different point [1990] 1 AC 637, HL); *Greater Nottingham Co-op Soc Ltd v Cementation Piling & Foundations Ltd* [1989] QB 71; *Reid v Rush & Tomkins Group plc* [1990] 1 WLR 212; *Johnstone v Bloomsbury HA* [1992] QB 333; *Scally v Southern Health & Social Services Board* [1992] 1 AC 294; *Robinson v PE Jones (Contractors) Ltd* [2011] EWCA Civ 9, [2012] QB 44; *Euroption Strategic Fund Ltd v Skandinaviska Enskilda Banken AB* [2012] EWHC 584 (Comm), [2013] 1 BCLC 125, at [132].
[19] This was particularly caused by influential obiter dicta of Lord Scarman giving the judgment of the Privy Council in *Tai Hing Cotton Mill Ltd v Liu Chong Hing Bank* [1986] AC 80, at 107. He said, 'Their Lordships do not believe that there is anything to the advantage of the law's development in searching for a liability in tort where the parties are in a contractual relationship.'
[20] [1995] 2 AC 145.   [21] ibid, at 193–194.
[22] See, generally, A Burrows, 'Comparing Compensatory Damages in Contract and Tort: Some Problematic Issues' in *Torts in Commercial Law* (eds S Degeling, J Edelman, and J Goudkamp, Thomson Reuters 2011) 367.

In contract, the aim is to put the claimant into as good a position as if the contract had been performed. In contrast, the aim of the damages for, for example, the tort of misrepresentation is to put the claimant into as good a position as if no contract had been made. The former will yield a higher measure than the latter if the claimant made a good bargain but a lower measure if the claimant made a bad bargain.[23] Again, some of the principles limiting compensatory damages are not applied in the same way to claims for breach of contract as they are to claims in tort.[24] For example, the rules on remoteness are traditionally more favourable to claimants in tort than in contract. And contributory negligence does not apply to reduce damages for many claims in contract, whereas it nearly always applies as a possible defence in tort. There may also be greater restrictions on the recoverability of certain types of loss, such as mental distress and loss of reputation, in contract than in tort.[25] It may also be that certain types of damages, for example, punitive damages,[26] are available for torts but not for breach of contract.

Secondly, the claimant may be entitled to a longer limitation period for commencing one cause of action rather than another. This may be because the statutory time period is longer. Or it may be because the different causes of action accrue at different dates so that the statutory time period starts running at different dates. Or it may be because of the application of the discoverability test for latent damage (other than personal injury) in the Limitation Act 1980 s 14A, which applies to the tort of negligence but not to breach of contract.[27]

7. Should one continue to distinguish torts and breach of contract?

The acceptance of concurrent liability and the expansion of the tort of negligence to allow the recovery of pure economic loss in some situations raise the question whether the traditional division between torts and breach of contract (ie tort and contract) can be sensibly maintained. In particular, one interpretation of some of the cases allowing the recovery of pure economic loss in the tort of negligence[28] is that the courts are recognising that a negligent breach of promise is a tort, enabling the recovery of damages, even by a third party, to fulfil expectations engendered by the promisor.[29] If this is so, the rationale of the division between torts and breach of contract is largely undermined. That rationale is that contract alone deals with liability for breach of a binding promise; and that such separate treatment is sensible because liability for breach of a binding promise rests on what, by convention, is treated as a voluntarily undertaken obligation whereas liability for all other wrongs (primarily comprising the different torts) has no such voluntary basis and is simply imposed. Promissory liability therefore rests on, and respects and upholds, the parties' private intentions and arrangements; in this sense it may be thought to be more directly in line with 'laissez-faire' thinking than are tortious liabilities.

However, despite these developments in tort, this book continues to use the distinction between torts and breach of contract for a number of reasons:

(i) The judges continue to think and talk in terms of distinct actions for torts and breach of contract.

---

[23] See below, p 39.   [24] See below, ch 7.   [25] See below, chs 13 and 14.
[26] See below, ch 20.
[27] *Iron Trade Mutual Ins Co Ltd v JK Buckenham Ltd* [1990] 1 All ER 808; *Islander Trucking Ltd & Hogg Robinson v Gardner Mountain (Marine) Ltd* [1990] 1 All ER 826. See below, ch 16.
[28] Eg, *Midland Bank Trust Co Ltd v Hett, Stubbs and Kemp* [1979] Ch 384; *White v Jones* [1995] 2 AC 207.
[29] A Burrows, *Understanding the Law of Obligations* (Hart Publishing 1998) 26–40. See similarly S Whittaker, 'The Application of the "Broad Principle of Hedley Byrne" as between Parties to a Contract' (1997) 17 Legal Studies 169.

(ii) As regards remedies, while there are clearly many similarities between remedies for torts and breach of contract—for example, damages and injunctions are both available for torts and breach of contract, and most of the principles governing their grant are common to both causes of action—there remain significant differences. For example, remedies such as specific performance and the award of an agreed sum are available only for breach of contract. And, as has been referred to above, some principles of compensatory damages, such as remoteness and contributory negligence, and some types of loss, like mental distress and loss of reputation, are dealt with differently for torts than for breach of contract. Furthermore, punitive damages can sometimes be awarded for torts but not for breach of contract.

(iii) The view that some tort cases rest on recognising that a negligent breach of promise is a tort may not be their only possible explanation. Certainly where the defendant is liable to the claimant for breach of contract it may be thought odd to recognise a concurrent tortious liability resting on what is, on this view, essentially the same basis, ie breach of promise.

(iv) Even if the 'negligent breach of promise as a tort' interpretation is correct, an action for breach of contract still formally differs from the tort action for negligence in that it accrues before 'damage', making it less favourable for the claimant as regards limitation periods. Furthermore a non-negligent breach of promise can still only be sued on by an action for breach of contract. In particular, this means that it will still only be for breach of contract that one can recover pure economic loss for non-negligent breach of an obligation, at least where that obligation is a positive one. Indeed strict liability, breach of a positive obligation, and pure economic loss are the standard features of most actions for breach of contract.

(v) Even if the courts are treating a negligent breach of promise as a tort, one can of course argue that it is unsatisfactory for them to do so. Indeed, one can strongly argue that the reason why the courts may have done so is to evade some of the unsatisfactory differences between contract and tort (in particular, as a means of allowing the claimant the more favourable limitation regime operating in tort and as a means of avoiding the traditional privity doctrine in contract). In other words, to treat a negligent breach of promise as a tort is a pragmatic, rather than a logical or principled, development.[30] The strictly logical development would be to effect reforms (eg to the law on limitation periods) so as to eliminate any unwarranted distinctions between contract and tort, thereby removing the incentive to use tort to overcome the deficiencies of contract.

8. The primary functions of judicial remedies for torts and breach of contract

The primary functions of the judicial remedies for torts and breach of contract can be expressed as follows: compensation, restitution (sometimes referred to as disgorgement), punishment, compelling performance of positive obligations, preventing a wrong, compelling the undoing of a wrong, declaring rights. A table (see below) is helpful to indicate which remedies correspond to which function.

These functions underpin the structure of this book and will be referred to throughout. This is not meant to suggest that there is no other way of expressing the primary

---

[30] A Burrows, *Understanding the Law of Obligations* (Hart Publishing 1998) 26–34.

functions; eg, one can equally well regard most of the remedies for breach of contract as having the common function of fulfilling expectations engendered by the contractual promise. But taking into account all judicial remedies for torts and breach of contract, the scheme below is considered the most helpful for understanding the role of and links between the remedies.

Remedies for Torts and Breach of Contract	
Primary Function	Remedies
Compensation	Compensatory damages.
Restitution	Account of profits. Award of money had and received.
Punishment	Punitive damages.
Compelling performance (of positive obligations)	Specific performance. Award of an agreed sum. Mandatory enforcing injunction. Appointment of a receiver.
Preventing a wrong	Prohibitory injunction. Delivery up for destruction or destruction on oath.
Compelling the undoing of a wrong	Mandatory restorative injunction. Delivery up of goods.
Declaring rights	Declaration. Nominal damages. Contemptuous damages.

Zakrzewski has argued that this classification, which he terms 'goal-based', is inadequate.[31] This is because one would need to unpack the goals of the rights triggering, for example, 'compelling performance' or 'preventing a wrong' and to do this would make the goals too diverse. With respect, this depends on the level of detail one uses to define the goals and there is nothing analytically impure in a classification of function that combines, for example, 'compensation' with 'preventing a wrong'. Even if there were an analytical impurity, it is submitted that this type of classification remains the most practically useful and illuminating one to adopt in understanding judicial remedies (for civil wrongs). In particular, as has been indicated above,[32] judges and practitioners are unlikely to find helpful Zakrzewski's view that the details of the law on specific performance and injunctions are within the law of remedies but the details of the law on damages are not.

9. Legal and equitable remedies

References will be made throughout to remedies being either legal or equitable. This is historical labelling indicating that the remedy was developed in the common law courts or in the Court of Chancery prior to the fusion of the courts by the 1873–75 Judicature Acts. It should be noted that, as a legacy of history, legal remedies, in contrast to equitable remedies, are almost all monetary.

Does it now matter whether the remedy for a tort or breach of contract is common law or equitable? For those who resist the fusion of common law and equity, the answer is 'yes'.

---

[31] R Zakrzewski, *Remedies Reclassified* (OUP 2005). [32] Above, p 4.

They would seek to emphasise and retain the historical differences between common law and equitable remedies. In particular, they would point to equitable remedies being discretionary, and being subject to discretionary defences (such as 'clean hands', hardship, and laches) in contrast to common law remedies being subject to clear rules and being available as of right. It is submitted that that approach is misleading. Both common law and equitable remedies are granted or refused in accordance with clearly established rules and principles. Some of the principles, including at common law, allow considerable discretion to the courts (eg the principles limiting compensatory damages and the availability of punitive damages) so that it is false to equate common law remedies with 'no discretion'.[33] True it is that there are some differences; for example, common law damages, in contrast to equitable damages awarded as a substitute for an injunction, cannot yet be awarded for an anticipated, rather than an accrued, wrong; and where a breach of contract or tort has been established, it appears that a court, if asked to do so, must at least award nominal damages whereas a claimant seeking an equitable remedy may simply be refused it. But it is submitted that the similarities far outweigh the differences; that the differences are relatively minor; that rationally there is no good reason for the differences; and that nothing would be lost, and some simplicity and rationality would be gained, if one took the small steps necessary to move to a fully fused system of remedies where it would be unnecessary to use the labels common law or equitable.[34]

Certainly it is a grave error of some books and courses to perpetuate the historical division by treating equitable remedies separately from legal remedies as if they have no connection with each other. One of the purposes of this book is to emphasise that both legal and equitable remedies may be available to a claimant for a legal wrong, whether a tort or breach of contract. Indeed, in certain situations, the legal and equitable remedies perform the same or similar functions, eg an account of profits and the award of money had and received effect restitution (sometimes referred to as disgorgement), and specific performance and the award of an agreed sum compel performance of positive contractual obligations.

10. Equitable wrongs

A useful classification within the civil law, articulated particularly by Peter Birks, is between causes of action that are wrongs and causes of action that are not wrongs.[35] Birks argued that a (civil) wrong means 'conduct ... whose effect in creating legal consequences is attributable to its being characterised as a breach of duty'.[36] Moreover, it appears that, with the conceivable exception of some statutory duties, a sure test for whether that definition is satisfied (ie whether the law is characterising particular conduct as constituting a breach of duty) is that compensation must be an available remedial measure for the conduct in question if loss is caused to the claimant by that conduct. Applying that test, torts and breach of contract are civil wrongs. In contrast, unjust enrichment triggering the restitution of money

---

[33] The sort of discretion in play has been called 'weak' rather than 'strong', which goes back to a distinction drawn by R Dworkin, *Taking Rights Seriously* (rev edn, Duckworth 1978) 31–39. There is a school of thought that remedies should be decided by a strong discretion, which would allow the judge to choose the most appropriate remedy on the particular facts. For powerful criticism of this 'discretionary remedialism', see P Birks, 'Rights, Wrongs and Remedies' (2000) 20 OJLS 1, 22–24; P Birks, 'Three Kinds of Objection to Discretionary Remedialism' (2000) 29 UWALR 1.

[34] A Burrows, 'We Do This at Common Law but That in Equity' (2002) 22 OJLS 1; A Burrows, *Fusing Common Law and Equity: Remedies, Restitution and Reform*, Hochelaga Lecture 2001 (Sweet & Maxwell 2002).

[35] Eg, P Birks, 'Misnomer' in *Restitution: Past, Present and Future* (eds W Cornish, R Nolan, J O'Sullivan, and G Virgo, Hart Publishing 1998) 1, 8–9; P Birks, 'Rights, Wrongs and Remedies' (2000) 20 OJLS 1, 25–36.

[36] P Birks, *An Introduction to the Law of Restitution* (Clarendon Press 1989) 313.

(or non-money benefits) rendered by mistake or for a failed consideration or under duress is a cause of action that is not a wrong. Restitution of the value of the enrichment conferred by the claimant is the only available remedial measure; compensation for loss is not available for the unjust enrichment.

It also then becomes clear that, alongside torts and breach of contract, which are common law wrongs (because they were developed in the common law courts), there are equitable wrongs (developed in the Court of Chancery). Applying the above test, the equitable civil wrongs are breach of fiduciary duty, breach of confidence, dishonestly procuring or assisting a breach of fiduciary duty, and those forms of estoppel that constitute causes of action, in particular proprietary estoppel.[37]

It further follows from this analysis that the primary focus in this book on remedies for torts and breach of contract is on the common law wrongs. On the face of it, one is putting to one side the analogous equitable wrongs merely because of their historical roots and not for rational reasons. Moreover, while it is still essentially true, as those wishing to perpetuate the historical divisions between common law and equity tend to stress, that only equitable remedies are available for equitable wrongs, it is also true that the same, or similar, functions are performed by the remedies for equitable wrongs as by the remedies for torts and breach of contract. In other words, there is a coherence in remedial function for civil wrongs that transcends the common law/equity divide.

In the first two editions of this book, the importance of seeing that the functions of the remedies for equitable and common law wrongs are coherent was emphasised in the introductory chapter;[38] and the equitable wrong of breach of confidence (because so close to being treated as a tort) was dealt with throughout the book.

Developments since then—and, in particular, the increased number of cases of 'professional negligence' against, for example, solicitors, in which claimants have sought equitable compensation for breach of fiduciary duty as an alternative to damages for the tort of negligence or breach of contract—suggest that a more detailed treatment of remedies for equitable wrongs is required. One way forward would have been to examine remedies for equitable wrongs alongside torts and breach of contract under each of the four parts of this book devoted to different remedial functions. The possible disadvantage of that approach is in making the issues less accessible, and the text less easy to use, not least because our understanding of equitable wrongs, and the basic law on the central remedy of equitable compensation, is still developing. It was therefore decided for the last edition of this book, and this is retained in this edition, that the better approach is to devote the last part and chapter to remedies for equitable wrongs where the parallels—and contrasts—with remedies for torts and breach of contract can conveniently be explored. One should add that the inclusion of a chapter on remedies for equitable wrongs means that the coverage of this book comes close to dealing with remedies for all civil wrongs.[39]

However, it is important to add that a significant development since the last edition of this book has been the recognition that, out of the equitable wrong of breach of confidence and catalysed by Article 8 of the European Convention on Human Rights (given effect to in the UK by the Human Rights Act 1998), there has emerged a modern tort of misuse of

---

[37] Undue influence (as the equitable creation of the judges and therefore putting to one side statutory undue influence under Part 4A of the Consumer Protection from Unfair Trading Regulations 2008) is not an equitable wrong because it does not trigger compensation: see P Birks, 'Unjust Factors and Wrongs: Pecuniary Rescission for Undue Influence' [1997] RLR 72 which discusses *Mahoney v Purnell* [1996] 3 All ER 61.

[38] (2nd edn, Butterworths 1994) 9–11.

[39] But this book does not purport to cover any specialised remedies for particular statutory wrongs (eg, the remedies that may be awarded by an employment tribunal for unfair dismissal).

private information. This can alternatively be referred to as a tort of privacy. This tort is seen as closely linked to, but now distinct from, the equitable wrong of breach of confidence. In other words, there are two different causes of action protecting two different interests: the equitable cause of action for breach of confidence, protecting confidential information, and the common law cause of action for misuse of private information, protecting privacy. The leading case on this is *Vidal-Hall v Google Inc*.[40] The main question at issue was whether there could be service out of the jurisdiction[41] for the cause of action for misuse of private information. That would be possible if that cause of action were a tort but would apparently not be possible if it were an equitable cause of action. In their joint judgment, Lord Dyson MR and Sharp LJ said the following:[42]

> '[T]here are problems with an analysis which fails to distinguish between a breach of confidentiality and an infringement of privacy rights protected by art 8, not least because the concepts of confidence and privacy are not the same and protect different interests.... [T]here are now two separate and distinct causes of action: an action for breach of confidence; and one for misuse of private information.... [T]he action for misuse of private information has been referred to as a tort by the courts.'

They clarified that the speeches of Lord Nicholls in *Campbell v Mirror Group Newspapers Ltd*[43] and *OBG Ltd v Allan*[44] supported this bifurcation; and they distinguished the earlier case of *Kitetechnology BV v Unicor GmbH Plastmaschinen*[45] in which the Court of Appeal had decided that there could be no service out of the jurisdiction, under the tort gateway, in an action for breach of confidence because that was an equitable cause of action not a tort. Lord Dyson MR and Sharp LJ accepted that that decision was binding on them but clarified that it was dealing with an action for breach of confidence and not one for misuse of private information. They concluded that 'misuse of private information should now be recognised as a tort for the purposes of service out of the jurisdiction.'[46]

Of course, in line with the long-standing debate as to whether breach of confidence should be differentiated from tort, one can argue that it makes no sense in policy terms to differentiate, for the purposes of service out, between an equitable wrong and a tort. And subsequent to the *Vidal* case the Civil Procedure Rules have been amended so that there can be service out for breach of confidence. But for the present, our law continues to regard breach of confidence as an equitable wrong that is not a tort. In contrast, misuse of private information has been carved out of breach of confidence and is now a tort.

It follows that, within this book, breach of confidence falls within Part Six dealing with equitable wrongs, while misuse of private information falls within Parts Two to Five as a tort.

11. Combining remedies

The question of the extent to which a claimant can combine judicial remedies for the same, or more than one, cause of action is a very difficult one. It has escaped the attention of commentators that it deserves.[47]

---

[40] [2015] EWCA Civ 311, [2016] QB 1003. [41] Under Civil Procedure Rules PD 6B, para 3.1(9).
[42] [2015] EWCA Civ 311, [2016] QB 1003, at [21].
[43] [2004] UKHL 22, [2004] 2 AC 457, at [13]–[17]. [44] [2007] UKHL 21, [2008] 1 AC 1, at [255].
[45] [1995] FSR 765. [46] [2015] EWCA Civ 311, [2016] QB 1003, at [51].
[47] An exception is the excellent article by S Watterson, 'Alternative and Cumulative Remedies: What is the Difference?' [2003] RLR 7. See also S Watterson, 'An Account of Profits or Damages? The History of Orthodoxy' (2004) 24 OJLS 471.

One should initially put to one side situations where a claimant invokes a self-help remedy and an inconsistent judicial remedy. For example, one cannot rescind ab initio a contract at the same time as claiming damages for breach of contract;[48] nor can one terminate a contract for breach of contract and seek specific performance of it.[49] The effect of the claimant's election to invoke the self-help remedy in these situations is akin to a claimant being barred from a remedy for an infringement of his or her rights because the claimant has affirmed, waived, or acquiesced in the infringement. All rest on the justifiable policy that, where the defendant has relied on the claimant taking one course of action, it would unfairly upset the defendant's expectations for the claimant to change his or her mind.

But where judicial remedies are being sought the concerns about combining remedies are rather different. One is barely concerned, if at all, about the other party's expectations being disappointed. Rather it is the avoidance of the claimant having 'double recovery' or otherwise excessive recovery that is in mind. Labelling judicial remedies as inconsistent, and requiring the claimant to elect between them, is designed to avoid such double (or excessive) recovery.[50] Where there is no such problem, the claimant has a free choice to combine remedies.

So, for example, an injunction to prevent the continuation of a tort can be combined with compensatory damages for the tort that has already been committed. There is no double recovery problem.

In contrast, one cannot combine damages protecting the expectation interest for breach of contract with damages protecting the reliance interest for a tortious misrepresentation inducing that contract. Where the bargain was a good one, the former swallows up the latter and, where the bargain was a bad one, the latter swallows up the former. To allow both would give double recovery. As alternatively expressed, it would be inconsistent: one cannot at the same time put the claimant into as good a position as if the contract had been performed and into as good a position as if no contract had been made. Again, it is clear law that a claimant cannot combine compensatory damages and an account of profits for, for example, an intellectual property tort. So, for example, if D, by committing a wrong to C, has made a net gain of £1,000 and by the same wrong has caused loss to C of £2,000, the effect of requiring D to pay C £3,000 would be that C is neither *just* compensated for its loss (but instead receives a windfall of £1,000) nor is D *just* stripped of its wrongly acquired gain (but rather has an extra £2,000 stripped away). An award of £3,000 would therefore be inconsistent with either of the remedial purposes being pursued and would constitute double recovery.

Where the law requires a claimant to make a choice, or election, of judicial remedy, the choice need not be made until judgment; and, even then, it can be changed if the defendant fails to comply with the judgment.[51]

One may question, however, whether the fear of double recovery necessitates the claimant making an election between judicial remedies. Provided one takes account of the other, double recovery can be avoided without requiring an election. In Watterson's words,

---

[48] E Peel, *Treitel on The Law of Contract* (14th edn, Sweet & Maxwell 2015) para 9-087.

[49] *Johnson v Agnew* [1980] AC 367, at 392. Lord Wilberforce said, '[I]f the vendor treats the purchaser as having repudiated the contract and accepts the repudiation, he cannot thereafter seek specific performance. This follows from the fact that, the purchaser having repudiated the contract and his repudiation having been accepted, both parties are discharged from further performance.'

[50] S Watterson, 'Alternative and Cumulative Remedies: What is the Difference?' [2003] RLR 7, esp 18–21, argues that the most appropriate label to describe the objection is neither 'inconsistency' nor 'double recovery' but rather 'excessive remedial cumulation'.

[51] See, generally, *United Australia Ltd v Barclays Bank Ltd* [1941] AC 1, 19, 21, 30. See also below, p 439 (specific performance).

'English law's election orthodoxy is not a logical necessity.'[52] In the above examples, what is objectionable is *full* protection of the expectation interest and *full* protection of the reliance interest; or *full* compensation and *full* restitution. But there would be no objection to combining damages for the expectation interest and damages for the reliance interest if one modified the award protecting the expectation interest to take account of what one is awarding to protect the reliance interest. Similarly, the correct award of £2,000 in the second example above could be justified as restitution (£1,000) plus partial compensation (£1,000).

Viewed in this way, it can be seen that the great merit of requiring an election between judicial remedies is that, in a clear and straightforward way, it avoids double (or excessive) recovery. It avoids the courts having to decide, in assessing quantum, whether, and the extent to which, a particular combination of remedies gives double recovery. The disadvantage of requiring an election is that it is conceivable that a claimant may be deprived of its full entitlement by making an inappropriate election.

12. Breach of European Union law

Subject to the impact of Britain (at the time of writing, almost certainly) leaving the European Union,[53] there are two situations where an individual has a cause of action for damages for breach of EU law. The first is 'state liability' as established in the leading case of *Francovich and Bonifaci v Italy*.[54] 'State liability' is concerned to impose liability for harm directly caused to individuals by a 'sufficiently serious' breach of EU law by the state where the relevant provision is best interpreted as conferring rights on individuals. 'State liability' extends from non-implementation of a directive to misimplementation, legislative acts and omissions, judicial decisions, and administrative decisions.[55] The second situation is where there has been breach of a 'directly effective'[56] provision of EU law, which operates horizontally to give a person rights against other individuals.[57]

English law has characterised the cause of action for damages for breach of EU law as a tort. It has usually been straightforwardly treated as an example of the tort of breach of statutory duty[58] although, perhaps because the link to an English statute (European Communities Act 1972, s 2(1)) is rather indirect, it has sometimes also been labelled a 'eurotort'.[59] As a tort, it falls within the scope of this book.

---

[52] S Watterson, 'Alternative and Cumulative Remedies: What is the Difference?' [2003] RLR 7, 21.

[53] Eg, under Schedule 1, para 4, of the European Union Withdrawal Act 2018, 'There is no right in domestic law on or after exit day to damages in accordance with the rule in *Francovich*'. The rule in *Francovich* is explained below.

[54] Case C-6&9/90, [1991] ECR I-5357. See also, eg, *Brasserie du Pêcheur SA v Germany, R v Secretary of State for Transport, ex p Factortame Ltd* Case C-46 & 48/93, [1996] QB 404; *R v HM Treasury, ex p British Telecommunications plc* Case C-392/93, [1996] QB 615; *Dillenkofer v Germany* Case C-178-9/94, 188–190/194, [1996] ECR I-4845; *Denkavit International v Bundesamt für Finanzen* Case C-283, 291, and 292/94, [1996] ECR I-5063; *R v Secretary of State for Transport, ex p Factortame Ltd (No 5)* [2000] 1 AC 524 (HL); *EnergySolutions EU Ltd v Nuclear Decommissioning Authority* [2017] UKSC 34, [2017] 1 WLR 1373.

[55] Eg, *Köbler v Austria* Case C-224/01, [2004] QB 848, ECJ (dealing with judicial decisions).

[56] See, eg, *NV Algemene Transporten Expeditie Onderneming van Gend en Loos v Nederlandse Administratie der Belastingen* Case 26/62, [1963] ECR 1; *Defrenne v Société Anonyme Belge de Navigation Aérienne* Case 43/75, [1976] ECR 455.

[57] See, eg, *Courage v Crehan* Case C-453/99, [2001] ECR I-6297.

[58] *Garden Cottage Foods Ltd v Milk Marketing Board* [1984] AC 130; *R v Secretary of State for Transport, ex p Factortame Ltd (No 6)* [2001] 1 WLR 942 (for the purposes of the Limitation Act 1980); *Phonographic Performance Ltd v Department of Trade and Industry* [2004] EWHC 1795 (Ch), [2004] 1 WLR 2893. An earlier view that the tort in question was best viewed as misfeasance in public office (see, eg, *Bourgoin SA v Ministry of Agriculture, Fisheries and Food* [1986] QB 716) was rejected in the *Brasserie du Pêcheur* case [1996] QB 404.

[59] *Clerk and Lindsell on Torts* (22nd edn, Sweet & Maxwell 2018) para 1–09; M Lunney, D Nolan, and K Oliphant, *Tort Law: Text and Materials* (6th edn, OUP 2017) 627. See, generally, P Giliker, *The Europeanisation of English Tort Law* (Hart Publishing 2014) ch 4.

In terms of remedies, it has been established that the basic EU law principle is one of national 'procedural autonomy'.[60] This means that the remedies available, and the rules and principles applicable to them, are a matter for the national legal system. However, this is qualified by two additional important EU principles.[61] First, the remedies must be effective for the breach in question (the 'principle of effectiveness').[62] They must not render virtually impossible or excessively difficult the exercise of the EU rights: in so far as they do, the domestic remedies must be modified or new remedies must be created. Secondly, the remedies must not be applied less favourably than those applying to similar domestic causes of action (the 'principle of equivalence').

In practice, the remedies for a 'eurotort', and the principles governing those remedies, have been no different from those applicable to domestic torts. One possible exception (although there is some difficulty in reconciling this with the general principle of equivalence) is that punitive damages may not be available (even if the case falls within the categories where they would be available for domestic torts).[63]

13. Economic analysis, bargaining around non-monetary remedies, and the consumer surplus

Over the past 50 years or so, there has been widespread interest by academic lawyers, especially in the US, in the economic analysis of law, which examines how far the law promotes economic efficiency. Indeed a good deal of economic analysis writing has focused on the civil law remedies considered in this book. Some commentators even seem to come close to using efficiency as the only important criterion for critically assessing the law, but this surely overplays its importance. The common law is best regarded as a complex system of principles, based on 'moral rights' reasoning, modified and tempered by the desire to pursue certain long-term policies. One important policy is efficiency; but its place is alongside, not as a replacement for, moral rights reasoning, and this is how it is used in this book.

On a more detailed level, several other criticisms can be levelled at traditional economic analysis. To understand these, it is as well to set out very briefly how economists have tended to look at tort and contract.[64] There can be said to be three important steps in the reasoning. The first is that a system is efficient where those who place the highest value on resources have the use of those resources. Free-market voluntary exchanges, by which resources are moved to successively more valued uses, are therefore the necessary means for efficiency. The second step is the Coase Theorem,[65] stating that in the absence of transaction costs it does not matter what legal rights and remedies there are because the parties as rational maximisers of value will negotiate round them to produce the most efficient result. Say, for example, A's factory produces smoke ruining B's enjoyment of her land. If the value of the factory to A as it is (that is, the value attributable to the smoke) is £100,000 and the enjoyment of B's land is worth £70,000 to her, the efficient allocation of resources is to allow A to

---

[60] *Rewe-Zentralfinanz and Rewe-Zentral v Landwirtschaftskammer für das Saarland* Case 33/76, [1976] ECR 1989.
[61] See, eg, *Amministrazione delle Finanze dello Stato SpA San Giorgio* Case 199/82, [1983] ECR 3595.
[62] For an example of EU law requiring a 'remedy', which has been rationalised in English law as restitution of an unjust enrichment, see *Metallgesellschaft Ltd v IRC, Hoescht AG v IRC* Cases C-397-410/98, [2001] Ch 620. There have been many subsequent English unjust enrichment tax cases applying *Hoescht*: see, eg, *Test Claimants in the FII Group Litigation v HMRC* [2012] UKSC 19, [2012] 2 AC 337.
[63] See below, pp 369–370.
[64] See also D Harris, *Remedies in Contract and Tort* (1st edn, Weidenfeld & Nicolson 1988) 6–14 (that introductory section was deleted in the 2nd edn, Butterworths 2002).
[65] R Coase, 'The Problem of Social Cost' (1960) 3 J Law & Econ 1.

continue polluting. According to the Coase Theorem, even if A is legally ordered to stop the factory emitting such smoke, A will carry on as before, by paying B £70,000, or indeed up to £99,999. If we reverse the figures, then by the same reasoning the smoke will be stopped even if B is given no injunction because, according to Coase, B will pay A between £70,000 and £99,999 to stop the smoke. The final step is then economic analysis confronting the fact that in the real world there are transaction costs. Hence the allocation of legal rights and remedies can be expected to affect efficiency. Free bargaining will not necessarily take place to correct 'errors' and, even if it does, transaction costs will be incurred. The courts should therefore strive to promote efficiency by deciding on legal rights and remedies that on a general level promote voluntary exchanges, and more specifically mimic the voluntary exchanges that the parties as rational maximisers of value would make.

This economic approach is troubling in several respects. First, the methodology being used is most unappealing to lawyers, who are used to dealing at a specific level with concrete facts and issues. In particular, lawyers are likely to be unhappy with individuals being portrayed as solely concerned to maximise value, when this does not correspond to the reality of human motivation. Secondly, it can be argued that efficiency is not a value-free notion, and that the approach outlined above rests on nothing more than right-wing, free-market ideology. Thirdly, even though applying the same general approach, economists differ as to whether particular legal rules are efficient or not. To give an example from the law in this book, it has been argued that it is efficient for specific performance to remain a secondary remedy to damages, but the opposing view has also been fervently put forward. It should not be thought, therefore, that the law can always turn to clearly agreed conclusions as to what is and what is not efficient. Finally, many of the arguments turn on the extent of transaction or other costs and yet there is little empirical data to support the views expressed.

For reasons such as these it is arguable that there is little to be gained from detailed economic analysis.[66] Moreover it should be reiterated that even where used at a general and relatively uncontroversial level, efficiency should in no sense be regarded as the sole criterion for assessing the law. Indeed it can be argued that, in the remedies field, the most significant contribution of the economic analysis movement lies not in showing that particular legal principles do or do not promote efficiency but rather in highlighting two legally important notions that might otherwise not have received the attention they deserve.

One is what economists term the 'consumer surplus', namely the subjective value that a consumer places on particular property or services, over and above the objective market value.[67] This is a useful way of explaining, for example, why a person having a wall built for privacy is, in the event of breach, unlikely to be put into as good a position as if the contract had been performed if she is simply awarded damages reflecting the difference in market value of her land with and without the wall; or why it is essential for the courts to award mental distress damages to compensate fully for a ruined holiday; or why specific performance is a preferable remedy to damages for someone buying a particular home.

The other notion is that the parties may well bargain around non-monetary remedies, like injunctions and specific performance, whether pre- or post-judgment.[68] Two views can be suggested as to the effect this should have on the remedies awarded.

---

[66] For a different view see, eg, S Bray, 'Remedies, Meet Economics; Economics, Meet Remedies' (2018) 38 OJLS 71.

[67] D Harris, A Ogus, and J Phillips, 'Contract Remedies and the Consumer Surplus' (1979) 95 LQR 581; S Mullen, 'Damages for Breach of Contract: Quantifying the Lost Consumer Surplus' (2016) 36 OJLS 83.

[68] R Sharpe, *Injunctions and Specific Performance* (5th edn, Thomson Reuters 2017) paras 1.150–1.180; B Thompson, 'Injunction Negotiations: An Economic, Moral and Legal Analysis' (1975) 27 Stan LR 1563.

First, there is the view that the possibility of post-judgment bargaining should have no effect on a court's reasoning. The court should rather reach a decision according to what it thinks is just, and should regard it as entirely a matter for the parties if they then prefer a different solution. After all, the court cannot know in advance whether the parties will embark on post-judgment bargaining. Alternatively, it can be argued that the courts should be wary of granting non-monetary remedies, precisely because the claimant, who has been or will be awarded an injunction or specific performance, is placed in too strong a position in pre- or post-judgment bargaining; for to the extent that the defendant's gains from the wrong will exceed the claimant's loss, it will be in each party's interest to negotiate a deal whereby the claimant takes a share in the defendant's gains in return for the defendant being free to commit the 'wrong'. Moreover, there will be every incentive for the claimant to demand a huge share of those gains, going far beyond the compensation needed to cover the value to him of the right infringed. Both the consumer surplus and bargaining around the remedies are ideas that will be returned to at various stages in this book.

14. Corrective justice, civil recourse, and rights

Perhaps as a reaction against the economic analysis of law, the last 30 years have seen attempts by scholars to explain private law, especially tort law, by high-level 'rights' theories.[69] Among the best known are Ernest Weinrib's version of 'corrective justice',[70] John Goldberg and Ben Zipursky's theory of 'civil recourse',[71] and Robert Stevens' 'rights-based' theory of tort.[72] There are close links between all three accounts and all purport to be primarily concerned with explaining private law as it is and not as it ought to be.[73]

Taking first Weinrib's corrective justice approach, this attempts to explain a number of central features of the private law of civil wrongs.

First, private law is concerned to restore parties to the position they were in, in relation to rights held, prior to the infringement of those rights. Private law corrects an injustice and is not concerned to redistribute rights afresh. In Aristotle's terminology, one is concerned with corrective, not distributive, justice.

Secondly, there is 'correlativity' between the parties in private law. The claimant and defendant are inseparably linked in the sense that infringement of the claimant's right by the defendant constitutes the breach of a duty owed by the defendant to the claimant. The claimant's right and the defendant's duty are two sides of the same coin. Furthermore, the

---

[69] For a very different philosophical account of private law, which sees it as helpfully understood as mirroring central issues in our personal lives, see J Gardner, *From Personal Life to Private Law* (OUP 2018).

[70] Although there are many articles by Weinrib on this theme, I have found most helpful the short article 'Corrective Justice in a Nutshell' (2002) 52 U Toronto LJ 349. An earlier full version of the theory, albeit modified since, was set out in *The Idea of Private Law* (Harvard UP 1995). See further E Weinrib, *Corrective Justice* (OUP 2012).

[71] B Zipursky, 'Rights, Wrongs and Recourse in the Law of Torts' (1998) 51 Vanderbilt LR 1; J Goldberg and B Zipursky, 'Unrealized Torts' (2002) 88 Virginia LR 1625, 1641–1649; B Zipursky, 'Civil Recourse, Not Corrective Justice' (2003) 91 Georgia LJ 695; J Goldberg and B Zipursky, 'Seeing Tort Law from the Internal Point of View: Holmes and Hart on Legal Duties' (2006) 75 Fordham LR 1563; J Goldberg and B Zipursky, 'Torts as Wrongs' (2010) 88 Texas LR 917, esp 960–963, 971–978.

[72] R Stevens, *Torts and Rights* (OUP 2007). See also A Beever, *Rediscovering the Law of Negligence* (Hart Publishing 2007).

[73] J Goudkamp and J Murphy, 'The Failure of Universal Theories of Tort Law' (2015) 21 Legal Theory' 47 argue that Posner's economic analysis, Weinrib's corrective justice approach, and Stevens' 'torts and rights' thesis fail because they purport to be 'universal theories of tort law' and yet they cannot explain several central aspects of tort in the common law world.

defendant is bound to pay damages to the claimant (not to the state) and the claimant can proceed only against the defendant and no one else. It is this correlativity that gives private law its structural coherence.

Thirdly, the law is concerned only with matters that concern the parties as between themselves and not matters that affect third parties or the legal system generally. In other words, policy goals, such as encouraging efficiency or deterrence or punishment or avoiding the floodgates of litigation or encouraging insurance, are irrelevant to private law.

Fourthly, and most importantly for this book, there is a principle of 'continuity' between right and remedy.[74] By this, the remedies for civil wrongs flow on naturally as a continuum from the breach of duty in question. The law does not set up remedies that can be chosen by the parties or the court as a 'smorgsmabord' irrespective of the particular wrong in question. The remedy and the right infringed are inextricably linked and the idea is that the remedy should as closely as possible replicate, or substitute for, or be the 'next best thing to', the right infringed.

While of great interest, this theory is problematic. Even if accurate, it operates at such a high level of generality that it is hard to translate it into distinctive arguments that can be run before the courts: law is a practical discipline and, if its theories are set at such a high level that they cannot answer the practical questions addressed by courts, they are of marginal help.[75] The theory also contradicts vast swaths of private law in so far as it indicates that policy concerns ought to be irrelevant. Private law is best understood as a mix of principle and policy. So, for example, it is hard to see how the theory can explain properly the law on remoteness or mitigation or the general non-recovery of mental distress in contract law where the courts rightly invoke policy concerns external to the parties in developing and explaining the law. Corrective justice similarly cannot explain any of the law on punitive damages. The principle of continuity is appealing—and indeed at one level is in line with a basic tenet of this book, namely that it is misleading to look at remedies without the context of the particular wrong in question—but, stated at such a high level of generality, it leaves open all the difficult questions that the law has to answer. For example, on the face of it, the best remedy for breach of contract should be specific performance, as the next best to performance, but that is clearly not the law (and this is for reasons of policy such as avoiding waste and respecting individual autonomy by avoiding forcing a party to do something for someone else on pain of contempt). Even cost of cure damages are not readily available unless reasonable (ie not wasteful) and the claimant intends to effect the cure. In short, the law on remedies, including the relationship between specific remedies and monetary remedies, cannot be explained simply by reference to the range of possible remedies: there are other policy factors that come into play and without reference to them the law cannot be properly understood.

Goldberg and Zipursky's theory of civil recourse is similar to corrective justice but emphasises that the primary importance of the infringement of the claimant's right is that it gives the claimant standing to sue and thereby the power to invoke the machinery of the state in providing recourse against the defendant. In contrast to criminal law, it is the person whose right has been infringed who can insist on bringing the wrongdoer to court

---

[74] J Gardner, 'What is Tort Law For? Part 1: The Place of Corrective Justice' (2011) 30 Law and Philosophy 1, at 33 first coined the phrase the 'continuity thesis'. See also J Gardner, *From Personal Life to Private Law* (OUP 2018) esp 98–124. For Weinrib's clear adoption of it, see E Weinrib, 'Civil Recourse and Corrective Justice' (2011) 39 Florida State University LR 273.

[75] See J Stapleton, 'Comparative Economic Loss: Lessons from Case-Law Focused "Middle Theory"' (2002-3) 50 UCLA Rev 531. Stapleton, in my view correctly, criticises 'high theorists of tort law' for not providing practical answers to the issues faced by courts.

both to establish that the wrong occurred and to invoke judicial remedies. It would appear that, unlike corrective justice, those advocating 'civil recourse' are not against policy reasoning in determining rights and remedies so that, for example, punitive damages are regarded as acceptable. Given that the emphasis is on the infringement of a right, the theory is principally focused on tort law and it is not clear, for example, how it is seen as applying to other areas of private law, such as unjust enrichment where there is no infringement of a right in play.

It would appear that another significant difference between civil recourse and corrective justice, which is directly relevant to this book, is that civil recourse takes the view that the remedies given are not controlled by the right in question but cover a range of options which it is for the claimant and/or the court to choose from as they consider appropriate. In other words, civil recourse appears to reject the principle of continuity. The issue of whether there is a right of action is distinct from the issue of what the remedy should be. As Weinrib has explained it, 'For corrective justice, the plaintiff's remedy is continuous with the right that the defendant infringed. For civil recourse, the wrong and remedy are distinct.'[76] Hence Zipursky argues that, after the infringement of its right, the claimant has a power (not a right) to choose a particular remedy and the defendant has a liability in relation to that remedy. Civil recourse is therefore a distinctive power in private law that a claimant has, consequent on infringement of its right which gives the claimant standing, to choose a judicial remedy. However, this is open to the criticism that, as a description of the law, it is clear that remedies are not simply matters for the courts' discretion, or the claimant's choice, but rest on established principles which severely confine that discretion or choice. Moreover, it is not entirely clear why the idea of civil recourse is thought to be a distinctive aspect of private law as opposed to public law. Judicial review of administrative action has standing rules that give a party the power to invoke the machinery of the state in providing recourse against the state.

Stevens' 'rights-based' analysis of torts is very much more practically orientated than the above two theories and painstakingly analyses almost the whole of the English law of torts through the lens of the infringement of a right, which is contrasted with loss-based analyses of tort focused on accidents. The theory seeks to draw a sharp line between principle and policy and, with respect, unrealistically—for the reasons that have been set out above in relation to Weinrib's views—regards policy as a matter solely for the elected Legislature and not the courts. Nevertheless there are many useful insights to be derived from Stevens' account. We analyse in depth in chapter 3 his fascinating, albeit flawed, approach to remedies, especially damages.

15. Approach and methodology

The approach to the law adopted in this book is avowedly doctrinal. This rests on the belief that practical legal scholarship and reasoning are of central importance in understanding the law; and, without wishing to deny the importance of other more theoretical approaches, it can be powerfully argued that, not least because law is a practical discipline, doctrine should lie at the core of legal research and training.[77]

---

[76] E Weinrib, 'Civil Recourse and Corrective Justice' (2011) 39 Florida State University LR 273, 275.
[77] See, generally, A Burrows, 'Challenges for Private Law in the Twenty-First Century' in *Private Law in the 21st Century* (eds K Barker, K Fairweather, and R Grantham, Hart Publishing 2017) 29, 34–40.

A valid criticism of many doctrinal scholars—although this is a charge that can be levelled at other types of academic lawyer as well—is that the methodology being applied is sometimes not thought through let alone articulated. Very few history students would now study history without serious consideration of historiography. Yet we rarely find doctrinal scholars analysing the precise methodological approach that they are adopting.

It is therefore worthwhile explaining, albeit briefly, that this book adopts an interpretative methodology which seeks to set out the best interpretation of the content of the law on remedies. The criteria that are being applied in determining whether one interpretation is better than another include fit, coherence, accessibility, practical workability, and normative validity. Perhaps most importantly, one's model should fit the vast bulk of the rules and principles (one cannot simply say that a significant proportion of the rules and principles cannot be explained and must be ignored); it should do so in a way that is coherent or rational by treating like cases alike and unlike cases differently; the interpretation should be as simple to understand—as accessible—as possible; the account of the law must be one that works in practice because law is pre-eminently a practical discipline; and the interpretation should be one that can be morally justified even if that moral justification goes no deeper than relying on what are perceived to be widely shared moral values. It should be added that a useful technique for testing some of these criteria is to look not only at existing legal rules and principles but also at hypothetical examples that have not yet come before the courts.

16. The layout of the book

This book is primarily structured according to, first, the functions of the remedies for torts and breach of contract and, secondly, the particular remedies concerned to effect those functions. So, after the Introduction (with the next chapter looking at the impact of the Human Rights Act 1998), there are four parts corresponding to the remedial functions set out above[78] (compensation; restitution and punishment; compelling performance or preventing (or compelling the undoing of) a wrong; and declaring rights). Within each part, the particular remedy or remedies for torts and breach of contract concerned to effect those functions are examined. A final part and chapter, for reasons set out above,[79] looks at remedies for equitable wrongs.

---

[78] Above, pp 9–10.   [79] Above, p 12.

2
The impact of the Human Rights Act 1998

1. Introduction	22
2. A non-tortious public wrong	23
3. The assessment of damages for the HRA cause of action	26

1. Introduction

The enactment of the Human Rights Act 1998 (HRA 1998) has raised a number of novel issues for English law. But the impact of the Act on the subject matter of this book has been limited. That impact is best understood by clarifying that there are two main respects in which the Act is relevant to civil wrongs.[1]

First, as the definition of a public authority in HRA 1998, s 6(3) includes a court, the HRA 1998 can have some 'horizontal' effect (that is, in actions between 'private parties').[2] While the HRA 1998 does not require the courts to develop new civil wrongs, it has led to the courts modifying existing common law or equitable wrongs to take account of Convention rights. One example of this is the reluctance to accept 'blanket immunities' from liability.[3] Another example is that, as we have seen in chapter 1,[4] the HRA 1998, through its enactment of Article 8 of the ECHR, has been the stimulus for the courts to develop a tort of privacy out of the equitable wrong of breach of confidence. The remedies for that new tort are the same as for any other tort.

Secondly, and most obviously, HRA 1998, s 6(1) has 'vertical effect' by creating a new statutory cause of action constituted by a public authority's infringement of a person's Convention rights. Although commentators initially viewed this new statutory cause of action as a tort,[5] it is now clear that the English courts have instead treated it as a sui generis public law wrong.[6] That is, it is a statutory wrong but it is not a tort. This is consistent with the way in which the Privy Council has for decades analysed claims for damages for breach of constitutional rights in Commonwealth countries. For example, in *Maharaj v A-G of Trinidad and Tobago (No 2)* Lord Diplock contrasted 'the existing law of torts' with the

---

[1] That HRA 1998, s 3(1) requires statutes to be interpreted, where possible, in accordance with Convention rights, may also, albeit very rarely, be relevant to the subject matter of this book: see, eg, below, p 257 n 14. On HRA 1998, s 12(3), see below, pp 479–480.

[2] For a clear recognition of this (contrary to the early doubts of some commentators) see, eg, *Campbell v Mirror Group Newspapers Ltd* [2004] UKHL 22, [2004] 2 All ER 995, at [132]–[133] (per Baroness Hale of Richmond).

[3] But the very significant impact indicated by the European Court of Human Rights in *Osman v United Kingdom* (1998) 5 BHRC 293 was backtracked from in, eg, *Z v United Kingdom* (2001) 34 EHRR 97.

[4] Above, pp 12–13.

[5] See, eg, A Lester and D Pannick, 'The Impact of the Human Rights Act on Private Law: The Knight's Move' (2000) 116 LQR 380, 382 ('new public law tort of acting in breach of the victim's Convention rights'); *Clerk and Lindsell on Torts* (18th edn, Sweet & Maxwell 2000) paras 1-04, 12-75–12-81 ('constitutional tort') (cf 22nd edn, Sweet & Maxwell 2018, para 14-74).

[6] Eg, *R (on the application of Greenfield) v Secretary of State for the Home Department* [2005] UKHL 14, [2005] 1 WLR 673.

claim for breach of a constitutional right in issue which he said was 'concerned with public law not private law'.[7]

It follows that the main vertical cause of action (hereinafter referred to as the 'HRA cause of action') falls outside the subject matter of this book. Nevertheless as that cause of action is a civil wrong, albeit not a tort, and as the main remedy for that wrong is 'damages' it has been thought important to say more about it in this introductory chapter.

Before proceeding further, it may be helpful to set out the central provisions of section 8 of the HRA which is headed 'judicial remedies'. Section 8(1)–(4) reads as follows:

'(1) In relation to any act (or proposed act) of a public authority which the court finds is (or would be) unlawful, it may grant such relief or remedy, or make such order, within its powers as it considers just and appropriate.
(2) But damages may be awarded only by a court which has power to award damages, or to order the payment of compensation, in civil proceedings.
(3) No award of damages is to be made unless, taking account of all the circumstances of the case, including—
    (a) any other relief or remedy granted, or order made, in relation to the act in question (by that or any other court), and
    (b) the consequences of any decision (of that or any other court) in respect of that act,
    the court is satisfied that the award is necessary to afford just satisfaction to the person in whose favour it is made.
(4) In determining—
    (a) whether to award damages, or
    (b) the amount of an award,
    the court must take into account the principles applied by the European Court of Human Rights in relation to the award of compensation under Article 41 of the Convention.'

2. A non-tortious public wrong

Why is it accurate to regard the vertical cause of action as a 'non-tortious public wrong' rather than a tort? Six reasons may be given. The first three of these are at the level of *describing* differences between tort and the HRA cause of action whether laid down in the HRA 1988 or by the English courts in applying the Act.[8] The remaining three are at a deeper level.

(i) There is no right to damages for the HRA cause of action. In other words, establishing the cause of action does not necessarily mean that an award of damages will be made.[9] This follows not only from the wording of section 8(3)—damages are not to be awarded unless 'necessary to afford just satisfaction'—but also from the jurisprudence of the Strasbourg Court which must be taken into account under section 8(4). In contrast a

---

[7] *Maharaj v A-G of Trinidad and Tobago (No 2)* [1979] AC 385, at 396.
[8] A further difference suggested by the Law Commission, *Damages under the Human Rights Act 1998* (Law Com No 266, 2000) para 4.64, is that Strasbourg damages are more generous in respect of mental distress. For example, loss of love and companionship are compensated by the Strasbourg court, whereas they are not compensated in England. This is misleading. Once a tort has been established, there appears to be no bar in English law to recovering such damages consequent on a personal injury or even in a claim for false imprisonment. It has also sometimes been suggested that Strasbourg has a looser approach to causation: see, eg, *Van Colle v Chief Constable of the Hertfordshire Police* [2008] UKHL 50, [2009] 1 AC 225, at [138] (Lord Brown). But again this seems misleading: in particular, loss of a chance damages, even free-standing, are often available in English law: see below, ch 5.
[9] So, eg, in *Dennis v Ministry of Defence* [2003] EWHC 793 (QB), [2003] NLJR 634, at [31] damages for infringement of a Convention right were not awarded because compensatory damages were being awarded, irrespective of the Human Rights Act 1998, for the tort of nuisance.

characteristic of all torts is that there is a right to damages. For torts actionable only on proof of damage, the damage proved will entitle the claimant to compensatory damages; and for torts actionable per se if actionable damage is proved there is an entitlement to compensatory damages but, in any event, nominal damages will be awarded even if no damage is proved.

(ii) Punitive damages cannot be awarded for the HRA cause of action. This is in line with the words—'just *satisfaction*' to the claimant—in section 8(3). Punitive damages do not fall happily within that phrase and in any event have never been (overtly) awarded by the Strasbourg Court.[10] That punitive damages cannot be awarded under section 8(3) was confirmed in *Anufrijeva v Southwark London BC*[11] and *Watkins v Secretary of State for the Home Department*.[12] In contrast, after *Kuddus v Chief Constable of Leicestershire Constabulary*,[13] one can say that, provided the facts fall within one of the *Rookes v Barnard*[14] categories, it is a characteristic of all torts that punitive damages may be awarded.

(iii) In the leading case of *R (on the application of Greenfield) v Secretary of State for the Home Department*[15] it was made clear that, contrary to the view of the Law Commission and the approach advocated in some earlier cases,[16] the quantum of compensatory damages for non-pecuniary loss should be fixed in line with the jurisprudence of the Strasbourg Court and not in line with domestic torts.[17] Although not an easy comparator, because the Strasbourg jurisprudence is notoriously flexible, it would seem that this will almost always mean that an award will be no higher and will commonly be lower for the HRA cause of action than for a domestic tort.[18] In Lord Bingham's words in *Watkins*, 'monetary compensation awarded at Strasbourg tends, in comparison with domestic levels of award, to be ungenerous'.[19]

(iv) At a deeper level, one can say that the rights protected are different. The HRA cause of action is concerned only with protecting rights that are rights against the state. They are not rights against any other person. They are public law rights not private law rights. While we know that private law rights can be invoked against public authorities (ie one can use any tort, most obviously trespass to the person or negligence or nuisance, against a public authority) that is on the basis that the rule of law demands that public authorities should not be treated any more favourably than other defendants. The reverse proposition does not hold true: the HRA cause of action can only be invoked against a public authority.

(v) Lord Bingham, giving the leading speech in *Greenfield*, reasoned that the functions of the remedies for the HRA cause of action and tort differ. He saw the primary function of

---

[10] See, eg, *BB v United Kingdom* (2004) 39 EHRR 635, at [36].
[11] [2003] EWCA Civ 1406, [2004] 2 WLR 603, at [55].
[12] [2006] UKHL 17, [2006] 2 AC 395, at [26], [32], [64].
[13] [2001] UKHL 29, [2002] 2 AC 122. See below, ch 20.   [14] [1964] AC 1129.
[15] [2005] UKHL 14, [2005] 1 WLR 673.
[16] Law Commission, *Damages under the Human Rights Act 1998*, Law Com No 266 (2000); *R (KB) v Mental Health Review Tribunal* [2003] EWHC 193 (Admin), [2003] 2 All ER 209; *R (Bernard) v Enfield London BC* [2002] EWHC 2282 (Admin), [2003] HRLR 4; *Anufrijeva v London Borough of Southwark* [2003] EWCA Civ 1406, [2004] 1 All ER 833.
[17] But see *Alseran v Ministry of Defence* [2017] EWHC 3289 (QB), [2018] 3 WLR 95, discussed below, pp 28–29.
[18] But the amount of bereavement damages awarded in the Strasbourg court may be higher than under the Fatal Accidents Act 1976 which imposes a fixed sum and is recoverable only by a very limited class. See *Rabone v Pennine Care NHS Foundation Trust* [2012] UKSC 2, [2012] 2 AC 72; *Smith v Lancashire Teaching Hospitals NHS Foundation Trust* [2017] EWCA Civ 1916, [2018] QB 804; below, p 264.
[19] [2006] UKHL 17, [2006] 2 AC 395, at [26].

remedies in tort as being to compensate whereas the primary function of remedies for the HRA cause of action is the vindication of rights. He said: '[T]he 1998 Act is not a tort statute. Its objects are different and broader. Even in a case where a finding of violation is not judged to afford the applicant just satisfaction, such a finding will be an important part of his remedy and an important vindication of the right he has asserted.'[20] While Lord Bingham would no doubt have accepted that both compensation and vindication are important functions in relation to both types of action, so that this is a matter of degree rather than kind, his fundamental point was that the balance between them is different in relation to tort and the HRA cause of action.

(vi) A possible further reason why the English courts may be particularly keen to treat the HRA cause of action as being different from a tort is that this more easily allows the traditions of the common law to be maintained. Had it been accepted that the HRA cause of action was a tort, this would have required accepting that the approach of the courts to the tortious liability of public authorities had been transformed by the HRA 1998. So, for example, the rejection of liability in negligence in many claims against public authorities[21] and the non-acceptance of a tort of loss caused by an ultra vires action would have been outflanked. That would not merely have been a radical change but would appear to have involved accepting that the development of the common law as regards tort claims against public authorities had hitherto not been fully compliant with human rights. Not surprisingly that is not an analysis that the judges would wish to accept. Adopting the analysis that the HRA cause of action belongs outside, albeit alongside, the liability in tort of public authorities—what has been termed 'the separate channels approach'[22]—may be thought to allow the courts their traditional freedom in deciding how the tortious liability of public authorities should be developed. Indeed, one might even say—and this has been borne out in the cases—that, because the claimant now has the HRA cause of action to fall back on within domestic law, any previous pressure to amend the domestic tortious liability of public authorities has been removed.[23] At the very least, the judges regard themselves as free to apply and develop the domestic liability in tort of public authorities in the same way as they traditionally have done, taking into account the jurisprudence of the Strasbourg court as a relevant, but not decisive, factor. The main impact of the HRA 1998 on the development

---

[20] [2005] UKHL 14, [2005] 1 WLR 673, at [19]. See also his comments in *Watkins v Secretary of State for the Home Department* [2006] UKHL 17, [2006] 2 AC 395, at [9]. See also Waller LJ, giving the judgment of the Court of Appeal, in *Dobson v Thames Water Utilities Ltd* [2009] EWCA Civ 28, [2009] 3 All ER 319, at [42]; *DSD v Metropolitan Police Commissioner* [2018] UKSC 11, [2018] 2 WLR 895, at [63]–[65] (per Lord Kerr).

[21] The ECHR has recognised positive protective duties requiring state intervention to protect individuals against harm from other private individuals (as shown, eg, by *DSD v Metropolitan Police Commissioner* [2018] UKSC 11, [2018] 2 WLR 895) whereas the common law still denies a general positive duty of care upon public authorities to protect members of the public (as shown, eg, in *Michael v Chief Constable of South Wales* [2015] UKSC 2, [2015] AC 1732: see J Morgan, 'Parallel Lines that Never Meet: Tort and the ECHR Again' [2018] CLJ 244.

[22] J Morgan, 'Parallel Lines that Never Meet: Tort and the ECHR Again' [2018] CLJ 244.

[23] So, for example, in *Watkins v Secretary of State for the Home Department* [2006] UKHL 17, [2006] 2 AC 395, at [26], Lord Bingham said, in relation to the tort of misfeasance in public office, 'It may reasonably be inferred that Parliament intended infringement of the core human (and constitutional) rights protected by the Act to be remedied under it and not by the development of parallel remedies.' See similarly in that case Lord Rodger, at [64]. See also in *Van Colle v Chief Constable of the Hertfordshire Police* [2008] UKHL 50, [2009] 1 AC 225 in which Lord Brown said, at [138]–[139], '[C]ertainly in the present context your Lordships should not feel tempted to develop the common law in harmony with Convention rights.... Clearly, the violation of a fundamental right is a very serious thing and happily, since the 1998 Act, it gives rise to a cause of action in domestic law. I see no sound reason, however, for matching this with a common law claim also.' In contrast, Lord Bingham, dissenting and adopting an approach that is not easy to reconcile with his comments in *Watkins*, said at [58] that he thought that 'the common law should develop in the light of Convention rights and in harmony with a Convention right concerning the same ground'.

of the tortious liability of public authorities has been to provide an alternative fall-back position which previously would have involved the claimant going off to Strasbourg (having exhausted her domestic remedies) but can now be relied on in the English courts. Put shortly, it is not surprising that the HRA cause of action has been viewed by the judges as a non-tortious public law wrong because that view more readily allows the traditional incremental development of the tortious liability of public authorities to continue as before.

It is submitted that, for all these reasons, it would be misleading to regard the HRA cause of action as a tort. It is best viewed, and is clearly being viewed by the courts, as a sui generis public law wrong.

3. The assessment of damages for the HRA cause of action

In the light of what has just been said, the judicial remedies for the HRA cause of action fall outside the scope of this book. Nevertheless, by section 8(1), a court may grant any remedy 'within its powers as it considers just and appropriate'. It follows that the remedies available for the HRA cause of action are the same as that applicable to a tort. So, for example, a declaration or an injunction or damages can be awarded.

If we focus on damages, if damages are awarded—and in contrast to tort there is no right to damages[24]—section 8(4) HRA 1998 requires the English courts to take into account the principles applied by the European Court of Human Rights. While these principles are notoriously unclear, there is no doubt that the basic aim of damages is compensation and that that means that the award is concerned, as in English domestic law, to put the claimant into as good a position as if his or her Convention rights had not been infringed. Both pecuniary loss and non-pecuniary loss can be compensated. Similar limitations on compensatory damages, such as remoteness, legal causation, and mitigation, apply as in domestic law.[25]

Where pecuniary loss has been suffered, the assessment will presumably be the same as for a domestic tort. However, as we have indicated in the last section,[26] it is in relation to the scale of non-pecuniary loss for the HRA cause of action that the English courts have regarded themselves as applying a Strasbourg rather than a domestic approach. We will now explain this in more detail.[27]

In *R (on the application of Greenfield) v Secretary of State for the Home Department*[28] case the applicant was a prisoner who, at a hearing before the deputy Governor, had been given an additional 21 days of imprisonment for taking drugs contrary to the prison rules. By the time the case reached the House of Lords the Secretary of State accepted that the prisoner's

---

[24] Above, p 23.
[25] In *DSD v Metropolitan Police Commissioner* [2014] EWHC 2493 (QB), [2015] 1 WLR 1833, at [56]–[65] damages were awarded under s 8(3) HRA even though there had been a settlement by the claimants with another concurrent wrongdoer and some payments had also been made by the Criminal Injuries Compensation Board. But while Green J said, at [63], that tort principles 'may not be entirely to the point' it would appear that much the same approach would have been applied under a domestic tort claim because Green J's reasoning was that the settlement and awards covered different harm and were recognised to be against someone who was unlikely to be able fully to meet all claims. This point was one of those appealed to, and Green J upheld by, the Supreme Court: [2018] UKSC 11, [2018] 2 WLR 895, at [63]–[65].
[26] Above, p 24.
[27] See also the first instance decision in *DSD v Metropolitan Police Commissioner* [2014] EWHC 2493 (QB), [2015] 1 WLR 1833 (not appealed on quantum as such).
[28] [2005] UKHL 14, [2005] 1 WLR 673.

Convention right to a fair trial under Article 6 had been infringed. This was because the proceedings involved a criminal charge and the applicant was therefore entitled to an independent tribunal—which the deputy Governor was not—and to legal representation, which had been denied to him. It was accepted that the applicant was entitled to declarations that the Secretary of State had acted unlawfully, contrary to Article 6, in those two respects. The dispute was about damages.

The House of Lords decided that the applicant was not entitled to any damages because the declarations in the applicant's favour afforded just satisfaction and an award of damages was not necessary. The applicant sought damages for non-pecuniary loss on two grounds. First, that by being denied legal representation he had been deprived of the opportunity of a more favourable outcome (thereby avoiding all or some of the extra days of imprisonment). This was, in any event, held to be too speculative. Secondly, he argued that he had suffered anxiety and frustration because he did not think that he would be fairly tried given that the tribunal was not independent. There was held to be no special feature in this case warranting damages on that basis.

The major importance of the case, however, is that the House of Lords used it as an opportunity to deal with the issue of whether the scale of damages for non-pecuniary loss in English tort law should apply where damages are being awarded for the HRA cause of action. In what was technically obiter dicta Lord Bingham, with whom the other Lords agreed, reasoned that that domestic tort scale for non-pecuniary loss should not apply. He stated that English courts 'should not aim to be significantly more or less generous than the [Strasbourg] court might be expected to be, in a case where it was willing to make an award at all'.[29]

Lord Bingham gave three reasons for his view. First, as we have seen, he argued that 'the 1998 Act is not a tort statute. Its objects are different and broader.'[30] Secondly, Lord Bingham said that: 'the purpose of incorporating the Convention in domestic law through the 1998 Act was not to give the victims better remedies at home than they could recover in Strasbourg but to give them the same remedies without the delay and expense of resort to Strasbourg.'[31] Thirdly, he argued that section 8(4) clearly indicates that 'courts in this country should look to Strasbourg and not to domestic precedents'.[32]

One can criticise this approach and reasoning as a matter of both principle and workability.[33] The principled objection can be expressed as follows. The rights protected by the HRA cause of action are fundamental rights. They are at least as important as the rights protected by the law of tort. If a victim suffers, and is being compensated for, a loss as a result of a breach by a public authority of his or her Convention rights, he or she should receive at least the same compensation as he or she would be entitled to in tort for suffering the same loss. One is otherwise treating a breach of a Convention right less seriously than the breach of a right protected in tort. As regards workability, it is very difficult to find a consistent line of Strasbourg authority on quantum and, in any event, the quantum will reflect the cost of living in the different jurisdictions in play so that it cannot straightforwardly be applied across to the UK.

---

[29] [2005] UKHL 14, [2005] 1 WLR 673, at [19].   [30] ibid.   [31] ibid.   [32] ibid.
[33] See A Burrows, 'Damages and Rights' in *Rights and Private Law* (eds D Nolan and A Robertson, Hart Publishing 2012) 275, 296–303. See also J Steele, 'Damages in Tort and under the Human Rights Act: Remedial or Functional Separation?' (2008) 67 CLJ 606; J Varuhas, 'A Tort-Based Approach to Damages under the Human Rights Act 1998' (2009) 72 MLR 750; J Varuhas, *Damages and Human Rights* (Hart Publishing 2016). See also J Edelman, *McGregor on Damages* (20th edn, Sweet & Maxwell 2018) ch 43 (written by J Varuhas).

However, with some relatively minor modifications designed to overcome any problems in practice, the Supreme Court affirmed the general approach in *Greenfield* in *R (on the application of Faulkner) v Secretary of State for Justice*.[34] The case concerned violations of Article 5(4) of the ECHR (ie the right to speedy determination of the lawfulness of detention). There had been delays by the Parole Board (consequent on delays by the Ministry of Justice) in assessing whether prisoners, who had been given life imprisonment or imprisonment for public protection, were safe to release after they had served the minimum time specified. Lord Reed, giving the leading judgment, said that, in line with the general approach in *Greenfield* (which was not being challenged in this case), damages under s 8 of the HRA should broadly reflect the level of awards made by the Strasbourg court in comparable cases brought by applicants from the UK or other countries with a similar cost of living. Lord Reed explained that, according to *Greenfield*, the correct approach was to regard the HRA 'as introducing into our domestic law an entirely novel remedy, the grant of which is discretionary and which is described as damages but is not tortious in nature ... Reflecting the international origins of the remedy and its lack of any native roots, the primary source of the principles which are to guide the courts in its application is ... the practice of the international court that is its native habitat.'[35] Nevertheless, Lord Reed indicated that over time one would expect the remedy to become absorbed into the domestic system through domestic appellate decisions.

As regards damages for infringement of the Convention right under Article 5(4) (in contrast to Article 5(1)), it was laid down that these could not be awarded for loss of liberty unless the prisoner established on the balance of probabilities that he would have been released earlier. Otherwise there is a strong, albeit rebuttable, presumption that the delay has caused the prisoner feelings of frustration and anxiety which, unless insufficiently severe (unlikely where the delay was three months or more), should be reflected in an award of damages. Applying the Strasbourg scale, derived from the relevant Strasbourg case law, the awards for non-pecuniary loss in respect of the two claimants being considered should be £6,500 in one case (which included damages for loss of liberty) and £300 in the other (as damages for frustration and anxiety).

All this now needs to be read in the light of the inspiring and radical judgment at first instance in *Alseran v Ministry of Defence*.[36] Leggatt J here accepted the powerful argument of principle that has been outlined above and, while purporting to follow *Greenfield* and *Faulkner*, as he was bound to do, he in effect departed from the approach there laid down. The case concerned the false imprisonment and ill-treatment in custody by British soldiers of Iraqi civilians during the Iraq War. It was held in relation to four lead cases that the claimants had claims in tort for assault and battery and false imprisonment but that those claims were time-barred; and that they also had claims for infringement of Convention rights (in Articles 3 and 5) under the Human Rights Act 1998 which were not time-barred. Leggatt J pointed out that to apply the scale of damages for non-pecuniary loss awarded by the Strasbourg court was problematic because that court approached each case on its facts and was not attempting to apply a consistent approach, and the awards were not intended to have precedential effect. In an important passage, dealing with where the claims in tort and under the Human Rights Act 1998 overlap in covering the same injury and damage, Leggatt J said this:

---

[34] [2013] UKSC 23, [2013] 2 WLR 1157. [35] ibid, at [29].
[36] [2017] EWHC 3289 (QB), [2018] 3 WLR 95.

'In such cases the same basic right—to bodily integrity or to liberty—is protected both by the law of tort and by the Human Rights Act 1998. There is a powerful argument of principle that where, in such cases, a victim is being compensated under section 8 of the Human Rights Act for the defendant's unlawful act, he or she should receive similar compensation for the harm suffered to that which would be awarded on a parallel claim in tort. To award less compensation would be to treat the breach of a fundamental human right guaranteed by the Convention as less serious than breach of the equivalent right protected by the common law of tort. Unless some good reason is shown for taking a different approach, the amount of compensation awarded for the same injury caused by the same wrongful conduct should in principle be the same in each case. This principle seems to me to carry particular weight in the case of non-pecuniary damage for which any amount awarded in compensation can only be symbolic of the value which our society attributes to harm of the relevant kind.'[37]

According to Leggatt J, therefore, the correct approach (at least in cases where there are overlapping claims in tort and under the 1998 Act) is first to take the level of awards that would be made in English law for the non-pecuniary losses in question. Then one should consider whether there should be any departure from such awards because of any particular facts of the case. On the facts of these cases, it was an important factor that the claimants were all living in Iraq where the cost of living was low so that the purchasing power of money was much higher than that in this country. For this reason, Leggatt J thought that awards of approximately half of those which would be awarded under English law would be equitable. Finally one should cross-check to awards in Strasbourg to ensure that the amount of damages to be awarded would not, as far as can be judged, be considered inadequate or excessive by that court.[38] Here there was nothing in the Strasbourg cases to indicate that any alteration to the awards needed to be made.

It can be seen from this that, by carefully applying first principles, Leggatt J has turned the approach in *Greenfield* on its head. Far from being inappropriate, the domestic scale for non-pecuniary loss is of primary importance and the Strasbourg level is of secondary importance as a cross-check even assuming that one can work out what the Strasbourg level would be. It remains to be seen whether this enlightened approach will be accepted by the higher courts.

---

[37] ibid, at [931].   [38] ibid, at [937]–[948].

PART TWO
COMPENSATION

Section One

General Principles in Assessing Compensatory Damages

3
Introduction to compensatory damages

1. Compensation, compensatory damages, and types of loss	35
2. The compensatory aims	38
3. Theoretical underpinnings of compensation	39
4. Damages valuing the right infringed?	46
5. A non-compensatory cost of cure?	48

This chapter, by way of introduction to compensatory damages, looks at the different types of loss, the compensatory aims, and the theoretical underpinnings of compensation. It goes on to examine, albeit to reject, the thesis that the primary function of damages is not compensation but is rather to value the right infringed. It also examines the controversial view that a standard measure of damages is a non-compensatory cost of cure.

1. Compensation, compensatory damages, and types of loss

Compensation means the award of a sum of money which, so far as money can be so, is equivalent to the claimant's loss. The loss may be pecuniary (that is, a loss of wealth) where the equivalence to the claimant's loss can be precise; or non-pecuniary (for example, pain, suffering, and loss of amenity; loss of reputation; and mental distress generally) where the sum to be awarded as compensation cannot be precisely equivalent to the loss and where the only way to ensure consistency of awards is through conventionally accepted tariffs of value.

The remedy concerned to achieve compensation for torts and breach of contract is compensatory damages (that is, damages concerned to compensate). This is almost always a common law remedy although, as we shall see in chapter 17 below, equitable compensatory damages awarded in addition to, or in substitution for, specific performance or an injunction, may also be awarded for a tort or breach of contract.

By an award of damages a sum of money assessed by the court is required to be paid by the defendant to the claimant.[1] The usual function of damages is compensation; that is, damages are usually compensatory. But it would be a mistake to imagine that damages and compensation are synonymous. This is because some awards of damages are non-compensatory: ie damages may also be punitive or nominal or contemptuous. In this part of this book, we are solely concerned with compensatory damages.

This and the following 15 chapters examine in detail the law on compensatory damages. The first seven chapters (chapters 3 to 9) cover the general principles of assessment and equip one with all that is basically needed to assess compensatory damages, whatever the type of loss in question. The subsequent five chapters (chapters 10 to 14) then put flesh on those bare bones by examining compensatory damages for the different types of loss. Chapters 15

---

[1] Strictly speaking, this refers to unliquidated damages. For 'liquidated damages' for breach of contract, see below, ch 21.

and 16 deal with two factors of relevance to, while not concerning the assessment of, compensatory damages, namely, awards of interest and limitation periods. Chapter 17 looks at equitable compensatory damages for torts and breach of contract. Finally, chapter 18 explores 'negotiating damages' which the Supreme Court regards as compensatory.

It is convenient to consider in a little more depth here the fundamental division between pecuniary and non-pecuniary loss and to explain the further division of types of loss adopted in chapters 10 to 14.

So starting with the fundamental division between pecuniary and non-pecuniary loss, money can be complete compensation for the former but not for the latter. As Lord Diplock said in *Wright v British Railways Board*,[2] '[Non-pecuniary] loss is not susceptible of *measurement* in money. Any figure at which the assessor of damages arrives cannot be other than artificial …'.

This distinction does not mean that there are never any difficulties in assessing pecuniary loss; for while in some cases compensation for monetary loss is mathematically obvious and exact (for example, pre-trial expenditure), in most instances the uncertainties of what would have happened but for the wrong, and of what will happen in the future, make the assessment of even the loss of monetary income (eg loss of earnings) problematical. Similarly, while reliance on market values is often the most accurate method of assessing pecuniary loss for, for example, property damage, any attempt to put a value on anything, other than money itself, involves some approximation. So the distinction is not between losses where the compensation is precise and losses where it is imprecise. Rather it is between losses which are of wealth, and can therefore be readily translated into money, and other losses.

But as non-pecuniary losses are not losses of wealth, how exactly are they viewed and compared? The traditional judicial approach is to treat some heads of non-pecuniary loss, namely loss of amenity, physical inconvenience, and loss of reputation, as analogous to proprietary losses and as losses over and above the claimant's distress or loss of happiness; such heads of loss, in contrast to pain and suffering and mental distress, are therefore assessed objectively (in the sense of being assessed irrespective of the claimant's own awareness) with the severe distress of the claimant or the claimant's unconsciousness being regarded as irrelevant. On this approach, while pain and suffering and mental distress are compared in terms of the degree of distress suffered by the claimant, the other non-pecuniary losses are compared by examining the extent of the interference with, and the importance of, the 'personal asset' affected.

An alternative view is that to treat any non-pecuniary loss as analogous to a property loss is unrealistic and that ultimately all non-pecuniary loss is concerned with the claimant's distress or loss of happiness. Taking this approach the different heads of non-pecuniary loss must simply be regarded as different types of distress with the head of 'mental distress' being a residual category. In practice this approach would rarely lead to different results than the traditional judicial one for the courts would need to treat a particular personal injury or physical inconvenience or loss of reputation as affecting individuals' happiness in essentially the same way, just as they already do, for example, in assessing pain and suffering damages. So adoption of the alternative approach would not mean that the claimant who has made the best of his or her misfortune would be likely to recover less than the claimant who has not, nor that a claimant would be encouraged to present a long face to the court. But the alternative view does provide a sound theoretical explanation for non-pecuniary

---

[2] [1983] 2 AC 773, at 777. For similar judicial statements, see *The Mediana* [1900] AC 113, at 116; *West & Son Ltd v Shephard* [1964] AC 326, at 346; *Fletcher v Autocar and Transporters Ltd* [1968] 2 QB 322, at 335, 339–340, 363; *Heil v Rankin* [2001] QB 272, at 293.

loss and hence for why, for example, some non-pecuniary losses are regarded as more serious than others. Moreover, there would be at least two practical differences. First, severe distress suffered by the claimant would merit higher damages under any of the heads of non-pecuniary loss and, secondly, an unconscious claimant would recover nothing for non-pecuniary loss.

Whichever of the two approaches is taken—and as yet there is little judicial support for any departure from the first traditional view—there ought to be uniformity between awards. In other words, similar awards should be made for similar non-pecuniary losses and more serious losses should be compensated by higher awards. This is dictated by the essential justice of like cases being treated alike. It also gives some certainty to the law which in turn aids out-of-court settlements.

Since the virtual elimination of jury trials in personal injury cases, uniformity has indeed become the prime feature of damages for pain and suffering and loss of amenity, with judges relying on a tariff system. Similarly in Fatal Accidents Act 1976 cases there is a fixed statutory sum for bereavement. It has also been recognized in cases on, for example, the torts of defamation, false imprisonment, and malicious prosecution that awards for non-pecuniary loss should not be out of line with those given in personal injury cases; and this drive towards uniformity has been made easier by the abolition through s 11 of the Defamation Act 2013 of the right to trial by jury in defamation cases.

Of course the emphasis on uniformity in no sense explains how the level of award is reached in the first place. Why, for example, should damages for loss of amenity and pain and suffering resulting from blindness be assessed at (say) £140,000 rather than £1,000? The courts are generally content to say merely that the level of awards must be fair and reasonable,[3] should keep pace with the times,[4] and should in no sense reflect the claimant's wealth.[5] This may be all that can be sensibly said. However, economists have suggested that a value can be put on injury or life by, for example, asking what people would be prepared to pay to avoid incurring that injury, or what they would be willing to accept to incur it.[6] But in general it is hard to see how either question can produce anything more than further guesswork and the latter would, in any event, produce astronomically high awards. Perhaps more hopeful is to think in terms of the cost of substitute pleasures; that is, a claimant should be enabled to buy whatever can in some sense be regarded as making up for the loss the claimant has suffered or will suffer so that, to use rather hackneyed examples, a blind person should at the very least be able to buy music and speakers and the person disabled from skiing should be able to buy holidays in the sun.

It follows from this discussion that one way to divide the types of loss for the purposes of examining compensatory damages is simply to divide between pecuniary and non-pecuniary loss. But ultimately it has been considered preferable in this book to make a different and more detailed division of types of loss which, it is believed, accords more with the way lawyers are used to confronting and thinking about compensatory damages. The division adopted is therefore as follows: pecuniary loss (except consequent on personal injury, death, or loss of reputation); personal injury losses; losses on death; loss of reputation; and mental distress or physical inconvenience (except consequent on personal injury or death).

It should be emphasised finally that this book's approach to compensation is novel in not dividing torts and breach of contract and then examining compensatory damages for

---

[3] Eg *Rowley v London and North Western Rly Co* (1873) LR 8 Exch 221, at 231; *Scott v Musial* [1959] 2 QB 429, at 443; *Gardner v Dyson* [1967] 1 WLR 1497, at 1501; *Heil v Rankin* [2001] QB 272, at 294, 297.
[4] Below, pp 171–172. [5] *Fletcher v Autocar and Transporters Ltd* [1968] 2 QB 322, at 340–341.
[6] See P Cane and J Goudkamp, *Atiyah's Accidents, Compensation and The Law* (9th edn, CUP 2018) 150.

different torts and contracts respectively. There are many common approaches to compensation, whether the cause of action be tort or breach of contract, and in order to bring these out it has been considered preferable to examine compensatory damages in respect of the different types of loss with the tort/breach of contract divide then being recognised, where helpful, under each of those types.

2. The compensatory aims

The aim of compensatory damages for breach of contract is to put the claimant into as good a position as it would have been in if the contract had been performed. For tort the aim of compensatory damages is to put the claimant into as good a position as it would have been in if no tort had been committed.

These compensatory aims are of fundamental importance. They guide the whole process of assessment. They clarify in general terms—subject to the limiting principles considered in chapter 7—the losses which compensatory damages are concerned to cover.

The classic contract case laying down the aim of compensatory damages is *Robinson v Harman*[7] in which Parke B said:

'The rule of common law is that where a party sustains a loss by reason of a breach of contract he is, so far as money can do it, to be placed in the same situation with respect to damages as if the contract had been performed.'

Lord Blackburn's statement in *Livingstone v Rawyards Coal Co*,[8] a case concerning trespass to goods, is the most cited tort authority on this. He said that the measure of damages was:

'… that sum of money which will put the party who has been injured, or who has suffered, in the same position as he would have been in if he had not sustained the wrong for which he is now getting his compensation or reparation.'

Many subsequent cases contain equally clear expressions of these central aims.[9]

For shorthand purposes, the two aims can be linked by saying that the aim of compensation is to put the claimant into as good a position as if no wrong had been committed. However, if one does combine the two aims in that way, one must be aware that very different results may ensue depending on whether the duty broken was a positive or a negative one; and that typically contractual duties are positive (hence the separate formulation of the aim as being to put the claimant into as good a position as if the contract had been performed) while tort duties are typically negative (hence the separate formulation of the aim as being to put the claimant into as good a position as if no tort had been committed).

---

[7] (1848) 1 Exch 850, at 855.   [8] (1880) 5 App Cas 25, at 39.
[9] Eg for breach of contract, *Wertheim v Chicoutimi Pulp Co* [1911] AC 301, at 307; *British Westinghouse Co v Underground Electric Rlys Co of London Ltd* [1912] AC 673, at 689; *Monarch SS Co Ltd v Karlshamns Oljefabriker* [1949] AC 196, at 220; *The Heron II* [1969] 1 AC 350, at 414; *Doyle v Olby (Ironmongers) Ltd* [1969] 2 QB 158, at 167; *Tito v Waddell (No 2)* [1977] Ch 106, at 328–334; *Radford v De Froberville* [1977] 1 WLR 1262, at 1268; *Rees v Darlington Memorial Hospital NHS Trust* [2003] UKHL 52, [2003] 4 All ER 987, at [130]; *Golden Strait Corpn v Nippon Yusen Kubishika Kaisha (The Golden Victory)* [2007] UKHL 12, [2007] 2 AC 353, at [36]; *Bunge SA v Nidera NV* [2015] UKSC 43, [2015] Bus LR 987, at [14]; *Morris-Garner v One Step (Support) Ltd* [2018] UKSC 20, [2018] 2 WLR 1353, at [31]–[32]. For torts, see, eg, *Shearman v Folland* [1950] 2 KB 43, at 49; *British Transport Commission v Gourley* [1956] AC 185, at 187; *Lim Poh Choo v Camden and Islington Area Health Authority* [1980] AC 174, at 186ff; *Dodd Properties (Kent) Ltd v Canterbury City Council* [1980] 1 WLR 433, at 456; *Swingcastle Ltd v Alastair Gibson* [1991] 2 AC 223; *Rees v Darlington Memorial Hospital NHS Trust* [2003] UKHL 52, [2003] 4 All ER 987, at [130]; *Knauer v Ministry of Justice* [2016] UKSC 9, [2016] AC 908, at [1]; *Tiuta International Ltd v De Villiers Surveyors Ltd* [2017] UKSC 77, [2017] 1 WLR 4627, at [6]; *Morris-Garner v One Step (Support) Ltd* [2018] UKSC 20, [2018] 2 WLR 1353, at [25] and [31].

The difference in results—between compensation for breach of positive contractual duties and for breach of negative tort duties—is best illustrated by reference to tortious misrepresentations inducing contracts. Say, for example, the claimant buys a car. The seller falsely misrepresents to her, and gives a contractual warranty, that the car is only one year old. In fact it is four years old. The claimant pays £5,000. The market value of a one-year-old car (but with the other characteristics—apart from the age—of the car the claimant buys) is £5,500 but the value of the car she actually receives (given its real age) is £4,000.

If the claimant keeps the car and brings a claim for damages for the tortious misrepresentation (whether for the tort of deceit or the tort of negligent misrepresentation), the aim is to put her into as good a position as if she had never entered into the contract. Her damages will be £5,000 – £4,000 = £1,000. But if she brings an action for breach of contract, that is, for breach of the contractual warranty as to the age of the car, the aim is to put her into as good a position as if the statement had been true. Her damages will be £5,500 – £4,000 = £1,500.

If the claimant made a bad bargain, so that the market value of a one-year-old car of that type is £4,500, not £5,500, she would be better off suing for tortious misrepresentation. Her damages in contract would be £4,500 – £4,000 = £500 whereas in tort they would be £5,000 – £4,000 = £1,000.

3. Theoretical underpinnings of compensation

(1) Breach of contract

Fuller and Perdue in their seminal article 'The Reliance Interest in Contract Damages'[10] labelled the principle of putting the claimant into as good a position as if the contract had been performed as that of protecting the claimant's expectation interest. They regarded this, on the face of things, as an odd kind of compensation since it often puts the claimant into a better position than if no contract had been made. Hence the central question raised by Fuller and Perdue was, why should contractual damages usually protect the claimant's expectation interest? Why, for example, should damages not be restricted to ensuring that the claimant is made no worse off than if the contract had not been made—in Fuller and Perdue's terminology why should not damages be restricted to protecting the claimant's reliance interest?

A famous illustration of the distinction between damages protecting the claimant's expectation and reliance interests is provided by the US case of *Hawkins v McGee*.[11] The claimant had burnt his hand and the defendant, who was a surgeon interested in skin grafting, contractually promised the claimant to restore his hand to a perfect condition by an operation. The operation went wrong and, instead of having a perfect hand, the claimant's hand was made worse than it was before the operation. Two possible ways in which the damages for the breach of contract could be assessed were examined. The first was to deduct from the value of the hand before the operation the value of the hand as it was after it—in Fuller and Perdue's terminology this would protect the claimant's reliance interest. The second was to deduct from the value of a perfect hand the value of the hand after the operation—this would protect the claimant's expectation interest. The court held that for breach of contract the claimant was entitled to be put into as good a position as if the contract had been performed; hence the second measure of damages was awarded. In other words the claimant's expectation interest was protected.

---

[10] L Fuller and W Perdue, 'The Reliance Interest in Contract Damages' (1936–37) 46 Yale LJ 52 and 373.
[11] 84 NH 114, 146 A 641 (1929).

Fuller and Perdue ultimately thought that at least for bargain promises—promises supported by consideration—protection of the expectation interest could be justified on two main grounds. First, that the expectation interest is the best measure of the claimant's reliance interest given that the latter is difficult to prove, particularly with regard to the forgoing of opportunities to enter other bargains.[12] But this seems a weak argument[13] since it is often just as difficult to prove what position the claimant would have been in if the contract had been performed as it is to prove what position it would have been in if no contract had been made. Moreover, difficulty of proof does not justify picking what on this reasoning would be an arbitrary measure.

Fuller and Perdue's second justificatory argument is, in contrast, a forceful one. This is, in essence, that protecting the claimant's expectation interest for promises supported by consideration ensures that parties reap the benefit of their bargains and thereby encourages the practice of bargaining. This in turn upholds the working of the market economy under which, through bargains, goods and services find their way to where they are most wanted.[14]

A similar approach is taken by the economics and law theorists, like Posner,[15] who argue that contract law is a system of rules and principles furthering economic efficiency and hence overall social welfare. As expectation damages for bargain promises give the claimant no less and no more than the value it has placed on the defendant's performance, they provide the defendant with an incentive to exchange resources with those who place the highest value on them; the efficient result is thereby promoted. Say, for example, A contracts to sell to B for £100,000 a machine that is worth £110,000 to B (ie that would yield him a profit of £10,000). Before delivery C comes to A and offers him £109,000 for that machine. A would be encouraged to break the contract with B were he not liable to pay B £10,000 expectation damages. Given that damages do protect the expectation rather than the reliance interest, C will not be able to induce a breach of As contract with B unless he offers A more than £110,000 thereby indicating that the machine really is worth more to him than to B. The expectation rule thus ensures that the machine ends up where it is most valuable.

In contrast to the above justification is Fried's theory of 'Contract as Promise'[16] according to which, contract rests on the moral bindingness of a promise.[17] This is essentially a revival of the will theory of contract whereby a contractual obligation as against, for example, a tortious obligation is regarded as resting on the defendant's voluntary acceptance of that obligation; and a promise, as a matter of convention,[18] is a voluntarily undertaken obligation. On this approach the expectation interest is the obvious and natural measure of damages for all promises, even if gratuitous, since it represents the monetary equivalent of the defendant's promised performance. Fried expresses this as follows:

> 'If I make a promise to you, I should do as I promise: and if I fail to keep my promise, it is fair that I should be made to hand over the equivalent of the promised performance. In contract doctrine

---

[12] L Fuller and W Perdue, 'The Reliance Interest in Contract Damages' (1936–37) 46 Yale LJ 52, 60–61.

[13] For a similar persuasive criticism, see D Friedmann, 'The Performance Interest in Contract Damages' (1995) 111 LQR 628, 635–636, 638. See also S Smith, *Contract Theory* (OUP 2004) 78–96, 413–417.

[14] L Fuller and W Perdue, 'The Reliance Interest in Contract Damages' (1936–37) 46 Yale LJ 52, 60–62.

[15] R Posner, *Economic Analysis of Law* (9th edn, Wolters Kluwer 2014) ch 4. See also R Birmingham, 'Breach of Contract, Damages, Measures and Economic Efficiency' (1970) 24 Rutgers LR 273; H Beale, *Remedies for Breach of Contract* (Sweet & Maxwell 1980) 159–164.

[16] C Fried, *Contract as Promise* (2nd edn, OUP 2015); see A Burrows, 'The Will Theory of Contract Revived – Fried's "Contract as Promise"' [1985] CLP 141.

[17] S Smith, *Contract Theory* (OUP 2004) chs 3–4, esp 74–78, also supports a promissory rights-based justification of contract but for different reasons than Fried.

[18] C Fried, *Contract as Promise* (2nd edn, OUP 2015) ch 2.

this proposition appears as the expectation measure ... [it] gives the victim of a breach no more or less than he would have had had there been no breach ...'[19]

On this view, based as it is on moral 'rights' or 'principle', 'policy' and 'consequentialist' arguments put forward in Fuller and Perdue's market economy and Posner's economic efficiency explanations provide merely additional reasons for protecting the claimant's expectation interest, where the promise is a bargain promise.

In a superb article,[20] Friedmann has argued that, while synonymous, 'performance interest' is more appropriate terminology than 'expectation interest'; that the explanation for the law's protection of the performance interest is that it is the natural and obvious concomitant of there being a valid contract which confers a legal right to the promised performance; and that Fuller and Perdue's promotion of the 'reliance interest' (at the expense of the 'expectation interest') was misconceived and has had relatively little impact on the substantive law.

However, it should be stressed that all the above approaches, purporting to justify the protection of the expectation interest, run counter to many of the writings of one of the most influential English legal academics of the late twentieth century, Professor Patrick Atiyah.[21] A major thrust of Atiyah's work was that while protecting the expectation interest may have been justified in the nineteenth century, when people strongly believed in the moral bindingness of promises, and in upholding the free-market economy, it was far more difficult to justify in the late twentieth century. He therefore argued that protection of the reliance interest should be the normal rule and, while he did backtrack to some extent,[22] his predominant view was that traditional contract law protecting the expectation interest and built up on, what he regarded, as nineteenth-century laissez-faire values was dead or at least in its final death throes.

But his attack grossly overstated the position; for while the law does and should enable a promisor to escape from a contract more easily than in the past—reflecting a greater concern in today's age for the weak—there is still a large area where the expectation interest is and should be protected for breach of a binding promise. Indeed the development of promissory estoppel and the reform of privity potentially open the way for more promises to be legally enforced. Moreover, while in the US Second Restatement of Contracts, restriction to the reliance interest is suggested as a possibility under promissory estoppel or where there is a disproportion between the consideration and the defendant's liability,[23] there is no indication in England of the courts preferring to measure contractual damages by the reliance rather than the expectation interest.[24] Contract law, and its central protection of the promisee's expectation interest, remains fully alive and is in no sense dying. As Friedmann has written:

'[T]he main thrust of modern law has been in the very opposite direction ... [T]here are no signs of weakening of the performance interest. On the contrary, one of the major trends in

---

[19] ibid, at 17.
[20] D Friedmann, 'The Performance Interest in Contract Damages' (1995) 111 LQR 628.
[21] P Atiyah, *The Rise and Fall of the Freedom of Contract* (Clarendon Press 1979); P Atiyah, *Promises, Morals and Law* (Clarendon Press 1981); P Atiyah, *Essays on Contract* (Clarendon Press 1986) essays 2 and 7. Similar views are put forward by G Gilmore, *The Death of Contract* (Ohio State UP 1974). See also H Collins, *The Law of Contract* (4th edn, LexisNexis 2003) 405–422.
[22] P Atiyah, *An Introduction to the Law of Contract* (5th edn, Clarendon Press 1995) 27–34, 444–464. Cf S Smith, *Atiyah's Introduction to the Law of Contract* (6th edn, Clarendon Press 2005) 16–20, 399–408.
[23] Ss 87, 90, and 351(3). See also ss 158(2), 272(2) dealing with recovery of reliance loss where a contract is unenforceable. See, generally, W Young, 'Half Measures' (1981) 81 Col LR 19. On s 90, see W Slawson, 'The Role of Reliance in Contract Damages' (1990) 76 Cornell LR 197.
[24] This is so even for non-bargain promises; A Burrows, 'Contract, Tort and Restitution – a Satisfactory Division or Not?' (1983) 99 LQR 217, 241.

modern contract law is the strengthening of the protection accorded to the performance interest. Traditional limitations upon the availability of specific performance and upon the recovery of performance damages have either been removed or severely curtailed.'[25]

One final point, which concerns Fuller and Perdue's interest analysis, is that it does not seem particularly helpful and indeed may be confusing to subdivide the expectation interest into damages protecting the (subsidiary) reliance and expectation interests, although this is an approach often adopted by commentators. All possible confusion is best avoided by using the expectation and reliance interests to refer only to the overall interest that the damages are seeking to protect. If so confined, *there is no question of combining the different interests since they are mutually inconsistent.*[26]

(2) Torts

In the tort realm (with the exception of misrepresentation)[27] the theoretical underpinnings of compensation have not been discussed in relation to any controversy over what the compensatory aim should be. On the contrary it is accepted without dispute that the compensatory aim is and should be to put the claimant into as good a position as if no tort had been committed. Nevertheless the justification for tort compensation is hotly debated,[28] with attention being particularly concentrated on the most fundamental question of all—should tort compensation (at least in the realm of accidents) be abolished altogether?

Most of the theoretical discussion has had in mind the usual type of tortious obligation, which is the imposed *negative* obligation; that is, the obligation not to make the claimant worse off. However, not all tortious obligations are negative, and arguably there is a growing trend to impose positive tortious obligations, that is, obligations to benefit the claimant. This will be discussed later. For the present, sole concentration will be on the justification for imposing on a defendant negative obligations and corresponding compensatory damages.

One explanation is again offered by economics and law theorists, like Posner,[29] who argue that tort compensation promotes economic efficiency. By making a defendant responsible for costs he has caused, it encourages him to take precautions to prevent those

---

[25] D Friedmann, 'The Performance Interest in Contract Damages' (1995) 111 LQR 628, 648. For the trend in favour of specific performance, see below, ch 22. As regards a strengthening of 'performance' damages, Friedmann points to changes in relation to the date for assessment, the removal of the bar on damages consequent on impecuniosity, and the availability of damages for non-pecuniary loss.

[26] A Burrows, 'Contract, Tort and Restitution—a Satisfactory Division or Not?' (1983) 99 LQR 217, 223–224. See above, pp 13–15.

[27] Below, pp 223–226.

[28] In addition to the literature cited below in the text, see T Ison, *The Forensic Lottery* (Staples 1967); G Williams and B Hepple, *Foundations of the Law of Tort* (2nd edn, Butterworths 1984) ch 7; P Cane, 'Justice and Justifications for Tort Liability' (1982) 2 OJLS 30; L Klar, 'New Zealand's Accident Compensation Scheme: a Tort Lawyer's Perspective' (1983) 33 UTLJ 80; A Hutchinson and D Morgan, 'The Canengusian Connection: The Kaleidoscope of Tort Theory' (1984) 22 Osgoode Hall LJ 69; A Ogus, 'Do We Have a General Theory of Compensation?' (1984) 37 CLP 29; I Englard, *The Philosophy of Tort Law* (Dartmouth 1993) chs 1–6; J Stapleton, 'Tort, Insurance and Ideology' (1995) 58 MLR 820; J O'Connell and B Kelly, *The Blame Game* (Lexington Books 1987); P Atiyah, *The Damages Lottery* (Hart Publishing 1997); P Bell and J O'Connell, *Accidental Justice* (Yale UP 1997); P Cane, *The Anatomy of Tort Law* (Hart Publishing 1997); B Hepple, 'Negligence: The Search for Coherence' (1997) 50 CLP 69; G Schwartz, 'Mixed Theories of Tort Law' (1997) 75 Texas LR 1801; A Burrows, *Understanding the Law of Obligations* (Hart Publishing 1998) ch 6; D Harris, D Campbell, and R Halson, *Remedies in Contract and Tort* (2nd edn, Butterworths 2002) chs 18 and 24; J Morgan, 'Tort, Insurance and Incoherence' (2004) 67 MLR 384; Lord Sumption, 'Abolishing Personal Injuries Law—A Project', Personal Injuries Bar Association Annual Lecture 2017 (accessible on Supreme Court website).

[29] R Posner, *Economic Analysis of Law* (9th edn, Wolters Kluwer 2014) ch 6.

costs unless the costs of the precautions outweigh the costs caused to the claimant. The general tort standard of negligence precisely fixes liability on those who act inefficiently by not taking cost-justified precautions. The approach to negligence taken in *United States v Carroll Towing Co*[30] is particularly focused on as showing such economic reasoning. Judge Learned Hand there said, 'If the probability be called P: the injury L: and the burden B: liability depends upon whether B is less than L multiplied by P: ie whether B < PL.'[31] For Posner, then, the liability to pay compensation for negligence promotes economic efficiency by deterring uneconomical accidents.

A different and more elaborate economic efficiency justification has been advocated by Calabresi in his 'market deterrence' theory.[32] According to this, the costs of accidents will be reduced, and indeed, will reach the optimum level in terms of efficiency, where the cheapest cost avoider, who is a cause of an accident, is made strictly liable to compensate the injured party. It is essential to this theory that, while the defendant's ability to spread the loss is an important factor in deciding liability, the aim is not loss-spreading per se, but rather the reaching of the most efficient level of accidents by making the defendant bear the costs of the accident. So while for Calabresi 'non-fault enterprise liability' should replace the present legal emphasis on fault, the tort system of individual responsibility for accident compensation is preferable to a state compensation scheme. As Blum and Kalven put it, according to Calabresi: 'Social security "externalises" from the activities that produce accidents the costs of those accidents—bringing in its wake a loss of "general deterrence".'[33]

In contrast to such economic justifications for tort compensation is an explanation in terms of individualistic morality. It can be argued that it is a basic principle of corrective justice that, while one should generally be free to carry out one's own activities, one should generally not be free to interfere with or harm others by those activities; hence if one does cause harm, there is a good reason why one should compensate the injured party. This does not demand that the person causing the harm must actually pay the compensation but rather that that person must ensure that compensation is paid. Most obviously, there is no objection to a liability being met by liability insurance.[34] On this view, the traditional insistence on fault is arguably unnecessary and may merely add further moral weight to an already sufficient case for compensation: it is perhaps best explained (like consideration in contract) as being concerned to confine legal intervention in individuals' lives to the strongest cases.[35]

A leading modern theorist advocating a strict liability corrective justice approach to tort compensation has been Epstein.[36] He has stated his aim as being, '... to show how ... tort

---

[30] 159 F 2d 169 (1947).   [31] ibid, at 173.

[32] Eg G Calabresi, *The Costs of Accidents* (Yale UP 1970); see P Cane and J Goudkamp, *Atiyah's Accidents Compensation and the Law* (9th edn, CUP 2018) 389–433.

[33] W Blum and H Kalven, 'The Empty Cabinet of Dr Calabresi: Auto Accidents and General Deterrence' (1967) 34 U of Chi LR 239, 243.

[34] A Burrows, *Understanding the Law of Obligations* (Hart Publishing 1998) 122–123.

[35] For a corrective justice theory requiring fault, see E Weinrib, 'The Special Morality of Tort Law' (1989) 34 McGill LJ 403; E Weinrib, *The Idea of Private Law* (Harvard UP 1995) chs 6–7; E Weinrib, *Corrective Justice* (OUP 2012). We have examined Weinrib's general corrective justice approach, as underpinning private law, in chapter 1. See also J Coleman, *Risks and Wrongs* (CUP 1992) ch 18 (albeit that he argues that true strict liability can sometimes be a matter of corrective justice).

[36] R Epstein, *A Theory of Strict Liability* (Cato Institute 1980). Cf R Epstein, 'Causation in Context: An Afterword' (1987) 63 Chicago Kent Law Review 653. See also G Fletcher, 'Fairness and Utility in Tort Theory' (1972) 85 Harv LR 537. For a different moral explanation of strict liability, which rests on the fairness of bearing responsibility for the results of bad luck, see T Honoré, 'Responsibility and Luck' (1988) 104 LQR 530. For criticisms of Epstein's theory, and strict liability in general, see S Stoljar, 'Concerning Strict Liability' in *Essays on Torts* (ed P Finn, Law Book Co 1989) ch 11; and E Weinrib, 'The Special Morality of Tort Law' (1989) 34 McGill LJ 403, 411–412; E Weinrib, *The Idea of Private Law* (Harvard UP 1995) 171–177.

law can be viewed usefully as a system of corrective justice appropriate for the redress of private harms'.[37] His central proposition has been that he who causes harm by affirmative action should be strictly liable to compensate the victim, subject to certain limited defences. On this view causation is crucial and, while not developing any general theory of causation, Epstein has offered four examples of sufficient causal connections; A hit B; A frightened B; A made B hit C; A created a dangerous condition that resulted in B's harm. Epstein's approach is both simple and clear, but its prime importance, as far as we are here concerned, is that it emphasises that tort compensation can be justified on the basic moral principle of corrective justice albeit that, contrary to the present law, strict liability rather than negligence is regarded as the central standard of liability.

Strict liability for accidents has also been widely advocated by those who view loss distribution as a justification in itself for tort compensation.[38] Stemming directly from dissatisfaction with the fault system, this approach calls upon the courts to take into account insurance and other methods of spreading losses such as a manufacturer charging higher prices for its goods. Strict liability should then fall on whichever of the parties was most capable of spreading the loss or, as it can alternatively be expressed, on the party who was better able to guard against the risk of damage. The underlying rationale is that, while it is fair that individuals who have suffered loss from the activities of others should be compensated, it is also fair that the burden of compensation should not fall on one pair of shoulders but should be distributed. Fleming explained this as follows:

> '[I]f a certain type of loss is looked upon as the more or less inevitable by-product of a desirable but dangerous activity, it may well be just to distribute its costs among all who benefit from that activity, although it would be unfair to impose it upon each or any one of those individuals …'[39]

Although the courts have traditionally purported to ignore insurance considerations, advocates of this theory regard some areas of traditional tort law, most notably vicarious liability, as best justified by loss distribution.

The major problem with this approach, as a justification for tort compensation, is that to apply it fully would undermine tort compensation altogether; for if loss distribution is the sole objective, a state compensation scheme where the loss can be widely distributed among, for example, all taxpayers would be the best way forward. In other words, the 'fairness' underlying loss distribution is that of distributive justice but, followed to its true conclusion, distributive justice requires compensation by the state, and to leave it to tort compensation is to adopt an unsatisfactory half-way house.

This leads finally to those who consider that a state compensation scheme on the lines, for example, of the industrial injuries scheme, should replace tort compensation for accidents at least where causing personal injury or death.[40] In contrast to all the above theories, this approach considers that distributive justice dictates state compensation, and that there is here no justification for the tort system based as it is on individual responsibility. Support for this is particularly sought in the vagaries and expense of the present fault system. But

---

[37] R Epstein, *A Theory of Strict Liability* (Cato Institute 1980) 71.
[38] Eg JA Jolowicz, 'Liability for Accidents' [1968] CLJ 50.
[39] 'Introduction' in *Fleming's The Law of Torts* (eds C Sappideen and P Vines, 10th edn, Law Book Co 2011) 11.
[40] This was most famously the view of Patrick Atiyah expressed in his *Accidents, Compensation and the Law* (3rd edn, Weidenfeld and Nicolson 1980) ch 25. He subsequently dramatically changed his views so that, while still favouring the abolition of tort, he did not favour its replacement by a social welfare system but rather favoured leaving individuals to choose whether to take out personal accident insurance protection: P Atiyah, *The Damages Lottery* (Hart Publishing 1997) ch 8. Atiyah's original (rather than his later) views find more favour with Cane and Goudkamp: see P Cane and J Goudkamp, *Atiyah's Accidents Compensation and the Law* (9th edn, CUP 2018) ch 18.

arguably the tort system would be harder to attack if strict liability were to replace negligence as the general standard of liability for accidents. Moreover, it should be realised that a state compensation scheme would have no deterrent effect at all on harmful actions or activities (though if this were considered a defect it could perhaps be overcome by, for example, extending the criminal law); nor would a state scheme fulfil the 'ombudsman' role of tort in helping to establish the true facts of a particular accident, which may be of benefit both to the public at large and to the immediate victims and their families.

All in all, within the realm of accidents (and few would ever seek to deny the need for tort compensation outside that realm, for example, in the area covered by intentional torts) it is submitted that the basic moral corrective justice principle of compensating those whom one has wrongfully harmed, has traditionally justified, and provides a convincing reason for continuing to impose on a defendant, negative tort obligations and corresponding compensation. This is to justify tort as a system of individual responsibility.[41] However, there is room for debate as to whether fixing the general standard of liability at negligence is an unsatisfactory cut-off point short of strict liability.

So far our discussion has been confined solely to negative tort obligations. But some tortious obligations, particularly those imposed by the torts of negligence or breach of statutory duty, are positive; that is, the obligation is to put the claimant into a better position than he would have been in if the defendant had done nothing. For example, there is often a tortious obligation to use reasonable care to ensure that a person within your control,[42] or property belonging to you,[43] does not cause personal injury or property damage to others. Again, there is often a tortious obligation to use reasonable care to ensure that a person within your control does not himself suffer personal injury or property damage;[44] and there is sometimes an obligation to use reasonable care to perform properly services that are beneficial to a claimant with whom one is in a relationship of close proximity.[45]

What then is the justification for positive tortious obligations, and hence for the compensatory damages for breach of them? There has been relatively little consideration of this. What there has been has tended to concentrate on the classic hypothetical example of whether there should be a duty of care to rescue a drowning child. Posner[46] considers that there should be such a duty, wherever the costs of the intervention are less than the costs of the injury, ie wherever it is economically efficient to confer the benefit. Epstein, confining himself to corrective justice, considers that there should be no such duty.[47] But perhaps the courts' approach is best regarded as applying, albeit to a very limited extent, the moral notion that one should 'look after one's neighbour'. In most of the situations where a positive duty of care has been imposed, the defendant has been in a particularly good position to prevent personal injury or property damage being suffered by the claimant, and it is not merely efficient, but also accords with the idea of looking after one's neighbour, that the defendant should use reasonable care to prevent such harm. Applying this, a defendant in a particularly good position to rescue a drowning child should be under a legal duty of care to do so.

---

[41] A Burrows, *Understanding the Law of Obligations* (Hart Publishing 1998) ch 6.
[42] Eg *Carmarthenshire County Council v Lewis* [1955] AC 549; *Home Office v Dorset Yacht Co Ltd* [1970] AC 1004. Cf *Smith v Littlewoods Organisation Ltd* [1987] AC 241.
[43] Eg *Goldman v Hargrave* [1967] 1 AC 645; *Leakey v National Trust* [1980] QB 485; Occupiers' Liability Act 1957.
[44] Eg *Kasapis v Laimos Bros* [1959] 2 Lloyd's Rep 378; *McCallion v Dodd* [1966] NZLR 710.
[45] Eg *Midland Bank Trust Co Ltd v Hett Stubbs and Kemp* [1979] Ch 384; *White v Jones* [1995] 2 AC 207.
[46] R Posner, *Economic Analysis of Law* (9th edn, Wolters Kluwer 2014) 221–223.
[47] R Epstein, *A Theory of Strict Liability* (Cato Institute 1980) ch 4.

Where pure economic loss is in issue the justification for imposing positive obligations seems less obvious. One possible explanation of the cases is that the courts are recognising that a negligent breach of promise is a tort, and that the promisee's expectations are being fulfilled as in an action for breach of contract. If so, it may be thought preferable to recognise the action as one for breach of contract and not for tort.[48]

4. Damages valuing the right infringed?

In *Torts and Rights*,[49] Professor Robert Stevens has argued that the basic award of damages in all cases of tort and breach of contract is non-compensatory. Rather, the basic award of damages is to provide a substitute for, and hence to vindicate, the right that has been infringed. They are what Stevens labels 'substitutive damages'.[50] They are concerned to value the right infringed and will be assessed by the market value of the right (if necessary by constructing a reasonable hypothetical bargain between the parties). It is irrelevant to these damages whether a claimant has suffered any loss although, where it has, consequential compensatory damages can be added (as sometimes, where gains have been made by the defendant, can consequential restitutionary damages).

Therefore, applying Stevens' approach, every infringement of a right triggers an award of damages for the value of that right and compensatory damages are merely additional consequential damages in so far as losses have been suffered. So, for example, a personal injury award in the tort of negligence is seen as awarding damages for the value of the infringed right to bodily integrity plus consequential compensatory damages for any financial or non-financial losses, such as pain and suffering. Damages for false imprisonment are awarded for the value of the infringed right to freedom plus consequential compensatory damages for any financial or non-financial loss caused. Damages for breach of contract are awarded for the value of the contractual right infringed plus consequential compensatory damages for any financial or non-financial losses caused.

Stevens' thesis cannot, and does not, stop short of seeking to alter the whole of our conventional understanding of damages which has seen compensation as lying at the heart of damages. By any standards, therefore, his substitutive damages thesis constitutes a radical, novel, and fascinating re-interpretation of the law. With respect, it does not stand up to close scrutiny whether as a matter of principle or authority. There are at least six objections to it:

(i) The Stevens thesis appears to contradict the law on the duty to mitigate, mitigation, and compensating advantages. Take the leading case on mitigation in contract, *British Westinghouse Electric and Manufacturing Co Ltd v Underground Electric Railways Co of London Ltd*.[51] The defendant had delivered defective turbines which the claimant had replaced by turbines that turned out to be more efficient and profitable than the old turbines would have been even if non-defective. The principle laid down by the House of Lords was that, in assessing the purchaser's damages, one should take into account, to reduce damages, the greater efficiency of the replacement turbines. In other words, one is concerned to compensate the overall loss, having deducted all mitigating gains, and it would follow that if

---

[48] Above, p 9; A Burrows, *Understanding the Law of Obligations* (Hart Publishing 1998) 24–40.
[49] R Stevens, *Torts and Rights* (OUP 2007) ch 4.
[50] Other commentators have preferred to use the label 'vindicatory damages'. See, eg, D Pearce and R Halson, 'Damages for Breach of Contract: Compensation, Restitution and Vindication' (2008) 28 OJLS 73. But that label has primarily been used for damages awarded for infringement of a constitutional right: see below, ch 20.
[51] [1912] AC 673. See below, ch 8.

all the losses (including those in purchasing the replacements) were outweighed by the mitigating gains, no substantial damages at all would be awarded. Yet on Stevens' approach, substantial damages should still be awarded in that situation for the infringement of the right to delivery of non-defective turbines (presumably measured by the difference in market price between the turbines delivered and those that should have been delivered). Similarly, in *Uzinterimpex JSC v Standard Bank Plc*[52] it was accepted by the Court of Appeal that the duty to mitigate applies to the tort of conversion in the same way that it applies to other legal wrongs. So if the owner unreasonably turns down an offer by the tortfeasor for the goods to be returned, or for deteriorating goods to be sold off and the sale proceeds paid into a joint account pending resolution of the dispute, no damages may be recovered in the tort of conversion for subsequently being deprived of the goods or for the deterioration in the value of the goods. Yet according to Stevens' thesis, damages should be awarded for conversion assessed according to the market value of the goods converted and irrespective of a failure in the duty to mitigate.

(ii) The approach contradicts the standard approach to causation of loss. To use the example put forward by James Edelman,[53] say D1 negligently crashes into the claimant's car denting a panel which will therefore need replacing. The claimant is entitled to damages for the cost of that replacement. Say before that work has been carried out, D2 negligently crashes into the claimant's car and puts a second dent into the same panel. Applying the traditional law, D2 will not be liable to pay substantial damages because it has caused the claimant no loss.[54] The panel needed repairing anyway. But on Stevens' thesis, there ought to be a substantial award of damages against D2 because D2 has infringed the claimant's right not to be crashed into just as much as D1. The same basic damages ought therefore to be awarded against both.

(iii) Closely linked to the last two points is that the courts take account of events subsequent to the breach of contract or tort as this may increase or reduce the claimant's loss.[55] A rigid 'date of breach' or 'date of tort' rule for the date of assessment for damages has been replaced by a more flexible approach that seeks to ensure true compensation while not undermining the duty to mitigate. As Oliver J said in *Radford v De Froberville*, 'the proper approach is to assess the damages at the date of the hearing unless it can be said that the plaintiff ought reasonably to have mitigated by seeking an alternative performance at an earlier date.'[56] Yet for Stevens it would appear that there is never a good reason for assessing the value of the right infringed other than at the date of the infringement.

(iv) Applying the logic of Stevens' approach, it is not clear that one can avoid an unacceptable overlap between the damages for the value of the right infringed and the consequential compensatory damages. If my car is damaged beyond repair by your negligence, but the next day I spend £10,000 to replace it with a new car, one surely would not wish to award the market value of the right infringed—which is presumably the market value of the destroyed car—plus the £10,000 replacement cost. Yet, if these are two different types of damages, then they ought to be cumulative rather than alternative and there can be no

---

[52] [2008] EWCA Civ 819, [2008] 2 Lloyd's Rep 456. See below, pp 128–129.
[53] J Edelman, 'The Meaning of Loss and Enrichment' in *Philosophical Foundations of the Law of Unjust Enrichment* (eds R Chambers, C Mitchell, and J Penner, OUP 2009) 211, 220.
[54] *Performance Cars Ltd v Abraham* [1962] 1 QB 33.
[55] Two leading decisions of the House of Lords on the date of assessment in contract are *Johnson v Agnew* [1980] AC 367 and *Golden Strait Corp v Nippon Yusen Kabishika Kaisha (The Golden Victory)* [2007] UKHL 12, [2007] 2 AC 353. See below, ch 9.
[56] *Radford v De Froberville* [1977] 1 WLR 1262 (Ch) 1286.

justification for requiring an election between them. The logic of Stevens' approach would allow both to be recovered.

(v) It is not clear that there is any role for 'nominal damages'[57] in Stevens' scheme. Every infringement of a right would seem to require a substantial sum of damages assessed according to the market value of the right infringed. The idea of a nominal sum for wrongs actionable per se, not reflecting any loss suffered, would appear to be redundant. This may be no bad thing because there is a strong argument that nominal damages are unnecessary given that one can always seek a declaration that one's rights have been infringed. However, under the present law, for better or worse, nominal damages do exist and Stevens' thesis cannot account for them.

(vi) Underpinning several of the above difficulties is that Stevens' approach falls down in imagining that, across the board, we would want to put a value on the right that has been infringed rather than the consequential impact of that infringement. As Edelman points out,[58] if one were truly concerned to value the right, the nature of the infringement and its consequences should be irrelevant. So, for example, the value of the right to the integrity of one's car is the same whether the right is infringed by a tiny dent or a colossal crash.[59] But it cannot be correct for the basic award of damages to be the same in both situations and that is because one is not concerned with the value of a right infringed but rather with the consequences of the infringement for the victim; and that is what the traditional compensatory approach focuses on.

Having said all that, it is true that there is a type of damages, now referred to as 'negotiating damages', which may be thought to come close to valuing the right infringed. We shall examine negotiating damages in detail in chapter 18. Suffice it to say here that in the leading decision in *Morris-Garner v One Step (Support) Ltd*[60] the Supreme Court has taken an approach to negotiating damages that contradicts Stevens' thesis in two central respects. First, negotiating damages are not being seen as a standard award but are rather regarded as available in only a limited range of cases. Secondly, and most importantly, negotiating damages have been rationalized by the Supreme Court as compensating for a loss of the claimant. While one may reasonably disagree with the Supreme Court on this, it is submitted that the best alternative explanation is one that focuses on the gains made by the wrongdoer (ie a restitutionary analysis) rather than Stevens' radical thesis.

5. A non-compensatory cost of cure?

David Winterton in his book, *Money Awards in Contract Law*,[61] accepts many of Stevens' insights, in the context of contract law, but with important modifications. So, like Stevens, he argues that one must distinguish between two separate measures of contractual

---

[57] See below, ch 25.
[58] J Edelman, 'The Meaning of Loss and Enrichment' in *Philosophical Foundations of the Law of Unjust Enrichment* (eds R Chambers, C Mitchell, and J Penner, OUP 2009) 211, 219.
[59] One might be able to divide up certain rights into more important and less important rights. Eg, it may be realistic to divide up a right to bodily integrity so that the right to see or hear is distinguished from the right to the use of a toe. But the point remains that the same right might be infringed in a more or less serious way depending on the consequences for the claimant (eg the right to the use of a toe may be infringed by a cut or by being cut off).
[60] [2018] UKSC 20, [2018] 2 WLR 1353.
[61] D Winterton, *Money Awards in Contract Law* (Hart Publishing 2015). For somewhat similar views to those of Winterton, see B Coote, 'Contract, Damages, *Ruxley* and the Performance Interest' [1997] CLJ 537; C Webb, 'Performance and Compensation: An Analysis of Contract Damages and Contractual Obligation' (2006) 26 OJLS

damages: substitutionary damages and compensatory damages. The former measure is not concerned with loss, in the sense of the claimant's position being factually worse off, whereas the latter is. The former is a monetary substitute for the performance to which the claimant was entitled and is most closely analogous to an order of specific performance (or, at common law, the award of an agreed sum). But, in contrast to Stevens, Winterton argues that the primary example of substitutionary damages is not an award of the market value of the right infringed but the cost of substitute performance (referred to in this book as the 'cost of cure')[62] whether by repair or replacement.[63] This links in to his view that it is more accurate to say that one is valuing the performance not the right to performance. The reasonable minimum cost of cure will be awarded irrespective of whether the claimant intends to effect the cure or whether it has already effected the cure. No restrictions, such as remoteness or the duty to mitigate, apply to cost of cure damages (ie substitutionary damages) in contrast to compensatory damages. The only restrictions on choosing cost of cure damages are that it must be reasonable to make such an award and the claimant must be unconditionally entitled to performance (so the cost of cure cannot be awarded if conditional on the claimant's own performance which has not been carried out). According to Winterton, there is no problem about double recovery because compensatory damages cover only the factual loss that has not been made good by the cost of cure damages.

This is a powerful analysis which subtly avoids some of the objections to Stevens' approach. Although Winterton confines his examination to contract, it is equally applicable to tort cases (in so far as repair or replacement is a possible option). Of course, the cost of cure very often is a true compensatory measure as where the claimant has effected the cure or will do so; but Winterton argues that, just as specific performance and the award of an agreed sum are not concerned with the loss of the claimant, there is room for a non-compensatory cost of cure. According to Winterton, the justification for such an award is analogous to the justification for specific performance. Indeed, as a monetary award does not entail the infringement of individual liberty that ordering the defendant to peform does, one may regard the non-compensatory cost of cure measure as less controversial than an order of specific performance.

Attractive as this thesis may be, it is submitted that it should be rejected for at least two reasons. The first is that the link to specific performance (or the award of an agreed sum) may be said to break down unless the claimant has cured or intends to cure. The courts will not order specific performance where performance cannot be carried out and the assumption of such an order is that it will be complied with. The direct analogy is therefore to the compensatory cost of cure—dependent on the claimant effecting or intending to effect cure—rather than the non-compensatory cost of cure, where the intention to cure is irrelevant.

41; S Smith, 'Substitutionary Damages' in *Justifying Private Law Remedies* (ed C Rickett, Hart Publishing 2008) 93 (although Smith argues, at 103, that the intention to cure is essential which contradicts the non-compensatory analysis to which he otherwise adheres); J Edelman, 'Money Awards of the Cost of Performance' (2010) 4 J Eq 122 (controversially arguing that equitable 'substitutive compensation'—as opposed to equitable 'reparative compensation'—is the equivalent of a common law non-compensatory cost of cure measure: see below, p 515 n 36). See further below, pp 189–190.

[62] See below, ch 9.

[63] Winterton argues that another example of damages substituting for performance are 'reasonable release fee' damages (what are now referred to as 'negotiating damages' and were often in the past referred to as '*Wrotham Park* damages': see below, ch 18) which he argues are available where cost of cure damages are not because there can be no cure.

Secondly, it is not clear how Winterton can account for there being a 'reasonableness' restriction on the cost of cure.[64] On the face of it, it is hard to see why, applying Winterton's approach, one should ever deny a claimant a cost of cure award even if it is very much higher than the difference in value. The idea that it must be reasonable to effect cure makes sense as part of the 'duty to mitigate' but that contradicts Winterton's view that the duty to mitigate is relevant only to compensatory damages.

Andrew Summers, in his Oxford doctorate,[65] soon to be published as a book,[66] may also be regarded as providing support for a non-compensatory cost of cure measure of damages. However, unlike Winterton, he arrives at that position by the very different route of a detailed analysis of the contract and tort case law on mitigation. He sees that measure as being a corollary of the duty to mitigate and as ensuring symmetry in the law on mitigation. Although he does not express it in quite this way, one simple way of understanding his basic idea is as follows. Had the claimant effected the cure, and it was reasonable to do so, the claimant would indisputably have been entitled to the cost of cure as compensatory damages; it would therefore be inconsistent to deny that measure—and the defendant cannot complain if that measure is awarded—just because the claimant has not effected the cure and does not intend to do so. While, in contrast to Winterton's thesis, this neatly explains the reasonableness restriction on the cost of cure as being an aspect of the law on mitigation, the underlying justification for the non-compensatory cost of cure is left somewhat unclear. Summers seeks to offer a causation justification but it is hard to see how one can regard the defendant as having caused the cost of a cure that has not been, and will not be, effected. Another possible justification is that the approach comes close to saying that 'it does not lie in the mouth of a wrongdoer' to deny such a claim. But that appears to come close to a punitive justification. The defendant can perfectly reasonably assert that it makes all the difference whether or not the claimant has effected the cure or intends to do so and the fact that the defendant would have had to pay had the cure been incurred is irrelevant and deals with a different factual situation.

In conclusion, it should be emphasised that English law has certainly not committed itself to accepting a non-compensatory cost of cure. On the contrary, it is strongly arguable that it remains important in English law that the claimant has effected the cure or intends to do so; and, if that remains a requirement, the cost of cure is best viewed as a compensatory rather than a non-compensatory measure. Moreover, it may be that a willingness of the courts to award a cost of cure, irrespective of loss, can be seen as nothing more than a preference for a clear, easily provable, and standard objective measure rather than a measure that is finely tuned to the claimant's own position and loss. In other words, in awarding a cost of cure, the courts may not see themselves as departing from compensation but are instead merely taking a pragmatic approach to the assessment of that compensation. In so far as that is not the case, and one is required to explain a non-compensatory analysis, the approach of Summers has much to commend it.

---

[64] D Winterton, *Money Awards in Contract Law* (Hart Publishing 2015) 199–201. Perhaps the best way of explaining the restriction, within the logic of Winterton's approach, is by drawing the analogy to restrictions on the award of an agreed sum or specific performance. A primary restriction on specific performance is that compensatory damages are inadequate; and similarly in relation to an award of an agreed sum, a claimant cannot keep a contract open to earn the agreed sum where it has no legitimate interest in so doing. Both restrictions may be said to ensure that the claimant cannot choose specific relief where economically wasteful. It may be that, if fully fleshed out, those ideas could help Winterton best explain what is otherwise a problematic 'reasonableness' qualification on his non-compensatory cost of cure.

[65] A Dyson, 'Mitigation in the Law of Damages', Oxford D Phil thesis (2016).

[66] A Summers, *Mitigation in the Law of Damages* (OUP, 2019).

4

Factual causation

1. Introduction	51
2. The 'but for' test	52
3. Additional sufficient events	52
4. Material increase of risk	55

1. Introduction

A requirement that can be regarded as inherent in the compensatory aims is that the defendant's tort or breach of contract has been *a* cause of the claimant's loss. So the words, '... as if the tort or breach of contract had not been committed' correlate to the usual 'but for' or *sine qua non* test of factual causation; that is, the claimant must establish that but for the tort or breach of contract she would not have suffered the loss.

It should be emphasised that for torts actionable only on proof of damage, factual causation is a factor more often concerned with whether a tort has been committed than with damages.[1] But to provide a rounded analysis of the courts' approach, examples of factual causation are included even where they do go to liability rather than damages.

The approach to factual causation does not differ whether the claimant is suing for a tort or breach of contract. Nevertheless nearly all the important cases concern torts. This is because factual causation is usually a disputed issue only in respect of damages for personal injury or property damage, and such damages are generally sought in tort.

There is a huge literature on factual causation.[2] Much of the academic writing is concerned to deal with where the standard 'but for' test fails to produce satisfactory outcomes (as, most obviously, where there is more than one sufficient event).[3] An influential example in academia—although not yet considered by the English courts—is the work of Professor Richard Wright[4] who has developed the NESS test (is the breach a Necessary Element in a Set of conditions Sufficient for the outcome?) to establish factual causation where the 'but for' test is inadequate. The work of Professor Jane Stapleton has also been influential. She has argued that factual causation, concerned as it is with the historical connection between the breach and the damage, should be sharply distinguished from what have traditionally

---

[1] For the tort of deceit, it is sufficient that the misrepresentation was a reason or 'present to his mind' or 'influenced' the claimant, even if the claimant would have done the same (eg, entered into the same contract) had there been no misrepresentation: *Edgington v Fitzmaurice* (1885) 29 Ch D 459 (where the claim was for damages for the tort of deceit). Indeed it may be that, for the tort of deceit, the burden of proof in respect of that less stringent test lies on the defendant: see, eg, *Barton v County Natwest Bank Ltd* (1999) Lloyd's Rep Banking 408. In *Hayward v Zurich Insurance Co Ltd* [2016] UKSC 48, [2017] AC 142, it was held that, to satisfy the required element of causation, in the context of rescission of a contract for fraudulent misrepresentation (and the same would apply to damages for deceit) it was not necessary for the claimant to believe the truth of the representations.

[2] For two helpful books on causation in tort, see S Green, *Causation in Negligence* (Hart Publishing 2015); S Steel, *Proof of Causation in Tort Law* (CUP 2015).

[3] The 'but for' test may also fall short in situations where something contributes to an outcome without being necessary or sufficient (J Stapleton, 'Unnecessary Causes' (2013) 129 LQR 39 gives several helpful hypothetical examples, which include a voting example and an example of adding weights to a railway bridge).

[4] R Wright, 'Causation in Tort Law' (1985) 73 California Law Review 1737.

been called intervening causation and remoteness, which are concerned with the appropriate scope of liability for consequences of the breach of duty.[5] That in itself is a relatively uncontroversial proposition although it should be noted that Stapleton regards issues concerning successive sufficient events (such as the facts of *Baker v Willoughby*)[6] as falling within the latter and not the former. Linked to this is that, very controversially, she thinks that factual causation as a matter of liability should be distinguished from the 'no better off' principle in damages.[7] This seems misconceived once one looks across all torts (and breach of contract). Essentially the same causal issues are in play whether they go to liability or to damages and it does not help to treat the causal enquiries as different.[8]

2. The 'but for' test

The best-known case showing a straightforward application of the 'but for' test is *Barnett v Chelsea and Kensington Hospital Management Committee*.[9] A night-watchman, the claimant's husband, called early in the morning at the defendant's hospital complaining of vomiting after drinking tea. The nurse on duty consulted a doctor by telephone and he said that the night-watchman should go home and consult his own doctor in the morning. Five hours later he was dead as a result of arsenic poisoning. In failing to examine the deceased the doctor was in breach of his duty of care but the claimant's action failed because she could not establish on a balance of probabilities that the doctor's negligence had been a cause of the death since, even if the deceased had been properly examined and treated, he would almost certainly still have died.

It has sometimes been suggested[10] that the 'material contribution to the damage' test, put forward in *Bonnington Castings v Wardlaw*[11] and applicable to cumulative or dose-related diseases, is an exception to the 'but for' text. But the better view is to the contrary: 'material contribution' means that the disease would not have been suffered at the time it was but for the defendant's breach of duty.[12]

3. Additional sufficient events

Where a tort or breach of contract was sufficient in its own right to bring about the loss and yet there was an additional sufficient event, application of the 'but for' test to each event would produce the result that neither was a cause of the loss. That result offends common sense. In this situation, therefore, the courts have departed from simply applying the 'but

---

[5] J Stapleton, 'Cause-in-Fact and the Scope of Liability for Consequences' (2003) 119 LQR 388.
[6] [1970] AC 467. See below, p 53.   [7] J Stapleton, 'Unnecessary Causes' (2013) 129 LQR 39.
[8] See S Green, *Causation in Negligence* (Hart Publishing 2015) 20–22.
[9] [1969] 1 QB 428. Personal injury cases, discussed in the next chapter, denying damages for loss of a less than 50% chance of avoiding an injury or disease, are also good examples of the application of the 'but for' test provable on the balance of probabilities: see, eg, *Hotson v East Berkshire Health Authority* [1987] AC 750 and *Gregg v Scott* [2005] UKHL 2, [2005] 2 AC 176. For other good examples of the application of the 'but for' test, outside the context of personal injury, see *JEB Fasteners Ltd v Marks Bloom & Co* [1983] 1 All ER 583; *Tate & Lyle Industries Ltd v Greater London Council* [1983] 2 AC 509; *Rigby v Chief Constable of Northamptonshire* [1985] 1 WLR 1242. In *Messenger Newspapers Group Ltd v National Graphical Association* [1984] IRLR 397, expenditure incurred in anticipation of a tort was held recoverable: the 'but for' test shows that this cannot be correct.
[10] See, eg, *Bailey v Ministry of Defence* [2008] EWCA Civ 883, [2009] 1 WLR 1052.
[11] [1956] AC 613.
[12] For a superb article making this point, see S Bailey, 'Causation in Negligence: What Is a Material Contribution?' (2010) 30 Legal Studies 167. For his follow-up article, in the light of *Williams v The Bermuda Hospitals Board* [2016] UKPC 4, [2016] AC 888, see S Bailey, '"Material contribution" after *Williams v The Bermuda Hospitals Board*' (2018) 38 Legal Studies 411.

'for' test and have relied on other reasoning to decide that each event, or one or other, was a cause of the loss. This therefore represents a minor qualification to the compensatory aim being to put the claimant into as good a position as if the tort or breach of contract had not been committed.

Additional sufficient events may be either concurrent or successive. The classic hypothetical illustration of the former is where two independent fires, negligently started by D1 and D2 respectively, converge on a house and demolish it, each being sufficient on its own to demolish it. Applying the 'but for' test neither defendant's breach of duty would be regarded as a cause because each could say that the claimant's home would have been burnt down even if he had not committed his breach of duty.

However, it has been established that the 'but for' test is not applied in situations of concurrent sufficient events and that D1 and D2 and can both be held liable for the loss. For example, in *Crossley & Sons v Lightowler*[13] it was held to be no defence to an action for nuisance against the defendant for wrongfully polluting a river that the river was also being wrongfully polluted by others so that the claimants would not have had water in a fit state for use even if the defendant had not polluted it. One can say that the justification for this is that there is no more reason to pin the loss on one tortfeasor than on the other, and hence both should be liable.

Although there is no direct authority, analogous reasoning from successive sufficient events[14] suggests that where the concurrent event is not a breach of duty but rather a natural event—for example, if one of the fires in the above example started naturally—the 'but for' test will be applied to the breach of duty so that the defendant will not be liable for the loss.

The facts of *Baker v Willoughby*[15] beautifully illustrate the problem of successive sufficient events. As a result of D1's negligence the claimant suffered an injury to his left leg. Later he was the victim of an armed robbery during which he was shot in the left leg by D2. The leg had to be amputated. D1 argued that he was liable only for loss suffered from having an injured leg until the date of the robbery: after that time D1's breach could not be regarded as a factual cause of that loss. But the House of Lords rejected that argument and held that as regards an action against D1 in a situation of successive sufficient causes the 'but for' test should not be applied; D1 should therefore be liable for the loss suffered from having an injured leg without any reduction on the ground of D2's breach. In other words, D1 was held liable to pay full compensation for the difference between a good and an injured leg. On the other hand, the House of Lords did consider that D2 would only have been liable for depriving the claimant of an already damaged leg, which represents an acceptance of the 'but for' test in relation to D2. This aspect is further supported by the earlier case of *Performance Cars Ltd v Abraham*.[16] The claimant's car was involved successively in two collisions brought about by the negligence of D1 and D2 respectively, and each necessitated a respray of the lower part of the bodywork. The car had not had this work done to it in between the two collisions. D2 was held not liable because he had not caused any additional loss in relation to what was an already damaged car.

The *Baker* approach in respect of D1 again shows the rejection of the 'but for' test. Of the three possible solutions left of pinning the relevant loss (that is, the loss for which D1's

---

[13] (1867) 2 Ch App 478.   [14] Below, p 54.
[15] [1970] AC 467. See H McGregor and D Strachan, 'Variations on an Enigma' (1970) 33 MLR 378. *Baker v Willoughby* was distinguished (but, with respect, not altogether convincingly) in *Heil v Rankin (No 2)* [2001] PIQR Q16 in holding that the deduction for the vicissitudes of life, in assessing future loss of earnings in a personal injury case, did include vicissitudes of life that might be caused by a future tort.
[16] [1962] 1 QB 33. See also *Murrell v Healy* [2001] EWCA Civ 486, [2001] 4 All ER 345; *Halsey v Milton Keynes General NHS Trust* [2004] EWCA Civ 576, [2004] 1 WLR 3002.

and D2's acts were sufficient—here the loss suffered from an injured leg after the date of the robbery) either on D1 alone, or on D2 alone, or on both D1 and D2, the Lords in *Baker* were taking the first alternative. This seems correct. It cannot be right for the claimant to be worse off, as regards damages, by being the victim of two torts than if he had suffered just the first of them. And to hold D2 liable for more than the *additional* injury would infringe the normal principle, applied in *Performance Cars Ltd v Abraham*, that whether for better or worse one takes one's victim as one finds him, a principle that attaches greater importance to events that happen first in time.

On the facts, a further possible reason for favouring the first alternative was that D2 was insolvent. But as a matter of principle that should be irrelevant: *Baker* should still have been decided in the same way even if D1 had been insolvent.

But what if one of the successive sufficient events is a natural event rather than a breach of duty? In *Jobling v Associated Dairies Ltd*[17] the defendants' breach of statutory duty had caused the claimant to suffer a back injury which meant that he could thereafter do only light work. Three years later and before trial he was found to be suffering from a spinal disease (myelopathy) unrelated to and arising after the accident but which in itself rendered him wholly unfit to work. The defendants argued that the onset of the myelopathy ended their liability for his loss of earnings resulting from the back injury; applying the 'but for' test to the breach of duty it could not be said that the claimant would not have suffered the loss of earnings but for the defendants' breach of duty. Moreover, they argued that this approach is implicitly accepted in the courts' practice of reducing damages for future pecuniary loss to take account of the 'vicissitudes of life'. The claimant, on the other hand, contended that *Baker v Willoughby* should be analogously applied, so that the defendants remained liable for the loss of future earnings as if no spinal disease had occurred.

The House of Lords found for the defendants. Much of the reasoning in *Baker v Willoughby* was heavily criticised, but it was left open whether that decision may remain valid for successive sufficient breaches of duty.[18] All their Lordships accepted the 'vicissitudes of life' argument and in effect therefore accepted the 'but for' test as applied to the breach of duty, but not to the natural event. But most of them also emphasised that at root the question was one of policy, and that it was only fair that the defendants' liability should here be cut down. Unfortunately there was little clear articulation of why this solution was considered fair. Lord Wilberforce thought it relevant whether or not the claimant would be compensated from other sources. But irrespective of that, it would seem that the fairness of the decision rests on the notion, firmly embedded in the common law, that an individual has no right to compensation for natural injury and disease. In the words of McGregor and Strachan:

> 'It is one thing to protect the victims of multiple torts from falling between two stools: it is quite another to afford protection from non-tortious loss while our legal system continues to adhere to the principle that adequate compensation for injury and disease should be available only to those whose injury or disease has been tortiously inflicted.'[19]

---

[17] [1982] AC 794.

[18] See also *Rahman v Arearose Ltd* [2001] QB 351 where it was said, at 367, per Laws LJ, that there was no inconsistency between *Baker v Willoughby* and *Jobling v Associated Dairies Ltd* because the essential principle is that 'every tortfeasor should compensate the injured claimant in respect of that loss and damage for which he should justly be held responsible'. The complex facts raised an issue that was analogous to the *Baker* case. A psychiatric illness had been caused by D1 but that psychiatric illness had been made very much worse by D2 (who had been solely responsible for the loss of the claimant's eye). It was held that (as regards non-pecuniary loss) D1 was responsible as to one-quarter for C's psychiatric illness and D2 as to three-quarters.

[19] H McGregor and D Strachan, 'Variations on an Enigma' (1970) 33 MLR 378, at 382–383.

Where the successive sufficient events comprise a natural event followed by the defendant's breach of duty, the 'but for' test will be applied to the breach of duty so that the defendant will not be liable. This follows from the notion of taking one's victim as one finds him and is consistent with *Baker* and *Jobling*. It is directly supported by *Kerry v England*[20] where a druggist supplied tartar emetic (a fatal poison), instead of bismuth, to a fatally sick patient for an attack of 'flu. Damages were reduced to nil on the basis that the tartar emetic had not accelerated to any appreciable extent an already imminent death.

In an important examination of the role and limits of the 'but for' test in the context of the tort of conversion, the House of Lords in *Kuwait Airways Corpn v Iraqi Airways Co*[21] clarified that one should not apply the 'but for' test in respect of multiple conversions (actual or hypothetical) of the claimant's property. The claimant was therefore entitled to damages for the defendant's conversion of six aeroplanes even though those aeroplanes would have been seized and converted by the Iraqi government had they not been converted by the defendant. Lord Nicholls, giving the leading speech, explained that, in respect of multiple wrongdoers, 'the but for test is over-exclusionary'.[22] He went on to deal specifically with conversion and to hold that each tortfeasor is liable for damages for the claimant's loss of possession of the goods. He said:[23]

> 'By definition, each person in a series of conversions wrongfully excludes the owner from possession of his goods. This is the basis on which each is liable to the owner. That is the nature of the tort of conversion. The wrongful acts of a previous possessor do not therefore diminish the plaintiff's claim in respect of the wrongful acts of a later possessor. Nor, for a different reason, is it anything to the point that, absent the defendant's conversion, someone else would wrongfully have converted the goods. The likelihood that, had the defendant not wronged the plaintiff, somebody would have done so is no reason for diminishing the defendant's liability and responsibility for the loss he brought upon the plaintiff.'

4. Material increase of risk

The 'but for' test (provable by the claimant on the balance of probabilities) has also been departed from in a few other exceptional cases. These appear to be situations where: (i) the defendant has broken its duty to the claimant; (ii) by so doing the defendant has materially increased the risk of the type of injury or disease that the claimant has in fact suffered; (iii) not least because of the present state of scientific knowledge, the claimant cannot prove—but nor can the defendant disprove—that it was that breach of duty that caused the injury or disease; (iv) there is a very restricted number of causes of the claimant's injury or disease other than the defendant's breach of duty. Where all these factors are present, the courts in seeking to do justice to claimants have been prepared to accept that factual causation is proved even though the claimant cannot satisfy the 'but for' test.

This was explained by Lord Nicholls in *Fairchild v Glenhaven Funeral Services Ltd*.[24] He said:

> 'The law habitually *limits* the extent of the damage for which a defendant is held responsible, even when the damage passes the threshold "but for" test. The converse is also true. On occasions the threshold "but for" test of causal connection may be over-exclusionary. Where justice so requires, the threshold itself may be lowered. In this way the scope of a defendant's liability

---

[20] [1898] AC 742. See also *The Ferdinand Retzlaff* [1972] 2 Lloyd's Rep 120, at 128.
[21] [2002] UKHL 19, [2002] 2 AC 883.   [22] At [73].   [23] At [82].
[24] [2002] UKHL 22, [2003] 1 AC 32, at [40].

may be *extended*. The circumstances where this is appropriate will be exceptional, because of the adverse consequences which the lowering of the threshold will have for a defendant. He will be held responsible for a loss the plaintiff might have suffered even if the defendant had not been involved at all.'

Three main examples of where this approach has been applied may be given. The first is the well-known Canadian case of *Cook v Lewis*.[25] The two defendants had negligently fired in the direction of the claimant, who was hit by one shot. Although the claimant could not prove which of the two defendants had fired the shot that hit the claimant, both defendants were held liable.

The second example is *McGhee v National Coal Board*[26] where the defendants had failed to comply with their duty of care by failing to provide showers for their employees who had been working inside a very dusty and sweaty brick kiln. The claimant employee had contracted dermatitis. He succeeded in his negligence claim against the defendants even though he could not prove on the balance of probabilities that he would not have suffered dermatitis had showers been provided. It was just as likely, for example, that the dermatitis might already have been inevitable before showering rather than being contracted in the period between when a shower would have been taken and showering at home. Nevertheless it was held sufficient that the defendants had materially increased the risk of dermatitis by negligently failing to provide showers. Although there are passages in some of the speeches in the House of Lords that treat the approach taken as an application of the 'but for' balance of probabilities test (which was plainly incorrect) or as reversing the burden of proof of the 'but for' test (which is an unhelpful description given that it was known that the defendants could not discharge that burden), the better view is that the 'material increase of risk' approach is a departure from the normal 'but for' test of factual causation.

The third, and leading example, is *Fairchild v Glenhaven Funeral Services Ltd*[27] itself. Here the claimant was suffering (or, in the claims by estates, had died) from mesothelioma. This was caused by exposure to asbestos dust at work. The complication was that the claimant or the deceased had worked for more than one employer, each of whom, in breach of its duty of care, had failed to take measures to prevent the employees from inhaling asbestos dust. The claimants could not establish, applying the 'but for' balance of probabilities test, which employer had caused the mesothelioma. Nevertheless it was held that, as each of the employers had negligently materially increased the risk of the employees contracting mesothelioma, they should each be regarded as causally responsible for it. Their Lordships openly recognised that they were departing from the normal 'but for' test as a matter of policy in order to ensure justice for claimants. As Lord Bingham said:

'[T]here is a strong policy argument in favour of compensating those who have suffered grave harm, at the expense of their employers who owed them a duty to protect them against that very harm and failed to do so, when the harm can only have been caused by breach of that duty and when science does not permit the victim accurately to attribute, as between several employers, the precise responsibility for the harm he has suffered. I am of the opinion that such injustice as may be involved in imposing liability on a duty-breaking employer in these circumstances is heavily outweighed by the injustice of denying redress to a victim.'[28]

---

[25] [1951] SCR 830.   [26] [1973] 1 WLR 1.
[27] [2002] UKHL 22, [2003] 1 AC 32. For an interesting case-note see J Morgan, 'Lost Causes in the House of Lords: *Fairchild v Glenhaven Funeral Services*' (2003) 66 MLR 277. For the application of the 'but for' test, and the rejection of *Fairchild* outside its narrow facts, see, eg, *Clough v First Choice Holidays and Flights Ltd* [2006] EWCA Civ 15, [2006] PIQR P22 (which concerned an accident in a swimming pool).
[28] [2002] UKHL 22, [2003] 1 AC 32, at [33].

While *Fairchild* made good sense, in policy terms, as a rare exception to the 'but for' test of causation, the rationale for the decision was subsequently removed—and the common law set on a different and difficult path—by the majority of the House of Lords (Lord Rodger dissenting) in *Barker v Corus (UK) Plc*.[29] Here the deceased had died of mesothelioma. He had been negligently exposed to asbestos for a short period when employed by the defendant but also when employed by another employer and when self-employed. Even though this was not a case of two or more negligent defendants, it was held that *Fairchild* should be applied. However, the House of Lords reinterpreted *Fairchild* as a case where the relevant damage was the material increase in risk of contracting the mesothelioma rather than the mesothelioma. The importance of this was that, rather than being liable for full damages for mesothelioma, the defendant was liable only for damages proportionate to the material increase in risk brought about by its negligence. In other words, *Fairchild* was reinterpreted as a 'loss of a chance' case rather than as being a rare exception to factual causation of the damage/disease.

With respect, this was a false move that watered down the helpful impact of *Fairchild* for claimants.[30] It was quickly reversed by statute. In cases of mesothelioma, the Compensation Act 2006, s 3, restores *Fairchild* as it was originally understood before *Barker*.[31] Where s 3 applies, a defendant will be jointly and severally liable for the full damages for mesothelioma although there may be a reduction for contributory negligence (and of course the defendant is entitled to contribution from other defendants who are also liable to the claimant for materially increasing the risk of mesothelioma). It is also clear that s 3 applies to all cases where there is one negligent defendant who has materially increased the risk (and a risk is material if it is more than de minimis) even if other innocent factors have also materially increased that risk.[32] The Act is confined to mesothelioma and does not therefore save the *McGhee* case, the status of which is now in doubt but which, in line with *Barker*, may survive only as a loss of a chance case awarding proportionate damages. We consider in the next chapter exactly how *Barker* fits with other cases on damages for loss of a chance.

---

[29] [2005] UKHL 20, [2006] 2 AC 572.

[30] Writing extra-judicially, Lord Hoffmann, '*Fairchild* and After' in *Judge and Jurist: Essays in Memory of Lord Rodger of Earlsferry* (eds A Burrows, D Johnston, and R Zimmermann, OUP 2013) 63 has argued that *Fairchild* was a mistake and that the courts should have left matters to Parliament. I disagree. The wrong turn was made in *Barker v Corus*. Note also that treating the relevant damage as the material increase in risk of contracting the mesothelioma does not sit easily with the wording of the Fatal Accidents Act 1976 which applies where the person has died from the mesothelioma and requires that the defendant must have caused the death.

[31] In construing an employer's liability insurance policy, covering an employer for a breach of duty *causing* mesothelioma, the Supreme Court in *Durham v BAI (Run Off) Ltd* [2012] UKSC 14, [2012] 1 WLR 867, effectively ignored *Barker* by holding that the policy covers the employer against *Fairchild* liability with the necessary causal requirement being satisfied by the employer having materially increased the risk of mesothelioma. Subsequently, however, in dealing with the liability of insurers, and contribution between them, under Guernsey law (where there has been no equivalent to the Compensation Act 2006 so that the position is the same as under English common law), the Supreme Court in *International Energy Group Ltd v Zurich Insurance plc UK Branch* [2015] UKSC 33, [2016] AC 509, stressed that *Barker* remains good law at common law.

[32] *Sienkiewicz v Greif (UK) Ltd* [2011] UKSC 10, [2011] 2 AC 229.

5
Proof of loss and loss of a chance

1. Introduction	58
2. Uncertainty about past fact: balance of probabilities	58
3. Future or hypothetical events: assessment proportionate to the chances?	60
4. Miscellaneous points	73

1. Introduction

A word is merited about the terminology of damages for loss of a chance. While it may be possible to distinguish conceptually between damages for loss of a chance and damages for the chance of a loss,[1] this chapter draws no such distinction. Rather it uses the terminology of loss of a chance in a wide sense which covers both the lost chance of acquiring a benefit and the lost chance of avoiding a detriment. Increasing the chance of a loss equates to the lost chance of avoiding a detriment and this explains why a case like *Barker v Corus (UK) Plc*[2]—where, as we have seen in the previous chapter, the courts awarded damages proportionately to the 'material increase in risk' of a disease—is equally well viewed as a loss of a chance case. Materially increasing the risk of a disease or injury means that the claimant has lost the chance of avoiding the disease or injury. As Lord Walker said in the *Barker* case, '"increase in risk" [has, as] its mirror image, "loss of a chance".'[3] The important underlying point is that this chapter's reference to damages for loss of a chance is intended to embrace all situations where the courts assess compensatory damages proportionately according to the chances. So through the terminology of loss of a chance the central question addressed in this chapter is this: when is it that the courts award compensatory damages in proportion to the relevant chances rather than applying an all-or-nothing balance of probabilities approach?[4]

2. Uncertainty about past fact: balance of probabilities

The area of controversy about damages for loss of a chance concerns uncertainty as to hypothetical events or the future. It does not concern uncertainty as to past fact. All uncertainty as to what happened in the past is resolved in the civil law by a balance of probabilities all-or-nothing approach.

---

[1] That distinction is drawn in the excellent article by K Cooper, 'Assessing Possibilities in Damages Awards—The Loss of a Chance of the Chance of a Loss?' (1973) 37 Sask L Rev 193. However, as in this chapter, nothing in the analysis in that article turns on that distinction and the central question the article addresses is the underlying one of whether the law should adopt what is termed a 'simple probability' approach to contingencies in assessing damages (ie damages assessed proportionately according to the chances).

[2] [2006] UKHL 20, [2006] 2 AC 572. Above, p 57.   [3] ibid, at [114].

[4] This chapter draws on A Burrows, 'Uncertainty about Uncertainty: Damages for Loss of a Chance' (2008) 1 Journal of Personal Injury Law 31.

Say, for example, in a road traffic accident, there is uncertainty as to the speed at which the defendant was travelling and hence whether the damage to the claimant's car was caused by any negligence of the defendant. Let us further assume, somewhat simplistically, that had the defendant been travelling 40mph or less his driving would not have been negligent; whereas had he been driving at over 40mph, his driving would have been negligent. The court has to decide the question of the speed that the defendant was travelling one way or the other. If the claimant cannot prove on the balance of probabilities that the defendant was travelling at more than 40mph the claim will fail. There can be no question of the court coming to the view that, if there is a 70% chance that the defendant was travelling at more than 40mph, the claimant should be entitled to 70% of the damages; nor is there any question of the court awarding 25% of the damages if the claimant has satisfied it only to a 25% degree of probability that the defendant was so negligent. The matter has to be decided on a balance of probabilities provable by the claimant in an all-or-nothing manner.

The classic exposition of the distinction between past fact on the one hand, and hypothetical or future events on the other, was given by Lord Diplock in the Fatal Accidents Act case of *Mallett v McMonagle*.[5] He said:

> 'In determining what did happen in the past a court decides on the balance of probabilities. Anything that is more probable than not it treats as certain. But in assessing damages which depend upon its view as to what will happen in the future or would have happened in the future if something had not happened in the past, the court must make an estimate as to what are the chances that a particular thing will or would have happened and reflect those chances, whether they are more or less than even, in the amount of damages which it awards.'

Similar observations were made by Lord Nicholls in his dissenting speech in *Gregg v Scott*.[6] He said:

> 'In the normal way proof of the facts constituting actionable damage calls for proof of the claimant's present position and proof of what would have been the claimant's position in the absence of the defendant's wrongful act or omission. As to what constitutes proof, traditionally the common law has drawn a distinction between proof of past facts and proof of future prospects. An event happening in the past either occurred or it did not. Whether an event happened in the past is a matter to be established in civil cases on the balance of probability. If an event probably happened no discount is made for the possibility it did not. Proof of future possibilities is approached differently. Whether an event will happen in the future calls for an assessment of the likelihood of that event happening, because no one knows for certain what will happen in the future.'[7]

Having then explained that an assessment of likelihood is also generally applied to hypothetical events[8] he concluded:

> 'The theory underpinning the all-or-nothing approach to proof of past facts appears to be that the past fact either happened or it did not and the law should proceed on the same footing. But

---

[5] [1970] AC 166, at 176. [6] [2005] UKHL 2, [2005] 2 AC 176. [7] ibid, at [9].

[8] However, it should be noted that Lord Nicholls drew a distinction between hypothetical future events and hypothetical past events in that he thought that, while a chances approach applied to the former, the balance of probabilities all-or-nothing approach normally applied to the latter. But, although this is a very difficult issue, it appears to be misleading to equate the approach to past facts with the approach to hypothetical past events. The cases relied on by Lord Nicholls as showing an all-or-nothing balance of probabilities approach were ones where a chances approach would only be applied to the assessment of damages once the claimant had established, on the balance of probabilities, that there had been an actionable personal injury or death. But once such a personal injury or death had been established, a chances approach would be applied in assessing damages whether one was dealing with uncertainty as to the future, uncertainty as to a hypothetical event in the future or uncertainty as to a hypothetical event in the past (eg, what would the claimant have earned pre-trial had he not been injured).

the underlying certainty, that a past fact happened or it did not, is absent from hypothetical facts. By definition hypothetical events did not happen in the past, nor will they happen in the future. They are based on false assumptions. The defendant's wrong precluded them from ever materializing.'[9]

Therefore, the initial question that must always be asked in this area is whether the relevant uncertainty that is in issue is about a past fact or not. If the uncertainty is about what did happen in the past or what the state of affairs was in the past, a balance of probabilities approach applies. A 'loss of a chance' approach is only on the agenda if the uncertainty in issue is as to the future (that is, what will the claimant's position be after trial) or is as to a hypothetical event (that is, what would have happened to the claimant, in the past or in the future, had there been no breach of duty).

It should be noted that, although English law clearly applies an all-or-nothing balance of probabilities approach to past fact, this is not an approach that is immune from criticism. For example, it can be argued that, where the uncertainty about past facts turns on the state of medical and scientific knowledge, one should treat uncertainty about those past facts in the same way as future events. That is, as in practice, as opposed to theoretically, it is just as impossible to be certain of some past facts as it is to be certain of the future, there is an argument that one should apply the same approach (of assessment according to the chances) to both. In his dissenting judgment in *Commonwealth of Australia v Amann Aviation Pty Ltd*,[10] which concerned reliance damages for breach of contract, Deane J said the following:

> 'It is true that Lord Reid's reasons for rejecting the balance of probability test in the circumstances of *Davies v Taylor* could be applied equally to some categories of case in which a court is concerned with the determination of past facts. That does not mean, however, that the traditional approach for determining past facts should be applied to a case requiring the assessment of damages on the basis of what would have happened or will happen. To the contrary, it lends support for the view that there is a need for modification or reassessment in some categories of case of the conventional approach that, in assessing damages for what has occurred in the past, a court decides on the balance of probabilities and assumes certainty where none in truth exists.'

But there has, as yet, been no sign of the English courts considering it necessary to carve out exceptions to the all-or-nothing approach to past facts. Indeed it may be doubted whether it is possible to recognise exceptions without shattering the conventional approach altogether.

3. Future or hypothetical events: assessment proportionate to the chances?

(1) Introduction

Having established in the last section that it is only where the uncertainty in issue is as to future or hypothetical events that a proportionate damages approach may be appropriate,

---

[9] [2005] UKHL 2, [2005] 2 AC 176, at [14].
[10] (1991) 66 ALJR 123, at 147. See also, eg, J Fleming, 'Probabilistic Causation in Tort Law: A Postscript' (1991) 70 CBR 136, 140–141.

we must now make clear that, even in this area, a proportionate damages approach will not always be applied.[11]

Very importantly—although one might say that this falls outside the scope of this book—a proportionate damages approach will not normally be applied in personal injury and death cases unless and until it has been determined that there is an actionable personal injury or death.[12] In other words, at the liability stage—rather than at the assessment of damages stage—the courts have normally applied an all-or-nothing balance of probabilities approach and the loss of a chance of avoiding an injury or disease has not itself been actionable. For example, in *Barnett v Chelsea and Kensington Hospital Management Committee*[13] where, as we have seen in the last chapter, the claimant's husband died of arsenic poisoning, the question asked was whether on the balance of probabilities the deceased would have lived had the defendant doctor properly examined and treated him.

Similarly, in *Hotson v East Berkshire Health Authority*[14] and *Gregg v Scott*[15] the claimants' attempts to found their actions on the less than 50% chance of recovery both failed.

In the former case, the claimant injured his hip in a fall. The medical staff at the defendant's hospital incorrectly diagnosed his injury and he was sent home. After five days of severe pain he returned to the hospital where the medical staff realised its earlier mistake. The claimant developed a permanent hip disability and brought an action for negligence against the defendant claiming that, if his injury had been properly diagnosed at the start, his permanent disability would have been avoided. Simon Brown J found that, even if the defendant had treated the claimant properly, there was still a 75% chance that his disability would have developed. Nevertheless he awarded the claimant damages (25% of the full damages) for being deprived by the defendant's negligence of the 25% chance of avoiding the disability. The House of Lords overturned that award. Although the central uncertainty was surely as to a hypothetical event (would the claimant's permanent hip disability have been avoided had the defendant complied with its duty) rather than a past fact (what was the state of the claimant's hip prior to the negligence) the House of Lords reasoned that it was the latter. The all-or-nothing balance of probabilities standard of proof was therefore applied. Applying that standard, the claim failed because the claimant had not established that the negligence of the defendant had caused his permanent hip disability. No damages could be awarded for the negligent material increase in risk of not avoiding the permanent hip disability: ie for loss of the 25% chance of avoiding the disability. It is submitted that the best interpretation of the case is that because one was concerned with whether there was an actionable personal injury (ie had the negligence caused the permanent hip disability) the balance of probabilities test was applicable even though one was concerned with a hypothetical event rather than a past fact.

In the latter case, a doctor negligently diagnosed a lump under the claimant's left arm as benign when it was in fact cancerous. This led to a delay of nine months in the claimant receiving proper treatment. It was found that, on the balance of probabilities, the claimant would not have been 'cured' of cancer (with 'cure' meaning surviving for more than ten years) even if there had been no delay. It was also found that the delay had reduced the

---

[11] A loss of the chance approach, as regards the hypothetical decision of a tribunal, has been rejected by the European Court of Human Rights: see the discussion in *R (KB) v Mental Health Review Tribunal* [2003] EWHC 193 (Admin), [2004] QB 936.
[12] It appears that the same applies to establishing actionable property damage. Say the question is whether, had the defendant driven in a particular way, the damage to the claimant's car would have been avoided: it would seem that that question (which concerns uncertainty as to a hypothetical event in the past) is to be resolved applying an all-or-nothing balance of probabilities test.
[13] [1969] 1 QB 428.   [14] [1987] AC 750.   [15] [2005] UKHL 2, [2005] 2 AC 176.

claimant's chances of cure from 42% to 25%. The majority of the House of Lords (Lord Hoffmann, Lord Phillips, and Baroness Hale) refused to award the claimant damages for the reduction in the chances of cure. In other words, even though this was a case where it was accepted that one could not clearly isolate the uncertainty as relating to a past fact as opposed to the hypothetical or future medical condition of the claimant, the House of Lords held that no substantial damages should be awarded for being deprived of a 17% chance of being cured of cancer by the defendant's negligent failure to diagnose that cancer. On the balance of probabilities, the personal injury in question (not being cured of cancer) had not been caused by the breach of duty.

The standard approach, therefore, is that the breach of duty must be shown on the balance of probabilities to have caused the personal injury or death.

Barker v Corus (UK) Ltd,[16] which we have examined in the previous chapter on causation, should be regarded as a limited and problematic exception to that standard approach (and in cases of mesothelioma the effect of the decision has, in any event, been reversed by the Compensation Act 2006, s 3). In that case, the relevant damage in question (in applying and interpreting the 'material increase of risk' exception to causation recognised in *Fairchild v Glenhaven Funeral Services Ltd*)[17] was controversially treated as the material increase of risk of contracting mesothelioma (ie the loss of the chance of avoiding the disease). Even if that was a correct interpretation of *Fairchild*, and even putting to one side that in respect of mesothelioma it has been statutorily reversed, the decision is best regarded as having a relatively limited application because it was stressed that this 'loss of a chance' recovery applied only where, first, there was a single causative agent (asbestos) and, secondly, the outcome was known, that is, the relevant disease had been contracted. The second of those two restrictions explains why the decision has clearly not opened the door to the recovery of damages for loss of a chance simply because a defendant has negligently materially increased the risk of a claimant suffering a particular disease or injury. Take the example of a radiation leak from a power station that has occurred as a result of negligence (or a breach of statutory duty). Plainly *Barker* does not allow a claim just because a person can show that, as a result of that leak, his or her risk of contracting cancer has been materially increased. Rather claims could only be brought by those who have contracted cancer. The outcome must be known.

This is not to deny that *Barker* has left some serious interpretative difficulties as regards cases such as *Hotson* and *Gregg* considered above in this chapter and *McGhee v National Coal Board*[18] considered in the previous chapter. Most of the difficulty turns on what is meant by the 'single causative agent' restriction. In *Barker* the House of Lords was clear that *Barker* and *Fairchild* were single agent cases in that the single causative agent was asbestos. As an example of multiple agents, to which the loss of a chance approach was inapplicable, their Lordships pointed to lung cancer possibly caused by negligent exposure to asbestos and smoking. They were also clear that *Wilsher v Essex Area Health Authority*[19] was a multiple agent case because the blindness of the baby could have been caused by five possible agents, only one of which was the excess oxygen negligently administered by the defendant. Their Lordships indicated that *McGhee* was a single agent case, whereas *Hotson* and *Gregg* were not. The difficulty is that in all three of those cases it can plausibly be argued that there was a single agent and that the defendants had materially increased the risk of that single agent causing the relevant disease or injury. That is, the single agents can be respectively

---

[16] [2006] UKHL 20, [2006] 2 AC 572.   [17] [2002] UKHL 20, [2003] 1 AC 32.
[18] [1973] 1 WLR 1.   [19] [1988] AC 1074.

said to have been: in *McGhee*, the brick dust that led to the dermatitis; in *Hotson*, the cutting off of the blood supply that led to the boy's hip disability; and in *Gregg*, the pre-existing cancerous cells that led to the spread of the cancer.

Perhaps in retrospect *Gregg v Scott* is best re-analysed as a case where the outcome had not eventuated, ie as it happened, the claimant was still alive and had been cured of cancer in the sense that he had survived for more than ten years. But the case was certainly not argued, or reasoned, on that basis. That is, the case proceeded on the assumption that the claimant had suffered the relevant outcome.

It is also worth stressing that, while the express reasoning in *Hotson* was that the uncertainty involved a past fact, that analysis was unconvincing and cannot stand as a valid distinguishing feature. If *Hotson* was a case of uncertainty about a past fact, so was *McGhee* in the sense that one did not know the state of the claimant's skin at the time when he should have been provided with a shower.

It is submitted, therefore, that *Barker v Corus* should be viewed as a problematic and limited departure from the standard approach; and the standard approach is that, even though the uncertainty is in relation to hypothetical or future events, a proportionate damages approach will not be applied in personal injury and death cases unless and until it has been determined that there is an actionable personal injury or death. As we shall see, a proportionate damages approach is also inapplicable, even though the uncertainty is as to a hypothetical event, where the uncertainty is as to the claimant's or the defendant's hypothetical conduct.

On the other hand, there are many examples of where proportionate damages—damages for loss of a chance—have been awarded. They can principally be divided into three main categories of case as set out in the next section.

(2) Examples of damages for loss of a chance

(a) Loss of profits in contract

A first category is damages for loss of profits, or other lost economic benefits, consequent on a breach of contract. The leading case is *Chaplin v Hicks*.[20] The defendant, a theatrical manager, ran a newspaper beauty competition in which he offered theatrical engagements to those 12 contestants whom he should choose after interview from the 50 who secured the greatest number of votes of the newspaper's readers. Six thousand women entered the contest and the claimant succeeded in being voted as one of the 50 to be interviewed. However, because of the defendant's breach of contract, the claimant was not informed of the interview in time and the 12 winners were chosen in her absence from the remaining 49. This was a case where the uncertainty was as to the hypothetical actions of the interviewing panel: that is, would it have chosen the claimant at interview?[21] The Court of Appeal held that, while the claimant could not recover for the loss of a theatrical engagement, since she could not establish to the required degree of proof that she would have been one of the 12, nevertheless she should be given contractual damages for the loss of the chance of being

---

[20] [1911] 2 KB 786.
[21] Although the Court of Appeal treated the interviewing panel as if it were independent of the defendant, careful examination of the facts shows that the competition rules had been changed and that the sole decision-maker was the defendant himself. There is therefore a problem with reconciling this approach with the 'minimum obligation' principle applied to hypothetical conduct of the defendant (although one might say that here the minimum obligation, as a matter of construction, coincided with the most accurate assessment of the chances: see generally below, pp 68–73).

one of the 12 (ie about a 25% chance, although the court did not need to be precise on this because the damages had been fixed by a jury and the court was simply concerned to confirm that substantial, rather than nominal, damages were appropriate). In other words, she was entitled to damages scaled down proportionately in accordance with what the chances of gain were thought to be.

It would be a major mistake to regard *Chaplin v Hicks* as an isolated example. On the contrary, almost all loss of profit awards in contract involve an assessment of damages according to the contingencies. A good more recent example is *Jackson v Royal Bank of Scotland plc*[22] where one question at issue was whether the claimant and the third party customer would have continued to make contracts with each other had there not been the breakdown in the relationship caused by the defendant bank's breach of contract in disclosing certain confidential information to the third party customer. In assessing the appropriate damages for loss of profits it was held that the parties would otherwise have continued to make contracts for a further period of four years but that the amount of damages awarded for the lost benefits of those contracts should be reduced towards the end of the four years to reflect the increased uncertainties that the contracts would have been concluded. Another straightforward example is *Ministry of Defence v Wheeler*[23] where a number of women had been wrongfully dismissed from the army because of their pregnancy. In assessing their damages for wrongful dismissal, the Court of Appeal took into account the chances that they would have left the army in any event.

(b) Pure economic loss in the tort of negligence

A second main category of case where the courts award damages for loss of a chance is for pure economic loss in the tort of negligence.[24] Of course, the situations in which pure economic loss is recoverable in the tort of negligence are limited. Without going into the details, one can summarise the law by saying that those situations are limited to where there is a contractual relationship between the parties or a similar close relationship in which the defendant has assumed responsibility to the claimant. Where there is such a relationship, so that we are in the sphere of recoverable pure economic loss, loss of a chance damages are clearly recoverable.

The most common examples are actions against negligent solicitors where a client's claim has become time-barred. The courts assess damages in tort and contract according to the chances that the claim would have otherwise been successful. For example, in *Kitchen v Royal Air Forces Association*[25] the claimant's husband had been electrocuted and died while preparing tea in the kitchen of his home. In respect to the wife's possible action against the relevant electricity company under the Fatal Accidents Act, her solicitors appeared to take the extraordinary decision of deliberately letting the limitation period run out in the vague hope of obtaining a satisfactory ex gratia payment. Lord Evershed MR was scathing of the solicitors' conduct:

> '[The] solicitors proceeded to adopt the line of least possible effort. It is not merely that they never applied their minds at all to what their duties were and what the possible rights of the plaintiff might be, but they never applied their minds … to the question of who their client was.'[26]

---

[22] [2005] UKHL 3, [2005] 1 WLR 377.   [23] [1998] 1 WLR 637.
[24] For an example of loss of a chance damages being awarded for the tort of deceit, see *4 Eng Ltd v Harper* [2008] EWHC 9, [2009] Ch 91. See below, p 227.
[25] [1958] 1 WLR 563.   [26] ibid, at 568.

However, the important point for us is that the Court of Appeal upheld an award of £2,000 damages on the basis that the claimant was entitled to damages assessed proportionately according to the chances that she would have had of winning a Fatal Accidents Act claim. Another well-known example of loss of a chance damages being held applicable for solicitors' negligence is *Allied Maples Group Ltd v Simmons & Simmons*[27] but as the principal point of that leading case is to distinguish, very importantly, between claimant and third party uncertainty this is dealt with in more detail below.[28] There are many other examples in the law reports of analogous awards for loss of a chance in professional negligence actions, primarily against solicitors in litigation or other work,[29] but also against, for example, surveyors[30] and accountants.[31]

In case it is thought that the only examples are ones involving concurrent liability in tort and contract, it is helpful to refer to *Spring v Guardian Assurance Co*.[32] Here the House of Lords held that a former employer owes a duty of care to its former employee in writing a reference that was an essential requirement for employment with a new employer. Referring to the authority of *Chaplin v Hicks*, Lord Lowry said:

> 'Once the duty of care is held to exist and the defendant's negligence is proved, the plaintiff only has to show that by reason of that negligence he has lost a reasonable chance of employment (which would have to be evaluated) and has thereby suffered loss … He does not have to prove that, but for the negligent reference, [the new employer] *would* have employed him.'[33]

(c) Loss consequent on an actionable personal injury or death

We have seen above that a loss of a chance approach is not applied in deciding whether there is an actionable personal injury or death.[34] In contrast, once there is an actionable personal injury, uncertainties as to what the claimant's future will be and/or what the claimant's position would have been had he or she not been injured are dealt with by the courts quantifying proportionate damages according to the chances. Analogously in Fatal Accident Act 1976 claims, the courts quantify damages proportionately in line with their assessment of what a dependant's future will be and/or what the deceased's and dependant's position would have been but for the death. Such chances are reflected proportionately in the damages awarded: in other words, although not traditionally phrased in this way, the courts are standardly awarding damages for loss of a chance when assessing damages for personal injury or death. So in calculating future pecuniary loss, the multipliers in the Ogden Tables take account of the statistical chances of death prior to normal retirement age

---

[27] [1995] 1 WLR 1602.   [28] See p 67–68.
[29] Eg, *Hall v Meyrick* [1957] 2 QB 455 (rvsd on other grounds); *Sharif v Garrett & Co* [2001] EWCA Civ1269, [2002] 1 WLR 3118; *Normans Bay Ltd v Coudert Brothers* [2003] EWCA Civ 215; *Dudarec v Andrews* [2006] EWCA Civ 256, [2006] 1 WLR 3002; *Whitehead v Searle* [2008] EWCA Civ 285, [2009] 1 WLR 549. A particularly interesting example is *Dixon v Clement Jones* [2004] EWCA Civ 1005, [2005] PNLR 6, in which the CA upheld an award of 30% damages against a solicitor for loss of a claim against accountants albeit that the trial judge found that, on the balance of probabilities, the claimant would not have relied on the accountants' negligent advice so that her claim against them would have failed: it appears that the important point justifying this decision is that the trial judge's view as to the claimant's reliance was not a finding at the trial of the action against the accountants (where that question would have been decided on all the evidence) and was therefore not caught by the all-or-nothing approach taken to a claimant's hypothetical actions (see below, pp 67–68); a proportionate chances approach was therefore appropriate.
[30] *First Interstate Bank of California v Cohen Arnold* [1996] PNLR 17 (negligent misstatement by accountant).
[31] *John D Wood & Co Ltd v Knatchbull* [2002] EWHC 2822 (QB), [2003] 8 EG 131 (in a contract and tort claim for professional negligence against a surveyor, damages of £120,000 were awarded for the loss of a 60% chance of selling property for an extra £200,000).
[32] [1995] 2 AC 296.   [33] ibid, at 327.   [34] Above, pp 61–62.

and the courts make a further adjustment for the contingencies of life (that is, for the fact that the claimant might in any event have been unemployed or sick).[35]

In some cases on the assessment of damages for future loss of earnings consequent on a personal injury, the courts have expressly referred to the award as being for loss of a chance. For example, in *Doyle v Wallace*[36] the 19-year-old claimant suffered brain damage in a road accident. In quantifying her loss of past and future earnings, the main uncertainty was whether she would have otherwise qualified and worked as a drama teacher. The chances of this were assessed at 50/50. Dismissing the defendant's argument that, as she had failed to prove on the balance of probabilities that she would be a teacher, this possibility should be ignored, the Court of Appeal awarded her damages for the 50% chance of becoming a teacher. This was subsequently followed in, for example, *Langford v Hebran*[37] in assessing the loss of earnings that the claimant would have made from professional kick-boxing; and in *Brown v Ministry of Defence*[38] in which, in quantifying damages for loss of pension, the chances of the claimant completing 22 years of service, which would have entitled her to an immediate pension, were assessed at 30%.

It is also trite law that in considering a claimant's future position, one includes the risk of deterioration (or it could be improvement) consequent on the actionable personal injury. Classic examples are damages awarded for the 10% risk that the claimant who has suffered a head injury will develop epilepsy or that the claimant who has suffered a hand injury has a 20% chance of suffering from osteoarthritis.[39]

(3) The scale of proportionate damages

If the case is one in which proportionate damages (damages for loss of a chance) are being awarded, what is the scale of assessment proportionate to the chances? Does the scale run from 1% to 99% or is it less finely tuned than that?

The answer is that the scale runs from reasonable certainty down to more than a mere speculative possibility. So at the top end of the scale full damages can be awarded for a loss that is proved to a standard of reasonable certainty. In *Ratcliffe v Evans*[40] Bowen LJ said:

> 'As much certainty and particularity must be insisted on, both in pleading and proof of damage, as is reasonable, having regard to the circumstances and to the nature of the acts themselves by which the damage is done. To insist upon less would be to relax old and intelligible principles. To insist upon more would be the vainest pedantry.'

This means that full damages may be awarded for a loss even though there is some doubt whether that loss will be incurred or would have been incurred irrespective of the breach of duty. Reasonable certainty is therefore a notch down from absolute certainty.

In the US in the nineteenth century some types of loss, especially contractual loss of profits, had to be proved with certainty. As such, and in contrast to England, certainty played a vigorous role in restricting damages alongside limiting principles, such as remoteness and the duty to mitigate. During the twentieth century this high standard was relaxed so that, in the US too, the standard required is now one of reasonable certainty.[41]

---

[35] See below, p 244.
[36] [1998] PIQR Q146. See also *Mulvaine v Joseph* (1968) 112 Sol Jo 927 (lost prize money consequent on personal injury).
[37] [2001] EWCA Civ 361, [2001] PIQR Q13.
[38] [2006] EWCA Civ 546, [2006] PIQR Q9.
[39] *Jones v Griffiths* [1969] 1 WLR 795, at 801.
[40] [1892] 2 QB 524, at 532–533.
[41] A Farnsworth, *Farnsworth on Contracts* (3rd edn, Aspen 2004) para 12.15; C McCormick, *Handbook on the Law of Damages* (West Pub Co 1935) ch 4.

Coming down the scale, if the loss cannot be proved with reasonable certainty, damages are awarded in proportion to the chance of loss. However, the claimant cannot recover any damages if it cannot establish that the chance of the loss is more than very small, ie if the chance is entirely speculative. The classic old-fashioned hypothetical example was given by Erle CJ in *Priestley v Maclean*:[42] '... supposing a lady to have been injured and disfigured in a railway accident, she could not say that she ought to recover damages because she was prevented from going to a ball, at which she might have met a rich husband.' In *Davies v Taylor*[43] the principle was applied in relation to a claim under the Fatal Accidents Act by a wife who had deserted the deceased husband, and the latter had begun divorce proceedings against her. It was held that she had no claim because she could show nothing more than a 'speculative possibility'[44] of a reconciliation, and hence a pecuniary gain, had the husband lived.

(4) The claimant's hypothetical conduct

Even though one is in the realm of hypothetical events, to which a proportionate damages approach is normally applied, that will not be so where one is considering the hypothetical conduct of the claimant. For example, the claimant must establish all or nothing on the balance of probabilities that, had there been no breach, it would itself have been able to perform. This was laid down in clear and emphatic terms in *Flame SA v Glory Wealth Shipping PTE Ltd, The Glory Wealth*.[45] Under a contract for the carriage of coal by sea, between the defendant charterers and the claimant shipowners, the charterers committed a repudiatory breach by failing to 'declare laycans' (ie they failed to specify the loading dates). The owners accepted that repudiation and sought damages. The charterers argued that no damages were payable because, in the light of a collapse in the freight market, had the charterers complied with the contract by declaring laycans, the owners would not have been able to provide the required ships. The owners denied that that was a matter that they had to prove. Teare J held that the charterers were correct on this question. He said: 'The innocent party is claiming damages and therefore the burden lies on that party to prove its loss. That requires it to show that, had there been no repudiation, the innocent party would have been able to perform the obligations under the contract.'[46] But, as it was further held that there was no reason to overturn the arbitrators' finding that, on the facts, the owners had proved that they would have been able to perform the contract if it had gone ahead, the owners were entitled to substantial damages.

Similarly, in the earlier important case of *Allied Maples Group Ltd v Simmons & Simmons*,[47] which was a professional negligence claim against a solicitor brought in contract and tort

---

[42] (1860) 2 F & F 288, at 289.
[43] [1974] AC 207. See also *Fielding v Variety Inc* [1967] 2 QB 841—the Court of Appeal reduced damages for injurious falsehood from £10,000 to £100 because the loss was almost entirely speculative. See also several contract cases in which damages for loss of a chance would have been awarded but were not because the chances were entirely speculative: *Obagi v Stanborough (Developments) Ltd* (1993) 69 P & CR 573 (upheld 7 April 1999, CA) (denying substantial damages for breach of a contractual obligation to use best endeavours to obtain planning permission because the chance of obtaining such permission was merely speculative); *North Sea Energy Holdings v Petroleum Authority of Thailand* [1999] 1 All ER (Comm) 173; *Bank of Credit & Commerce Int SA v Ali (No 2)* [2002] 3 All ER 750 (albeit that the reasoning in the last case is not easy to interpret).
[44] [1974] AC 207, at 219 (per Viscount Dilhorne).
[45] [2013] EWHC 3153 (Comm), [2014] QB 1080.   [46] ibid, at [85].
[47] [1995] 1 WLR 1602. For (an uncharacteristically unconvincing) criticism of the *Allied Maples* case, see J Stapleton, 'Cause-in-Fact and the Scope of Liability for Consequences' (2003) 119 LQR 388, 402–411. For a clear application of the distinction drawn in the *Allied Maples* case, see *4 Eng Ltd v Harper* [2008] EWHC 915 (Ch), [2009] Ch 91 (tort of deceit). See also the very recent important confirmation of the *Allied Maples* distinction in *Perry v Raleys Solicitors* [2019] UKSC 5.

in relation to the drawing up of a contract, the uncertainty was as to whether the claimant client would have acted on the solicitor's advice, had proper advice been given, and whether the other party to the contract (the third party) would then have agreed to the different clauses in the contract. The Court of Appeal drew a distinction between the hypothetical conduct of the third party, to which the normal chances approach applied, and the hypothetical conduct of the claimant to which it was held that an all-or-nothing 'balance of probabilities' approach should apply. No explanation for that distinction was offered. *McGregor on Damages*[48] explained it on the basis that the claimant can be expected to satisfy the court (on the all-or-nothing balance of probabilities civil standard of proof) as to how it would itself have behaved if it wished to have damages assessed on the basis that it would have behaved in that way. McGregor wrote:

> 'While at first glance it may seem somewhat strange to have different tests applicable to hypothetical acts of the claimant and hypothetical acts of third parties, it can be seen to make sense, with nothing at all arbitrary about it and with no need to bring in public policy to justify it. For a claimant can hardly claim for the loss of the chance that he himself *might* have acted in a particular way; he must show that he *would* have; it cannot surely be enough for a claimant to say that there was a *chance* that he would have so acted. The onus is on a claimant to prove his case and he therefore must be able to show how he would *in fact* have behaved. There is no such onus on third parties.'

In other words the courts equate uncertainty about how the claimant would have acted with uncertainty as to past fact because it can expect the claimant to provide as good evidence about its own conduct as it can provide about past fact. The court either believes the claimant's evidence as to how it would have acted or it does not. A balance of probabilities test seems appropriate even though one is in a context where loss of a chance damages are normally recoverable. In contrast, third parties may not be before the court and, at least generally, therefore, one is in the realm of greater uncertainty as regards the hypothetical conduct of third parties so that an all-or-nothing balance of probabilities approach seems less appropriate than the normal chances approach.

(5) The defendant's hypothetical conduct: the minimum obligation principle

A chances approach is also not taken in relation to the defendant's hypothetical conduct. Rather the starting assumption is that the defendant would not have broken the relevant duty. Hence the mantra that the aim of compensation is to put the claimant into as good a position as if the duty had not been broken, ie as if the defendant had complied with its duty.

Even where the defendant had a choice of different modes of contractual performance, a chances approach has generally not been applied in assessing damages for breach of contract and instead a minimum obligation principle has been applied. There is a rich case law on this principle, and arguably some movement away from it in recent cases, which must now be examined in some detail.

---

[48] H McGregor, *McGregor on Damages* (19th edn, Sweet & Maxwell 2014) para 10-060 (and the same wording is in the current edition: J Edelman, *McGregor on Damages* (20th edn, Sweet & Maxwell 2018) para 10-062). See also Mance LJ in *Gregg v Scott* [2002] EWCA Civ 1471, [2003] Lloyd's Rep Med 105, at [71]: '[T]he rationale of the distinction ... must, I would think, be the pragmatic consideration that a claimant may be expected to adduce persuasive evidence about his own conduct (even though hypothetical), whereas proof of a third party's hypothetical conduct may often be more difficult to adduce.'

Where a contract entitles the defendant to perform in alternative ways or, as it is sometimes expressed, the defendant has a discretion as to the contractual benefits to be conferred on the claimant, damages are generally assessed on the basis that the defendant would have performed in the way most favourable to herself. As Maule J said in *Cockburn v Alexander*,[49] 'Generally speaking, where there are several ways in which the contract might be performed, that mode is adopted which is the least profitable to the plaintiff and the least burthensome to the defendant'; and in *Lavarack v Woods of Colchester Ltd*,[50] Diplock LJ said, 'The first task of the assessor of damages is to estimate as best he can what the plaintiff would have gained … if the defendant had fulfilled his legal obligation and had done no more.'[51]

The cases provide a number of illustrations of the application of this principle. As shown in *Kaye Steam Navigation Co v W & R Barnett*,[52] for example, if in a contract for the carriage of goods by sea the cargo-owner has the right to choose between a number of different ports for the cargo to be unloaded, damages for its failure to provide the cargo to the carrier will be based on the assumption that it would have chosen the most distant port for unloading. In *Re Thornett & Fehr and Yuills Ltd*,[53] it was held that in a contract for the sale of goods, where the seller has an option as to the exact quantity to be delivered (in this case, '200 tons, 5% more or less'), damages for non-delivery are based on the assumption that it would have delivered the smallest quantity, ie here 190 tons. Wrongful dismissal actions provide a particularly helpful range of examples.[54] So, as held in *British Guiana Credit v Da Silva*,[55] where an employee could have been dismissed with notice, but has been dismissed without notice, damages for his loss of earnings are restricted to the period of notice. Again where it is at the employer's discretion to make certain payments, no damages should be awarded for them in a wrongful dismissal action: so, in *Lavarack v Woods of Colchester Ltd*, no damages were awarded (Lord Denning dissenting) in relation to bonuses, to which the employee had no contractual entitlement, under a service contract that still had two years eight months to run; and in *Beach v Reed Corrugated Cases Ltd*[56] no damages were awarded for the fees that the employee, a director, could have been paid. Similarly in *Withers v General Theatre Corpn Ltd*,[57] an actor who had been wrongfully dismissed recovered no damages for the loss of the opportunity to enhance his reputation by appearing at a famous theatre, because the defendant had the option as to the theatres at which the claimant should appear.

Another excellent illustration of the application of the minimum obligation principle is provided by the Supreme Court of Canada's decision in *Hamilton v Open Window Bakery Ltd*.[58] The claimant had a three-year contract to act as the defendant's exclusive agent for the marketing and selling of certain goods in Japan. Provided 18 months of the contract had run, it permitted termination on three months' notice. The defendant terminated, without notice, after 16 months. The trial judge, applying a loss of the chance approach, had considered how likely it was that the contract would have run its full three-year course had the defendant not terminated at 16 months. He awarded 75% of what the claimant would have

---

[49] (1848) 6 CB 791, at 814.   [50] [1967] 1 QB 278.   [51] ibid, at 294.
[52] (1932) 48 TLR 440. See also *Phoebus D Kyprianou Co v Wm Pim Jnr & Co* [1977] 2 Lloyd's Rep 570; *The Rijn* [1981] 2 Lloyd's Rep 267; *Spiliada Maritime Corpn v Louis Dreyfus Corpn* [1983] Com LR 268; *Kurt A Becher GmbH v Roplak Enterprises SA, The World Navigator* [1991] 2 Lloyd's Rep 23.
[53] [1921] 1 KB 219.
[54] But as shown in *Rigby v Ferodo Ltd* [1988] ICR 29 the principle has no application where the defendant has continued to employ the claimant, while underpaying him. It would contradict the facts to postulate that it would have been cheaper for the defendant to have dismissed the claimant.
[55] [1965] 1 WLR 248.   [56] [1956] 1 WLR 807.   [57] [1933] 2 KB 536.
[58] (2004) 235 DLR (4th) 193. See also *Janciuk v Winerite Ltd* [1998] IRLR 63 (EAT, in a wrongful dismissal case, rejected a loss of the chance approach in favour of the traditional minimum legal obligation approach).

earned in that full remaining period up to three years. This was overturned by the Ontario Court of Appeal whose decision was upheld by the Supreme Court. The claimant was held entitled to damages assessed on the basis that the contract would have been in force for 21 months. That was the minimum legal obligation of the defendant.

A very difficult question is whether the usual principle is infringed by the courts' assessment of damages in hire-purchase agreements where the debtor repudiates the contract. As established in *Yeoman Credit v Waragowski*,[59] damages are assessed on the assumption that the debtor would have gone on to pay off the instalments, albeit without exercising its option to purchase. So the creditor is entitled to recover the unpaid balance of the hire-purchase price, less the sum fixed as the fee for exercise of the option to purchase, the proceeds of resale of goods repossessed or their value, and a discount to allow for acceleration of payment.[60]

It can be argued that that contradicts the usual principle: as the debtor had the option to terminate the contract lawfully at any time, the creditor's damages should be restricted to those to which it would have been entitled if the debtor had terminated.[61] But the difficulty is that usually in such contracts the debtor in choosing to terminate (other than for the creditor's breach) would be bound by a minimum payment clause that would dictate payment of a sum at least as great as judicially assessed damages. It follows that, unless the minimum payment clause is invalid as a penalty (even though there is no breach in issue),[62] the assessment in *Waragowski* does not normally exceed the defendant's minimum contractual obligation.

In applying the usual minimum obligation principle there are two qualifications that must be borne in mind. The first is that, while a particular performance may be the least burdensome to the defendant when judged solely according to the contract, this may not be the basis upon which damages are assessed because the courts judge the defendant's least burdensome performance by taking all other potential losses into account. The classic expression of this was in *Lavarack v Woods of Colchester Ltd*,[63] where Diplock LJ said, '… one must not assume that he [the defendant] will cut off his nose to spite his face and so [act] as to reduce his legal obligations to the plaintiff by incurring greater loss in other respects.'[64] The decision in *Bold v Brough, Nicholson and Hall Ltd*[65] is probably best explained on this basis. There the claimant, who had been wrongfully dismissed by the defendant, claimed for the loss of pension rights. Phillimore J held that the claimant should be compensated for this loss even though the defendant had the right to terminate the pension scheme on

---

[59] [1961] 1 WLR 1124.
[60] This follows from the *Waragowski* case, as modified by *Overstone Ltd v Shipway* [1962] 1 WLR 117.
[61] See *Financings v Baldock* [1963] 2 QB 104, at 113 (per Lord Denning MR). But the decision in *Baldock* distinguished between the creditor accepting a repudiatory breach or terminating for breach of condition (*Waragowski* damages recoverable based on unpaid instalments, *future* as well as past) and the creditor terminating under a power given by an express term (where the creditor is entitled to recover only past unpaid instalments and damages for any breach prior to termination). That difficult distinction has been applied in subsequent cases: see, eg, *Charterhouse Credit Co Ltd v Tolly* [1963] 2 QB 683; *Lombard North Central plc v Butterworth* [1987] QB 527. But in the latter case the distinction was regarded as unsatisfactory because skilled draftsmen can easily sidestep it. See generally B Opeskin, 'Damages for Breach of Contract Terminated Under Express Terms' (1990) 106 LQR 293 (cf G Treitel, 'Damages on Rescission for Breach of Contract' [1987] LMCLQ 143); R Goode, *Hire Purchase Law and Practice* (2nd edn, Butterworths 1970) 400–402; J Edelman, *McGregor on Damages* (20th edn, Sweet & Maxwell 2018) paras 26-017-26.022.
[62] Below, pp 397–400. [63] [1967] 1 QB 278. [64] ibid, at 295.
[65] [1964] 1 WLR 201. See also *Commonwealth of Australia v Amann Aviation Pty Ltd* (1991) 66 ALJR 123 (in assessing reliance damages it was assumed by all their Honours, with the exception of Toohey J, that the defendants would have exercised an option to renew the contract so that there was no need for a discount for the chance of non-renewal).

notice because it was unlikely that it would have taken 'a step so disastrous to its relations with all its employees solely to defeat a claim by this plaintiff'.[66]

The second qualification is that where, on the construction of the contract or by reason of an implied term, the defendant's discretion should be exercised reasonably, damages will be assessed on the basis of the defendant's minimum *reasonable* performance. In *Abrahams v Herbert Reiach Ltd*,[67] the defendants, a firm of publishers, agreed with the claimants, authors of a series of articles on athletics, to publish the articles in a book, paying the authors 4d for every copy of the book sold. The number of copies to be printed and other details regarding the publication were left to the publishers' discretion. They refused to publish the book. In an action for breach of contract, the Court of Appeal seems to have held that damages should be assessed on the basis not that the defendants would have published the minimum number of copies that could be described as a publication, but rather that they would have printed the minimum number that was reasonable in all the circumstances. Similarly in *Paula Lee Ltd v Robert Zehil & Co Ltd*[68] the claimants, who were dress manufacturers, entered into a contract by which they appointed the defendants the sole distributors for the sale of their garments in a certain territory. The defendants undertook to purchase not less than 16,000 garments each season. The defendants repudiated the contract with two seasons left to run. In an action for that breach of contract, Mustill J held that there was an implied term that the garments would be selected in a reasonable manner and that it would not have been reasonable for the defendants to select the 32,000 cheapest garments because some variation of style, size, and colour would be necessary to fulfil buyers' desires. Damages should therefore be assessed, applying *Abrahams v Herbert Reiach Ltd*, in terms of that reasonable selection which would be the cheapest for the defendants to buy.

Similarly, in line with the general movement in contract law, whereby there is an implied term (of fact) that an express contractual discretion should be exercised in good faith and must not be exercised arbitrarily, capriciously, or irrationally, there have been a number of wrongful dismissal cases distinguishing *Lavarack* as regards discretionary bonuses. Most importantly, in *Horkulak v Cantor Fitzgerald International*[69] it was held that damages should be assessed on the basis that the defendant employer would have exercised, in good faith and rationally, its discretion to award a bonus, which was an important element of the salary structure. Indeed, one might say that, in contrast to *Lavarack*, the employee was contractually entitled to a bonus and that it was the amount that lay in the employer's discretion.

Again, as a matter of construction, it is important to stress that, in order for the usual principle to apply, it is necessary for the defendant to have had a choice as to how to perform. Where there is no such choice, the damages must be assessed on the basis that the defendant would have performed in the one contracted-for way. This was the point that underlay the Privy Council's decision in *Lion Nathan Ltd v C-C Bottlers Ltd*.[70] The question here related to the correct measure of damages for the defendant's breach of warranty in failing to use reasonable care in providing a profit forecast for the business that the defendant was selling to the claimant. In working out what price the claimant would have paid had the warranty

---

[66] [1964] 1 WLR 201, at 212.   [67] [1922] 1 KB 477.
[68] [1983] 2 All ER 390. Both the *Abrahams* and *Paula Lee* cases were distinguished in *Baird Textiles Holdings Ltd v Marks & Spencer plc* [2002] 1 All ER (Comm) 737, where the lack of objective criteria by which the court could assess what would be reasonable either as to the quantity of garments or price meant that the alleged contract was invalid for uncertainty. In contrast, in the *Abrahams* and *Paula Lee* cases the existence of a contract was not in doubt.
[69] [2004] EWCA Civ 1287, [2005] ICR 402. See also *Clark v BET plc* [1997] IRLR 348 and *Clark v Nomura Ltd* [2000] IRLR 766.
[70] [1996] 1 WLR 1438.

been accurate (with the damages being awarded for the difference between that price and the higher price the claimant had actually paid) it was argued by the defendant that the court should take the highest profit forecast (and hence the highest price) within the range of possible forecasts compatible with reasonable care having been used. This was argued to be in line with the minimum obligation principle of, for example, *Lavarack* and *Paula Lee*. The Privy Council disagreed and held that the court should take the forecast which the defendant would be most likely to have given had reasonable care been used. In the absence of contrary evidence, this was taken to be the forecast that, as events subsequently turned out, was correct. Lord Hoffmann distinguished *Lavarack* and *Paula Lee* because they were concerned with predicting how the defendant would have performed outstanding contractual obligations which gave a choice of what to do. This case was different because the defendant was not entitled to choose from a range of figures. Rather it was required to make its best forecast in good faith using reasonable care. There was no reason to think that that figure would have been at the higher rather than the lower end of the range.

The rationale for giving no damages beyond the defendant's minimum contractual obligation is that that is all that the claimant is legally entitled to. Had the contract been on foot, the claimant could not have complained if the defendant had merely performed its bare contractual obligation. Had it wanted a greater legal entitlement, the claimant could have contracted for it (presumably at an increased price). But it did not do so.

In his dissenting judgment on this point in *Lavarack v Woods of Colchester Ltd*,[71] Lord Denning adopted a different approach. As we have seen, the majority held that damages should not be awarded in respect of lost bonuses. But Lord Denning would have awarded damages to the claimant for his lost chance of gaining the bonuses: '... the compensation is to be based on the probabilities of the case—on the remuneration which the plaintiff might reasonably be expected to receive—and not on the bare minimum necessary to satisfy the legal right.'[72] Lord Denning was therefore adopting a loss of the chance approach rather than the usual minimum legal obligation principle.

Although the rationale (as set out in the penultimate paragraph) for the traditional view is a powerful one, it would appear that the courts are moving towards Lord Denning's position. In particular, what we have described above as the second qualification on the minimum obligation principle operates to limit significantly its scope. At the level of principle, there is much to be said for assessing the factual evidence as to what the defendant *would* have done rather than considering merely what the defendant *could* legally have done.[73]

Perhaps the best way forward, which goes some way to reconciling the two approaches, is to say that, while one is concerned with what the defendant *would* have done, the 'minimum obligation' principle is a helpful default rule.[74] In general, it reflects the defendant's most likely performance (that is, a party does not in general exceed its minimum legal obligation). But that default rule may be departed from where the claimant can establish to the required standard of certainty (ie applying the approach set out earlier in this chapter, on

---

[71] [1967] 1 QB 278.   [72] ibid, at 288.
[73] This proposition may be said to derive some support from *Durham Tees Valley Airport Ltd v Bmibaby* [2010] EWCA Civ 485, [2011] 1 Lloyd's Rep 68 in which Patten LJ, with whom Toulson and Mummery LJJ agreed, said, at [79], 'The court ... has to conduct a factual enquiry as to how the contract would have been performed had it not been repudiated.' However, the approach taken to the 'minimum obligation' principle was not at all clear and the decision primarily laid down that a long-term obligation to fly two planes from an airport was sufficiently certain to be contractually binding.
[74] Cf D Pearce, 'Of Ceilings and Flaws: An Analytical Approach to the Minimum Performance Rule in Contract Damages' (2016) 36 OJLS 781, who argues that the minimum performance rule has no role to play and should be abandoned.

the balance of probabilities or, for loss of a chance damages, proportionately in line with the chances) that the defendant *would* have exceeded its minimum obligation.

An analogous (or, on another view, the same) principle as that being discussed in this section applies where the claimant would itself have committed a repudiatory breach had the contract continued and one is considering what the defendant would then have done. In *The Mihalis Angelos*[75] charterers were entitled to cancel a charterparty if the ship was not ready to load by 20 July. On 17 July, when it was clear that the ship would not be ready to load by 20 July, the charterers purported to terminate the contract. It was held that they were entitled to do so and were therefore not liable in damages. But in obiter dicta the Court of Appeal discussed what the position would have been had that termination by the charterers constituted an anticipatory repudiation which had been accepted by the owners. It was thought that the owners' damages would have been nominal because the charterers would otherwise have exercised their option to terminate on 20 July. In Edmund Davies LJ's words:

'The assumption has to be made that, had there been no anticipatory breach, the defendant would have performed his legal obligation and no more ... [I]t is beyond dispute that, on the belated arrival of the Mihalis Angelos at Haiphong, the charterers not only could have elected to cancel the charterparty, but would certainly have done so. The rights lost to the owners by reason of the assumed anticipatory breach were thus certain to be rendered valueless.'[76]

4. Miscellaneous points

(1) Sometimes loss is presumed

In several types of case English law eases the burden on the claimant by presuming that loss has been suffered: in other words, damages are sometimes 'at large'. The tort of defamation is probably the most important in this respect,[77] but the same applies, for example, to trespass to goods,[78] and inducing breach of contract.[79] Very similar is the tort of injurious falsehood where, although loss will not be presumed, proof of general loss of business is sufficient and the claimant does not need to prove the loss of any particular customer or contract.[80] The one clear case of loss being presumed for breach of contract is in respect of pecuniary loss of reputation, caused by the defendant's failure to honour the claimant's cheques.[81]

(2) Difficulty of assessment is not a bar

Where loss or a more than speculative chance of loss has been proved or is presumed, a court will do its best to assess damages even if the assessment is difficult and is necessarily imprecise. So in *Chaplin v Hicks*[82] Vaughan Williams LJ said:

'[I]t may be that the amount [of damages] ... will really be a matter of guesswork. But the fact that damages cannot be assessed with certainty does not relieve the wrongdoer of the necessity of paying damages for his breach of contract.'

---

[75] [1971] 1 QB 164. In *Commonwealth of Australia v Amann Aviation Pty Ltd* (1991) 66 ALJR 123, in assessing reliance damages it was held by the majority that the *Mihalis Angelos* principle did not affect the result because there was merely a 20% chance that the defendants would otherwise have validly cancelled the contract for the claimants' own breach: see below, p 80.
[76] [1971] 1 QB 164, at 203.
[77] *Tripp v Thomas* (1824) 3 B & C 427; *Ley v Hamilton* (1935) 153 LT 384; *Jameel v Wall Street Journal Europe SPRL* [2003] EWHC 2945 (QB), [2004] 2 All ER 92.
[78] *GWK Ltd v Dunlop Rubber Co Ltd* (1926) 42 TLR 376.
[79] *Exchange Telegraph Co Ltd v Gregory & Co* [1896] 1 QB 147; *Goldsoll v Goldman* [1914] 2 Ch 603.
[80] *Ratcliffe v Evans* [1892] 2 QB 524.
[81] *Rolin v Steward* (1854) 14 CB 595; *Wilson v United Countries Bank Ltd* [1920] AC 102.
[82] [1911] 2 KB 786, at 792.

The most obvious example of difficulty of assessment is in respect of damages for non-pecuniary loss, such as loss of amenity or pain and suffering. Lord Halsbury LC emphasised the point in *The Mediana*:[83]

> 'How is anybody to measure pain and suffering in moneys counted? Nobody can suggest that you can by arithmetical calculation establish what is the exact sum of money which would represent such a thing as the pain and suffering which a person has undergone by reason of an accident ... But nevertheless the law recognises that as a topic upon which damages may be given.'

But the same sort of approach applies also to pecuniary loss. For example, in *Simpson v London and North Western Rly Co*[84] the claimant was a manufacturer who displayed samples of his goods at shows in order to attract custom. The defendants in breach of contract failed to deliver the samples in time for a particular show. The claimant recovered damages from the defendants for loss of custom and the defendants' argument that damages for the loss of custom could not be awarded because the amount of damages could not be precisely assessed was rejected.

---

[83] [1900] AC 113, at 116.   [84] (1876) 1 QBD 274.

6
Contractual reliance damages

1. Introduction	75
2. Protection of the reliance interest where direct protection of the expectation interest is barred	76
3. Protection of the reliance interest even when direct protection of the expectation interest is not barred	77
4. No escape from a known bad bargain	78
5. Pre-contractual expenses	81

1. Introduction

The term 'reliance interest' was coined by Fuller and Perdue, whose classic article 'The Reliance Interest in Contract Damages'[1] first clarified and explored the different possible objectives of damages for breach of contract. The aim of damages protecting the reliance interest is, according to Fuller and Perdue, '... to put the plaintiff in as good a position as he was in before the promise was made'.[2] This can alternatively and preferably be expressed as aiming to put the claimant into as good a position as she would have been in if no contract had been made.

For many years the debate concerning the reliance interest, in line with Fuller and Perdue's article, was whether the protection of the reliance interest for breach of contract was a more obvious measure of compensation than the usual protection of the claimant's expectation interest. But it now seems clear that that debate has tended to mislead and that the idea that protection of the reliance interest is an alternative measure of damages is a myth. The protection of the expectation interest is the sole, obvious, and justified measure of compensation for breach of contract.[3] In this respect, breach of contract is to be contrasted with tortious misrepresentation where the wrong in question justifies reliance, not expectation, damages.[4] Where the courts have awarded reliance damages for breach of contract, this is *not* best justified as showing that reliance protection is as well-merited an aim of compensation as expectation protection. Rather the single overall aim remains the protection of the claimant's expectation interest. True it is that a claimant, instead of directly seeking its lost gains, can alternatively claim its reliance loss. But, as the aim is still to put the claimant into as good a position as if the contract had been performed, two features of the law follow (as we explore below): (i) a claimant cannot escape from what the defendant proves to be a bad bargain and (ii) even pre-contractual expenses may be recoverable. Neither of those features of the law is readily explicable if one takes the view that the reliance interest is an alternative separate measure to the expectation interest.

In most contracts (where the aim is financial gain) it is helpful to think of the claimant who seeks reliance damages as having the benefit of a presumption, rebuttable by the defendant, that reliance expenses (including pre-contractual expenses) would have been

---

[1] L Fuller and W Perdue, 'The Reliance Interest in Contract Damages' (1936–37) 46 Yale LJ 52 and 373.
[2] ibid, at 54.   [3] Above, pp 39–42.   [4] Above, p 39. Below, pp 79–80, 223–228.

recouped had the contract been performed. However, the notion of 'recoupment' is difficult to apply where profit is not the aim as, for example, where mental satisfaction is the main purpose of the contract. Take a contract between A and B, a musician, to perform at a concert held in memory of a friend of A's. Let us say, A incurs expenses of £2,000 for the hire of a hall. In breach of contract, B fails to turn up. In seeking to put A into as good a position as if the contract had been performed, A is entitled to 'reliance damages' of £2,000. This is so even though one cannot sensibly talk of A recouping those expenses had the contract been performed because this is not a commercial contract. In so far as it is thought helpful to regard there as being a presumption, it is preferable to express the presumption as being that the claimant has made a good bargain so that the reliance losses would not have been wasted had the contract been performed. It is then for the defendant to rebut that presumption by proving that the claimant made a bad bargain so that the reliance losses would have been wasted had the contract been performed.

In the first two editions of this book, damages for breach of contract protecting the reliance interest were treated after examining the details of the law's standard protection of the expectation interest. However, in recognition of the preferable view that reliance interest protection in contract is not full-blown protection of the reliance interest (in contrast to a claim for tortious misrepresentation) but is rather a means of protecting the expectation interest—by which the claimant may be said to have the benefit of a rebuttable presumption that the bargain was a good one—it was thought preferable in the last edition, and this has been followed through in this edition, to deal with it here immediately following the general chapter on proof of loss.

2. Protection of the reliance interest where direct protection of the expectation interest is barred

While the English courts have generally not adopted Fuller and Perdue's interest terminology, there are decisions which may be viewed as protecting the claimant's reliance interest for breach of contract.

First, there are those cases to which the (now abolished) rule in *Bain v Fothergill*[5] applied. By this if, because of a defect in his title, a vendor without fault broke a contract for the sale of land by failing to complete or delaying in completion, the purchaser could not recover damages for the difference between the market value of the land and the contract price. Rather the purchaser was restricted to damages in respect of at least some expenses incurred in relation to the contract; and those damages could be viewed as at least partially protecting the claimant's reliance interest.

Secondly, there are cases where the claimant cannot directly recover damages protecting its expectation interest because it cannot prove what position it would have been in if the contract had been performed.[6] The Australian case of *McRae v Commonwealth Disposals Commission*[7] affords an excellent illustration. The claimants bought from the defendants an oil tanker together with its contents which the defendants had advertised as lying off a named reef. The claimants went to considerable expense to reach and salvage the tanker but it turned out that neither tanker nor reef existed. The claimants successfully sued the defendants for breach of contract, it being held that the contract contained a term that the tanker and reef existed. The claimants were not given damages based on the

---

[5] (1874) LR 7 HL 158. Abolished by the Law of Property (Miscellaneous Provisions) Act 1989, s 3.
[6] See above, ch 5.   [7] (1950) 84 CLR 377.

value of the ship and its contents, for this was considered too speculative. Rather they were given damages in respect of the price paid for the tanker and for what it had cost to send out a salvage expedition to look for the tanker. Such damages may be viewed as protecting the claimants' reliance interest.

A similar English authority is *Anglia Television Ltd v Reed*.[8] Here the claimants, with the intention of mounting the film production of a play, sought to engage the defendant for the main part. For the purposes of the production they incurred expenditures to the extent of some £2,750, including fees for a director, designer, stage manager, and supporting artists. The contract between the claimants and the defendant was made but a few days later he repudiated. In an action for breach of contract, the claimants did not claim profits that the play would have made since they conceded that these could not be ascertained. They sought instead to recover the £2,750 expenditure in organising the production. The Court of Appeal affirmed the lower court's judgment awarding the full £2,750. This may again be viewed as the award of the reliance loss to claimants who could not directly prove their expectation loss.

3. Protection of the reliance interest even when direct protection of the expectation interest is not barred

Dicta of the majority of the Court of Appeal in *Cullinane v British Rema Manufacturing Co Ltd*[9] and of the unanimous Court of Appeal in *Anglia Television Ltd v Reed* supported the view that the claimant is always free to claim protection of its reliance interest. As Lord Denning said in the latter case, '... the plaintiff ... has an election; he can either claim for loss of profits or for his wasted expenditure.'[10] The decision in *Lloyd v Stanbury*[11] could also be regarded as supporting this although it concerned a contract for the sale of land and such contracts could, arguably, be regarded as special particularly given the (now abolished) *Bain v Fothergill* rule. But the answer to this question was put beyond doubt by Hutchison J's comments in *CCC Films (London) Ltd v Impact Quadrant Films Ltd*.[12] The defendants had there granted a licence to the claimants to exploit three films and the claimants had paid the agreed consideration of $12,000 for that licence. By the contract the defendants were to send to the claimants video tapes of the films and were to insure them. In breach of contract the defendants sent the video tapes by ordinary post and uninsured and they were lost. The defendants were also in breach of contract in failing to deliver replacement tapes. The claimants could not prove any loss of profits and instead claimed damages in respect of the expenses of $12,000. Hutchison J held that they could recover those damages. Moreover he squarely addressed the question of whether a claimant's choice to claim reliance expenses is unfettered and said:

'... the plaintiff has an unfettered choice; it is not only where he establishes by evidence that he cannot prove loss of profit or that such loss of profit as he can prove is small that he is permitted to frame his claim as one for wasted expenditure ... I consider that those cases [*Cullinane v British Rema Manufacturing Co Ltd* and *Anglia Television Ltd v Reed*] are authority for the proposition that a plaintiff may always frame his claim in the alternative way if he chooses.'[13]

---

[8] [1972] 1 QB 60. See also *Nurse v Barns* (1664) T Raym 77.   [9] [1954] 1 QB 292.
[10] [1972] 1 QB 60, at 63–64. Clearly the profits referred to were gross and not net.
[11] [1971] 1 WLR 535. The damages awarded here extended beyond 'wasted expenses', strictly construed, to include a sum for the claimant's loss of earnings.
[12] [1985] QB 16.   [13] ibid, at 32.

4. No escape from a known bad bargain

Once one recognizes that the claimant has a free choice to claim protection of the reliance interest, the crucial question that arises is whether this means that the courts will thereby allow a claimant to escape from what is clearly a bad bargain. The answer, as laid down in *C & P Haulage v Middleton*,[14] *CCC Films (London) v Impact Quadrant Films Ltd*, and *Omak Maritime Ltd v Mamola Challenger Shipping Co, The Mamola Challenger*,[15] is that they will not.

In the first of these three cases, the respondents had granted a contractual licence to the appellant to use their yard for his car-repair business. With ten weeks remaining of a second six-month licence the respondents, in breach of contract, terminated the licence. Proceedings were begun by the respondents but the real controversy centred on the appellant's counterclaim for reimbursement of £1,767.51 to cover labour and material used in building a wall enclosing the yard, laying on electricity, and transferring a telephone. The Court of Appeal refused to award the appellant anything beyond nominal damages. If we adopt the reliance interest interpretation, the reasoning was that a court will not award damages protecting a claimant's reliance interest if this will knowingly put him in a better position than he would have been in if the contract had been performed. To have awarded the appellant the damages he claimed would have contravened this because the respondents could have lawfully terminated the licence at the end of the next ten weeks and presumably the appellant could not during that period of time, nor indeed during a full six months, have recouped in profits his expenditure on the yard: but, in any case, as the local authority had permitted him to work from home the appellant had been able fully to mitigate his loss of profits during those ten weeks. Indeed his profits would be higher working at home since he was spared paying for the use of the yard.

In deciding that a claimant cannot escape from a known bad bargain by claiming protection of his reliance interest, the Court of Appeal took the same view as that prevailing in the US and Canada. Indeed Ackner LJ, giving the principal judgment, relied heavily on the decision of the British Columbia Supreme Court in *Bowlay Logging Ltd v Dolmar Ltd*[16] which in turn had cited with approval *L Albert & Son v Armstrong Rubber Co*[17] the classic US authority on this point. In the former, Berger J admirably summarised the underlying rationale of these cases in the following passage:

> 'Where it can be seen that the plaintiff would have incurred a loss on the contract as a whole, the expenses he incurred are losses flowing from entering into the contract, not losses flowing from the defendant's breach ... The principle contended for ... would entail the award of damages not to compensate the plaintiff but to punish the defendant.'[18]

C & P Haulage v Middleton was applied in *CCC Films*, where Hutchison J went on to stress, relying on the same Canadian and US authorities, that where the claimant claims reliance damages, the burden of proving that he has made a bad bargain, that is that he would not have recouped his expenses if the contract had been performed, is on the defendant.

The leading case is now *Omak Maritime Ltd v Mamola Challenger Shipping Co, The Mamola Challenger*.[19] Charterers, under a long-term charterparty, repudiated that contract even though the contract was for them a good one with the charter rate being below

---

[14] [1983] 1 WLR 1461.
[15] [2010] EWHC 2026 (Comm), [2011] 1 Lloyd's Rep 47.
[16] (1978) 4 WWR 105.
[17] 178 F 2d 182 (1949).
[18] (1978) 4 WWR 105, at 117.
[19] [2010] EWHC 2026 (Comm), [2011] 1 Lloyd's Rep 47. For an excellent note on this case, see D McLauchlan, 'The Redundant Reliance Interest in Contract Damages' (2011) 127 LQR 23.

the market rate (by about $7,500 per day). The owners accepted that repudiatory breach and thereby became able to trade the ship at the higher market rate. The owners nevertheless claimed, and were awarded by the arbitrators, substantial damages based on the expenses they had incurred in preparing to perform the charterparty. The owners' argument was that they were entitled to the expenses incurred as reliance damages and that it was irrelevant to those damages that they had entirely mitigated the loss of hire because, so it was said, reliance damages were not concerned with the owners' position had the contract been performed. Rather, reliance damages were concerned with the position the owners would have been in had no contract been made. Had no contract been made, the owners would not have incurred those reliance expenses and would also not have lost the opportunity to enter into other contracts at the market rate. While the owners' freedom to trade at the market rate after breach went to mitigate the loss of hire, it did not mitigate the expenses incurred. That argument of the owners was firmly rejected by Teare J. In a very clear judgment, he reasoned that reliance damages are not based on a separate principle from the protection of the expectation interest laid down by *Robinson v Harman*. The expectation interest is the one and only compensatory principle to be applied so that, as the owners' loss assessed according to that principle had been entirely mitigated, there was no other loss to be compensated. The recovery of wasted reliance expense is merely an indirect method, supported by a reverse burden of proof, of protecting the expectation interest.

Subsequently, in *Yam Seng Pte Limited v International Trade Corporation Limited*,[20] Leggatt J praised Teare J's 'masterly judgment'[21] and continued as follows: 'The advantage of claiming damages on the "reliance" basis is not that the claimant can recover expenditure which would have been wasted even if the contract had been performed but that, where such a claim is made, the burden of proof lies on the defendant to show that the expenditure would not have been recouped and would have been wasted in any event.'[22] He went on to award damages compensating the claimant for its wasted expenditure (ie its net expenditure in performing the agreement) where the defendant could not prove that such expenses would not have been recouped.

The upshot of all this is that where the defendant (D) cannot prove that the claimant (C) has made a bad bargain and C's reliance loss exceeds the expectation loss that C can prove, it will be to C's advantage to claim reliance damages. But where D can prove that C has made a bad bargain C's 'free choice' to claim protection of the reliance interest is of no advantage to C because C will be confined to the lower expectation damages.

Ultimately, then, the reliance interest bows to the expectation interest. This is only right since it is the breaking of the promise, disappointing the claimant's expectations, that renders the defendant's conduct wrongful.[23] As such, damages for tortious misrepresentation provide an interesting contrast.[24] The very objection to misrepresentation is that the defendant ought not to have induced the claimant to rely on an untrue statement. If in reliance on the misrepresentation the claimant has, for example, entered into what is a bad bargain, she can and ought to be able to escape from it by recouping all her losses because if the defendant had not wrongfully made the representation the claimant would not have entered into the contract. In other words, unlike a contract-breaker who acts wrongfully when he breaks his contractual promise and not when he induces the claimant to enter into the contract,

---

[20] [2013] EWHC 111 (QB), [2013] 1 Lloyd's Rep 526.   [21] ibid, at [186].   [22] ibid, at [187].
[23] See above, pp 39–42.   [24] See above, p 39. Below, pp 223–228.

the misrepresentor commits a wrong when he induces the claimant by his statement to act to her detriment by, for example, entering into a losing contract.

In the difficult Australian case of *Commonwealth of Australia v Amann Aviation Pty Ltd*[25] the primary question in issue was the standard of proof faced by a defendant who seeks to discharge the burden of showing that the claimant has made a bad bargain (ie that the claimant would not have recouped his reliance loss).

The claimant had won a contract to conduct aerial coastal surveillance for the defendant. It committed large sums of money in acquiring the necessary specially equipped aircraft. Several months after the contract commenced, and at a time when the claimant was itself in breach by having insufficient aircraft available, the defendant committed a repudiatory breach by serving an invalid termination notice. That breach entitled the claimant to terminate the contract and sue for damages, which it did. The majority of the High Court of Australia (Mason CJ, Dawson J, Brennan J, Gaudron J) held that it was entitled to full reliance damages of some $5.5 million (plus interest). Although the defendant had shown that there was a 20% chance that the defendant would otherwise have validly terminated the contract for the claimant's own breach, in which event the claimant's reliance losses would not have been recouped, the majority felt that no discount should be made for that chance because it was unlikely. A balance of probabilities, all-or-nothing, standard of proof therefore seems to have been applied. In contrast, the three minority judges thought that a discount should be made. Intriguingly each of them adopted different reasoning and conclusions. Deane J thought the appropriate discount from full reliance damages should be the 20% chance that the defendant would have validly terminated. Toohey J considered that, taking account of all the contingencies in the case, the discount should be 50%. On the other hand, McHugh J thought that reliance damages were inappropriate and that instead normal expectation damages, reduced by the 20% chance, should be awarded.

It follows that, as the courts will not knowingly award reliance damages which put the claimant into a better position than if the contract had been performed, the best interpretation of the cases awarding reliance damages is that they are concerned to protect the claimant's expectation interest, albeit in a different way than the expectation interest is normally protected. That is, one can say that the law accepts an alternative way of putting the claimant into as good a position as if the contract had been performed, because it allows the claimant the benefit of a presumption, rebuttable by the defendant, that the claimant has made a good bargain. Hence where the claimant can prove its reliance expenses, this rebuttable presumption enables it to recover that amount on the ground that if the contract had been performed it would at the very least have made financial gains to cover those expenses or, in a non-commercial contract, the claimant would have reaped mental benefits so that those expenses would not have been wasted.

This analysis provides the only convincing explanation for why the courts do not allow claimants to escape from a known bad bargain by claiming reliance damages. If one were concerned to protect the reliance interest because that provides an alternative and valid aim of compensation for breach of contract (as suggested by Fuller and Perdue), it is hard to see why it should be limited by a known lower expectation interest.

---

[25] (1991) 66 ALJR 123; G Treitel, 'Damages for Breach of Contract in the High Court of Australia' (1992) 108 LQR 226.

On the other hand, it may at first sight appear puzzling why, on this interpretation, the courts are willing to give the claimant the benefit of a rebuttable presumption that it made a good bargain. But it is submitted that this is simply a consequence of the fact that the defendant is a contract-breaker. It is as a result of breach by the defendant that one does not know what the position would have been had the contract been performed. It is therefore only fair and proper that the problems of proving what the position would have been had the contract been performed should fall on the contract-breaker and not on the innocent claimant.

One should also note that, as Berger J stressed in the passage cited above,[26] there is simply no causal link between a breach of contract and damages protecting the reliance interest. The expenses would have been incurred even if there had been no breach. This is another way of expressing the point that expectation, and not reliance, protection is the natural measure of compensation for breach of contract.

5. Pre-contractual expenses

A further reason to prefer the 'rebuttable presumption of a good bargain' explanation is that pre-contractual reliance expenses have been held recoverable. In *Lloyd v Stanbury* pre-contractual expenditure was recovered, and Brightman J said that this should be so, so long as the costs were of '… performing an act required to be done by the contract'.[27] Given doubts about whether contracts for the sale of land are exceptional, however, the clearest authority is *Anglia Television Ltd v Reed*. Here many of the expenses recovered were pre-contractual. Lord Denning, with whom the other two judges agreed, said:

> 'If the plaintiff claims the wasted expenditure, he is not limited to the expenditure incurred after the contract was concluded. He can claim also the expenditure incurred before the contract, provided it was such as would reasonably be in the contemplation of the parties as likely to be wasted if the contract was broken. Applying that principle here, it is plain that, when Mr Reed entered into this contract, he must have known perfectly well that much expenditure had already been incurred on directors' fees and the like. He must have contemplated—or at any rate, it is reasonably to be imputed to him—that if he broke his contract, all that expenditure would be wasted, whether or not it was incurred before or after the contract. He must pay damages for all the expenditure so wasted and thrown away.'[28]

The recovery of pre-contractual expenses is perfectly explicable if one adopts the view that the claimant has the benefit of a rebuttable presumption that the claimant has made a good bargain so that, in a commercial contract, it would at least have recouped its expenses had the contract been performed. In deciding whether a claimant has made a good or a bad bargain, one would naturally take into account pre-contractual as well as post-contractual expenses. Put another way, in a commercial contract, a claimant could not be said to have 'broken even', if it recouped only post-contractual expenses.[29]

---

[26] Above, p 78.   [27] [1971] 1 WLR 535, at 546.
[28] [1972] 1 QB 60, at 64. Note also that Lord Denning was here applying a normal 'reasonable contemplation' remoteness limitation to the 'wasted expenses'.
[29] *Commonwealth of Australia v Amann Aviation Pty Ltd* (1991) 66 ALJR 123, at 161 (per Gaudron J); S Waddams, *The Law of Damages* (6th edn, Thomson Reuters) paras 5.200–5.250; M Owen, 'Some Aspects of the Recovery of Reliance Damages in the Law of Contract' (1984) 4 OJLS 393, 396–399; D McLauchlan, 'Damages for Pre-Contract Expenditure' (1984–5) 11 NZULR 346.

In contrast, if one applies the view that the reliance interest is awarded as a valid alternative aim of compensation, it is hard to see why pre-contractual expenses are recoverable. They would in any event have been wasted if no contract had been made with the defendant. The defendant has not induced the claimant to incur them.[30] And if one were to allow the claimant to recover some pre-contractual expenses, it is hard to see how far back one would go or where one would rationally stop.[31]

---

[30] In *Chicago Coliseum Club v Dempsey* 256 Illinois App 542 (1932) it was held that reliance damages for breach of contract did not extend to pre-contractual expenses.

[31] Cf A Ogus, *The Law of Damages* (Butterworths 1973) 350 who writes, 'Perhaps the best solution would be for the reliance interest award to comprise those expenses incurred as from the time when there was substantial agreement between the parties.'

7
Principles limiting compensatory damages

1. Introduction	83
2. Remoteness	86
3. Intervening cause	107
4. The *SAAMCO* principle	117
5. The duty to mitigate	127
6. Contributory negligence	132
7. The demise of impecuniosity as a limitation	144

1. Introduction

There can be said to be five[1] principles limiting compensatory damages (ie which reduce the damages that full adherence to the compensatory aims would dictate)[2] for both torts and breach of contract, and the role played by each can be briefly described as follows:

Remoteness—A claimant cannot succeed if the loss was too remote from the breach of duty.[3] The principal tests for remoteness centre on reasonable foreseeability or contemplation of the loss.

Intervening cause—A claimant cannot succeed if an intervening cause is so much more responsible for the loss than the defendant's breach of duty that it breaks the chain of causation between the breach of duty and the loss.

The SAAMCO principle—The House of Lords in *South Australia Asset Management Corpn v York Montague Ltd*,[4] in the context of a claim for negligent valuation, held that the lenders' loss consequent on a fall in the property market was not recoverable from the valuer. This exclusion was justified on the principle (the *SAAMCO* principle) that the loss

---

[1] Consent, *volenti non fit injuria*, and illegality (including the dismissal of claims for personal injury because of 'fundamental dishonesty' under the Criminal Justice and Courts Act 2015, s 57) are not considered because these defences are practically always concerned with liability rather than with damages (but for illustrations of illegality barring damages rather than the cause of action see, eg, *Burns v Edman* [1970] 2 QB 541; *Hunter v Butler* [1996] RTR 396; *Hewison v Meridian Shipping Pte* [2002] EWCA Civ 1821, [2003] PIQR P252). Exclusion and limitation clauses are also omitted because, taken together, they are not purely concerned with restricting remedies and, in any event, space prevents an adequate examination of them. See, generally, E Peel, *Treitel on The Law of Contract* (14th edn, Sweet & Maxwell 2015) ch 7. Also not examined are special statutory provisions limiting damages: eg, Carriage by Air Act 1961, Sch 1, art 22; Carriage of Passengers by Road Act 1974, Sch 1, art 13(1); Merchant Shipping Act 1995, s 185. Note also that, as between the parties, the costs of litigating (eg, in relation to a tort or breach of contract) are only recoverable as 'costs' and not damages subject to some exceptions: see, eg, *Berry v British Transport Commission* [1962] 1 QB 306; *Union Discount Co Ltd v Zoller* [2002] 1 WLR 1517; *National Westminster Bank Plc v Rabobank Nederland (No 3)* [2007] EWHC 1742 (Comm), [2008] 1 All ER (Comm) 243; L Merrett, 'Costs as Damages' (2009) 125 LQR 468.

[2] Subject to the limiting principles considered in this chapter, compensation for both torts and breach of contract aims to be full compensation. This is sometimes referred to, in the context of personal injury compensation, as 'the 100% principle'. See P Cane and J Goudkamp, *Atiyah's Accidents, Compensation and the Law* (9th edn, CUP 2018) 131–149, esp 143–145. See also *Wells v Wells* [1999] 1 AC 345, at 363, 382–383, 398.

[3] Breach of duty is throughout used as shorthand for breach of contract, tort actionable per se, or in the case of a tort actionable only on proof of damage, breach of duty.

[4] [1995] QB 375.

was outside the scope of the duty. This principle was treated by their Lordships as distinct from remoteness and intervening cause. The validity and scope of this principle are controversial.

Duty to mitigate—A claimant cannot succeed if subsequent to the tort or breach of contract he or she could reasonably have avoided the loss.

Contributory negligence—Damages may be reduced where the claimant's negligence has contributed to, ie been a partial cause of, the claimant's loss. But this principle is not applicable to some torts and is inapplicable to breach of contract (other than of a contractual duty of care where there is concurrent liability in tort).

A further limiting principle—that, as established in *The Liesbosch*,[5] loss flowing from the claimant's impecuniosity is irrecoverable—was authoritatively removed from the law, after 70 years of doubtful existence, by the House of Lords in *Lagden v O'Connor*.[6] We shall briefly examine its demise at the end of this chapter.

Five introductory points need to be made regarding these principles.

(i) For torts actionable only on proof of damage, such as negligence, and in contrast to torts actionable per se and breach of contract, remoteness, intervening cause and the SAAMCO principle are often concerned with establishing whether a tort has been committed (ie liability) rather than with damages. But in order to provide a full picture of the courts' approach to those principles they will here be examined even when they are concerned with establishing tort liability.

(ii) Since all these principles are concerned to limit compensatory damages it is not at all surprising that the same result may often be reached by applying more than one of them. So, for example, in *Compania Financiera Soleada SA v Hamoor Tanker Corpn Inc, The Borag*,[7] where the issue was the recoverability of interest charges paid on a loan taken out by the claimant as a consequence of the defendant's breach of contract, Templeman LJ said, '... in the present case if the interest charges were unreasonable, they were too remote: they were not caused by the breach; they were not part of a reasonable form of mitigation; all these matters hang together.'[8] But normally just one of these principles will be used to limit damages.

(iii) The distinction between remoteness and intervening cause is often not drawn and both principles are dealt with under the one head, whether labelled 'remoteness' or 'legal causation' or 'proximate cause'. This is perfectly acceptable since both principles are essentially concerned with the same policy, namely that, as explained by Lord Wright in *The Liesbosch*, '... the law cannot take account of everything that follows a wrongful act: it regards some subsequent matters as outside the scope of its selection ... In the varied web of affairs, the law must abstract some consequences as relevant not perhaps on grounds of pure logic, but simply for practical reasons.'[9] In Ogus' words, 'A line has to be drawn somewhere so that the burden of liability will not crush those who have to pay the bill.'[10] However, in this book it has been considered helpful to separate remoteness and intervening cause for not only does each have a different focus of attention but also the principles applied to each are not the same.

(iv) Where the claimant's unreasonable conduct subsequent to the tort or breach of contract has been a cause of her suffering loss, both the duty to mitigate and intervening cause

---

[5] *Owners of the Dredger Liesbosch v Owners of SS Edison* [1933] AC 449.
[6] [2003] UKHL 64, [2004] 1 AC 1067.　　[7] [1981] 1 WLR 274.　　[8] [1981] 1 WLR 274, at 864.
[9] [1933] AC 449, at 460.　　[10] A Ogus, *The Law of Damages* (Butterworths 1973) 67.

can be regarded as denying damages for exactly the same reason. Hence in this situation the courts sometimes use the principles interchangeably.[11] But generally they are distinguished by using the duty to mitigate for the claimant's unreasonable *inaction*, ie her failure to minimise loss, while using intervening cause breaking the chain of causation for the claimant's unreasonable *action*, ie her augmenting of loss.[12] However, where the unreasonable action comprises incurring expense, this is generally viewed as an aspect of the duty to mitigate rather than intervening cause. These general usages are adopted in this book.

The role of contributory negligence (if applicable to the tort or breach of contract in question) also needs to be clarified in this situation. In particular it should be realised that contributory negligence has been applied to the claimant's negligence occurring subsequently to, as well as prior to or contemporaneously with, a tort.[13] What, then, is the essential distinction between contributory negligence, on the one hand, and intervening cause and the duty to mitigate on the other? One way of explaining this is to say that the former is a partial defence while the latter two are total defences. So one cannot recover any damages for a loss that was not caused by the breach or that should reasonably have been avoided; whereas, if there has been contributory negligence in relation to a loss, damages for that loss are merely reduced to the extent that this is thought just and equitable.[14] But that explanation does not seek to deny that, where there has been an intervening cause or a failure to mitigate, damages can still be awarded for that part of the loss that would have been suffered even if the claimant had acted reasonably. An alternative explanation of the difference—which avoids the possible ambiguity in describing a defence as total even though some damages may be awarded—is that the recoverable loss is reduced for different reasons. In respect of contributory negligence, damages are reduced according to the comparative blameworthiness and causal potency of the claimant and defendant. In respect of intervening causation/ the duty to mitigate the damages are reduced down to the loss (which may be zero) that, applying a counterfactual approach, the claimant would have suffered even if it had acted reasonably.

(v) The burden of proof in relation to these limiting principles (provided liability has been established) is on the defendant.[15] That is, once the claimant has proved a breach of duty, factual causation and his loss—that is, once he has shown that prima facie he merits compensation—it is, and should be, for the defendant to prove that one of these limiting

---

[11] Eg *Compania Naviera Maropan SA v Bowaters Lloyd Pulp and Paper Mills Ltd* [1955] 2 QB 68; *The Borag* [1981] 1 WLR 274 (per Templeman LJ); *Emeh v Kensington and Chelsea and Westminster Area Health Authority* [1985] QB 1012; *Schering Agrochemicals Ltd v Resibel NV SA* (26 November 1992, unreported) (per Purchas LJ); *Standard Chartered Bank v Pakistan National Shipping Corpn* [2001] EWCA Civ 55, [2001] 1 All ER (Comm) 822, at [41]; *Morris v Richards* [2003] EWCA Civ 232, [2004] PIQR Q3; *Borealis AB v Geogas Trading SA* [2010] EWHC 2789 (Comm), [2011] 1 Lloyd's Rep 482.

[12] For express recognition of this, see *Schering Agrochemicals Ltd v Resibel NV SA* (26 November 1992, unreported) (per Nolan LJ). A different distinction was drawn by Scott LJ in that case and by Phillips J in *Youell v Bland Welch & Co (No 2)* [1990] 2 Lloyd's Rep 431, at 461–462 to the effect that a duty to mitigate only arises once the claimant has actual knowledge of the breach: for criticism of that, see A Burrows, 'Contributory Negligence in Contract: Ammunition for the Law Commission' (1993) 109 LQR 175.

[13] *The Calliope* [1970] P 172.

[14] It is for this reason that *Tennant Radiant Heat Ltd v Warrington Development Corpn* [1988] 1 EGLR 41 is controversial as a decision on causation (as opposed to contributory negligence).

[15] *SS Heranger (Owners) v SS Diamond (Owners)* [1939] AC 94, at 104 (contributory negligence); *Philco Radio and Television Corpn of Great Britain Ltd v Spurling Ltd* [1949] 2 KB 33 (intervening cause); contra *SS Singleton Abbey (Owners) v SS Paludina (Owners)* [1927] AC 16 (burden of proving not an intervening cause on claimant); *Roper v Johnson* (1873) LR 8 CP 167; *Garnac Grain Co Inc v Faure & Fairclough Ltd* [1968] AC 1130n; *Standard Chartered Bank v Pakistan National Shipping Corpn* [2001] EWCA Civ 55, [2001] 1 All ER (Comm) 822, at [33]–[41]; *Geest plc v Lansiquot* [2002] UKPC 48, [2002] 1 WLR 3111; *LE Jones (Insurance Brokers) Ltd v Portsmouth City Council* [2002] EWCA Civ 1723, [2003] 1 WLR 427, at [26] (all duty to mitigate).

principles applies to reduce the damages. But the burden of proof in respect of the *SAAMCO* principle has been held to be on the claimant.[16]

2. Remoteness

A principal restriction on compensatory damages is that the loss must not be too remote from the breach of duty. The tests formulated for deciding on this have centred on whether the loss was (in contract) reasonably contemplated or (in tort) reasonably foreseeable by the defendant. While broadly similar these tests have, in their detail, been traditionally regarded as having significant differences. The full recognition of concurrent liability, and the expansion of the recovery of pure economic loss in the tort of negligence, have rendered these differences particularly interesting, important, and controversial. The issue of whether the tests are different will be examined in depth in the contract section.[17]

In policy terms the remoteness restriction is based on the view that it is unfair to a defendant, and imposes too great a burden, to hold it responsible for losses that it could not have reasonably contemplated or foreseen. It has also been regarded as having an economic efficiency rationale in encouraging the disclosure of information regarding unusual potential losses, so that the defendant with full knowledge of the risks involved can plan and act rationally.[18]

(1) Torts

(a) The Wagon Mound 'reasonable foreseeability' test

Remoteness for torts has been primarily discussed judicially in relation to the tort of negligence; but as is explained below, it seems that with the exception of deceit and other torts that have been committed dishonestly or intentionally, the test applied to negligence applies to all other torts.

The old test for remoteness was that laid down in *Re Polemis and Furniss Withy & Co*:[19] according to this, a defendant was liable for all the direct consequences of its negligence suffered by the claimant whether a reasonable man would have foreseen them or not. But *Re Polemis* was effectively overruled by *Overseas Tankship (UK) Ltd v Morts Dock & Engineering Co Ltd, The Wagon Mound*,[20] which established that consequences are too remote if a reasonable man would not have foreseen them. Here the defendants carelessly discharged oil from their ship into a harbour. Over two days later, molten metal from the claimant's welding operations on the wharf set fire to the oil on the water. The claimant's wharf was severely damaged. The Privy Council held that the defendants were not liable in negligence because, while they could have reasonably foreseen damage to the wharf by fouling, they could not have reasonably foreseen that the wharf would be damaged by fire when they carelessly discharged the oil. Viscount Simonds said: 'It is the foresight of the reasonable man which alone can determine responsibility. The *Polemis* rule by substituting

---

[16] BPE Solicitors v Hughes-Holland [2017] UKSC 21, [2018] AC 599.
[17] See, generally, J Cartwright, 'Remoteness of Damage in Contract and Tort: A Reconsideration' [1996] CLJ 488.
[18] R Posner, *Economic Analysis of Law* (9th edn, Wolters Kluwer 2014) 138–140; H Beale, *Remedies for Breach of Contract* (Sweet & Maxwell 1980) 180; D Harris, D Campbell, and R Halson, *Remedies in Contract and Tort* (2nd edn, Butterworths 2002) 310–313.
[19] [1921] 3 KB 560; M Davies, 'The Road from Morocco: *Polemis* Through *Donoghue* to No-Fault' (1982) 45 MLR 534.
[20] [1961] AC 388. See M Stauch, 'Risk and Remoteness of Damage in Negligence' (2001) 64 MLR 191.

"direct" for "reasonably foreseeable" consequence leads to a conclusion equally illogical and unjust.'[21] The illogicality he was referring to was that under *Re Polemis* the test for the extent of the defendant's liability (directness) differed from that for the existence of liability (reasonable foreseeability).

(b) The application of the 'reasonable foreseeability' test

In applying the *Wagon Mound* the courts have chosen not to restrict the defendant's liability to the degree indicated by the reasoning of Viscount Simonds. Rather 'reasonable foreseeability' has been loosely adhered to, so that the results produced differ little from those that would have been reached under *Re Polemis*. This represents a policy view that fairness to the defendant does not dictate quite such a rigid cutting off point as that favoured by Viscount Simonds. Five features of this loose case-law application of the *Wagon Mound* merit particular consideration.

(i) So long as the type of physical damage which has resulted was reasonably foreseeable at the time of the negligence, neither the actual manner in which it came about nor its actual extent needs to have been reasonably foreseeable.[22] *Hughes v Lord Advocate*[23] is the classic illustration. Post Office workmen left an open manhole, in which they had been working, covered by a shelter tent and surrounded by warning paraffin lamps. The claimant, aged eight, was playing with one of the lamps when he stumbled over it and knocked it into the hole. An explosion followed and the claimant was thrown into the manhole and was severely burned. The defendants were held liable because, while it was not reasonably foreseeable that a child would be burned as a result of the actual sequence of events that had occurred, it was reasonably foreseeable that a child could be burned by playing with one of the gas-lamps. Nor did it matter that the burns were more serious than those that were reasonably foreseeable. Similarly in *Vacwell Engineering Co Ltd v BDH Chemicals Ltd*,[24] the defendants supplied a chemical and carelessly failed to attach a warning that it was liable to explode in water. A scientist working for the claimants placed a consignment in a sink and a violent explosion ensued causing extensive damage. The defendants were held liable because a minor explosion causing some property damage was reasonably foreseeable, and it did not matter that the magnitude of the explosion and the actual extent of the damage could not reasonably have been foreseen. Again in *Jolley v Sutton London BC*[25] a 13-year-old boy was severely injured when a boat, which had been left on the defendant council's land, collapsed on him while he was under it. The type of accident and injury (personal injury from meddling with the boat)[26] were reasonably foreseeable. It did not matter, applying *Hughes v Lord Advocate*, that the precise manner in which the injury came about (the boy with a friend had jacked the boat up to 'work' on it and it fell off the jack) or its extent (the boy was rendered paraplegic) may not have been reasonably foreseeable.

---

[21] [1961] AC 388, at 424.
[22] *Doughty v Turner Manufacturing Co Ltd* [1964] 1 QB 518 is difficult to reconcile with this principle, as is acknowledged in *A-G of the British Virgin Islands v Hartwell* [2004] UKPC 12, [2004] 1 WLR 1273, at [29].
[23] [1963] AC 837.   [24] [1971] 1 QB 88.
[25] [2000] 1 WLR 1082. See also *Hadlow v Peterborough CC* [2011] EWCA Civ 1329.
[26] 'Meddling with the boat' was emphasised by Lord Hoffmann as being the relevant type of accident. In contrast, Lord Steyn went so far as to accept the trial judge's finding that the precise accident—the collapse of the propped-up boat—was reasonably foreseeable.

Goff LJ's judgment in the negligence case of *Muirhead v Industrial Tank Specialities Ltd*[27] contains an excellent passage stressing the need for only the type of physical damage to be reasonably foreseeable:

> '... the true question to which the judge should have addressed his mind was simply whether damage of the relevant *type* was reasonably foreseeable by the manufacturers, ie physical harm to fish stored in a tank at a fish farm ... If he had found that damage of that type was reasonably foreseeable, then the fact that, by reason of the full stocking of the relevant tank, the fish died more quickly or in greater quantity was of no relevance, unless it could be said that overstocking of the tank constituted the sole or contributory cause of the disaster which took place.'[28]

Applying this, the manufacturers of defective circulation pumps were held liable for the loss of the claimant's entire stock of lobsters.

(ii) The notion that it is the type of physical damage that needs to be reasonably foreseeable allows the courts considerable discretion in how wide to extend the defendant's liability, for opinions can differ as to how to divide up types of damage. Two cases can be usefully contrasted. In *Bradford v Robinson Rentals Ltd*[29] the defendant employers exposed the claimant van driver to extreme cold in the course of his duties and in consequence he suffered frostbite. It was held that a common cold, pneumonia or chilblains were reasonably foreseeable and since frostbite was of the same type of harm as these the defendants were liable. On the other hand, in *Tremain v Pike*,[30] the rat population on the defendants' farm was allowed to become unduly large and the claimant, a herdsman on the farm, contracted a rare disease, Weil's disease, through coming into contact with rat's urine. Payne J held that the defendants were not liable, for while the effects of a rat bite or food poisoning from contaminated food were reasonably foreseeable, Weil's disease was not and was 'entirely different in kind'[31] from such consequences.

(iii) The 'thin skull' principle, that the defendant takes the victim in the physical condition that he or she is already in, survives. A good example of it is *Smith v Leech Brain & Co Ltd*[32] in which a negligently inflicted burn on the claimant's husband's lip resulted in his dying of cancer because he was suffering from pre-malignant cancer and this was caused to develop by the burn. The defendants were held liable for his death. Lord Parker CJ's reasoning suggests that the thin-skull principle is merely an aspect of the principle looked at above: that so long as the type of damage which has resulted was reasonably foreseeable, its actual extent need not have been; but it is probably preferable, so as to avoid deciding whether the type of damage is the same as that which could have been reasonably foreseen, to regard the thin-skull principle as separate.

(iv) The *Wagon Mound* has not affected the principle that it is no bar to recovery that the pecuniary value of property damage or the loss of earnings/dependency resulting from personal injury or death is far greater than could reasonably have been foreseen.[33] So if the defendant negligently injures a multi-millionaire or negligently damages an antique vase, it is no defence that she could not reasonably have foreseen that the loss of earnings or pecuniary value would be so great and she will be liable so long as the personal injury or property damage was reasonably foreseeable. One *can* say that this follows logically because the damage itself is foreseeable, and it is merely the quantum that is unexpectedly high.

---

[27] [1986] QB 507. See also *Ogwo v Taylor* [1988] AC 431, at 444–445.
[28] [1986] QB 507, at 532.   [29] [1967] 1 WLR 337.   [30] [1969] 1 WLR 1556.
[31] ibid, at 1561.   [32] [1962] 2 QB 405. See also *Brice v Brown* [1984] 1 All ER 997.
[33] The usually cited authority is the dictum in Scrutton LJ's dissent in *The Arpad* [1934] P 189, at 202.

But the line between damage and quantum is not an easy one to draw. Ultimately then the principle may be best seen as accepting that such loss should not be regarded as too remote, even though unforeseeable. It is not clear whether this principle extends to profits consequent on physical damage or to other pecuniary loss.[34] However, much the same result will be reached by applying the different principle—plainly relevant, as we have seen, to physical damage—that the precise extent, and manner in which it has occurred, of the pecuniary loss consequent on physical damage is not too remote provided that the type of pecuniary loss was reasonably foreseeable.[35]

(v) What degree of likelihood of the loss occurring is required under the *Wagon Mound* test? This has rarely been discussed in the tort cases themselves. The main exception was *The Wagon Mound (No 2)*,[36] which arose out of the same fire that produced *The Wagon Mound*. In this case, however, the claimants were the owners of the damaged ship rather than the wharf owners, and they sued in nuisance and negligence. Somewhat different evidence was presented than in the first case and the Privy Council decided that the damage to the ship by the fire was not too remote, since it was reasonably foreseeable. One can distinguish the two *Wagon Mound* decisions because of the different facts found, but it does appear from the use of phrases like 'real risk' that in the second case, in contrast to the first, the Privy Council considered that only a low degree of likelihood of the loss occurring need be reasonably foreseeable in order for the loss to be recoverable. Thus Smith has written that *The Wagon Mound (No 2)*, 'makes a substantial change in *The Wagon Mound* rule in that it limits … the test of foreseeability of damage to possibility rather than to probability'.[37] Furthermore the House of Lords in *The Heron II*[38] (a contract case), in contrasting the contract and tort remoteness tests, emphasised that the tort test requires only a low degree of likelihood of the loss to be reasonably foreseeable. Similarly, in *H Parsons Ltd v Uttley & Co Ltd*[39] (a contract case) Lord Denning MR said that the *Wagon Mound* test was reasonable foreseeability at the time of the breach of the type of loss occurring *as a slight possibility*.

(c) Is 'reasonable foreseeability' the test for remoteness for all torts?

The *Wagon Mound* test was applied to the tort of nuisance in *The Wagon Mound (No 2)*. It was also applied by the House of Lords to liability under *Rylands v Fletcher*[40] in *Cambridge Water Co v Eastern Counties Leather plc*.[41] These cases strongly suggest that the *Wagon Mound* test is the appropriate remoteness test for all unintentional torts even though the liability is strict (as under *Rylands v Fletcher* and, arguably, nuisance) in the sense that the defendant may be held liable despite the fact that it has taken all reasonable care to avoid harm to others.[42]

---

[34] But see *The Liesbosch* [1933] AC 449, at 463–464; *The Argentino* (1889) 14 App Cas 519, at 523.
[35] For support for this principle being applicable to pecuniary loss consequent on physical damage, see *Network Rail Infrastructure Ltd v Conarken Group Ltd* [2011] EWCA Civ 644, [2012] 1 All ER (Comm) 692 (pecuniary loss—albeit that its precise manner of occurrence could not have been reasonably foreseen—was held to be not too remote because the type of loss, loss of revenue, consequent on damage to the claimant's railtracks, was reasonably foreseeable).
[36] *Overseas Tankship, (UK) v Miller SS Co Pty Ltd (The Wagon Mound No 2)* [1967] 1 AC 617.
[37] J Smith, 'The Limits of Tort Liability in Canada: Remoteness, Foreseeability and Proximate Cause' in *Studies in Canadian Tort Law* (ed A Linden, Butterworths 1968) 102.
[38] *Koufos v Czarnikow Ltd, The Heron II* [1969] 1 AC 350.   [39] [1978] QB 791.
[40] (1868) LR 3 HL 330.   [41] [1994] 2 AC 264.
[42] This is also supported by E Peel and J Goudkamp, *Winfield & Jolowicz on Tort* (19th edn, Sweet & Maxwell 2014) paras 16.035, 17.026–17.027; and *Clerk & Lindsell on Torts* (22nd edn, Sweet & Maxwell 2018) paras 2-145–2-146.

However, as far as the tort of deceit is concerned, the Court of Appeal in *Doyle v Olby (Ironmongers) Ltd*[43] considered that reasonable foreseeability was too restrictive a test. Lord Denning said: 'the defendant is bound to make reparation for all the actual damages directly flowing from the fraudulent inducement ... All such damages can be recovered: and it does not lie in the mouth of the fraudulent person to say that they could not reasonably have been foreseen.'[44] This was confirmed as the correct approach by the House of Lords in *Smith New Court Securities Ltd v Scrimgeour Vickers (Asset Management) Ltd*.[45] It can be regarded as the survival of the *Polemis* test for the tort of deceit. Indeed one can strongly argue that the same should apply to other dishonestly committed, or intentional, torts on the ground that there is less justification for showing leniency and limiting compensatory damages where the defendant committed the tort dishonestly or intentionally (in the sense that the consequences were intended).[46] This is supported by obiter dicta of Lord Nicholls, giving the leading speech, in *Kuwait Airways Corpn v Iraqi Airways Co (Nos 4 & 5)*:[47] his Lordship thought that, although the tort of conversion is a strict liability tort, the *Doyle v Olby* 'direct' test of remoteness should be applied if the conversion was committed dishonestly. Otherwise the *Wagon Mound* test of reasonable foreseeability should be applied to the tort of conversion.[48] Lord Nicholls said, 'I can see no good reason why the remoteness test of "directly and naturally" applied in cases of deceit should not apply in cases of conversion where the defendant acted dishonestly.'[49]

Unfortunately the remoteness test laid down in *Doyle v Olby* was applied by the Court of Appeal in *Royscot Trust Ltd v Rogerson*[50] to a claim for negligent misrepresentation brought under the Misrepresentation Act 1967, s 2(1). This was on the ground that the 'fiction of fraud' wording used in the subsection left the court with no alternative but to apply the same test of remoteness as for deceit. This is a most unsatisfactory approach for it cannot be sensible to apply a different remoteness test under the Act than to the closely analogous common law tort of negligent misrepresentation. And the rejection of the *Wagon Mound* only seems justifiable where, as in deceit, there is a high degree of blameworthiness attached to the tortfeasor. Moreover the words in s 2(1) do not need to be read as dictating that the rules applicable to assessing damages for deceit apply in exactly the same way in every respect to claims under s 2(1).[51]

In a controversial decision in *Essa v Laing Ltd*[52] the majority of the Court of Appeal (Pill and Clarke LJJ, Rix LJ dissenting) held that it was sufficient in an action for the statutory tort of racial discrimination that the psychiatric illness suffered by the claimant was a direct consequence of the defendant's offensive racist remark even if a psychiatric illness was not a reasonably foreseeable consequence of that remark. Yet the majority did not think it necessary to consider the intentions of the defendant in making that remark. This, it is submitted, is to extend the realm of the exceptional 'directness' test too far. The analogy with

---

[43] [1969] 2 QB 158.   [44] ibid, at 167.   [45] [1997] AC 254.

[46] For an excellent clarification that intentional (as distinct from deliberate) conduct in tort refers to consequences, see P Cane, *The Anatomy of Tort Law* (Hart Publishing 1997) 32–33.

[47] [2002] UKHL 19, [2002] 2 AC 883.

[48] See *Saleslease Ltd v Davis* [1999] 1 WLR 1664: discussed below, pp 250–251. See also *Sandeman Coprimar SA v Transitos y Transportes Integrates SL* [2003] EWCA Civ 113, [2003] QB 1270, where the claimant's loss (from having to pay guarantees to the Spanish tax authorities when paper tax seals for bottles were lost) was held too remote in the torts of negligence and conversion.

[49] [2002] UKHL 19, [2002] 2 AC 883, at [104].

[50] [1991] 2 QB 297. It was left open by the House of Lords in *Smith New Court* whether *Royscot* was correctly decided on this point: [1997] AC 254, at 267, 283.

[51] For an historical argument to the contrary, written before the *Royscot* case, see J Cartwright, 'Damages for Misrepresentation' [1987] Conv 423.

[52] [2004] EWCA Civ 2, [2004] ICR 746.

dishonestly committed torts required that the defendant must have intended (or possibly been reckless as to) the consequences of his remark. But it should have been insufficient to trigger the wider remoteness test that the defendant deliberately made the remark. The majority went on to indicate—and, with respect, this is again controversial—that injury to feelings and psychiatric illness were the same type of harm for the purposes of the remoteness test so that, even applying a reasonable foreseeability test, the psychiatric illness in question was not too remote given that injury to feelings was clearly reasonably foreseeable.

Essa v Laing was relied on by the Court of Appeal in *Jones v Ruth*[53] in applying a similar approach to the statutory tort of harassment under the Protection from Harassment Act 1997. While stressing that harassment depends on deliberate conduct, there was again no examination of whether the injury in question (here psychiatric illness) was intended. Rather it was held that, once harassment had occurred, the defendant was liable for the consequences that flowed from that conduct irrespective of foreseeability.

(d) A stricter test where there is concurrent contractual liability

After many years of academic debate, and some indication of this in the cases, it was finally decided in *Wellesley Partners LLP v Withers LLP*[54] that, in a case of concurrent liability, at least for negligently caused pure economic loss, the stricter so-called 'contract' remoteness test applies even to the tort claim. As a matter of policy this must be correct. This is discussed and explained further below once we have examined the contract remoteness test.

(2) Breach of contract[55]

(a) The traditional test for remoteness in contract

The traditional contract remoteness test has been dealt with in three leading cases. The first, and probably the most famous case in English contract law, was *Hadley v Baxendale*.[56] The claimant's mill was brought to a standstill by a broken crank-shaft. The claimant engaged the defendant carrier to take it to Greenwich as a pattern for a new one, but in breach of contract the defendant delayed delivery. The claimant sought damages for loss of profit arising from the fact that the mill was stopped for longer than it would have been if there had been no delay. All the carrier knew was 'that the article to be carried was the broken shaft of a mill and that the plaintiffs were millers of that mill'.[57] The court held that the loss of profit was too remote and that therefore the carriers were not liable for it.

The test for remoteness was laid down in two rules by Alderson B. He said:

'Where two parties have made a contract which one of them has broken, the damages which the other party ought to receive in respect of such breach of contract, should be such as may fairly and reasonably be considered, either arising naturally, ie according to the usual course of things from such breach of contract itself, or such as may reasonably be supposed to have been in the contemplation of both parties, at the time they made the contract as the probable result of the breach of it.'[58]

---

[53] [2011] EWCA Civ 804, [2012] 1 All ER 490.   [54] [2015] EWCA Civ 1146, [2016] Ch 529.
[55] For an excellent discussion, see H Beale, *Remedies for Breach of Contract* (Sweet & Maxwell 1980) 179–187. For a comparative account, see G Treitel, *Remedies for Breach of Contract* (Clarendon Press 1988) 150–162.
[56] (1854) 9 Exch 341. R Danzig, '*Hadley v Baxendale*: A Study in the Industrialisation of the Law' (1975) 4 J Legal Studies 249.
[57] (1854) 9 Exch 341, at 355.   [58] ibid, at 354.

On the facts neither of these two rules was satisfied; the loss was not the natural consequence because it was felt that in the great multitude of cases the absence of a shaft would not cause a stoppage at a mill as usually a mill-owner would have another shaft in reserve or be able to get one; nor was the loss in the contemplation of both parties because the special circumstance that the mill could not restart until the shaft came back was not known to the defendant.

In the second case of the trio, *Victoria Laundry (Windsor) Ltd v Newman Industries Ltd*,[59] the claimants, launderers and dyers, decided to extend their business and contracted to buy a boiler from the defendants. The defendants knew that the claimants wanted the boiler for immediate use in their business, but in breach of contract delivered the boiler five months late. The claimants sought damages for the loss of profits that would have resulted from using the boiler, including damages for the exceptional loss of profits that they would have been able to gain from contracts made with the Ministry of Supply. The Court of Appeal held, applying *Hadley v Baxendale*, that damages should be awarded for ordinary loss of profits but not for the exceptional loss of profits. The exceptional profits were too remote because they did not arise naturally and were not in the contemplation of the parties at the time of contracting since the defendants knew nothing about the Ministry of Supply contracts.

Asquith LJ, giving the Court of Appeal's judgment, correctly reasoned that the two rules of *Hadley v Baxendale* could be regarded as comprising a single rule, centring on reasonable contemplation or, as he preferred, reasonable foreseeability. If in applying the second rule one includes as important what the defendant should have reasonably contemplated or foreseen if he had thought about the breach at the time of contracting, then it can swallow up the first rule; for something arising naturally is something that should have been reasonably contemplated by the defendant if he had thought about the breach.

Since *Victoria Laundry*, while the courts have sometimes continued to talk of two rules of remoteness, they have tended, like Asquith LJ, to think in terms of one rather than two rules.[60] Indeed Lord Reid in *Heron II* (which we shall examine below) specifically said, 'I do not think that it was intended that there were to be two rules or that two different standards or tests were to be applied.'[61] And in *The Pegase*[62] Robert Goff J said:

> '*Hadley v Baxendale* is now no longer stated in terms of two rules, but rather in terms of a single principle—though it is recognised that the application of the principle may depend on the degree of relevant knowledge held by the defendant at the time of the contract in a particular case. This approach accords to what actually happens in practice; the courts have not been over-ready to pigeon-hole the cases under one or other of the so-called rules in *Hadley v Baxendale*, but rather to decide each case on the basis of the relevant knowledge of the defendant.'

It is hard to see that anything of substance should turn on whether one formulates the test in two rules or one; and some of the leading contract texts do provide illustrations of the two rules taken separately.[63] In particular, where one is talking about special circumstances that must have been communicated to the defendant in order for particular loss to be non-remote, it can be convenient to say that one is talking about the second rule in *Hadley v Baxendale*.

---

[59] [1949] 2 KB 528.
[60] See, eg, Lord Denning in *Robophone Facilities Ltd v Blank* [1966] 1 WLR 1428; *Parsons v Uttley Ingham* [1978] QB 791.
[61] [1969] 1 AC 350, at 385.   [62] [1981] 1 Lloyd's Rep 175, at 182.
[63] Eg E McKendrick, *Contract Law* (12th edn, Palgrave 2017) para 21.11.

But what is incorrect is to treat the two rules as providing mutually exclusive, rather than overlapping, tests. This is not least because what occurs naturally will almost always be within the contemplation of the parties. Yet some courts have approached the rules as if they were mutually exclusive so that the first gives the remoteness test for 'general damages' and the second gives the remoteness test for 'special damages'.[64] This requires one to embark initially on an unnecessary, unhelpful and largely circular categorisation of loss as being either general or special. In truth, one shades into the other.

Perhaps the best clarification of this in the case law was provided by the Court of Appeal in *Kpohraror v Woolwich Building Society*.[65] The case was concerned with what damages were recoverable for the wrongful dishonour of a cheque where the defendant bank's error had been corrected, and the claimant informed that the cheque would be honoured, later the same day. The claimant sought compensation for the damage to his credit and reputation and for the trading loss caused by being unable, as a consequence of the breach, to pay for and hence resell a particular shipment of goods. The Court of Appeal upheld the master's judgment awarding £5,500 for the injury to the claimant's credit and reputation but refusing damages for the particular trading loss. The reasoning was that there was no 'traders only' rule denying the claimant damages for the injury to his credit and reputation and that loss was not too remote. In contrast, the specific trading loss was too remote because the defendant bank had not been informed, and did not know, that a short delay in payment would cause the loss of a transaction. In particular, the bank had not been given notice of the need for immediate clearance.

The important point for us here is that in respect of remoteness the case had been argued by making a rigid distinction between the general damage to the claimant's credit and reputation which was presented as being entirely a matter for the first rule in *Hadley v Baxendale*; and the specific trading loss which had been presented as being entirely a matter for the second rule in *Hadley v Baxendale*. As the Court of Appeal clarified, the correct approach should have been to apply both rules to both types of loss. Evans LJ, with whom Waite LJ and Sir John May agreed, said:

'The contentions for both parties were presented as if in a straitjacket imposed by the strict application of the rule in *Hadley v Baxendale* so as to require the separate consideration of each of the two limbs ... I would prefer that the starting point for any application of *Hadley v Baxendale* is the extent of the shared knowledge of both parties when the contract was made (... including the possibility that knowledge of the defendant alone is enough). When that is established, it

---

[64] See, eg, *Monarch SS Company v A/B Karlshamns Oljefabriker* [1949] AC 196, at 221 (per Lord Wright); *President of India v La Pintada Compania Navigacion SA* [1985] AC 104. A rigid distinction has also been drawn between the two rules in *Hadley v Baxendale* for the rather different purpose of construing 'indirect or consequential loss' in exclusion clauses: *Croudace Construction Ltd v Cawoods Concrete Products Ltd* [1978] 2 Lloyd's Rep 55; *British Sugar plc v Projects Ltd* (1997) 87 BLR 42; *Deepak Fertilisers & Petrochemicals Ltd v Davy McKee (London) Ltd* [1999] 1 All ER (Comm) 69; *BHP Petroleum Ltd v British Steel plc* [1999] 2 All ER (Comm) 544; *Hotel Services Ltd v Hilton International Hotels (UK) Ltd* [2000] 1 All ER (Comm) 750; *Watford Electronics Ltd v Sanderson CFL Ltd* [2001] 1 All ER (Comm) 696. Cf *Caledonia North Sea Ltd v British Telecommunications Plc* [2002] UKHL 4, [2002] 1 Lloyd's Rep 553, at [99]–[100] (per Lord Hoffmann). Construing exclusion clauses is, of course, a different matter from deciding when losses are, and are not, too remote and one should not reason back from these cases to say that, for the purposes of remoteness, there is a sharp line between the two rules in *Hadley v Baxendale*. As Sedley LJ said in *Hotel Services Ltd v Hilton International Hotels (UK) Ltd* [2000] 1 All ER (Comm) 750, at 755, having referred to the rules in *Hadley v Baxendale*: 'This is not a dichotomous but a continuous classification, bringing into the region of recoverability all loss which the parties must in the nature of things or for known reasons have anticipated. It is the framing of exclusion clauses which has made it necessary to divide up its elements ...'

[65] [1996] 4 All ER 119. See also *International Mineral and Chemical Corpn v Carl O'Helm AG* [1986] 1 Lloyd's Rep 81 (per Hobhouse J).

may often be the case that the first and the second parts of the rule overlap, or at least that it is unnecessary to draw a clear line of demarcation between them.'[66]

Returning to our trio of leading cases, we come finally to *Heron II*[67] in which the House of Lords was concerned with the degree of likelihood of the loss occurring that needs to be in the reasonable contemplation of the defendant in order for the loss to be non-remote. The claim was being brought by charterers of a ship against the defendant shipowner for delivering sugar at Basrah, nine days late. During those nine days, 8,000 tons of sugar had arrived at Basrah with the result that the market price for sugar at Basrah had fallen. The shipowner had not known that the charterer intended to sell the sugar as soon as it reached Basrah but had known that there was a market for sugar at Basrah. The House of Lords held that, applying *Hadley v Baxendale*, as refined by *Victoria Laundry*, the loss of profit from the fall in the market was not too remote and was recoverable. The argument that the remoteness test for carriage of goods by sea was more restricted than that of *Hadley v Baxendale* was rejected. The Law Lords agreed that a higher degree of likelihood of the loss occurring was required in contract than under the tort remoteness test of reasonable forseeability laid down in the *Wagon Mound*[68] so that losses may be too remote in contract that would not be too remote in tort. Unfortunately, there was no clear consensus as to how the degree of likelihood required in contract should be expressed. However, perhaps the clearest way of expressing the essence of their Lordships' reasoning[69] is that, while a slight possibility of the loss occurring is required in tort, a serious possibility of the loss occurring is required in contract. So, on the facts, the loss of profit from the market fall was not too remote because the defendant should have reasonably contemplated that loss as a serious possibility had it thought about the breach at the time the contract was made.

(b) Type of loss or damage

We have seen that in applying the *Wagon Mound* reasonable foreseeability test it is the type of loss not the actual loss that one is focusing on. Is that also the case in applying the traditional contract remoteness test? This was the main issue in *Parsons v Uttley Ingham & Co Ltd*[70] in which it was held that the supplier of a defective pig hopper was liable in contract for the loss of 254 pigs that had died from a rare intestinal disease after eating nuts that had gone mouldy in the hopper. The Court of Appeal decided unanimously that the loss of the pigs was not too remote but the judges found this difficult to reconcile with the traditional *Hadley v Baxendale* approach and there was a sharp distinction between the reasoning of Lord Denning, on the one hand, and Scarman and Orr LJJ on the other. Lord Denning took the novel view which, at least overtly, has not enjoyed any subsequent judicial support, that there were different remoteness tests in contract depending on whether the loss in question was a loss of profit or physical damage.[71] More significant, as the law has subsequently developed, was the judgment of the majority, Scarman and Orr LJJ. They disagreed with Lord Denning's reasoning because they did not think that his distinction between the remoteness test for loss of profit and for physical damage was supported by the authorities. Rather, they

---

[66] [1996] 4 All ER 119, at 127–128.   [67] [1969] 1 AC 350.   [68] [1961] AC 388.
[69] This fits in with Lord Denning's interpretation in *Parsons v Uttley Ingham* [1978] QB 791.
[70] ibid.
[71] Lord Denning drew his analysis from HLA Hart and T Honoré, *Causation in the Law* (1st edn, Clarendon Press 1959) 281–287. It seems safe to assume—particularly given his express reliance on the distinction drawn in the tort of negligence between pure economic loss and other economic loss—that Lord Denning's reference to loss of profit is to 'pure' loss of profit (as was in issue in *Hadley v Baxendale*, *Victoria Laundry*, and *Heron II*) and not to loss of profit consequent on personal injury or damage to one's property.

considered that *Heron II* provides the single test for remoteness in contract but stressed that, in applying it, it is the type and not extent of loss that must be reasonably contemplated as a serious possibility at the time of contracting. Scarman LJ said:

> 'It does not matter … if they thought that the chance of physical injury, loss of profit, loss of market, or other loss as the case may be, was slight or that the odds were against it, provided they contemplated as a serious possibility the type of consequence, not necessarily the specific consequence, that ensued on breach.'[72]

Applying that test to the facts, as it was reasonably contemplated by the parties at the time of the contract that, by reason of the failure to provide a hopper fit for storing pig food, there was a serious possibility that the pigs would become ill, and since illness could be said to be the same type of loss as death, it did not matter that the extent of that illness (that is the death of many pigs) was not reasonably contemplated as a serious possibility. The death of the 254 pigs was therefore not too remote.

This decision, and the reasoning of all three judges, pushed the contract and tort remoteness tests closer together. Indeed the majority judges indicated that, where a claim may be brought in contract or tort, it would be desirable if one equated the remoteness tests in contract and tort. Hence Scarman LJ said:

> '… the law must be such that in a factual situation where all have the same actual or imputed knowledge … the amount of damages recoverable does not depend on whether, as a matter of legal classification, the plaintiff's cause of action is breach of contract or tort. It may be that the necessary reconciliation is to be found, notwithstanding the strictures of Lord Reid in *Heron II*, in holding that the difference between "reasonable foreseeability" (the test in tort) and "reasonably contemplated" (the test in contract) is semantic not substantial. Certainly Asquith LJ in *Victoria Laundry v Newman Industries* and Lord Pearce in *Heron II* thought so; and I confess I think so too.'[73]

However, the difference between the *Heron II* and the *Wagon Mound* tests is not to do with the terms foreseeable or contemplation; ie we can agree that the difference in these terms is semantic and not substantial. Even accepting that it is the type of loss or damage that one is focusing on, the *Heron II* test still differs significantly from the *Wagon Mound* as to the degree of likelihood of loss required—the *Heron II* test requiring a higher degree—and as to the time at which the contemplation or foreseeability is judged, being at the time the contract is made under the *Heron II* and at the time of the breach of duty under the *Wagon Mound*.[74] It is submitted therefore that this possible 'reconciliation' between the tort and contract tests was nothing of the kind.

It is also noteworthy that Scarman LJ's approach differed from Lord Denning's in that in applying his test to the facts, he regarded the breach not as that of supplying a hopper with inadequate ventilation but rather that of supplying a hopper unfit for the purpose of storing pig food. So that instead of asking, 'was it reasonably contemplated at the time

---

[72] [1978] QB 791, at 813. This might be said to derive some support from Megarry J's earlier holding in *Wroth v Tyler* [1974] Ch 30 that the extraordinary and uncontemplated rise in the market price of houses was not too remote because the type of loss—a difference between the market and contract prices—had been contemplated. But it can be argued that the case is better regarded as turning on the fact that the claimants were 'consumers', who wanted the house to live in, rather than businessmen. As such their loss was most accurately described as the loss of a home of a certain standard rather than a loss of profit. Viewed in this way, the loss was clearly contemplated, and remoteness and the type/extent distinction were not in issue.

[73] [1978] QB 791, at 807.

[74] This 'timing' difference was stressed in *Jackson v Royal Bank of Scotland plc* [2005] UKHL 3, [2005] 1 WLR 377, at [36].

of contracting as a serious possibility that supplying a hopper with inadequate ventilation would make the pigs ill?' to which the answer was clearly 'no', Scarman LJ asked, 'was it reasonably contemplated at the time of contracting as a serious possibility that supplying a hopper unfit for the purpose of storing pig food would make the pigs ill?' to which he was able to answer 'yes'. In other words, Scarman LJ's approach shows that, by defining the breach more generally, the loss is less likely to be judged too remote.

Very importantly, the Court of Appeal has subsequently approved and applied the approach of the majority in *Parsons*. In *Brown v KMR Services Ltd*,[75] one of the questions, in claims by Lloyd's names against their members' agents for breach of contract (and the tort of negligence), was whether the loss was too remote. The defendants' argument was that the magnitude of the financial disasters that had struck, and the consequent scale of the loss, was unforeseeable and uncontemplatable. The Court of Appeal held that the loss was not too remote because it was the type and not the extent of the loss that needed to be foreseen or contemplated and here there was one relevant type of loss which was clearly foreseeable. Hobhouse LJ, with whom Peter Gibson LJ agreed, said that the only type of loss in question was that suffered by being a member of a high-risk syndicate. Stuart-Smith LJ similarly regarded there as being only one type of loss in issue although he described that as underwriting loss. The majority's view in *Parsons v Uttley Ingham* was cited with approval.

The importance of the *Brown* case was that it put beyond doubt that the traditional remoteness test in contract, as in tort, focuses on the type of loss in question and not the specific loss that occurred. The difficult issue is now not whether the emphasis on the type of loss is correct but how types of loss should be divided up. If, as the *Parsons* and the *Brown* cases indicate, the courts are taking a broad view of types of loss, it may well be that the distinction drawn in the *Victoria Laundry* case, between recoverable loss of ordinary profits and irrecoverable loss of exceptional profits, can no longer stand: for one could argue that the type of loss in issue there was loss of profits and that the exceptional profits were merely a greater extent of that same type of loss. However, the *Victoria Laundry* case was distinguished in the *Brown* case. Stuart-Smith LJ said:

> 'I accept that difficulty in practice may arise in categorisation of loss into types or kinds, especially where financial loss is involved. But I do not see any difficulty in holding that loss of ordinary business profits is different in kind from that flowing from a particular contract which gives rise to very high profits, the existence of which is unknown to the other contracting party who therefore does not accept the risk of such loss occurring.'[76]

This suggests that, at least in some cases, the courts regard it as acceptable to divide up types of pure economic loss in a more precise way than they divide up types of physical damage (although even in relation to personal injury, we have seen in the context of the tort remoteness test, that there has been some inconsistency in the cases in dividing up types of damage).[77]

---

[75] [1995] 4 All ER 598. For contract cases on remoteness since *Parsons*, which failed to clarify the issues raised by that decision, see, eg, *Rumsey v Owen, White and Catlin* (1978) 245 Estates Gazette 225; *The Pegase* [1981] 1 Lloyd's Rep 175; *Kemp v Intasun Holidays Ltd* [1987] 2 FTLR 234; *Seven Seas Properties Ltd v Al-Essa (No 2)* [1993] 3 All ER 577. Cf *The Borag* [1981] 1 All ER 856 (in which Lord Denning relied on his own judgment in *Parsons*); *The Rio Claro* [1987] 2 Lloyd's Rep 173 (in reliance on *Parsons*, the type of loss was stressed, albeit that the loss was held too remote); *The Forum Craftsman* [1991] 1 Lloyd's Rep 81 (in which an argument that the loss was not too remote, based on the 'type' emphasis in *Parsons*, was rejected). See also the very interesting Scottish case of *Balfour Beatty Construction (Scotland) Ltd v Scottish Power Plc* 1994 SLT 807 in which it was explicitly left open whether *Parsons* was correctly decided. For discussion of that case, see H MacQueen, 'Remoteness and Breach of Contract' [1996] Jur Rev 295; A Burrows, *Understanding the Law of Obligations* (Hart Publishing 1998) 160–163.

[76] [1995] 4 All ER 598, at 621.   [77] See above, p 88.

This discretion and flexibility, in dividing up 'types' of loss or damage, may be thought desirable: but it plainly comes at the expense of certainty.

(c) The principle in Cory v Thames Ironworks Co

Where the claimant's actual loss of profit is too remote, and hence irrecoverable, it is still entitled to recover a lesser sum measured by the loss of profit that would have been non-remote. The leading authority on this often overlooked principle is *Cory v Thames Ironworks Co*[78] in which the defendants were in breach of contract in failing to deliver the hull of a boat on time. The claimants, who were coal merchants, intended to use the hull in a novel way unknown to the defendants. The defendants assumed that the claimants intended to use the hull for the usual purpose of storing coal. It was held that, while the loss of profit flowing from the special use was too remote, the lesser profit that would have been lost from applying the hull for usual purposes was recoverable. That was so even though the claimants had suffered no such loss in the sense that they would not have used the hull for storage.[79] Cockburn J said:

> 'The buyer has lost the larger amount, and there can be no hardship or injustice in making the seller liable to compensate him in damages so far as the seller understood and believed that the article would be applied to the ordinary purposes to which it was capable of being applied.'[80]

This must be correct. To overcome the objection that the claimant recovers for a loss that it has not suffered, the principle is best rationalised by saying that the claimant recovers that part of its actual loss of special profit that is *equivalent* to the ordinary profit that would have been lost.

(d) Disproportionate loss compared to the contractual consideration: the US approach

An argument can be made that the contract test is too harsh on defendants in that it does not directly take into account the amount of the contractual consideration to be received by the defendant. In other words, the fact that the claimant's losses are out of all proportion to what the defendant was to receive under the contract is an irrelevant factor in judging remoteness. For example, in *Hadley v Baxendale* itself, the fact that the claimant's loss of profits from delay was out of all proportion to the price to be paid to the defendant for carrying the mill-shaft was irrelevant. In the US this point has led commentators and courts frequently to suggest that the *Hadley v Baxendale* test does not restrict liability enough.[81] In accordance with this, the Second Restatement of Contracts, s 351(3) states: 'A court may limit damages for foreseeable loss … if it concludes that in the circumstances justice so requires in order to avoid disproportionate compensation'; and by comment (f) 'disproportionate' means 'an extreme disproportion between the loss … and the price charged by the party whose liability for that loss is in question'.[82]

---

[78] (1868) LR 3 QB 181.
[79] *Victoria Laundry (Windsor) Ltd v Newman Industries Ltd* [1949] 2 KB 528, above, p 92, was significantly different in that the claimants had suffered a loss of both ordinary and exceptional profits.
[80] (1868) LR 3 QB 181, at 190.
[81] Eg *Lamkins v International Harvester Co* 182 SW 2d 203 (1944); A Farnsworth, 'Legal Remedies for Breach of Contract' (1970) 70 Col LR 1145, 1209.
[82] See M Kniffin, 'A Newly Identified Contract Unconscionability: Unconscionability of Remedy' (1988) 63 Notre Dame LR 247; see also above, p 41 n 23.

It is strongly arguable that the traditional English approach is to be preferred. Once the defendant has been given notice of unusual potential losses, the defendant can act accordingly, whether by refusing to contract, or by raising the price, or by reducing the probability of breach, or by excluding liability. Given such a choice, it seems perfectly fair and not unduly harsh to hold the defendant responsible for reasonably contemplated losses flowing from what, after all, was the defendant's breach of contract. In any event, an approach like that advocated in the Second Restatement inevitably creates uncertainty. However, as we shall now see, the disproportionality of the loss may have crept in to English law as one factor in applying the qualification required by *The Achilleas*.[83]

(e) The qualification of the traditional contract test required by The Achilleas

The law on contractual remoteness that has so far been set out (as derived from *Hadley v Baxendale*, *Victoria Laundry*, and *Heron II* and with *Parsons* and *Brown* emphasising that it is the 'type of loss' that matters) requires qualification in the light of the decision of the House of Lords in *The Achilleas*. In short, that decision lays down that the traditional 'reasonable contemplation' contract test is the general test only and that it requires qualification in line with whether or not the defendant has 'assumed responsibility' for the loss.

(i) The rejection of a test of acceptance of liability as a term of the contract

Even prior to *The Achilleas* there had been a strand of English cases, particularly concerning carriers, in which the courts applied a different, more restrictive, test than that of *Hadley v Baxendale*. For example, in *British Columbia and Vancouvers Island Spar, Lumber and Saw-Mill Co Ltd v Nettleship*[84] it was held that a carrier would not be liable even if told of special circumstances unless the carrier agreed to accept liability for the unusual risk as a term of the contract. Willes J said:

> 'Take the case of a barrister on his way to practise at the Calcutta bar, where he may have a large number of briefs awaiting him; through the default of the Peninsular and Oriental Company he is detained in Egypt or in the Suez boat, and consequently sustains great loss: is the company to be responsible for that, because they happened to know the purpose for which the traveller was going?'[85]

The answer was considered to be 'no' applying the approach that one needs both knowledge and actual acceptance of the risk of loss as a contractual term.

Similarly in *Horne v Midland Rly Co*,[86] a carrier failed to deliver shoes on time so that the claimants lost a lucrative contract with the French army. Notice had been given that the shoes had to be delivered by the fixed date otherwise the claimants would be 'thrown on their hands'. It was held by a five–two majority that the loss of profits on the lucrative contracts was too remote. All of the judges reasoned that one needed notice plus acceptance of the liability and the minority merely differed from the majority on the application of that approach to the facts. In Kelly CB's words one needed an 'expressed or implied contract by the company to be liable to these damages'.[87] Martin B required 'something equivalent to a contract on his part to be liable to such damages';[88] and Blackburn J inclined to the view that 'in order that the notice may have any effect, it must be given under such circumstances as that an actual contract arises on the part of the defendant to bear the exceptional loss'.[89]

---

[83] *Transfield Shipping Inc v Mercator Shipping Inc, The Achilleas* [2008] UKHL 48, [2009] 1 AC 61.
[84] (1868) LR 3 CP 499. See also *Horne v Midland Rly Co* (1873) LR 8 CP 131.
[85] (1868) LR 3 CP 499, at 510.   [86] (1873) LR 8 CP 131.
[87] ibid, at 137.   [88] ibid, at 140.   [89] ibid, at 140.

However, that narrower approach in *Nettleship* and *Horne* was subsequently rejected. Although not dealing with special loss, none of their Lordships in *The Heron II* thought it necessary to go beyond determining what degree of likelihood of the loss needed to be reasonably contemplated applying *Hadley v Baxendale*. Lord Upjohn expressly denied that there was a further test that needed to be applied over and above reasonable contemplation. He said:[90]

> 'In *British Columbia Saw Mill Co. Ltd v Nettleship* it was decided on the second branch of the rule that there must not only be common knowledge of some special circumstances but liability for damages resulting therefrom must be made a term of the contract. This was followed in *Horne v Midland Railway Co*. I do not see why that should be so. If parties enter into the contract with knowledge of some special circumstances, and it is reasonable to infer a particular loss as a result of those circumstances that is something which both must contemplate as a result of a breach. It is quite unnecessary that it should be a term of the contract. I agree with the learned editor of the *Halsbury's Laws of England*, 3rd ed., Vol. II (1955), p 243, that those authorities ought not to be followed.'

The same view was taken by both Lord Denning MR and Bridge LJ in *GKN Centrax Gears Ltd v Matbro Ltd*,[91] in deciding that a manufacturer's loss of repeat orders of fork-lift trucks, consequent on their suppliers' breach of contract in supplying defective axles for those trucks, was not too remote. Each expressly rejected the view that one needed to ask a further question, over and above reasonable contemplation, as to whether the defendant had expressly or impliedly undertaken to pay damages for such loss. Lord Denning expressly said that the narrower approach in the *Nettleship* case could not survive *The Heron II*; and Bridge LJ said that that narrower approach in *Nettleship* and *Horne* had either been overruled in *The Heron II* or had been shown to add nothing.

However, it is significant in the light of *The Achilleas* that, while rejecting the need for there to be any express or implied term (of fact) to this effect, a watered-down version of acceptance of liability or assumption of risk continued to be supported in several texts even after *The Heron II* and before *The Achilleas* (see, eg, the books by Treitel;[92] McGregor;[93] and Harris, Campbell, and Halson[94]). Admittedly though, it was far from clear what precisely, if anything, this watered-down version was seen as adding to the reasonable contemplation test.

Certainly it is correct that awkward hypothetical examples remained unresolved. A classic was the taxi-driver example. This example is referred to in books and articles in various forms. Its essence is captured in the following formulation. A books a taxi for £50 with B, a taxi-driver. A explains to B when booking that it is essential for him to reach his specified destination on time as he is meeting a business client there to clinch a highly lucrative deal.

---

[90] [1969] 1 AC 350, at 422. [91] [1976] 2 Lloyd's Rep 555.

[92] E Peel, *Treitel on The Law of Contract* (12th edn, Sweet & Maxwell 2007) para 20-088 (and the same wording is in the current edition (14th edn, Sweet & Maxwell 2015) para 20-107).

[93] J Edelman, *McGregor on Damages* (20th edn, Sweet & Maxwell 2018) paras 8-206–8-207: 'However a defendant will still only be liable for damages resulting from special circumstances when those special circumstances have been brought home to him in such a way as to show that he has accepted, or is taken to have accepted, the risk. Not only must the parties contemplate that the damage resulting from the special circumstances may occur. But they must further contemplate that the defendant is taking the risk of being liable for such consequences should they occur.'

[94] D Harris, D Campbell, and R Halson, *Remedies in Contract and Tort* (2nd edn, Butterworths 2002) 97: 'The test is whether the reasonable man in D's position would have realised that, by making the promise in these special circumstances, he was *assuming responsibility* for the risk of causing this unusual type of loss.' See similarly Robert Goff J's words in *The Pegase* [1981] 1 Lloyd's Rep 175, at 184 asking whether it was 'within the reasonable contemplation of the defendant that he was assuming responsibility for the risk of such loss in the event of late delivery'.

In breach of contract, B takes the wrong route so that A arrives late at his destination. As a consequence, A loses the lucrative deal (worth an estimated £10m net profit). The unresolved question was (and is) whether A is entitled to damages of £10m from B and, if not, why not? Applying the traditional contract remoteness test it would appear that the loss is not too remote. We shall return to this after considering *The Achilleas*.

(ii) *The Achilleas*

Transfield Shipping Inc v Mercator Shipping Inc, The Achilleas[95] concerned loss consequent on a delay in returning a ship at the end of a time charter. Under the time charter, the defendant charterers should have redelivered the ship to the claimant owners by 2 May 2004. In breach of contract, they did not redeliver to the owners until 11 May. The owners had entered into a follow-on time charter under which they were bound to deliver the ship to the new charterers by 8 May. When they were unable to do so as a result of the defendants' breach, the owners renegotiated the follow-on charter and, because rates had fallen, they agreed to reduce the rate of hire on that follow-on charter from $39,500 to $31,500 a day, a loss of $8,000 a day. The defendants accepted that they were liable for damages of the difference between the market rate and the charter rate for the nine-day overrun period between 2 May and 11 May. That came to $158,301. However, the claimant owners sought damages for their full loss, namely $8,000 a day for the whole period of the follow-on fixture. That came to $1,364,584. It was held by the House of Lords, unanimously, that the claimants were limited to $158,301. The rest of the loss was too remote.

In the House of Lords, two distinct lines of reasoning were taken by, on the one hand, Lord Rodger and Baroness Hale and, on the other hand, Lord Hoffmann and Lord Hope. What makes it difficult to determine the ratio is that Lord Walker agreed with both.

Lord Rodger and Baroness Hale applied the conventional 'reasonable contemplation' test. Surprisingly, they concluded that, applying that test, the loss on the follow-on charter was too remote. It is hard to see how that could be a correct application of the conventional test. That late delivery would lead to loss on a follow-on charter was surely reasonably contemplatable and the fact that the scale of that loss, consequent on volatile market movements during the days of the overrun period, was not contemplatable should have been irrelevant. That went to the quantum of the loss not to its type. Extra-judicially, Lord Hoffmann has described applying *Hadley v Baxendale* to reach the result that the loss on the follow-on charter was too remote as involving 'an intellectual sleight of hand'.[96]

In contrast, Lord Hoffmann and Lord Hope—and Lord Hoffmann's judgment is the fuller of the two and the one we all focus on—reasoned that what was ultimately important in deciding on remoteness in contract was whether the defendant had assumed responsibility (or accepted liability) for the loss. Although the *Hadley v Baxendale* test normally provided the answer to whether there had been that assumption of responsibility, satisfaction of the 'reasonable contemplation' test was not sufficient. On these facts, the charterers had not assumed responsibility for the loss beyond the overrun period so that the loss on the follow-on charter was too remote.

Why did Lord Hoffmann (and Lord Hope) think that the charterers had not assumed responsibility for the loss even though it was a loss that was reasonably contemplated as a serious possibility in the event of late delivery?

---

[95] [2008] UKHL 48, [2009] 1 AC 61. For general discussion of the impact of the case, see, eg, P Wee, 'Contractual Interpretation and Remoteness' [2010] LMCLQ 150; M Stiggelbout, 'Contractual Remoteness, Scope of Duty and Intention' [2010] LMCLQ 97.

[96] Lord Hoffmann, '*The Achilleas*: Custom and Practice or Foreseeability?' (2010) 14 Edinburgh LR 47, 54.

We can put disproportionate liability to one side. As we have seen, this has been a concern in the USA. But neither Lord Hoffmann nor Lord Hope mentioned disproportion as being the problem in *The Achilleas*. This is understandable because, on the facts, the loss claimed was less than 25% of the cost of the charter.

In contrast, two factors (or linked series of factors) were mentioned by their Lordships and appear to have been uppermost in their minds in deciding that the charterers had not assumed responsibility.

First, the loss was 'something over which they had no control'[97] and, at the time of contracting, was 'completely unquantifiable'[98] and 'completely unpredictable'.[99] With respect, reliance on these linked factors is difficult to understand. Of course, one could not know at the time of contracting how the owner would deal with late delivery of the ship and nor could one quantify or predict market movements. But there was no suggestion that the owners' conduct was unreasonable so as to break the chain of causation or to constitute a failure in the owners' duty to mitigate; and such unpredictability or unquantifiability has often been present in past cases and has not led to the loss being too remote. So, for example, in *The Heron II* the drop in prices in the sugar market in Basrah was unpredictable and unquantifiable at the time the contract was made and was out of the control of the carriers. Yet that loss was held, by the House of Lords, to be not too remote. Similarly in *Brown v KMR Services Ltd*[100] the magnitude of the underwriting loss was unpredictable, unquantifiable and out of the control of the underwriters. Yet the loss was held to be not too remote.

Secondly, reliance was placed on the view of the law in the industry being that, in this situation, the liability was limited to the difference between the (higher) market rate and the charter rate for the overrun period. In Lord Hoffmann's words, relying on the finding of the arbitrators, 'The general understanding in the shipping market was that liability was restricted to the difference between the market rate and the charter rate for the overrun period …';[101] and later he said that one must consider 'what these parties, contracting against the background of market expectations found by the arbitrators, would reasonably have considered the extent of the liability they were undertaking … '.[102] Yet there was no previous decision that had laid down that the damages in this situation were limited to the overrun period. Surely the industry had not taken a view on what the position was where the owners' loss was much higher than that represented by the difference in value during the overrun period. Indeed one might make exactly the same argument about the decision in *The Heron II* where there was the earlier long-established decision in *The Parana*[103] that a sea-carrier's liability for delay was limited to damages for the interest on the invoice value of the cargo during the period of delay. Yet the House of Lords in *The Heron II* did not regard that understanding of the law as dictating that, on the facts of that case, the market fall was too remote. Even if there was a clear industry view about the facts in *The Achilleas*, it would seem odd for the House of Lords to have regarded what may have been a mistaken view of the law as overriding what might otherwise have been the correct solution. In this

---

[97] [2008] UKHL 48, [2009] 1 AC 61, at [34] (per Lord Hope). Lord Hoffmann at [23] pointed out that the owners under a time charterparty have the contractual right to refuse instructions if the last voyage is bound to overrun: but it is hard to see why that should affect the position on remoteness (the charterers are still in breach by late redelivery) not least in a case where there was no suggestion on the facts that there was an inevitability that the last voyage would overrun. (In the Court of Appeal [2007] 2 Lloyd's Rep 555, at [13] Rix LJ stated that it would seem that the last voyage was 'a last minute spot charter, but we are told nothing otherwise about its date or rate'.)
[98] ibid, at [23] (per Lord Hoffmann).   [99] ibid, at [34] (per Lord Hope).
[100] [1995] 4 All ER 598.   [101] [2008] UKHL 48, [2009] 1 AC 61, at [6].   [102] ibid, at [23].
[103] (1877) 2 PD 118.

respect, it is noteworthy that the majority arbitrators themselves put to one side the legal understanding in the industry precisely because, in their view, it was mistaken as to the law.

It is submitted, therefore, that even accepting that there is an additional 'assumption of responsibility' test, over and above the traditional reasonable contemplation test, the charterers had assumed responsibility for the loss claimed by the owners. With respect, Lords Hoffmann and Hope therefore reached the wrong conclusion (as, for the different reasons mentioned above, did Lord Rodger and Baroness Hale). The majority arbitrators, the first instance judge (Christopher Clarke J), and the Court of Appeal (Ward, Tuckey and Rix LJJ) were correct that the loss claimed was not too remote.

Nevertheless, the reasoning of Lord Hoffmann has had an important beneficial effect. His clear recognition of the additional 'assumption of responsibility' test has marked an important step forward in the law of remoteness in contract. What is now essential is that we properly understand that additional test. It is to that task that we now turn.

(iii) Understanding 'assumption of responsibility'

Several cases subsequent to *The Achilleas* have had to grapple with what exactly the 'assumption of responsibility' test entails. A very useful summary was put forward by Hamblen J in *Sylvia Shipping Co Ltd v Progress Bulk Carriers Ltd*.[104] He said:

> 'The orthodox approach remains the general test of remoteness applicable in the great majority of cases. However, there may be "unusual" cases, such as *The Achilleas* itself, in which the context, surrounding circumstances or general understanding in the relevant market make it necessary specifically to consider whether there has been an assumption of responsibility. This is most likely to be in those relatively rare cases where the application of the general test leads or may lead to an unquantifiable, unpredictable, uncontrollable or disproportionate liability or where there is clear evidence that such a liability would be contrary to market understanding and expectations.'

It is noteworthy that Hamblen J here included reference to disproportionate liability albeit that, as we have explained above, that concern did not actually feature in the reasoning of Lords Hoffmann or Hope.

Hamblen J's summary was dealing with the situations in which the traditional test might be cut back so as to hold a loss too remote that would otherwise be regarded, applying the traditional approach, as not too remote. That of course was the question in *The Achilleas* itself. It can usefully be referred to as the 'exclusionary effect' of the assumption of responsibility.

However, although not expressly mentioned by Lord Hoffmann, it is clear that applying the assumption of responsibility test might have the opposite effect to that in *The Achilleas* and render loss that would otherwise be too remote, not too remote. This can usefully be referred to as the 'inclusionary effect' of the assumption of responsibility. This was what was in issue in the leading case, since *The Achilleas*, of *Supershield Ltd v Siemens Building Technologies FE Ltd*.[105] In the context of deciding that a settlement reached by the parties was reasonable, Toulson LJ (with whom Richards and Mummery LJJ agreed) said that, while *Hadley v Baxendale* remains the standard rule, it can be overridden if, on examining the contract and the commercial background, the loss in question was within or outside the scope of the contractual duty. In other words, the approach in *The Achilleas* might override the standard rule by making loss that would be recoverable under *Hadley v Baxendale* too

---

[104] [2010] EWHC 542 (Comm), [2010] 2 Lloyd's Rep 81, at [40].
[105] [2010] EWCA Civ 7, [2010] 1 Lloyd's Rep 349.

remote (an 'exclusionary' effect)[106] or by making loss that would be non-recoverable under *Hadley v Baxendale* not too remote (an 'inclusionary effect').[107] On the facts, it was unlikely that loss by flooding would occur as a consequence of the defendant's breach in failing properly to install a float valve in a fire-sprinkler water storage system because normally the drains would have taken away the overflow water but here the drains were blocked. Applying *Hadley v Baxendale*, the loss would have been too remote. But the loss was held to be not too remote because the installer had assumed responsibility for that loss and it was within the scope of the installer's duty.

One can readily think of other analogous situations where the assumption of responsibility might have an inclusionary effect. So, for example, Lord Walker in *The Achilleas* gave the example of a lightning conductor. His Lordship said: 'If a manufacturer of lightning conductors sells a defective conductor and the customer's house burns down as a result, the manufacturer will not escape liability by proving that only one in a hundred of his customers' buildings had actually been struck by lightning.'[108]

It has become clear, therefore, that *The Achilleas* requires us to accept that the traditional reasonable contemplation test is not the sole test of remoteness. There are exceptional situations where that test is overridden, whether in an exclusionary or inclusionary way. However, to explain the exceptions as ones where the defendant has or has not assumed responsibility for the loss is in itself extremely vague.

Moreover, to talk, as Lord Hoffmann did, of the answer being 'agreement-centred' and as turning on the contract, as objectively and contextually interpreted, adds little, if any, light.[109] The better view is that the law on remoteness, like the law of damages generally, is externally imposed. The relevance to remoteness of the parties' intentions and the construction of the contract is limited to the standard law on remoteness being excludable by the parties whether expressly or impliedly. So, for example, in many contracts there is an express clause excluding liability for consequential loss. The correct approach is that of Professor Andrew Robertson who writes, '[T]he remoteness rule is not an agreement-based rule, which is concerned with identifying an implicit allocation of risk made by the contacting parties, but a gap-filling device, which is concerned with ensuring that a contract breaker is not subjected to an unreasonable burden.'[110]

Applying the external view of remoteness enables one to clarify why, exceptionally, one would wish to depart from the standard reasonable contemplation test. In this analysis, remoteness is seen as a rule of policy designed to ensure that the award of damages (to put the claimant into as good a position as if the contract had been performed) does not impose an unreasonable burden of liability on a defendant. In essence, where the parties' intentions run out, the law must decide who should bear the risk of the loss that has occurred. It must allocate the risk in a fair and reasonable way. Applying that approach, it is in general fair and reasonable to allocate the risk of loss to the contract-breaker if the defendant, at the time of the contract, could contemplate that type of loss as a serious possibility of the breach.

---

[106] These were Toulson LJ's words at [43]. [107] ibid.
[108] [2008] UKHL 48, [2009] 1 AC 61, at [78]. Another example is that given by Lord Hoffmann, 'The Achilleas: Custom and Practice or Foreseeability?' (2010) 14 Edinburgh LR 47, 55, of the builder's liability for a roof collapsing on someone's head, however unlikely.
[109] See also *John Grimes Partnership Ltd v Gubbins* [2013] EWCA Civ 37, [2013] PNLR 17 (decision that loss of profits was not too remote was clearly correct; but, with respect, Sir David Keene's preference for the language of an implied term to explain *The Achilleas* is unhelpful).
[110] A Robertson, 'The Basis of the Remoteness Rule in Contract' (2008) 28 Legal Studies 172, 172. Note also that in *Supershield Ltd v Siemens Building Technologies FE Ltd* [2010] EWCA Civ 7, [2010] 1 Lloyd's Rep 349, at [40], Toulson LJ referred to the law on remoteness in contract as grounded on policy.

That explains the force of the traditional test. However, that general risk allocation must be qualified in two main situations.

The first is where the whole purpose of the duty broken is to guard against the risk of the type of loss that has occurred. In that situation, it is fair for the risk of that loss to be allocated to the defendant however unlikely the loss. This is the proper explanation for the so-called inclusionary effect of *The Achilleas*. It explains the lightning conductor and water valve situations mentioned above.

The second is where the type of loss is so exceptional in relation to the standard purpose of the duty that the only reason why it was reasonably contemplated as a serious possibility by the defendant at the time of the contract was that the claimant informed the defendant of the special risk. This is the taxi-driver example.[111] Or, as another illustration, let us assume that in *Hadley v Baxendale* the mill-owner *had* informed the carrier that the mill was stopped. The essential question here is whether mere knowledge of the special risk (and hence the opportunity to limit the liability) is sufficient for the law to allocate that risk to the defendant. It would seem not and that further relevant factors should be taken into account in deciding on a fair and reasonable allocation of the risk. These may include whether there has been an adjustment to the price to take account of the risk, how disproportionate the loss is to the price, and the extent to which the parties are insured against, or could be expected to insure against, that loss.[112] If we apply these factors to the taxi-driver example we arrive at the conclusion that, because the loss is wholly disproportionate to the price and because one could not expect a taxi-driver to insure against this sort of liability, the loss will be too remote unless, for example, the price has been significantly adjusted to reflect that risk. It is submitted that it is this balancing of factors to reach a fair risk allocation that provides the true explanation for the so-called exclusionary effect of *The Achilleas*. But in *The Achilleas* itself, in contrast to the taxi-driver example, the type of loss was not so exceptional in relation to the standard purpose of the duty; and, in any event, the loss was not disproportionate to the price. There was therefore no good reason for cutting back the normal allocation of risk, laid down by the standard remoteness rule, and according to which the loss should have been fairly borne by the charterers.[113] One *could* feed in to the balance of factors the two articulated by Lords Hoffmann and Hope but, for the reasons already given,[114] they do not seem of great relevance to the fair allocation of risk in that case. In particular, it is for the courts to decide what was a fair allocation of risk in a situation that had plainly neither been thought through by the parties themselves nor, it is submitted, by the market in which they operated.

It may be that Lord Hoffmann would accept much of what has been said above, but would argue that the relevant factors articulated above as going to a fair and reasonable risk allocation are best seen as going to whether, objectively, the defendant agreed to accept

---

[111] See above, pp 99–100.

[112] Andrew Robertson's articulation of factors similarly includes whether the defendant had a reasonable opportunity to limit his or her liability; the degree of disproportion between loss and benefit; and the insurance arrangements. But he also adds as potentially relevant the defendant's culpability which seems alien to the English approach in contract law.

[113] In the Court of Appeal [2007] 2 Lloyd's Rep 555, at [96] Rix LJ also points out that, '[I]n taking the risk of a delay on a last legitimate voyage, the charterers were of course seeking to squeeze the last drop of profit from what … was a particularly strong market … They may or may not have calculated that, if the delay which they had put in motion caused their owners to lose their next fixture, this would happen just at a time when there was a sudden crack in market rates. But if they had considered that possibility, they ought to have appreciated that, barring any unusual features of the subsequent fixture, the risk of that loss should fairly fall on themselves rather than the owners. Why should it fall on the owners?'

[114] See above, p 101.

responsibility for the loss. The objection to that is that it masks what is an externally imposed rule as if it were agreement-centred. It expands and fictionalises the role of the parties' intentions (albeit objectively construed) when it is cleaner and more transparent to list the policy factors.

(f) Assimilation of the contract and tort tests where there is a contractual relationship

Moving on from the impact of *The Achilleas* to other issues, we have seen above that the emphasis on it being the type and not the actual loss or damage that matters in the contract, as well as the tort, remoteness test has brought those tests closer together. But, as we have also seen, while it was plain that the majority of the Court of Appeal in *Parsons v Uttley Ingham* desired assimilation of the two tests, the majority failed to explain how they could be assimilated given that they significantly differ (in terms of the likelihood of the loss and their time of application). As made clear in *Heron II*, the contract test is a stricter test than that applied in tort so that losses may be too remote in contract that would not be too remote in tort; and that remains the case after *The Achilleas*.

In terms of policy, at least where the parties are in a contractual relationship, the best way to achieve assimilation is to recognise that the stricter contract test should be applied even to a claim in the tort of negligence. The policy behind having different tests rests on there being an opportunity for a contracting party to inform the other party of unusual risks. That other party can then exclude or limit its liability or can negotiate a higher price. This is not an opportunity that a party suing in tort normally has because the defendant prior to the commission of the tort is a stranger. The classic judicial exposition of this policy was in Lord Reid's speech in *Heron II*. He said:

> 'In contract, if one party wishes to protect himself against a risk which to the other party would appear unusual, he can direct the other party's attention to it before the contract is made, and I need not stop to consider in what circumstances the other party will then be held to have accepted responsibility in that event. In tort however, there is no opportunity for the injured party to protect himself in that way and the tortfeasor cannot reasonably complain if he has to pay for some very unusual but nevertheless foreseeable damage which results from his wrongdoing.'[115]

But where the claim is being brought in tort in the context of a contractual relationship the parties are not strangers and plainly the claimant has had the same opportunity to inform the defendant of risks—and this can be reflected in the terms of the contract—vis-à-vis the tort claim as the claimant has had vis-à-vis the contract claim. In that context, therefore, there is good reason to apply the stricter contract test to the claim in tort.

This assimilation of remoteness tests where the parties are in a contractual relationship derived some support from *Brown v KMR Services Ltd*[116] because it is arguable that the contract test was applied even in relation to the concurrent claim in the tort of negligence. Admittedly both Gatehouse J and the Court of Appeal used only the language of breach of contract in expressing their conclusions; and, at the time of Gatehouse J's judgment, the House of Lords' decision in *Henderson v Merrett Syndicates Ltd*,[117] authoritatively accepting

---

[115] [1969] 1 AC 350, at 385–386. See similarly at 411 (per Lord Hodson) and at 422–423 (per Lord Upjohn). See also *Jackson v Royal Bank of Scotland plc* [2005] UKHL 3, [2005] 1 WLR 377, at [36].

[116] [1995] 4 All ER 598. See also *Berryman v London Borough of Hounslow* [1997] PIQR P83 where the contractual remoteness test was applied to deny damages for a personal injury where the claim was framed in both contract and tort.

[117] [1995] 2 AC 145.

concurrent liability, had not yet been laid down. But the claims in *Brown* were for both breach of contract and the tort of negligence and the appeal in *Brown* was heard, and the judgment of the Court of Appeal was given, almost a year after *Henderson v Merrett*.

However, whatever one's interpretation of the *Brown* case on this point, it has been superseded by the leading case of *Wellesley Partners LLP v Withers LLP*.[118] Here the defendant solicitors were negligent in drafting a partnership agreement for the claimant partnership. Instead of giving an option to an investor in the partnership to withdraw after 42 months, the agreement allowed the investor to withdraw within the first 41 months. An investor exercised that option after only 12 months. The claimant as a result did not have the funds that it otherwise would have had to take a lucrative opportunity to expand the business in the USA. In an action in contract and the tort of negligence against the solicitors, the claimant sought damages for those lost US profits and these were awarded at trial. Even if too remote in contract, that loss of profits was held, by Nugee J at first instance, to be not too remote in tort applying the tort *Wagon Mound* test. The defendants appealed, arguing that the stricter contract remoteness test should be applied even to the tort claim and that, applying that test, the loss of profit was too remote. The Court of Appeal accepted that the contract test here applied but that, even applying that stricter test, the loss was not too remote.

Floyd LJ said:

'I am persuaded that where ... contractual and tortious duties to take care in carrying out instructions exist side by side, the test for recoverability of damage for economic loss should be the same, and should be the contractual one. The basis for the formulation of the remoteness test adopted in contract is that the parties have the opportunity to draw special circumstances to each other's attention at the time of formation of the contract ... [T]here exists the opportunity for consensus between the parties, as to the type of damage (both in terms of its likelihood and type) for which it will be able to hold the other responsible. The parties are assumed to be contracting on the basis that liability will be confined to damage of the kind which is in their reasonable contemplation. It makes no sense at all for the existence of the concurrent duty in tort to upset this consensus, particularly given that the tortious duty arises out of the same assumption of responsibility as exists under the contract.'[119]

After *Wellesley*, we can set out the relationship between the contract and tort remoteness tests, based on sound policy, in the following three points.[120] First, subject to an 'assumption of responsibility' to the contrary, the contract test of remoteness lays down that losses are too remote if, at the time the contract was made, the defendant did not contemplate and could not reasonably have contemplated that type of loss as a serious possibility. Secondly, the normal tort test, applicable in standard tort claims where the parties are not in a contractual relationship, is that losses are too remote if at the time of the breach of duty the defendant did not foresee and could not reasonably have foreseen that type of loss as a slight possibility. Thirdly, where the parties are in a contractual relationship, the above contract test applies even where the claim is being brought in tort because of the equal opportunity that the claimant has had to inform the other party of unusual risks.[121]

---

[118] [2015] EWCA Civ 1146, [2016] Ch 529.
[119] ibid, at [80]. See similarly Roth LJ at [151] and [157]; Longmore LJ at [186]–[187].
[120] For a different approach, see R Cooke, 'Remoteness of Damages and Judicial Discretion' [1978] CLJ 288 (advocating a wide judicial discretion, albeit with articulated considerations to be taken into account).
[121] One can strongly argue that, wherever there is a pre-existing relationship, even if non-contractual, between the parties, the 'contract' test should apply even where the claim is being brought in tort because the claimant has had the opportunity, and should be encouraged, to inform the other party of unusual risks. Admittedly the scope for the defendant to deal with that information is more restricted than where there is a contractual relationship: in particular there is no price to modify. But the defendant can exclude or limit its tortious liability (eg, for negligent advice) by a non-contractual disclaimer.

3. Intervening cause[122]

Even though the defendant's breach of duty is a cause of the claimant's loss, the claimant may not recover damages for it because an intervening cause,[123] combining with it to produce the loss,[124] is regarded as breaking the chain of causation between the defendant's breach of duty and the loss. The underlying policy behind this restriction is that, where an intervening cause is much more responsible for the loss than is the defendant's breach of duty, it is considered unfair on the defendant and is imposing too great a burden on her to hold her liable for the loss.

The principles upon which the decisions in this area are based have rarely been clearly articulated, and some judges have even resorted to saying that it is simply a matter of instinct or common sense.[125] However, unarticulated common sense or instinct is hardly a satisfactory basis for legal decision-making and therefore an attempt will be made to indicate the main principles that underlie the decisions in relation to each of the three main types of intervening cause: namely natural events (that is, where the event is not caused by any identifiable person); conduct of a third party; and conduct of the claimant.[126]

(1) Intervening natural events

In general, a natural event only breaks the chain of causation if the sole contribution that the defendant's breach of duty makes to the claimant's loss is that the claimant or his property is in the place where, at the time when, the natural event intervenes. Even then the natural event will not break the causal chain if it was likely to intervene.

This is illustrated by the well-known hypothetical examples of the claimant who, having been injured by the defendant's negligence and while on the way to hospital, is further injured by a falling tree or roof-tile or, while in hospital, suffers further injury because of a fire there.[127] In each of these situations the sole contribution of the breach of duty to the further loss is that the claimant is at the place where, at the time when, the natural event intervenes; since, in addition, none of these natural events was likely to intervene the causal chain is broken. Similarly in *Carlslogie SS Co Ltd v Royal Norwegian Government*[128] the claimant's ship was damaged in a collision for which the defendant was wholly responsible. After temporary repairs rendering the ship seaworthy, she set out on a voyage to the US. On that voyage she suffered extensive damage due to heavy weather. The House of Lords considered

---

[122] The leading discussion on causation is HLA Hart and T Honoré, *Causation in the Law* (2nd edn, Clarendon Press 1985). The analysis in this book is in agreement with theirs that causal limits should be kept distinct from other limits on responsibility such as remoteness; but it differs from theirs in regarding intervening cause as depending on a policy decision rather than on the largely factual question of whether there is causation in the ordinary commonsense meaning of that term.
[123] Ie a factual cause subsequent to the breach of duty. A factual cause prior to or contemporaneous with the defendant's breach of duty cannot be correctly described as intervening so as to come within this section. But such a factual cause does not merit separate treatment elsewhere since it is very rarely regarded as the sole legal cause of the damage.
[124] Contrast sufficient causes, above, pp 52–55.
[125] Watkins LJ in *Lamb v Camden London Borough Council* [1981] QB 625, at 647; Glidewell LJ in *Galoo Ltd v Bright Grahame Murray* [1994] 1 WLR 1360, at 1374–1375.
[126] In *Normans Bay Ltd v Coudert Brothers* [2003] EWCA Civ 215 the rare question arose of whether the *defendant's* own wrongful conduct (which was not actionable because of limitation) broke the chain of causation between the wrongful conduct of the defendant being sued for and the claimant's loss. Not surprisingly, it was held that, as a matter of principle and policy, it did not.
[127] See *Hogan v Bentinck West Hartley Collieries (Owners) Ltd* [1949] 1 All ER 588, at 601 (per Lord Macdermott).
[128] [1952] AC 292.

that there was certainly no question of the defendant being liable for the heavy weather damage. Viscount Jowitt said that it '… was not in any sense a consequence of the collision, and must be treated as a supervening event occurring in the course of a normal voyage'.[129] More specifically it can be said that the chain of causation was broken because the sole contribution of the breach of duty to the heavy weather damage was that the claimant's ship was in the Atlantic at the time of that heavy weather, and moreover that heavy weather was unlikely to intervene.

An alternative way of expressing the central idea is to say that the natural event breaks the chain of causation if it was coincidental to the breach of duty. The damage from the falling tree or falling roof-tile, or the heavy weather, is a coincidence for which the defendant should not be held responsible.

In contrast, let us suppose that the defendant negligently sets fire to the claimant's field and later, fanned by gale-force winds, the fire spreads to and destroys the claimant's house; the winds do not break the chain of causation because the contribution of the defendant's negligence to the burning down of the house clearly has nothing to do merely with the claimant's property being in the place where, at the time when, the natural event intervenes. On the contrary without the defendant's breach of duty there would have been no fire at all.

A further example of a natural event not breaking the causal chain is provided by *Monarch SS Co Ltd v A/B Karlshamms Oljefabriker*.[130] The defendant's breach of contract in failing to provide a seaworthy ship for the carriage of the claimant's cargo of soya beans meant that the voyage was delayed, and that the ship could not reach her destination in Sweden before the Second World War broke out. The ship was ordered by the Admiralty to discharge the soya beans at Glasgow. The claimants thereupon had to pay for the beans to be forwarded to Sweden in neutral ships. They claimed damages for the cost of that transhipment. One issue was whether that transhipment was too remote in the sense discussed in the last section, but another was whether the intervening events, in particular the outbreak of war, broke the causal connection between the defendant's breach and the transhipment. It was held that the chain of causation was not broken. Although the sole contribution of the defendant's breach to the transhipment was that the ship was within waters patrolled by the British Navy when the war broke out, that intervention, as Lord Porter stressed, was likely.[131]

This principle for natural events sets a fairly high standard for establishing that the chain of causation is broken; that is, it is relatively rare for a natural event to break the chain of causation. This should be contrasted with the approach to wrongful intervention by a third party or the claimant's own unreasonable conduct. The difference reflects sound policy; a defendant cannot attach blame to anyone else in the case of natural events.

Although concerning initial liability, and not damages for an established liability, the decision of the House of Lords in *Chester v Afshar*[132] represents a departure from the principles of intervening causation here set out. The defendant doctor advised the claimant to have an operation to relieve her back pain but, in breach of his duty of care, he failed to warn her of the very small risk of paralysis connected with the operation. The claimant went ahead with the operation and, although it was properly performed, she sustained paralysis. The claimant could not prove on the balance of probabilities that, if properly warned, she would not have had the operation at some stage but she could prove that she would have delayed the operation. It was held by a three–two majority that she was entitled to

---

[129] ibid, at 299.   [130] [1949] AC 196.   [131] ibid, at 215.
[132] [2004] UKHL 41, [2005] 1 AC 345. See the excellent case-note by R Stevens, 'An Opportunity to Reflect' (2005) 121 LQR 189. See also the illuminating analysis of the Court of Appeal in *Duce v Worcestershire Acute Hospitals NHS Trust* [2018] EWCA Civ 1307, [2018] PIQR P18.

damages for her paralysis. The majority controversially accepted that they were departing from normal causation principles but nevertheless thought that damages were justified here in order to vindicate the patient's right to be warned of the risks of the operation. That seems incorrect—one is not talking here about a tort actionable per se or the award of a conventional sum to vindicate a right—and there was a powerful dissent by Lords Bingham and Hoffmann. It is important to appreciate that, although the contrary has sometimes been suggested, the departure from normal causation principles was not a departure from the factual 'but for' causation test. This was because, had the claimant delayed the operation, she would not, on the balance of probabilities, have suffered the paralysis. But although 'but for' causation was satisfied, the normal approach would have been that the chain of causation was broken by the paralysis. The failure to warn merely meant that the claimant was in the place where, at the time when, the natural event of the paralysis occurred. Like the falling tree example, the paralysis was essentially coincidental to the breach of duty because the claimant could not prove that she would never have had the operation and the same small risk of paralysis applied whenever the operation was performed.

Mention should be made here of one final puzzling case. In *Galoo Ltd v Bright Grahame Murray*,[133] which we shall consider in more detail below, the Court of Appeal held that a company could not recover for trading losses subsequent to a negligent audit by the defendant of the company's accounts on the reasoning that there was a break in causation between the auditor's negligence and the trading losses. In so far as the Court of Appeal was treating the market falls as intervening natural events which broke the chain of causation, the decision is difficult to reconcile with the standard approach to intervening causation. One is left with the somewhat unsatisfactory conclusion that the decision rests on a specific policy of protecting professionals (here auditors) against liability in negligence for market losses (unless, perhaps, the whole purpose of the duty is to guard against those losses as where, for example, the professional's duty is to give reasonable advice as to whether to make a particular investment). In this respect, *Galoo* is in line with the subsequent *SAAMCO* case,[134] in which the House of Lords held that market fall losses were not recoverable from a negligent valuer because they fell outside the scope of the valuer's duty of care to his client. But, as we shall see, the decision and reasoning in *SAAMCO* is highly controversial.

(2) Intervening conduct of a third party

(a) *The duty was to guard against such a third party intervention*

Clearly in this situation the third party should not be regarded as having broken the chain of causation, and this is shown in a number of contract cases. In *London Joint Stock Bank v Macmillan*,[135] for example, the defendant customer of the claimant bank, in breach of his contractual duty to the claimant not to draw cheques so as to facilitate fraud, signed for a trusted clerk a cheque for £2 drawn in such a way as to enable the clerk readily to alter the amount to £120; the clerk then obtained this sum from the bank and absconded. The House of Lords held that the defendant was liable to the claimant for the forged sum. Lord Finlay LC said, 'The fact that a crime was necessary to bring about the loss does not prevent it being the natural consequence of the carelessness.'[136] More specifically, one can say that the reason why the intervening acts of the third party, albeit criminal, did not break the chain of

---

[133] [1994] 1 WLR 1360. See below, p 115.   [134] [1997] AC 191. See below, pp 117–127.
[135] [1918] AC 777. See also *De La Bere v Pearson* [1908] 1 KB 280.   [136] [1918] AC 777, at 794.

causation was that the duty broken was to guard against a third party fraudulently obtaining money from the bank.

Stansbie v Troman,[137] in which the cause of action is probably best rationalised as breach of contract,[138] is a further and very clear example. A decorator was at work in a house and left it for two hours to get wallpaper. He was alone and had been told by the claimant householder to lock the front door if he ever left. Instead he left the door unlocked and during his absence a thief entered and stole some jewellery and clothes. The Court of Appeal held that the defendant was liable for the loss: the third party intervention did not break the chain of causation because the duty broken was clearly to prevent what had occurred. As Tucker LJ said, '... the act of negligence itself consisted in the failure to take reasonable care to guard against the very thing that in fact happened.'[139]

Similarly in *Home Office v Dorset Yacht Co Ltd*[140] the majority of their Lordships, with the notable exception of Lord Reid, framed the issue in terms of whether a duty of care in the tort of negligence was owed by borstal officers to the owners of nearby yachts damaged by escaping borstal boys. Having decided that there was such a duty, and that it had been breached, it obviously followed that the chain of causation was not broken by the intervention of the borstal boys. As Oliver LJ said in *P Perl (Exporters) Ltd v Camden London Borough Council*[141] in which the defendant was held to owe no duty of care to a neighbour whose premises had been burgled by thieves gaining access through the defendant's premises:

> '... the question of the existence of a duty and that of whether the damage brought about by the act of a third party is too remote are simply two facets of the same problem: for if there be a duty to take reasonable care to prevent damage being caused by a third party then I find it difficult to see how damage caused by the third party consequent on the failure to take such care can be too remote a consequence of the breach of duty.'[142]

The same sentiment was expressed by Lord Goff in *Smith v Littlewoods Organisation Ltd*[143] in which it was decided that no duty of care was owed to neighbours whose property had been damaged as a result of vandals setting fire to the defendant's derelict cinema. 'Of course, if a duty of care is imposed to guard against deliberate wrongdoing by others, it can hardly be said that the harmful effects of such wrongdoing are not caused by such breach of duty.'[144]

The controversial decision in *Weld-Blundell v Stephens*[145] seems to be out of line with the principle being discussed and it is submitted that, for this reason alone, the minority view is to be preferred. The claimant, when employing the defendant accountant to investigate the affairs of the company, libelled certain officials of the company in his letter of instructions to the defendant. The defendant negligently left the letter at the company's office, where it was read by a third party who related its contents to the officials, who successfully sued the claimant for libel. The claimant brought an action against the defendant for breach of contract, claiming compensation for those damages and the costs. The House of Lords held by a bare majority that the third party's act broke the chain of causation and that the claimant could therefore recover no more than nominal damages. The main ground of reasoning was expressed as follows by Lord Sumner:

---

[137] [1948] 2 KB 48.
[138] See *P Perl (Exporters) Ltd v Camden London Borough Council* [1983] 3 All ER 161, at 170.
[139] [1948] 2 KB 48, at 52.   [140] [1970] AC 1004.   [141] [1984] QB 342.   [142] ibid, at 353.
[143] [1987] AC 241.   [144] ibid, at 272.
[145] [1920] AC 956. The case was distinguished in *Slipper v BBC* [1991] 1 QB 283.

'In general ... even though A is in fault he is not responsible for injury to C which B, a stranger to him, deliberately chooses to do. Though A may have given the occasion for B's mischievous activities, B then becomes a new and independent cause ... It is hard to steer clear of metaphors. Perhaps one may be forgiven for saying that B snaps the chain of causation; that he is no mere conduit pipe through which consequences flow from A to C, no mere part of a transmission gear set in motion by A; that in a word, he insulates A from C.'[146]

Such a generalisation is misleading and did mislead the majority in the case, for it fails to indicate that where, as on the facts of this case, the duty broken is to guard against such a third party intervention as occurred, even a criminal act of the third party, let alone a non-wrongful act as here, does not break the chain of causation. In the dissenting words of Viscount Finlay, '... the very thing happened which it was [the defendant's] duty to guard against'.[147]

(b) Third party intervention other than where there was a duty to guard against it

Rationalisation of the case law is here particularly difficult. However, it would seem that where the third party's intervention comprises wrongdoing it breaks the chain of causation unless it was a likely, or in the case of intentional wrongdoing, a very likely consequence of the defendant's breach of duty. Non-wrongful conduct of a third party will probably only break the chain on the same principle as for natural events. The policy is therefore one of showing more leniency towards the defendant if a third party's intervening conduct has been wrongful, so that the claimant can claim against him, than if non-wrongful. Moreover, the greater the culpability of the third party's wrong, the greater the leniency.

Two cases involving multiple collisions can be used to illustrate a third party's non-intentional wrongdoing. In *Rouse v Squires*[148] D1 negligently jack-knifed his lorry across a motorway. D2 driving his lorry negligently, collided into D1's lorry and killed the claimant's husband who was assisting at the scene. D2 was held liable to the claimant. D2 now brought third party proceedings against D1. The question that arose was whether that intervening negligence of D2 broke the chain of causation between D1's negligence and the death of the claimant's husband. The Court of Appeal held that that chain of causation was not broken. Cairns LJ said that where a driver:

'... so negligently manages his vehicle as to cause it to obstruct the highway and constitute a danger to other road users, including those who are driving too fast or not keeping a proper look-out, but not those who deliberately or recklessly drive into the obstruction,[149] then the first driver's negligence may be held to have contributed to the causation of an accident of which the immediate cause was the negligent driving of the vehicle which because of the presence of the obstruction collides with it.'[150]

Moreover, on these facts, once D1 had negligently jack-knifed, it was likely that another negligently driven vehicle would collide causing injury or death to those on the scene.

On the other hand, in *Knightley v Johns*[151] D1 negligently overturned his car thereby blocking a tunnel. D2, a police inspector, was held to be negligent in not immediately closing the tunnel and in ordering the claimant, a constable, to ride back along the tunnel against the traffic in order to close it. While doing so, the claimant collided with D3's oncoming car and

---

[146] [1920] AC 956, at 986.   [147] ibid, at 974.   [148] [1973] QB 889.
[149] These words were expressly relied on by the Court of Appeal in *Wright v Lodge* [1993] 4 All ER 299 in holding that the *reckless* driving in question broke the chain of causation.
[150] [1973] QB 889, at 898.   [151] [1982] 1 WLR 349.

was injured. The primary question was whether the intervening negligent acts of D2 broke the chain of causation between D1's negligence and the claimant's injuries. Stephenson LJ said that the test to be applied was '... reasonable foreseeability, which I understand to mean foreseeability of something of the same sort being likely to happen'.[152] Applying that the Court of Appeal, not surprisingly, reached the conclusion that D2's negligent acts broke the chain of causation and that therefore D1 was not liable for the claimant's injuries. Some types of risk-taking and even negligence by the police were likely to intervene; but the same could not be said of the acts of negligence that D2 had actually committed.

The well-known case of *The Oropesa*[153] concerned non-wrongful intervention. A ship of that name negligently caused a collision with another ship. The master of the latter ship decided to cross to The Oropesa in a small boat. The boat overturned and the claimant's son was killed. The question was whether the death was caused by the negligence of The Oropesa or whether the master's action in taking to the boat broke the chain of causation. It was held that the chain of causation was not broken. Lord Wright said:

> 'To break the chain of causation it must be shown that there is something which I will call ultroneous, something unwarrantable, a new cause which disturbs the sequence of events, something which can be described as either unreasonable or extraneous or extrinsic.'[154]

This is typical of reasoning in the area of intervening cause in not articulating the exact principle; but it does indicate that non-wrongful conduct will rarely break the chain. It is submitted that in accordance with this and with the approach to natural events, the underlying general principle is that third party non-wrongful acts will only break the chain if the sole contribution that the defendant's breach of duty makes to the claimant's loss is that the claimant is in the place where, at the time when, the third party intervenes. Even then the causal chain will not be broken if the intervention was likely. Applying this to the facts of *The Oropesa* the causal chain was not broken because the defendant's breach of duty contributed to the master taking out the boat, and its contribution was therefore not solely that the claimant was in the boat when it overturned. Similarly it is submitted that, had the events considered above under natural events[155] been caused by a third party's non-wrongful act, the same decisions on causation would be reached.

Where the third party's conduct comprises intentional wrongdoing, the intervention will break the chain of causation, unless it was a very likely consequence of the defendant's breach of duty. In *Home Office v Dorset Yacht Co Ltd*[156] Lord Reid who, unlike the majority, regarded the primary issue as one of intervening cause rather than as one of duty, said:

> '... where human action forms one of the links between the original wrong-doing of the defendant and the loss suffered by the plaintiff, that action must at least have been something very likely to happen if it is not to be regarded as *novus actus interveniens* breaking the chain of causation. I do not think that a mere foreseeable possibility is or should be sufficient, for then the intervening human action can more properly be regarded as a new cause than as a consequence of the original wrongdoing.'[157]

---

[152] ibid, at 366.
[153] [1943] P 32. For a colourful example of non-wrongful intervention of a third party being held not to break the chain of causation in the context of the tort of defamation, see *McManus v Beckham* [2002] EWCA Civ 939, [2002] 1 WLR 2982 (publication of defendant's slander did not break chain of causation).
[154] [1943] P 32, at 39.   [155] Above, pp 107–109.
[156] [1970] AC 1004. For an excellent illustration, see the Supreme Court of Alberta case of *Duce v Rourke* [1951] 1 WWR 305 (theft of tools from car by third party after accident broke the chain of causation). For the intentional wrongful act of a third party breaking the chain of causation in a claim for breach of statutory duty, see *Horton v Caplin Contracts Limited* [2002] EWCA Civ 1604, [2003] PIQR P180.
[157] [1970] AC 1004, at 1030.

Since on these facts it was very likely that as a result of the defendant's negligence the boys would escape and damage nearby yachts, the chain of causation was not broken.

Lord Reid's dictum was subsequently applied by Oliver LJ in *Lamb v Camden London Borough Council*,[158] albeit that he recast Lord Reid's test in terms of 'reasonable forseeability' and regarded intervening cause as an aspect of remoteness. The defendants had negligently caused the subsidence of the claimant's house with the result that the claimant had to leave it unoccupied. The question was whether in addition to their admitted liability in nuisance for the subsidence the defendants should be held responsible for the loss caused by the action of squatters occupying and looting the home. The Court of Appeal unanimously held that the defendants should not be liable for that further loss. Oliver LJ, applying Lord Reid's test, in effect held that as the third party's intervention was unlikely the chain of causation was broken. On the other hand the reasoning of the other judges is unhelpful with regard to intervention by a third party. Least satisfactory was Watkins LJ who regarded the loss as too remote because his instinct told him so. Rather more satisfactory was Lord Denning's primary reasoning by which he in effect decided the issue in terms of the claimant's failure to act (that is, the duty to mitigate) rather than intervening third party conduct; the claimant had unreasonably failed to secure adequately the empty house even after an initial intrusion by squatters.

Unfortunately even Oliver LJ thought that Lord Reid's test might not be stringent enough, and he said, 'There may … be circumstances in which the court would require a degree of likelihood amounting almost to inevitability before it fixes a defendant with a responsibility for the act of the third party over whom he has and can have no control.'[159] The hypothetical example worrying the Court of Appeal was that of an escaping borstal boy stealing a car and committing a burglary hundreds of miles from the borstal. While this was thought very likely, it was considered that the Home Office ought not to be held liable for it. But there is surely no need to qualify or reject Lord Reid's test to reach that result for it can be argued that the Home Office would owe no duty of care to the claimant in that situation. In other words Lord Reid regarded *Dorset Yacht* as raising particular difficulties over intervening cause rather than the duty of care, but he could still have regarded the duty of care as the problem issue on other facts.

In *Ward v Cannock Chase District Council*[160] there was no such qualification of Lord Reid's dictum which was applied, along with Oliver LJ's reasoning in *Lamb*, to reach the decision that the defendant council (which admitted negligence) was liable for damage to the claimant's house resulting initially from vandalisation of the defendant's empty house next door and later from direct vandalisation of the claimant's then unoccupied house. The chain of causation was held to be unbroken as it was very likely that unoccupied houses in that area would be vandalised.

(3) Intervening conduct of the claimant

The position here seems to be that, where there has been a tort[161] or breach of contract, unreasonable conduct of the claimant breaks the chain of causation (unless the duty was to

---

[158] [1981] QB 625.   [159] ibid, at 644.   [160] [1986] Ch 546.
[161] Separate consideration is not given to the claimant's conduct subsequent to a breach of duty but prior to a tort (that is, where there is as yet no damage and the tort is not actionable per se) because here even unreasonable conduct rarely breaks the chain of causation and usually amounts to contributory negligence. Exceptions are *Rushton v Turner Bros Asbestos* [1960] 1 WLR 96, and *Jayes v IMI Ltd* [1985] ICR 155 (in the latter the incorrect term '100% contributory negligence' was used); *Galoo Ltd v Bright Grahame Murray* [1994] 1 WLR 1360 (as regards the tort claim).

guard against that intervention)¹⁶² whereas reasonable conduct does not.¹⁶³ In accordance with the distinction explained above,¹⁶⁴ cases where the claimant has unreasonably failed to take action, or has unreasonably incurred expenses, are not discussed here but under the duty to mitigate.¹⁶⁵

(a) Unreasonable acts

The classic case is *McKew v Holland and Hannen and Cubitts*.¹⁶⁶ The claimant had suffered an injury for which the defendants were tortiously liable, and as a result he occasionally lost control of his left leg. Some days after the accident he was descending a steep staircase without a handrail and without the available assistance of his wife and brother-in-law when he lost control of his left leg and, in jumping to save himself falling, broke his ankle. The House of Lords held that the further injury was brought about by the claimant's own actions because, in placing himself unnecessarily in a position where he might be injured, the claimant was acting unreasonably; and even though unreasonable conduct was not unlikely or unforeseeable, it nevertheless broke the chain of causation. Lord Reid said, '… it is not at all unlikely or unforeseeable that an active man who has suffered such a disability will take some quite unreasonable risk but if he does, he cannot hold the defender liable for the consequences.'¹⁶⁷

Two contract cases similarly illustrate the principle. In *Quinn v Burch Bros (Builders) Ltd*¹⁶⁸ the defendants in breach of contract failed to supply a step-ladder to the claimant, a sub-contractor. The claimant injured himself when he fell from an unfooted trestle which he had made use of in the absence of a step-ladder. The Court of Appeal held that the defendants were not liable for the claimant's injuries because their breach of contract did not cause them: the claimant's own unreasonable acts broke the chain of causation between the breach of contract and his injuries.

Again in *Lambert v Lewis*¹⁶⁹ a dealer supplied a defective trailer coupling to a farmer, who negligently went on using it after it was obviously broken. There was an accident resulting in injuries to other parties, when the coupling gave way. The farmer was found liable for those injuries and in an action for breach of contract against the dealer sought to recover an indemnity for the damages he had had to pay. The House of Lords held, however, that

---

¹⁶² Eg *Reeves v Metropolitan Police Commissioner* [2000] 1 AC 360 where it was held that suicide did not break the chain of causation because the duty of the police was precisely to take reasonable care to prevent suicide. (Note that, as a case on the tort of negligence, this is also consistent with the general rule referred to in the previous note.) That the duty in question was to guard against the claimant's conduct is also probably the best explanation of *British Racing Drivers' Club Ltd v Hextall Erskine & Co* [1996] 3 All ER 667 (distinguishing the *Galoo* case discussed below, at p 115) where there was held to be no break in the chain of causation between solicitors' negligent advice to a company that its directors could go ahead with a transaction without reference to its members and loss caused to the company by that transaction.

¹⁶³ Cf *Borealis AB v Geogas Trading SA* [2010] EWHC 2789 (Comm), [2011] 1 Lloyd's Rep 482, esp at [45], where Gross LJ (sitting in the High Court) took the view that mere unreasonable conduct does not necessarily break the chain of causation: rather the underlying highly fact-specific test is whether the defendant's breach remains an effective cause of the loss.

¹⁶⁴ Above, pp 84–85.

¹⁶⁵ Where the chain of causation has been broken by the claimant's unreasonable conduct, it would appear that damages can still be awarded for the loss that, counterfactually, the claimant would have suffered had it acted reasonably. Although no clear causation case on this has been found, the close link to the duty to mitigate indicates that this must be so; and for the application of this approach to the duty to mitigate, see below, pp 131–132.

¹⁶⁶ [1969] 3 All ER 1621. See also *Spencer v Wincanton Holdings Ltd* [2009] EWCA Civ 1404, [2010] PIQR P8.

¹⁶⁷ [1969] 3 All ER 1621, at 1623.

¹⁶⁸ [1966] 2 QB 370. See also *Beoco Ltd v Alfa Laval Co* [1995] QB 137; *Young v Purdy* [1996] 2 FLR 795; *Clay v TUI UK Ltd* [2018] EWCA Civ 1177, [2018] 4 All ER 672.

¹⁶⁹ [1982] AC 225.

he should not be so indemnified because his negligence in continuing to use the coupling knowing of its condition had broken the chain of causation between the dealer's breach of contract and the accident.

At least at first sight, it may be thought that the principle that unreasonable intervening conduct of the claimant breaks the chain of causation is the best explanation of the well-known decision in *Galoo Ltd v Bright Grahame Murray*.[170] A claim was brought by a company for trading losses against its auditors. The claimant company argued that, had the auditors drawn up the company's accounts using reasonable care, they would have revealed that the company was insolvent. The company would thereupon have stopped trading. The auditors were therefore liable in contract and tort to the company for its continued trading losses after that time. But the Court of Appeal dismissed this claim on the basis that there was a break in the chain of causation between the auditors' negligence and the company's trading losses. Rather unhelpfully Glidewell LJ said the following: '[H]ow does the court decide whether the breach of duty was the cause of the loss or merely the occasion for the loss? ... The answer in the end is, "By the application of the court's common sense."'[171] It is arguable that behind this opaque reasoning lay the idea that the company's trading losses were essentially a result of its own poor decisions.[172] That 'unreasonable conduct' broke the chain of causation between the auditors' breach of duty to the company and those losses. But a difficulty with that argument is that the tenor of Glidewell LJ's judgment is that there would still have been a break in the chain of causation even if the trading losses were essentially attributable to market forces rather than poor decisions. Given that applying usual principle, natural events or the non-wrongful conduct of third parties relatively rarely break the chain of causation,[173] one may be led to the conclusion that the approach to intervening causation in *Galoo* is inconsistent with normal principle; and that in this case intervening causation was being used to reflect a specific policy decision that an auditor's liability (in contract or tort) should be severely limited.[174]

(b) Reasonable acts

The contract case of *Compania Naviera Maropan v Bowaters*[175] illustrates that the chain of causation will not be broken by reasonable intervening acts of the claimant.[176] The defendant charterers were in breach of contract with the claimants by nominating an unsafe loading place for their ship. The master of the claimants' ship thought that the place nominated was unsafe, but placed reliance on the assurance of safety given by the defendants' experienced pilot. The

---

[170] [1994] 1 WLR 1360. See also *Moore v Zerfahs* [1999] Lloyd's Rep PN 144 (unwise investment of a loan in a company, which fails, breaks the chain of causation between the defendant's breach of duty of care owed in tort in organising the loan and the claimant's loss).
[171] [1994] 1 WLR 1360, at 1374–1375.
[172] This derives some support from Laddie J's analysis of the Australian negligent audit case of *Alexander v Cambridge Credit Corpn* (1987) 9 NSWLR 310 in *Bank of Credit and Commerce International v Price Waterhouse (No 3)*, *The Times*, 2 April 1998: Alexander's breach of duty was not regarded as the cause, in the legal sense, of the losses which arose simply from continuing trading. What caused those losses were the dangers inherent in the marketplace and the directors' management decisions which, with the benefit of hindsight, could be seen to have been the wrong decisions to take.
[173] Above, pp 107–109, 111–112.   [174] See above, p 109.   [175] [1955] 2 QB 68.
[176] A relatively minor degree of carelessness by the claimant may be insufficient to break the chain of causation. See, eg, *County Ltd v Girozentrale* [1996] 3 All ER 834: chain of causation between broker's breach of contract (to claimant bank, which was underwriting an issue of shares, in telling potential investors of bank's intention to proceed on an 'all or nothing' basis) and claimant's loss not broken by claimant carelessly accepting indicative commitments from an investor which then pulled out.

ship was damaged and the question that arose was whether the master's actions had broken the chain of causation between the breach of contract and the damage to the ship. It was held that they had not because he had acted reasonably in the circumstances. Hodson LJ said:

> 'The question is one of causation. If the master by acting as he did, either caused the damage by acting unreasonably in the circumstances in which he was placed or failed to mitigate the damage, the charterers would be relieved accordingly, from the liability which would otherwise have fallen upon them.'[177]

Similarly in *Wieland v Cyril Lord Carpets Ltd*[178] the defendants negligently inflicted neck injuries on the claimant so that she had to wear a collar. She later fell down some stairs because she could not use her bifocal spectacles with her usual skill. Eveleigh J held that she was entitled to recover for her further injuries from the defendants because her own acts did not break the chain of causation. Again we can say this was because the claimant was not acting unreasonably when she fell down the stairs.

(c) Contributory negligence?

The all or nothing division between reasonable and unreasonable acts leaves out of account the possibility that contributory negligence subsequent to the tort or breach of contract might not break the chain of causation while allowing a reduction of damages in line with the comparative blameworthiness and causal potency of the claimant and defendant. For breach of contract this mid-position is often unavailable because the Law Reform (Contributory Negligence) Act 1945 often does not apply to breach of contract.[179] But there is no such reason for forcing tort cases into the all or nothing straitjacket and contributory negligence has been applied to acts subsequent to a tort. In *The Calliope*,[180] a ship of that name sustained damage in a collision in the river Seine with another ship, attributable to the negligence of both. In view of the damage she had sustained it was decided to turn the 'Calliope' round and proceed up river to an anchorage to await the ebb-tide. The next day she was to be turned round again to proceed down river. Unfortunately, when the ship was being turned round for the second time she sustained further damage. Brandon J found that this would not have occurred but for the negligence of the 'Calliope' but he held that this negligence did not break the chain of causation between the other ship's negligence and the further damage; rather, some damages for that further damage should be given, albeit of a reduced amount for the contributory negligence of the 'Calliope'.[181] He said:

> 'Looking at the question from the point of principle, I cannot see any logical reason for denying to the court the right to apportion ... liability in the circumstances contemplated. Where all relevant negligence on both sides precedes the original casualty the fact that A's negligence occurs later than B's negligence, and possibly also in a different place, does not prevent an apportionment of liability for such casualty. The view that it did so was enshrined in the so-called last-opportunity rule, which is, to this extent, dead and buried. I find it difficult to see why, as a matter of principle, it should make any difference that, in relation to a particular part of the damage arising or alleged to arise, from the casualty, the later negligence of B should follow

---

[177] [1955] 2 QB 68, at 99.   [178] [1969] 3 All ER 1006.
[179] Below, pp 138–144.   [180] [1970] P 172.
[181] As the 'Calliope' had been contributorily negligent in relation to the original accident, there was a sub-apportionment.

rather than precede the casualty itself. Why should later negligence of B before the casualty be held not necessarily to break the chain of causation but later negligence of his after the casualty be held necessarily to do so?'[182]

This is an eminently sensible approach, and it is therefore surprising that contributory negligence was not even discussed, let alone applied, in the *McKew* case.[183]

4. The *SAAMCO* principle

(1) Introduction

The House of Lords in *South Australia Asset Management Corpn v York Montague Ltd*[184] ('*SAAMCO*'), in the context of a claim for negligent valuation, laid down what was arguably a new principle restricting damages, namely that loss is irrecoverable if outside the scope of the duty broken. This principle ('the *SAAMCO* principle') has subsequently been applied to various examples, in tort and contract, of negligent misrepresentation or negligent failure to provide information. To that extent it may be regarded as a general restriction on damages although the House of Lords in *SAAMCO* saw the principle as going to the initial question, prior to considering damages, of whether a duty was owed in respect of that loss.[185] And in *BPE Solicitors v Hughes-Holland*,[186] in which the Supreme Court affirmed the correctness of the *SAAMCO* principle, Lord Sumption held that the legal burden of proof in relation to the *SAAMCO* principle lies on the claimant not the defendant.

So controversial is the *SAAMCO* principle that there was thought to be a realistic possibility that it would be departed from in the *BPE* case. But that did not happen. Rather, for better or worse, it has been cemented into English law and there now appears to be no prospect of going back. It seems inevitable, however, that difficulties will remain. This is because *SAAMCO* ultimately rests on the novel assertion that the liability of a professional person providing information, as opposed to advice (although the distinction between 'information' and 'advice' was regarded as a blunt, rather than a precise, description of the two categories by Lord Sumption in *BPE Solicitors v Hughes-Holland*[187]) is restricted to only those consequences that flow from the information being incorrect. This is so even though the other consequences would not normally be too remote and there would be no break in the chain of causation. The proposition appears to rest on the belief that the other consequences are properly borne by the client who has to take responsibility for the decision taken.[188] But the question that the House of Lords failed to answer is why there should be that cut-off. No reasons at all were given and nor were any given in *BPE*. There was a bare assertion (that the loss fell outside the scope of the duty) disguised as an application of a straightforward principle.

---

[182] [1970] P 172, at 181–182.
[183] M Millner, 'Novus Actus Interveniens: The Present Effect of Wagon Mound' (1971) 22 NILQ 168, 178–179.
[184] [1997] AC 191. See, generally, J Stapleton, 'Negligent Valuers and Falls in the Property Market' (1997) 113 LQR 1; E Peel, 'SAAMCO Revisited' and R Butler, 'SAAMCO in Practice' in *Commercial Remedies* (eds A Burrows and E Peel, OUP 2003) 55–87.
[185] For clarification that the *SAAMCO* scope of duty principle should follow the application of the basic compensatory aim—and be seen as a limitation on it—rather than preceding it, as Lord Hoffmann confusingly suggested ([1997] AC 191, at 210–211), see J Edelman, *McGregor on Damages* (20th edn, Sweet & Maxwell 2018) para 2-002.
[186] [2017] UKSC 21, [2018] AC 599.   [187] ibid. See below, p 125.
[188] There is a parallel here with *The Achilleas* [2008] UKHL 48, [2009] 1 AC 61 in which, as we have seen above at pp 100–102, it was decided that the charterers had not 'assumed responsibility' for the full losses suffered by the owners but only for the losses in the overrun period. Although that decision seems wrong at least some reasons were given for why there was thought to be no assumption of responsibility.

(2) *SAAMCO* and the *SAAMCO* principle

The question at issue in the various cases being decided in *SAAMCO* was the extent to which, if at all, valuers who had negligently overvalued property provided as security for loans were liable in contract or tort for the losses suffered by lenders consequent on the collapse of the property market in the early 1990s. For example, let us assume that claimants had advanced £11 million on the security of a property valued by defendants at £15 million. The property's actual value at the time of valuation was £5 million and the claimants ultimately realised £2.5 million on resale. At first instance, Phillips J held that the claimants were entitled to be put into as good a position as if they had not entered into the loan transaction but that, on grounds of causation, they were not entitled to damages for the fall in the property market.[189] They were therefore entitled to the money lent (£11 million in the above example) minus the actual value of the property at the date of valuation (£5 million in the above example) plus interest from the date the money was lent. This was reversed by the Court of Appeal which held that, applying a 'no transaction' approach, the claimants were entitled to damages for the fall in the market.[190] They were therefore entitled to the money lent (£11 million in the above example) minus the value ultimately realised (£2.5 million in the above example) plus interest from the date the money was lent.

The House of Lords took a mid-position. Unfortunately Lord Hoffmann's speech, with which the other Law Lords agreed, is difficult to interpret. At one level, the reasoning can be expressed quite simply. A lender will be entitled to be put into as good a position as if it had not entered into the loan transaction but can never recover a greater measure than the difference between the represented value of the property and its actual value at the date of the valuation (plus interest). So in the above example the claimants would be entitled to the £8.5 million (£11 million minus £2.5 million) plus interest because that falls within the outer limit of £10 million (£15 million minus £5 million) plus interest. But had the property been valued at £13 million rather than £15 million, the outer limit would have been £8 million (£13 million minus £5 million) so that only £8 million (plus interest) would have been recoverable.

The puzzle lies in determining whether and, if so, why that is the correct measure. Lord Hoffmann reasoned that this followed from carefully analysing at the outset the scope of the valuer's duty of care. The scope of that duty did not extend to protecting the lender against a loss that would have been a consequence of the transaction even if the representation had been true. Or, put another way, the scope of the duty extended only to the consequences of the information being wrong so that there was no liability for losses which would still have been incurred even if the information had been correct. In Lord Hoffmann's words in the *SAAMCO* case:

> '[A] person under a duty to take reasonable care to provide information on which someone else will decide upon a course of action is, if negligent, not generally regarded as responsible for all the consequences of that course of action. He is responsible only for the consequences of the information being wrong. A duty of care which imposes upon the informant responsibility for losses which would have occurred even if the information which he gave had been correct is not in my view fair and reasonable as between the parties. It is therefore inappropriate either as an implied term of contract or as a tortious duty arising from the relationship between them.'[191]

---

[189] [1995] 2 All ER 769.
[190] [1995] QB 375. Five other decisions, some contrary to Phillips J's, were also on appeal.
[191] [1997] AC 191, at 214.

It is also of central importance that in *Nykredit plc v Edward Erdman Group Ltd (No 2)*[192] Lord Hoffmann clarified that the 'scope of the duty' concept was distinct from—and that the *SAAMCO* decision was not based on—remoteness or causation (or a cap on liability). In Lord Hoffmann's words, in the *Nykredit* case:

> 'It was not suggested that the possibility of a fall in the market was unforeseeable or that there was any other factor which negatived the causal connection between lending and losing the money. There was, for example, no evidence that if the lender had not made the advance in question, he would have lost his money in some other way. Nor, if one started from the proposition that the valuer was responsible for the consequences of the loan being made, could there be any logical basis for limiting the recoverable damages to the amount of the overvaluation. The essence of the decision was that this is not where one starts and that the valuer is responsible only for the consequences of the lender having too little security.'[193]

At first sight it might appear that, contrary to Lord Hoffmann's view, the same decision excluding liability for the fall in the market could have been reached applying the law on remoteness or intervening cause. As regards remoteness, we have seen that the courts have a wide degree of discretion in dividing up types of loss, perhaps especially so as regards economic loss.[194] The same conclusion as in the *SAAMCO* case could perhaps have been reached by deciding that the loss consequent on the fall in the property market was too remote because it was a different type of loss (and could not have been reasonably contemplated as a serious possibility at the time of contracting) from the 'ordinary lending loss' suffered because the property did not provide the security that the claimant had been led to expect. Alternatively, one might have reached the same decision as in *SAAMCO* by the sort of reasoning that was subsequently adopted in *The Achilleas*: ie that the valuers had not 'assumed responsibility' for the loss consequent on the fall in the property market.[195]

Similarly, as regards intervening cause, we have seen that the principles are flexible.[196] One could say that the fall in the property market was a natural event that broke the chain of causation between the valuers' negligence and the actual loss suffered by the claimant. The claimant was therefore merely entitled to recover for the direct loss consequent on the security being inadequate and not the indirect loss consequent on the fall in the property market.[197]

The difficulty with both these approaches—and ultimately supporting Lord Hoffmann's view that a different concept was in play—is that the approaches involve straining or rejecting the principles that have been developed for remoteness and intervening causation. To divide, for the purpose of the conventional contractual remoteness test, the loss consequent on the fall in the property market from the other economic loss consequent on the negligent valuation would, at the very least, be highly controversial. Applying the

---

[192] [1997] 1 WLR 1627. This is also supported by the Court of Appeal's reasoning in the *SAAMCO* case that the fall in the property market was neither too remote nor a new intervening cause: [1995] 2 All ER 769, at 841, 842–855.
[193] [1997] 1 WLR 1627, at 1638.   [194] Above, pp 88, 94–97.
[195] See similarly, prior to *The Achilleas*, J Wightman, 'Negligent Valuations and a Drop in the Property Market: the Limits of the Expectation Loss Principle' (1998) 61 MLR 68, 75–76.
[196] Above, pp 107–109.
[197] At first instance, [1995] 2 All ER 769, 809, Phillips J reached a similar (but not identical) conclusion as the House of Lords using the language of causation: 'I do not see how the negligent adviser can fairly be said to have caused that loss unless his advice has been relied upon as providing protection against the risk of that loss.' In his extra-judicial lecture, given to the Chancery Bar Association on 15 June 1999 entitled 'Common Sense and Causing Loss' Lord Hoffmann conceded that one might say causation was relevant to the *SAAMCO* principle: but this was only in the trivial sense that, once outside the scope of the duty, the loss was not 'legally caused' by the breach.

'assumption of responsibility' idea from *The Achilleas* in an 'exclusionary' way is only justified in exceptional circumstances; and it is hard to see that there were exceptional circumstances justifying cutting back the normal allocation of risk, laid down by the standard remoteness rule, according to which the loss should have been fairly borne by the valuers. Similarly, as regards intervening cause, we have seen that normally natural events do not break the chain of causation. Indeed, it is ironic that, in the context of intervening cause, the language of 'scope of duty' has been used to explain why what would otherwise have broken the chain of causation did not do so; that is, it has been used to extend normal liability. In contrast, the *SAAMCO* 'scope of duty' principle operates to limit liability.

The best conclusion is that Lord Hoffmann was correct to regard the *SAAMCO* principle as different from remoteness and intervening cause. It appears to add another separate limitation on compensatory damages. But this conclusion only serves to highlight how controversial the *SAAMCO* principle is. Rather than being a standard application of remoteness or intervening cause, it represents a novel development. So the question remains, is the *SAAMCO* principle justified?

(3) Is the *SAAMCO* principle justified?

It is important to clarify that factual causation was not the basis of the *SAAMCO* decision. As was made clear in the *Nykredit* case,[198] there was no evidence that, had it not loaned money secured on the particular property in question, the lender would have loaned money secured on another property and would therefore have suffered the same 'property market loss' in any event. Similarly, as was made clear in the Court of Appeal in the *SAAMCO* case,[199] the finding of fact in relation to all the cases considered was that, had the valuers not overvalued the land, no loan would have been made (ie to use the old language frowned upon by the House of Lords, these were treated as 'no transaction' rather than 'successful-transaction' cases).

Much discussion has turned on Lord Hoffmann's celebrated mountaineer example. According to this, a mountaineer goes to the doctor about his knee and is negligently told that he is fit to go on an expedition. Had the doctor used reasonable care he would have informed the mountaineer that the knee was unfit and the mountaineer would not have gone on the expedition. He goes on the expedition and suffers an injury which is an entirely foreseeable consequence of mountaineering but has nothing to do with his knee. According to Lord Hoffmann, the doctor ought not to be liable and the justification for this is that the mountaineering injury is outside the scope of the doctor's duty. More specifically, if the representation had been true (so that his knee was fit to go on the expedition), the mountaineer would still have suffered the mountaineering injury.

However, it is important to note—and this weakens the force of the example—that the same conclusion would follow from a standard application of the principles of intervening cause. Assuming that the accident was the consequence of a natural event (eg, a rock-fall or avalanche) the chain of causation would be broken by that intervening cause. This is because the sole contribution that the doctor's breach of duty made to the claimant's loss was that the claimant was in the place where, at the time when, the natural event intervened: ie the injury was coincidental to the breach of duty.[200]

---

[198] [1997] 1 WLR 1627, at 1638.   [199] [1995] 2 All ER 769, at 841a.
[200] See above, pp 107–109. See also E Peel and J Goudkamp, *Winfield & Jolowicz on Tort* (19th edn, Sweet & Maxwell 2014) paras 7.060–7.061.

Moreover, one would still need to apply intervening cause to reach desired results even if the injury were within the scope of the doctor's duty of care. Say, for example, having received the doctor's 'all-clear' on his knee, the mountaineer goes on the expedition. While there, his knee swells up requiring him to be carried down on a stretcher. While being carried down, he is hit by a rock-fall. Applying Lord Hoffmann's approach, it would seem that the rock-fall injury is within the scope of the doctor's duty of care because, had the representation as to the mountaineer's knee been true, his knee would not have swollen up and he would not have been hit by the rock-fall. Yet, applying standard principles, the rock-fall is essentially coincidental to the doctor's breach of duty and would break the chain of causation.

The point to emerge, therefore, is that Lord Hoffmann's mountaineering example does not justify or explain the need for his 'scope of duty' restriction. Standard principles of intervening cause are sufficient and, in relation to variations of the example, are necessary in order to achieve the correct result.

A more fundamental criticism is that Lord Hoffmann's approach undermines the traditional link between the duty broken and the measure of damages, thereby upsetting the standard view that damages for negligent misrepresentation allow escape from a bad bargain. In comparing damages for breach of contract with damages for the tort of misrepresentation, it has been trite law that the former enables the claimant to reap the benefits of a good bargain (putting the claimant into as good a position as if the contract had been performed) while the latter enables the claimant to escape from a bad bargain (by putting the claimant into as good a position as if no representation had been made). In chapter 2, we gave the following simple example to illustrate that the so-called tort measure of damages for misrepresentation may exceed the so-called contract measure of damages for breach of warranty.[201] A, in selling his car to B, makes a misrepresentation about the age of the car. The car is four years old but A tells B that it is one year old. B pays £5,000 for the car. The market value of a one-year-old car which otherwise has the same characteristics as the car A is selling is £4,500. The market value of the car, however, given that it is in fact four years old, is £4,000.

In this situation, B's damages for the tortious misrepresentation (including negligent misrepresentation) would be £1,000 (£5,000 – £4,000) whereas the damages for breach of warranty would be only £500 (£4,500 – £4,000). Yet it appears that this basic proposition, known to all law students, is inconsistent with Lord Hoffmann's approach. According to Lord Hoffmann one should put the claimant into as good a position as if no representation had been made only to the extent that this does not put the claimant into a better position than if the representation had been true. This is because the (normal) scope of the representor's duty is confined to protecting the claimant against the consequences of the information being wrong. It appears therefore that damages for the tort of negligent misrepresentation in the above example would be cut back from £1,000 to £500. The claimant could not escape from a bad bargain; or to use well-known academic terminology, the reliance interest would be limited by a lower expectation interest. That Lord Hoffmann was assimilating damages for negligent misrepresentation with damages for breach of contract in bad bargains meets his argument that 'it would seem paradoxical that the liability of a person who warranted the accuracy of the information should be less than that of a person who gave no such warranty but failed to take reasonable care'.[202]

Yet, in principle, this seems incorrect. Where one is suing for breach of contract, it is correct to measure damages according to the expectation interest. This is because the very

---

[201] See above, p 39.   [202] [1997] AC 191, at 213–214.

duty broken was one to fulfil a promise that would have put the claimant in the promised position whether for good (under a good bargain) or bad (under a bad bargain). But misrepresentation (or breach of a contractual duty of care in giving information) rests on a duty not to induce the claimant to act in a particular way. Reflecting that duty, the aim of the damages should be to put the claimant into the position it would have been in if it had not been induced to act in that way (including not entering into a bad bargain). The protection of the reliance interest is therefore the natural measure of recovery for misrepresentation and there is no principled reason why it should be limited by the expectation interest.

Jane Stapleton made a similar criticism in her excellent case-note on *SAAMCO*.[203] She wrote:

'[Lord Hoffmann's] is not the correct approach to determining the scope of the duty of care. What makes the valuation wrongful is that it is careless, not that it is not true. The wrong is that the defendant did not use care: he valued the property at V when he should have valued it at V*. When dealing with liability for breach of an obligation of care the correct test is one based on the approach of the Court of Appeal: determining ... what were the consequences of the information being given carelessly and therefore asking where the plaintiff would have been had he received a careful valuation ... In contrast, Lord Hoffmann sees the wrong as V not being accurate. He therefore focuses on the consequences of the information being wrong, and asks where the plaintiff would have been had the valuation which was given been accurate ... Lord Hoffmann's approach in effect allows a defendant to take advantage of the fact that the plaintiff made a bad bargain, but in circumstances where it is inappropriate to allow the defendant to take such advantage.'

Nor, as a matter of principle, can it make a difference whether the negligent misrepresentation is made by a professional person, who the claimant has approached for that information, or by a non-professional person such as a person selling his or her car. Yet it appears that the motivation behind *SAAMCO* was to protect professionals.

(4) Scope of application and difficulties in applying *SAAMCO*

The flawed basis of the *SAAMCO* decision perhaps explains the difficulties the courts have subsequently encountered in applying it. Four such difficulties are adverted to below. Before examining these, it is worth clarifying the scope of the *SAAMCO* principle as applied in subsequent cases. The case itself, and the two House of Lords' decisions following on it,[204] concerned negligent valuations and losses consequent on falls in the property market. However, subsequent cases have made clear that the scope of the *SAAMCO* principle is not so confined. Even putting to one side cases where the 'scope of duty' language has been used in traditional ways (eg, to determine the type of loss for which a claim for breach of statutory duty could be brought),[205] the *SAAMCO* principle has been applied to a variety of negligent misrepresentations or negligent failures to give correct information. For example, the *SAAMCO* principle has been applied to information given by solicitors

---

[203] J Stapleton, 'Negligent Valuers and Falls in the Property Market' (1997) 113 LQR 1, 3. For another excellent critical case-note, see J O'Sullivan, 'Negligent Professional Advice and Market Movements' [1997] CLJ 19. The SAAMCO case was distinguished, but without casting doubt on the decision, by the High Court of Australia in *Kenny v Good Pty Ltd v MGICA (1992) Ltd* (1999) 163 ALR 611. For a case-note pointing out the difficulties of interpreting the judgments in that case, see D McLauchlan and C Rickett, '*SAAMCO* in the High Court of Australia' (2000) 116 LQR 1.
[204] *Nykredit Mortgage Bank plc v Edward Erdman Group Ltd (No 2)* [1997] 1 WLR 1627; *Platform Home Loans Ltd v Oyston Shipways Ltd* [2000] 2 AC 190.
[205] *Blue Circle Industries plc v MOD* [1999] Ch 289; for traditional use of this idea in this context, see, eg, *Gorris v Scott* (1874) LR 9 Exch 125.

to lenders[206] or to purchasers;[207] to statements made by a vendor to a purchaser as regards the time within which the transaction could be finalised and the title registered;[208] to an architect's failure to warn of the consequences of his design;[209] and to statements made by a public or quasi-public body (the Intervention Board for Agricultural Produce) to a farmer as regards milk quotas.[210] One must also recall that Lord Hoffmann relied on his hypothetical example of a doctor making a negligent misrepresentation to his patient. It seems, therefore, that the *SAAMCO* principle has been treated as a principle of general application in contract or tort to negligent misrepresentation and negligent failure to provide information. In contrast, the tort of deceit was put to one side by Lord Hoffmann as raising different considerations where the *SAAMCO* limitation was inappropriate.[211]

A first difficulty encountered in applying the *SAAMCO* principle has been in ascertaining when the cause of action accrues (for the purposes of a tortious claim for negligent valuation) and from when interest should be paid. This was the issue for the House of Lords in *Nykredit Mortgage Bank plc v Edward Erdman Group Ltd (No 2)*.[212] Under the Supreme Court Act 1981, s 35A, a court can award simple interest on damages from the time when the cause of action arises. The standard approach to negligent valuation pre-*SAAMCO* was that the date of accrual of the cause of action in tort—and the date from when interest should be paid—was normally when the lender entered into the losing transaction.[213] While there may be variations on this,[214] the *SAAMCO* principle has made this basic position more complex because the relevant loss is now regarded not as that suffered by entering into the transaction as such but rather as that suffered because of the overvaluation. In *Nykredit* it was therefore decided that, while the cause of action in tort did accrue at the time of the transaction,[215] interest was not payable until the claimant had suffered its full allowable loss (within what we may for shorthand purposes call the *SAAMCO* 'cap') which was not sustained until nine months later. Not only does *Nykredit* therefore require an unusual separation between the date of accrual of the cause of action in tort and the date from when interest is payable, it requires a difficult and time-consuming exercise plotting when it is that the *SAAMCO* 'cap' is reached.

---

[206] *Bristol and West Building Society v Mothew* [1996] 4 All ER 698; *Bristol and West Building Society v Fancy & Jackson* [1997] 4 All ER 582; *Portman Building Society v Bevan Ashford* [2000] 1 EGLR 81; *Lloyds Bank Plc v Crosse & Crosse* [2001] PNLR 34; *Haugesund Kommune v Depfa ACS Bank (No 2)* [2011] EWCA Civ 33, [2011] 3 All ER 655; *LSREF III Wight Ltd v Gateley LLP* [2016] EWCA Civ 359, [2016] PNLR 21; *BPE Solicitors v Hughes-Holland* [2017] UKSC 21, [2018] AC 599. The second and fourth of those cases was criticised by Lord Sumption in the *BPE* case for having failed to apply *SAAMCO* correctly.

[207] *Cottingham v Attey Bower & Jones* [2000] PNLR 557; *Peterson v Personal Representatives of Cyril Rivlin* [2002] EWCA Civ 194, [2002] Lloyd's Rep PN 386. See also *Main v Giamborne & Law* [2017] EWCA Civ 1193, [2018] PNLR 2 (where *SAAMCO* was considered applicable to a claim for equitable compensation for breach of trust against a solicitor although, controversially, the facts were held to be within the advice rather than information category so that the *SAAMCO* limitation did not apply: see below, p 519).

[208] *Green v Turner* [1999] PNLR 28.

[209] *HOK Sport Ltd v Aintree Racecourse Co Ltd* [2002] EWHC 3094 (TCC), [2003] Lloyd's Rep PN 148.

[210] *Leidig v Intervention Board for Agricultural Produce* [2000] Lloyd's Rep PN 144.

[211] This has subsequently been confirmed, and the Court of Appeal's contrary approach in *Downs v Chappell* [1996] 3 All ER 344, at 361–362 disapproved, by the House of Lords in *Smith New Court Securities Ltd v Scrimgeour Vickers (Asset Management)* [1997] AC 254. The 'fiction of fraud' language used in the Misrepresentation Act 1967, s 2(1) may mean that the SAAMCO principle does not apply to s 2(1) damages as well as damages for deceit itself: *Avon Insurance plc v Swire Fraser Ltd* [2000] 1 All ER (Comm) 573.

[212] [1997] 1 WLR 1627.

[213] Eg *Forster v Outred & Co* [1982] 1 WLR 86; *Bell v Peter Browne & Co* [1990] 2 QB 495.

[214] Eg *First National Commercial Bank v Humberts* [1995] 2 All ER 673.

[215] Surprisingly there was very little mention in *Nykredit* of the cause of action in contract which clearly accrued at the date of the valuer's breach irrespective of any damage caused. The decision that interest would be payable only from when the claimant sustained its full allowable loss would presumably apply equally to a claim for breach of contract.

A second difficulty is in the application of contributory negligence. In principle, one would have expected contributory negligence to be applied to the legally recoverable loss (ie the loss recoverable under *SAAMCO*) and not to a higher irrecoverable loss. If one considers the analogy of remoteness, contributory negligence is applied to reduce damages for non-remote loss. It is not applied to reduce damages for remote loss. So, for example, if contributory negligence were applicable in contract to a case like *Victoria Laundry (Windsor) Ltd v Newman Industries Ltd*[216] it would surely apply to reduce damages for the recoverable ordinary profits and would not first be applied to the irrecoverable exceptional profits. Yet in *Platform Home Loans Ltd v Oyston Shipways Ltd*[217] the majority of the House of Lords (Lord Cooke dissenting) held that a 20% reduction for contributory negligence applied to the claimant's overall loss attributable to negligent overvaluation and not to the claimant's legally recoverable loss under the *SAAMCO* principle. So where the claimant's overall loss (ie reliance loss) was £611,750 and the recoverable loss under *SAAMCO* (ie reliance loss limited by expectation) was £500,000, a 20% reduction for contributory negligence was applied to the first figure (giving damages of £489,400) and not to the second figure (which would have given damages of £400,000). This decision seems correct. But, applying the *SAAMCO* principle, this is only because, as Lord Millett explained, the contributory negligence (in not checking adequately the creditworthiness of the borrower and in having a general policy of lending 70% of the secured value) did not directly relate to the overvaluation as opposed to the overall loss. As Lord Millett said, 'Where the lender's negligence has caused or contributed directly to the overvaluation, then it may be appropriate to apply the reduction to the amount of the overvaluation as well as to the overall loss.'[218] It is not obvious that this qualification will be easy to apply in practice. Above all, the point to stress is that the *SAAMCO* principle has required the development of a novel approach to contributory negligence which requires a departure from the usual starting point of applying contributory negligence to legally recoverable loss only. Prior to *SAAMCO*, the same decision in *Platform Homes* would have been simply and straightforwardly reached without any departure from normal legal principle.

A third difficulty is that one can think of examples where, on the face of it, Lord Hoffmann's approach appears to produce clearly unacceptable results. Say, for example, a representation is made which the claimant relies on to forgo profits that would otherwise have been obtained. More specifically, let us assume that a claimant was given negligent legal information to the effect that developing a particular product (that would have been very profitable) would infringe a third party's intellectual property rights.[219] Relying on that information, the claimant did not develop the product and thereby lost profits. In this type of situation, to limit the claimant to the position he would have been in if the representation had been true would mean that the claimant could not recover for the lost profits (because had the representation been true the claimant would not have had the right to develop the product). That result is plainly unacceptable. The lost profits should be straightforwardly recoverable to protect the claimant's reliance interest. No doubt Lord Hoffmann would seek to arrive at the same result by distinguishing the *SAAMCO* case and by arguing that the loss of profit in this example was within the scope of the duty. But it is not obvious wherein the distinction lies.

A fourth difficulty is the distinction drawn by Lord Hoffmann between providing information and advice. His Lordship said:

---

[216] [1949] 2 KB 528: see above, p 92.   [217] [2000] 2 AC 190.   [218] ibid, at 215.
[219] This example was discussed in *Green v Turner* [1999] PNLR 28.

'The principle thus stated distinguishes between a duty to *provide information* for the purpose of enabling someone else to decide upon a course of action and a duty to *advise* someone as to what course of action he should take. If the duty is to advise whether or not a course of action should be taken, the adviser must take reasonable care to consider all the potential consequences of that course of action. If he is negligent, he will therefore be responsible for all the foreseeable loss which is a consequence of that course of action having been taken. If his duty is only to supply information, he must take reasonable care to ensure that the information is correct and if he is negligent, he will be responsible for all the foreseeable consequences of the information being wrong.'[220]

But it is hard to see the principled difference between these two situations and, as a matter of practice, one surely shades into the other. This is supported by *Aneco Reinsurance Underwriting Ltd v Johnson & Higgins Ltd*[221] in which all of their Lordships sought to explain the distinction being drawn by Lord Hoffmann in a way that was not dependent on the labels 'advice' or 'information'. For, as Lord Millett said, '[the distinction] between a duty to provide information and a duty to give advice ... is a distinction without a difference, for the terms are interchangeable.'[222]

How to distinguish the two categories was returned to by the Supreme Court in *BPE Solicitors v Hughes-Holland*.[223] Here the claimant had lent £200,000 to a developer believing that the developer was also putting money into the development. That was incorrect and the developer used the money lent to discharge a debt. The development did not go ahead and the claimant lost all the money lent. The claimant sued the defendant solicitor who had negligently drawn up the legal documentation for the loan in such a way that it contained statements that confirmed the claimant's incorrect belief that the developer was also contributing money. The defendant solicitor also negligently failed to inform the claimant that that was the position. Had the information been true (that the developer was also putting money in) the claimant would still have lost his money. It was held that *SAAMCO* applied and that no damages were recoverable. Lord Sumption recognised 'the descriptive inadequacy'[224] of the labels 'information' and 'advice' and clarified that the underlying distinction was between a case where the professional is 'responsible for guiding the whole decision-making process' as against where the professional 'contributes a limited part of the material on which his client will rely in deciding whether to enter into a prospective transaction'.[225] The *SAAMCO* limitation applies to the latter but not the former.

In the light of these continuing difficulties in application—as well as the argument set out above that the basis of the *SAAMCO* principle is flawed—it is not surprising that the *SAAMCO* principle remains very controversial. This is borne out by the different views taken in the House of Lords' in *Aneco Reinsurance Underwriting Ltd v Johnson & Higgins Ltd*.[226] Here the claimant insurance company sought reinsurance. This was arranged for them by the defendant brokers. Unfortunately the brokers failed properly to present the risk to the reinsurers who were able to avoid the reinsurance contract, and did so, for material non-disclosure. Under the insurance contract (the 'Bullen Treaty'), for which the insurers were seeking reinsurance, the claimant suffered a loss of $35 million. Had the reinsurance been valid, the claimant would have recovered about $11 million. That is, even if

---

[220] [1997] AC 191, at 214. The former (providing information) has been referred to as a category one case and the latter (advising) as a category two case.
[221] [2001] UKHL 51, [2001] 2 All ER (Comm) 929.   [222] ibid, at [62].
[223] [2017] UKSC 21, [2018] AC 599.   [224] ibid, at [39].   [225] ibid, at [40]–[41].
[226] For an excellent discussion of this case see E Peel, '*SAAMCO* Revisited' and R Butler, '*SAAMCO* in Practice' in *Commercial Remedies* (eds A Burrows and E Peel, OUP 2003) 55, 60–63, 71, 81–86.

the reinsurance had been valid the claimant would still have lost $24 million. The claimant brought an action in contract and tort against the brokers on the basis that the brokers had negligently informed them that reinsurance for the Bullen Treaty was available in the market whereas, in fact, it was never available. Had the claimant known the truth it would never have entered into the Bullen Treaty insurance. It therefore sought damages for its full loss of $35 million. This claim succeeded (Lord Millett dissenting).

The majority of the House of Lords considered that *SAAMCO* was distinguishable. Here the scope of the duty of care was not confined to obtaining reinsurance and informing the claimant that reinsurance had been obtained. Rather it was a wider duty and extended to advising the claimant generally on what course of action to take (including whether to enter into the Bullen Treaty). In the words of Lord Steyn, the facts here fell on the other 'side of the line drawn in *SAAMCO*'.[227] In the light of that wider duty, the wider measure of damages—putting the claimant into as good a position as if it had not entered into the transaction—was appropriate.

It is noteworthy that Lord Steyn presented the issue as one of disputed fact not law. He thereby avoided re-examining the correctness of the *SAAMCO* principle. While essentially adopting the same approach, Lord Lloyd suggested that *SAAMCO* was laying down a narrow principle for a special class of case (typically, but not exclusively, concerning valuers). That special class of case is where the scope of the duty is confined to the giving of specific information. Lords Slynn and Browne-Wilkinson agreed with Lords Lloyd and Steyn.

Lord Millett gave a powerful dissenting speech. In his view, this case was indistinguishable from *SAAMCO*. The defendants were not under a duty to advise in relation to the claimant's decision to enter into the Bullen Treaty. The defendants were brokers, not underwriters, and their only duty was to take reasonable care to ensure that the information which they did supply was correct. This was directly covered by *SAAMCO* so that the defendants were responsible only for the consequences of that information being wrong. Had the information been correct, the claimant would have had reinsurance of $11 million but would still have lost $25 million. The correct measure of damages, in Lord Millett's opinion, was therefore $11 million not $35 million.

It is submitted that, applying *SAAMCO*, Lord Millett's speech is correct. The brokers could not be classed as general advisers. They were concerned with a specific task and had made a specific representation. On the other hand, the decision of the majority is to be welcomed in confining—albeit artificially—the application of *SAAMCO*. In most cases, there is no clear difference between a duty to give general advice and a duty to give specific information. This is shown by the fact that all general advice may be regarded as comprising a number of specific pieces of information. Albeit contrary to the *SAAMCO* principle, the important issue *should* be whether the claimant relied on the representation in entering into the whole transaction; if he did, damages for having entered the whole transaction should be recoverable. It is in contradicting that, that the *SAAMCO* principle is flawed. In this respect, it is again noteworthy that, prior to *SAAMCO*, the decision in *Aneco* would have been straightforward.[228]

It seems inevitable that the *SAAMCO* principle will continue to generate litigation as the courts struggle with it. It is not clear why Lord Hoffmann, followed by Lord Sumption in the *BPE* case, should wish to protect professionals from the full consequences of their provision of incorrect information. But if that is the policy, it needs to be stated openly and clearly.

---

[227] [2001] UKHL 51, [2001] 2 All ER (Comm) 929, at [43].
[228] As was exemplified by the concession of counsel for the brokers in the similar case of *Youell v Bland Welch & Co Ltd (No 2)* [1990] 2 Lloyd's Rep 431.

5. The duty to mitigate

The duty to mitigate is a further restriction on compensatory damages.[229] On the one hand a claimant should not sit back and do nothing to minimise loss flowing from a wrong but should rather use its resources to do what is reasonable to put itself into as good a position as if the contract had been performed or the tort not committed. On the other hand, it should not unreasonably incur expense subsequent to the wrong. The policy is one of encouraging the claimant, once a wrong has occurred, to be to a reasonable extent self-reliant or, in economists' terminology, to be efficient, rather than pinning all loss on the defendant.[230]

The term 'duty to mitigate' should not be thought to indicate that the claimant can itself be sued for failure to comply with its duty: rather the consequence of such a failure is simply that no damages are given for the avoidable loss.[231] In so far as the language of 'duty' is thought misleading, one can avoid it by describing this restriction as one whereby loss, that should reasonably have been avoided, cannot be recovered. The restriction is best regarded as comprising two principles, the first focusing on unreasonable inaction, the second on unreasonable action.

(1) The first principle—unreasonable inaction

A claimant must take all reasonable steps to minimise its loss so that it cannot recover for any loss which it could reasonably have avoided but has failed to avoid. The classic judicial formulation of this is Viscount Haldane LC's in *British Westinghouse Electric v Underground Electric Rlys Co of London Ltd*[232] (a contract case), who said that the principle '... imposes on a plaintiff the duty of taking all reasonable steps to mitigate the loss consequent on the breach and debars him from claiming any part of the damage which is due to his neglect to take such steps'.

Clearly whether steps should reasonably have been taken to minimise loss depends on the particular facts in question. However, some indication can be given of the sort of factors that have been considered important in past cases in deciding this:

(i) Where the claimant has been wrongfully dismissed he need not accept an offer of re-employment from his former employer *if* factors like the following are present: the new work would involve a reduction in status, employment elsewhere would be more likely to be permanent, or the claimant has no confidence in his employers because of their past treatment of him. Such factors were present in *Yetton v Eastwoods Froy Ltd*,[233] and it was therefore held that the claimant had not failed in his duty to mitigate by refusing his former

---

[229] The duty to mitigate is also sometimes used as a positive reason for awarding damages, ie one can recover reasonable expenses incurred in seeking to minimise loss. But it is simpler to view this proposition as a natural consequence of there being no relevant restriction limiting the compensatory principle.

[230] M Bridge, 'Mitigation of Damages in Contract and the Meaning of Avoidable Loss' (1989) 105 LQR 398 argues that several policies are at play in explaining the duty to mitigate.

[231] Theoretically, contributory negligence should apply as a mid-position to *reduce* damages but no case has been found allowing contributory negligence as a mid-position alternative to the duty to mitigate: cf above, pp 116–117.

[232] [1912] AC 673, at 689.   [233] [1967] 1 WLR 104.

employer's offer of re-employment. The opposite decision was reached in *Brace v Calder*,[234] where such factors were not present.

(ii) In relation to a contract of sale, if the defendant makes an offer of alternative performance, it will generally be unreasonable for the claimant to turn it down if acceptance would reduce its loss. So in *Payzu Ltd v Saunders*[235] the defendants, who had contracted to deliver goods to the claimants in instalments, refused to deliver the second and subsequent instalments unless the claimants would pay cash on delivery. The claimants refused this offer and sued the defendants for breach, claiming damages based on the difference between the market and contract prices, the market having risen. It was held that although the defendants were in breach, the claimants had failed in their duty to mitigate, and they recovered merely £50 damages for the period of credit they would have lost by paying the cash on delivery rather than when stipulated in the contract. Contrasting with this is *Strutt v Whitnell*,[236] where the defendants offered to repurchase from the claimant a house, which they could not transfer to him with vacant possession. The claimant's refusal of the offer was held not to amount to a failure to mitigate; the offer was not of an alternative performance but of no performance at all and was in effect merely equivalent to an offer by the defendants to pay the claimant damages.

(iii) The claimant's conduct is unreasonable if she refuses an operation contrary to firm medical advice. In *McAuley v London Transport Executive*[237] the claimant, having been injured by the defendants, refused to have an operation strongly recommended by a doctor which, if successful, would have restored him to his previous earning capacity. It was held that his refusal was unreasonable, and the claimant was therefore able to recover his loss of earnings only until the time when he would have recovered had he undergone the operation. On the other hand in *Selvanayagam v University of West Indies*[238] the Privy Council upheld the trial judge's decision that the claimant had not been unreasonable in refusing to undergo a neck operation. A doctor had recommended the operation but, given the claimant's diabetic condition, the recommendation had not been a strong one. Similarly in *Geest plc v Lansiquot*[239] it was held that the claimant had not been unreasonable in not going ahead with an operation on her back where the doctor had made plain that surgery could not guarantee a cure and where he was clearly ready to respect her decision if she decided against the operation.

(iv) It will generally be unreasonable for the claimant to refuse offers of help which would have prevented further property damage. In *Anderson v Hoen, The Flying Fish*[240] the claimant's ship was damaged by the negligence of those in charge of the defendant's vessel. After the collision, the claimant's captain refused aid and in consequence the ship was destroyed. The claimant was able to recover for the damage caused by the collision but not for the additional loss when the ship was destroyed. Somewhat similarly in *Uzinterimpex JSC v Standard Bank Plc*,[241] in the context of applying the duty to mitigate to the tort of conversion, an owner was held to have failed in that duty by unreasonably turning down

---

[234] [1895] 2 QB 253.
[235] [1919] 2 KB 581. See also *Sotiros Shipping Inc v Sameiet Solholt, The Solholt* [1983] 1 Lloyd's Rep 605. These decisions are criticised by M Bridge, 'Mitigation of Damages in Contract and the Meaning of Avoidable Loss' (1989) 105 LQR 398.
[236] [1975] 1 WLR 870.   [237] [1957] 2 Lloyd's Rep 500.
[238] [1983] 1 All ER 824. Note that in putting the burden of proof in relation to the duty to mitigate on the claimant this decision was disapproved by the Privy Council in *Geest plc v Lansiquot* [2002] UKPC 48, [2002] 1 WLR 3111: see above, pp 85–86.
[239] [2002] UKPC 48, [2002] 1 WLR 3111.   [240] (1865) 3 Moo PCCNS 77.
[241] [2008] EWCA Civ 819, [2008] 2 Lloyd's Rep 456.

an offer by the tortfeasor for the goods to be returned or for deteriorating goods to be sold off and the sale proceeds paid into a joint account pending resolution of the dispute. No damages could therefore be recovered in the tort of conversion for subsequently being deprived of the goods or for the deterioration in the value of the goods.

(v) The claimant need not take action which will put its commercial reputation or good public relations at risk. In *James Finlay & Co Ltd v Kwik Hoo Tong*[242] the seller under a cif contract tendered to the buyer a bill of lading which incorrectly stated the date of shipment. The buyer was unaware of this and entered into sub-contracts but the sub-purchasers, realising the error on the bill of lading, refused in breach of contract to take delivery. The buyer sued the seller for breach of contract and recovered substantial damages, the Court of Appeal holding that the buyer was not bound to reduce its loss by suing the sub-purchasers because to do so, when knowing of the error on the bill of lading, might seriously injure its commercial reputation. Similarly in *London and South of England Building Society v Stone*[243] borrowers from the claimant building society had covenanted to keep the house being purchased in good repair. In fact the house suffered from serious subsidence and was valueless and the claimant undertook repairs at a cost to itself of £29,000. The claimant had made the loan on the strength of the defendant valuer's report which had negligently failed to disclose the subsidence. In an action brought in contract and tort against the defendant valuer the claimant recovered as damages the sum lent (£11,880). The Court of Appeal rejected the defendant's argument that there should be a deduction of £3,000, as the amount the claimant could have recovered from the borrowers by enforcing the repair covenant, because, to maintain its good public relations, it was reasonable for the claimant not to call upon the borrowers to pay for any part of the repairs.

(vi) The claimant need not take steps which would involve the claimant in complicated litigation. In *Pilkington v Wood*[244] the claimant bought a house but when he came to sell it he discovered that his vendor had given him a defective title. The claimant sued the defendant, his solicitor, for contractual negligence and recovered damages based on the difference in value between the property with and without good title. The defendant's argument that the claimant should have mitigated by suing his vendor was rejected by Harman J because, '... the so-called duty to mitigate does not go so far as to oblige the injured party ... to embark on a complicated and difficult piece of litigation against a third party'.[245] But as a rare exception to this, the Court of Appeal in *Walker v Medlicott*[246] held that the claimant, who was suing a solicitor for negligent will-drafting, had failed in his duty to mitigate his loss by not first seeking rectification of the will. This rare exception appears to stem from the courts' belief that a negligence action against a solicitor is a less satisfactory solution to the problem of an incorrectly drawn-up will than is rectification of the will. The duty to mitigate is therefore being used as a means of ensuring that a claim for negligent will-drafting is used as a last resort.

(vii) The claimant need not take steps which it cannot financially afford, ie impecuniosity is an excuse for failure to mitigate. This is examined in a later section.[247]

---

[242] [1929] 1 KB 400.   [243] [1983] 1 WLR 1242.   [244] [1953] Ch 770.
[245] [1953] Ch 770, at 777. *Pilkington v Wood* was distinguished in *Western Trust & Savings Ltd v Clive Travers & Co* [1997] PNLR 295 (lenders had failed in their duty to mitigate by failing to enforce their security by a straightforward possession action).
[246] [1999] 1 All ER 685. This was distinguished in *Horsfall v Haywards* [1999] 1 FLR 1182, which was another negligent will-drafting case.
[247] Below, p 145.

(2) The second principle—unreasonable action

Unreasonable action subsequent to a wrong is normally regarded as an aspect of intervening cause. But the unreasonable incurring of expense subsequent to the wrong is generally viewed as an aspect of the duty to mitigate.[248]

The principle is that a claimant should not unreasonably incur expense subsequent to the wrong. As with the first principle, what is unreasonable depends on the facts, but a number of illustrations can be given in most of which the expense was held to be reasonably incurred.

So, for example, in *Holden Ltd v Bostock & Co Ltd*,[249] the defendants had sold sugar to the claimants for brewing beer. Unfortunately the sugar had contained arsenic. To prevent any loss of business the claimants advertised that they had changed their brewing methods. In an action against the defendants for breach of contract, the claimants were awarded, inter alia, the advertising costs. Again in *Bacon v Cooper (Metals) Ltd*[250] the high hire-purchase interest charges paid for a rotor to replace that damaged beyond repair because of the defendants' breach of contract were held to be reasonably incurred and recoverable. No doubt the most common example of recoverable reasonable expenses are the medical, hospital and nursing expenses undertaken following personal injury.[251]

A particularly colourful illustration is provided by *Banco de Portugal v Waterlow & Sons Ltd*.[252] Here the defendants contracted to print banknotes for the claimant bank. In breach of contract they delivered a large number of these to a criminal, who put them into circulation in Portugal. On discovering this, the bank withdrew the issue. It then undertook to exchange all the notes illegally circulated for others. In an action brought against them for breach of contract the defendants argued that they were only liable for the cost of printing new notes, which amounted to £8,922, and that the further heavy loss was due to the bank's own act in giving value for the notes. But the House of Lords, by a majority, rejected this argument and held the defendants liable for the further loss because the conduct of the bank was reasonable, having regard to its commercial obligations towards the public. Lord MacMillan emphasised that no great weight should be attached to the defendant's argument that cheaper measures could have been taken:

> '[T]he measures which [the claimant] may be driven to adopt in order to extricate himself ought not to be weighed in nice scales at the instance of the party whose breach of contract has occasioned the difficulty. It is often easy after an emergency has passed to criticise the steps which have been taken to meet it, but such criticism does not come well from those who have themselves created the emergency … [The claimant] will not be held disentitled to recover the cost of such measures merely because the party in breach can suggest that other measures less burdensome to him might have been taken.'[253]

---

[248] Above, p 85.   [249] (1902) 18 TLR 317.
[250] [1982] 1 All ER 397. See also *Mattocks v Mann* [1993] RTR 13 and *Burdis v Livsey* [2002] EWCA Civ 510, [2003] QB 36, where the cost of hiring a replacement car, while the claimant's car was being repaired, was considered reasonable and recoverable even though those repairs, through no fault of the claimant, had taken longer than they should have done (and the hire charges were therefore higher than they should have been). For a further illustration of reasonably incurred costs being recovered—here the costs in paying a landlord for releasing a forfeiture clause so as to increase the value of the claimant lender's security over the property—see *LSREF III Wight Ltd v Gateley LLP* [2016] EWCA Civ 359, [2016] PNLR 21.
[251] Below, p 239.
[252] [1932] AC 452. For an argument that the bank, by issuing and transferring new notes, suffered no loss other than the printing costs, see F Oditah, 'Takeovers, Share Exchanges and the Meaning of Loss' (1996) 112 LQR 424, 437–441. See also below, p 513 n 23.
[253] [1932] AC 452, at 506. This passage was cited with approval in *Bacon v Cooper* [1982] 1 All ER 397, at 399; *London and South of England Building Society v Stone* [1983] 3 All ER 105, at 121; *LE Jones (Insurance Brokers) Ltd v Portsmouth City Council* [2002] EWCA Civ 1723, [2003] 1 WLR 427, at [26]; *Borealis AB v Geogas Trading*

On the other hand, in *Compania Financiera Soleada SA v Harmoor Tanker Corpn Inc, The Borag*,[254] the claimants in seeking to gain the release of a ship detained in breach of contract took out a loan requiring very high interest charges. It was held by the Court of Appeal that such high interest charges should not be compensated since the claimants had not acted reasonably in incurring them.

It should also be stressed that the fact that the incurring of expense has overall augmented the loss, rather than minimised it, ie it has not been a success, does not mean that it was unreasonably incurred and is irrecoverable. A statement to this effect in the twelfth edition of *Mayne and McGregor on Damages* was cited with approval in *Lloyds and Scottish Finance Ltd v Modern Cars and Caravans (Kingston) Ltd*.[255] *Esso Petroleum Co Ltd v Mardon*[256] may be said to illustrate it. Here the claimant had been induced to enter into a tenancy agreement for a petrol station by the defendant's false estimates of the potential throughput of petrol. In an action for negligent misrepresentation, or breach of a warranty that the estimate was made using reasonable care, the claimant was held able to recover all the loss he had suffered, until he gave up possession. This included the loss after he had entered into a fresh tenancy agreement. In the Court of Appeal's opinion, in view of the loss already suffered, the claimant was acting reasonably in attempting to mitigate some of that loss by entering into that new agreement: the fact that he actually suffered further loss as a result did not prevent recovery.

(3) Loss that would have been suffered even if the claimant had complied with the 'duty' to mitigate

Although sometimes overlooked, it is important to appreciate that, even if the claimant cannot recover for loss because of a failure to mitigate (ie it is loss that the claimant could reasonably have avoided), the claimant is still entitled to recover for the loss that would have been suffered even if the claimant had complied with the 'duty' to mitigate. For example, in *Payzu Ltd v Saunders*,[257] where the claimants unreasonably turned down the contract-breaker's offer of alternative performance, the claimants still recovered £50 damages for the loss that would have been incurred even if they had acted reasonably by accepting that offer. Scrutton LJ plainly regarded it as uncontroversial that the claimants were still entitled to damages for the loss that they would have suffered had the claimants acted reasonably when he said that a claimant can 'recover no more than he would have suffered even if he had acted reasonably'.[258]

Although at first sight this may seem strange, in that the claimant may appear to be compensated for a loss that it did not in fact suffer, it is best to view this as compensation for that part of the claimant's actual loss equivalent to what could not have been avoided even if the claimant had acted reasonably. In other words, the approach is analogous to that applied in respect of remoteness under the principle of *Cory v Thames Ironworks Co*.[259]

The point is well-illustrated by *Herrmann v Withers LLP*.[260] Here the claimants were awarded damages for breach of the defendant solicitor's duty of care in incorrectly advising

---

SA [2010] EWHC 2789 (Comm), [2011] 1 Lloyd's Rep 482, at [50]; *Thai Airways International Public Co Ltd v KI Holdings Co Ltd* [2015] EWHC 1250 (Comm), [2016] 1 All ER (Comm) 675, at [38].
[254] [1981] 1 WLR 274.   [255] [1966] 1 QB 764.
[256] [1976] QB 801. See also *Hoffberger v Ascot International Bloodstock Bureau Ltd* (1976) 120 Sol Jo 130. *Banco de Portugal v Waterlow & Sons Ltd* [1932] AC 452 may be a further example, depending on what was regarded as the value of the bank's commercial obligations to the public. Somewhat similar is *Gebrüder Metalmann GmbH & Co KG v NBR (London) Ltd* [1984] 1 Lloyd's Rep 614.
[257] [1919] 2 KB 581.   [258] ibid, at 589.   [259] See above, p 97.
[260] [2012] EWHC 1492 (Ch), [2012] PNLR 28.

them that, in relation to a house that they were purchasing, they had a statutory right to access a communal garden without charge. While the claimants were prima facie entitled to damages for the difference in value between the purchase price and the actual value of the property, they were held to have failed in their duty to mitigate because they had refused to accept the offer of paying for a licence to access that garden. Nevertheless they were held entitled to damages for the cost of such a licence and the legal expenses that would have been incurred in acquiring it. Although they did not incur such costs, Newey J made clear that one should regard this as equivalent to that part of the loss (the difference in value) that could not reasonably have been avoided. Newey J said the following:[261]

'Where a claimant has failed to mitigate, he is not entitled to recover more than the loss he would have sustained had he done so. The extent to which he is compensated for the loss he has suffered is reduced because, had he mitigated, there would have been less loss. He may or may not have incurred loss in quite the way he would have done had he mitigated; that is immaterial. It is not a matter of compensating for "costs which ought to have been incurred but weren't" but of limiting the damages he receives for the (larger) loss he has in fact sustained. He is compensated for loss he has suffered, but only up to the amount of loss he would have suffered had he mitigated. An example may help. Suppose that the victim of a wrong stands to suffer loss of £100,000 but could readily avoid that loss by spending £75,000. If he unreasonably fails to do so, and so loses the £100,000, he can be held responsible for increasing his loss by £25,000 (£100,000 less £75,000) but he should receive damages of £75,000. It could not be right for him to be denied damages altogether.'

(4) When does the duty to mitigate arise in relation to the anticipatory repudiation of a contract?

Indisputably there is a duty to mitigate once there has been an actual breach of contract. This is reflected, for example, in the general rule that one assesses the market value of property at the date of the breach of contract. But the traditional approach is that, following an anticipatory repudiation, there is no duty to mitigate,[262] unless the claimant chooses to accept the anticipatory repudiation.[263] It is submitted that the better view is that economic efficiency should override the wishes of the innocent party to hold the contract alive and that, as in the US,[264] the duty to mitigate should arise once there has been an anticipatory repudiation. Such a reform is supported by departures from *White & Carter (Councils) Ltd v McGregor*[265] regarding the analogous question of the extent to which a claimant is entitled to outflank the duty to mitigate by an action for the agreed price.

6. Contributory negligence

At common law, although it was unclear whether it applied as such to breach of contract, contributory negligence was a complete defence to many torts. In other words, where

---

[261] ibid, at [92]–[93].
[262] *Tredegar Iron & Coal Co v Hawthorn Bros & Co* (1902) 18 TLR 716; *Shindler v Northern Raincoat Co Ltd* [1960] 1 WLR 1038.
[263] As in *Melachrino v Nickoll & Knight* [1920] 1 KB 693. See also *Gebrüder Metalmann GmbH & Co KG v NBR (London) Ltd* [1984] 1 Lloyd's Rep 614; *Kaines (UK) Ltd v Osterreichische Warrenhandelsgesellschaft Austrowaren Gesellschaft mbH* [1993] 2 Lloyd's Rep 1.
[264] Uniform Commercial Code, ss 2–610a, 2–723(1). But see C Goetz and R Scott, 'The Mitigation Principle: Towards a General Theory of Contractual Obligation' (1983) 69 Vir LR 967, 993–995.
[265] [1962] AC 413. See below, pp 383–387.

applicable, it nullified the causal potency of the defendant's breach of duty.[266] However, the Law Reform (Contributory Negligence) Act 1945 (LR(CN)A 1945) made contributory negligence a partial defence, by which damages are reduced but not completely denied. Section 1(1) of that Act provides:

> 'Where any person suffers damage as a result partly of his own fault and partly of the fault of any other person or persons, a claim in respect of that damage shall not be defeated by reason of the fault of the person suffering the damage, but the damages recoverable in respect thereof shall be reduced to such extent as the court thinks just and equitable having regard to the claimant's share in the responsibility for the damage.'

As far as breach of contract is concerned, the crucial question is whether the Act, and hence the defence of contributory negligence, applies at all. This will be examined after looking at the operation of the defence for torts, where generally it is clear that the Act applies.

(1) Torts

(a) What must the defendant establish?

In order for the defence to apply the defendant must establish three points. First, the claimant must have been at fault or negligent towards himself or herself. To illustrate this by reference to cases of personal injury or death, the claimant is most obviously negligent towards himself if he negligently causes an accident (involving himself) or puts himself in an inherently dangerous position or renders an inherently non-dangerous position dangerous by failing to take safety precautions. The first situation is illustrated by the commonest of contributory negligence examples, where two motorists negligently collide. Examples of the second situation are riding on the towbar at the back of a 'traxcavator', as in *Jones v Livox Quarries Ltd*,[267] accepting a lift with someone who you know to have been drinking heavily, as in *Owens v Brimmell*,[268] or accepting a lift in a car knowing that the brakes are defective, as in *Gregory v Kelly*.[269] The classic examples of the third situation are failing to wear a seatbelt while travelling in the front seat of a car, as in *Froom v Butcher*,[270] or failing to wear a crash helmet while riding a motor-bike, as in *O'Connell v Jackson*.[271] It should be added that the courts are reluctant to find that a child has been negligent towards himself—and the younger the child the greater the reluctance.[272]

Secondly, the claimant's negligence must have been a factual cause of the claimant's loss. The usual 'but for' test is used to decide this. So, for example, where two motorists negligently collide, as each person's negligent driving is a factual cause of the collision, so necessarily it is a factual cause of the loss suffered by each. A case like *Froom v Butcher* stressed that while not wearing a seat-belt could of course not be said to be a factual cause of the collision, it was a factual cause of the loss, and this was what was important. On the other hand in *Owens v Brimmell*[273] the claimant's negligence in not wearing his seat-belt was not established to be a factual cause of his injuries—they were no worse than if he had been wearing one.

---

[266] Where subsequent to the breach of duty contributory negligence was therefore indistinguishable from saying that the intervening conduct of the claimant broke the chain of causation or, where a negligent failure to act followed a tort, from saying that the claimant failed in his duty to mitigate.
[267] [1952] 2 QB 608.   [268] [1977] QB 859.   [269] [1978] RTR 426.   [270] [1976] QB 286.
[271] [1972] 1 QB 270.
[272] Eg *Yachuk v Oliver Blais Co Ltd* [1949] AC 386; *Gough v Thorne* [1966] 1 WLR 1387.
[273] See also *UCB Corporate Services Ltd v Clyde* [2000] 2 All ER (Comm) 257 (claimant bank's own negligence not causative of its loss).

Thirdly, the claimant's negligence must have exposed the claimant to the particular risk of the type of damage suffered. In the standard negligent driving case there is no difficulty in establishing this since in driving negligently or in not wearing his seat-belt the claimant is clearly exposing himself to a particular risk of suffering personal injury in a crash. This principle, which can be regarded as analogous to remoteness, was discussed in some detail in *Jones v Livox Quarries Ltd*. There the claimant was riding on the towbar at the back of a quarry vehicle. Another vehicle belonging to the defendants was negligently driven into him and the claimant was injured. By so riding, the claimant exposed himself not only to the particular risk of falling off the vehicle but also to the particular risk of being crushed—as had happened. The claimant was therefore found to be contributorily negligent, although Denning LJ said that this would not have been the case if, whilst riding on the towbar, the claimant had, for example, been hit in the eye by a shot from a negligent sportsman—he was not exposing himself to a particular risk of suffering that type of damage by riding on the towbar.

Finally, it should be noted that, as has been discussed above,[274] in *The Calliope*[275] Brandon J applied contributory negligence in respect of the claimant's conduct subsequent to the tort. In terms of policy this is a sensible approach and there seems to be nothing in LR(CN)A 1945 to restrict the defence to contributory negligence prior to or contemporaneously with the tort.

(b) How do the courts decide the extent to which the damages should be reduced?

The LR(CN)A 1945, s 1(1) says that where contributory negligence applies, the damages '... shall be reduced to such extent as the court thinks just and equitable having regard to the claimant's share in the responsibility for the damage'. How exactly the courts apply these words is difficult to clarify; but what can be said, as stressed by, for example, Denning LJ in *Davies v Swan Motor Co (Swansea) Ltd*,[276] and confirmed more recently by the Supreme Court in *Jackson v Murray*,[277] is that the courts consider both the causal potency and the comparative blameworthiness of the parties' conduct.[278]

Where the defendant is held strictly liable, it might be thought difficult to apply comparative blameworthiness, since the defendant is not blameworthy at all. But Ogus[279] thinks that one can still talk in terms of comparative blameworthiness by asking how far short of the standard imposed by law did the conduct of each party fall.

In *Froom v Butcher*[280] Lord Denning, recognising the difficulty of deciding to what extent to reduce damages and in a desire to avoid prolonging cases, suggested standard figures for reducing damages where the claimant has been contributorily negligent by not wearing a seat-belt. If the damage would have been prevented altogether a reduction of 25% should be made and if it would have been considerably less severe a reduction of 15% should be made. To have standard figures for very common instances of contributory negligence sensibly produces certainty and uniformity but it can only be adopted where, as with seat-belts, the blameworthiness of the contributory negligence varies hardly at all from case to case.

---

[274] Above, p 116.   [275] [1970] P 172.   [276] [1949] 2 KB 291, at 326.
[277] [2015] UKSC 5, [2015] 2 All ER 805, at [19]–[26]. See also *Stapley v Gypsum Mines Ltd* [1953] AC 663, at 682; *Eagle v Chambers* [2003] EWCA Civ 1107, [2004] RTR 115.
[278] For a suggested principled approach in applying these criteria, see N Gravells, 'Three Heads of Contributory Negligence' (1977) 93 LQR 581.
[279] A Ogus, *The Law of Damages* (Butterworths 1973) 105.   [280] [1976] QB 286.

In *Capps v Miller*[281] the claimant moped-driver was severely brain-damaged when a car negligently ran into him. The claimant was wearing a crash helmet but, contrary to the Motor Cycles (Protective Helmet) Regulations 1980, the chin strap was unfastened and the helmet came off before the claimant's head struck the ground. Damages were reduced by 10% for contributory negligence in not fastening the strap. In arriving at that figure Lord Denning's guidelines were relied on but it was felt (Croom-Johnson LJ *dubitante*) that the true analogy to not fastening a seat-belt was not wearing a helmet at all. Wearing a helmet but not fastening the chin-strap was less blameworthy than not fastening a seat-belt (or not wearing a helmet at all) so that 10% rather than 15% was the appropriate reduction. In deciding on the appropriate reduction contributory negligence must be kept distinct from the issue of contribution between tortfeasors. In *Fitzgerald v Lane*[282] the claimant was hit by two cars one after the other on a pelican crossing. The claimant and each of the drivers was found to have been equally to blame for the claimant's injuries. It was held by the House of Lords that the appropriate reduction for contributory negligence should have been 50% and not 33 1/3%. In Lord Ackner's words:

'… the determination of the extent of each of the defendants' responsibility for the damage is not made in the main action but in the contribution proceedings between the defendants, inter se, and this does not concern the plaintiff.'[283]

What has to be contrasted is the claimant's conduct on the one hand with the totality of the tortious conduct of the defendants on the other.[284]

Although there has been little discussion of this, it is clear that, in general, contributory negligence is applied once it has been determined what loss is (otherwise) legally recoverable. For example, one would not apply contributory negligence to loss that is legally irrecoverable because too remote. This has been discussed above in the context of the *SAAMCO* principle and the decision of the House of Lords in *Platform Home Loans Ltd v Oyston Shipways Ltd*.[285]

Finally, it was clarified by the Supreme Court in *Jackson v Murray*[286] that an appellate court will not interfere with a lower court's apportionment unless there has been an identifiable error or the apportionment was outside the range of reasonable determinations. On the facts, the Supreme Court reduced from 70% (found by the appellate court which was itself a reduction from 90% at first instance) to 50% the contributory negligence of a 13-year-old girl who had stepped from behind a school minibus into the path of a car that was being driven too fast by the defendant.

Goudkamp and Nolan have carried out two useful empirical surveys of cases on contributory negligence in England and Wales at first instance and in the Court of Appeal.[287] Among their more interesting conclusions are the following:

---

[281] [1989] 1 WLR 839. For consideration of whether a pedal cyclist's failure to wear a helmet comprises contributory negligence see, eg, *Smith v Finch* [2009] EWHC 53 (QB); *Reynolds v Strutt and Parker LLP* [2011] EWHC 2263 (QB).
[282] [1989] AC 328.   [283] ibid, at 345.
[284] See also the Australian case of *Barisic v Devenport* [1978] 2 NSWLR 111. For criticism of *Fitzgerald v Lane* as being too pro-defendant see, eg, P Chandler and J Holland, 'Apportionment of Loss: Collisions and Contributions' [1989] LMCLQ 30. See generally, A Burrows, 'Should One Reform Joint and Several Liability?' in *Torts Tomorrow* (eds N Mullany and A Linden, LBC Information Services 1998) 102, 115–117.
[285] [2000] 2 AC 190. See above, p 124.   [286] [2015] UKSC 5, [2015] 2 All ER 805.
[287] J Goudkamp and D Nolan, 'Contributory Negligence in the Twenty-First Century: An Empirical Study of First Instance Decisions' (2016) 79 MLR 575; J Goudkamp and D Nolan, 'Contributory Negligence in the Court of Appeal: An Empirical Study' (2017) 37 Legal Studies 437. See also, including cases in Northern Ireland and Scotland, J Goudkamp and D Nolan, 'Contributory Negligence and Professional Negligence: An Empirical Perspective' in *Apportionment in Private Law* (eds K Barker and R Grantham, Hart Publishing 2019) 161–195.

(i) Where a finding of contributory negligence was made at first instance, the average discount was 40.5%. Where there has been an appeal, the average post-appeal discount was 50%.

(ii) The most popular discounts both at first instance and after appeal were fractions that are commonly used in everyday life, namely, one-half, one-third, and one-quarter. Although judges use essentially the full spectrum of discounts, discounts at the higher end of the spectrum are relatively infrequent.

(iii) Judges are very slow to find contributory negligence in professional negligence claims. However, when contributory negligence is found in such claims, the discount tends to be relatively high.

(iv) Judges treat children (aged over 10) more harshly than adult claimants, both when deciding whether to make a finding of contributory negligence and when determining the discount where contributory negligence has been found.

(c) Is contributory negligence applicable to all torts?[288]

The crucial words are those in LR(CN)A 1945, s 4 which define fault in LR(CN)A 1945, s 1(1) as meaning '... negligence, breach of statutory duty or other act or omission which gives rise to a liability in tort, or would, apart from this Act, give rise to the defence of contributory negligence'.

For reasons discussed under 'breach of contract',[289] it is best to read this as comprising two limbs, the first—'... negligence, breach of statutory duty or other act or omission which gives rise to a liability in tort'—referring to the defendant's fault and the second—any act or omission which '... would apart from this Act, give rise to the defence of contributory negligence'—referring to the claimant's fault. In the context of torts, this two-limbed interpretation of LR(CN)A 1945, s 4 has now been authoritatively accepted by the House of Lords in *Standard Chartered Bank v Pakistan National Shipping Corpn (No 2)*.[290]

In this context, the first limb creates no difficulties; the defendant is at fault whenever liable for a tort and it makes no difference which tort. So whether contributory negligence is inapplicable to some torts turns solely on the second limb of LR(CN)A 1945, s 4. One interpretation of the second limb is that it all depends whether, in relation to the tort for which the claimant is now suing, the claimant's conduct would have given rise to the total defence of contributory negligence at common law. Since contributory negligence was probably not a defence at common law to intentional torts, like deceit and intentional trespass to the person, this view means that contributory negligence continues not to apply to such torts. That was the approach adopted by the House of Lords in *Standard Chartered Bank v Pakistan National Shipping Corp (No 2)* in deciding that contributory negligence is not a defence to the tort of deceit.[291] It was also the approach taken by the Court of Appeal in

---

[288] See G Williams, *Joint Torts and Contributory Negligence* (Stevens 1951) 318–319, 326–328; A Hudson, 'Contributory Negligence as a Defence to Battery' (1984) 4 Legal Studies 332.
[289] Below, p 139.
[290] [2002] UKHL 43, [2003] 1 AC 959, at [11]. See also *Reeves v Metropolitan Police Commissioner* [2000] 1 AC 360.
[291] The House of Lords approved the decision to the same effect of Mummery J in *Alliance & Leicester Building Society v Edgestop Ltd* [1993] 1 WLR 1462. See also *Corporacion Nacional del Cobre de Chile v Sogemin Metals Ltd* [1997] 1 WLR 1396 in which contributory negligence was held inapplicable where the defendants had bribed the claimant's employee and the claims extended beyond deceit to include conspiracy, inducing breach of contract and the equitable wrong of assisting a breach of fiduciary duty.

Pritchard v Co-operative Group Ltd,[292] which applied the *Standard Chartered Bank* case in deciding that contributory negligence (comprising provocation) is not a defence to the tort of trespass to the person (ie assault and battery).

Lord Hoffmann, giving the leading speech in the *Standard Chartered Bank* case, pointed to past cases where the fault of the claimant had been no answer to a claim to rescind a contract or damages for fraudulent misrepresentation.[293] Moreover, he thought that such a rule was based upon sound policy. 'It would not seem just that a fraudulent defendant's liability should be reduced on the grounds that, for whatever reason, the victim should not have made the payment which the defendant successfully induced him to make.'[294]

In terms of policy, this denial of contributory negligence is a response to the dishonesty of the defendant. A dishonest defendant ought not to have its liability cut back by reason of the claimant's own fault. In this respect, the approach is consistent with the application of a wider-than-usual remoteness test for the tort of deceit.[295]

A similar policy may be said to underpin the denial of contributory negligence in relation to the intentional tort of trespass to the person (ie assault and battery) in *Pritchard v Co-operative Group Ltd*,[296] and ought also to extend to other intentional torts. Although Lord Denning MR in *Murphy v Culhane*[297] indicated that a widow's claim for damages for the death of her husband might fall to be reduced under LR(CN)A 1945, because it had resulted from a criminal affray in which he had participated, this was expressly said to be incorrect by the Court of Appeal in the *Pritchard* case.[298]

What it is certainly important to avoid is the wider view that contributory negligence is inapplicable to negligent misrepresentation. *Standard Chartered Bank* concerned only fraudulent misrepresentation. The non-availability of contributory negligence must be distinguished from the separate rule, originating in *Redgrave v Hurd*[299] and applicable to all misrepresentations, whether fraudulent or not, that one should not attach blame to a claimant who has relied on a misrepresentation without taking an opportunity to check the truth of the representation. This is a rule that that conduct of the claimant, in the context of misrepresentation, should be treated as non-blameworthy. As Lord Hoffmann made clear, this is not to deny that other negligent conduct of the claimant may reduce damages for negligent misrepresentation on the ground of contributory negligence. This is supported by *Gran Gelato Ltd v Richcliff (Group) Ltd*[300] in which Sir Donald Nicholls V-C held that contributory negligence can apply to the statutory tort of negligent misrepresentation in the Misrepresentation Act 1967, s 2(1)[301] albeit that there was no contributory negligence on

---

[292] [2011] EWCA Civ 329, [2012] QB 320.
[293] Eg *Redgrave v Hurd* (1881) 20 Ch D 1; *Edgington v Fitzmaurice* (1885) 29 Ch D 459.
[294] [2003] 1 AC 959, at [16]. [295] See above, p 90. [296] [2011] EWCA Civ 329, [2012] QB 320.
[297] [1977] QB 94.
[298] [2011] EWCA Civ 329, [2012] QB 320, at [49]. In the *Standard Chartered Bank* case, at [45], Lord Rodger had expressly left open whether Lord Denning MR's suggestion should be regarded as sound. In the *Pritchard* case, Smith LJ, at [82], thought that there might be cases—the facts of *Pritchard* being one—where contributory negligence *ought* to be available to reduce damages for trespass to the person. But she concluded, 'I do not think the law permits me so to hold.'
[299] (1881) 20 Ch D 1.
[300] [1992] Ch 560. One possible, albeit unattractive, argument against the applicability of contributory negligence to liability under the Misrepresentation Act 1967, s 2(1) is the 'fiction of fraud' wording of that subsection. This might be read as laying down that contributory negligence cannot apply to s 2(1) if it does not apply to the tort of deceit. Cf *Royscot Trust Ltd v Rogerson* [1991] 2 QB 297 discussed above, p 90.
[301] Sir Donald Nicholls V-C thought it important that the defendant was also concurrently liable for the tort of negligence at common law and drew an analogy with the approach to contributory negligence as a defence to breach of contract laid down in *Forsikringsaktieselskapet Vesta v Butcher* [1989] AC 852. On the face of it, this was to focus on the *defendant* being at fault within the first limb of LR(CN)A 1945, s 4. But there would be no need to find concurrent liability if one took the view that the Misrepresentation Act 1967, s 2(1) itself creates a liability in tort (ie that s 2(1) is a 'statutory tort').

the facts because the claimant had merely failed to take an opportunity to check the truth, thereby falling within the rule in *Redgrave v Hurd*.

One should note that the interpretation given in the *Standard Chartered Bank* case by the House of Lords to the second limb of LR(CN)A 1945, s 4 is not an inevitable one. This is because one could interpret that second limb as meaning that the conduct of the claimant must be of the sort that at common law would have given rise to the total defence of contributory negligence, if the claimant had been suing for a tort to which the defence indisputably applied, for example the tort of negligence. But if that alternative interpretation of the second limb had been taken, the House of Lords would have had no scope to deny the applicability of contributory negligence to the tort of deceit because plainly, under the first limb, a liability in deceit is a liability in tort.

On the other hand, the interpretation taken of the second limb by the House of Lords might be thought to produce the oddity that the applicability of contributory negligence to torts would be entirely controlled by the state of the common law prior to 1945. The better view, which avoids this 'freezing of the common law' problem, is that when their Lordships referred to the common law they were hypothetically assuming the continuation of a common law of contributory negligence after 1945; and were deciding—as a matter of the normal interpretation and development of the common law based on sound policy—that contributory negligence was and should be inapplicable to the tort of deceit.

Whatever the correct interpretation of LR(CN)A 1945, it is important to add that the Torts (Interference with Goods) Act 1977, s 11, specifically lays down that contributory negligence is not a defence to conversion[302] or intentional trespass to goods. While the exclusion of intentional trespass is in line with the sound policy underpinning *Standard Chartered Bank* it is hard to see the justification for contributory negligence not applying to non-intentional conversion.

(2) Breach of contract—does contributory negligence apply?[303]

The correct approach to construing LR(CN)A 1945, s 4 in relation to breach of contract was first put forward judicially as late as 1989 in obiter dicta of the Court of Appeal, confirming Hobhouse J's reasoning, in *Forsikringsaktieselskapet Vesta v Butcher*.[304]

The case concerned the reinsurance of underlying insurance that the claimants had given in respect of fish lost on a fish farm in Norway. The claimants asked their brokers, who were the defendants, to sort out the reinsurance for them. They specifically told them in a telephone call that they did not want one of the terms in the underlying insurance (requiring a 24-hour watch over the fish) to be relevant to the reinsurance contract. But in breach of their contractual (and tortious) duty of care to the claimants, the defendants failed to delete that term in the offer of reinsurance.

Ultimately it was held by the Court of Appeal, and upheld by the House of Lords, that the reinsurers were liable to pay the claimants for what they had had to pay out in respect

---

[302] This is qualified by the Banking Act 1979, s 47 so that contributory negligence does apply in favour of a banker being sued for non-intentional and non-negligent conversion.

[303] J Swanton, 'Contributory Negligence as a Defence to Actions for Breach of Contract' (1981) 55 ALJ 278; N Palmer and P Davies, 'Contributory Negligence and Breach of Contract – English and Australian Attitudes Compared' (1980) 29 ICLQ 415; P Chandler, 'Contributory Negligence and Contract: Some Underlying Disparities' (1989) 40 NILQ 152; G Williams, *Joint Torts and Contributory Negligence* (Stevens 1951) 318, 328–332.

[304] [1989] AC 852; affd by the House of Lords on a different point [1989] AC 880. Authoritative confirmation of the obiter dicta in *Vesta v Butcher* has been given by the Court of Appeal in, eg, *Barclays Bank plc v Fairclough Building Ltd* [1995] QB 214; *UCB Bank plc v Hepherd Winstanley and Pugh* [1999] Lloyd's Rep PN 963.

of a loss of fish irrespective of the '24-hour watch' term. The defendants' breach of contract did not therefore cause the claimants any loss. But if that term had been crucial the claimants would have had an action for substantial damages against the defendants for breach of contract. And it was in relation to that action that contributory negligence was discussed, as obiter dicta, by the Court of Appeal (there was no examination of the point by the Lords): for the defendants argued that the claimants were contributorily negligent in relying on just the one telephone call to bring about the deletion of an important contract term, especially as the claimants had asked for confirmation that the deletion was acceptable to the reinsurers and the defendants had never given that confirmation.

The Court of Appeal thought that, had the breach of contract caused loss, contributory negligence would have here applied—and Hobhouse J's reduction of damages by 75% at first instance was supported—because the defendants would have been liable not only for breach of a contractual duty of care but also in the tort of negligence. Hobhouse J's threefold classification of cases for dealing with contributory negligence was approved.

A 'category one' case is where the defendant is in breach of a strict contractual duty. A 'category two' case is where the defendant is in breach of a contractual duty of care. A 'category three' case is where the defendant is in breach of a contractual duty of care and is also liable for the tort of negligence (or would be so liable, if pleaded). In terms of that classification, this was a category three case and hence contributory negligence would have applied.[305] And according to the Court of Appeal it is in a category three case only that LR(CN)A 1945, s 4 allows contributory negligence to be a defence to breach of contract.

How does one arrive at that conclusion in interpreting LR(CN)A 1945, s 4?[306]

The initial problem is whose fault does LR(CN)A 1945, s 4, or the different parts of s 4, refer to? The view taken by Pritchard J in his influential judgment in the New Zealand case of *Rowe v Turner, Hopkins and Partners*,[307] which was in effect approved by the Court of Appeal in *Vesta v Butcher*[308]—and is an approach that, in the context of the tort of deceit, has subsequently been applied by the House of Lords in *Standard Chartered Bank v Pakistan National Shipping Corpn (No 2)*[309]—was as follows.

The first limb of LR(CN)A 1945, s 4—'... negligence, breach of statutory duty or other act or omission, which gives rise to a liability in tort'—refers to the defendant's fault: while the second limb—any act or omission which '... would apart from this Act, give rise to the defence of contributory negligence'—refers to the claimant's fault. To divide s 4 in this way is sensible: for on the one hand, it is hard to see how any act or omission which 'would apart from this Act, give rise to the defence of contributory negligence' can refer to the defendant's fault, since such an act or omission might not even be actionable; and on the other hand, it seems irrelevant to establishing the claimant's fault whether his acts or omissions give rise to a liability in tort.

But so to divide LR(CN)A 1945, s 4 does not end the problem of statutory interpretation, for each of the two limbs can be interpreted in various ways.

---

[305] The Court of Appeal considered itself bound so to hold in a category three case by *Sayers v Harlow Urban District Council* [1958] 1 WLR 623: but there was no detailed reasoning on this point in that case and it is possible to interpret the reasoning as supporting the application of contributory negligence in category two as well as category three. For other relevant decisions, prior to *Vesta v Butcher*, see the second edition of this book at pp 82–83.
[306] LR(CN)A 1945, s 4 has been set out above, p 136.
[307] [1980] 2 NZLR 550; rvsd on liability [1982] 1 NZLR 178.
[308] But, while stressing that the practical effect would be the same, O'Connor LJ preferred to regard both parts of LR(CN)A 1945, s 4 as applying to the *claimant's* fault: [1989] AC 852, at 862.
[309] [2003] 1 AC 959: see above, p 136.

Taking first the second limb defining the claimant's fault, on one interpretation the essential issue is whether the claimant's conduct would have given rise to the total defence of contributory negligence at common law had the claimant been suing, as he is now is, for breach of contract. Assuming, as seems correct, that contributory negligence was not a defence at common law, this interpretation concludes that the Act does not apply to breach of contract.

However, there are at least two alternative interpretations according to which the second limb sometimes does apply to breach of contract, even accepting that contributory negligence was not a defence to breach of contract at common law. One of these, or an equivalent, must have been adopted in *Rowe v Turner* and *Vesta v Butcher*.

The first is that where the defendant is concurrently liable in tort, then if the claimant's conduct would have been a total defence at common law to that tort, had the claimant framed its action in tort, the Act applies even though the claimant has now framed its action in contract.[310] The second interpretation is that it is irrelevant to consider the defendant's actual conduct, or what the claimant is suing for in the instant case. Rather the second limb refers to the claimant's conduct being of the sort that at common law would have given rise to the total defence of contributory negligence, if the claimant had been suing for a cause of action to which the defence indisputably applied, eg, the tort of negligence. On this second interpretation, the claimant's fault in the second limb is kept rigidly distinct from the defendant's fault in the first limb.

The common feature of these alternative interpretations is that the second limb of LR(CN)A 1945, s 4 does sometimes apply to breach of contract, so that the applicability of contributory negligence rests on the first limb of s 4 defining the defendant's fault. So turning now to the first limb (which was primarily focused on in *Rowe v Turner* and *Vesta v Butcher*) does 'negligence, breach of statutory duty, or other act or omission which gives rise to a liability in tort', include the defendant's breach of contract?

One possibility is to regard the first limb as comprising three separate clauses, ie 'which gives rise to a liability in tort' does not qualify 'negligence'.

But such an approach seems to ignore the word 'other', and in *Rowe v Turner* and *Vesta v Butcher* it was considered that 'negligence' (and 'breach of statutory duty') is qualified by 'which gives rise to a liability in tort'. One might then think that, as breach of contract is not liability in tort, the Act does not apply to breach of contract. But in *Rowe v Turner* and *Vesta v Butcher* it was considered that the words do cover where the defendant is being sued only for the breach of a contractual duty of care provided he would also be liable for the tort of negligence on the ground that that is then 'negligence ... which gives rise to a liability in tort'.

Whatever the technicalities in construing LR(CN)A 1945, it has now been confirmed in a number of subsequent cases—and is therefore now clear law in England[311]—that, in line with *Vesta v Butcher*, contributory negligence applies as a defence to breach of contract in category three but not in categories one and two.

The leading case on category three is *UCB Bank plc v Hepherd Winstanley and Pugh*[312] in which, confirming the obiter dicta in *Vesta v Butcher*, the Court of Appeal applied

---

[310] N Palmer and P Davies, 'Contributory Negligence and Breach of Contract – English and Australian Attitudes Compared' (1980) 29 ICLQ 415, 445; cf J Swanton, 'Contributory Negligence as a Defence to Actions for Breach of Contract' (1981) 55 ALJ 278, 280–281.

[311] In *Astley v Austrust Ltd* (1999) 197 CLR 1, the High Court of Australia (Callinan J dissenting) held that the identical Australian legislation should be construed as meaning that contributory negligence can never apply to breach of contract even in a category three case.

[312] [1999] Lloyd's Rep PN 963.

contributory negligence to reduce damages. The claimant bank sought damages from its solicitors in relation to loans made by the bank. It was held that the solicitors had been negligent and in breach of their contractual duty of care in failing, contrary to the wishes of the bank, to ensure that full collateral security for the loans was obtained. As a consequence, when the borrower defaulted and the security was enforced, the bank received £107,151 less than it would have done had it had full collateral security. The Court of Appeal nevertheless reduced the damages by 25% because of the bank's own fault constituted by the failure of its relevant employee to read properly the letter sent by the solicitors. Chadwick LJ said:

> 'Properly understood this is a category (3) case within [the] classification in *Vesta v Butcher*. Accordingly the damages which UCB may recover in respect of HWP's breach of duty must be reduced to such extent as the court thinks just and equitable having regard to UCB's own share in the responsibility for its loss. In my view, the appropriate reduction in the present case is 25%.'[313]

In contrast, contributory negligence was held to be inapplicable by the Court of Appeal in *Barclays Bank Plc v Fairclough Building Ltd*[314] because this was a category one case. The defendant had been in breach of contract in cleaning the roofs of the claimant bank's storage warehouse. The roofs were made of asbestos cement sheeting and the result of the defendant's cleaning, without proper precautions being taken, was that the warehouse was contaminated with asbestos fibres and dust requiring remedial work of £4 million. The defendants alleged that the claimant bank was partly responsible, through its property division, for proper precautions not having been taken and that therefore there should be a reduction for contributory negligence. It was held that contributory negligence could not here apply so that full damages were awarded. This was because the facts fell within category one. The claimant's loss followed from the breach of the defendant's strict obligations to carry out the work in accordance with the specifications and to achieve the standard specified. The breach was not merely one of a duty of care. While the Court of Appeal accepted that contributory negligence could apply in a category three case, it was emphatically laid down that it should not apply in a category one case. Indeed Nourse LJ went so far as to say the following:

> 'It ought to be a cause of general concern that the law should have got into such a state that a contractor who was in breach of two of the main obligations expressly undertaken by him in a standard form building contract was able to persuade the judge in the court below that the building owner's damages should be reduced by 40% because of its own negligence in not preventing the contractor from committing the breaches. In circumstances such as these release, waiver, forbearance or the like are the only defences available to a party to a contract who wishes to assert that the other party's right to recover damages for its breach has been lost or diminished. It ought to have been perfectly obvious that the Law Reform (Contributory Negligence) Act 1945 was never intended to obtrude the defence of contributory negligence into an area of the law where it has no business to be.'[315]

Since the House of Lords' acceptance of concurrent liability in *Henderson v Merrett Syndicates Ltd*[316] it will be very rare to find a case that falls within category two but outside

---

[313] [1999] Lloyd's Rep PN 963, at 971.   [314] [1995] QB 214.
[315] ibid, at 234. In third and fourth party proceedings in *Barclays Bank Plc v Fairclough Building Ltd (No 2)* (1995) 44 Con LR 35, the sub-sub-contractors, who had actually carried out the cleaning work, were held liable for breach of a contractual duty of care to the sub-contractors. Ironically there was a 50% reduction because of the sub-contractor's contributory negligence, this being a category three case. *Vesta v Butcher* was applied.
[316] [1995] 2 AC 145. Above, p 7.

category three. *Raflatac Ltd v Eade*[317] is such a rare case. Here the defendant head-contractor had broken its contractual duty of care as regards acts of a sub-contractor in negligently damaging the claimant's property. Although the defendant head-contractor was in breach of its contractual duty of care it was held that it had no personal or vicarious liability in tort for those acts of the sub-contractor. This was therefore a category two case and contributory negligence was held to be inapplicable.

But while the law is now clear, how satisfactory is the 'category three only' approach? Two main criticisms can be made.

The first is that it encourages an odd reversal of roles in that a blameworthy claimant will be better off, as regards contributory negligence, if it can establish that the defendant was merely liable for breach of a contractual duty of care (or the breach of a strict contractual duty) and was not also liable for the tort of negligence. In other words, as far as contributory negligence is concerned, the claimant will be trying to show that the defendant was not also liable in the tort of negligence, while the defendant will be trying to show that it was also liable in the tort of negligence.

Secondly, it would seem that contributory negligence ought to apply as a defence to breach of contract, irrespective of whether the defendant is concurrently liable in the tort of negligence and even if the duty broken was strict. If the claimant's unreasonable conduct can sometimes result in its recovering no damages for a loss, through the principles of intervening cause or the duty to mitigate, it must be sensible for there to be a mid-position where its negligence results in a mere reduction of damages. This is most obviously so where the defendant is in breach of a contractual duty of care, for then the claimant's and the defendant's fault are both in the same range, ie there is clear negligence/blameworthiness on both sides. But the same argument applies even where there is the breach of a strict contractual duty. After all, contributory negligence is applicable to torts of strict liability.[318]

The unreported decision of the Court of Appeal in *Schering Agrochemicals Ltd v Resibel NV SA*[319] constitutes a classic illustration of the injustice that the present law can cause. The claimants manufactured and bottled certain inflammable chemicals. The defendants supplied them with equipment that heat-sealed caps onto bottles. The equipment contained a safety alarm system whereby the heat sealer would be switched off if a bottle was stationary for too long and thereby exposed to excessive heat. Two months after the equipment was operational, there was a serious fire at the claimants' premises owing to a defect in the safety system of the heat sealer. On appeal, the defendants accepted that they were in breach of a strict contractual duty in supplying equipment that was not reasonably fit for its purpose, contrary to the Sale of Goods Act 1979, s 14(3). The crucial fact, in what would otherwise have been a simple case, was that three weeks before the fire there had been an incident, observed by two of the claimants' employees and reported to a supervisor, in which the safety system did not switch off when it should have done, resulting in a small explosion in one or more of the bottles and an orange flash. The supervisor took no action in response to that report.

The Court of Appeal held that the claimants' unreasonable failure to investigate that incident (which would have revealed the defect) or to close down the bottling line pending investigations meant that damages should not be awarded for the loss caused by the fire: the claimants had failed in their duty to mitigate their loss or had broken the chain of

---

[317] [1999] 1 Lloyd's Rep 506.
[318] See, eg, *Cork v Kirby MacLean Ltd* [1952] 2 All ER 402; *Mullard v Ben Line Steamers Ltd* [1970] 1 WLR 1414 (breach of statutory duty).
[319] (26 November 1992, unreported).

causation.[320] This seems a harsh result which could have been avoided had the court been able to award damages reduced for the claimants' contributory negligence.

With the increased interest in a European Contract Code, it is noteworthy that in the *Principles of European Contract Law*,[321] edited by Lando and Beale, contributory negligence is applicable to all three categories. Article 9: 504 reads as follows: 'The non-performing party is not liable for loss suffered by the aggrieved party to the extent that the aggrieved party contributed to the non-performance or its effects.' One of the main illustrations given is a category one case.[322] Similarly Article 7.4.7 of the UNIDROIT Principles of International Commercial Contracts[323] reads:

> 'Where harm is due in part to an act or omission of the aggrieved party or to another event as to which that party bears the risk, the amount of damages shall be reduced to the extent that these factors have contributed to the harm, having regard to the conduct of the parties.'

Given the controversy as to whether the present law is unsatisfactory, and given that it is not open to the courts to 'amend' the LR(CN)A 1945, it is unsurprising that the Law Commission carried out a project in this area in the late 1980s and early 1990s. In its Working Paper it provisionally recommended that the 1945 Act should be reformed so that contributory negligence would apply to all three categories of case.[324] However, in its final report it instead recommended (contrary to the views of the majority of its consultees who supported its wider provisional recommendation) that contributory negligence should be extended only to category two and not also to category one.[325] What primarily worried the Law Commission in back-tracking from its provisional recommendation—and was stressed to it by some consultees—was the uncertainty that contributory negligence might cause.[326] The fear was that what are at present straightforward damages claims for breach of contract would become complex disputes as to comparative blameworthiness. This would potentially increase litigation and hamper out-of-court settlements. The recommendation to move the law marginally forward to include category two as well as category three was a pragmatic compromise which would not significantly increase uncertainty in commercial litigation.[327]

---

[320] Above, p 85. But at first instance, unreported (QB) 4 May 1991, Hobhouse J applied a counterfactual assessment of the loss that would have been suffered even if the claimants had taken reasonable steps to avoid the loss. He therefore awarded the claimants the cost of bringing the alarm and safety system up to specification and the loss of profit that could have resulted from the bottling line being out of production while the work was carried out. This was correct and in line with the standard approach to the duty to mitigate: see above, pp 131–132. Cf for the contrary view that this loss was not recoverable, see *Beoco Ltd v Alfa Laval Co* [1995] QB 137 (where Stuart Smith LJ, with respect incorrectly, equated the position where the chain of causation was broken by the claimant's unreasonable conduct with the position where broken by natural events or by a third party).

[321] (Kluwer 2000).

[322] 'A leases a computer which under the terms of the contract is to be ready for use in England where the voltage is 240v. The computer supplied is capable of operating on various voltages and, in breach of contract, is actually set for 110v. A prominent sign pasted on the screen warns the user to check the voltage setting before use. A ignores this and switches on without checking the setting. The computer is extensively damaged and repairs will cost A £1,500. The court may take the view that the loss was at least half A's fault and award only £750 damages.'

[323] (International Institute for the Unification of Private Law 2016).

[324] *Contributory Negligence as a Defence in Contract*, Law Commission Working Paper No 114 (1990).

[325] *Contributory Negligence as a Defence in Contract*, Law Com 219 (1993).

[326] ibid, paras 3.39–3.40, 4.6.

[327] The Law Commission also expressed concerns that extending contributory negligence to category one might operate to the disadvantage of consumers and others in weaker bargaining positions: *Contributory Negligence as a Defence in Contract*, Law Com 219 (1993) paras 3.39–3.40, 4.6. But this argument was effectively repudiated in the Working Paper No 114, para 4.45(e) (eg, 'apportionment will improve the position of the consumer whose conduct, under the present law, is held to break the chain of causation and so results in no recovery'.) The Report, paras 4.2–4.5, also relies on what was termed a reason of principle namely that a claimant should be able to rely on the defendant fulfilling a strict obligation and should not have to take precautions against the possibility that a breach might occur. But that argument had been comprehensively answered in the

This compromise reform would have the merit of removing the reversal of role oddity referred to above: and, unlike the provisional recommendation, it would limit the risk of complicating straightforward damages claims. But it would leave in play the injustice forced upon courts in cases like *Schering*. And it should be stressed that, subsequent to the acceptance of concurrent liability in *Henderson v Merrett Syndicates Ltd*,[328] very few cases fall within category two and not category three so that the proposed reform would be largely cosmetic.[329]

Perhaps a better compromise would have been a recommendation to extend contributory negligence to category one as well as category two, while restricting to a few fixed percentages (say 25%, 50%, and 75%) the possible reductions for contributory negligence. It is hard to believe that such a reform would have produced the significant increase in litigation that the Law Commission feared.

7. The demise of impecuniosity as a limitation

The House of Lords in *Owners of Dredger Liesbosch v Owners of Steamship Edison, The Liesbosch*[330] appeared to lay down that loss resulting from the claimant's weak financial position is irrecoverable. Here the dredger, 'Liesbosch', was fouled and sunk by the negligent navigation of the 'Edison'. The owners of the 'Liesbosch' were under contract to complete work within a certain time. Although a substitute dredger could have been bought and fairly quickly adapted for use, the owners of the 'Liesbosch' could not afford to buy a substitute at once and had to hire a replacement. This was more expensive to use than a substitute dredger would have been, as it required the attendance of a tug and two barges. The House of Lords held that the claimants could recover the market price of a comparable dredger, the expenses that would have been incurred in adapting the dredger for use, and the loss on the contract between the date of the sinking and the date on which the substitute dredger could reasonably have been ready for work. But they could not recover their greater actual loss including, in particular, the hire fee and expenditure incurred in using the hire vessel, because that resulted from their impecuniosity. Lord Wright rationalised this decision on grounds of either intervening cause or remoteness. He said that the extra loss arose from the claimant's '... impecuniosity as a separate and concurrent cause, extraneous to and distinct in character from the tort', and, '... if the financial embarrassment is to be regarded as a consequence of the tort, I think it is too remote, but I prefer to regard it as an independent cause.'[331] However, since by applying normal principles of causation (and more arguably remoteness) to the facts the loss from impecuniosity should have been recoverable, it appears that Lord Wright was in reality treating impecuniosity as a reason in itself for limiting damages.

Working Paper No 114 Part II by clarifying that, in deciding whether the claimant has been at fault, one must take into account the contractual context. In particular the Working Paper stressed that normally a claimant should not be regarded as being at fault in relying on the defendant to perform his (strict or reasonable care) contractual obligation and by not checking up that he has done so. Eg if C takes a car to a garage for work to be done on the brakes, C should not be regarded as being at fault if he fails to check that the work has been properly done and as a consequence has an accident.

[328] [1995] 2 AC 145.
[329] This appears to be the main reason why the recommended reform has not been implemented.
[330] [1933] AC 449. P Davies, 'Economic Stringency and the Recovery of Damages' (1982) JBL 21. For detailed criticism of *The Liesbosch*, as being inconsistent with legal principle, see B Coote, 'Damages, the Liesbosch, and Impecuniosity' [2001] CLJ 511.
[331] [1933] AC 449, at 460.

At the same time Lord Wright accepted Lord Collins' dictum in *Clippens Oil Co Ltd v Edinburgh and District Water Trustees*[332] to the effect that if a claimant failed to mitigate its loss because of impecuniosity this did not act to reduce the amount of damages it would recover, ie no argument based on mitigation could prevent full recovery by an impecunious claimant. Lord Collins had there said, '... the wrongdoer must take his victim *talem qualem*, and if the position of the latter is aggravated because he is without the means of mitigating it, so much the worse for the wrongdoer.'[333]

The denial of recovery for loss flowing from impecuniosity was unjustified in terms of policy. As Sir Patrick Bennett QC said at first instance in *Perry v Sidney Phillips & Son*:[334]

'I find it difficult to understand why, if you harm somebody who is a millionaire and thereby increase the damages you have to pay, or a talented musician whose hands are damaged, which also increases the damages you have to pay, when the victim is impecunious ... that fact is used via *The Edison* decision to reduce the damages.'

Moreover it is mystifying how Lord Wright could have regarded the whole issue as being treated differently if viewed in terms of the duty to mitigate.

It is therefore no surprise that the courts rarely followed[335] *The Liesbosch* and chose instead to distinguish[336] or ignore it.[337] This finally culminated in the decision of the House of Lords in *Lagden v O'Connor*[338] that the *Liesbosch* rule on impecuniosity should no longer be regarded as good law. All of their Lordships agreed on the removal of that rule. In Lord Hope's words:[339]

'It is not necessary for us to say that the *Liesbosch* case was wrongly decided. But it is clear that the law has moved on, and that the correct test of remoteness today is whether the loss was reasonably foreseeable. The wrongdoer must take his victim as he finds him ... This rule applies to the economic state of the victim in the same way as it applies to his physical and mental vulnerability. It requires the wrongdoer to bear the consequences if it was reasonably foreseeable that the injured party would have to borrow money or incur some other kind of expenditure to mitigate his damages. For these reasons I would reject [the defendant's] argument that we should apply the rule that was laid down in the *Liesbosch* case that loss due to the claimant's pre-existing impecuniosity is too remote and cannot be recovered as damages. I would hold that this rule should now be departed from.'

And in the words of Lord Walker:[340]

'In the light of the development of the law in the 70 years since the *Liesbosch* case was decided, it has in my view become apparent that Lord Wright's sharp distinction between mitigation of

---

[332] [1907] AC 291.   [333] ibid, at 303.   [334] [1982] 1 All ER 1005, at 1013.
[335] A rare exception was *Ramwade Ltd v W J Emson & Co Ltd* [1987] RTR 72. See the second edition of this book, pp 91–92.
[336] Eg *Dodd Properties v Canterbury City Council* [1980] 1 WLR 433; *Perry v Sidney Phillips* [1982] 1 WLR 1297; *Archer v Brown* [1984] 2 All ER 267; *Mattocks v Mann* [1993] RTR 13; *Alcoa Minerals of Jamaica Inc v Herbert Broderick* [2002] 1 AC 371. See also in Australia and New Zealand, respectively, *Burns v MAN Automotive (Aust) Pty Ltd* (1986) 161 CLR 653; *Attorney-General v Geothermal Produce NZ Ltd* [1987] 2 NZLR 348. See the second edition of this book, pp 90–91.
[337] Eg *Muhammad Issa El Sheikh Ahmed v Ali* [1947] AC 414; *Trans Trust SPRL v Danubian Trading Co Ltd* [1952] 2 QB 297 (both contract cases). Note that there was no reason in principle why *The Liesbosch* rule should be any less applicable in contract than tort; and in purporting to reconcile the *Muhammad v Ali* case with *The Liesbosch* Lord Wright in *Monarch SS Co v A/B Karlshamns Oljefabriker* [1949] 1 All ER 1, at 14, did say that '... the difference in result did not depend on the difference (if any) between contract and tort'. See the second edition of this book, p 89.
[338] [2003] UKHL 64, [2004] 1 AC 1067. See A Tettenborn, 'Compensating the Cash-strapped: the Sinking of the *Liesbosch*' [2004] LMCLQ 135.
[339] [2003] UKHL 64, [2004] 1 AC 1067, at [61]–[62].   [340] ibid, at [102].

damage and measure ... of damage is not helpful. Nor do I think his general classification of impecuniosity as "extraneous" or "extrinsic" is consistent with the modern state of the law (although loss attributable to impecuniosity, on a claim in contract or tort, may on examination prove to be too remote). Many recent cases, both in England and in the Commonwealth, have noted that the *Liesbosch* case has been distinguished so often that its authority has been greatly attenuated ... In my view the time has now come to say that the law has moved on from Lord Wright's exposition in the *Liesbosch* case ...'

The majority of their Lordships (Lord Nicholls, Slynn, and Hope) went on to hold that where a claimant, whose car has been tortiously damaged, reasonably wishes to hire a replacement car but, because of lack of funds, has no real choice other than to hire through an accident-hire scheme, he or she can recover the costs incurred in so doing. This is so even though those costs are higher (and include incidental benefits) than the normal costs of hiring a replacement car. In other words, viewed as an aspect of the duty to mitigate, an impecunious claimant will be acting reasonably in incurring the higher costs of an accident-hire scheme; whereas an affluent claimant will be acting unreasonably in incurring such high costs and will instead be compensated only for the normal hiring costs.

In practice one would expect that defendants will find it difficult to challenge a claim for the higher costs of an accident-hire scheme that have been (or will be) incurred by the claimant. But Lord Nicholls suggested that insurers and credit hire companies should be able to agree on standard inquiries to assess a claimant's impecuniosity. And as a test of impecuniosity, he suggested, '[An] inability to pay car hire charges without making sacrifices the plaintiff could not reasonably be expected to make.'[341]

The minority (Lords Scott and Walker) held that the approach in *Dimond v Lovell*[342] could not be distinguished and that therefore only the normal hiring costs (ie the 'spot-rate' of hire) could be recovered and not the higher costs of an accident-hire scheme (which includes additional benefits).

---

[341] ibid, at [9]. For the application of this in another 'credit hire' case, in which it was held that the claimant was impecunious and could not therefore pay the 'spot-rate' of hire, see *W v Veolia Environment Services (UK) Plc* [2011] EWHC 2020 (QB), [2012] 1 All ER (Comm) 667. Cf *Stevens v Equity Management Ltd* [2015] EWCA Civ 93, [2015] 4 All ER 458 (see below, p 215).

[342] [2002] 1 AC 384. See below, p 214 n 166.

8

Compensating advantages

1. Introduction	147
2. Indirect compensating advantages are not deducted	148
3. Some compensating advantages provided by third parties are not deducted	152

1. Introduction

The compensatory aims require the courts to assess not only the position the claimant would have been in if the breach of contract or tort had not been committed but also its actual position as a result of the tort or breach of contract, so that damages can make up the difference. Where the claimant's actual position has been, or will be, improved by benefits acquired subsequent to and as a result of the tort or breach of contract, one might expect (in accordance with the compensatory aims) that such benefits would be taken into account—if they are ignored the claimant will be left in a better position than if the contract had been performed or if no tort had been committed. In a nutshell, one might expect 'compensating advantages'[1] to be deducted or, as it is sometimes alternatively expressed, that losses mitigated would not be compensated. But in fact compensating advantages are often not deducted. Our concern here is to indicate when this is so.

However, it is first essential to stress that to be a compensating advantage the benefit in question must arise from the breach of contract or tort; that is, the breach of contract or tort must be a cause of the benefit according to the 'but for' test of factual causation. So, for example, if the claimant is injured by the defendant's negligence but completes his or her football pools coupon as usual, and wins the pools, that benefit is not a compensating advantage since he or she would have won the pools even if there had been no tort. Upjohn J in *W L Thompson Ltd v Robinson (Gunmakers) Ltd*[2] can similarly be viewed as applying the 'but for' causation test in deciding that a subsequent gain was not a compensating advantage. The issue was whether a purchaser who had broken his contract to buy a car should be made to pay damages for the vendor's loss of profit on the sale even though the vendor had since sold the car at the same price to someone else. It was held that, because supply exceeded demand, if the purchaser had not broken the contract the vendor would have made two profits and not one; hence the subsequent sale was not a compensating advantage and the purchaser had to pay damages for the vendor's lost profit on his sale.

Having stressed the factual causation inherent in the notion of a compensating advantage, we can now attack the question: when are compensating advantages ignored?

---

[1] Lawyers tend to use the phrase 'collateral benefits' rather than 'compensating advantages'. This is especially so where the benefit is provided from a source other than the claimant or defendant (ie from a collateral source). But the disadvantage of that term is that it may be taken to imply that the benefit is in some sense unrelated to the tort or breach of contract, when the opposite is true. The term 'compensating advantage', coined by A Ogus, *The Law of Damages* (Butterworths 1973) 93–94, has therefore been preferred in this book.

[2] [1955] Ch 177.

Leaving aside claims under the Fatal Accidents Act 1976,[3] there are two general principles of non-deduction: first, indirect compensating advantages are not deducted; and, secondly, some compensating advantages provided by third parties are not deducted. We shall look at each in turn. It can be taken that a compensating advantage that does not fall within either principle is normally deducted in accordance with the compensatory aims,[4] common examples being the expenses of performance saved by a claimant because of the defendant's breach of contract and the earnings the claimant has acquired under a new job following a wrongful dismissal or dismissal necessitated by personal injury.

2. Indirect compensating advantages are not deducted

'Directness' puts a limit on the extent to which compensating advantages are deducted on the policy ground that it is unfair that a claimant should have its damages reduced by a benefit that is far removed from the wrong and is essentially coincidental to it. Directness therefore plays an analogous but reverse role to remoteness and intervening cause; they counter a rigid adherence to the compensatory principle by limiting the claimant's damages, whereas directness here counters compensation, as strictly applied, by increasing the claimant's damages.

A useful hypothetical example, illustrating an indirect and non-deductible compensating advantage, is of a claimant who, because he has more time on his hands as a result of his wrongful dismissal or negligently caused injuries, fills in a winning football pools coupon, which he would otherwise not have had time to do. Even though the defendant's tort or breach of contract has been a factual cause of the claimant's pools win, that benefit should not be deducted because it was too indirectly related to the tort or breach of contract.

Turning to the cases, it is submitted that those dealing with compensating advantages provided by third parties shed little light on the directness principle since the judges have used the terminology of directness for decisions that are clearly better justified on other grounds.[5] This leaves as prime examples cases where the compensating advantages have been gained from actions taken by the claimant subsequent to the tort or breach of contract; and here the test for directness appears to turn on whether the compensating advantage derived from actions taken by the claimant *to avoid* the consequences of the wrong. As it is expressed in *McGregor on Damages*, '… the basic rule is that the benefit to the claimant, if it is to be taken into account in mitigation of damages, must arise out of the act of mitigation itself.'[6]

A leading case, albeit that the advantage was considered direct and therefore deductible, is *British Westinghouse v Underground Electric Rlys Co of London Ltd*.[7] The defendants in breach of contract supplied to the claimants turbines which were defective. The claimants

---

[3] Compensating advantages following the death are almost entirely covered by the Fatal Accidents Act 1976, s 4, ordering non-deduction. For full discussion see below, pp 265–267.

[4] A good example is *Westwood v Secretary of State for Employment* [1985] AC 20. One exception is the non-deduction of the price at which goods have been resold, above the market price, in cases like *Slater v Hoyle and Smith Ltd* [1920] 2 KB 11 and *Campbell Mostyn (Provisions) Ltd v Barnett Trading Co* [1954] 1 Lloyd's Rep 65, criticised below, pp 193–196.

[5] Below, p 153.

[6] J Edelman, *McGregor on Damages* (20th edn, Sweet & Maxwell 2018) para 9-120. Applying Andrew Dyson's views, 'Mitigation of Damages' (unpublished Oxford D Phil 2016), esp para 7.2, this might more accurately be expressed as saying that the benefit must arise out of the claimant's attempt to restore its non-breach position.

[7] [1912] AC 673. See also *Erie County Natural Gas & Fuel Co Ltd v Carroll* [1911] AC 105; *Bellingham v Dhillon* [1973] QB 304; *Techno Land Improvements Ltd v British Leyland (UK) Ltd* (1979) 252 Estates Gazette 805; *Cerberus Software Ltd v Rowley* [2001] ICR 376; *Dimond v Lovell* [2002] 1 AC 384, at 402–403. See generally A Dyson, '*British Westinghouse* Revisited' [2012] LMCLQ 412.

subsequently replaced them with other turbines. The replacement turbines turned out to be more efficient and profitable than the old turbines would have been if non-defective. In fact the extra profit gained from the replacement turbines being more efficient amounted to more than the losses caused by the original turbines being defective. The House of Lords held that the claimants were entitled only to nominal damages for the defendants' breach of contract because their losses had been completely mitigated by the extra profit gained from the claimants' steps taken to avoid the consequences of the breach. Viscount Haldane LC said:

> 'When in the course of his business he [the plaintiff] has taken action arising out of the transaction, which action has diminished his loss, the effect in actual diminution of the loss he has suffered may be taken into account even though there was no duty on him to act.'[8]

An excellent illustration of the distinction between direct and indirect compensating advantages is provided by *Lavarack v Woods of Colchester Ltd.*[9] The claimant was wrongfully dismissed from his employment with the defendants and so freed from a provision in his contract with them that he should not, without their written consent, be engaged or interested in any other business. After his dismissal the claimant took employment with a company called Martindale at a lower salary than he had earned with the defendants, acquired half the shares in the Martindale company, and bought shares in a company called Ventilation. The value of both the Martindale and Ventilation shares increased. The Court of Appeal held that while his new salary and the profit from the Martindale Co shares should be deducted, the profits from the Ventilation Co shares should not be. Lord Denning said:

> 'I realise that the plaintiff was only at liberty to invest in Ventilation because his employment was terminated. But nevertheless the benefit from that investment was not a direct result of his dismissal. It was an entirely collateral benefit ... for which he need not account to his [former] employers ... [his shareholding in] Martindale stands on a little different footing ... it looks as if he was getting a concealed remuneration by a profit on his shares in the company.'[10]

In other words, while the profit on the Ventilation shares was a compensating advantage, it should not be deducted because it was too indirectly related to the breach, as it did not follow from action taken to avoid its consequences. On the other hand, the profit on the Martindale shares was more directly related, as it followed from actions taken to avoid being without employment, and could not be clearly distinguished from the claimant's salary with Martindale.

Profit on shares was also not deducted, because regarded as too indirect a compensating advantage, in *Needler Financial Services Ltd v Taber*.[11] In 1990 the financial adviser of a company negligently advised Mr Taber to transfer the deferred benefits to which he was entitled under an occupational pension scheme to a personal pension plan with a mutual

---

[8] [1912] AC 673, at 689.

[9] [1967] 1 QB 278. See also *Hodge v Clifford Cowling & Co* [1990] 2 EGLR 89 (compensating advantage not deducted because the mitigating conduct, in acquiring another ship, was not connected with the wrong); *Mobil North Sea Ltd v PJ Pipe & Valve Co* [2001] 2 All ER (Comm) 289 (compensating advantage not deducted because it did not arise from an act of mitigation by the claimant but from a separate settlement agreement between the claimant and another party); *Thai Airways International Public Co Ltd v KI Holdings Co Ltd* [2015] EWHC 1250 (Comm), [2016] 1 All ER (Comm) 675, at [46]–[62] (third year of jet lease not deducted because the choice of a three-year, rather than a two-year, lease term was driven by independent commercial considerations).

[10] [1967] 1 QB 278, at 290–291.

[11] [2002] 3 All ER 501. See also *Primavera v Allied Dunbar Assurance Plc* [2002] EWCA Civ 1327, [2003] PNLR 12 (increased value, five years later, of an executive retirement plan, which the claimant had been negligently advised to take out, not deducted). In both these cases the controversial decision in *Hussey v Eels* [1990] 2 QB 227, discussed below, p 150, was applied.

life assurance society. Seven years later, because of his pension-holding, Mr Taber was given shares in the company to which the society had transferred its business on its demutualisation. He sold those shares for £7,815 net. In 1998, when Mr Taber was 65, he discovered that his pension was less valuable than it would have been had he not transferred it in 1990. While the advising company accepted liability in negligence to compensate Mr Taber for the difference in the value between the two pensions, it argued that the profit on shares (£7,815) should be deducted as a compensating advantage. Sir Andrew Morritt V-C disagreed. He held that the profit from demutualisation was not directly caused by the breach of duty. He said:

> 'It is true that but for the negligence of Needler Mr Taber would not have taken out the personal pension plan (PPP). It is also true that but for the PPP Mr Taber would not have received any demutualisation benefit. Even allowing for these factors the demutualisation benefit was not caused by and did not flow, as part of a continuous transaction, from the negligence. In causation terms the breach of duty gave rise to the opportunity to receive the profit but did not cause it ... The link between the negligence and the benefit was broken by all these events in the mid 1990s and later which led to the directors of the Society formulating ... the transfer of the long-term insurance business of the Society ...'[12]

A more difficult example of a compensating advantage that was not deducted is provided by *Hussey v Eels*.[13] The claimants were induced to buy a bungalow from the defendants by a negligent misrepresentation that the property had not been subject to subsidence. It was estimated that the claimants had paid £17,000 more than the bungalow was worth given its actual subsidence problems. Rather than effecting repairs or reselling straightaway, the claimants sought planning permission to replace the bungalow with two new ones. After two-and-a-half years they finally succeeded in obtaining that permission and sold the bungalow and land with planning permission for nearly £23,000 more than they had paid for it. The trial judge held that the claimants were not entitled to any damages for the negligent misrepresentation because they had fully mitigated their loss by the favourable resale. But that decision was overturned by the Court of Appeal which awarded £17,000 damages. The reasoning of Mustill LJ, giving the leading judgment, was that the resale profit was too indirect a consequence of the tort:

> 'Did the negligence which caused the damage also cause the profit, if profit there was? I do not think so. It is true that in one sense there was a causal link between the inducement of the purchase by misrepresentation and the sale two-and-a-half years later, for the sale represented a choice of one of the options with which the plaintiffs had been presented by the defendants' wrongful act. But only in that sense ... It seems to me that when the plaintiffs unlocked the development value of their land they did so for their own benefit, and not as part of a continuous transaction of which the purchase of land and bungalow was the inception.'[14]

This is controversial because, although there was a considerable time lag, the seeking and obtaining of planning permission and subsequent sale were clearly actions taken to avoid the subsidence problems. It is difficult to accept that those actions were too indirectly

---

[12] [2002] 3 All ER 501, at 511–512.
[13] [1990] 2 QB 227. This decision was controversially applied by the majority of the Court of Appeal (Peter Gibson LJ dissenting) in *Gardner v Marsh & Parsons* [1997] 1 WLR 489: damages in respect of defects in a building were awarded against a negligent surveyor even though those defects had been repaired by the landlord at no cost to the claimant tenant. For support for Peter Gibson LJ's dissent, see D Allen and M Thompson, 'Surveyor's Negligence and Collateral Benefits' [1998] Conv 303.
[14] [1990] 2 QB 227, at 241.

related. While the claimants might have been entitled to damages because of the general increase in prices over that two-and-a-half-year period (ie the loss of opportunity to buy an equivalent bungalow that would have increased in value), they had not produced evidence supporting such a claim. Certainly there is no reason to think that the £17,000 bore any relationship to such price increases.

An equally controversial decision, and even more significant, because made by the Supreme Court, is *Fulton Shipping Inc of Panama v Globalia Business Travel SAU of Spain, The New Flamenco*.[15] Here charterers had committed a repudiatory breach of a charterparty by returning the ship two years early. In response, the owners decided to sell the ship which, as was common ground between the parties, was a reasonable response to the breach because, at the time, and unusually, there was no suitable replacement charter for the ship. Subsequently the market value of ships fell dramatically so that this sale turned out to be very good news for the owners. They ended up far better off than they would have been had there been no breach by the charterers. The question was whether that compensating advantage (of having sold the ship before values fell) should be deducted in assessing the damages for the loss of profit on the charter.

The Supreme Court, overturning the Court of Appeal, held that that compensating advantage should not be deducted on the ground that the benefit from selling the ship was not caused by the breach in the relevant sense. The decision to sell the ship had not been necessitated by the breach but was rather a decision to speculate by the owner and did not represent the replacement of the income stream lost. This reasoning is puzzling. It was clear that 'but for' causation (as between the gain and the breach) was satisfied because the owners would not have sold the ship had there been no breach. Moreover, the sale was in direct response to the breach and was an attempt to reduce the losses from the breach. So it is hard to understand why the sale was treated as too indirect. In contrast, the purchase of the Ventilation shares in *Lavarack*[16] was an investment decision by the claimant where the assets invested had nothing to do with the breach (the only link being the claimant's freedom from a clause precluding investment in a different company). There was also no clear analogy with the long-accepted non-deduction of insurance proceeds where a claimant has precisely chosen to cover itself against the risk that has eventuated. Nor was it correct to say, as Lord Clarke did,[17] that had market prices gone the other way (ie up rather than down), those losses would have had to be borne by the owners. On the contrary, the fact that in that situation the sale would have increased the owners' loss would not have mattered given that selling the ship was a reasonable option to pursue: it is a well-established principle that there is no failure to mitigate if, in pursuing a reasonable course of action, the claimant increases its loss.

The straightforward conclusion to be reached is that, applying a true compensatory analysis, *Hussey v Eels* and *The New Flamenco* were wrongly decided. The compensating advantages should have been deducted. But if one were to try to justify those decisions, how

---

[15] [2017] UKSC 43, [2017] 1 WLR 2581. See also the fascinating decision of the High Court of Australia in *Clark v Macourt* [2013] HCA 56, (2013) 88 ALJR 190, criticised by K Barnett, 'Contractual Expectations and Goods' (2014) 130 LQR 387, in which, on the sale of a fertility business, the defendant seller supplied the claimant purchaser with 1996 fewer straws of usable sperm than warranted. It was held (Gageler J dissenting) that the claimant was entitled to the cost ($1.02m) of replacement sperm straws from a third party even though the claimant had not purchased the full number of replacement straws and even though the claimant had fully recouped the increased costs from her customers. Although the full cost of cure appeared to over-compensate the claimant, so that one might simply conclude that the decision is wrong, one might perhaps justify this decision on the same reasoning as is set out in the text below.

[16] Above, p 149.   [17] [2017] UKSC 43, [2017] 1 WLR 2581, at [33].

might one do so? It is submitted that, looked at alongside some other leading cases,[18] there are two main possibilities.

The first is that the courts, while at root favouring a compensatory analysis, have been willing to apply an objective or standard measure (what a reasonable claimant in that situation would have lost) even though, on the facts, this over-compensated the particular claimant. This may be thought to have the pragmatic virtue of being clear and simple to apply and corresponds with what is generally a just outcome.

The second possible justification, closely connected to the first, is that the defendant should pay damages according to the measure which, had the claimant acted reasonably, would most closely put the claimant into as good a position as it would have been in had the contract been performed or the wrong not been committed.[19] This may produce symmetry with the duty to mitigate by which a claimant cannot recover loss which it could reasonably have avoided: the corollary might be said to be that the defendant cannot complain if it has to compensate for loss that the claimant would have suffered if it had acted reasonably even if that loss has not actually been suffered. For example, in *Hussey v Eels* the claimant could reasonably have sold the bungalow and that would have most closely restored the claimant to the position it would have been in had there been no misrepresentation. So the claimant was entitled to £17,000 as the difference in value between the purchase price paid and the value of the bungalow at the time of purchase. It did not matter that, on the facts, the claimant chose not to sell the bungalow but to replace it profitably with two new ones. The compensating advantages from doing so were irrelevant. Again in *The New Flamenco* it would appear that the claimant owners could reasonably have entered into short-term charterparties for the two-year period and that would most closely have restored them to the position they would have been in had there been no breach. The owners were therefore entitled to the difference between the profits under the original charterparty and what could reasonably have been earned from those short-term replacement charters. The compensating advantages gained as a consequence of the owners' choosing to sell the ship were irrelevant.

Although either of these justifications might possibly explain the courts' thinking, any departure from applying the true measure of compensation for the particular claimant on the facts is not easy to support. Certainly what is disappointing is that the courts in cases like *Hussey v Eels* and *The New Flamenco* are not making clear in any convincing way why it is thought acceptable to overcompensate the claimant.

3. Some compensating advantages provided by third parties are not deducted

(1) General factors influencing the courts

The compensating advantages in issue here may be provided by the state in the form, for example, of social security benefits; or by an insurance company or employer by the terms of an existing contract with the claimant; or gratuitously by the claimant's relatives, friends, employer, trade union, or indeed by the public at large. Usually arising in respect of personal

---

[18] See, eg, *William Bros v Agius Ltd* [1914] AC 510; *Slater v Hoyle & Smith Ltd* [1920] 2 KB 11. See the discussion of these cases in chapter 10. See also the discussion in chapter 3 rejecting Stevens' theory, and Winterton's modification, of 'substitutive damages'.

[19] This is the approach favoured by Andrew Summers: see chapter 3. But as we have explained in chapter 3, there may be a punitive element in this.

injury, it is the deduction or non-deduction of this type of compensating advantage that has given rise to the most discussion and controversy.[20] Before looking at the details of the law, it is helpful to examine the factors that influence the courts.[21]

(i) Traditionally, the commonest explanation offered for the non-deduction of this type of compensating advantage is that it was too indirectly related to the tort or breach of contract. For example, in relation to accident insurance it has been said that the contract of insurance, rather than the accident, was the cause of the compensating advantage.[22] The same idea is often alternatively expressed by saying that the compensating advantage is a *res inter alios acta* or is collateral,[23] although the latter term invites confusion since all compensating advantages provided by third parties are commonly labelled collateral, whether deductible or not.[24] But the essential objection to this traditional reasoning is that a compensating advantage provided in response to the consequences of a tort or breach of contract cannot realistically be said to be too indirect so as to be non-deductible under the first principle examined above. In *Parry v Cleaver*,[25] the usage of remoteness and causation in this context was criticised and overall it is clear that the terminology of cause, collateral, and *res inter alios acta* is here merely a shroud for decisions really justified on other grounds.

(ii) Much of the traditional inconsistency in this area of the law appears to stem from the courts' willingness to punish the defendant, rather than merely to compensate the claimant. Hence there is often reference to the defendant being a wrongdoer who ought to pay and who does not deserve to be benefited by the compensating advantage.[26] But, if punishment is desired, it is surely better to administer it through punitive damages, where the punishment is explicit and where the amount awarded can be fixed in accordance with the extent to which it is felt the defendant deserves punishment. Note, however, that under the present law punitive damages can only be awarded in tort within the categories laid down in *Rookes v Barnard*;[27] and, it appears, cannot be awarded for breach of contract.

(iii) Parliament has sometimes laid down whether these compensating advantages are or are not to be deducted. For example, the Social Security (Recovery of Benefits) Act 1997 basically lays down that social security benefits paid as a result of an injury, or likely to be so paid, for up to five years from the accident are to be deducted from damages for personal injury; but that the state (through the Compensation Recovery Unit) is entitled to recoup the amount of benefits paid from the tortfeasor. However, there is to be no deduction from

---

[20] 'Unreason in the Law of Damages: The Collateral Source Rule' (1964) 77 Harv LR 741; H McGregor, 'Compensation Versus Punishment in Damages Awards' (1965) 28 MLR 629; P Cane and J Goudkamp, *Atiyah's Accidents, Compensation and the Law* (9th edn, CUP 2018) 365–374; J Fleming, *International Encyclopaedia of Comparative Law* vol XI (Mohr 1971); Law Commission, *Damages for Personal Injury: Collateral Benefits* (1997) Consultation Paper No 147; Law Commission, *Damages for Personal Injury: Medical, Nursing and Other Expenses; Collateral Benefits* (1999) Report No 262; R Lewis, *Deducting Benefits from Damages for Personal Injury* (OUP 1999). For an economic analysis, see R Posner, *Economic Analysis of Law* (9th edn, Wolters Kluwer 2014) 233–234.

[21] In Consultation Paper No 147, *Damages for Personal Injury: Collateral Benefits* (1997) paras 4.30–4.51, the Law Commission referred to the factors (ii), (iv), (v), and (vi) below as, respectively, the 'wrongdoer should not be relieved' argument, the 'paid for' argument, the 'provider's intentions' argument, and the 'incentive' argument. Its conclusion, at para 4.51, was that 'it is open to debate whether the policy arguments put for non-deduction of some collateral benefits withstand close scrutiny'.

[22] *Bradburn v Great Western Rly Co* (1874) LR 10 Exch 1.

[23] *Parsons v BNM Laboratories Ltd* [1964] 1 QB 95, at 143; J Edelman, *McGregor on Damages* (20th edn, Sweet & Maxwell 2018) para 9-111.

[24] See above, p 147 n 1.   [25] [1970] AC 1.   [26] Eg *Yates v Whyte* (1838) 4 Bing NC 272, at 283.

[27] [1964] AC 1129. See below, ch 20.

damages for non-pecuniary loss;[28] and benefits after the five years are not to be deducted.[29]

(iv) The courts sometimes regard the fact that the claimant has paid for, and in that sense earned, the advantage as a reason for not deducting it. In *Parry v Cleaver*, for example, this was part of Lord Reid's justification for not deducting a disability pension. If this were not so, it would mean that, as events have turned out, the claimant's payments would be rendered unnecessary, since he or she would have recovered the same compensation without those payments. Put another way, the person who has been a spendthrift should not be treated as well as someone who has used his or her money to guard against the unfortunate event that has occurred.

(v) The purpose of the compensating advantage is often regarded as relevant; for example, in *Parry v Cleaver* this partly underlay Lord Reid's explanation of why gratuitous payments are not deducted. But it is questionable whether this factor does provide much real assistance. In relation to any of these compensating advantages one can say that the purpose is to benefit the claimant as opposed to relieving the wrongdoer. But the real question is whether the purpose is to overcompensate the claimant and the answer to that is generally unclear. Indeed to answer it properly would require analysing the intention of, for example, each gratuitous donor or each insured claimant, and clearly the courts do not attempt this.

(vi) A factor that has been influential in relation to gratuitous payments—and provides the best explanation for their non-deduction—is that one would not wish to discourage benevolence. In the words of Andrews CJ in *Redpath v Belfast and County Down Rly*,[30] which were approved by Lord Reid in *Parry v Cleaver*, 'I would only add that if the proposition contended for by the defendants is sound the inevitable consequence in the case of future disasters of a similar character would be that the springs of private charity would be found to be largely if not entirely dried up.'

(vii) Leaving aside an indemnity insurer's subrogation rights,[31] there is rarely any question at common law of the third party (X) recovering the value of the benefit conferred on the claimant (C) from C, assuming the compensating advantage has not been deducted, or from the defendant (D), assuming the deduction has been made.

X has no restitutionary claim against C in that he has rendered the benefit, either as a volunteer, or under a valid contractual or statutory obligation owed to the claimant. Therefore the only possibility of recovery is where there is an undertaking by C to reimburse X in the event of recovering damages. At present, that undertaking is only generally exacted by an employer providing sick pay, and significantly, in this situation, the courts do indeed appear to depart from the general approach to sick pay by not deducting it from the damages.[32] The

---

[28] By the Social Security (Recovery of Benefits) Act 1997, s 8, and Sch 2, recoupment shall only be against compensation for loss of earnings, cost of care, and loss of mobility, and then only 'like for like.'
[29] ibid, ss 3 and 17.   [30] [1947] NI 167, at 170.
[31] H Street, *Principles of the Law of Damages* (Sweet & Maxwell 1962) 105. Property insurance is indemnity insurance, accident insurance is not. An indemnity insurer's subrogation rights ensure that the normal rule of not deducting insurance payments can apply without there being any double compensation: *Arab Bank Plc v John Wood (Commercial) Ltd* [2000] 1 WLR 857. See analogously *Bristol and West Building Society v May May & Merrimans (No 2)* [1998] 1 WLR 336.
[32] *Browning v War Office* [1963] 1 QB 750, at 770; *IRC v Hambrook* [1956] 2 QB 641, at 656–657. See also *Berriello v Felixstowe Dock & Rly Co* [1989] 1 WLR 695 (payments from Italian state welfare fund held not deductible because under Italian law the state would recover from C if C recovered the same loss from D); *Cosemar SA v Marimarna Shipping Co Ltd* [1990] 2 Lloyd's Rep 323 (owners able to recover voyage expenses from time charterers even though paid by third party because, on recovery from time charterers, owners bound to reimburse third party). Cf *Design 5 v Keniston Housing Assoc* (1986) 34 BLR 92 in which it was thought that a state grant given by the Department of the Environment was non-deductible: the best explanation for that otherwise controversial view was that the grant would probably have to be repaid.

possibility of the court itself exacting an undertaking from C to use part of the damages to reimburse X has generally not found favour, being contrary to the usual rule that damages must be awarded unconditionally.[33]

Where a deduction has been made, it appears that X does not have a restitutionary claim at common law against D, even where there is an 'unjust factor' in the law of unjust enrichment (such as where X was acting under a mistake or for a failed consideration or under 'legal compulsion'), because, as laid down in *Metropolitan Police District Receiver v Croydon Corpn*,[34] X has not discharged any liability of D, since if the damages were reduced by the compensating advantage D was not liable to pay any higher amount. Moreover, even if one could say that D's liability has been discharged (or that D has otherwise been enriched), that enrichment may be an 'incidental benefit' and therefore not 'at the claimant's expense' in the sense required by the law of unjust enrichment.[35]

The importance of X rarely having any rights at common law against C or D is that the courts almost always regard the question of deducting these compensating advantages, as solely involving C and D, so that the choice is either to overcompensate C or to relieve D. Hence, in the leading case of *Parry v Cleaver*, there was no mention of X's rights. It can be argued that, while more expensive (for example, extra litigation would be likely),[36] it might be better to deduct these compensating advantages, other than gratuitous payments, and to allow X to recover from D the value of that benefit deducted by, for example, allowing X a tort claim for pure economic loss against D or reversing *Metropolitan Police v Croydon Corpn* so as, in some circumstances (where there is an unjust factor and the benefit is direct rather than incidental), to grant X restitution from D in the law of unjust enrichment.[37]

It is arguable that this approach to reform has been accepted by the Legislature vis-à-vis state benefits. The basic strategy of the Social Security (Recovery of Benefits) Act 1997 is precisely for there to be full deduction of compensating benefits provided by the state (X) but for the state to be able to recoup the value of those benefits from D.[38]

Having examined the factors influencing the courts, we can now look at whether particular benefits provided by third parties are deducted, not deducted, or partly deducted.

---

[33] Below, p 168–169. Contra, eg, is *Dennis v London Passenger Transport Board* [1948] 1 All ER 779.

[34] [1957] 2 QB 154. *Croydon Corpn* was distinguished, with respect unconvincingly, by Sachs J in *Land Hessen v Gray & Gerrish* (31 July 1998, unreported). See generally A Burrows, *The Law of Restitution* (3rd edn, OUP 2011) 452–455; *Goff and Jones The Law of Unjust Enrichment* (eds C Mitchell, P Mitchell and S Watterson, 9th edn, Sweet & Maxwell 2016) paras 4-38–4-42.

[35] This is ultimately the best explanation for why there was no unjust enrichment claim by X against D, through subrogation, in *Swynson Ltd v Lowick Rose LLP* [2017] UKSC 32, [2018] AC 313. See A Burrows, '"At the Expense of the Claimant": A Fresh Look' [2017] RLR 167, 180–182.

[36] For other objections, see P Cane and J Goudkamp, *Atiyah's Accidents, Compensation and the Law* (9th edn, CUP 2018) 360–365; H Street, *Principles of the Law of Damages* (Sweet & Maxwell 1962) 106.

[37] While being critical of the Court of Appeal's view in *Croydon Corpn* that the tortfeasor was not enriched, the Law Commission did not recommend a new statutory right for the provider of a deductible collateral benefit to recoup its value from the tortfeasor. See Law Commission, *Damages for Personal Injury: Medical, Nursing and Other Expenses; Collateral Benefits* (1999) Report No 262, paras 10.68–10.72, 12.28–12.32.

[38] See A Burrows, *The Law of Restitution* (3rd edn, OUP 2011) 453–454.

(2) Social security benefits

In respect of damages for personal injury the law on the deduction of social security benefits has been transformed by the radical and complex provisions contained in the Social Security (Recovery of Benefits) Act 1997, accompanied by the Social Security (Recovery of Benefits) Regulations 1997.[39] The 1997 Act builds on, but significantly modifies, the state recoupment scheme first introduced in 1989. The following seven points explain the general operation of the Act:[40]

(i) The defendant (the 'compensator') must reimburse the state for the total amount of listed social security benefits received by the claimant during the 'relevant period' in respect of the injury or disease.[41]

(ii) The 'relevant period' is five years or, if shorter, the period to a final settlement payment from the day following the accrual of the cause of action (or, in the case of disease, from the claimant's first claim for a listed benefit).[42]

(iii) The listed social security benefits are: universal credit, benefits under the Social Security Contributions and Benefits Act 1992,[43] a jobseeker's allowance, an employment and support allowance, personal independence payment, or mobility allowance.[44]

(iv) Subject to significant limitations, the compensator may deduct the amount of the listed benefits, for which he must reimburse the state, from the compensation payable to the claimant.[45] The significant limitations are as follows. First, a benefit can only be deducted 'like for like'; that is, against an equivalent head of compensation.[46] For example, a benefit listed as being paid in respect of lost earnings can only be deducted from compensation for lost earnings and not from compensation for cost of care. Secondly, the heads of compensation from which there can be deduction are loss of earnings, cost of care, and loss of mobility (all during the 'relevant period').[47] There can therefore be no deduction from damages for pain, suffering, and loss of amenity. These limitations mean that, in contrast to the earlier recoupment scheme, a compensator is liable to reimburse the state in respect of a social security benefit even though that benefit may not be deductible from the damages payable. This marks an important theoretical shift because while, arguably, the original

---

[39] SI 1997/2205.
[40] See, generally, R Lewis, *Deducting Benefits from Damages for Personal Injury* (OUP 1999) Pt II.
[41] Social Security (Recovery of Benefits) Act 1997, s 6. This applies, without any reduction, even if the claimant was contributorily negligent: see s 1(2)(a) referring to 'liable to any extent'. Payments under the Fatal Accidents Act 1976 are exempted from the statutory scheme: Social Security (Recovery of Benefits) Regulations 1997, SI 1997/2205, reg 2(2)(a).
[42] Social Security (Recovery of Benefits) Act 1997, s 3.
[43] Eg incapacity benefit, attendance allowance, disability living allowance, or disablement pension.
[44] Social Security (Recovery of Benefits) Act 1997, s 29 and Sch 2. As regards relevant social security benefits not listed in the 1997 Act the common law will apply to determine whether there should be deduction or not. *Hodgson v Trapp* [1989] AC 807 (in which, prior to the legislative recoupment regime, the House of Lords held that attendance and mobility allowance were fully deductible in assessing damages for personal injury) suggests that there should be deduction of such non-listed benefits from damages: and this is supported by *Clenshaw v Tanner* [2002] EWCA Civ 1848 in which housing benefit (which is not listed in the 1997 Act) was deducted from the claimant's loss of earnings. See also *Ballantine v Newalls Insulation Co Ltd* [2001] ICR 25 (payment made under Pneumoconiosis etc (Workers' Compensation) Act 1979 deducted in full from damages for personal injury, applying *Hodgson v Trapp*).
[45] Social Security (Recovery of Benefits) Act 1997, s 8. The deduction is from the compensation payable after any reduction for contributory negligence (or because of other factors). Contrary to the normal principle that interest is awarded for the claimant being kept out of his money, the statutory scheme has been construed by the House of Lords as dictating that interest should be payable on the whole amount of damages irrespective of the deduction of social security benefits: *Wadey v Surrey County Council* [2000] 1 WLR 820.
[46] Social Security (Recovery of Benefits) Act 1997, s 8 and Sch 2.
[47] ibid. Loss of mobility is not defined but presumably refers to, eg, the cost of a wheelchair.

scheme could have been entirely explained on the basis that the state's recoupment was in respect of relieving a liability of the defendant's the new scheme goes beyond that and in effect holds the defendant liable for the pure economic loss caused to the state by the tort.[48]

(v) A central feature of the administration of the scheme is a certificate of recoverable benefits furnished to the compensator by the Secretary of State (ie by the Compensation Recovery Unit).[49]

(vi) The compensator is not liable to reimburse the state for listed benefits payable after five years: such benefits are not to be deducted from damages.[50] This is unfortunate. There is no good policy reason not to apply the basic principle that compensation dictates deduction: punishment is not justified, the claimant has not directly paid for such benefits, and there is no question of deduction discouraging private benevolence. The Pearson Commission recommended that social security benefits should be fully deducted[51] and this is strongly supported by the reasoning of the House of Lords in *Hodgson v Trapp*[52] dealing with social security benefits prior to the legislative recoupment regime.

(vii) In contrast to the earlier recoupment scheme, there is no exclusion for 'small payments'.[53] There is provision for regulations to be made for the disregarding of small payments but no such regulations have yet been made (or appear likely to be made).

In *Hassall v Secretary of State for Social Security*[54] it was decided by the Court of Appeal that the former recoupment scheme applied (and the same can be said of the Social Security (Recovery of Benefits) Act 1997), even though the claimant was receiving approximately the same amount of social security benefits prior to the accident. This was because the benefits paid after the accident were paid on the different basis that the claimant was no longer fit for work and were therefore clearly paid in consequence of the accident. The fact that the claimant would be left undercompensated was regarded as flowing not from a defect in the recoupment scheme but from his failure to claim damages for the loss of the non-recoupable benefits. Following this, damages for loss of non-recoupable benefits have been awarded.[55] But under the 1997 Act, it is no longer possible to deduct benefits from damages for non-pecuniary loss, and as a result there is now much less scope for such an award.[56]

In the light of the Social Security (Recovery of Benefits) Act 1997, the common law approach to the deductibility of social security benefits is now largely of relevance only to claims for wrongful dismissal. The cases establish that social security benefits paid as a result of the dismissal (eg unemployment benefit) are fully deducted.[57] This is to be supported for, as has been said in relation to social security benefits above in criticising non-deduction after five years, there is no good policy reason not to apply the basic principle that compensation dictates deduction.

---

[48] See analogously the right of hospital authorities to charge to tortfeasors the costs of treatment of their victims under the Health and Social Care (Community Health and Standards) Act 2003, Pt 3.
[49] Social Security (Recovery of Benefits) Act 1997, ss 4–5.   [50] ibid, ss 3, 17.
[51] Pearson Report, paras 467–498; cf para 494. See also the more radical argument in P Cane and J Goudkamp, *Atiyah's Accidents, Compensation and the Law* (9th edn, CUP 2018) 371: 'tort damages and social security benefits ... are paid for by much the same group of people (that is, a significant section of the public), and there is no rational justification for paying double compensation for the same loss at the expense of the same group.'
[52] [1989] AC 807. See above, n 44.
[53] The half-deduction for five years of certain social security benefits laid down in the Law Reform (Personal Injuries) Act 1948, s 2(1) no longer has any application, even to damages of £2,500 or less. By Social Security (Recovery of Benefits) Act 1997, s 33 and Sch 3, the Law Reform (Personal Injuries) Act 1948, s 2(1) is repealed.
[54] [1995] 1 WLR 812.   [55] *Neal v Bingle* [1998] QB 466.
[56] R Lewis, *Deducting Benefits from Damages for Personal Injury* (OUP 1999) 219–222.
[57] *Parsons v BNM Laboratories Ltd* [1964] 1 QB 95; *Westwood v Secretary of State for Employment* [1985] AC 20. See also *Chan v Hackney LBC* [1997] ICR 1014 (EAT deducted invalidity benefit in assessing compensation for loss of earnings for race discrimination).

(3) Non-state payments

In an important speech in *Hussain v New Taplow Paper Mills Ltd*[58] (which concerned the deductibility of sick pay paid under an employer's health insurance scheme), Lord Bridge summarised the law on the deductibility of non-state benefits in personal injury cases. He clarified that the basic rule is that 'prima facie the only recoverable loss is the net loss'.[59] He then went on to explain that there are two well-established exceptions. First, money from an insurance policy paid for by the claimant and, secondly, money received from the benevolence of a third party. It is helpful to look at each of these two exceptions in turn before turning to benefits that are deducted in line with the prima facie rule.

As regards insurance,[60] it was held in *Bradburn v Great Western Rly Co*[61] that sums received under an accident insurance policy, paid for by the claimant, should not be deducted. More recently, in *Parry v Cleaver*,[62] the House of Lords decided, by a three–two majority, that sums received under a disability pension scheme should also not be deducted (in assessing damages for loss of earnings).[63] In essence this rested on the view that such a pension scheme is more akin to insurance than to wages and hence, in accordance with *Bradburn*, no deduction should be made. Lord Reid said:

> 'As regards moneys coming to the plaintiff under a contract of insurance, I think that the real and substantial reason for disregarding them is that the plaintiff has bought them and that it would be unjust and unreasonable to hold that the money which he prudently spent on premiums and the benefit from it should enure to the benefit of the tortfeasor ... Then I ask—why should it make any difference that he insured by arrangement with his employer rather than with an insurance company?'[64]

But while the analogy drawn between the disability pension and accident insurance is justified, the controversial issue is whether accident insurance payments should be non-deductible. It is arguable that *Bradburn* is right on this because a claimant who has paid for benefits in the event of misfortune has earned those benefits over and above full damages from a defendant.[65]

In *Smoker v London Fire and Civil Defence Authority*[66] the House of Lords held that the non-deduction principle of *Parry v Cleaver* remained good law (subsequent to the *Hussain* case) and was applicable even where the employer operating the disablement pension

---

[58] [1988] AC 514. See also his very similar subsequent comments in *Hodgson v Trapp* [1989] AC 807 (which concerned state benefits: see above, p 156 n 44) and *Hunt v Severs* [1994] 2 AC 350 (which concerned gratuitous care).

[59] [1988] AC 514, at 527.

[60] The insurance exception does not produce double recovery in respect of indemnity insurance, as opposed to non-indemnity insurance, because of an indemnity insurer's subrogation rights: see above, p 154 n 31.

[61] (1874) LR 10 Exch 1.   [62] [1970] AC 1.

[63] The question as to whether a pension (whether a disability or retirement pension) should be deducted from damages *for loss of pension* is more complex. In *Parry v Cleaver* [1970] AC 1 it was held that the pension should be deducted after normal retirement age in the assessment of damages for lost retirement pension. See also *Auty v National Coal Board* [1985] 1 All ER 930; *West v Versil Ltd, The Times*, 31 August 1996; *Longden v British Coal Corpn* [1998] AC 653.

[64] [1970] AC 1, at 14.

[65] For a contrary argument—that the claimant was not paying for overcompensation—see Law Commission, *Damages for Personal Injury: Collateral Benefits* (1997) Consultation Paper No 147, para 4.40. See also below, p 161.

[66] [1991] 2 AC 502.

scheme was the tortfeasor. And in *Hopkins v Norcross plc*[67] the same principles were applied by the Court of Appeal in holding that a retirement pension was not to be deducted in assessing damages for a wrongful dismissal.

Gratuitous payments are not deducted.[68] Non-deduction here is fully supported by *Parry v Cleaver* where Lord Reid said:

'It would be revolting to the ordinary man's sense of justice and therefore contrary to public policy, that the sufferer should have his damages reduced, so that he would gain nothing from the benevolence of his friends or relatives or the public at large, and that the only gainer would be the wrongdoer.'[69]

At a deeper level, as suggested earlier,[70] the best explanation for this non-deduction is that the courts do not want to discourage benevolence.

But, if that is the correct justification, gratuitous payments *made by the tortfeasor* should normally be deducted. This was accepted by the Court of Appeal in *Williams v BOC Gases Ltd*,[71] where the defendant employer had made an *ex gratia* payment to its employee, the claimant, which was expressed to be 'an advance against damages that may be awarded to you in respect of any claim you may have against the company'. After referring to Lord Bridge's approach in *Hussain* (and other cases), Brooke LJ said the following:[72]

'The "benevolence" exception is limited in terms to gifts arising from the benevolence of third parties, and does not cover benevolent gifts made by the wrongdoer himself, for which allowance ought prima facie to be made against any compensation he might have to pay. Neither of the justifications for the benevolence exception apply to the tortfeasor. Deductibility will encourage him to make benevolent payments in future to injured employees, rather than the reverse. And it certainly cannot be said that in making the gift, his intention was to benefit the plaintiff rather than to relieve himself of liability *pro tanto*: he would have been happy to achieve both purposes at once. *A fortiori* in a case in which he said in terms, at the time he made the gift, that it was to be treated as an advance against any damages he might have to pay.'

In *Williams,* the apparently contrary decision of the Court of Appeal in *McCamley v Cammell Laird Shipbuilders Ltd*[73]—where money from an accident insurance policy taken out by the defendant employer for employees was held non-deductible on the supposed application of the benevolence exception—was said to be a case that should be confined to its own facts.

Subsequently the Court of Appeal in *Gaca v Pirelli General plc*[74] approved *Williams* and, in an excellent decision, took the opportunity formally to overrule *McCamley* on the ground that it was inconsistent with, for example, Lord Bridge's reasoning in the House of Lords in *Hussain v New Taplow Paper Mills*.[75] In *Gaca*, the claimant was seriously injured at work in an accident for which the defendant employers were responsible. The defendants paid him an ill-health gratuity and he also received disability payments under the defendants' group accident insurance policy. The Court of Appeal held that the benevolence exception to the 'net loss' principle did not apply to either of those two types of payment because they were

---

[67] [1994] ICR 11.
[68] *Redpath v Belfast & County Down Rly* [1947] NI 167 (public appeal). See also *Liffen v Watson* [1940] 1 KB 556 (charitable gifts in kind, in the shape of housing, food, or clothing, ignored in assessing damages).
[69] [1970] AC 1, at 14.   [70] See above, p 154.
[71] [2000] PIQR Q253. Obiter dicta of Lloyd LJ to this effect in *Hussain v New Taplow Paper Mills Ltd* [1987] 1 All ER 417, at 428, were approved.
[72] [2000] PIQR Q253, at Q261.   [73] [1990] 1 WLR 963.
[74] [2004] EWCA Civ 373, [2004] 1 WLR 2683.   [75] [1988] AC 514.

provided by the tortfeasor.[76] They should therefore be deducted in assessing damages. Not to deduct gratuitous payments where made by the tortfeasor would tend to discourage benevolence by the tortfeasor, which would be contrary to the purpose of the exception. In any event, the payments made under the group insurance policy were not paid by benevolence. The exception was concerned with payments made out of sympathy or charity whereas these payments were arranged, and made, in order to promote good working relations between the employers and employees. This decision constitutes a long overdue and welcome clarification of the law on the benevolence exception generally and on benevolence provided by tortfeasors specifically.

Wages, salary, and sick pay are generally deducted in assessing damages for loss of earnings[77] and rightly so, for there is here no reason not to apply the 'compensation dictates deduction' (or 'net loss') principle. In *Hussain v New Taplow Paper Mills Ltd*[78] the injured claimant was entitled under his contract of employment to full sick pay for 13 weeks and thereafter to half pay under his employers' permanent health insurance scheme. The House of Lords held that payments under the scheme should be deducted in assessing damages for loss of earnings. They were indistinguishable from the sick pay paid during the first 13 weeks and were the antithesis of the pension in *Parry v Cleaver* which was payable only after employment ceased. Moreover it was the employers, not the claimant, who had paid the insurance premiums under the scheme. Lord Bridge said:

> 'It positively offends my sense of justice that a plaintiff, who has certainly paid no insurance premiums as such, should receive full wages during a period of incapacity to work from two different sources, his employer and the tortfeasor. It would seem to me still more unjust and anomalous where, as here, the employer and the tortfeasor are one and the same.'[79]

The same approach was taken in *Page v Sheerness Steel Plc*,[80] where the claimant was entitled to half pay for life under a permanent health insurance policy taken out and paid for by his employers. This was deducted in assessing his loss of earnings. Similarly in *Gaca v Pirelli General plc*[81] the Court of Appeal held that the payments made to the injured employee under the employers' group personal accident insurance policy did not fall within the 'insurance exception' to the general principle of deducting compensating advantages because the premiums were paid by the employers and not by the claimant employee.

An exception to the deduction of sick pay is where the claimant is under an obligation to refund the sick pay to his employer in the event of recovering full damages. In such a situation the courts do not make a deduction, and this seems a sensible way of both compensating the claimant and reimbursing his employer.[82]

In accordance with the general principle of deduction, where the claimant has been made redundant as a result of his injuries and has received a redundancy payment that payment is deducted.[83]

Outside the context of personal injury, an excellent illustration of the general rule of deduction (or net loss) is provided by *Swynson Ltd v Lowick Rose LLP*.[84] Swynson had made

---

[76] Dyson LJ pointed out that, of course, the position would be different if the tortfeasor has spelt out explicitly that ex gratia payments are not to be deducted from any damages.
[77] *Parry v Cleaver* [1970] AC 1; *Turner v Ministry of Defence* (1969) 113 Sol Jo 585.
[78] [1988] AC 514.   [79] ibid, at 532.   [80] [1999] 1 AC 345.
[81] [2004] EWCA Civ 373, [2004] 1 WLR 2683.   [82] Above, p 154 n 32.
[83] *Colledge v Bass Mitchells & Butlers Ltd* [1988] 1 All ER 536. See also *Wilson v National Coal Board* 1981 SLT 67. Cf *Mills v Hassall* [1983] ICR 330 where the claimant would have been made redundant irrespective of his injury.
[84] [2017] UKSC 32, [2018] AC 313. Given that the payments were deducted, the question then arose whether Hunt had a claim in unjust enrichment (through subrogation) against the negligent accountants for having 'discharged' their liability: see for the failure of that claim, above, p 155 n 35. For a somewhat similar example of the general rule of deduction, in the context of a negligent valuation, see *Tiuta International Ltd v De Villiers Surveyors Ltd* [2017] UKSC 77, [2017] 1 WLR 4627.

three loans to a borrower (Evo Medical Solutions Ltd ('EMSL')), on which EMSL defaulted. The purpose of the loans had been for EMSL to buy a company called EVO and, before making the loans, Swynson had relied on a negligent report about EVO by the defendant accountants. Swynson brought an action in contract and the tort of negligence against the accountants for the losses on the three loans. However, subsequently to the defaults, the owner of Swynson (Hunt), as part of a refinancing deal, had lent EMSL the money to repay two of the loans to Swynson and those repayments were made. The Supreme Court held that Hunt's payments, which enabled Swynson to pay off its loans to EMSL, were not *res inter alios acta* and therefore reduced the damages payable to Swynson by the negligent defendant accountants. Those payments were sufficiently direct and were not motivated by benevolence—but rather by commercial considerations—and were not paid under an insurance contract.

The Law Commission completed a Report in 1999 which included detailed consideration of the common law on compensating advantages in personal injury cases. In its earlier Consultation Paper, the Law Commission put forward several options (including leaving the law unchanged) on which it sought the views of consultees.[85] The most radical option for reform was, in effect, to deduct all compensating advantages from damages meeting the same loss including charitable payments, personal accident insurance, and disablement pensions. A second, still radical, option was to deduct all compensating advantages from damages meeting the same loss except charitable payments. A third, and less radical, option was to leave the present law as it is, except that disablement pensions would be deducted: it was argued that this would remove the greatest anomaly in the present law, namely that if a person is paid long-term sick pay that will be deducted from damages for loss of earnings, but if he or she is paid a disablement pension that will not be deducted.

The Law Commission indicated that there are strong arguments for favouring greater deduction of compensating advantages than is achieved under the present law. First, the basic notion that damages are to compensate the claimant, and not to punish the defendant, indicates that prima facie compensating advantages should be deducted. That is, compensation equals deduction. Secondly, to deduct compensating advantages would reduce damages and would therefore reduce the cost of the tort system without unduly prejudicing victims, who will be fully compensated in any event. Thirdly, the main policy reasons for non-deduction of, say, insurance payments that have been put by judges—in particular Lord Reid in *Parry v Cleaver*[86]—may not withstand close scrutiny. For example, to the argument that deduction would act as a disincentive for parties to take out insurance, it can be counter-argued that it is unlikely that the law is known about by those who are about to take out insurance and, even if it were, deduction would not act as a real disincentive because a prudent person would take out insurance anyway. In particular, it would guarantee payment even where the injury is not caused by a legal wrong. Similarly, to the argument that non-deduction ensures that the claimant receives back what he or she has paid for, one can equally well argue that the claimant has not paid for double recovery but has rather paid to ensure that he or she receives full compensation, including in situations where there would be no legal claim for compensation.

---

[85] Law Commission, *Damages for Personal Injury: Collateral Benefits* (1997) Consultation Paper No 147, paras 4.79–4.105.
[86] [1970] AC 1.

In its Report,[87] the Law Commission felt unable to make any recommendation for statutory reform of the law on compensating advantages in personal injury cases. No single suggested option received majority support from its consultees and, when it came to working out the details of even the limited reform of reversing *Parry v Cleaver* and equating disablement pensions with long-term sick pay, severe difficulties were encountered in trying to distinguish disablement pensions from some types of insurance. The overall message to emerge was that, while the present common law in this difficult area may not be perfect, it has reached satisfactory compromises that are difficult to improve upon.

---

[87] Law Commission, *Damages for Personal Injury: Medical, Nursing and Other Expenses; Collateral Benefits* (1999) Report No 262.

9

Form of compensatory damages, date for assessment, taxation

1. The form of compensatory damages	163
2. The date for the assessment of compensatory damages	169
3. Taxation	182

1. The form of compensatory damages

(1) Once-and-for-all assessment: the general rule and its exceptions

(a) The general rule

The general rule can be expressed as follows: a court must assess in a lump sum all past, present, and future loss resulting from the particular tort or breach of contract being sued for, because no damages can be later given for a cause of action on which judgment has already been given. The classic authority is *Fitter v Veal*,[1] where the claimant had been awarded £11 damages against the defendant in an action for assault and battery. His injuries proved to be more serious than at first thought and he had to undergo an operation on his skull. It was held that he could not recover for this further loss in a new action.

Naturally, this rule does not prevent a different cause of action later being brought, and in deciding what amounts to a different cause of action it should be remembered that a single act may give rise to more than one cause of action. A leading case is *Brunsden v Humphrey*,[2] which involved a road accident injuring the claimant and damaging his vehicle. It was held that the claimant had two separate causes of action, one for his personal injury and another for his property damage.

(b) Arguments for and against the once-and-for-all rule

The purpose of the once-and-for-all rule is to prevent continual litigation. But it carries with it the problem of the court having to make an assessment of future loss, which must necessarily involve guesswork and usually produces inaccuracy. As Lord Scarman said in

---

[1] (1701) 12 Mod Rep 542. For more recent examples, see *Buckland v Palmer* [1984] 1 WLR 1109; *Burke v Tower Hamlets HA*, The Times, 10 August 1989.
[2] (1884) 14 QBD 141. See also *Darley Main Colliery Co v Mitchell* (1886) 11 App Cas 127; *O'Sullivan v Williams* [1992] 3 All ER 385. The decision in *Brunsden* has been criticised in, eg, *Talbot v Berkshire CC* [1993] 4 All ER 9; cf *The Indian Endurance* [1993] AC 410, at 420 (per Lord Goff). For continuing wrongs (even apparently where the defendant commits no further acts) a fresh cause of action accrues *de die in diem* and hence future loss is irrecoverable (at common law) as being caused by a future rather than an already committed tort or breach of contract: eg *Battishill v Reed* (1856) 18 CB 696. In *Deeny v Gooda Walker Ltd* [1995] 4 All ER 289 Phillips J held that the special features of the Lloyd's litigation meant that, as an exception to the general once-and-for-all rule, names at Lloyd's were entitled to contractual and tortious damages for past losses and could later claim damages for anticipated losses.

Lim Poh Choo v Camden and Islington Area Health Authority,[3] 'Knowledge of the future being denied to mankind, so much of the award as is to be attributed to future loss and suffering ... will almost surely be wrong. There is really only one certainty: the future will prove the award to be either too high or too low.' While an assessment of compensatory damages generally involves some speculation in judging what position the claimant would have been in if no tort or breach of contract had been committed, to have to assess once-and-for-all what position the claimant will from now on be in requires additional speculation about the uncertain.

For personal injury and death, future loss is often an important head of assessment, and it is here that the question of whether the once-and-for-all rule should be departed from to allow the award of periodic payments has been hotly debated over several decades.[4] This has finally resulted in the introduction of a regime for reviewable periodical payments.[5] The difficulties of assessing the future are particularly obvious in this field—common questions that arise, for example, are whether further operations will be necessary, whether brain damage will lead to epilepsy, when the claimant will die, or when the claimant will be fit to return to work. In all such instances, reviewable periodic payments make the courts' task easier and enable them to put the claimant more closely into the position she would have been in if the tort or breach of contract had not been committed.

A rather different criticism of the once-and-for-all rule in relation to future pecuniary loss following on personal injury or death is that the lump sum award, which is intended to be sufficient to provide for the claimant's pecuniary needs over the years, may be quickly and foolishly dissipated and may hence not fulfil its purpose. Periodic payments tend to remove this problem. Moreover, periodic payments correspond more closely than does a lump sum to the continuing loss of income, for which the damages are generally intended to compensate.

However, it is misleading to think that, even confining one's attention to personal injury cases, the arguments are all one way or that there is no argument against periodic payments being standardly ordered. The finality produced by the once-and-for-all rule enables the defendant and his or her insurers to be certain where they stand and minimises judicial expense and time. Furthermore, a once-and-for-all award contains no disincentive for the claimant to recover from an injury, puts an end to any 'compensation neurosis' (which is a recognised psychiatric illness), rules out any difficulties produced by the defendant's (or his or her insurer's) subsequent insolvency, and renders unnecessary continued investigation of the claimant's condition and lifestyle, sometimes possible only by intrusive 'spying'. The precise extent to which reviewability should be allowed is particularly problematic. Finally, if both claimants and defendants prefer lump sums, giving the courts the power to award periodic payments does not of course prevent the parties opting for a lump sum by settling out of court.

---

[3] [1980] AC 174, at 183.
[4] See, eg, Law Commission, *Report on Personal Injury Litigation—Assessment of Damages* (1973) Report No 56, paras 231–244; *Royal Commission on Civil Liability and Compensation for Personal Injury* (chaired by Lord Pearson) (1978) Vol 1, ch 14; Law Commission, *Report on Structured Settlements and Interim and Provisional Damages* (1994) Report No 224; Lord Chancellor's Department, Consultation Paper on *Periodical Payments* (2002).
[5] See below, pp 166–167.

(c) Provisional damages

The first relatively minor break with lump sums was the introduction in 1982, implementing the Law Commission's recommendation of 1973, of provisional damages.[6] By the Senior Courts Act 1981, s 32A, and the Civil Procedure Rules, Pt 41, the High Court has power to award provisional damages in actions:

> 'for damages for personal injuries in which there is proved or admitted to be a chance that at some definite or indefinite time in the future the injured person will, as the result of the act or omission which gave rise to the cause of action, develop some serious disease or suffer some serious deterioration in his physical or mental condition.'[7]

In such a case the court is able to assess the damages on the assumption that the injured person will not develop the disease or suffer the deterioration but then to award further damages at a future date if the risk should in fact materialise.[8] However, the power can only be used if the particulars of claim include a claim for provisional damages.[9] The provisional order must specify the disease or type of deterioration as to which an application for further damages may be made and will normally specify the period within which such application must be made, although the period may be extended on an application by the claimant.[10] Only one application for further damages may be entertained in relation to each disease or type of deterioration specified in the provisional order.[11] In *Willson v Ministry of Defence*[12] provisional damages were refused on the ground that 'serious deterioration' refers to a clear and severable event rather than an ordinary continuing deterioration, as in a typical osteoarthritic case. It was further said by Scott Baker J that the Supreme Court Act 1981, s 32A is concerned with a 'measurable rather than a fanciful' chance.[13] In awarding provisional damages in *Chewings v Williams*[14] it was held that a 2% risk of an ankle amputation was more than fanciful.

Provisional damages marked an important theoretical break with the once-and-for-all lump sum system. However, they represented only a small departure from the traditional approach and are very different from a system of reviewable periodic payments. In practice, most claimants do not claim provisional damages. That is, they choose to forgo the possibility of higher damages in the long term, by taking what at trial is a higher award under the traditional once-and-for-all approach.

(d) Structured settlements

Although a development in relation to out-of-court settlements of personal injury and death cases, rather than awards made by the courts, it is important here to mention structured

---

[6] Law Commission, *Report on Personal Litigation—Assessment of Damages* (1973) Report No 56. Cf the 'recommendation of the *Royal Commission on Civil Liability and Compensation for Personal Injury* (chaired by Lord Pearson) (1978) Vol 1, ch 14, favouring reviewable periodic payments for future pecuniary loss in cases of serious or lasting injury or death.

[7] Senior Courts Act 1981, s 32A(1).   [8] ibid, s 32A(2).

[9] CPR 41.2. Examples have been rare: but see *Cronin v Redbridge London Borough Council*, The Times, 20 May 1987; *Chewings v Williams* [2009] EWHC 2490 (QB), [2010] PIQR Q1.

[10] CPR 41.2. For provisional damages ordered without trial (ie following a settlement), see also *Hurditch v Sheffield HA* [1989] QB 562.

[11] CPR 41.3.

[12] [1991] 1 All ER 638. Provisional damages do not cover a potential improvement in the claimant's condition (which could have resulted in higher expenditure for the claimant's special needs in the community): *Adan v Securicor Custodial Services Ltd* [2004] EWHC 394 (QB), [2005] PIQR P6.

[13] [1991] 1 All ER 638, at 642.   [14] [2009] EWHC 2490 (QB), [2010] PIQR Q1.

settlements.[15] If the defendant's insurer purchased an annuity for the claimant it was accepted by the Inland Revenue in the late 1980s that the payments received by the claimant from the annuity were tax free (i.e. they were treated as capital not income). The defendant therefore had to pay less to produce the same (or a greater) stream of money for the claimant (the rate of discount, which presumably included the defendant's insurer's costs as well as the tax saving, appeared to run at 10% to 15%). Such a settlement was also in the interests of claimants, who were guaranteed a stream of 'income', and of the state, which was saved having to support those who squander lump sums of damages. A structured settlement was also more true to the aim of compensation than a lump sum. Self-financing structured settlements (that is, not involving insurers) were also entered into by public sector defendants, such as NHS trusts.

Structured settlements related to future pecuniary loss only: non-pecuniary loss and past pecuniary loss was paid in the usual form of a lump sum. Flexibility was possible in the sense that part of the future pecuniary loss could be paid in a lump sum or into a contingency fund to deal with unforeseen events; and more than one annuity could be bought depending on the claimant's likely future needs. Most annuities were index-linked and precise estimation of the claimant's life expectancy was not necessary; but otherwise structured settlements were as prone to inaccuracy as a lump sum for they were not reviewable. Although an annuity would normally cease on the claimant's death, it was usual to incorporate a guaranteed minimum time period of payments so that, as under the lump sum system, dependants would be guaranteed a (windfall) sum in the event of the claimant's unexpected death.

Structured settlements could not be imposed by the courts, although court approval was sometimes required because of, for example, the claimant's disability or infancy.[16] Since 1 April 2005, structured settlements have been absorbed within the wider concept of (reviewable) periodical payments and the Damages Act 1996, as amended by the Courts Act 2003, no longer refers to structured settlements. Structured settlements were therefore the forerunners of the new system of (reviewable) periodical payments.

(e) (Reviewable) periodical payments

On 1 April 2005 a fundamental departure from lump sums was introduced[17] by the Courts Act 2003, ss 100–101 (amending the Damages Act 1996), the Damages (Variation of Periodical Payments) Order 2005[18] and accompanying Civil Procedure Rules.[19] In the case of damages for future pecuniary loss in respect of personal injury or death, the courts are empowered (and are required to consider whether) to make an order that the damages are to take the form of periodical payments.[20] By s 2(8) of the Damages Act 1996, a periodical payments order ('PPO') shall be updated by reference to the retail prices index unless, under

---

[15] See generally R Lewis, *Structured Settlements: The Law and Practice* (Sweet & Maxwell 1993); Law Commission, *Structured Settlements and Interim and Provisional Damages* (1994) Report No 224 Pt III; N Bevan and H Gregory, 'Structured Settlements' (2004) 154 NLJ 1280, 1388, 1658. For the impact of structured settlements on a claimant's entitlement to social security benefits, see R Lewis, 'Structured Settlements and State Benefits' (2001) 151 NLJ 1066.

[16] As in *Kelly v Dawes*, The Times, 27 September 1990.

[17] See, generally, N Bevan and H Gregory, 'Periodical Payments' (2005) 155 NLJ 565, 907, 980; R Lewis, 'The Politics and Economics of Tort Law: Judicially Imposed Periodical Payments of Damages' (2006) 69 MLR 418.

[18] SI 2005/841.   [19] CPR 41.4–41.10.

[20] Damages Act 1996, s 2(1), as substituted by the Courts Act 2003, s 100. In *Godbold v Mahmood* [2005] EWHC 1002, [2006] PIQR Q5, a periodical payments order was made in respect of future care costs but not future lost earnings.

s 2(9), the court making the PPO specifies that a different index should be used (such as an average earnings index for future care costs).[21] Moreover, the periodical payments order may be made variable so that it can be reviewed by the courts.[22] These provisions, therefore, give the courts the power to order (reviewable) periodical payments. It is clear that a particularly influential political factor driving the reform was that, in respect of litigation against the National Health Service, periodical payments are more attractive to the NHS (at least in the short term) than having to find large capital sums.[23] However, before such an order can be made, a court has to be satisfied that the continuity of payment is reasonably secure.[24] Other than in respect of public sector defendants, this will essentially be so where the defendant's insurer purchases an annuity as under a structured settlement. Protection for claimants in the event of an insurer's insolvency or a public body's non-existence is provided by the Damages Act 1996, ss 4 and 6, as amended by the Courts Act 2003, s 101.

Of particular interest are the provisions that enable the variation of periodical payments.[25] The extent to which periodical payments can be reviewed is the most difficult and controversial aspect of this reform. The reviewability provisions closely match the law on 'provisional damages'. The original court can make a variable order but only to deal with the development of some serious disease or the suffering of some serious deterioration or significant improvement in the claimant's condition. Moreover, only one application to vary a variable order can be made in respect of each specified disease or type of deterioration or improvement.

(f) Interim payments

Although not concerned with the problems of predicting the future—and not contradicting the general rule that damages *after trial* must be awarded once-and-for-all—it is convenient here to mention interim payments. This is because they constitute an exception to the general rule that damages are awarded once-and-for-all: obviously they do not prevent further damages being awarded at trial for the same cause of action.

In accordance with Rules of Court[26] and the Senior Courts Act 1981, s 32 (and the County Courts Act 1984, s 50), the claimant may apply for an interim payment of the damages which the defendant may be held liable to pay him or for his benefit. Although originally confined to personal injury and death cases, interim payments may now be made in any type of case. The court may order an interim payment of such amount as it thinks just, not exceeding a reasonable proportion of the damages[27] which it considers are likely to be recovered by the claimant,[28] after taking into account any contributory negligence and any counterclaim.

---

[21] *Tameside and Glossop Acute Services NHS Trust v Thompstone* [2008] EWCA Civ 5, [2008] 1 WLR 2207 (updating future care costs by reference to the Annual Survey of Hours and Earnings, 'ASHE 6115', was approved in this case). See also *Flora v Wakom (Heathrow) Ltd* [2006] EWCA Civ 1103, [2007] 1 WLR 482. See, generally, H Trusted, 'Periodical Payments after the Court of Appeal decision in *Thompstone*' [2008] JIPL 44; R Lewis, 'The Indexation of Periodical Payments of Damages in Tort: the Future Assured?' (2010) 30 Legal Studies 391.

[22] Damages Act 1996, s 2B, as substituted by the Courts Act 2003, s 100; and Damages (Variation of Periodical Payments) Order 2005, SI 2005/841.

[23] The Explanatory Notes to the Act make this clear.

[24] Damages Act 1996, s 2(3). See, eg, *YM v Gloucester Hospitals NHS Foundation Trust* [2006] EWHC 820, [2006] PIQR P27.

[25] Damages (Variation of Periodical Payments) Order 2005, authorised under Damages Act 1996, s 2B.

[26] CPR 25.6–25.9.

[27] In *Eeles v Cobham Hire Services Ltd* [2009] EWCA Civ 204, [2010] 1 WLR 409, it was held that the damages likely to be recovered by the claimant are, for these purposes, the damages payable as a lump sum and do not include damages which may be payable as a periodical payment order.

[28] This involves an estimate of the damages that are likely to be recovered. But the court's investigation should not turn into a long consideration of the issues in dispute; rather a broad approach should be taken: *Newport (Essex) Engineering Co v Press and Shear Machinery Co* (1984) 24 BLR 71.

Before making an order, however, the court must be satisfied that one of the three following conditions is fulfilled: (i) that the defendant has admitted liability; or (ii) that the claimant has obtained judgment against the defendant for damages to be assessed;[29] or (iii) that if the action proceeded to trial the claimant would obtain judgment against the defendant[30] for substantial damages.[31]

By CPR 25.9, the fact that an order for an interim payment has been made must not be disclosed to the court at trial until all questions of liability and quantum of damages have been determined, unless the defendant agrees. By CPR 25.8, in giving final judgment the court may make any order with respect to the interim payment that proves to be necessary by way of adjustment and, in particular, if the interim payment exceeds the amount for which the defendant is held liable, may order repayment of the appropriate amount, plus interest,[32] by the claimant.

The policy behind interim payments is that, if he or she so wishes, the claimant should be relieved of immediate financial worries where there is a strong case on liability.[33]

(2) Damages must be awarded unconditionally

The leading case is *Banbury v Bank of Montreal*,[34] where the defendant was held liable for negligently advising the claimant to invest in certain securities. The jury's verdict on damages was 'for £25,000 and all securities to be returned to the defendant bank'. The finding of liability was overturned by the House of Lords, but three of their Lordships considered that in any event the award was improper because of the condition attached. Similarly, in *Patel v Hooper & Jackson*[35] the Court of Appeal overturned an award of damages against a negligent surveyor where the damages were 'to be reduced by £14,200 in the event of the plaintiffs electing to treat the endowment policy as their own free standing long-term investment'. In the words of Nourse LJ, 'the powers of the court in a case of this kind are confined to making a once and for all award of damages.'[36]

The main reason for having this principle is that it brings finality to litigation. Another possible explanation is the inappropriateness of sanctions in the event that the claimant fails to comply with a condition imposed. But in some personal injury cases involving gratuitous nursing services rendered or expenses incurred by a relative, or gratuitous payments made by an employer, damages have been made conditional on the claimant paying them over

---

[29] An interim payment can be ordered even though an appeal is pending: *Halvanon Insurance Co v Central Reinsurance Corp* [1984] 2 Lloyd's Rep 420.

[30] Or, where there is more than one defendant, against at least one of the defendants (even if the court has not yet determined which of them is liable) provided all the defendants are insured in respect of the claim; or the defendants' liability will be met by an insurer under s 151 of the Road Traffic Act 1988 or by an insurer acting under the Motor Insurers Bureau Agreement, or by the Motor Insurers Bureau where it is acting itself; or all the defendants are public bodies. Interim payments comprising different fractions of the total amount thought to be 'just' may be ordered against the different defendants provided the claimant does not overall recover more than the just amount (which, in the case of damages, cannot exceed a reasonable proportion of the damages likely to be recovered): *Schott Kem Ltd v Bentley* [1991] 1 QB 61.

[31] The court must be satisfied of this applying the civil standard of proof: *Shearson Lehman Brothers Inc v Maclaine, Watson & Co Ltd* [1987] 1 WLR 480, at 489. The necessary standard is not met—and hence no interim payment can be awarded—where summary judgment has been refused and *unconditional* leave to defend has been given; *British and Commonwealth Holdings Plc v Quadrex Holdings Inc* [1989] QB 842; *Andrews v Schooling* [1991] 1 WLR 783.

[32] *Mercers Co v New Hampshire Insurance Co* [1991] 1 WLR 1173. But the decision that the interim sum should be repaid was reversed on appeal: [1992] 1 WLR 792. Interest (or other profit) gained from the use of the interim payment is to be ignored in deciding on the final judgment applying the principle that it is irrelevant what the claimant does with his 'damages': *Parry v North West Surrey HA, The Times*, 5 January 2000.

[33] Winn Committee, *Report of the Committee on Personal Injuries Litigation* (1968) Cmnd 3691, paras 71–110.

[34] [1918] AC 626. [35] [1999] 1 WLR 1792. [36] ibid, at 1800.

to,[37] or holding them on trust for,[38] the relative or employer. Unfortunately, despite the convenience of these techniques in this sort of case, the force of these decisions is diminished by there having been no discussion of the principle against unconditional awards.

2. The date for the assessment of compensatory damages

This heading, although commonly used, is rather ambiguous and in order to understand the issues involved, it is helpful to distinguish two questions raised by it. Is there a time after which the court assessing damages is barred from taking into account events that have already occurred? Which value of money, property, or services do the courts apply in assessing damages?

(1) Is there a time after which the court assessing damages is barred from taking into account events that have already occurred?

As regards a court of first instance the answer to this question is in the negative; a trial judge can take into account evidence of all events that occur *prior to the date of judgment*. One of the clearest judicial statements on this is that of Lord Macnaughten in *Bwllfa and Merthyr Dare Steam Collieries Ltd v Pontypridd Waterworks Co*,[39] albeit that he was there dealing with an arbitrator's assessment of statutory compensation. He said:

'... the arbitrator's duty is to determine the amount of compensation payable. In order to enable him to come to a just and true conclusion, it is his duty ... to avail himself of all information at hand at the time of making his award which may be laid before him. Why should he listen to conjecture on a matter which has become an accomplished fact?'[40]

For contractual pecuniary loss relevant events commonly arising subsequent to breach but prior to judgment include payments that the claimant has had to make to a third party because of the breach, or subsequent 'mitigation' of a loss, for example by obtaining another job having been wrongfully dismissed. In the field of personal injuries, illustrations include a deterioration of the claimant's medical condition after the initial injury, a wage rise in the job that the claimant would have been in but for his injuries, and the death of the injured person (in a claim by the estate).

By CPR 52.21 the Court of Appeal (and by analogy the Supreme Court) will not receive evidence which was not before the lower court 'unless it orders otherwise'. The appellate court therefore has the power to admit evidence of events occurring since the trial (as well as evidence of events prior to the trial).[41] But so as not to undermine finality in litigation, some restraint is exercised in using this power. As regards evidence of events occurring since trial, Lord Wilberforce laid down a few guidelines in *Mulholland v Mitchell*:[42]

'Negatively, fresh evidence ought not to be admitted when it bears upon matters falling within the field or area of uncertainty, in which the trial judge's estimate has previously been made.

---

[37] Eg *Dennis v London Passenger Transport Board* [1948] 1 All ER 779; *Schneider v Eisovitch* [1960] 2 QB 430.
[38] Eg *Cunningham v Harrison* [1973] QB 942; *Hunt v Severs* [1994] 2 AC 350.   [39] [1903] AC 426.
[40] ibid, at 431.
[41] The leading case in relation to the admission of fresh evidence of events prior to trial remains *Ladd v Marshall* [1954] 1 WLR 1489. See also *Noble v Owens* [2010] EWCA Civ 224, [2010] 1 WLR 2491 (where the issue was whether the claimant had been fraudulent at trial in feigning the extent of his injuries).
[42] [1971] AC 666.

Positively, it may be admitted if some basic assumptions, common to both sides have clearly been falsified by subsequent events, particularly, if this has happened by the act of the defendant.[43] Positively, too, it may be expected that courts will allow fresh evidence where to refuse it would affront common sense, or a sense of justice. All these are only non-exhaustive indications ...'[44]

A good example of where fresh evidence was admitted was *Lim Poh Choo v Camden and Islington Area Health Authority*.[45] There the trial judge had assessed damages on the assumption that the claimant would be looked after abroad by her mother but, since then, her mother had become ill and the claimant had been transferred to a nursing home in England. The House of Lords admitted such fresh evidence, so that the cost of future care was reassessed. Lord Scarman's comments are of interest. He said:

'The device of granting the parties leave to adduce fresh evidence at the appellate stages of litigation can, as in the present case, mitigate the injustices of a lump sum system by enabling the appellate courts to bring the award into line with what has happened since trial. But it is an unsatisfactory makeshift, and of dubious value in any case where the new facts are themselves in issue.'[46]

(2) Which value of money, property, or services do the courts apply in assessing damages?

It is this question that is usually in mind when one refers to the date for the assessment of damages. The traditional general rule has been stated in one of two ways. Either that damages are assessed (that is the value is taken) at the date of the loss for which the damages are being awarded, or at the date of the accrual of the cause of action. So in *Philips v Ward*[47] Denning LJ said, 'The general principle of English law is that damages must be assessed as at the date when the damage occurs',[48] whereas in *Dodd Properties (Kent) v Canterbury City Council*[49] Donaldson LJ commented that '... the general rule is that damages fall to be assessed as at the date when the cause of action arose'.[50] The two often correspond but for some losses, for example, expenses or loss of earnings in personal injury cases, the former formulation seems to be the more accurate.

However, the important point is that the modern trend (triggered by periods of high inflation and of declines in the external value of sterling) has been to recognise exceptions to the rule. Indeed the exceptions are such that it is now arguable that assessment at the date of loss/date of the cause of action no longer represents the general rule. Instead, one might say that the general rule has now become assessment at the date of trial/judgment unless the claimant could reasonably have mitigated its loss at some earlier date (and, very commonly, the claimant could have mitigated its loss at, or shortly after, the date of the cause of action).[51] In examining the details of the law it is convenient to consider separately changes in the value of property or services or in the internal value of money and changes in the external value of money.

---

[43] Eg *Murphy v Stone-Wallwork (Charlton) Ltd* [1969] 1 WLR 1023.   [44] [1971] AC 666, at 679–680.
[45] [1980] AC 174. See also *Curwen v James* [1963] 1 WLR 748; *Jenkins v Richard Thomas and Baldwin Ltd* [1966] 1 WLR 476; *Perry v Sidney Phillips & Son* [1982] 1 WLR 1297; *Whitehead v Searle* [2008] EWCA Civ 285, [2009] 1 WLR 549; cf *Hunt v Severs* [1993] 4 All ER 180.
[46] [1980] AC 174, at 183.   [47] [1956] 1 WLR 471.   [48] ibid, at 474.
[49] [1980] 1 WLR 433.   [50] ibid, at 457.
[51] For support for this as the new general rule in the context of breach of contract, see A Dyson and A Kramer, 'There is No "Breach Date Rule": Mitigation, Difference in Value and Date of Assessment' (2014) 130 LQR 259.

(a) Changes in the value of property or services or in the internal value of money

In the late 1960s and the 1970s, the major relevant factor shaping the law here was the dramatic fall in the internal value of money because of high inflation. But of course the value of property or services may additionally fluctuate because of ordinary market movements.

(i) Non-pecuniary loss

Looking first at non-pecuniary loss, it would seem that until fairly recently the traditional general rule applied, so that any internal fall in the value of money between loss and judgment was ignored. So, for example, in *Bishop v Cunard White Star Co Ltd v The Queen Mary*,[52] Hodson J did not think that the conventional figure of £200 laid down for loss of expectation of life in *Benham v Gambling*[53] should be altered despite the fall in the value of the pound since that decision and since the accident in the case. But the courts' approach has since changed. In *Yorkshire Electricity Board v Naylor*,[54] the conventional figure for loss of expectation of life was raised to £500 because of inflation. That head of loss has now been abolished but the same approach is shown in the application of the tariff system for loss of amenity and pain and suffering. There are several judicial statements recognising this. In *Mitchell v Mulholland (No 2)*[55] Widgery LJ said:

> 'No one doubts that an award of damages must reflect the value of the pound sterling at the date of the award' and conventional sums attributed to, say the loss of an eye, have been adjusted in recent years on that account. Inflation which has reduced the value of money at the date of the award must, thus, be taken into account.'[56]

Again, in *Walker v John McLean & Sons Ltd*,[57] where the issue was the level of damages for non-pecuniary loss because of paraplegia, Cumming-Bruce LJ said:

> 'We cannot distinguish any principle recognised in the law of damages which suggests that damages for non-pecuniary loss are in this regard different from damages for pecuniary loss. And in the case of damages for future pecuniary loss the award is assessed by reference to the value of money at the date of trial, and not some other lower sum calculated by reference to an earlier and higher value of the pound.'[58]

In *Wright v British Railways Board*[59] Lord Diplock, in deciding that interest on personal injury non-pecuniary loss should be kept at a low rate, regarded the judges as having a duty to assess damages for such loss '… in the money of the day at the date of the trial'.[60] Finally, in *Heil v Rankin*[61] the Court of Appeal said that, having reset the appropriate level of award for pain, suffering, and loss of amenity in personal injury cases, the standard approach of '[a]ppropriate guideline cases updated by the RPI [retail prices index] should be used to find the appropriate level of award'.[62] It rejected an argument that the more accurate way of updating for inflation was to apply the GDP (gross domestic product) or average earnings index.[63]

Although there is no express authority, it can be assumed that awards for other non-pecuniary loss, such as mental distress, similarly reflect the value of money at the date of judgment, rather than any earlier value. Analogously, the Lord Chancellor has used his

---

[52] [1950] P 240.   [53] [1941] AC 157.   [54] [1968] AC 529.   [55] [1972] 1 QB 65.
[56] ibid, at 83.   [57] [1979] 1 WLR 760.   [58] ibid, at 765.
[59] [1983] 2 AC 773. See also *Cookson v Knowles* [1977] QB 913, at 921; *Dodd Properties v Canterbury City Council* [1980] 1 All ER 928, at 939; *Housecroft v Burnett* [1986] 1 All ER 332, at 337.
[60] [1983] 2 AC 773, at 782.   [61] [2001] QB 272.   [62] ibid, at 312.
[63] See also favouring continuation of updating by use of the RPI, Law Commission, *Damages for Personal Injury: Non-Pecuniary Loss* (1999) Report No 257, paras 3.171–3.176.

discretion to keep the sum for bereavement under the Fatal Accidents Act 1976 (at present £12,980)[64] in line with inflation.

All such adjustments are necessary in order that the claimant be fully compensated for the loss he or she has suffered. Although money can never be perfect compensation for non-pecuniary loss, it is the best that the law can offer. If £X was the right compensation for a particular non-pecuniary loss, when £1 was worth 10% more than at the date of trial, it must be right to award £X + 10% for that loss at the later time.

(ii) Pecuniary loss

Turning to pecuniary loss, past recurring pecuniary loss, such as loss of earnings and medical expenses in personal injury cases, is assessed according to the value of money at the date of the loss. So if £50 was spent on medical expenses, £50 will be awarded, irrespective of whether £50 is worth less at the date of judgment than at the date when spent. Future pecuniary loss has to be assessed according to the value of money at the date of judgment since there is no sound basis for choosing any other date. The question of whether future inflation is taken into account in assessing personal injury damages for future pecuniary loss is discussed in chapter 11 below.[65]

In relation to other pecuniary loss, the application of the traditional rule is shown, for example, in the prima facie rules for assessing damages under the Sale of Goods Act 1979, which take the market value of the goods at the date of the breach of contract, and by cases such as *General and Finance Facilities Ltd v Cooks Cars (Romford) Ltd*[66] and *Chubb Cash Ltd v John Crilley & Son*,[67] which show that for conversion, the value of the goods is generally to be assessed at the time of the conversion. On the other hand in several cases the traditional rule has been departed from.

Starting with examples of breach of contract, in *Wroth v Tyler*,[68] for example, Megarry J was concerned to assess damages given in lieu of specific performance[69] for the breach of a contract to sell a bungalow. Applying the usual formula of market price minus contract price, the question arose whether the market price should be that at the date of the breach (£7,500) or that at the date of judgment (£11,500). Megarry J considered that where damages were being given in lieu of specific performance the usual date of breach rule did not necessarily apply, and here, since the claimants in view of their lack of funds could not have been expected to mitigate their loss by going into the market, the market price at the date of judgment was chosen. Furthermore, Megarry J indicated in dicta that even for ordinary common law damages the date of breach rule might not be inflexible.

In *Radford v De Froberville*[70] the defendant in breach of contract failed to build a wall. In assessing the claimant's damages one issue was the date at which the cost of building a wall should be assessed. Oliver J considered that the decision in *Wroth v Tyler* was equally applicable to ordinary common law damages, and indeed went so far as to say that '… the proper approach is to assess the damages at the date of the hearing unless it can be said that the plaintiff ought reasonably to have mitigated by seeking an alternative performance at an earlier date'.[71] Ultimately, however, Oliver J did not reach a decision as to which date was

---

[64] The sum was most recently raised by the Damages for Bereavement (Variation of Sum) (England and Wales) Order 2013, SI 2013/510.
[65] Below, p 245.   [66] [1963] 1 WLR 644.
[67] [1983] 1 WLR 599. See also, eg, *BBMB Finance (Hong Kong) Ltd v Eda Holdings Ltd* [1990] 1 WLR 409. See, generally, A Tettenborn, 'Conversion Damages Clarified' (1991) 141 NLJ 452.
[68] [1974] Ch 30.   [69] Ie equitable damages; see below, ch 17.   [70] [1977] 1 WLR 1262.
[71] ibid, at 1286.

appropriate because there was insufficient evidence to enable him to decide whether the claimant should have mitigated earlier.

This move in favour of fixing the date for assessment more flexibly, so as to accord with when the claimant ought reasonably to have, or has, mitigated its loss has been authoritatively confirmed by the House of Lords in *Johnson v Agnew*,[72] where it was the vendor of land who was claimant in a situation where mortgagees had sold the land off at a low value subsequent to the date of breach. The vendor had initially obtained an order for specific performance but the defendant purchaser had delayed in complying with the order with the consequence that the vendor could not pay off his mortgage and his mortgagee became entitled to sell off his land. The vendor therefore now sought damages for the purchaser's breach of contract. Having emphasised that damages in lieu of specific performance and ordinary common law damages should be assessed on the same basis, Lord Wilberforce went on to say the following:

> 'The general principle for the assessment of damages is compensatory, ie that the innocent party is to be placed, so far as money can do it, in the same position as if the contract had been performed. Where the contract is one of sale, this principle normally leads to assessment of damages as at the date of breach—a principle recognised and embodied in s 51 of the Sale of Goods Act 1893. But this is not an absolute rule; if to follow it would give rise to injustice, the court has power to fix such other date as may be appropriate in the circumstances. In cases where a breach of contract for sale has occurred, and the innocent party reasonably continues to try to have the contract completed, it would to me appear more logical and just rather than tie him to the date of the original breach to assess damages as at the date when otherwise than by his default the contract is lost.'[73]

Accordingly, it was decided that the market value of the land should be assessed not at the date of the purchaser's original breach but rather when the vendor's reasonable attempts to have the contract enforced failed: ie when the mortgagees, as they were entitled to do, contracted to sell the land to another party hence making it impossible for the claimant vendor to comply with his side of the contract.

Johnson v Agnew was applied,[74] and its approach very clearly summarised, in *Suleman v Shahsavari*.[75] This concerned actions by a prospective purchaser of a house against the vendors for specific performance or, in the event of the contract for purchase being held invalid, against the vendors' solicitor for damages for breach of a warranty that he had authority to bind the vendors. Andrew Park QC, sitting as a deputy judge of the High Court, held that the contract was invalid because the vendors' solicitor had had no authority to sign the contract on their behalf. Specific performance against the vendors was therefore denied. The question then arose whether the damages for the solicitor's breach of warranty of authority should be calculated according to the difference between the contract price and the market price on the completion date (£9,500 plus interest) or the difference between the contract price and the market price at the date of judgment, nearly two-and-a-half years later, which was £29,500. On a straightforward application of *Johnson v Agnew* the judge awarded £29,500.

---

[72] [1980] AC 367.   [73] ibid, at 401.
[74] See also *Hooper v Oates* [2013] EWCA Civ 91, [2014] Ch 287.
[75] [1988] 1 WLR 1181. This decision was applied in *Habton Farms v Nimmo* [2003] EWCA Civ 68, [2004] QB 1: in assessing a seller's damages (for breach of an agent's warranty of authority) the majority correctly refused to deduct from the agreed purchase price the value of the horse—which had died in the seller's possession four weeks after the failed sale—because the seller had not failed in its duty to mitigate by failing to resell the horse before it died.

In the leading case of *Golden Strait Corp v Nippon Yusen Kubishika Kaisha, The Golden Victory*[76] the House of Lords, by a majority, assessed the value of a charterparty at the date of trial not at the date of breach. The case concerned a seven-year charterparty made in December 1998. After three years, there was a repudiatory breach by the defendant charterers which was accepted by the claimant shipowners a few days later (on 17 December 2001). Some 15 months later, in March 2003 (after arbitration on liability and failed negotiations between the parties for another charter of the vessel), the Second Gulf War broke out which, under a war clause in the charterparty, would have entitled the charterers to cancel the contract in any event and it was assumed that they would have done so. The question was whether the shipowners' damages should be assessed as at the date of breach on the basis of the value of a four-year remaining charterparty, ie ignoring the outbreak of war, or as at the date of trial on the basis of a 15-month remaining charterparty, ie taking into account the known outbreak of war. The arbitrator, albeit with reluctance, Langley J, and the Court of Appeal decided that it should be the second of those, ie assessment as at the date of trial. That was upheld by the House of Lords, by a three–two majority.

Although this decision has been criticised,[77] it is clearly correct if one is applying a true compensatory approach. Indeed, if one takes the view that the law has departed from assessment at the date of the cause of action (the breach of contract) to a general rule of assessment at the time of trial/judgment, unless the claimant could reasonably have mitigated its loss at some earlier date, the decision in the case was straightforward because, on the facts, the duty to mitigate was essentially irrelevant. The owners had not gone out into the market and made substitute charters; and their delay—while arbitration and negotiation were pursued—had the consequence that, because of the outbreak of war, their actual loss was reduced from the loss of a four-year contract to the loss of a 15-month contract.

The majority's view in *The Golden Victory* was emphatically reaffirmed in *Bunge SA v Nidera BV*.[78] This concerned a contract for the sale of wheat. In breach of contract, the sellers prematurely invoked a cancellation clause in the contract, fearing a Russian export embargo. The buyers accepted that repudiation as terminating the contract and sought damages. At that date the difference between the market price of the wheat and the contract price was $3,602,500. The buyers did not buy in substitute wheat. Shortly afterwards Russia did impose an export embargo which would have entitled the sellers to cancel the contract. It was held that, as it was known at trial that the buyers had suffered no loss, given that the contract would have been cancelled because of the Russian embargo, the compensatory principle dictated that nominal damages only should be awarded. *The Golden Victory* was applied and the argument was rejected that that case was inapplicable to a one-off sales contract rather than a contract for the supply of goods or services over a period of time such as a charterparty.

We see the same sort of departure from the date of the cause of action as being the date of assessment in cases on tortious misrepresentation. For example, in *Naughton v O'Callaghan*[79] Waller J relied on *Johnson v Agnew* in awarding damages (for a negligent

---

[76] [2007] UKHL 12, [2007] 2 AC 353.
[77] R Stevens, 'Damages and the Right to Performance: a *Golden Victory* or Not?' in *Exploring Contract Law* (eds J Neyers, R Bronaugh and S Pitel, Hart Publishing 2009) 171; F Reynolds, 'The *Golden Victory*—A Misguided Decision' (2008) 38 HKLJ 333.
[78] [2015] UKSC 43, [2015] 2 Lloyd's Rep 469. See also *Ageas (UK) Ltd v Kwik-Fit (GB) Ltd* [2014] EWHC 2178 (QB) (breach of warranty in share sale agreement: events subsequent to breach to be taken into account so as to give effect to the overriding compensatory principle).
[79] [1990] 3 All ER 191. Although this decision seems correct, it is arguable that, applying the controversial *SAAMCO* principle—see above, pp 117–127—damages might be restricted to the difference between the horse's value had the representation been true and its then actual value (ie £26,000 – £23,500 = £3,500).

misrepresentation and breach of a contractual warranty) calculated according to the price paid for a horse (26,000 guineas) minus its value (£1,500) nearly two years later after it had proved a failure on the racecourse and hence lost most of its value. The claimants would not have bought the horse but for the vendor's misrepresentation as to its pedigree and had they discovered the error straightaway they would have sold the horse at its then value. Moreover, and in line with the crucial importance to the date of assessment of the duty to mitigate, it is clear that the claimants could not reasonably have mitigated their loss until they discovered the error nearly two years after purchase.

Similarly in *Smith New Court Securities Ltd v Scrimgeour Vickers (Asset Management) Ltd*,[80] in an action for the tort of deceit, the claimant was held entitled to the difference in value between the contract price paid for shares and the price for which the claimant had sold them several months later. As the share price had plummeted, that difference was far higher at the date of resale than at the date when the claimant had bought the shares. The House of Lords stressed that assessment at the later date was necessary to give the claimant full compensation; that the flexibility introduced by cases such as *Johnson v Agnew* would often allow assessment for the tort of deceit at a date later than that of the original transaction (which was 'only prima facie the right date');[81] and that here the claimant had not acted unreasonably in holding onto the shares for several months and then reselling them.

In *Dodd Properties v Canterbury City Council*[82] a similar approach was adopted in relation to the time at which the cost of repairing damaged property should be assessed in an action for tortious negligence or nuisance. Having said that the general rule was that the cost of repairs should be assessed at the date of the tort, the Court of Appeal went on to emphasise that this was not an inflexible rule, and that here the cost of repairs should be assessed at the date of the hearing. The reason for preferring this later date was that, having regard to all the circumstances and in particular the claimant's impecuniosity, it was the date when it was first reasonable for the claimant to have undertaken the repairs.

The same decision was reached in the closely analogous case of *Alcoa Minerals of Jamaica Inc v Herbert Broderick*.[83] In the light of *Johnson v Agnew*[84] it was held that the normal rule of assessment at the date of the cause of action could be departed from. Here the cost of repairing property damaged because of the defendant's nuisance (which had increased dramatically because of inflation in Jamaica) was assessed as at the date of the first instance judgment because the claimant, who could not afford to pay for the repairs, had acted reasonably in waiting for that judgment. The claimant needed to be sure that the defendant would pay or be liable before he carried out the repairs.

It should further be noted that apart from these important departures from the traditional general rule, the earlier decision in *Sachs v Miklos*,[85] while leaving the date of conversion as the date for assessing the value of the chattel, apparently accepted that subsequent increases in the market value of the converted chattel could be recovered as consequential loss. The defendant, having gratuitously stored the claimant's goods from 1940 to 1943, twice wrote to the claimant requesting their removal. Receiving no reply he sold them for

---

[80] [1997] AC 254. See also *Khakshouri v Jiminez* [2017] EWHC 3392 (QB) (tort of deceit).
[81] [1997] AC 254, at 284 (per Lord Steyn).
[82] [1980] 1 WLR 433. See also *Forster v Silvermere Golf & Equestrian Centre Ltd* (1981) 42 P & CR 255 (breach of contract).
[83] [2002] 1 AC 371; see above, p 145 n 336.   [84] [1980] AC 367.
[85] [1948] 2 KB 23. See also *Empresa Exportadora De Azucar v Industria Azucarera National, The Playa Larga* [1983] 2 Lloyd's Rep 171, at 181; *IBL Ltd v Coussens* [1991] 2 All ER 133 (conversion damages for value of cars—under what would previously have been an action for detinue—to be assessed at a date fixed flexibly, although prima facie at the date of judgment); *Trafigura Beheer BV v Mediterranean Shipping Co SA* [2007] EWCA Civ 794, [2008] 1 All ER (Comm) 385 (conversion damages assessed at date of judgment).

£15. In 1946 the claimant demanded the goods. The defendant tendered the £15 but the market value having risen to £115, the claimant sought, and was seemingly held able to recover, the extra £100 as consequential damages for conversion (on the assumption that he had never received the letters). In essence this again was a departure from the general rule albeit by a different route.

Waddams criticises the modern more flexible approach and considers that it would be preferable to stick more rigidly to assessment at (or shortly after) the date of the loss.[86] He offers several arguments in support: postponement of assessment hampers desirable finality to litigation; it encourages the claimant to be inefficient; interest awarded on the damages acts as an adequate counter to inflation; and assessment at an early date tends to reduce the total cost of litigation. But finality of litigation in the sense, seemingly intended, of litigation not going on beyond trial is no more achieved by a date of loss than a date of trial assessment; and the second argument is countered by the fact that the courts would consider that a claimant who had unreasonably delayed allowing values to rise could have mitigated earlier, and its damages would therefore be assessed at that earlier date.[87] While it is true that interest rates do reflect inflation, so that assessment of damages at an early date plus full interest will often achieve much the same result as assessment at a later date plus reduced or no interest until that date,[88] interest rates reflect price rises only very roughly and clearly they are not attuned to fluctuations (whether up or down) in the value of particular property. Finally, although rigid adherence to the date of loss rule may save litigation costs, because that approach is clear and simple (but without empirical data the extent of the cost-saving is unclear) this is at the expense of effecting true compensation.

The above discussion on pecuniary loss has assumed that it is advantageous for the claimant to have damages assessed at a later date than that of loss/the cause of action. But what if it is disadvantageous? Say, for example, the claimant is a buyer and that the value of property has fallen since the date of the vendor's breach; or that the defendant has converted the claimant's goods, which have since fallen in value. In these situations, assessment at the date of the breach of contract or conversion would be more advantageous to the claimant than assessment at a later date. Although the few cases on this[89] assess damages at the date of loss/cause of action, they do predate the recent developments. It is submitted that logical symmetry, avoidance of overcompensation, and adherence to the duty to mitigate dictate that the same flexibility should be adopted as where assessment at a later date is to the claimant's advantage. Waddams again disagrees and in particular focuses on a situation where the claimant buyer or owner of converted goods may wish to establish that he would have mitigated against a fall in the value of the property by, for example, selling off the goods at an early date. He writes, 'The cost of inquiry into how the plaintiff would have used his property had the defendant not deprived the plaintiff of it outweighs the cost of overcompensation ...'[90] Once more therefore Waddams is expressing a preference for rough-and-ready often inaccurate compensation produced by rigid adherence to the date of loss/cause of action rule as against the true compensation produced by the more flexible approach, on the ground that the former is much cheaper, albeit that no empirical data is offered to indicate the extent of the cost-saving.

---

[86] S Waddams, 'The Date for the Assessment of Damages' (1981) 97 LQR 445; S Waddams, *The Law of Damages* (6th edn, Thomson Reuters 2017) paras 1.650–1.1100, 7.60–7.70.
[87] As in *Malhotra v Choudhury* [1980] Ch 52.
[88] For the relationship between date for assessment and interest, see below, pp 306–308.
[89] *Aronson v Mologa Holzindustrie A/G Leningrad* (1927) 32 Com Cas 276; *Solloway v McLaughlin* [1938] AC 247.
[90] S Waddams, *The Law of Damages* (6th edn, Thomson Reuters 2017) para 1.660.

(b) Changes in the external value of money—foreign money liabilities

It should be stressed at the outset that the law here applies to the award of an agreed sum,[91] as well as to damages. Indeed the important legal change made in 1975 was initially concerned solely with the former remedy. In order to provide a coherent exposition, the law will be looked at as a whole, rather than simply examining the damages aspect of it.[92]

The traditional assessment date rule meant that the conversion into sterling of agreed sums payable or damages calculable in foreign money was made according to the rates applicable at the time of the loss/cause of action.[93] Also of relevance in understanding this area of the law was the rule that a money judgment had to be expressed in sterling.[94] The Law Commission[95] has referred to these two rules taken together as the sterling-breach-date rule.

The problem with that rule was that, where the value of sterling had changed in relation to the relevant foreign currency between the date of loss/cause of action and the date of judgment, the claimant was left under- or overcompensated. This began to bother the courts when sterling weakened as a currency, so that claimants were being undercompensated.[96] An example will make this clearer. Say D owes C 1,000 units of foreign currency and at the date of loss/cause of action those units are worth £100 (ie £1 = 10 units) but at the date of judgment they are worth £200 (ie £1 = 5 units). In other words, the value of sterling has declined. Clearly if C is given only £100 it is undercompensated. But assessment at the date of loss/cause of action will overcompensate C if the value of sterling has increased. Say the units at the date of judgment are worth £50 (ie £1 = 20 units). By being given £100 C is overcompensated.

Given this defect with conversion at the date of loss/cause of action, what were the alternatives? One obvious alternative was to convert at the date of judgment. But this would leave injustice where the value of sterling changed between judgment and actual payment of the agreed sum or damages. The ideal solution was therefore for conversion to be made at the rates prevailing at the date of payment. But the rule that judgment had to be in sterling was here a stumbling-block, for it was very difficult to see how one could have the judgment expressed in sterling, while converting into sterling at the date of payment. On the other hand, if judgments could be expressed in foreign currency this would free the way for the ideal solution of conversion into sterling at the date of payment: ie the order could then be for the defendant to pay the claimant X units of the foreign currency or the sterling equivalent at the time of payment. It should be stressed that, for two reasons, to allow judgment in a foreign currency would not prevent the need for a conversion date rule: first, English execution necessarily yields value in sterling; secondly, there seems no reason why a defendant should not have the option of satisfying an English court's judgment in sterling.

Miliangos v George Frank (Textiles) Ltd[97] is the classic case in which the House of Lords departed from the 'sterling-breach-date' rule and held that for some foreign agreed sums a judgment can be expressed in foreign currency, and that conversion into sterling can be

---

[91] Below, ch 21.
[92] See, generally, J Knott, 'A Quarter of a Century of Foreign Currency Judgments' [2004] LMCLQ 325.
[93] Eg *Di Fernando v Simon, Smits & Co* [1920] 3 KB 409 (contractual damages); *SS Celia (Owners) v SS Volturno (Owners)* [1921] 2 AC 544 (tort damages); *Tomkinson v First Pennsylvania Banking and Trusts Co* [1961] AC 1007 (agreed sum).
[94] Eg *Manners v Pearson & Son* [1898] 1 Ch 581, at 587.
[95] Law Commission, *Private International Law—Foreign Money Liabilities* (1983) Report No 124, Cmnd 9064.
[96] As A Briggs has written in *The Conflict of Laws* (3rd edn, OUP 2013) 194–195, 'When sterling went into a period of relentless depreciation it was apparent that this rule would do injustice to claimants, as well as endangering England as a centre for commercial litigation, and all for no obvious reason.'
[97] [1976] AC 443.

made at the date of payment, meaning the date of actual payment or, if earlier, the date on which the court authorises enforcement of the judgment. The facts concerned the non-payment of a contract price for yarn. The money of account (ie the currency by which the debtor's obligation was measured) and the money of payment (ie the currency in which the payment was to be tendered) was Swiss francs, and the proper law of the contract was Swiss. The defendants were ordered to pay in Swiss francs or the equivalent in sterling at the time of payment.

Lord Wilberforce explained that because of the instability of sterling:

'... instead of a situation in which changes of relative value occurring between the "breach date" and the date of judgment or payment being the exception, so that a rule which did not provide for this case could be generally fair, this situation is now the rule. So the search for a formula to deal with it becomes urgent in the interest of justice.'[98]

But Lord Wilberforce confined his departure from the long-established rule to agreed sums: 'In my opinion, it should be open for future discussion whether the rule applying to money obligations, which can be a simple rule should apply as regards claims for damages for breach of contract or for a tort.'[99] However, the policy underlying *Miliangos* did not differ whether one was talking of agreed sums or damages, and in *Services Europe Atlantique Sud v Stockholms Rederiaktiebolag SVEA, The Folias*[100] and *The Despina R*,[101] *Miliangos* was extended to claims for contractual and tortious damages respectively. It is therefore now clear law that a foreign currency liability should be expressed in foreign currency and that the date for conversion into sterling is the date of payment.

Having said that, there were some comments made by Lord Goff in the House of Lords in *The Texaco Melbourne*[102] that are, at first sight, puzzling. The case applied *The Folias* with the central question being whether the appropriate currency for contractual damages for breach of a contract for the carriage of oil between two Ghanaian ports was the US dollar or the Ghanaian cedi. This made a huge difference to the claimants because the Ghanaian currency had collapsed catastrophically since the breach of contract and, by the time of trial, it was worth less than 1% (against the US dollar) of what it had been worth at the date of breach. The House of Lords decided that, nevertheless, the appropriate currency—the currency in which the claimants felt their loss—was Ghanaian cedis essentially because this was the currency in which they carried on their business and was the currency they would have received for reselling the fuel oil. That decision was plainly correct.[103] But, in the course of his speech, Lord Goff said the following:

'We have at all times to bear in mind that fluctuations in the relevant currency between the date of breach and the date of judgment are not taken into account. The award of damages is assessed as at the date of breach ... Delay between the date of breach and the date of judgment is compensated for by an award of interest ... But, as I have said, no account is taken of fluctuations in the relevant currency as against other currencies between the date of breach and the date of judgment.'[104]

---

[98] ibid, at 463. [99] ibid, at 468. [100] [1979] AC 685. [101] ibid.

[102] A-G of the Republic of Ghana v Texaco Overseas Tankships Ltd, The Texaco Melbourne [1994] I Lloyd's Rep 473; noted by J Knott, 'The Currency of Damages in Contract' [1994] LMCLQ 311.

[103] However, *The Texaco Melbourne* was distinguished in *Milan Nigeria Ltd v Angeliki B Maritime Co* [2011] EWHC 892 (Comm) (loss, comprising damage to cargo, held by arbitrators to be felt in US dollars rather than Nigerian naira and Gloster J refused the defendants permission to appeal on that issue).

[104] [1994] 1 Lloyd's Rep 473, at 476.

At first sight, this passage may be thought to contradict the departure in *Miliangos* from the sterling-breach-date rule. But that is not so.[105] The point flowing from *Miliangos* about conversion at the date of payment not breach meant that any conversion from Ghanaian cedis to sterling would be made according to the value of sterling at the date of judgment or payment not the date of breach. Rather what Lord Goff was concerned with was that, in deciding the amount of damages, expressed in Ghanaian cedis, the court should take the value of the oil at the date of the breach of contract in accordance with the traditional (albeit, as we have seen, not inflexible) rule for the date of assessing the value of goods.

It is important to realise that, although the *Miliangos* reform was triggered by claimants being undercompensated where sterling had declined in value since the date of loss/cause of action, it was not solely concerned with preventing undercompensation. Rather it was concerned that judgment should be expressed in the most appropriate currency, whether this was to the benefit or detriment of the claimant in comparison with the sterling-breach-date rule. Thus in *Miliangos* Lord Wilberforce explained: 'The creditor has no concern with pounds sterling: for him what matters is that a Swiss franc *for good or ill* should remain a Swiss franc.'[106] And in *The Despina R*, he said:

'To fix such a plaintiff with sterling commits him to the risk of changes in the value of a currency with which he has no connection; to award him a sum in the (appropriate) currency ... gives him exactly what he has lost and commits him only to the risk of changes in the value of that currency.'[107]

It follows that where the appropriate foreign currency loses value in relation to sterling, the claimant should not be able to resort to the sterling-breach-date rule. This point was firmly expressed by the Law Commission:

'Although there is little authority on the point it is clear that to allow the plaintiff to seek judgment in sterling in the case of a foreign-currency claim would be contrary to the principle in *Miliangos* ... [therefore] a plaintiff should not be able to obtain judgment in sterling in the case of the enforcement of a claim which ought properly to be expressed in a foreign currency.'[108]

However, the Law Commission accepted that, where the claimant can show that it would have converted the appropriate foreign currency into sterling, and thereby reaped the benefit of the increase in sterling's value, it should be able to recover damages for such exchange losses, subject to remoteness.[109] This was the basis of the Law Commission's interpretation of the difficult case of *Ozalid Group (Export) Ltd v African Continental Bank Ltd*.[110] Here the defendant had delayed in paying a contract price of US dollars to the claimants. By exchange control regulations the claimants were obliged to convert US dollars into sterling and would have done so if the money had been paid. During the period of delay sterling rose in value against the dollar. The claimants sought the difference in value between sterling at the time payment should have been made and when it was made. Donaldson J held that the claimants were entitled to that amount.

The Law Commission's interpretation of the decision was that damages were being awarded for non-remote exchange losses consequent on the defendant's delay in making

---

[105] See J Edelman, *McGregor on Damages* (20th edn, Sweet & Maxwell 2018) paras 20-043–20-045.
[106] [1976] AC 443, at 466 (italics inserted).   [107] [1979] AC 685, at 697.
[108] Law Commission, *Private International Law—Foreign Money Liabilities* (1983) Report No 124, Cmnd 9064, para 3.9. See also para 2.5.
[109] ibid, paras 2.34–2.35, 3.58–3.61.
[110] [1979] 2 Lloyd's Rep 231; cf *International Minerals & Chemical Corpn v Karl O Helm AG* [1986] 1 Lloyd's Rep 81, at 105.

payment. This was therefore an example of the *Wadsworth v Lydall*[111] 'special damages' exception to the old *London, Chatham & Dover Rly Co v South Eastern Rly Co*[112] rule that no damages can be awarded for breach of an obligation to pay money. But an alternative interpretation was that the appropriate currency was not US dollars at all but was sterling; and that where a claimant's loss was really suffered in sterling rather than a foreign currency—and that sterling loss was not too remote—conversion according to the sterling-breach-date rule was appropriate.

Both interpretations seem acceptable: indeed they are simply different legal analyses of the same ideas. The crucial common point is that the claimant does not have a free choice to have the sterling-breach-date rule applied; rather it must have suffered a non-remote loss of sterling.

Some commentators criticise the *Miliangos* reform. Waddams, for example, suggests that it neglects the fact that many claimants can perfectly well mitigate against a decline in sterling.[113] But surely there is nothing in *Miliangos* to undermine normal mitigation principles so that, if the defendant can show a failure to mitigate, the claimant would not be entitled to full loss assessed according to *Miliangos*. More forceful are the arguments first, that introducing flexibility as against the certainty of the sterling-breach-date rule is paid for by higher litigation costs; and secondly, that the injustice to claimants of the sterling-breach-date rule has been overstated, since interest rates will generally increase in response to a decline in the currency's value; hence the sterling-breach-date rule plus interest at sterling rates will produce much the same result as expressing judgment in foreign currency, converted at the date of payment, plus interest at the rate for that foreign currency.[114] In similar vein, Waddams argues that, as regards an increase in the home currency's value, it is better to risk overcompensation than to encourage costly investigation of how the claimant would have used the foreign currency.[115] Analogous arguments have been considered earlier[116] and again it is submitted that the courts are right to effect true compensation rather than favouring a potentially less costly approach (and the extent of the cost-saving is unclear) of rough-and-ready justice.

Finally, while not concerning the date for assessment as such, it is convenient to consider briefly two further questions of central importance. When is sterling considered a less appropriate currency than a foreign currency? And where more than one foreign currency is involved, which is the more appropriate foreign currency? Assuming that, as a matter of English private international law, English law applies to answer these questions (either because it is the *lex fori* and these are matters of procedure or because English law is the applicable law that should be applied because of the private international rules applicable to contractual and non-contractual obligations),[117] there are five principal points to note.

---

[111] [1981] 1 WLR 598. Below, pp 296–298, esp n 11.   [112] [1893] AC 429.
[113] S Waddams, *The Law of Damages* (6th edn, Thomson Reuters 2017) paras 7.250–7.300.
[114] R Bowles and C Whelan, 'Law Commission Working Paper No 80, Private International Law Foreign Money Liabilities' (1982) 45 MLR 434, 442, 444. For the relationship between foreign currency judgments and interest, see below, pp 307–308.
[115] S Waddams, *The Law of Damages* (6th edn, Thomson Reuters 2017) paras 7.180–7.200.
[116] See above, p 176.
[117] If one applies the traditional approach in English private international law (ie English conflict of laws), it would seem that English law, as the *lex fori*, applies to determine the appropriate currency in which judgment can be expressed because that is treated as an issue concerning 'procedure'. That is so, irrespective of the law applicable to the contract or tort (or other cause of action) in question. But it is not entirely clear whether that traditional approach remains applicable in the light of the Rome I and Rome II Regulations. This depends on the scope of those Regulations which, in the context of the currency of an award, is obscurely worded. The Rome I Regulation, Reg 593/2008, lays down that the scope of the applicable law for contractual obligations

(i) For the judgment to be expressed in foreign currency the loss in question must be pecuniary loss. As laid down in *Hoffman v Sofaer*[118] non-pecuniary loss, such as pain and suffering and loss of amenity in a personal injury action, does not raise foreign currency problems; rather such a loss is calculated and expressed in sterling whatever the claimant's nationality or wherever the injury or loss occurred.

(ii) In *Miliangos,* Lord Wilberforce confined departure from the sterling-breach-date rule to where the proper law of the contract was foreign, but in subsequent cases *Miliangos* has been applied to contracts whose proper law was English.[119]

(iii) As regards agreed sums where the money of account and payment are of the same foreign money, as in *Miliangos* itself, it is clearly appropriate for judgment to be expressed in that foreign currency. Lord Wilberforce confined departure from the old approach to this situation, but in *Veflings Rederi A/S v President of India, The Bellami,*[120] Donaldson J at first instance held that where the money of payment and account are of different countries, and even if the money of payment is English, judgment can be expressed in the currency of the money of account.

(iv) As laid down in *The Folias,*[121] for contract damages, unless there is a 'currency of the contract'—that is, an appropriate currency expressly laid down in the contract—the appropriate currency will be that in which the loss was felt or which most truly expresses the claimant's loss. This may or may not be the currency in which the loss first and immediately arose and depends on ordinary principles of proof and remoteness.

(v) A similar approach to that adopted in *The Folias* was applied for tort damages in *The Despina R.*[122] The only main difference is that with no contract in play, the currency of the contract is obviously not a possibility.

---

includes 'within the limits of the powers conferred on the court by its procedural law, the consequences of breach, including the assessment of damages in so far as it is governed by rules of law' (Article 12(c)). In working out what is the money of account or payment (see above, p 178 for explanation of these terms) see also Art 12(1)(a) and Art 12(2). The same obscurity of scope, as regards the currency of an award, is also to be found in the Rome II Regulation, Reg 864/2007 which applies to non-contractual obligations. Under Article 15(c) and (d), the law applicable to the non-contractual obligation includes within its scope 'the execution, nature and the assessment of damages or the remedy claimed' and 'within the limits of powers conferred on the courts by its procedural law, the measures which a court may take ... to ensure the provision of compensation'. For criticism of the traditional *lex fori* approach as regards remedies, see A Briggs, 'Conflict of Laws and Commercial Remedies' in *Commercial Remedies* (eds A Burrows and E Peel, OUP 2003) 271–286. See generally AV Dicey, JHC Morris, and LA Collins, *Dicey, Morris and Collins on the Conflict of Laws* (15th edn, Sweet & Maxwell 2012) ch 37; *Harding v Wealands* [2006] UKHL 32, [2007] 2 AC 1; *Cox v Ergo Versicherung AG* [2014] UKSC 22, [2014] AC 1379; *Alseran v Ministry of Defence* [2017] EWHC 3289 (QB), [2018] 3 WLR 95, at [872]–[874], [900]–[903].

[118] [1982] 1 WLR 1350.
[119] *Barclays Bank International Ltd v Levin Bros (Bradford) Ltd* [1977] QB 270; *Federal Commerce and Navigation Co v Tradax Export, The Maratha Envoy* [1977] QB 324; *Veflings Rederi A/S v President of India* [1979] 1 WLR 59; *The Folias* [1979] AC 685.
[120] [1978] 1 WLR 982. On appeal the Court of Appeal held that the US dollar was the money of account and payment: [1979] 1 WLR 59.
[121] [1979] AC 685. Followed in, eg, *President of India v Taygetos Shipping Co SA, The Agenor* [1985] 1 Lloyd's Rep 155 (cf *President of India v Lips Maritime Corpn* [1985] 2 Lloyd's Rep 180, at 187–188 (per Staughton J), [1988] AC 395, at 426); *Société Française Bunge SA v Belcan NV, The Federal Huron* [1985] 3 All ER 378; *Metaalhandel JA Magnus BV v Ardfields Transport Ltd* [1988] 1 Lloyd's Rep 197; *A-G of the Republic of Ghana v Texaco Overseas Tankships Ltd, The Texaco Melbourne* [1994] 1 Lloyd's Rep 473; *Verani Ltd v Manuel Revert y Cia SA* [2003] EWCA Civ 1651, [2004] 2 Lloyd's Rep 14.
[122] [1979] AC 685. Followed in *The Lash Atlantico* [1987] 2 Lloyd's Rep 114; *The Transoceanica Francesca and Nicos V* [1987] 2 Lloyd's Rep 155.

3. Taxation

The question here is, in assessing damages for the gains that the claimant has been prevented from making by the defendant's tort or breach of contract, do the courts deduct income tax or corporation tax[123] that the claimant would have paid on those gains?

(1) The *Gourley* principle

Applying the usual compensatory aims it would seem that tax that would have been paid on the gains should be deducted since, if liabilities which the claimant would have otherwise incurred are ignored, the claimant will be put into a better position than it would have been if the contract had been performed or the tort not committed.

However, until 1955, it was considered that, other than in Fatal Accidents Act actions,[124] tax considerations should be ignored. But in that year in the now famous case of *British Transport Commission v Gourley*,[125] the House of Lords held that, in assessing damages in a personal injuries action for loss of earnings, the tax which the claimant would have paid if he had been working for those earnings must be deducted. In Lord Goddard's words:

> 'I cannot see on what principle of justice the defendants should be called upon to pay [the plaintiff] more than he would have received, if he had remained able to carry out his duties... Damages which have to be paid for personal injuries are not punitive, still less are they a reward. They are simply compensation.'[126]

The *Gourley* principle has since been applied to actions for wrongful dismissal,[127] for trespass and conversion,[128] and for libel,[129] and it can therefore be regarded as a general principle in assessing compensatory damages.

In *Gourley* itself, however, it was emphasised that the deduction should apply only if the damages themselves were not to be taxed, on the basis that otherwise the claimant would be taxed twice.[130] This has created particular difficulties in wrongful dismissal actions, where awards of damages of less than a certain amount, at present £30,000, are exempt from income tax, whereas awards over that amount are taxable. The approach traditionally adopted is that where the award (not having applied *Gourley*) is less than £30,000, *Gourley* must then be applied to reduce the damages, but that where the award of damages (not having applied *Gourley*) is greater than £30,000, *Gourley* must be applied to £30,000 of it but not to the excess.[131] In *Shove v Downs Surgical plc*[132] Sheen J adopted a more satisfactory approach. He took the view that whether the damages are themselves to be taxed or not, one should apply *Gourley* to work out first the claimant's loss, net of tax. The damages award is then the sum, taking into account the tax to be paid on the damages, which ensures that the claimant receives that amount of net loss. So on the facts of the case the claimant's net loss, applying

---

[123] Corporation tax is a tax on a company's income. For discussion of capital gains tax, explaining why it does not in practice raise problems in relation to damages, see J Edelman, *McGregor on Damages* (20th edn, Sweet & Maxwell 2018) paras 20-063–20-077.
[124] *Zinovieff v British Transport Commission*, The Times, 1 April 1954.   [125] [1956] AC 185.
[126] ibid, at 207–208.   [127] *Beach v Reed Corrugated Cases Ltd* [1956] 1 WLR 807.
[128] *Hall & Co Ltd v Pearlberg* [1956] 1 WLR 244.
[129] *Rubber Improvement Ltd v Daily Telegraph Ltd* [1964] AC 234.
[130] There was therefore no *Gourley* deduction in *Deeny v Gooda Walker Ltd* [1996] 1 WLR 426 (names at Lloyd's bringing claims in the tort of negligence for pure economic loss).
[131] *Parsons v BNM Laboratories Ltd* [1964] 1 QB 95, and particularly *Bold v Brough, Nicholson & Hall Ltd* [1964] 1 WLR 201.
[132] [1984] 1 All ER 7. See also *Stewart v Glentaggart* 1963 SLT 119.

Gourley, was £60,729. To ensure that the claimant recovered that loss, given that the damages were themselves taxable, the claimant was awarded £83,477.

A similarly welcome move towards greater accuracy, in preference to the application of a blunt rule of there being no *Gourley* deduction if the damages are themselves taxable, was taken by Judge Humphrey Lloyd QC in *Amstrad plc v Seagate Technology Inc*.[133] Contractual damages were being awarded for loss of profits from the sale of some 67,500 computers. The corporation tax on the damages when received would be at a rate of 31%. But the corporation tax on the profits, had they been received at the proper time, would have been at rates of 33–35%. A *Gourley* deduction was made so as to ensure that the claimants were not overcompensated by the lowering of the tax rate. Although the difference in rates was small in percentage terms, in real terms the difference was some £3.4 million. That is, the damages were subject to £3.4 million less tax than the lost profits would have been.

(2) Is the *Gourley* principle satisfactory?

It should not be thought that the *Gourley* principle has been accepted as satisfactory by everyone. On the contrary, there has been a good deal of criticism of it, and the Canadian courts,[134] for example, have refused to follow it.

Apart from the clearly unsatisfactory punitive view that the defendant does not deserve to be benefited by a reduction in damages, three main arguments have been put against deducting tax.[135] First, it means that judges and practitioners, who are not tax experts, are required to argue and decide complex questions of how much tax the claimant would have paid, and on the *Shove* approach, what grossed-up amount is now needed to ensure that the claimant is compensated for his loss net of tax. But if *Gourley* has justice on its side, such an argument of impracticality can hardly be regarded as a good reason for not applying it. Moreover, there has been little evidence post-*Gourley* of lawyers being unable to cope with its consequences, and nowadays there is, in any event, greater legal education in tax matters.

Secondly, *Gourley* means that the Inland Revenue loses tax revenue that it would otherwise have gained. But as this was also true pre-*Gourley* it is not an argument against *Gourley* in itself but is rather an argument for legislation to be introduced ordering tax to be paid on all damages awards.[136] In any case, the point does not necessarily hold true; for example, a defendant employer may have replaced the injured or dismissed claimant employee.

A third argument is that without further adjustment *Gourley* would leave the claimant undercompensated. Damages awards are reduced where the claimant would not otherwise have had a capital sum to invest. But if he does invest the damages he will have to pay tax on the investment income. The pre-*Gourley* approach was a rough-and-ready way of taking this tax liability into account. So Waddams writes:

> 'The Canadian rule of ignoring income tax is … justified as a short-cut to the complex and uncertain process of deducting first, the tax that the plaintiff would have had to pay on his income,

---

[133] (1998) 86 BLR 34. This approach was approved and applied in *BSkyB Ltd v HP Enterprise Services UK Ltd* [2010] EWHC 862 (TCC), (2010) 131 Con LR 42.
[134] *R v Jennings* (1966) 57 DLR (2d) 644; *Cunningham v Wheeler* (1994) 113 DLR (4th) 1, at 21–3. See also *North Island Wholesale Groceries Ltd v Hewin* [1982] 2 NZLR 176. But *Australia Atlas Tiles v Briers* (1978) 144 CLR 202, which had rejected *Gourley*, was overturned by *Cullen v Trappell* (1980) 146 CLR 1.
[135] A Ogus, *The Law of Damages* (Butterworths 1973) 113–115.
[136] This is strongly advocated by W Bishop and J Kay, 'Taxation and Damages: the Rule in Gourley's Case' (1987) 103 LQR 211.

and then adding back the tax the plaintiff will presumably have to pay on the income from the investment of the award.'[137]

But the objection to this short-cut is that it cannot hope to be as accurate as applying *Gourley* and also taking account of the presumed tax payable on the investment income. That standard rate tax will be paid on investment income is assumed in the fixing of the appropriate multiplier for assessing future pecuniary loss. In *Hodgson v Trapp*[138] the House of Lords in overruling *Thomas v Wignall*[139] held that, normally, there should be no increase in the multiplier to take account of higher rate tax payable on the investment income from large awards (ie there should be no '*Gourley* in reverse' as Lord Reid termed it in *Taylor v O'Connor*).[140] The main reasons given for this were the uncertainty of future higher tax rates and that it would be rare for the investment income from damages for future pecuniary loss alone to attract higher rate tax. But, as clarified by Lord Steyn in *Wells v Wells*,[141] Lord Oliver's speech in *Hodgson v Trapp* is best interpreted as accepting that there will be exceptional cases in which the courts may accept that a lower discount rate should be applied, and hence a higher multiplier chosen, where it is likely that higher rate tax will be payable on the income from a large award.

It is submitted, therefore, that *Gourley* should remain good law. There is little force in objections put to it and, despite the greater complexity involved in the assessment of damages, the *Gourley* principle adheres to the compensatory aims and is fully justified.

---

[137] S Waddams, *The Law of Damages* (6th edn, Thomson Reuters 2017) para 3.980.
[138] [1989] AC 807.   [139] [1987] QB 1098.   [140] [1971] AC 115, at 129.
[141] [1999] 1 AC 345, at 388.

Section Two

Damages for the Different Types of Loss

10

Pecuniary loss (except consequent on personal injury, death, or loss of reputation)

1. Breach of contract—basic pecuniary loss	187
2. Breach of contract—additional pecuniary loss	205
3. Torts—damage to property, including destruction	206
4. Torts—wrongful interference with goods or land, other than causing property damage	219
5. Torts—pure economic loss	222

Breach of contract damages are normally sought and awarded for this type of loss. It is therefore not surprising that there is a host of different ways of analysing and subdividing it. Here the approach adopted will be to divide between basic pecuniary loss, which will be primarily concentrated on, and which focuses on the benefit to which the claimant was contractually entitled and of which it has been wholly or partially deprived by the defendant's breach, and additional pecuniary loss.[1]

On the other hand, for torts, where the central focus is on wrongful interference rather than a failure to benefit, it has been considered more helpful to adopt a division which gives some flavour of the interference in question. This type of tortious pecuniary loss is therefore examined under three heads:[2] damage to property, including destruction; wrongful interference with goods or land, other than causing property damage; and pure economic loss.[3]

1. Breach of contract—basic pecuniary loss

(1) The content of the promise

It is crucial to keep constantly in mind what the defendant contractually promised, so as not to put the claimant in a better or worse economic position than if the contract had been performed.

---

[1] This is similar to Farnsworth's analysis in A Farnsworth, 'Legal Remedies for Breach of Contract' (1970) 70 Col LR 1145, 1160–1175. See also the distinction between basic or normal, and consequential, pecuniary loss drawn in J Edelman, *McGregor on Damages* (20th edn, Sweet & Maxwell 2018) paras 3-008–3-012, 4-002–4-023, 4-050–4-062.

[2] Other examples of such pecuniary loss are the expenses of gaining release from a false imprisonment in *Prichet v Boevey* (1833) 1 Cr & M 775, and the legal costs of defending a malicious prosecution in *Savile v Roberts* (1699) 1 Ld Raym 374 and *Berry v British Transport Commission* [1962] 1 QB 306.

[3] A specialised issue, which is not discussed below, is whether a company and a shareholder in that company can both recover for economic loss caused by a breach of duty (whether in contract or tort) to both the company and the shareholder See, generally, C Mitchell, 'Shareholders' Claims for Reflective Loss' (2004) 120 LQR 457; R Lee, 'Creditors' Claims for Reflective Loss' [2008] JBL 479; S Griffin, 'Shareholder Remedies and the No Reflective Loss Principle' [2010] JBL 529. Leading cases include *Prudential Assurance v Newman Industries (No 2)* [1982] 1 Ch 204; *Johnson v Gore Wood & Co* [2002] 2 AC 1; *Carlos Sevilleja Garcia v Marex Financial Ltd* [2018] EWCA Civ 1468, [2019] QB 173 (in which the 'no reflective loss' rule was extended to creditors of the company).

A good illustration of how easy it is to drift away from the basic compensatory principle is where a surveyor contracts to survey a house for a prospective house purchaser. Subject to any express term, the surveyor will be taken to have promised contractually to use reasonable care in making the survey. The surveyor will not be taken to have warranted either that the house is worth any particular price or that it is free from any defects other than those reported. It follows that if in reliance on the survey the purchaser goes ahead and buys the house and it transpires that the survey was made in breach of contract, because the surveyor did not report reasonably discoverable defects, the aim of damages will be to put the claimant into as good a position as if reasonable care had been used in making the survey and the report; they are not aimed at putting the claimant into any (other) warranted position. There are two possible positions the claimant may argue that he would have been in if reasonable care had been used in making the survey and report. Either he would not have bought the house at all or he would have bought it but for less than he paid. Applying the former, the claimant's basic loss will be the purchase price paid minus the house's actual value. Applying the latter, the basic loss will be the same if one assumes that the claimant would have paid the actual value of the house. Alternatively, the court might take the cost of repairs as a convenient starting point for the deduction in price the purchaser would actually have made from the purchase price if he had known of the defects.

These principles were clearly and correctly applied by the Court of Appeal in cases such as *Perry v Sidney Phillips & Son*[4] and *Watts v Morrow*[5] but in other cases concerning negligent surveys the court's failure to reason from the basic compensatory principle is shown not so much by wrong decisions but rather by statements suggesting that damages are to be calculated according to the warranted value or condition of the property minus its actual value.[6]

One might argue that the effect of the controversial *SAAMCO* principle is that the house purchaser could not recover more than the difference between the value of the house, had the report been accurate, and its actual value. But even if that were the law (and it has been argued above that the *SAAMCO* principle is flawed)[7] it is submitted that one should regard *SAAMCO* as a restriction (because of the 'scope of the duty') on the damages that would otherwise be awarded applying the compensatory aim. One must first apply the compensatory aim correctly by bearing in mind what the defendant contractually promised.

Another good illustration of the need to keep constantly in mind what the defendant contractually promised—so as to avoid awarding an erroneous measure of compensatory damages—is provided by breach of an agent's warranty of authority. This occurs where an agent, who does not have its principal's authority (for example, to conclude a contract), contractually warrants to the claimant that it does have that authority. If the claimant sues for breach of the agent's contractual warranty of authority, the aim, bearing in mind the contractual promise, must be to put the claimant into as good a position as if the agent did have the principal's authority. And if the agent did have that authority, the claimant would, for example, have had a valid contract with the principal so that the damages against the agent must ultimately be based on the claimant's position had there been a valid contract between the principal and the claimant.[8]

---

[4] [1982] 1 WLR 1297.
[5] [1991] 1 WLR 1421. See similarly *Swingcastle Ltd v Alastair Gibson (a firm)* [1991] 2 AC 223; *Gardner v Marsh & Parsons* [1997] 1 WLR 489; *Patel v Hooper & Jackson* [1999] 1 WLR 1792.
[6] Eg *Philips v Ward* [1956] 1 WLR 471, at 473; *Simple Simon Catering Ltd v Binstock Miller & Co* (1973) 117 Sol Jo 529.
[7] Above, pp 117–127.
[8] For a careful application of these principles, see *Habton Farms v Nimmo* [2003] EWCA Civ 68, [2004] QB 1.

(2) Difference in value or cost of cure

There is often a choice between awarding the difference in value or the cost of cure. The former directly awards the claimant the financial advantage it has lost by being deprived, partially or wholly, of the benefit to which it was contractually entitled. The cost of cure, on the other hand, seeks to award the claimant the additional financial sacrifice it would have to incur to put itself into as good a position as if it had received the benefit to which it was contractually entitled.

In many situations the difference in value is in practice the only possible measure because no replacement benefit is available at any cost: for example, the party in breach may alone be capable of performing the contract or the delay may have made the performance impossible. Where both are possible measures, which will be awarded is a central question of interest and will be constantly referred to when looking at examples of the measures of basic pecuniary loss applied. But it is useful here to point to three of the factors that should and do influence the courts in making this choice. First, the claimant's duty to mitigate means that it will recover the cost of cure where it has, or ought to have, incurred that cost in reasonably seeking to minimise its losses. Secondly, the fact that the claimant has cured or intends to cure may be a decisive factor favouring the cost of cure. Thirdly, the claimant's purpose for wanting performance may be relevant; so if the claimant wanted performance primarily to reap economic gain, the difference in value will fully compensate the claimant; that is, it will obtain the intended profits. But if performance was wanted for other reasons (eg for pleasure), difference in value will not, or not as fully, compensate the claimant.

It is important to note that this long-standing choice in the law of contract damages (which also applies in analogous areas of tort damages)[9] has recently been the subject of academic and judicial scrutiny. The cornerstone of this debate was an article by Brian Coote entitled 'Contract Damages, *Ruxley* and the Performance Interest'.[10] In it, Coote took Friedmann's terminology of 'performance interest', which Friedmann had himself regarded as merely synonymous with 'expectation interest',[11] and used it as a label to describe 'cost of cure' damages. Performance interest damages were contrasted with 'difference in value' damages which Coote saw as 'mere compensation for the economic consequences of breach'[12] or as being 'to compensate for the loss of the economic benefits of performance'.[13] Coote then suggested that there has been a tendency in the law of damages for the 'performance interest' to be subordinated to the 'compensation approach'.[14]

It is submitted that Coote's terminology is unhelpful. Both 'difference in value' and 'cost of cure' are concerned to compensate the claimant by putting him or her into as good a position as if the contract had been performed. Both are measures of pecuniary loss. The one is concerned with the loss of financial advantage, the other with the cost (ie the out-of-pocket loss) that the claimant must now incur. It is erroneous to treat only difference in value as compensating pecuniary loss. The overall interest normally protected by contractual damages is usefully labelled the expectation interest or performance interest. It is at a lower,

---

[9] See below, pp 206, 219.
[10] B Coote, 'Contract Damages, *Ruxley*, and the Performance Interest' [1997] CLJ 537. For somewhat similar views to those of Coote, see C Webb, 'Performance and Compensation: An Analysis of Contract Damages and Contractual Obligation' (2006) 26 OJLS 41; S Smith, 'Substitutionary Damages' in *Justifying Private Law Remedies* (ed C Rickett, Hart Publishing 2008) 93; and D Winterton, *Money Awards in Contract Law* (Hart Publishing 2015). See further above, pp 48–50.
[11] D Friedmann, 'The Performance Interest in Contract Damages' (1995) 111 LQR 628: see above, p 37.
[12] B Coote, 'Contract Damages, *Ruxley*, and the Performance Interest' [1997] CLJ 537, 557.
[13] B Coote, 'Contract Damages, *Ruxley*, and the Performance Interest' [1997] CLJ 537, 544.
[14] ibid, 547, 569–570.

more specific, level that one must then go on to choose, in protecting that expectation/performance interest, between difference in value or cost of cure.

Moreover, it is misleading to indicate that English law has been more committed to 'difference in value' than 'cost of cure'. As we shall see throughout this chapter, various factors have influenced the courts in deciding between those two measures. Neither is dominant over the other.

Coote's arguments are, arguably, more powerful in so far as he argues that 'cost of cure' (using that traditional terminology) should be even more widely favoured than it traditionally has been. In particular, he would favour 'downgrading' the importance attached to the claimant's intention to cure in favour of a single 'reasonableness' test albeit that he would clothe the reasonable person with the needs and tastes of the actual promisee.[15] Coote argues that in contracts made for the benefit of third parties, this approach would lead to 'cost of cure' damages being naturally recoverable by the contracting party as its own 'loss', irrespective of whether that party has cured or intends to cure.[16]

As we shall see, that approach apparently found favour with Lords Goff and Millett (dissenting) and, to an extent, Lord Browne-Wilkinson in *Alfred McAlpine Construction Ltd v Panatown Ltd*,[17] which concerned a construction contract for a third party's benefit. But, with respect, the traditional reliance on the claimant's intention to effect cure makes good sense in avoiding overcompensation of the claimant; and in the context of a contract for the benefit of a third party it also avoids unacceptable double liability to both the contracting party and the third party.[18] We shall return to these matters when discussing the *Panatown* case.

This is not to deny that there are some cases, considered at various points in this chapter, where the courts have awarded damages which appear to overcompensate the claimant. One might argue that those cases are simply wrong for that reason. Alternatively they can perhaps be justified, while maintaining the view that the damages are compensatory, by recognising that, for pragmatic reasons, the courts may prefer a simple and certain objective or standard measure of damages. A further justification might be that such cases are treating the damages as a corollary of the 'duty to mitigate': that is, that the defendant cannot complain that the claimant is being overcompensated by cost of cure damages in a situation where such damages would indisputably have been recoverable as reasonably incurred had the claimant chosen to incur the cost of cure (even if it has not done so and will not do so).[19]

(3) The general formulae for assessing basic pecuniary loss

From what has already been said it can readily be seen that, taking into account the advantages as well as the disadvantages resulting from the breach, the claimant's basic pecuniary loss can be represented as follows: the value to the claimant of the benefit it should have received (minus the value of any benefits gained under the contract or that have, or ought to

---

[15] ibid, 563, 570. See also S Rowan, 'Cost of Cure Damages and the Relevance of the Injured Promisee's Intention to Cure' [2017] CLJ 616.

[16] B Coote, 'Contract Damages, *Ruxley*, and the Performance Interest' [1997] CLJ 537, 549–552.

[17] [2001] 1 AC 518: see below, pp 202–203.

[18] E McKendrick, 'The Common Law at Work: The Saga of *Alfred McAlpine Construction Ltd v Panatown Ltd*' (2003) 3 OUCLJ 145, 175, agrees that the intention to cure is a critical factor. But, with respect, intention to cure shows the need for (an actual or anticipated) financial loss which contradicts McKendrick's general argument (on which see also E McKendrick, 'Breach of Contract and the Meaning of Loss' (1999) 52 CLP 37) similar to Coote's, that the courts should not be so concerned about financial loss.

[19] For the same analysis, see above, p 50. As there explained, the latter approach is that advocated by Andrew Summers.

have, been gained as a result of the breach) minus the cost it has, or ought to have, avoided as a result of the breach; *or* the cost required to put the claimant into as good a position as if it had received the benefit minus the cost it has, or ought to have, avoided as a result of the breach; put shortly, *difference in value minus cost avoided* or *cost of cure minus cost avoided.*

The beauty of such formulae is that they can be applied whatever the nature of the benefit contracted for: that is, whether it comprised the delivery of goods, the transfer of land, the rendering of services, or the payment of money.

(4) Examples of the measures of basic pecuniary loss applied

These examples show the above general formulae in operation in respect of two of the most common types of contract—contracts for the sale of goods (examples (a)–(g))[20] and contracts for the building or repairing of real property (examples (h)–(j)).

(a) Breach by seller failing to deliver goods wanted for resale

The buyer's duty to mitigate generally dictates that it should buy substitute goods in the market so as to make its resale profit. Therefore, as laid down in the Sale of Goods Act 1979, s 51(3), the generally appropriate measure is market price at time fixed for delivery minus contract price, with the market price here referring to the market buying price.[21] This is a cost of cure rather than a difference in value measure, with the contract price, assuming unpaid or recovered, being deducted as a cost avoided.

A higher resale price (that is, the price at which the buyer has contracted to sell the goods) clearly does not displace the market price, since it does not affect the buyer's duty to mitigate. More controversial is a lower resale price. Several cases indicate that this should also be ignored. The leading one is *William Bros Ltd v Agius Ltd*[22] where the defendant contracted to sell coal to the claimant at 16s 3d per ton. The claimant agreed to resell the coal to a third party for 19s per ton. The defendant failed to deliver. The market price at the date of breach was 23s 6d. The claimant was awarded damages of 7s 3d per ton, that is 23s 6d minus 16s 3d. The defendant's argument that the damages should have been only 2s 9d per ton, that is 19s minus 16s 3d, was rejected. Although some commentators support this decision,[23] it would seem that ignoring the resale overcompensated the claimant. True, it is often reasonable, given the claimant's potential liability to the sub-buyer, to buy at a higher market price. But on the facts the claimant had not done so; and there was no question of liability on the resale contract because the sub-buyer had assigned its rights to the defendant. Nor is it satisfactory to say that, if the contract had been performed, other goods

---

[20] Analogous rules apply in relation to contracts for the carriage of goods. See, eg, *Rodocanachi v Milburn* (1886) 18 QBD 67; *Coastal (Bermuda) Petroleum Ltd v VTT Vulcan Petroleum SA (No 2), The Marine Star (No 2)* [1994] 2 Lloyd's Rep 629 (non-delivery of goods by carrier); *The Heron II* [1969] 1 AC 350; *The Pegase* [1981] 1 Lloyd's Rep 175 (late delivery of goods by carrier). Note also *White Arrow Express Ltd v Lamey's Distribution Ltd* (1995) 15 Tr LR 69 in which an inferior delivery service was provided than that contracted for: it was held that the claimant was entitled as damages to the difference between the market value of the services it had contracted for minus the market value of the services obtained but, as the claimant had produced no evidence of that difference in value (nor evidence of any other loss), nominal damages only were awarded.

[21] A Ogus, *The Law of Damages* (Butterworths 1973) 324.

[22] [1914] AC 510. In relation to carriage contracts, the classic case laying down that one should ignore resale prices, whether higher or lower than the market price, is *Rodocanachi v Milburn* (1886) 18 QBD 67. Lord Esher MR said, at 77, '[T]he value is to be taken independently of any circumstances peculiar to the plaintiff.'

[23] Eg S Waddams, *The Law of Damages* (6th edn, Thomson Reuters 2017) paras 1.30–1.40, 1.1940, and more generally D Simon and G Novack, 'Limiting the Buyers' Market Damages to Lost Profits: A Challenge to the Enforceability of Market Contracts' (1979) 92 Harv LR 1395.

could still have been bought to fulfil the resale, leaving the claimant free to sell the goods that should have been delivered by the defendant at the market selling price; for those other goods would still have to be bought at the higher market price and resold at the lower resale price, thereby producing an identical loss. So, it is submitted that, applying a compensatory analysis, a lower resale price should displace the market buying price, except where the claimant has reasonably bought substitute goods to fulfil the resale (or there is liability on the sub-sale), in which case damages should be the price paid for the substitutes minus the original contract price (or the amount of damages the buyer has to pay the sub-buyer).

It should be recognised, however, that *William Bros Ltd v Agius Ltd* is one of several leading cases[24] in which the courts have overcompensated the claimant. On the face of it, this seems wrong. However, it might perhaps be justified simply as a pragmatic preference for a clear and certain objective measure (ie what a reasonable claimant would have lost). Alternatively, as a corollary of the 'duty to mitigate', it might be said that the defendant cannot complain if damages are based on what the defendant would have had to pay as damages if the claimant had acted reasonably by buying in substitute goods.[25] So on the facts of *William Bros Ltd v Agius Ltd*, the claimant, to put itself most closely into as good a position as if the contract had been performed, could reasonably have bought in substitute goods at 23s 6d. Applying this analysis, it did not matter that it had not in fact done so.

Where the claimant cannot mitigate by buying substitute goods in the market, it is entitled to a difference in value measure. A good example is *Re R & H Hall and W H Pim, Jr & Co's Arbitration*.[26] The claimants could not mitigate because they had contracted to resell the specific cargo of grain, and no other, to be delivered by the defendant. They were held entitled, subject to remoteness, to the actual resale price, which was higher than the market price, minus the contract price.

(b) Breach by seller failing to deliver goods wanted for use

The buyer's duty to mitigate means that it should generally buy substitute goods in the market so as to make its user profit and again, therefore, as laid down in the Sale of Goods Act 1979, s 51(3), the generally appropriate measure is market buying price at time fixed for delivery minus contract price. However, where the buyer cannot so mitigate and cannot mitigate in other ways, for example by having substitute goods manufactured and adapted,[27] it will generally be awarded its lost user profit as the difference in value measure.[28]

Exceptionally, a buyer is awarded the market resale price of goods (minus the contract price if unpaid or recovered). This will be so where the cost of replacing the goods exceeds that resale value, the claimant has no intention of replacing the goods, and there is no obvious lost user profit. In *Sealace Shipping Co Ltd v Oceanvoice Ltd, The Alecos M*[29] the defendants contracted to sell a ship, including its spare parts, to the claimants. However, when it was delivered, the defendants failed to deliver also its spare propeller. The arbitrator

---

[24] See also, eg, *Rodocanachi v Milburn* (1886) 18 QBD 67 (non-delivery of goods by carrier); *Slater v Hoyle and Smith Ltd* [1920] 2 KB 11 (seller delivering defective goods).

[25] This is the approach advocated by Andrew Summers: see above, p 50.

[26] (1928) 139 LT 50. However, Viscount Haldane's judgment is misleading on remoteness; see E McKendrick, *Goode on Commercial Law* (5th edn, Penguin 2016) 415–416. See also *Coastal (Bermuda) Petroleum Ltd v VTT Vulcan Petroleum SA (No 2), The Marine Star (No 2)* [1994] 2 Lloyd's Rep 629 (lost resale profits awarded as damages for breach of contract of carriage by carrier's non-delivery where no available market).

[27] See, by analogy, *Hall Ltd v Barclay* [1937] 3 All ER 620; below, p 220.

[28] See, by analogy, *Cullinane v British Rema Manufacturing Co Ltd* [1954] 1 QB 292.

[29] [1991] 1 Lloyd's Rep 120. The decision seems correct but it is criticised by G Treitel, 'Damages for Non-Delivery' (1991) 107 LQR 364.

awarded $1,100 for that breach on the grounds that the claimants were not interested in buying a replacement spare propeller (which would cost $121,000) and that, as there was no commercial market in second-hand propellers, the resale value of a propeller was its scrap value of $1,100. Steyn J disagreed and awarded $121,000 but the Court of Appeal allowed an appeal by the defendants and restored the lower award made by the arbitrator.

(c) Breach by seller delivering defective goods wanted for resale[30]

While one can imagine situations[31] in which the duty to mitigate would dictate that the buyer should render the goods non-defective before reselling, hence entitling it to the cost of cure, a difference in value measure is here generally applied. As laid down in the Sale of Goods Act 1979, s 53(3) the buyer is generally awarded the market price that the goods would have had if of the contracted-for quality, less the market price of the goods actually delivered, and it is clear that the market price here refers to the market selling price.[32] The contract price is not deducted because it is payable by the buyer and is therefore not a cost avoided.

Resale prices here seem relevant in two senses. First, if prior to the breach the buyer had made a resale contract of the goods, one would expect the resale selling price to displace the market selling price of the goods had they been of contracted-for quality. Secondly, if after breach the buyer had sold the goods, one would expect the resale price to displace the market selling price of the goods actually delivered if the former was higher. But in *Slater v Hoyle and Smith Ltd*,[33] where a resale concluded prior to breach had been carried through after breach, resale prices were considered irrelevant, whether prior or subsequent, and the claimant was held entitled to the normal measure under the Sale of Goods Act 1979, s 53(3). The claimant bought cotton cloth from the defendant to fulfil a contract of sale already made. The cloth delivered was of inferior quality than warranted, although the claimant was able to use it as intended to fulfil his sub-contract and received the full contract price from the sub-buyer. The price paid by the sub-buyer was greater than the market selling price of the cloth delivered but less than the market selling price of the cloth as warranted. The defendant contended that the claimant's damages should be nominal because the resale contract price concluded prior to breach minus the resale contract price received subsequent to breach amounted to nil. But the Court of Appeal rejected this, considered cases like *Williams Bros v Agius Ltd*[34] to be correct, and awarded the claimant damages assessed according to s 53(3). Again while some commentators support this approach,[35] there are difficulties in justifying it on compensatory reasoning because it appears to leave the claimant in a better position than if the contract had been properly performed.

If it is to be justified, it is submitted that, as has been explained above in relation to *William Bros Ltd v Agius Ltd*,[36] it is best viewed either as representing a pragmatic preference for a simple and certain objective or standard measure or as a corollary of the 'duty to mitigate' (it would have been reasonable for the claimant to have bought in replacement goods so as to fulfil the sub-contract and the defendant cannot complain if damages are based on that reasonable conduct).

---

[30] It is assumed here and in examples (d)–(f) that the buyer has reasonably accepted the goods. If not, the damages are assessed as for non-delivery.
[31] Eg where the cost of cure is much lower than the difference in market value.
[32] A Ogus, *The Law of Damages* (Butterworths 1973) 324.   [33] [1920] 2 KB 11.
[34] [1914] AC 510.
[35] Eg S Waddams, *The Law of Damages* (6th edn, Thomson Reuters 2017) paras 1.2570–1.2580.
[36] [1920] 2 KB 11: above, p 192.

There is strong support in *Bence Graphics Int Ltd v Fasson UK Ltd*[37] for the view that *Slater v Hoyle and Smith Ltd* was incorrect to disregard the resale price. Here the defendants supplied vinyl film to the claimants for £564,328.54. As the defendants knew, this film was to be used, and was so used, by the claimants to manufacture many thousands of 'decals' (that is, self-adhesive transfers) for use in identifying bulk containers. The decals were sold to various customers who owned bulk containers. The film supplied was defective so that some decals became illegible more quickly than they should have done. The essential question at issue was whether, applying the Sale of Goods Act 1979, s 53(3), the claimants were entitled to £564,328.54 as the difference between the market price of the film as it should have been and as it was; or were the claimants merely entitled to damages indemnifying them for the (apparently relatively minor) claims against them by their customers consequent on the decals being defective. The majority (Thorpe LJ dissenting) held that the latter was the appropriate measure. Contrary to *Slater v Hoyle and Smith Ltd*, the sales by the claimants to their customers should not be ignored. They meant that the claimants had not suffered a loss from being unable to sell on the film. Auld LJ, in an enlightened judgment, boldly said that the *Slater* case should be reconsidered not least because it awarded a buyer more than the evidence clearly showed he had lost. Otton LJ preferred to distinguish the *Slater* case on the grounds—rather unconvincing as he himself seemed inclined to recognise—that in that case, in contrast to *Bence*, the same goods were sub-sold without any manufacturing process and the defendant sellers did not know of the particular sub-sale.

(d) Breach by seller delivering defective goods wanted for use

While one can imagine situations[38] where the duty to mitigate would dictate that the buyer should render the goods non-defective, hence entitling it to the cost of cure, a difference in value measure is here generally applied whereby the buyer is normally entitled to its lost user profit. For example, in *Cullinane v British Rema Manufacturing Co Ltd*,[39] the defendants sold and delivered to the claimant a clay pulverising machine warranting that it would process clay at six tons per hour. In fact it could process clay at only two tons per hour. The claimant sought damages, inter alia,[40] for his lost user profit and throughout the judgments it was taken for granted that the buyer was so entitled.[41] Jenkins LJ said:

> 'The plant having been supplied in contemplation by both parties that it should be used by the plaintiff in the commercial production of pulverised clay, the case is one in which the plaintiff can claim as damages for the breach of warranty, the loss of the profit he can show that he would have made if the plant had been as warranted.'[42]

(e) Breach by seller making late delivery of goods wanted for resale

A difference in value formula is generally applied whereby, as laid down in *Elbinger Aktiengesellschaft v Armstrong*,[43] the claimant is entitled to the market selling price at the

---

[37] [1998] QB 87. See also J Edelman, *McGregor on Damages* (20th edn, Sweet & Maxwell 2018), paras 9-179, 25-069. For the contrary view, that the majority in the *Bence* case was incorrect, see G Treitel, 'Damages for Breach of Warranty of Quality' (1997) 113 LQR 188.
[38] Eg where the cost of cure is much lower than the lost user profits.
[39] [1954] 1 QB 292. See also *Gull v Saunders* (1913) 17 CLR 82.
[40] The claimant also claimed damages for some of his wasted expenses. The majority (Morris LJ dissenting) refused these. But this seems wrong since the profits awarded were not gross; see A Ogus, *The Law of Damages* (Butterworths 1973) 352–354; J Macleod, 'Damages: Reliance or Expectancy Interest' [1970] JBL 19.
[41] [1954] 1 QB 292, at 303, 308, 316.   [42] ibid, at 308.
[43] (1874) LR 9 QB 473. See, analogously, *The Heron II* [1969] 1 AC 350 (damages for late delivery by a carrier).

time when the goods should have been delivered minus the market selling price at the time when they were actually delivered.

As regards resale prices, in *Wertheim v Chicoutimi Pulp Co*[44] a resale after breach was taken into account but a resale prior to breach was not; ie the higher resale price received subsequent to breach displaced the market selling price of the goods when actually delivered but the lower resale price concluded prior to breach did not displace the market selling price of the goods at the time when they should have been delivered. The case concerned a contract for the sale of a number of tons of wood pulp. Applying the normal measure of market selling price at the time when the goods should have been delivered (70s per ton) minus the market selling price when actually delivered (42s 6d), the claimant would have been entitled to damages of 27s 6d per ton. However, the Privy Council awarded damages of 5s per ton on the ground that the claimants had subsequently resold the same goods at 65s per ton (ie 70s minus 65s). It would seem, however, that the Privy Council was taking an unsatisfactory mid-position. Either the *Slater v Hoyle and Smith Ltd*[45] approach of ignoring resale prices applies, in which case the claimants should have been entitled to 27s 6d per ton or, and preferably, applying a compensatory approach, resale prices of goods both prior and subsequent to breach are taken into account—in which case the claimants should have been entitled to merely nominal damages (ie 65s minus 65s).[46]

(f) Breach by seller making late delivery of goods wanted for use

A difference in value measure is here generally applied, whereby the buyer is normally entitled to its lost user profit. An illustration of this is provided by one of the classic cases on remoteness, *Victoria Laundry (Windsor) Ltd v Newman Industries*,[47] where the claimants were awarded damages for loss of their ordinary (but not exceptional) user profit following the defendants' breach of contract in delivering five months late a boiler to be used in the claimants' business.

(g) Breach by buyer refusing to accept the goods

The duty to mitigate generally dictates that the seller should sell the goods to another buyer. Therefore, as laid down by the Sale of Goods Act 1979, s 50(3), the general measure is the contract price minus the market price at the date of breach.

This is a difference in value measure—the contract price represents the value to the claimant of the defendant's performance as it should have been and the market price is the market selling price[48] and represents the benefit the seller has or ought to have gained by selling the goods to another buyer.

If the seller resells the goods at a price higher than the market selling price, one would expect that this resale price—being the benefit gained—would displace the market selling price as the sum deducted from the contract price. However, in *Campbell Mostyn (Provisions) Ltd v Barnett Trading Co*[49] (as we have seen, analogously, in relation to a buyer's damages for non- or defective delivery) it was held that the resale price should

---

[44] [1911] AC 301. See, analogously, *The Pegase* [1981] 1 Lloyd's Rep 175 (lost resale profit awarded as damages where late delivery of goods by carrier and no available market).
[45] [1920] 2 KB 11.
[46] This is also the approach preferred by J Edelman, *McGregor on Damages* (20th edn, Sweet & Maxwell 2018) para 9-180.
[47] [1949] 2 KB 528.   [48] A Ogus, *The Law of Damages* (Butterworths 1973) 324.
[49] [1954] 1 Lloyd's Rep 65. See also *AKAS Jamal v Moolla Dawood Sons & Co* [1916] 1 AC 175.

be ignored. The defendants had refused to accept 350 cases of tinned ham, which they had contracted to buy from the claimants. The claimants were awarded damages of the contract price minus the market price at the date of breach, even though they had subsequently sold the goods at or above the contract price. This approach leaves a claimant in a better position than if the contract had been performed and therefore runs contrary to the avowed compensatory goal.

If it is to be justified, it is submitted that, as has been explained above in relation to *William Bros Ltd v Agius Ltd*,[50] it is best viewed either as representing a pragmatic preference for a simple and certain objective or standard measure or as a corollary of the 'duty to mitigate' (it would have been reasonable for the claimant to have sold the goods to another buyer at the market price and the defendant cannot complain if damages are based on that reasonable conduct).

Where the seller cannot mitigate by selling in the market—for example, where supply exceeds demand—the Sale of Goods Act 1979, s 50(3) does not apply, and the claimant will instead be basically entitled to its loss of profit on that sale (ie contract price minus cost avoided) without any deduction of the market selling price.[51] This is shown by *W L Thompson Ltd v Robinson (Gunmakers) Ltd*[52] in which there was a contract to sell a Vanguard car. The supply of those cars exceeded the demand and therefore when the buyer refused to take the car the seller was held entitled to his loss of profit on the sale even though there was no difference between the contract price and the market selling price at the date of breach. A particularly clear analysis of *Thompson v Robinson* was made by Jenkins LJ in *Charter v Sullivan*.[53] There, because demand exceeded supply, *Thompson v Robinson* was distinguished and s 50(3) applied entitling the seller of a Hillman Minx car to merely nominal damages. Jenkins LJ said:

> 'The number of sales he [the plaintiff] can effect and consequently the amount of profit he makes, will be governed, according to the state of the trade, either by the number of cars he is able to obtain from the manufacturers or by the number of purchasers he is able to find. In the former case demand exceeds supply, so that the default of one purchaser involves him in no loss, for he sells the same number of cars as he would have sold if that purchaser had not defaulted. In the latter case, supply exceeds demand so that the default of one purchaser may be said to have lost him one sale...'[54]

and later he went on to say:

> 'Upjohn J's decision in favour of the plaintiff dealers in *Thompson's* case was essentially based on the admitted fact that the supply of the cars in question exceeded the demand and his judgment leaves no room for doubt that if the demand had exceeded the supply, his decision would have been the other way.'[55]

It should further be added that, as laid down in *Lazenby Garages Ltd v Wright*,[56] *Thompson v Robinson* cannot be applied to sales of second-hand cars, because one cannot say of such cars that supply exceeds demand, or that a subsequent sale does not mitigate the seller's loss of profit. As Lord Denning said, '... it is entirely different in the case of a secondhand car. Each second-hand car is different from the next, even though it is the same make.'[57]

---

[50] [1920] 2 KB 11: above, p 192.
[51] See similarly US Uniform Commercial Code, s 2-708(2); C Goetz and R Scott, 'Measuring Sellers' Damages: The Lost-Profits Puzzle' (1979) 31 Stan LR 323.
[52] [1955] Ch 177. Above, p 147.   [53] [1957] 2 QB 117.   [54] [1957] 2 QB 117, at 124–125.
[55] ibid, at 130.   [56] [1976] 1 WLR 459.   [57] ibid, at 462.

(h) Breach by builder refusing to carry out work or carrying it out defectively

One obvious possibility is that the owner will here be awarded the difference in value (ie difference in market selling price) between his property as it should have been if the contract had been performed and its actual value.[58] However, the cost of cure, ie the cost of engaging someone to complete the work, is often awarded instead. This may be because the cost of cure is less than the difference in the property's value and hence the owner's duty to mitigate dictates that she should recover only the cost of cure. But even where the cost of cure greatly exceeds the difference in the property's value, the owner has been held entitled to that cost provided she has cured or intends to cure. Three main cases repay examination.[59]

In *Tito v Waddell (No 2)*[60] a British company mining for phosphate on Ocean Island, a small island in the Pacific, had contractually promised to restore the land mined by replanting trees but had failed to do so. One of the questions that arose was whether the islanders would be entitled as damages to the cost of cure (ie the cost of replanting the land) which ran into thousands of pounds, or merely to the difference in value between the land as it was and as it would be if replanted, which at most ran to a few hundred pounds. Megarry V-C thought that the fundamental issue was whether the claimant had already cured or intended to cure. If so, the higher cost of cure would be awarded. He said, '... if the plaintiff establishes that the contractual work has been or will be done, then in all normal circumstances, it seems to me that he has shown that the cost of doing it is, or is part of, his loss and is recoverable as damages.'[61] Of course, where the court is basing itself on the claimant's intention to cure it cannot be absolutely sure that this is what the claimant will do but Megarry V-C thought that probable intention would be sufficient. He further suggested that in cases of doubt the court might be satisfied if the claimant gave an undertaking to do the work;[62] but such an undertaking might produce problems of enforcement and satellite litigation and was subsequently rejected as an idea by the House of Lords in *Ruxley Electronics and Construction Ltd v Forsyth*.[63] On the facts of *Tito v Waddell* it was held that there was not a sufficiently clear intention on the part of the islanders to use the damages to replant Ocean Island. In particular this was because they were now living on a different island. Damages based on the lower difference in the property's value were therefore awarded.

In *Radford v De Froberville*[64] the claimant had sold a plot of land to the defendant on terms, inter alia, that the defendant would erect a wall on the plot so as to divide it from the claimant's land. The defendant had failed to do so. One question was whether the claimant was entitled to damages assessed according to the cost of cure (ie the cost of building a wall on his land), which at the time of trial would have cost £3,400 and at the time of breach £1,200, or according to the difference in the land's value with and without the wall, which

---

[58] Where the owner intended to use the property to make a profit, the difference in value measure could alternatively (at least in theory) refer to the owner's loss of user profits.
[59] See also, eg, *Dean v Ainley* [1987] 1 WLR 1729; *Alfred McAlpine Construction Ltd v Panatown Ltd* [2001] 1 AC 518 (per Lords Goff and Millett), discussed below, at pp 227–228. There has been much academic discussion of this situation: eg A Farnsworth, 'Legal Remedies for Breach of Contract' (1970) 70 Col LR 1145, 1167–1175; A Tettenborn, 'Damages for Breach of Positive Covenants' (1978) 42 Conv 366; D Harris, A Ogus and J Phillips, 'Contract Remedies and the Consumer Surplus' (1979) 95 LQR 581, 589–594, 601–603; P Marschall, 'Wilfulness: A Crucial Factor in Choosing Remedies for Breach of Contract' (1982) 24 Ariz LR 733; T Muris, 'Cost of Completion or Diminution in Market Value: the Relevance of Subjective Value' (1983) 12 J Legal Studies 379; S Rowan, 'Cost of Cure Damages and the Relevance of the Injured Promisee's Intention to Cure' [2017] CLJ 616; H Beale, *Remedies for Breach of Contract* (Sweet & Maxwell 1980) 173–177. See also the articles and book referred to above, p 189 n 10.
[60] [1977] Ch 106, at 328–338.   [61] ibid, at 333.   [62] Cf above, p 168.
[63] [1996] AC 344. See below, pp 198–199.
[64] [1977] 1 WLR 1262. See also *Mertens v Home Freeholds Co* [1921] 2 KB 526.

was almost nil. Oliver J, applying *Tito v Waddell* (*No 2*), held that the claimant was entitled to the cost of cure. He said, 'In the instant case, I am entirely satisfied that the plaintiff genuinely wants this work done, and that he intends to expend any damages awarded on carrying it out.'[65]

In the leading case of *Ruxley Electronics and Construction Ltd v Forsyth*[66] the claimant contracted to have a swimming pool built with the depth at the deep end of 7ft 6ins. When built the pool was in fact only 6ft 9ins at the deep end. Nevertheless, it was still perfectly safe for swimming and diving so that the difference in resale value of the property was not affected by the admitted breach of contract. To increase the depth of the pool to the agreed depth would cost £21,460 (nearly a third of the total price of the pool). Overturning the Court of Appeal, the House of Lords refused to award the claimant the cost of cure of £21,560; that would be unreasonable, because of the contrast with the nil difference in value. Moreover the first instance judge had found that the claimant had no intention to use the damages to rebuild the pool. But rather than awarding the claimant no damages at all for the breach the House of Lords upheld the first instance judge's award of damages of £2,500 for loss of amenity. Although there has been disagreement as to the basis of such damages,[67] it appears that they fall within the well-recognised category of damages for mental distress where the predominant (or an important) object of the contract is mental satisfaction. Mr Forsyth's diving was not as pleasurable as it would have been had the pool been of the depth contracted for.[68]

The House of Lords took account both of reasonableness and the claimant's intentions. On the facts, both pointed in the same direction: the claimant did not intend to have the pool rebuilt and it was thought unreasonable (given the disparity with the difference in value) to have done so. The same is true of *Tito v Waddell*. Where 'reasonableness' and 'intention' point in different directions, it is submitted that the 'intention' test is the more important.[69] Indeed the best approach is that the courts will award a higher cost of cure if the claimant intends to effect the cure unless effecting the cure would be contrary to the claimant's standard duty to mitigate his or her loss. So had Mr Forsyth already rebuilt the pool to the specified depth, or had he intended to do so, he should have been entitled to the cost of cure of £21,560. For a consumer to expend money to ensure that a swimming pool is of the depth he contracted for (because, for example, as on these facts, he is a tall man who wants to feel entirely comfortable when diving) should not be regarded as contrary to his duty to mitigate. In contrast, Mr Forsyth would have been acting contrary to his duty to mitigate if he had been a property speculator, who was intending to sell the property, and

---

[65] [1977] 1 WLR 1262, at 1284. In *Minscombe Properties Ltd v Sir Alfred McAlpine & Son Ltd* (1986) 279 Estates Gazette 759 an intention to effect the cure was held sufficient even though it was conditional on obtaining planning permission.

[66] [1996] AC 344.

[67] See J O'Sullivan, 'Loss and Gain at Greater Depth: The Implications of the *Ruxley* Decision' in *Failure of Contracts* (ed F Rose, Hart Publishing 1997) 1, 14–16; A Burrows and E Peel, 'Compensatory Damages: Review of Discussion' in *Commercial Remedies* (ed A Burrows and E Peel, OUP 2003) 25.

[68] This was clearly Lord Lloyd's approach: see [1996] AC 344, at 363, 373–374. Staughton LJ's judgment in the Court of Appeal sets out the judge's indication that Mr Forsyth's pleasure in diving was affected: see [1994] 1 WLR 650, at 654. See below, p 278.

[69] This derives strong support from Lord Lloyd's speech: [1996] AC 344, at 372–373. But note that one interpretation of the minority's reasoning in *Alfred McAlpine Construction Ltd v Panatown Ltd* [2001] 1 AC 518 is that intention is downplayed and a higher cost of cure is presumptively to be awarded unless that is unreasonable: see below, p 203. Note also the views at first instance, in analogous services cases, in *De Beers UK Ltd v Atos Origin IT Services UK Ltd* [2010] EWHC 3276, at [324] (per Edwards-Stuart J) and *Van der Garde BV v Force India Formula One Team* [2010] EWHC 2373 (QB), at [484] (per Stadlen J), that the cost of replacement services can be awarded if reasonable even though that cost has not been incurred and there is no intention to do so.

yet insisted on rebuilding the pool to the required depth even though that made no difference to the property's value.

It is sometimes suggested that this emphasis on the claimant's intention is unacceptable because it runs counter to the rule that the courts are not concerned with the use to which damages are put. This is a misleading objection. In assessing damages, the courts commonly have to assess the likely future costs of the claimant on the assumption that damages will cover those costs (for example, damages for the cost of care in a personal injury claim). The true rule is that, once awarded, the courts are not concerned with how the damages are used. That is, the damages are not clawed back if the claimant chooses to spend them inappropriately. But nothing that is here being said about the importance of the claimant's 'intention' in a case like *Ruxley* contradicts that 'no claw-back' rule.

Earlier cases support the 'intention' approach. For example, while the Landlord and Tenant Act 1927, s 18 lays down that, for a tenant's breach of a covenant to repair, the measure of damages is the extent by which the market value of the reversion at the end of the lease is diminished by the want of repair,[70] cases like *Smiley v Townshend*[71] and *Haviland v Long*[72] have awarded the cost of repairs that have been or are intended to be carried out, albeit under the pretence that the cost of repair represented the diminution in value. In *Haviland v Long* Denning LJ said:

> 'The measure of damage is the extent by which the market value of the reversion at the end of the lease was diminished by the want of repair. That depends on whether the repairs are going to be done or not. In cases where they have been or are going to be done the cost of repair is usually the measure of damage…'[73]

Clearly the danger of this approach, where the claimant has not yet effected cure, is that he may not use the damages as he appears to intend, and will thereby end up with a windfall. But the main alternative of awarding difference in value if the cost of cure is far higher and therefore deemed to be unreasonable or, in the language used in the US, 'economically wasteful',[74] fails to compensate a claimant fully, wherever he has contracted for a purpose not reflected in the objective market value, ie this often fails to recognise properly the 'consumer surplus'[75] such as the claimant's interest in privacy in *Radford* or pleasure in diving in *Ruxley*. For this reason the reliance on the claimant's intention seems preferable. However, it should be reiterated that where the claimant wanted the contractual performance solely to make a profit (so that the difference in value can fully compensate him) and the cost of cure is far higher than the difference in value, the standard duty to mitigate should override the claimant's intention to effect cure and the lower difference in value only should be awarded.

It finally remains to consider three further approaches that have been advocated for this situation where the cost of cure far exceeds the difference in value.

The first is to abandon the traditional compensatory analysis and to treat the cost of cure as the primary and non-compensatory measure. On this approach, while the

---

[70] This was a statutory departure from the rule at common law, as laid down in *Joyner v Weeks* [1891] 2 QB 31, that the prima facie measure of damages for the tenant's breach was the cost of repair (irrespective of any intention by the landlord to carry out the repair). *Joyner v Weeks* was relied on in the important Australian case of *Tabcorp Holdings Ltd v Bowen Investments Pty Ltd* [2009] HCA 8, (2009) 236 CLR 272 in which a commercial tenant had cynically broken its covenant not to make alterations to the property without the landlord's consent: the very much higher cost of cure was awarded ($1.38m) rather than the difference in value ($34,820) because it would be reasonable to effect the cure (and the High Court of Australia did not mention as important whether the landlord intended to effect the cure or not).
[71] [1950] 2 KB 311.   [72] [1952] 2 QB 80.   [73] ibid, at 84.
[74] Eg *Peevyhouse v Garland Coal Mining Co* 382 P 2d 109 (1962).
[75] D Harris, A Ogus, and J Phillips, 'Contract Remedies and the Consumer Surplus' (1979) 95 LQR 581.

reasonableness requirement is still relevant (although it is hard to see why) the intention of the claimant should be irrelevant. We have examined this approach, albeit to reject it, in chapter 3.[76]

The second is to award as damages a figure representing what the claimant would have reasonably accepted to release the defendant from its contractual obligation.[77] These are now referred to as 'negotiating damages'.[78] But in this context this approach was specifically rejected in *Tito v Waddell* and, after *Morris-Garner v One Step (Support) Ltd*,[79] it would appear that negotiating damages are not available in a standard breach of contract situation.

The third is to award a restitutionary remedy assessed by the cost the defendant has saved by not performing. Restitutionary remedies are discussed in chapter 19.[80] It is there explained that a restitutionary remedy for a breach of contract is very rare (even assuming that the courts recognise an 'expense saved' restitutionary measure as opposed to a stripping of profits).

(i) Breach by builder in carrying out work late

There are no authorities on the measure of damages in this situation, but presumably the owner is entitled to either the value (market selling price) of the property at the time the work should have been completed minus its value at the time the work was actually completed, or if it intended to use the property for profit, the loss of user profit in the interim period of delay.

(j) Breach by owner refusing to allow work to proceed

There are again no cases on the measure of damages in this situation.[81] However, applying the general difference in value formula (and assuming no other profitable work has or should have been taken on in the time now left free) the builder should be entitled to the contract price minus the cost avoided because of the breach. So, for example, if a house owner has contracted with a builder for the building of an extension for £2,000 payable on completion, and it will cost the builder £800 for materials and £1,000 on labour to complete the job, and the owner repudiates when the job is three-quarters of the way through, the builder will be basically entitled to damages of £1,550, ie contract price (£2,000) minus cost avoided (£200 + £250).[82]

---

[76] Above, pp 48–50.
[77] See, eg, A Farnsworth, 'Legal Remedies for Breach of Contract' (1970) 70 Columbia LR 1145, 1175, advocating the award of the reasonable fee. A variation on this is to focus on the alteration to the price that, at the time of contracting, the claimant would have reasonably accepted for the relevant contractual obligation to have been omitted: see H Beale, *Remedies for Breach of Contract* (Sweet & Maxwell 1980) 177.
[78] See below, ch 18.
[79] [2018] UKSC 20, [2018] 2 WLR 1353. It is an interesting question whether the facts of *Ruxley* would fall within the limited range of cases in which the Supreme Court in *Morris-Garner* would allow negotiating damages to be awarded.
[80] Below, pp 352–359.
[81] For an analogous example, outside the building context, see *Western Web Offset Printers Ltd v Independent Media Ltd* [1995] 37 LS Gaz R 24. In breach of contract, the owners of a newspaper cancelled an order for printing with the claimants which had 48 weeks still to run. The claimants were, reasonably, unable to find other orders to fill that gap. They were held entitled to the gross profits lost on the contract minus the costs of paper and printing which had been saved. Overhead costs were not deducted because these had not been saved.
[82] Simplistically this assumes that the builder at the time of breach has used three-quarters of the required materials and labour.

(5) Contracts for the benefit of third parties

Subject to exceptions, perhaps most importantly now the Contracts (Rights of Third Parties) Act 1999, the doctrine of privity prevents actions for breach of contract by third parties. But what is the measure of damages if the promisee chooses to sue on a contract made for another's benefit?

Applying the normal expectation principle, the claimant is entitled to be put into as good a position as *it* would have been if the contract had been performed; ie the relevant loss is the claimant's not the third party's. This has been accepted as the generally correct approach and Lord Denning's reasoning to the contrary in *Jackson v Horizon Holidays Ltd*[83] (allowing the promisee to recover the third party's loss) has been rejected.[84]

However—and again as the authorities have made clear—this does not mean (even putting to one side the possibility of specific performance[85] and looking just at damages) that the promisee is necessarily restricted to nominal damages.[86] On the contrary, one would expect that in many contracts made for a third party's benefit, the defendant's failure to benefit the third party will constitute a substantial pecuniary loss to the promisee.[87] This may be, for example, because the promisee required the defendant to pay the third party in order to pay off a debt owed by the promisee to the third party. Or the promisee may have stood to gain from the use to be made by the third party of the promised benefit. And, by analogy to the cases allowing a cost of cure in excess of a difference in value,[88] the claimant should be entitled to substantial damages (measured by the cost of cure) where it has subsequently conferred the benefit on the third party or intends to do so.[89]

Moreover, the courts have recognised an important exception to the general rule (that the promisee recovers for its own loss not the third party's).[90] Developed from *The Albazero*[91] through *Linden Gardens Trust Ltd v Lenesta Sludge Disposals Ltd*[92] to *Darlington BC v Wiltshier Northern Ltd*[93] it has been laid down that a promisee can recover a third party's loss on a contract relating to property (whether goods or land) where it was contemplated that the property in question would be transferred to the third party or where it was otherwise contemplated that loss in respect of that property would be suffered by the third party. Having recovered the damages the promisee is then bound to account for them to the third party.

The rationale of this exception is that, on the assumption that the third party cannot itself sue, the exception prevents a defeating of the parties' intentions where it was clearly anticipated that the real loss would be suffered by the third party rather than the promisee. The exception prevents damages disappearing down a 'black hole' where the promisee can sue but has suffered no loss and the third party who has suffered the loss cannot sue.

---

[83] [1975] 1 WLR 1468.

[84] *Woodar Investment Development Ltd v Wimpey Construction UK Ltd* [1980] 1 WLR 277. See also *Coulls v Bagot's Executor and Trustee Co Ltd* [1967] ALR 385, at 410–411 (per Windeyer J); *Beswick v Beswick* [1968] AC 58; *White v Jones* [1995] 2 AC 207.

[85] As was ordered in *Beswick v Beswick* [1968] AC 58: see below, p 410.

[86] See the first two cases cited above in n 84; and Lord Pearce's judgment in *Beswick v Beswick* [1968] AC 58.

[87] This leaves aside the additional possibility of mental distress damages being awarded on the ground that an important object of the contract is the claimant's mental satisfaction: below, pp 277–279. One rationalisation of *Jackson* given in *Woodar* was that the damages were purely for the claimant's mental distress.

[88] See, eg, above, pp 197–199.

[89] A Briggs, 'Privity Problems in Damages for Breach of Contract' [1981] NLJ 343.

[90] Another exception is that a 'trustee' (B) suing for breach of a contract by A to create a trust in favour of a 'beneficiary' (C), can recover substantial damages as C's loss. In *St Albans City and District Council v International Computers Ltd* [1996] 4 All ER 481, the Court of Appeal drew an analogy between a local authority, recovering contractual damages for the loss suffered by its inhabitants, and a trustee.

[91] *Albacruz v Albazero* [1977] AC 774.   [92] [1994] 1 AC 85.   [93] [1995] 1 WLR 68.

The scope of this exception (the so-called *Albazero* exception) came before the House of Lords in the controversial and difficult case of *Alfred McAlpine Construction Ltd v Panatown Ltd*.[94] Panatown entered into a construction contract with McAlpine for McAlpine to design and construct an office building on land owned by Unex Investment Properties Ltd (UIPL). The building was defective and delayed and Panatown sought damages for the cost of repair, loss of use, and delay. These losses were actually suffered by UIPL not by Panatown so that, at least on the face of it, the claim was by a promisee to recover damages suffered by a third party. It should be noted that Panatown was in the same group of companies—the Unex Group—as UIPL; and that the reason the contract was made with Panatown rather than UIPL was as a means of avoiding value added tax.

Judge Thornton QC, as official referee, had held that Panatown could recover only nominal and not substantial damages. The Court of Appeal had overturned that and, by extending the *Albazero* exception to the normal rule that a promisee can recover only its own loss, had held that Panatown was entitled to substantial damages for UIPL's loss. By a three–two majority, the House of Lords restored Judge Thornton's decision. Panatown was not here entitled to substantial damages.

The approach of the majority (Lords Clyde, Jauncey, and Browne-Wilkinson) was to accept the *Albazero* exception while holding that it did not here apply because UIPL was not merely a third party beneficiary of the main construction contract but had also been given a direct contractual right against the promisor. That is, UIPL had been given a contractual warranty comprising a duty of care deed which gave UIPL direct contractual rights against McAlpine for breach of the latter's contractual duty of care. In Lord Clyde's words, 'the express provision of the direct remedy for the third party is fatal to the application of *The Albazero* exception.'[95] And according to Lord Browne-Wilkinson, 'If the contractual arrangements between the parties in fact provide the third party with a direct remedy against the wrongdoer the whole rationale of [the *Albazero*] rule disappears.'[96]

The difficulty with this is that the direct contractual right given to UIPL was not co-extensive with the promisee's rights under the main contract. For example, liability under the collateral warranty was for negligence and not for strict liability and, moreover, there were liquidated damages and arbitration clauses in the main contract but not in the duty of care deed. It followed that the third party might be worse off under its direct collateral contract than if the promisee sued and recovered the third party's loss under the main contract. Moreover, it appears that the purpose of the collateral warranty was to replace the tort liability that would have existed pre-*Murphy v Brentwood DC*;[97] it was surely not intended to prevent Panatown, as contracting party, recovering damages on behalf of UIPL as the known first owner of the building. It is submitted, therefore, that in this case the fact that the third party had a direct contractual right was not a good ground for excluding the *Albazero* exception.

But it is not only the decision of the majority that has proved controversial. The minority judges (Lords Goff and Millett) took a different starting point. Rather than regarding there as being a valid exception to the general rule (that the promisee recovers its own loss, not the third party's) they considered that, applying what was referred to as Lord Griffiths' 'broad ground' in the *Linden Gardens* case, the promisee is recovering its own loss in these cases. The broad ground is that a promisee itself suffers loss where services are not performed for which it has contracted even though those services are for the benefit of a third

---

[94] [2001] 1 AC 518. For the author's full analysis of this case, see A Burrows, 'No Damages for a Third Party's Loss' (2001) 1 OUCLJ 107.
[95] [2001] 1 AC 518, at 532. [96] ibid, at 577. [97] [1991] 1 AC 398.

party. So here, according to the minority, Panatown was entitled to substantial damages for its own loss.

The difficulty with this is that, as Lords Clyde and Jauncey persuasively argued, it seems fictional. There is no (pecuniary) loss to the promisee (other than the reliance loss constituted by the contract price paid) where the promisor has broken its contract with the promisee to render services to a third party. To award substantial damages to the promisee would therefore overcompensate the promisee (or, to put it another way, would give the promisee a windfall). In contrast, there would be a true loss to the promisee if the promisee had paid for the 'cost of cure' or intended to do so. But on the facts Panatown had not itself carried out the repairs nor did it intend to do so. Even if one were to say that the minority's speeches are best interpreted[98] as loosening the normal requirements for the recovery of a higher 'cost of cure' (as against a lower or nil difference in value)—so that, for example, a higher 'cost of cure' will be awarded, irrespective of the claimant's intention to cure, unless the defendant satisfies the court that such an award would be unreasonable—this could not account for the fact that damages for loss of use and delay were also claimed (and regarded as recoverable by the minority) even though they would not be covered by the 'cost of cure'.

A further problem with the minority's reasoning is that, on the face of it, it produces problems of double liability. If one says that the repair cost is the promisee's own loss, irrespective of whether it incurs that cost, and that it does not need to account for those damages to the third party, then in a situation, as on the facts of this case, where the third party also has direct contractual rights, it is hard to see how one can avoid saying that both the promisee and the third party are entitled to the repair costs. Admittedly Lords Goff and Millett suggested ways round this although, with respect, neither is entirely convincing.

Although problematic,[99] the reasoning of Lords Goff and Millett cannot simply be dismissed as being merely a minority view. This is not only because of the stature of Lords Goff and Millett. It is also because Lord Browne-Wilkinson, while agreeing with the majority's decision, was prepared to assume that the 'broad ground' was correct and disagreed with Lords Goff and Millett only because he thought that the broad ground was inapplicable where, as on these facts, the third party had been given a direct contractual right against the promisor.

In summary, therefore, *McAlpine v Panatown* raises several difficult issues. It is submitted that, contrary to the reasoning of all their Lordships, the *Albazero* exception should have been applied so that Panatown should have been entitled to substantial damages for which it was bound to account to UIPL.

A final question in relation to contracts for the benefit of third parties concerns the *third party's* measure of damages where, under an exception to privity, the third party has a right to sue the promisor. For example, in relation to assignment the general rule has been that, as an assignee takes 'subject to equities', an assignee cannot recover more from the debtor than the assignor could have done had there been no assignment.[100] Say, for example, a building is sold at full value along with an assignment to the purchaser of claims in contract

---

[98] This interpretation is consistent with the approach of B Coote, 'Contract Damages, *Ruxley,* and the Performance Interest' [1997] CLJ 537 which appeared to be especially influential on Lord Goff. See above, pp 189–190.

[99] See also above, p 190. For somewhat similar (but more detailed) criticisms of the reasoning of Lords Goff and Millett, see H Unberath, *Transferred Loss* (Hart Publishing 2003) 59–82. For views supporting, or sympathetic to, the reasoning of Lords Goff and Millett, see B Coote, 'The Performance Interest, *Panatown* and the Problem of Loss' (2001) 117 LQR 81; and E McKendrick, 'The Common Law at Work: The Saga of *Alfred McAlpine Construction Ltd v Panatown Ltd*' (2003) 3 OUCLJ 145 (although McKendrick ultimately regards the 'intention to cure' as critical: see above, p 190 n 18). See also above, p 50 n 61.

[100] *Chitty on Contracts* (33rd edn, Sweet & Maxwell 2018) paras 19-075–19-077.

or tort in relation to the building. The building turns out to need repairs as a result of a breach of the builder's contract with the assignor (whether that breach is prior, or subsequent, to the sale to the assignee) or of a tort (damaging the building prior to the sale). The assignee pays for the repairs. It might be argued that the assignor in that situation has suffered no loss so that, applying the governing principle that the assignee cannot recover more than the assignor, the assignee has no substantial claim. If correct, '… the claim to damages would disappear … into some legal black hole, so that the wrongdoer escaped scot-free'.[101] Acceptance of the argument would also nullify the purpose of the governing principle which is to avoid prejudice to the debtor and not to allow the debtor to escape liability. Perhaps not surprisingly, therefore, that argument was rejected in *Offer-Hoar v Larkstore Ltd*.[102] The Court of Appeal said that, in applying the principle that the assignee cannot recover more than the assignor, one should be asking what damages the assignor could itself have recovered had there been no assignment and *had there been no transfer of the land* to the assignee. Substantial damages were, therefore, recoverable where an assignor had sold its land to an assignee along with, or prior to, the assignment of the relevant cause of action relating to the land.

In any event, the problem could normally be circumvented by the courts' recognition of the *Albazero* exception. In other words, as we have seen,[103] where a third party is, or will become, owner of the defective or damaged property, there is an exception to the general rule that a contracting party can recover damages only for its own loss and not the loss of the third party. Where the *Albazero* exception applies, the contracting party (the assignor) is entitled to substantial damages for the loss suffered by the third party (the assignee): by the same token, where the third party (the assignee) is itself suing, an award of substantial damages to the assignee does not infringe the principle that the assignee cannot recover more than the assignor.

Similar questions may arise where third parties are given rights to sue under the Contracts (Rights of Third Parties) Act 1999.[104] In contrast to assignment, the Act is not based on the third party taking over the promisee's rights. Rather both the promisee and the third party are regarded as having separate rights to sue and as suffering separate losses. But to avoid injustice to the promisor one could not always simply award the third party damages for its own loss without taking into account the position as between the promisor and the promisee. In particular, it may be unfair to the promisor on an unexecuted contract to award the third party its own full loss without taking into account the promisee's own saved cost of performance. It would appear, therefore, that in construing the Contracts (Rights of Third Parties) Act 1999, s 1(5),[105] the third party's damages should be assessed in an analogous, but not necessarily identical, way to those of the promisee.

---

[101] *GUS Property Management Ltd v Littlewoods Mail Order Stores Ltd* 1982 SLT 533, at 538 (per Lord Keith).
[102] [2006] EWCA Civ 1079, [2006] 1 WLR 2926. *Offer-Hoar v Larkstore Ltd* was applied in *Landfast (Anglia) Ltd v Cameron Taylor One Ltd* [2008] EWHC 343 (TCC).
[103] Above, p 201.
[104] See R Stevens, 'The Contracts (Rights of Third Parties) Act 1999' (2004) 120 LQR 292, 301–302.
[105] Contracts (Rights of Third Parties) Act 1999, s 1(5), reads: 'For the purpose of exercising his right to enforce a term of the contract, there shall be available to the third party any remedy that would have been available to him in an action for breach of contract if he had been a party to the contract (and the rules relating to damages, injunctions, specific performance and other relief shall apply accordingly).'

2. Breach of contract—additional pecuniary loss

To put the claimant into as good a position as if the contract had been performed, all other pecuniary loss caused to the claimant by the defendant's breach and not ruled out by limiting principles, such as remoteness and the duty to mitigate, must be added to the basic measures of pecuniary loss so far discussed (unless already covered by the basic measure).

Loss of user profit may be an additional pecuniary loss: for example, where the claimant is basically awarded the costs of replacing and adapting goods, it is also entitled to any interim loss of user profit. Additional pecuniary loss may also comprise—albeit fairly rarely—damage to or destruction of the claimant's property. So, for example, in *Harbutt's Plasticine Ltd v Wayne Tank and Pump Co Ltd*[106] the defendant's breach of contract in installing an unsuitable heating system and insulating the pipes with unsafe material led to the claimant's factory burning down. Such damage to property is directly analogous to tortious damage to property and it has therefore been considered preferable to discuss the few contract cases in that tort subsection.[107]

However, the commonest form of additional pecuniary loss is expenses caused by the breach, other than those that have been awarded within a cost of cure measure.[108] These expenses are referred to in the US Uniform Commercial Code as giving rise to 'incidental damages'. By the Uniform Commercial Code, s 2-710 a seller's incidental damages include 'any commercially reasonable charges, expenses or commissions incurred in stopping delivery, in the transportation, care and custody of the goods after the buyer's breach, in connection with return or resale of the goods or otherwise resulting from the breach'. By the Uniform Commercial Code, s 2-715 a buyer's incidental damages include '… expenses reasonably incurred in inspection, receipt, transportation and care and custody of goods rightfully rejected, any commercially reasonable charges, expenses or commissions in connection with effecting cover and any other reasonable expense incident to the delay or other breach'. Two common examples following a seller's breach are compensation paid to a sub-buyer and the costs incurred in defending a sub-buyer's claim. *Henry Kendall & Sons v William Lillico & Sons Ltd*[109] provides an example of the former. The buyer bought groundnut extractions from the seller, which were then used for making a poultry food, that the buyer sold to a game farm. The groundnut extractions were contaminated and many of the game farm's poultry died or grew up stunted. The buyer was liable to pay damages to the game farm but it successfully claimed compensation in respect of those damages from the seller. An example of the latter is the award in *Hammond & Co v Bussey*.[110] There the claimants bought coal from the defendants and resold it with the same description to X who used it for steamships. The defendants knew that it was the claimants' business to supply coal to steamships. The coal delivered by the defendants was, however, not of the

---

[106] [1970] 1 QB 447. See also *Bacon v Cooper (Metals) Ltd* [1982] 1 All ER 397.
[107] Below, pp 206–218.
[108] One can regard expenses *wasted* because of breach as an additional loss. But in directly protecting the expectation interest (as opposed to the reliance interest—above, ch 6) such expenses are only recoverable if the basic measure has been calculated according to net rather than gross difference in value. Since the basic measure can always therefore take wasted expenses into account it seems unnecessarily complex to consider them separately here. But for claims framed in this way, see *Hydraulic Engineering Co Ltd v McHaffie, Goslett & Co* (1878) 4 QBD 670; *Cullinane v British Rema Manufacturing Co Ltd* [1954] 1 QB 292.
[109] [1969] 2 AC 31. See also *Re Hall Ltd and Pim* (1928) 139 LT 50. As made clear in, eg, *Total Liban SA v Vitol Energy SA* [2001] QB 643 (where defective gasoline was being sold to, and sub-sold by, the claimant) the seller is liable in damages even before the buyer has paid compensation to the sub-buyer: the incurring of a legal liability (to the sub-buyer) is itself a compensatable loss.
[110] (1887) 20 QBD 79. See also *Agius v Great Western Colliery Co* [1899] 1 QB 413.

warranted quality. The defendants admitted responsibility in respect of the claimants' liability to pay damages to X, but disputed that they should also have to pay damages for the claimants' legal costs in defending X's action against the claimants. The Court of Appeal held, however, that the defendants were liable to pay such damages, because not only were those costs not too remote, but also the claimants had not failed in their duty to mitigate by defending X's action, since the defect in the coal was discoverable only by X's using the coal and not by mere inspection, and hence there was some doubt as to X's claim.

3. Torts—damage to property, including destruction

This section is concerned with where the defendant's tort (such as trespass to land or goods, negligence, nuisance, or conversion)[111] has caused damage to the claimant's existing property, whether real or personal. Cases where damage to property is an additional pecuniary loss consequent on a breach of contract will also be considered.[112] Whether for torts or breach of contract, the general compensatory aims dictate that the claimant should be put into as good a position as if its property had not been damaged. This was emphasised in relation to tortious damage to a ship in *The Liesbosch*,[113] where Lord Wright said:

> '... the owners of the vessel are entitled to what is called *restitutio in integrum* which means that they should recover such sum as will replace them, as far as can be done by compensation in money, in the same position as if the loss had not been inflicted on them ...'[114]

A basic choice is generally presented between awarding diminution in value of the property or cost of cure. The former compensates the claimant for its loss of financial advantage in being deprived of its property, while the latter compensates for the cost of putting the claimant into as good a position as if its property had not been damaged. This choice is analogous to that presented in assessing compensation for tortious interference with goods by misappropriation or loss and in assessing basic pecuniary loss for breach of contract (the damaged property corresponds to a deprivation of the contractual benefit). The decision therefore similarly rests on factors such as the claimant's duty to mitigate, whether it intends to cure, and for what purpose it owned the property.

The details of the law are best examined by dividing between damage to real and personal property. Separate consideration will also be afforded to the so-called 'betterment' question.

(1) Damage to real property

The diminution in value of real property is normally assessed by taking the difference between the market selling price of the damaged and undamaged property, while the cost of cure normally comprises the cost of repair or, as a more appropriate term where a building has been destroyed, the cost of reinstatement. The cost of cure might alternatively comprise the market cost of buying or building replacement property elsewhere, minus the selling value of the claimant's damaged property, but in view of the nature of real property, this is rarely a realistic option in practice.[115]

---

[111] In respect of goods the relevant torts come within the Torts (Interference with Goods) Act 1977. Liability under the Consumer Protection Act 1987, Pt I extends, under s 5, to property damage subject to restrictions (eg that the property is for private use and that the damages exceed £275).
[112] Above, p 205.   [113] [1933] AC 449.   [114] ibid, at 459.
[115] An exception, on unusual facts, was *Ward v Cannock Chase District Council* [1985] 3 All ER 537, at 561–563. See also *Dominion Mosaics and Tile Co Ltd v Trafalgar Trucking Co Ltd* [1990] 2 All ER 246.

A useful dictum on the choice between diminution in value and cost of cure is Donaldson LJ's in *Dodd Properties v Canterbury City Council*,[116] a case where the claimant's building had been damaged by the defendants' pile-driving. In an action for negligence and nuisance, the defendants conceded that they were liable for the cost of repairs. Donaldson LJ, however, took the opportunity to explain the law on damages for property damage. Having said that there are two possible measures he went on:

'The first is to take the capital value of the property in an undamaged state and to compare it with its value in a damaged state. The second is to take the cost of repair or reinstatement. Which is appropriate will depend on a number of factors, such as the plaintiff's future intentions as to the use of the property and the reasonableness of those intentions. If he reasonably intends to sell the property in its damaged state, clearly the diminution in capital value is the true measure of damages. If he reasonably intends to continue to occupy it and to repair the damage, clearly the cost of repairs is the true measure. And there may be in-between situations.'[117]

There have been several cases in which a decision between the two measures has had to be made. In *Hollebone v Midhurst and Fernhurst Builders Ltd*[118] the claimant's dwelling house had been damaged by fire due to the admitted negligence of the defendant. The claimant was awarded the cost of repairs (£18,991 5s 8d) rather than the difference between the value of the house in its undamaged and damaged state (£14,850). This was an undoubtedly correct decision as the claimant had already carried out the repairs and it was reasonable for him to have done so given that he owned the house for living in. Similarly in *Harbutt's Plasticine Ltd v Wayne Tank and Pump Co Ltd*,[119] the claimants' factory was burnt down as a result of the defendant's breach of contract. The claimants were awarded the cost of building and equipping a new factory (£146,581) rather than the diminution in value (£116,785). Again the claimants had already had the factory rebuilt and, given that the factory was owned for business, it was not only reasonable to do so but, as stressed by the Court of Appeal, necessary in order to keep their business going.

The cost of reinstatement was also preferred, though subject to an important qualification, in *Ward v Cannock Chase District Council*.[120] Here the defendant council's negligence in failing to maintain their houses in a particular terrace had led, through the activities of vandals, to the destruction of the claimant's two houses where he had been living with his large family. Scott J held that the cost of reinstatement should be awarded, provided that the claimant could obtain planning permission to rebuild the houses. If not, and if permission was also refused to convert another of the claimant's houses nearby,[121] he should instead be awarded the diminution in value of the properties.

Again in *Dominion Mosaics and Tile Co Ltd v Trafalgar Trucking Co Ltd*,[122] in which the claimants' business premises had been burnt down because of the defendants' negligence, the Court of Appeal followed *Harbutt's Plasticine* and awarded a cost of cure measure (albeit the cost of leasing property elsewhere rather than the cost of reinstatement). Salient points were that the claimants had leased other property, that it was reasonable for them to do so to mitigate their loss of use, and that the cost of the lease was significantly less than the cost

---

[116] [1980] 1 WLR 433. [117] ibid, at 456–457.
[118] [1968] 1 Lloyd's Rep 38. See also *Heath v Keys*, *The Times*, 28 May 1984. Analogously, an owner of land is entitled to damages for the cost of abating a nuisance: *Delaware Mansions Ltd v Westminster City Council* [2001] UKHL 55, [2001] 1 AC 321; *Abbahall Ltd v Smee* [2002] EWCA Civ 1831, [2003] 1 WLR 1472.
[119] [1970] 1 QB 447. [120] [1985] 3 All ER 537.
[121] Above, n 115. The issue was being tried as a preliminary question of law: had Scott J been awarding damages he could not have left open the question of planning permission because of the rule that damages must be awarded unconditionally (above, p 168).
[122] [1990] 2 All ER 246.

of rebuilding. The claimants were awarded £390,000, as the cost of the lease, even though the diminution in the value of the site was estimated at merely £60,000.

Contrasting with those four decisions is *CR Taylor (Wholesale) Ltd v Hepworths Ltd*,[123] where the claimants' disused billiard hall was destroyed by fire. The cost of reinstating it was agreed at £28,957. The diminution in value of the site was notionally £2,500, although in the event of sale for redevelopment this would be completely offset by the beneficial effect of the fire in saving the expense of clearing the site. May J held that the diminution in value measure should here be preferred (and hence no damages were awarded under this head). This was because the site and billiard hall were owned by the claimants as an investment, which in time would be sold off for redevelopment. The claimants had no intention, prior or subsequent to the fire, of rebuilding the billiard hall.

A further issue, that arose at first instance in the *Dodd Properties* case,[124] is what exactly is meant by repair (or reinstatement). Cantley J said:

> 'The plaintiffs are entitled to the reasonable cost of doing reasonable work of restoration and repair. They are, of course, not bound to accept a shoddy job or put up with an inferior building for the sake of saving the defendants expense. But I do not consider that they are entitled to insist on complete and meticulous restoration when a reasonable building owner would be content with the less extensive work which produces a result which does not diminish to any or any significant extent the appearance, life or utility of the building, and when there is also a vast difference in the cost of such work and the cost of meticulous restoration.'[125]

Applying this, the lower cost of non-meticulous repair was awarded and there was no appeal against this. So, in other words, while generally repair or reinstatement means to produce as close a restoration to the original condition as is reasonably possible, it will mean a lesser restoration where this will serve the claimant's purposes just as well and will cost far less.

What happens where repairs (or reinstatement) have been carried out but a third party has paid for them? This raises the issue of how compensating advantages are dealt with.[126] In line with the general approach adopted in personal injury cases, the coherent position is that, assuming the compensating advantage is sufficiently direct, it should prima facie be deducted. But there are two well-recognised exceptions to this, namely benevolence and insurance.[127] The issue arose in the context of tortious damage to real property in *Jones v Stroud BC*.[128] The cost of repairs to a house, consequent on a local authority's negligent inspection, was awarded to the claimant even though he had not paid for the repairs. Rather the repairs had been paid for by the claimant's company which had not invoiced him for them. Neill LJ made a sweeping statement to the effect that who paid for the repairs was irrelevant.[129] With respect, that is too wide. But the actual decision may have been justified on the ground that the third party here was in effect acting out of benevolence in not invoicing the claimant and therefore fell within one of the two recognised exceptions to deduction. This was in line with Neill LJ's reliance on the statement in *The Endeavour*,[130] a damaged ship case, where it was said, 'If somebody out of kindness were to repair the injury and make no charge for it, the wrongdoer would not be entitled to refuse to pay as part of the damages the cost of the repairs to the owner.'

---

[123] [1977] 1 WLR 659. See also *Jones v Gooday* (1841) 8 M & W 146; *Moss v Christchurch RDC* [1925] 2 KB 750; *Munnelly v Calcon Ltd* [1978] IR 387; *Farmer Giles Ltd v Wessex Water Authority* [1988] 2 EGLR 189.
[124] [1980] 1 WLR 433. [125] ibid, at 441. [126] See, generally, above, ch 8.
[127] See above, pp 158–160. [128] [1986] 1 WLR 1141. See also below, pp 213–214.
[129] ibid, at 1150–1151. [130] (1890) 6 Asp MC 511, at 512.

Finally, in addition to the diminution in value or cost of cure, all other pecuniary losses resulting from the property damage should be recoverable subject to the usual limiting principles, such as remoteness and mitigation. So, for example, in *Grosvenor Hotel Co v Hamilton*,[131] the claimants' expenses in moving their hotel business from the damaged property were recovered; in the *Dodd Properties* case[132] the claimants were awarded the potential loss of profits on their car business for the time during which the repairs would be carried out; and in *Network Rail Infrastructure Ltd v Conarken Group Ltd*[133] the claimant was awarded damages not only for the cost of repairing its rail tracks damaged by the defendants' negligent driving but also the payments it became legally liable to make under contracts with the train-operating companies who could not use the tracks.

(2) Damage to goods

As in relation to damage to real property there is a basic choice between, on the one hand, awarding the diminution in value of the property—normally the market selling price of the goods as undamaged minus, if the goods are still in existence, their market selling price as damaged—and, on the other hand, the cost of cure, comprising the cost of replacing or, if possible, repairing the goods.[134]

But damage to goods does differ from damage to land or buildings in that here the cost of replacement is often a realistic cost of cure measure. Indeed it is convenient to distinguish between the destruction of goods (including 'constructive total loss') where the cost of replacement *is* the cost of cure measure, repair being out of the question, and mere damage to goods, where both cost of replacement and cost of repair are potential cost of cure measures. Although most of the cases concern ships, it has been said on several occasions that the same principles of assessment apply to all goods.[135]

(a) Destruction of goods

Although the measure of damages chosen has sometimes been obscured by the courts' ambiguous references to damages being assessed according to the value of the chattel, early cases generally seemed to prefer the market selling price (ie diminution in value), while more modern cases have generally preferred the market replacement cost (ie cost of cure). In either case, if anything is left of the chattel, its salvage value (ie market selling price in its present condition) must be deducted.[136]

Illustrative of the earlier cases is *The Clyde*,[137] in which the market selling price was applied. In Dr Lushington's words, 'It is the market price which the Court looks to, and nothing else, as the value of the property. It is an old saying, "the worth of a thing is the price it will bring."'[138] But for goods owned for use rather than sale (such as ships) this is generally a less appropriate measure than the market replacement cost, which was awarded in *The Liesbosch*.[139] There the claimants were using their dredger 'The Liesbosch' to carry out

---

[131] [1894] 2 QB 836. [132] [1980] 1 All ER 928.
[133] [2011] EWCA Civ 644, [2012] 1 All ER (Comm) 692. See also *Rust v Victoria Graving Dock Co* (1887) 36 Ch D 113; *Ehmler v Hall* [1993] 1 EGLR 137.
[134] For what is meant by replacement or repair, see above, p 208.
[135] Eg *The Hebridean Coast* [1961] AC 545, at 562 (per Devlin LJ).
[136] See, eg, *The Fortunity* [1961] 1 WLR 351. [137] (1856) Sw 23. [138] ibid, at 25.
[139] [1933] AC 449. See also *Clyde Navigation Trustees v Bowring SS* (1929) 34 Ll L Rep 319; *Jones v Port of London Authority* [1954] 1 Lloyd's Rep 489; *Dominion Mosaics and Tile Co Ltd v Trafalgar Trucking Co Ltd* [1990] 2 All ER 246 (paternoster machines).

work at Patras harbour, when it was sunk owing to the defendants' negligence. The claimants were awarded, inter alia, the market price of a replacement dredger, and the costs of adapting it for their use and of transporting it to Patras.

It is now clear, however, that whatever has been the historical preference, the choice between the market selling price and the market replacement cost turns, in relation to the tortious destruction of goods, on the same factors that we have looked at in relation to, for example, damage to real property and breach of a building contract. Relevant factors therefore include the claimant's duty to mitigate (and hence the reasonableness of a claim for the higher sum), whether the claimant intends to replace the goods, and for what purpose the goods were owned.

So in *The Maersk Colombo*,[140] where the claimants' crane had been demolished by the defendants' negligence, it was decided by the Court of Appeal that the claimants were entitled as damages to the resale value of the crane (£665,000) and not its replacement value (£2,359,484). The replacement value was so much higher because a second-hand crane would have had to be modified in the US and transported from there to Southampton. The crucial factor in determining that that higher sum should not be awarded was that the claimants, prior to the accident, had already ordered a larger crane to replace the one demolished and therefore had no intention, after the accident, of buying another crane to replace the demolished one. In an excellent leading judgment, Clarke LJ analysed the main contract and tort cases on the question of difference in value or cost of care and explained that, in deciding between them, the important factors included reasonableness and intention. In rejecting an argument that there are distinct rules applying to tortious destruction of goods, he said, 'In my opinion a similar approach applies to the measure of damages for the tortious destruction of chattels as it applies to the measure of damages for both the tortious destruction of real property and for breach of contract in circumstances such as those in *Ruxley*.'[141]

Where damages are based on the chattel's market selling price at the time of destruction, additional damages for loss of use should not be recoverable: this theory of assessment rests on the assumption that the claimant could have otherwise sold his chattel at the time of destruction and clearly he could not both have sold it and used it. As Lord Wright said in *The Liesbosch*:

> 'The value of prospective freights cannot simply be added to the market value but ought to be taken into account in order to ascertain the total value for purposes of assessing the damage, since if it is merely added to the market value of a free ship, the owner will be getting pro tanto his damages twice over. The vessel cannot be earning in the open market, while fulfilling the pending charter or charters.'[142]

However, these principles have not always been correctly adhered to and in some cases loss of profit on the voyage the ship was on,[143] or even on all other engagements already

---

[140] [2001] EWCA Civ 717, [2001] 2 Lloyd's Rep 275. This was followed in *Ali Reza-Delta Transport Co Ltd v United Arab Shipping Co* [2003] EWCA Civ 86, [2003] 2 Lloyd's Rep 450: damages were based on the market selling price (of similar goods in Saudi Arabia where they had been tortiously destroyed) rather than the replacement costs; there was no evidence that the claimants had replaced, or would replace, the destroyed goods. In *Aerospace Publishing Ltd v Thames Water Utilities* [2007] EWCA Civ 3, [2007] NPC 5, the principles in *The Maersk Colombo* were applied, albeit that a different conclusion was reached, in holding that, following the destruction of a photographic archive by flood water, damages should be awarded based on the cost of reinstating the archive rather than its diminution in value.
[141] [2001] EWCA Civ 717, [2001] 2 Lloyd's Rep 275, at [43].   [142] [1933] AC 449, at 464.
[143] *The Llanover* [1947] P 80.

fixed,[144] has been awarded in addition to the market selling price at the date of the destruction.

On the other hand, where damages are based on the cost of replacement, damages for loss of use during the period until use could be made of the replacement are and should be recoverable subject to the usual limiting principles. As Street wrote, 'The rationale of … claims for loss of profits is that they are allowable for that period which would elapse before a replacement is procurable.'[145] So in *The Liesbosch*[146] the House of Lords held that additional damages should be awarded for the loss of user profit for the period between the dredger's sinking and the time at which the substitute dredger could reasonably have been available for use in Patras. In Lord Wright's words, 'The true rule seems to be that the measure of damages in such cases is the value of the ship to her owner as a going concern at the time and place of loss.'[147] He then regarded the combination of replacement costs and loss of user profit, as opposed to the market selling price, as representing that value.

The other most obvious consequential losses that are prima facie recoverable are the reasonable hiring charges of a substitute chattel in the interim period before the replacement chattel can be used.[148] These costs will often mitigate any loss of use and, indeed, where they ought to have been incurred to mitigate such loss of use, they will presumably be awarded instead of damages for loss of use.

(b) Mere damage to goods

(i) Replacement or repair costs?

No case has been traced in which diminution in value (ie market selling price as undamaged minus market selling price as damaged) has here been awarded although if the goods were owned for sale rather than use and the repair or replacement costs are a lot higher, the diminution in selling price should be the preferred measure.[149]

Under the cost of cure, there is a decision to be made here between awarding the replacement cost (minus the market selling price of the damaged chattel) and the cost of repairs.[150] Two pairs of cases may be contrasted to illustrate the courts' approach.

In *O'Grady v Westminster Scaffolding Ltd*,[151] the claimant's MG car was damaged by the defendant's admitted negligence. The claimant repaired the car at a cost of £253 and also incurred costs of about £208 in hiring a substitute car in the interim. The defendant argued that the claimant should have written the car off and replaced it which, according to the defendant, would have cost him about £145, ie market price of replacement (£180) minus scrap value of MG (£35). But Edmund Davies J held that the claimant was entitled to damages based on the cost of repair (plus hiring charges) because he had acted reasonably in

---

[144] *The Philadelphia* [1917] P 101; *The Fortunity* [1961] 1 WLR 351 (cf A Hudson, 'Money Claims for Misuse of Chattels' in *Interests in Goods* (eds N Palmer and E McKendrick, 2nd edn, LLP 1998) 839, fn 16 who appears to construe the latter case as having awarded the cost of replacement rather than the market selling price).
[145] H Street, *Principles of the Law of Damages* (Sweet & Maxwell 1962) 195. See, generally, J Knott, 'Loss of Profit Caused by the Total Loss of a Ship: its Relationship to Value and Interest' [1993] LMCLQ 502.
[146] [1933] AC 449.   [147] ibid, at 464.
[148] But such costs were held not recoverable in *The Liesbosch* because they flowed from impecuniosity—see above, pp 144–146. See also *Moore v DER Ltd* [1971] 3 All ER 517, where no replacement cost was being awarded.
[149] At first sight, it might be thought that *Derby Resources AG v Blue Corinth Marine Co Ltd, The Athenian Harmony* [1998] 2 Lloyd's Rep 410 is such an example. But on closer inspection—see especially at 417, 419—the market value of sound (ie uncontaminated) kerosene was regarded as the market buying price of such kerosene so that the damages (against a carrier for negligent damage to goods) were assessed using a replacement cost (ie cost of cure) measure.
[150] For what is meant by replacement or repair, see above, p 208.   [151] [1962] 2 Lloyd's Rep 238.

carrying out the repairs; this was particularly because the car, lovingly named 'Hortensia' by the claimant, was his pride and joy, which he had spent a lot of time and effort maintaining and it could not really be replaced.

On the other hand in *Darbishire v Warran*[152] the claimant, who had repaired his car for £192 (plus hiring charges) preferring to keep a car he knew to be reliable and suitable for his needs, was restricted to damages based on the market cost of a replacement, namely £85 (plus hiring charges). The Court of Appeal held that the claimant had failed to take reasonable steps to mitigate his loss by buying a replacement and *O'Grady v Westminster Scaffolding* was distinguished on the ground that there, unlike here, the car in question was unique.

Another contrasting pair of cases concerns damaged ships. In *Italian State Rlys v Minnehaha*[153] the claimants' ship was damaged. They had it repaired for about £37,000 (and had also incurred some relatively minor consequential expenses during the repairing period). It was decided that the value of the ship when repaired, which it was assumed equalled the market cost of replacement, was £53,000. Its value, that is its market selling price, in its damaged condition had been £20,000. The Court of Appeal held that the claimants were only entitled to the replacement cost minus market selling price, which equalled £33,000. It had been unreasonable to incur the greater expense of repair, for the claimants had failed to establish that there was anything particularly special about the ship. Instead they should have sold it off in its damaged state. Lord Sterndale MR said, '... unless there is some circumstance to justify him the shipowner does not act reasonably in repairing the ship if the repaired value is very much less than the cost of repairing her.'[154]

In contrast in *Algeiba v Australind*,[155] the cost of repairing the ship was awarded which, including lost profits during repair, amounted to £31,000. This was so even though this exceeded the cost of a replacement (£30,000) minus the selling price as damaged (£6,000), amounting to £24,000. It was held to have been reasonable to repair because it was not easy to obtain a replacement at that time and the ship was particularly well equipped for the claimant's work.

These pairs of cases show that the duty to mitigate dictates that whichever is the cheaper of the cost of repair and the replacement cost (also taking into account consequential loss) will generally be preferred. However, if the claimant has chosen to repair and there is good reason for him to have done so—because of the special value to him of the chattel and the difficulty of replacing it—the repair cost will be awarded even if well in excess of the replacement cost. There must, however, be some limit to the discrepancy between repair and replacement cost that will be tolerated. Admittedly, in *O'Grady v Westminster Scaffolding* the cost of repairs and consequential loss was three times the replacement cost, but this was still only a matter of hundreds and not thousands of pounds.

In the light of the above cases *The London Corpn*,[156] which is often cited for there being a general rule that the cost of repairs will be awarded, must be approached with caution. There the damaged ship had been sold off and not repaired yet the cost of repairs was awarded. Greer LJ said, 'Prima facie, the damage occasioned to a vessel is the cost of repairs.'[157] But assuming that a replacement had been bought, or was intended to be, the measure should have been the replacement cost, unless the cost of repairs was cheaper.

In *Burdis v Livsey*[158] the question at issue was whether damages for the cost of repairs to a car, damaged by the defendant's negligence, should be awarded where the claimant had

---

[152] [1963] 1 WLR 1067.　[153] (1921) 6 Ll L Rep 12.　[154] ibid, at 13.
[155] (1921) 8 Ll L Rep 210.　[156] [1935] P 70.　[157] ibid, at 77.
[158] [2002] EWCA Civ 510, [2003] QB 36.

not itself incurred those costs because they had been paid for under what, it transpired, was an unenforceable consumer credit agreement. In other words, could the claimant recover damages for the cost of repairs where a third party had paid for those repairs (and had done so neither benevolently nor in accordance with a valid insurance contract which are the two recognised exceptions to the general principle that compensating advantages are deducted)? The Court of Appeal held that the claimant was entitled to recover damages for the cost of repairs. *Jones v Stroud District Council*,[159] where the cost of repairing real property was awarded, even though it had been paid for by a third party, was applied; and it was thought that one could distinguish the decisions of the House of Lords in *Dimond v Lovell*,[160] where damages for hire costs that would not be incurred were held irrecoverable, and *Hunt v Severs*,[161] where the costs of nursing services were only recoverable as a loss to the third party who provided them. This was said to be because those cases dealt with consequential or potential future loss whereas one was here concerned with direct loss. That is, the damage to the car, causing a diminution in value, was a direct loss which was measured by the cost of repairs.

It is submitted, with respect, that this reasoning and decision are incorrect. The Court of Appeal invoked a novel approach to the long-debated issue of how to deal with compensating advantages which has no support in authority or principle or policy (ie that there is a different treatment of compensating advantages dependent on whether one is concerned with direct loss or consequential loss).[162] In truth the hire costs in *Dimond v Lovell* could not be validly distinguished and that House of Lords' decision should have directly dictated the deduction of the repair costs in this case.

Furthermore, it was misleading to say, as the Court of Appeal said, that the claimant suffers a diminution in value when her car is damaged and that the prima facie measure of damages for that diminution is the cost of repairs. The true approach is that the cause of action accrues when the claimant's car is damaged. The claimant's pecuniary loss as a consequence of that damage may comprise either the diminution in value of her car (ie the difference in its value before and after the damage) or the cost of repairs (or indeed the cost of replacement minus the car's present value). In addition to the cost of repairs the claimant may be entitled to compensation for loss of use or hire charges incurred while the damaged car is awaiting repair or being repaired. The distinction between the difference in value measure and the cost of repair/replacement measure is to be found throughout the law of damages (whether one is dealing with personal or real property and indeed whether the claim is in contract or tort). The central concepts in deciding whether the courts will award the difference in value or the cost of repair are whether the claimant has had the repairs carried out—or whether the claimant intends to do so—and reasonableness. But where it is known that the claimant has not, and will not, incur the costs of repair (or has not, and will not, incur hire charges) those costs do not constitute a loss to the claimant. It is a fiction to pretend that the claimant has suffered such a loss.

On the facts of the case, the payment by the third party of the repair costs was not too indirect—on the contrary, it was in direct response to the tort—and did not fall within the benevolence and insurance exceptions to the deduction of compensating advantages. This was because the third party was not acting out of benevolence; and it paid for the repairs under an unenforceable consumer credit agreement with the claimant (and not a valid insurance contract). Moreover, as Gray J stressed at first instance, there was no good specific

---

[159] [1986] 1 WLR 1141. See above, p 208.
[160] [2002] 1 AC 384. See below, p 215.
[161] [1994] 2 AC 350. See below, pp 240–241.
[162] For the approach to compensating advantages generally, see above, ch 8.

policy reason to ignore the compensating advantage provided by the third party in this situation. Finally, as we have seen,[163] while the wide reasoning in *Jones v Stroud DC* cannot be supported, the actual decision may have been correct because the facts may have fallen within the well-established benevolence exception to non-deduction: the claimant's own company had incurred the expense but had not invoiced him for it.

Despite these criticisms, there was subsequent support in *Coles v Hetherton*[164] for the approach taken in *Burdis*. It was there held that, where it is reasonable to repair a damaged car, a claimant is entitled to damages for the reasonable cost of repairing the car even though the actual cost of the repairs, whether incurred by the claimant or his insurer, are lower. The Court of Appeal's reasoning was that the reasonable cost of repair represents the diminution in value of the car; and that while the duty to mitigate applies to a consequential loss, it is irrelevant to that direct loss (the diminution in the value of the car), which is suffered as soon as the car is damaged and cannot be mitigated. Again this can be criticised and is controversial because the decision appears to be awarding damages to the claimant for more than the loss suffered.

(ii) Additional loss, including loss of use?

In addition to the cost of repair or replacement, all other pecuniary losses resulting from the property damage are recoverable, subject to the usual limiting principles like remoteness and mitigation. For example, in *Aerospace Publishing Ltd v Thames Water Utilities Ltd*,[165] where the claimant's archive had been damaged by flooding caused by the defendant's breach of statutory duty, the claimant was held able to recover for payments made to staff to deal with the consequences of the flood in addition to the cost of reinstatement of the archive. And, as already briefly mentioned, in *O'Grady v Westminster Scaffolding Ltd*,[166] damages were awarded for the charges of hiring a car while the claimant's car was being repaired, as they were in *Darbishire v Warran*[167]—although this was presumably on the basis that the claimant would have had to incur such charges even if he had bought a replacement.

But are reasonable hiring charges, during the period of repair, recoverable by the claimant even where a hire car has been supplied without any cost to the claimant? For example, the car may have been supplied by the claimant's insurers under an unenforceable insurance contract or by a company providing replacement cars under what transpire to be unenforceable consumer credit agreements. In these situations, the claimant has no legal liability to pay for the hire car. Initially the view taken in *McAll v Brooks*[168] was that the reasonable hiring costs were still recoverable. Just as in the personal injury case of *Donnelly v Joyce*[169] the claimant could recover the costs of nursing care even though gratuitously rendered by a third party, so the claimant could recover the costs of hire even though those costs were borne by a third party. But that approach was departed from by the House of Lords in

---

[163] Above, p 208.   [164] [2013] EWCA Civ 1704, [2015] 1 WLR 160.
[165] [2007] EWCA Civ 3, [2007] NPC 5.
[166] [1962] 2 Lloyd's Rep 238. See also *Giles v Thompson* [1994] 1 AC 142 (claimant able to recover because legally liable to pay hire costs albeit not yet paid). In *Dimond v Lovell* [2002] 1 AC 384, at 402–403 there were obiter dicta to the effect that, if the hiring charges had been recoverable (it was decided that they were not) one should deduct the cost of additional services, over and above the hiring of the car, that were provided as part of the hiring package. In other words, the 'spot rate' of hire and not the higher costs of an accident-hire scheme were recoverable. But in *Lagden v O'Connor* [2003] UKHL 64, [2004] 1 AC 1067, it was decided that an impecunious claimant could recover those higher costs: see above, p 146. In *Burdis v Livsey* [2002] EWCA Civ 510, [2003] QB 36, it was clarified that the claimant could only recover for the costs of hiring (a Vauxhall Vectra) actually incurred even though higher hire charges (for a replacement sports car) might reasonably have been incurred. For the position where, without the claimant being at fault, the period of hiring is extended see above, p 130 n 250.
[167] [1963] 1 WLR 1067.   [168] [1984] RTR 99.   [169] [1974] QB 454. See below, p 240.

Dimond v Lovell.¹⁷⁰ The earlier approach was said to be based on an approach in personal injury cases that had been departed from in *Hunt v Severs*¹⁷¹ where the House of Lords recognised that the loss was the third party's and not the claimant's. To ignore the fact that the costs were being borne by the third party and not the claimant could only be justified if there was an exception to the deduction of compensating advantages. But neither of the well-recognised exceptions (of benevolence or insurance) applied here. In Lord Hoffmann's words, 'The only way … in which Mrs Dimond could recover damages for the notional cost of hiring a car which she actually had for free is if your Lordships were willing to create another exception to the rule against double recovery. I can see no basis for doing so.'¹⁷² As we have seen, it is difficult to understand how the later decision of the Court of Appeal in *Burdis v Livsey*¹⁷³ (dealing with repair, rather than hire, costs) can be reconciled with their Lordships' decision in *Dimond v Lovell*.

In contrast to *Dimond v Lovell*, in *Bee v Jensen*¹⁷⁴ hire costs incurred *by the claimant's insurer*¹⁷⁵ were held recoverable by the claimant from the tortfeasor because they were reasonable costs for a car that had been reasonably hired. This was so even though some of those costs included payments which went beyond the strict hire costs and included a sum paid by the hiring company to an affiliated company of the insurer. In another of the 'credit hire' cases, *Stevens v Equity Syndicate Management Ltd*,¹⁷⁶ it was held that a claimant who is not impecunious is entitled only to the basic hire rate (ie the locally available rate for cars in the same group as the claimant's car) and not a higher rate, which confers additional benefits, charged by a credit hire company.

Loss of user profit for the period while the goods are being repaired or replaced is also recoverable.¹⁷⁷ But if the chattel would have been operating at a loss during that period no such damages should be awarded.¹⁷⁸

As regards the duty to mitigate, it was held in *Beechwood Birmingham Ltd v Hoyer Group UK Ltd*¹⁷⁹ that the claimant company should have mitigated its loss by replacing the damaged car from its stock, rather than hiring in a replacement, during the period while the car was being repaired. But while the cost of hire could not therefore be recovered, damages for loss of use were awarded and these were to be measured by the interest on the capital value of a car of the type damaged, plus depreciation, over the repair period.

Similarly, in *West Midlands Travel Ltd v Aviva Insurance UK Ltd*,¹⁸⁰ where a bus company was able to replace the damaged bus, during the repair period, from its spare capacity (ie it operated its buses in such a way that a damaged bus could be replaced), it was held that

---

[170] [2002] 1 AC 384. [171] [1994] 2 AC 350. See below, pp 240–241.
[172] [2002] 1 AC 384, at 400. [173] [2002] EWCA Civ 510, [2003] QB 36. See above, pp 212–214.
[174] [2007] EWCA Civ 923, [2007] 4 All ER 791. In *Copley v Lawn* [2009] EWCA Civ 580, [2009] PIQR P21 it was controversially (and with respect incorrectly) held that claimants, whose cars had been negligently damaged and had been supplied with temporary replacement cars by their insurers, did not fail in their duty to mitigate by refusing or ignoring the offer of replacement cars from the defendants' insurers. Even more controversially it was said in obiter dicta that, even if this did constitute a failure in their duty to mitigate, they would still be entitled as damages to the cost of hire of those replacement cars. Perhaps not surprisingly the trial judge (the highly respected Judge Charles Harris QC) in *Sayce v TNT (UK) Ltd* [2011] EWCA Civ 1583, [2012] 1 WLR 1261, refused to follow *Copley v Lawn* although he was strongly criticised for departing from precedent by the Court of Appeal in that case (a criticism which he could perhaps have avoided by arguing that the reasoning was inconsistent with House of Lords authority and was therefore *per incuriam*).
[175] Applying the normal approach to insurance, established in *Bradburn v Great Western Ry* (1874) LR 10 Ex1, the fact that it was the insurer, rather than the claimant, who bore the hire costs was irrelevant to the assessment of the damages.
[176] [2015] EWCA Civ 93, [2015] 4 All ER 458.
[177] *The Argentino* (1889) 14 App Cas 519; *The World Beauty* [1970] P 144.
[178] *The Bodlewell* [1907] P 286. [179] [2010] EWCA Civ 647, [2011] QB 357.
[180] [2013] EWCA Civ 887, [2014] RTR 10. See also *Birmingham Corpn v Sowsbery* [1970] RTR 84.

damages for loss of use should be assessed during the repair period according to the capital tied up in the damaged bus, the wasted expenses, and depreciation.

Particularly interesting are the cases allowing damages for loss of use where non-profit-earning ships have been damaged. In *The Greta Holme*,[181] for example, the damage was to a dredging boat owned by a harbour authority for removing silt from the sea bed and in *The Mediana*[182] the damage was to a harbour authority's lightship. In addition to the cost of repairing these service ships the claimants were held entitled to damages for the loss of their use. In the latter case, this was held to be so even though the claimants always maintained a substitute lightship as cover in the event of damage to the main ship. The justification for such damages for loss of use is not at all obvious. In *The Mediana* Lord Halsbury LC drew an analogy with tortious misappropriation: '... supposing a person took away a chair out of my room and kept it for 12 months, could anybody say you had a right to diminish the damages by showing I did not usually sit on that chair, or that there were plenty of other chairs in the room?'[183] That analogy is misleading. In misappropriation cases, 'negotiating damages' can be awarded and the justification for those damages can be said to be either compensatory (that they compensate for, for example, the loss of the fee that the claimant would have charged if it had been approached by the defendant) or, more controversially, restitutionary (in that they reverse the defendant's wrongful gains).[184] But in the case of damage to chattels, negotiating damages and those justifications are not in play. Furthermore, even though the claimants would have been entitled to damages to compensate for the additional costs of hiring a temporary replacement if incurred, they could not be said to have suffered that loss where not incurred. Nor had the claimants suffered a loss in terms of the depreciation of the ships or the costs incurred (for example, the crew's wages) during repair or replacement, because there would have been that depreciation and those costs would have been incurred even if the ships had not been damaged.

Reflecting these problems of justification is the difficulty of how to assess damages for loss of use in this type of case. In *The Marpessa*[185] the House of Lords held that damages should be assessed according to the costs of working and maintaining the dredger that would have been incurred, plus its depreciation, during the period of repairs. In *The Hebridean Coast*[186] the House of Lords awarded a reasonable rate of interest on the value of the ship, as if it had been invested as capital money for the repair period, plus a sum of depreciation. A further possibility would be to award what it would have cost to hire a temporary replacement.[187]

Overall, however, the approach of the courts to loss of use in these 'damage to non-profit-earning ship' cases is difficult to justify. The truth may be that no pecuniary loss had been suffered by the claimants. This was particularly clear in *The Mediana* where there was a cover ship. Might it be said that, even if there was no pecuniary loss, there was a non-pecuniary loss that was being compensated? One might argue, for example, that the loss suffered by the harbour authority in *The Mediana* was the upsetting of its peace of mind because in having to use the spare lightship it no longer had the security of there being a spare in the event that that lightship was damaged.[188] The background facts indicated that

---

[181] [1897] AC 596. See also *The Marpessa* [1907] AC 241; *Admiralty Comrs v SS Susquehana* [1926] AC 655; *The Hebridean Coast* [1961] AC 545.
[182] [1900] AC 113. [183] ibid, at 117.
[184] Below, ch 18. In the leading case of *Morris-Garner v One Step (Support) Ltd* [2018] UKSC 20, [2018] 2 WLR 1353, it was reasoned that negotiating damages are compensatory not restitutionary.
[185] [1907] AC 241. *Birmingham Corpn v Sowsbery* [1970] RTR 84.
[186] [1961] AC 545. *Admiralty Comrs v SS Chekiang* [1926] AC 637.
[187] Suggested in *The Bodlewell* [1907] P 286, at 292 (per Bargrave Deane J).
[188] For a similar analysis—which focuses on the 'undesired' non-pecuniary consequence of the damage to the lightship—see J Edelman, 'The Meaning of Loss and Enrichment' in *Philosophical Foundations of the Law of Unjust Enrichment* (eds R Chambers, C Mitchell, and J Penner, OUP 2009) 211, esp 215–218.

damage to lightships was not an unusual occurrence and it was precisely for that reason that a spare was maintained. Moreover, if we do think in terms of 'peace of mind' one can understand why the parties applied the cost of maintaining the spare as the way to measure the damages. That was precisely what the harbour authority was paying for its 'peace of mind'. However, the main difficulty with that analysis is that the traditional view is that a non-human person, such as a company or public authority, is incapable of incurring non-pecuniary loss.[189] The logic is that non-pecuniary loss, which is not a loss of wealth, is ultimately concerned with the claimant's mental distress or loss of happiness and that is not something that a non-human person can experience. But this restriction may be thought unsatisfactory given that a public authority and many private companies are concerned with the pursuit of non-profit-making goals. These include, as in *The Mediana*, the safety of the public.

In so far as a compensatory analysis fails, no damages should have been awarded for loss of use in these 'damage to non-profit-earning ship' cases and the claimants should have been confined to recovering the cost of repair or replacement.

(3) The betterment question

The courts have sometimes been criticised[190] for purportedly leaving the claimant overcompensated by not deducting from the full repair or replacement cost of property damaged or destroyed by the defendant's tort or breach of contract an amount for 'betterment'; that is, for the fact that the replacement or repaired property is in a better condition than the property before it was damaged or destroyed. So, for example, in *The Gazelle*[191] the claimant's ship was damaged in a collision with the defendant's ship caused by the defendant's negligence. In the claimant's action for damages for the costs of repairing his ship and replacing items destroyed, the assessors of the damages had deducted one-third from those costs because the claimant was getting new for old. But Dr Lushington overruled this. He said, '... if that party derives incidentally a greater benefit than mere indemnification, it arises only from the impossibility of otherwise effecting such indemnification without exposing him to some loss of burden, which the law will not place upon him.'[192] Again, in *Harbutt's Plasticine Ltd v Wayne Tank and Pump Co Ltd*,[193] where the claimants' factory was burnt down as a result of the defendants' breach of contract, it was held that the claimants were entitled to the cost of building and equipping a new factory and that no deduction would be made for the fact that the new factory would be better than the old one. Similarly, in *Bacon v Cooper (Metals) Ltd*,[194] where the defendants were in breach of contract in supplying the claimants with the wrong kind of scrap metal which then broke the rotor of the claimants' fragmentiser, the claimants were held entitled to the hire-purchase cost of a new rotor and no deduction was made for the fact that the new rotor

---

[189] See below, p 288. Where the owner is an individual, there is in principle no difficulty in regarding the damages for loss of use as compensating for non-pecuniary loss, ie physical inconvenience or mental distress. In *Alexander v Rolls Royce Motor Cars Ltd* [1996] RTR 95, damages for loss of use of a Rolls Royce car were refused because the claimant had other cars and there was no evidence of inconvenience or loss of enjoyment while repairs to the car were being carried out (or awaited).

[190] A Ogus, *The Law of Damages* (Butterworths 1973) 134.   [191] (1844) 2 Wm Rob 279.
[192] (1844) 2 Wm Rob 279, at 281.
[193] [1970] 1 QB 447. See also *Hollebone v Midhurst and Fernhurst Builders Ltd* [1968] 1 Lloyd's Rep 38; *Dominion Mosaics and Tile Co Ltd v Trafalgar Trucking Co* [1990] 2 All ER 246.
[194] [1982] 1 All ER 397.

had an expected life of seven years, whereas the old rotor had had only three and three-quarter years' expected life left.

But it is submitted that these cases do not contradict the compensatory principle because it is not at all clear that the betterment represented a real benefit to the claimant. In *The Gazelle* and *Harbutt's Plasticine* the claimant would only realise a gain from the betterment if the ship and factory respectively were to be sold, and there was little likelihood of that. Similarly, in *Bacon v Cooper* there was no certainty that having a new rotor would benefit the claimant more than the old one since by the time the old rotor would have worn out, the fragmentiser itself might have become outmoded. So these cases should not be read as an unjustifiable commitment to not deducting for a true benefit; and where the claimant has clearly benefited from the new for old—and it should probably be for the defendant to show this—an appropriate deduction should be made. That this will be so is supported by Cantley J's view in *Bacon v Cooper* that it would be absurd to allow the full cost of replacing a rotor that had only a few days of useful life left.

This principled approach derives strong support from the Court of Appeal in *Voaden v Champion, The Baltic Surveyor*.[195] The claimant's pontoon had been sunk and lost by reason of the defendant's negligence. At first instance Colman J had awarded £16,000 in respect of the pontoon on the basis that a replacement would have cost £60,000 and had a life of 30 years but the old pontoon only had eight years of life left in it. He therefore awarded 8/30ths of £60,000. That deduction for 'betterment' was upheld by the Court of Appeal as being correct in principle (albeit that Colman J's view that this approach only applied to where one was concerned with replacement rather than repair was doubted). Provided the new for old constituted a true (pecuniary) benefit to the claimant, it should be deducted. Having examined cases such as *The Gazelle*, *Harbutt's Plasticine*, and *Bacon v Cooper*, Rix LJ said:[196]

> 'I suspect ... that the true principle is that in the relevant cases[197] the betterment has conferred no corresponding advantage on the claimant. Take the ordinary case of the repair of some part of a machine. Where only a new part can be fitted or is available, the betterment is likely to be purely nominal: for unless it can be posited that the machine will outlast the life left in the damaged part just before it was damaged, the betterment gives the claimant no advantage; and in most cases any such benefit is likely to be entirely speculative. So in the case of replacement buildings: the building may be new, but buildings are such potentially long-lived objects that the mere newness of a building may be entirely by the way ... Even where the replacement is of a moderately bigger size ... in the absence of any reason for thinking that the bigger size is of direct benefit to the claimant, he has merely mitigated as best he can. If, however, it were to be shown that the bigger size (or some other aspect of betterment) were of real pecuniary advantage to the claimant, as where, for instance, he was able to sublet the 20 per cent extra floor space he had obtained in his replacement building, I do not see why that should not have to be taken into account. It is after all a basic principle that where mitigation has brought measurable benefits to a claimant, he must give credit for them ...'

---

[195] [2002] EWCA Civ 89, [2002] 1 Lloyd's Rep 623. [196] ibid, at [85].
[197] Ie where betterment appeared to be ignored.

4. Torts—wrongful interference with goods or land, other than causing property damage

(1) Goods

Wrongful interference with the claimant's goods, without causing property damage, comprises misappropriation or loss of those goods whether by conversion[198] trespass to goods or negligence.[199]

In aiming to put the claimant into as good a position as it would have been in if no misappropriation or loss had occurred, as the general compensatory aim dictates, then where the goods have been permanently misappropriated or lost the courts are generally content to say simply that damages are assessed according to the value of the goods.[200] But this is a rather ambiguous phrase. For example, even if there is a market for the goods there may be a variation between the market selling and buying prices. Indeed there is often a basic choice between directly awarding the claimant its lost financial advantage from not having the goods (diminution in value) and, on the other hand, awarding it the costs of acquiring substitute goods (cost of cure). This choice is analogous to that presented in assessing compensation for damage to goods and in assessing basic pecuniary loss for breach of contract (the lost property corresponds to a deprivation of the contractual benefit).

It is also noteworthy that in some of the leading cases the defendant had contracted to deliver the goods in question to the claimant, and the claimant's action in conversion (property in the goods having passed) was therefore alternative to that for breach of contract for non-delivery. Subject to differences in limiting principles, like remoteness and contributory negligence, the damages do not differ according to which action is chosen.

So the claimant's duty to mitigate means that normally the value of the goods is the market buying price of replacements. However, if there is no such market and if the claimant's purpose in having the goods was to sell them, the goods' value will be represented by the profit that would have been made on sale, ie by the market selling price or the actual resale price. The market selling price was awarded in *The Arpad*.[201] There the claimants had bought a quantity of wheat and had resold it at 36s 6d a quarter. The market price had since fallen considerably. The defendant shipowners failed to deliver some 47 tons. In an action for conversion (and breach of contract) the claimants were awarded damages only for the market selling price of the 47 tons at the time fixed for delivery, ie 23s 6d per ton, on the ground that the actual resale price was too remote. On the other hand, in *France v Gaudet*[202] the actual resale price was awarded in a situation where the defendant had failed to deliver champagne. It is submitted that the latter decision is to be preferred since if there is no market for buying replacements, as in these two cases, an award of the actual resale price puts the claimant more closely into the position it would have been in if the goods had not been

---

[198] Conversion was extended and detinue abolished by the Torts (Interference with Goods) Act 1977, s 2.
[199] See above, p 206 n 111.
[200] Eg *Re Simms* [1934] Ch 1; *Caxton Publishing Co Ltd v Sutherland Publishing Co* [1939] AC 178, at 192 (per Lord Roche). The relevant date for assessing the value has been in issue in several conversion cases: see above, pp 172, 175–176. For the damages recoverable by those with a limited interest in the goods, see J Edelman, *McGregor on Damages* (20th edn, Sweet & Maxwell 2018) paras 38-050-33-065; eg the creditor under a hire-purchase agreement is restricted to the unpaid instalments if lower than the goods' value: *Wickham Holdings Ltd v Brooke House Motors Ltd* [1967] 1 WLR 295; *Chubb Cash Ltd v John Crilley & Son* [1983] 1 WLR 599.
[201] [1934] P 189.   [202] (1871) LR 6 QB 199.

misappropriated or lost; moreover it is hard to see why the resale loss was regarded as too remote in *The Arpad*.[203] Significantly, Scrutton LJ dissented in that case although it appears that his willingness to take account of the actual resale price was confined to where, as on these facts, there was no available market at the port of discharge.

Where the claimant's purpose in having the goods was for use, and there is no market for buying replacements, the claimant is likely to be awarded the cost of manufacturing a replacement plus adaptation costs. This was awarded, for example, in *J and E Hall Ltd v Barclay*,[204] where the defendant converted the claimant's machinery and there was no market for buying such machinery. Where the claimant cannot even mitigate by replacement manufacture he will presumably be awarded his lost user profits.

In addition to the diminution in value or cost of cure, all other pecuniary losses resulting from the misappropriation or loss of the goods should be recoverable, subject to the usual limiting principles. So, most obviously, where the claimant is having replacement goods manufactured, any loss of interim user profit or any charge reasonably incurred in hiring a temporary replacement should be recoverable.

Where the claimant gets its goods back it will still be entitled to some damages for having been temporarily deprived of them. So, for example, in *Hillesden Securities Ltd v Ryjak Ltd*,[205] where the claimant's car had been returned at the commencement of the trial, the claimant was awarded damages under the Torts (Interference with Goods) Act 1977, s 3 for the temporary loss of use based on the commercial hire fee that it would otherwise have gained during the weeks between the date of the conversion and the date of the car's return. *Strand Electric and Engineering Co Ltd v Brisford Entertainments Ltd*[206] was followed. There the defendants had wrongfully detained the claimants' electrical theatrical equipment. In a detinue action, the defendants were ordered to return the goods or pay their value (at the time of judgment) and additionally the claimants were awarded damages assessed according to a reasonable hiring charge for the period until judgment. The trial judge found, however, that the claimants would not themselves have realised the full hire during that period. Therefore the decision may be best viewed as compensating the claimants for loss of the fee that they would have charged the defendants for legitimate use of their goods or, as Denning LJ but not the majority preferred, as reversing the defendants' wrongful enrichment rather than compensating the claimants' loss of use.[207] A compensatory analysis of these 'negotiating damages' has been preferred by the Supreme Court in *Morris-Garner v One Step (Support) Ltd*.[208]

In *Saleslease Ltd v Davis*[209] the claimant recovered an MOT testing machine that had been wrongfully detained by the defendant. On its return, the claimant sold the machine for its market value. But during the period of wrongful detention, the claimant had lost an unusual opportunity to lease the machine to a third party. That lease would have allegedly given the claimant £8,194 more than the market selling price of the machine. The majority of the Court of Appeal (Walker and Butler-Sloss LJJ) held that, applying *The Arpad*[210] and *The Wagon Mound*[211] tests of remoteness, that loss could not have been reasonably anticipated by the defendant and was too remote. Nominal damages only could be recovered for the tortious conversion. Schiemann LJ, dissenting, thought that the defendant had been put on notice by the claimant of the potential unusual loss if it persisted with the detention and

---

[203] But the analogous decisions ignoring resales in *William Bros Ltd v Agius* [1914] AC 510 and *Rodocanachi v Milburn* (1886) 18 QBD 67 were applied: see above, pp 191–192.
[204] [1937] 3 All ER 620.   [205] [1983] 1 WLR 959.   [206] [1952] 2 QB 246.
[207] Below, pp 324–325.   [208] [2018] UKSC 20, [2018] 2 WLR 1353. See, generally, ch 18.
[209] [1999] 1 WLR 1664.   [210] [1934] P 189.   [211] [1961] AC 388.

that the loss claimed was, therefore, not too remote and was recoverable. It is submitted that Schiemann LJ's dissenting judgment is to be preferred. Applying *The Wagon Mound*, the claimant had given the defendant clear notice of the particular loss that it would suffer by a continuation of the conversion. But, in any event, one might argue that the continued conversion was dishonest and that, applying the enlightened view of Lord Nicholls in *Kuwait Airways Corpn v Iraqi Airways Co (Nos 4 & 5)*,[212] the relevant remoteness test should have been that of directness rather than reasonable foreseeability.

(2) Land

Wrongful interference with land is mainly covered by the torts of trespass and nuisance. Normally a claimant is concerned with a temporary loss of use of his land, either because of wrongful occupation or use (and here the damages are often referred to as 'mesne profits')[213] or because the defendant's activities off the land have prevented the claimant using the land as desired.

Damages for the temporary loss of use of land attempt to compensate the claimant's lost user profit (a diminution in value measure). This will often comprise the rent or fee which would have been obtained if the defendant had not wrongfully interfered. For example, in *Hall & Co Ltd v Pearlberg*,[214] where the defendant had wrongfully occupied the claimants' two farms, the claimants were awarded, inter alia, £650 damages for trespass, representing the one year's rent that they would otherwise have been able to charge an incoming tenant. In other cases damages have been given for the loss of custom caused by the defendant's wrongful interference. For example, in *Fritz v Hobson*[215] damages were awarded for the claimant's loss of custom caused by the defendant's nuisance in carrying on building operations which prevented free access along a public passage to the claimant's shop. Similarly, in *Andreae v Selfridge & Co Ltd*[216] damages were awarded, inter alia, for the claimant's loss of hotel custom attributable to those building operations of the defendant which constituted a nuisance. Of course the loss of user profit is only recoverable to the extent that it does not infringe limiting principles, like remoteness and the duty to mitigate.

Sometimes, however, damages are based on what is regarded as a reasonable rent or fee irrespective of whether the claimant would have otherwise acquired that sum by letting to a third party.[217] Those damages can be straightforwardly regarded as compensating loss of use if it is realistic to think that the claimant would have charged the defendant that sum for legitimate use of the land. Alternatively, those damages might be viewed as restitutionary, reversing the defendant's wrongful enrichment. The Supreme Court in *Morris-Garner v One Step (Support) Ltd*[218] has taken the view that such 'negotiating damages' are best analysed as compensatory not restitutionary.

Where a claimant has been and *will be* prevented from using his land or using it as desired (that is, the deprivation is permanent)—for example, where no injunction is granted to restrain smells or noise or to remove buildings blocking lights—equitable damages (in lieu of an injunction) will normally be measured by the diminution in the market selling price of the land.[219]

---

[212] [2002] UKHL 19, [2002] 2 AC 883. See above, p 90.
[213] Eg *Clifton Securities Ltd v Huntley* [1948] 2 All ER 283; *Morris v Tarrant* [1971] 2 QB 143.
[214] [1956] 1 WLR 244.   [215] (1880) 14 Ch D 542.   [216] [1938] Ch 1.
[217] Eg *Whitwham v Westminster, Brymbo, Coal & Coke Co* [1896] 1 Ch 894; *Swordheath Properties Ltd v Tabet* [1979] 1 WLR 285.
[218] [2018] UKSC 20, [2018] 2 WLR 1353. Below, ch 18.
[219] Eg *Griffith v Clay & Sons Ltd* [1912] 2 Ch 291. For equitable damages, see below, ch 17.

But in *Bracewell v Appleby*,[220] *Carr-Saunders v Dick McNeil Associates Ltd*,[221] and *Jaggard v Sawyer*[222] the courts have assessed damages according to what would have been a fair sum for the claimants to have accepted for granting the defendants, in the first and third case, a right of way and, in the second case, a right to obstruct light. In the first two cases the judges spoke of the damages being awarded for the claimant's 'loss of amenity'.[223] But in *Bracewell v Appleby* Graham J's emphasis on the profits the defendant had made from building his home (which was accessible only by using the claimant's road) might be thought to make it preferable to regard the damages in that case as restitutionary, reversing the defendant's wrongful enrichment.[224] But again, all this must now be read in the light of *Morris-Garner v One Step (Support) Ltd*[225] in which the Supreme Court has taken the view that such 'negotiating damages' are compensatory not restitutionary.

5. Torts—pure economic loss

The term 'pure economic loss' is well-known in the realm of tortious negligence where it refers to economic loss that is not consequent on physical damage. Physical damage most obviously comprises personal injury or property damage but its 'spirit' also includes death, damage to reputation, and wrongful interference with goods or land (apart from property damage). Hence, for our purposes, pure economic loss will be taken to comprise economic loss not consequent on any of the above kinds of 'physical damage'.

In looking at compensatory damages for pure economic loss it is convenient to divide between four general heads of tortious liability: misrepresentation, wrongful infringement of intellectual property rights, wrongful interference with business or contract, and acts or omissions under the tort of negligence.

It is important to realise that the recovery of damages for pure economic loss was, until 40 years ago, severely restricted in that, other than for infringement of intellectual property rights, there was no liability for negligently inflicted pure economic loss; deceit and the torts concerning interference with contract or business require intentional or reckless conduct. But this restriction has been eased, initially by the development of the tort of negligent misrepresentation allowing the recovery of pure economic loss in *Hedley Byrne & Co Ltd v Heller & Partners Ltd*[226] and later by the recognition that, in some limited situations, a defendant can be liable in the tort of negligence for acts or omissions causing pure economic loss.

---

[220] [1975] Ch 408. [221] [1986] 1 WLR 922.
[222] [1995] 1 WLR 269. See also *Severn Trent Water Ltd v Barnes* [2004] EWCA Civ 570 where damages of £610 were upheld as compensating the claimant's loss of opportunity to negotiate compensation in a case where the defendant had trespassed under a corner of the claimant's land by laying a water pipe. Of particular interest was the CA's rejection of the trial judge's additional award of £1,560 'restitutionary damages', based on the gains made by the defendant in using the pipe, on the reasoning that that overlapped with, or was inconsistent with, the compensatory award. For an analysis of the quantum of equitable damages in trespass (and breach of restrictive covenant) cases, in which the author tends to assume a compensatory rather than a restitutionary approach, see D Halpern, 'Damages in Lieu of an Injunction: How Much?' [2001] Conv 453.
[223] [1975] Ch 408, at 420; [1986] 1 WLR 922, at 931.   [224] Below, p 325 n 15.
[225] [2018] UKSC 20, [2018] 2 WLR 1353. Below, ch 18.
[226] [1964] AC 465. In *Caparo Industries Plc v Dickman* [1990] 2 AC 605 it was held that no duty of care was owed by auditors of a company to investors in that company who had relied on the auditors' accounts in making their investments. It was stressed by the House of Lords that liability for misrepresentation under *Hedley Byrne* required the representation to be claimant-specific and purpose-specific. See similarly *Banca Nazional del Lavoro SpA v Playboy Club London Ltd* [2018] UKSC 43, [2018] 1 WLR 4041 (no duty of care, as regards reference as to credit-worthiness, owed to undisclosed principal of the company asking for the reference).

(1) Misrepresentation

A misrepresentation is the basis of a cause of action in tort where made fraudulently, as in the tort of deceit, or negligently, as in the tort of negligent misrepresentation. Similarly a negligent misrepresentation inducing the making of a contract between the parties is a statutory tort under s 2(1) of the Misrepresentation Act 1967.

(a) What is the aim of the damages?

Most discussion regarding damages for tortious misrepresentation has centred on what the compensatory principle here requires. As the tort consists of fraudulently or negligently making a false statement misleading the claimant, the aim should be to put the claimant into as good a position as if no statement misleading it had been made. Although the contrary has sometimes been suggested,[227] the aim is not and should not be to put the claimant into as good a position as it would have been in if the statement had been true, for this would go beyond the essence of the tort. The claimant's reliance, and not expectation, interest is therefore being protected.[228]

Damages for tortious misrepresentation are therefore fundamentally distinct from damages for breach of contract, where the claimant's expectations are fulfilled by putting it into as good a position as if the contract had been performed. At a deeper level the distinction between the two rests on the difference between lying and breaking one's promise, with the latter, unlike the former, generally comprising the breaking of a positive rather than a negative obligation. It is hence essential to distinguish between mere representations, where the sole action is for tortious misrepresentation, and warranties, where the claimant can sue for breach of contract; or, to put it another way, between statements merely inducing the making of a contract and the terms of the contract.

A number of cases show that the aim of damages for tortious misrepresentation is indeed to put the claimant into as good a position as if no statement had been made, rather than as if the statement had been true. For fraudulent misrepresentation an important case is *Doyle v Olby (Ironmongers) Ltd*.[229] The claimant had bought a business from the defendant company. He was induced to do so by various fraudulent misrepresentations. The critical one was that the trade of the business was 'all over the counter', when in fact half of it was obtained by a traveller going out to canvass customers. The judges, particularly Lord Denning, indicated that there is a difference between damages for the tort of deceit and for breach of contract. Lord Denning said:

'It appears therefore that the plaintiff's counsel submitted and the judge accepted that the proper measure of damages was the "cost of making good the representation" or what came to the same thing, "the reduction in value of the goodwill" due to the misrepresentation. In so doing, he treated the misrepresentation as if it were a contractual promise, that is, as if there were a contractual term to the effect, "The trade is all over the counter. There is no need to employ a traveller." I think it was the wrong measure. Damages for fraud and conspiracy are assessed differently from damages for breach of contract ... On principle, the distinction seems to be this: in contract, the defendant has made a promise and broken it. The object of damages is to put the

---

[227] As we have seen above, at pp 117–127, the *SAAMCO* principle is flawed in its insistence that damages for breach of an obligation to use reasonable care in making a statement should be restricted by the position the claimant would have been in had the statement been true.
[228] See above, pp 39, 79–80.
[229] [1969] 2 QB 158. See also *East v Maurer* [1991] 1 WLR 461, below, p 227.

plaintiff in as good a position as far as money can do it, as if the promise had been performed. In fraud, the defendant has been guilty of a deliberate wrong by inducing the plaintiff to act to his detriment. The object of damages is to compensate the plaintiff for all the loss he has suffered, so far again, as money can do it.'[230]

Winn and Sachs LJJ agreed with Lord Denning, and Winn LJ specifically approved the passages in the 12th edition of *Mayne and McGregor on Damages*[231] which emphasised that damages for deceit aim to put the claimant into the position he would have been in if no statement had been made. The author there relied, as Lord Denning did in *Doyle v Olby*, on cases such as *McConnel v Wright*[232] and *Clark v Urquhart*[233] which had established that, when the claimant is induced to buy shares by a fraudulent misrepresentation, the measure of damages is not the value of the shares if the representation had been true less their actual value but rather the purchase price paid less their actual value.

Doyle v Olby was approved and applied in the leading case of *Smith New Court Securities Ltd v Scrimgeour Vickers (Asset Management) Ltd*.[234] The claimant bought shares in F Inc that were pledged to the defendant bank. In reliance on false representations by representatives of the bank that there were rival bids close to the price offered by the claimant, the claimant went ahead and bought the shares at 82.25p per share at a total price of £23,141. A couple of months later, F Inc revealed that it had been the victim of a massive fraud and its share price dropped dramatically. The claimant sold the shares over several months at prices of between 30p and 40p for £11,788 (at a loss of £11,353). In an action for the tort of deceit, it was held by the House of Lords, approving *Doyle v Olby*, that the claimant was entitled to be put into as good a position as if no false representations had been made; that the claimant was not restricted to the loss as assessed at the date of the transaction; and that all direct consequential loss, even if not reasonably foreseeable, was recoverable. The claimant was therefore held entitled to damages for the difference between the contract price and the amount actually realised by the sale of the shares (ie its full loss of £11,353).

Doyle v Olby was also applied but, it is submitted, the wrong result reached on the particular peculiar facts in the earlier case of *Smith Kline & French Laboratories Ltd v Long*.[235] The claimant was induced by the deceit of the defendant, the managing director of Swift Exports Ltd, to sell to Swift 16,800 packs of tablets at a price of £56.66 per pack. The fraudulent misrepresentation was to the effect that Swift would sell the tablets in Central Africa. In fact they were sold in Holland. Swift paid all but £157,028 of the agreed contract price but then became insolvent. Whitford J dismissed the claim on the ground that the claimant had suffered no loss as a result of the fraud. The Court of Appeal reversed that decision and awarded £157,028.

Subject to any argument that fraud overrides normal rules as to mitigation of loss,[236] that award would only have been correct if the claimant would have sold the tablets at the same price to someone else had it not been induced to sell to Swift. Yet the claimant conceded that it could have supplied whatever quantity of tablets was needed to meet demand (and that it could be assumed that the tablets had cost nothing to produce). It should have followed that the contract with Swift could not be treated as having deprived the claimant of the

---

[230] [1969] 2 QB 158, at 166–167.
[231] H McGregor, *Mayne and McGregor on Damages* (12th edn, Sweet & Maxwell 1961) paras 955 ff.
[232] [1903] 1 Ch 546. [233] [1930] AC 28. [234] [1997] AC 254.
[235] [1989] 1 WLR 1. In the *Smith New Court* case [1997] AC 254, 283, Lord Steyn referred to this criticism of the *Smith Kline* decision but left open whether he regarded this criticism as correct. See also *Inter Export LLC v Lasytsya* [2018] EWCA Civ 2068, at [59]–[67].
[236] An analogy might be drawn with, eg, remoteness where a special more extensive 'directness' rule applies to the tort of deceit: see above, p 90.

opportunity to sell those tablets (at the same price) to someone else: and that there was no true analogy with cases on wrongful interference with goods which have awarded damages based on the value of the goods.[237]

Moving on to the tort of negligent misrepresentation, as established in *Hedley Byrne & Co v Heller & Partners Ltd*,[238] *Esso Petroleum Co Ltd v Mardon*[239] shows the application of the same principle. Here a tenant was induced to take a lease of a petrol station from an oil company by a statement made by an experienced salesman on the company's behalf, as to the potential throughput of petrol at that station. The Court of Appeal held that the defendant was liable, inter alia, for its salesman's pre-contractual negligent misrepresentation. As regards the damages, Lord Denning said:

> 'Mr Mardon is not to be compensated for "loss of a bargain". He was given no bargain that the throughput would amount to 200,000 gallons a year. He is only to be compensated for having been induced to enter into a contract which turned out to be disastrous for him. Whether it be called breach of warranty or negligent misstatement, its effect was not to warrant the throughput, but only to induce him to enter into the contract. So the damages in either case are to be measured by the loss he suffered … It is to be measured in a similar way as the loss due to a personal injury. You should look into the future so as to forecast what would have been likely to happen if he had never entered into the contract; and contrast it with his position as it now is, as a result of entering into it.'[240]

Shaw LJ agreed with Lord Denning over these principles, and while Ormrod LJ did not clearly adopt this approach his comments on the computation of damages are consistent with it.

Similarly in *Box v Midland Bank Ltd*,[241] which concerned a negligent misrepresentation made by a bank's employee regarding the claimant's chances of getting a large loan from the bank, Lloyd J had the following to say on the question of how to assess the damages:

> 'The damages claimed amount to just under £250,000 but a very large part of that represents the gains that the plaintiff would have made if the Manitoban contract had been successfully carried through and the Churchman Newton group saved. Once the claim in contract had been abandoned, Mr Box could not hope to recover for loss of his bargain and [his counsel] rightly abandoned that part of the claim. Instead he says that Mr Box is entitled to be put in the position he would have been in if the negligent misstatement had not been made. That always involves questions of the greatest difficulty. It was difficult in *Doyle v Olby*; it was difficult in *Esso v Mardon*; it is even more difficult here.'[242]

Applying this principle Lloyd J ultimately assessed damages at £5,000.

With regard to statutory liability under the Misrepresentation Act 1967, s 2(1), it is also now clear (contrary to early cases suggesting that the claimant should be put into as good a position as if the representation had been true)[243] that the basic principle is to put the claimant into the position it would have been in if no statement has been made. In *F & B Entertainments Ltd v Leisure Enterprises Ltd*,[244] Walton J ordered an inquiry as to damages under s 2(1) saying that, 'The measure of damages, quite clearly, is the same as those in an action for damages for deceit'.[245] In *André & Cie SA v Ets Michel Blanc & Fils*[246] Ackner J

---

[237] Above, pp 219–221.   [238] [1964] AC 465.   [239] [1976] QB 801.   [240] ibid, at 820–821.
[241] [1979] 2 Lloyd's Rep 391. See also *Naughton v O'Callaghan* [1990] 3 All ER 191, at 196–198.
[242] [1979] 2 Lloyd's Rep 391, at 399.
[243] *Gosling v Anderson* (1972) 223 Estates Gazette 1743; *Davis & Co (Wines) Ltd v Afa-Minerva (EMI) Ltd* [1974] 2 Lloyd's Rep 27; *Watts v Spence* [1976] Ch 165.
[244] (1976) 240 Estates Gazette 455.   [245] ibid, at 461.   [246] [1977] 2 Lloyd's Rep 166.

similarly said of s 2(1), 'To my mind, the subsection puts the victim of the innocent misrepresentation in the same position, relative to his claim for damages, as the victim of the fraudulent misrepresentation. To his claim, the measure of damages appropriate to claims in tort has to be applied.'[247] In *McNally v Welltrade International Ltd*[248] Sir Douglas Franks QC, in assessing damages under s 2(1), applied *Doyle v Olby* and said, 'The plaintiff's position before the inducement should be compared with his position at the end of the transaction.'[249] And in *Cemp Properties (UK) Ltd v Dentsply Research & Development Corpn*,[250] in which the Court of Appeal awarded damages under s 2(1) to a purchaser of land, Bingham LJ regarded it as 'the cardinal rule of damages in this field that the plaintiff should be put in the same financial position as if the misrepresentation had not been made'. Furthermore Balcombe LJ in *Royscot Trust Ltd v Rogerson*[251] expressly disapproved the early cases describing them as 'initial aberrations' and said, '[I]t is difficult to see how the measure of damages under [s 2(1)] could be other than the tortious measure and ... that is now generally accepted.'

This must be correct. As has been explained above, it follows from the very nature of the wrong of misrepresentation. Moreover, it would be irrational to award the claimant the expectation measure under the Misrepresentation Act 1967, s 2(1) when it is confined to being put into as good a position as if no statement had been made under the very similar tort of negligent misrepresentation and under the more blameworthy tort of deceit.

It follows from the above reasoning that damages that can be awarded for even a purely innocent misrepresentation in lieu of rescission under the Misrepresentation Act 1967, s 2(2)[252] should not go beyond putting the claimant into as good a position as if no statement had been made.[253]

(b) Expenses caused and gains forgone

To put the claimant into as good a position as if no representation had been made it can recover damages for all the expenses caused by and gains forgone because of the misrepresentation, subject to the usual limiting principles.

Dealing first with expenses caused, a useful example is *Richardson v Silvester*.[254] The defendant inserted in a newspaper an advert for the letting of a farm which, as he knew, he had no power to let. In reliance on the advert the claimant incurred expenses by himself inspecting the property and in employing other persons to inspect and value it. It was held that the claimant had an action for deceit enabling him to recover his expenses.

Where the expenses take the form of a contract price paid under a contract induced by a misrepresentation, the damages are assessed according to the contract price paid minus

---

[247] ibid, at 181.   [248] [1978] IRLR 497.   [249] ibid, at 499.   [250] [1991] 2 EGLR 197, at 201.
[251] [1991] 2 QB 297, at 304–305. See also *Chesneau v Interhome Ltd* [1983] CLY 988; *Sharneyford Supplies Ltd v Edge* [1987] Ch 305, at 323 (per Balcombe LJ); *Naughton v O'Callaghan* [1990] 3 All ER 191, at 196–198; *Gran Gelato Ltd v Richcliff (Group) Ltd* [1992] Ch 560, at 574–575.
[252] The discretion to award damages in lieu of rescission is dependent on rescission otherwise being available and not being barred by one of the standard bars to rescission, such as *restitutio in integrum* being impossible: *Salt v Stratstone Specialist Ltd* [2015] EWCA Civ 745, [2016] RTR 285. This is because the purpose of the Misrepresentation Act 1967, s 2(2) is not to add to the misrepresentee's remedies but to give the courts a discretion to cut back the remedy of rescission where the misrepresentation has been trivial and rescission would cause undue hardship to the misrepresentor.
[253] See generally *William Sindall plc v Cambridgeshire CC* [1994] 1 WLR 1016: in obiter dicta the Court of Appeal indicated that, whether recoverable under the Misrepresentation Act 1967, s 2(1) or not, loss due to the sharp fall in the market value of the land subsequent to its purchase by the claimant could not be included within damages under the Misrepresentation Act 1967, s 2(2).
[254] (1873) LR 9 QB 34.

the value of what has been received under the contract. This is well illustrated by cases where the misrepresentation induced the purchase of shares. So, for example, in *Smith New Court Securities Ltd v Scrimgeour Vickers (Asset Management) Ltd*,[255] as we have seen, the claimant was awarded damages of the difference between the price paid for shares (£23,141) and the price at which they were sold (£11,788). And in the earlier case of *Archer v Brown*[256] the purchase price of £30,000 was recovered as damages because the claimant received no shares in return, the defendant having already sold them to someone else. The claimant also received damages of £13,528 in respect of the interest payable on a bank loan taken out to buy the shares. Similarly in *Naughton v O'Callaghan*,[257] in which the claimants had been induced to buy a horse by a negligent misrepresentation as to its true pedigree, the damages awarded were the difference between the price paid (26,000 guineas) and the horse's value nearly two years later when the misrepresentation was discovered and the horse had proved a failure on the racecourse (£1,500); plus £9,820 expenses incurred in training and keeping the horse.

A more complex illustration of damages based on expenses caused minus benefits accruing is provided by *Doyle v Olby*.[258] The expenses amounted to £12,500, and comprised the purchase of business and stock (£9,500) and interest on a loan and overdraft plus rates (£3,000). The benefits amounted to £7,000 and comprised the sale of the business and stock (£4,300) and salary and living accommodation (£2,700). The damages awarded were therefore £5,500 (£12,500 minus £7,000).

Turning to gains forgone, in *Burrows v Rhodes*[259] the claimant joined a private army invading the South African Republic in reliance on the defendant's fraudulent misrepresentations that protection was needed for women and children, that the invasion would be reinforced by other lawful troops, and that the plan had the sanction of HM Government. It was held that the claimant had a good action in deceit enabling him to recover, inter alia, his loss of earnings while involved in the invasion. Another example is *East v Maurer*,[260] in which the claimant had been induced to buy a hair salon by the vendor's fraudulent misrepresentation that he would not be continuing to run a competing salon. In an action for deceit, the claimant was awarded not only the price paid minus the selling price, plus the trading losses, plus the expenses incurred in buying and selling and carrying out improvements, but also £10,000 for profits forgone. It was explained by the Court of Appeal (in reducing the sum that had been awarded under the last head by the trial judge) that the recoverable profits forgone were what the claimant might have been expected to make in another similar hairdressing business and not the profits that would have been made in this particular business had the vendor's representation been true. The latter could only have been justified in an action for breach of a contractual warranty. *East v Maurer* was followed in *4 Eng Ltd v Harper*.[261] Here the claimant company had been induced to buy a company (Ironfirm Ltd) from the defendants by fraudulent misrepresentations made by the defendants. In an action for the tort of deceit, the damages awarded covered not only the purchase price paid for Ironfirm, and costs incurred in the purchase, but also the loss of the chance of making profit from purchasing another company which the claimants would have purchased had they not bought Ironfirm. Again, in *Parabola Investments Ltd v Browallia Cal Ltd*[262] the deceit had resulted in the claimant having a reduced fund with which to trade in stocks, shares, and derivatives. It was held that the claimant was entitled to damages in

---

[255] [1997] AC 254. See also, eg, *McConnel v Wright* [1903] 1 Ch 546; *Clark v Urquhart* [1930] AC 28.
[256] [1985] QB 401.   [257] [1990] 3 All ER 191. See also above, pp 174–175.
[258] [1969] 2 QB 158.   [259] [1899] 1 QB 816.   [260] [1991] 1 WLR 461.
[261] [2008] EWHC 915 (Ch), [2009] Ch 91.   [262] [2010] EWCA Civ 486, [2011] QB 477.

the tort of deceit for the loss of investment opportunity (ie the loss of profit) which was a loss that continued after discovery of the fraud. A final and particularly interesting example of the recovery of gains forgone is provided by *Clef Aquitaine SARL v Laporte Materials (Barrow) Ltd*.[263] The claimant had entered into two profitable distributorship contracts with the defendant. The defendant had induced the claimant to agree to the particular terms by a fraudulent misrepresentation. Had that fraudulent misrepresentation not been made, the claimant would have entered into the contracts with the defendant on more favourable terms and would have made greater profits than it in fact did make. In an action for deceit, it was held by the Court of Appeal that the claimant was entitled to those gains forgone (that is, the greater profits lost). It was no bar to awarding damages for those lost profits that the claimant had still entered into profitable, rather than loss-making, contracts with the defendant.

(2) Wrongful infringement of intellectual property rights[264]

The torts concerned with the wrongful infringement of intellectual property rights[265] are the infringement of a trade mark, patent, design, performer's property right, or copyright and passing-off.[266] To put the claimant into as good a position as if there had been no wrongful infringement it can recover damages for all the expenses caused by and gains forgone because of the infringement, subject to the usual limiting principles.

There are no clear examples of cases in which expenses caused by the defendant's infringement of the claimant's intellectual property rights have been compensated. However, in *A-G Spalding Bros v AW Gamage Ltd*[267] the defendants had sold some of the claimants' old and discarded footballs as their new goods and in a passing-off action the claimants were awarded damages, inter alia, for what it would have cost to counter-advertise. It clearly follows that if they had incurred expenses in counter-advertising these would have been recoverable.

In contrast there have been numerous cases compensating for the claimant's lost profits. The profits that have most commonly been lost have been from the reduction in sales of goods or materials as a result of the defendant's unlawful competition.[268] The assessment

---

[263] [2001] QB 488.
[264] See A Brown, 'Damages and Account of Profits in Trademark, Trade Secrets, Copyright and Patent Law' (1977) 3 Auck Univ LR 188.
[265] Alongside these intellectual property torts, a claimant whose intellectual property rights have been infringed can claim damages under regulation 3 of the Intellectual Property (Enforcement etc) Regulations 2006 which gives effect to Article 13 of the Intellectual Property Rights Enforcement Directive, 2004/24/EC. For discussion, see *Hollister Inc v Medik Ostomy Supplies Ltd* [2012] EWCA Civ 1419, [2013] Bus LR 428; C Waelde et al., *Contemporary Intellectual Property* (OUP 2016) 976–978.
[266] A non-negligent wrongdoer is not liable for damages (but may be subject to an injunction) for infringement of a patent or copyright or performers' property right or primary infringement of a design right: see the Patents Act 1977, s 62(1); the Copyright, Designs and Patents Act 1988, ss 97(1), 191J(1), 233(1). In contrast, damages (and an injunction) may be awarded for the common law torts of infringement of a trade mark and passing off on a strict liability basis: *Gillette UK Ltd v Edenwest Ltd* [1994] RPC 279. The standard of liability applied in respect of an account of profits for the intellectual property torts is even more inconsistent as between the different torts: see below, pp 342–343. Under regulation 17 of the Copyright and Related Rights Regulations 1996 (SI 1996/2967) and regulation 23 of the Copyright and Rights in Databases Regulations 1997 (SI 1997/3032), a person with, respectively, a publication right and a database right has the same rights and remedies as a copyright owner under, eg, ss 96–98 of the Copyright, Designs and Patents Act 1998.
[267] (1918) 35 RPC 101.
[268] *United Horse-Shoe and Nail Co Ltd v Stewart & Co* (1888) 13 App Cas 401 (patent infringement); *Draper v Trist* [1939] 3 All ER 513 (passing-off); *Aktiebolaget Manus v Fullwood & Bland Ltd* (1954) 71 RPC 243, at 250 (infringement of trademark); *Catnic Components Ltd v Hill & Smith Ltd* [1983] FSR 512 (patent infringement); *Gerber Garment Technology Inc v Lectra Systems Ltd* [1997] RPC 443 (patent infringement). In *Sutherland Publishing Co Ltd v Caxton Publishing Co Ltd* [1936] Ch 323, at 336, Lord Wright said that for copyright infringement, 'The

of those lost profits is often very difficult and the courts frequently resort to rough estimation. Certainly it cannot simply be assumed that the sales made by the defendant from selling infringing goods or materials correspond to the claimant's lost sales, that is, that there is equivalence between the diversion of customers from the claimant and the customers buying from the defendant.[269] In particular one is concerned only with profits lost from (that is, factually caused by) the infringement and not the profit that would in any event have been lost because of lawful competition. Furthermore, the defendant's profits may have resulted from special exertions which the claimant would not have undertaken.

Some lost sale profits may also have been the result of the claimant lowering its prices to counter the defendant's unlawful competition. Damages for such losses were awarded in the patent infringement case of *American Braided Wire Co v Thomson*,[270] but were denied in *United Horse-Shoe and Nail Co Ltd v Stewart*[271] on the ground that the claimants would have lowered their prices irrespective of the patent infringement.

However, the claimant may not have lost sales profits; rather it may have lost the profits from licensing its intellectual property. This loss is assessed by determining the lump sum or royalties the claimant would have received for granting a licence to the defendant. A detailed examination of the assessment of such damages was made by the House of Lords in *General Tire Co v Firestone Tyre Co Ltd*,[272] an infringement of patent case. Ultimately damages were assessed on the basis of a royalty rate of 3/8th of a US cent, the Lords holding that there was sufficient evidence indicating that this 'going rate' (that is the rate at which other licences for the patent had been granted) was the rate for which the claimants would have granted the patent licence to the defendants. Lord Wilberforce did, however, stress that:

'Before a "going rate" of royalty can be taken as the basis on which an infringer should be held liable, it must be shown that the circumstances in which the going rate was paid are the same as or at least comparable with those in which the patentee and the infringer are assumed to strike their bargain.'[273]

Lord Wilberforce went on to say:

'Given that the respondents were not claiming an account of profits, the consequence of departing from the conception of loss can only be to discover a *tertium quid* defined, it seems, by reference to what the infringer ought fairly to have paid. But there is no warrant for this on authority or principle.'[274]

However, in the earlier case of *Watson, Laidlaw & Co v Pott, Cassels & Williamson*,[275] an infringement of patent case, Lord Shaw suggested that even where the claimant can show neither loss of sales profit, because, for example, it could not have sold patented machines in the particular area where the defendant has sold them, nor loss of licensing profit, because it would not have granted a patent licence, it can still recover substantial damages. Lord

---

measure of damages is the depreciation caused by the infringement to the value of the copyright, as a chose in action.' Taking this approach the lost sale profits represent the depreciation in value.

[269] *United Horse-Shoe and Nail Co Ltd v Stewart & Co* (1888) 13 App Cas 401. But there was taken to be this equivalence in *American Braided Wire Co v Thomson* (1890) 44 Ch D 274.

[270] (1890) 44 Ch D 274. *Alexander v Henry* (1895) 12 RPC 360 (infringement of trademark); *Gerber Garment Technology Inc v Lectra Systems Ltd* [1997] RPC 443 (patent infringement).

[271] (1888) 13 App Cas 401.

[272] [1975] 1 WLR 819. *Meters Ltd v Metropolitan Gas Meters Ltd* (1911) 28 RPC 157, at 164–165 (patent infringement); *Scovin-Bradford v Valpoint Properties Ltd* [1971] Ch 1007 (infringement of copyright); *Catnic Components Ltd v Hill & Smith Ltd* [1983] FSR 512 (patent infringement); *Irvine v Talksport Ltd* [2003] EWCA Civ 423, [2003] 2 All ER (Comm) 141 (passing-off).

[273] [1975] 1 WLR 819, at 825.   [274] ibid, at 833.   [275] (1914) 31 RPC 104.

Shaw drew an analogy with taking someone's horse, using it and returning it in the same condition, and said:

> 'Each of the infringements was an actionable wrong, and although it may have been committed in a range of business or of territory which the patentee might not have reached, he is entitled to hire or royalty in respect of each unauthorised use of his property. Otherwise, the remedy might fall unjustly short of the wrong.'[276]

One might argue that it is difficult to view this approach as being concerned to put the claimant into as good a position as if no tort had been committed, and it looks rather as if it is restitutionary based on reversing the defendant's wrongful enrichment, with the royalties representing either the expense the defendant saved in not having to acquire an equivalent patent licence or a fair proportion of the defendant's profits.[277] But all this must now be read in the light of *Morris-Garner v One Step (Support) Ltd*[278] in which the Supreme Court has taken the view that such 'negotiating damages' are compensatory not restitutionary.

(3) Wrongful interference with business or contract

Wrongful interference with the claimant's business or contract is the basis of several torts, for example, inducing breach of contract, intimidation, interference by unlawful means, conspiracy, and injurious falsehood. To put the claimant into as good a position as if there had been no such interference it can recover damages for all the expenses caused by and gains forgone because of the interference, subject to the usual limiting principles.

As regards expenses caused, *British Motor Trade Association v Salvadori*[279] provides a good example. The claimant trade association, in an attempt to keep down the price of certain cars, required all purchasers of those cars to covenant not to resell within 12 months. The defendants with the intention of breaking the system induced certain purchasers to break the covenant. In an action for inducing breach of contract and conspiracy Roxburgh J held that the claimants could recover, inter alia, the expenses incurred in 'unravelling and detecting the unlawful machinations of the defendants'.[280]

But where the defendant has interfered with the claimant's business or contract, the claimant is usually primarily concerned to recover damages for the profit lost as a result of such interference. So, for example, in *Goldsoll v Goldman*[281] the defendant induced an employee of the claimant to break his contract with the claimant by setting up a rival jewellery business close to the claimant's. In an action for inducing breach of contract damages were awarded for the claimant's general loss of business.

Less commonly the gains forgone may comprise a loss of earnings. In *Morgan v Fry*[282] the claimant lockman had been dismissed by his employers under pressure from the defendant.

---

[276] ibid, at 120.   [277] Below, pp 324–326.
[278] [2018] UKSC 20, [2018] 2 WLR 1353. Below, ch 18.   [279] [1949] Ch 556.
[280] ibid, at 569. This case was distinguished in *Admiral Management Services Ltd v Para-Protect* Ltd [2002] EWHC 233 (Ch), [2002] 1 WLR 2722, where no extra expenses had been incurred by the claimant in investigating the torts; rather the employees carrying out the investigation work had simply been paid the salaries that the claimant would have paid them in any event.
[281] [1914] 2 Ch 603. See also *Admiral Management Services Ltd v Para-Protect Ltd* [2002] EWHC 233 (Ch), [2002] 1 WLR 2722: loss of revenue recoverable in principle but no evidence of this provided. Stanley Burnton J also indicated (and see further, in support of this, *Pearson v Sanders Witherspoon* [2000] PNLR 110, a solicitor's negligence case, and *Standard Chartered Bank v Pakistan National Shipping Corpn* [2001] EWCA Civ 55, [2001] 1 All ER (Comm) 822, at [48]–[49], a deceit case) that 'damages for management time', caused by the tort, accepted in principle by Forbes J in *Tate & Lyle Food and Distribution Ltd v Greater London Council* [1982] 1 WLR 149, were recoverable only if there was a loss of revenue (or, presumably, extra expenditure).
[282] [1968] 1 QB 521; rvsd on liability [1968] 2 QB 710.

In an action for intimidation the claimant was at first instance awarded the earnings he would have made as a lockman (and it was assumed that he would not have continued in that job for more than another five years) minus his present wages working in a different job.

It should be noted that damages awarded for tortious interference with contract will not necessarily be the same as for breach of that contract. In particular, principles like remoteness and contributory negligence do not apply in the same way.

(4) Acts or omissions under the tort of negligence

The courts over the last 50 or so years have struggled to decide on the extent to which pure economic loss caused by negligent acts or omissions is recoverable in the tort of negligence. In general, a narrow approach to liability in this area has been taken with the courts traditionally fearing an indeterminate liability to an indeterminate number and undermining contractual terms.[283] Various concepts have been utilised by the courts in trying to draw a coherent boundary of liability, for example, 'assumption of responsibility', 'reliance', 'proximity', and whether imposition of a duty of care is 'fair and reasonable'. But in truth these concepts give relatively little guidance and one tends to be forced back to incremental reasoning from the facts of past decisions.[284]

In looking at how damages should be assessed for negligently caused pure economic loss, it seems helpful to divide between (a) negligent interference with contract or business and (b) negligent performance of services beneficial to the claimant.[285]

(a) Negligent interference with contract or business

No English case has yet allowed the recovery of damages for pure economic loss caused by a negligent interference with contract or business. The situation is exemplified by the pure economic loss claim in *Spartan Steel and Alloys v Martin & Co (Contractors) Ltd*.[286] In that case, the defendants had negligently damaged an electricity cable, thereby cutting off the electricity supply to the claimants' factory for 14 hours. As a result the 'melt' then in the furnace was damaged. The claimants were able to recover damages for the damaged melt (£368) and the loss of profit that would have been made on that melt (£400), but not for the profit on four further melts (£1,767) that would have been put through the furnace if the electricity supply had not been cut off. The last head was denied because it amounted to pure economic loss.

As regards the assessment of damages, the important point is that if negligently caused pure economic loss were to be recoverable in English law in this situation, it should be seen alongside the earlier section on wrongful (intentional) interference with business or contract and damages should be assessed in basically the same way; ie in aiming to put the claimant into as good a position as if the defendant had not negligently interfered, expenses

---

[283] Important cases denying a duty of care in respect of negligent acts or omissions causing pure economic loss include *Candlewood Navigation Corpn Ltd v Mitsui OSK Lines Ltd* [1986] AC 1; *Muirhead v Industrial Tank Specialities Ltd* [1986] QB 507; *Leigh and Sillavan Ltd v Aliakmon Shipping Co Ltd* [1986] AC 785; *Murphy v Brentwood District Council* [1991] 1 AC 398; *Customs and Excise Commissioners v Barclays Bank plc* [2006] UKHL 28, [2007] 1 AC 181.

[284] For an excellent attempt to give a succinct account of this turbulent area of the law, see E Peel and J Goudkamp, *Winfield & Jolowicz on Tort* (19th edn, Sweet & Maxwell 2014) paras 5.049–5.064.

[285] For a similar division, see M MacGrath, 'The Recovery of Economic Loss in Negligence – an Emerging Dichotomy' (1985) 5 OJLS 350.

[286] [1973] QB 27.

caused,[287] and particularly gains forgone, as claimed for in *Spartan Steel*, should be compensated in so far as not ruled out by limiting principles such as remoteness. In the same vein, it should be added that this aspect of pure economic loss recovery for tortious negligence does not raise problems for the distinction between tort and contract because it is within traditional tort reasoning in imposing a negative obligation, not to interfere making someone worse off, rather than imposing a positive obligation to confer a benefit.

(b) Negligent performance of services beneficial to the claimant

Most of the cases on negligently inflicted pure economic loss have so far been concerned with this situation. It occurs, for example, where a professional person, such as a solicitor,[288] surveyor,[289] or an engineer,[290] fails to advise a client properly. The client has an action against the professional defendant in the tort of negligence to compensate for the pure economic loss caused. Similarly in *Henderson v Merrett Syndicates Ltd*[291] Names at Lloyd's were held entitled to damages for pure economic loss in the tort of negligence against the managing agents of syndicates of which they were members.

The client will also almost always have a prima facie concurrent claim for breach of the professional's contractual duty of care[292] although in several cases the tortious claim was relied on because the contractual action was time-barred. Subject to differences in limiting principles, such as remoteness, the assessment of damages will be the same for breach of the tortious as for the breach of the contractual duty of care with the basic aim being to put the claimant into as good a position as if the defendant had performed the services using reasonable care. For example, in *Perry v Sidney Phillips & Son*,[293] if the survey had been properly carried out, the purchaser would not have bought the house or at least would not have paid more for it than its true market value. Hence damages for both breach of contract and the tort of negligence were assessed according to the purchase price of the house minus its actual market value (difference in value measure); and Lord Denning, having said that the aim of damages for breach of contract is 'to put the plaintiff in the same position as he would have been in if the contract had been properly performed' continued, 'Even if the claim be laid in tort against the surveyor, the damages should be on the same basis.'[294] It is important to realise that while one can see this as being in line with the usual compensatory aim of putting the claimant into as good a position as if no tort had been committed, the tortious obligation here is a positive one to benefit the claimant by performing the services non-negligently.

---

[287] An example of damages compensating for expenses caused in this context is provided by the Australian case of *Caltex Oil (Australia) Pty Ltd v Dredge 'Willemstad'* (1976) 136 CLR 529: the claimants were awarded damages compensating for the costs of transporting oil by other means when the defendants' dredger negligently damaged an underwater pipeline used, but not owned, by the claimants.

[288] Eg *Midland Bank Trust Co Ltd v Hett, Stubbs & Kemp* [1979] Ch 384; *Forster v Outred & Co* [1982] 1 WLR 86.

[289] Eg *Perry v Sidney Phillips & Son* [1982] 1 WLR 1297.

[290] Eg *Pirelli General Cable Works Ltd v Oscar Faber & Partners* [1983] 2 AC 1.

[291] [1995] 2 AC 145. See above, p 7. See also *Spring v Guardian Assurance Plc* [1995] 2 AC 296 (duty of care owed to one's former employee in writing a reference that was an essential requirement for the claimant's employment by a new employer).

[292] Above, pp 6–8. In so far as the basis of the tort liability is breach of promise, it is strongly arguable that the use of tort is a pragmatic, not a principled, development designed to evade deficiencies in contract: see above, p 9.

[293] [1982] 1 WLR 1297. See also, eg, *Nykredit Mortgage Bank plc v Edward Erdman Group Ltd (No 2)* [1997] 1 WLR 1627; *Tiuta International Ltd v De Villiers Surveyors Ltd* [2017] UKSC 77, [2017] 1 WLR 4627.

[294] [1982] 1 WLR 1297, at 1302.

But the tortious action may also be available where the defendant is performing the services under a contract with a party other than the claimant, so that (subject to an exception applying) privity prevents the claimant suing for breach of contract.[295] The best example is *White v Jones*.[296] Here delay by a solicitor in carrying out his client's instructions to draw up a new will meant that the client died without that new will having been executed. It was held (Lord Keith and Mustill dissenting) that a duty of care was owed by the solicitor to the claimants who would have benefited under the new will. Lord Goff based his reasoning on the concept of an 'assumption of responsibility' and on there being no other satisfactory way of filling the gap whereby the person who had suffered the loss could not otherwise sue and the person who could sue had suffered no loss. Note also that the claimants were a small number of identified people and there would otherwise have been no sanction in respect of the solicitor's breach of professional duty. Assuming that a defendant is held tortiously liable (and in a book on remedies this is the starting point) then, as where the parties are in a contractual relationship, the damages should be assessed according to the position the claimant would have been in if the services had been performed non-negligently. In other words, subject to differences in limiting principles, the approach should be the same as for contractual pecuniary loss. For example, in *White v Jones* the claimants were held entitled to the £9,000 each that they would have received under the amended will had the solicitor carried out his instructions properly.

---

[295] In so far as the basis of the tort liability is breach of promise, it is strongly arguable that the use of tort is here a pragmatic, not a principled, development designed to evade an excessively restrictive privity doctrine in contract: see above, p 9.

[296] [1995] 2 AC 207. This decision approved *Ross v Caunters* [1980] Ch 297. See also the claims of the *indirect* names in *Henderson v Merrett Syndicates Ltd* [1995] 2 AC 145; and *Gorham v British Telecommunications plc* [2000] 1 WLR 2129 (duty of care owed to dependants in their own right for defendant's negligent failure to advise the deceased who had opted out of a better pension scheme than the one he had opted into).

11

Personal injury losses

1. Claims by the injured person	234
2. Claims by the deceased's estate	253

Personal injury includes disease and physical illness as well as, for example, cuts, bruises, broken bones, loss of limbs or loss of the use of limbs, blindness, deafness, and brain damage.[1] Recognised psychiatric illnesses[2] are included. Damages have also been awarded for the physical and mental effects of a rape or sexual assault.[3]

Claims for personal injury are nearly always founded on a tort (and usually the tort of negligence or breach of statutory duty) but they can also be founded on a breach of contract.[4] Subject to differences in relation to some of the limiting principles, like remoteness, the principles applied are and should be the same whether founded on tort or breach of contract.

1. Claims by the injured person

The general compensatory aims dictate that damages should put the claimant into as good a position as if the personal injury had not occurred. In so doing, damages are awarded for several heads of loss, both pecuniary and non-pecuniary. Before examining these, three introductory points should be made.

First, as laid down in *Jefford v Gee*,[5] awards must be itemised, at least into non-pecuniary loss, pre-trial pecuniary loss, and future pecuniary loss. This itemisation was held to be required, because of the differing awards of interest payable or non-payable under these three

---

[1] Pleural plaques, which are a symptomless thickening of the blood from inhaling, eg, asbestos dust, are not classed as actionable personal injury: *Grieves v FT Everard & Sons* (also referred to as *Rothwell v Chemical and Insulating Co Ltd*) [2007] UKHL 39, [2008] 1 AC 281. But platinum sensitisation, which may lead to allergic reactions if the person is further exposed to platinum salts, does constitute actionable personal injury: *Dryden v Johnson Matthey plc* [2018] UKSC 18, [2018] 2 WLR 1109. Cf *Cartledge v Jopling* [1963] AC 758 (on the question when does a cause of action accrue for pneumoconiosis). See, generally, J Stapleton, 'The Gist of Negligence' (1988) 104 LQR 213; D Nolan, 'Damage in the English Law of Negligence' (2013) 4 Journal of European Tort Law 259.

[2] *Hinz v Berry* [1970] 2 QB 40, at 42 (morbid depression); *McLoughlin v O'Brian* [1983] 1 AC 410, at 418, 431 (organic depression and a change of personality); *Brice v Brown* [1984] 1 All ER 997, at 1005–1006 (hysterical personality disorder); *Alcock v Chief Constable of South Yorkshire Police* [1992] 1 AC 310 (post-traumatic stress disorder); *Walker v Northumberland County Council* [1995] 1 All ER 737 (nervous breakdown consequent on workplace stress); *Page v Smith* [1996] AC 155 (chronic fatigue syndrome); *Vernon v Bosley* [1997] 1 All ER 577 (pathological grief disorder); *Frost v Chief Constable of South Yorkshire Police* [1998] QB 254 (post-traumatic stress disorder); *Hatton v Sutherland* [2002] EWCA Civ 76, [2002] 2 All ER 1; and *Barber v Somerset County Council* [2004] UKHL 13, [2004] 1 WLR 1089 (depressive illness or nervous breakdown consequent on workplace stress). See, generally, Law Commission, *Liability for Psychiatric Illness* (1998) Report No 249, esp Part III. See also *Malyon v Lawrence, Messer & Co* [1968] 2 Lloyd's Rep 539 (compensation neurosis).

[3] *W v Meah* [1986] 1 All ER 935; *Griffiths v Williams*, The Times, 24 November 1995; *JXL v Britton* [2014] EWHC 2571 (QB).

[4] *Summers v Salford Corpn* [1943] AC 283; *Matthews v Kuwait Bechtel Corpn* [1959] 2 QB 57; *Kralj v McGrath* [1986] 1 All ER 54; *Berryman v London Borough of Hounslow* [1997] PIQR P83; *Giambrone v JMC Holidays Ltd (No 2)* [2004] EWCA Civ 158, [2004] 2 All ER 891.

[5] [1970] 2 QB 130.

heads.[6] So, as regards non-pecuniary loss, interest on damages is awarded at the rate of 2% from the date of service of the claim form to the date of trial.[7] Interest on pre-trial pecuniary loss awards is normally payable from the date of the accident until trial and the normal rate is half the average rate on the special account over that period.[8] No interest is payable on damages for future pecuniary loss.[9]

An undoubted consequence of itemisation has been an increase in the damages awarded for personal injury. Indeed in a number of cases awards of several million pounds have been made to claimants requiring constant care. But as rightly stressed in *Lim Poh Choo v Camden and Islington Area Health Authority*[10] it is no ground for appeal that the global award is too high; rather rationality dictates that a particular item of damages should be challenged.

A second point is that reference is often made to a distinction between special and general damages. The traditional view has been that 'special damages' refer to losses that are capable of substantially exact calculation, that is, pre-trial pecuniary loss; whereas 'general damages' refer to non-pecuniary loss and future pecuniary loss. However, in respect of personal injury claims, the relevant pleading rule under the Civil Procedure Rules makes no reference to special damages. Rather it simply states, 'The claimant must attach to his particulars of claim a schedule of details of any past and future expenses and losses which he claims.'[11]

Finally, the necessity for an award to be made once-and-for-all in a lump sum has been departed from in this field; the courts have power to award provisional damages and to make periodic payment orders.[12]

(1) Non-pecuniary loss

(a) Pain, suffering, and loss of amenity

In the context of damages for personal injury, the non-pecuniary losses, for which the claimant is entitled to compensation, are almost invariably referred to as pain, suffering, and loss of amenity. The amount of such damages—which is not susceptible to mathematical proof and accuracy—is awarded in accordance with a tariff system whereby the courts are guided by awards made for similar personal injuries in other cases. This system has depended on the publication (in, for example, *Current Law* and *Kemp & Kemp on The Quantum of Damages*) of judicial awards listed under the different types of personal injury (such as deafness, loss of thumb, loss of leg, quadriplegia) with brief details of the claimant's circumstances. The past awards must then be uplifted for inflation by taking into account changes in the retail price index since the past award was made.[13] The tariff or bracket of damages for that injury, which the previous cases have laid down (adjusted upwards for inflation), will provide the basic award (or range of award) in the instant case; but it will be adjusted flexibly by the courts to take account of the claimant's particular circumstances. For example, the injury (or treatment) may have been accompanied by a great deal of pain in one case but not so in another. And higher awards may be made in respect of younger,

---

[6] Interest is discussed below, ch 15.   [7] *Wright v British Railways Board* [1983] 2 AC 773.
[8] *Jefford v Gee* [1970] 2 QB 130; *Cookson v Knowles* [1979] AC 556. As regards the special account, see below, p 306 n 61.
[9] *Jefford v Gee* [1970] 2 QB 130. In Australia non-pecuniary loss is further itemised into pre-trial and future loss, with no interest being payable on the latter: see *Fire and All Risks Insurance Co Ltd v Callinan* (1978) 140 CLR 427.
[10] [1980] AC 174.   [11] CPR 16 PD.4.2.   [12] See above, pp 163–168.
[13] *Wright v British Railways Board* [1983] 2 AC 773; *Heil v Rankin* [2001] QB 272.

rather than older, claimants because the injury (if permanent) will be suffered for longer.[14] There may also be particular deprivations brought about by the injury: for example, that the claimant who has lost a hand was a pianist;[15] that the injury prevents sexual intercourse;[16] that, as a consequence of the injury, the claimant is unlikely to marry;[17] that, because of the injury, the claimant is unable to look after a terminally ill spouse as much as the claimant would have liked;[18] that the claimant was injured on holiday so that he was deprived of the enjoyment of that holiday;[19] or that, as a result of the injury, the claimant will not be able to obtain as satisfying a job as he previously had.[20]

In an attempt to produce greater consistency of awards, and in generally seeking to make the judicial tariff of values more accessible, the Judicial Studies Board in 1992 produced *Guidelines for the Assessment of General Damages in Personal Injury Cases*. The fourteenth edition of the *Guidelines* was published in 2017 and was updated to the end of May 2017. They set out, in easily understood form, the range of awards for various injuries. In that fourteenth edition, the range runs from a few hundred pounds for minor cuts and bruises through to £354,260[21] for the most serious injuries. This range takes account of the important decision of *Heil v Rankin*.[22] The Court of Appeal there partly implemented a recommendation of the Law Commission[23] by uplifting on a tapered scale awards over £10,000 so that the top end of the scale was increased from £150,000 to £200,000 (as at that date). This was on the basis that awards for more serious injuries had fallen behind what was considered fair, just, and reasonable.

The *Guidelines* also take into account[24] that, from 1 April 2013, when the legislative changes to the costs regime recommended by Sir Rupert Jackson came into force, damages for pain, suffering, and loss of amenity (and indeed all awards of damages for non-pecuniary loss) were increased by 10%. This uplift was essentially designed to compensate claimants who are funding litigation under a conditional fee agreement for the loss of their right to recover the success fee from the defendant (so that the 10% uplift does not apply where such a success fee is ordered under s 44(6) of the Legal Aid, Sentencing and Punishment of Offenders Act 2012).[25]

It is theoretically, and occasionally practically, important to clarify that the loss of amenity aspect of the award is assessed objectively in the sense that it is made irrespective of the claimant's own appreciation of her condition.[26] In contrast, pain and suffering is assessed

---

[14] Cf *Rose v Ford* [1937] AC 826 where £2 only was awarded for amputation of the deceased's leg the day before she died.

[15] *Moeliker v Reyrolle and Co Ltd* [1977] 1 WLR 132 (fishing).

[16] *Cook v JL Kier and Co Ltd* [1970] 1 WLR 774.   [17] *Hughes v McKeown* [1985] 1 WLR 963.

[18] *Rourke v Barton*, The Times, 23 June 1982.   [19] *Ichard v Frangoulis* [1977] 2 All ER 461.

[20] *Hale v London Underground Ltd* [1993] PIQR Q30 (this is commonly referred to as a 'loss of congenial employment'). In *Meah v McCreamer* [1985] 1 All ER 367 a substantial sum was awarded for the non-pecuniary loss of being imprisoned, where the claimant suffered a severe personality change (consequent on being brain-damaged in a car accident) which led to the claimant being imprisoned for sexual offences on women. But this can no longer be regarded as good law as the claim should have been barred by illegality: *Clunis v Camden and Islington HA* [1998] QB 978; *Gray v Thames Trains* [2009] UKHL 33, [2009] 1 AC 1339. See also *Meah v McCreamer (No 2)* [1986] 1 All ER 943 where the claimant was refused damages, indemnifying him against his liability to victims of his sex attacks, on the grounds of remoteness and public policy.

[21] This figure includes the 10% uplift explained below.

[22] [2001] QB 272. For an excellent case-note, see L Barmes, 'Damages for Pain and Suffering and Loss of Amenity: Is This Enough?' (2000) 116 LQR 548. For a different view, see R Lewis, 'Increasing the Price of Pain: Damages, The Law Commission and *Heil v Rankin*' (2001) 64 MLR 100.

[23] Law Commission, *Damages for Personal Injury: Non-Pecuniary Loss* (1999) Report No 257, esp para 3.110. For criticism of the Law Commission's approach, see D Harris, D Campbell, and R Halson, *Remedies in Contract and Tort* (2nd edn, Butterworths 2002) 375–376.

[24] The figures with and without the 10% uplift are both given.

[25] *Simmons v Castle* [2012] EWCA Civ 1039, [2012] EWCA Civ 1288, [2013] 1 WLR 1239.

[26] See, generally, A Ogus, 'Damages for Lost Amenities: For a Foot, a Feeling or a Function?' (1972) 35 MLR 1.

subjectively so that if the claimant is not capable of experiencing the pain or suffering no damages will be awarded for them.

Hence a majority of the Court of Appeal in *Wise v Kaye*[27] and of the House of Lords in *West & Son Ltd v Shephard*[28] upheld a loss of amenity award of £15,000, and a loss of amenity and pain and suffering award of £17,500 respectively, for claimants who had been very seriously injured and brain-damaged and were totally, or almost totally, incapable of appreciating their loss. Similarly, in *Lim Poh Choo v Camden and Islington Area Health Authority*[29] the House of Lords refused to overrule *West v Shephard* and upheld an award of £20,000 under loss of amenity and pain and suffering for the claimant's brain damage even though she was largely unaware of her deprivation. As Lord Morris said in *West v Shephard*:

> 'An unconscious person will be spared pain and suffering and will not experience the mental anguish which may result from knowledge of what has in life been lost or from knowledge that life has been shortened. The fact of unconsciousness is therefore relevant in respect of and will eliminate those heads or elements of damages which can only exist by being felt or thought or experienced. The fact of unconsciousness does not, however, eliminate the actuality of the deprivations of the ordinary experiences and amenities of life which may be the inevitable result of some physical injury.'[30]

Such an approach has been criticised[31] and there were strong dissenting judgments by Diplock LJ in *Wise v Kaye* and by Lords Devlin and Reid in *West & Son Ltd v Shephard*.[32] A main line of criticism is that for loss of amenity the courts should be seeking to compensate for the claimant's distress or loss of happiness and hence where the claimant cannot feel any distress or unhappiness no damages should be awarded under this head. In other words, critics of these decisions are mainly advocating what has been referred to above[33] as the alternative view of non-pecuniary loss, by which all such loss is ultimately viewed in terms of distress or of loss of happiness. This contrasts with the traditional judicial approach by which the heads of loss of amenity, loss of reputation, and physical inconvenience are regarded as analogous to proprietary losses, and as losses over and above any distress caused.

Where the claimant's expectation of life has been reduced by the injury an objective fixed sum, additional to loss of amenity and pain and suffering, used to be awarded for 'loss of expectation of life'. This was abolished by the Administration of Justice Act 1982, s 1(1)(a), although by s 1(1)(b) the courts are ordered to take into account in assessing damages for the claimant's pain and suffering, '… any suffering caused or likely to be caused to him by awareness that his expectation of life has been reduced'.

In *Shaw v Kovac*,[34] there had been medical negligence comprising a failure to obtain the patient's consent to an operation and the patient had died following the operation. It was held by the Court of Appeal that there could be no separate award for 'loss of autonomy' over and above personal injury damages for pain, suffering, and loss of amenity.

---

[27] [1962] 1 QB 638.   [28] [1964] AC 326. Also see *Andrews v Freeborough* [1967] 1 QB 1.
[29] [1980] AC 174.   [30] [1964] AC 326, at 349.
[31] See *Skelton v Collins* (1966) 115 CLR 94; *Knutson v Farr* (1984) 12 DLR (4th) 658; and *Royal Commission on Civil Liability and Compensation for Personal Injury* (chaired by Lord Pearson) (1978) Vol I, paras 393–398. The Law Commission, *Damages for Personal Injury: Non-Pecuniary Loss* (1999) Report No 257, paras 2.8–2.24 explained that, while it had initially favoured reversing *Wise v Kaye* and *West v Shephard*, the majority of its consultees were against this and it therefore made no recommendation for such a change.
[32] Illogically these minority judges still thought that some damages should be awarded for loss of amenity to an unconscious claimant.
[33] Above, pp 36–37.
[34] [2017] EWCA Civ 1028, [2017] 1 WLR 4773. The conventional award made in *Rees v Darlington Memorial Hospital NHS Trust* [2003] UKHL 52, [2004] 1 AC 309 (see below, pp 251–252) was distinguished as concerning the very different facts of a wrongful birth.

(b) Should there be a threshold for the recovery of damages for non-pecuniary loss?

The Pearson Commission recommended that no damages should be awarded for non-pecuniary loss suffered during the first three months after the injury.[35] Its reasoning was, first, that the primary concern of the tort system should be with compensating pecuniary loss and, secondly, that excluding such damages would save the system a great deal of expense.

But that recommendation has not been implemented; and when the Law Commission revisited the question of whether there should be a threshold for the recovery of damages for non-pecuniary loss, it came out firmly against such an idea.[36] It gave several main reasons for this. First, even if the tort system is too expensive, there are better ways to reduce costs (especially through procedural reforms) than interfering with basic common law principles. Secondly, a threshold might encourage potential claimants to exaggerate or prolong their symptoms in order to cross the threshold. Thirdly, since minor injuries typically cause little or no pecuniary loss, to refuse damages for non-pecuniary loss would lead to some wrongs going unremedied. Fourthly, the Pearson Commission's recommendation had to be seen in the context of its view that the role of the tort system should be as a mere supplement to no-fault compensation provided by the state. Fifthly, an exclusion of damages for non-pecuniary loss in the first three months after the accident would in many cases exclude compensation when a victim's pain is at its worst. Finally, a large majority of its consultees (93%), who responded on this issue, agreed with the Law Commission's provisional view that no such threshold should be introduced.

However, in a limited area, a similar idea to a threshold for non-pecuniary loss has been accepted in the Civil Liability Act 2018, Part 1 (which has not yet been brought into force). One of the purposes of the Act is to crack down on fraudulent whiplash claims thereby reducing motor insurance premiums. It allows for regulations imposing a low fixed tariff of damages for pain, suffering, and loss of amenity in respect of whiplash injuries, with a duration of up to two years, caused by negligent driving.

(2) Pecuniary loss

(a) The different types of recoverable pecuniary loss

The claimant is entitled to recover his or her *loss of net earnings*.[37] To calculate the net earnings, one deducts from the loss of gross earnings, the tax,[38] national insurance contributions,[39] and pension payments[40] that would have been paid from the gross earnings. In principle, the expenses involved in earning, which have been saved (eg the costs of travelling to work), should be deducted, although in general this appears not to be the practice.[41]

---

[35] *Royal Commission on Civil Liability and Compensation for Personal Injury* (chaired by Lord Pearson) (1978) Vol I, paras 362, 382–389.

[36] Law Commission, *Damages for Personal Injury: Non-Pecuniary Loss* (1999) Report No 257, paras 2.25–2.28.

[37] Loss of earnings includes all classes of earnings whether, eg, wages or professional fees or partnership profits (on which see *Ward v Newalls Insulation Co Ltd* [1998] 1 WLR 1722). Benefits in kind (eg a company car) are included alongside earnings: see, eg, *Kennedy v Bryan, The Times*, 3 May 1984. Illegality may rule out a claim for loss of earnings: *Hewison v Meridian Shipping PTE* [2002] EWCA Civ 1821, [2003] PIQR P252. For loss of a chance in relation to loss of earnings see, eg, *Doyle v Wallace* [1998] PIQR Q146; see above, p 66.

[38] *British Transport Commission v Gourley* [1956] AC 185. See above, ch 9.

[39] *Cooper v Firth Brown Ltd* [1963] 1 WLR 418. [40] *Dews v National Coal Board* [1988] AC 1.

[41] *Dews v National Coal Board* [1988] AC 1, at 12–13. Cf *Eagle v Chambers* [2004] EWCA Civ 1033, [2004] 1 WLR 3081, at [66]–[68].

The injured claimant may alternatively (or additionally) be awarded damages for being *handicapped in the labour market*. These are often described as 'Smith v Manchester Corp damages', that being the leading case.[42] The loss primarily in mind is that, as a result of the injury, the claimant may find it more difficult to find another equally well-paid job if he or she loses the present one. This head of damages has most commonly been used where a working claimant is still in the same job despite the injury. But it has also been used, for example, for the situation where the range of future jobs open to a child has been narrowed because of the injury.[43]

As a result of the injury, the claimant may have suffered a *loss of pension rights*: that is, the claimant may have lost all rights to a pension or may be entitled merely to a lower pension. *Lim Poh Choo v Camden and Islington Area Health Authority*[44] and *Auty v National Coal Board*,[45] for example, show that the claimant is entitled to damages for this loss. The courts appear to put a present value on it by taking the price an insurance company would demand for a pension providing equivalent rights to those lost.

The claimant can also recover all *medical, nursing, and hospital expenses* which have been, or will be, reasonably incurred.[46] It follows that if the claimant does not incur these expenses because she makes use of the NHS, she cannot recover what she would have had to pay if she had had private treatment.[47] Similarly, if it appears to the court to be likely that the claimant will be unable to obtain privately all the nursing services that will be needed, so that the claimant will eventually have to enter an NHS hospital, an appropriate deduction will be made.[48] So as not to overcompensate, ordinary living expenses saved are deducted from the cost of staying in a private hospital or home;[49] and by the Administration of Justice Act 1982, s 5, any saving to the claimant, which is or will be attributable to his maintenance by the NHS, is to be set off against his loss of earnings.[50] In *Rialas v*

---

[42] (1974) 17 KIR 1. See also, eg, *Moeliker v Reyrolle & Co Ltd* [1977] 1 WLR 132; *Foster v Tyne and Wear CC* [1986] 1 All ER 567; *Robson v Liverpool CC* [1993] PIQR Q78; *Brown v Ministry of Defence* [2006] EWCA Civ 546, [2006] PIQR Q9; *Ronan v Sainsbury's Supermarkets Ltd* [2006] EWCA Civ 1074; *Billett v Ministry of Defence* [2015] EWCA Civ 773, [2016] PIQR Q1 (while in some cases it would be appropriate to use a multiplicand and multiplier and the Ogden Tables to assess 'Smith v Manchester Corp damages' that was not an appropriate approach where, as on the facts of this case, the disability was of a minor kind that was causing the claimant no present loss of earnings; instead a relatively broad brush approach should be taken and, applying that approach, the judge's assessment of these damages at £99,062 using the Ogden Tables was reduced by the Court of Appeal to £45,000).

[43] *Mitchell v Liverpool Area Health Authority*, The Times, 17 June 1985.   [44] [1980] AC 174.

[45] [1985] 1 All ER 930. See also *Dews v National Coal Board* [1988] AC 1 (where there was no loss of pension); *Longden v British Coal Corpn* [1998] AC 653. For loss of a chance in relation to loss of pension rights, see *Brown v Ministry of Defence* [2006] EWCA Civ 546, [2006] PIQR Q9.

[46] These include the costs of appliances, eg a wheelchair. In *Briody v St Helens and Knowsley Health Authority* [2001] EWCA Civ 1010, [2002] QB 856, where the claimant had been deprived of her womb because of the defendant's negligence and therefore could not have children, it was held that surrogacy costs would be unreasonably incurred and were therefore irrecoverable. But this was confined to the facts where the child would not be genetically linked to the claimant (ie where neither the baby nor the pregnancy would be hers).

[47] *Cunningham v Harrison* [1973] QB 942; *Lim Poh Choo v Camden and Islington Area Health Authority* [1980] AC 174.

[48] ibid; *Eagle v Chambers* [2004] EWCA Civ 1033, [2004] 1 WLR 3081 (the same factual test should be applied to services provided by social services as to services provided by the NHS; and where a private care regime is needed, the burden of proving that services will be provided by the NHS or social services lies on the defendant); *Walton v Calderdale Healthcare NHS Trust* [2005] EWHC 1053 (QB), [2006] PIQR Q3; *Freeman v Lockett* [2006] EWHC 102 (QB), [2006] Lloyd's Rep Med 151. Applying the basic principle that benefits should be deducted from damages (see *Hodgson v Trapp* [1989] AC 807; see above, p 157) where a court finds that a claimant will receive direct payments from a local authority for care, they must be deducted in assessing damages for the cost of care: *Crofton v NHS Litigation Authority* [2007] EWCA Civ 71, [2007] 1 WLR 923.

[49] *Shearman v Folland* [1950] 2 KB 43; *Lim Poh Choo v Camden and Islington Area Health Authority* [1980] AC 174.

[50] Administration of Justice Act 1982, s 5 was enacted following the recommendation of the *Royal Commission on Civil Liability and Compensation for Personal Injury* (chaired by Lord Pearson) (1978) Vol 1, paras 510–512, that *Daish v Wauton* [1972] 2 QB 262 should be reversed. As the section requires the set off to be against loss of earnings, there can be no set off where the claimant has suffered no loss of earnings. The policy behind restricting

Mitchell[51] it was held that, where the claimant continues to live at home, the fact that it would be much cheaper to provide medical and nursing expenses in a private institution does not prevent the full recovery of such expenses. In *Sowden v Lodge*[52] it was stressed that the relevant test is one of reasonableness not one of what is in the claimant's best interests: but, even if unreasonable for the claimant to live in her own home, rather than in local authority residential accommodation, it might be workable and reasonable to have extra services in such accommodation thereby requiring a 'top-up fee' paid for by the defendant. By the Law Reform (Personal Injuries) Act 1948, s 2(4), the possibility that the claimant could have avoided expenses by using the facilities of the NHS is to be disregarded. The Pearson Commission recommended the repeal of s 2(4) so that private medical expenses should be recoverable only if it was reasonable on medical grounds for the claimant to incur them.[53] But private treatment may offer advantages which are more than merely medical in nature (eg speed and comfort) and it is hard to see how it can ever be unreasonable for a claimant to opt for it. In any event, a merit of s 2(4) is that it avoids the courts having to make difficult and invidious comparisons between the respective merits of NHS and private care. For these reasons, the Law Commission recommended that s 2(4) should not be repealed or amended.[54]

There is a valid claim for nursing expenses even though the services have been rendered gratuitously by a third party.[55] In *Donnelly v Joyce*[56] the Court of Appeal attempted to fit this within the normal principle that one is compensating the claimant's loss, by regarding the claimant's loss not as the incurring of nursing expenses but rather as the need for care. There was no legal obligation on the claimant to reimburse the third party but it was considered essential that sufficient should be awarded to allow the claimant to pay the third party reasonable recompense, including making up for any lost wages, the commercial rate of nursing services providing the ceiling. However, in *Hunt v Severs*[57] the House of Lords recognised that, in reality, it was not the claimant but the gratuitous carer who suffered the loss. Damages could be recovered in respect of the services rendered but the claimant must hold them on trust for the third party.[58] In *Hunt v Severs* itself, the gratuitous carer was also

---

the scope of the set off was presumably that it would not be deducting like from like to allow the set off against damages for non-pecuniary loss. In *O'Brien v Independent Assessor* [2007] UKHL 10, [2007] 2 AC 312 the same approach as that taken in s 5 of the 1982 Act was applied in the different context of the statutory compensation scheme for those whose conviction has been quashed for a miscarriage of justice: the saved cost of food, clothing, and accommodation while in prison was held to be deductible from the compensation for loss of earnings.

[51] (1984) 128 Sol Jo 704.

[52] [2004] EWCA Civ 1370, [2005] 1 WLR 2129. In *Peters v East Midlands SHA* [2009] EWCA Civ 145, [2010] QB 48 the disabled claimant would, on the balance of probabilities, be cared for and accommodated by a local authority in a residential home. It was held that she was entitled as of right to damages for the cost of self-funding that residential care even though the local authority would provide it for free if she did not self-fund. It was decided—with respect, controversially—that the duty to mitigate had no role to play here but that, even if it did, the claimant's preference to be self-funded, and not to be reliant on the state, was reasonable. It was thought that there was here no risk of double recovery (ie being awarded damages for self-funding and then being provided with free residential care) because the claimant's affairs were controlled by the Court of Protection.

[53] *Royal Commission on Civil Liability and Compensation for Personal Injury* (chaired by Lord Pearson) (1978) Vol 1, para 342.

[54] Law Commission, *Damages for Personal Injury: Medical, Nursing and Other Expenses; Collateral Benefits* (1999) Report No 262, paras 3.1–3.18.

[55] Provided more than *de minimis*, there is no lower threshold of seriousness that needs to be crossed before gratuitous nursing care can be compensated: see *Giambrone v JMC Holidays Ltd* (*No 2*) [2004] EWCA Civ 158, [2004] 2 All ER 891.

[56] [1974] QB 454. See also, eg, *Housecroft v Burnett* [1986] 1 All ER 332.

[57] [1994] 2 AC 350. See P Matthews and M Lunney, 'A Tortfeasor's Lot is not a Happy One?' (1995) 58 MLR 395; L Hoyano, 'The Dutiful Tortfeasor in the House of Lords' (1995) 3 Tort L Rev 63. *Hunt v Severs* was rejected by the High Court of Australia in *Kars v Kars* (1996) 71 AJLR 107, the approach in *Donnelly v Joyce* [1974] QB 454 being preferred.

[58] This was the view of Lord Denning in *Cunningham v Harrison* [1973] QB 942.

the tortfeasor; no damages for the care were recoverable, since the defendant would otherwise have been paying damages only for those damages to be returnable to the defendant under the trust.

In Part III of its Report, *Damages for Personal Injury: Medical, Nursing and Other Expenses; Collateral Benefits*,[59] the Law Commission approved the adoption of the view in *Hunt v Severs* that the loss is the carer's, not the claimant's. However, it recommended that the actual decision in the case should be reversed by legislation for several reasons. First, it was undesirable either to encourage the making of contracts with friends and relatives for the provision of care, or to provoke arguments as to whether or not a particular contract should be seen as a sham. Secondly, there should be no disincentive to accept care from the person in the best position to provide it, particularly as an increased liability in damages would usually arise if the claimant adopted the alternative of engaging professional care rather than relying on the care provided by the tortfeasor. Thirdly, the situation in which the gratuitous carer was only partially liable for the claimant's injuries presented problems. The Law Commission also rejected the use of a trust to ensure recompense for the gratuitous carer, preferring a personal liability on the claimant to account to the third party as regards damages for past (but not future) care. For future care it considered that the damages should be paid to the claimant without any duty to pay across to the carer, whether through a trust or personal liability.

The principle established in *Hunt v Severs*, that a claimant can recover damages for the loss incurred by a third party in gratuitously caring for the claimant, was applied in *Drake v Foster Wheeler Ltd*[60] so as to allow the cost of care provided by a charitable hospice to be compensated. The claimant was the estate of the deceased who had been cared for, prior to his death, by the hospice. As the damages awarded for that care were subject to a trust in favour of the hospice, it was ordered that the tortfeasor should pay the damages direct to the hospice.

Hunt v Severs was distinguished by the Court of Appeal in *Hardwick v Hudson*,[61] in which the injured claimant's wife provided gratuitous clerical services to his business. No damages were awarded in respect of those services. This was because the policy considerations favouring recompense for a gratuitous carer (such as encouraging effective and economical care) did not apply to the provision of those services, and the decision not to contract for them had been commercially motivated.

It was also recognised in *Hunt v Severs*[62] that *visiting costs* reasonably incurred by third parties in gratuitously visiting the claimant in hospital are recoverable by the claimant and are held on trust for the third party. In other words, they are treated in a similar way to nursing services. Correspondingly, the Law Commission recommended that the claimant should be under merely a personal obligation to account for the damages awarded in respect of past visits to the claimant and under no legal liability at all to the visitor in respect of damages awarded for future visits.[63] The main question in *Walker v Mullen*[64] was whether the claimant could recover damages in respect of his father's lost earnings, where his father had not gone back to his job in Jordan so as to be with his wife and the claimant while the

---

[59] Law Commission, *Damages for Personal Injury: Medical, Nursing and Other Expenses; Collateral Benefits* (1999) Report No 262. The report has been criticised, for compounding existing errors of legal classification, by S Degeling, 'Carers' Claims: Unjust Enrichment and Tort' [2000] RLR 172.
[60] [2010] EWHC 2004 (QB), [2011] 1 All ER 63.   [61] [1999] 1 WLR 1770.
[62] [1994] 2 AC 350, at 356–357.
[63] Law Commission, *Damages for Personal Injury: Medical, Nursing and Other Expenses; Collateral Benefits* (1999) Report No 262, para 3.68.
[64] *The Times*, 19 January 1984.

latter was in hospital. Comyn J reluctantly refused such damages on the ground that the loss was too remote. But surely that type of loss was foreseeable; and the father's loss of earnings was reasonably incurred. Nevertheless, taking the view that the loss in these sorts of cases is really the third party's, and hence that allowing the claimant to recover is highly exceptional, the decision is perhaps justified as confining recovery to a narrow range of claims.

The claimant can further recover the *cost of buying, fitting out, and moving to special accommodation*. But the capital cost of a new house (as opposed to the cost of the capital) is not awarded since the claimant still has that capital in the form of the house.[65] In *Roberts v Johnstone*[66] it was laid down that the claimant can recover 2% per annum of the capital cost of the purchase as the cost of the capital. More recently, in *Wells v Wells*[67] the House of Lords decided that the appropriate interest rate, for the purposes of applying *Roberts v Johnstone*, is that on index-linked government stock (ILGS) and for the time being that rate was regarded as being 3%. As we shall see below, the appropriate discount rate in assessing future pecuniary loss has subsequently been reduced by the Lord Chancellor, acting under the powers conferred on him by the Damages Act 1996, s 1, to minus 0.75%. The effect of this negative discount rate on a *Roberts v Johnstone* award for the cost of the capital is unclear but it can be powerfully argued that the logical consequence is that there should now be no sum payable as the cost of the capital under *Roberts v Johnstone*. A claimant can also recover for *loss of ability to do work in and around the home*, such as housekeeping, gardening, and carrying out repairs. Unfortunately, in the leading case of *Daly v General Steam Navigation Co Ltd*[68] the Court of Appeal appeared to adopt an inconsistent approach to whether this was a pecuniary loss depending on whether one was concerned with past or future loss. That is, for the future, loss of housekeeping capacity was considered to be a pecuniary loss, irrespective of whether any expenses in employing someone else to do the work would be incurred and irrespective of whether a third party would gratuitously carry out the work. In contrast, it was held that such a loss was only a recoverable pecuniary loss for the past where the claimant had actually employed someone, or where a third party, in this case the husband, had given up earnings so as to carry out the housekeeping work. Otherwise it was thought that past loss of housekeeping capacity should be regarded as a non-pecuniary loss, which was recoverable at least where the claimant had struggled on with her housekeeping despite her injury. But this approach seems hopelessly inconsistent: it criticises the artificiality of regarding the 'housewife' as having always suffered a past pecuniary loss in respect of housekeeping incapacity, while applying that artificiality to the future.

It is submitted therefore that the correct compensatory principles are as follows[69] (assuming that, in line with the nursing services cases, the claimant can recover for a third party's loss in gratuitously carrying out the housekeeping): the claimant may herself suffer a recoverable pecuniary loss by incurring the expense of employing someone to carry out her housekeeping work; even if not, she can recover a third party's loss where a third party gratuitously carries out that work, especially if the third party suffers a loss of earnings;[70]

---

[65] *George v Pinnock* [1973] 1 WLR 118; *Cunningham v Harrison* [1973] QB 942; *Moriarty v McCarthy* [1978] 1 WLR 155; *Roberts v Johnstone* [1989] QB 878.
[66] [1989] QB 878. [67] [1999] 1 AC 345.
[68] [1981] 1 WLR 120. See also *Hoffman v Sofaer* [1982] 1 WLR 1350, at 1355–1356 (recovery in respect of 'do-it-yourself' work around the home); *Lowe v Guise* [2002] EWCA Civ 197, [2002] QB 1369 (recovery for the fact that the injury prevented the claimant carrying out as many hours as before of gratuitous care for his disabled brother, the difference being made up by his mother).
[69] This was supported by the Law Commission which made a recommendation to the same effect in *Damages for Personal Injury: Medical, Nursing and Other Expenses; Collateral Benefits* (1999) Report No 262, para 3.91.
[70] Applying *Hunt v Severs* [1994] 2 AC 350 by analogy, the claimant would be bound to hold such damages on trust for the third party at least as regards damages for past loss. The Law Commission in *Damages for Personal Injury: Medical, Nursing and Other Expenses; Collateral Benefits* (1999) Report No 262, para 3.91, recommended

the claimant is entitled to damages for loss of housekeeping capacity as a non-pecuniary loss, at the very least where she struggles on with the housekeeping despite her injury; these principles are just as applicable to the past as to the future.

Most other pecuniary losses consequent on the injury are recoverable, provided they are not too remote or do not infringe the duty to mitigate.[71] An exception is loss consequent on a divorce caused by the personal injury. Departing from earlier authority,[72] the Court of Appeal in *Pritchard v JH Cobden Ltd*[73] held that, even though a divorce has foreseeably resulted from the claimant's injury, pecuniary 'loss' on that divorce is irrecoverable. There were three main grounds for this decision. The first was that where the financial consequences of a divorce have not yet been decided on in the Family Division, a judge in a personal injury action would be placed in the invidious position of having to make an assessment of the outcome of those proceedings. Secondly, it was thought that to allow compensation for this sort of loss would produce 'infinite regress' because, in deciding on the orders to be made after divorce, the potential assets of the parties, including any claims for damages, are taken into account in making those orders. Finally, talk of loss on divorce was in any case thought inapt on the ground that the financial consequences of a divorce are based on a distribution of the parties' assets taking into account various factors.

The Law Commission looked in detail at the arguments for and against the decision in *Pritchard v Cobden*.[74] In recommending that the law should not be reformed on this issue, the Law Commission stressed that, apart from the objections referred to by the Court of Appeal, there are real difficulties in establishing whether an injury did cause a divorce. Moreover, this might require distressing and distasteful inquiries into the personal lives of the married couple. Nor rationally could one confine such recovery only to the breakdown of marriage; if allowed for divorce, one ought rationally to extend recovery to pecuniary (and non-pecuniary) losses consequent on the breakdown, because of the injury, of any personal relationship.

(b) Calculating damages for pecuniary loss

Having identified the different types of recoverable pecuniary loss, we can now turn to the question of how damages for those pecuniary losses are calculated.

The calculation of damages for pre-trial pecuniary loss is relatively straightforward. It is essentially merely a question of adding together the expenses that the claimant has incurred; or multiplying the claimant's pre-injury monthly earnings by the number of months during which the claimant could not work. The latter calculation clearly depends upon the assumption that, but for the injury, the claimant would have continued to earn at the same rate. If this assumption is not justified (for example, because the claimant would have been promoted and had higher earnings)[75] an adjustment must be made.

---

that the claimant should be under a personal liability to account for damages, awarded in respect of past work, to the person (including the tortfeasor) who performed the work; but no legal obligation should be imposed in respect of damages awarded for work to be done in the future.

[71] For example, a widow can recover damages for the diminution in value of her dependency right under the Fatal Accidents Act 1976 as a result of the defendant having negligently injured, or caused a disease to, the widow, which reduces her life expectancy (and hence reduces the damages she can recover for loss of dependency under the 1976 Act on the tortious death of her husband): *Haxton v Philips Electronics UK Ltd* [2014] EWCA Civ 4, [2014] 1 WLR 2721.

[72] *Jones v Jones* [1985] QB 704. See also *Oakley v Walker* (1977) 121 Sol Jo 619.   [73] [1988] Fam 22.

[74] Law Commission, *Damages for Personal Injury: Medical, Nursing and Other Expenses; Collateral Benefits* (1999) Report No 262, Part IV.

[75] See, eg, *Anderson v Davis* [1993] PIQR Q87.

The calculation of damages for future pecuniary loss is more complex. Elements of uncertainty inevitably enter into the calculation, such as the claimant's life expectancy, and what would have happened to the claimant had he or she not been injured. The standard method of assessment (the so-called 'multiplier' method) is to multiply the assessed net annual loss by a multiplier. The starting point for the multiplier is the number of years during which the loss is likely to endure and thus, in a claim for loss of future earnings, the remaining period that the claimant would have worked. This figure is then reduced to take account of the fact that the claimant receives a lump sum which can be invested. There may then be a further (normally small)[76] reduction for the 'contingencies of life' other than mortality (for example, because the claimant might in any event have been unemployed or sick). The basis of the award is that the total sum will be exhausted at the end of the period contemplated; that, during the period, the claimant will draw upon both the income derived from the investment of the sum awarded and the capital; and that the income and withdrawals of capital will produce a stream of payments equal to the claimant's lost earnings or cost of care (or other loss in question). The courts conventionally used multipliers based on a discount of about 4.5%. But in *Wells v Wells*[77] the House of Lords held that this was incorrect and that the claimant was entitled to be treated as risk-averse. It was therefore appropriate that the (relatively low) rate of interest on ILGS should be taken as the appropriate discount rate for calculating multipliers. At the time of the decision, the ILGS rate was 3% (net of tax) and this was therefore laid down as the appropriate basis for multipliers for the time being. This meant that significantly higher multipliers would be used than where the discount rate was 4.5%. As we shall see shortly, the discount rate has since been reduced further, first to 2.5% and then to a negative discount rate of minus 0.75%.

After a long fight to overcome judicial resistance to actuarial evidence, it was also laid down in *Wells v Wells* that it is appropriate in working out the correct multiplier to make use of the 'Ogden Tables'. Over 20 years earlier, Oliver LJ had famously said in *Auty v National Coal Board*[78] that in this context, '… the predictions of an actuary can be only a little more likely to be accurate (and will almost certainly be less entertaining) than those of an astrologer'. Commentators long criticised this approach[79] and in 1982 a joint working party of lawyers and actuaries was set up, under the chairmanship of Sir Michael Ogden QC, to produce tables specifically geared to the assessment of damages for future pecuniary loss in personal injury and death actions. The seventh edition of the Ogden Tables, as they have become known, was published in 2011.[80] The Ogden Tables give actuarially accurate multipliers, applying various discount rates, according to the age of the claimant at the date of the trial. The acceptance of the Ogden Tables was spelt out by Lord Lloyd in *Wells v Wells*.[81] He said:

'I do not suggest that the judge should be a slave to the tables. There may well be special factors in particular cases. But the tables should now be regarded as the starting-point, rather than a

---

[76] In *Herring v Ministry of Defence* [2003] EWCA Civ 528, [2004] 1 All ER 44 Potter LJ said that the level of reduction for contingencies traditionally applied by the judiciary has been too high.
[77] [1999] 1 AC 345.   [78] [1985] 1 All ER 930, at 939.
[79] Eg J Prevett, 'Actuarial Assessment of Damages: The Thalidomide Case' (1972) 35 MLR 140, 257.
[80] *Actuarial Tables for Use in Personal Injury and Fatal Accident Cases* (7th edn, TSO 2011) (hereinafter cited as Ogden Tables). See also (Ogden) Supplementary Tables (March 2017) (accessible at www.gov.uk) which have the tables for the discount rate of minus 0.75% that was set in March 2017.
[81] [1999] 1 AC 345, at 379. The tables were designed for use in personal injury and fatal accident cases. But in *Kingston Upon Hull City Council v Dunnachie (No 3)* [2003] IRLR 843 the Employment Appeal Tribunal held that, in rare cases, where there was established to be a career-long loss, it would be appropriate to use the Ogden Tables in calculating loss of future earnings in a claim for unfair dismissal.

check. A judge should be slow to depart from the relevant actuarial multiplier on impressionistic grounds, or by reference to "a spread of multipliers in comparable cases" especially when the multipliers were fixed before actuarial tables were widely used.'

The standard multipliers assume that standard rate tax will be paid on the investment income but, according to the controversial decision of the House of Lords in *Hodgson v Trapp*,[82] there should normally be no further uplift of the multiplier to account for any higher rate tax that the claimant has to pay.

There is no adjustment made for future inflation. Now that the discount rate is essentially based on ILGS rates this follows inevitably (ie the ILGS rate automatically takes into account inflation). But even prior to the adoption of ILGS rates the courts took the same approach of making no adjustment for inflation on the reasoning that either it was too speculative to estimate what any future rate of inflation would be or that sensible investment of the damages could, to a large extent, counter the effect of inflation.[83]

Under the Damages Act 1996, s 1, the Lord Chancellor was given power to set the discount rate to be applied in assessing damages for personal injury and death (subject to a party showing that a different rate is more appropriate in the case in question). By the Damages (Personal Injury) Order 2001[84] the Lord Chancellor exercised that power to set a discount rate of 2.5%; and by the Damages (Personal Injury) Order 2017[85] the Lord Chancellor set a negative discount rate of minus 0.75% for assessing damages as from 20 March 2017. These changes have reflected the lower ILGS returns in the last two decades although the adjustments were very slow in being made so that claimants in personal injury cases were for many years being undercompensated (assuming that the *Wells v Wells* approach to compensation is correct).

In setting a rate of 2.5% in 2001 the Lord Chancellor saw himself as basically applying the principles set out in *Wells v Wells* and updating the rate in the light of the changed ILGS rates.[86] But he also took into account three further reasons, the last two of which cut against the principles in *Wells*. The first further reason was that, in his view, the ILGS yields appeared to have been artificially low in the three years prior to June 2001. Secondly, the Court of Protection, even after *Wells v Wells,* had continued to invest, on behalf of claimants, in multi-asset portfolios which enabled them to achieve a real rate of return at 2.5% or above, without their being unduly exposed to risk in the equity markets. Thirdly, the Lord Chancellor thought it likely that, in reality, claimants who sought investment advice would not be advised to invest solely or even primarily in ILGS but rather in a mixed portfolio.

There continues to be considerable controversy as to whether the ILGS rates are the best way of assessing the discount rate and hence arriving at the correct amount of compensation. Those representing the interests of defendant insurers argue that the present negative discount rate of minus 0.75% overcompensates claimants because they can readily invest to obtain higher returns. Those representing personal injury victims counterargue that one should not be treating personal injury victims as normal investors and that, in any event, empirical historical evidence shows that personal injury victims have certainly not been overcompensated.[87] In 2017, the Ministry of Justice, following a

---

[82] [1989] AC 807; see above, p 184. See also *Wells v Wells* [1999] 1 AC 345, at 388.
[83] *Cookson v Knowles* [1979] AC 556, esp at 577; *Lim Poh Choo v Camden and Islington Area Health Authority* [1980] AC 174, esp at 193; *Auty v National Coal Board* [1985] 1 All ER 930.
[84] SI 2001/2301. [85] SI 2017/206.
[86] *Setting the Discount Rate, Lord Chancellor's Reasons*, 27 July 2001 (www.lcd.gov.uk/civil/discount.htm).
[87] See, eg, note 95 below.

consultation exercise, proposed[88] that, while full compensation should remain the aim of damages, the discount rate should not be set on what it considered to be the unrealistic basis that claimants will invest in ILGS. Rather it should be assumed that, while claimants are low-risk investors, they will invest (and would be professionally advised to invest) in a mixed portfolio which will enable them to achieve higher rates of return. It is also proposed that, while the Lord Chancellor should set the rate, he or she should be advised by an independent expert panel; and that there should be a review of the discount rate at least once every three years. These proposals (but substituting five years for three years) have been carried through into the Civil Liability Act 2018 (inserting a new Schedule 1 into the Damages Act 1996).

Applying a present discount rate of minus 0.75%, the basic multiplier[89] for calculating loss of future earnings for a male who is 16 years old (at the date of trial) and who would have worked until 65 but will now not be able to do so, is 57.67; for a 30-year-old male it is 38.71.[90] Applying a discount rate of minus 0.75%, the basic multiplier for calculating the cost of care for life of a male who is 16 years old (at the date of trial) is 96.45; for a 30-year-old male it is 71.43.[91]

The courts are bound by the rate set by the Lord Chancellor unless, applying s A1(2) of the Damages Act 1996,[92] any party to the proceedings shows that a different rate of interest is 'more appropriate in the case in question'. When does this exception apply? In *Warriner v Warriner*[93] it was said that, in the interests of certainty, a departure from the rate set would probably be rare. In the instant case, there was nothing unusual justifying a lower rate than that set by the Lord Chancellor (which at that time was 2.5%). In *Cooke v United Bristol Health Care*,[94] the Court of Appeal rejected a different line of attack by the claimants on the conventional method for assessing future pecuniary loss. The claimants wanted to adduce evidence that the cost of care, and indeed earnings, had increased, and could be expected to increase, at a substantially higher rate than the retail price index.[95] The claimants therefore sought to argue that the conventional method undercompensated claimants, especially where there were high future costs of care, and that, to prevent such undercompensation, there should be adjustments to the multiplicands. But the Court of Appeal refused to allow such evidence to be adduced on the basis that, in reality, the claimants were arguing for a departure from the discount rate for multipliers set by the Lord Chancellor; and in line with *Warriner v Warriner* such a departure was thought to be unjustified. Although not mentioned by the Court of Appeal, it is perhaps worth adding, as a further reason for rejecting the claimants' specific arguments in *Cooke*, that, in adopting the ILGS rate in *Wells v Wells*, the House of Lords assumed that it is the retail price index that is the correct measure of

---

[88] *The Personal Injury Discount Rate: How it Should be Set in Future* (Draft Legislation, Ministry of Justice, September 2017, Cm 9500).

[89] This figure is then subject to a further (normally small) adjustment for the 'contingencies of life' other than mortality. See Ogden Tables (7th edn, TSO 2011) Section B.

[90] Ogden Tables (7th edn, TSO 2011) and (Ogden) Supplementary Tables (March 2017) (accessible at www.gov.uk) Table 9. Applying the former discount rate of 2.5% the multipliers were, respectively, 27.92 and 22.84.

[91] Ogden Tables (7th edn, TSO 2011) and (Ogden) Supplementary Tables (March 2017) (accessible at www.gov.uk) (March 2017) Table 1. Applying the former discount rate of 2.5% the multipliers were, respectively, 32.94 and 29.60.

[92] Inserted by the Civil Liability Act 2018, s 10. [93] [2002] EWCA Civ 81, [2002] 1 WLR 1703.

[94] [2003] EWCA Civ 1370, [2004] PIQR Q2.

[95] For the view that, in comparison to the 'labour market' approach in the US, the traditional English approach to calculating loss of future earnings undercompensates claimants (principally because it underestimates the earnings growth claimants would have enjoyed if not injured and overestimates the earnings of claimants after injury) see R Lewis, R McNabb, H Robinson, and V Wass, 'Court Awards of Damages for Loss of Future Earnings: An Empirical Study and an Alternative Method of Calculation' (2002) 29 J Law & Soc 406.

inflation and this is also the index used for updating awards for non-pecuniary loss in personal injury cases.[96]

Closely linked to the discount rate is the question of whether damages can be recovered for the costs of investment advice. Logically if the assumption is ILGS investment, such costs should not be recoverable because that sort of investment is straightforward and does not require the sort of advice that investing in gilts and equities would do. This logic was accepted in *Page v Plymouth Hospital NHS Trust*.[97] There a claim for damages for the costs of investment advice and fund management charges was rejected as inconsistent with the assumption of ILGS investment and as being another attempt indirectly to depart from the (then) 2.5% discount rate. In *Eagle v Chambers*[98] the Court of Appeal approved the reasoning in *Page* and held that the same approach applied where the claimant was a patient subject to the Court of Protection. So just as the cost of investment advice was irrecoverable generally, the cost of a Court of Protection's panel broker's fees was irrecoverable in respect of a patient of the Court of Protection. The discount rate assumed standard investment in ILGS without the need for investment advice. Claimants, including patients through the agency of the Court of Protection, were free to invest more broadly for higher returns. But to avoid overcompensation, the fees for those investments must be set off against the higher gains made.

In calculating loss of future earnings, the multiplier applicable to an injured young woman has sometimes in the past been reduced to take account of the workless years that she would in any event have had, bringing up a family.[99] However, this was then largely balanced out by an award for loss of marriage prospects as a pecuniary loss: ie the loss of the economic support, during the years raising a family, of the never-to-be-husband.[100] Not surprisingly, therefore, in *Hughes v McKeown*[101] Leonard J took the simpler approach of making no deduction from the multiplier while also making no award for loss of marriage prospects (as a pecuniary loss). This approach was approved by the Court of Appeal in *Housecroft v Burnett*[102] provided that there was a reasonable equivalence between the loss of earnings of the woman and the economic support that a husband would have given. There might be no such equivalence, for example, where the woman was a particularly high earner. However, one can strongly argue that, in the light of changes in working practices, attitudes, and maternity rights, the old (pre-*Hughes v McKeown*) approach would, in any event, now be considered inaccurate and inappropriate.

In so far as a multiplier approach is used,[103] low multipliers are applied in respect of young children, since they might never have become wage earners. For example, in *Croke v Wiseman*,[104] where the claimant was aged seven at trial and was expected to live until 40, a multiplier of five was applied for loss of future lifetime earnings. As there was no present loss of earnings in that case, it was held acceptable to take the national average earnings during early working years as the multiplicand (or the basis for working out the multiplicand).

---

[96] See above, p 171.
[97] [2004] EWHC 1154, [2004] 3 All ER 367. This logical position is also supported by the Law Commission, *Damages for Personal Injury: Medical, Nursing and Other Expenses; Collateral Benefits* (1999) Report No 262, paras 5.11–5.15.
[98] [2004] EWCA Civ 1033, [2004] 1 WLR 3081.
[99] *Harris v Harris* [1973] 1 Lloyd's Rep 445; *Moriarty v McCarthy* [1978] 1 WLR 155.
[100] [1973] 1 Lloyd's Rep 445.   [101] [1985] 1 WLR 963.   [102] [1986] 1 All ER 332.
[103] Cf *Joyce v Yeomans* [1981] 1 WLR 549; see below, p 249.
[104] [1982] 1 WLR 71. See P Davies, 'Damages for Severely Injured Children' (1982) 45 MLR 333.

Where the injury has reduced the number of years which the claimant is expected to live, the multiplier and hence the damages are calculated according to his or her life expectancy prior to the accident, with a deduction for the living expenses which the claimant would have incurred during those 'lost years' that he or she will no longer live through. That damages can be recovered for the 'lost years' was laid down by the House of Lords in *Pickett v British Rail Engineering Ltd*,[105] overruling *Oliver v Ashman*.[106]

What is the reason for allowing a lost years claim when the claimant will not be alive to suffer any financial deprivation? The formal answer is to say that, by analogy to, for example, *Wise v Kaye*,[107] the claimant's subjective enjoyment of his or her earnings is irrelevant. The claimant has still *objectively* suffered a loss. An alternative explanation is that a lost years claim is granted not so much because the claimant has lost out, but rather because the claimant's dependants will otherwise lose out. This is highlighted, as in *Pickett*, where the victim dies from his injuries having settled or obtained judgment, thus preventing any Fatal Accidents Act claim by his dependants.[108] But this alternative explanation can only be valid so long as the claimant has dependants. In any event it is rather confusing to represent the loss as the claimant's, if it is in reality the dependants'. As such, the main problem could be better solved, without relying on lost years awards, if dependants under the Fatal Accidents Act could be awarded damages even though the victim had settled or obtained judgment. But this would not prevent the dependants losing out if the claimant were to live on but with life expectancy and earnings reduced. So perhaps the best solution of all, albeit a rather radical one, would be to abolish the lost years award, and for legislation to be passed allowing dependants a claim for pecuniary loss where the person on whom they are dependent has been injured as well as where he or she has been killed.

No award for the lost years is likely to be made where the claimant is a young child. So for example, in *Connolly v Camden and Islington Area Health Authority*[109] a four-year-old with over 20 years' life expectancy was given nothing for the lost years; nor was the seven-year-old with a life expectancy of 40 in *Croke v Wiseman*.[110] On a formal level, the justification for such decisions is that to assess the value of the lost years claim in respect of young children involves too much speculation. On a deeper level, as stressed particularly by Griffiths LJ in *Croke v Wiseman*, they are justified by the fact that where a child's injuries render it unlikely that there will ever be any dependants, the policy reason for awarding the lost years damages is non-existent.

How the deductible living expenses in a lost years claim are to be calculated has given rise to controversy which reflects the tension between the formal objective reason and the alternative policy justification for the lost years award. In some first instance decisions[111] it was held that the same approach should be adopted as where calculating damages under the Fatal Accidents Act 1976, ie living expenses are what the claimant would have spent *exclusively* on herself (the theory being that the dependants would have benefited from the rest of the claimant's money). But these decisions were overruled in *Harris v Empress Motors Ltd*[112] where the Court of Appeal considered that one should deduct as living expenses what the claimant would have spent in maintaining himself at the standard of living appropriate to his case (the theory being that he would have the rest of his income free to spend as he

---

[105] [1980] AC 136. [106] [1962] 2 QB 210. [107] [1962] 1 QB 638.
[108] Below, p 258. See also *McCann v Sheppard* [1973] 2 All ER 881. [109] [1981] 3 All ER 250.
[110] [1982] 1 WLR 71. See also *Iqbal v Whipps Cross University Hospital NHS Trust* [2007] EWCA Civ 1190, [2008] PIQR P9.
[111] Eg *Benson v Biggs Wall & Co Ltd* [1982] 3 All ER 300; *Clay v Pooler* [1982] 3 All ER 570.
[112] [1983] 1 WLR 65.

wished). In contrast to an assessment under the Fatal Accidents Act 1976, a pro rata amount of his family expenditure, eg expenditure on housing, heat, and light, should therefore be deducted. This decision takes the objective approach. On the alternative view, as the justification for allowing the claimant damages for the lost years is to benefit his dependants, who are the ones who will otherwise lose out, calculation of the living expenses should be on the same basis as under the Fatal Accidents Act 1976.[113]

In *Housecroft v Burnett*,[114] where a 16-year-old girl was very badly injured, the Court of Appeal considered that a simpler way to proceed than deducting notional living expenses from notional earnings, and multiplying by the lost years multiplier, was to add one or half to the multiplier for the lost years and then to multiply the full multiplicand with no living expenses deduction.

Finally, it should be noted that a multiplier approach is not always appropriate for calculating future pecuniary loss. For example, '*Smith v Manchester Corp* damages'[115] are normally assessed without first trying to fix a multiplicand. Similarly, in assessing the loss of future earnings of an injured child, the courts have occasionally preferred to estimate directly in a lump sum the loss of earnings without the use of a multiplicand.[116] These are situations—and there are others[117]—where the assessment is particularly speculative and where the more precise multiplier approach may, therefore, be thought inappropriate.

(3) Compensating advantages provided by third parties in response to the personal injury ('collateral' benefits)

The important question of whether these benefits should be deducted in assessing the damages has been fully dealt with in chapter 8.[118]

(4) Addendum—damages for wrongful birth[119]

'Wrongful birth' claims are made where a child, who was originally unwanted, has been born as a result of a doctor's or health authority's civil wrong (be it the tort of negligence or breach of contract). Although the losses are not quite the same as personal injury losses, they are sufficiently similar to be included as an addendum to personal injury.

When first recognised, the approach in this area was to apply the general compensatory principle and to permit recovery of all pecuniary and non-pecuniary loss suffered by the parents as a result of the wrongful birth, subject to the usual restrictions like remoteness and mitigation. So, for example, in *Emeh v Kensington Area Health Authority*,[120] where a sterilisation operation had been performed negligently, the mother was awarded damages for the pain and suffering and loss of amenity of having and looking after the child, who had congenital abnormalities, plus the pecuniary loss of maintaining her. Similarly, in *Thake v*

---

[113] D Evans and K Stanton, 'Valuing the Lost Years' (1984) 134 NLJ 515.   [114] [1986] 1 All ER 332.
[115] See above, p 239, esp n 42.   [116] *Joyce v Yeomans* [1981] 1 WLR 549.
[117] See, eg, *Blamire v South Cumbria HA* [1993] PIQR Q1; *Ward v Allies & Morrison Architects* [2012] EWCA Civ 1287, [2013] PIQR Q1. In line with the more impressionistic approach to the assessment in this type of case, the courts sometimes refer to the loss in these cases as a loss of earning capacity rather than a loss of earnings.
[118] Above, pp 152–162.
[119] See generally A Taylor, 'Compensation for Unwanted Children' (1985) 15 Fam Law 147; C Symmons, 'Policy Factors in Actions for Wrongful Birth' (1987) 50 MLR 269; A Stewart, 'Damages for the Birth of a Child' (1995) 40 JLSS 298; R Scott, 'Reconsidering "Wrongful Life" in England after 30 Years' [2013] CLJ 115.
[120] [1985] QB 1012.

Maurice[121] the defendant surgeon had failed to warn the claimants, in breach of his contractual and tortious duty of care, that the vasectomy operation would not be a 100% guarantee against pregnancy. Consequently the mother had not sought an abortion at an early stage. The parents were awarded damages for their pecuniary loss (loss of earnings and the cost of the child's upkeep) and antenatal pain and suffering, subject to a deduction from the latter for the fact that the pain and suffering of an abortion had not been suffered. But postnatal non-pecuniary loss (ie the time and trouble in bringing up the child) was not claimed, and was in any event non-recoverable since it had been fully mitigated by the joy of a having a (healthy) child.

However, the scope of damages recoverable in a 'wrongful birth' claim was considerably narrowed by the House of Lords in *McFarlane v Tayside Health Board*,[122] a failed vasectomy case. A surgeon negligently advised a husband and wife that the vasectomy had rendered the husband infertile; the couple ceased to use contraceptives and the wife became pregnant, giving birth to a healthy child. The House of Lords held (Lord Millett dissenting on this point) that the mother's non-pecuniary and pecuniary losses directly consequent on the pregnancy and giving birth were recoverable; they were regarded as equivalent to personal injury losses. But all their Lordships were in agreement that the parents could not recover for their economic loss in maintaining the child, which was regarded as pure economic loss. Lords Slynn, Steyn, and Hope saw the issue as one of liability, rather than the extent of liability, and held that no duty of care was owed to the parents as regards the pure economic loss because, in line with the standard approach to that sort of loss, it was not fair, just, and reasonable for there to be such a duty. Lord Steyn, in particular, relied on what he termed considerations of distributive, rather than corrective, justice; that is, 'on the just distribution of burdens and losses among members of a society'.[123] And in determining that just distribution, Lord Steyn thought it relevant that, in his opinion, popular morality would be against holding the doctor or hospital liable for the costs of bringing up a child.

Two main matters were left unresolved by their Lordships in *McFarlane*. The first and more important was whether the position would have been any different if the child had been disabled. The previously leading case of *Emeh v Kensington Area Health Authority* concerned a disabled child. That decision was not expressly overruled and Lord Steyn specifically left open what the position would have been in such a case. The second, more conceptual, point is what the position would have been if the parents could have sued for breach of contract. Lord Steyn expressly confined his views to claims in delict or tort; and certainly in respect of breach of contract one could not regard the issue as going to liability rather than the extent of liability.

It was not long before the question of the disabled child came before the appellate courts. In *Parkinson v St James and Seacroft University Hospital NHS Trust*[124] a negligent sterilisation operation led to the birth of a disabled child. The Court of Appeal took a mid-position. The mother was awarded damages for the upbringing costs attributable to the disability. It

---

[121] [1986] QB 644. See also *Gold v Haringey Health Authority* [1988] QB 481; *Benarr v Kettering Health Authority* [1988] NLJR 179; *Salih v Enfield Health Authority* [1991] 3 All ER 400; *Allen v Bloomsbury Health Authority* [1993] 1 All ER 651; *Fish v Wilcox* (1993) 13 BMLR 134.
[122] [2000] 2 AC 59. This was a Scottish case, but their Lordships made it clear that on this issue the same law should apply in both England and Scotland. By a four–three majority, the High Court of Australia in *Cattanach v Melchior* (2003) 77 AJLR 1312 went the other way from *McFarlane* and awarded the costs of maintaining the child.
[123] [2000] 2 AC 59, at 82.
[124] [2001] EWCA Civ 530, [2002] QB 266. See also *Rand v East Dorset Health Authority* (2000) 50 BMLR 39; *Hardman v Amin* [2000] Lloyd's Med Rep 448; *Lee v Taunton and Somerset NHS Trust* [2001] 1 FLR 419; *Groom v Selby* [2001] EWCA Civ 1522, [2002] PIQR P201; O Quick, 'Damages for Wrongful Conception' (2002) 10 Tort LR 5.

was held that such damages had not been ruled out by *McFarlane*. On the other hand, damages for the costs which would be incurred in bringing up any child (healthy or disabled) were disallowed. Those damages, it was held, had been ruled out by *McFarlane* and to this extent, *Emeh*, in which all the costs of bringing up a disabled child were held recoverable, had been impliedly overruled by *McFarlane*.

But that was not the end of the story. On the contrary, a further factual twist—the birth of a healthy child, following a negligently conducted sterilisation operation, to a disabled mother—brought the whole question back to a seven-man House of Lords in *Rees v Darlington Memorial Hospital NHS Trust*.[125] All their Lordships decided that *McFarlane* had been correctly decided and should basically be followed. By a four–three majority (Lords Bingham, Nicholls, Millett, and Scott in the majority, Lords Steyn, Hope, and Hutton dissenting) it was then decided that the majority of the Court of Appeal in the instant case had been incorrect, as being inconsistent with *McFarlane*, to award damages to the mother for the additional upbringing costs attributable to the mother's disability.[126] On the other hand, a 'gloss' (as it was termed by Lords Bingham and Nicholls)[127] was placed on *McFarlane* by the majority in holding that a conventional sum of £15,000 should be awarded to the mother (or jointly to the parents) where there has been an unwanted birth attributable to a civil wrong. Such a conventional sum is to be awarded irrespective of whether the child or the parents are healthy or disabled. Although Lord Bingham at one point said that this conventional award 'would not be, and would not be intended to be, compensatory',[128] he had earlier spoken of 'the real loss … [of being] denied … the opportunity to live her life in the way that she wished and planned' and that there should be 'a conventional award to mark the injury and loss'.[129] And in Lord Millett's words, '[T]he parents have lost the opportunity to live their lives in the way that they wished and planned to do. The loss of this opportunity, whether characterised as a right or a freedom, is a proper subject for compensation by way of damages.'[130] Similarly, Lord Scott referred to *Farley v Skinner*[131]—a leading contractual case on mental distress—and spoke of the award as compensating the mother for being deprived of her expected benefit. It is submitted, therefore, that the conventional sum is best viewed as an award to compensate for non-pecuniary loss, namely a mother's mental distress consequent on having her lifestyle plans disrupted. Admittedly, a *fixed* conventional award—as opposed to a bracket of awards—for non-pecuniary loss is unusual but it is the approach used for bereavement damages under the Fatal Accidents Act 1976 and it is the approach that used to be applied to non-pecuniary loss of expectation of life.

Although three of the majority would have overruled *Parkinson*, Lord Millett explicitly left open whether *Parkinson* had been correctly decided.[132] Without a majority for or against that decision, it technically remains good law.[133] Applying the majority's approach, therefore, in a wrongful birth case, a mother is entitled to all pecuniary and non-pecuniary loss directly attributable to the pregnancy and giving birth *and* a conventional sum of £15,000 for disruption of planned lifestyle. In so far as *Parkinson* remains good law, where the child

---

[125] [2003] UKHL 52, [2004] 1 AC 309.
[126] In a powerful dissenting judgment in the Court of Appeal [2002] EWCA Civ 88, [2002] 2 All ER 177, at [53]–[54], Waller LJ pointed to some of the anomalies that might be thought to arise from 'picking out' the disabled mother; eg the contrast between the rich, very well assisted, disabled mother and the poor, unassisted, healthy mother.
[127] [2003] UKHL 52, [2004] 1 AC 309, at [7] and [17]. [128] ibid, at [8]. [129] ibid, at [8].
[130] ibid, at [123]. [131] [2001] UKHL 49, [2002] 2 AC 732.
[132] [2003] UKHL 52, [2004] 1 AC 309, at [112].
[133] In *Farraj v King's Healthcare NHS Trust* [2006] EWHC 1228, [2006] PIQR P29, at [39] Swift J said as much: 'for the present, the decision in *Parkinson* represents the law.'

is disabled, a mother will additionally be entitled to the upbringing costs attributable to the disability.

While agreeing that *McFarlane* was correctly decided, the minority judges (Lords Steyn, Hope, and Hutton) disagreed with the majority's 'gloss' on it and would have upheld not only *Parkinson* but also the majority of the Court of Appeal's decision in *Rees* that the extra upbringing costs attributable to the mother's disability were recoverable.

The approach of the majority of their Lordships in *Rees* has much to commend it. It represents a fair and relatively clear answer to an intractable problem, albeit that it is unfortunate that there was no majority either way on *Parkinson*. Moreover, it should be appreciated—as Lord Hope explained with great clarity in his dissenting speech—that the conventional award is unique because, in contrast to damages for personal injury and death, it compensates mental distress in a situation where, for reasons of legal policy, the courts have decided that pecuniary loss is non-compensatable.[134] To place non-pecuniary loss above pecuniary loss is certainly odd. To that extent, it is clear that the majority have adopted a pragmatic compromise rather than a principled solution.

The same basic policy approach to wrongful birth claims is applicable whether the claim is brought in tort or for breach of contract. That point was strongly affirmed in the context of the breach of a strict contractual obligation in *ARB v IVF Hammersmith*.[135] A private IVF clinic acted in breach of its contract with the claimant by thawing and implanting an embryo containing the claimant's gametes into his ex-partner without his consent. This ultimately resulted in the birth of a healthy daughter. The claimant sought damages for that breach of contract to cover the costs to him of bringing up the daughter.[136] It was held by the Court of Appeal that, applying *McFarlane* and *Rees*, such damages were not recoverable on policy grounds and that it did not matter that the claim was for breach of contract (comprising the breach of a strict duty) rather than the tort of negligence. In the words of Nicola Davies LJ:[137]

'At the core of the legal policy which prevented recoverability of the identified loss in *Rees* and *McFarlane* was the impossibility of calculating the same loss given the benefits and burdens of bringing up a healthy child. If it is impossible for a court to calculate the value to be attributed to the benefit of a child, so as to set off such value against the financial cost of the child's upbringing as a matter of legal policy in tort, how is the task possible for a court if such loss results from a breach of contract? Added to this is the sense, reflected in the judgments in *Rees* and *McFarlane*, that it is morally unacceptable to regard a child as a financial liability.'

Finally, although not involving a wrongful birth, the controversial decision in *Kralj v McGrath*[138] can also be conveniently mentioned here. The defendant doctor's negligence during the birth of one of the claimant's twins had caused the baby's death. The claimant wanted three children and hence would have to undergo another pregnancy and workless years which would not have been necessary had that baby not died. Inter alia, Woolf J awarded the claimant mother damages for the non-pecuniary and pecuniary loss of another pregnancy and childbirth and the pecuniary loss of initial workless years looking after another child. But the force of this decision is diminished because the only objection to those

---

[134] [2003] UKHL 52, [2004] 1 AC 309, at [73].   [135] [2018] EWCA Civ 2803.
[136] As made clear at first instance, [2017] EWHC 2438 (QB), [2018] 2 WLR 1223, at [288], the claimant did not seek a conventional award for non-pecuniary loss.
[137] [2018] EWCA Civ 2803, at [33].
[138] [1986] 1 All ER 54. See also *Kerby v Redbridge Health Authority* [1993] 4 Med LR 178 (damages awarded for the non-pecuniary rigours of an additional pregnancy).

damages that was examined in the judgment was remoteness and there was no discussion of the fact that this claim was entirely novel and that the loss could not really be regarded as consequent on the personal injury to the mother. If followed to its logical conclusion the decision would mean that a mother whose baby is killed by the defendant's negligent driving should also be awarded damages for the non-pecuniary and pecuniary loss of pregnancy and workless years if she will want to have another child to replace the one lost. Yet such damages are presumably irrecoverable in a claim under the Fatal Accidents Act 1976 where the most the mother would be awarded would be bereavement damages (plus any funeral expenses incurred).

2. Claims by the deceased's estate

The Law Reform (Miscellaneous Provisions) Act 1934, s 1(1), provides that on the death of any person all causes of action vested in him, subject to certain exceptions,[139] survive for the benefit of his estate. The most important consequence of this, and the one with which we are here concerned, is that the deceased's action for personal injury survives for the benefit of his estate. It should be stressed that the action brought by the estate is not for death caused by the defendant. The defendant may or may not have been responsible for the deceased's death. Rather the action is for the deceased's personal injury caused by the defendant.[140]

Thus the estate can be awarded damages for all the deceased's recoverable loss,[141] both non-pecuniary and pecuniary, but only until the time of her death, applying the normal principle that all events up to trial are taken into account. So in *Rose v Ford*,[142] *Murray v Shuter*,[143] and *Andrews v Freeborough*[144] damages for the deceased's loss of amenity were awarded, and in the first two of these cases for his pain and suffering: in *Murray v Shuter* damages for the deceased's loss of earnings were recovered and in *Rose v Ford* for the medical expenses he had incurred.

It has sometimes been argued that a damages claim for non-pecuniary loss should not survive for the benefit of the deceased's estate, as such loss is personal to the deceased. But while the estate clearly cannot itself suffer any non-pecuniary loss, there is still good reason for allowing the estate's claim in that the deceased died without having recovered the compensation for non-pecuniary loss to which he was entitled and which would have enured to the estate's benefit. Not surprisingly, therefore, the Law Commission recommended that there should be no change to the law on the survival of damages for non-pecuniary loss.[145] Indeed the Law Commission was strengthened in its view by the fact that Scottish law, which had excluded damages for non-pecuniary loss from survival actions between 1976 and 1992, was brought back into line with English law on this issue by the Damages (Scotland) Act 1993.[146]

---

[139] Ie defamation (Law Reform (Miscellaneous Provisions) Act 1934, s 1(1)) and the right to bereavement damages (Law Reform (Miscellaneous Provisions) Act 1934, s 1(1A) as inserted by Administration of Justice Act 1982, s 4(1)).
[140] A Ogus, *The Law of Damages* (Butterworths 1973) 116.
[141] Ie subject to the usual principles, eg contributory negligence. Interest can also be awarded according to the usual principles.
[142] [1937] AC 826   [143] [1976] QB 972.   [144] [1967] 1 QB 1.
[145] Law Commission, *Damages for Personal Injury: Non-Pecuniary Loss* (1999) Report No 257, paras 2.59–2.64.
[146] Amending the Damages (Scotland) Act 1976.

In one respect, however, the principles governing compensatory[147] damages for the deceased's estate differ from those governing the injured claimant's damages. By the Administration of Justice Act 1982, s 4(2), amending the Law Reform (Miscellaneous Provisions) Act 1934, s 1(2), no damages may be awarded for loss of income in respect of any period after the death of the injured person; that is, the claim for loss of earnings in the 'lost years' does not survive for the benefit of the estate and *Gammell v Wilson*[148] is thereby overruled. This is a sensible reform.[149] Other than on a formal 'objective' view, the justification for allowing a lost years claim is that the claimant's dependants will otherwise lose out. But where the victim has already died from his injuries prior to trial, the dependants are satisfactorily compensated by their Fatal Accidents Act claim and to allow his estate also to claim damages for the lost years potentially benefits persons other than his dependants, who take under his estate, thus providing a 'windfall' to those whom the lost years claim is not intended to benefit. Similarly, to allow the lost years claim to survive means that potentially the defendant may have to pay large damages under both the 1934 and 1976 Acts. Section 4(2) removes such problems.[150] It should also be realised that an effect of this reform is that where the deceased dies instantly, no claim for damages for personal injury survives for the benefit of her estate.[151]

Where 'provisional damages' have been awarded under the Supreme Court Act 1981, s 32A,[152] does the right of the injured claimant to return to court for further damages survive for the benefit of her estate? And is it caught by the 'lost years' bar? Tentative dicta of the Court of Appeal in *Middleton v Elliott Turbomachinery Ltd*[153] suggest that the claim is treated as if a judgment for damages to be assessed. Consequently, in assessing those damages the court would be able to take account of the worsening of the claimant's condition, including death caused by that condition. The position has been clarified by the Damages Act 1996, s 3. This implicitly accepts that the claim for further damages does survive. But by the Damages Act 1996, s 3(4), no award of further damages made after the death is to include any amount for loss of income in respect of any period after the death (ie the 'lost years' bar applies).

By the Law Reform (Miscellaneous Provisions) Act 1934, s 1(2)(c), where the deceased's death has been caused by the act or omission which gives rise to the cause of action, damages recoverable by the estate 'shall be calculated without reference to any loss or gain to his estate consequent on his death, except that a sum in respect of funeral expenses may be included'. The main part of this is intended to emphasise that, even where the defendant has been responsible for the death, the estate can recover only what the deceased could have

---

[147] Exemplary damages cannot be claimed by the estate—Law Reform (Miscellaneous Provisions) Act 1934, s 1(2).

[148] [1982] AC 27.

[149] Cf P Cane and D Harris, 'Administration of Justice Act 1982, section 4(2): A Lesson in How Not to Reform the Law' (1983) 46 MLR 478. They criticise the reform, inter alia, because if the victim dies other than from his injuries, the estate, and hence dependants, will lose out. But factual causation principles (see *Jobling v Associated Dairies Ltd* [1982] AC 794) dictate that they should lose out because they would have done so if there had been no wrong.

[150] S Waddams, 'Damages for Wrongful Death: Has Lord Campbell's Act Outlived its Usefulness?' (1984) 47 MLR 437 explores the alternative method of solving the overlap problem; ie to repeal the Fatal Accidents Act, to allow the lost years claim to survive, and to allow dependants to recover from the estate. See also *Gammell v Wilson* [1982] AC 27, at 80–81 (per Lord Scarman). In *Claims for Wrongful Death* (1999) Report No 263, paras 3.1–3.2, the Law Commission rejected Waddams' approach principally because the Fatal Accidents Act and survival claims may cover two different sets of losses. To abolish the former could therefore leave dependants undercompensated.

[151] Furthermore, in *Hicks v Chief Constable of the South Yorkshire Police* [1992] 1 All ER 690, affirmed by the House of Lords [1992] 2 All ER 65, it was held that where injury, pain, and suffering are in reality part of the death itself, albeit endured for a very short time before death, no damages are recoverable.

[152] Above, p 165.   [153] *The Times*, 29 October 1990.

recovered and hence neither loss, such as cessation of an annuity, nor gain, such as insurance payment consequent on the death, is of any relevance. However, where the defendant has been responsible for the death, the courts are empowered to award the estate funeral expenses incurred. This is exceptional in that it does not represent the survival of a claim the deceased would have had.

12

Losses on death

1. Dependants	256
2. Actionability by injured person	257
3. The three heads of recoverable loss	258
4. Fatal Accidents Act 1976, section 4	265
5. The relationship between actions under the Law Reform (Miscellaneous Provisions) Act 1934 and the Fatal Accidents Act 1976 where the wrong has caused death	267

At common law no action could be brought for loss suffered through the killing of another. But this was altered by the Fatal Accidents Acts 1846–1959, now the Fatal Accidents Act 1976 (FAA 1976) (as amended by the Administration of Justice Act 1982, s 3) which gives a statutory action '… if death is caused by any wrongful act, neglect or default …'.[1] Most such statutory actions are founded on a tort by the defendant but the basis may be breach of contract.[2]

1. Dependants

As laid down in FAA 1976, s 1(2), the action under the 1976 Act is for the benefit of the dependants of the deceased (subject to a narrower restriction on who can be awarded bereavement damages). The meaning of 'dependant' is statutorily laid down in a list that has been enlarged on several occasions.

By s 1(3) the list now comprises the wife or husband[3] or civil partner or former spouse or former civil partner of the deceased, including a person whose marriage or civil partnership has been annulled or declared void;[4] any person who was living as the husband or wife or civil partner[5] of the deceased in the same household immediately before the date of the death and had been so living for at least two years before the death;[6] any parent or other ascendant of the deceased; any person who was treated by the deceased as his parent; any

---

[1] Special statutory regimes differing from FAA 1976 (eg under the International Transport Conventions Act 1983) are not examined here.
[2] *Grein v Imperial Airways Ltd* [1937] 1 KB 50.
[3] As a result of the Marrriage (Same Sex Couples) Act 2013, s 11 and Sch 3, the references in FAA 1976 to marriage and its effects (for example, 'wife or husband') must now be read as including a same sex marriage.
[4] S 1(4)–(4A).
[5] This therefore meets the long-standing criticism of the previous law that same sex partners were excluded. Even if not a civil partner, the same sex partner is included because he or she is living 'as a civil partner'.
[6] In *Pounder v London Underground Ltd* [1995] PIQR P217, it was held that a brief absence from the home during the two-year period prior to death did not give rise to a break in continuity in the context of a 10-year relationship. For a restrictive interpretation of the two-year requirement, see *Kotke v Saffarini* [2005] EWCA Civ 221, [2005] PIQR P26. In *Swift v Secretary of State for Justice* [2013] EWCA Civ 193, [2014] QB 373 the claimant's partner, with whom she had been living for about six months, was killed as a result of an admitted tort. While their son, who was born after that death, had a claim for pecuniary loss under FAA 1976, the claimant did not. This was because she had not been living with the deceased for two years prior to the death. She argued unsuccessfully that, in denying her a claim, the 1976 Act was incompatible with her right to family life under Article 8 of the ECHR as protected by the Human Rights Act 1998. Note however that a claimant who, as a victim of an infringement of the right to life under Article 2 of the ECHR, has a claim under the Human Rights Act 1998 may conceivably outflank

child or other descendant of the deceased;[7] any person who was treated by the deceased as a child of the family in relation to any marriage or civil partnership of the deceased; and any person who is, or is the issue of, a brother, sister, uncle, or aunt of the deceased.[8] A relationship by marriage or civil partnership is treated as a relationship by consanguinity, a relationship of the half-blood as a relationship of the whole blood, and the stepchild of any person as his child.[9] An illegitimate person is to be treated as the legitimate child of his mother and reputed father[10] or, in the case of a person who has a female parent by virtue of s 43 of the Human Fertilisation and Embryology Act 2008, the legitimate child of his mother and that female parent.[11]

Although the list of dependants is now a wide one, it is still capable of causing hardship, which calls into question the need for a restriction beyond (non-business) financial dependency. For example, the financially dependent friend and companion of the deceased remains excluded. This criticism is reflected in the Court of Appeal's judgment in *Shepherd v The Post Office*[12] where it was said that a simpler approach would be a provision to the effect that any person who could show a relationship of dependence on the deceased should be entitled to make a claim. In similar vein, the Law Commission in its report, *Claims for Wrongful Death*,[13] recommended that there should be added to the present list a generally worded class of claimant whereby any other individual who 'was being wholly or partly maintained by the deceased immediately before the death or who would, but for the death, have been so maintained' would be able to bring an action. And a person would be treated as being wholly or partly maintained by another if that person 'otherwise than for full valuable consideration, was making a substantial contribution in money or money's worth towards his reasonable needs'.

By FAA 1976, s 2(1), 'The action shall be brought by and in the name of the executor or administrator of the deceased', but by FAA 1976, s 2(2), where there is no such personal representative, or no action is brought by him within six months, the action may be brought by and in the name of all or any of the persons for whose benefit a personal representative could have brought it. Although the loss and damages must ultimately be separately assessed for each dependant, the usual practice is first to determine the total liability of the defendant and then to apportion the damages between the dependants. By FAA 1976, s 2(3) only one action may be brought in respect of the death.[14]

2. Actionability by injured person

By FAA 1976, s 1(1), an action can only succeed if the wrongful act, neglect or default which caused the death '… is such as would (if death had not ensued) have entitled the person injured to maintain an action and recover damages in respect thereof …' Therefore if the

---

the restrictive definition of dependants under FAA 1976: *Rabone v Pennine Care NHS Foundation Trust* [2012] UKSC 2, [2012] 2 AC 72; see below, p 264.

[7] Including a child *en ventre sa mère*: J Edelman, *McGregor on Damages* (20th edn, Sweet & Maxwell 2018) para 41-006.
[8] Quaere, does this mean children only, or all descendants.   [9] S 1(5)(a).   [10] S 1(5)(b)(i).
[11] S 1(5)(b)(ii). This amendment was made by the Marriage (Same Sex Couples) Act 2013 (Consequential and Contrary Provisions and Scotland) Order 2014, SI 2014/560.
[12] *The Times*, 15 June 1995.
[13] Law Commission, *Claims for Wrongful Death* (1999) Report No 263, para 7.7 and Draft Bill, clause 1.
[14] 'Action' is, by the Human Rights Act 1998, ss 3(1) and 6(1), to be interpreted as 'served process' so that the existence of a previous unserved writ does not bar a new claim brought within the limitation period: *Cachia v Faluyi* [2001] EWCA Civ 998, [2001] 1 WLR 1966.

deceased was killed entirely through his own fault,[15] if the defendant had validly excluded all liability to the deceased, if the deceased's action had become time-barred before his death, or if the deceased had settled his claim or obtained judgment against the defendant,[16] the dependants will have no action. Similarly by FAA 1976, s 5, where the deceased was contributorily negligent in relation to his death, and hence his damages would have been reduced by a certain amount under the Law Reform (Contributory Negligence) Act 1945, the damages recoverable by the dependants under the 1976 Act are to be reduced to a proportionate extent.[17]

By the Damages Act 1996, s 3, an award of provisional damages does not operate as a bar to an action in respect of the injured person's death under FAA 1976: but such part of the provisional damages or further damages awarded before the injured person's death, as was intended to compensate him for pecuniary loss in a period which in the event falls after his death, shall be taken into account in assessing the amount of any loss of support suffered by dependants.

3. The three heads of recoverable loss

(1) The first head—pecuniary loss attributable to the non-business relationship between deceased and dependant

(a) Pecuniary loss

This most obviously refers to the loss of support from the deceased's earnings.[18] But it is important to realise that it also includes the loss of a mother's or wife's 'services'.[19] So in *Berry v Humm & Co*[20] a husband was able to recover damages for the loss of his wife's housekeeping 'services' which she had performed gratuitously.[21] Similarly, in *Hay v Hughes*,[22] children were able to recover damages for the loss of their mother's 'services' calculated according to the cost of engaging a housekeeper or nanny, even though on the facts this expense was not incurred because the children's grandmother was looking after them gratuitously. In *Regan v Williamson*[23] Watkins J stressed that a mother's 'services' should be widely interpreted

---

[15] But claims have succeeded for the deceased's suicide: see, eg, *Corr v IBC Vehicles Ltd* [2008] UKHL 13, [2008] 1 AC 884. See also *Reader v Molesworth Bright Clegg* [2007] EWCA Civ 169, [2007] 1 WLR 1082 in which it was held that, where the deceased's action in negligence for personal injury, that had subsequently resulted in his death (from suicide), had been (negligently) discontinued after his death by his solicitors, that was not a bar to an action under the Fatal Accidents Act 1976. At the date of the death the deceased could still have maintained an action. The position would have been different had the action been discontinued prior to the death.

[16] It was this that produced the injustice to the dependants of denying the 'lost years' claim to an injured claimant, who then died from his injuries: see above, p 248. In *Jameson v Central Electricity Generating Board* [2000] 1 AC 455, a settlement, satisfying a claim against one joint and several tortfeasor, on its true construction extinguished the cause of action (so that no action could be brought under FAA 1976) against the other joint and several tortfeasor. See also *Thompson v Arnold* [2007] EWHC 1875 (QB), [2008] PIQR P1 (deceased's settlement of a claim prior to her death precluded a subsequent action by her dependants under the Fatal Accidents Act 1976).

[17] In accordance with normal principle a dependant who has been contributorily negligent in relation to his tortious loss (ie was partly responsible for the death) should have his damages reduced. See *Mulholland v McCrea* [1961] NI 135.

[18] It can also include loss of support from the deceased's future retirement pension, as in *Auty v National Coal Board* [1985] 1 WLR 784; and a loss of support because of a reduction in state benefits consequent on the death, as in *Cox v Hockenhull* [2000] 1 WLR 750.

[19] See, analogously, *Clay v Pooler* [1982] 3 All ER 570 compensating for the loss of a husband and father's services as a handyman around the house.

[20] [1915] 1 KB 627.

[21] This has not been affected by the Administration of Justice Act 1982, s 2, abolishing the action for loss of the wife's services.

[22] [1975] QB 790. See below, pp 265–266.   [23] [1976] 1 WLR 305.

to take into account the fact that a mother is not just a housekeeper; on the other hand he reluctantly accepted that no damages could be given simply for the loss of a mother's love and care for this was not a pecuniary loss. As laid down in *Spittle v Bunney*,[24] a deduction must be made from the notional commercial cost of a full-time nanny (which was taken to be the net wages a nanny would receive rather than the expense of engaging her) because older children do not require the same looking-after as young children. In *Mehmet v Perry*[25] the loss to the family of the deceased's 'services' as wife and mother was mainly calculated according to the wages lost by the father by giving up work to look after the children. And, as established in *Stanley v Saddique*,[26] lower damages should be awarded if the mother was unreliable and unlikely to have looked after the child properly. In some cases, an extra sum for lost services has been awarded to reflect the fact that those services would have been performed by a family member rather than, less conveniently, by a commercial provider (in other words, the awards reflected the fact that the services provided by a family member were, in that sense, more valuable than those provided by a commercial provider).[27]

(b) Business pecuniary loss

The pecuniary loss caused to the dependant by the deceased's death is not recoverable if it flows from the business relationship between them;[28] business pecuniary loss is clearly outside the Act's scope for otherwise there would be no sense in the restriction of claims to dependants which excludes, for example, an employer's claim for the pecuniary loss caused by the wrongful death of his employee. So in *Burgess v Florence Nightingale Hospital For Gentlewomen*[29] a husband could not recover damages for his loss of income as a dancer resulting from the death of his dancing-partner wife. Similarly, in *Malyon v Plummer*,[30] a wife who had been employed by her husband could not recover that part of her lost salary, which represented a true commercial payment for her services.

(c) Proof of loss

In accordance with general principle there will be no award if the loss is entirely speculative or if there is no 'reasonable expectation of pecuniary benefit as of right, or otherwise, from the continuance of the life'.[31] So in *Barnett v Cohen*[32] the parent of a four-year-old child was held to have no cause of action under this head and in *Davies v Taylor*,[33] where a wife had deserted her husband five weeks before his death and he had instructed a solicitor to begin divorce proceedings, she was held to have no action as she had failed to prove that there was a significant prospect of reconciliation with her husband and hence a reasonable expectation of pecuniary benefit. On the other hand, in *Taff Vale Rly Co v Jenkins*,[34] a parent recovered damages under the Act when his 16-year-old daughter died having almost completed her unpaid dressmaking apprenticeship and in *Kandalla v British Airways Board*[35]

---

[24] [1988] 1 WLR 847.
[25] [1977] 2 All ER 529. See also *Cresswell v Eaton* [1991] 1 WLR 1113 (value of mother's services based on wages given up by children's aunt to look after them).
[26] [1992] QB 1.
[27] *Beesley v New Century Group Ltd* [2008] EWHC 3033 (QB); *Wolstenholme v Leach's of Shudehill Ltd* [2016] EWHC 588 (QB).
[28] A further restriction is where the deceased's earnings were illegally made: *Burns v Edman* [1970] 2 QB 541; *Hunter v Butler* [1996] RTR 396.
[29] [1955] 1 QB 349.   [30] [1964] 1 QB 330.
[31] *Franklin v South Eastern Rly Co* (1858) 3 H & N 211, at 213–214. Above, p 67.
[32] [1921] 2 KB 461.   [33] [1974] AC 207.   [34] [1913] AC 1.   [35] [1981] QB 158.

the elderly parents of two young women doctors were awarded damages on proof that the doctors had intended to flee from Iraq (where they had been working) to England, where they would have supported their parents.

(d) Multiplier method

As with future pecuniary loss for personal injury, the calculation of damages for loss of dependency is not easy. Again the courts' approach is generally[36] to use the multiplier method.

In this context, it was previously the law that, in contrast to personal injury claims, the multiplier was used to assess all the pecuniary loss and not merely the post-trial pecuniary loss. The leading case was *Cookson v Knowles*[37] in which the House of Lords laid down that the dependants' pecuniary loss prior to trial should be assessed separately from that after the trial. This was essentially because the former was less speculative and because no interest was to be paid on the future loss but was payable on the pre-trial loss, normally from the date of death until the time of trial at half the average rate on the special account over that period.[38] In *Graham v Dodds*[39] it was clarified that that itemisation did not mean that the multiplier method should be abandoned for pre-trial loss. Rather the multiplier should continue to be calculated from the date of death (rather than from the date of trial) on the basis that, in contrast to a personal injury case, there could be no certainty even that the deceased would have survived until trial. So if, for example, the multiplier was 14, and four years had elapsed between death and trial, the pre-trial loss was calculated using a multiplier of four and the post-trial loss, using a multiplier of 10. But a separate pre-trial and post-trial *multiplicand* was generally appropriate to take account of facts known at trial: eg the rate of wages for the job that the deceased had.[40]

In the light of the House of Lords' decision in *Wells v Wells*,[41] it was argued in the last edition of this work that, contrary to the approach in *Cookson v Knowles* and *Graham v Dodds*, the multiplier should be calculated from the date of trial. Although *Wells v Wells* was itself a personal injury case, it was clear that its approach was intended to apply to fatal accident claims as well. So the relevant discount rate for assessing the multiplier should be based on ILGS (Index Linked Government Stock) rates; and, more generally, a sound actuarial approach should be taken using the Ogden Tables as a starting point. But as the Law Commission pointed out, it was difficult to see how the Ogden Tables could be properly used where one is calculating a multiplier from the date of death rather than from trial.[42] Subsequent editions[43] of the Ogden Tables were produced with this criticism by the Law Commission in mind.[44] The Ogden Working Party argued that, in the light of *Wells v Wells*, multipliers for post-trial pecuniary loss should be calculated from the date of trial. In contrast, pre-trial loss should be calculated in much the same straightforward way as in personal injury cases, with the qualification that there would need to be a general discount for the uncertainty as to whether the deceased would have lived to trial.

---

[36] But this might not be appropriate, for example, where there is as yet no dependency.
[37] [1979] AC 556.   [38] *Jefford v Gee* [1970] 2 QB 130: see below, pp 304–306.
[39] [1983] 1 WLR 808.
[40] See, especially, Lord Fraser's speech in *Cookson v Knowles* [1979] AC 556, at 575–576.
[41] [1999] 1 AC 345.
[42] Law Commission, *Claims for Wrongful Death* (1999) Report No 263, paras 4.1–4.23.
[43] *Actuarial Tables for Use in Personal Injury and Fatal Accident Cases* (5th edn, TSO 2005).
[44] The Ogden Tables, *Actuarial Tables for Use in Personal Injury and Fatal Accident Cases*, are now in their 7th edn (TSO 2011).

Those criticisms were accepted by the Supreme Court in *Knauer v Ministry of Justice*,[45] which finally took the opportunity, applying the 1966 Practice Direction, to overrule *Cookson v Knowles* and *Graham v Dodds*. It is therefore now the law that the multiplier (for post-trial loss) in death cases is to be calculated from the date of trial not the date of death. It was recognised that the problem with not doing this is that the calculation of damages requires the courts to ignore facts known at trial and is therefore less accurate than it should be; and there should only be a discount for the early receipt of damages in respect of post-trial, not pre-trial, loss. According to the correct approach, therefore, as established by *Knauer*, post-trial pecuniary loss should be assessed using a multiplier calculated from the date of trial; whereas pre-trial losses should be calculated in much the same straightforward way as in personal injury cases (taking as the 'multiplier' the number of years between the date of death and the trial) albeit with the qualification that there may need to be a discount for the uncertainty as to whether the deceased would have lived to trial.

In applying the multiplier method to assess the dependant's pre-trial or post-trial loss, one will commonly take as the multiplicand the deceased's notional annual net[46] earnings and deduct the deceased's living expenses; and living expenses here means expenses for the deceased's own purposes exclusively.[47] There should then be an adjustment to take account, for example, of the prospects of promotion that the deceased had.

But one has to be careful not to include what may at first sight appear to be a loss but on closer analysis turns out not to be. Two cases can be used to illustrate this. In *Auty v National Coal Board*[48] one of the claimants was a widow claiming under FAA 1976. She claimed as part of her loss of dependency the lost chance of gaining a widow's 'death-after-retirement' pension, and argued that the widow's 'death-in-service' pension that she was actually receiving was non-deductible under FAA 1976, s 4(1) (not then amended though the same argument would hold under the new wording). The Court of Appeal rejected this argument and held that, as she was only ever entitled to one or other pension and was receiving one, it was false to say that she had lost the chance of gaining the other. As Waller LJ said, '... she cannot claim for loss of an opportunity to obtain a widow's pension because she is already in receipt of a widow's pension.'[49]

Again in *Malone v Rowan*[50] Russell J held that in assessing a widow's pecuniary loss on the death of her husband the courts should not take into account that the couple planned to have a family so that, on giving up work, the wife's pecuniary dependency on her husband would have increased from the position at his death. Russell J was reluctant to so hold and did so only because he felt bound by the unreported Court of Appeal decision in *Higgs v Drinkwater*. But it is submitted that the decisions are correct and that Russell J's reluctance was ill-founded: for the increase in dependency that would have occurred was offset by the change of circumstances brought about by the death, namely that the claimant would now not suffer a loss of earnings in giving birth to and bringing up the deceased's children.

There is also some confusion on the authorities as to whether the dependant's (typically a widow's) own earning capacity should be taken into account to reduce the pecuniary loss.[51] Applying the duty to mitigate plus the principle that direct compensating advantages should

---

[45] [2016] UKSC 9, [2016] AC 908.
[46] Eg tax is deducted—*Zinovieff v British Transport Commission*, The Times, 1 April 1954; *British Transport Commission v Gourley* [1956] AC 185.
[47] *Harris v Empress Motors Ltd* [1984] 1 WLR 212, at 216–217; *Crabtree v Wilson* [1993] PIQR Q24.
[48] [1985] 1 WLR 784.   [49] ibid, at 799.
[50] [1984] 3 All ER 402. See M Jones, 'Calculating the Widow's Dependency' (1985) 101 LQR 20.
[51] *Howitt v Heads* [1973] QB 64 (ignored); *Cookson v Knowles* [1977] QB 913 (taken into account). Presumably FAA 1976, s 4 is irrelevant to this sort of 'benefit'.

be deducted, subject to a good policy reason to the contrary (such as not discouraging private benevolence), earning capacity should be taken into account provided, first, it is sufficiently likely that the dependant will work or it is reasonable for her to do so; secondly, she would not have worked but for the death; and thirdly, it is reasonable to suppose that her earnings would have reduced the pecuniary benefit from the deceased had he lived.

The starting point for the *multiplier* for post-trial loss is the estimated number of years (taking into account, for example, the deceased's and dependant's life expectancies) from the date of trial that the dependant would have received the deceased's pecuniary support. When the deceased was unmarried and supporting his parents, account must also be taken of the possibility of the deceased's marriage.[52]

The starting figure is then adjusted. In particular, there is a reduction because the claimant is receiving a capital sum now, which can be invested, rather than periodical payments over the years. A further small reduction may also be made for the contingencies of life, other than mortality, such as the deceased's possible unemployment. The aim is to award a capital sum, which when invested will produce an income in terms of interest and withdrawals of capital, equal to the dependant's lost income over the period intended to be covered (ie the post-trial period of dependency).[53] In *Wells v Wells*[54] the House of Lords held that the appropriate discount rate (ie the rate of return on investing the capital sum) for calculating personal injury multipliers should be based on the ILGS rate. Although fatal accident multipliers were not expressly mentioned, it is clear that the reasoning was equally applicable to them. In line with the principles laid down in that decision, and with other factors that he considered relevant, the Lord Chancellor has set a discount rate of minus 0.75% under the power conferred on him by the Damages Act 1996, s 1(2). That rate applies to fatal accident as well as personal injury cases. The reforms made by the Civil Liability Act 2018 (which mark a move away from the ILGS rate as an underpinning principle) apply to the discount rate in fatal accident claims just as they do in personal injury claims.[55]

In *Owen v Martin*[56] it was held that the prospects of a divorce between a claimant widow and the deceased are to be taken into account in assessing the widow's damages. And FAA 1976, s 3(4), as amended by the Administration of Justice Act 1982, lays down that in the case of a claim by a cohabitee, the court must take into account '… the fact that the dependant had no enforceable right to financial support by the deceased as a result of their living together'. This is presumably designed to impress upon the courts that there is even less certainty of continued future support in the case of cohabitees than in the case of married couples, particularly since legal obligations of support continue after the breakdown of marriage. But both *Owen v Martin* and s 3(4) have been criticised by the Law Commission primarily because it was thought distasteful for judges to reach speculative conclusions about intimate aspects of people's lives. It was therefore recommended[57] that s 3(4) should be repealed and replaced by a provision to the effect that the prospect of breakdown in the relationship between the deceased and his or her partner should not be taken into account (although the fact of such a breakdown would continue to be relevant);

---

[52] *Dolbey v Goodwin* [1955] 2 All ER 166.
[53] *Taylor v O'Connor* [1971] AC 115; *Cookson v Knowles* [1979] AC 556, at 576–577; *Robertson v Lestrange* [1985] 1 All ER 950, at 955–958. Analogously to the assessment of damages for future pecuniary loss consequent on personal injury, there is no adjustment for future inflation nor, normally, for higher rate tax payable by the claimant on the investment income: see above, pp 184, 245.
[54] [1999] 1 AC 345.
[55] See above, p 246. For the interpretation of a claim for personal injury, as including a claim under the FAA 1976, see the Damages Act 1996, s 7.
[56] [1992] PIQR Q151.
[57] Law Commission, *Claims for Wrongful Death* (1999) Report No 263, paras 4.54–4.71; Draft Bill, cl 4.

and that, overruling *Owen v Martin,* the prospect of divorce or breakdown in the relationship between the deceased and his or her spouse should not be taken into account when assessing damages for the purposes of any claim under FAA 1976 unless the couple were no longer living together at the time of death, or one of the couple had petitioned for divorce, judicial separation, or nullity.

By FAA 1976, s 3(3), as amended by the Administration of Justice Act 1982, in assessing a widow's claim in respect of her husband's death, 'there shall not be taken into account the re-marriage of the widow or her prospects of re-marriage'. Parliament introduced this provision to put a stop to the degrading judicial 'guessing game' of assessing a widow's prospects of re-marriage. But this is at the expense of not deducting what is a direct compensating advantage and the effect can be grotesque; eg a widow who marries a multi-millionaire, even prior to trial, is still entitled to a large sum of damages in respect of the death of her former husband. Certainly there is no good reason why a marriage that has already taken place should not be taken into account, since no guessing is then required. It should further be noted that the provision applies only to a widow's claim and therefore a mother's prospects of re-marriage must still be taken into account in assessing a child's claim. Similarly, where the claim is brought by a 'common-law wife' her prospects of marriage are to be taken into account. In addition, a widower's prospects of remarriage are relevant. All in all it is hard to dissent from Atiyah's view that this law reform 'must be one of the most irrational … ever passed by Parliament'.[58]

Not surprisingly, the Law Commission has recommended that FAA 1976, s 3(3) should be repealed.[59] Nevertheless it saw force in the argument that assessing the prospects of a widow or widower remarrying or entering into a relationship of financially supportive cohabitation would involve distressing and distasteful inquiries that should be avoided. It therefore recommended a new provision[60] to the effect that, unless a person is engaged to be married at the time of trial, the prospect that he or she will marry, remarry, or enter into financially supportive cohabitation with a new partner, should not be taken into account when assessing any claim for damages under FAA 1976. In contrast, the fact of a marriage and, as appears to be the present law, the fact of financially supportive cohabitation should be taken into account.

(2) The second head—damages for bereavement

By FAA 1976, s 1A, as inserted by the Administration of Justice Act 1982 and as subsequently amended by the Civil Partnership Act 2004, damages for death are to be awarded for the mental distress, eg the sorrow, grief, and loss of society and enjoyment, consequent on the death.[61] Called 'damages for bereavement', a fixed sum, of at present £12,980,[62] can by FAA 1976, s 1A(2), be claimed for the benefit:

---

[58] P Cane and J Goudkamp, *Atiyah's Accidents, Compensation and the Law* (9th edn, CUP 2018) 122.
[59] Law Commission, *Claims for Wrongful Death* (1999) Report No 263, paras 4.27–4.53; Draft Bill, cl 4. For earlier recommendations for reform, see Law Commission, *Report on Personal Injury Litigation—Assessment of Damages* (1973) Report No 56, paras 251–252; and *Royal Commission on Civil Liability and Compensation for Personal Injury* (chaired by Lord Pearson) (1978) paras 409–412, 414. See also *De Sales v Ingrilli* (2002) 212 CLR 338, High Court of Australia.
[60] Law Commission, *Claims for Wrongful Death* (1999) Report No 263, paras 4.27–4.53 and Draft Bill, cl 4.
[61] For cases denying such damages prior to the Administration of Justice Act 1982, see *Franklin v South Eastern Rly Co* (1858) 3 H & N 211; *Davies v Powell Duffryn Associated Collieries Ltd* [1942] AC 601, at 617.
[62] The Lord Chancellor's power to alter the amount, most recently exercised by the Damages for Bereavement (Variation of Sum) (England and Wales) Order 2013, SI 2013/510, is conferred by FAA 1976, s 1A(5). In principle,

'(a) of the wife or husband or civil partner of the deceased; and
(b) where the deceased was a minor who was never married or a civil partner—
  (i) of his parents, if he was legitimate;[63] and
  (ii) of his mother, if he was illegitimate.'

This rightly brought English law into line with most other countries, although not all have a fixed award, nor restrict so severely those entitled to claim.

In *Rabone v Pennine Care NHS Foundation Trust*[64] the claimant parents of a deceased adult, who had committed suicide while on home release from hospital, were held to be entitled to damages, and were awarded £5,000, under the Human Rights Act 1998 as victims of the infringement of the right to life under Article 2 of the ECHR. In this respect, a claim under the Human Rights Act 1998 may be regarded as outflanking the Fatal Accidents Act 1976 because the parents would have had no claim for bereavement damages under the 1976 Act.[65]

In answering a slightly different question, it was held by the Court of Appeal in a bold judgment in *Smith v Lancashire Teaching Hospitals NHS Foundation Trust*[66] that the exclusion from the limited list of those who can claim bereavement damages, under s 1(2)(b) of the 1976 Act, of a cohabitee who had been living with the deceased for two years as his wife (and the same reasoning applies to a cohabitee living as the deceased's husband or civil partner) infringed the cohabitee's Article 8 and Article 14 convention rights under the Human Rights Act 1998. A declaration of incompatibility was made under s 4 of the 1998 Act.

In its Report *Claims for Wrongful Death*, the Law Commission recommended that the list of those who can claim bereavement damages should be widened (so as to include parent, child, sibling, fiancé(e), and co-habitee of the deceased) but that there should be a maximum payable (of £30,000 as at that time) in respect of any one death.[67] The decision of the Court of Appeal in the *Smith* case adds further support for the long overdue implementation of the Law Commission's recommendations.

(3) The third head—funeral expenses

By FAA 1976, s 3(5), as amended by the Administration of Justice Act 1982, 'If the dependants have incurred funeral expenses in respect of the deceased, damages may be awarded in respect of those expenses.' Case law has established that, to be recoverable, the expenses must have been reasonably incurred in all the circumstances, including the deceased's station in life, religion, and racial origin.[68]

---

interest should be payable as for personal injury non-pecuniary loss: ie 2% from the date of the service of the claim form until trial. In practice it has been awarded at the full special account rate from the date of death until trial: *Kemp and Kemp on The Quantum of Damages* (4th edn, Sweet & Maxwell) paras 16-031–16-032.

[63] By FAA 1976, s 1A(4), if both parents claim, the fixed sum is to be divided equally between them.
[64] [2012] UKSC 2, [2012] 2 AC 72.
[65] A Tettenborn, 'Wrongful Death, Human Rights and the Fatal Accidents Act' (2012) 128 LQR 327.
[66] [2017] EWCA Civ 1916, [2018] QB 804.
[67] Law Commission, *Claims for Wrongful Death* (1999) Report No 263, Part VI.
[68] *Gammell v Wilson* [1982] AC 27 where the funeral expenses were held to include the cost of a gravestone. Although in this case these damages were being awarded under the Law Reform (Miscellaneous Provisions) Act 1934, s 1(2)(c), the same would apply under FAA 1976.

4. Fatal Accidents Act 1976, section 4

By FAA 1976, s 4, inserted by the Administration of Justice Act 1982, 'In assessing damages in respect of a person's death in an action under this Act, the benefits which have accrued or will or may accrue to any person from his estate or otherwise as a result of his death shall be disregarded.'

Under the former FAA 1976, s 4(1) any benefit—defined to mean social security benefit, or payment by a trade union or friendly society—insurance money, pension, or gratuity was not to be deducted. This was criticised by the Law Commission[69] and the Pearson Commission[70] for not also ordering the non-deduction of benefits derived from the deceased's estate; the benefits in mind being the acceleration and certainty of the inheritance of the deceased's property and awards for non-pecuniary loss[71] under the Law Reform (Miscellaneous Provisions) Act 1934. The new s 4 was passed in response to that criticism. This is unfortunate since that criticism lacked force. Compensation dictates the deduction of compensating advantages, the benefits in mind arise directly from the death, and there is no question of deduction discouraging benevolence or undermining the deceased's prudent spending of money in providing for his dependants after death.

The new FAA 1976, s 4 (as well as the old s 4(1)) is also inconsistent with the approach advocated in chapter 8 for compensating advantages rendered by third parties in response to the consequences of a tort or breach of contract.[72] According to that, while life assurance payments, gratuitous payments, and probably pensions should continue not to be deducted, social security benefits should be deducted. This was a further reform of s 4(1) recommended by the Pearson Commission[73] and there seems no good reason why the provisions for the recoupment of social security benefits contained in the Social Security (Recovery of Benefits) Act 1997[74] have not been made applicable to damages under FAA 1976.

A further difficulty is the actual wording of FAA 1976, s 4. For the natural interpretation of 'benefits [accruing] ... as a result of his death' is that all compensating advantages (that is, all benefits factually caused by the death applying the 'but for' test) are covered. But if so, a widow's remarriage or her earnings from starting work after the death or gratuitous services rendered by a relative may all be benefits accruing as a result of the death and therefore non-deductible under the Act. Yet the purpose of s 4 was clearly not to introduce such a wide reform.[75] Indeed if it had been, FAA 1976, s 3(3) ordering remarriage to be ignored in assessing a widow's damages would now be unnecessary and criticism of that provision for not also applying to a child's claim, and for not being matched by an equivalent provision regarding a widower's remarriage, would now be unfounded.

Of course the way out of this difficulty is to take a narrow interpretation of FAA 1976, s 4. Indeed, somewhat ironically, the same narrow construction has often been taken at common law—a good example being *Hay v Hughes*[76] concerning gratuitous services

---

[69] Law Commission, *Report on Personal Injury Litigation—Assessment of Damages* (1973) Report No 56, paras 254–256.
[70] *Royal Commission on Civil Liability and Compensation for Personal Injury* (chaired by Lord Pearson) (1978) paras 537–539.
[71] Below, p 267. [72] Above, pp 152–162.
[73] *Royal Commission on Civil Liability and Compensation for Personal Injury* (chaired by Lord Pearson) (1978) paras 480–483.
[74] Above, pp 156–157. For a recommendation that the scheme of the Social Security (Recovery of Benefits) Act 1997 should be expanded so as to apply to benefits received by a claimant under FAA 1976, see Law Commission, *Claims for Wrongful Death* (1999) Report No 263, paras 5.56–5.69.
[75] See, eg, 428 HL Official Report (5th series) col 28.
[76] [1975] QB 790. See also, eg, *Peacock v Amusement Equipment Co Ltd* [1954] 2 QB 347.

rendered by a relative—in deciding that benefits did not result from the death and were therefore *non-deductible* under the general principle of *deduction* laid down in *Davies v Powell Duffryn Associated Collieries Ltd*.[77] But it seems clear that the narrow interpretation taken in cases like *Hay v Hughes* is artificial and that the decisions were really justified on policy grounds such as not discouraging private benevolence. Yet now that s 4 has used similar wording, that artificial narrow construction must live on if the section is not to have a far wider effect than intended.[78]

This exact dilemma has surfaced in the apparently contradictory interpretations of FAA 1976, s 4 taken in two Court of Appeal decisions. In *Stanley v Saddique*[79] it was held that, in assessing a child's damages for the death of his mother, the advantages to the child from the father's marriage to a woman who provided excellent motherly services to the child (and better care than the child's natural mother would have provided had she lived) were benefits accruing as a result of the death under s 4 and were to be disregarded. Section 4 was not to be given a narrow interpretation. In contrast, the majority of the Court of Appeal in *Hayden v Hayden*[80] (McCowan LJ dissenting) decided that, where the tortfeasor was the father of the infant claimant and had given up his paid work to look after the claimant, the value of his services was not a benefit accruing as a result of the death under s 4 and was to be deducted in assessing the claimant's damages for the death of her mother.

The Divisional Court followed *Stanley v Saddique* in *R v Criminal Injuries Compensation Board, ex p K*.[81] This case concerned the assessment of compensation under the old Criminal Injuries Compensation Scheme for children whose mother had been murdered and who had then been well looked after by their uncle and aunt. On a judicial review application, it was held that the gratuitous services of the uncle and aunt fell to be disregarded under s 4. *Hayden v Hayden* was distinguished as a case on its special facts, namely that the provider of the gratuitous services was the tortfeasor who was only carrying out his parental duty.

Stanley v Saddique was also applied but with an important additional qualification in *H v S*.[82] The mother of infant children had been killed. Their father, who was not the tortfeasor, and had not previously provided them with any care or support, cared for them thereafter. The Court of Appeal held that the father's care and support was a benefit accruing as a result of the death and that, applying FAA 1976, s 4, it should therefore be disregarded in assessing damages. However, it was also held that *Hunt v Severs*[83]—the leading personal injury case on gratuitous services—should be applied to this Fatal Accidents Act claim. The

---

[77] [1942] AC 601.
[78] See, eg, *Cameron v Vinters Defence Systems Ltd* [2007] EWHC 2267 (QB), [2008] PIQR P5 (payment made to the dependant of the deceased under the Pneumoconiosis etc (Worker's Compensation) Act 1979 held not to be a benefit within s 4 of the Fatal Accidents Act 1976 and should therefore be deducted in assessing the dependant's damages: but this resulted from a purposive construction of s 4 and was designed to ensure that dependants did not gain by tactically delaying the commencement of proceedings under the 1976 Act until after payments had been made under the 1979 Act).
[79] [1992] QB 1. For more straightforward applications of FAA 1976, s 4, leading to the non-deduction of benefits, see, eg, *Pidduck v Eastern Scottish Omnibuses Ltd* [1990] 1 WLR 993 (widow's pension); *Wood v Bentall Simplex Ltd* [1992] PIQR P332 (inheritance of the deceased's assets); *Harland & Wolff Plc v McIntyre* [2006] EWCA Civ 287, [2006] 1 WLR 2577 (retirement payments that had accrued to the deceased and, on his death, were paid by his employers to his estate, were held to be non-deductible, in a claim brought for loss of retirement benefits under FAA 1976); *Arnup v White Ltd* [2008] EWCA Civ 447, [2008] ICR 1064 (payments under the defendant employer's death-in-service and life insurance schemes were held to be non-deductible in assessing damages under FAA 1976).
[80] [1992] 1 WLR 986. FAA 1976, s 4 was not discussed in *Watson v Willmott* [1991] 1 QB 140 where a child's loss of dependency was treated as the difference between the pecuniary support that the claimant's natural father (as bread-winner) would have provided and that provided by his adoptive father.
[81] [1999] QB 1131.   [82] [2002] EWCA Civ 792, [2002] 3 WLR 1179.
[83] [1994] 2 AC 350. See above, pp 240–241.

Fatal Accident Act damages in respect of the lost gratuitous services were therefore here given only on the basis that they would be used to reimburse the voluntary carer (the father) for his services; and they were therefore to be held on a trust for the carer, which the court could enforce.

In addition to recommending the integration of the central reasoning in *Hunt v Severs* into the Fatal Accidents Act regime[84]—along the lines now applied in *H v S*—the Law Commission has recommended the replacement of FAA 1976, s 4 by a new provision making clearer which benefits are, and are not, to be deducted.[85] This would be far preferable to the current rule of complete non-deduction, which depends in order to achieve its purpose on a narrow and questionable interpretation of 'benefits [accruing] … as a result of his death'.

5. The relationship between actions under the Law Reform (Miscellaneous Provisions) Act 1934 and the Fatal Accidents Act 1976 where the wrong has caused death

It seems appropriate finally to clarify this relationship because, where the defendant's tort or breach of contract has caused death, an action may be brought under both the Law Reform (Miscellaneous Provisions) Act 1934 and FAA 1976 and the two are commonly combined. The former is for the benefit of the deceased's estate and the latter for the benefit of her dependants. Usually, however, a person benefiting from the estate and hence from the 1934 Act will also be a dependant under FAA 1976. The former law, embodied in *Davies v Powell Duffryn Associated Collieries Ltd*, was that an award made or likely to be made under the 1934 Act to a dependant was to be deducted from the Fatal Accidents Act damages, although not vice versa. But, as held in *Murray v Shuter*,[86] an award under the 1934 Act for pre-death loss of earnings (and analogous reasoning applied to awards for other pre-death pecuniary loss) should not be deducted because the dependants would have benefited from those earnings. In other words such an award compensates the dependants for their pre-death loss consequent on the deceased's injury and does not constitute a compensating advantage. Under the old law therefore it was, in any event, only awards for non-pecuniary loss (and, while they lasted, 'lost years' earnings awards) that were deducted. The new FAA 1976, s 4 now means that even non-pecuniary loss awards under the 1934 Act are not to be deducted.

Thus where the death is not instantaneous the action under the Law Reform (Miscellaneous Provisions) Act 1934 enables the estate to recover damages for the deceased's pre-death personal injury losses, both pecuniary and non-pecuniary (plus any property damage), while the action under FAA 1976 enables dependants to recover their pecuniary loss as a result of the death and a spouse or parent(s) to recover damages for bereavement. Damages to cover the funeral expenses may be awarded under either Act[87] depending on whether incurred by the estate or by the dependants (though clearly the courts would not award them twice over). On the other hand, where the death is instantaneous and there has been no property damage, there is no point bringing an action under the 1934 Act, other than where the estate (and not a dependant) has incurred the funeral expenses.

---

[84] Law Commission, *Claims for Wrongful Death* (1999) Report No 263, paras 5.47–5.55; Draft Bill, cl 3.
[85] ibid, paras 5.21–5.46; Draft Bill, cl 5.   [86] [1976] QB 972.
[87] The relevant provision in the Law Reform (Miscellaneous Provisions) Act 1934 is s 1(2)(c). The relevant provision in FAA 1976 is s 3(5): see above, p 264.

13

Loss of reputation

1. When are damages awarded for loss of reputation?	268
2. Assessing damages for loss of reputation	273

Loss of reputation is a non-pecuniary loss, which is traditionally regarded as distinct from mental distress in that it deals with society's feelings towards the claimant, rather than with the claimant's own feelings. But often mental distress consequent on loss of reputation is not clearly separated from the award for loss of reputation itself. Indeed on an alternative view, alternative to that traditionally taken by the courts, all non-pecuniary loss, including loss of reputation, is ultimately regarded as a loss only in terms of the distress or loss of happiness caused to the claimant.[1] However, where a claimant complains of a loss of reputation she is generally concerned not only about loss of reputation itself, but also and often primarily about the pecuniary loss flowing from it and both will be considered.

In order to put the claimant into as good a position as if the tort or breach of contract had not occurred, as the general compensatory aims dictate, damages should be awarded, subject to the usual limiting principles, wherever loss of reputation and consequential pecuniary loss result from a tort or breach of contract. But the courts have taken a more restrictive approach especially where the claimant is suing for breach of contract.

1. When are damages awarded for loss of reputation?

(1) Breach of contract

Addis v Gramophone Co Ltd[2] is the leading authority for the rule that no damages can be given for loss of reputation for breach of contract. In that case the House of Lords held that in the claimant's action for wrongful dismissal he should be confined to damages for his direct pecuniary loss, such as loss of salary, and should not be compensated for any loss of his reputation or for the fact that the dismissal might make it more difficult for him to get another job. So the decision appears to deny damages both for loss of reputation in itself—ie as a non-pecuniary loss—and for the pecuniary loss flowing from it. Lord Atkinson said:

> 'I can conceive nothing more objectionable and embarrassing in litigation than trying in effect an action of libel or slander as a matter of aggravation in an action for illegal dismissal, the defendant being permitted, as he must in justice be permitted, to traverse the defamatory sense, rely on privilege, or raise every point which he could raise in an independent action brought for the alleged libel or slander itself.'[3]

---

[1] See above, pp 36–37. On this view too, only a person and not, eg, a company, would be able to recover for loss of reputation as a non-pecuniary loss: a company would be solely concerned with the pecuniary loss flowing from a loss of reputation.
[2] [1909] AC 488.
[3] ibid, at 496.

When are damages awarded for loss of reputation? 269

Yet in many cases subsequent to *Addis*, while damages for loss of reputation in itself have continued to be denied—for example, in *Groom v Crocker*[4] damages were held irrecoverable for any loss of the claimant's reputation as a careful driver, caused by his defendant solicitor's breach of contract in wrongfully admitting that the claimant had been negligent in his driving—pecuniary loss flowing from loss of reputation has been held recoverable. This distinction was particularly clearly applied in *Aerial Advertising Co v Batchelors Peas Ltd*.[5] There the defendants had contracted with the claimants to advertise their peas by trailers from a plane. In breach of contract the claimants flew the plane with the advertising trailers over a city centre during minutes of silence in armistice services. The public was horrified and the defendants' sales dropped. Atkinson J held that, while following *Groom v Crocker* the defendants were not entitled to damages for loss of reputation in itself, they were entitled to damages for loss of sales following on that loss of reputation.

There are several groups of cases in which damages for pecuniary loss flowing from loss of reputation have been awarded for breach of contract.

First, where the defendant's breach comprises a refusal to allow an actor's appearance or to publish an author's book, the actor or author has been held able to recover for the lost income flowing from the loss of the chance to enhance his reputation or, as it is often termed, the 'loss of publicity'. The leading cases are *Marbé v George Edwardes (Daley's Theatre) Ltd*[6] and *Herbert Clayton v Oliver*,[7] which concerned actors, and *Tolnay v Criterion Film Productions Ltd*[8] and *Joseph v National Magazine Co*[9] concerning authors. In *Withers v General Theatre Corpn Ltd*[10] the Court of Appeal stressed that while an actor can recover income lost from the loss of a chance to enhance his reputation he cannot recover that lost from damage to his existing reputation. This distinction is not only very difficult to justify in terms of policy but also in *Marbé v George Edwardes* the Court of Appeal had earlier specifically said that damages could be given for lost income flowing from damage to the actor's existing reputation.[11] Since *Marbé* was later applied by the House of Lords in *Herbert Clayton v Oliver*, and since it seems preferable in principle, it is submitted that the *Withers* distinction should be regarded as incorrect.

Secondly, where the breach of contract comprises a mismanagement of advertising, the claimant can recover for pecuniary loss flowing from the loss of reputation. This is particularly well illustrated by the *Aerial Advertising v Batchelors Peas* case. Similarly in *Marcus v Myers and Davis*,[12] where the defendant in breach of contract failed to insert an advert in a newspaper, the claimant was awarded damages for loss of business. Although loss of reputation was not mentioned, the loss of business can be regarded as analogous to pecuniary loss flowing from the loss of a chance to enhance one's reputation.

Thirdly, where a bank in breach of contract refuses to honour the claimant trader's cheque, as in *Rolin v Steward*,[13] or fails to supervise the claimant's business as agreed so that the claimant goes bankrupt, as in *Wilson v United Counties Bank Ltd*,[14] the claimant can recover damages for the pecuniary loss flowing from the damage to his credit and reputation.

Fourthly, where in breach of contract the defendant supplies goods or provides services that are not of the standard required by the claimant's customers, the claimant can recover damages for the pecuniary loss flowing from the loss of reputation. In *Anglo-Continental Holidays Ltd v Typaldos Lines (London) Ltd*,[15] travel agents were awarded damages for loss

---

[4] [1939] 1 KB 194; *Bailey v Bullock* [1950] 2 All ER 1167.   [5] [1938] 2 All ER 788.
[6] [1928] 1 KB 269.   [7] [1930] AC 209.   [8] [1936] 2 All ER 1625.   [9] [1959] Ch 14.
[10] [1933] 2 KB 536.   [11] [1928] 1 KB 269, at 281, 288.   [12] (1895) 11 TLR 327.
[13] (1854) 14 CB 595. See also, eg, *Kpohraror v Woolwich Building Society* [1996] 4 All ER 119: above, p 93.
[14] [1920] AC 102.   [15] [1967] 2 Lloyd's Rep 61.

of goodwill when the shipowner, with whom they had arranged a cruise, substituted a smaller less attractive ship and a less satisfactory timetable of ports of call. Similarly in *GKN Centrax Gears Ltd v Matbro Ltd*,[16] where the claimants had supplied defective drive axles for fork-lift trucks that the defendants had then sold to their customers, the defendants, on their counterclaim, were awarded damages for the loss of repeat orders. Somewhat similar is *Foaminol Laboratories v British Artid Plastics Ltd*[17] where the claimants, who were putting a sun-tan cream on the market in attractive containers, had secured the co-operattion of certain editors of ladies' magazines. The claimants had ordered ten thousand of the containers from the defendants who, however, failed to deliver most of them. Hallett J held that damages for loss of profit flowing from the loss of future co-operation with the editors could in theory be recovered, although here they would not be because the pecuniary loss was, first, too speculative and, secondly, too remote. Neither of these grounds of denial is convincing and in the *GKN Centrax* case Lord Denning doubted the actual decision in this case.[18]

The courts have therefore been prepared to compensate pecuniary loss flowing from loss of reputation. Indeed, in terms of policy there is no good reason why those four groups should be regarded as exhaustive: whatever one may say about loss of reputation as a non-pecuniary loss there is no convincing argument for leaving the claimant undercompensated by refusing to recognise this kind of pecuniary loss. As Hallett J said in *Foaminol*, '... if pecuniary loss be established, the mere fact that the pecuniary loss is brought about by the loss of reputation caused by a breach of contract is not sufficient to preclude the plaintiffs from recovering in respect of that pecuniary loss.'[19]

That that is a correct statement of the law has been authoritatively established in the leading modern case of *Malik v Bank of Credit and Commerce International SA*.[20] Former employees of the corrupt bank, BCCI, claimed damages from the bank for loss of reputation: that is, they sought compensation (so-called 'stigma damages') for their handicap in the labour market flowing from the dishonesty stigma that attached to employees of BCCI. It was laid down by the House of Lords that damages were recoverable for the pecuniary loss of reputation flowing from the employer's breach of the implied term not to undermine the employee's trust and confidence. Lord Nicholls specifically cited with approval Hallett J's statement in *Foaminol* set out above. The *Addis* case was not followed albeit that it was recognised that, on the facts of *Malik*, the relevant loss of reputation did not flow from the wrongful nature of the dismissal but rather from a breach of the implied term of mutual trust and confidence.

One might have thought that *Malik* had cleared the way for there to be a departure from *Addis*, allowing damages for financial loss consequent on a loss of reputation, even where the claim is for wrongful dismissal. But in *Johnson v Unisys Ltd*[21] (which did not directly concern a loss of reputation) the House of Lords decided that statute prevented them departing from *Addis* in a case where the claimant alleged that the manner of his (wrongful) dismissal had caused him a psychiatric illness which made it impossible for him to find another job. In the realm of wrongful dismissal, there has been, since 1971, a special statutory compensation scheme for unfair dismissal. It is now contained in the Employment

---

[16] [1976] 2 Lloyd's Rep 555.   [17] [1941] 2 All ER 393.   [18] [1976] 2 Lloyd's Rep 555, at 573.
[19] [1941] 2 All ER 393, at 400.   [20] [1998] AC 20.
[21] [2001] UKHL 13, [2003] 1 AC 518. *Johnson v Unisys* was distinguished by the House of Lords, without reopening its correctness, in *Eastwood v Magnox Electric plc* [2004] UKHL 35, [2004] 3 WLR 322. The so-called '*Johnson* exclusion zone'—where the statutory regime alone applies and the common law does not—was further entrenched in *Edwards v Chesterfield Royal Hospital NHS Foundation Trust* [2011] UKSC 58, [2012] 2 AC 22.

Rights Act 1996. Their Lordships reasoned that to allow employees to recover damages for pecuniary loss (or indeed for non-pecuniary loss) beyond the salary that they were owed, and were not paid, for the notice period would conflict with that statutory compensation scheme. In particular, had the claimant sued for unfair dismissal, the statutory maximum sum that he could have recovered was £11,000 whereas he was here claiming damages for loss of earnings of £400,000. In the words of Lord Nicholls,[22]

> '[A] common law right embracing the manner in which an employee is dismissed cannot satisfactorily co-exist with the statutory right not to be unfairly dismissed. A newly developed common law right of this nature, covering the same ground as the statutory right, would fly in the face of the limits Parliament has already prescribed on matters such as the classes of employees who have the benefit of the statutory right, the amount of compensation payable and the short time limits for making claims. It would also defeat the intention of Parliament that claims of this nature should be decided by specialist tribunals, not the ordinary courts of law.'

Lord Steyn dissented from the other Law Lords on this reasoning and agreed with the decision only because he thought that the psychiatric illness was too remote.[23] It should be emphasised that none of their Lordships supported the decision in *Addis* as such. The reasoning was rather that common law principle—allowing pecuniary loss consequent on a psychiatric illness (or a loss of reputation) caused by a breach of contract—should not be applied to a wrongful dismissal because of the clash with the unfair dismissal legislation.

What about the continued denial of damages for loss of reputation in itself, that is, as a non-pecuniary loss? This was not in issue in the *Malik* case and is closely linked to the question of whether, and when, mental distress damages can be awarded for breach of contract. While less crucial than the denial of pecuniary loss consequent on a loss of reputation, the blanket refusal of damages for non-pecuniary loss of reputation is unjustified. Adherence to full compensation dictates recovery, and although proof of this loss may be difficult, as may assessing damages, these are not reasons for a blanket refusal, particularly given the judicial willingness to compensate other types of non-pecuniary loss. Nor, if allowed, is there any reason to think that the courts would be swamped with claims. Furthermore, Lord Atkinson in *Addis* was misguided in fearing that the intricacies of defamation law would be incorporated into breach of contract claims, for the simple reason that the issue here concerns damages, not liability. Defences of privilege, truth and so on, are thus irrelevant. It is therefore to be hoped that, just as the courts (with the exception of a claim for wrongful dismissal) have departed from *Addis* as regards pecuniary loss consequent on loss of reputation, and as regards mental distress,[24] they will also feel able to depart from it as regards damages for loss of reputation in itself.

(2) Torts

Although the term 'loss of reputation' is often not referred to, and although the damages are generally not itemised, loss of reputation in itself, and pecuniary loss flowing from it, are both recoverable for some torts.

---

[22] [2001] UKHL 13, [2003] 1 AC 518, at [2]. For criticism, see below p 282.
[23] In *Eastwood v Magnox Electric plc* [2004] UKHL 35, [2004] 3 WLR 322, Lord Steyn, in powerful obiter dicta, gave several reasons for doubting the approach of the majority in the *Johnson* case.
[24] Below, pp 277–283.

The tort of defamation, for example, largely exists in order to protect reputations, and damages there can compensate for both the non-pecuniary and pecuniary loss caused.[25] In *McCarey v Associated Newspapers Ltd*,[26] for example, £9,000 damages had been awarded by the jury in a libel action. The Court of Appeal overturned this as being too high; no punitive damages could here be awarded, and as the claimant had not proved any consequent pecuniary loss, he should be restricted to general loss of reputation as a non-pecuniary loss, plus mental distress damages for grief and annoyance. The judgments do recognise, however, that pecuniary loss flowing from the loss of reputation, as well as the non-pecuniary loss itself, can be compensated. Diplock LJ said, for example:

> 'Under head (1)—that is to say, the consequences of the attitude adopted towards the plaintiff by other persons—it may be possible to prove pecuniary loss, such as loss of practice or employment, or inability to obtain fresh appointment ... But the major consequences under head (1) may be purely social and lie in the attitude adopted towards the plaintiff by persons with whom he comes into social or professional contact.'[27]

Damages for loss of reputation and for consequential pecuniary losses have further been awarded for the tort of privacy[28] and false imprisonment[29] and have been recognised to be recoverable for malicious prosecution.[30]

In other cases damages for pecuniary loss consequent on loss of reputation have been awarded without any question being raised as to compensating the non-pecuniary loss.[31] For example, damages have been held recoverable where goods infringing the claimant's intellectual property rights are so inferior to the claimant's that his reputation was diminished and sales were lost.[32] And in *Mulvaine v Joseph*,[33] where a professional golfer was injured in a car accident, his damages for negligence included compensation for the lost opportunity to enhance his golfing prestige by competing in a number of European tournaments.

In contrast it was held by the Court of Appeal in *Lonrho plc v Fayed* (*No 5*)[34] that, while consequential pecuniary loss is recoverable for lawful means conspiracy, loss of reputation itself is not. And, although this is essentially an issue going to liability rather than damages, there is no liability in the tort of negligence for inflicting a loss of reputation (that is not consequent on the claimant's personal injury).[35]

So, to summarise, assuming a tort has been established and one is simply concerned with the question of damages, there appear to be no particular restrictions on tortious recovery for pecuniary loss consequent on a loss of reputation; but, for some torts, damages for loss of reputation in itself are irrecoverable. This latter restriction can be criticised for the same

---

[25] There is some doubt whether loss of reputation in itself is recoverable for slander actionable only on proof of damage. But once liability is established it would seem that it is: *Dixon v Smith* (1860) 5 H & N 450.
[26] [1965] 2 QB 86.   [27] ibid, at 108.   [28] *Sir Cliff Richard v BBC* [2018] EWHC 1837 (Ch).
[29] *Childs v Lewis* (1924) 40 TLR 870; *Walter v Alltools Ltd* (1944) 61 TLR 39; *White v Metropolitan Police Commissioner*, The Times, 24 April 1982.
[30] *Savile v Roberts* (1699) 1 Ld Raym 374; *Childs v Lewis* (1924) 40 TLR 870; *Clark v Chief Constable of Cleveland Constabulary* [1999] 21 LS Gaz R 38.
[31] In addition to the cases cited below, see *GWK Ltd v Dunlop Rubber Co Ltd* (1926) 42 TLR 593 (inducing breach of contract); *E Worsley & Co Ltd v Cooper* [1939] 1 All ER 290 (injurious falsehood).
[32] *Sykes v Sykes* (1824) 3 B & C 541 (passing-off). See similarly *AG Spalding & Bros v Garnage Ltd* (1918) 35 RPC 101 (passing-off).
[33] (1968) 112 Sol Jo 927.
[34] [1993] 1 WLR 1489. Cf *Pratt v British Medical Association* [1919] 1 KB 244, at 282 (unlawful means conspiracy).
[35] See, eg, *Calveley v Chief Constable of Merseyside* [1989] AC 1228, at 1238, where Lord Bridge said, speaking of the type of injury protected by the tort of negligence, 'The submission that "anxiety, vexation and injury to reputation may constitute such an injury" needs only to be stated to be seen to be unsustainable.'

reasons as have been put forward above in relation to the denial of compensation for non-pecuniary loss of reputation caused by breach of contract.

2. Assessing damages for loss of reputation

Pecuniary loss consequent on loss of reputation generally comprises lost earnings—as, for example, in *McCarey v Associated Newspapers Ltd* or *Marbé v George Edwardes*—or lost profits, as in the *Aerial Advertising* or *Anglo-Continental Holidays* cases. It is usually not possible to offer precise proof of those losses, although of course the more precise the proof the less the court (be it judge or jury) needs to resort to educated guesswork.

Loss of reputation in itself is, like all non-pecuniary losses, very difficult to assess and all that the courts can aim for is a fair and reasonable sum and some degree of uniformity between awards.[36] Clearly the greater the loss of reputation the greater the damages should be,[37] and in order to prove anything other than general loss of reputation a claimant would presumably need to bring evidence to indicate the difference between his or her present and former reputations. Where an 'offer of amends' has been made, under the Defamation Act 1996 procedure, there will be a discount from the damages (for non-pecuniary loss) that would otherwise have been awarded to reflect the public apology (and the removal, or at least significant reduction, of the stress of litigation).[38]

It is submitted that one of the best statements relating to the assessment of damages for loss of reputation is that of Diplock LJ in *McCarey v Associated Newspapers Ltd*,[39] where he made the point that there should be some degree of uniformity not only between loss of reputation damages but also between damages for all non-pecuniary losses. He said:

'In putting a money value on these kinds of injury, as the law requires damage-awarding tribunals to do, they are being required to attempt to equate the incommensurable. As in the case of damages for physical injuries, it is impossible to say that any answer looked at in isolation is right, or that any answer is wrong. But justice is not justice if it is arbitrary or whimsical, if what is awarded to one plaintiff for an injury bears no relation at all to what is awarded to another plaintiff for an injury of the same kind, or, I would add, if what is awarded for one kind of injury shows a wrong scale of values when compared with what is awarded for injuries of a different kind which are also incommensurable with pounds, shillings and pence.'[40]

And he later went on:

'If, as I have said, figures much lower than that awarded in this case are the proper compensation for the loss of an eye or limb, or for other life-long disabling injuries, a sum of £9,000 as compensation for this injury … is a figure that no reasonable jury, applying correct principles which included a proper scale of value, could have reached.'[41]

---

[36] It would appear that past awards (ie prior to 1 April 2013) for loss of reputation as a non-pecuniary loss should be uplifted by 10% in the light of *Simmons v Castle* [2012] EWCA Civ 1039, [2012] EWCA Civ 1288, [2013] 1 WLR 1239: see above, p 236.

[37] In *Sir Cliff Richard v BBC* [2018] EWHC 1837 (Ch) an award of £190,000 for loss of reputation and mental distress plus £20,000 aggravated damages were awarded for a serious infringement of privacy (by televising the entry by the police of Cliff Richard's home investigating alleged child sexual abuse for which he was not subsequently charged).

[38] *Cairns v Modi* [2012] EWCA Civ 1382, [2013] 1 WLR 1015 (in which a very high discount of 50% was upheld). Litigation may not be avoided altogether because the parties may not be able to agree on the quantum of damages.

[39] [1965] 2 QB 86. See also *Coyne v Citizen Finance Ltd* (1991) 172 CLR 211, at 221 (per Mason CJ and Deane J dissenting).

[40] [1965] 2 QB 86, at 108.   [41] ibid, at 110.

Although that approach, of seeking consistency with personal injury awards, was for many years rejected[42]—primarily because damages for defamation were normally decided by juries and it was felt inappropriate for juries to be referred to awards in personal injury cases—it was approved by the Court of Appeal in *John v MGN Ltd*.[43] In substituting a figure of £35,000 compensatory damages for the 'excessive' £75,000 damages awarded by the jury,[44] the Court of Appeal laid down that in defamation cases the scale of awards for non-pecuniary loss in personal injury cases could be drawn to the attention of juries and that the level of an appropriate award could be indicated by the judge.[45] In Sir Thomas Bingham MR's words:

> 'It is in our view offensive to public opinion, and rightly so, that a defamation plaintiff should recover damages for injury to reputation greater, perhaps by a significant factor, than if that same plaintiff had been rendered a helpless cripple or an insensate vegetable.'[46]

This marked an important step forward but even more significant—and no doubt a response not only to the remaining risk of jury awards being unpredictable and inconsistent but also to the expense and length of a jury trial—was the removal of the right to jury trial in defamation cases by the Defamation Act 2013, s 11. This means that, under the Senior Courts Act 1981, s 69 and the County Courts Act 1984, s 66, the right to a jury trial in a civil case is now confined to claims for malicious prosecution or false imprisonment or where there is a charge of fraud.[47] Otherwise trial is by judge alone, unless the court exercises its discretion to order trial by jury.

In thinking about the assessment of damages for loss of reputation for the torts of malicious prosecution and false imprisonment, there is no good reason for the right to jury trial to continue even in that very limited class of case. Jury assessment has declined since the middle of the twentieth century. In *Ward v James*[48] the Court of Appeal held that personal injury cases should almost always be tried by a judge and this was confirmed and strengthened in *H v Ministry of Defence*,[49] where the Court of Appeal reversed a decision to order trial by jury in a case where a major part of the claimant's penis had been amputated. Lord Donaldson MR said, '[T]rial by jury is normally inappropriate

---

[42] See, eg, *Cassell & Co Ltd v Broome* [1972] AC 1027, at 1070; *Blackshaw v Lord* [1984] QB 1; *Sutcliffe v Pressdram Ltd* [1991] 1 QB 153; *Rantzen v Mirror Group Newspapers Ltd* [1994] QB 670.
[43] [1997] QB 586. See also *Cairns v Modi* [2012] EWCA Civ 1382, [2013] 1 WLR 1015.
[44] The Court of Appeal's power to substitute such sum as appears to the court to be 'proper' for that of the jury is conferred by the Courts and Legal Services Act 1990, s 8: see also CPR Sch 1 r 59.11. Formerly, where damages were excessive or inadequate, the Court of Appeal merely had power to order a new trial. In *Kiam v MGN Ltd* [2002] EWCA Civ 43, [2003] QB 281, a defamation case, it was held (by a majority) that the 'proper' award is 'the highest award which the jury could reasonably have thought necessary', and that the jury's award should not be disturbed unless it substantially exceeds that sum. The bracket suggested by the judge was £40,000 to £80,000 and the jury awarded £105,000; this was not 'out of all proportion to what could sensibly have been thought appropriate' given the deference to be shown to jury awards in defamation cases. Guidance on the use of brackets in directing juries was also given.
[45] This was in line with the majority of the High Court of Australia in *Carson v John Fairfax & Sons Ltd* (1993) 178 CLR 44. It was also the position advocated in the second edition of this book, at p 228. In *Cairns v Modi* [2012] EWCA Civ 1382, [2013] 1 WLR 1015, a further comparison—with the so-called '*Vento* tariff' for the assessment of injured feelings in discrimination cases (see below, pp 289–290)—was rejected.
[46] [1997] QB 586, at 614.
[47] But there is no right to jury trial where 'the court is of the opinion that the trial requires any prolonged examination of documents or accounts or any scientific or local investigation which cannot conveniently be made with a jury': Senior Courts Act 1981, s 69(1).
[48] [1966] 1 QB 273.   [49] [1991] 2 QB 103.

for any personal injury action in so far as the jury is required to assess compensatory damages, because the assessment of such damages must be based upon or have regard to conventional scales of damages.'[50] The same can be said in relation to all types of action, including malicious prosecution and false imprisonment, where damages for non-pecuniary loss are being awarded.

---

[50] ibid, at 112.

14

Mental distress or physical inconvenience (except consequent on personal injury or death)[1]

---

1. When are damages awarded for mental distress or physical inconvenience? 277
2. Assessing damages for mental distress or physical inconvenience 288

Mental distress covers, for example, disappointment, worry, anxiety, fear, upset, and annoyance. On the traditional approach taken by the courts, mental distress, along with 'pain and suffering' consequent on a personal injury and 'bereavement', compensated under the Fatal Accidents Act 1976, are the heads of non-pecuniary loss covering the claimant's loss of happiness and distress in contrast to the other 'objective' non-pecuniary losses (such as 'loss of amenity' consequent on a personal injury and 'loss of reputation'). On an alternative view,[2] all non-pecuniary loss is regarded as ultimately dealing with distress or loss of happiness and 'mental distress' is seen as a residual head for distress not falling within any of the other heads.

Traditionally, and especially in the contract realm, physical inconvenience has been regarded as distinct from mental distress and as an objective loss analogous to loss of amenity in a personal injuries claim. But even leaving aside the point made at the end of the previous paragraph, the distinction between mental distress and physical inconvenience has become less important as the courts have become more willing to award mental distress damages for breach of contract. In particular, as we shall see, a now well-recognised category of recovery for non-pecuniary loss in contract is physical inconvenience and mental distress directly consequent on it. It has therefore been thought more helpful to look at physical inconvenience alongside mental distress in this chapter rather than separating it out into a different chapter.

It should be emphasised that mental distress has to be distinguished from a psychiatric illness, such as depression or post-traumatic stress disorder. The law regards psychiatric illness as a type of personal injury[3] and the restrictions on damages for mental distress do not apply to damages for psychiatric illness.[4]

In order to put the claimant into as good a position as if the tort or breach of contract had not occurred, as the general compensatory aims dictate, damages for mental distress or physical inconvenience should be awarded, subject to the usual limiting principles, whenever mental distress or physical inconvenience result from a tort or breach of contract.

---

[1] For damages for pain and suffering consequent on personal injury and for bereavement see above, pp 235–238, 263–264. Damages for loss of amenity in a personal injury case will usually include some damages for physical inconvenience.
[2] See above, pp 36–37.   [3] See above, p 234 n 2.
[4] So, for example, in *Hatton v Sutherland* [2002] EWCA Civ 76, [2002] 2 All ER 1 and *Barber v Somerset County Council* [2004] UKHL 13, [2004] 1 WLR 1089, which are leading cases on psychiatric illness consequent on stress at work, there was no mention of the leading case on contractual damages for mental distress, *Addis v Gramophone Co Ltd* [1909] AC 488.

Traditionally, however, the courts have been reluctant to award mental distress damages, particularly for breach of contract, and despite recent developments they are still sometimes irrecoverable for both torts and breach of contract.

1. When are damages awarded for mental distress or physical inconvenience?

(1) Breach of contract[5]

Traditionally *Addis v Gramophone Co Ltd*[6] was regarded as barring any damages for mental distress in an action for breach of contract. There the claimant had been wrongfully dismissed. The House of Lords confined damages to his direct pecuniary loss and refused to award any damages for the injury to the claimant's feelings following the 'harsh and humiliating manner'[7] in which he had been treated. Similarly in *Groom v Crocker*,[8] in which a solicitor in breach of contract had wrongly admitted negligent driving on the part of the claimant, the claimant's action for damages for the humiliation of being branded a negligent driver was denied and *Addis* applied. Further illustrations of the traditional denial of damages for mental distress are provided by cases on physical inconvenience, which drew a distinction between recoverable damages for physical inconvenience and non-recoverable damages for mental distress. For example, in *Hobbs v London and South Western Rly Co*[9] Mellor J said, 'For the mere inconvenience, such as annoyance and loss of temper or vexation … you cannot recover damages. That is purely sentimental and not a case where the word inconvenience, as I here use it, would apply.'[10]

This traditional denial was departed from by the Court of Appeal in *Jarvis v Swan's Tours*,[11] where the claimant was compensated for his disappointment at not getting as good a holiday as he had contracted for. Since then, mental distress damages have been awarded in many cases, primarily but not only for ruined holidays. But Lord Denning said that mental distress damages were recoverable only in a 'proper case'; and the Court of Appeal in *Watts v Morrow*,[12] as confirmed and expanded by the House of Lords in *Farley v Skinner*,[13] has clarified that there are only two exceptional categories of case where mental distress damages are recoverable. In Bingham LJ's words, neatly summarising the position, in *Watts v Morrow*:[14]

> 'A contract-breaker is not in general liable for any distress, frustration, anxiety, displeasure, vexation, tension or aggravation which his breach of contract may cause to the innocent party. The rule is not, I think founded on the assumption that such reactions are not foreseeable, which they surely are or may be, but on considerations of policy. But the rule is not absolute. Where the very object of a contract is to provide pleasure, relaxation, peace of mind or freedom from molestation, damages will be awarded if the fruit of the contract is not provided or if the contrary result is procured instead. If the law did not cater for this exceptional category of case it would be defective. A contract to survey the condition of a house for a prospective purchaser does not, however, fall within this exceptional category. In cases not falling within this exceptional category, damages are in my view recoverable for physical inconvenience and discomfort caused by the breach and mental suffering directly related to that inconvenience and discomfort.'

---

[5] See generally E Veitch, 'Sentimental Damages in Contract' (1977) 16 UWOLR 227. For a comparative account, see G Treitel, *Remedies for Breach of Contract* (Clarendon Press 1988) 194–201.
[6] [1909] AC 488.   [7] ibid, at 493 (per Lord Atkinson).   [8] [1939] 1 KB 194.
[9] (1875) LR 10 QB 111.   [10] ibid, at 122. Also see *Bailey v Bullock* [1950] 2 All ER 1167.
[11] [1973] QB 233.   [12] [1991] 1 WLR 1421.   [13] [2001] UKHL 49, [2002] 2 AC 732.
[14] [1991] 1 WLR 1421, at 1445.

The first category, therefore, is where the very, or predominant, object of the contract, from the claimant's point of view, was to obtain mental satisfaction, whether enjoyment or relief from distress. The ruined holiday cases, such as *Jarvis v Swan's Tours* and *Jackson v Horizon Holidays*,[15] most obviously fall within this. So does *Heywood v Wellers*,[16] where the defendant solicitors, in breach of their contractual duty of care, had failed to gain an injunction to stop molestation of the claimant by her former boyfriend. She was awarded damages for the mental distress resulting from being further molested. The same principle can also be said to underpin the influential Scottish case of *Diesen v Samson*[17] in which mental distress damages were awarded for the defender's breach of contract in failing to appear at a wedding to take photographs. Although not everyone agrees about this,[18] it is submitted that the decision of the House of Lords in *Ruxley Electronics and Construction Ltd v Forsyth*[19] also falls within this category. The damages of £2,500 for so-called 'loss of amenity' are best rationalised as flowing from the fact that the claimant's primary object in specifying the particular depth of the deep end of a swimming pool was mental satisfaction. That is, damages were being given for Mr Forsyth's loss of pleasure in diving into a deep pool rather than diving into a merely safe pool.[20]

In *Farley v Skinner*,[21] the House of Lords examined the width of this first category and decided that it extended to where *an important object* of the contract was mental satisfaction or freedom from distress even though that was not the very, or predominant, object. The claimant was considering buying a house 15 miles from Gatwick Airport. He engaged the defendant to survey the property and specifically asked him to investigate whether the property was affected by aircraft noise. After buying the property and moving in, the claimant discovered that aircraft bound for Gatwick flew directly over, or nearly over, the house and that the noise substantially affected the property and was 'a confounded nuisance'. Nevertheless he decided not to sell. Moreover, he was found to have suffered no financial loss in that he had paid the market value of the property where that value took into account the aircraft noise. Nevertheless he sought mental distress damages because his enjoyment of the property was detrimentally affected. The House of Lords upheld the first instance judge's award of £10,000 because an important object of the contract, albeit not the very object of the contract, was peace of mind in relation to the aircraft noise. No doubt the major point of the survey contract was to help ensure that the claimant paid the right price for the property. But given that he had made an express request for the aircraft noise to be investigated, it was an important object of the contract for him to be satisfied as to the aircraft noise.

It is significant that an express specific request was made in this case. This enables the concept of 'an important object of the contract being mental satisfaction' to be narrowly construed. Without that controlling feature, there would be a danger that this first category has been expanded to cover most consumer contracts; for one can say that mental satisfaction is an important object of most consumer contracts even if not the predominant object. For example, the purchaser of a new kitchen or a person who contracts for a standard house

---

[15] [1975] 1 WLR 1468. See also *Hunt v Hourmont* [1983] CLY 983.
[16] [1976] QB 446. See also *McLeish v Amoo-Gottfried & Co* (1993) 137 Sol Jo LB 204. Cf *Dickinson v Jones Alexander & Co* [1990] Fam Law 137 (which is controversial because the wife's mental distress consequent on the negligent handling of her *financial* claims surely fell outside this first category).
[17] 1971 SLT 49. See also *Reed v Madon* [1989] 2 All ER 431 (contract for exclusive burial rights); *Yearworth v North Bristol NHS Trust* [2009] EWCA Civ 37, [2009] 2 All ER 986 (mental distress damages recoverable, by analogy to the first of the two exceptional categories in contract, where the claimants' sperm had perished because of the defendant's breach of its duty of care as a bailee).
[18] See above, p 198 n 67.   [19] [1996] AC 344.   [20] See above, p 198 n 68.
[21] [2001] UKHL 49, [2002] 2 AC 732.

survey or even a person who pays for financial advice has mental satisfaction and peace of mind as an important object of the contract. Yet it is clear that the House of Lords did not intend the concept of an important object to be so widely construed given that it treated an ordinary surveying contract as not falling within this category.

A case that was held to fall within the first category, as expanded by *Farley v Skinner*, was *Hamilton Jones v David & Snape*.[22] Here a claim was brought against solicitors in contract and tort for having negligently failed to renew 'agency notifications' of the risk of the claimant's twin sons being taken out of England by her former husband. The children had been taken to Tunisia and, as a consequence, the mother had lost custody of them. Neuberger J held that the claimant was entitled to £20,000 mental distress damages for breach of contract (and concurrently for the tort of negligence). While the primary object of the contract between the claimant and her solicitors was the welfare of the children, an important factor was to ensure, so far as possible, that the claimant retained custody of the children for her own pleasure and peace of mind. Applying the approach to the first category taken in *Farley v Skinner*, damages for the mental distress consequent on losing custody of her children were therefore recoverable.

A second situation in which mental distress damages can be awarded is where the claimant's mental distress is directly consequent on physical inconvenience caused by the defendant's breach of contract. That damages for the physical inconvenience itself can be awarded has long been established.

In *Burton v Pinkerton*,[23] for example, a sailor left a ship at a foreign port, when in breach of his contract of employment, the captain of the ship decided to take it into war. The sailor was able to recover damages for the non-remote physical inconvenience caused by the captain's breach of contract. Similarly in *Hobbs v London and South Western Rly Co*,[24] a man and his family were set down at the wrong station by the defendant railway company in breach of contract. As it was late at night, there was no available transport or accommodation and so, despite rain, they had to walk five miles home. They were able to recover damages for that physical inconvenience. Again damages have long been awarded for the physical inconvenience of living in a house requiring repairs (including the inconvenience while the repairs are carried out) when the house would not have been bought, or at least not in that condition, but for a breach of the contractual duty of care by the purchaser's surveyor or solicitor.[25] A solicitor was also held liable for physical inconvenience damages in *Bailey v Bullock*[26] where he had delayed in bringing an action for possession of a house. As a result the claimant and his family were forced to live in one room of his parents-in-law's small house. A final example is *Perera v Vandiyar*,[27] where the defendant landlord, in an attempt to evict the claimant tenant, cut off the supply of gas and electricity to his flat, leaving the claimant without alternative means of heat or light. After two days' discomfort, the claimant left with his wife and child to stay with friends for five days until the gas and electricity supply were restored. The claimant was awarded physical inconvenience damages for breach by the landlord of his tenancy agreement.

But, subsequent to the development of the law in *Jarvis v Swan's Tours* (although that case did not concern physical inconvenience), the courts have clarified that damages for

---

[22] [2003] EWHC 3147 (Ch), [2004] 1 WLR 924.   [23] (1867) LR 2 Exch 340.
[24] (1875) LR 10 QB 111.
[25] Eg *Hill v Debenhams Tewson & Chinnock* (1958) 171 Estates Gazette 835; *Moss v Heckingbottom* (1958) 172 Estates Gazette 207; *Hipkiss v Gaydon* [1961] CLY 9042 (where the defendant was the vendor-builder); *Sinclair v Bowden* (1962) 183 Estates Gazette 95; *Collard v Saunders* [1971] CLY 11161. *Piper v Daybell Court-Cooper & Co* (1969) 210 Estates Gazette 1047 and *Trask v Clark & Sons* [1980] CLY 2588 are analogous (lack of privacy).
[26] [1950] 2 All ER 1167.   [27] [1953] 1 WLR 672.

mental distress directly consequent on the physical inconvenience are also recoverable. For example, in *Perry v Sidney Phillips & Son*[28] the claimant bought a house on the faith of a survey report prepared by the defendants, a firm of chartered surveyors. The report had been negligently made, in breach of the defendants' contractual and tortious duty of care, and did not mention several serious defects including a leaking roof and a septic tank which produced an offensive smell. The claimant was held entitled to mental distress damages for the 'anxiety, worry and distress'[29] caused and this mental distress is best viewed as directly consequent on the physical inconvenience of having to live in a house that was in a poor condition; for having emphasised that the mental distress here was recoverable because reasonably foreseeable, Lord Denning, with whom Oliver LJ apparently agreed, went on to cite with approval that part of the judgment at first instance where no clear distinction was drawn between physical inconvenience and mental distress consequent on it. Sir Patrick Bennett QC had there said:

> 'I think it was reasonably foreseeable that, if Mr Perry bought the house in such a condition that he was exposed to the incursion of water, the anxiety resulting from the question of when the repairs should be done and the odour and smell from the defective septic water tank would cause him distress and discomfort which I have gathered together under the term "vexation"... In my view, the plaintiff is entitled ... to damages for such discomfort, distress and the like ...'[30]

Furthermore, Kerr LJ, in upholding the trial judge's decision on damages for vexation and inconvenience, emphasised that those damages were recoverable because, '... the physical consequences of the breach were all foreseeable at the time'.[31]

Similarly in *Watts v Morrow*[32] a husband and wife were each awarded £750 for the physical inconvenience and directly related mental distress of living (at weekends) in a house undergoing extensive repairs. The repairs were necessitated by defects that had been negligently omitted from the defendant's survey report upon which the claimants had relied in buying the house. As we have seen, Bingham LJ clarified that, in addition to the first exceptional category considered above, damages are 'recoverable for physical inconvenience and discomfort caused by the breach and mental suffering directly related to that inconvenience and discomfort'.[33] Damages were therefore awarded within this second category whereas they could not have been awarded within the first category (the contract being for an ordinary house survey).

In *Farley v Skinner*,[34] the facts of which we have considered above, the House of Lords held that mental distress damages could be awarded within this second category as well as within the first. Aircraft noise causes 'physical inconvenience' because that term should be interpreted in a wide sense to include all matters detrimentally affecting sight, hearing, smell, or touch. In Lord Scott's words, '[I]f the cause of the inconvenience or discomfort is a sensory (sight, touch, hearing, smell etc) experience, damages can, subject to the remoteness

---

[28] [1982] 1 WLR 1297. See also *McCall v Abelesz* [1976] QB 585 (landlord's breach of tenancy agreement); *Buckley v Lane Herdman & Co* [1977] CLY 3143, *Wapshott v Davis Donovan & Co* [1996] PNLR 361 (both concerning breach by a solicitor); *Calabar Properties Ltd v Stitcher* [1984] 1 WLR 287, *Lubren v London Borough of Lambeth* (1988) 20 HLR 165, *Wallace v Manchester CC* (1998) 30 HLR 1111 (all concerning breach of landlord's repairing obligations); *Cross v David Martin & Mortimer* [1989] 1 EGLR 154, *Bigg v Howard Son & Gooch* [1990] 1 EGLR 173 (both concerning surveyors' breach).

[29] [1982] 1 WLR 1297, at 1303 (per Lord Denning). [30] [1982] 1 All ER 1005, at 1016–1017.

[31] [1982] 1 WLR 1297, at 1307.

[32] [1991] 1 WLR 1421. See also *Patel v Hooper & Jackson* [1999] 1 WLR 1792 (damages of £2,000 each for the relative discomfort of having to live in less desirable rented accommodation until the uninhabitable house bought as a result of the defendant's negligent survey could be sold).

[33] [1991] 1 WLR 1421, at 1445. See above, p 277. [34] [2001] UKHL 49, [2002] 2 AC 732.

rules, be recovered.'[35] It is arguable that this definition of 'physical inconvenience' is so wide that there is no distinction left between 'physical inconvenience' and 'inconvenience': but, if so, that would vastly expand the range of the second category so as to include almost every example of mental distress. For that reason, it would seem that Lord Scott's approach to 'inconvenience' needs to be approached with caution and certainly in subsequent cases the courts have continued to speak in terms of 'physical inconvenience'.[36]

Beyond the two exceptional categories, mental distress damages remain irrecoverable for breach of contract.

For example, in *Bliss v South East Thames Regional Health Authority*,[37] the defendant health authority in breach of contract had suspended the claimant, a consultant surgeon, on the unfounded grounds that he was mentally unfit for his job. At first instance, Farquharson J awarded £2,000 mental distress damages. This was overturned by the Court of Appeal, which held that, until altered by the House of Lords, *Addis* largely remains good law.

In *Hayes v James & Charles Dodd*,[38] the claimants were a husband and wife in the motor car repair business and they bought a yard and workshop on the faith of their solicitors' advice that there was a right of access to the rear of the workshop. This was untrue. The yard and workshop were therefore useless for the claimants' business plans and they were forced to sell them. In an action against the solicitors for breach of their contractual duty of care the claimants were awarded £92,000 for their pecuniary losses. But the Court of Appeal overturned Hirst J's award of £1,500 each for mental distress (largely comprising the anxiety and vexation of the dispute itself). *Bliss* was applied and it was stressed that mental distress damages were inappropriate where the contract was merely a commercial one entered into with a view to profit. Reflecting a widely held fear that, unless heavily restricted, mental distress damages would feature in almost every award of contractual damages, Staughton LJ said:

'I would not view with enthusiasm the prospect that every shipowner in the Commercial Court, having successfully claimed for unpaid freight or demurrage, would be able to add a claim for mental distress suffered while he was waiting for his money.'[39]

In *Johnson v Gore Wood & Co*,[40] which involved claims for professional negligence against the defendant solicitors in connection with the purchase of land by the claimant and the claimant's company, the claimant sought damages for the mental distress and anxiety, and for the financial embarrassment and deterioration in his family relationships, caused by the protracted litigation. Although the case primarily concerned other issues, the House of Lords (Lord Cooke dissenting)[41] struck out the claim for damages for non-financial loss. This was on the basis that *Addis* largely remains good law and the facts of this case did not fall within the two exceptional categories recognised in *Watts v Morrow*.[42]

---

[35] ibid, at [85]. [36] See, eg, *Milner v Carnival Plc* [2010] EWCA Civ 389, [2011] 1 Lloyd's Rep 374.
[37] [1985] IRLR 308. In addition to the cases denying mental distress damages discussed in the text below, see *Rae v Yorkshire Bank plc* [1988] BTLC 35 (dishonouring of cheque); *O'Laoire v Jackel International Ltd (No 2)* [1991] ICR 718 (wrongful dismissal); *Branchett v Beaney* [1992] 3 All ER 910 (breach of covenant of quiet enjoyment).
[38] [1990] 2 All ER 815. [39] ibid, at 823. [40] [2002] 2 AC 1.
[41] While agreeing that damages for the mental distress and anxiety were irrecoverable, Lord Cooke dissented because he thought that damages for the financial embarrassment and deterioration in family relationships could be recovered as being akin to physical inconvenience and discomfort within the second category in *Watts v Morrow*. He was also anxious to assert that he doubted the correctness of *Addis* in laying down that mental distress damages are irrecoverable for wrongful dismissal.
[42] [1991] 1 WLR 1421.

It is submitted, therefore, that the present law on the recoverability of mental distress damages in contract is relatively clear. Outside the two exceptional categories, at least the first of which has been 'loosened' by the House of Lords in *Farley v Skinner*,[43] mental distress damages are irrecoverable.

Before considering an alternative analysis, favoured by Lord Scott in *Farley v Skinner*, it should be noted that, in relation to the facts of *Addis* itself, which concerned a wrongful dismissal, the House of Lords in *Johnson v Unisys Ltd*[44] has controversially held that, whatever the normal position at common law, wrongful dismissal is a special case because of the need to avoid undermining the statutory regime of unfair dismissal (which, for example, includes a statutory cap on compensation of, at present, £83,682).[45] In other words, there is, so it has been laid down, a special reason for denying mental distress damages for wrongful dismissal.[46] This is controversial because the statutory unfair dismissal legislation can sit perfectly well with a full common law regime for damages for the manner of a wrongful dismissal. They can be viewed as simply concurrent causes of action albeit that only employment tribunals, and not the courts, have jurisdiction in respect of unfair, as opposed to wrongful, dismissal. Any idea that the purpose of the unfair dismissal legislation was to halt the development of normal contractual rights is a false reading of history: the aim was to add protection to employees not to freeze their contractual rights.

In *Farley v Skinner* Lord Scott put forward an alternative approach to that which sees there as being a general bar to mental distress damages and two main exceptions.[47] Part of his reasoning was to distinguish between loss of expected mental benefits and mental distress as a consequential loss. With respect, this is an unworkable distinction (not least because where one has lost a mental benefit, there is an inevitable consequential suffering of mental distress) and required Lord Scott to adopt forced classifications of past cases.[48] But ultimately, the essential thrust of his approach appears to be that mental distress (but, peculiarly, with the apparent exception of disappointment) should be recoverable if not too remote. While, as we shall see in a moment, this reliance on remoteness has much to commend it as a matter of principle and policy, it is plainly inconsistent with past cases. Indeed it was specifically rejected by the Court of Appeal in *Bliss v South East Thames Regional*

---

[43] [2001] UKHL 49, [2002] 2 AC 732.

[44] [2001] UKHL 13, [2003] 1 AC 518. See above, pp 270–271. *Johnson v Unisys* was distinguished, without reopening its correctness, in *Eastwood v Magnox Electric plc* [2004] UKHL 35, [2005] 1 AC 503.

[45] Employment Rights (Increase of Limits) Order 2018, SI 2018/194. Compensation for unfair dismissal is awarded by employment tribunals under the Employment Rights Act 1996, ss 112(4), 117(3)(a), 118–27. Prior to *Johnson v Unisys Ltd* it had been decided by the National Industrial Relations Court in *Norton Tool Co Ltd v Tewson* [1972] ICR 501 that the loss compensated for unfair dismissal was limited to pecuniary loss: this has been approved as still good law, so that there can be no unfair dismissal compensation for injured feelings (or psychiatric illness), by the House of Lords in *Dunnachie v Kingston-upon-Hull County Council* [2004] UKHL 36, [2005] 1 AC 226. See also *Santos Gomes v Higher Level Care Ltd* [2018] EWCA Civ 418, [2018] 2 All ER 740 (no compensation for injured feelings for breach of the Working Time Regulations 1998, SI 1998/1833).

[46] As shown by the facts of *Johnson* case itself, the *Johnson* bar to damages for mental distress for wrongful dismissal applies also to bar damages for psychiatric illness. For the drawing of the line between wrongful dismissal and a breach of the employment contract (including causing psychiatric illness) that is sufficiently distinct from wrongful dismissal as to fall outside the *Johnson* bar to damages (or, as it was termed, the '*Johnson* exclusion area'), see *Eastwood v Magnox Electric plc* [2004] UKHL 35, [2005] 1 AC 503: the House of Lords there pointed to the unsatisfactory but, as the majority saw it, unavoidable consequences of its own decision in *Johnson* and called for legislative reform to be considered as a matter of urgency. That has not happened and, instead, the Supreme Court has further entrenched the position in *Edwards v Chesterfield Royal Hospital NHS Foundation Trust* [2011] UKSC 58, [2012] 2 AC 22.

[47] For a more favourable view of Lord Scott's speech than that taken here, see D Capper, 'Damages for Distress and Disappointment—Problem Solved?' (2002) 118 LQR 193. See also E McKendrick and M Graham, 'The Sky's the Limit: Contractual Damages for Non-Pecuniary Loss' [2002] LMCLQ 161.

[48] Eg he regarded *Hobbs v London and South Western Rly Co* (1875) LR 10 QB 111 as a loss of expected benefit case but *Heywood v Wellers* [1976] QB 446 as a consequential mental distress case.

Health Authority;[49] and in his classic statement in *Watts v Morrow* Bingham LJ emphasised that the law on mental distress damages was concerned to place restrictions over and above the normal restriction of remoteness. If remoteness is the test, surely *Bliss, Hayes v Dodd,* and *Johnson v Gore Wood*—and many other cases—would have been decided differently.

Having said that, a strong argument can be made (supporting the general thrust of Lord Scott's speech) that English courts should be more willing to award mental distress damages than they presently are. For while the first exceptional category perhaps presents the strongest claim for such relief, since mental distress damages there reflect the 'consumer surplus'[50] (namely the particular value to the claimant of the contractual performance over and above its objective market value), the compensatory principle indicates that mental distress caused by the breach of contract should always be compensated, subject to the usual limiting principles, such as remoteness. After all, the confusion between punitive and mental distress damages has been clearly exposed in cases like *Rookes v Barnard*[51] and, while assessing damages is difficult for mental distress, it is no more difficult than for other non-pecuniary losses. Similarly, the fact that mental distress is difficult to prove should not deter the courts, since applying normal principle if the claimant cannot establish that he or she has suffered mental distress that is not *de minimis*, he or she should recover no damages. Although it has been suggested that parties to commercial contracts accept the risk of mental distress consequent on a breach of contract,[52] it is hard to see why this should be thought to be so. While parties plainly accept the strains and stresses of commercial life, it is hard to see why they are regarded as accepting the risk of mental distress consequent on contract-breaking any more than they accept the risk of financial loss consequent on contract-breaking. If the risks of 'losses' consequent on contract-breaking were truly accepted, no damages at all would be payable. Certainly in many other jurisdictions there has been a greater willingness to award mental distress damages.[53] Finally it should be realised that, even if mental distress damages were freely available, it would not be correct to imagine that they would figure in almost every contractual damages claim, for often the claimant is not a human person but is a company which is incapable of experiencing mental distress.

(2) Torts

Looking first at physical inconvenience, it appears that, as in contract so in tort, damages for physical inconvenience have long been recoverable and are not subject to special restrictions. Moreover, in contrast to the position taken until recently in contract, it would seem that in tort cases damages for mental distress consequent on physical inconvenience have not been separated out as being irrecoverable.

So, while usually not classified under the head of physical inconvenience, damages for the tort of false imprisonment must always include some compensation for the claimant's

---

[49] [1985] IRLR 308. This overruled *Cox v Philips Industries Ltd* [1976] 1 WLR 638 in which Lawson J had said, at 644, that there was '… no reason in principle why, if a situation arises which within the contemplation of the parties would have given rise to vexation, distress and general disappointment and frustration, the person who is injured by a contractual breach, should not be compensated in damages for that breach'. For a similar approach to Lawson J's see the excellent dissenting judgment of Thomas J in the New Zealand Court of Appeal in *Bloxham v Robinson* (1996) 7 TCLR 122.
[50] D Harris, A Ogus and J Phillips, 'Contract Remedies and the Consumer Surplus' (1979) 95 LQR 581; S Mullen, 'Damages for Breach of Contract: Quantifying the Lost Consumer Surplus' (2016) 36 OJLS 83.
[51] [1964] AC 1129.
[52] Cf Lord Cooke's statement in *Johnson v Gore Wood & Co* [2002] 2 AC 1, at 49: 'Contract-breaking is treated as an incident of commercial life which players in the game are expected to meet with mental fortitude.'
[53] For Canadian cases, see S Waddams, *The Law of Damages* (6th edn, Thomson Reuters 2017) paras 3.1310–3.1450. For the US, see J Chmiel, 'Recovery for Mental Suffering from Breach of Contract' (1957) 32 Notre Dame LR 482; Second Restatement of Contracts, s 353.

physical inconvenience (which, in that context, equates to the loss of liberty).[54] The same must generally be true for nuisance. In *Bone v Seale*,[55] for example, two owners of neighbouring property were awarded damages for the 'inconvenience, discomfort and annoyance'[56] caused by the smells from the defendant's pig farm which constituted a nuisance; and in *Hunter v Canary Wharf Ltd*[57] Lord Goff said, 'If a nuisance should occur, then the spouse who has an interest in the property can ... recover any damages in respect of the discomfort or inconvenience caused by the nuisance'. In *Mafo v Adams*,[58] damages for physical inconvenience were expressly awarded to a tenant in an action for deceit against his landlord, who had induced him to leave protected premises, and in *Millington v Duffy*[59] a tenant was awarded damages for inconvenience and distress primarily for trespass to land, his landlord having wrongfully evicted him. In *Saunders v Edwards*[60] damages for inconvenience and disappointment were awarded to the tenants of a flat who had been induced to buy the lease by the defendant vendor's fraudulent misrepresentation that it included the roof terrace. And in *Perry v Sidney Phillips & Son*[61] and *Watts v Morrow*[62] damages for the physical inconvenience (and consequent distress) of living in a house with defects (or while repairs were being made to remedy those defects) that had been negligently omitted from the defendant surveyor's report were awarded in an action brought for both the tort of negligence and breach of contract. Finally, in *Ward v Cannock Chase District Council*[63] damages were awarded for the discomfort and consequent distress of living initially in a house with a hole in the roof and later in overcrowded temporary accommodation, all of which was caused by the defendants' tortious negligence in leaving neighbouring houses derelict.

Turning to mental distress itself (irrespective of any physical inconvenience), the law has traditionally been more favourable to the distressed claimant in tort than in contract. So there has been compensation, often under the head of 'aggravated damages',[64] for mental distress caused by torts such as false imprisonment,[65] malicious prosecution,[66] assault and battery,[67]

---

[54] *Prison Officers Association v Iqbal* [2009] EWCA Civ 1312, [2010] QB 732; *Alseran v Ministry of Defence* [2017] EWHC 3289 (QB), [2018] 3 WLR 95, at [876]. See also the discussion of damages for loss of liberty in the context of the tort of misfeasance in public office in *Karagozlu v Commissioner of Police of the Metropolis* [2006] EWCA Civ 1691, [2007] 1 WLR 1881.
[55] [1975] 1 WLR 797.   [56] ibid, at 804.
[57] [1997] AC 655, at 694. See similarly the references to 'damages for loss of amenity value' (per Lord Lloyd, at 696); 'compensation for the diminution in the amenity value of the property during the period for which the nuisance persisted' (per Lord Hoffmann, at 706); damages for 'loss of amenity' (per Lord Hope, at 724). But, as their Lordships recognised, because the landowner alone has the right to sue in private nuisance, the discomfort and inconvenience of others living at the property is irrelevant except in so far as it affects the landowner's own enjoyment of his land. See also *Dobson v Thames Water Utilities Ltd* [2009] EWCA Civ 28, [2009] 3 All ER 319.
[58] [1970] 1 QB 548.   [59] (1984) 17 HLR 232.   [60] [1987] 1 WLR 1116.
[61] [1982] 1 WLR 1297. See also, eg, *Roberts v J Hampson & Co* [1990] 1 WLR 94 (compensation for disruption of having to live with wife's mother consequent on negligence of surveyor engaged by building society).
[62] [1991] 1 WLR 1421. See also *Patel v Hooper & Jackson* [1999] 1 WLR 1792: above, p 329 n 12.
[63] [1986] Ch 546.   [64] Below, pp 287–288.
[65] Eg *Walter v Alltools Ltd* (1944) 61 TLR 39; *White v Metropolitan Police Commissioner*, The Times, 24 April 1982; *Thompson v Metropolitan Police Commissioner* [1998] QB 498; *Metropolitan Police Commissioner v Gerald*, The Times, 26 June 1998; *Prison Officers Association v Iqbal* [2009] EWCA Civ 1312, [2010] QB 732; *Alseran v Ministry of Defence* [2017] EWHC 3289 (QB), [2018] 3 WLR 95, at [878].
[66] Eg *Savile v Roberts* (1698) 1 Ld Raym 374; *White v Metropolitan Police Commissioner*, The Times, 24 April 1982; *Thompson v Metropolitan Police Commissioner* [1998] QB 498; *Metropolitan Police Commissioner v Gerald*, The Times, 26 June 1998.
[67] Eg *White v Metropolitan Police Commissioner*, The Times, 24 April 1982; *Ballard v Metropolitan Police Commissioner* (1983) 133 NLJ 1133; *Barbara v Home Office* (1984) 134 NLJ 888; *George v Metropolitan Police Commissioner*, The Times, 31 March 1984; *W v Meah* [1986] 1 All ER 935; *Griffiths v Williams*, The Times, 24 November 1995; *Appleton v Garrett* [1996] PIQR P1; *Metropolitan Police Commissioner v Gerald*, The Times, 26 June 1998; *JXL v Britton* [2014] EWHC 2571 (QB); *Alseran v Ministry of Defence* [2017] EWHC 3289 (QB), [2018] 3 WLR 95, at [878].

defamation,[68] nuisance,[69] trespass to land,[70] deceit,[71] trespass to goods,[72] and now privacy.[73] The Copyright, Designs and Patents Act 1988, s 97(2) (formerly the Copyright Act 1956, s 17(3)) appears to empower the award of mental distress damages for copyright infringement.[74] The Equality Act 2010, s 119 empowers the courts (or, under s 124 of the Act, in the employment field, employment tribunals) to award damages (or, in the employment field, compensation) for 'injured feelings' for breach of the statutory duty against non-discrimination laid down in the 2010 Act.[75] And under the Protection from Harassment Act 1997 a claimant who suffers a course of conduct[76] which amounts to harassment (which is defined to include 'causing the person alarm or distress')[77] may be awarded damages for, among other things, 'any anxiety caused by the harassment'.[78]

It has also been accepted that damages for mental distress may be awarded under the Human Rights Act 1998 for the infringement by a public authority of a person's Convention rights.[79]

However—and although one can strongly argue (analogously to the arguments put forward in respect of breach of contract) that, once liability in tort has been established and one is purely concerned with damages, the law should always be willing to award damages for mental distress subject to the usual limitations such as remoteness—the above decisions do not mean that damages for mental distress are now always recoverable in tort.[80] Most importantly, although this is usually an issue going to liability rather than damages, there

---

[68] Eg *McCarey v Associated Newspapers Ltd* [1965] 2 QB 86 (libel); *Khodaparast v Shad* [2000] 1 All ER 545 (malicious falsehood).

[69] Eg *Bone v Seale* [1975] 1 WLR 797; *Dunton v Dover District Council* (1977) 76 LGR 87. The damages for 'loss of amenity' in *Carr-Saunders v Dick McNeil Associates Ltd* [1986] 1 WLR 922 presumably also included some compensation for mental distress. But private nuisance does not protect against interference with television reception caused by a building: *Hunter v Canary Wharf Ltd* [1997] AC 655.

[70] In *Drane v Evangelou* [1978] 1 WLR 455 and *McMillan v Singh* (1984) 17 HLR 120 aggravated damages were awarded to a tenant for his landlord's trespass to land (or nuisance) in wrongfully evicting him. In the former, the Court of Appeal emphasised the worry and stress of being deprived of a roof over one's head and, in the latter, Sir John Arnold stressed also the tenant's outrage at the landlord's actions. See also *Merest v Harvey* (1814) 5 Taunt 442; *Millington v Duffy* (1984) 17 HLR 232; *Guppys (Bridport) Ltd v Brookling and James* (1984) 269 Estates Gazette 846, at 942; *Ashgar v Ahmed* (1984) 17 HLR 25. See also, somewhat analogously, the award of mental distress damages for breach of the statutory duty not to infringe exclusive burial rights in *Reed v Madon* [1989] 2 All ER 431.

[71] *Archer v Brown* [1984] 2 All ER 267 (Peter Pain J here used both the terminology of 'injured feelings' and 'aggravated damages'); *Saunders v Edwards* [1987] 2 All ER 651.

[72] *Owen and Smith v Reo Motors (Britain) Ltd* (1934) 151 LT 274. See also *Piper v Darling* (1940) 67 Ll L Rep 419 (sentimental value taken into account in fixing the value of the claimant's yacht, destroyed by the defendant's negligence); *Yearworth v North Bristol NHS Trust* [2009] EWCA Civ 37, [2009] 2 All ER 986 (mental distress damages recoverable where consequent on perishing of the claimant's sperm by reason of the defendant's negligence).

[73] *Gulati v MGN Ltd* [2015] EWCA Civ 1291, [2017] QB 149; *Sir Cliff Richard v BBC* [2018] EWHC 1837 (Ch).

[74] *Nichols Advanced Vehicle Systems Inc v Rees and Oliver* [1979] RPC 127; *Henderson v All Around the World Recordings Limited* [2014] EWHC 3087 (IEPC); *Absolute Lofts South West London Ltd v Artisan Home Improvements Ltd* [2015] EWHC 2608 (IPEC), [2017] ECDR 6. The latter two cases also looked at damages for infringement of an IP right under reg 3 of the Intellectual Property (Enforcement etc) Regulations 2006, which gives effect to Art 13 of the Intellectual Property Rights Enforcement Directive, 2004/24/EC, and which refers to damages for 'moral prejudice'. As to whether s 97(2) authorises punitive damages, see below, ch 20.

[75] See, eg, *Alexander v Home Office* [1988] 2 All ER 118, *Deane v Ealing London Borough Council* [1993] ICR 329, *Armitage, Marsden and HM Prison Service v Johnson* [1997] ICR 275 (racial discrimination); *Vento v Chief Constable of West Yorkshire Police (No 2)* [2002] EWCA Civ 1871, [2003] IRLR 102 (sex discrimination). In these cases, aggravated damages were awarded as well as compensation for injured feelings. See further below, pp 287–288.

[76] Protection from Harassment Act 1997, s 1(1). [77] ibid, s 8(3).

[78] ibid, s 3(2). See, eg, *Levi v Bates* [2015] EWCA Civ 206, [2016] QB 91.

[79] *R (on the application of Bernard) v Enfield London Borough Council* [2002] EWHC 2282 (Admin), [2003] HRLR 4; *R (on the application of KB) v Mental Health Review Tribunal* [2003] EWHC 193 (Admin), [2003] 2 All ER 209. But in the latter case, which concerned infringement of a mental patient's right to speedy determination of whether correctly detained, Stanley Burnton J held that to be compensatable the distress had to be of sufficient intensity to justify an award. For his view that breach of a Convention right might trigger aggravated damages, see [2003] EWHC 193 (Admin), at [50].

[80] In addition to the restriction discussed below in this paragraph, see *Lonrho plc v Fayed (No 5)* [1993] 1 WLR 1489 (no damages for injured feelings for lawful means conspiracy). E Descheemaeker, 'Rationalising Recovery for

is no liability in the tort of negligence[81] for the 'mere' infliction of mental distress (ie not consequent on death[82] or the claimant's personal injury)[83] as opposed to a recognisable psychiatric illness. In *McLoughlin v O'Brian*,[84] Lord Bridge said, '[T]he first hurdle which a plaintiff claiming damages of the kind in question must surmount is to establish that he is suffering, not merely grief, distress or any other normal emotion, but a positive psychiatric illness.' In *Hicks v Chief Constable of the South Yorkshire Police*[85] Lord Bridge said, 'Those trapped in the crush at Hillsborough who were fortunate enough to escape without injury have no claim in respect of the distress they suffered in what must have been a truly terrifying experience.' It follows that fear of impending death felt by the victim of a fatal injury before that injury is inflicted cannot by itself give rise to a cause of action which survives for the benefit of the victim's estate. Again in *Page v Smith*,[86] Lord Jauncey said, 'The ordinary emotions of anxiety, fear, grief or transient shock are not conditions for which the law gives compensation.' Finally, in *White v Chief Constable of the South Yorkshire Police*[87] Lord Hoffmann said, '[A] "recognised psychiatric illness" ... is distinguished from shock, fear, anxiety or grief which are regarded as normal consequences of a distressing event and for which damages are not awarded.'

However, it should be added here that the extension of tortious negligence to the negligent performance of services causing pure economic loss, and the acceptance of concurrent liability,[88] presumably means that mental distress damages are recoverable in the tort action provided they would be recoverable in that situation for breach of contract. In other words, mental distress damages will be recoverable provided one can show that an important object of the services was to provide mental satisfaction or freedom from distress, or that the mental distress is directly consequent on physical inconvenience. This is illustrated by one of the leading cases on the recovery of mental distress damages in contract,

---

Emotional Harm in Tort Law' (2018) 134 LQR 627 argues that there is, and should be, no particular restriction on recovery for emotional harm once a tort has been established.

[81] For the denial of mental distress damages for a tort other than negligence, see the denial of damages for fear for oneself, in respect of liability for animals, in *Behrens v Bertram Mills Circus Ltd* [1957] 2 QB 1. The claimant was in a booth when an elephant went out of control and knocked the booth over, terrifying the claimant. Devlin J, at 28, said that damages could not be given '... infringing the general principle embedded in the common law that suffering caused by grief, fear, anguish and the like is not assessable'. Note also that there is no liability under *Wilkinson v Downton* [1897] 2 QB 57 for even intentionally inflicted mental distress (as opposed to psychiatric illness): *Wong v Parkside Health NHS Trust* [2001] EWCA Civ 1721, [2003] 3 All ER 932. Cf *Hunter v Canary Wharf Ltd* [1997] AC 655, at 707 (per Lord Hoffmann); *Wainwright v Home Office* [2003] UKHL 53, [2003] 3 WLR 1137, at [41]–[47] (per Lord Hoffmann); *OPO v Rhodes* [2015] UKSC 32, [2016] AC 219, at [63]–[67], [73]. See F Trindade, 'The Intentional Infliction of Purely Mental Distress' (1986) 6 OJLS 219; P Handford, N Mullany, and P Mitchell, *Mullany and Handford's Tort Liability for Psychiatric Damage* (2nd edn, Law Book Co 2006) 699–716.
[82] Bereavement damages may be awarded to a spouse or parent of the deceased under the Fatal Accidents Act 1976: see above, pp 263–264.
[83] See also, alongside but distinct from personal injury, the conventional sum of £15,000 awarded for 'wrongful birth' in *Rees v Darlington Memorial Hospital NHS Trust* [2003] UKHL 52, [2004] 1 AC 309, discussed above, at pp 251–252.
[84] [1983] 1 AC 410, at 431. In addition to the cases cited below, see *Hinz v Berry* [1970] 2 QB 40, at 42; *Calveley v Chief Constable of the Merseyside Police* [1989] AC 1228, at 1238; *F v Wirral Metropolitan Borough Council* [1991] Fam 69, esp at 104 (mother had no claim in negligence against a local authority for the mental distress of 'losing' her child to long-term foster parents); *Alcock v Chief Constable of South Yorkshire Police* [1992] 1 AC 310, at 401, 409–10, 416; *Kerby v Redbridge Health Authority* [1994] PIQR Q1 (no damages recoverable for 'dashed hopes' of claimant in respect of death of newborn baby caused by defendants' negligence); *Reilly and Reilly v Merseyside Regional Health Authority* [1995] 6 Med LR 246 (claustrophobia and fear suffered when trapped in a lift for over an hour did not give rise to a cause of action). Cf *Whitmore v Euroways Express Coaches Ltd*, The Times, 4 May 1984, in which a wife was awarded damages, against a holiday coach firm for negligent driving, for the 'ordinary shock', falling short of a recognised psychiatric illness, suffered at seeing her husband's injuries both at the time of the accident and in the weeks afterwards; and in *Robinson v St Helens Metropolitan Borough Council* [2002] EWCA Civ 1099, [2003] PIQR P128 (and see also *Adams v Bracknell Forest Borough Council* [2004] UKHL 29, [2005] 1 AC 76) emotional or psychological harm, falling short of a recognised psychiatric illness, caused by a negligent failure to diagnose dyslexia, was held to be actionable (and to constitute personal injury for the purposes of the Limitation Act 1980).
[85] [1992] 2 All ER 65, at 69.
[86] [1996] AC 155, at 171.
[87] [1999] 2 AC 455, at 501.
[88] See above, pp 6–8.

Perry v Sidney Phillips & Son,[89] where the claim was alternatively framed in the tort of negligence. Similarly in *Hamilton Jones v David & Snape*,[90] where a claim for a solicitor's negligence was brought in contract and tort, Neuberger J held that, while there was no claim for the mental distress of losing the custody of a child in the tort of negligence standing alone, that did not prevent such an award in contract or, apparently, concurrently in tort. After referring to the reasoning of the Court of Appeal in *Verderame v Commercial Union Assurance Co plc*,[91] to the effect that there could be no liability in the tort of negligence for mental distress where there would have been no such liability had there been a contract (because the *Watts v Morrow* exception did not apply), Neuberger J said the following:[92]

> '[I]f a head of claim, in a case such as this, is recoverable in contract, the fact that it may not normally be recoverable in tort should not prevent it being recoverable in contract. The logic of the reasoning in *Verderame* suggests, if anything, that the approach to damages in tort in a case such as this is governed by the approach to damages in contract.'

However, outside a contractual relationship, to expand liability in the tort of negligence to cover mere mental distress would be highly controversial[93] for that would be to expand enormously the scope of that tort and would raise legitimate fears of 'opening the floodgates of litigation'. One can also argue that mere mental distress is a transient and less significant type of harm than personal injury, property damage, or economic loss and that, for that reason, one should not expand liability in the tort of negligence to cover it.[94]

A final word is merited on 'aggravated damages'.[95] In *Rookes v Barnard*[96] those damages were stressed to be compensatory—albeit compensating for mental distress—and not punitive. Nevertheless the confusion between the two lingers on. For example, it has been held that aggravated damages cannot be awarded for the tort of negligence or breach of contract:[97] but it is hard to see the justification for this once one accepts that aggravated damages are not punitive and that mental distress damages can sometimes be awarded for breach of contract (and concurrently in the tort of negligence). This continued confusion is not surprising given that aggravated damages are regarded as a sub-category of mental distress damages to be awarded only where the defendant's behaviour has been particularly reprehensible.[98] Now that mental distress damages are more freely recoverable this link to the especially bad conduct of the defendant seems unhelpful and unnecessary. It is submitted that the law would be improved in terms of clarity if aggravated damages were regarded as nothing more than 'mental distress damages' or 'damages for injured feelings' and

---

[89] [1982] 1 WLR 1297. See also *Wood v Law Society*, The Times, 2 March 1995; *Johnson v Gore Wood & Co* [2002] 2 AC 1, at 49 (per Lord Cooke).
[90] [2003] EWHC 3147 (Ch), [2004] 1 WLR 924.   [91] [1992] BCLC 793, at 803.
[92] [2003] EWHC 3147 (Ch), [2004] 1 All ER 657, at [51].
[93] But some jurisdictions in the US have expanded the tort of negligence to cover severe mental distress: see P Handford, N Mullany, and P Mitchell, *Mullany and Handford's Tort Liability for Psychiatric Damage* (2nd edn, Law Book Co 2006) 89–90; Law Commission, *Liability for Psychiatric Illness* (1995) Consultation Paper No 137, 115–116. In principle, French law, through Code Civil art 1382, protects against negligently caused mental distress (as 'dommage moral').
[94] For discussion, see P Handford, N Mullany, and P Mitchell, *Mullany and Handford's Tort Liability for Psychiatric Damage* (2nd edn, Law Book Co 2006) 79–82, 99–101.
[95] See, generally, Law Commission, *Aggravated, Exemplary and Restitutionary Damages* (1997) Report No 247, Part II; J Murphy, 'The Nature and Domain of Aggravated Damages' [2010] CLJ 353.
[96] [1964] AC 1129.
[97] *Kralj v McGrath* [1986] 1 All ER 54, approved in *AB v South West Water Services Ltd* [1993] QB 507; *Levi v Gordon*, 12 November 1992 (unreported CA). See also the clear confusion in *Messenger Newspapers Group Ltd v National Graphical Association* [1984] IRLR 397.
[98] The Law Commission in its Report, *Aggravated, Exemplary and Restitutionary Damages* (1997) Report No 247, paras 2.18–2.20, referred to this as the 'exceptional conduct' requirement.

if the very term 'aggravated damages' was replaced by either of those phrases.[99] Certainly the relationship between aggravated damages and damages that are awarded for injured feelings irrespective of aggravating conduct is not straightforward.[100] In *Rowlands v Chief Constable of Merseyside Police*[101] it was laid down that, as aggravated damages are compensatory and not punitive, a judge and/or jury must be careful to ensure that there is no double recovery between 'basic' and 'aggravated' damages for assault, false imprisonment, and malicious prosecution by the police. So in principle where damages for distress, humiliation, and injury to feelings have been fully compensated as part of the 'basic' damages, they should not be the subject of further compensation in the form of an award of aggravated damages.[102]

It should also be borne in mind that, because aggravated damages are to compensate for a person's injured feelings and mental distress, they cannot be awarded to a company.[103]

2. Assessing damages for mental distress or physical inconvenience

As with all non-pecuniary losses the aim must be to award a fair and reasonable sum, which is in line with other awards for mental distress or physical inconvenience. It would also be sensible to maintain 'external consistency', most obviously with damages for non-pecuniary loss in personal injury cases.[104]

In *Thompson v Metropolitan Police Commissioner*[105] the Court of Appeal held that an analogy should be drawn with personal injury damages in assessing compensatory damages for false imprisonment and malicious prosecution. Lord Woolf MR said that this was even more apt than in defamation cases where, as we have seen in the previous chapter, it was decided in *John v MGN Ltd*[106] that the scale of damages for non-pecuniary loss in personal injury cases was thought relevant. In Lord Woolf's words in *Thompson*, '[W]here what is being calculated is the proper compensation for loss of liberty or the damaging effect of a malicious prosecution the analogy with personal injuries is closer than it is in the case of defamation. The compensation is for something which is akin to pain and suffering.'[107] Lord

---

[99] This was recommended by the Law Commission in its Report, *Aggravated, Exemplary and Restitutionary Damages* (1997) Report No 247, para 2.42; Draft Bill, cl 13. Cf Crime and Courts Act 2013, s 39, which retains the term 'aggravated damages' while clarifying that they are only to compensate for mental distress and are not to punish.

[100] For the view that (contrary to *Appleton v Garrett* [1996] PIQR P1 and the discrimination cases referred to above, at p 285 n 75) there can be no separate award of aggravated damages over and above a general award for injury to feelings, see *McConnell v Police Authority for Northern Ireland* [1997] IRLR 625, at 629; *Gbaja-Biamila v DHL International (UK) Ltd* [2000] ICR 730, at [32]. See also *Richardson v Howie* [2004] EWCA Civ 1127, [2005] PIQR Q3, where it was said, in an assault and battery case, that a court should not characterise as aggravated damages an award of damages for injury to feelings, including for any indignity, humiliation, or anger caused by an attack, except possibly in a wholly exceptional case. See further *Martins v Choudhary* [2007] EWCA Civ 1379, [2008] 1 WLR 617: while normally it is better to separate out damages for psychiatric harm from damages for injury to feelings, it is usually preferable, following *Richardson v Howie*, not to separate out damages for injury to feelings from aggravated damages. For an enlightened and rigorous examination of these issues in the context of an award of damages for victimisation of a 'whistleblower', see *Commissioner of Police of the Metropolis v Shaw* [2012] ICR 464.

[101] [2006] EWCA Civ 1773, [2007] 1 WLR 1065.

[102] On the facts of the case, it was held that an award of aggravated damages might have been appropriate so that the trial judge should have left that question to the jury.

[103] *Collins Stewart Ltd v The Financial Times Ltd* [2005] EWHC 262 (QB), [2006] EMLR 5; *Eaton Mansions (Westminster) Ltd v Stinger Compania de Inversion SA* [2013] EWCA Civ 1308, [2014] HLR 4.

[104] It would appear that the guidelines or tariffs for non-pecuniary loss, referred to in the text below, should generally be uplifted by 10% in the light of *Simmons v Castle* [2012] EWCA Civ 1039, [2012] EWCA Civ 1288, [2013] 1 WLR 1239: see above, p 236.

[105] [1998] QB 498.   [106] [1997] QB 586. See above, p 274.   [107] [1998] QB 498, at 512.

Woolf went on to lay down some specific figures as part of the guidance to be given to juries in assessing damages in cases of false imprisonment and malicious prosecution. What was said is, of course, equally helpful in a case where a judge alone is assessing damages. Lord Woolf said:

> 'In a straightforward case of wrongful arrest and imprisonment the starting point is likely to be about £500 for the first hour during which the plaintiff has been deprived of his or her liberty. After the first hour an additional sum is to be awarded, but that sum should be on a reducing scale so as to keep the damages proportionate with those payable in personal injury cases and because the plaintiff is entitled to have a higher rate of compensation for the initial shock of being arrested. As a guideline we consider, for example, that a plaintiff who has been wrongly kept in custody for 24 hours should for this alone normally be regarded as entitled to an award of about £3,000. For subsequent days the daily rate will be on a progressively reducing scale … In the case of malicious prosecution the figure should start at about £2,000 and for prosecution continuing for as long as two years, the case being taken to the Crown Court, an award of about £10,000 could be appropriate.'[108]

To these 'basic' compensatory damages could then be added aggravated damages where appropriate. These would rarely be less than £1,000 or greater than double the basic damages.

One can argue that, having gone so far in guiding juries as to the correct quantum of damages in cases of false imprisonment and malicious prosecution, the logical next step would be to remove the assessment of damages from juries. Indeed this is what the Law Commission recommended. In Part IV of its Report on *Damages for Personal Injury: Non-Pecuniary Loss*[109] its recommendation was that the assessment of damages for all actions (except defamation) should always be a matter for a judge not a jury.

In *Vento v Chief Constable of West Yorkshire (No 2)*[110] the Court of Appeal emphasised the need for some consistency with awards for non-pecuniary awards in personal injury cases in deciding the appropriate level of compensation for injured feelings in sex and race discrimination cases. This was also a point made by Smith J in *Armitage, Marsden and HM Prison Service v Johnson*[111] in her statement of principles for the assessment of such damages in discrimination cases, which was approved by the Court of Appeal in *Vento*. The Court of Appeal went on to lay down a tariff for injured feelings in discrimination cases with a top band of £15,000–£25,000 for the most serious cases, £5,000–£15,000 for serious cases, and £500–£5,000 for less serious cases. Additional sums could be awarded for aggravated damages (and for psychiatric illness) although the overall global sum must be in line with conventional wisdom on levels of compensation for non-pecuniary loss

---

[108] [1998] QB 498, at 515. In *Clark v Chief Constable of Cleveland Constabulary* [1999] 21 LS Gaz R 38, a jury's award of £500 for malicious prosecution was increased to £2,000 in line with *Thompson*. In *R v Governor of Brockhill Prison, ex p Evans (No 2)* [1999] QB 1043, the Court of Appeal increased damages from £2,500 to £5,000 for false imprisonment where the wrongful imprisonment was for 59 days but was as a result of a mistake (upheld by the House of Lords [2001] 2 AC 19). But in *Prison Officers Association v Iqbal* [2009] EWCA Civ 1312, [2010] QB 732, if it had been decided that there had been a false imprisonment, a low sum of £120 (for six hours' imprisonment) would have been awarded. See further *R (on the application of Bernard) v Enfield London Borough Council* [2002] EWHC 2282 (Admin), [2003] HRLR 4 where a local authority had failed, in breach of the Human Rights Convention, Art 8, to provide suitable accommodation to a severely disabled wife and her carer husband so that they had to live in deplorable conditions for about 20 months. The damages awarded under the Human Rights Act 1998 were £8,000 to the wife and £2,000 to the husband. The awards in *R (on the application of KB) v Mental Health Review Tribunal* [2003] EWHC 193 (Admin), [2004] QB 936 to claimants for breach of their Convention rights (under Art 5(4)) to a speedy determination of whether they should continue to be detained under powers conferred by the Mental Health Act 1983 ranged from £750 to £4,000.

[109] Law Commission, *Damages for Personal Injury: Non-Pecuniary Loss* (1999) Report No 257. The right to jury trial in defamation cases has since been removed: see above, p 274.

[110] [2002] EWCA Civ 1871, [2003] IRLR 102.   [111] [1997] ICR 275.

generally. On the facts of *Vento*, which was a very serious case of persistent sexual discrimination against a female police officer, the Court of Appeal reduced the sums awarded by the Employment Tribunal and the Employment Appeal Tribunal to £18,000 for injured feelings plus £5,000 aggravated damages (and £9,000 for psychiatric damage).[112] In the *Armitage* case, the Employment Appeal Tribunal had upheld an award of £21,000 for injured feelings plus £7,500 aggravated damages in a case of very serious race discrimination which had gone on over a period of 18 months. The move in these cases to try to ensure greater consistency, both 'internally' between awards for injured feelings for discrimination and 'externally' with awards for non-pecuniary loss, is to be welcomed. But there are two points of concern. The first is the separation out of aggravated damages from the tariff for injured feelings. It would have been preferable to have absorbed aggravated damages within the tariff. Secondly, the tariff does appear high. More specifically, it is hard to see why damages for injured feelings in a discrimination case should exceed those awarded for moderate or minor general psychiatric damage in a personal injury case, where the bracket (at the time of the *Vento* case))[113] was £750–£10,000.

In *Alseran v Ministry of Defence*,[114] the *Vento* tariff was applied to the assessment of damages for injured feelings in cases of assault and battery and false imprisonment.[115] Leggatt J updated the tariff for increases in the retail prices index since *Vento* so that the figures (in December 2017) were £23,000 to £38,000 for the top band; £7,500 to £23,000 for the middle band; and £750 to £7,500 for the lower band.

Again in *Gulati v MGN Ltd*,[116] which was a phone-hacking breach of privacy case, it was held that damages for non-pecuniary loss should bear a 'reasonable relationship'[117] to the scale of damages for non-pecuniary loss in personal injury cases. The damages were to compensate for the mental distress and the infringement of the right to privacy itself (and aggravated damages might also be awarded). However, it is very surprising that the damages actually awarded by the judge at first instance, admittedly for many different infringements of privacy suffered by each of several claimants, were held by the Court of Appeal not to be wholly out of line with the scale of damages for personal injury. Those damages in eight cases, in none of which was there any pecuniary loss in issue, ranged from £72,500 to £280,250. Given that, at the time of *Gulati*, the bracket for non-pecuniary loss for the worst personal injuries (without the 10% uplift which did not apply in *Gulati*)[118] was a bracket of £246,750 to £307,000 for tetraplegia and £214,350 to £307,000 for very severe brain damage,[119] it is very hard to understand how the awards could have

---

[112] The *Vento* tariff has also been applied by the EAT, outside sex and race discrimination, to discrimination against trade union members (contrary to the Trade Union and Labour Relation (Consolidation) Act 1992, s 146) in *London Borough of Hackney v Adams* [2003] IRLR 402; and to discrimination against 'whistle-blowers' (contrary to the Employment Rights Act 1996, s 47B) in *Virgo Fidelis Senior School v Boyle* [2004] IRLR 268. In the latter case, a separate award of £10,000 aggravated damages was also made.
[113] See Judicial Studies Board, *Guidelines for the Assessment of General Damages in Personal Injury Cases* (6th edn, OUP 2002). The 2017 edition was the 14th.
[114] [2017] EWHC 3289 (QB), [2018] 3 WLR 95, at [891]–[893].
[115] See also the assault and battery cases of *BDA v Quirino* [2015] EWHC 2974 (QB) and *Mohidin v Commmissioner of Police for the Metropolis* [2015] EWHC 2740 (QB). But in *Cairns v Modi* [2012] EWCA Civ 1382, [2013] 1 WLR 1015, the *Vento* tariff was thought inappropriate for libel awards.
[116] [2015] EWCA Civ 1291, [2017] QB 149. See also *Sir Cliff Richard v BBC* [2018] EWHC 1837 (Ch) in which the claimant in an action for the tort of privacy (there was live television coverage of the arrival of police to search his home in relation to allegations of child sexual abuse for which he was never charged) was awarded £190,000 for loss of reputation and mental distress plus £20,000 as aggravated damages.
[117] [2015] EWCA Civ 1291, [2017] QB 149, at [63].
[118] For explanation of the 10% uplift, see above, p 236.
[119] See Judicial College, *Guidelines for the Assessment of General Damages in Personal Injury Cases* (13th edn, OUP 2015).

As regards the tort of private nuisance, the majority of the Court of Appeal in *Bone v Seale*,[120] in assessing 'loss of amenity'[121] damages for 'inconvenience, discomfort and annoyance'[122] caused by offensive smells from a pig farm, drew an analogy with assessing damages for loss of amenity in a personal injury action. But in *Hunter v Canary Wharf Ltd*[123] Lord Hoffmann disagreed with this. Certainly the fact that the tort of private nuisance is actionable only by a person with an interest in the land means that one has to be careful not to compensate others without such an interest. But the real difficulty here is that the courts see 'loss of amenity' in the nuisance context as being best assessed by reference to the notional loss of rental value and that makes comparison with personal injury awards (and other awards for non-pecuniary loss) potentially problematic.

Milner v Carnival Plc[124] is the leading case on the level of contractual damages for mental distress and physical inconvenience. The claimants' luxury cruise was ruined as a result of structural noise problems in their cabin. In awarding contractual damages for 'physical inconvenience, discomfort and mental distress'[125] of £4,000 to Mr Milner and £4,500 to Mrs Milner, the Court of Appeal helpfully emphasised that the level of such damages should be fixed not only by looking at other holiday awards for breach of contract but also at 'comparable awards for psychiatric damage in personal injury cases, for injury to feelings in cases of sex and race discrimination and damages for bereavement ...'.[126]

In respect of discomfort and inconvenience consequent on a landlord's breach of repairing obligations, the Court of Appeal in *Wallace v Manchester City Council*[127] assumed, without deciding, that there was an unofficial tariff of £1,000–£2,750 per annum (as at July 1998). But it was also suggested in that case, and has subsequently been reaffirmed,[128] that a judge should cross-check the award by reference to the rent payable for the duration of the landlord's breach of obligation on the rationale that the award relates to the tenant not receiving proper value for the rent. It follows that any tariff seems misleading because, plainly, rents vary so significantly depending on the type of property and the location.

In general, the courts have not regarded mental distress (or physical inconvenience) as that serious (although of course the worse the distress or inconvenience the higher the damages should be) and have often stressed that awards should be kept at a moderate level.[129] To give some other miscellaneous examples of awards that have been mentioned earlier in this chapter, £750 was awarded to each of the two claimants for the physical inconvenience and consequent distress of living in a house that was in a poor condition in *Watts v Morrow*;

---

[120] [1975] 1 WLR 797. [121] ibid, at 803. [122] [1975] 1 WLR 797, at 804.
[123] [1997] AC 655, at 706. See above, p 284. See also *Dobson v Thames Water Utilities Ltd* [2009] EWCA Civ 28, [2009] 3 All ER 319.
[124] [2010] EWCA Civ 389, [2011] 1 Lloyd's Rep 374. [125] ibid, at [31], [32], and [47] (per Ward LJ).
[126] [2010] EWCA Civ 389, [2011] 1 Lloyd's Rep 374, at [57] (per Ward LJ).
[127] (1998) 30 HLR 1111.
[128] See *English Churches Housing Group v Shine* [2004] EWCA Civ 434, [2004] HLR 42; *Earle v Charalambous* [2006] EWCA Civ 1092, [2007] HLR 8. In *Moorjani v Durban Estates Ltd* [2015] EWCA Civ 1252, [2016] 1 WLR 2265, the Court of Appeal held that a tenant was still entitled to some damages, albeit significantly reduced, for 'loss of amenity' even though he had chosen, for reasons unconnected to the disrepair, to live elsewhere. This was because the damages (for non-pecuniary loss) were not entirely for the discomfort, inconvenience, and distress actually suffered by the tenant (in the words of Briggs LJ, at [35], they were the 'symptoms' of the underlying 'impairment to the rights of amenity').
[129] Eg *Perry v Sidney Phillips & Son* [1982] 1 WLR 1297; *Archer v Brown* [1985] QB 401; *Watts v Morrow* [1991] 1 WLR 1421; *Farley v Skinner* [2001] UKHL 49, [2002] 2 AC 732.

£2,500 'loss of amenity' damages was awarded in *Ruxley Electronics and Construction Ltd v Forsyth* for the lost pleasure of diving and swimming in a deeper pool; and £10,000 was awarded for the disturbance from aircraft noise in *Farley v Skinner* albeit that the House of Lords recognised that this was at the very top end of what could possibly be regarded as appropriate.[130]

---

[130] Cf *Dennis v Ministry of Defence* [2003] EWHC 793 (QB), [2003] NLJR 634, where £50,000 was awarded for long-term loss of amenity caused by aircraft noise. See below, p 447.

Section Three

Miscellaneous Issues Relevant to Compensatory Damages

15

Interest as damages and interest on damages

1. Introduction	295
2. Interest as damages	296
3. Interest on damages: statutory interest under section 35A Senior Courts Act 1981	301

1. Introduction

The law on interest in English law is a tangled web.[1] This is principally because the common law traditionally set itself against awards of interest and this has resulted in the piecemeal intervention of statutes which allow the award of interest in specific situations. In the leading modern case of *Sempra Metals Ltd v IRC*[2] the House of Lords reformed the common law as regards awards of interest as compensatory damages for a tort or breach of contract (although the part of the decision that was concerned with interest as restitution of an unjust enrichment, which was the direct claim in question, was overruled by the Supreme Court in *Prudential Assurance Co Ltd v HMRC*).[3] *Sempra Metals* was concerned with an award of *compound* interest (as damages or as restitution) which contrasts with the relevant statutes which allow awards of *simple* interest only.

In understanding the law, it is helpful to differentiate between 'interest as damages'—that is, an award of damages for loss of the use of money—and 'interest on damages'—that is, an award of statutory interest on damages. In general, statutory interest can be awarded on debts as well as on damages so that it is convenient to consider statutory interest on debts, as well as on damages, in this chapter.

It is being assumed in this chapter that there is no contractual agreement as to the payment of interest. But where the claim is for a contractual debt (or even damages for breach of contract) it is commonplace for contracting parties to agree that interest, at a certain rate, shall be payable on the unpaid debt (or damages). The agreement may be for post-judgment as well as pre-judgment interest and it may specify whether simple or compound interest is to be paid. Contractually agreed interest is, and always has been, enforceable in the same way as any other contractually agreed sum. Nothing special applies to it or needs to be said about it.

However, following on from this, and although it concerns only debts and not damages, it is convenient at this point to mention that the Late Payment of Commercial Debts (Interest) Act 1998 gives a creditor a right to simple interest on an unpaid commercial debt,

---

[1] See A Burrows, 'Interest' in *Commercial Remedies: Resolving Controversies* (eds G Virgo and S Worthington, CUP 2017) 247.
[2] [2007] UKHL 34, [2008] 1 AC 561.
[3] [2018] UKSC 39, [2018] 3 WLR 652. The Supreme Court decided that, in principle, there was no claim in the law of unjust enrichment to interest (compound or simple) because there was no relevant transfer of value from the claimant to the defendant and hence the 'at the expense of the claimant' element needed for a successful unjust enrichment claim could not be established. The law of unjust enrichment falls outside the scope of this book.

which starts to run from the day after 'the relevant day'.[4] The Act applies to contracts for the supply of goods or services (other than excluded contracts, such as a consumer credit agreement) where the purchaser and supplier each act in the course of a business. The rate of interest has been fixed at the base rate plus 8%. The interest may be remitted, wholly or in part, because of the creditor's conduct;[5] and the right to interest may be ousted or varied by the agreement of the parties.[6] The basis for interest under the Act builds from the idea of a contractual term for interest. The statute implies a term into a contract to which the Act applies to the effect that simple interest shall be payable; and the relationship to other statutes is dealt with by saying that the interest shall be treated as if it were provided for under an 'express contract term'. That apparent contradiction between saying, on the one hand, that the term is implied and yet, on the other, that it should be treated as 'express' seems unnecessary. The essential point is that the interest is treated as if contractually agreed so that, for example, it is not inconsistent with s 35A of the Senior Courts Act 1981 (which by s 35A(4) lays down that interest in respect of a debt is not to be awarded under the 1981 Act for a period during which interest on the debt already runs as, for example, under a contractual term).

2. Interest as damages

(1) The old rule of no damages for a failure to pay

London, Chatham and Dover Rly Co v South Eastern Rly[7] was traditionally regarded as House of Lords authority for the rule that, where the only obligation broken is to pay money, no damages can be awarded and the sole remedy is the award of the agreed sum (ie the payment of the debt). Interest paid or lost could not be recovered as damages because there could be no damages for a failure to pay.

The rationale for the *London Chatham and Dover Railway* rule was unclear. It may have been linked to the common law's traditional refusal to compensate losses consequent on one's own impecuniosity as most famously illustrated by the (now overruled) decision in *The Liesbosch*.[8] Given its uncertain basis, it is not surprising that, even before *Sempra Metals*, exceptions had been recognised at common law to the *London Chatham and Dover Railway* rule.

Perhaps the best known example was *Wadsworth v Lydall*.[9] Here the defendant failed to pay all of a sum of money owing to the claimant. As a result, the claimant had to take out a loan in order to finance a contract to purchase some land. The claimant was awarded damages for interest charges paid on the loan (and legal costs) even though these followed from the defendant's failure to pay the sum of money. The Court of Appeal distinguished

---

[4] The period from when the statutory interest runs—which turns on the definition of the 'relevant day'—is extremely complex. It is principally laid down in s 4 (and for advance payments in s 11) of the 1998 Act but complexity has been added by the amendments to s 4 by the Late Payment of Commercial Debts Regulations 2013, SI 2013/395, and the Late Payment of Commercial Debts (Amendment) Regulations 2015, SI 2015/1336. By s 4 it appears that where no date for payment has been agreed, the interest normally runs from 30 days after the date (which, for shorthand, may be referred to as the 'performance/notice date') on which the creditor performed or on which the debtor had notice of the amount of the debt, whichever is the later: but if the parties have agreed a date for payment, interest runs from the day after that date or, if earlier than the agreed payment date, 60 days from the performance/notice date (or if the debtor is a public authority 30 days from the performance/notice date). By reason of s 3(2) interest under this Act does not run after there is a judgment debt because then the Judgments Act 1838, s 17 applies.
[5] Section 5.   [6] Sections 8–9.   [7] [1893] AC 429.
[8] [1933] AC 449, departed from in *Lagden v O'Connor* [2003] UKHL 64, [2004] 1 AC 1067. See above, pp 145–146.
[9] [1981] 1 WLR 598.

London Chatham and Dover Railway on the ground that, while it prevented general damages for failure to pay a sum of money, it did not prevent 'special damages'. What was meant by special damages was unclear. One interpretation was that, apart from the general loss of the use of money (as dealt with by awards of statutory interest on damages under s 35A of the Senior Courts Act 1981), all other losses (most obviously specific interest charges paid) were recoverable as damages. However, while approving *Wadsworth v Lydall* the House of Lords in *President of India v La Pintada Compania Navigacion SA*[10] applied a different interpretation according to which 'general' and 'special' damages correlated to the first and second rules of remoteness in *Hadley v Baxendale*.[11] Bizarrely, this meant that interest paid or lost could only be recovered as damages if it did not arise naturally or in the normal course of things and yet, because of the defendant's special knowledge, was not too remote.

In the light of *Sempra Metals* we no longer need to concern ourselves with what was here meant by general or special damages. *La Pintada*, in which the House of Lords had refused to depart from the rule in *London Chatham and Dover Railway* in a context where statutory interest could not be awarded,[12] was overruled in *Sempra Metals* and the rule (although not the actual decision) in *London Chatham and Dover Railway* was disapproved. Although the decision in *Sempra Metals* concerned an award of restitution for money paid,[13] and not damages, part of the central reasoning was that interest, including compound interest, can be awarded as damages.[14]

The impact of the rule in *London Chatham and Dover Railway* has also been ameliorated over the years by the intervention of statute. Most importantly, s 35A of the Senior Courts Act 1981 permits the award of interest on damages or debts. But statutory intervention has not filled all the gaps. For example, s 35A permits the award of simple interest only, and not compound interest, and it does not apply unless there are proceedings for damages or a debt so that where the debt or damages is paid before proceedings, albeit after a delay, no statutory interest can be awarded.

Before turning to examine *Sempra Metals* more closely, it may be helpful to make the perhaps obvious point that the *London Chatham and Dover Railway* rule has never been regarded as affecting the claimant's right to terminate a contract and sue for damages for the defendant's repudiatory breach. This is because a repudiatory breach always goes beyond merely being the breach of an obligation to pay money: one is not seeking damages for the non-payment of a debt. So of course, a seller of goods can sue the buyer for non-acceptance, and a wrongfully dismissed employee can sue for lost earnings. Similarly damages are

---

[10] [1985] AC 104.
[11] (1854) 9 Exch 341. See above, pp 91–93. See also *International Mineral & Chemical Corpn v Karl O Helm AG* [1986] 1 Lloyd's Rep 81 and *Hartle v Laceys* [1999] Lloyd's Rep PN 315, where currency exchange losses, and compound interest and bank charges paid, were respectively held recoverable as special damages applying *Wadsworth v Lydall* and the *La Pintada* case.
[12] There was, and is, no power to award any interest under Senior Courts Act 1981, s 35A where the sum was paid *before proceedings started*: in *Tehno-Impex v Gebr van Weelde Scheepvartkantoor BV* [1981] QB 648 the Court of Appeal held that arbitrators at least could get round this by awarding damages to compensate for the loss of the use of the money in this situation but this was overruled in *La Pintada* which applied *London, Chatham and Dover Rly*. For criticism of *La Pintada*, see F Wooldridge and R Insley, 'The Award of Interest for the Late Payment of Debts: Orthodoxy Prevails' (1985) 4 CJQ 97. See, generally, F Mann, 'On Interest, Compound Interest and Damages' (1985) 101 LQR 30.
[13] That decision on restitution was overturned in *Prudential Assurance Co Ltd v HMRC* [2018] UKSC 39, [2018] 3 WLR 652.
[14] The High Court of Australia in *Hungerfords v Walker* (1989) 171 CLR 125 and the Supreme Court of Canada in *Bank of America Canada v Mutual Trust Co* (2002) 211 DLR (4th) 385 have also departed from the *London, Chatham and Dover Railway* case by awarding lost compound interest as damages.

recoverable for a debtor's failure to pay so many hire-purchase instalments as to constitute a repudiation of the contract.[15]

(2) What did *Sempra Metals* decide?

In general terms, the claimants in *Sempra Metals* were seeking a remedy for the premature payment of corporation tax paid to HMRC that had been obtained (as advanced corporation tax) contrary to EU law. The question was how, applying the notion of procedural autonomy, the undisputed right to 'repayment' (the EU right required by the *San Giorgio* case)[16] was to be translated into a cause of action recognised by English domestic law. Ultimately it was recognised by the House of Lords that there were three possible causes of action for the repayment of the unlawfully levied tax: (i) compensatory damages for (a serious) breach of statutory duty; (ii) restitution for unjust enrichment under the principle laid down in *Woolwich Equitable Building Society v IRC*;[17] (iii) restitution for unjust enrichment for payments made by mistake of law.

It would appear that it was not until part way through the hearing in the House of Lords that the claimants made clear that they were seeking restitution for mistake of law, so as to take the benefit of the postponement of the limitation period under s 32(1)(c) of the Limitation Act 1980, rather than either of the other two causes of action. This partly explains why so much time was spent in the leading speech of Lord Nicholls in considering the law on damages for loss of interest even though the main claim was recognised as being one for restitution of unjust enrichment. As it was, Lord Nicholls saw that discussion as useful background to understanding the restitutionary claim for interest that was directly in issue but it is nevertheless correct that there is some issue as to whether, strictly speaking, everything said about damages and the rule in *London Chatham and Dover Railway* was obiter dicta. Lord Hope's speech made clear that that was not the issue: 'In my opinion a decision on this point [on damages for interest losses] is not essential to the resolution of the question which is at issue in this case, as the cause of action with which we are concerned here is different.'[18] However, it would seem that Lord Nicholls did regard the damages discussion as part of the ratio because he stressed that the judge's order on damages awarding compound interest should be upheld.[19] In truth, this debate about the ratio is no longer of practical importance because, not surprisingly, in the light of the careful consideration given to that rule and to the law on damages for interest, *Sempra Metals* has inevitably been treated as binding in respect of the law of damages (as well as in relation to the law on unjust enrichment although, ironically, the decision on restitution as interest in the law of unjust enrichment has subsequently been overruled in *Prudential Assurance Co Ltd v HMRC*).[20] In practice, *Sempra Metals* has been interpreted as having overruled *La Pintada* and as having rid the law of the rule in *London Chatham and Dover Railway*.

It is submitted that, in a nutshell, what *Sempra Metals* decided as regards damages was that, subject to any clash with s 35A, no special rules apply to deny or restrict the recovery of interest, including compound interest, as damages for a tort or breach of contract. The special rule of denial in *London Chatham and Dover Railway* no longer applies. So, subject to any clash with s 35A, if applying normal common law principles—on, for example, proof of

---

[15] *Yeoman Credit Ltd v Waragowski* [1961] 3 All ER 145. In addition, the rule does not prevent a promisee recovering damages where the promise is to pay money to a third party: below, pp 382–383.
[16] *Amministrazione delle Finanze dello Stato v SpA San Giorgio*, Case 199/82 [1983] ECR 3595.
[17] [1993] AC 70.   [18] [2007] UKHL 34, [2008] 1 AC 561, at [16].   [19] ibid, at [127].
[20] [2018] UKSC 39, [2018] 3 WLR 652.

loss, remoteness, or the duty to mitigate—interest as damages would be awarded for a tort or breach of contract, that interest should be awarded. In other words, normal rules apply when considering the question of interest at common law.

It would appear, therefore, that the correct approach is to ask whether, applying the normal rules of compensatory damages for a tort or breach of contract, the claimant has suffered a loss that is best measured by interest (whether simple or compound) and which is not ruled out by standard limiting principles: so, for example, that loss must not be too remote and must not be a loss that could reasonably have been avoided applying the 'duty to mitigate'. Such a loss will cover, most obviously, interest charges on borrowings incurred or interest that would have been earned but has not been. These losses may include compound interest paid or forgone that would not be recoverable under s 35A. As with all awards of compensatory damages, the loss has to be pleaded and proved in the normal way.

If that analysis is correct, it is perhaps surprising that there appear to have been very few reported cases since *Sempra Metals* in which damages for a loss of compound interest have been awarded.[21]

The two most important post-*Sempra* damages cases reveal a disagreement about the standard of proof required. *Equitas Ltd v Walsham Brothers & Co Ltd*[22] concerned an arrangement that had been entered into to deal with some of the fall-out from the huge losses suffered by Names at Lloyds in the 1990s. The claimant was entitled, either in its own right or as an assignee, to certain premiums and claims that should have been paid across by the defendant brokers before and after 1996. In addition to the principal sums (most of which had now been paid) the claimant sought damages (in contract and tort) for their loss of investment income from not having had those payments. Even though the claimant did not seek to provide precise details of that loss, it was held that, applying *Sempra Metals*, the claimant was entitled to damages for that loss calculated at the LIBOR rate plus 1% and compounded. Faced with the argument that the claimant had not provided proof of that compound interest loss, Males J said the following:[23]

'[I]t is not necessary for the claimant to produce specific evidence of what it would have done with the money or what steps if any it took to borrow or otherwise to replace the money of which it was deprived.... [I]t may often be impossible or at any rate extremely difficult to produce such evidence, especially if that would mean attempting to disentangle a claimant's overall business operations in an artificial attempt to attribute specific activity such as borrowing to the non-remittance of specific funds. Instead, at any rate in commercial cases and unless there is some positive reason to do otherwise, the law will proceed on the basis that the measure of the claimant's loss is the cost of borrowing to replace the money of which the claimant has been deprived regardless of whether that is what the claimant actually did. A conventional rate will be used which represents the cost to commercial entities such as the claimant and is not necessarily the rate at which the claimant itself could have borrowed or did in fact borrow. This avoids the need for protracted investigation of the particular claimant's financial affairs. As with other conventional measures (for example, the assessment of damages by reference to a market price in sale of goods cases) this approach has the advantage of certainty and predictability which is always important in the commercial context, as well as being broadly fair in the great majority of cases and avoiding expensive and often ultimately unproductive litigation.... If a conventional

---

[21] In addition to the two cases considered in the text see, eg, *Xena Systems Ltd v Cantideck* [2013] EWPCC 1 (HHJ Birse QC awarding compound interest at 8% as damages); *Sainsbury's Supermarkets Ltd v Mastercard Incorporated* [2016] CAT 11 (compound interest awarded as damages on the basis that it had been sufficiently pleaded and proved).
[22] [2013] EWHC 3264 (Comm), [2014] PNLR 8.   [23] ibid, at [123].

borrowing cost is to be adopted in this way, the question whether interest should be simple or compound answers itself. While simple interest has the virtue of simplicity ... it also has the certainty of error and injustice ... it is impossible to borrow commercially on simple interest terms. I respectfully agree with Lord Nicholls that the law must recognise and give effect to this reality if it is to achieve a fair and just outcome when assessing financial loss. To conclude that, at least in a typical commercial case, the normal and conventional measure of damages for breach of an obligation to remit funds consists of compound interest at a conventional rate is therefore both principled and predictable, as well as being in accordance with what was actually awarded in *Sempra Metals*.'

Yet six months earlier in *JSC BTA Bank v Ablyazov*,[24] which was not cited to or mentioned by Males J, a different approach to this question of proof was taken by Teare J in applying *Sempra Metals*. His decision was that the loss, represented by compound interest, must be explicitly proved and that one could not presume a loss based on compound interest rates so that the claim for compound interest failed. The claim was for damages for fraud and the claimant bank sought interest on the sums paid away at compound interest rates applying *Sempra Metals* or, alternatively, at simple interest rates under s 35A. It was held that only the latter could be awarded because the claim for compound interest had not been sufficiently pleaded and proved: the claimant had not alleged what it would otherwise have used the money for or any borrowing that it had now had to make because of the loss of the money paid out. In a very clear judgment, Teare J said:[25]

> 'It is to be observed that in none of the actions is there any allegation of the use to which the monies paid away as a result of the Defendants' fraud would have been put had there been no fraud. There is no allegation of losses the Bank had suffered in addition to having paid away the principal sums. Thus the Bank, in my judgment, has not alleged "its actual interest losses". It may be that the monies paid away would have been lent to bona fide borrowers but that has not been alleged. It may be that the sums would have been used to augment the Bank's capital base and so reduced the extent of the Bank's own borrowings but whether that was done and if so what savings would have been made (and therefore lost) has not been alleged. It may be that but for the fraud the monies would not have been borrowed by the Bank in the first place and so the interest it paid has been thrown away but that has not been alleged. [Counsel for the Bank] submitted that the pleadings, whilst not perhaps perfect, nevertheless were sufficient to entitle the Bank to claim interest as damages. I am unable to accept that submission. There has been, no doubt for very good reason, no attempt to plead as damages the Bank's actual interest losses over and above the paying away of the principal sums. There has merely been a claim for damages. But that, as was clearly stated by Lord Nicholls in *Sempra Metals*, is insufficient for the purpose of claiming actual interest losses.'

And later he concluded:

> 'To require actual interest losses to be specifically pleaded might be regarded by the Bank as unrealistic and unduly formalistic. But Lord Nicholls expressly accepted this "reproach" to the common law and said that in the absence of a specific plea of actual interest losses the remedy lay in the statutory provisions for interest. This is clear guidance for trial judges which I must follow. I have therefore concluded that there has been no plea of actual interest losses. It follows that the Bank can only claim simple interest pursuant to s 35A of the Senior Courts Act 1981.'

It is possible that one can reconcile these apparently conflicting decisions by saying that in the former the loss had been pleaded and proved and it was merely the quantum that was

---

[24] [2013] EWHC 867 (Comm).   [25] ibid, at [12]–[13], [18]–[19].

in dispute whereas in the latter it was the loss that had not been pleaded or proved. But that is a strained distinction.

3. Interest on damages: statutory interest under section 35A Senior Courts Act 1981

We are here principally concerned with pre-judgment interest on damages (or debts) under s 35A of the Senior Courts Act (or under s 69 of the County Courts Act 1984, which is the equivalent for claims in the county courts). For shorthand this interest will be referred to in this section as 'statutory interest'.

However, prior to examining such pre-judgment interest, it should be quickly noted that a court's award of damages or an agreed sum constitutes a 'judgment debt'; and under s 17(1) of the Judgments Act 1838 simple[26] interest automatically runs post-judgment on a 'judgment debt' at a rate of what, since 1993,[27] has been 8%.[28] By the Civil Procedure Rules, CPR 40.8, the interest on a judgment debt runs from the date of the judgment unless the court orders otherwise.[29] Under s 17(2) of the 1838 Act, rules of court may provide for the court to disallow all or part of any interest otherwise payable.[30] There is no discretion for a court to award judgment debt interest at a different rate than 8% (other than where the award is being made in a currency other than sterling).[31]

(1) Section 35A Senior Courts Act 1981

The award of pre-judgment statutory interest on damages (or debts) under s 35A of the Senior Courts Act (or under s 69 of the County Courts Act 1984) is commonplace and will almost always be claimed in addition to the damages (or debt).[32]

Prior to 1934 the courts had no power to award interest on damages but this was altered first by the Law Reform (Miscellaneous Provisions) Act 1934 and subsequently by the Administration of Justice Act 1982. The 1934 and 1982 provisions were then consolidated in what is now the Senior Courts Act 1981, s 35A.[33] By s 35A(1), the High Court has discretion to award simple interest on damages (and debts);[34] and by the Supreme Court Act 1981, s 35A(2) the High Court must award simple interest on damages for personal injuries or death (exceeding £200) unless satisfied that there are 'special reasons' why it should not do so.

---

[26] Although not explicitly stated, it has always been assumed that this Act merely permits simple interest. This is not least because, as the statute fixes a rate per annum, it must have in mind simple interest because if compound interest were in mind one would need to specify the periods of rest.
[27] Judgment Debts (Rate of Interest) Order 1993, SI 1993/564.
[28] From 1838 until 1971 the rate was fixed at 4%. It was then raised to 7.5% and went to a high of 15% in 1985 before being reduced to the present rate of 8% in 1993.
[29] Where, eg, there is a split trial, the judgment debt rate of interest runs from the damages judgment and not from the liability judgment: *Thomas v Bunn* [1991] 1 AC 362.
[30] Eg CPR 47.8 (sanction for failure to commence detailed costs assessment proceedings in time).
[31] This is provided for in s 44A of the Administration of Justice Act 1970. See below, p 308.
[32] Interest (and its rate and period) may be provided for by a contract term, but it is being assumed here that there is no such term: see above, p 295 .
[33] Inserted by the Administration of Justice Act 1982, Sch 1. Analogous provisions are contained in the County Courts Act 1984, s 69. Generally speaking, the same principles apply to interest on an agreed sum.
[34] But s 35A does not allow interest to be awarded on 'damages' or debts paid (eg under a settlement) before the commencement of proceedings: as regards damages, see *IM Properties plc v Cape & Dalgleish* [1999] QB 297.

(2) The compensatory purpose of statutory interest

That statutory interest under s 35A of the Senior Courts Act is intended to be compensatory was made clear by Robert Goff J's statement (albeit in the context of a claim for a restitutionary debt not damages) in *BP Exploration Co (Libya) Ltd v Hunt (No 2)*:[35] 'The fundamental principle is that interest is not awarded as punishment but simply because the plaintiff has been deprived of the use of the money which was due to him.' Similarly Forbes J in *Tate and Lyle Food and Distribution Ltd v Greater London Council*[36] said: 'One looks ... not at the profit which the defendant wrongfully made out of the money he withheld ... but at the cost to the plaintiff of being deprived of the money which he should have had.'[37]

In the context of damages, the money due to the claimant comprises either the money that the claimant would have had but for the defendant's wrong or, where the wrongful loss was not of money, the damages themselves which it is felt the defendant should have paid to compensate the loss as soon as it occurred. In commercial cases it is then generally assumed that as a result of being deprived of that money the claimant has had to borrow it (ie this is a cost of cure measure), whereas in non-commercial cases the assumption is generally simply that the claimant has lost the interest from investing that money.[38] We look in more detail below at how far the rates that have been chosen in commercial cases take account of the individual claimant involved.[39]

How precisely does one justify the compensatory approach to statutory interest? Compensation is easy to justify where there is a civil wrong. So in justifying the compensatory approach to interest under the 1981 Act, one naturally searches for a civil wrong. But is there always a civil wrong in play?

Where the sum is contractually owed, the failure to pay that sum will constitute a breach of contract and one might therefore regard the interest as compensation for that breach of contract. Again, where the interest is payable on damages, at least for a pecuniary loss, one may regard the interest as another layer of pecuniary loss consequential on the wrong (eg the tort or breach of contract) that triggered the damages.

But it is hard to see how interest on damages for a non-pecuniary loss (eg pain, suffering, and loss of amenity in a personal injury action) can be regarded as compensating for an extra loss caused by the wrong that triggered those damages.

Again, at least at first sight, there is no wrong involved where the interest is being paid on a restitutionary remedy for unjust enrichment (as in *BP Exploration v Hunt*).

One might conclude from this that, where there is no underlying civil wrong or, even if there is, where the loss is non-pecuniary, there is no principled explanation for the award of statutory interest under the 1981 Act; that the compensation that the courts say underpins the award of interest is *sui generis* because it does not involve a civil wrong; and that one does not need to agonise further because this is all a matter for the discretion of the courts as conferred by statute. However, coherence in the law demands that, if it all possible, the exercise of a statutory discretion ought to adopt a principled approach.

---

[35] [1982] 1 All ER 925, at 974. See also *Jefford v Gee* [1970] 2 QB 130, at 146; *Tate & Lyle Food and Distribution Ltd v Greater London Council* [1981] 3 All ER 716, at 722; *Wentworth v Wiltshire County Council* [1993] 2 All ER 256, at 269.
[36] [1982] 1 WLR 149.   [37] ibid, at 154.
[38] For this distinction see especially *Tate & Lyle Food and Distribution Ltd v Greater London Council* [1981] 3 All ER 716, at 722–723.
[39] Below, p 305.

With that in mind, it is submitted that the best explanation (on the assumption that the interest is indeed compensating a loss of the claimant) is that the failure to pay a sum that is legally due (whether a debt or damages) *is in itself being treated as a wrong for the purposes of the 1981 Act*.[40] It is a wrong that, under the statute, triggers compensation for loss of the use of money caused by the failure to pay the sum legally owed with the wrong being committed at the date of the accrual of the cause of action for the debt or damages (ie at the date when the debt or damages were payable). The recognition of that wrong readily explains why statutory interest compensating the claimant is being awarded not only on damages for a pecuniary loss but also on damages for a non-pecuniary loss. It further explains how it is that one can regard interest on restitutionary remedies as compensatory.[41]

(3) Simple interest only

The Supreme Court Act 1981, s 35A empowers a court to award simple interest only. In some circumstances, especially in commercial cases, the claimant's loss will be best reflected in the compound interest rate at which it has had to borrow replacement funds or at which it has had to forgo lending, or otherwise investing, the funds. To confine the interest to simple interest may therefore leave the commercial claimant undercompensated. Admittedly there has long been power in equity to award compound interest but it appears that this equitable jurisdiction is restricted to where necessary to strip away gains made by breach of fiduciary duty or fraud.[42] More significantly, after the decision in *Sempra Metals v IRC*[43] it appears that this deficiency may have been cured in the sense that a claimant can now claim compound interest as damages, subject to satisfying normal rules applicable to compensatory damages. However, some caution may be necessary here as the apparent clash between this development and section 35A has not yet been faced up to and resolved.

Certainly there is a strong case for statutory reform of s 35A so as to empower the courts to award compound interest. Indeed, arbitrators have been given the power to award compound interest by the Arbitration Act 1996, s 49. In a Report in 2004, the Law Commission recommended a reform of the Senior Courts Act 1981, s 35A (and the County Courts Act 1984, s 69) so that the courts would be permitted to award compound, rather than just simple, interest.[44] It recommended that there should be a rebuttable presumption that awards of £15,000 or more would attract compound interest whereas sums of less than

---

[40] One might go on to say that a similar explanation applies to explain the award of interest under the Judgment Debts Act 1838. As this statute imposes a fixed rate of award, there has been no real discussion of the justification for the interest. However, if it is seen as compensating a loss of the claimant—even though the award is highly objective and not finely tuned to the position of the claimant—there is again the apparent objection that compensation is normally triggered only by a wrong. As with the 1981 Act, one might therefore suggest that the failure to pay a judgment debt (including an award of damages) is itself a type of wrong, for the purposes of the 1838 Act, which triggers compensation for the loss of use of the judgment debt owed.

[41] Cf S Smith, 'Why Courts Make Orders (and What This Tells us About Damages)' (2011) 64 CLP 51, 72 and S Smith, 'A Duty to Make Restitution' (2013) 26 Can JL Juris 157, 166, arguing that one reason why one cannot regard the legal requirement to pay damages or to make restitution as a 'duty' is precisely because there is no compensation for the loss of use from not being paid the damages or restitutionary sum. That is, as the mirror image of the argument made here in the text, Smith is arguing that there is no wrong because interest is not being awarded as compensation for that loss of use. But this of course is contradicted by the judicial interpretation of s 35A (albeit correct at common law).

[42] *President of India v La Pintada Compania* [1985] AC 104; *Westdeutsche Landesbank Girozentrale v Islington London Borough Council* [1996] AC 669. See below, pp 542–543.

[43] See above, pp 298–299.

[44] Law Commission, *Pre-Judgment Interest on Debts and Damages* (2004) Report No 287.

£15,000 would attract simple interest. The Commission further recommended that tables should be published by the Court Service so as to make it easy to calculate compound interest at a particular rate. Unfortunately, although those eminently sensible recommendations were included in a Civil Justice Bill in 2011, they were ultimately rejected by Government.

(4) Is statutory interest always awarded?

As regards personal injury and death, the statute leaves no discretion—interest must be awarded subject to special reasons. But in *Jefford v Gee*[45] and *Cookson v Knowles*[46] it has been held that the different types of loss must be itemised, since no interest is payable on damages for future pecuniary loss for the reason that that loss has not yet been suffered and hence the claimant has not been deprived of the use of money due.

Outside the realm of personal injury and death, the award of interest is discretionary but in practice the courts are generally willing to exercise their discretion to award interest on damages for pecuniary loss:[47] but interest on damages for non-pecuniary loss is generally denied. So in an action for deceit in *Saunders v Edwards*[48] the Court of Appeal refused to award interest (even at the low 2% rate used in personal injury cases)[49] on damages for inconvenience and disappointment. Contrary to the argument that has been put forward above—that the failure to pay the damages is itself a wrong—this denial was thought to be correct in principle because in Bingham LJ's words, 'the damages [cannot] be realistically seen as having accrued due to the plaintiff at a certain time in the past and as having thereafter been wrongly withheld from him.'[50] It was also pointed out that no interest has traditionally been awarded on damages for non-pecuniary loss in defamation cases. The inconsistency with the approach to non-pecuniary loss in personal injury cases was put to one side as a product of the statutory requirement of awarding interest in such cases.

(5) For what period is statutory interest payable?

Under section 35A, the courts have the discretion to choose the period for which interest is payable, although the maximum is between the date when the cause of action arose and the date of judgment (or the date of payment in respect of a sum paid before judgment). The date *to which* interest is payable causes little difficulty and is almost always fixed as the date of judgment or trial. More interesting is the date *from which* interest is payable. This was carefully examined by Robert Goff J in *BP Exploration v Hunt (No 2)*,[51] albeit in the context of a restitutionary award under the Law Reform (Frustrated Contracts) Act 1943 rather than an award of damages. His conclusion was that the general rule is that interest runs from the date of loss, but that there are three main exceptions to this. The first is where it would be unfair on the defendant to make it pay interest from the date of loss: for example, '… if the defendant neither knew, nor reasonably could have been expected to know, that the plaintiff was likely to make a claim, and so was in no position to tender payment,

---

[45] [1970] 2 QB 130.   [46] [1979] AC 556.
[47] In *Metal Box Ltd v Currys Ltd* [1988] 1 WLR 175 interest was awarded on damages for loss of goods that were not income-producing. But in *Giles v Thompson* [1994] 1 AC 142 interest on damages for the costs of hiring a replacement car was denied because the claimant was not obliged to pay these costs until judgment so that she was not 'kept out of' any money while the claim was being litigated.
[48] [1987] 1 WLR 1116. See also *Holtham v Metropolitan Police Comr*, The Times, 28 November 1987.
[49] Below, pp 306–307.   [50] [1987] 1 WLR 1116, at 1135.   [51] [1982] 1 All ER 925.

or even to make provision for payment if the money should be found due'.[52] The second is where the claimant's conduct is such that it should not have interest awarded from the date of loss: for example, where it has unreasonably delayed in pursuing its claim.[53] Finally interest will not be awarded from the date of loss where it would otherwise be unjust in all the circumstances of the case to do so. The most obvious example of this is that, as laid down in *Jefford v Gee*,[54] interest on damages for non-pecuniary loss in a personal injury action is payable from the date of the service of the claim form until trial, the reasoning being that, as the loss is spread over a long period of time, it is more just to award interest from when the damages were first formally demanded.

It should further be noted that interest on damages for pre-trial pecuniary loss in personal injury and Fatal Accident Act cases is normally payable from the date of the accident or death until trial, as laid down in *Jefford v Gee* and *Cookson v Knowles*[55] respectively. But this is not an exception to the date of loss rule. Rather it represents half of a formula, considered more fully below, designed as a rough substitute for detailed calculations of the interest on each pecuniary loss from the date it was suffered.

(6) What is the rate of statutory interest?

In commercial cases, where the focus is generally on the claimant having to borrow replacement money,[56] the courts usually take the average clearing bank base rate plus 1%, this being the borrowing rate for big companies.[57] Smaller less prestigious companies, or individual businessmen, may be awarded more, corresponding to the higher borrowing rate charged to them.[58] Rix LJ explained the position as follows in *Jaura v Ahmed*:[59]

> 'The history in the business context of the movement in recent decades [has been] away from a purely conventional rate to one which more closely reflects the claimant's costs of borrowing... Thus a rate of 1% above base rate prevailing from time to time has become the practice of the Commercial Court, albeit this is only a presumption and can be varied up or even down to meet the fairness of the parties' particular situation. It is right that defendants who have kept small businessmen out of money to which a court ultimately judges them to have been entitled should pay a rate which properly reflects the real cost of borrowing incurred by such a class of businessmen.'

Of course, the statute only permits simple not compound interest so that, to that extent, even the more careful consideration of the class of borrower to which the claimant belongs does not end up with an award of statutory interest that reflects the 'real cost of borrowing'.

---

[52] ibid, at 975. See *Allied London Investments Ltd v Hambro Life Assurance Ltd* [1985] 1 EGLR 45; *Kuwait Airways Corpn v Kuwait Insurance Co SAK (No 2)* [2000] 1 All ER (Comm) 972; *Quorum A/S v Schramm (No 2)* [2002] 2 All ER (Comm) 179.
[53] See *Quorum A/S v Schramm (No 2)* [2002] 2 All ER (Comm) 179.   [54] [1970] 2 QB 130.
[55] [1979] AC 556.   [56] See above, p 302.
[57] *BP Exploration v Hunt (No 2)* [1982] 1 All ER 925; *Tate & Lyle Food and Distribution Ltd v Greater London Council* [1981] 3 All ER 716; *International Military Services Ltd v Capital & Counties plc* [1982] 1 WLR 575; *Polish SS Co v Atlantic Maritime Co* [1985] QB 41; *Metal Box Ltd v Currys Ltd* [1988] 1 WLR 175; *Shearson Lehman Hutton Inc v Maclaine Watson & Co Ltd (No 2)* [1990] 3 All ER 723; *Kuwait Airways Corpn v Kuwait Insurance Co SAK (No 2)* [2000] 1 All ER (Comm) 972; *Fiona Trust and Holding Corp v Privalov* [2011] EWHC 664 (Comm), at [13]–[16], [31].
[58] *Catnic Components Ltd v Hill & Smith Ltd* [1983] FSR 512 (2% above base); *Jaura v Ahmed* [2002] EWCA Civ 210 (3% above base); *West v Ian Finlay* [2014] EWCA Civ 316, [2014] BLR 324 (4.5% above base).
[59] [2002] EWCA Civ 210, at [20] and [26].

In personal injury and death cases (and in rare commercial cases where it is unrealistic to think that the claimant has had to borrow) the focus is on the lost interest from investment. So for personal injury non-pecuniary loss[60] interest is payable at a fixed rate of 2%, as is examined further below. For pre-trial pecuniary loss, interest on the whole amount of loss is normally payable from the date of the accident or death until trial at half the average rate on the special account[61] over that period.[62] This represents a rough substitute for awarding interest on each pecuniary loss for the period from when it was suffered until trial at the full average rate (on the special account) over that period. As recognised in *Dexter v Courtaulds Ltd*,[63] it may be more appropriate in exceptional cases, for example where all the loss has been incurred years before trial, to award interest on the whole amount of loss for a period from half-way through the time when the loss was suffered until trial at the full average rate (on the special account) over that period. But, as stressed, it would be for the claimant to plead and prove that such an alternative method of calculation is more appropriate than the normal method.

(7) What is the relationship between the date of assessment of damages and statutory interest?

(a) Liabilities other than foreign currency liabilities

Traditionally the date for assessing damages, ie the date at which the value of money, goods, or services is assessed, is the date of loss/date of the cause of action. But more recently, particularly in response to inflation, the courts have assessed damages at a later date.[64] What effect does this have on the award of statutory interest?

The main judicial discussion of this has been in relation to non-pecuniary loss in personal injury actions. One view is that since interest rates contain a large inflationary element (an element to preserve the real value of money) it would overcompensate the claimant to award both damages assessed according to the internal value of sterling at the date of judgment plus full interest on those damages from the date of service of the claim form. Put another way, in times of high inflation an investor cannot generally expect to do much more than maintain the real value of its money; an award of statutory interest designed to compensate for the claimant being kept out of money to which it is entitled should therefore not be given if damages are already based on the real value of money. This lay behind the decision of the Court of Appeal in *Cookson v Knowles*:[65] since damages for non-pecuniary loss, in contrast to, for example, damages for pre-trial loss of earnings, are now based on the value of money at the time of judgment, it was held that no interest should be awarded on them. But in *Pickett v British Rail Engineering Ltd*[66] the House of Lords overruled this and considered that a clear distinction could be drawn between maintaining the real value of money, to which interest was thought to be irrelevant, and being kept out of money, which was the reason for an award of interest. Lord Wilberforce said:

'Increase for inflation is designed to preserve the "real" value of money, interest to compensate for being kept out of that "real" value. The one has no relation to the other. If the damages

---

[60] For interest on bereavement damages, see above, p 263 n 62.
[61] The special account (sometimes referred to as the special investment account) is an investment account used for court funds: see Court Funds Rules 2011, SI 2011/1734. It was formerly called the short-term investment account. Since 1 July 2009, the rate of interest on the special account has been 0.5%.
[62] *Jefford v Gee* [1970] 2 QB 130; *Cookson v Knowles* [1979] AC 556.   [63] [1984] 1 WLR 372.
[64] See above, pp 171–176.
[65] [1977] QB 913 (appealed on a different point to the House of Lords [1979] AC 556).
[66] [1980] AC 136.

claimed remained nominally the same ... because there was no inflation, interest would normally be given. The same should follow if damages remain in real terms the same.'[67]

In *Birkett v Hayes*,[68] while he accepted that *Pickett* meant that some interest must be awarded on damages for the non-pecuniary losses, Lord Denning considered in the spirit of his approach in *Cookson v Knowles* that a low rate of interest of 2% was appropriate and this was agreed with by the two other judges. Eveleigh LJ said that, where interest rates have a large inflationary element:

> '... it cannot be right to apply such interest rates to an award which already takes into account the need for preserving the value of money. We must look for some other rate of interest.'[69]

This low 2% rate of interest was confirmed as correct by the House of Lords in *Wright v British Railways Board*.[70]

Although the rate for awarding statutory interest was not in issue in *Wells v Wells*,[71] one might argue that their Lordships' preference for the rate of return on Index Linked Government Stock (ILGS), as the most accurate indicator of the rate of interest on a low-risk investment, means that the ILGS rate (which was taken to be 3% in *Wells v Wells*)[72] should be the rate of interest applied on damages for non-pecuniary loss. But this argument was rejected by the Court of Appeal in *Lawrence v Chief Constable of Staffordshire*.[73] May LJ said that there was no reason why the guideline rate for calculating future pecuniary loss should be the same as the guideline rate of interest on damages for non-pecuniary loss. This was, not least, because damages for non-pecuniary loss take account of inflation up until the date of judgment. In any event, 'since general damages in personal injury cases are awarded on amounts which are conventional, and since an award of interest is discretionary, a rigid mathematical approach to the calculation of interest is less appropriate than in an actuarial calculation of future loss.'[74]

There has been little other discussion of the effects on statutory interest of assessing damages at a date later than the date of loss.[75] But the clear message from the above cases is that wherever damages are assessed at a date later than the date of loss, the courts must be careful not to award statutory interest at a rate which will overcompensate the claimant.

(b) Foreign currency liabilities

Under the former sterling-breach-date rule, interest was awarded on an agreed sum or damages at sterling rates. But what effect has the reversal of that rule in *Miliangos v George Frank (Textiles) Ltd*[76] had on the award of statutory interest?

In *Shell Tankers (UK) Ltd v Astro Comino Armadora SA, The Pacific Colocotronis*[77] the Court of Appeal held that, where *Miliangos* applies and judgment is expressed in a foreign currency, statutory interest should be awarded, prima facie, at the rate applicable to that currency. Judgment had there been expressed in US dollars and the rate of interest applied was therefore the dollar rather than the sterling rate. This approach should be supported

---

[67] [1980] AC 136, at 151. [68] [1982] 1 WLR 816. [69] ibid, at 822.
[70] [1983] 2 AC 773. [71] [1999] 1 AC 345.
[72] This is now at a negative rate of minus 0.75%. [73] [2000] PIQR Q349. [74] ibid, at [26].
[75] But see obiter dicta in *Perry v Sidney Phillips & Son* [1982] 1 WLR 1297, at 1302.
[76] [1976] AC 443. Above, pp 177–181.
[77] [1981] 2 Lloyd's Rep 40, at 45, 77. See also *Miliangos v George Frank (No 2)* [1976] 2 Lloyd's Rep 434.

as effecting true compensation; for example if sterling has declined in value, then since interest rates generally increase in response to a decline in the value of currency, it would usually overcompensate the claimant to express judgment in foreign currency (with a conversion into sterling at the date of payment) and then to award statutory interest at the sterling rate.[78]

---

[78] For similar reasons the courts have also been given a wide discretion to award a different interest rate, than the usual fixed rate, on judgment debts expressed in a foreign currency: s 44A of the Administration of Justice Act 1970.

16
Limitation periods

1. Introduction	309
2. The normal time limits	310
3. The main exceptions to the normal time limits	311

1. Introduction

Although, strictly speaking, the law of limitation is separate from the law of remedies, the two are closely connected. Moreover, it has been said to be '... trite law that the English Limitation Acts bar the remedy and not the right'.[1] It has therefore been thought helpful to include here a very brief outline of limitation periods for claims for damages, albeit with the warning that this chapter does not attempt to deal with all the details of the law.[2]

For the purposes of limitation, no distinction has been drawn between compensatory and non-compensatory damages. So, for example, the limitation period for punitive damages for a tort is the same as for compensatory damages. Indeed, although there are significant departures from this, the Limitation Act 1980 basically fixes the limitation periods according to the cause of action (breach of contract or tort) rather than the remedy.

Before proceeding to the details of the law on limitation in relation to damages, there is an initial and very important general question. Why is there a limitation defence at all? The most obvious answer is that the limitation defence is there to protect defendants in two main senses. First, fairness to defendants indicates that, after a certain period of time, defendants should be free from the worry and uncertainty of having a legal action hanging over them. In Lady Hale's words, defendants should 'not be harassed with stale claims'.[3] To respect their autonomy to lead their lives as they would wish, defendants should be secure in the knowledge that they are free from litigation relating to particular conduct and are not going to have to find the assets (or maintain liability insurance) to satisfy claims against them dating back many years. Secondly, the deterioration in evidence over time—especially oral evidence—may mean that there is a difficulty in the defendant denying the claim. It may be that the defendant had a perfectly good riposte or defence but that there is now no good evidence that it can rely on to make out its case. In other words, part of the reason for the law of limitation is to ensure that the defendant has a fair civil trial.

Aside from the principal concern with protecting defendants, the law of limitation also has benefits for claimants and for the state. As regards the former, the law of limitation provides an incentive for claimants to act relatively quickly once they realise that they may have a claim and that, in turn, may mean that good evidence for the claimant is preserved and

---

[1] *Ronex Properties Ltd v John Laing Construction Ltd* [1982] 3 WLR 875, at 879 (per Donaldson LJ). But this is not always the case; see, eg, the Limitation Act 1980, s 11A(3).
[2] For detailed accounts, see, eg, A McGee, *Limitation Periods* (8th edn, Sweet & Maxwell 2018); *Clerk and Lindsell on Torts* (22nd edn, Sweet & Maxwell 2018) ch 32; *Chitty on Contracts* (32nd, Sweet & Maxwell 2015) ch 28. Albeit rejected by the Government, see also the extensive reforms recommended by the Law Commission in *Limitation of Actions* (2001) Report No 270.
[3] In *AB v Ministry of Defence* [2012] UKSC 9, [2013] 1 AC 78, at [164].

not lost. Moving swiftly may also keep down costs. And for the state, the more reliable the evidence, the more likely it is that its dispute resolution process will be non-arbitrary and fair, thereby complying with the rule of law.

However, at least some of these 'policies' could be dealt with by considering the fairness of the trial (taking into account the quality of the evidence) on a case by case basis. Indeed, irrespective of the limitation defence, under the Civil Procedure Rules the courts have the power to strike out a claim for abuse of process under CPR 3(4)(2)(b).[4] It is clear, therefore, that the law of limitation acts as a somewhat blunt instrument (albeit that it has the merit of certainty) to achieve the goal of a fair trial. Moreover, one may question just how strong the policies are for protecting defendants against claims many years after particular conduct. If we know that the defendant had no possible defence, and the claimant can prove its case, one might argue that the defendant should not escape liability simply because of the effluxion of time.

However, all legal systems appear to regard it is as essential to have limitation periods for civil claims and no-one seriously suggests that limitation periods should be abolished. Nevertheless, standing back and considering the underlying reasons for the defence does indicate that the defence operates in a somewhat blunt manner; and this suggests that where, for example, the rules of limitation do allow discretion to the courts in deciding whether to allow a claim to proceed or not,[5] the courts ought to err on the side of allowing the claim to proceed provided time has not so diminished the quality of the evidence as to render the trial unfair.

It is a separate point that, *if* there is to be a limitation defence, it should be one that seeks to recognise the interests of claimants as well those of defendants and the state. In particular, in relation to latent injury and damage it has been perceived as unfair that a claimant may be out of time before it could reasonably have known that it had a claim. As the Law Commission expressed it, in seeking to articulate the policy interests that should underpin any proposals for reform of the limitation regime:[6]

> '[A]ny limitation system must balance the interests of the defendant, the state and the plaintiff.... [A]ny limitation system will involve some injustice either to the plaintiff who does not have sufficient time to bring a claim, or to the defendant, who is asked to defend a claim after several years of the plaintiff's inaction. Any limitation system must attempt to minimise this injustice, and reconcile, as far as possible, the conflicting interests involved.'

2. The normal time limits

By the Limitation Act 1980, s 5, 'An action founded on simple contract shall not be brought after the expiration of six years from the date on which the cause of action accrued.' By s 8(1), 'An action upon a specialty shall not be brought after the expiration of twelve years from the date on which the cause of action accrued.' The reason for this difference is not obvious but perhaps it relates to a contract by deed being easy to prove.

The date of the cause of action accruing for breach of contract, and hence the date from which the six or 12 years run, is the date of the breach of contract.[7]

---

[4] By this rule, 'The Court may strike out a statement of case if it appears to the court— ... (b) that the statement of case is an abuse of the court's process or is otherwise likely to obstruct the just disposal of the proceedings.'
[5] See the discussion of s 33 of the Limitation Act 1980 below, pp 312–313.
[6] Law Commission, *Limitation of Actions* (1998) Consultation Paper No 151, para 1.38.
[7] The same periods apply to an action for an agreed sum: below, ch 21.

By the Limitation Act 1980, s 2, 'An action founded on tort shall not be brought after the expiration of six years from the date on which the cause of action accrued.' The date of the cause of action accruing for torts, and hence the date from which the six years run, is the date of the tort.[8]

One issue of particular practical importance stems from the expansion of the tort of negligence to cover pure economic loss (in certain situations) combined with the acceptance of concurrent liability between tortious negligence and breach of contract: for these developments mean that, for example, where a professional person has negligently performed services beneficial to her claimant client causing pure economic loss, the latter is now generally given a longer period in which to sue for the tort of negligence (time running from the date of damage) rather than for breach of contract (time running from the date of breach).[9]

3. The main exceptions to the normal time limits[10]

(1) Damages for personal injury and death

The law on limitation periods for damages for personal injury and death is now contained in the Limitation Act 1980, ss 11–14, which contain the basic time limits, and s 33 of that Act, which gives the courts a discretion to disapply the basic time limits.

(a) Basic time limits for personal injury—s 11

Where the action is brought by the injured person the limitation period, as laid down in the Limitation Act 1980, s 11(4), is three years from either the date on which the cause of action accrued or, if later, the date of knowledge of the person injured.

By the Limitation Act 1980, s 14(1), the date of knowledge means the date on which the person first had knowledge (including constructive knowledge as dealt with by s 14(3)) of all the following facts: that the injury was significant (as defined in s 11(2)); that the injury was attributable in whole or in part to the act or omission which is alleged to constitute negligence, nuisance, or breach of duty; the identity of the defendant; and if it is alleged that the act or omission was that of a person other than the defendant, the identity of that person and the additional facts supporting the bringing of an action against the defendant.

Where the estate is bringing the action under the Law Reform (Miscellaneous Provisions) Act 1934 the limitation period laid down in the Limitation Act 1980, s 11(5) is three years from the date of death or the date of the personal representative's knowledge, whichever is

---

[8] For full discussion (including the difficult questions that have arisen in, eg, *Forster v Outred & Co* [1982] 1 WLR 86 and *Law Society v Sephton & Co* [2006] UKHL 22, [2006] 2 AC 543, as to when the cause of action accrues—ie when is there actionable damage—in the tort of negligence) see *Clerk and Lindsell on Torts* (22nd edn, Sweet & Maxwell 2018) paras 32-06–32-18. Where there is more than one conversion of the same chattel time runs from the date of the original conversion: Limitation Act 1980, s 3(1). For patent infringement the action can accrue before proceedings can be instituted; *Sevcon Ltd v Lucas CAV Ltd* [1986] 2 All ER 104.

[9] See, eg, *Midland Bank Trust Co Ltd v Hett, Stubbs & Kemp* [1979] Ch 384; *Henderson v Merrett Syndicates Ltd* [1995] 2 AC 145.

[10] Special provisions of the Limitation Act 1980 deal with the defendant's fraud or deliberate concealment or the claimant's mistake (s 32) and the claimant's disability (s 28). See also s 4A, introduced by the Defamation Act 1996, reducing the basic period for defamation and malicious falsehood actions to one year (although, by s 32A, this is subject to the court's discretion to disapply that period); and s 11A which, inter alia, imposes a three-year basic period and a ten-year long-stop for actions under the Consumer Protection Act 1987, Pt 1. Other special limitation periods for damages claims are laid down in, eg, the Merchant Shipping Act 1995, s 190; the Carriage by Air Act 1961, Sch 1, art 29; and the Human Rights Act 1998, s 7(5).

the later. Section 14(1) again applies to define the date of knowledge. It should also be remembered that a precondition of a claim by the estate is that there is a valid personal injury action surviving. Hence no action can be brought if the deceased's action would have been time-barred.

(b) Basic time limits for death—s 12

By the Limitation Act 1980, s 12(2), the limitation period for a claim under the Fatal Accidents Act 1976 is three years from either the date of death or the date of knowledge of the person for whose benefit the action is brought, whichever is the later. The date of knowledge is again defined by s 14(1).

By the Fatal Accidents Act 1976, s 1(1), an action can only succeed if the deceased would have been entitled to damages. Hence, if the deceased's action was time-barred, no Fatal Accidents Act claim lies, and this is reiterated in the Limitation Act 1980, s 12(1).

(c) The discretion to disapply the basic time limits for personal injury and death—s 33

In a novel development, the Limitation Act 1980, s 33(1) gave a court the discretion to disapply the basic time limits under ss 11 and 12 if equitable to do so having regard to the prejudice to the claimant of sticking to the limits and the prejudice to the defendant of extending them. In exercising this discretion the courts, by s 33(3), are to have particular regard to certain factors, such as the length of and reason for delay by the claimant, the extent to which the cogency of evidence will be impaired, and the defendant's conduct after the cause of action arose.

The discretion is also applicable vis-à-vis a deceased's action (with, by the Limitation Act 1980, s 33(5), references to the 'plaintiff' in s 33(3) being replaced by references to the deceased) so that a claim under the Law Reform Act 1934 or the Fatal Accidents Act 1976 can succeed even though the basic time limits would have barred the deceased's action.

There have been many legal decisions dealing with the Limitation Act 1980, s 33 discretion.[11] Perhaps not surprisingly with such a wide-ranging discretion, different courts have taken markedly different views in applying section 33. So, for example, the predominant view until recently was that the claimant had a heavy burden to discharge for the s 33 discretion to be exercised in her favour. Put another way, the discretion was seen as one that should be exercised only in exceptional circumstances with the prima facie position being that the limitation period applied. However, in *Sayers v Hunters*[12] the Court of Appeal rejected the view that the burden on the claimant is a heavy one. Again in balancing the prejudice, it used to be assumed that the loss of the protection of the limitation period was included as relevant prejudice to the defendant. However in *Cain v Francis*,[13] the Court of Appeal decided that loss of the limitation defence does not in itself count as a relevant prejudice to the defendant. This was on the reasoning that a limitation defence should be seen as a windfall to a defendant who would otherwise be liable to pay damages. The relevant prejudice to the defendant should therefore be confined to asking whether the delay has disadvantaged the defendant in defending the claim. In the words of Smith LJ:[14]

---

[11] For full discussion, see *Clerk and Lindsell on Torts* (22nd edn, Sweet & Maxwell 2018) paras 32-54–32-66.
[12] [2012] EWCA Civ 1715, [2013] 1 WLR 1695.   [13] [2008] EWCA Civ 1451, [2009] QB 754.
[14] ibid, at [72].

'[T]he basic question to be asked is whether it is fair and just in all the circumstances to expect the defendant to meet his claim on the merits, notwithstanding the delay in commencement. The length of the delay will be important, not so much for itself as to the effect it has had. To what extent has the defendant been disadvantaged in his investigation of the claim and/or the assembly of evidence, in respect of the issues of both liability and quantum?'

It is submitted that these recent moves favouring claimants in the exercise of the discretion under s 33 should be supported. As has been explained earlier,[15] the major underlying policy behind having a limitation defence is to protect a defendant against an unfair civil trial: provided a fair trial is possible, the courts should err on the side of allowing the claim to proceed.[16]

(2) Damages for latent damage (other than personal injury) in the tort of negligence

By definition, latent damage occurs, and hence for the tort of negligence the cause of action begins to run, at a time when the claimant has no reasonable opportunity of knowing of the damage. Indeed the normal time period may have run out before the claimant ever had a reasonable opportunity to discover the damage. While for latent personal injury this problem was solved by the provisions examined above, the expansion of the tort of negligence in the 1970s led to a revival of concern over latent damage this time particularly (although not exclusively)[17] in relation to negligently constructed or designed buildings.

In *Sparham-Souter v Town and Country Developments*[18] the Court of Appeal, in seeking to do justice to claimants, held that the cause of action accrued, and hence time began to run, only when the claimant discovered or ought to have discovered the damage (or possibly the defect). But this decision was overruled by the House of Lords in *Pirelli General Cable Works Ltd v Oscar Faber and Partners*,[19] which said that, by analogy to the common law rule for personal injury, time begins to run only from when damage to the building occurs, whether reasonably discoverable or not. However, the House of Lords recognised the injustice that such an approach can cause to claimants and called for legislative reform.

The calls in *Pirelli* for legislative reform were soon answered. Following the proposals of the Law Reform Committee[20] the Latent Damage Act 1986 was enacted, amending the Limitation Act 1980 in respect of negligently caused latent damage (other than personal injury).[21] By the Limitation Act 1980, s 14A(4)(a), the normal six-year limit running from the date of the cause of action (ie the *Pirelli* approach) remains but is now subject to two crucial

---

[15] Above, p 310.
[16] In *AB v Ministry of Defence* [2012] UKSC 9, [2013] 1 AC 78, the majority of the Supreme Court held that the claim was time-barred and went on to decide briefly that the Court of Appeal had been correct to refuse to exercise its s 33 discretion to disapply the limitation period. This was in particular because the claims had no real prospect of success. But this was an exceptional case where the merits of the case on causation had been meticulously examined by the Court of Appeal. Although in other less exceptional cases, the courts have regarded the strength of the claim as relevant under s 33 (see, eg, *Forbes v Wandsworth HA* [1997] QB 402, at 417) the courts should be astute to avoid mini-trials, involving detailed considerations of the evidence. Indeed one might argue that the strength of the claim should not be assessed at all under s 33 because there is a more appropriate procedure for hopeless claims, namely striking out or (reverse) summary judgment.
[17] The problem has also arisen in claims against, eg, negligent solicitors or accountants.
[18] [1976] QB 858.
[19] [1983] 2 AC 1. *Pirelli* has not been followed in New Zealand: *Invercargill City Council v Hamlin* [1996] AC 624.
[20] Law Reform Committee, *24th Report Latent Damage* (HMSO 1984) Cmnd 9390.
[21] Negligence here means the tort of negligence and not breach of a contractual duty of care: *Iron Trade Mutual Insurance Co Ltd v J K Buckenham Ltd* [1990] 1 All ER 808; *Société Commerciale de Réassurance v ERAS (International) Ltd* [1992] 2 All ER 82n.

qualifications: first, by s 14A(4)(b) and (5) a claimant can bring an action within three years from the date when the claimant first had the knowledge required for bringing an action, including constructive knowledge (as dealt with by s 14A(10)); and secondly, by s 14B there is an absolute long-stop bar to actions 15 years from the date of the (alleged) negligent act or omission causing the relevant damage.

These provisions appear to achieve a measure of fairness for both claimants and defendants: by the 15-year long-stop defendants are protected against actions being brought scores of years after their negligence, such actions being not only hard to defend but rendering insurance difficult and expensive; and on the other hand, in most situations, the discoverability qualification will allow a claimant to get to know of and hence to bring an action for the damage before the 15-year absolute limit expires.

Since these reforms, the overruling of *Anns v Merton London BC*[22] in *Murphy v Brentwood District Council*[23] has significantly narrowed the potential for liability in the tort of negligence for defective buildings. The scope of ss 14A and 14B has been correspondingly cut back leaving it as largely applying to latent pure economic loss in claims for professional negligence against, for example, solicitors and accountants.[24]

(3) Equitable damages[25]

It would appear that the question of what is the limitation period for equitable damages (for a tort or breach of contract) has never been dealt with in the cases.[26] By the Limitation Act 1980, s 36(1), none of the statutory time limits applies directly to specific performance, injunctions or 'other equitable relief'; and, as regards 'by analogy' limitation periods under s 36(1), it was held in *P & O Nedlloyd BV v Arab Metals Co*[27] that no 'by analogy' limitation period applies to specific performance and one can assume that the same applies to injunctions.[28] As such, the most obvious view is that whether equitable damages are time-barred or not depends in turn on whether the specific performance or injunction in substitution for, or in addition to, which the damages are potentially being given, would be barred under the laches doctrine.[29]

---

[22] [1978] AC 728.   [23] [1991] AC 398.
[24] See *Haward v Fawcetts* [2006] UKHL 9, [2006] 1 WLR 682; *Clerk and Lindsell on Torts* (22nd edn, Sweet & Maxwell 2018) paras 32-70–32-76.
[25] For equitable damages generally, see below, ch 17.
[26] For limitation periods for equitable remedies for equitable wrongs, see below, pp 543–544.
[27] [2006] EWCA Civ 1717, [2007] 1 WLR 2288.   [28] See below, pp 489–490.
[29] See below, pp 433–434, 489–491 (laches both under specific performance and injunctions). The contrary view was controversially taken by the Privy Council in *Pell Frischmann Engineering Co Ltd v Bow Valley Iran Ltd* [2009] UKPC 45, [2011] 1 WLR 2370: at [54] Lord Walker said, '[The claimant's] delay in commencing proceedings meant that it had no prospect at all of obtaining injunctive relief, but that is not fatal to an award of damages under Lord Cairns's Act.' This would suggest that, applying laches, a longer period of delay is permissible if the claim is for equitable damages than if one is seeking an injunction. But this links to Lord Walker's view, criticised in *Morris-Garner v One Step (Support) Ltd* [2018] UKSC 20, [2018] 2 WLR 1353, at [45], that equitable damages can be awarded even if no injunction or specific performance has been sought: see below, p 316. Admittedly, in terms of policy it is arguable that, if actions for common law damages are basically acceptable before but not after six years, the same should apply to equitable damages: but equitable damages are most likely to be sought where the tort or breach of contract is anticipated rather than accrued and, at least in that situation, the analogy with common law damages is weak.

17

Equitable (compensatory) damages

1. When may equitable damages be awarded?	315
2. When are equitable damages more advantageous than common law damages?	317
3. Non-compensatory equitable damages?	319

1. When may equitable damages be awarded?

Prior to 1858 there was probably some power, albeit very restricted, to award damages in equity in addition to specific performance.[1] But this is of merely historical interest, because by the Chancery Amendment Act 1858, s 2 (Lord Cairns's Act) the Court of Chancery was given power to award damages 'in addition to or in substitution for [an] injunction or specific performance'. This power to award what are commonly referred to as 'equitable damages' is now vested in the courts by the Senior Courts Act 1981, s 50. As regards damages in addition, the power is self-explanatory—whenever an injunction or specific performance is granted, damages can be added. But when may damages in substitution be awarded?

By the Senior Courts Act 1981, s 50, this will depend on whether the court 'has jurisdiction to entertain an application for an injunction or specific performance'. But there is difficulty in deciding when this is satisfied. The traditional approach has been to decide whether the particular reason for denying specific performance or the injunction is jurisdictional or discretionary and only if it is the latter can damages in substitution be awarded. For example, in *Price v Strange*[2] the Court of Appeal in obiter dicta considered that the want of mutuality bar to specific performance was discretionary so that damages in substitution could have been awarded had specific performance been refused. Both Buckley and Goff LJJ also thought that the denial of specific performance in contracts for the sale of non-unique goods was jurisdictional, but they disagreed as to whether the personal service bar was jurisdictional or discretionary, Buckley LJ thinking that it was the former and Goff LJ that it was the latter. This disagreement tends to support the view that, given that the bars to specific performance are nowadays rarely absolute,[3] the approach of categorising them as either jurisdictional or discretionary is unhelpful.

A simpler and preferable approach to the Senior Courts Act 1981, s 50 is to ask whether the claimant had an arguable case for specific performance or an injunction at the time the claim was brought; if so, equitable damages can be awarded.[4] This is consistent with obiter dicta of Lord Sumption in *Morris-Garner v One Step (Support) Ltd*[5] that what matters is

---

[1] *Todd v Gee* (1810) 17 Ves 273.   [2] [1978] Ch 337.   [3] Below, ch 22.
[4] There is also jurisdiction where specific performance was ordered but has since been abandoned because of the defendant's non-compliance: eg *Biggins v Minton* [1977] 1 WLR 701; *Malhotra v Choudhury* (1980) Ch 52
[5] [2018] UKSC 20, [2018] 2 WLR 1353, at [113] (per Lord Sumption). This was his Lordship's interpretation of the approach of Millett LJ in *Jaggard v Sawyer* [1995] 1 WLR 269, at 289–290.

whether the injunction or specific performance was available in principle at the time proceedings were commenced. It is also consistent with most past decisions.[6] In *Ferguson v Wilson*,[7] for example, specific performance of a contract for the allotment of shares to the claimant had been refused because, as the shares had already been allotted to third parties (in fact that had been done prior to the claim being brought) compliance would be impossible. It was further held that no equitable damages could be awarded and this can be best justified by saying that the claimant had no arguable case for specific performance at the time the claim was brought. On the other hand, in *Miller v Jackson*,[8] where the Court of Appeal refused an injunction but granted damages in substitution, the claimant clearly had an arguable case for an injunction—indeed Geoffrey Lane LJ dissented and considered that an injunction should be granted.

Two further points are noteworthy.

First, the fact that a court has power to award equitable damages does not mean that it will necessarily use that power. For example, where a claimant's conduct has debarred the claimant from specific relief, the court may refuse to award even damages in substitution.[9]

Secondly it has traditionally been thought that the Senior Courts Act 1981, s 50 does not allow the award of equitable damages in the case where the claimant would have been granted specific performance or an injunction had she claimed it but she has made no such claim (since she wants damages in substitution).[10] However, although this was doubted in obiter dicta of Lord Reed in the Supreme Court in *Morris-Garner v One Step (Support) Ltd*,[11] in *Pell Frischmann Engineering Co Ltd v Bow Valley Iran Ltd*[12] Lord Walker, giving the advice of the Privy Council, said that a court would have jurisdiction to award damages in substitution for an injunction, even if an injunction had not been sought. On the facts of the case, although no injunction had been sought, the Privy Council made an award of equitable damages assessed according to what the claimant could reasonably have charged for releasing the defendant from its obligations (ie these were so-called 'negotiating damages').[13] It seems odd to regard damages as available in equity but not at common law where the jurisdiction of equity has not been invoked by seeking specific relief. Moreover, on the facts of the *Pell Frischmann* case, where there had been a breach of a contractual joint venture agreement, it is hard to see why it made any difference whether the damages were equitable or common law: ie negotiating damages should either have been available at common law or unavailable both at common law and in equity.

---

[6] But in *Pell Frischmann Engineering Co Ltd v Bow Valley Iran Ltd* [2009] UKPC 45, [2011] 1 WLR 2370, at [48] and [54]—explicitly doubted in the obiter dicta of Lord Sumption in the *Morris-Garner* case, at [113]—Lord Walker controversially said that equitable damages could be awarded even if the claimant had no prospect of being granted an injunction at the time proceedings were commenced (eg because of delay).

[7] (1866) 2 Ch App 77. See also *Proctor v Bayley* (1889) 42 Ch D 390.   [8] [1977] QB 966.

[9] See below, p 488. For delay barring equitable damages, see above, p 314.

[10] *Horsler v Zorro* [1975] Ch 302. Also see G Jones, 'Restitution of Benefits Obtained in Breach of Another's Confidence' (1970) 86 LQR 463, 491. Contra is M Albery, 'Mr Cyprian Williams' Great Heresy' (1975) 91 LQR 337, 352–353.

[11] [2018] UKSC 20, [2018] 2 WLR 1353, at [45] (per Lord Reed). Cf the different approach of Lord Sumption at [113].

[12] [2009] UKPC 45, [2011] 1 WLR 2370, at [48]. See also *Jaggard v Sawyer* [1995] 1 WLR 269, at 285 (per Millett LJ).

[13] See below, ch 18.

2. When are equitable damages more advantageous than common law damages?

As the Supreme Court 1981, s 49, embodying the fusion provisions of the Judicature Acts 1873–1875, allows the claimant to combine a claim for common law damages with an action for specific performance or an injunction, equitable damages generally offer no advantage to a claimant. This is particularly so since *Johnson v Agnew*[14] in which it was laid down by Lord Wilberforce, following doubts in, for example, *Wroth v Tyler*,[15] that the assessment of equitable damages—and in this case the particular dispute concerned the time for assessing market value—is no different to that for common law damages.[16] Although the Supreme Court in *Morris-Garner v One Step (Support) Ltd*[17] has indicated that caution must be exercised in relation to what Lord Wilberforce said on this matter in *Johnson v Agnew*, it would appear that all that the Supreme Court had in mind is the obvious point that there are situations, as we shall now see, where equitable damages can be awarded and common law damages cannot (as, for example, in substitution for an anticipated wrong). Lord Wilberforce's comments were directed to where both common law and equitable damages are being awarded in respect of the same loss: where that is so, Lord Wilberforce was plainly correct that the principles for assessment should not differ as between common law and equity.

The one major advantage of equitable damages over common law damages[18] is that equitable damages may be awarded even though there is no cause of action at common law and hence no possible award of common law damages. A number of illustrations can be given of the application of this advantage in relation to torts and breach of contract.

(i) In *Eastwood v Lever*[19] it was first recognised that a third party can be awarded damages in addition to or in substitution for an injunction, available under the *Tulk v Moxhay*[20] principle, for the breach of a restrictive covenant concerning land, although the third party would have no cause of action at common law because of the privity of contract rule.[21] A more recent instance of this is *Wrotham Park Estate Co v Parkside Homes Ltd*,[22] where houses had been built by the defendants in breach of a restrictive covenant. While Brightman J refused to grant a mandatory injunction to demolish them, he did award substantial damages in substitution.

(ii) In *Hasham v Zenab*[23] it was held by the Privy Council that while an anticipatory breach that has not been accepted gives rise to no cause of action at common law, specific performance can be ordered. It had to follow that equitable damages could be awarded in this situation, even though common law damages could not, and this has since been confirmed by the decision in *Oakacre Ltd v Claire Cleaners (Holdings) Ltd*.[24]

---

[14] [1980] AC 367. See also *Surrey CC v Bredero Homes Ltd* [1993] 1 WLR 1361; *Jaggard v Sawyer* [1995] 1 WLR 269.
[15] [1974] Ch 30.
[16] So the law discussed in chs 3–15 applies analogously to equitable damages. See also *Malhotra v Choudhury* [1980] Ch 52 (the duty to mitigate and the old *Bain v Fothergill* restriction).
[17] [2018] UKSC 20, [2018] 2 WLR 1353, at [47].
[18] A minor advantage is that equitable damages may be awarded even though not claimed: *Betts v Neilson* (1863) 3 Ch App 429, at 441.
[19] (1863) 4 De GJ & Sm 114.   [20] (1848) 18 LJ Ch 83.
[21] It is conceivable that the third party would now have a claim for common law damages under the Contracts (Rights of Third Parties) Act 1999.
[22] [1974] 1 WLR 798. See below, pp 321, 354.   [23] [1960] AC 316.   [24] [1982] Ch 197.

(iii) In the classic case of *Leeds Industrial Co-operative Society v Slack*[25] it was held by the House of Lords that damages can be awarded in substitution for a *quia timet* injunction, which is an injunction to prevent a threatened wrong where no wrong has yet been committed. So on the facts damages were held recoverable in substitution for a *quia timet* injunction preventing the defendant constructing buildings which, when complete, would have obstructed the claimant's ancient lights but as yet were causing no obstruction. Similarly, in respect of continuing torts or a continuing breach of contract equitable damages in substitution for even an ordinary (ie not a *quia timet*) injunction are more advantageous than common law damages in compensating for an anticipated rather than just an accrued cause of action. Common law damages, in contrast, compensate only for loss (whether past or prospective) caused by a tort or breach of contract that has already been committed.[26] This means that where loss is continuing to be caused by a continuing tort or breach of contract, common law damages can be awarded only for the past continuing loss and not the future continuing loss so that many separate claims will need to be brought at common law in order to obtain full compensation. In contrast, equitable damages can be awarded in one action for all loss including future continuing loss. The explanation for this is that, as equitable damages are a substitute for an injunction or specific performance, and as those specific remedies can be granted to prevent an anticipated tort or breach of contract, equitable damages can instead be awarded in respect of the anticipated cause of action. As Sir Thomas Bingham MR said in *Jaggard v Sawyer*:[27]

> '[Lord Cairns' Act] also enabled the Chancery Court to award damages instead of granting an injunction to restrain unlawful conduct in the future. Such damages can only have been intended to compensate the plaintiff for future unlawful conduct, the commission of which, in the absence of any injunction, the court must have contemplated as likely to occur.'

So, for example, in *Bracewell v Appleby*[28] and *Jaggard v Sawyer*,[29] where damages were awarded in substitution for an injunction to prevent defendants continuing to trespass by using the claimant's road to reach their houses, there was no question of the equitable compensatory damages being assessed only for loss caused by past, as opposed to future, acts of trespass.

Although reversed on liability by the House of Lords,[30] there was an interesting discussion at first instance of this power to award equitable damages for an anticipated or continuing tort in *Marcic v Thames Water Utilities Ltd* (No 2).[31] The claimant owned property that was regularly subject to flooding. In an action against the defendant, a sewerage undertaker, the claimant sought damages and a mandatory injunction ordering the defendant to implement a scheme to stop the flooding. Judge Richard Havery QC held that the defendant was not liable in the tort of nuisance but was liable—it was this aspect of his decision that was held to be incorrect by the House of Lords—for the wrong of infringing the claimant's convention rights under the Human Rights Act 1998, s 6. However, he refused a mandatory injunction on the ground that this would require supervision by the

---

[25] [1924] AC 851. See also *Hooper v Rogers* [1975] Ch 43 (damages in lieu of *quia timet* mandatory injunction): D Nolan, 'Preventive Damages' (2016) 132 LQR 68, 72, uses this case as support for his powerful argument that common law damages should sometimes be awarded to cover the cost of preventing a tort.
[26] Above, p 163 n 2.   [27] [1995] 1 WLR 269, at 276–277.
[28] [1975] Ch 408. See also above, pp 221–222.
[29] [1995] 1 WLR 269. In this case there was held to be both a continuing trespass and breach of a restrictive covenant.
[30] [2003] UKHL 66, [2004] 2 AC 42.   [31] [2002] 2 WLR 1000.

court. As regards damages, he held that these should be awarded for both past and future wrongs. The claimant was therefore entitled to the difference between the value his property would have had if rendered non-susceptible to wrongful flooding minus its actual value. As regards the damages for future flooding caused by the future wrongs, these were being awarded in substitution for the mandatory injunction. The judge was satisfied that the defendant would commit the future wrongs because they intended not to carry out works necessary to remedy the flooding. Pressed with the argument that he should follow the common law and refuse equitable damages for the future wrongs, Judge Havery QC said, 'The common law would not afford the claimant just satisfaction. He would have to bring onerous proceedings from time to time to enforce his rights. Nor would he be able to recover any diminution in the value of his property caused by the prospect of future wrongs.'[32] In awarding equitable damages for future wrongs, he also rejected a novel argument that this would be contrary to the jurisprudence on the European Convention on Human Rights.

It is to be noted that Lord Upjohn's much-discussed statement in the classic mandatory injunctions case of *Redland Bricks Ltd v Morris*[33]—that Lord Cairns's Act had nothing to do with the case—plainly seems wrong. Damages could have been awarded in substitution for a mandatory injunction to restore the support to the claimant's land, albeit that on the facts it was arguably preferable to leave the claimant to bring fresh proceedings should a new cause of action arise, since the probability of further landslips and theirlord likely extent were both in doubt, and the claimant could not carry out effective preventive work on his own land.

In respect of the second and third illustrations ((ii) and (iii) above), the normal compensatory aims of putting the claimant into as good a position as if no tort or breach of contract had been committed must of course be modified (and nothing in Lord Wilberforce's speech in *Johnson v Agnew* denies this) to include the aim of putting the claimant into as good a position as if the threatened or continuing tort or breach of contract were not to be committed or continued.

3. Non-compensatory equitable damages?

In all that has been said so far in this chapter, the assumption has been that the equitable damages in question are compensatory. But it is arguable (despite the reasoning to the contrary in *Morris-Garner v One Step (Support) Ltd*[34]) that so-called 'negotiating damages'— that is, damages assessed according to the reasonable price for releasing the defendant from its obligations—are sometimes better analysed as restitutionary rather than compensatory. And while negotiating damages may be awarded at common law, they have mowarded as equitable damages in substitution for an injunction. The question as to whether negotiating damages (whether common law or equitable) are sometimes best analysed as restitutionary is considered in chapter 18 below.

There has been no case in which equitable punitive damages have been awarded. It is conceivable that a tort case might fall within the *Rookes v Barnard*[35] categories permitting

---

[32] ibid, at 1008.
[33] [1970] AC 652. Below, pp 463–464. J Jolowicz, 'Damages in Equity—A Study of Lord Cairns' Act' (1975) 34 CLJ 224, 242–245; P Pettit, 'Lord Cairns' Act in the County Court: A Supplementary Note' (1977) 36 CLJ 369.
[34] [2018] UKSC 20, [2018] 2 WLR 1353.   [35] [1964] AC 1129.

punitive damages and yet only equitable (and not common law) damages are available. But as regards anticipated wrongs it may be thought unattractive to punish a defendant in advance of the wrong having been committed. The most likely possibility for the award of equitable punitive damages is, therefore, for accrued equitable wrongs (such as breach of confidence). This lies outside the realm of torts and breach of contract and is considered in chapter 26 below.

18

Negotiating damages

1. Introduction	321
2. *Morris-Garner v One Step (Support) Ltd*	323
3. The purpose of negotiating damages	324
4. The availability of negotiating damages	328

1. Introduction

'Negotiating damages' are assessed according to the price which, prior to the wrong, the claimant could reasonably have charged the defendant for releasing the defendant from the duty that has been broken. In what is now the leading case of *Morris-Garner v One Step (Support) Ltd*,[1] the view of the Supreme Court was that damages assessed in that way are best labelled 'negotiating damages'.

It is because the Supreme Court has authoritatively ruled that 'negotiating damages' are compensatory that this chapter has been included as the last chapter in this Part (Part 2) on compensation. In the first three editions of this book, the view was taken that these damages are normally best viewed as restitutionary so that the relevant cases were considered in the chapter on restitutionary remedies.

Previously, the label most commonly used to describe 'negotiating damages' was '*Wrotham Park* damages'.[2] This reflected the fact that one of the best known cases in which damages were assessed in this way was *Wrotham Park Estate Ltd v Parkside Homes Ltd*.[3] In that case, houses had been built in breach of a restrictive covenant. Brightman J refused to grant a mandatory injunction ordering the houses to be pulled down because of the social waste that that would have involved. But he did make an award of substantial damages in substitution for the injunction under the judicial power conferred by what was previously Lord Cairns' Act 1858 and is now s 50 of the Senior Courts Act 1981. The important point is that the damages in substitution for an injunction were assessed not by the diminution in value of the claimant's land caused by the breach of covenant (which was nil) but by the price which the claimant could reasonably have demanded for releasing the defendant from the restrictive covenant had the defendant approached the claimant prior to building the houses.

There have been many subsequent cases in which damages (whether in substitution for an injunction under s 50 or not) have been assessed in the same way for a civil wrong, whether a tort or a breach of contract (or the equitable wrong of breach of confidence).[4] Moreover,

---

[1] [2018] UKSC 20, [2018] 2 WLR 1353.
[2] Several other labels have been used to describe these damages including, for example, 'hypothetical release damages' and 'reasonable licence fee' damages.
[3] [1974] 1 WLR 798.
[4] *Bracewell v Appleby* [1975] Ch 408, *Jaggard v Sawyer* [1995] 1 WLR 269, *Severn Trent Water Ltd v Barnes* [2004] EWCA Civ 570, *Field Common Ltd v Elmbridge BC* [2008] EWHC 2079 (Ch), [2009] 1 P & CR 1, *Stadium Capital Holdings (No 2) Ltd v St Marylebone Property Co Plc* [2010] EWCA Civ 952, *Eaton Mansions (Westminster) Ltd v Stinger Compania De Inversion SA* [2013] EWCA Civ 1308, [2014] HLR 4 (all tortious

there were earlier cases in which damages were assessed according to what was considered a reasonable fee for the wrongful use of property (whether real or personal property and including intellectual property).[5] These cases were effectively taking the same approach to the assessment of damages as was subsequently taken in *Wrotham Park*. Although often referred to as 'user damages' or damages applying the 'user principle', they can now all be labelled 'negotiating damages'.

The principal puzzles regarding negotiation damages have revolved around two main linked uncertainties. First, what is the purpose of such damages? This has spawned a large academic literature.[6] Are they compensatory (ie covering the claimant's loss)? Or is it more realistic to regard negotiating damages as restitutionary (ie reversing gains made by the defendant) rather than compensating loss? Or do they support Stevens' thesis—the so-called 'substitutive damages thesis'—that the central award of damages is always to value the right infringed, and compensatory and restitutionary damages are merely dealing with consequential gains and losses if any?[7] Secondly, when can such damages be awarded (ie what is their availability)?

In *Morris-Garner v One Step (Support) Ltd* the Supreme Court sought to answer both those questions in the context of a claim for breach of contract.

---

trespass to land); *Carr-Saunders v Dick McNeil Associates Ltd* [1986] 2 All ER 888, *Tamares (Vincent Square) Ltd v Fairpoint* [2007] EWHC 212, [2007] 1 WLR 2167 (both tort of nuisance by infringement of the right to light); *General Tire Co v Firestone Tyre Co Ltd* [1975] 1 WLR 819, *32Red Plc v WHG (International) Ltd* [2013] EWHC 815 (Ch) (both infringement of intellectual property rights, the former infringement of patent and the latter infringement of trade mark); *Amec Developments Ltd v Jury's Hotel Management (UK) Ltd* (2000) 82 P & CR 286 (breach of restrictive covenant over land); *Experience Hendrix LLC v PPX Enterprises Inc* [2003] EWCA Civ 323, [2003] 1 All ER (Comm) 830 (breach of contractual obligation restricting use of master tapes); *Lane v O'Brien Homes Ltd* [2004] EWHC 303 (breach of collateral contract restricting the development of land); *WWF-World Wide Fund for Nature v World Wide Wrestling Federation* [2006] EWHC 184 (reversed on appeal, [2007] EWCA Civ 286, [2008] 1 WLR 445) (breach of contractual obligation to restrict use of particular initials); *Lunn Poly Ltd v Liverpool and Lancashire Properties Ltd* [2006] EWCA Civ 430, [2006] 2 EGLR 29 (landlord's breach of covenant of quiet enjoyment); *Pell Frishmann Engineering Ltd v Bow Valley Iran Ltd* [2009] UKPC 45, [2011] 1 WLR 2370 (breach of obligations in joint venture); *Vercoe v Rutland Fund Management Ltd* [2010] EWHC 424 (Ch) (breach of obligation to purchase a company jointly); *Van der Garde v Force India Formula One Team Ltd* [2010] EWHC 2373 (QB), at [499]–[559], esp at [505]–[507] (breach of obligation to allow driving time); *Force India Formula One Team Ltd v 1 Malaysia Racing Team Sdh Bhd* [2013] EWCA Civ 780, [2013] RPC 36 (breach of contractual and equitable obligation of confidence); *Primary Group (UK) Ltd v Royal Bank of Scotland* [2014] EWHC 1082, [2014] 2 All ER (Comm) 1121 (breach of contractual obligation of confidence); *MVF 3 APS v Bestnet Europe Ltd* [2016] EWCA Civ 541, [2017] FSR 5 (breach of confidence); *Marathon Asset Management LLP v Seddon* [2017] EWHC 300 (Comm) (breach of contractual, and equitable, obligations of confidence).

[5] *Whitwham v Westminster, Brymbo, Coal & Coke Co* [1896] 2 Ch 538, *Penarth Dock Engineering Co Ltd v Pounds* [1963] 1 Lloyd's Rep 359 (both trespass to land by, respectively, tipping spoil on to the claimant's land and refusing to remove a floating pontoon from the claimant's dock); *Meters Ltd v Metropolitan Gas Meters Ltd* (1911) 28 RPC 157, at 164–165, *Watson, Laidlaw & Co v Pott, Cassels & Williamson* (1914) 31 RPC 104 (both patent infringement); *Strand Electric Engineering Co Ltd v Brisford Entertainments Ltd* [1952] 2 QB 246 (tort of detinue by retaining and using the claimant's theatre equipment); *Seager v Copydex Ltd (No 2)* [1969] 1 WLR 809 (breach of confidence).

[6] Eg, R Sharpe and S Waddams, 'Damages for the Lost Opportunity to Bargain' (1982) 2 OJLS 290; M McInnes, 'Gain, Loss and the User Principle' [2006] RLR 76; A Burrows, 'Are "Damages on the *Wrotham Park* Basis" Compensatory, Restitutionary, or Neither?' in *Contract Damages* (eds D Saidov and R Cunnington, Hart Publishing 2008) 165; C Rotherham, 'The Conceptual Structure of Restitution for Wrongs' [2007] CLJ 172; C Rotherham, '*Wrotham Park* Damages and Account of Profits: Compensation or Restitution?' [2008] LMCLQ 25; C Rotherham, 'Gain-based Relief in Tort after *Attorney-General v Blake*' (2010) 126 LQR 102; K Barker, '"Damages Without Loss": Can Hohfeld Help?' (2014) 34 OJLS 631; K Low, 'The User Principle: Roshomon Effect or Much Ado about Nothing?' (2016) 28 SAcLJ 984; J Edelman, *Gain-Based Damages* (Hart Publishing 2002); R Stevens, *Torts and Rights* (OUP 2007) ch 4; K Barnett, *Accounting for Profit for Breach of Contract* (Hart Publishing 2012).

[7] See R Stevens, *Tort Law and Rights* (OUP 2007) ch 4. We have examined his thesis in depth, albeit to reject it, in ch 3 above.

2. *Morris-Garner v One Step (Support) Ltd*

The claimant, One Step (Support) Ltd, was in the business of providing support for young people leaving care. Karen Morris-Garner, the first defendant, was a 50% shareholder and director of that company and the second defendant, Andrea Morris-Garner, was manager of that company. When both left the company, and the first defendant sold her shares in it, each entered into three-year covenants with the company promising not to compete with it or solicit the company's clients and to keep certain information about the company confidential. The defendants had in fact already set up a competing company (Positive Living Ltd) of which they were the sole shareholders and, after the defendants left One Step, Positive Living started to trade in competition with One Step. Through that trading, the defendants acted in breach of their non-competition and non-solicitation covenants, and the first defendant acted in breach of the confidentiality clause. Positive Living was very successful and was sold by the defendants, some three years after starting trading, for £12.8m. One Step, meanwhile, suffered a significant downturn in its business.

In the claimant's action for breach of contract, it was estimated by the claimant's expert that the loss to the claimant's business (ie the loss of profits) caused by the defendants' breach of the non-competition covenant (and, incidentally, the other covenants) was between £3.4m and £4.6m. But the claimant argued that it was entitled to '*Wrotham Park* damages' with the hypothetical release fee from the covenants being estimated by the claimant's expert as being between £5.6m and £6.3m.

So the claimants were seeking 'negotiating damages' in a situation where compensatory damages assessed in the ordinary way would yield a very substantial sum of damages. And this was because negotiating damages would give them an even higher sum. Why was that? There are several possible reasons. For example, applying a conventional approach, the loss of profits might have been difficult to prove especially given the need to take into account loss of goodwill. But, in any event, negotiating damages may yield more because, at the time just before breach, when it is assumed that the hypothetical bargain would have been struck, it might reasonably have been assumed that the claimant's losses from the competition, or the defendant's gains from being able to compete, would be far higher than they in fact turned out to be so that the reasonable release fee would be higher than loss as conventionally assessed.

While at first instance and in the Court of Appeal the claimant succeeded in its argument that it was entitled to elect for negotiating damages, that argument was unanimously rejected by the Supreme Court. In remitting the assessment of the damages back to the trial judge, it was held that negotiating damages were not here available as an alternative measure of damages albeit that a hypothetical release fee might be used as evidence in calculating the claimant's loss of business.[8]

Lord Reed, with whom Lady Hale, Lord Wilson, and Lord Carnwath agreed, gave the leading judgment. That judgment will therefore be focused on in this chapter. Lord Sumption gave a separate judgment concurring with the result and adopting broadly similar reasoning to Lord Reed. Lord Carnwath gave a separate judgment explaining, inter alia, why he preferred Lord Reed's judgment to that of Lord Sumption.

On our two puzzles, Lord Reed held as follows. The purpose of negotiating damages is to compensate the claimant for a loss. They are not restitutionary and they are not a non-compensatory measure of the value of the right infringed. As regards availability, Lord Reed

---

[8] This distinction between measure and evidence is explained below, p 331.

identified two categories of case in which negotiating damages can be awarded. First, where the damages are being given in substitution for an injunction (or specific performance) under the Supreme Court Act 1981, s 50; and secondly, where the wrong in question constitutes the infringement of a property right or a closely analogous right. On the facts, neither category was in play. Hence negotiating damages could not here be awarded.

The next two sections look in more depth at those two puzzles.

3. The purpose of negotiating damages

Lord Reed expressly or impliedly rejected both a restitutionary analysis—that these damages are really concerned to strip profit—and Robert Stevens' analysis that these damages are not compensatory but are concerned to value the right infringed.

Speaking of negotiating damages for wrongful use of property, Lord Reed said that, although the loss is 'not loss of a conventional kind', 'a compensatory analysis need not be regarded as strained or artificial'.[9] This was because:

> '[T]he person who makes wrongful use of [another's] property prevents the owner from exercising his right to obtain the economic value of the use in question, and should therefore compensate him for the consequent loss.'[10]

Extending this more broadly to cases of breach of contract, such as the breach of a restrictive covenant over land or breach of a contractual right of confidence, Lord Reed said:

> 'The claimant has in substance been deprived of a valuable asset, and his loss can therefore be measured by determining the economic value of the asset in question.'[11]

In viewing the damages as compensatory, we can therefore see that Lord Reed effectively says that the relevant loss is the loss of the right to obtain value or the loss of the value of the right/asset of which the claimant has been deprived. This most directly equates to the 'loss of opportunity to bargain' analysis put forward by Sharpe and Waddams in a famous article in 1982.[12]

Prior to *Morris-Garner*, several commentators, myself included, argued that it was often fictional to regard the claimant as having suffered a loss of bargaining opportunity (or a loss in value of a right) because the claimant would never have agreed to bargain away its rights or at least would not have done so at the reasonable fee fixed.[13] So several of us took the view that, while compensation for a loss of bargaining opportunity was sometimes a realistic analysis of negotiating damages, often it was not and that what the courts were often doing in awarding negotiating damages was stripping away some of the gains made by the defendant rather than compensating the claimant. And reference was made to explicit reasoning in many negotiating damages cases where the courts accepted that they were effecting restitution of gain rather than compensating loss.

For example, in **Strand Electric Engineering Co Ltd v Brisford Entertainments Ltd**,[14] concerned with a claim in the tort of detinue for the retention and use of theatre equipment,

---

[9] [2018] UKSC 20, [2018] 2 WLR 1353, at [30] and [66].   [10] ibid, at [30].
[11] ibid, at [92]. See similarly at [95] point (10): 'Negotiating damages can be awarded for breach of contract where the loss suffered by the claimant is appropriately measured by reference to the economic value of the right which has been breached, considered as an asset.'
[12] R Sharpe and S Waddams, 'Damages for the Lost Opportunity to Bargain' (1982) 2 OJLS 290.
[13] See, eg, the articles by Burrows and Rotherham, and the books by Edelman and Barnett, referred in n 6 above. See also the first three editions of this book.
[14] [1952] 2 QB 246.

and *Penarth Dock Engineering Co Ltd v Pounds*,[15] concerned with trespass to land by a floating pontoon, Lord Denning said that the damages were concerned not with what the claimants had lost but with the benefit the defendants had gained from their wrongful use of the claimant's goods or land. So in the former case, as Denning LJ, he said:

'If a wrongdoer has made use of goods for his own purposes, then he must pay a reasonable hire for them, even though the owner has in fact suffered no loss. It may be that the owner would not have used the goods himself, or that he had a substitute readily available, which he used without extra cost to himself. Nevertheless the owner is entitled to a reasonable hire ... The claim for a hiring charge is therefore not based on the loss to the plaintiff, but on the fact that the defendant has used the goods for his own purposes. It is an action against him because he has had the benefit of the goods. It resembles therefore, an action for restitution, rather than an action of tort.'[16]

In the latter case, sitting as a single judge in the Queen's Bench Division, Lord Denning said:

'... the Penarth company would not seem to have suffered any damage to speak of. They have not to pay any extra rent to the British Transport Commission. The dock is no use to them: they would not have made any money out of it. But ... in a case of this kind ... the test of the measure of damages is not what the plaintiffs have lost, but what benefit the defendant has obtained by having the use of the berth.'[17]

Damages were assessed at £32 5s a week. This was apparently based on the evidence that £37 10s a week was what the defendants would have had to pay for an alternative dock of that kind. Why there was some reduction is not made clear but perhaps the claimants' berth was inferior to the alternatives, or involved the defendants in some expense which the alternatives did not, so that to award the full £37 10s would have gone beyond reversing the defendants' benefit.

In *Ministry of Defence v Ashman*,[18] in which a tenant had wrongfully ignored a notice to quit RAF accommodation because she and her children had nowhere else to go, a majority of the Court of Appeal (Kennedy and Hoffmann LJJ) accepted that the claimant landlord was entitled to restitutionary damages for the trespass. The *Penarth Dock* case was relied on and it was held that the damages should be assessed according to what it would have cost the tenant to rent alternative local authority accommodation had any been available. Hoffmann LJ said:

'A person entitled to possession of land can make a claim against a person who has been in occupation without his consent on two alternative bases. The first is for the loss which he has suffered in consequence of the defendant's trespass. This is the normal measure of damages in the law of tort. The second is the value of the benefit which the occupier has received. This is a claim for restitution. The two bases of claim are mutually exclusive and the plaintiff must elect before judgment which of them he wishes to pursue. These principles are not only fair but, as

---

[15] [1963] 1 Lloyd's Rep 359. See also *Bracewell v Appleby* [1975] Ch 408 (in assessing damages in lieu of an injunction, to restrain trespass over land to reach the defendant's newly-built house, Graham J took into account, in fixing a fair sum for having granted a right of way, the profits the defendant had made from the house: £2,000 damages form a notional profit of £5,000 were awarded).
[16] [1952] 2 QB 246, at 254–255. The majority, Somervell and Romer LJJ, overall preferred to fit their decision within the normal conception of damages compensating the claimant's loss.
[17] [1963] 1 Lloyd's Rep 359, at 361–362.
[18] (1993) 66 P & CR 195. See also *Ministry of Defence v Thompson* [1993] 2 EGLR 107; *Gondall v Dillon Newsagents Ltd* [2001] RLR 221; *Ramzan v Brookwide Ltd* [2011] EWCA Civ 985, [2012] 1 All ER 903, at [67]. See, generally, E Cooke, 'Trespass, Mesne Profits and Restitution' (1994) 110 LQR 420. Cf *Inverugie Investments Ltd v Hackett* [1995] 1 WLR 713.

Kennedy LJ demonstrated, also well established by authority. It is true that in earlier cases it has not been expressly stated that a claim for mesne profit for trespass can be a claim for restitution. Nowadays I do not see why we should not call a spade a spade. In this case the Ministry of Defence elected for the restitutionary remedy.'[19]

In *Attorney-General v Blake*[20] the House of Lords laid down that an account of profits can be awarded, in exceptional circumstances, to strip a contract-breaker of profits. An account of profits is indisputably a restitutionary, not a compensatory, remedy but the important point here is that the reasoning of Lord Nicholls appeared to support a restitutionary analysis of tort 'user damages' and the damages awarded in *Wrotham Park*, which were used as a bridge to the account of profits in that case.

Following on from *Blake*, it was accepted that an award of 'negotiating damages' could be made on a restitutionary basis in *Experience Hendrix LLC v PPX Enterprises Inc*.[21] There had been a settlement in 1973 of a dispute between the rock star Jimi Hendrix and the defendant record company. By the terms of that contractual settlement, it was agreed that certain master tapes could be used for recording purposes by the defendant but that the rest should be delivered up to Jimi Hendrix. In breach of that contract, the defendant licensed the use of master tapes that should have been delivered up. The claimant, the estate of Jimi Hendrix, sought damages (or an account of profits) for that breach of contract. The claimant was held entitled to damages based not on compensating the claimant's loss but on what was a reasonable sum taking into account the gains made by the defendant from its use of the forbidden master tapes. Peter Gibson LJ's judgment, taking a restitutionary analysis, was particularly clear. He said:

'In my judgment, because (1) there has been a deliberate breach by PPX of its contractual obligations for its own reward, (2) the claimant would have difficulty in establishing financial loss therefrom, and (3) the claimant has a legitimate interest in preventing PPX's profit-making activity carried out in breach of PPX's contractual obligations, the present case is a suitable one (as envisaged by Lord Nicholls) in which damages for breach of contract may be measured by the benefits gained by the wrongdoer from the breach. To avoid injustice I would require PPX to make a reasonable payment in respect of the benefit it has gained.'[22]

But it would appear that Lord Reed has now said that all that is incorrect. Certainly, in relation to breach of contract he explicitly rejected the idea that, rather than being compensatory, negotiating damages are restitutionary, designed to strip the defendant of some of the wrongdoer's gains. In his Lordship's view, it is incorrect to think that there is a sliding scale by which an account of profits and negotiating damages are both gain-based with negotiating damages stripping away a proportion, rather than the whole, of the defendant's profits depending on, for example, whether the breach of contract was deliberate or whether the claimant had a 'legitimate interest' in preventing the profit-making activity.[23] This is a

---

[19] (1993) 66 P & CR 195, at 200–201.   [20] [2001] 1 AC 268. See below, pp 356–359.
[21] [2003] EWCA Civ 323, [2003] 1 All ER (Comm) 830. For a helpful case-note, see M Graham, 'Restitutionary Damages: The Anvil Struck' (2004) 120 LQR 26.
[22] [2003] EWCA Civ 323, [2003] 1 All ER (Comm) 830, at [58]. See also *Marathon Asset Management LLP v Seddon* [2017] EWHC 300 (Comm), [2017] ICR 791, in which Leggatt J, in a tightly reasoned judgment in which he surveyed most of the relevant authorities, concluded that a compensatory or a restitutionary analysis might be realistic depending on the facts. The case concerned breach of a contractual (or equitable) duty of confidence by electronically copying some files. The claimants were denied substantial damages and were instead awarded nominal damages. The claimant had not suffered a loss (because, for example, it would not have bargained away the right in question) and the defendant had not made a gain (because it had not used the electronic files and had certainly made no profits, nor would make any profits, from so doing). Importantly, Leggatt J regarded many of the past cases on 'negotiating damages' as having awarded restitutionary damages stripping a part of the defendant's profits. But on the facts of the instant case, 'negotiating damages' should not be awarded as they would neither compensate for loss nor strip gain.
[23] [2018] UKSC 20, [2018] 2 WLR 1353, at [90].

denial at the highest level that negotiating damages are restitutionary at least in the sense, which is the most realistic alternative to compensation, that they are concerned to strip away a proportion of the gain obtained by the wrongdoer.[24]

It follows from this that the fact that the breach of the no-competition clause in *Morris-Garner* was cynical and one by which the defendant made large profits, which they would now keep, was irrelevant. According to the Supreme Court, we are concerned with the claimant's loss not the defendant's cynically acquired gains.

However, it should be clarified, not least to balance the picture of authority that has so far been given, that Lord Reed is not the first highly respected judge to favour a compensatory analysis and to reject a restitutionary analysis. For example, in *Jaggard v Sawyer*[25] where the facts concerned a continuing trespass to land and breach of covenant by using the claimant's road as a right of way, Sir Thomas Bingham MR and Millett LJ were presented with obiter dicta of Steyn LJ who had said the following in *Surrey CC v Bredero Homes Ltd*: 'The object of the award in the *Wrotham Park* case was not to compensate the plaintiff for financial injury, but to deprive the defendants of an unjustly acquired gain.'[26] Sir Thomas Bingham MR and Millett LJ explicitly rejected that analysis. They said that *Wrotham Park* damages were compensatory not restitutionary and that the relevance of the reference to the profits made by the defendant was only that it helped to fix the reasonable fee that the claimant would reasonably have charged for the release of the defendant from its obligation. Millett LJ said:

> '[T]here is no reason why compensatory damages for future trespasses and continuing breaches of covenant should not reflect the value of the rights which she has lost, or why such damages should not be measured by the amount which she could reasonably have expected to receive for their release.'[27]

It should also be pointed out that in *Inverugie Investments Ltd v Hackett*[28] and *Pell Frischmann Engineering Ltd v Bow Valley Iran Ltd*[29] the courts made awards of negotiating damages that exceeded the profits actually made by the defendant. In the former case, the trespassing defendants had been running a hotel business on the land at a loss so that no profits at all were made; while, in the latter case, the damages awarded far exceeded the profits the defendant had made from the breach of its contractual obligations. There may be thought to be some difficulty in explaining those decisions on a restitutionary analysis.[30] In contrast, there is no difficulty in explaining them if one regards the claimant as having lost the release fee—lost the opportunity to bargain away the right infringed—that could

---

[24] Although perhaps 'clutching at straws', there are a few passages that might be interpreted as indicating that Lord Reed has not entirely shut the door on a restitutionary analysis. So his emphasis, at [30] and [92], on 'taking something for nothing' might be thought to indicate that it is important that the defendant has gained rather than that the claimant has lost. Again, at [79], Lord Reed accepted that in the wrongful use cases one might say that negotiating damages have been measured by the benefit gained by the wrongdoer provided the benefit was taken to be the objective value of the wrongful use: but, he said, 'The courts did not ... adopt a benefits-based approach, but conceived of the awards as compensating for loss.' Note that J Edelman, *Gain-Based Damages* (Hart Publishing 2002) has argued that 'restitutionary damages'—based on reversing a transfer of value from the claimant to the defendant—are to be distinguished from another type of 'gain-based damages' which comprise a monetary award (an account of profits) stripping the wrongdoer of profits made by the wrong which he terms 'disgorgement damages'. See below, pp 337–338.
[25] [1995] 1 WLR 269. See above, p 222. See also, eg, *Severn Trent Water Ltd v Barnes* [2004] EWCA Civ 570. See above, p 222 n 222.
[26] [1993] 1 WLR 1361, at 1369.   [27] [1995] 1 WLR 269, at 291.   [28] [1995] 1 WLR 713.
[29] [2009] UKPC 45, [2010] BLR 73.
[30] K Barnett, *Accounting for Profits for Breach of Contract* (Hart Publishing 2012) 158 argues that *Inverugie* can be explained as an 'expense saved' restitutionary measure. But is that correct? The claimant would not have sold its right (and, if so, a compensatory analysis would be straightforward); and there was nothing to indicate that equivalent property was available from a third party.

reasonably have been charged just prior to the commission of the wrong. At that time, the parties may well have reasonably over-estimated the likely profits that the defendant might make from the breach.[31]

Turning to principle, one might say, in favour of a compensatory analysis, that if one is unwilling to recognise that there has been a loss, where the claimant would not have been willing to release the rights, one appears to reach the paradoxical result that the more the claimant values the right infringed—such that it would never have been willing to release that right at a reasonable or indeed any price—the less one would say the claimant has lost (and the lower the compensatory damages would become).

It might also perhaps be argued that it is irrelevant whether or not in reality the claimant would have bargained away its rights. The fact that it could have done so and that it was reasonable to have done so is sufficient. After all, if we take the analogy of the permanent deprivation of the claimant's property—let's say that the claimant's goods have been stolen and disposed of and the claimant brings an action in the tort of conversion—we would assess damages according to the market value of the goods irrespective of whether it is realistic to think that the claimant would ever have sold the goods or is intending to replace them.

An alternative possible way of meeting the argument that a loss of bargaining opportunity is often fictional is to think of the counter-factual in mind when one is considering the claimant's loss. The relevant counter-factual that we apply in a conventional assessment of compensatory damages is the position the claimant would have been in *if the defendant had not carried out the relevant wrongful conduct*. But plainly that counter-factual is unrealistic in the sense that the defendant has precisely carried out that wrongful conduct. So in relation to negotiating damages, one might say that all one is doing is positing a different counter-factual, based on the claimant's opportunity to bargain away its legal rights, and it is equally irrelevant whether or not that counter-factual is realistic.

While it is disappointing that the Supreme Court has rejected a restitutionary analysis of negotiating damages—which on authority and in principle can be seen as a useful alternative measure of damages in many situations—it is fair to say that there are plausible arguments to justify the Supreme Court's compensatory analysis based in effect on a loss of bargaining opportunity.

4. The availability of negotiating damages

In *Morris-Garner v One Step*, Lord Reed can be interpreted as having identified two wide-ranging categories of case in which negotiating damages have been awarded and are appropriate.

The first is where 'equitable damages' are being given in substitution for an injunction or specific performance as in the *Wrotham Park* case itself. Lord Reed argued that the refusal to grant specific relief produces the same effect as if the claimant had given up its right so that measuring damages by what the claimant would have reasonably charged for giving up that right is particularly apt:

---

[31] This is not to deny that the conduct to which the payment is being related is the precise conduct of the defendant that was wrongful. This is an important point in meeting the objection that the remedy might not otherwise meet the wrong in question. One is thinking about permission for the defendant to commit the particular infringement that has occurred, not some hypothetical infringement.

'The rationale is that, since the withholding of specific relief has the same practical effect as requiring the claimant to permit the infringement of his rights, his loss can be measured by reference to the economic value of such permission.'[32]

However, all compensatory damages, whether common law or equitable, are in one sense a monetary substitute for the rights infringed and it is therefore not immediately obvious why one should be carving out negotiating damages as being especially apt where substituting for specific relief.

The approach linking negotiating damages to damages in substitution for specific relief may also mean, oddly, that the availability of negotiating damages may turn on the timing of the commencement of proceedings. Say, on the facts of this case, One Step had commenced proceedings seeking an injunction to restrain the breach of contract prior to the expiry of the three-year covenants. Even if the case came to court after the expiry of the three-year period, so that an injunction would not be granted because too late to have any effect, it would appear that negotiating damages could have been awarded in substitution for the injunction because, at the commencement of the proceedings, there was jurisdiction to grant an injunction. Indeed, although Lord Reed indicated some doubts about this,[33] Lord Walker in *Pell Frischmann Engineering Co Ltd v Bow Valley Iran Ltd*[34] controversially said that the court would have jurisdiction to award damages in substitution for an injunction—and hence to award negotiating damages—even if an injunction had not been sought.

It therefore seems misconceived to regard negotiating damages as more appropriate *just because* the damages are equitable rather than common law. However, although not articulated in this way by Lord Reed, there is a powerful argument that where equitable damages are being given as compensatory damages for a future or anticipated wrong, rather than for a wrong that has already been committed, negotiating damages, in contrast to compensatory damages assessed in the normal way, provide a very helpful technique for avoiding the need to speculate as to the future. Trying to put the claimant into as a good a position as it would have been in had a future or anticipated wrong not occurred is doubly speculative: not only are the losses all in the future but the actual wrong in question is in the future. In contrast, it may be thought much easier to assess a reasonable release fee on the basis that there would be no future or anticipated wrong.

But, on the facts of *Morris-Garner*, this first category—whether or not narrowed in the way just explained—was not in play. The damages were common law not equitable, and the wrong was in the past not the future. Plainly therefore the facts fell outside Lord Reed's first category.

The second category of case identified by Lord Reed comprises what, for shorthand (although his Lordship did not use this terminology) can be labelled 'interference with proprietary rights and closely analogous rights'. This covers proprietary and closely analogous rights whether created by operation of law or by contract. Lord Reed's judgment indicated that, prior to their more widespread use in breach of contract cases after *Attorney-General v Blake*, the main application of negotiating damages was in the following three types of case: wrongful use of another's real or personal property (the 'user' cases in tort); wrongful interference with intellectual property rights, whether by a tort or by the equitable wrong of breach of confidence; and breach of a restrictive covenant over land, as in *Wrotham Park* itself (although Lord Reed primarily saw the damages in the *Wrotham Park* case as being justified because they were awarded in substitution for an injunction under the first

---

[32] [2018] UKSC 20, [2018] 2 WLR 1353, at [95] point (4). [33] ibid, at [45].
[34] [2009] UKPC 45, [2011] 1 WLR 2370. See above, p 316.

category considered above). Lord Reed appeared to regard those three types of case as being relatively stable and defensible but that that stability had been undermined by the reasoning in *Attorney-General v Blake*: 'in *Blake* the wider availability of such awards was signalled, but the seeds of uncertainty were sown.'[35] Although the decision of the House of Lords in that case was to the effect that, very exceptionally, an account of profits can be awarded for a breach of contract so as to strip away the profits made by the contract-breaker, Lord Reed interpreted the reasoning of Lord Nicholls as having subsequently led, unacceptably, to common law negotiating damages being freely available for breach of contract. In that respect, while not challenging the decision as to the account of profits, his Lordship appeared to wish, in respect of common law negotiating damages, to turn the clock largely back to the position prior to *Attorney-General v Blake*. To put the point another way, it would appear that Lord Reed wanted to put an end to negotiating damages being used as a sort of discretionary jackpot which claimants could choose in most breach of contract cases.[36]

A central question is whether a primary focus on proprietary rights can be justified in principle. True it is that they may be said to have a market value and can be bought and sold. However, the same can be said of all assignable contractual rights. This difficulty of drawing a sharp line around proprietary rights perhaps explains why Lord Reed went on to include closely analogous rights. Hence he envisaged that such damages were appropriate provided 'the breach of contract results in the loss of a valuable asset created or protected by the right which was infringed';[37] or, expressed in a slightly different way, provided 'the contractual right is of such a kind that its breach can result in an identifiable loss equivalent to the economic value of the right, considered as an asset, even in the absence of any pecuniary losses which are measurable in the ordinary way'.[38]

Lord Reed used that reasoning to justify the award of negotiating damages in, for example, the *Experience Hendrix* case where, as we have seen, the defendant in breach of contract had licensed the use of certain master tapes which were in its possession. Lord Reed also indicated that the award of negotiating damages in *Pell Frischmann Engineering Co Ltd v Bow Valley Iran Ltd* might be justified on this basis because the relevant contractual right in a joint venture agreement—failing to afford the claimant the right to participate in a business opportunity—was 'treated ... as a commercially valuable asset, of which the claimant had been effectively deprived'.[39]

However, the limits of this idea become problematic. If *Pell Frischmann* was correctly decided, why could one not say on the facts of the *One Step* case that the purpose of the non-competition covenant was to protect the claimant against the loss of business profit, including goodwill, and hence to protect against 'the loss of a valuable asset ... protected by the right which was infringed'? Indeed if one just focused on the goodwill, surely one could have said that the no-competition clause was designed to protect that valuable asset. Again, why could one not say that the non-competition covenant was a 'contractual right of such a kind that its breach could result in identifiable loss equivalent to the economic value of the right'? Let us assume, for example, that, contrary to the facts, the claimant could not easily prove loss caused by the defendant's competition (not least if the loss was mainly loss of goodwill): why could it not instead focus on the economic value of the non-competition right, considered as an asset, as fixed by negotiating damages? Yet Lord Reed held that this kind of right fell on the wrong side of the line for an award of negotiating damages. What

---

[35] [2018] UKSC 20, [2018] 2 WLR 1353, at [48].
[36] See the reference to 'jackpot damages' in this context in *Marathon Asset Management LLP v Seddon* [2017] EWHC 300 (Comm), at [282].
[37] [2018] UKSC 20, [2018] 2 WLR 1353, at [92].   [38] ibid, at [93].   [39] ibid, at [83].

Lord Reed appears to have had in mind is the contractual creation of an asset or proprietary right distinct from the contractual right itself but, if so, it is not clear how one can justify that distinction in principle. Certainly this borderline has a 'fuzzy' edge which is likely to require fine-tuning in future cases.

So, in summary on this second category, it is very hard to see why, applying the explanatory logic of Lord Reed's reasoning, negotiating damages should not always be available where the right in question protects an economic rather than a personal right and why, indeed, negotiating damages were not available on the facts of *One Step* itself. The Supreme Court has sought to draw a distinction between some economic rights (those that are or are close to proprietary rights) and others. Ultimately that line-drawing appears to be based more on pragmatism than principle and to rest on a desire not to allow negotiating damages to be available at the claimant's election for every breach of contract. But it is hard to understand where the precise line is being drawn.

It is noteworthy that, in deciding on the availability of negotiating damages, Lord Reed found no role for the inadequacy of compensatory damages assessed in the conventional way. But one wonders whether this might be a helpful concept (even accepting Lord Reed's compensatory analysis of negotiating damages) where inadequacy refers to where the claimant may have difficulty in proving economic loss or where the claimant has a non-financial interest in upholding the right infringed that would not be reflected in a conventional award of damages.[40] The latter may particularly be in play where the claimant is barred from directly recovering 'mental distress' because the claimant is not a human person but is a company or a public authority. So, for example, in *Wrotham Park*, ordinary damages based simply on the diminution of value of the claimant's land were inadequate because they did not reflect the claimant's environmental interest in maintaining the land as it was without the buildings. It should be noted that this ties in with the first of Lord Sumption's three categories of case[41] where negotiating damages may be awarded, namely where the claimant has an 'interest extending beyond financial reparation'.

A final wrinkle with Lord Reed's judgment is that, as indicated above, he accepted—and Lord Sumption made a lot of this point in his judgment—that a reasonable release fee could be used by the judge in this case as evidence in assessing the claimant's loss of profit. In other words, a reasonable release fee could be used—and it would appear can always be used by a judge if thought helpful—not as an alternative measure to the conventional measure of compensation but as an evidential technique or tool, as Lord Sumption expressed it, in applying the conventional measure. This distinction between evidential tool and measure is not straightforward but, in practice, what it means is that a claimant by using the reasonable release fee evidence should not knowingly be put in a better position than the conventional measure would dictate. Therefore, in the *One Step* case, the claimant could not recover more than the loss of profit, known to have been suffered, by claiming a higher reasonable release fee. One sees here therefore a parallel with the relationship between the expectation measure and reliance loss.[42] In *One Step* the claimant had precisely sought negotiating damages as an alternative measure, not as an evidential tool in assessing loss of profit, so that it was claiming a higher sum as negotiating damages than the loss of profit applying a conventional measure. It was that which was impermissible.

---

[40] For this approach, in the context of deciding whether an account of profits should be awarded for breach of contract, see below, pp 356–359.

[41] His other two categories were 'damages in lieu of an injunction' and where the 'notional release fee is [evidence of the claimant's] pecuniary loss': [2018] UKSC 20, [2018] 2 WLR 1353, at [110]–[123].

[42] See above, ch 6.

Finally, it is of interest that in *Turf Club Auto Emporium Pte Ltd v Yeo Boong Hua*[43] the highest Singaporean court, the Singapore Court of Appeal, has also recently been grappling with the purpose and justification of '*Wrotham Park* damages' in the context of the breach of a settlement agreement of a commercial dispute. While agreeing with the Supreme Court that the purpose of those damages is compensatory not restitutionary, the Singaporean Court of Appeal was strongly critical of Lord Reed's approach to the availability of such damages and regarded the 'property or analogous rights' category as too uncertain. The Singaporean Court of Appeal's preference was, in part,[44] to focus on there being a 'remedial lacuna', which is similar to the above suggestion that the inadequacy of normal compensatory damages might be of help.

---

[43] [2018] SGCA 44.

[44] Two other criteria for the availability of '*Wrotham Park* damages' were laid down in addition to there being a 'remedial lacuna': (i) that, in general, there has been the breach of a negative, not a positive, covenant (but it is hard to see the force of this); and (ii) that the hypothetical bargain would not be illegal.

PART THREE

RESTITUTION AND PUNISHMENT

19

Restitutionary remedies (for torts and breach of contract)

1. Introduction	335
2. Restitution for torts	338
3. Restitution for breach of contract	352

1. Introduction

(1) Restitution for wrongs

In this book we are concerned with only a part of the law of restitution, namely restitutionary remedies—that is, remedies reversing gains—for a tort or breach of contract (or, in chapter 26, for an equitable wrong). We are, in other words, concerned with restitution for wrongs and not restitution of an unjust enrichment.[1]

Where the restitution is not based on a wrong, the claimant seeking restitution must establish that the defendant has been unjustly enriched 'at the claimant's expense' (and 'at the claimant's expense' means that there must have been a transfer of value from the claimant to the defendant). The claimant's payment of money, or rendering of services, to the defendant by mistake or under duress, or subject to a condition being fulfilled that has not been, are examples of the general cause of action of unjust enrichment which, subject to defences, will trigger restitution. But where there has been a wrongful enrichment, the law of restitution is concerned with the wrong as the cause of action not unjust enrichment. Hence the central distinction drawn in the law of restitution between restitution for wrongs and restitution of an unjust enrichment. In this chapter, we are solely concerned with restitution for wrongs where the wrong is a tort or breach of contract.[2]

---

[1] For the law of restitution, incorporating both restitution of an unjust enrichment and restitution for wrongs, see, generally, P Birks, *An Introduction to the Law of Restitution* (rev edn, Clarendon Press 1989); A Burrows, *The Law of Restitution* (3rd edn, OUP 2011); G Virgo, *The Principles of the Law of Restitution* (3rd edn, OUP 2016). For the law of unjust enrichment, see *Goff and Jones on the Law of Unjust Enrichment* (eds C Mitchell, P Mitchell, and S Watterson, 9th edn, Sweet & Maxwell 2016); P Birks, *Unjust Enrichment* (2nd edn, OUP 2004); A Burrows, *A Restatement of the English Law of Unjust Enrichment* (OUP 2012); J Edelman and E Bant, *Unjust Enrichment* (2nd edn, Hart Publishing 2016).

[2] Apart from the relevant chapters in the works cited in the previous note, see generally I Jackman, 'Restitution for Wrongs' [1989] CLJ 302; P Birks, 'Civil Wrongs: A New World' (*Butterworths Lectures 1990-91*, Butterworths 1992); Law Commission, *Aggravated, Exemplary and Restitutionary Damages* (1997) Report No 247 Pt III; J Edelman, *Gain-Based Damages* (Hart Publishing 2002); C Rotheram, 'The Conceptual Structure of Restitution for Wrongs' [2007] CLJ 172. For discussion of the problems of multiple defendants and multiple claimants in respect of restitution for wrongs, see A Burrows, 'Reforming Non-Compensatory Damages' in *The Search for Principle* (eds W Swadling and G Jones, OUP 1999) 295, 307-310. For a comparative examination of 'restitution for wrongs' across the world, see *Disgorgement of Profits: Gain-Based Remedies throughout the World* (eds E Hondius and A Janssen, Springer 2015).

As will become apparent, the main restitutionary remedies in issue in this chapter are an award of money in an action for money had and received and an account of profits.[3] In the light of *Morris-Garner v One Step (Support) Ltd*,[4] and contrary to the approach taken in previous editions of this book, 'negotiating damages' now find no place in this chapter. Although in the past it has been argued, both by commentators and judges, that awards of 'negotiating damages' (previously referred to as '*Wrotham Park* damages' and including damages based on the 'user principle') were often restitutionary as being concerned to strip a proportion of profits made by the wrongdoer, that restitutionary analysis has been rejected by the Supreme Court in *Morris-Garner*. We have explored this issue in depth in chapter 18 where there was full reference to the main cases supporting a restitutionary analysis. It is the view of this author that, despite what was said in the Supreme Court in *Morris-Garner*, a restitutionary analysis of many of the 'negotiating damages' cases remains convincing. If that is correct, 'negotiating damages' as a restitutionary remedy, with the main relevant cases being those set out in the last chapter as adopting a 'restitutionary analysis',[5] should be seen alongside the restitutionary remedies in this chapter. In particular, those damages would form a less extreme profit-stripping remedy (stripping a fair percentage of profits wrongfully made) alongside the remedies stripping all profits examined in this chapter.

(2) Alternative analysis

What complicates this chapter's concern solely with restitution for wrongs (whether by a tort or breach of contract) is that in some situations where a claim for restitution could be based on a tort or breach of contract, there is an alternative claim that does not rely on the wrong and rather is based on the cause of action of unjust enrichment. This 'alternative analysis' is best understood by reference to an example. Say the defendant has induced the claimant to give her £25 by a deliberate misrepresentation of fact. Irrespective of establishing the tort of deceit, and then going on to consider whether the law is willing to strip gains made by the tort of deceit, the claimant has an independent good reason for a restitutionary remedy based on an unjust enrichment; namely he has paid £25 to the defendant under an induced mistake of fact which taints the validity of the transfer of value. The fact that the defendant has deliberately lied causing the claimant loss is irrelevant to that.

It follows that, where a wrong does result in an unjust enrichment at the expense of the claimant, the fact that there may be some restriction, preventing restitutionary remedies based on the wrong, will not necessarily rule out restitutionary remedies for the cause of action of unjust enrichment, and vice versa. It also follows that, where attention is being focused solely on restitution for wrongs as in this chapter, some care must be taken not to include cases based instead on the cause of action of unjust enrichment.

(3) The terminology of disgorgement in preference to restitution?

We have explained that this book is concerned with what has been labelled 'restitution for wrongs' as opposed to restitution of an unjust enrichment at the expense of the claimant (where 'at the expense of the claimant' means that there has been a transfer of value by the

---

[3] For (pre-judgment) interest on restitutionary remedies, see A Burrows, *The Law of Restitution* (3rd edn, OUP 2011) 21–25 (although that must now be read in the light of *Prudential Assurance Co Ltd v HMRC* [2018] UKSC 39, [2018] 3 WLR 652). For limitation periods for restitution for torts or breach of contract, see pp 703–705 of the same title.
[4] [2018] UKSC 20, [2018] 2 WLR 1353.   [5] Above, pp 324–326.

claimant to the defendant). Terminologically, it is possible to sharpen the divide between the two by using the term 'disgorgement' instead of restitution where one is concerned with a gain-based remedy for a wrong.[6] In other words, it is arguable that restitution is the more natural terminology for 'giving back' to the claimant the value transferred by the claimant to the defendant whereas, in the context of restitution for wrongs, one is concerned not with a giving back of value transferred but rather with a 'giving up' of profits made by committing a wrong to the claimant.

It is clear, however, that restitution can be used in the wider sense of a giving up of benefits as well as a giving back of benefits; conversely disgorgement can be used to refer to the giving back, as well as the giving up, of benefits. After some hesitation, it has therefore been decided to maintain the terminology previously used in this book of restitution for wrongs rather than switching to disgorgement for wrongs.

However, it is important to stress that the view here being taken is that, in the context of restitution for wrongs, restitution and disgorgement are synonymous so that nothing substantive should turn on the terminology preferred.

(4) Edelman's thesis

James Edelman in his excellent book *Gain-Based Damages*[7] put forward the novel thesis that so-called restitution for wrongs in fact embodies two different remedial gain-based measures which should be kept distinct. The first is the reversal of a wrongful transfer of value from a claimant to a defendant. He terms this measure 'restitutionary damages'. The second is the stripping away of profits made by the defendant committing a wrong to the claimant. He calls this measure 'disgorgement damages'. The importance of this distinction, according to Edelman, is that the former rests on corrective justice, is analogous to unjust enrichment, is relatively uncontroversial, and should be available for every type of wrong. The latter, in contrast, is designed to deter a wrong where compensatory damages are inadequate to do so. Disgorgement damages are, and should therefore be, restricted to two main circumstances. First, where a wrong is committed cynically with a view to making material gain and the profit made exceeds the compensation payable; and, secondly, for breach of fiduciary duty (an equitable wrong) in order to protect the institution of trust inherent in the fiduciary relationship.

In previous editions of this book, Edelman's distinction was explored in some depth, albeit to question its validity.[8] One of the points made was that it was hard to reconcile that distinction with the law laid down in the cases so that, in particular, 'negotiating damages' were not standardly available for civil wrongs. In the light of the rejection of a restitutionary/gains-based analysis of negotiating damages by the Supreme Court in *Morris-Garner v One Step (Support) Ltd*,[9] the clash between Edelman's thesis and the present law is even more clear-cut than it was before.

Another point is that, despite the characteristic power of Edelman's reasoning, it is far from clear that, in the context of the gain having been made by a wrong, anything of importance turns (or should turn) on whether the gain made by the wrong represents a transfer of value from the claimant or not. Put another way, there are two separate causes

---

[6] This was the preferred approach of L Smith, 'The Province of the Law of Restitution' (1992) 21 Can BR 672.
[7] (Hart Publishing 2002).
[8] See the 3rd edition at pp 374–375. Edelman has carried through his distinction into the latest edition of J Edelman, *McGregor on Damages* (20th edn, Sweet & Maxwell 2018).
[9] [2018] UKSC 20, [2018] 2 WLR 1353. See above, ch 18.

of action—the wrong and the unjust enrichment—and one cannot add them together to increase the force of the claim. In line with this criticism, it is submitted that the best 'restitutionary' analysis of negotiating damages—albeit, as we have seen, rejected by the Supreme Court in *Morris-Garner v One Step (Support) Ltd* which has preferred a compensatory approach—is that they have often been concerned to strip a proportion of the profits made by the wrongdoer.[10] Put another way, using Edelman's terminology, we are only ever concerned with 'disgorgement damages' and not 'restitutionary damages'.

A final linked point is that, where the cause of action is a wrong, in contrast to unjust enrichment, compensation is a natural and uncontroversial measure of recovery. The courts will naturally gravitate towards any possible compensatory analysis of the remedial response to a wrong. In this respect, a difficulty with Edelman's thesis is that, where there has been a transfer of value from the claimant to the defendant, this will commonly mean that there has been a loss to the claimant and, in the context of wrongs, that loss will naturally be seen as triggering a compensatory remedy. In other words, a restitutionary analysis will often be no more realistic than a compensatory analysis.[11]

2. Restitution for torts[12]

(1) Introduction

We are here concerned with remedies that reverse gains because the defendant has acquired them by committing a tort against the claimant. This is often what is meant by 'waiver of tort', that is, the claimant sues on the tort but seeks a restitutionary remedy rather than usual compensatory damages. But it can be argued that 'waiver of tort' also refers to where the claimant ignores the tort, and bases its claim for restitution on the cause of action of unjust enrichment. It should further be realised that the judicial usage of 'waiver of tort' appears to be confined to where the restitutionary remedy in issue is the award of money had and received (or one of the other 'quasi-contractual' remedies, like a *quantum meruit*) rather than being an account of profits. The term 'waiver of tort' is therefore ambiguous and unhelpful and should be avoided wherever possible.

It is also convenient to stress at this initial stage that rescission of a contract for misrepresentation where enrichments gained are reversed[13] is better viewed as based on unjust enrichment, rather than a tort; that is, the reason for the remedy is essentially that the benefit has been rendered non-voluntarily because of induced mistake.[14] This non-wrong

---

[10] See above, ch 18.

[11] A plausible response to this might be that, often, a transfer of value equates only to an objective loss and not a loss that this claimant has itself suffered because, for example, it would never have sold its property or services; and that at least normally in relation to compensatory damages one is concerned with the loss to the particular claimant. One might add that, in contrast, the standard approach to benefits in the law of unjust enrichment is to take, as a starting point, an objective approach, which might then be modified by 'subjective devaluation': but that in the context of wrongs, a wrongdoer ought not to be permitted to deny that it is benefited by the objective benefit. The plausibility of this response may turn on whether it is coherent to approach benefits more objectively than loss. For discussion of the distinction between the claimant's loss and the defendant's gain in the context of unjust enrichment, see A Burrows, *The Law of Restitution* (OUP 2011) 64–65.

[12] See generally L Teller, 'Restitution as an Alternative Remedy for a Tort' (1956) 2 NY Law Forum 40; K York, 'Extension of Restitutional Remedies in the Tort Field' (1957) 4 UCLALR 499; J Hodder, 'Profiting from Tortious Use of Property: A Reply to the Lost Bargain Theory' (1984) 42 UT Fac LR 105; J Beatson, *The Use and Abuse of Unjust Enrichment* (Clarendon Press 1991) 206–243.

[13] Rescission may simply be concerned to allow escape from a contract. For the same reasons as those in the text such rescission is best viewed as not being a remedy for a tort and hence as being outside this book's scope.

[14] P Birks, *An Introduction to the Law of Restitution* (rev edn, Clarendon Press 1989) 167–171; A Burrows, *The Law of Restitution* (3rd edn, OUP 2011) 246–253.

analysis is supported by the facts that, first, rescission for misrepresentation is similar to that for undue influence, duress, mistake, and non-disclosure, where there is no tort (or wrong as such) involved; secondly, rescission was available for non-fraudulent misrepresentation, before the development of the tort of negligent misrepresentation or the passing of the Misrepresentation Act 1967; thirdly, rescission is an available remedy for a purely innocent misrepresentation which is not treated as a tort (or other wrong); and fourthly, for the torts involved, whether deceit, negligent misrepresentation, or under the Misrepresentation Act 1967, it is necessary to show damage resulting from the misrepresentation, that is, the torts are actionable only on proof of damage, whereas no damage needs to be proved for rescission.[15]

(2) Why should a claimant want a restitutionary remedy for a tort, rather than compensatory damages?

The main and most obvious advantage is that the claimant may obtain more by restitution than compensation, since the gain the defendant has made by the tort may exceed the loss caused to the claimant by the tort.

But there may be other advantages in that a common law rule or a statutory provision may be regarded as barring compensatory damages but not a restitutionary remedy for the tort. Birks has argued that there can only be an evasion of a bar where it is the remedy (compensation) and not the cause of action (tort) that is barred.[16] But whether illogical or not, the courts in the past have been willing to allow at least some restitutionary remedies for torts to evade bars on 'tort actions'. The major example concerned the *actio personalis* rule, or what was left of it in the Law Reform (Miscellaneous Provisions) Act 1934, s 1(3), whereby there was a six-month limitation period for 'tort actions' against a wrongdoer's personal representatives; for while this was regarded as barring tortious compensatory damages, it was considered not to be a bar to restitutionary remedies.[17]

It is worth adding as a postscript that, now that the Proceedings Against Estates Act 1970 has finally removed any trace of the unjust *actio personalis* rule, it is unlikely that the courts will see any reason to allow restitutionary remedies for a tort to avoid the six-year limitation period applicable to tortious compensatory damages.[18] Certainly nothing in the Limitation Act 1980 contradicts this. An award of money had and received is not mentioned and, by the Limitation Act 1980, s 23, an action for an account of profits '... shall not be brought after the expiration of any time limit under the Act which is applicable to the claim which is the basis of the duty to account', which does appear to mean that if the basis is tort, tort limitation periods should apply.

(3) When are restitutionary remedies available for torts?

There are a number of cases which have awarded restitution for a tort rather than the more usual compensatory damages.[19] These cases will be examined by dividing them according

---

[15] C Witting, *Street on Torts* (15th edn, OUP 2018) 339.
[16] P Birks, *An Introduction to the Law of Restitution* (rev edn, Clarendon Press 1989) 347. Cf A Burrows, *The Law of Restitution* (3rd edn, OUP 2011) 10–11.
[17] *Chesworth v Farrar* [1967] 1 QB 407, and reasoning in *Phillips v Homfray* (1883) 24 Ch D 439.
[18] A Burrows, *The Law of Restitution* (3rd edn, OUP 2011) 703–704.
[19] For influential cases in the US see, eg, *Federal Sugar Refining Co v US Sugar Equalisation Bd* 286 F 575 (1920) (profits from inducing breach of contract); *Edwards v Lee's Administrators* 96 SW 2d 1028 (1936) (account of profits for trespass to land); *Raven Red Ash Coal Co v Ball* 39 SE 2d 231 (1946) (value of use of land); *Olwell v Nye and Nissen Co* 26 Wash 2d 282 (1946) (reasonable value of use/expense saved by conversion of egg-washing

to whether the remedy given for the tort was money had and received or an account of profits.

(a) Money had and received

An award of money had and received is automatically restitutionary: ie by its very nature it is looking at the defendant's receipt and not just the claimant's loss (if any). It is submitted, therefore, that it would be sufficient in proving that restitution may be awarded for a tort to point to cases in which this remedy has been awarded *for* a tort. But if the defendant's gain correlates to the claimant's loss, as is usually the case with this remedy in unjust enrichment, there is the conceivable re-interpretation that one is concerned with the well-established principle of compensating for wrongful loss. It follows that the best proof lies in the fact that in several cases awarding money had and received it is at least strained to regard the measure of recovery as corresponding to the claimant's loss and it is more natural, either in the light of the amount awarded or the court's reasoning or both, to regard the measure as solely concerned to strip the tortfeasor of some or all of the gains made by the tort.

First, there are the cases of *Lamine v Dorrell*[20] and *Chesworth v Farrar*[21] on the tort of conversion. In the former, the defendant had wrongfully converted the claimant's Irish debentures by selling them off. It was held that the claimant could recover the actual sale price of the debentures. No investigation was made as to whether that sale had been at the market price. Had the claim been for compensatory damages the normal measure would have been the value of the goods assessed according to the market price at the date of the tort. It must be admitted, however, that the actual reasoning in the case weakens its authority as an example of restitution for the tort because, in justifying the measure, Holt CJ relied on an idea of 'extinctive ratification' agency reasoning which was later disapproved by the House of Lords in *United Australia Ltd v Barclays Bank Ltd*.[22]

In *Chesworth v Farrar* the deceased landlord had wrongfully converted, by selling off, property belonging to his tenant. The tenant successfully recovered the sale price of the goods from the deceased's administrators without any investigation of their value at the date of conversion. The central issue in the case concerned whether the claim was time-barred by the statutory remnant of the *actio personalis* rule laying down a six-month limitation period for an action in tort where the tortfeasor had died. In holding that it was not so time-barred Edmund Davies J reasoned that that limitation period only applied to an action for damages for the tort and not to a quasi-contractual or, as we would now say, restitutionary, remedy. In an important passage he said:

'A person upon whom a tort has been committed has at times a choice of alternative remedies, even though it is a *sine qua non* regarding each that he must establish that a tort has been committed. He may sue to recover damages for the tort, or he may waive the tort and sue in quasi-contract to recover the benefit received by the wrongdoer.'[23]

Turning to the tort of trespass to goods, in *Oughton v Seppings*[24] a sheriff's officer in executing a writ of *fieri facias* against a Mr Winslove had seized a horse belonging to the claimant. That horse had subsequently been sold by the sheriff and the proceeds of sale paid

---

machine). Cf *Hart v EP Dutton & Co Inc* 93 NYS 2d 871 (1949) (refusing restitution for libel). See, generally, G Palmer, *Law of Restitution* (Little, Brown & Co 1978) Vol I, 49–140, 157–166; *Restatement of the Law Third, Restitution and Unjust Enrichment* (American Law Institute 2011) ch 5.

[20] (1701) 2 Ld Raym 1216. [21] [1967] 1 QB 407. [22] [1941] AC 1.
[23] [1967] 1 QB 407, at 417. [24] (1830) 1 B & Ad 241.

to the officer. Again, without any investigation of the loss to the claimant, it was held that he could recover the sale proceeds from the officer in an action for money had and received.

Finally, there is *Powell v Rees*[25] which concerned the tort of trespass to land by the extraction of coal from the claimant's land. The claimant was held able to evade the *actio personalis* bar by suing the deceased tortfeasor's estate in an action for money had and received to recover the sale proceeds of the coal. But this case is somewhat weaker than the above three in that Lord Denman CJ did not seem concerned by the lack of direct evidence of the sale price and also indicated that a compensatory award would have yielded the same sum.

(b) Account of profits

This is an equitable remedy by which the defendant is required to draw up an account of, and then to pay the amount of, the net profits it has acquired by particular wrongful conduct. The remedy's label 'account of profits' is therefore shorthand for 'account and award of profits'. This is plainly a restitutionary remedy concerned with the stripping of profits.[26] The contrast with compensatory damages was clearly stressed in the typically superb judgment of Windeyer J in the Australian infringement of trade mark case, *Colbeam Palmer Ltd v Stock Affiliates Pty Ltd*:[27]

> 'The distinction between an account of profits and damages is that by the former the infringer is required to give up his ill-gotten gains to the party whose rights he has infringed; by the latter he is required to compensate the party wronged for the loss he has suffered. The two computations can obviously yield different results, for a plaintiff's loss is not to be measured by the defendant's gain, or a defendant's gain by the plaintiff's loss. Either may be greater, or less, than the other. If a plaintiff elects to take an inquiry as to damages the loss to him of profits which he might have made may be a substantial element of his claim ... But what a plaintiff might have made had the defendant not invaded his rights is by no means the same thing as what the defendant did make by doing so.'

As yet, an account of profits is only available for a tort if the tort involves an infringement of intellectual property rights,[28] whether by the infringement of a patent,[29] copyright,[30] design right,[31] performer's property right,[32] or trade mark,[33] or passing off.[34] Confinement of this equitable remedy to those torts is explicable historically because they have their roots

---

[25] (1837) 7 Ad & El 426.
[26] Chadwick LJ's obiter dicta in *WWF-World Wide Fund for Nature v World Wrestling Federation Entertainment Inc* [2007] EWCA Civ 286, [2008] 1 WLR 445, to the effect that an account of profits is compensatory, should be dismissed as confused (or as using the word 'compensation' in a loose and unhelpful sense to cover any monetary remedy for a wrong).
[27] (1968) 122 CLR 25, at 32.
[28] In *Hollister Inc v Medik Ostomy Supplies Ltd* [2012] EWCA Civ 1419, [2013] Bus LR 428, it was made clear that, despite its reference to 'any unfair profits made by the defendant' under the heading of 'assessment of damages' for infringement of an intellectual property right, regulation 3 of the Intellectual Property (Enforcement etc) Regulations 2006, which gives effect to Article 13 of the Intellectual Property Rights Enforcement Directive, 2004/24/EC, has not altered the approach in English law to an account of profits (and the need for a claimant to elect between an account of profits and damages).
[29] Patents Act 1977, s 61(1)(d); *Siddell v Vickers* (1892) 9 RPC 152. Presumably design infringement is analogous.
[30] Copyright, Designs and Patents Act 1988, s 96(2); *Delfe v Delamotte* (1857) 3 K & J 581; *Potton Ltd v Yorkclose Ltd* [1990] FSR 11. For those with a publication right or a database right having essentially the same rights as a copyright owner, see above, p 228 n 266.
[31] Copyright, Designs and Patents Act 1988, s 229(2).
[32] ibid, s 1911(2).
[33] *Edelsten v Edelsten* (1863) 1 De GJ & SM 185; *Slazenger & Sons v Spalding & Bros* [1910] 1 Ch 257; *Hollister Inc v Medik Ostomy Supplies Ltd* [2012] EWCA Civ 1419, [2013] Bus LR 428.
[34] *Lever v Goodwin* (1887) 36 Ch D 1; *My Kinda Town Ltd v Soll* [1982] FSR 147; rvsd on liability [1983] RPC 407.

in equity. But this is not a policy justification and it can be argued that the role of an account of profits should be expanded to reverse gains made by any dishonestly committed tort. Indeed, given that an account of profits is commonplace for the equitable wrong of breach of confidence,[35] it surely cannot be long before the question is litigated as to whether an account of profits can be awarded for the tort of privacy, which has grown out of breach of confidence.

Originally the courts would only award an account of profits if ancillary to an injunction. For example, in *Smith v London and South Western Rly Co*[36] and *Price's Patent Candle Co Ltd v Bauwen's Patent Candle Co Ltd*[37] it was held that no account of profits could be awarded because, as there would be no further patent infringement, there was no justification for an injunction. But while it is generally the case that an account of profits is awarded in addition to an injunction, this is no longer a requirement. Presumably as with an injunction, traditional equitable defences concerning the claimant's conduct, such as clean hands and acquiescence, will apply as bars to an account of profits.

There are four remaining issues of importance:

(i) Innocent wrongdoing

There is an interesting difference between these torts as to whether an account of profits will be refused because the defendant was an innocent wrongdoer. So by the Patents Act 1977, s 62(1), in proceedings for patent infringement, it is a defence to a claim for an account of profits or indeed damages (but not an injunction) that the defendant was not aware, and had no reasonable grounds for supposing, that the patent existed. In other words, a negligence standard is laid down for an account of profits (and damages).

At common law, an account of profits may be ordered for the torts of passing off[38] or infringement of trade mark[39] although it appears that dishonesty is here a pre-condition of an account of profits[40] (albeit not of a claim for damages).[41] Windeyer J explained this as follows in *Colbeam Palmer Ltd v Stock Affiliates Pty Ltd*:[42]

> 'By [the account of profits] a defendant is made to account for, and is then stripped of profits he has made which it would be unconscionable that he retain. These are profits made by him dishonestly, that is by knowingly infringing the rights of the proprietor of the trade mark.'

But in contrast to the above are the Copyright, Designs and Patents Act 1988, ss 97(1), 233(1), and 191J(1) whereby, for infringement of copyright, a primary infringement of a design right, and infringement of a performer's property right respectively, it is a defence to damages *but not to an account of profits* that the defendant did not know and had no reason to believe that copyright or the design right or performer's property right subsisted in the work to which the action relates. In other words, an account of profits is awarded on a strict liability basis.

There is no justification for such a difference of approach and the inconsistency should be removed. Whether this should be by adopting the standard of dishonest wrongdoing, as

---

[35] See below, ch 26.   [36] (1854) Kay 408.   [37] (1858) 4 K & J 727.
[38] *Lever v Goodwin* (1887) 36 Ch D 1; *AG Spalding & Bros v AW Gamage Ltd* (1915) 84 LJ Ch 449; *My Kinda Town Ltd v Soll* [1982] FSR 147, rvsd on liability [1983] RPC 407.
[39] *Edelsten v Edelsten* (1863) 1 De GJ & Sm 185; *Slazenger & Sons v Spalding & Bros* [1910] 1 Ch 257; *Colbeam Palmer Ltd v Stock Affiliates Pty Ltd* (1968) 122 CLR 25. Cf Trade Marks Act 1994, s 14(2): 'In an action for infringement [of a registered trade mark] all such relief by way of damages, injunctions, accounts or otherwise is available to him as is available in respect of the infringement of any other property right.'
[40] *Colbeam Palmer Ltd v Stock Affiliates Pty Ltd* (1968) 122 CLR 25.
[41] *Gillette UK Ltd v Edenwest Ltd* [1994] RPC 279.   [42] (1968) 122 CLR 25, at 34.

for the common law torts; or negligence, as for patent infringement; or strict liability, as for copyright, primary design infringement, and infringement of performer's property right, is a difficult policy issue which ultimately rests on the justification for applying restitution as a mid-position between compensation and punishment.

(ii) Account of which profits?

The courts' approach shows a veiled awareness that the wrong must have been a factual cause of the profits for which the account is ordered. Slade J affirmed the central principle in the following classic statement in *My Kinda Town Ltd v Soll*,[43] where the defendants were alleged to be liable for passing off by using a name similar to the claimants' for their own chain of restaurants:

> 'The purpose of ordering an account of profits in favour of a successful plaintiff in a passing off case is not to inflict punishment on the defendant. It is to prevent an unjust enrichment of the defendant by compelling him to surrender those ... parts of the profits, actually made by him which were improperly made and nothing beyond this.'

It followed that, as the alleged tort comprised confusing the public into thinking the defendants' restaurants were the claimants', the profits to be accounted for were only those additional profits caused by that confusion, and not all the profits made by the defendants from those restaurants.[44]

Again, in relation to infringement of a trade mark, it is not all the profits from the sale of infringing goods that are gained by the infringement and must be accounted for: rather it is only those made because the goods were sold under the trade mark. As Windeyer J said in *Colbeam Palmer v Stock Affiliates Pty Ltd*,[45] 'The profit for which the infringer of a trade mark must account is thus not the profit he made from selling the article itself but ... the profit made from selling it under the trade mark.'

Similarly, as Lord Watson pointed out in dicta in *United Horse-Shoe & Nail Co Ltd v Stewart & Co*,[46] it 'would be unreasonable to give the patentee profits which were not earned by the use of his invention'. So where the patent infringement comprises using a particular means of manufacturing goods, but there are other means, the profits to be accounted for are those made by using that particular means; that is, as suggested in *Siddell v Vickers*,[47] one should compare the profits actually made with those that would have been made if the next most likely means of manufacture had been adopted.

In *Celanese International Corpn v BP Chemicals Ltd*[48] Laddie J controversially held that, in assessing the sum to be awarded under an account of profits for patent infringement, no sum could be awarded if no profits (but instead losses) were made (even though the losses would have been greater but for the infringement). This is closely tied to the view that one cannot award an account of profits for an 'expense saved'[49] and, while unusual, there seems no reason in principle why that should be ruled out (although it will commonly be unrealistic to imagine that the defendant would have acquired the same benefit

---

[43] [1982] FSR 147, at 156; rvsd on liability [1983] RPC 407. See also *Potton Ltd v Yorkclose Ltd* [1990] FSR 11.
[44] *Lever v Goodwin* (1887) 36 Ch D 1, where the amount of profits included sales to non-confused customers, was distinguished on the unconvincing ground that the sales there were to middlemen.
[45] (1968) 122 CLR 25, at 37.   [46] (1888) 13 App Cas 401, at 412–413.   [47] (1892) 9 RPC 152.
[48] [1999] RPC 203, esp at [127].
[49] In Lord Nicholls's words in *Attorney-General v Blake* [2001] 1 AC 268, at 286: an expense saved (in the sense of a part refund of the price agreed for services) does 'not fall within the concept of an account of profits as ordinarily understood'. But it might help to think of the account of profits as an account of gains: and gains can be negative as well as positive. Note also that there is an analogy with the controversy in *Phillips v Homfray* (1883) 24 Ch D 439, discussed below at pp 347–348, as to whether an award of money had and received can include an expense saved.

from a third party). After all, in some situations, the expense saved precisely is the profit made by the wrong.[50] Moreover, it would be most odd if a defendant could be stripped of net profits but could not be deprived of an expense saved which would appear to represent a less draconian award. In relation to the equitable wrong of breach of confidence, Lord Denning thought that the expense saved of acquiring the information elsewhere (or from the claimant), depending on how special the information was, should be recoverable and clearly saw this as a less extreme remedy than stripping all the defendant's profits made by the wrong.[51] Ideally one should recognize that 'stripping' the expense saved is a useful mid-position to stripping all net profits: and that would appear to have been a role that was previously filled by 'negotiating damages'. However, that role appears to have been closed off by the compensatory analysis of negotiating damages favoured in *Morris-Garner v One Step (Support) Ltd*.[52]

In the *Celanese* case Laddie J also reasoned that, while causation was important, so that the profits must be ones made by the infringement, it was inappropriate to consider what profits the defendant would have made had it adopted the most likely non-infringing method of production.[53] On the face of it, this appears to contradict causation[54] but it may perhaps be justified in most situations as rendering the calculation of the account of profits more straightforward. An alternative approach might be to switch the burden of proof so that it would be for a defendant to prove the profits that it would have been made even if no wrong had been committed.[55] But in the context of an account of profits being awarded for the equitable wrong of dishonest assistance, the High Court of Australia in *Ancient Order of Foresters in Victoria Friendly Society Ltd v Lifeplan Australia Friendly Society Ltd*[56] has reasoned that, on the assumption that the account of profits is being given where the defendant has been dishonest, there is good reason in terms of deterrence not to allow the defendant to use such an argument to reduce the profits that must be disgorged. It can also be argued that, beyond applying factual cause, a court should restrict an account of profits by making an allowance to take into account the skill and effort expended by the defendant to make the profit. But in contrast to cases on an account of profits for equitable wrongs, there has as yet been no such restriction applied to an account of profits for a tort,[57] perhaps because the tort in issue has generally been intentional.

(iii) Difficulty of an account of profits

A point emphasised in many of the cases, particularly those of the nineteenth century, in which an account of profits has been ordered is the difficulty of working out the profits the defendant has wrongfully acquired. For example, in *Price's Patent Candle Co Ltd v Bauwen's*

---

[50] For general discussion, see J Edelman, *Gain-Based Damages* (Hart Publishing 2002) 73–76.
[51] Below, p 523. [52] [2018] UKSC 20, [2018] 2 WLR 1353: see above, ch 18.
[53] [1999] RPC 203, esp at [39]–[41].
[54] R Stevens, *Torts and Rights* (OUP 2007) 83–84 suggests, with respect unpersuasively, that this restriction tends to show that one is not here concerned with profit-stripping: rather the 'profits traceably represent the value of the right infringed'.
[55] Cf the trade mark infringement case of *Hollister Inc v Medik Ostomy Supplies Ltd* [2012] EWCA Civ 1419, [2013] Bus LR 428, in which the Court of Appeal, while not directly addressing this point about non-infringing production, did make clear that deductions from the defendant's profits should be made to reflect opportunity costs if the defendant could support such deductions by evidence. The precise point laid down was that it was too broad-brush an approach simply to deduct from the profits a proportion of the defendant's general overheads: rather it was for the defendant to prove by evidence that costs had been incurred that would not have been incurred but for the infringement and should therefore be deducted. See also, eg, *OOO Abbott v Design and Display Ltd* [2017] EWHC 932 (IPEC), [2017] FSR 43.
[56] [2018] HCA 43, (2008) 360 ALR 1. See below, p 536.
[57] But see, in support, Robert Goff J's dicta in *Redwood Music Ltd v Chappell & Co Ltd* [1982] RPC 109, at 132 (innocent copyright infringement).

Patent Candle Co Ltd[58] Sir Page Wood V-C said, '... the questions involved in taking accounts of the particular instances in which patents have been infringed, and of the profits thereby made, are questions of great nicety and difficulty and never tend to any satisfactory result.'[59] But particularly where all profits on the manufacture and sale of certain goods have to be accounted for, it is hard to see why this is regarded as that difficult. Even where only some of the profits from sales of goods have to be accounted for, it is not clear why it is thought more difficult to work out the profits the defendant has made from his wrong, than it is to calculate compensatory damages for, for example, the profits the claimant has lost as a result of the wrong.

Perhaps the explanation for this emphasis on difficulty is that traditionally the courts have taken the view that an account of profits requires a very precise calculation of the relevant profits, with an actual account having to be drawn up, showing gains and losses, whereas it has been accepted that damages can be calculated in a rough and ready manner. But there is no reason why an account of profits should not also be roughly rather than precisely calculated and in support of this are Slade J's comments in *My Kinda Town Ltd v Soll*:[60]

> '... the general intention of the Court in making the order [of an account of profits] ... has been to achieve a fair apportionment, so that neither party will have what justly belongs to the other. What will be required on the inquiry, if it has to be pursued, will not be mathematical exactness, but only a reasonable approximation.'

Similarly in the breach of contract case of *Attorney-General v Blake*[61] Lord Nicholls said: 'Despite the niceties and formalities once associated with taking an account, the amount payable under an account of profits need not be any more elaborately or precisely calculated than damages.'

(iv) Account of profits and damages

It has been laid down that a claimant cannot both be awarded damages and an account of profits.[62] In *Neilson v Betts*[63] Lord Westbury explained the rule on the ground that, 'The two things are hardly reconcilable, for if you take an account of profits you condone the infringement'. But this reasoning is unconvincing and it has been restrictively interpreted in *Codex Corpn v Racal-Milgo Ltd*,[64] where the actual decision was that the taking of an account of profits for infringement of patent does not amount to a 'franking' of the defendant's products so as to prevent future actions for patent infringement. Indeed Lord Westbury's view is reminiscent of the argument rejected in *United Australia Ltd v Barclays Bank Ltd*[65] that, having 'waived the tort' and sued for an action for money had and received,

---

[58] (1858) 4 K & J 727.
[59] ibid, at 730. See also *Crosley v Derby Gas Light Co* (1838) 3 My & Cr 428; *Siddell v Vickers* (1892) 9 RPC 152.
[60] [1982] FSR 147, at 159. See also *Potton Ltd v Yorkclose Ltd* [1990] FSR 11.
[61] [2001] 1 AC 268, at 288.
[62] *Neilson v Betts* (1871) LR 5 HL 1; *De Vitre v Betts* (1873) LR 6 HL 319; Patents Act 1977, s 61(2); *Colbeam Palmer Ltd v Stock Affiliates Pry Ltd* (1968) 122 CLR 25; *Island Records Ltd v Tring International plc* [1996] 1 WLR 1256, noted by P Birks, 'Inconsistency Between Compensation and Restitution' (1996) 112 LQR 375; *Spring Form Inc v Toy Brokers Ltd* [2002] FSR 276, noted by L Bently and C Mitchell, 'Combining Money Awards for Patent Infringement' [2003] RLR 79; *Hollister Inc v Medik Ostomy Supplies Ltd* [2012] EWCA Civ 1419, [2013] Bus LR 428, at [54]–[56]. See analogously *United Australia Ltd v Barclays Bank Ltd* [1941] AC 1 in which it was accepted that a claimant cannot recover both compensatory damages and an award of money had and received for a tort. See also on breach of fiduciary duty *Mahesan S/O Thambiah v Malaysian Government Officers Co-operative Housing Society* [1979] AC 374; *Tang Min Sit v Capacious Investments Ltd* [1996] AC 514. See, generally, M Tilbury, Civil Remedies (Butterworths 1990) paras 2015, 2027. See also above, pp 13–15.
[63] (1871) LR 5 HL 1, at 22.   [64] [1984] FSR 87.   [65] [1941] AC 1.

the claimant cannot switch to claiming damages for conversion if judgment on that prior action is unsatisfied.

Although that reasoning is unconvincing, the rule that a claimant cannot be awarded both compensation and restitution for a wrong may be thought to be justified on the basis that it prevents double recovery or 'inconsistency'.[66] For example, if D, by committing a tort against C has made a net gain of £2,000 and by the same tort has caused loss to C of £5,000, the effect of requiring D to pay C £7,000 would be that C is neither just compensated for its loss nor is D just stripped of its wrongly acquired gain. An award of £7,000 would therefore appear to be inconsistent with either of the remedial purposes being pursued and would constitute double recovery.

On the other hand, there would appear to be no objection to a combination of compensation and restitution provided one takes account of the other. So the correct award of £5,000 in the above example *could* be justified as an award of restitution (£2,000) plus partial compensation (£3,000).

At present the law requires a claimant to make an election or choice between these so-called 'inconsistent' remedies. That election need not be made until judgment and even then it can be changed if the judgment is unsatisfied.[67]

A requirement of election between 'inconsistent' remedies saves the court from having to become embroiled in the issue of the extent to which an award of both restitution and compensation would entail 'double recovery'. It may also remove the risk of defendants being pressurised into paying inappropriate measures of recovery. The disadvantage of requiring an election is that it is conceivable that a claimant may be deprived of its full entitlement by making an inappropriate election although normally a claimant will make the right choice by electing the remedy which, on the facts, yields the higher measure of recovery. The chance of injustice to claimants (by choosing a lower measure) has been further reduced by the decision in *Island Records Ltd v Tring International Plc*[68] to the effect that a claimant is entitled to defer election until after an inquiry as to the amount of profits.

(c) The relationship with punitive damages

In considering the extent to which restitution can be awarded for a tort, it is important to bear in mind the second of the three categories of punitive (otherwise known as exemplary) damages recognised in *Rookes v Barnard*.[69] This category is where 'the defendant's conduct has been calculated to make a profit for himself which may well exceed the compensation payable to the plaintiff'. Punitive damages go beyond restitution. But if the courts are willing to go to the lengths of punishing the profit-seeking deliberate tortfeasor, it arguably follows, and was accepted by the Law Commission,[70] that they ought to be prepared to go to the lesser length of awarding a restitutionary remedy stripping the deliberate tortfeasor of ill-gotten gains.

---

[66] See above, pp 13–15.
[67] *United Australia Ltd v Barclays Bank Ltd* [1914] AC 1; *Tang Min Sit v Capacious Investments Ltd* [1996] AC 514.
[68] [1996] 1 WLR 1256.   [69] [1964] AC 1129, at 1226. See below, ch 20.
[70] Law Commission, *Aggravated, Restitutionary and Exemplary Damages* (1997) Report No 247, paras 3.50–3.51.

(d) Some significant anti-restitution cases?

As a contrast to the picture that has so far been presented, which shows restitution (whether through an award of money had and received or an account of profits) being awarded for various torts, we must now consider five Court of Appeal decisions that stand as possible obstacles to the full or wide acceptance of restitution as a remedial measure for a tort.

(i) *Phillips v Homfray*[71]

In this case, the deceased had trespassed by using roads and passages under the claimants' land to transport coal. In an earlier action the claimants had won a judgment for 'damages' to be assessed against the then living tortfeasor.[72] After his death, the question at issue was whether the claimants could treat the judgment for damages for use of their land as one for a restitutionary remedy which would survive against the deceased's executors despite the *actio personalis* rule. The majority held not on the ground that for a restitutionary remedy, at least one that is to survive against the deceased's executors, it is necessary for the gain made by the tortfeasor to comprise the claimant's property or the proceeds of that property. On the facts that was not so: the deceased had gained by saving himself the expense of not paying the claimant for using the underground roads or alternatively by not paying for other methods of transporting the coal. Baggallay LJ, in a powerful dissenting judgment, could not see why the type of benefit should matter. He said:

> 'I feel bound to say that I cannot appreciate the reasons upon which it is insisted that although executors are bound to account for any accretions to the property of their testator derived directly from his wrongful act, they are not liable for the amount or value of any other benefit which may be derived by his estate from or by reason of such wrongful act.'[73]

This case can be, and has been, analysed in many different ways. Goff and Jones in their first three editions regarded it as an unfortunate decision on restitution for the tort of trespass to land which should be overruled. They wrote, 'In our view the principle of Baggallay LJ's dissent should be adopted and *Phillips v Homfray* overruled.'[74] Underpinning this view was that, while the issue in point was whether an action could be brought against the deceased's executors and was therefore bound up with the *actio personalis* rule which no longer applies, the reasoning appeared to be also directed to claims against the wrongdoer himself. For example, Bowen LJ said, 'The true test to be applied in the present case is whether the plaintiffs' claim against the deceased ... belongs to the category of actions *ex delicto* or whether any form of action against the executors of the deceased, *or the deceased man in his lifetime*, can be based upon any implied contract or duty.'[75]

Birks argued that the case presents no obstacle to restitution for wrongdoing because, given the *actio personalis* bar to tort actions then existing, the case could only be concerned with the cause of action of unjust enrichment (ie 'alternative analysis').[76] But while it might be *possible* to analyse the decision as being concerned purely with the cause of action of unjust enrichment, the judgments seemed principally geared towards enrichment by wrongdoing.

---

[71] (1883) 24 Ch D 439.   [72] (1871) 6 Ch App 770.   [73] (1883) 24 Ch D 439, at 471–472.
[74] R Goff and G Jones, *The Law of Restitution* (3rd edn, Sweet & Maxwell 1986) 611.
[75] (1883) 24 Ch D 439, at 460–461 (author's italics).
[76] Above, p 336. P Birks, *An Introduction to the Law of Restitution* (rev edn, Clarendon Press 1989) 323. See, similarly, G Virgo, *The Principles of the Law of Restitution* (3rd edn, OUP 2015) 450–452.

On another view, favoured more recently by Goff and Jones[77] and in a forceful article by Swadling, while the decision does deal with restitution for wrongs, it should be regarded as posing no difficulty for the modern law because of the abolition of the *actio personalis* rule. Swadling persuasively contends that, taking into account the earlier 1871 decision (which he calls *Phillips v Homfray (No 1)*), the 1883 decision (which he calls *Phillips v Homfray (No 2)*) was not denying that a court can award restitution for negative benefits against a living trespasser.[78] He writes:

> '*Phillips & Homfray (No 2)* is not the anti-restitutionary case it is painted to be. It should not be overruled, or banished to a dark corner of our law, but instead set out in lights. It is a decision concerned only with the operation of the maxim *actio personalis moritur cum persona*, and therefore tells us nothing of the restitutionary liability of living wrongdoers. And when read in conjunction with *Phillips v Homfray (No 1)*, it is in fact authority *against* the very proposition for which it is said to stand, namely, that a restitutionary claim in respect of the wrong of trespass to land yields only positive benefits, for in the first stage of the litigation Stuart V-C at first instance, and Lord Hatherley LC on appeal, allowed a restitutionary claim for expense saved by the then living defendants ... The only thing which needs to be buried is the myth in *Phillips v Homfray*, not the decision itself.'[79]

Even if one treats *Phillips v Homfray* as a problem case it must not be forgotten that it was not totally anti-restitution in that it indisputably did recognise that restitution could be given for a tort where the gain comprised the claimant's property or its proceeds.[80] It was therefore implicit in the majority's reasoning that the first part of the 'damages' to be assessed for the value of the coal taken (which the Court of Appeal in the later *Phillips v Homfray* appeal[81] construed as being for an equitable account of profits so that no interest could be added) was maintainable against the deceased's executors despite the *actio personalis* rule.

Moreover, it is noteworthy that the decision has had no impact outside actions for money had and received: the granting of an account of profits for intellectual property torts accepted at common law and in statutes conflicts with, while ignoring, the *Phillips v Homfray* restriction.

(ii) *Stoke-on-Trent City Council v W & J Wass Ltd*[82]

Here the defendants had deliberately committed the tort of nuisance by operating a market within a distance infringing the claimant's proprietary market right. The claimant was granted an injunction to restrain further infringement of its right. On the question of damages it was accepted by the claimant that it had not suffered any loss, in the sense of loss of custom. But at first instance Peter Gibson J awarded damages on the basis of an appropriate licence fee that the claimant could have charged the defendant for lawful operation of its market: that is, he awarded what are now called 'negotiation damages'. After *Morris-Garner v One Step (Support) Ltd*[83] these should be viewed as compensatory damages. In contrast,

---

[77] R Goff and G Jones, *The Law of Restitution* (7th edn, Sweet & Maxwell 2007) para 36-003: the reasoning 'may have been then valid but ... can no longer be supported'. See also S Hedley, 'Unjust Enrichment as the Basis of Restitution—an Overworked Concept' (1985) 5 Legal Studies 56, 64; W Gummow, 'Unjust Enrichment, Restitution and Proprietary Remedies' in *Essays on Restitution* (ed P Finn, Law Book Co 1990) 60–67.

[78] W Swadling, 'The Myth of *Phillips v Homfray*' in *The Search for Principle* (eds W Swadling and G Jones, OUP 1999) 277–294.

[79] W Swadling, 'The Myth of *Phillips v Homfray*' in *The Search for Principle* (eds W Swadling and G Jones, OUP 1999) 294.

[80] Taking account of all the stages of the litigation, Birks regarded the case as 'indisputably authority in favour of the proposition that an account does lie for the profits of a trespass': P Birks, 'Civil Wrongs: A New World' (*Butterworths Lectures 1990–91*, Butterworths 1992) 64–67.

[81] [1892] 1 Ch 465.   [82] [1988] 1 WLR 1406.

[83] [2018] UKSC 20, [2018] 2 WLR 1353. See above, ch 18.

the Court of Appeal restricted the claimant to nominal damages. This was odd given that negotiation damages have classically been awarded for the infringement of proprietary rights and this was just such a case. The tort in question was a proprietary tort. However, for the purposes of this chapter, the most important feature of the case is that the Court of Appeal ruled out any idea that there could be a restitutionary remedy for a tort. Most alarming was that the whole question was approached as if only compensatory damages could be awarded. It was only at the very end of Nourse LJ's judgment that there was any reference to restitution. He said:

> 'It is possible that the English law of tort, more especially of the so-called "proprietary torts" will in due course make a more deliberate move towards recovery based not on loss suffered by the plaintiff but on the unjust enrichment of the defendant—see Goff and Jones *The Law of Restitution* (3rd edn), pp 612–614. But I do not think that that process can begin in this case and I doubt whether it can begin at all at this level of decision.'[84]

This is to ignore the cases that we have earlier explored in this chapter. Unfortunately, as we shall see, rather than being put to one side and distinguished as an unusual case, *Wass* has been allowed to exercise a restrictive influence in some subsequent decisions.

(iii) *Halifax Building Society v Thomas*[85]

The importance of this case is that it appears to cast doubt on whether restitution is available for the tort of deceit. The defendant fraudulently misrepresented his identity and creditworthiness to obtain a loan from the claimant to finance the purchase of a flat. The loan was secured by a mortgage over the flat. When the defendant defaulted on the repayments, the claimant exercised its right to sell off the flat. The proceeds of sale exceeded the loan. The claimant sought a declaration that it was entitled to keep all the proceeds of sale (ie including the surplus of £10,504.90 plus interest) as restitution for the tort of deceit. If made out, such a restitutionary claim would have defeated the Crown's competing claim to confiscate the surplus in execution of a criminal confiscation order made when the defendant was found guilty of conspiring to obtain mortgage advances by deception.

The Court of Appeal held that the claimant was not entitled to restitution (whether personal or proprietary) for the tort of deceit.[86] The reasoning was that this was not a proprietary tort case. Nor did it involve a breach of fiduciary duty. Moreover, the claimant had affirmed the loan and mortgage, rather than rescinding it for misrepresentation, and had recovered all that, as a secured creditor, it was contractually entitled to under the loan agreement.

One may interpret this case as a significant block on restitution for a personal, non-proprietary tort. However, Peter Gibson LJ did stress that it was 'in the circumstances of the present case',[87] where the claimant had affirmed the contract of loan, that restitution should be denied. Moreover, it can be argued that, as the criminal convictions and confiscation order would ensure that the defendant would not profit from his wrong, there was no work needing to be done by the civil law of restitution.

---

[84] [1988] 1 WLR 1406, at 1415.   [85] [1996] Ch 217.
[86] At first instance in *Murad v Al-Saraj* [2004] EWHC 1235, at [342]–[347] Etherton J appeared to accept that an account of profits can be awarded for the tort of deceit but in the Court of Appeal, [2005] EWCA Civ 959, [2005] WTLR 1573, esp at [46], the award was recast as being a conventional award for breach of fiduciary duty.
[87] [1996] Ch 217, at 227.

(iv) *Forsyth-Grant v Allen*[88]

The claimant owned a hotel. The defendant built a pair of semi-detached houses on the land adjoining the hotel which infringed the claimant's right to light. The defendant was aware of this and sought to negotiate a way round it but the claimant unreasonably refused to communicate with the defendant or his architect. The claimant then sought damages or an account of profits for the tort of nuisance.

At first instance it was decided that the loss to the claimant as a result of the infringement of its right to light was £1,848. That sum was awarded as damages. The net profit to the defendant as a result of the nuisance was assessed at £6,767 being the profit that it would have had to forgo had the building had less floor space so as to avoid infringing the claimant's right to light. However, the judge at first instance held that an account of profits could not here be awarded.[89] That reasoning was upheld by the Court of Appeal. The majority (Patten J and Mummery LJ) laid down that an account of profits cannot be awarded for the tort of nuisance.[90] *Wass* was regarded as supporting that and it was reasoned that, even if the contract case of *Attorney-General v Blake*[91] were applicable to an account of profits in tort, the approach in that case required exceptional circumstances as a condition for restitution and there were none here. Toulson LJ, while agreeing with the result, took a slightly more flexible approach and was willing to accept that there might be cases where an account of profits could be awarded for the tort of nuisance: but here an account of profits would in any event have been inappropriate because of the claimant's own uncooperative attitude in refusing to communicate with the defendant.

(v) *Devenish Nutrition Ltd v Sanofi-Aventis SA*[92]

The defendants, who were the manufacturers of vitamins for animal feed, had been operating an illegal price-fixing cartel. As a consequence, the claimants had had to pay higher prices than they should have done to purchase those vitamins. The European Commission had imposed very significant fines on the defendants for operating the cartel. The claimants now sued the defendants in tort for breach of the statutory duty laid down in Article 81 of the EC Treaty prohibiting such cartels. On a preliminary issue the question was whether the claimants were entitled to restitution for the tort rather than the usual compensation. This was important for the claimants principally because it was thought likely that at least the direct purchasers of the vitamins would be regarded as having avoided their loss by absorbing the higher prices charged in the prices they had themselves charged to their customers.

It was held by a majority of the Court of Appeal (Arden and Tuckey LJJ) that a restitutionary award could not be made for the tort of breach of statutory duty in issue in this case because it was not a proprietary tort. *Wass* was held to be binding authority for refusing restitution except for proprietary torts; and that case was thought not to have been overruled by the wider reasoning of the House of Lords in *Attorney-General v Blake*. Even if incorrect on that, a restitutionary award could only be made if there were exceptional circumstances of the kind described in *Blake* and here that was not so because compensatory damages were an adequate remedy.

---

[88] [2008] EWCA Civ 505, [2008] Env LR 41. C Rotherham, 'Gain-Based Relief in Tort after *Attorney-General v Blake*' (2010) 126 LQR 102 is heavily critical of this case and the *Devenish* case, discussed below.

[89] And even if, applying *Wrotham Park*, a reasonable fee might have been awarded as damages, he assessed such a fee as being 15% of the profit (£1,050) which, being less than the sum awarded as compensation, was of no use to the claimant.

[90] See esp [2008] EWCA Civ 505, [2008] Env LR 41, at [32].

[91] [2001] 1 AC 268. See below, pp 356–358.

[92] [2008] EWCA Civ 1086, [2009] 3 WLR 198. For an excellent case-note, see O Odudu and G Virgo, 'Remedies for Breach of Statutory Duty' [2009] CLJ 32.

While agreeing with the result—because he did not think there was any good reason on these facts to extend the law on restitution for torts, especially where the claimant had passed on its loss to its customers—Longmore LJ disagreed with the majority that the *Wass* case stood as a blocking authority. He said: 'I do not consider that [*Wass*] is authority for the proposition that the categories of cause of action in which it is permissible to order an account of profits are necessarily confined to tortious claims for breach of a proprietary right.'[93]

Longmore LJ should be supported on this. With respect, the majority's approach to the *Wass* case is flawed because, in particular, *Wass* concerned a proprietary tort (the tort of private nuisance).[94] Therefore, the restriction on restitution in that case cannot have had anything to do with restitution being limited to proprietary torts. It is also arguable that, even if that analysis was correct, the reasoning of the House of Lords in *Attorney-General v Blake*, albeit a contract case, has subsequently moved the law of restitution on beyond a restriction to proprietary wrongs.

(e) Conclusion

It is submitted that, despite those five significant anti-restitution cases, the main picture emerging from all the cases is that, at least for proprietary torts, restitution (reversing the defendant's wrongful gains) is an available remedial response. That is, taking both types of restitutionary remedy together (whether an award of money had and received or an account of profits) the torts for which restitution has been awarded have involved interference with the claimant's property, whether that property be real or personal or intellectual. The cases therefore reveal a judicial desire firmly to deter even innocent interference with the claimant's property; that is, merely to compensate for any loss caused appears to be regarded as insufficient to deter that interference. This seems sensible. Applying Jackman's theory, restitution is justified as a means of deterring harm to the 'facilitative institution' of private property.[95]

A subsidiary feature exhibited in a few of the account of profits cases (eg for passing off and infringement of trade mark) is that the tort must be committed intentionally if restitution is to be awarded. It can be strongly argued (not least if one takes into account the contract case of *Attorney-General v Blake*)[96] that this category should be expanded[97] so that restitution should be awarded to reverse gains made by, eg, intentionally inducing a breach of contract or an intentional libel.[98] This is particularly so, if the courts can rid themselves of the former emphasis on an account of profits being mathematically exact. Indeed punitive damages can be awarded for these torts under the category of cynically exploiting wrongdoing to make a profit[99] and, since stripping the defendant of its unjust profits by restitution is less drastic than punishment,[100] it is arguable that restitution should follow on the reasoning that the greater should include the lesser. This was supported by the Law Commission. Irrespective of any other power to award restitution for torts (eg for

---

[93] [2008] EWCA Civ 1086, [2009] 3 WLR 198, at [145].   [94] [1998] 1 WLR 1406, at 1410.
[95] I Jackman, 'Restitution for Wrongs' [1989] CLJ 302.
[96] [2001] 1 AC 268: see the next section below.
[97] See P Birks, *An Introduction to the Law of Restitution* (rev edn, Clarendon Press 1989) 326–327.
[98] Street also gave examples for the tort of battery in H Street, *Principles of the Law of Damages* (Sweet & Maxwell 1962) 254.
[99] Below, pp 364–367.
[100] *Cassell & Co Ltd v Broome* [1972] AC 1027, at 1130 (per Lord Diplock); A Ashworth, *Sentencing and Penal Policy* (Weidenfeld & Nicolson 1983) 294.

proprietary torts) the Commission recommended that a claimant may be awarded restitution for any tort if the defendant's conduct showed a deliberate and outrageous disregard of the claimant's rights.[101]

3. Restitution for breach of contract[102]

(1) Restitution for breach of contract and unjust enrichment

We are here concerned with remedies that reverse gains because the defendant has acquired them by breach of a contract with the claimant.

It is initially important to stress that remedies, such as the recovery of money had and received for total failure of consideration and a *quantum meruit*, which an innocent party can claim once it has validly terminated a contract for breach, are better viewed as based on the cause of action of unjust enrichment, rather than being remedies for breach of contract.[103] Three main features of the law support this view. First, the claimant must have validly terminated the contract, before it can claim these remedies. If the remedies were simply for breach of contract, there would be no need for this; whereas on the view that the cause of action is unjust enrichment this is readily explicable on the ground that it is only where the contract is terminated that the direct shift of wealth from the claimant to the defendant is invalidated. Indeed traditionally there has been a further restriction on the recovery of money in that there must have been a total rather than merely a partial failure of consideration.[104]

Secondly, even though no breach is involved, the same restitutionary remedies governed by the same, or very similar, principles are available where the contract is unenforceable or is void (for example, for uncertainty) or is merely anticipated. Prior to the Law Reform (Frustrated Contracts) Act 1943 this was also true of the remedies available where the contract was frustrated.

Thirdly, it is no restriction on the recovery of money paid in an action for money had and received that the defendant had made a good bargain. Say, for example, the claimant contracts to buy a car from the defendant for £900 and pays £100 in advance; the defendant fails to deliver the car: the market price is £700: the claimant can recover £100 in an action for money had and received.[105] This cannot be sensibly explained if the recovery is regarded as a restitutionary remedy *for* the breach of contract: for the breach cannot be

---

[101] Law Commission, *Aggravated, Exemplary and Restitutionary Damages* (1997) Report No 247, para 3.51 and Draft Bill, cl 12.
[102] See, generally, G Jones, 'The Recovery of Benefits Gained From a Breach of Contract' (1983) 99 LQR 443; A Farnsworth, 'Your Loss or My Gain? The Dilemma of the Disgorgement Principle in Breach of Contract' (1985) 94 Yale LJ 1339; P Birks, 'Restitutionary Damages for Breach of Contract: *Snepp* and the Fusion of Law and Equity' [1987] LMCLQ 128; S Stoljar, 'Restitutionary Relief for Breach of Contract' (1989) 2 JCL 1; R O'Dair, 'Restitutionary Damages for Breach of Contract and The Theory of Efficient Breach: Some Reflections' (1993) 46(2) CLP 113; E Weinrib, 'Punishment and Disgorgement as Contract Remedies' (2003) 78 Chicago-Kent LR 55; G Palmer, *Law of Restitution* (Little, Brown & Co 1978) Vol I, 437–452; J Beatson, *The Use and Abuse of Unjust Enrichment* (Clarendon Press 1991) 15–17; *Restatement of the Law Third, Restitution and Unjust Enrichment* (American Law Institute 2011) 646–670. For discussion of the law in Scotland, but rejecting legislative reform (in relation to 'gain-based damages', whether an account of profits or a reasonable fee), see Scottish Law Commission, *Report on Review of Contract Law: Formation, Interpretation, Remedies for Breach, and Penalty Clauses* (2018) Report No 252, ch 17.
[103] P Birks, *An Introduction to the Law of Restitution* (rev edn, Clarendon Press 1989) 334; P Birks, 'Restitution and the Freedom of Contract' (1983) 36 CLP 141, 149 ff.
[104] The requirement that the failure of consideration be total has come under attack both in decisions and from commentators: see A Burrows, *The Law of Restitution* (3rd edn, OUP 2011) 322–324, 330–334.
[105] *Wilkinson v Lloyd* (1845) 7 QB 27.

regarded as a cause of the defendant's gain, since if there had been no breach, the defendant would still have made that gain from the contract. The same may also be the law regarding the claimant's *quantum meruit* claim. Certainly in *Lodder v Slowey*[106] on appeal from New Zealand, the Privy Council in assessing the claimant's *quantum meruit* considered it irrelevant that the defendant might have made a good bargain so that he would have retained some part of that gain if he had not broken the contract. Again, this aspect of the law is readily explicable if one regards such restitutionary remedies as reversing an unjust enrichment rather than being remedies for breach of contract; for if the basis is not breach of contract, but rather an invalidation of the shift of wealth from the claimant to the defendant, there is no necessary reason why the value of the defendant's contractual counter-performance should be regarded as relevant.[107]

But if the remedies just discussed are not restitutionary remedies for breach of contract, does the law ever award restitution *for* breach of contract?

(2) The law, and analysis, prior to *Blake*

The traditional view, prior to *Attorney-General v Blake*,[108] was that there can be no restitution *for* breach of contract. So, for example, in the Scottish case of *Teacher v Calder*,[109] the defendant financier broke a contract to invest £15,000 in the claimant's timber business, and instead invested the same sum in a distillery. It was held that the claimant's damages were to compensate for the loss to his business and were not concerned with a disgorgement of the much higher profits the defendant had gained from the distillery investment.

The same view applied in England. As Megarry V-C said in *Tito v Waddell (No 2)*:[110]

'... it is fundamental to all questions of damages that they are to compensate the plaintiff for his loss or injury by putting him as nearly as possible in the same position as he would have been in had he not suffered the wrong. The question is not one of making the defendant disgorge what he has saved by committing the wrong, but one of compensating the plaintiff.'

So in that case it was irrelevant that the defendants had saved themselves considerable expense by not replanting Ocean Island as they had covenanted to do. The claimant's loss was alone considered relevant and, as the islanders no longer intended to replant the island and were therefore not entitled to the cost of cure, only a small sum of damages for the trivial difference in value of the land was awarded.[111]

It is important to stress that while the cost of cure may, in some cases, be equivalent to the expense saved, there is no necessary correlation between the two: for example, where cheaper materials have been used in building, the cost of replacing them is likely to be far greater than the expense the defendant saved. In a nutshell, cost of cure damages are compensatory and not restitutionary. One should also clarify that, applying a standard 'difference in value' compensatory award for breach of contract, one is comparing the value of the services or goods that the claimant should have received and the value of the services or goods actually received. A breach of contract by 'skimped performance' leads naturally

---

[106] [1904] AC 442. See also *Boomer v Muir* 24 P 2d 570 (1933).
[107] This is not to deny that there may be other good reasons for thinking *Lodder v Slowey* incorrect: eg, it can be strongly argued that, given 'subjective devaluation', the contract price should often be relevant to unjust enrichment in assessing the services' value to the defendant.
[108] [2001] 1 AC 268.   [109] (1899) 1 F 39.   [110] [1977] Ch 106, at 332.
[111] An interim sum, which it was argued the claimants would have accepted for releasing the defendants from their obligation, was also rejected, ibid, at 319: see above, p 200.

to a standard difference in value compensatory award and it only serves to confuse matters to treat such an award as if it were granting restitution for the expense saved by breach.[112]

Again, prior to the *Blake* case, in *Surrey CC v Bredero Homes Ltd*[113] the Court of Appeal refused to award restitution for a breach of contract. The claimant councils had sold two adjoining parcels of land to the defendant for the development of a housing estate. The defendant covenanted to develop the land in accordance with the scheme approved by the claimants. In breach of that covenant it built more houses on the site than under the approved scheme, thereby making extra profit. Although aware of the breach, the claimants did not seek an injunction or specific performance but waited until the defendant had sold all the houses on the estate and then sought damages. Nominal damages only were awarded on the ground that the claimants had suffered no loss. A restitutionary award was thought inappropriate because this was an action for ordinary common law damages for breach of contract: it did not involve either a tort or an invasion of proprietary rights or equitable damages.

On one interpretation, *Wrotham Park Estate Co v Parkside Homes Ltd*[114] constituted a significant exception to this denial of a restitutionary remedy for breach of contract. We have looked at that case in the last chapter on 'negotiating damages'. Two points should be stressed about the award of damages in that case. First, Brightman J accepted that it was artificial to pretend that the claimant would ever have relaxed the covenant; and, secondly, in assessing the reasonable release fee, Brightman J looked at the defendant's profits from the breach of £50,000 and awarded 5% of those profits (£2,500). Both of those features might be thought to indicate that Brightman J was more concerned to strip the wrongdoer of part of its profits from breach than to compensate the claimant for a loss. But, as we have seen in the last chapter, attractive as a restitutionary analysis of that case might be thought to be, it has been rejected by the Supreme Court in *Morris-Garner v One Step (Support) Ltd*, which has taken a compensatory interpretation of 'negotiating damages'.

Assuming then that, prior to *Attorney-General v Blake*, there was no case law awarding restitution *for* breach of contract, was that state of the law satisfactory? Several commentators argued that it was not. For example, Jones wrote, 'It is difficult to accept the justice of the result of such cases as *Tito v Waddell* (No 2), where the defendant had saved himself considerable expense from failing to execute his promise but where the plaintiff's damages were trivial because he had suffered no "loss".'[115] Jones cited the Louisiana case of *City of New Orleans v Fireman's Charitable Association*[116] as a further striking example of injustice. The defendant had contracted with the claimant to provide a fire-fighting service over a number of years and had received the full contract price. After the expiry of the contract, the claimant discovered that the defendant had not had available the number of men or horses or the footage of pipe promised under the contract. As the claimant had suffered no loss—for example, there was no averment that the defendant had failed to extinguish any fires because of the breach—no substantial damages were recovered, despite the fact that the defendant had saved itself over $40,000 by the breach of contract.

---

[112] This was a point made by Lord Nicholls in *Attorney General v Blake* [2001] 1 AC 268, at 286, and, especially clearly, by Lord Reed in *Morris Garner v One Step (Support) Ltd* [2018] UKSC 20, [2018] 2 WLR 1353, at [80].
[113] [1993] 1 WLR 1361. See R O'Dair, 'Remedies for Breach of Contract: A Wrong Turn' [1993] RLR 31; A Burrows, 'No Restitutionary Damages for Breach of Contract' [1993] LMCLQ 453.
[114] [1993] 1 WLR 1361. See R O'Dair, 'Remedies for Breach of Contract: A Wrong Turn' [1993] RLR 31; A Burrows, 'No Restitutionary Damages for Breach of Contract' [1993] LMCLQ 453.
[115] G Jones, 'The Recovery of Benefits Gained from a Breach of Contract' (1983) 99 LQR 443, 459.
[116] So 486 (1891).

Birks, too, applying a cynical wrongdoing test, argued that restitution should be more widely available as a remedy for breach of contract.[117] As an example of cynical wrongdoing he pointed to *Tito v Waddell (No 2)*[118] as a case in which restitution, rather than nominal or a small sum of compensatory damages, should have been awarded. It was also a theme of Birks' work that, contrary to the picture of the law traditionally painted, sometimes the label 'breach of fiduciary duty' was merely acting as a mask for what were in reality already examples of restitution for breach of contract.[119]

Some expansion of restitution was also advocated by Beatson.[120] He saw restitution as 'in reality a monetised form of specific performance'. This is because if a person knows she will be stripped of her profits from breach there is no advantage for her in breaking the contract. Restitution is therefore justified in the rare cases where specific performance is available (or would have been available were it not now too late for such an order); most obviously where damages are inadequate. This theory has the attraction of building on existing principles of contract law. However, on closer inspection it is far from clear that one would want to apply principles of specific performance to restitution. For example, would general bars to specific performance, such as the bar to specific performance in contracts of personal service or the severe hardship bar, apply also to rule out restitution? And how would the theory apply to negative contractual promises where the prohibitory injunction is the primary remedy and damages are generally regarded as inadequate? It would be odd if restitution were widely available for the breach of negative but not positive promises.

In contrast, Jackman suggested that there may be no need for restitution to protect the facilitative institution of contract because protection is sufficiently afforded by the standard award of expectation damages.[121] In other words, one of the justifications for awarding expectation damages is to protect the institution of contract. On his view, *Wrotham Park* was a rare and acceptable exception because it was not a pure contract case. Breach of a restrictive covenant constitutes the infringement of a proprietary right and falls to be treated like a 'proprietary tort'.

Support for the denial of restitution is also derived from the 'efficient breach' theory that it is more economically efficient to allow breach of contract than to deter it, as restitution would prima facie do.[122] But this sort of argument has been considered in detail and rejected elsewhere in this book,[123] and here it is sufficient to point out that a restitutionary remedy will not necessarily deter the defendant from an efficient breach—namely one where the profits to be made from breach exceed the claimant's expectation loss—because it will be in both parties' interests to negotiate the defendant's release from the contract. Say D contracts to make a machine part for C for £10,000, which C values at £13,000. X offers D £15,000 for that part. The fact that C may be entitled to restitution of say £5,000 for breach,

---

[117] P Birks, 'Restitutionary Damages for Breach of Contract: Snepp and the Fusion of Law and Equity' [1987] LMCLQ 421.
[118] [1977] Ch 106.
[119] Birks relied on *Reading v Attorney-General* [1951] AC 507; *Reid-Newfoundland Co v Anglo-American Telegraph Ltd* [1912] AC 555; *Lake v Bayliss* [1974] 1 WLR 1073; and the dissenting judgment of Deane J in *Hospital Products Ltd v United States Surgical Corpn* (1985) 156 CLR 41.
[120] J Beatson, *The Use and Abuse of Unjust Enrichment* (Clarendon Press 1991) 15–17. See, similarly, P Maddaugh and J McCamus, *The Law of Restitution* (2nd edn, Canada Law Book 2004) para 19.16 tentatively favouring restitution where compensatory damages are inadequate and yet equitable relief is not available.
[121] I Jackman, 'Restitution for Wrongs' [1989] CLJ 302, 318–321. However, at the end of his analysis of breach of contract he very tentatively suggests that his secondary principle of the moral quality of the wrongdoing might justify restitution for cynical breach.
[122] For this general theory, see R Posner, *Economic Analysis of Law* (9th edn, Wolters Kluwer 2014) 128–138, 145–146. See also below, pp 412 n 88, 413 n 91.
[123] Below, pp 413–414.

would not deter the efficient result of D delivering the part to X, because it is in C's interest to accept between £3,000 and £5,000 to release D from the contract (because if D sticks to the contract, C will make only £3,000) and in D's interest to pay up to £5,000 to C to be released to transfer the part to X.

(3) *Attorney-General v Blake* and its aftermath

All previous writings and case law on restitution for breach of contract must now be read in the light of the fascinating and still controversial decision of the House of Lords in *Attorney-General v Blake*.[124]

The notorious spy, George Blake, had written his autobiography in 1989. The publishers had agreed to pay him, as an advance against royalties, three sums of £50,000 on signing the contract, delivery of the manuscript, and on publication. They had paid him £60,000 so that £90,000 was still owing. The Crown sought to stop him being paid that £90,000 and for that sum, instead, to be paid to the Crown. Their claims were brought in both public and private law. The Court of Appeal had upheld Sir Richard Scott V-C's decision at first instance that Blake was not acting in breach of fiduciary duty in publishing the book because there was no fiduciary duty owed by an ex-employee to the Crown. There was also no question of a breach of confidence claim succeeding because, by the time of publication, the information in the book was in the public domain and no longer confidential. But the Court of Appeal had decided that a public law claim should succeed: the Attorney-General, as an extension of his power to obtain injunctions in aid of the criminal law in furtherance of the public interest, was entitled to an order for payment so as to prevent Blake receiving money from his breach of the Official Secrets Act 1989.

The House of Lords firmly rejected that novel public law order on the ground that, without any established private law claim, it constituted a criminal confiscatory order that had not been expressly authorised by Parliament. Nevertheless the House of Lords (Lord Hobhouse dissenting) found in favour of the Crown not in public law but by revisiting obiter dicta of the Court of Appeal in relation to whether the Crown was entitled to the private law remedy of 'restitutionary damages' for breach of contract.

The argument that succeeded was based on the fact that, while there was no cause of action for breach of fiduciary duty or for breach of confidence, there was a cause of action for breach of contract. Blake had expressly undertaken at the beginning of his employment not to publish, during or after his employment with the Secret Service, any official information gained by him as a result of that employment. And, although the normal remedy for breach of contract is damages, compensating the claimant, this was regarded as an exceptional case where an account of profits,[125] aimed at a disgorgement of the gains made from the breach of contract, could, and should, be awarded.

Lord Nicholls, giving the leading speech, elegantly drew together the cases in which the courts have awarded restitution for, for example, proprietary torts, intellectual property torts, and breach of fiduciary duty, and—alongside the 'solitary beacon'[126] of the *Wrotham*

---

[124] [2001] 1 AC 268. For a useful case-note see D Fox, 'Restitutionary Damages to Deter Breach of Contract' [2001] CLJ 33. See, generally, E McKendrick, 'Breach of Contract, Restitution for Wrongs, and Punishment' in *Commercial Remedies* (eds A Burrows and E Peel, OUP 2003) ch 10. For a very hostile view of restitution for breach of contract, see D Campbell and D Harris, 'In Defence of Breach: a Critique of Restitution and the Performance Interest' (2002) 22 Legal Studies 208 and D Campbell and P Wylie, 'Ain't No Telling (Which Circumstances Are Exceptional)' [2003] CLJ 605.

[125] Lord Nicholls did not like the term 'restitutionary damages': [2001] 1 AC 268, at 284.

[126] ibid, at 283.

Park case as an example of restitution being awarded for breach of contract—his Lordship concluded that there was no good reason in principle why an account of profits should not be awarded for breach of contract.[127] However, as to when such an order would be made, his Lordship's speech is rather thin on detail and relies heavily on this being at the discretion of the court. He stressed that an award would be exceptional and should only be made where the standard remedies for breach of contract of compensatory damages or specific performance or an injunction were inadequate. He said:

> 'An account of profits will be appropriate only in exceptional circumstances. Normally the remedies of damages, specific performance and injunction, coupled with the characterisation of some contractual obligations as fiduciary, will provide an adequate response to a breach of contract. It will be only in exceptional cases, where those remedies are inadequate, that any question of accounting for profits will arise. No fixed rules can be prescribed. The court will have regard to all the circumstances, including the subject matter of the contract, the purpose of the contractual provision which has been breached, the circumstances in which the breach occurred, the consequences of the breach and the circumstances in which relief is being sought. A useful general guide, although not exhaustive, is whether the plaintiff had a legitimate interest in preventing the defendant's profit-making activity and, hence, in depriving him of his profit.'[128]

Later in his speech his Lordship said that three facts which, individually, would *not* constitute a good reason for ordering an account of profits are:

> 'the fact that the breach was cynical and deliberate; the fact that the breach enabled the defendant to enter into a more profitable contract elsewhere; and the fact that by entering into a new and more profitable contract the defendant put it out of his power to perform his contract with the plaintiff.'[129]

It is obvious that phrases like 'inadequacy'[130] and 'legitimate interest' are open-ended and import a wide degree of judicial discretion. They could be used to justify an account of profits in a wide or a narrow range of cases. The crucial point, therefore, is that the House of Lords regarded restitution as an exceptional remedy reserved for rare cases. However, we must then ask, how exceptional and how rare?

The *Blake* case itself was unusual. What Blake had done came very close to being, but was not quite, a breach of fiduciary duty and a breach of confidence. Moreover, the courts had no sympathy with a notorious traitor whose book profits would to some extent have derived from his crime of breaking the Official Secrets Act. One might therefore be tempted to dismiss this case as so exceptional that it is a 'one-off' that will not be repeated. That would be a mistake. It is submitted that there will be a limited range of cases where an account of profits will be awarded for a breach of contract. Certainly after *Blake* one must bear this in mind as a possibility whenever one is concerned with remedies for breach of contract. So, for example, although perhaps not formally overruled, it is clear that the House of Lords did not like the decision in *Surrey County Council v Bredero*.[131] If similar facts were to reoccur after *Blake*, it is strongly arguable that the defendant would be held liable to the claimant

---

[127] Lord Nicholls' interpretation of the 'wrongful use' cases in tort and the *Wrotham Park* case in contract as awarding restitution has subsequently been contradicted by the compensatory analysis of 'negotiating damages' favoured in *Morris-Garner v One Step (Support) Ltd* [2018] UKSC 20, [2018] 2 WLR 1353: see above, ch 18.
[128] [2001] 1 AC 268, at 285.   [129] [2001] 1 AC 268, at 286.
[130] It is noteworthy that the inadequacy referred to is in respect of specific remedies as well as damages. But if compensatory damages are considered inadequate, and profits have been made from a past breach, it is likely to be rare for an injunction or specific performance to be 'adequate' (given that they can only ensure that there is no future or continuing breach).
[131] [1993] 1 WLR 1361. See above, p 354.

to account for profits made from building the extra houses.[132] Although the loss to the claimant from the breach may have been minimal, *Blake* means that the claimant need not be limited to nominal damages. Again, one may draw on cases, which have traditionally been rationalised on the basis of a breach of fiduciary duty but which Lord Nicholls indicated are, in substance, examples of an account of profits being granted for breach of contract. For example, in *Reid-Newfoundland Co v Anglo-American Telegraph Co Ltd*[133] the defendant company agreed not to transmit any commercial messages, other than the claimant's messages, over a particular telegraph wire. The Privy Council held the defendant liable to account for the profits made in breach of that agreement. Similarly, Lord Nicholls indicated that the award of damages in *British Motor Trade Association v Gilbert*,[134] for breach of a covenant not to resell a car within a certain period of time, was in reality concerned to strip the defendant of the profits he had made by breaking that covenant.

In contrast, it is unlikely that, where the assessment of expectation damages is straightforward, the courts would wish to strip away the gains made by a defendant breaking one contract in order to enter into another more lucrative contract. Indeed, as we have seen, Lord Nicholls expressly said that such a fact alone would not justify an account of profits. To lock parties into less profitable contracts would be inconsistent with the general approach in English law whereby specific performance is not the primary remedy for breach of contract.

That *Blake* was not a one-off has been shown by *Esso Petroleum Co Ltd v Niad*[135] in which Sir Andrew Morritt V-C decided that the claimants were entitled, at their election, to compensatory damages or an account of profits or a 'restitutionary remedy' for breach of contract. Niad, who owned a petrol station, had entered into a pricing agreement (called 'Pricewatch') with Esso who supplied Niad with petrol. In breach of that agreement, Niad charged higher prices to its customers than had been agreed. This in turn meant that Niad was given 'price support' by Esso to which Niad was not entitled: that is, Niad paid less to Esso for its petrol than it would have done had Esso known that Niad was over-charging its customers. Applying *Blake*, Morritt V-C held that Esso was here entitled to an account of profits aimed at stripping away the gains Niad had made from breaking the contract. Compensatory damages were inadequate because it was almost impossible for Esso to establish that sales had been lost as a result of the breach by Niad. The breach undermined the whole Pricewatch scheme that Esso had agreed with all retailers in the area. Esso had complained to Niad on several occasions. And Esso had a legitimate interest in preventing Niad from profiting from its breach. Alternatively, Morritt V-C said that Esso was entitled to a 'restitutionary remedy' for the amount of the price support that, in breach of contract, it had obtained from Esso.

---

[132] This may be thought to derive support from *Lane v O'Brien Homes Ltd* [2004] EWHC 303 (QB) where the defendant developer built four houses, instead of three, in breach of a collateral contract with the claimant seller of the land. Applying the *Wrotham Park* case, David Clarke J upheld an award of damages of £150,000 based on the defendant's estimated profit from building the extra house of £280,000. But this must now be read in the light of the compensatory approach to 'negotiating damages' taken in *Morris-Garner v One Step (Support) Ltd* [2018] UKSC 20, [2018] 2 WLR 1353: see above, ch 18.

[133] [1912] AC 555. See also *Lake v Bayliss* [1974] 1 WLR 1073 (breach of a contract to sell land); and *CMS Dolphin Ltd v Simonet* [2001] 2 BCLC 704 in which Lawrence Collins J said that, had an account of profits for breach of fiduciary duty not been available, he would have awarded an account of profits for breach of the contractual duty of fidelity in line with *Blake*.

[134] [1951] 2 All ER 641.

[135] [2001] All ER (D) 324 (Nov). See also the comments of the Supreme Court of Canada in *Bank of America Canada v Mutual Trust Co* [2002] SCC 43 to the effect that restitution for breach of contract can be awarded but not where this would discourage efficient breach.

Although the distinction between an account of profits and the so-called 'restitutionary remedy' is a difficult one to draw on these facts (ie it is not clear what the difference is between the two) the great importance of the case is that it shows *Blake* being applied to a commercial contract far removed from the peculiar facts of *Blake* itself.[136]

In conclusion, it is tentatively suggested, in the light of *Blake*, that an account of profits is an appropriate remedy for a breach of contract where two factors are present. First, the breach of contract must be cynical, deliberately calculated to make gains. It is this that triggers the courts' wish to deter the breach by stripping the gains. The breach was cynical in *Blake* and in *Esso v Niad Petroleum*. The same can be said, although restitution was refused, of the earlier cases of *Tito v Waddell* and *Surrey County Council v Bredero Homes*. But, as Lord Nicholls stressed, this is not a sufficient condition. This is because there are many cynical breaches (for example, where a party to a commercial contract of sale breaks it in order to enter into a more lucrative contract with someone else) that the law does not wish to deter.[137] The second factor that must also be present, therefore, is that normal compensatory damages are 'inadequate' in the sense that difficulties of assessment, or bars to the recovery of certain types of damages, mean that compensatory damages will not put the claimant into as good a position as if the contract had been performed. In other words, compensatory damages will not properly protect the claimant's contractual expectations. In cases like *Surrey County Council v Bredero Homes* and *Tito v Waddell* and *Blake* the claimants had non-financial expectations which would not be protected by compensatory damages; their interests were in protecting the environment or in protecting national security. And in *Esso v Niad*, while the claimants entered into the contract for financial reasons, the assessment of damages compensating their financial losses would be highly problematic and prone to error.

---

[136] *Blake* was distinguished, so that an account of profits was refused for breach of contract because the facts were not sufficiently exceptional, in *Stretchline Intellectual Properties Ltd v H & M Hennes & Mauritz (UK) Ltd* [2016] EWHC 162 (Pat), [2016] RPC 15.

[137] See, eg, *AB Corpn v CD Company, The Sine Nomine* [2002] 1 Lloyd's Rep 805 in which an account of profits was refused by arbitrators for the withdrawal, and use, of a ship in breach of a charterparty.

20

Punitive damages

1. Are punitive damages awarded for breach of contract?	360
2. When are punitive damages awarded for torts?	361
3. The quantum of punitive damages	372
4. Should the law on punitive damages be reformed?	374

Punitive or exemplary damages are damages whose purpose is to punish the defendant for his or her wrongful conduct.[1] In *Broome v Cassell*[2] Lord Hailsham said that he preferred the term 'exemplary damages' to 'punitive damages' as better expressing the policy of the law. English courts have subsequently followed Lord Hailsham's preference. But in its Report on this area in 1997,[3] the Law Commission recommended that the pre-*Broome v Cassell* terminology of 'punitive damages' was clearer and more straightforward and did not accept that this label deflected attention from the deterrence and disapproval aims of such damages. As the Law Commission said, 'When one uses the term "punishment" in the criminal law, one does not thereby indicate that deterrence is not an important aim.'[4] Although nothing of substantive importance should turn on which label is adopted, the Law Commission's approach is persuasive and the term 'punitive damages' is therefore preferred in this chapter and book.

The fascinating and crucial question of policy is whether punitive damages are justified but, before examining that, we must look at the details of the present law.

1. Are punitive damages awarded for breach of contract?

As laid down in *Addis v Gramophone Co Ltd*,[5] no punitive damages can be awarded for breach of contract. There the claimant had been wrongfully dismissed. The House of Lords restricted damages to his pecuniary loss and refused to award any damages for the harsh manner in which he had been treated.

The same approach has been applied in several subsequent cases. In *Perera v Vandiyar*,[6] for example, the claimant was the tenant of the defendant's flat and in an attempt to get rid of him, the defendant cut off the supply of gas and electricity to the flat, leaving the claimant without alternative means of heat or light. A week later the gas and electricity supply was restored as a result of an interlocutory judgment granted by the county court, and the tenant was able to return. In an action for damages for breach of the defendant's covenant of quiet enjoyment the trial judge awarded, inter alia, £25 punitive damages, but the Court of Appeal overturned this; since damages were here being given for breach of

---

[1] See generally Law Commission, *Aggravated, Exemplary and Restitutionary Damages* (1997) Report No 247. Of the law on compensatory damages examined above in Part Two, the form of damages and foreign currency awards (ch 9), interest on damages (ch 15), and limitation periods (ch 16) are also relevant to punitive damages.
[2] [1972] AC 1027, at 1073.
[3] Law Commission, *Aggravated, Exemplary and Restitutionary Damages* (1997) Report No 247, para 5.39.
[4] ibid.   [5] [1909] AC 488.   [6] [1953] 1 WLR 672.

contract (and indeed no tort had been committed) no punitive damages could be awarded. Similarly in *Kenny v Preen*,[7] which also involved the breach by a landlord of his covenant of quiet enjoyment, punitive damages were refused, Pearson LJ saying, 'As the claim was only in contract and not tort, punitive or exemplary damages could not be properly awarded.'[8]

On the other hand in *McMillan v Singh*,[9] where again a landlord evicted a tenant, punitive damages of £250 were awarded. Although parts of Sir John Arnold's judgment seem to indicate that those damages were being given for breach of the covenant of quiet enjoyment, they are better viewed as being given for the tort of trespass or nuisance. This was not only because of his reliance solely on tort cases, but also because no mention was made of the traditional rule barring such damages for breach of contract.

Three relatively recent developments suggest that the rule in *Addis* that punitive damages can never be awarded for breach of contract may require reconsideration in the near future.

The first was the decision of the House of Lords in *Attorney-General v Blake*[10] to the effect that restitution, through an account of profits, can be awarded, albeit exceptionally, for breach of contract. This has been fully discussed in the previous chapter. Although punishment is a more extreme remedial response to a wrong than restitution, the importance of *Blake* for punitive damages is its recognition that, exceptionally, a substantial monetary remedy that is non-compensatory is appropriate for a breach of contract.

Secondly, there has been the decision of the House of Lords in *Kuddus v Chief Constable of Leicestershire Constabulary*[11] removing the former 'cause of action' restriction on punitive damages for torts. This is discussed below. Although their Lordships did not mention breach of contract, the removal of the 'cause of action' test for torts clearly leads on to the question whether it is satisfactory to rule out punitive damages because the cause of action is breach of contract rather than tort.

Thirdly, as is discussed below, punitive damages have been awarded for the first time in Canada for breach of contract by the Supreme Court in *Whiten v Pilot Insurance Co*.[12]

2. When are punitive damages awarded for torts?

(1) The three categories

The situations in which punitive damages can be awarded for torts were laid down in Lord Devlin's classic speech in *Rookes v Barnard*.[13] The case concerned the tort of intimidation, and at first instance Sachs J had ruled that punitive damages could be awarded. The House of Lords overturned that ruling.

The general tenor of Lord Devlin's speech, with which the other Law Lords agreed, was that awarding punitive damages tends to confuse unsatisfactorily the role of the civil and criminal law and that, while precedent and statute prevent their judicial abolition, the ambit of punitive damages should be restricted. Having extensively reviewed the relevant authorities, and having stressed that aggravated damages are compensatory and should therefore not be confused, as they often have been, with punitive damages,[14] Lord Devlin laid down the three sole categories in which punitive damages can be awarded: first, where

---

[7] [1963] 1 QB 499.
[8] ibid, at 513. Stephenson LJ cited these words in *Guppys (Bridport) Ltd v Brookling and James* (1984) 269 Estates Gazette 846, at 942. See also *Drane v Evangelou* [1978] 1 WLR 455.
[9] (1985) 17 HLR 120. See also *Warner v Clark* (1984) 134 NLJ 763 (CA dubiously finding a tort justification—inducing breach of contract—for punitive damages awarded at trial for breach of contract).
[10] [2001] 1 AC 268.   [11] [2001] UKHL 29, [2002] 2 AC 122. See below, pp 368–369.
[12] [2003] SCC 18. See below, p 378.   [13] [1964] AC 1129.   [14] Above, pp 287–288.

there is '… oppressive, arbitrary or unconstitutional action by the servants of the government';[15] secondly, where 'the defendant's conduct has been calculated by him to make a profit for himself which may well exceed the compensation payable to the plaintiff';[16] and thirdly, where expressly authorised by statute. As the facts of this case did not fall within any of these categories, Lord Devlin concluded that no punitive damages should have been awarded. Lord Devlin's speech was later confirmed by the House of Lords in *Cassell & Co Ltd v Broome*[17] following an attempt by the Court of Appeal in the case to outflank that restrictive approach. It is therefore now beyond argument that, applying the present law, for a claimant to be awarded punitive damages the tortious conduct must fall within one of the three categories. That, of course, is not the same as saying that the three categories are justified. It is submitted that they are not, as will be explained later when considering reform.[18]

(a) 'Oppressive, arbitrary or unconstitutional action by the servants of the government'

In *Cassell v Broome* it was made clear that 'servants of the government' is to be widely construed. As Lord Diplock said, 'It would embrace all persons purporting to exercise powers of government, central or local, conferred upon them by statute or at common law by virtue of the official status or employment which they hold.'[19] But the defendant must be exercising governmental power and in *AB v South West Water Services Ltd*[20] it was felt that that constituted a different idea in this context than in relation to whether a decision can be judicially reviewed or whether a body is an emanation of the state for the purposes of European Community law. The actions of a nationalised corporation in contaminating drinking water and failing to warn the public properly of this were therefore held not to fall within the first category.

In *Rookes v Barnard* Lord Devlin instanced three eighteenth-century cases within this category. The best known are the two concerning the printing of the *North Briton*.[21] In *Wilkes v Wood*[22] the claimant's house in which it was alleged that the paper had been printed was searched under an illegal general warrant issued by the Secretary of State. In the claimant's action for trespass, it was held that punitive damages could be awarded. Similarly, in *Huckle v Money*[23] the claimant was held entitled to punitive damages for false imprisonment, having been detained for six hours by a King's Messenger on suspicion of having printed the *North Briton*.

From the 1980s onwards, this category has found its sharpest ever cutting edge in actions against the police. So in *White v Metropolitan Police Commissioner*[24] £20,000 punitive damages were awarded to each of two claimants for false imprisonment, assault, and malicious prosecution by several police officers. In *George v Metropolitan Police Commissioner*[25]

---

[15] [1964] AC 1129, at 1226. [16] ibid. [17] [1972] AC 1027. [18] See below, p 374.
[19] [1972] AC 1027, at 1130.
[20] [1993] QB 507, overruled on other grounds by *Kuddus v Chief Constable of Leicestershire Constabulary* [2001] UKHL 29, [2002] 2 AC 122. See also *Virgo Fidelis Senior School v Boyle* [2004] IRLR 268 (school governors not acting as servants of government). Cf *Bradford City Metropolitan Council v Arora* [1991] 2 QB 507 where the public/private divide drawn for judicial review purposes was also rejected but so as to *award* punitive damages.
[21] The third was *Benson v Frederick* (1766) 3 Burr 1845. [22] (1763) Lofft 1.
[23] (1763) 2 Wils 205.
[24] *The Times*, 24 April 1982. This and the two following cases (but not the third where vicarious liability was denied) also show that vicarious liability may apply where punitive damages are being claimed, presumably on the ground that the employer deserves punishment and can best prevent future misconduct. See P Atiyah, *Vicarious Liability* (Butterworths 1967) 433–437; Law Commission, *Aggravated, Exemplary and Restitutionary Damages* (1997) Report No 247, paras 4.102–4.105, 5.209–5.230.
[25] *The Times*, 31 March 1984.

£2,000 punitive damages were awarded for trespass and assault where police officers had unlawfully searched the claimant's house looking for her son and had kicked and hit her. In *Connor v Chief Constable of Cambridgeshire*[26] there was an award of £500 punitive damages for 'assault' where a police officer had without justification hit the claimant over the head with his truncheon in the course of crowd trouble outside the entrance to a football ground and had persisted in a baseless defence to the claimant's action. And in *Makanjuola v Metropolitan Police Commissioner*[27] punitive damages of £2,000 were awarded for trespass to the person and intimidation where a police officer had sexually assaulted the claimant. Significantly this rebirth of the first category coincided with increased public criticism of the police, and a widespread belief that police powers are often abused at the expense of civil liberties.

Significant cases in the 1990s, falling within this first category, included *Treadaway v Chief Constable of West Midlands*[28] where, in addition to £10,000 compensatory damages, £40,000 punitive damages were awarded to the claimant who had had a confession extracted from him by police officers placing a bin bag over his head; and *Thompson v Metropolitan Police Commissioner*[29] where, as we shall see, £15,000 punitive damages was substituted by the Court of Appeal for a jury award of £200,000 for false imprisonment and assault by the police.

In *Muuse v Secretary of State for the Home Department*,[30] which concerned the tort of false imprisonment, it was stressed that it was the outrageous nature of the tortious conduct that made punitive damages appropriate within this first category but that there was no need to find additionally that the defendant had acted with malice. The trial judge's award of punitive damages for the tort of false imprisonment was therefore upheld.

In another case of false imprisonment, *R (on the application of Lumba) v Secretary of State for the Home Department*,[31] the claimants had been detained in breach of public law. The Supreme Court held that they were entitled to damages for the tort of false imprisonment but, as they would have been detained in any event had correct procedures been followed, the damages should be nominal only. For that and other reasons, including that there were multiple claimants some of whom were not before the court,[32] it was held that no punitive damages should here be awarded albeit that the conduct of the Home Office officials had been deplorable.

There is a close relationship between punitive damages under this first category and so-called 'vindicatory damages' for infringement of constitutional rights.[33] In a series of decisions of the Privy Council, 'vindicatory damages' for infringement of constitutional rights have been awarded in circumstances where punitive damages might otherwise have been awarded within the first of Lord Devlin's categories. So, for example, in *Attorney-General of Trinidad and Tobago v Ramanoop*,[34] there had been an unconstitutional arrest, assault, and detention by a police officer. It was held that there was jurisdiction under section 14 of the Constitution of Trinidad and Tobago to award the victim, in addition

---

[26] *The Times*, 11 April 1984. See also *Holden v Chief Constable of Lancashire* [1987] QB 380.
[27] *The Times*, 8 August 1989.   [28] *The Times*, 25 October 1994.
[29] [1998] QB 498: see below, p 372.   [30] [2010] EWCA Civ 453.
[31] [2011] UKSC 12, [2012] 1 AC 245. See also *Bostridge v Oxleas NHS Foundation Trust* [2015] EWCA Civ 79, [2015] Med LR 113; *Parker v Chief Constable of Essex* [2018] EWCA Civ 788.
[32] Below, pp 373–374.
[33] There is a wide-ranging debate as to whether 'vindicatory damages'—sometimes referred to as 'substitutive damages'—should be seen as a generally available non-compensatory measure of damages for torts and breach of contract: see above, pp 46–48.
[34] [2005] UKPC 15, [2006] 1 AC 328. See, similarly, *Merson v Cartwright* [2005] UKPC 38; *Inniss v Attorney-General for St Christopher and Nevis* [2008] UKPC 42.

to compensatory damages, damages for infringement of his constitutional rights. These additional damages were to vindicate the claimant's constitutional right, to emphasise the gravity of the breach, to reflect the sense of public outrage, and to deter further infringements. Although recognised as covering the same ground as punitive or exemplary damages, the Privy Council thought that, as punishment in the sense of retribution was not the object of this additional award, the expressions 'punitive damages' or 'exemplary damages' were here better avoided. In *Takitota v Attorney-General*[35] it was held that a court should not award both vindicatory damages and exemplary damages because of the overlap between them.

Although the nearest English law equivalent to such a constitutional wrong is an action for the infringement by the state of a person's rights under the Human Rights Act 1998 (ie for breach of the HRA cause of action),[36] it seems most unlikely that 'vindicatory damages' will be awarded for even that cause of action for two reasons. First, the wording of section 8(3) of the Human Rights Act 1998 stresses 'just satisfaction' which appears to equate to compensation; and, secondly, there appears to be nothing in the jurisprudence of the Strasbourg court, which the UK courts tend to follow in applying the 1998 Act, suggesting that vindicatory damages can be awarded.

It should be added that, while in *R (on the application of Lumba) v Secretary of State for the Home Department*[37] three of the nine Supreme Court Justices (Lord Walker, Lord Hope, and Baroness Hale) would have been willing to award 'vindicatory damages' for the tort of false imprisonment, the majority thought that such damages were inappropriate; and some of the judges, especially Lord Dyson giving the leading judgment, rightly cast severe doubt on whether vindicatory damages are ever justified as a remedy in tort (as opposed to being given for the infringement of a constitutional right where there is a written constitution).[38]

(b) 'The defendant's conduct has been calculated by him to make a profit for himself which may well exceed the compensation payable to the plaintiff'

This category, which until the 1980s was the only really important one of the three, was the focus of attention in *Cassell v Broome*.[39] The claimant, a distinguished retired naval officer, brought an action for libel against two publishers of a book presented as an authentic account of a war-time disaster when a British convoy had been destroyed. The jury had awarded the claimant £15,000 compensatory damages and £25,000 punitive damages. The defendants appealed against the award of punitive damages, but the House of Lords upheld it as falling within Lord Devlin's second category. In construing Lord Devlin's words it was held that while, on the one hand, the fact that the tortious act was committed in the course of carrying on a profit-making business is not sufficient to bring a case within the second category, on the other hand it is not necessary for the defendant actually to have calculated in arithmetical form that the profit to be made from the tort would exceed the damages and costs to which

---

[35] [2009] UKPC 11, (2009) 26 BHRC 578. [36] See above, ch 2.
[37] [2011] UKSC 12, [2012] 1 AC 245. See also *Bostridge v Oxleas NHS Foundation Trust* [2015] EWCA Civ 79, [2015] Med LR 113.
[38] See, similarly, A Burrows, 'Damages and Rights' in *Rights and Private Law* (eds D Nolan and A Robertson, Hart Publishing 2012) 275, 303–307. See, generally, N Witzleb and R Carroll, 'The Role of Vindication in Torts Damages' (2009) 17 Tort Law Review 16; J Edelman, 'Vindicatory Damages' in *Private Law in the 21st Century* (eds K Barker, K Fairweather, and R Grantham, Hart Publishing 2017) 343.
[39] [1972] AC 1027. See also *Manson v Associated Newspapers Ltd* [1965] 1 WLR 1038; *John v Mirror Group Newspapers Ltd* [1997] QB 586.

he would make himself liable. Indeed, as Lord Hailsham said, 'The defendant may calculate that the plaintiff will not sue at all.'[40] So, according to his Lordship, what is required is:

> '(i) knowledge that what is proposed to be done is against the law or a reckless disregard whether what is proposed to be done is illegal or legal and (ii) a decision to carry on doing it because the prospects of material advantage outweigh the prospects of material loss.'[41]

In the words of Lord Morris:

> 'The situation contemplated is where someone faces up to the possibility of having to pay damages for doing something which may be held to have been wrong but where nevertheless he deliberately carried out his plan because he thinks it will work out satisfactorily for him. He is prepared to hurt somebody because he thinks he may well gain by so doing even allowing for the risk that he may be made to pay damages.'[42]

Applying these approaches to the facts, punitive damages were justified because there was clear evidence that the defendants, in the knowledge that they might be defaming the claimant, were still prepared to sell the book in its sensational form.

A crucial additional point made by Lord Diplock is that damages under this second category are not concerned merely to reverse the defendant's unjust enrichment. He said:

> 'It ... may be a blunt instrument to prevent unjust enrichment by unlawful acts. But to restrict the damages recoverable to the gain made by the defendant if it exceeded the loss caused to the plaintiff, would leave a defendant contemplating an unlawful act with the certainty that he had nothing to lose to balance against the chance that the plaintiff might never sue him, or if he did, might fail in the hazards of litigation. It is only if there is a prospect that the damages may exceed the defendant's gain that the social purpose of this category is achieved—to teach a wrongdoer that tort does not pay.'[43]

The main use[44] of this second category has been in actions by tenants against landlords for wrongful harassment or eviction founded on the torts of trespass or nuisance. In *Drane v Evangelou*,[45] for example, the jury had awarded £1,000 damages for the landlord's wrongful eviction of his tenant, and the Court of Appeal held that this award was justified as including some punitive damages[46] for the tort of trespass under the second category. Both Lord Denning and Goff LJ cited that part of Lord Devlin's judgment where he said:

> 'This category is not confined to moneymaking in the strict sense. It extends to cases in which the defendant is seeking to gain at the expense of the plaintiff some object—perhaps some

---

[40] [1972] AC 1027, at 1079.
[41] ibid, at 1079. In *Borders (UK) Ltd v Commissioner of Police of the Metropolis* [2005] EWCA Civ 197, at [23], Sedley LJ said that 'calculated' meant 'likely' to make a profit beyond what would probably be recovered in cash or in kind by legal process. But, as made clear in *AXA Insurance UK Plc v Financial Claims Solutions Ltd* [2018] EWCA Civ 1330 it is preferable to adhere to Lord Hailsham's formulation.
[42] [1972] AC 1027, at 1094.   [43] ibid, at 1130.
[44] This is supported by J Goudkamp and E Katsampouka, 'An Empirical Study of Punitive Damages' (2018) 38 OJLS 90. They studied every electronically accessible judgment in England, Wales, and Northern Ireland between January 2000 and December 2015 in which punitive damages were sought (146 claims). Most claims were made for 'interference with property' (35.6%) and punitive damages were awarded in 53.8% of those claims. In contrast, for example, there were very few such claims for defamation and privacy (5.5%) and there were no awards of punitive damages in respect of those claims.
[45] [1978] 2 All ER 437. See also *Devonshire and Smith v Jenkins* [1979] LAG Bull 114; *McMillan v Singh* (1985) 17 HLR 120; *Millington v Duffy* (1984) 17 HLR 232; *Asghar v Ahmed* (1985) 17 HLR 25; *Ramdath v Daley* [1993] 1 EGLR 82 (also illustrating the point that there can be no punitive damages under this category where the defendant is acting for another's benefit); *Ramzan v Brookwide Ltd* [2011] EWCA Civ 985, [2012] 1 All ER 903 (punitive damages awarded for the tort of trespass to land).
[46] Confusingly, Lord Denning appears to use the term 'exemplary damages' to describe an award of both compensatory and exemplary damages.

property which he covets—which either he could not obtain at all or not obtain except at a price greater than he wants to put down.'[47]

And Lord Denning said:

'... this category includes cases of unlawful eviction of a tenant. The landlord seeks to gain possession at the expense of the tenant, so as to keep or get a rent higher than that awarded by the rent tribunal, or to get possession from a tenant who is protected by the Rent Acts.'[48]

Similarly in *Guppys (Bridport) Ltd v Brookling and James*[49] landlords had set about converting a building occupied by tenants into self-contained flats. They had no intention of offering alternative accommodation to the tenants and wanted to be rid of them as soon as possible. During the building work they removed all the internal sanitary and washing facilities, discontinued the supply of water to the external toilets, and cut off the electricity. The trial judge awarded £1,000 'exemplary damages' to each of the two claimant tenants. The Court of Appeal upheld this as awarded not for the tort of trespass, which was here difficult to make out, but rather for the tort of nuisance. The case fell within Lord Devlin's second category as the claimants were content to ignore the rights of the tenants in order to pursue their own profit-seeking alterations. It should be added, however, that the trial judge and the Court of Appeal were almost certainly accepting that part of the £1,000 included compensatory damages: if so, to refer to it all as 'exemplary damages' was unnecessarily confusing.[50]

Analogously, in *Design Progression Ltd v Thurloe Properties Ltd*[51] punitive damages were awarded against a landlord for breach of its statutory duty under the Landlord and Tenant Act 1988, s 1(3) in failing to give a decision, within a reasonable time, on a tenant's application for a licence to assign. Peter Smith J explained that, following the removal of the cause of action test in *Kuddus v Chief Constable of Leicestershire Constabulary*,[52] it was possible for punitive damages to be awarded for breach of statutory duty under the 1988 Act. And here the facts fell within the second category in *Rookes v Barnard* because the landlord had behaved in a cynical way designed to frustrate the tenant's legitimate expectation of being able to assign the premises. The landlord's aim had been to force the tenant out of the premises and then to be able itself to rent the premises out at a higher rent. In addition to compensatory damages (the amount of which was not fixed but appeared to be approximately £111,000), the judge awarded £25,000 punitive damages. He made clear that this went beyond any profit that the landlord had actually made and was designed to deter similar conduct by the landlord in the future and to mark the court's disapproval of its past conduct.[53]

Punitive damages have occasionally been awarded under this second category for tortious interference with the claimant's business. The case Lord Devlin principally relied on within his second category—*Bell v Midland Rly Co*[54]—can be regarded as an early example of this. There the defendants had wrongfully prevented trains running to the claimant's wharf so as to divert trade to themselves. A jury award of £1,000 was upheld, Willes J saying:

'... if ever there was a case in which the jury were warranted in awarding exemplary damages, this is that case. The defendants have committed a grievous wrong ... for the purpose of destroying the plaintiff's business and securing gain for themselves.'[55]

---

[47] [1964] AC 1129, at 1227.   [48] [1978] 1 WLR 455, at 459.   [49] (1983) 269 Estates Gazette 846.
[50] See also above, n 46.   [51] [2004] EWHC 324 (Ch), [2005] 1 WLR 1.
[52] [2001] UKHL 29, [2002] 2 AC 122. See below, pp 368–370.
[53] Although not mentioned by the judge, the breach of statutory duty can be classified as a statutory tort.
[54] (1861) 10 CBNS 287.   [55] (1861) 10 CBNS 287, at 307.

In *Borders (UK) Ltd v Commissioner of Police of the Metropolis*[56] the Court of Appeal held that punitive damages were appropriate in a case where tens of thousands (possibly hundreds of thousands) of new books had been stolen from the claimants by shoplifters and sold by the defendant from his market stalls. More controversially, in *Messenger Newspaper Group Ltd v National Graphical Association*[57] punitive damages were awarded against a trade union under the second category for the torts of interference with business by unlawful means, intimidation, and public and private nuisance, committed in the course of a dispute over the claimants' refusal to operate a closed shop. But this is hard to justify given that the defendants were not directly seeking any material gain from their conduct. Nor did Caulfield J satisfactorily overcome the objection, considered below, that the NGA had already been heavily fined for its conduct, so that the award of punitive damages amounted to double punishment.

A recent trend has been for punitive damages to be awarded for insurance fraud.[58] A good example was *AXA Insurance UK Plc v Financial Claims Solutions Ltd*[59] where fictitious motor accident claims, alleged to involve insureds of AXA, were brought and initially succeeded but were ultimately thwarted when the sophisticated fraud was exposed. Punitive damages of £20,000 (in addition to compensatory damages) were awarded within Lord Develin's second category for the tort of deceit and unlawful means conspiracy.

Finally, in *AT v Gavril Dulghieru*[60] punitive damages were awarded under this second category for the torts of unlawful conspiracy, false imprisonment, and assault by forcing several women from Moldova to work as prostitutes.

(c) Express authorisation by statute

In *Rookes v Barnard* Lord Devlin mentioned the Reserve and Auxiliary Forces (Protection of Civilian Interests) Act 1951, s 13(2), as a statutory provision expressly authorising punitive damages. Another clear example now, in the context of outrageous infringement of rights by the Press, is contained in the Crime and Courts Act 2013, ss 34–39. A controversial question is whether what was formerly the Copyright Act 1956, s 17(3), and is now the Copyright, Designs and Patents Act 1988, s 97(2) (and the parallel provisions for breach of design right and performer's property right in s 229(3) and s 191J(2) respectively), authorise punitive damages.[61] Prior to *Rookes v Barnard* the Court of Appeal in *Williams v Settle*[62] held that punitive damages could be awarded for breach of copyright either at common law or as authorised by what is now the Copyright, Designs and Patents Act 1988, s 97(2).

---

[56] [2005] EWCA Civ 197.
[57] [1984] IRLR 397, noted M Jones and A Morris, 'Picketing, The Closed Shop, and Enforcement of the Employment Acts' (1985) 14 ILJ 46. See also *Warner v Islip* (1984) 134 NLJ 763 (inducing breach of contract).
[58] The study by J Goudkamp and E Katsampouka, 'An Empirical Study of Punitive Damages' (2018) 38 OJLS 90 (see above, n 44) shows that, where sought, punitive damages are very commonly awarded in respect of insurance fraud (for the tort of deceit). As they say, at 114, 'The award of punitive damages for insurance fraud, which has been possible only since the demise of the cause-of-action test, constitutes a new trend in the case law ...'
[59] [2018] EWCA Civ 1330. [60] [2009] EWHC 225 (QB).
[61] By s 97(2): 'The court may in an action for infringement of copyright having regard to all the circumstances, and in particular to (a) the flagrancy of the infringement, and (b) any benefit accruing to the defendant by reason of the infringement, award such additional damages as the justice of the case may require.' For consideration of the close relationship between 'additional damages' and damages (available for the infringement of all IP rights) under regulation 3 of the Intellectual Property (Enforcement etc) Regulations 2006 which gives effect to Article 13 of the Intellectual Property Rights Enforcement Directive, 2004/24/EC, see *Absolute Lofts South West London Ltd v Artisan Home improvements Ltd* [2015] EWHC 2608 (IPEC), [2017] ECDR 6.
[62] [1960] 1 WLR 1072.

There the defendant, a professional photographer, following the murder of the claimant's father-in-law, sold to the Press certain photographs taken by him at the claimant's wedding which were then published in two national newspapers. Punitive damages of £1,000 were awarded in the claimant's action for breach of copyright. However, in *Rookes v Barnard* Lord Devlin left open whether punitive damages can be awarded under what is now the Copyright, Designs and Patents Act 1988, s 97(2),[63] and said that the decision in *Williams v Settle* was more easily justified as an example of aggravated rather than punitive damages.[64] In *Cassell v Broome* Lord Hailsham agreed with Lord Devlin that the question was an open one,[65] but Lord Kilbrandon considered that what is now s 97(2) did not authorise punitive damages.[66] Similarly, in *Beloff v Pressdram Ltd*[67] Ungoed-Thomas J considered that, since the subsection is directed to providing 'effective relief' for the claimant, it empowers the award of purely compensatory and not punitive damages. Again in *Redrow Homes Ltd v Bett Brothers plc*,[68] Lord Clyde suggested, without having to decide, that additional damages under s 97(2) were 'more probably' aggravated rather than punitive damages.[69] In *Nottinghamshire Healthcare NHS Trust v News Group Newspapers Ltd*[70] Pumfrey J held that additional damages under s 97(2) were not punitive but might be aggravated and might include an element of restitution. It should be clarified that, after the decision in *Kuddus v Chief Constable of Leicestershire Constabulary*[71]—which, as we shall see below, has removed the cause of action test for punitive damages—there is no bar to awarding punitive damages for the statutory tort of breach of copyright irrespective of s 97(2). But for claimants, the advantage of establishing that s 97(2) does authorise punitive damages is that it would obviate the need to show that the facts fall within one of Lord Devlin's (other) two categories (most obviously, the cynical profit-making category).

(2) The demise of the 'cause of action' test

Prior to the decision of the House of Lords in *Kuddus v Chief Constable of Leicestershire Constabulary*[72] a very important restriction, over and above whether the facts fell within Lord Devlin's three categories, was the 'cause of action test', which had been laid down by the Court of Appeal in *AB v South West Water Services Ltd*.[73] It was decided in the latter case that *Cassell v Broome* required that the tort be one for which punitive damages had been awarded prior to *Rookes v Barnard* in 1964. This was thought to be the view not only of Lords Hailsham and Diplock but also of Lords Wilberforce and Kilbrandon and, possibly,

---

[63] [1964] AC 1129, at 1225.   [64] ibid, at 1229.   [65] [1972] AC 1027, at 1080.
[66] ibid, at 1134.
[67] [1973] 1 All ER 241, at 265. But the words 'effective relief' in the Copyright Act 1956, s 17(3) have not been repeated in the Copyright, Designs and Patents Act 1988, s 97(2).
[68] [1999] 1 AC 197. The decision of their Lordships was that, as a matter of statutory interpretation, additional damages under the Copyright, Designs and Patents Act 1988, s 97(2) could not be added to an account of profits as opposed to an award of damages.
[69] In *Nichols Advanced Vehicle Systems Inc v Rees* [1979] RPC 127 it was held that damages should be awarded under what is now the Copyright, Designs and Patents Act 1988, s 97(2) but without clarifying whether punitive or not. See also *ZYX Music GmbH v King* [1995] 3 All ER 1.
[70] [2002] EWHC 409, [2002] RPC 49, esp at [51].   [71] [2001] UKHL 29, [2002] 2 AC 122.
[72] ibid.
[73] [1993] 1 All ER 609. The state of the law had previously been uncertain: see, inter alia, *Cassell v Broome* [1972] AC 1027, at 1076, 1130–1131 (Lords Hailsham and Diplock); *Mafo v Adams* [1970] 1 QB 548; *Metall & Rohstoff AG v Acli Metals (London) Ltd* [1984] 1 Lloyd's Rep 598, at 612 (Purchas LJ); *Archer v Brown* [1984] 2 All ER 267, at 281 (Peter Pain J); *Morton-Norwich Products v Intercen (No 2)* [1981] FSR 337; *Catnic Components v Hill & Smith Ltd* [1983] FSR 512; *Bradford City Metropolitan Council v Arora* [1991] 3 All ER 545 (where the point was not taken).

Lord Reid and therefore of the majority of the seven Law Lords sitting in that case.[74] There could therefore be no award of punitive damages for the tort of public nuisance in supplying contaminated drinking water to inhabitants of Camelford, Cornwall, since public nuisance was not a tort for which punitive damages had been awarded prior to *Rookes v Barnard*. The result of the decision was that punitive damages were only available for malicious prosecution, false imprisonment, assault and battery, defamation, trespass to land or to goods, private nuisance, and tortious interference with business. Other torts, such as negligence, deceit, misfeasance in public office, and unlawful discrimination, failed the cause of action test and did not qualify for the award of punitive damages.

In *Kuddus*, in which it was decided that punitive damages could be awarded for the tort of misfeasance in public office under the first category, the House of Lords held unanimously that the cause of action test should be removed. It was noted that the need to search through old authorities to find a pre-1964 award of punitive damages for a particular tort was unfortunate, especially as, since aggravated and punitive damages have only been clearly distinguished since *Rookes v Barnard* itself, it may well be difficult to determine the characterisation of an award of damages in an older case. Argument was not heard on the wider question of whether punitive damages should be retained at all, although three of their Lordships expressed their opinion on the subject.[75]

The demise of the cause of action test in *Kuddus* means that, subject to what is said below about eurotorts and infringement of human rights, punitive damages can now be awarded for any tort (provided the facts fall within one of the three categories of *Rookes v Barnard*).[76]

It is an unresolved issue whether punitive damages can be awarded for a eurotort (eg for breach of a directly effective EU directive).[77] The main judicial analysis of this was at first instance in *R v Secretary of State for Transport, ex p Factortame (No 5)*[78] where the availability of punitive damages was denied. But an important part of the Divisional Court's reasoning was that this denial would not discriminate against claimants for eurotorts, in comparison to claimants under English domestic law, because punitive damages could not be awarded for an analogous breach of statutory duty under English domestic law: applying the 'cause of action' test, punitive damages could not be awarded for breach of a post-1964 statute (and had not been expressly authorised by the European Communities Act 1972). Since that decision the 'cause of action' test has been abolished by the House of Lords in *Kuddus v Chief Constable of Leicestershire Constabulary*.[79] This has therefore undermined that part of the Divisional Court's reasoning. But this does not necessarily mean that the Divisional Court would have reached a different conclusion. The judgment is hostile in general terms to punitive damages in this context and stressed that, as no other EU state has punitive damages, uniformity within the EU supported the view that such damages were not available. The Law Commission considered that the arguments for and against

---

[74] In *Kuddus* Lords Slynn, Mackay, and Hutton found that *Cassell v Broome* did not support the cause of action test, whereas Lords Nicholls and Scott held that the interpretation of that case adopted in *AB v South West Water Services Ltd* was correct.

[75] Lords Nicholls and Hutton favoured their retention; Lord Scott took the opposite view. For discussion of this issue see below, pp 374–378.

[76] The decision in *Mosley v News Group Newspapers Ltd* [2008] EWHC 1777 (QB), [2008] EMLR 20 that no exemplary damages can be awarded for breach of confidence/privacy cannot now stand in so far as it may be interpreted as denying exemplary damages for the tort of privacy (as opposed to breach of confidence). It was decided at a time before it had been made clear that privacy is a tort as opposed to an equitable wrong: see ch 1.

[77] For the term 'eurotort', see above, p 15.

[78] [1997] Eu LR 475. On appeal, there was no discussion of punitive, as opposed to compensatory, damages: [2000] 1 AC 524.

[79] [2001] UKHL 29, [2002] 2 AC 122.

'seem finely balanced'.[80] But if English domestic law would award punitive damages for an analogous tort, the 'equivalence' principle of EU law may be thought more important than uniformity in the EU. If that is so, then subsequent to the *Kuddus* case, punitive damages should be available for eurotorts.

We have seen in chapter 2 that breach of a Convention right under the Human Rights Act 1998 is not a tort but is a sui generis public law wrong. As such, it strictly speaking falls outside the scope of this book. Moreover, the reasoning in the *Kuddus* case was confined to allowing punitive damages for any tort and would therefore not apply to the HRA cause of action. But even if punitive damages could be awarded for a non-tortious wrong, and even if the facts were to fall within one of the *Rookes v Barnard* categories (most obviously category one), it seems clear that no punitive damages are to be awarded for the HRA cause of action. This is because the Human Rights Act 1998, s 8(3) refers to the award being necessary to afford 'just satisfaction' to the claimant, which appears to be a reference to compensation alone. Moreover, by s 8(4) the courts are required to take into account in deciding whether to award damages the principles applied by the European Court of Human Rights; and the Strasbourg court has never awarded punitive damages. That this is the correct interpretation of the Human Rights Act 1998—that no punitive damages can be awarded under that Act—has been supported in obiter dicta of Stanley Burton J in *R (KB) v Mental Health Review Tribunal*[81] and the Court of Appeal in *Anufrijeva v London Borough of Southwark*.[82]

(3) Other factors to be considered in deciding whether to award punitive damages

Punitive damages will not be awarded just because there has been a tort and the facts fall within one of the three categories in *Rookes v Barnard*. There are three other factors to consider (as well as factors that go solely or primarily to the quantum of the award and will be discussed later).

(a) Compensatory damages adequate

As stressed in *Rookes v Barnard*[83] and *Cassell v Broome*[84] there should be no punitive damages if it is considered that the compensatory damages awarded are adequate to punish the defendant. This has been referred to as the 'if but only if' test because Lord Devlin in *Rookes v Barnard* said that, if a case fell within one of the categories, a jury should be directed that:

> 'if, but only if, the sum which they have in mind to award as compensation (which may, of course, be a sum aggravated by the way in which the defendant has behaved to the plaintiff) is inadequate to punish him for his outrageous conduct ... then it can award some larger sum.'[85]

---

[80] Law Commission, *Aggravated, Exemplary and Restitutionary Damages* (1997) Report No 247, para 5.69.
[81] [2003] EWHC 193 (Admin), [2003] 2 All ER 209.
[82] [2003] EWCA Civ 1406, [2004] 1 All ER 833, at [55]. [83] [1964] AC 1129, at 1228.
[84] [1972] AC 1027, at 1062, 1089, 1096, 1104, 1118, 1121–1122, 1134.
[85] [1964] AC 1129, at 1227–1228. In *Borders (UK) Ltd v Commissioner of Police of the Metropolis* [2005] EWCA Civ 197, the Court of Appeal considered that an award of punitive damages would probably still leave the claimants undercompensated for theft of their property on a massive scale: but the fact that there was an element of compensation did not prevent the award from falling within Lord Devlin's second category. In *Ramzan v Brookwide Ltd* [2011] EWCA Civ 985, [2012] 1 All ER 903, the Court of Appeal, while upholding an award of punitive damages for the tort of trespass to land as being justified to deter similar conduct, reduced the quantum of punitive damages that had been awarded at first instance by two-thirds to £20,000: confusingly,

(b) Criminal punishment

It is not entirely clear whether the fact that the defendant has been punished by the criminal law is an absolute bar to an award of punitive damages or merely a factor to be taken into account so as to ensure that the overall punishment is not excessive. As laid down in *Devonshire and Smith v Jenkins*[86] and *Archer v Brown*,[87] where a defendant has already been punished by the criminal law in respect of the facts upon which the claimant now founds his tortious action, no punitive damages should be awarded since a person should not be punished twice for the same offence. In the first of these cases the defendant had already been fined and, in the second, imprisoned for the conduct in question.

In contrast, in *Borders (UK) Ltd v Commissioner of Police of the Metropolis*[88] the Court of Appeal considered that the fact that the defendant had been sentenced to 30 months' imprisonment and that his assets were likely to be subject to a confiscation order under the Criminal Justice Act 1988 did not preclude an award of punitive damages.[89]

Perhaps the best view, therefore, is that the prior imposition of criminal sanctions should be taken into account rather than operating as a complete bar to punitive damages. This is further supported by *AT v Gavril Dulghieru*[90] in which punitive damages were awarded even though there had been criminal proceedings and confiscation orders made against the defendants.

(c) The claimant's conduct

In *Rookes v Barnard*[91] Lord Devlin said that the court should take into account all mitigating circumstances. So most obviously, punitive damages may be refused (or reduced) if the claimant has brought the defendant's conduct upon himself. Indeed this is analogous to the principles of causation and contributory negligence applied in relation to compensatory damages. A rare example of its application is *O'Connor v Hewitson*[92] where punitive damages were refused for trespass to the person under the first category because the claimant had provoked the defendant policeman's assault. Conduct by the claimant which is not a cause of the offending behaviour is not relevant; thus, a refusal to co-operate in a complaints procedure will not affect an award of punitive damages.[93]

---

the Court of Appeal reasoned that one had to be careful to ensure that the award of punitive damages did not infringe the principle, in relation to the concurrent claim for breach of trust, that the claimant must elect for either compensation or an account of profits.

[86] [1979] LAG Bulletin 114.

[87] [1985] QB 401 (tort of deceit). See also *Loomis v Rohan* (1974) 46 DLR (3d) 423; *Daniels v Thompson* [1998] 3 NZLR 22, upheld on appeal as *W v W* [1999] 2 NZLR 1 (but abrogated by what is now the Injury Prevention, Rehabilitation and Compensation Act 2001, NZ, s 319). Similarly in *Gray v Motor Accident Commission* (1999) 73 AJLR 45 it was held by the High Court of Australia that, where a defendant had been imprisoned for the conduct in question (deliberately injuring the claimant by driving a car at him), there was an automatic bar against the claimant being awarded punitive damages in an action for negligence.

[88] [2005] EWCA Civ 197. See also *AXA Insurance UK Plc v Financial Claims Solutions Ltd* [2018] EWCA Civ 1330.

[89] The facts of this case were peculiar in the sense that the punitive award in practice covered the claimants' loss and Sedley LJ commented, at [28], that the unusual situation in which an award of punitive damages was, in practice, compensatory 'has to make up in justice what it lacks in logic'.

[90] [2009] EWHC 825 (QB). See also *Devenish Nutrition Ltd v Sanofi-Aventis SA (France)* [2007] EWHC 2394 (Ch), at [58]–[64] (upheld on appeal on a different point, [2008] EWCA Civ 1086, [2009] Ch 390).

[91] [1964] AC 1129, at 1228.

[92] [1979] Crim LR 46. See also *Bishop v Metropolitan Police Commissioner* [1990] 1 LS Gaz R 30.

[93] *Thompson v Metropolitan Police Commissioner* [1998] QB 498.

3. The quantum of punitive damages

Assuming punitive damages are to be awarded (and hence under the present law we are here dealing solely with tort cases) how does the court, be it judge or jury, assess them? While Lord Devlin did stress that awards should be moderate,[94] the basic answer has traditionally been that there is almost total discretion to award whatever sum is felt necessary to punish the defendant and to set an example to others.[95]

There have, however, been three main developments in respect of a jury's assessment of punitive damages.

Firstly, there have been cases in which the Court of Appeal[96] has substituted a very much lower figure for an award of punitive damages made by a jury. In *John v MGN Ltd*[97] the jury awarded £275,000 in punitive damages for defamation, which on appeal was reduced to £50,000. Similarly, in *Thompson v Metropolitan Police Commissioner*[98] £15,000 was substituted for an award of £200,000 punitive damages for false imprisonment and assault.

Secondly, in cases of jury assessment the judge is now encouraged to give guidance on the quantum of the punitive award, and a guideline 'tariff' is emerging. In *Thompson v Metropolitan Police Commissioner* the Court of Appeal stated that, in a case of false imprisonment or assault against the police, unless the figure for punitive damages is at least £5,000 the case is unlikely to be suitable for the award of such damages.[99] For a punitive award of £25,000 to be appropriate in such a case 'the conduct must be particularly deserving of condemnation', and £50,000 'should be regarded as the absolute maximum', the example given being a case where officers of at least the rank of superintendent were directly involved.[100]

Thirdly, the right to jury trial in defamation cases was removed by the Defamation Act 2013, s 11. This means that, under the Senior Courts Act 1981, s 69, and the County Courts Act 1984, s 66, the right to a jury trial in a civil case is now confined to claims for malicious prosecution or false imprisonment or where there is a charge of fraud.[101] While not removing the role of juries in relation to punitive damages, the removal of the right to a jury in defamation cases has reduced the range of cases in which the quantum of punitive damages (and whether they should be awarded) is a matter for a jury.

These developments do not remove the risk of jury awards being inconsistent with each other or with awards made by judges.[102] Moreover, there is no convincing reason why the quantum of punitive damages should ever be decided by a jury rather than a judge even if the civil trial is by jury. After all, it is for a judge and not a jury to decide on the appropriate sentence in a criminal trial. It is therefore submitted that, as the Law Commission

---

[94] [1964] AC 1129, at 1227–1228.
[95] The study by J Goudkamp and E Katsampouka, 'An Empirical Study of Punitive Damages' (2018) 38 OJLS 90 (see above, n 44) indicated, at 115, that, in the sample cases, there was a surprising level of uniformity in the quantum of punitive damages: 'there was considerable uniformity in punitive damages awards, with most cases falling within a relatively narrow bracket (£588 to £33,851).'
[96] In the exercise of its powers under the Courts and Legal Services Act 1990, s 8(2).
[97] [1997] QB 586.   [98] [1998] QB 498.
[99] But in *Watkins v Secretary of State for the Home Department* [2004] EWCA Civ 966 it was said that a lower minimum figure of punitive damages could be appropriate for a case of malicious prosecution where there was no jury.
[100] [1998] QB 498, at 517.   [101] See above, p 274.
[102] The study by J Goudkamp and E Katsampouka, 'An Empirical Study of Punitive Damages' (2018) 38 OJLS 90 (see above, n 44) indicates, at 116, that 'judges and juries do not differ substantially from each other in determining whether to award punitive damages or in assessing the quantum of such awards'.

recommended,[103] the assessment of punitive damages should be made the sole preserve of the judges, whose first priority should be consistency of awards.

There are three further important points on assessment. First, Lord Devlin said that the parties' means and all mitigating circumstances should be taken into account.[104] The latter most obviously refers to the claimant's own contributory blameworthy conduct, and has already been considered. The former is presumably in line with the criminal sentencing principle that there is no sense in fining someone beyond what that person can pay.[105] Following some debate as to whether, in vicarious liability cases, reference should be made to the means of the wrongdoer employee or only to those of the defendant employer, it was held in *Thompson v Metropolitan Police Commissioner*[106] that the means of the employee are irrelevant and do not limit the award against the vicariously liable employer. In *Rowlands v Chief Constable of Merseyside Police*[107] the question of whether a chief officer of police can be vicariously liable for punitive damages was carefully considered. It was held that for policy reasons such an award should be possible (even though this meant that the financial means of the 'servant' joint tortfeasor would be irrelevant). In Moore Bick LJ's words: 'Only by this means can awards of an adequate amount be made against those who bear public responsibility for the officers concerned.'[108] On the facts, punitive damages of £7,500 were awarded in addition to compensatory (including aggravated) damages of £12,350.

Secondly, as laid down in *Cassell v Broome*,[109] where there are joint defendants punitive damages must not exceed the lowest sum that any of the defendants ought to pay; so that if damages are not justified against any one of the defendants, they should not be awarded at all. It follows that if he or she can be identified the claimant is best advised to sue the most blameworthy defendant alone.

Finally, where there are multiple claimants *Riches v News Group Newspapers*[110] makes clear that the total amount of punitive damages considered fair for the defendant to pay should first be decided on. Then that amount can be divided among the claimants. The Court of Appeal therefore set aside a total award of £250,000 punitive damages to ten

---

[103] Law Commission, *Aggravated, Exemplary and Restitutionary Damages* (1997) Report No 247, paras 5.44, 5.81–5.90. The Law Commission further recommended in these paragraphs that the question of whether punitive damages should be awarded should also be for the judge and not the jury.

[104] [1964] AC 1129, at 1228.

[105] It can be argued that a defendant ought not to be able to insure against punitive damages just as he cannot insure against criminal fines. In *Lancashire County Council v Municipal Mutual Insurance Ltd* [1997] QB 897, however, it was decided that there is no public policy objection to insurance against a liability to pay punitive damages where they are awarded against a defendant on the basis of vicarious liability for another's tort. Stuart-Smith LJ also considered the issue in relation to personal liability, and suggested that insurance would be acceptable where it covers conduct which is not also criminal. The Law Commission recommended that insurance against punitive damages should never be regarded as against public policy: Law Commission, *Aggravated, Exemplary and Restitutionary Damages* (1997) Report No 247, paras 5.234–5.269.

[106] [1998] QB 498. But see the comments of Lord Mackay in *Kuddus v Chief Constable of Leicestershire Constabulary* [2001] UKHL 29, [2002] 2 AC 122, at [47]. The decision causes difficulty where the employer seeks contribution or an indemnity from the employee in respect of the punitive damages award. The court solved this pragmatically by holding that contribution disproportionate to the employee's means should not be ordered.

[107] [2006] EWCA Civ 1773, [2007] 1 WLR 1065.

[108] ibid, at [47]. For the Law Commission's detailed reasoning on this, coming to the same conclusion, see *Aggravated, Exemplary and Restitutionary Damages* Report (1997) No 247, paras 5.209–5.230.

[109] [1972] AC 1027, at 1063. See also *Francis v Brown* (1998) 30 HLR 143 (no punitive damages for unlawful eviction under the Housing Act 1998, ss 27–28 because one of the joint defendants did not merit punishment). The Law Commission recommended that a separate assessment of punitive damages should be made against each defendant, who would be severally liable to pay it: Law Commission, *Aggravated, Exemplary and Restitutionary Damages* (1997) Report No 247, paras 5.186–5.208.

[110] [1986] QB 256.

claimants for libel because, inter alia, there had been no direction on this point by the judge and there was the possibility (and on the face of it, surely a high probability) that the jury had considered that £25,000 rather than £250,000 (£2,500 rather than £25,000 to each claimant) should be the total amount of punitive damages. More generally, in *R (on the application of Lumba) v Secretary of State for the Home Department*[111] one of the reasons for not awarding punitive damages was that there were others in the same position as the claimants who were not before the court.

4. Should the law on punitive damages be reformed?[112]

To echo Stephenson LJ's words in the *Riches* case,[113] the law on punitive damages '... cries aloud ... for parliamentary intervention'. Although the law has become less artificial following the abolition of the cause of action test, reform is still desirable. Lord Devlin's categories in *Rookes v Barnard*[114] lack satisfactory rationale in principle or policy. As regards category one, why, for example, should a private store detective who maliciously falsely imprisons an alleged shoplifter be immune from punitive damages when a police officer, who does exactly the same, is not? And as regards category two, why, for example, should it make all the difference as regards the availability of punitive damages, whether a person who attacked an old lady was paid to do so or not? In essence, the categories represent an unhappy compromise between the desire to rid the law of punitive damages altogether and the belief that precedent is too firmly entrenched to allow this.

But what form should reform take? There are two main options: the abolition of punitive damages or their retention and extension on a principled basis.

---

[111] [2011] UKSC 12, [2012] 1 AC 245, at [167]. See also *Devenish Nutrition Ltd v Sanofi-Aventis SA (France)* [2007] EWHC 2394 (Ch), at [68] (upheld on appeal on a different point, [2008] EWCA Civ 1086, [2009] Ch 390). There are practical difficulties in deciding who are the multiple claimants on any particular facts. For the Law Commission's recommendations for dealing with those difficulties, based on the principle that 'the first past the post take all', see Law Commission, *Aggravated, Exemplary and Restitutionary Damages* (1997) Report No 247, paras 5.159–5.185.

[112] H Street, *Principles of the Law of Damages* (Sweet & Maxwell 1962) 34–36 (arguing that an empirical study of the effectiveness of punitive damages in attaining their stated goals is a necessity in order to decide whether they should be retained or abolished); A Ogus, *The Law of Damages* (Butterworths 1973) 32–34; S Waddams, *The Law of Damages* (6th edn, Thomson Reuters 2017) paras 11.10–11.100; R Posner, *Economic Analysis of Law* (9th edn, Wolters Kluwer 2014) 223; H Collins, *The Law of Contract* (4th edn, LexisNexis 2003) 422–427; J Stone, 'Double Count and Double Talk: The End of Exemplary Damages?' (1972) 46 ALJ 311; T Sullivan, 'Punitive Damages in the Law of Contract: The Reality and the Illusion of Legal Change' (1977) 61 Minn LR 207; J Mallor and B Roberts, 'Punitive Damages: Towards a Principled Approach' (1980) 31 Hastings LJ 639; D Owen, 'The Moral Foundations of Punitive Damages' (1989) 40 Alabama LR 705; B Chapman and M Trebilcock, 'Punitive Damages: Divergence in Search of a Rationale' (1989) 40 Alabama LR 741; B Perlstein, 'Crossing the Contract-Tort Boundary: An Economic Argument for the Imposition of Extracompensatory Damages for Opportunistic Breach of Contract' (1992) 58 Brooklyn LR 877; N McBride, 'A Case for Awarding Punitive Damages in Response to Deliberate Breaches of Contract' (1995) 24 Anglo-American LR 369; N McBride, 'Punitive Damages' in *Wrongs and Remedies in the Twenty-First Century* (ed P Birks, Clarendon Press 1996) 175–202; A Ogus, 'Exemplary Damages and Economic Analysis' in *The Human Face of Law: Essays in Honour of Donald Harris* (ed K Hawkins, Clarendon Press 1997) 85–102; J Edelman, *Gain-Based Damages* (Hart Publishing 2002) ch 1; A Beever, 'The Structure of Aggravated and Exemplary Damages' (2003) 23 OJLS 87; E Weinrib, 'Punishment and Disgorgement as Contract Remedies' (2003) 78 Chicago-Kent LR 55; S Smith, *Contract Theory* (OUP 2004) 417–420; E McKendrick, 'Breach of Contract, Restitution for Wrongs, and Punishment' in *Commercial Remedies* (eds A Burrows and E Peel, OUP 2003) 93; R Cunnington, 'Should Punitive Damages by Part of the Judicial Arsenal in Contract Cases?' (2006) 26 Legal Studies 369; S Rowan, 'Reflections on the Introduction of Punitive Damages for Breach of Contract' (2010) 30 OJLS 495. For a detailed examination of the arguments, see Law Commission, *Aggravated, Exemplary and Restitutionary Damages* (1997) Report No 247 Pt V.

[113] [1985] 2 All ER 845, at 850.   [114] [1964] AC 1129.

(1) Arguments for the abolition of punitive damages[115]

(i) Most importantly, it is argued that punitive damages, because their primary aim is punishment, confuse the role of the criminal and the civil law and that this is unsatisfactory for several reasons. First, punishment is an extreme sanction justifiable only if a law designated as criminal has been broken. Secondly (as under present criminal proceedings), the defendant should have the benefit of more protective procedures, evidential rules and rights of appeal if punishment rather than, say, compensation is in issue. In *Cassell v Broome*[116] Lord Reid was particularly critical of jury awards of punitive damages on the ground that in criminal cases it is never left to a jury to decide the punishment. Thirdly, punishment requires a state–individual relationship rather than being for one individual to demand against another. It follows that the rightful recipient of monetary punishment should be the state, and not a claimant. Of course all this in no sense denies that the criminal courts are justified in awarding compensation or restitution to the victim of a crime, for there is no objection to less drastic remedies than punishment being ordered for a crime. The objection is to the more drastic sanction of punishment being used for civil wrongs.

(ii) It may also be contended that any useful purpose served by tortious punitive damages within Lord Devlin's categories could be achieved by other satisfactory means. For example, all the cases on actions against the police within the first category also involved crimes, and a criminal prosecution would serve equally well to punish and deter police misconduct. Similarly, within the second category there are already adequate criminal sanctions against landlords for wrongful eviction under the Protection from Eviction Act 1977.[117] Moreover, and irrespective of whether criminal punishment is felt justified, the civil law in respect of the second category can justifiably go beyond compensation by awarding restitutionary remedies stripping the defendant of her profits.[118] Compensation alone does not and need not underpin tortious or, more controversially, contractual monetary remedies; restitution, occupying a mid-position between compensation and punishment, is an acceptable remedial function for a civil wrong. Arguably, therefore, cases within the second category like *Cassell v Broome* could be satisfactorily dealt with by awarding a restitutionary remedy to the claimant. Indeed that there is dispute over the extent of even restitutionary remedies for torts could be said to make pursuit of the more drastic aim of punishment doubly surprising.

(2) Arguments for extending punitive damages on a principled basis

There are strong arguments in favour of retaining punitive damages, while removing the illogicalities in the present law by giving punitive damages an extended ambit based on principle to replace the artificial categories test. In addition to the two main arguments set out below, support for this is derived from the experience in other Commonwealth countries where punitive damages continue to be awarded for a wide range of torts.[119] Tortious punitive damages are also freely recoverable in the US.[120]

---

[115] It has also been argued that punitive damages would deter an efficient breach of contract. As discussed below, pp 413–415, this is an unsatisfactory argument given the opportunity to bargain round the remedy. Note also that punitive damages are almost unknown in civil law systems.
[116] [1972] AC 1027, at 1087.   [117] As amended by the Housing Act 1988.   [118] Above, ch 19.
[119] *Uren v John Fairfax & Sons Pty Ltd* (1966) 117 CLR 118; *Taylor v Beere* [1982] 1 NZLR 81; *Paragon Properties Ltd v Magna Envestments Ltd* (1972) 24 DLR 156, at 167 cited with approval in *Vorvis v Insurance Corp of British Columbia* [1989] 1 SCR 1085, at 1108; *ACB v Thomson Medical Pte Ltd* [2017] SGCA 20, [2017] 1 SLR 918, esp at [175].
[120] Second Restatement of Torts, para 908. See, also, *Exxon Shipping Co v Baker* 554 US 471 (2008), at 496.

(i) The primary argument is encapsulated in the following passage from Lord Wilberforce's judgment (dissenting on some points) in *Cassell v Broome*:

> 'It cannot lightly be taken for granted, even as a matter of theory, that the purpose of the law of tort is compensation, still less that it ought to be ... or that there is something inappropriate or illogical or anomalous in including a punitive element in civil damages, or, conversely, that the criminal law, rather than civil law, is in these cases the better instrument for conveying social disapproval, or for redressing a wrong to the social fabric, or that damages in any case can be broken down into the two separate elements. As a matter of practice English law has not committed itself to any of these theories ...'[121]

There is no logical reason why punishment should not be a response available to the civil law. Moreover, it is not intended to be, and is not, identical to criminal punishment. In particular, civil punishment can be demanded by an individual, the victim of the wrongdoing, whereas criminal punishment is sought by or on behalf of the state; civil punishment also lacks the stigma of criminal punishment.

(ii) Even if illogical, punitive damages can serve a useful purpose. This is supported by the following passage from the speech of Lord Devlin himself:

> '... there are certain categories of case in which an award of exemplary damages can serve a useful purpose in vindicating the strength of the law and thus affording a practical justification for admitting into the civil law a principle which ought logically to belong to the criminal.'[122]

These words were echoed by Lord Nicholls in *Kuddus v Chief Constable of Leicestershire Constabulary*:

> 'From time to time cases do arise where awards of compensatory damages are perceived as inadequate to achieve a just result between the parties. The nature of the defendant's conduct calls for a further response from the courts. On occasion conscious wrongdoing by a defendant is so outrageous, his disregard of the plaintiff's rights so contumelious, that something more is needed to show that the law will not tolerate such behaviour. Without an award of exemplary damages, justice will not have been done ... [T]he underlying rationale lies in the sense of outrage which a defendant's conduct sometimes evokes, a sense not always assuaged fully by a compensatory award of damages, even when the damages are increased to reflect emotional distress.'[123]

Punitive damages represent another means of protection for the victim of wrongdoing and an additional deterrent to engaging in such conduct. Aggravated damages and a restitutionary award cannot cover the whole field. For instance, D may have libelled C in order to make a profit, but if any profit cannot be identified there will be no appropriate response to D's blameworthy motivation in the absence of punitive damages. Moreover, the criminal law offers incomplete protection; for example, its substantive scope does not cover all wrongs deserving of punishment.[124] In addition, the resources and priorities of the state determine whether the wrongdoer is caught and prosecuted, and this may be felt to be particularly inappropriate where the state itself has committed the wrongdoing; punitive damages have perhaps been most useful in protecting civil liberties.[125]

---

[121] [1972] AC 1027, at 1114. [122] [1964] AC 1129, at 1226.
[123] [2001] UKHL 29, [2002] 2 AC 122, at [63]–[65].
[124] There may indeed be persuasive objections to criminalising certain wrongs, for example because they are not thought to warrant the stigma of criminal punishment.
[125] See, eg, Lord Hutton's speech in *Kuddus v Chief Constable of Leicestershire Constabulary* [2001] UKHL 29, [2002] 2 AC 122, at [75]–[79].

(3) The Law Commission's recommendations

The latter arguments persuaded the Law Commission,[126] it is submitted correctly, to recommend the retention of punitive damages and a redefinition of the cases in which they could be awarded so as to put them on a sound principled basis. In particular, it recommended that the cause of action test should be abolished (as has subsequently been brought about judicially in the *Kuddus* case)[127] and that, instead of Lord Devlin's three categories, punitive damages should be available for any civil wrong (except breach of contract) where 'the defendant's conduct shows a deliberate and outrageous disregard of the [claimant's] rights'.[128] Such a principled approach (albeit without the emphasis on 'deliberate') replacing the categories derives strong support from obiter dicta of Lord Nicholls in the *Kuddus* case.[129] It also underpins his comment in the Privy Council in *A v Bottrill*[130] that English law is 'still toiling in the chains of *Rookes v Barnard*'.

The Law Commission recommended the retention of several of the current features of the law: for example, that punitive damages should not be awarded unless other possible remedies (and the Law Commission highlighted not merely compensation but also restitution) do not go far enough to punish the defendant. Other factors to guide the judge's discretion were listed, such as the harm caused or intended to the claimant, any benefit the defendant derived or intended to derive from the conduct, the nature of the right infringed, and the defendant's state of mind. An important change recommended was that, in a jury trial, the judge, rather than the jury, should decide whether punitive damages should be awarded and their quantum.[131] Unfortunately the Law Commission's recommendations on punitive (and other non-compensatory) damages have not been accepted by the Government[132] and there seems little chance in the foreseeable future of legislative reform dealing generally with punitive damages. Having said that, in the limited context of the outrageous infringement of rights by news publishers who are not members of an approved regulator, the Crime and Courts Act 2013, ss 34–39[133] has implemented the core recommendations on punitive damages of the Law Commission and that provides a limited but interesting indication of how those recommendations can be enshrined in legislation.

The Law Commission recommended that the law should not be changed to allow the award of punitive damages for breach of contract.[134] It is certainly more difficult to envisage cases of breach of contract in which an award of punitive damages would be merited, particularly as the damage suffered is usually purely economic. Yet the same considerations which support the award of punitive damages in a tort case—deterrence, for example—may equally apply in an exceptional case of breach of contract. This may be illustrated by

---

[126] Law Commission, *Aggravated, Exemplary and Restitutionary Damages* (1997) Report No 247 Pts IV and V.
[127] Above, pp 368–369.
[128] The Law Commission thought that intention or subjective recklessness should be required (hence the inclusion of the word 'deliberate'). This is also the view now taken in New Zealand (where punitive damages are not confined to the *Rookes v Barnard* categories): *Couch v Attorney General (No 2)* [2010] NZSC 27, [2010] NZLR 149 holding that subjective recklessness is a necessary minimum requirement for punitive damages albeit that the cause of action may be the tort of negligence (overruling *A v Bottrill* [2002] UKPC 44, [2003] 1 AC 449 on this point).
[129] [2001] UKHL 29, [2002] 2 AC 122, at [65]–[68].
[130] [2002] UKPC 44, [2003] 1 AC 449, at [41].
[131] See above, p 373 n 103.
[132] Hansard (HC Debates), 9 November 1999, col 502, citing the absence of a clear consensus on the way ahead, and anticipating future judicial clarification of the position.
[133] These sections were implemented following the recommendations (drawing in turn on the Law Commission's recommendations) of B Leveson, *An Inquiry into the Culture, Practices and Ethics of the Press: Report* (TSO 2012).
[134] For equitable wrongs, see below, pp 536–537.

reference to the facts of *Whiten v Pilot Insurance Co*,[135] the case which clearly established that in Canada punitive damages may in certain circumstances be awarded for a breach of contract where no tortious conduct is involved. An accidental fire destroyed the claimant's home, and she claimed under the insurance policy issued to her by the defendant company. However, the defendant alleged that the claimant had started the fire deliberately and paid hardly any of the sum due under the policy. The allegation of arson was contradicted by the local fire chief and by the company's own expert investigator and initial expert; it was made in bad faith (and pursued through an eight-week trial) in order to try to force the claimant, who was in a very poor financial position, into an unfairly low settlement. This was held by the Supreme Court of Canada to justify an award of $1 million punitive damages. Although there had been no tort in addition to the breach of contract, the defendant had committed an 'actionable wrong' in breaching the duty to act in good faith which, as the other party to an insurance contract, it owed to the claimant. In such a case, punitive damages are an appropriate legal response, and it appears unduly restrictive to allow them only if a tort has also been committed.

---

[135] (2002) 209 DLR (4th) 257. For a useful case-note, see G Fridman, 'Punitive Damages for Breach of Contract—A Canadian Innovation' (2003) 119 LQR 20. See also *Royal Bank of Canada v W Got & Associates Electric Ltd* (2000) 178 DLR (4th) 385 (punitive damages awarded for breach of contract but, on the facts, a tort had also been committed) noted by J Edelman, 'Exemplary Damages for Breach of Contract' (2001) 117 LQR 539. Punitive damages in contract were set aside by the Supreme Court of Canada in an insurance case, *Fidler v Sun Life Assurance Co of Canada* (2006) 271 DLR (4th) 1, and in a wrongful dismissal case, *Keays v Honda Canada Inc* (2008) 294 DLR (4th) 577, because the defendants had not acted in bad faith.

PART FOUR

COMPELLING PERFORMANCE OR PREVENTING (OR COMPELLING THE UNDOING OF) A WRONG

21

The award of an agreed sum

1. General points 382
2. Award of an agreed price 383
3. Award of an agreed sum payable on breach—liquidated damages 388
4. Award of an agreed sum (other than an agreed price) payable on an event other than breach 397

The award of an agreed sum is a remedy which protects the promisee's expectations by enforcing the defendant's contractual promise to pay a sum of money. As such, its justification ultimately rests on the morality of promise-keeping.[1] The remedy can be regarded as a hybrid, being like damages in that it is common law and monetary but like specific performance in that its function is to compel performance of a positive contractual obligation.[2]

The most important agreed sum, and the commonest remedy for breach of contract,[3] is the sum to be paid in return for the agreed contractual performance by the other party.[4] It directly enforces the debt owed under the contract so that this is often referred to as an action in debt.[5] The sum owed may be the price of goods or land sold, or remuneration for work or services, or rent payable by a tenant to a landlord, or the repayment of a loan. In a wide sense, which will be used from here on, the money owing in all these situations can be described as the 'price'.

Despite its practical importance, an action for the price is not afforded separate treatment in some standard works on contract, where references to it are rather uncomfortably contained in sections on damages or discharge.[6] This chapter further differs from most analyses in including liquidated damages and related sums (generally treated under damages)[7] alongside an agreed price, on the ground that they are also agreed sums awarded by the courts.[8] Admittedly there is an underlying fundamental difference between them in that the award of an agreed price compels performance of a primary contractual obligation whereas the award of liquidated damages compels performance of a secondary contractual obligation (triggered by breach of a primary contractual obligation).

---

[1] Above, pp 40–41.
[2] For judicial confusion—so that this remedy was incorrectly treated as if it were specific performance and hence subject to, eg, a want of mutuality bar—see *Ministry of Sound (Ireland) Ltd v World Online Ltd* [2003] EWHC 2178 (Ch), [2003] 2 All ER (Comm) 823.
[3] H Beale, *Remedies for Breach of Contract* (Sweet & Maxwell 1980) 144; Ministry of Justice, *Civil Justice Statistics Quarterly 2018* accessed at https://www.gov.uk/government/collections/civil-justice-statistics-quarterly#2018
[4] If the amount has not been expressly agreed, but there is a valid contract for goods or services, a reasonable sum is payable and is awarded in a (contractual) action for *quantum valebant*, where goods, or *quantum meruit*, where services. See the Sale of Goods Act 1979, s 8(2); Supply of Goods and Services Act 1982, s 15(1); E Peel, *Treitel on The Law of Contract* (14th edn, Sweet & Maxwell 2015) para 22-020.
[5] The concept of an action in debt can also extend to non-contractual demands for a certain sum based on unjust enrichment.
[6] Eg M Furmston, *Cheshire, Fifoot & Furmston's Law of Contract* (17th edn, OUP 2017) 778–781.
[7] Eg E Peel, *Treitel on The Law of Contract* (14th edn, Sweet & Maxwell 2015) paras 20-129–20-146.
[8] For a similar approach see S Waddams, *The Law of Damages* (6th edn, Thomson Reuters 2017) paras 7.10–7.20, 8.10–8.30.

To analyse the main issues raised, each of the three principal types of agreed sum will be examined in turn, after looking at some points that apply whichever type of agreed sum is in question.

1. General points

The defendant must be in breach of a valid contractual obligation to pay the agreed sum. So the contract must not be void or unenforceable, and must not have been rescinded; neither must the obligation be one that has been wiped away by termination of the contract for frustration or breach.[9] Also the sum must be due. So an agreed sum payable on breach will only be awarded once that breach has occurred and an agreed sum payable on an event other than breach only when that specified event has taken place.[10] An agreed price is only regarded as due, in the absence of any express provision as to advance payment, where the claimant has completed or substantially completed what the claimant is being paid for: for example, a seller of goods is generally not entitled to the agreed price until property in the goods has passed to the buyer, as laid down in the Sale of Goods Act 1979, s 49(1),[11] and a builder generally not until it has completed or substantially completed the stage of the building to which the payment relates.[12]

Agreed sums are normally awarded after trial of the action. However, by the Senior Courts Act 1981, s 32 and CPR 25.6–25.9, a court has power in certain circumstances to award an interim payment pre-trial in respect of an agreed sum (or indeed any other monetary sum, including damages).[13] Generally speaking, the court must be satisfied that, if the claim went to trial, the claimant would obtain judgment for a substantial amount of money (other than costs).

The law governing interest payable on an agreed sum and the limitation period for claiming agreed sums[14] has already been dealt with in chapters 15 and 16.[15]

A difficult question is whether a promisee can enforce a contractual obligation to pay a sum of money to a third party by an action for an agreed sum. In principle there seems no objection to this. The defendant's promise is simply being enforced albeit that, subject to exceptions, the doctrine of privity prevents an action by the third party beneficiary. Yet there is no clear support for this, nor indeed direct discussion of it, in the cases or in academic writings.[16] What has been discussed is whether the promisee can sue for an agreed

---

[9] In *Hyundai Heavy Industries Co Ltd v Papadopoulos* [1980] 1 WLR 1129, and *Stocznia Gdanska SA v Latvia Shipping Co* [1998] 1 WLR 574, the claimants, builders, and sellers of a ship, were held able to recover an agreed sum, payable before termination for the defendant's breach, because the right to that part payment had already accrued and the defendant had no set-off for restitution (because there had been no total failure of consideration).

[10] Eg in *Damon Cia Naviera SA v Hapag-Lloyd International SA, The Blankenstein* [1985] 1 All ER 475, the 10% deposit was not recoverable as a debt because it was only payable on the buyers' signing of the contract.

[11] By s 49(2) the agreed price is also payable where, irrespective of the passing of property, it is payable 'on a day certain'. In *PST Energy 7 Shipping LLC v OW Bunker Malta Ltd, The Res Cogitans* [2016] UKSC 23, [2016] AC 1034, at [40]–[58], there were important obiter dicta to the effect that, contrary to *Caterpillar (NI) Ltd v John Holt & Co (Liverpool) Ltd* [2013] EWCA Civ 1232, [2014] 1 WLR 2365, s 49 is not an exclusive code so that, at common law, there may be an action for the price outside s 49, albeit that this will be rare. E Peel, *Treitel on The Law of Contract* (14th edn, Sweet & Maxwell 2015) para 21-007 takes the view that the Sale of Goods Act 1979, s 49(1) adds a requirement to the sum being due and that this is explicable as encouraging mitigation. But see also E McKendrick, *Goode on Commercial Law* (5th edn, Penguin 2016) 429–431.

[12] *Hoenig v Isaacs* [1952] 2 All ER 176; *ICE Architects Ltd v Empowering People Inspiring Communities* [2018] EWHC 281 (QB).

[13] See above, pp 167–168.

[14] But for agreed sums ('any debt or other liquidated pecuniary claim') time runs afresh from an acknowledgment or part payment—Limitation Act 1980, s 29(5).

[15] For agreed sums payable in a foreign currency, see above, pp 177–181.

[16] However, passages in *Beswick v Beswick* [1968] AC 58, at 81, 88, 97 may be thought to suggest that the administratrix could sue for arrears to be paid *to the widow* in her personal capacity.

sum to be paid to the promisee, which should have been paid to a third party. The objection in that situation is that (unless on a true construction of the contract the promisee can insist on the defendant paying the promisee rather than the third party)[17] the award of the agreed sum would no longer be specifically enforcing the defendant's promise to pay the third party. Windeyer J's dicta rejecting this idea in *Coulls v Bagot's Executor and Trustee Co Ltd*[18] therefore seems correct. If the promisee wishes to recover a monetary sum for itself it should instead sue for (unliquidated) damages.

2. Award of an agreed price

The main issue and one of burning controversy is whether an action for the agreed price may fail where the defendant has clearly repudiated the contract[19] but the claimant, instead of accepting the repudiation and suing for damages, has kept the contract open. For example, a builder may have gone on to complete a building even though the owner has repudiated, or a seller of goods, where property in them has passed to the buyer, may have kept the goods for the buyer even though the buyer has refused to take delivery of them.

There are two major and contradictory approaches to this issue. First, one might say that the claimant has an unfettered option to hold the contract open and recover the agreed price: that is, that the duty to mitigate never applies to an action for the agreed price[20] and that it is no bar that damages are adequate. The alternative view is that the claimant may not be entitled to hold the contract open and recover the agreed price; the duty to mitigate can apply to an action for the agreed price and, where damages are adequate to compensate a claimant for its loss, it is contrary to that duty for the claimant to carry on with its own unwanted performance and to claim the agreed price: rather, it should accept the repudiation, claim damages, and make substitute contracts.

The leading case is *White and Carter (Councils) Ltd v McGregor*.[21] The claimants supplied to local authorities litterbins on which they let advertising space. The defendants contracted to pay for the display of adverts, advertising their garage business, but later that day they repudiated the contract, which had been concluded by their sales manager contrary to the wishes of the proprietor. The claimants refused to accept the repudiation, went ahead, and displayed the adverts for a period. There was an accelerated payment clause in the contract which, on failure to pay, entitled the claimants to the agreed contract price without displaying the adverts for the full three-year period and, applying that clause, they claimed the agreed price of £196 4s. The House of Lords held, by a three–two majority, that they were entitled to the agreed price. Two of the majority (Lords Hodson and Tucker) simply adopted the first of the two views examined above. The third, Lord Reid, while basically taking that view, suggested a possible qualification:

'... it may well be that, if it can be shown that a person has no legitimate interest, financial or otherwise, in performing the contract, rather than claiming damages, he ought not to be allowed to saddle the other party with an additional burden with no benefit to himself.'[22]

---

[17] As in *Tradigrain SA v King Diamond Shipping SA, The Spiros C* [2000] 2 Lloyd's Rep 319, at 331.
[18] [1967] ALR 385, at 411. Cf *Cleaver v Mutual Reserve Fund Life Association* [1892] 1 QB 147; E Peel, *Treitel on The Law of Contract* (14th edn, Sweet & Maxwell 2015) para 14-022.
[19] The repudiation will almost always, but not necessarily, be anticipatory.
[20] For a standard non-application of the duty to mitigate and mitigation to the award of agreed remuneration see, eg, *Abrahams v Performing Right Society Ltd* [1995] ICR 1028: 'damages', which an employer was bound to pay in lieu of notice following a dismissal, were a debt and therefore not limited by the duty to mitigate (cf *Cerberus Software Ltd v Rowley* [2001] EWCA Civ 78, [2001] IRLR 160).
[21] [1962] AC 413. [22] ibid, at 431.

384   *The award of an agreed sum*

But Lord Reid failed to clarify what having 'no legitimate interest' means. Presumably, though, he had a very narrow notion in mind, since despite the fact that damages would surely have been adequate for the claimants, so that they had nothing to gain by continuing performance, Lord Reid did not think it established that they had no legitimate interest in continuing. On the other hand, Lords Morton and Keith, dissenting, took the second of the two views above. Lord Keith said:

> 'I find the argument advanced for the appellants a somewhat startling one. If it is right it would seem that a man who has contracted to go to Hong Kong at his own expense and make a report, in return for remuneration of £10,000, and who, before the date fixed for the start of the journey and perhaps before he has incurred any expense, is informed by the other contracting party that he has cancelled or repudiated the contract, is entitled to set off for Hong Kong and produce his report in order to claim in debt the stipulated sum. Such a result is not, in my opinion, in accordance with principle or authority, and cuts across the rule that where one party is in breach of contract, the other must take steps to minimise the loss sustained by the breach.'[23]

It is interesting to contrast immediately the leading US case on this issue. In *Clark v Marsiglia*[24] a restorer of paintings, who had completed the restoration contracted for, despite an earlier repudiation of the contract by the owner, was held not to be entitled to the agreed price and was rather restricted to damages. Similarly by the Uniform Commercial Code, s 2–709(1)(b), the seller of goods may only recover their price if he is '… unable after reasonable effort to resell them at a reasonable price or the circumstances reasonably indicate that such effort will be unavailing.'[25]

White & Carter has been both attacked and defended by academics,[26] and the judicial reaction has also been mixed.[27] In *Hounslow London Borough Council v Twickenham Garden Developments Ltd*[28] Megarry J explained, as Lord Reid had himself observed, that *White & Carter* can only apply where the claimant is able to carry on with his performance without the defendant's co-operation. But it is particularly significant, and reveals an underlying antipathy towards *White & Carter*, that Megarry J included passive co-operation within this: he therefore held that *White & Carter* did not apply to the facts before him since an owner of land on which building work is being carried out is required to co-operate with the builder in that the owner has to allow him to enter the land.[29]

The Court of Appeal also distinguished *White & Carter* in *Attica Sea Carriers v Ferrostaal*.[30] This concerned a demise charterparty. On the assumption that the charterers were bound to repair the vessel before redelivery, it was held that, following repudiation by the charterers, the owners should have taken redelivery and were not entitled to insist on holding the contract open and receiving the agreed hire until the ship was repaired. Most

---

[23] ibid, at 442. [24] 1 Denio 317 (NY 1845).
[25] See C Twigg-Flesner, R Canavan, and H MacQueen, *Atiyah and Adams' Sale of Goods* (13th edn, Pearson 2016) 420–422.
[26] A Goodhart, 'Measure of Damages when a Contract is Repudiated' (1962) 78 LQR 263; P Neinaber, 'The Effect of Anticipatory Repudiation: Principle and Policy' [1962] CLJ 213; E Tabachnik, 'Anticipatory Breach of Contract' [1972] CLP 149.
[27] It was followed very soon after in *Anglo-African Shipping Co of New York Inc v J Mortner Ltd* [1962] 1 Lloyd's Rep 81.
[28] [1971] Ch 233. See also *Finelli v Dee* (1968) 76 DLR (2d) 393 (Ont CA).
[29] In dismissing an application for summary judgment, Nicholas Strauss QC in *Ministry of Sound (Ireland) Ltd v World Online Ltd* [2003] EWHC (Ch) 2178, [2003] 2 All ER (Comm) 823, held that a firm that provided packaging and distribution services for CDs supplied by the defendant could perform without the defendant's co-operation—and had done so thereby entitling it to the final payment of £200,000—even though, for the last 18 months of the two-year agreement, the defendant, in breach of contract, had supplied no CDs.
[30] [1976] 1 Lloyd's Rep 250.

radical was Lord Denning. He did not think *White & Carter* should be followed except in a case on all fours with it. 'It has no application whatever in a case where the plaintiff ought in all reason to accept the repudiation and sue for damages—provided that damages would provide an adequate remedy for any loss suffered by him.'[31] An analogy was then drawn with specific performance to emphasise, in contradiction of *White & Carter*, that, when damages are adequate, specific relief (including the action for the agreed sum) should not be granted. Lord Denning went on to emphasise that what made the claimants' refusal particularly unreasonable on these facts was that the repairs would cost four times as much as the difference in value between the repaired and unrepaired ship. The owners' refusal to accept repudiation was, therefore, doubly wasteful. Orr LJ, with whom Browne LJ concurred, while saying that he agreed with Lord Denning, distinguished *White & Carter* on the grounds that here co-operation was needed from the defendants, and the claimants had no legitimate interest in holding the contract open. Unfortunately, no explanation of these points was forthcoming. One can safely assume, however, that on the latter point the majority was also influenced by the cost of repairs being uneconomic; it was this that made the facts *of Attica* so extreme.

There were no such unusual facts in *The Odenfeld*.[32] Charterers had repudiated a charterparty but the owners had refused to accept this and had kept the vessel at their disposal. The claimants, assignees of money due under the charterparty, now claimed the agreed hire for the period in question. Kerr J distinguished *Attica Sea Carriers* and considered that it was only in extreme cases like that that *White & Carter* did not apply. In a statement resembling Lord Reid's, Kerr J said, '... any fetter on the innocent party's right of election whether or not to accept a repudiation will only be applied in extreme cases, viz where damages would be an adequate remedy and where an election to keep the contract alive would be wholly unreasonable.'[33] Kerr J went on to say that on the facts of the case there was doubt about the adequacy of damages because of the difficulty in their assessment and that, since the owners had obligations to the claimants to keep the charterparty in existence, they were not acting unreasonably in refusing to accept the repudiation.

However, it would seem that an important, albeit veiled, departure from *White & Carter* and *The Odenfeld* was made by Lloyd J in *Clea Shipping Corpn v Bulk Oil International Ltd*.[34] The facts were straightforward and again concerned a charterparty: the charterers had repudiated, but the owners had refused to accept this and had kept the vessel at the charterers' disposal until the expiry of the charter. The charterers in fact paid the hire for the full period, but now sought to recover it on the ground that the owners should have accepted the repudiation and were restricted to damages. The arbitrator's decision in favour of the charterers was upheld by Lloyd J. After a masterly survey of the case law he said the following:

'Whether one takes Lord Reid's language which was adopted by Orr and Browne LJJ in *The Puerto Buitrago*, or Lord Denning MR's language in that case ("in all reason") or Kerr J's language in *The Odenfeld* ("wholly unreasonable ...") there comes a point at which the court will cease, on general equitable principles, to allow the innocent party to enforce his contract according to its strict legal terms. How one defines that point is obviously a matter of some difficulty for it involves drawing a line between conduct which is merely unreasonable ... and conduct which is *wholly* unreasonable. But however difficult it may be to define the point, that there *is* such a point seems to me to have been accepted ...'[35]

---

[31] ibid, at 255. [32] [1978] 2 Lloyd's Rep 357. [33] ibid, at 374. [34] [1984] 1 All ER 129.
[35] ibid, at 136–137.

Applying this approach to the case before him, Lloyd J considered that the arbitrator could not be said to have been wrong to conclude that the relevant point had been reached, and hence that the owners should be restricted to damages. But ultimately, it is hard to see how this decision can be squared with *White & Carter* and *The Odenfeld*. True, Lord Reid and Kerr J recognised a point at which the claimant should accept the repudiation, but what is crucial is that that point was regarded as being reached only on extreme facts, like those in *Attica Sea Carriers*. Yet the facts in *Clea Shipping* were in no sense extreme. It would seem, therefore, that Lloyd J's decision represents a move towards the minority approach in *White & Carter* and the second of the two views set out above.

It should also be noted that in dicta Lloyd J did express tentative 'first blush' support for the view, accepted by the majority in *Attica Sea Carriers* but rejected in *The Odenfeld*, that a charterparty requires such co-operation as to fall outside *White & Carter*. Again this approach cannot be sensibly reconciled with *White & Carter*, and if adopted would similarly undermine that decision.

In *Ocean Marine Navigation Ltd v Koch Carbon Inc, The Dynamic*[36] Simon J has usefully summarised the above main cases as follows:

'These cases establish the following exception to the general rule that the innocent party has an option whether or not to accept a repudiation: (i) The burden is on the *contract-breaker* to show that the innocent party has no legitimate interest in performing the contract rather than claiming damages. (ii) The burden is not discharged merely by showing that the benefit to the other party is small in comparison to the loss to the contract-breaker. (iii) The exception to the general rule applies only in extreme cases: where damages would be an adequate remedy and where an election to keep the contract alive would be unreasonable.'

Cooke J similarly emphasized that Lord Reid's exception applied only in extreme cases in yet another charterparty case, *Isabella Shipowner SA v Shagang Shipping Co Ltd, The Aquafaith*.[37] He said:

'With only 94 days left of a 5 year time charter in a difficult market where a substitute time charter was impossible, and trading on the spot market very difficult, it would be impossible to characterize the owners' stance in wishing to maintain the charter and a right to hire as unreasonable, let alone beyond all reason, wholly reasonable or perverse.... [T]his is not an extreme or unusual case and in such circumstances the exception to the *White and Carter* principle cannot apply.'

The most recent case to consider these issues, *MSC Mediterranean Shipping Co SA v Cottonex Anstalt*,[38] concerned a contract for the carriage of cotton by sea. The shipper repudiated the contract but the carrier refused to accept that repudiation so as to claim the continuing money owing (as 'demurrrage') under the contract which was higher than it would have been entitled to as damages (ie the demurrage was in excess of the lost income). It was held that, after some four months, the commercial purpose of the contract had gone and it was then no longer open to the carrier to hold the contract open and claim demurrage. However, instead of saying that, from that point, the *White and Carter* 'no legitimate interest' or 'wholly unreasonable' qualification applied, the Court of Appeal muddied matters by indicating that, at that point, the contract was automatically terminated so that there

---

[36] [2003] EWHC 1936 (Comm), [2003] 2 Lloyd's Rep 693, at [23].
[37] [2012] EWHC 1077 (Comm), [2012] 2 Lloyd's Rep 61.
[38] [2016] EWCA Civ 789, [2016] 2 Lloyd's Rep 494.

was no need to rely on *White and Carter*. This reasoning cuts across the conventional view[39] that a contract is never automatically terminated for breach so that termination for breach is always at the election of the innocent party (albeit subject to the *White and Carter* qualification). More conventionally, the Court of Appeal disagreed with Leggatt J's reasoning at first instance[40] that it was helpful to regard the 'no legitimate interest' or 'wholly unreasonable' qualification, alongside the law on implied terms restricting contractual discretions, as an aspect of good faith in contractual dealings.

Before moving on to consider the merits or otherwise of *White and Carter*, it is worth stressing that, while the majority of cases in which the principle has been applied have involved charterparties or contracts for the carriage of goods by sea, the principle is applicable to all types of contract. In *Reichman v Beveridge*[41] there was an interesting application of *White and Carter* to the common situation of a tenant giving up an expired lease. The claimants let out offices to the defendant solicitors on a five-year lease. About half-way through, the defendants ceased to practise and, having no need for the offices, stopped paying rent. Nine months later, the claimants sued for the arrears of rent then due. Although the claimants knew of the defendants' circumstances, they had not instructed agents to find new tenants, had refused the offer of a prospective new tenant, and had refused the defendants' offer to negotiate a payment for surrender of the lease. The defendants argued that the claimants had therefore failed in their duty to mitigate and so were not entitled to the arrears. That argument was rejected by the Court of Appeal. It held that, applying Lord Reid's speech in *White and Carter*, as developed in the subsequent cases, damages were not adequate, because a landlord was probably not entitled to damages from a tenant who had given up a lease, and the claimants had not acted wholly unreasonably.

Should *White & Carter* be supported, or is that decision justified? This depends on the extent to which it is felt that economic efficiency, as represented by the duty to mitigate, should counter the claimant's wish for specific enforcement of the promise to pay the claimant money. Under *White & Carter* that wish is given overriding importance where the claimant can go ahead and fulfil its obligations. It is submitted that that is unsatisfactory. Where the claimant can be adequately compensated by damages, so that it is of no real benefit to the claimant to carry on with its side of the contract, the claimant's wishes should be outweighed by the pure waste of its carrying on with an unwanted performance. Put shortly, where damages are adequate, economic efficiency dictates that the claimant should be required to mitigate, by stopping performance and making substitute contracts, rather than holding the contract open and claiming the agreed sum.[42] Indeed it should be realised, as clearly Lord Denning did in *Attica Sea Carriers*, that the *White & Carter* approach runs counter to the traditional approach to specific performance, where if damages are adequate, specific performance will not be granted. The importance of upholding the duty to mitigate, which is the primary argument used in chapter 22 to support the traditional subsidiary role of specific performance,[43] is therefore equally valuable for criticising *White & Carter*.

---

[39] Affirmed, even for employment contracts where this has sometimes been disputed, in *Société Générale v Geys* [2012] UKSC 63, [2013] 1 AC 523: see A Burrows, 'What is the Effect of a Repudiatory Breach of a Contract of Employment?' (2013) 42 ILJ 281–288.
[40] [2015] EWHC 283 (Comm), [2015] 1 Lloyd's Rep 359, at [97]–[98].
[41] [2006] EWCA Civ 1659, [2007] 1 P & CR 20.
[42] The same argument has been used to criticise the damages principle—analogous to *White & Carter*, but arising only where the repudiation is anticipatory—that there is no duty to mitigate unless the claimant chooses to accept an anticipatory repudiation. See above, p 132.
[43] Below, pp 412–415.

3. Award of an agreed sum payable on breach—liquidated damages[44]

(1) The distinction between liquidated damages and penalties

Although the award of liquidated damages is conventionally treated as an aspect of contractual damages, it is in reality the same type of judicial remedy as the award of an agreed price, in that it is a common law monetary remedy which specifically enforces the defendant's promise to pay a sum of money. Where it differs fundamentally from the award of an agreed price is that the promise enforced represents the parties' agreed remedy for the (primary) breach of contract, and the important question is whether the courts should uphold what the parties have themselves agreed should be paid for breach rather than assessing what should be paid according to the usual principles of damages. Although strictly speaking this question is concerned with the validity of the promise, rather than the judicial remedy itself, examination of it is essential to understand what is meant by an award of liquidated damages. Moreover, it must be relevant to one's general understanding of damages to know whether the courts do award such an agreed sum, rather than damages assessed according to the usual principles.

Clauses by which the parties agree how much should be paid for breach are commonplace in many different types of contract. They include, for example, payments for delay in building contracts, the 'demurrage' which the charterer of a vessel agrees to pay for detention of the ship for unloading or loading beyond the 'lay-days', and sums payable by a debtor under a hire-purchase or conditional sale agreement where the debtor has defaulted in paying instalments leading the creditor to terminate the contract for breach.

The courts will award the agreed sum if it is liquidated damages; but if it is a penalty, the promise to pay is invalid (ie unenforceable or, arguably, void) and the courts will instead award normal (unliquidated) damages. How, then, does one decide whether the agreed sum is liquidated damages or a penalty?

In looking at this an initial point to note is that the label 'penalty clause' is often a neutral description used to refer to an agreed damages clause without meaning to suggest that the clause is a penalty rather than liquidated damages.

The traditional approach, as laid down by Lord Dunedin in *Dunlop Pneumatic Tyre Ltd v New Garage and Motor Co Ltd*,[45] was that liquidated damages were a sum which represented a genuine pre-estimate of the claimant's loss from the breach;[46] whereas a penalty was a sum which was greater than such a genuine pre-estimate and was inserted to deter the defendant from breaking the contract. As Lord Dunedin said, 'the essence of a penalty is a payment of money stipulated as in terrorem of the offending party; the essence of liquidated damages is a genuine covenanted pre-estimate of damage.'[47] He also indicated that the 'genuine pre-estimate of loss' test should be flexibly applied saying that a sum was a penalty if it was 'extravagant and unconscionable in amount in comparison with the greatest loss that could conceivably be proved'.[48] Lord Dunedin also made clear that the parties' own use of the label 'liquidated damages' or 'penalty' was not conclusive.

---

[44] For a comparative account, see G Treitel, *Remedies for Breach of Contract* (Clarendon Press 1988) 208–234.
[45] [1915] AC 79.
[46] Or the loss of a third party in a situation where the law allows the promisee to recover a third party's loss: see above, pp 201–204.
[47] [1915] AC 79, at 86. [48] ibid, at 87.

In the case itself, the defendants bought tyres from the claimants under an agreement that they would neither tamper with the manufacturer's markings on the tyres, nor sell the tyres to the public below list price, nor sell them to persons whose supplies the claimants had decided to suspend, nor exhibit or export them without the claimants' consent. £5 was made payable for every tyre 'sold or offered' in breach of the agreement. The House of Lords held that this sum was liquidated damages. Although there were several ways in which tyres could be 'sold or offered' in breach of the agreement, the loss likely to result from any such breach was difficult to assess and £5 represented a genuine attempt to do so.

A particularly rich source of examples of the application of the traditional 'genuine pre-estimate of loss' test has been provided by cases on hire-purchase and conditional sale agreements. In *Bridge v Campbell Discount Co Ltd*,[49] for example, there was a minimum payment clause in the hire-purchase agreement whereby if the debtor was in breach of contract (or chose to terminate lawfully the contract) it should return the goods to the creditor and make up the payments already paid to two-thirds of the hire-purchase price. This sum was expressed to be 'compensation for depreciation'. The debtor, having made several payments, refused to pay any more and returned the car. The House of Lords, having held that the debtor was in breach of contract, decided that the sum payable under the minimum payment clause was penal and irrecoverable because it did not represent a genuine pre-estimate of loss. In particular, the amount stated could not be regarded as compensation for depreciation because, in Lord Radcliffe's words, the clause:

> '... produces the result, absurd in its own terms, that the estimated amount of depreciation becomes progressively less the longer the vehicle is used under the hire. This is because the sum agreed upon diminishes as the total of cash payments increases. It is a sliding scale of compensation but a scale that slides in the wrong direction ...'[50]

On the other hand, in *Wadham Stringer Finance Ltd v Meaney*[51] an accelerated payments clause in a conditional sale agreement—whereby on default of payment in two or more monthly instalments, the creditor was entitled to call for the unpaid balance of the purchase price plus certain charges, in return for title in the car passing to the debtor—was held to be a valid liquidated damages clause. It did represent a genuine pre-estimate of the creditor's loss, given that title was to pass to the debtor.

A particularly influential decision in the application of the 'genuine pre-estimate of loss' test, which showed the willingness of the courts to stretch the law so as to hold clauses valid, was *Philips Hong Kong Ltd v Attorney-General of Hong Kong*.[52] Lord Woolf, giving the judgment of the Privy Council upholding as liquidated damages a clause in a road construction contract, considered that the courts should not be too zealous in knocking down clauses as penal. '[W]hat the parties have agreed should normally be upheld.'[53] More specifically it was stressed that a clause could be a genuine pre-estimate of loss even though hypothetical situations could be presented in which the claimant's actual loss would be substantially lower. To hold otherwise would be to render it very difficult to draw up valid liquidated damages clauses in complex commercial contracts. Moreover it was thought acceptable to take account of the fact that, as it happened, the actual loss was not much greater than the agreed damages. Although the matter had to be judged as at the date the contract was made, what actually happened 'can provide valuable evidence as to what could reasonably be expected to be the loss at the time the contract was made'.[54]

---

[49] [1962] AC 600.　[50] ibid, at 623.　[51] [1981] 1 WLR 39, at 48.　[52] (1993) 61 BLR 41.
[53] ibid, at 59.　[54] ibid, at 59.

(2) The new law

In the conjoined appeals in *Cavendish Square Holding BV v Talal El Makdessi* ('*Makdessi*') and *ParkingEye Ltd v Beavis* ('*ParkingEye*'),[55] the Supreme Court, while retaining the distinction between valid liquidated damages (or an analogous valid sanction for breach) and invalid penalties, has departed from the traditional 'genuine pre-estimate of loss' test for deciding whether an agreed sum is liquidated damages or a penalty. This was a landmark ruling for the law on penalties in English law and represents the most important judgment of the Supreme Court on remedies for breach of contract since its creation in 2009. It is submitted that the decision is to be warmly welcomed as retaining the power to strike down penalties while rendering it less likely that that power will be exercised in the context of commercial contracts.

In *Makdessi*, the defendant agreed to sell to the claimant a controlling interest in the advertising and marketing company which he had founded. The contract provided for payments of up to $147m depending on profits. After the sale, the defendant agreed not to compete with his old business and that, if he did, he would not be entitled to any further payments (clause 5.1) and that the claimant would acquire an option to buy his remaining shares at a price which disregarded goodwill (clause 5.6). The defendant broke that non-competition provision. The claimant sought a declaration that the defendant was therefore not entitled to any further payments and was obliged to sell his shares to the claimant. The Court of Appeal decided that the clauses were unenforceable as penalties because they were not genuine pre-estimates of loss and were designed to deter breach. But that was overturned by the Supreme Court which held that neither clause was unenforceable as a penalty.

In *ParkingEye* the defendant parked his car in a shopping centre car park managed by the claimant. Notices at the entrance and around the car park prominently stated that the maximum permitted stay was for two hours, that parking was free up to that time, but that £85 would be charged to those who stayed longer. The defendant drove out of the car park having stayed for nearly three hours and was charged £85 by the claimant. The defendant refused to pay and the claimant brought proceedings to recover the £85. The defendant argued that he should not have to pay because the charge was a penalty (and/or an unfair term and therefore not binding on the consumer under what was then the Unfair Terms in Consumer Contracts Regulations 1999 and is now the Consumer Rights Act 2015, Part 2). The charge was held not to be a penalty (and the term was fair).

In deciding that in neither of these cases was there a penalty, the Supreme Court stressed that, even if a stipulated sum (or another sanction for breach) is not a genuine pre-estimate of loss, it is not a penalty if it protects a legitimate interest of the claimant (in the performance of the contract) and is not out of all proportionate in doing so. In other words, the traditional focus on (non-excessive) compensation is only one of the legitimate interests that the claimant may protect. In departing from the 'genuine pre-estimate of loss' test, Lords Neuberger and Sumption (with whom Lord Carnwath agreed) restated the law as follows:

> 'The true test is whether the impugned provision is a secondary obligation which imposes a detriment on the contract-breaker out of all proportion to any legitimate interest of the innocent party in the enforcement of the primary obligation.'[56]

---

[55] [2015] UKSC 67, [2016] AC 1172.
[56] See the similar formulations of Lord Mance at [152] and Lord Hodge at [255] supported by Lord Toulson at [293].

So, on the facts of the cases, the legitimate interests included maintaining the goodwill of the company (in *Makdessi*) and encouraging the prompt turnover of car parking space and funding the claimant's business as car park managers (in *ParkingEye*). As the detriment on the defendants imposed by the clauses was not out of all proportion to those legitimate interests of the claimants, the clauses were not penalties and were therefore enforceable.

In clarifying the law in this way, the Supreme Court may be regarded as having built on the approach articulated in *Lordsvale Finance plc v Bank of Zambia*[57] (and followed in a number of subsequent cases) where Colman J said that a clause would be upheld if it was 'commercially justifiable, provided always that its dominant purpose was not to deter the other party from breach'. However, the Supreme Court stressed that it is unhelpful to regard deterrence as objectionable; and the notion of 'commercial justification' has been replaced by the emphasis on protecting a legitimate interest and doing so proportionately. Even prior to *Makdessi* the courts in recent times, in line with Colman J's approach, had tended to be reluctant to decide that a clause in a commercial contract was a penalty; and it seems likely that, following *Makdessi* and having clarified that there is nothing objectionable about seeking to deter breach, it will now be even rarer for a clause in a commercial contract to be struck down as a penalty. In other words, while not abolishing the power to strike down penalties, the Supreme Court has rendered it less likely that that power will be exercised. It is important to add that, as regards consumer contracts, the term may in any event be invalid if it is unfair under what was is now the Consumer Rights Act 2015, Part 2. Although not quite the same enquiry, it seems likely that the courts will apply the statute consistently with the law on penalties so that, if the sum is a penalty, it would in any event be unfair under the statute and vice versa (for example, on the facts of *ParkingEye*, it was decided that the term was not a penalty and was fair under the statute).

In *Makdessi* the clauses in question did not actually require the defendants to pay a sum of money. One allowed the claimant to stop paying money otherwise owed; and the other gave the claimant an option to buy shares at a low price. Previous cases had applied the law on penalties to such clauses. So, for example, in *Gilbert-Ash (Northern) Ltd v Modern Engineering (Bristol) Ltd*[58] the House of Lords had applied the law on penalties to a clause which, in the event of breach, allowed the claimant to hold back a payment that it would otherwise have been bound to make. And in *Jobson v Johnson*[59] the law on penalty clauses was extended to a clause to transfer shares, in the event of breach, rather than to pay money. As Dillon LJ said in the latter case:

> 'In principle, a transaction must be just as objectionable and unconscionable in the eyes of equity if it requires a transfer of property by way of penalty on a default in paying money as if it requires a payment of an extra, or excessive, sum of money.'[60]

In applying the law on penalties to such clauses, *Makdessi* has made clear that those extensions of the law on penalties were correct. It further follows that, as one cannot accurately describe such clauses as providing for liquidated damages, the correct distinction is between penalties, on the one hand, and liquidated damages *or other valid sanctions for breach*, on the other. This is not to deny that normally the relevant sanction is the payment of a stipulated sum.

---

[57] [1996] QB 752, at 764.   [58] [1974] AC 689.   [59] [1989] 1 WLR 1026.   [60] ibid, at 1034.

(3) What is a legitimate interest?

In applying the new test, a crucial question is what is here meant by a legitimate interest? We have articulated above what were included as legitimate interests in *Makdessi* and *ParkingEye*. More generally, if we focus on the usual case of a clause requiring the payment of money, it may be helpful to think about the aim of judicial monetary remedies for breach of contract. In summary, these aim to compensate for loss or, exceptionally, to strip gains. But, at least in English law, punitive damages cannot be awarded for breach of contract. It would seem to follow that the claimant has a legitimate interest in compensating loss, including loss that may not be legally recoverable, and in stripping profits but has no legitimate interest in a sanction that is simply designed to punish the defendant for the breach. In other words, whether the clause is protecting a legitimate interest of the claimant will to some extent be assessed in line with the judicial remedies available. The further the clause strays from what the courts would themselves award, the more likely it is that the agreed remedy will be regarded as penal.

If this is correct, then we have an answer to an interesting question that has not so far been answered by the judges and has barely been touched on by commentators.[61] In the light of *Attorney-General v Blake*,[62] in which the House of Lords accepted that, in exceptional circumstances, an account of profits could be awarded for breach of contract, what is the status of a contractual clause which requires the defendant, in the event of a profitable breach, to disgorge some or all of the profits made? Clearly, applying the traditional approach, this is not a 'liquidated damages' clause because it does not constitute a genuine pre-estimate of loss. On the other hand, even before *Makdessi*, it might have been thought odd to knock out such a clause as a penalty at least in a situation where the courts would otherwise have been willing to award an account of profits. Let us assume, for example, that in *Blake* itself, there had been a contractual clause to the effect that, in the event of breach, Blake would pay over all his profits from writing a book to the Crown.[63] After *Makdessi* it is surely clear that such a clause would be enforceable because the claimant is protecting a legitimate interest in stripping profit which has been recognized as such by the courts. In contrast, if such a clause were to be inserted in a standard commercial contract, where the courts would not be willing to award an account of profits, one might be more inclined to knock out such a clause as a penalty.

If also follows that, if it is correct that an interest protected by the courts through judicial remedies must be a legitimate interest under *Makdessi*, then it will often remain pertinent to consider whether the sum to be awarded is a genuine attempt to pre-estimate the loss. A clause attempting to ensure that the claimant is fully compensated must be regarded as protecting a legitimate interest. In this sense, Lord Dunedin's approach remains useful albeit that it must now be seen as helping to decide whether the claimant was proportionately protecting a legitimate interest. This explains why Lords Neuberger and Sumption said that Lord Dunedin's classic test will continue to be useful in simple damages clauses in standard contracts.[64]

---

[61] But see S Rowan, 'For the Recognition of Remedial Terms Agreed Inter Partes' (2010) 126 LQR 448 (reprinted, with light amendments, in her *Remedies for Breach of Contract* (OUP 2012) ch 5): she criticises, as being too conservative, my approach that validity should to a large extent turn on whether the clause matches the remedial response that would be available in any event.

[62] [2001] 1 AC 268. See above, pp 356–359.

[63] Cf *R v Attorney-General for England and Wales* [2003] UKPC 22, [2003] EMLR 24, in which the Privy Council upheld the 'enforcement' by an account of profits and damages of a clause whereby a member of the SAS had promised to assign to the Crown any rights acquired (eg by writing a book) in breach of a confidentiality clause. No question of this being a 'penalty' clause was raised either in the Privy Council or in the courts below.

[64] [2015] UKSC 67, [2016] AC 1172, at [22].

Award of an agreed sum payable on breach—liquidated damages

(4) Three controversial issues

Under the previous law, there were a number of controversial issues in applying the genuine pre-estimate of loss test. Was it the actual or legally recoverable loss that one was concerned with? Could one use liquidated damages to limit damages? What if the recoverable loss was greater than the penalty? Under the new law, these remain pertinent questions to ask albeit that the answer to the first question now appears to be clearer than before *Makdessi*.

(a) Actual or legally recoverable loss

It was argued in the previous edition of this book that the 'best approach is to say that the yardstick for assessing whether the damages are a genuine pre-estimate is actual, not legally recoverable, loss'.[65] The argument proceeded on the basis that, since an accepted important function of liquidated damages is to avoid difficulties of assessment, it must be the case that the loss that needs to be genuinely pre-estimated includes loss that is legally irrecoverable because it falls foul of the required standard of proof. It was then pointed out that there were conflicting views as to whether other limiting factors, such as remoteness and the duty to mitigate, could be outflanked. But now that the focus is on the claimant's legitimate interest, it seems even clearer that the yardstick should be the claimant's actual loss, irrespective of factors that would limit the legally recoverable damages, such as remoteness, the duty to mitigate, and contributory negligence. The claimant has a legitimate interest in ensuring that its actual loss is compensated and a genuine pre-estimate of that loss cannot be regarded as disproportionate in protecting that interest.

(b) Liquidated damages used to limit damages[66]

In the leading case of *Cellulose Acetate Silk Co v Widnes Foundry Ltd*[67] a contract for the construction of an acetone recovery plant provided that if completion was delayed the contractor should pay 'by way of penalty the sum of £20 per working week'. The work was completed 30 weeks late and the owners suffered losses of £5,850 as a result. It was held by the House of Lords that the owners were restricted to £20 per week (that is £600) the clause being held valid albeit that its purpose was to limit rather than pre-estimate loss. It is important to realise that, while such a clause looks like a limitation clause, the House of Lords was treating it as a type of liquidated damages clause, the difference being that under a liquidated damages clause a defendant is bound to pay the agreed sum, even if the claimant's loss is less, whereas under a limitation clause, the defendant is bound to pay only the claimant's loss up to the limit fixed. So Lord Atkin said, 'I entertain no doubt that what the parties meant was that in the event of delay the damages and the only damages were to be £20 a week, no less and no more.'[68] This is further supported by Lord Upjohn's speech in *Suisse Atlantique Société d'Armement Maritime SA v Rotterdamsche Kolen Centrale NV*[69] where he said that, even if the demurrage clause in question represented an underestimate of loss, the sum agreed was valid liquidated damages rather than a limitation of liability.

There is no reason to think that a different approach to such clauses will be applied after *Makdessi*. This is not only because the 'genuine pre-estimate of loss' test no longer holds

---

[65] 3rd edition, at pp 446–447. But it was noted that one would need to exclude legal costs from the estimate of loss because costs are recoverable in the normal way in addition to liquidated damages.
[66] W Fritz, '"Underliquidated" Damages as Limitation of Liability' (1954) 33 Tex LR 196.
[67] [1933] AC 20. See also *Diestal v Stevenson* [1906] 2 KB 345.
[68] [1933] AC 20, at 25 (author's emphasis).   [69] [1967] 1 AC 361, at 421.

sway but also because the Supreme Court was clearly keen to uphold, rather than to knock down, clauses in commercial contracts. Admittedly there is some difficulty in saying that an 'underliquidated' damages clause protects a legitimate interest *of the innocent party* although one might say that the clause could operate in the interests of even the innocent party because, although designed to limit damages, it fixes a sum that will be payable even if the claimant's loss is less than the agreed sum. Of course, if such a clause is unfair to a consumer it can be struck down under the Consumer Rights Act 2015.

(c) Loss greater than penalty

A further difficult question of interest is what if the agreed sum is a penalty but it is the claimant not the defendant contract-breaker who wishes to assert that it is a penalty because the claimant's recoverable loss (ie unliquidated damages) would be higher than the penalty? In other words, to refuse to enforce the penalty would actually be to the claimant's advantage. Can the claimant insist on the penalty being invalid and thereby recover its actual loss? It may be that this is less likely to occur after *Makdessi* than before because it will be less common for a payment to be regarded as a penalty. In *Wall v Rederiaktiebolaget Luggude*[70] it was held that charterers could disregard what was construed as a penalty clause (rather than as a liquidated damages or limitation clause) and sue for their greater actual loss. But this is rather weak authority since it is hard to see why the clause in question was penal. In *Cellulose Acetate Silk Co Ltd v Widnes Foundry Ltd*[71] the issue was expressly left open by the House of Lords, and Diplock LJ similarly regarded it as 'by no means clear' in *Robophone Facilities Ltd v Blank*.[72]

What is the best approach? On the one hand, it can be argued that, as matters are, in principle judged at the time the contract is made, the penalty clause should be held invalid even where this is to the claimant's advantage. As against that, and as Hudson has forcefully pointed out,[73] since it is well-settled that where the claimant's loss is greater than the liquidated damages, the claimant is confined to the liquidated damages,[74] to allow the claimant to recover more than a penalty wrongly treats the claimant who has acted unfairly by inserting the penalty clause more favourably than the claimant who has acted fairly by inserting a liquidated damages clause. It also encourages the inclusion of penalty clauses, since the claimant can take the advantage of having the clause, without suffering any disadvantage. So in this situation it does indeed seem preferable to uphold the penalty clause (ie to treat the penalty as valid) and, significantly, this was the view taken in the important Canadian case of *Elsley v JG Collins Ins Agencies Ltd*.[75]

(5) Relief against forfeiture

A difficult question, expressly left open by the Supreme Court in *Makdessi*,[76] is the precise relationship between the penalty doctrine and the (equitable) power to relieve from forfeiture. Plainly the courts' power to relieve against a forfeiture clause, requiring the forfeiture of money paid,[77] raises somewhat analogous problems to that raised by penalties.

---

[70] [1915] 3 KB 66, approved in *Watts Watts & Co Ltd v Mitsui & Co Ltd* [1917] AC 227. See also *Jobson v Johnson* [1989] 1 WLR 1026.
[71] [1933] AC 20.   [72] [1966] 1 WLR 1428, at 1446.
[73] A Hudson, 'Penalties Limiting Damages' (1974) 90 LQR 31; (1975) 91 LQR 25; (1985) 101 LQR 480.
[74] See above, p 393.   [75] (1978) 83 DLR (3d) 1, at 14–15.
[76] [2015] UKSC 67, [2016] AC 1172, at [16]–[18].
[77] The jurisdiction to relieve against forfeiture clauses extends beyond the forfeiture of money paid to the forfeiture of proprietary or possessory rights. Important cases dealing with the scope of that jurisdiction include

But, normally, the obvious difference is that the money has already been paid whereas, in relation to penalties, the dispute is as to a payment (or a transfer of property) that has yet to be made. This leads to the important point that the underlying cause of action is generally different because, in relation to the forfeiture of money paid, one is generally concerned with the cause of action of unjust enrichment rather than breach of contract. It would not therefore be appropriate in this book to deal with the forfeiture of money paid in any detail.[78] But it is helpful to appreciate that the Privy Council in *Workers Trust and Merchant Bank Ltd v Dojap Investments Ltd*[79] decided that a clause allowing the forfeiture of money paid could be and, on the facts, would be struck down as a 'penalty'; and, in this context, given that deposits are generally not concerned to pre-estimate loss, the test applied to decide whether the sum to be forfeited was penal or not was one of reasonableness. It was indicated that in a contract for the sale of land, repudiated by the buyer, the standard forfeiture of 10% of the purchase price paid was reasonable: in contrast, the actual clause in question was to the effect that a deposit of 25% of the purchase price was to be forfeited. It was therefore unreasonable and unenforceable.

Obiter dicta in *Makdessi* suggest that both the law on penalties and the law on relief against forfeiture may be applied to the same clause albeit that the relationship between the two is 'not entirely easy'.[80] It was also said that a case like *Workers Trust v Dojap* may now be best rationalized as applying the modern law on penalties (looking at legitimate interest and proportionality) rather than a different law on relief against forfeiture.

It should also be borne in mind that, in a consumer contract, a term allowing forfeiture may be unfair and not binding on the consumer under Part 2 of the Consumer Rights Act 2015.[81]

(6) Should penalties, like liquidated damages, be valid?

One of the arguments raised in the Supreme Court in *Makdessi* was that the power to strike down penalties should be abolished given that consumers are protected in any event against unfair terms under the Consumer Rights Act 2015. The Supreme Court rejected that argument while restating the law in such a way as to make it less likely that a clause will be struck

---

Shiloh Spinners Ltd v Harding [1973] AC 691 (power to relieve against a landlord's termination of a lease but not exercised on the facts); *The Scaptrade* [1983] 2 AC 694 (no power to relieve against a shipowner's withdrawal of a ship in a time charterparty because a time-charterer has no proprietary or possessory right in the ship). For further decisions that there was no power to relieve, see *Sport International Bussum BV v Inter-Footwear Ltd* [1984] 1 WLR 776 (contractual licence) and *Celestial Aviation Trading 71 Ltd v Paramount Airways Private Ltd* [2010] EWHC 185, [2011] 1 Lloyd's Rep 9 (aircraft operating lease). For an example of the exercise of the power, see *BICC plc v Burndy Corp* [1985] Ch 232; and for the recognition that relief would have been granted had the relevant goods not been sold, see *On Demand Information plc v Michael Gerson (Finance) plc* [2002] UKHL 13, [2003] 1 AC 368. See E Peel, *Treitel on The Law of Contract* (14th edn, Sweet & Maxwell 2015) paras 18-066–18-073; L Smith, 'Relief against Forfeiture: a Restatement' [2001] CLJ 178.

[78] For the details, see E Peel, *Treitel on The Law of Contract* (14th edn, Sweet & Maxwell 2015) paras 20-147–20-155.

[79] [1993] AC 573. For other cases on the forfeiture of money paid, see *Stockloser v Johnson* [1954] 1 QB 476 (Somervell and Denning LJJ indicating that repayment would have been required if unconscionable for the money to be forfeited); *Amble Assets LLP v Longbenton Foods Ltd* [2011] EWHC 3774 (Ch), [2012] 1 All ER (Comm) 764, at [62]–[82] (Andrew Sutcliffe QC, sitting as a Deputy High Court Judge, regarding the test as being whether it was unconscionable to allow the forfeiture to take effect): cf, for a different, more restrictive, view of the courts' power to relieve against forfeiture of money paid, Romer LJ in the *Stockloser* case and Sachs J in *Galbraith v Mitchenall Estates Ltd* [1965] 2 QB 473.

[80] [2015] UKSC 67, [2016] AC 1172, at [16]–[18], [156], [160]–[161], [230], [291].

[81] See esp s 63, Sch 2, para 4.

down as a penalty in a commercial contract. Was the Supreme Court correct to do so or should penalties be valid?

Let us think first about a standard liquidated damages clause that is seeking to pre-estimate the claimant's loss. Should such a clause oust the judicial assessment and awarding of damages? The primary answer is that liquidated damages have a number of advantages. They make it less likely that there will be a serious dispute between the parties. They enable the defendant to know in advance what its exact liability will be. From the administration of justice angle, they save judicial time and expense in deciding what the claimant's damages should be and, from the claimant's point of view, they avoid such problems as the cost of litigation, the risk of inaccurate assessment by the courts, the need to prove one's loss according to the judicially imposed standard, and probably restrictions such as remoteness and the non-recoverability of certain types of loss. Further to these advantages, the courts have not been hostile to clauses seeking to estimate loss because they reflect the compensatory aim of judicially assessed damages: that is, they are a genuine pre-estimate of the sum needed to put the claimant into as good a position as if the contract had been performed.

In contrast, what about a clause that is purely designed to punish the defendant for breach? Such a clause runs counter to the central principle that contractual damages are for compensating the claimant and not punishing the defendant. They are therefore regarded as substantively unfair. However, in other areas the courts almost always require some procedural unfairness before they will undermine the freedom of the parties to fix their own terms, and hence their refusal to enforce penalty clauses is rather exceptional. This is one of the points made by those who argue that even penalty clauses should be upheld, subject to standard factors invalidating a contract (in particular, exploitation of weakness).[82] Indeed this point has arguably been strengthened by the enactment of the Consumer Rights Act 2015, Part 2 (formerly the Unfair Terms in Consumer Contracts Regulations 1999)[83] which allows the courts to protect consumers against unfair terms (including penalty clauses) without the need for a special rule against penalties. Additionally, it is said that there would be important advantages in making all agreed damages clauses prima facie valid. There would be less need for judicial assessment of damages with its attendant expense and, because parties would be more certain as to the validity of an agreed damages clause, litigation costs in testing validity would be reduced and contract-making would be encouraged.

On the other hand it has been argued by some adherents of 'economic analysis' that to uphold penalty clauses would encourage defendants to stick to contracts, which it would be economically efficient for them to break.[84] In other words, the 'efficient breach' theory is against upholding penalty clauses. This theory is discussed in more detail in chapter 22[85] and it will be sufficient here to give an example and to make a general criticism. Say D contracts to make a machine part for C for £10,000. If X offers D £15,000 for that part, breach by D is efficient if X values the part more than C, and inefficient if X values the part less than C. Let us assume, therefore, that C values the part at £13,000 so that efficiency dictates that

---

[82] C Goetz and R Scott, 'Liquidated Damages, Penalties and the Just Compensation Principle' (1977) 77 Col LR 554; P Kaplan, 'A Critique of the Penalty Limitation on Liquidated Damages' (1977) 50 Southern Californian LR 1055; H Beale, *Remedies for Breach of Contract* (Sweet & Maxwell 1980) 60–61; S Rea, 'Efficiency Implications of Penalties and Liquidated Damages' (1984) 13 JLS 147; G Muir, 'Stipulations for the Payment of Agreed Sums' (1985) 10 Syd LR 503; A Ham, 'The Rule Against Penalties in Contract: an Economic Perspective' (1990) 17 Melb ULR 649; T Downes, 'Rethinking Penalty Clauses' in *Wrongs and Remedies in the Twenty-First Century* (ed P Birks, Clarendon Press 1996) 249–269; and M Chen-Wishart, 'Controlling the Power to Agree Damages' in the same publication, 271–299.

[83] SI 1999/2083. See especially Consumer Rights Act 2015, s 63, Sch 2 para 6, below, p 400.

[84] J Fenton, 'Liquidated Damages as Prima Facie Evidence' (1975) 51 Ind LJ 189, 191.

[85] Below, pp 413–415.

D breaks the contract, pays C £3,000 damages, and transfers the part to X for £15,000. The argument is that a penalty clause of, let us say, £6,000 in the contract between C and D will prevent the efficient breach, since D will no longer be better off by breaking the contract. However, the flaw in this is that it ignores the possibility of bargaining round the clause. It is in C's interests to accept between £3,000 and £5,000 to release D from the contract (because if D sticks to the contract C will make only £3,000) and in D's interest to pay up to £5,000 to C to be released to transfer the part to X. In other words, the validity of a penalty clause will only undermine efficiency where no bargaining round the clause will take place because the transaction costs are too high. As the transaction costs are unlikely to be high, the efficient breach theory is an unsatisfactory argument for knocking down penalty clauses. As Goetz and Scott write:

> '... the existence of an overcompensation provision is never per se evidence of an efficiency impediment. Absent significant negotiation costs, the pre-stipulation of a penalty still permits ... efficient solutions in which the efficiency gains are divided between the breacher and the non-breacher in a bargained for manner.'[86]

But while the efficient breach theory seems defective, there may be some validity in the argument of Clarkson, Miller, and Muris, that in many cases to uphold penalty clauses will act as an incentive for the claimant wastefully to direct resources to induce the defendant to break the contract.[87] More straightforwardly, it is submitted the strongest argument for knocking down penalty clauses is that this would contradict the traditional approach to damages according to which punitive damages are not available for breach of contract.[88] That is, while the courts should and do allow the parties to make their own assessment of compensation, it would contradict normal judicial remedies for the claimant to enforce a clause purely aimed at punishing the defendant for breach of contract. If English law were to be reformed so that punitive damages could be awarded, this would weaken the argument for knocking out penalties. It would then be particularly hard to justify denying validity to a proportionate agreed penalty clause between parties of equal bargaining power who have negotiated the contract in question. In other words, applying the language of *Makdessi*, it would then be difficult to regard such a clause, provided proportionate, as not protecting a legitimate interest of the claimant. But as the law on punitive damages stands, there seems good reason to rule as invalid agreed punishment.

4. Award of an agreed sum (other than an agreed price) payable on an event other than breach

This sort of agreed sum occupies a position between an agreed price and an agreed sum payable on breach. Traditionally it is treated like an agreed price, so that once the event has occurred the sum can be recovered without any type of liquidated damages/penalty analysis. However, the main controversy is whether it is always sensible so to distinguish these agreed sums from those payable on breach.[89]

---

[86] C Goetz and R Scott, 'Liquidated Damages, Penalties and the Just Compensation Principle' (1977) 77 Col LR 554, 568.
[87] K Clarkson, R Miller, and T Muris, 'Liquidated Damages v Penalties: Sense or Nonsense?' (1978) 54 Wisconsin LR 351.
[88] For the contrary view that there is no good reason to link the purpose of common law damages with agreed damages, see T Downes, 'Rethinking Penalty Clauses' in *Wrongs and Remedies in the Twenty-First Century* (ed P Birks, Clarendon Press 1996) 249, 265–266.
[89] See, generally, L Gullifer, 'Agreed Remedies' in *Commercial Remedies* (eds A Burrows and E Peel, OUP 2003) 191, 198–205.

In Australia in *Andrews and New Zealand Banking Group Ltd*[90] the penalty doctrine was extended to cover sums payable on events other than breach. This approach was strongly rejected for English law by the Supreme Court in *Makdessi*[91] not only because this would require a departure from authority but also because one would be creating uncertainty in relation to a whole range of contractual clauses that have traditionally been governed by mutual agreement. It is submitted that, although retaining this line may sometimes permit clever drafting to evade the penalty doctrine, the Supreme Court was correct to resist extending the penalty doctrine in this way.

What sort of clauses are we therefore talking about?

A colourful example is *Alder v Moore*,[92] where the defendant, a professional footballer, was injured and certified as unable to play football. Under an insurance policy the claimants paid him £500, subject to his agreement to the following term:

> 'In consideration of the above payment I hereby declare and agree that I will take no part as a playing member of any form of professional football and that in the event of infringement of this condition I will be subject to a penalty of the amount stated above.'

Four months later, the defendant began to play professional football again, and the claimants sought payment of the £500, which the defendant resisted on the ground that it was a penalty. The majority of the Court of Appeal held that the claimants were entitled to the £500. The liquidated damages/penalty distinction did not apply since the defendant had made no promise not to play football again. In any case, even if the sum was payable on breach, £500 was a genuine pre-estimate of loss and was therefore liquidated damages rather than a penalty. Devlin LJ dissented because he thought that the sum was payable on breach and was not a genuine pre-estimate of loss, but rather a penalty.

Agreed sums payable on events other than breach (as well as on breach) are particularly common in hire-purchase and conditional sale agreements. The conventional approach—that the liquidated damages/penalty distinction does not apply if the sum is payable on an event other than breach—is shown in a case such as *Associated Distributors Ltd v Hall*,[93] where the agreed sum was payable on the debtor exercising his option to terminate the contract. In *Bridge v Campbell Discount Co Ltd*,[94] however, some doubt was cast on this where the sum is payable either on breach[95] or on lawful termination by the debtor. It was held that, as on the facts the debtor was in breach and hence the accelerated payment was payable on breach, the liquidated damages/penalty distinction was applicable in accordance with normal principles, and the sum was held to be a penalty. But Lords Denning and Devlin considered that, even if the debtor had lawfully terminated the contract, so that on the facts the sum was payable on an event other than breach, the liquidated damages/penalty approach should still be applied. The reasoning behind this is that otherwise, as Lord Denning put it, 'It means that equity commits itself to this absurd paradox: it will grant relief to a man who breaks his contract but will penalise the man who keeps it.'[96]

Clearly Lord Denning's approach has some force. Like agreed sums payable on breach, the purpose of many agreed sums payable on an event closely allied to breach is either to

---

[90] (2012) 247 CLR 20.   [91] [2015] UKSC 67, [2016] AC 1172, at [40]–[43].   [92] [1961] 2 QB 57.
[93] [1938] 2 KB 83.   [94] [1962] AC 600.
[95] It has been accepted that the law on penalty clauses applies where the creditor has terminated the contract, under an express power of termination, for a breach by the debtor even though that power extends to events other than the debtor's breach: *Cooden Engineering Co Ltd v Stanford* [1953] 1 QB 86. This was also assumed, without discussion, in *Lombard North Central plc v Butterworth* [1987] QB 527 (see above, p 70 n 61).
[96] [1962] AC 600, at 629.

pre-estimate the claimant's loss caused by the 'event' or to punish the defendant for failure to perform. To distinguish them from agreed sums payable on breach does, therefore, produce some difficult distinctions and what are, arguably, unsatisfactory paradoxes. In line with this, the Law Commission provisionally recommended that the liquidated damages/penalty distinction should be applied to agreed sums payable on events closely allied to breach.[97]

On the other hand, it can be powerfully argued that, as the refusal to uphold penalty clauses is a somewhat unusual intrusion into freedom of contract, in that it does not rest on inequality of bargaining power, it is not sensible to extend it, particularly since to uphold an agreed sum payable on an event other than breach would not directly oust judicial compensation because there is no liability to pay unliquidated damages for an event that does not amount to a breach. Moreover, there is statutory protection for consumers under, for example, the Consumer Rights Act 2015.

The House of Lords' decision in *Export Credits Guarantee Department v Universal Oil Products Co*[98] made clear that the English law position is that the liquidated damages/penalty distinction will not be extended at the expense of freedom of contract. To simplify the complex facts, a Newfoundland company engaged the defendant building company to construct an oil refinery. Financing of the project was by arrangement between the Newfoundland company and a consortium of bankers. By this, the Newfoundland company were to issue promissory notes to the bankers, in return for their paying the defendants for the work as it proceeded. Payment on the promissory notes by the Newfoundland company was guaranteed by the claimants. The claimants made this guarantee in consideration of a premium paid to them by the defendants, under an agreement, which by clause 7 provided that where the Newfoundland company dishonoured promissory notes at a time when the defendants were in breach of contract the defendants would reimburse the claimants for any sums paid to the bankers under the guarantee. The Newfoundland company subsequently dishonoured many promissory notes and the claimants paid the bankers £39 million under their guarantee. They then claimed £39 million from the defendants under clause 7, as the defendants had been in breach of contract at the relevant time. The defendants argued that clause 7 was invalid as a penalty clause, since it imposed an obligation to repay the claimants no matter how trivial the defendants' breach of contract and the loss caused by it.

On the facts, such an argument could never hope to succeed for the simple reason that clause 7 only ever insisted on reimbursement of the claimants' payment to the bankers. So here the claimants had indeed lost the £39 million claimed, and therefore, as stressed by the House of Lords, even if a penalty/liquidated damages analysis were to be applied, the clause had to be valid as liquidated damages. The fact that the defendants would as a result be doing the work for a smaller sum than agreed, such that the Newfoundland company would ultimately benefit excessively, was of no consequence to the claimants, who could not be said to be linked to the Newfoundland company, so as to reap the benefit. The defendants were therefore held bound to pay the £39 million.

However, the House of Lords thought that the penalty/liquidated damages distinction was in any case irrelevant because the sum was to be paid on an event other than breach of

---

[97] Law Commission, *Penalty Clauses and Forfeiture of Monies Paid* (1975) Working Paper No 61, para 26. Lord Denning's approach is also strongly supported by Deane J, dissenting, in *AMEV-UDC Finance Ltd v Austin* (1986) 162 CLR 170, at 197–201.

[98] [1983] 2 All ER 205. See also *Euro London Appointments Ltd v Claessens Int Ltd* [2006] EWCA Civ 385, [2006] 2 Lloyd's Rep 436.

a contractual obligation owed to the claimants. Lord Roskill, giving the principal speech, confirmed the lower courts' reasoning that:

> 'The clause was not a penalty clause because it provided for payment of money on the happening of a specified event other than a breach of a contractual duty owed by the contemplated payer to the contemplated payee.'[99]

This confirms the traditional common law position of confining the power to strike down terms by a penalty clause analysis. The judiciary's attitude is well summed up in the observation of Diplock LJ in *Philip Bernstein (Successors) Ltd v Lydiate Textiles Ltd*[100] which Lord Roskill cited with approval:[101]

> 'I, for my part, am not prepared to extend the law by relieving against an obligation in a contract entered into between two parties which does not fall within the well-defined limits in which the court has in the past shown itself willing to interfere.'

As we have seen, the same approach has most recently been emphatically confirmed by the Supreme Court in *Makdessi*.[102]

It should be emphasised, however, that in order to protect consumers, statutory provisions have been enacted which do allow (or require) the courts to 'knock out' some sums payable on an event other than breach. For example, there is the Consumer Credit Act 1974, s 100 dealing with regulated hire-purchase and conditional sale agreements: where a debtor exercises her statutory right to terminate, her maximum liability, despite a higher agreed sum payable on termination (assuming she has taken reasonable care of the goods), is to pay what is needed to bring her payments up to half the purchase price, and the court can further reduce this if the creditor's loss is less.

Most importantly, and applicable to consumer contracts generally, there is the Consumer Rights Act 2015, Part 2.[103] One of the listed examples of a term that may be unfair is one 'requiring a consumer who fails to fulfil his obligation under the contract to pay a disproportionately high sum in compensation'.[104] Although that is referring to a traditional penalty payable on breach, the list is 'an indicative and non-exhaustive list' of terms that may be regarded as unfair. If unfair to the consumer, a similar term, albeit not triggered by breach, could equally be held to be non-binding on the consumer.[105]

---

[99] [1983] 2 All ER 205, at 223.
[100] Sub nom *Sterling Industrial Facilities Ltd v Lydiate Textiles Ltd* (1962) 106 Sol Jo 669.
[101] [1983] 2 All ER 205, at 224.   [102] Above, p 398.
[103] The controls apply to consumer contracts (ie a contract between a trader and a consumer) for goods, services, and digital content.
[104] Consumer Rights Act 2015, s 63, Sch 2 para 6.
[105] E Peel, *Treitel on The Law of Contract* (14th edn, Sweet & Maxwell 2015) para 20-146.

22

Specific performance

1. Introduction	401
2. The bars to specific performance	402
3. Other issues	436

1. Introduction

Specific performance is an equitable remedy which enforces a defendant's positive contractual obligations: that is, it orders the defendant to do what he or she promised to do. It is therefore a remedy protecting the claimant's expectation interest, the justification for such protection resting ultimately on the morality of promise-keeping.[1] Prohibitory injunctions also enforce contractual promises, but differ in that the promises in question are there negative. However, if what is in form a prohibitory injunction, in substance orders specific performance, or if the courts consider that in practice the injunction amounts to specific performance, it is governed by specific performance principles and is dealt with in this chapter.[2]

Strictly speaking, it is not an essential prerequisite of specific performance that the defendant is in breach of contract. Rather as McGhee says: '... an action for specific performance is based on the mere existence of the contract, coupled with circumstances which make it equitable to grant a decree.'[3] But in practice, it is a breach of contract, actual or threatened,[4] that renders it 'equitable' to grant the decree.[5]

However, in contrast to damages, specific performance is not available for every breach of contract. Indeed, as in this chapter, specific performance is best approached negatively, that is by examining the numerous restrictions on its availability. Positively, it then follows that if the remedy is not barred by such restrictions, a claimant who applies for it will succeed.[6]

Three other introductory points should be made. First, no order of specific performance can be made at the interim stage, where instead the appropriate remedy to enforce positive

---

[1] Above, pp 40–41.
[2] For further discussion of indirect specific performance see below, pp 456–460.
[3] J McGhee, *Snell's Equity* (33rd edn, Sweet & Maxwell 2015) para 17-003.
[4] *Hasham v Zenab* [1960] AC 316; R Maudsley, '*Hasham v Zenab*' (1960) 76 LQR 200 (note). See also *Zucker v Tyndall Holdings plc* [1992] 1 WLR 1127. The term 'threatened' is here preferred to 'anticipatory' so as to avoid the technicalities of the English doctrine of 'anticipatory breach'. According to that doctrine, an anticipatory breach does not constitute a breach unless and until it is accepted by the innocent party as terminating the contract. The better approach would be to say that an anticipatory breach is automatically a breach of contract because it constitutes a breach of the implied promise to be ready, able, and willing to perform. As, on that better approach, a threatened breach of contract is itself a breach of contract, it would seem inappropriate ever to label specific performance '*quia timet*' (cf J Heydon, M Leeming, and P Turner, *Meagher Gummow and Lehane's Equity, Doctrines and Remedies* (5th edn, LexisNexis 2015) para 20-025). For that labelling generally, see below, pp 442–443, 468–469.
[5] An exception is *Bass v Clivley* (1829) Taml 80, but it is unclear why it was there equitable to grant the order.
[6] In addition to the bars discussed in this chapter, specific performance cannot be ordered against the Crown: Crown Proceedings Act 1947, s 21(1)(a).

contractual obligations is the interim mandatory injunction. In so far as the availability of a final order is relevant to the grant of such an interim mandatory injunction, it is of course the principles governing specific performance that are applied.

Secondly, it is often said that, unlike damages, specific performance is a discretionary remedy. This is a misleading contrast.[7] It is misleading not only because the courts have a wide discretion (through, for example, intervening cause, remoteness, and the duty to mitigate) in deciding on the losses to be compensated by compensatory damages or in deciding on whether to award, and the quantum of, punitive damages, but also because the law on specific performance is relatively clear and certain. In truth, the description 'discretionary' makes the essentially trivial point that, while there are no bars on damages, which are therefore available as of right for breach of contract (or a tort),[8] there are numerous, albeit clearly established, bars to specific performance. The same trivial contrast can be made of all common law, as against equitable, remedies for breach of contract (and torts).

Finally, a commonly-drawn contrast is between English law's regard of specific performance as a secondary remedy to damages and the allegedly reverse situation under civil law systems. What does this mean? It cannot mean that specific performance is as freely available in civil law systems as damages, for this is plainly not true. It could mean that the bars to specific performance are not as wide-ranging in civil law systems as here, but that this is so is hardly sensibly expressed by referring to specific performance as a primary remedy. It seems rather that the contrast is based on the fact that, deriving from the historical role of equitable remedies as supplementary to those of the common law, a claimant in English law will not be awarded specific performance unless the claimant has shown that damages are inadequate whereas in civil law systems there is no such major hurdle.[9] Some recent cases indicate a weakening of this bar, and it has even been argued that specific performance is now the primary remedy in England. This seems exaggerated. However, a fascinating theme throughout this chapter is the recent apparent weakening not only of this, but of several other of the traditional bars, so that specific performance may be more freely available now than it was in the past.[10]

2. The bars to specific performance

(1) The primary restriction—adequacy of damages

Leaving aside a consumer's remedies under Part 1 of the Consumer Rights Act 2015,[11] specific performance will not be ordered unless damages (and the common law remedy of the award of an agreed sum) are inadequate. This is the major hurdle that a claimant seeking specific performance must overcome, but, even having done so, it may still fail because of one of the several other bars.

---

[7] See above, p 11. [8] Cf damages under the Human Rights Act 1998, s 8(3), above, pp 23–24.
[9] *Co-operative Insurance Society Ltd v Argyll Stores (Holdings) Ltd* [1998] AC 1, at 11 (per Lord Hoffmann).
[10] For a similar trend in the US, see M Van Hecke, 'Changing Emphases in Specific Performance' (1961) 40 North Carolina LR 1; Comment, 'Specific Performance: A Liberalization of Equity Standards' (1964) 49 Iowa LR 1290. For a general comparative account of 'enforced performance', see G Treitel, *Remedies for Breach of Contract* (Clarendon Press 1988) ch 3. See also S Rowan, *Remedies for Breach of Contract: A Comparative Analysis of the Protection of Performance* (OUP 2012) esp 37–55 and 237–242. For the law in Asia, see *Studies in the Contract Laws of Asia: Remedies for Breach of Contract* (eds M Chen-Wishart, A Loke, and B Ong, OUP 2016).
[11] See below, p 412.

(a) Availability of substitute—uniqueness

The most important factor in determining whether damages are adequate is whether money can buy a substitute for the promised performance. Most discussion of this has been in relation to a seller's obligation under a contract of sale, where the issue has often been expressed as one of the 'uniqueness' of the subject matter.

(i) Breach of a contract to sell land

Here specific performance is almost invariably granted where it is sought,[12] the traditional reasoning being that each piece of land is unique and cannot be replaced in the market. However, specific performance is ordered even where this does not reflect reality, for example in the case of a contact for the sale of identical new houses on a housing estate. Nor is the claimant's purpose in buying the land considered relevant. In other words, it makes no difference that the purchaser bought the land for resale or long-term investment rather than as a home.[13] The courts are therefore not confining specific performance to where the claimant places a subjective consumer value on the land over and above that reflected in the objective market price.[14] Assuming that there is no true substitute land, specific performance for the long-term investor is justified because of the acute difficulty of accurately assessing his profits. But there is no such obvious justification where the claimant was intending a quick resale, particularly where the resale contract has already been concluded. All in all, it seems clear that specific performance has simply taken over as the primary remedy for breach of an obligation to sell land, and that the adequacy of damages hurdle is in effect ignored. This is unfortunate as, for reasons later discussed, the adequacy of damages restriction rests on a sound footing.

The seller of an interest in land is also readily awarded specific performance ordering the buyer to accept title and to pay the contract price.[15] Since the seller's interest is purely monetary, damages or, where title has already passed, the remedy of the award of the agreed price would be perfectly adequate, except in a rare case where damages could not be accurately assessed. Nor is it an explanation to say that as the buyer can get specific performance, it is only just, in accord with 'affirmative mutuality',[16] for the seller to be so entitled, since no injustice would be caused by the grant of the common law remedies. In truth it seems that on this side of the contract too, the adequacy of the common law remedies is ignored and specific performance is the primary remedy.

(ii) Breach of a contract to sell goods

The Sale of Goods Act 1979, s 52 expressly gives the courts a discretion to order the specific performance of the sale of 'specific or ascertained' goods; but the courts have not interpreted this section as removing the adequacy of damages hurdle or as altering their traditional approach to it. Specific performance therefore continues not to be ordered for the sale of most

---

[12] *Sudbrook Trading Estate Ltd v Eggleton* [1983] 1 AC 444, at 478. Specific performance is also ordered of contracts to dispose of lesser interests in land: in *Verrall v Great Yarmouth Borough Council* [1981] QB 202, it was even ordered of a short-term contractual licence.

[13] For discussion see P Brenner, 'Specific Performance of Contracts for the Sale of Land Purchased for Resale or Investment' (1978) 24 McGill LJ 513, esp 545–548; G Jones and W Goodhart, *Specific Performance* (2nd edn, Butterworths 1996) 130–132; R Sharpe, *Injunctions and Specific Performance* (5th edn, Thomson Reuters 2017) paras 8.30–8.90. Cf *Semelhago v Paramadevan* (1996) 136 DLR (4th) 1, at 9–11 (Supreme Court of Canada); M McInnes, 'Specific Performance and Mitigation in the Supreme Court of Canada' (2013) 129 LQR 165.

[14] D Harris, A Ogus, and J Phillips, 'Contract Remedies and the Consumer Surplus' (1979) 95 LQR 581, 588.

[15] *Walker v Eastern Counties Rly Co* (1848) 6 Hare 594; *Eastern Counties Rly Co v Hawkes* (1855) 5 HL Cas 331; *Maskell v Ivory* [1970] Ch 502; *Johnson v Agnew* [1980] AC 367.

[16] R Sharpe, *Injunctions and Specific Performance* (5th edn, Thomson Reuters 2017) paras 7.820–7.880, 8.160.

goods, whether 'specific or ascertained' or not, on the ground that money enables substitutes to be bought in the market.[17] On the other hand, specific performance is ordered where the goods are unique.

Goods are most obviously unique where substitutes cannot be bought because the goods possess significant physical characteristics that very few, if any, other goods have. That the courts will order specific performance for the sale of physically unique goods is well-established. So in *Falcke v Gray*,[18] although specific performance was refused on other grounds, the court would have been prepared to order specific performance of a contract to sell two china jars on the ground that the jars were of 'unusual beauty, rarity and distinction';[19] and in *Thorn v Public Works Commissioners*[20] specific performance was ordered of a contract to sell the arch-stone, the spandrill stone, and the Bramley Fall stone of the old Westminster Bridge, which had been pulled down. Again the courts are often willing to order specific performance of a contract to sell a ship, because a ship often has characteristics shared by very few, if any, other ships. So, for example, in *Behnke v Bede Shipping Co Ltd*[21] Wright J, in ordering specific performance of a contract to sell the ship *City*, said, 'the *City* was of peculiar and practically unique value to the plaintiff ... A very experienced ship's valuer has said that he knew of only one other comparable ship but that may now have been sold.'[22] On the other hand, in *CN Marine Inc v Stena Line A/B and Regie Voor Maritiem Transport, The Stena Nautica (No 2)*,[23] specific performance was refused because the ship was not sufficiently different from other ships.

While there are few other cases in which the specific performance of the sale of physically unique goods has been ordered, there are analogous examples. First, there are cases where specific performance was ordered of contracts relating to such goods. In *Lingen v Simpson*,[24] for example, in breach of a contract dissolving a partnership one partner failed to release for copying a book of ornamental plates that had been used in the business. The court ordered him to release the book and, although there was no discussion of inadequacy, we can assume that damages were thought inadequate because each of the two books was physically unique. Again, when in *Phillips v Lamdin*[25] the defendant, who had contracted to sell his home to the claimant, was in breach of that contract by removing an Adam-style door from one of the rooms he was ordered to replace it. Croom-Johnson J said, 'You cannot make a new Adam door. You cannot in these times refashion a door or make a copy ... I do not see how damages can be an adequate remedy.'[26] Secondly, there are several oft-cited and particularly good examples of the analogous remedy of delivery up for wrongful detention being ordered in respect of physically unique goods, such as antiques, heirlooms, and works of art.[27]

Analogously to their approach to land, the courts appear not to be concerned with the purpose for which the claimant is buying the physically unique goods. In other words, no distinction appears to be drawn between the consumer, with a non-monetary interest, and the businessman who wants the goods for profitable use or resale.[28] The same criticism can be made as in relation to land contracts: namely, that for the reseller damages are adequate,

---

[17] An extreme example is *Cohen v Roche* [1927] 1 KB 169, refusing the analogous remedy of delivery up in relation to Hepplewhite chairs.
[18] (1859) 4 Drew 651. [19] ibid, at 658. [20] (1863) 32 Beav 490.
[21] [1927] 1 KB 649. See also *The Oro Chief* [1983] 2 Lloyd's Rep 509, at 521; and *Bristol Airport plc v Powdrill* [1990] Ch 744, at 759 (lease of an aircraft).
[22] [1927] 1 KB 649, at 661. [23] [1982] 2 Lloyd's Rep 336. [24] (1824) 1 Sim & St 600.
[25] [1949] 2 KB 33. [26] [1949] 2 KB 33, at 41. [27] Below, p 494.
[28] Eg in *Falcke v Gray* and *Thorn v Public Works Commissioners*, the claimants seemed to have merely a commercial interest in the goods. Contra is R Sharpe, *Injunctions and Specific Performance* (5th edn, Thomson Reuters 2017) para 8.350 citing *Cohen v Roche* [1927] 1 KB 169 and *Dowling v Betjemann* (1862) 2 John & H 544.

since the reseller's interest is purely monetary and, unlike the long-term investor, they can generally be readily assessed.

Will specific performance be ordered for the sale of commercially unique goods? Goods can be said to be commercially unique, a term coined by Treitel,[29] where, although the goods may not be physically unique, buying substitutes would be so difficult or would cause such delay that the claimant's business would be seriously disrupted.

Until fairly recently, no case could be confidently cited in which specific performance had been ordered on this ground,[30] although, in *Behnke v Bede Shipping,* Wright J did appear to regard it as relevant that the buyer needed the ship immediately for the purposes of his business. There was also Lord Hardwicke's dictum in *Buxton v Lister*[31] that in a supply contract the close vicinity of the goods to the buyer can make damages inadequate. Furthermore, in *North v Great Northern Rly Co*[32] it was accepted that the analogous remedy of delivery up could be ordered for commercially unique goods, here 54 coal waggons; and the interim order for delivery up of 500 tons of steel, made more recently in *Howard Perry Ltd v British Railways Board,*[33] can also be said to have been based on this reasoning.

But commercial uniqueness as a ground for specific performance was radically accepted in *Sky Petroleum Ltd v VIP Petroleum Ltd.*[34] Here, an interim injunction amounting to temporary specific performance was granted to enforce the supply of petrol to the claimants' filling stations, at a time when the petrol market was in such an unusual state that the claimants would be unlikely to find an alternative supply and as a result would be forced to stop trading. The reason why this is particularly radical is that petrol is not even 'specific or ascertained' goods within the Sale of Goods Act 1979, s 52. In *Re Wait,*[35] the majority of the Court of Appeal thought that the Act meant that specific performance could not be ordered of non-specific or unascertained goods and any application of commercial uniqueness to such goods was therefore clearly rejected. But in *Sky Petroleum* Goulding J adopted a different approach. He said:

> 'I come to the most serious hurdle in the way of the plaintiffs, which is the well-known doctrine that the court refuses specific performance of a contract to sell and purchase chattels not specific or ascertained … The ratio behind the rule is, as I believe, that under the ordinary contract for the sale of non-specific goods, damages are a sufficient remedy. That to my mind, is lacking in the circumstances of the present case. The evidence suggests, and indeed it is common knowledge, that the petroleum market is in an unusual state in which a would-be buyer cannot go into the market and contract with another seller, possibly at some sacrifice as to the price. Here the defendants appear for practical purposes to be the plaintiffs' sole means of keeping their business going, and I am prepared so far to depart from the general rule as to try to preserve the position under the contract until a later date.'[36]

It is noteworthy here that the US Uniform Commercial Code, para 2.716(1) has sought to encourage acceptance of the notion of 'commercial uniqueness' in relation to goods that are not specific or ascertained. The comment to that section reads:

> 'The test of uniqueness must be made in terms of the total situation, which characterises the contract. Output and requirements contracts involving a particular or peculiarly available source or

---

[29] G Treitel, *The Law of Contract* (11th edn, Sweet & Maxwell 2003) 1022 (repeated in the 14th edn: E Peel, *Treitel on Contract* (14th edn, Sweet & Maxwell 2015) para 21-024); G Treitel, 'Specific Performance in the Sale of Goods' [1966] JBL 211.
[30] But see in Australia, *Dougan v Ley* (1946) 71 CLR 142 (licensed taxi-cab).
[31] (1746) 3 Atk 383, at 385. But the correctness of this was specifically doubted in *Pollard v Clayton* (1855) 1 K & J 462.
[32] (1860) 2 Giff 64.   [33] [1980] 1 WLR 1375.   [34] [1974] 1 WLR 576.
[35] [1927] 1 Ch 606.   [36] [1974] 1 WLR 576, at 578–579.

market present today the typical contractual specific performance situation, as contrasted with contracts for the sale of heirlooms or priceless works of art, which were usually involved in the older cases.'[37]

But while the acceptance of commercial uniqueness for non-specific goods in the *Sky Petroleum* case is important, a degree of caution must be exercised in assessing its effects. Apart from the fact that it was a first instance decision that has not yet been followed or approved, doubt has been cast on the courts' acceptance of commercial uniqueness, even in relation to specific or ascertained goods, by the Court of Appeal decision in *Société des Industries Métallurgiques SA v Bronx Engineering Co Ltd*.[38] Here it was held that an interim injunction restraining the sellers from removing certain machinery from the jurisdiction should not be granted since, even if the sellers were in breach of contract, there was no likelihood of the claimant buyers being granted specific performance at the trial, because damages were adequate. This was held to be so, even though the court accepted that the delay of nine to 12 months in obtaining substitute machinery might substantially disrupt the claimants' business. While one might try to reconcile the cases by saying, for example, that the degree of disruption threatened in *Bronx Engineering* was not as great as in *Sky Petroleum* (or the analogous *North v Great Northern Rly*) the plain truth seems to be that the Court of Appeal was here rejecting commercial as opposed to physical uniqueness. Although *Howard Perry* has since been decided, without any reference being made to *Bronx Engineering*, it is still too early to say that such a rejection will be disregarded. As yet, therefore, even if the goods are specific or ascertained, it cannot be confidently asserted that specific performance will be ordered of a contract to sell goods that are commercially unique for the buyer.

In terms of policy, commercial uniqueness should be accepted, for while theoretically damages for the substantial disruption to a business are adequate, since it is ultimately only money that the claimant is losing, in practice in this situation, an accurate assessment of the claimant's losses is so difficult that the claimant is likely to be incorrectly compensated; and this high risk of incorrect compensation is a strong justification for accepting commercial uniqueness, whether the goods in question are specific or ascertained or not. Nor, it should be added, is there any need as a matter of construction to take the restrictive exhaustive interpretation of the Sale of Goods Act 1979, s 52 adopted in *Re Wait*.

It should further be noted that our courts, in contrast again to those in the US, may not recognise sentimental uniqueness. In Treitel's words, 'It is ... uncertain whether sentimental attachment to otherwise ordinary goods makes them unique.'[39] If this is so, it represents an unfortunate failure to take into account the consumer interest, for damages do not enable a satisfactory substitute to be bought for such goods.

Finally, can specific performance ever be obtained by the vendor of goods? The Sale of Goods Act 1979 makes no provision for specific performance being granted against a buyer so as to order the taking of and paying for goods and there is little authority to suggest

---

[37] M Nichols, 'Remedies—Specific Performance and Long Term Supply Contracts' (1976) 30 Ark LR 65. Output and requirements contracts are the major types of long-term supply contracts. Even where, in contrast to *Sky Petroleum*, there are substitute goods readily available at the time of the suppliers' breach, goods in such contracts are typically commercially unique, because the claimant is very often unsure of obtaining a substitute supply during the full contract period, and is thereby threatened with disruption to his business.

[38] [1975] 1 Lloyd's Rep 465.

[39] G Treitel, 'Specific Performance in the Sale of Goods' [1966] JBL 211, 214.

that a vendor of goods can be awarded specific performance at common law.[40] Normally, as the vendor's interest is purely monetary, damages or the award of the agreed price will be adequate. However, in long-term requirements contracts, specific performance may be merited because of the difficulty in assessing the vendor's damages, particularly in view of uncertainty as to the exact quantity of goods being sold and as to the future state of the market.[41] Certainly, prohibitory injunctions are commonly granted in respect of such contracts to restrain the purchaser from buying goods other than from the vendor.[42] But as the courts in such cases have not regarded themselves as in effect ordering specific performance, it is probably misleading to regard such cases as authorities on specific performance.

(iii) Breach of a contract to sell shares or stocks

Where the shares or stocks are freely available on the market, specific performance will generally not be ordered, since damages enable substitutes to be bought. For example, in *Cud v Rutter*,[43] specific performance of a contract to sell South Sea stock was refused, Lord Parker LC saying:

> '... a court of equity ought not to execute any of these contracts, but to leave them to law, where the party is to recover damages, and with the money may if he pleases buy the quantity of stock agreed to be transferred to him; for there can be no difference between one man's stock and another's.'[44]

But in the converse situation, where substitute shares are not readily available, an extreme case being where the breach deprives the claimant of a majority holding, damages are regarded as inadequate and specific performance will be ordered.[45] Generally this approach is fully justified, although one can imagine situations, for example where the purchaser has bought for a quick resale, where damages can be accurately assessed, and would be adequate.[46] A vendor of such shares has also been awarded specific performance,[47] but as with contracts for the sale of land there rarely seems any justification for this, and at root it probably rests on the unsatisfactory notion of 'affirmative mutuality'.[48]

(b) *Difficulty in assessing damages*

This head and the previous one (uniqueness) are inextricably linked; difficulty in assessing damages—whether in putting a value on a consumer's interest, or in calculating possible investment profit, or in putting a figure on the serious disruption to a business—lies as the root justification for specific performance, where the contractual subject matter is unique.[49] But the question now to be examined is, does difficulty in assessing damages in itself render damages inadequate?

The answer would appear to be that it does not for while there are eighteenth- and nineteenth-century cases relying on this, such as *Taylor v Neville*,[50] which concerned a contract for the sale of 800 tons of iron involving delivery in instalments over a number of

---

[40] But see *Shell-Mex Ltd v Elton Cop Dyeing Co Ltd* (1928) 34 Com Cas 39; *Elliott v Pierson* [1948] 1 All ER 939.
[41] G Treitel, 'Specific Performance in the Sale of Goods' [1966] JBL 211, 229–230.
[42] Below, pp 460–461.
[43] (1720) 1 P Wms 570. Also *Re Schwabacher* (1907) 98 LT 127; *Chinn v Hochstrasser* [1979] Ch 447, at 462, 470.
[44] (1720) 1 P Wms 570, at 571.
[45] *Duncuft v Albrecht* (1841) 12 Sim 189; *Langen and Wind Ltd v Bell* [1972] Ch 685; *Harvela Investments Ltd v Royal Trust Co of Canada* [1985] 2 All ER 966.
[46] See analogously above, pp 403, 404–405. [47] *Odessa Tramways Co v Mendel* (1878) 8 Ch D 235.
[48] Above, p 403. [49] A Kronman, 'Specific Performance' (1978) 45 U of Chi LR 351, 362.
[50] Unreported but cited in *Buxton v Lister* (1746) 3 Atk 383.

years, and *Adderley v Dixon*,[51] which dealt with a contract for the sale of debts proved in bankruptcy, later cases, such as *Fothergill v Rowland*,[52] denied the relevance of the difficulty of assessing damages. Indeed this concerned an output contract, where, irrespective of any commercial uniqueness, one would have expected difficulties of assessment to be particularly problematical because not only is there the usual difficulty in long-term contracts of judging future market prices but, in addition, as with requirements contracts, one cannot state in advance the exact quantity of goods to be supplied. Yet Sir G Jessel MR said:

> 'To say that you cannot ascertain the damage in a case of breach of contract for the sale of goods, say in monthly deliveries extending over three years … is to limit the power of ascertaining damages in a way which would rather astonish gentlemen who practise on what is called the other side of Westminster Hall. There is never considered to be any difficulty in ascertaining such a thing. Therefore I do not think it is a case in which damages could not be ascertained at law.'[53]

That the difficulty of assessing damages is irrelevant gains further and more recent support from the judgments in the *Bronx Engineering* case.[54] This approach is most unfortunate, for where there is grave doubt about whether damages will put the claimant into as good a position as if the contract had been performed, specific performance is prima facie a better remedy.[55] Certainly, the difficulty of assessing damages has been expressly regarded as a factor rendering damages inadequate in respect of interim prohibitory injunctions restraining defendants from selling goods other than to or through the claimant, their exclusive agent, or distributor.[56] But the courts in these cases did not regard themselves as in effect ordering specific performance, and this, plus the ease with which the adequacy of damages hurdle has been traditionally overcome with regard to prohibitory injunctions restraining the breach of negative contractual obligations, probably renders it misleading to use such cases as authorities on specific performance.[57]

(c) Inability to pay the damages

The question of whether the defendant's inability to pay the damages renders them inadequate has traditionally received surprisingly little attention in the cases. In *Re Wait*[58] though, the Court of Appeal clearly did not consider the defendant's insolvency sufficient to render damages inadequate for failure to deliver wheat, and Goulding J appeared to take the same view in *Anders Utkilens Rederi A/S v Lovisa Stevedoring Co A/B*:[59] 'Commercial life would be subjected to new and unjust hazards if the court were to decree specific performance of contracts normally sounding only in damages simply because of a party's threatened insolvency.' On the other hand, in the *Bronx Engineering* case, which in all other respects is so anti-specific performance, Lord Edmund Davies did think it relevant in relation to adequacy that the defendants would be able to pay; and in *The Oro Chief*,[60] Staughton J said

---

[51] (1824) 1 Sim & St 607.
[52] (1873) LR 17 Eq 132. The injunction sought was regarded as amounting to specific performance—see below, p 461.
[53] ibid, at 140.   [54] [1975] 1 Lloyd's Rep 465, at 468, 469–470.
[55] Similarly, it is arguable that damages are inadequate where some of the loss is irrecoverable because of a particular type (eg mental distress) or too remote. But see *The Stena Nautica (No 2)* [1982] 2 Lloyd's Rep 336, at 342 (per Parker J).
[56] *Evans Marshall & Co v Bertola SA* [1973] 1 WLR 349; *Decro-Wall International SA v Practitioners in Marketing Ltd* [1971] 2 All ER 216. Below, p 461.
[57] Contra is E Peel, *Treitel on The Law of Contract* (14th edn, Sweet & Maxwell 2015) para 21-020.
[58] [1927] 1 Ch 606.   [59] [1985] 2 All ER 669, at 674.
[60] [1983] 2 Lloyd's Rep 509, at 521. See also *Doloret v Rothschild* (1824) 1 Sim & St 590, at 598.

in dicta that even if a ship was not unique '... it may be that in special circumstances, such as when the seller is insolvent and can pay no damages, [the buyer] will still obtain an order for specific performance'. There are also prohibitory injunction cases, expressly stating that damages are inadequate where the defendant is unable to pay,[61] but again it is probably misleading to use them as authorities on specific performance.

In general, the former view is correct. If one focuses on a contract for the sale of goods, to allow a claimant to obtain specific performance simply because of the defendant's insolvency or imminent insolvency would, in effect, turn all unsecured creditors into secured creditors. In other words, it would undermine our present law of insolvency by entitling unsecured creditors to 'take out' particular goods from the insolvent's assets. Exceptionally, however, our insolvency system would not be undermined by such an order; for example, where the claimant is the defendant's only creditor or where the performance will not reduce the defendant's assets. In such (unusual) circumstances it is clearly right that an inability to pay damages renders them inadequate and justifies specific performance.

(d) Contractual obligation to pay money

The common law remedies, being monetary orders, are normally adequate where the breach is of a contractual obligation to pay money. However, specific performance has been ordered of a contract to pay an annuity.[62] In dicta in *Adderley v Dixon*[63] this was justified on the ground of the difficulty of here assessing a lump sum of damages. An alternative justification, put forward in *Beswick v Beswick*,[64] is that specific performance avoids the inconvenience of bringing numerous actions to recover the agreed sum. Specific performance can also be granted to enforce the purchaser's payment obligation in a contract for the sale of land, or for the sale of shares that cannot be replaced in the market,[65] but there rarely seems any justification for here regarding the common law remedies as inadequate.[66]

(e) Contracts that can be immediately terminated

A leading case is *Sheffield Gas Consumers' Co v Harrison*,[67] where specific performance was refused of a contract to allow the claimant to join a partnership. In Sir John Romilly's words:

> '... this Court will not enforce the specific performance of a contract to enter into a partnership, which, so far as the defendant is concerned, he may dissolve immediately afterwards. To specifically perform a contract of this description would be merely nugatory.'[68]

But if the order would be futile because the contract can be immediately terminated, it would seem that a fortiori damages are adequate, and that the case fails at this initial hurdle.[69]

---

[61] *Evans Marshall & Coy v Bertola SA* [1973] 1 WLR 349; *Associated Portland Cement Manufacturers Ltd v Tiegland Shipping A/S* [1975] 1 Lloyd's Rep 581. Analogously to these see *Hodgson v Duce* (1856) 28 LTOS 155 (injunction for trespass).

[62] *Ball v Coggs* (1710) 1 Bro Parl Cas 140; *Beswick v Beswick* [1968] AC 58.

[63] (1824) 1 Sim & St 607.   [64] [1968] AC 58, at 81, 88, 97.

[65] Further examples are the payment obligations in a contract to take up and pay for debentures, in a contract to discharge another's debt, and in a loan agreement collateral to a specifically enforceable agreement. See G Jones and W Goodhart, *Specific Performance* (2nd edn, Butterworths 1996) 154–161.

[66] Above, pp 403, 407.

[67] (1853) 17 Beav 294. See also *Hercy v Birch* (1804) 9 Ves 357; *Tito v Waddell (No 2)* [1977] Ch 106, at 326–327.

[68] (1853) 17 Beav 294, at 297.

[69] The same reasoning applies to a contract for a lease that has already expired by trial, see *Turner v Clowes* (1869) 20 LT 214.

However, one should not regard specific performance of such contracts as necessarily being ruled out, for one can imagine situations where damages are inadequate and where there is some point from the claimant's point of view in being granted specific performance even though the defendant can terminate the contract almost immediately. For example, specific performance of a contract of employment terminable at short notice may be important so as to give the claimant an extra period of employment necessary for the accrual of certain rights (eg to maternity leave or to a pension).

(f) Nominal damages and privity

In *Beswick v Beswick*[70] a coal merchant transferred his business to his nephew, who in return promised that, after his uncle's death, he would pay £5 a week to his widow. The uncle died and his widow brought an action for specific performance of the nephew's promise, suing both personally and as administratrix. The House of Lords, upholding the doctrine of privity, held that while the widow could not maintain a successful action suing personally, she could as administratrix succeed in suing for the estate's loss, though not her own personal third party loss. Crucially, however, the Lords held that as administratrix she should be granted specific performance of the nephew's promise rather than being confined to damages.

One aspect of the decision—that specific performance can be granted for failure to pay an annuity—has already been dealt with, and the wider implications of their Lordships' speeches will be considered shortly. But the decision is probably principally well known for laying down that specific performance can be granted to avoid the injustice that the privity rule can produce. The reasoning was as follows: if a party sues on a contract made for the benefit of a third party his damages, which are assessed according to his own loss, are usually going to be nominal; where this produces injustice, as here where the nephew had got the business and would end up paying almost nothing for it, nominal damages should be regarded as inadequate, enabling specific performance to be granted to enforce the defendant's promise. Only Lord Pearce thought that the administratrix could have recovered substantial damages but, if wrong on this, he too considered nominal damages 'manifestly useless'.[71] Two points should be added. First, while usually regarded as a pioneering manoeuvre around the doctrine of privity, there were earlier cases ordering specific performance of a contract for the benefit of a third party,[72] and these were relied on by the House of Lords. Secondly, the reform of the doctrine of privity by the Contracts (Rights of Third Parties) Act 1999 means that, on the facts of *Beswick v Beswick*, the third party (ie the widow in her personal capacity) would probably now have a direct right of action against the nephew.

(g) Beswick v Beswick—the radical interpretation

On a narrow view, *Beswick* lays down merely that damages may be inadequate, and specific performance can be ordered, for breach of a contract to pay an annuity or to benefit a third party.[73] But there is an alternative wide view of *Beswick*, which focuses on the fact that each of their Lordships at some stage described the relationship between damages and specific performance in terms other than the adequacy of damages. Thus Lord Reid, with whom

---

[70] [1968] AC 58.   [71] ibid, at 89.
[72] *Keenan v Handley* (1864) 2 De GJ & Sm 283; *Peel v Peel* (1869) 17 WR 586; *Hohler v Aston* [1920] 2 Ch 420.
[73] On this, *Beswick* was followed in *Gurtner v Circuit* [1968] 2 QB 587.

Lord Guest agreed, was concerned with ordering specific performance to produce '... a just result'.[74] Lord Upjohn said, 'Equity will grant specific performance when damages are inadequate to meet the justice of the case.'[75] Lord Hodson talked of deciding which was the more appropriate remedy and concluded that, as there had been an unconscionable breach of faith, the equitable remedy was 'apt'.[76] Lord Pearce too said that specific performance was 'the more appropriate remedy',[77] and it is particularly significant that he cited with approval sections of Windeyer J's judgment in *Coulls v Bagot's Executor and Trustee Co Ltd*[78] including the following: 'It is ... a faulty analysis of legal obligations to say that the law treats the promisor as having a right to elect either to perform his promise or to pay damages. Rather ... the promisee has "a legal right to the performance of the contract".'[79]

The wide view is that, given such terminology, the Lords were concerned to effect a general change in the relationship between damages and specific performance so that, to use conventional terminology, damages are inadequate in a far wider range of circumstances than in the past. Indeed Lawson thought that *Beswick* could be interpreted as saying that specific performance replaces damages as the primary remedy in English law. He wrote:

> '... it is not unreasonable to see in it an acknowledgement of a right to specific performance of all contracts where there is no adequate reason for the courts to refuse it. If this is so, we have already in England reached the Scottish principle that specific performance is the normal remedy for breach of contract, and a refusal of it must be justified in specific types of case or on special grounds. In other words ... the choice between specific performance and damages should in principle rest with the plaintiff, not the court ...'[80]

While *Beswick* can be given such a wide interpretation, and it is hard to interpret Lord Pearce's judgment in any other way, the courts have taken the narrow view, for they have continued to apply the adequacy of damages bar without even mentioning *Beswick*.

In *The Stena Nautica (No 2)*[81] May LJ, while not referring to *Beswick*, also preferred a different terminology than adequacy, and cited Sachs LJ's statement in *Evans Marshall & Co v Bertola SA*[82] (a prohibitory injunction rather than a specific performance case)[83] that, 'The standard question ... are damages an adequate remedy? might perhaps, in the light of authorities of recent years, be rewritten: is it just in all the circumstances that the plaintiff should be confined to his remedy in damages?'[84] Like *Beswick*, May LJ's approach can be interpreted widely as advocating that damages will be held inadequate in a far wider set of circumstances than in the past. But again a narrow view has prevailed so that May LJ's terminology has not heralded a substantive change. Indeed May LJ himself went on to apply seemingly traditional reasoning in denying specific performance: that is, the ship in question was not unique. The majority reached the same result by the same reasoning without advocating any change of terminology.

---

[74] [1968] AC 58, at 77. [75] ibid, at 102. [76] ibid, at 83. [77] ibid, at 88.
[78] (1967) 119 CLR 460. [79] ibid, at 504, citing *Alley v Deschamps* (1806) 13 Ves 225, at 228.
[80] F Lawson, *Remedies of English Law* (2nd edn, Butterworths 1980) 223–224.
[81] [1982] 2 Lloyd's Rep 336, at 346–347. E Macdonald, 'The Inadequacy of Adequacy: the Granting of Specific Performance' (1987) 38 NILQ 244 supports this approach. See also Goulding J in *Anders Utkilens Rederi A/S v O/Y Lovisa Stevedoring Co A/B* [1985] 2 All ER 669, at 674, referring to what 'good conscience' requires; and Lawrence Collins QC in *Rainbow Estates Ltd v Tokenhold Ltd* [1999] Ch 64, at 73: 'Subject to the overriding need to avoid injustice or oppression, the remedy should be available when damages are not an adequate remedy or, in the more modern formulation, when specific performance is the appropriate remedy.'
[82] [1973] 1 WLR 349. [83] Below, p 461.
[84] [1973] 1 WLR 349, at 379. It is unclear which 'authorities of recent years' Sachs LJ was referring to.

(h) A consumer's remedies under Part 1 of the Consumer Rights Act 2015

There are special remedies provided for a consumer in Part 1 of the Consumer Rights Act 2015. By sections 19 and 23 and 42–43 of the 2015 Act, these include that a consumer, who has a contract for the supply of goods (or digital content) by a trader, has a right to the repair or replacement, within a reasonable time, of goods (or digital content) which do not conform to the contract terms,[85] unless repair or replacement is impossible or disproportionate (compared to the other of those two rights). Similarly, by ss 54–55 of the 2015 Act a consumer, who has a contract for the supply of a service by a trader, has a right to require repeat performance, within a reasonable time and unless impossible, where the performance has not been in conformity with the contract terms.[86] By s 58 (which is headed 'powers of the courts'), the courts are expressly given the power to enforce these special remedies—the right to repair or replacement, or the right to repeat performance—by an order of specific performance. It is important to appreciate that this approach in s 58 to specific performance, enforcing a consumer's statutory right to repair or replacement, or the right to repeat performance, represents a move away in this area from the normal requirement for specific performance that damages must be inadequate. Since the regime of consumer remedies in the 2015 Act is implementing an EC Directive, it is perhaps not surprising that, in the primacy apparently afforded to specific performance, it reflects a civilian rather than a common law approach. It appears that (subject to the court's discretion under s 58(3) to decide that the exercise of another right is appropriate) a court should only refuse specific performance (ordering repair or replacement of goods (or digital content) or ordering the repeat performance of services) if impossible or, as between repair and replacement, disproportionate to the other.[87] One may therefore regard the law on specific performance under the 2015 Act as departing not only from the adequacy of damages requirement but also, on the face of it, from several other of the normal bars to specific performance considered below (for example, the bars concerning constant supervision, personal services, and want of mutuality).

(i) Is it satisfactory to maintain an adequacy of damages hurdle?

It is a complex policy question whether the primacy traditionally given to damages by the adequacy of damages rule is justified other than historically.[88] On the one hand, it might be said that, subject to other bars, a claimant ought to be entitled to specific performance if it so chooses, since in accordance with the morality of promise-keeping, this most closely fulfils its expectations. In particular, specific performance satisfies a consumer's non-monetary interest in performance and does not run the risk of inaccurate assessment or the defendant's inability to pay. Moreover, it saves the costs of a judicial assessment of damages.

---

[85] As defined in Consumer Rights Act 2015, ss 19(1)–(2) and 42(1).
[86] As defined in Consumer Rights Act 2015, s 54(2).
[87] See Consumer Rights Act 2015, ss 23(3), 43(3), and 55(3).
[88] A Kronman, 'Specific Performance' (1978) 45 U of Chi LR 351; A Schwartz, 'The Case for Specific Performance' (1979) 89 Yale LJ 271; P Linzer, 'On the Amorality of Contract Remedies—Efficiency, Equity and the Second Restatement' (1981) 81 Col LR 111; E Yorio, 'In Defence of Money Damages for Breach of Contract' (1982) 82 Col LR 1365; T Ulen, 'The Efficiency of Specific Performance: Towards a Unified Theory of Contract Remedies' (1984) Mich LR 341; A Ogus, 'Remedies' in *Contract Law Today* (eds D Harris and D Tallon, Clarendon Press 1989) 243–263; D Harris, D Campbell, and R Halson, *Remedies in Contract and Tort* (2nd edn, Butterworths 2002) 221–227; H Collins, *The Law of Contract* (4th edn, LexisNexis 2003) 399–405. See also D Laycock, *The Death of the Irreparable Injury Rule* (OUP 1991) esp ch 11.

On the other hand, a claimant entitled to specific performance has an incentive to be idle and inefficient, for while a claimant seeking damages has a duty to mitigate its loss, so that its damages will be reduced if it fails to do so, specific performance requires no reasonable steps to be taken by the claimant to put itself into as good a position as if the contract had been performed. Specific performance is also more of an infringement of individual liberty in that ordering people to stick to their promises is more coercive of their behaviour than requiring them to pay damages. Similarly it may be thought relevant that the sanction to enforce specific performance is more drastic with disobedience amounting to a contempt of court, potentially punishable by imprisonment. Indeed it was one of Dawson's[89] main arguments that specific performance might be more widely used if, as in Germany, the consequences of non-compliance were less severe and more varied. A further argument against specific performance is that it potentially generates undesirable future friction between the parties. Moreover, there is the view that non-monetary remedies generally are less satisfactory than damages because they give the claimant too much of an advantage in pre- and post-judgment bargaining.[90]

Consideration must also be given to probably the most discussed argument against specific performance, namely the economic analysis theory of 'efficient breach'.[91] The basis of this is that in a contract in which the claimant is to receive a contractual performance from the defendant in return for the payment of money, the claimant places a certain value on that contractual performance. This value most simply accords with the profits expected to be made from the performance. The free market produces economic efficiency by moving resources to those who place the highest value on them. In order to support this the law must permit and indeed encourage a defendant to break a contract where this will lead to resources passing to those who place higher values on them while at the same time discouraging breach where the claimant has a higher value use than others. The right encouragement and discouragement to breach is produced by awarding, where possible to estimate, expectation damages in preference to specific performance. An example will make this clearer.[92] Say D contracts to make a machine part for C for £10,000. If X offers D £15,000 for that part, breach by D is efficient if X values the part more than C, and is inefficient if X values the part less than C. The regime of expectation damages in preference to specific performance produces the efficient result: if C values the part at more than £15,000, D will not breach, since it will have to pay C expectation damages which, together with the contract price lost, will not exceed the £15,000 offered by X; on the other hand, if C values the part at less than £15,000, D will breach, since by paying C expectation damages and transferring the part to X, it will be better off. The machine part therefore passes to whichever party, C or X, places the higher value on it.

As it stands, this theory can be challenged on the ground that even if the claimant were entitled to specific performance, this would not necessarily prevent the machine part passing

---

[89] J Dawson, 'Specific Performance in France and Germany' (1959) 57 Mich LR 495, 538.
[90] Above, pp 17–18.
[91] In addition to the writings cited above, p 412 n 88, see R Birmingham, 'Breach of Contract, Damages Measures and Economic Efficiency' (1970) 24 Rutgers LR 273; C Goetz and R Scott, 'Liquidated Damages, Penalties and the Just Compensation Principle' (1977) 77 Col LR 554; D Farber, 'Reassessing the Economic Efficiency of Compensatory Damages for Breach of Contract' (1980) 66 Va LR 1443; I Macneil, 'Efficient Breach of Contract: Circles in the Sky' (1982) 68 Va LR 947; R Craswell, 'Contract Remedies, Renegotiation and the Theory of Efficient Breach' (1988) 61 So Cal LR 629; D Friedmann, 'The Efficient Breach Fallacy' (1989) 18 JLS 1; R Posner, *Economic Analysis of Law* (9th edn, Wolters Kluwer 2014) 128–138, 145–146; H Beale, *Remedies for Breach of Contract* (Sweet & Maxwell 1980) 13–14, 142; D Harris, D Campbell, and R Halson, *Remedies in Contract and Tort* (2nd edn, Butterworths 2002) 5–21, esp 11–13; S Smith, *Contract Theory* (OUP 2004) chs 4 and 11.
[92] It is assumed in economic analysis examples that the parties are rational maximisers of value.

to the highest value user. Indeed, according to the Coase theorem,[93] if transaction costs are absent, market forces will ensure that resources go to the person placing the highest value on them, irrespective of the initial assignment of legal rights and remedies. So in the above situation, assuming no transaction costs, D would negotiate from C a release from the specific performance so as to transfer the part to X, if X places a higher value on it than £15,000. Of course, in order to succeed in gaining a release, D will have to offer C more than the latter's expectation damages: as such, it is the distribution of wealth, but not overall efficiency, that is affected by ordering specific performance in the absence of transaction costs.

Ultimately, therefore, the efficient breach theory has to take account of the fact that in the real world there are transaction costs; and it becomes the theory either that the transaction costs of D gaining release from C are often so high as to prevent that release, so that the efficient transfer to X does not result, or that, even if the transaction costs are not so high as to prevent release, nevertheless the efficient transfer to X is more costly under specific performance than damages because of the transaction costs required.[94]

The defect of the former is that, since the parties are already known to each other, the transaction costs are unlikely to be so high as to prevent a release bargain. The latter is also flawed in that it pays insufficient attention to the costs associated with damages. Even though damages allow D to break the contract with C without bargaining for a release, D still has to pay and deciding on the amount will in itself involve transaction costs, or the costs of a judicial assessment of damages, with its attendant risk of inaccurate assessment. Such costs may be greater than the transaction costs associated with specific performance. So for this form of the efficient breach theory to have force empirical data would be needed to prove that the transaction costs of specific performance outweigh the transaction (and other) costs of damages.[95]

Finally, brief mention must be made of Professor Kronman's 'intention justification' theory,[96] that the present restrictive approach to specific performance is economically efficient because rational parties stipulating remedies in their contracts would agree to specific performance only where the subject matter was unique. As the law is in accord with this, initial transaction costs are thereby minimised. But there seems no necessary reason why it cannot be equally plausibly argued that rational parties would stipulate specific performance in a far wider range of cases, particularly where irrespective of uniqueness, damages are difficult to assess.[97] In short, it seems that Kronman's argument could be used for and against the present primacy of damages.

In conclusion, it is submitted that damages should remain the primary remedy: especially convincing is the duty to mitigate objection to specific performance. This conclusion is strengthened by the modern improvements in damages awards from a claimant's point of view, brought about, for example, by the modification of the time for assessment and the expansion of compensation for non-pecuniary loss, such as mental distress. Having said that, there is still room for the courts to show a more realistic awareness of when damages will not put the claimant into as good a position as if the contract had been performed. As such, the decision in *Sky Petroleum*[98] must be supported. Moreover, difficulty in assessing

---

[93] Above, pp 16–17.
[94] R Posner, *Economic Analysis of Law* (9th edn, Wolters Kluwer 2014) 145–146; H Beale, *Remedies for Breach of Contract* (Sweet & Maxwell 1980) 14.
[95] I Macneil, 'Efficient Breach of Contract: Circles in the Sky' (1982) 68 Va LR 947.
[96] A Kronman, 'Specific Performance' (1978) 45 U of Chi LR 351, 365–369.
[97] Kronman's theory is criticised by A Schwartz, 'The Case for Specific Performance' (1979) 89 Yale LJ 271, 278–284.
[98] [1974] 1 WLR 576.

damages should in itself be regarded as rendering damages inadequate, thereby opening the door to wider specific performance, particularly of long-term supply obligations and of obligations in which the claimant has a subjective consumer interest.

(2) The constant supervision objection

Traditionally, specific performance has not been ordered where this would require what is termed constant supervision. This is not an easily understood notion, but what it appears to mean is that, irrespective of the uncertainty bar,[99] specific performance will be denied where too much judicial time and effort would be spent in seeking compliance with the order. In the words of Lord Hoffmann in *Co-operative Insurance Society Ltd v Argyll Stores (Holdings) Ltd*:[100]

> '[S]upervision would in practice take the form of rulings by the court, on applications made by the parties, as to whether there had been a breach of the order. It is the possibility of the court having to give an indefinite series of such rulings in order to ensure the execution of the order which has been regarded as undesirable.'

Such an objection clearly does not arise where there is an easy method of enforcement without the defendant's co-operation, for example by nominating a person to effect a conveyance of land. It is rather where continuous acts are required of the defendant that the objection bites. In contrast, a lump sum of damages always requires merely a single act and, as Sharpe succinctly puts it, 'enforcement is left to the administrative rather than the judicial machinery of the court.'[101]

The long-standing classic authority is *Ryan v Mutual Tontine Westminster Chambers Association*.[102] Here the lease of a service flat to the claimant lessee included an obligation on the part of the defendant lessor to provide a resident porter who would be 'constantly in attendance'. The lessor in fact appointed as resident porter someone who absented himself every weekday for several hours. The claimant brought an action claiming specific performance of that obligation. The Court of Appeal held that specific performance should be denied because this would involve constant supervision by the courts. Lord Esher MR said:

> 'The contract is that these services shall be performed during the whole term of the tenancy: it is therefore a long-continuing contract to be performed from day to day and under which the circumstances of non-performance might vary from day to day. I apprehend, therefore, that the execution of it would require that constant superintendence by the court, which the court in such cases has always declined to give.'[103]

In Lopes LJ's words:

> '... it is clear that it is such a contract, that, in order to give effect to it by an order for specific performance, the court would have to watch over and supervise its execution. But it is a recognised rule that the court cannot enforce a contract by compelling specific performance where the execution of the contract requires such watching over and supervision by the court.'[104]

---

[99] For a clear recognition of the difference between these bars, see *Greenhill v Isle of Wight Rly Co* (1871) 23 LT 885.
[100] [1998] AC 1, at 12.
[101] R Sharpe, *Injunctions and Specific Performance* (5th edn, Thomson Reuters 2017) para 7.480.
[102] [1893] 1 Ch 116.   [103] ibid, at 123.   [104] ibid, at 125.

Kay LJ also considered that the court could not here order specific performance because the case fell within the general rule that '… the court will not enforce specific performance of works, such as building works, the prosecution of which the court cannot superintend'.[105]

In addition to *Ryan*, there have been numerous cases in which the constant supervision objection to specific performance has been applied.[106] However, this has not always been so. An important example is *Wolverhampton Corpn v Emmons*,[107] where the Court of Appeal laid down that specific performance could be ordered of contracts to build, provided the order was certain, damages were inadequate, and, in accordance with the contract, the defendant had already gained the land on which the work was to be done—that is, the bargain was for the claimant to transfer land to the defendant in return for the defendant building something wanted by the claimant, such as a road across the land. Traditionally this approach has been explained away by saying that it is a valid exception to the otherwise clearly established rule. But it is hard to see on what rational ground this 'exception' is based. After all, the first two conditions must always be satisfied if specific performance is to be ordered; and the fact that the defendant has already received its part of the bargain, while of relevance to mutuality, in no sense counters the constant supervision objection. Not surprisingly the third requirement has since been modified so that it is now sufficient that the defendant has possession of the land, thereby rendering it possible to carry out the work.[108] But again the possibility of complying with the order is a normal requirement of specific performance. Hence a better explanation of the *Emmons* approach than that traditionally offered is that at root it rests on the view that there is no validity in the constant supervision objection. Certainly this is supported by dicta of Collins LJ and Sir Archibald Smith MR in *Emmons*, the latter, for example, saying quite bluntly that he had never been able to see the force of that objection.

Whatever one's explanation of the *Emmons* approach, it has been the *general* rule that the courts have refused to order specific performance where this involves constant supervision.

More recently, however, the validity of the constant supervision objection has been directly attacked in several cases.[109] In *Giles & Co Ltd v Morris*,[110] although the actual decision did not turn on the supervision bar, Megarry V-C thought that the refusal of specific performance of contracts for personal service or involving the continuous performance of

---

[105] ibid, at 128.
[106] *Pollard v Clayton* (1855) 1 K & J 462; *Blackett v Bates* (1865) 1 Ch App 117; *Phipps v Jackson* (1887) 56 LJ Ch 550; *Dominion Coal Co Ltd v Dominion Iron & Steel Co Ltd* [1909] AC 293; *Dowty Boulton Paul Ltd v Wolverhampton Corpn* [1971] 1 WLR 204. And see, most importantly, *Co-operative Insurance Society Ltd v Argyll Stores (Holdings) Ltd* [1998] AC 1, discussed below, pp 418–419. See also *Gravesham Borough Council v British Railways Board* [1978] Ch 379, below, pp 540–541 (mandatory injunction).
[107] [1901] 1 KB 515. Prior cases applying the same approach include: *Storer v Great Western Rly Co* (1842) 2 Y & C Ch Cas 48; *Wilson v Furness Rly Co* (1869) LR 9 Eq 28; *Greene v West Cheshire Rly Co* (1871) LR 13 Eq 44; *Wolverhampton & Walsall Rly Co v London and North Western Rly Co* (1873) LR 16 Eq 433; *Fortescue v Lostwithiel and Fowey Rly Co* [1894] 3 Ch 621. *Emmons* has been followed, with the modification discussed below in the text, in *Carpenters Estates Ltd v Davies* [1940] Ch 160 and most importantly in *Jeune v Queen's Cross Properties Ltd* [1974] Ch 97 applying the principles to a landlord's repair covenant, since confirmed and extended, as regards dwellings, in the Landlord and Tenant Act 1985, s 17.
[108] *Carpenters Estates Ltd v Davies* [1940] Ch 160.
[109] In addition to the cases discussed below one can argue that two important cases on the adequacy of damages bar, *Beswick v Beswick* [1968] AC 58 and *Sky Petroleum Ltd v VIP Petroleum Ltd* [1974] 1 WLR 576, support the view that the constant supervision objection is invalid. This is because the obligations in question were specifically enforced though they involved continuous acts. Admittedly, however, there was no discussion of this objection (unless Lord Pearce had this in mind in his comments at [1968] AC 58, at 90). See also *Luganda v Service Hotels Ltd* [1969] 2 Ch 209 where *Ryan* was distinguished. Note also that specific performance ordering repair (or replacement) of non-conforming goods appears to be the primary remedy for a consumer (who wants it) under Part 1 of the Consumer Rights Act 2015: see above, p 412.
[110] [1972] 1 WLR 307.

services could not '... be based on any narrow consideration such as difficulties of constant superintendence by the courts'.[111] In *Tito v Waddell (No 2)*[112] his criticisms were expressed even more firmly. One of the many issues raised was whether specific performance should be ordered of a contractual obligation to replant land that had been mined. While Megarry V-C ultimately refused specific performance he thought that it was no longer a valid objection that the order involved constant supervision by the court. He said:

> 'In cases of this kind, it was at one time said that an order for the specific performance of the contract would not be made if there would be difficulty in the court supervising its execution: see, for example, *Ryan v Mutual Tontine Westminster Chambers Association*. Sir Archibald Smith MR subsequently found himself unable to see the force of this objection (see *Wolverhampton Corpn v Emmons*): and after it had been discussed and questioned in *Giles v Morris*, the House of Lords disposed of it (I hope finally) in *Shiloh Spinners Ltd v Harding*.[113] The real question is whether there is a sufficient definition of what has to be done in order to comply with the order of the court.'[114]

Megarry V-C also stressed that the courts were particularly willing to overcome such an objection where, as on the facts, the defendants had some or all of the benefit to which they were entitled under the contract; but as has been commented in relation to the *Emmons* case, it is hard to see the relevance of this in undermining the constant supervision objection. Importantly, however, Megarry V-C's reliance on *Shiloh Spinners* seems unjustified:[115] for in that case, Lord Wilberforce appeared to accept the traditional constant supervision objection to specific performance of a contract to do work and was rather stressing that the objection was irrelevant to the requested relief against forfeiture for breach of such a covenant, since all the court had to do was to satisfy itself *ex post facto* that the covenanted work had been done.

Further support for the removal of this bar is provided by *Regent International Hotels (UK) Ltd v Pageguide Ltd*[116] where the Court of Appeal granted an interim injunction, amounting to temporary specific performance, preventing the defendant company from terminating or hindering the claimants in carrying out their management of the defendant's hotel. In so doing, the constant supervision objection was apparently rejected, reliance being placed on Megarry V-C's comments in *Giles v Morris* and *Tito v Waddell (No 2)*.

Megarry V-C's comments were also cited with approval by Mervyn Davies J in *Posner v Scott-Lewis*.[117] The facts were almost identical to those in *Ryan*. The defendant landlord had broken his covenant to have a resident porter at a block of flats for the purposes of removing rubbish, opening the main door, and controlling the central heating etc. The claimant, a tenant of one of the flats, sued for and was granted specific performance ordering the defendant to employ a resident porter for those purposes. Although the actual decision did not contradict the constant supervision objection—since the defendant was not as such ordered to perform, or to ensure performance of, continuous acts but was merely ordered to employ the porter—the judge did indicate his support for the removal of that bar.

Finally, in *Rainbow Estates Ltd v Tokenhold Ltd*[118] Lawrence Collins QC, in holding that, exceptionally, a tenant's (as well as a landlord's) repairing obligation can be specifically enforced, said the following: '[T]he problems of defining the work and the need for

---

[111] ibid, at 318. [112] [1977] Ch 106. [113] [1973] AC 691.
[114] [1977] Ch 106, at 321–323.
[115] This point is supported by Lord Hoffmann in *Co-operative Insurance Society Ltd v Argyll Stores (Holdings) Ltd* [1998] AC 1, at 14.
[116] *The Times*, 13 May 1985. [117] [1987] Ch 25. [118] [1999] Ch 64.

supervision can be overcome by ensuring that there is sufficient definition of what has to be done in order to comply with the order of the court.'[119]

Lest it be thought, however, that this clutch of more recent cases means that the constant supervision objection will no longer be applied, we must now turn to consider the leading modern case. In *Co-operative Insurance Society Ltd v Argyll Stores (Holdings) Ltd*[120] the House of Lords reaffirmed the constant supervision objection in refusing to order specific performance of a covenant in a lease. The defendants were the lessees of the largest shopping unit in the claimants' shopping centre. Sixteen years of the 35-year lease had expired when the defendants closed their supermarket. The claimants, concerned that the closure would have an adverse effect on the rest of the shopping centre, sought specific performance of the defendants' covenant to keep the premises open for retail trade during usual hours of business. This order was refused.

Lord Hoffmann, giving the leading speech, said that there had been some misunderstanding about what is meant by continued superintendence. 'It is the possibility of the court having to give an indefinite series of rulings in order to ensure the execution of the order which has been regarded as undesirable.'[121] He added that it was oppressive (and, moreover, put the claimant in an undesirably strong position) to have to run a business under the threat of proceedings for contempt. His Lordship drew a distinction between orders to carry on activities and orders to achieve results (building contracts, for example, were regarded as falling within the latter category), arguing that the possibility of repeated applications for rulings on compliance with the order which arises in the former type of case does not exist to anything like the same extent in relation to the latter type of case. His Lordship further thought that, in the case at hand, the order could not be drawn up with sufficient precision to avoid arguments over whether it was being complied with.

With respect, Lord Hoffmann's reasoning is unconvincing. In particular, it is hard to see why the order could not be drawn up with sufficient precision; and nor is it clear why the constant supervision objection should be thought valid in respect of orders to carry on activities but not orders to achieve results. This is not to say that the decision in this case was wrong. To force a defendant to carry on with a business that is losing money may well fall foul of the severe hardship bar or a separate specific bar.[122] But this should have been addressed separately rather than being confused with the constant supervision objection.

In terms of policy, it is submitted that the constant supervision objection has little to commend it. In all but a few cases, the fact that the court has ordered specific performance will be sufficient to ensure compliance. In other words in almost all cases defendants do obey these court orders. It is hardly sensible to deny the claimant the remedy because of problems which arise only occasionally. Even in a case of non-compliance or alleged non-compliance, there is no need for full judicial machinery to be invoked: for example, a person could be appointed as an officer of the court to ensure enforcement or to investigate the allegations.[123] And even if judicial time and effort are involved, it is still strongly arguable that this is outweighed by the fact that justice otherwise requires the claimant to

---

[119] ibid, at 73.
[120] [1998] AC 1. See D Pearce, 'Remedies for a Keep-Open Covenant' (2008) 24 JCL 199.
[121] [1998] AC 1, at 12.
[122] Analogous mandatory injunction cases indicate that a separate bar, albeit not absolute, is where the order would require the defendant to carry on a business, requiring the continuous employment of people, especially where the business is a losing concern: *Attorney-General v Colchester Corpn* [1955] 2 QB 207; *Gravesham BC v British Railways Board* [1978] Ch 379. See below, p 465.
[123] E Peel, *Treitel on The Law of Contract* (14th edn, Sweet & Maxwell 2014) para 21-040; A Schwartz, 'The Case for Specific Performance' (1979) 89 Yale LJ 271, 293–294. The court could also use the power in RSC Ord 45, r 8 (see CPR Sch 1) to direct another to do the work at the defendant's expense.

be granted specific performance. In other words, it should be clearly understood that the constant supervision objection rests on denying a remedy to the claimant not because as between the parties it is less appropriate than damages but because the costs to society are regarded as too great. Clearly the resources to be devoted to achieving justice between the parties must have some limit, but it may be doubted whether that limit is even approached by the few problematical specific performance cases involving further judicial time and effort. This is particularly so when one bears in mind that specific performance may also save judicial time and effort, namely that involved in the often-complex task of assessing damages. Certainly it is unsatisfactory to deny justice on an unsubstantiated hunch about the costs of specific performance[124] and, in any event, it has to be explained why this area should be treated differently from, for example, family law, where the cost of continuing judicial involvement in supervising maintenance, access, and custody orders is considered acceptable. In short, the policy justifications for the constant supervision objection to specific performance seem particularly weak and the attempts by some judges, but, alas, not the House of Lords, to remove this bar should therefore be supported.

(3) Contracts for personal service[125]

It is traditionally a well-established rule that the courts will not order specific performance of such a contract, of which the prime example is the contract of employment.[126] Assuming that damages are inadequate (and this assumption cannot be made too readily, particularly since many contracts for personal service are terminable at short notice) and that the constant supervision objection is at best very weak, what are the reasons for this rule?[127]

One general reason often given is that such a contract creates a relationship of mutual confidence and respect and that where that has broken down, it cannot be satisfactorily rebuilt by a court order: on the contrary, to force the relationship to continue is only likely to lead to friction between the parties, or at least between the employee and the employer's representative. Another reason suggested by Megarry J in *Giles & Co Ltd v Morris*[128] is that where services are of an artistic kind, like opera-singing, it would not be possible to judge whether an order of specific performance against the employee was being properly complied with:

'... if ... the singer sang flat, or sharp, or too fast, or too slowly, or too loudly, or too quietly, or resorted to a dozen of the manifestations of temperament traditionally associated with some singers ... who could say whether the imperfections of performance were natural or self-induced?'[129]

---

[124] A Kronman, 'Specific Performance' (1978) 45 U of the Chi LR 351, 373–374; A Schwartz, 'The Case for Specific Performance' (1979) 89 Yale LJ 271, 292–294.

[125] This is shorthand for contract of service or contract for personal services.

[126] Specific performance was refused against an employee in *Clark v Price* (1819) 2 Wils Ch 157; *De Francesco v Barnum* (1890) 45 Ch D 430; *Ehrman v Bartholomew* [1898] 1 Ch 671 (injunction amounting to specific performance). And against an employer in *Johnson v Shrewsbury and Birmingham Rly Co* (1853) 3 De GM & G 914; *Brett v East India and London Shipping Co Ltd* (1864) 2 Hem & M 404; *Rigby v Connol* (1880) 14 Ch D 482; *Page One Records Ltd v Britton* [1968] 1 WLR 157 (injunction amounting to specific performance).

[127] It is sometimes said that repudiatory breach automatically terminates an employment contract and that this is a reason for no specific performance. But rightly this 'automatic' theory was firmly rejected in *Thomas Marshall Ltd v Guinle* [1979] Ch 227 (per Megarry V-C) because, for example, injunctions enforcing negative obligations are still available. See also *Gunton v Richmond-upon-Thames London Borough Council* [1981] Ch 448 (per Buckley LJ); *Dietman v Brent London Borough Council* [1987] ICR 737 (affirmed [1988] ICR 842); *Marsh v National Autistic Society* [1993] ICR 453. Indeed apparent automatic termination is a consequence of rather than a reason for there being no specific performance. Cf *Boyo v Lambeth London Borough Council* [1995] IRLR 50.

[128] [1972] 1 WLR 307. [129] ibid, at 318.

But whether such reasons are in play or not, more fundamental objections to specific performance may be suggested. From the employee's point of view specific performance would result in involuntary servitude. Thus in *De Francesco v Barnum*[130] Fry LJ said that the courts were afraid of turning 'contracts of service into contracts of slavery'.[131] From the employer's side the analogous rationale, seemingly implicitly accepted by the courts, is that as the employer has to organise and pay for the work the employer should have the prerogative to decide who remains employed in its employment.

As regards an employee being ordered to carry out a contract of service, the bar still applies in full force, being enshrined in the Trade Union and Labour Relations (Consolidation) Act 1992, s 236, which provides that:

'No court shall, whether by way of – a) an order for specific performance ... of a contract of employment, or b) an injunction ... restraining a breach or threatened breach of such a contract, compel an employee to do any work or attend at any place for the doing of any work.'

However, on the other side of the relationship, there have been some interesting modern developments.[132] For a full appreciation of these, private law, public (ie administrative) law, and the unfair dismissal legislation must all be examined.

(a) Private law

In *Hill v CA Parsons & Co Ltd*[133] the Court of Appeal confirmed the granting of an interim injunction which amounted to temporary specific performance of a contractual obligation to employ the claimant. The defendant employers had made a closed shop agreement with a trade union and gave the claimant one month to join that union. When he failed to do so, he was given one month's notice of termination of employment. The claimant sought an interim injunction restraining the defendants from implementing their notice of termination. The court held that the defendants were in breach of contract by giving only one month's notice, but the crucial point is that the majority held, Stamp LJ dissenting, that the interim injunction should be granted, even though this amounted to temporary specific performance of a contract for personal service. Both Lord Denning and Sachs LJ stressed that the rule barring specific performance against an employer in a contract for personal service was not absolute. Lord Denning said:

'The rule is not inflexible. It permits of exceptions. The court can in a proper case grant a declaration that the relationship still subsists and an injunction to stop the master treating it as at an end ... It may be said that ... the court is indirectly enforcing specifically a contract for personal services. So be it.'[134]

The majority thought that an exception to the general rule was justified because damages were inadequate and by granting the injunction the claimant would remain an employee until the coming into effect of the Industrial Relations Act 1971 by which he would be protected if dismissed for not joining the union. Sachs LJ also stressed that there was no

---

[130] (1890) 45 Ch D 430.   [131] ibid, at 438.
[132] See, generally, H Carty, 'Dismissed Employees: the Search for a More Effective Range of Remedies' (1989) 52 MLR 449; K Ewing, 'Remedies for Breach of the Contract of Employment' [1993] CLJ 405; M Freedland, *The Personal Employment Contract* (OUP 2003) 369–376.
[133] [1972] Ch 305. See also the comments of Megarry J in *Giles v Morris* [1972] 1 WLR 307, cited with approval in dicta of Goff LJ in *Price v Strange* [1978] Ch 337, at 359–360. The actual decision in *Giles* was that the traditional rule is no bar to ordering the employer to make, rather than to perform, a contract for personal service.
[134] [1972] Ch 305, at 314–315.

breakdown in mutual confidence between employer and employee. On the other hand, Stamp LJ in his dissent thought that there was no justification for departing from the rule that specific performance should not be granted in a contract for personal service.

Hill v Parsons can be and, in some cases,[135] was viewed as a 'freak' case, showing merely that there may be a very rare exception to the usual rule; after all, unfair dismissal legislation has been in force for decades, and so there is now no question of continuing employment to catch those provisions. Having said that, there are indications that the majority regarded the case as one of numerous exceptions. Lord Denning spoke of the rule as applying only in the '... ordinary course of things'[136] and Sachs LJ thought that, as there had been a recent marked trend towards '... shielding the employee', courts must be prepared to modify the traditional rule so as to conform '... to the realities of the day'.[137]

That less restrictive interpretation of *Hill v Parsons* has subsequently prevailed. For example, in *Irani v Southampton and South West Hampshire Health Authority*,[138] the claimant was an ophthalmologist employed on a part-time basis by the defendants at an eye clinic. Following disagreements between the claimant and the consultant in charge of the clinic, the defendants gave the claimant six weeks' notice of dismissal. As the defendants had failed to go through the disputes procedure laid down in the claimant's contract of employment, the dismissal was in breach of contract. The claimant sought an interim injunction restraining implementation of the dismissal notice until that disputes procedure had been complied with. This amounted to a claim for temporary specific performance of his contract of employment and, as Warner J described, the defendants had contended that:

> '... there was a clear rule that the court would not grant specific performance of a contract of employment, or in general, grant an injunction to restrain breach of it and that there were no special circumstances which would justify my granting an injunction, the effect of which would compel the defendant authority to continue to employ Mr Irani ...'[139]

Warner J disagreed, applied *Hill v Parsons*, and granted the interim injunction sought. Damages would plainly be inadequate at the pre-trial stage because the six weeks' notice of dismissal would probably have elapsed by trial; in any event, dismissal would make it difficult for the claimant to get another job in the Health Service. Warner J was particularly liberal in his application of the two other justifying reasons given in *Hill v Parsons*. He thought that there was still complete confidence between employer and employee in the sense that the defendants had perfect faith in the claimant's honesty, integrity, and loyalty, and merely considered him an incompatible colleague of the consultant at the clinic; and the fact that the claimant was seeking protection under the disputes procedure was regarded as analogous to the protection sought by Mr Hill under the then imminent Industrial Relations Act 1971.

It should be noted, however, that the temporary specific performance granted did not extend to ordering the defendants to allow the claimant to attend work (let alone to provide work for him) albeit that this was arguably one of the defendants' contractual obligations.[140]

---

[135] Eg *GKN (Cwmbran) Ltd v Lloyd* [1972] ICR 214; *Sanders v Ernst A Neale Ltd* [1974] ICR 565.
[136] [1972] Ch 305, at 314.   [137] ibid, at 321.
[138] [1985] ICR 590. See also *Jones v Lee and Guilding* [1980] ICR 310 (injunction amounting to temporary specific performance preventing school managers dismissing a teacher in breach of procedures established in his contract) and *Regent International Hotels (UK) Ltd v Pageguide Ltd The Times*, 13 May 1985 (injunction granted amounting to temporary specific performance of a hotel management agreement: but it was doubted that this was analogous to a contract for personal service).
[139] [1985] ICR 590, at 597.
[140] M Freedland, *The Personal Employment Contract* (OUP 2003) 129–140.

Indeed the claimant undertook as a condition of specific performance that he would not present himself for work at any of the defendants' establishments. As such the primary obligations enforced were those of paying the claimant his full salary and retaining him on the books as an employee. It would seem that specific performance was similarly limited in *Hill v Parsons & Co Ltd*.[141]

The most important case subsequent to *Hill v Parsons* has been *Powell v Brent London BC*.[142] The claimant was appointed principal benefits officer for the defendant local authority. A few days after starting work, she was told that her appointment was invalid because there might have been a breach of the defendant's equal opportunity code of practice in appointing her. She sought an interim injunction requiring the defendant to treat her as if she was properly employed as principal benefits officer and, even though that would amount to temporary specific performance, the Court of Appeal granted it. Ralph Gibson LJ, giving the leading judgment, relied on *Hill v Parsons* and especially Sachs LJ's judgment, to justify a departure from the general bar to specific performance. In an important statement of principle, he said:

'Having regard to the decision in *Hill v Parsons* and the long-standing general rule of practice to which *Hill v Parsons* was an exception, the court will not by injunction require an employer to let a servant continue in his employment, when the employer has sought to terminate that employment and prevent the servant carrying out his work under the contract, unless it is clear on the evidence not only that it is otherwise just to make such a requirement but also that there exists sufficient confidence on the part of the employer in the servant's ability and other necessary attributes for it to be reasonable to make the order. Sufficiency of confidence must be judged by reference to the circumstances of the case, including the nature of the work, the people with whom the work must be done and the likely effect upon the employer and the employee's operations if the employer is required by injunction to suffer the plaintiff to continue in the work.'[143]

On the facts there was held to be sufficient mutual confidence between the parties in that the claimant had been doing the job satisfactorily, and without complaint, for over four months before the hearing.

Powell has been followed—and interim injunctions, amounting to temporary specific performance, ordered—in *Hughes v London Borough of Southwark*[144] and *Wadcock v London Borough of Brent*.[145] Both concerned attempts by local authorities to reorganise the duties of social workers and, in both, an injunction was granted primarily because there was no breakdown of mutual confidence. The employees were clearly competent at their jobs.

More radical still was the decision in *Robb v Hammersmith and Fulham London Borough Council*[146] in which a director of finance was dismissed without his employers going through the disciplinary procedures required under his contract. As in *Irani*, an injunction was granted requiring the defendants to continue to employ and pay the claimant unless and until the procedure had been properly complied with (the claimant undertaking not to attend for work unless instructed to do so). Morland J accepted that the claimant had lost the trust and confidence of the defendants but regarded the important point as being that the order proposed was perfectly workable. To refuse the injunction would be to allow the defendants to snap their fingers at the rights of the claimant.

Lest it be thought that, in the light of such cases, specific performance is now the rule rather than the exception, it is helpful to refer to *Alexander v Standard Telephones and Cables*

---

[141] [1972] Ch 305, at 314 (per Lord Denning). [142] [1988] ICR 176. [143] ibid, at 194.
[144] [1988] IRLR 55. [145] [1990] IRLR 223.
[146] [1991] ICR 514. See also *Jones v Gwent County Council* [1992] IRLR 521.

plc[147] in which *Powell* and *Irani* were distinguished. The defendants had made the claimants redundant preferring to keep more skilled employees than applying a 'last in, first out' selection. Even if that action by the defendants had constituted a breach of contract, Aldous J held that there was no real prospect of an injunction being granted at trial because, in the context of the rationalisation of the workforce, the employers did not have sufficient confidence in those employees made redundant.

Finally, in the interesting case of *Ashworth v Royal National Theatre*[148] it was held that there was no 'sufficiency of confidence' so that specific performance should be refused. Specific performance had been sought requiring the National Theatre to continue employing musicians in the performance of the play *War Horse*. But this was denied because 'loss of confidence is fact-specific'[149] and there was 'clearly an absence of personal confidence on the part of the National Theatre which considered that the musicians could not contribute positively to the play'.[150] Cranston J also stated[151] that such an order would have interfered with the National Theatre's right of artistic freedom under Article 10 of the European Convention on Human Rights[152] to which the court must have particular regard.

(b) Public law

A further battle-ground on which the bar has been attacked concerns the use of the 'public law' principle whereby certain types of public employee—commonly labelled 'office-holders'—are protected against wrongful dismissal. Traditionally it has been recognised that such a dismissal, particularly where in breach of natural justice, can be declared invalid and may be restrained by an injunction;[153] that is, an 'office' may be specifically protected by the courts.[154] This has traditionally been reconciled with the rule against specific performance by simply regarding an office-holder as not really being an 'employee' under an ordinary or 'pure' contract of personal service.

Since the late 1950s the courts have applied this 'public law' principle to an increasingly wide range of dismissed 'employees' with the result that the area of pure contracts of personal service has been narrowed.[155] But two cases have developed this even further by intimating that the very distinction between office-holders and employees under ordinary contracts of personal service is no longer helpful.

In *Stevenson v United Road Transport Union*[156] a regional officer of a trade union was dismissed by the union's executive committee. The Court of Appeal confirmed a declaration that the dismissal was void because the committee had acted in breach of natural justice. While the case could presumably have been decided on the traditional principle that the claimant held an office, Buckley LJ giving the decision said, '... it does not much help ... to try to place the plaintiff in the category of a servant on the one hand, or an officer, on the other', and he went on to apply the following test:

---

[147] [1990] ICR 291. See also *Marsh v National Autistic Society* [1993] ICR 453. The traditional rule was also reaffirmed by the House of Lords in *Scandinavian Trading Tanker Co AB v Flota Petrolera Ecuatoriana, The Scaptrade* [1983] 2 AC 694, at 701.
[148] [2014] EWHC 1176 (QB), [2014] 4 All ER 238.   [149] ibid, at [23].   [150] ibid, at [25].
[151] ibid, at [27] and [33].   [152] See s 12 of the Human Rights Act 1998.
[153] On the face of it, an officer could alternatively seek a 'mandatory order', a 'prohibiting order', or a 'quashing order' under CPR Pt 54.
[154] Early cases are *Willis v Childe* (1851) 13 Beav 117; *Fisher v Jackson* [1891] 2 Ch 84.
[155] Eg *Vine v National Dock Labour Board* [1957] AC 488 (a registered dock-worker); *Malloch v Aberdeen Corpn* [1971] 1 WLR 1578 (a Scottish schoolmaster).
[156] [1977] ICR 893.

'Where one party has a discretionary power to terminate the tenure or employment by another of an employment or an office or a post or a privilege, is that power conditional on the party invested with the power being first satisfied on a particular point which involves investigating some matter on which the other party ought in fairness to be heard or to be allowed to give his explanation or put his case? If the answer to the question is Yes, then unless, before the power purports to have been exercised, the condition has been satisfied after the other party has been given a fair opportunity of being heard or of giving his explanation or putting his case, the power will not have been well exercised.'[157]

This test was further applied in *R v BBC, ex p Lavelle*.[158] Here Woolf J held that a tape examiner, employed under what would traditionally have been regarded as an ordinary contract of personal service, had the right to be heard, and could be protected by a declaration and injunction, particularly because the employer was required to go through various disciplinary procedures before dismissal, and this took the case out of the pure master and servant category. As such disciplinary procedures are probably incorporated into the contracts of several millions of workers, this approach is clearly of great importance, although on the facts no remedy was granted since Miss Lavelle had in effect waived her rights with regard to the initial disciplinary meeting.

However, it is important to note that Woolf J did not consider Miss Lavelle's case an appropriate one for judicial review under RSC Ord 53 (now CPR Pt 54) since the BBC was exercising private and not public powers in dismissing her. Therefore the public law notions of an officer and the right to be heard were being relied on, but the procedure for reviewing the exercise of public powers was not.

Of even wider potential significance for the personal service bar was Woolf J's dictum that:

'... the employment protection legislation has substantially changed the position at common law so far as dismissal is concerned. In appropriate circumstances the statute now provides that an industrial tribunal can order the reinstatement of an employee. It is true that the order cannot be specifically enforced. However, the existence of that power does indicate that even the ordinary contract of master and servant now has many of the attributes of an office, and the distinctions which previously existed between pure cases of master and servant and cases where a person holds an office are no longer clear.'[159]

In other words, Woolf J seemed to consider that, irrespective of the contractual incorporation of disciplinary procedures, unfair dismissal legislation has elevated ordinary employees to the status of office-holders, thereby paving the way for their specific protection on traditional principles, But this is clearly a controversial view of the impact of the unfair dismissal legislation, particularly as the legislature there shied away from providing the equivalent of full specific performance.

Perhaps not surprisingly, therefore, this dictum has not been approved since and in the leading case of *R v East Berkshire Health Authority, ex p Walsh*[160] there was an apparent back-tracking from *Stevenson* and *Lavelle*. The question arising was whether a senior nursing officer could apply for judicial review under RSC Ord 53 (now CPR Pt 54) to quash his dismissal as being in breach of natural justice. The Court of Appeal answered this in the negative on the ground that it was only if the public law officer principle applied

---

[157] ibid, at 902. [158] [1983] 1 WLR 23. [159] ibid, at 34.
[160] [1985] QB 152. See also, eg, *R v Home Secretary, ex p Broom* [1986] QB 198; *McClaren v Home Office* [1990] ICR 824 (judicial review unavailable for prison officers); *R v Derbyshire County Council, ex p Noble* [1990] ICR 808 (judicial review unavailable for police surgeon).

to this claimant that he could proceed under Ord 53, and there was no such public law element in his employment, although, like *Lavelle*, there were disciplinary procedures engrafted onto the contract of employment. Without mentioning them, the approach in *Stevenson* and *Lavelle* was impliedly rejected, a narrow view of who is an officer was taken, and the reasoning sought to restore a clear distinction between public officers and private employees.

While on the one hand such a decision prevents the unfair dismissal regime being supplemented, or even by-passed, by judicial review for procedural unfairness,[161] on the other hand a clear distinction between public officers and private employees is difficult to maintain. In any event cases like *Irani* and *Powell* supplement the unfair dismissal regime irrespective of the officer principle.

It is also of interest that while insisting on a consistency between RSC Ord 53 and the officer principle, which *Lavelle* had rejected, *Walsh*, in contrast to *Lavelle*, freed the right to be heard from its public law confinement to officers. As Purchas LJ said in *Walsh*, commenting on the decision at first instance:

> 'The importation by direct reference or by implication into a contract of employment of the rules of natural justice does not of itself import the necessary element of public interest which would convert the case from [the pure master and servant category] into one in which there was an element of public interest created as a result of status of the individual or the protection or support of his position as a public officer. With great respect to the judge, it is this distinction which seems to have escaped him.'[162]

(c) Unfair dismissal legislation

In providing a full picture of the recent challenges to the rule against specific performance of an employer's contractual obligations, it would be a mistake to leave out of account the unfair dismissal legislation, introduced in the Industrial Relations Act 1971 and now embodied in the Employment Rights Act 1996. By the Employment Rights Act 1996, ss 113–117 an employment tribunal can order the reinstatement or reengagement of an employee who has been unfairly dismissed. Indeed these remedies are treated in the legislation as the primary remedies although in practice, and presumably for the same reasons as the traditional rule against specific performance, tribunals usually prefer to award compensation, irrespective of the employee's wishes.[163] But even where made, an order of reinstatement or reengagement is not the same as specific performance for breach of contract: an unfair dismissal is not necessarily a breach of contract, and reinstatement or reengagement does not correspond to full specific performance since non-compliance does not constitute contempt and is instead dealt with by an award of extra compensation to the employee. In other words, the legislature accepted that an employer who is prepared to pay can always get rid of an employee. However, the regime is clearly very similar to specific performance for breach, and indeed the sanction of a monetary penalty is somewhat similar to the French 'astreinte' which is there the way of enforcing specific performance.[164]

---

[161] It is unclear whether an application for judicial review may be refused simply on the ground that proceedings before an industrial tribunal would be more appropriate: *R v Civil Service Appeal Board, ex p Bruce* [1989] ICR 171.
[162] [1985] QB 152, at 180.
[163] P Davies and M Freedland, *Labour Law* (2nd edn, Weidenfeld & Nicolson 1984) 493–497.
[164] B Nicholas, *French Law of Contract* (2nd edn, Clarendon Press 1992) 221–224.

(d) Conclusion

From the above examination, and particularly in the light of *Hill v Parsons*, *Irani*, *Powell*, and *Robb*, it is safe to say that the rule barring specific performance against an employer is less absolute than it once was. But the claim should not be exaggerated. Specific performance will generally still be denied. Moreover, some of the cases carrying the attack on the traditional position have not been concerned to ensure that the employer allows the employee to work or provides work for him,[165] and have primarily been concerned that the correct procedures are complied with before dismissal. In short, the view still holds sway that it is an employer's prerogative to decide ultimately who remains employed in its workforce.

As a matter of policy one might wish to challenge this view, and to support a greater move towards specific performance, which would secure more fully an employee's status.[166] But specific performance can only ever go as far as the contractual terms allow: that is, it can only ensure that dismissal is implemented without a breach of contract. As such, full security of employment can only be brought about by statute. The preference for increased compensation rather than contempt sanctions in the unfair dismissal regime shows that the legislature has as yet been prepared to travel only part way down that road.

(4) Want of mutuality[167]

Fry, in his book on specific performance first published in 1858, stated a rule of mutuality to the effect that a court will not in general order specific performance against the defendant unless from the time the contract was made the defendant could have got specific performance against the claimant had the claimant been in breach. To use Fry's exact words, 'A contract to be specifically enforced by the court must, as a general rule, be mutual, that is to say, such that it might at the time it was entered into have been enforced by either of the parties against the other of them.'[168] Over the years many exceptions to such a rule have been recognised and indeed, on close examination, the rule has not *necessarily* been supported by any authority. This has lent support to Ames's view[169] that Fry's formulation overstated the position and that the true rule is that the defendant will not be ordered to perform unless there is adequate assurance that the claimant will in turn perform. In Ames's words, 'Equity will not compel specific performance by a defendant if after performance the common law remedy of damages will be his sole security for the performance of the plaintiff's side of the contact.'[170] On this approach, in contrast to Fry's, there is no need to view as exceptional the fact, for example, that a vendor who acquires the property to be sold subsequent to the making of the contract can be granted specific performance against the buyer, or that a claimant who has performed personal services in return for a promised transfer of land can compel conveyance. On the other hand, like Fry's rule, Ames's will support the

---

[165] Above, pp 421–423. The exact effect of nullifying the dismissal of an officer is unclear; but in *Chief Constable of North Wales Police v Evans* [1982] 3 All ER 141 mandamus to coerce reinstatement was refused.

[166] G Clark, 'Unfair Dismissal and Reinstatement' (1969) 32 MLR 532; D Cohen, 'The Relationship of Contractual Remedies to Political and Social Status: A Preliminary Inquiry' (1982) 32 U Tor LJ 31; R Brown, 'Contract Remedies in a Planned Economy' in *Studies in Contract Law* (eds B Reiter and A Swan, Butterworths 1980) 94, 100–107.

[167] Sometimes referred to as negative mutuality, this is to be contrasted with affirmative mutuality, which is the unsound notion that specific performance will be granted to the claimant, simply because it could have been granted against him. See R Sharpe, *Injunctions and Specific Performance* (5th edn, Thomson Reuters 2017) paras 7.820–7.880, 10.430–10.570.

[168] E Fry, *Fry on Specific Performance* (6th edn, Stevens & Sons 1921) 219.

[169] J Ames, 'Mutuality in Specific Performance' (1903) 3 Col LR 1.

[170] ibid, 2–3, 12.

refusal of specific performance where the claimant's performance is to be subsequent to the defendant's and will not be specifically enforceable.[171]

The leading case is *Price v Strange*,[172] where the Court of Appeal rejected Fry's rule. The defendant, the head lessee of some flats in a house, orally agreed to grant the claimant a new underlease of his flat in return for the claimant's promise to carry out certain repairs to the house. The claimant did half the repairs but the defendant refused to allow him to complete them, had them done at her own expense, and refused to grant the underlease. The claimant brought an action for specific performance of the promise to grant the underlease and this was granted by the Court of Appeal, subject to the claimant compensating the defendant for the expense she had incurred in having the remaining repair work done. The defendant had argued that, in accordance with Fry's rule, specific performance should not be granted because she could not from the time the contract was made have obtained specific performance against the claimant, since his obligation to repair was not specifically enforceable. But Fry's rule was held to be wrong and as on these facts there could be no risk of the claimant not performing (since the work had already been completed) specific performance was granted. As regards what the correct rule is, however, there appears to be a slight difference between the views of Goff LJ and Buckley LJ: for while the former would seemingly have applied Ames's formulation, the latter tentatively indicated that, even if the defendant could not be assured of actual performance by the claimant, specific performance might still be granted so long as damages would be an adequate remedy to the defendant for any default on the claimant's part. So Buckley LJ's formulation of the true rule was as follows:

'The court will not compel a defendant to perform his obligation specifically if it cannot at the same time ensure that any unperformed obligations of the plaintiff will be perfectly performed, unless, perhaps, damages would be an adequate remedy to the defendant for any default on the plaintiff's part.'[173]

This formulation (with 'perhaps' omitted) is to be preferred to Ames's; the defendant can have no complaints so long as it is assured of a satisfactory remedy against the claimant for any non-performance and it should not be necessary for the defendant to be assured of actual performance; after all, the risk of subsequent non-performance is one that the defendant has contractually undertaken.

Indeed even this watered-down version of mutuality may be too kind to a defendant because, rather than refusing specific performance, the courts could grant it on terms that ensure adequate monetary security to the defendant or otherwise provide an incentive for the claimant to perform. Even more radical, and yet highly persuasive, is the argument that the defendant merits no such concern at all.[174] A fortiori damages will inadequately compensate the claimant, and hence by denying specific performance, the claimant is, as a matter of certainty, being denied a more appropriate remedy. In contrast, mutuality protects

---

[171] As in *Flight v Bolland* (1828) 4 Russ 298 (infant claimant); *Ogden v Fossick* (1862) 4 De GF & J 426 (claimant to employ defendant).

[172] [1978] Ch 337. This was applied in *Rainbow Estates Ltd v Tokenhold Ltd* [1999] Ch 64 where Lawrence Collins QC said, at p 69, '[I]t is now clear that it does not follow from the fact that specific performance is not available to one party that it is not available to the other: want of mutuality is a discretionary, and not an absolute, bar to specific performance.'

[173] [1978] Ch 337, at 367–368.

[174] W Lewis, 'The Present Status of the Defence of Want of Mutuality in Specific Performance' (1903) 51 Univ of Penn LR 591, 625–629; A Schwartz, 'The Case for Specific Performance' (1979) 89 Yale LJ 271, 301–303. E Durfee, 'Mutuality in Specific Performance' (1921) 20 Mich LR 289 takes a mid-position: the defence is justified where the defendant's potential hardship is greater than the claimant's hardship.

the defendant against a mere *risk* of the claimant subsequently not performing, and that is after all a risk which the defendant accepted by entering into that contract.[175]

(5) Uncertainty

The terms must satisfy a test of certainty for there to be a valid contract. But even if this is so, and damages are therefore recoverable for breach, specific performance may still be denied where the terms are too vague to allow a clear order to be made. A good example is provided by *Joseph v National Magazine Co*,[176] where the defendants contracted to publish an article by the claimant on the subject of jade. In breach of contract, they later refused to publish it without major amendments. It was held that, while the claimant was entitled to damages, specific performance should be refused because the terms of publication were too vague to allow a clear order to be made. This is also a reason why many building contracts are not specifically enforceable: for example, damages for breach of contract to build a house of a certain value can be readily assessed, but no specific performance will be ordered without building specifications.[177]

Again, in *Co-operative Insurance Society Ltd v Argyll Stores (Holdings) Ltd*[178] one of the reasons given by the House of Lords for refusing to enforce specifically a business tenant's covenant to keep premises in a shopping centre open for retail trade was that the order could not be drawn up with sufficient precision. In Lord Hoffmann's words:

> 'The fact that the terms of a contractual obligation are sufficiently definite to escape being void for uncertainty, or to found a claim for damages ... does not necessarily mean that they will be sufficiently precise to be capable of being specifically performed ... Precision is of course a question of degree and the courts have shown themselves willing to cope with a certain degree of imprecision in cases of orders requiring the achievement of a result in which the plaintiffs' merits appeared strong; ... it is, taken alone, merely a discretionary matter to be taken into account. It is, however, a very important one.'[179]

And later he concluded, 'I do not think that the obligation [in question] can possibly be regarded as sufficiently precise to be capable of specific performance.'[180] This conclusion is a surprising one on the facts and it was bound up with their Lordships' controversial (and, with respect, incorrect) application in this case of the constant supervision objection to specific performance.

There are several reasons for this uncertainty restriction. Most obviously it is only fair to the defendant that it should know precisely what it has to do to comply with the order and avoid being held in contempt. As Lord Hoffmann said in the *Co-operative Insurance* case, 'If the terms of the court's order, reflecting the terms of the obligation, cannot be precisely drawn ... [there is an increase in] the oppression caused by the defendant having to do things under threat of proceedings for contempt.'[181] The courts too must be able to enforce an order and to judge whether there has been compliance with it. Furthermore,

---

[175] Under the Landlord and Tenant Act 1985, s 17, specific performance can be ordered of a dwelling landlord's repairing covenant 'notwithstanding any equitable rule restricting the scope of the remedy, whether on the basis of a lack of mutuality or otherwise'. The courts also allow waiver of the defence—*Price v Strange* [1978] Ch 337 at 358, applied in *Sutton v Sutton* [1984] Ch 184. Also contrast injunctions where want of mutuality is not a defence (see H Beale, *Remedies for Breach of Contract* (Sweet & Maxwell 1980) 138), although the courts may grant an injunction on terms that the defendant can apply for dissolution if the claimant does not perform, see below, p 460 n 150.
[176] [1959] Ch 14. See also *South Wales Rly Co v Wythes* (1854) 5 De GM & G 880; *Greenhill v Isle of Wight Rly (Newport Junction) Co* (1871) 23 LT 885.
[177] *Brace v Wehnert* (1858) 25 Beav 348.   [178] [1998] AC 1. See above, pp 418–419.
[179] ibid, at 14.   [180] ibid, at 16.   [181] ibid, at 13.

there may be a fear that in complying with an unclear order the defendant will perform in a way that does not match the claimant's expectations. Finally it can be argued that, as in relation to the constant supervision objection, an unclear order is likely to give rise to future disputes, which will take up judicial time and effort. In Lord Hoffmann's words in the *Co-operative Insurance* case, 'If the terms of the court's order, reflecting the terms of the obligation, cannot be precisely drawn, the possibility of wasteful litigation over compliance is increased.'[182] But this problem in itself could be overcome by appointing a court officer to deal with any subsequent dispute if and when it arises and in any case it is not a strong argument where justice otherwise requires the order.

Despite the decision in the *Co-operative Insurance* case, it is reasonable to expect that the increased willingness of courts to imply terms will, in cases of doubt, normally enable them to make clear orders of specific performance and thereby overcome the uncertainty objection. This is supported by *Sudbrook Trading Estate Ltd v Eggleton*[183] where the House of Lords held that if the agreed machinery for valuation breaks down in a contract for the sale of land a court will ascertain the fair and reasonable price, thereby rendering the contract specifically enforceable.

(6) Contracts not supported by valuable consideration

While the common law remedies are granted for breach of a contract made by deed or supported merely by nominal consideration—that is where there is no true bargain but rather a gratuitous promise—specific performance is not.[184] This is essentially what is meant by the maxim 'Equity will not assist a volunteer.'

It is hard to see any rational reason for this distinction between the approach at common law and in equity and it is best regarded as a legacy of history. Moreover, since underlying morality justifies upholding gratuitous promises it is submitted that the common law is here to be preferred and that this bar to specific performance should be removed.

Indeed there is some support for an undermining of this restriction. *Mountford v Scott*[185] concerned an attempt by the defendant to withdraw an option to purchase land granted to the claimant for £1. Brightman J regarded the claimant as seeking specific performance not only of the contract to sell but also of the option contract and granted the remedy even though the consideration supporting the option was nominal. He said, 'It is not the function of equity to protect only those equitable interests which have been created for valuable consideration.'[186] However, it would be dangerous to place too much weight on this as the Court of Appeal,[187] while upholding the decision, adopted a different analysis under which the question of specific enforcement of the option did not arise; that is, it regarded the grantee of an option as being able to exercise that option, and hence create a valid contract for the sale of the land, without any need for the defendant's co-operation.

---

[182] ibid, at 13.
[183] [1983] 1 AC 444. In *Regent International Hotels (UK) Ltd v Pageguide Ltd*, The Times, 13 May 1985, the Court of Appeal suggested that any certainty problems could be avoided by insisting on arbitration of any bona fide disputes prior to court action.
[184] *Cannon v Hartley* [1949] Ch 213; *Lister v Hodgson* (1867) LR 4 Eq 30. But it would be surprising, applying usual equitable principles, if specific performance were to be refused where the promisee has detrimentally relied on the promise.
[185] [1975] Ch 258, at 263. See also *Gurtner v Circuit* [1968] 2 QB 587, at 596.
[186] [1975] Ch 258, at 262.   [187] ibid.

(7) Contract unfairly obtained

Specific performance may be denied where there has been procedural unfairness, whether misrepresentation, mistake induced by or known to the claimant, undue pressure, or unfair advantage taken of the defendant's weak position. So, for example, in *Walters v Morgan*[188] the defendant contracted to grant the claimant a mining lease over land which he had just bought; but specific performance was refused because the defendant had been hurried into signing the agreement in ignorance of the true value of his property. Similarly, in *Webster v Cecil*[189] the defendant, due to an arithmetical error, offered his property to the claimant for £1,250 instead of £2,250. The claimant accepted this, although since his previous offer of £2,000 had been refused, he must have known of the mistake. His action for specific performance was dismissed. Furthermore, while it appears that inadequacy of consideration is not in itself a ground for refusing specific performance,[190] that is, substantive unfairness is insufficient, this will probably tip the balance against specific performance, where there is any hint of procedural unfairness.[191] Finally it should be stressed that *Tamplin v James*[192] lays down the 'modem' approach that unilateral mistake, neither known to nor induced by the claimant, is not a defence to specific performance.

However, these days it may be doubted whether a defendant needs to rely on unfairness in obtaining the contract as a defence to specific performance; for, given the expansion of doctrines, such as duress, undue influence, misrepresentation, and, though more arguably, unilateral mistake and exploitation of weakness, the defendant will generally be able to escape from all contractual liability where there is a defence to specific performance because of procedural unfairness. For example, on the facts of *Walters v Morgan*, it may be that the defendant could now escape from the contract, and avoid all remedies for breach, by invoking unilateral mistake or exploitation of weakness. One can argue that such assimilation is to be supported, on the ground that it is only separate historical development that has led to procedural unfairness that is sufficient to deny specific performance being insufficient to rule out damages.[193] But perhaps some distinction can be rationally defended on the basis that the reasons that justify damages retaining their primacy, under the adequacy hurdle, also justify the courts being more willing to accept wider versions of particular defences where specific performance rather than damages is being claimed.

(8) Impossibility

Specific performance will not be ordered where performance is physically impossible, for there is clearly no sense in ordering the defendant to do something on pain of contempt, which he or she simply cannot do. So, for example, specific performance will not be ordered against a person who has agreed to sell land which that person does not own and cannot compel the owner to convey.[194] Similarly, where the defendant has sold property

---

[188] (1861) 3 De GF & J 718.
[189] (1861) 30 Beav 62. If damages were available at common law (but cf *Hartog v Colin and Shields* [1939] 3 All ER 566), there would be no advantage here in resisting specific performance, ie damages would probably be £1,000.
[190] *Colliery Brown* (1788) 1 Cox Eq Cas 428.
[191] *Griffith v Spratley* (1787) 1 Cox Eq Cas 383, at 389.
[192] (1880) 15 Ch D 215. Contrasting with earlier cases, such as *Malins v Freeman* (1836) 2 Keen 25.
[193] A Schwartz, 'The Case for Specific Performance' (1979) 89 Yale LJ 271, 300–301. Cf E Sherwin, 'Law and Equity in Contract Enforcement' (1991) 50 Maryland LR 253.
[194] *Castle v Wilkinson* (1870) 5 Ch App 534.

to a third party whose title is unaffected by the claimant's prior interest, the claimant will not be granted specific performance.[195] Analogous is *Wroth v Tyler*,[196] where specific performance of a contract to sell a home with vacant possession was refused because it would require the defendant to embark upon uncertain litigation in an attempt to force his wife to leave the house.

Specific performance will also be refused where this would require the defendant to do something the defendant is not lawfully competent to do. In *Warmington v Miller*,[197] for example, the defendant, a lessee of business premises, agreed to grant an underlease to the claimant, even though he was prohibited by his lease from sub-letting. He failed to grant the underlease but specific performance was refused because it would necessitate the defendant breaking the terms of his lease.

Sometimes in these situations, a defendant can escape from the contract and avoid all remedies for breach, by invoking doctrines such as common mistake, frustration, or illegality. But those doctrines are clearly narrower than the impossibility bar to specific performance, so that a claimant may be able to recover damages if denied specific performance.

(9) Severe hardship

Specific performance will be refused where it would cause severe hardship to the defendant.[198] It was on this ground that, in *Denne v Light*,[199] the court refused to order specific performance against the buyer of farming land which was apparently landlocked: that is, there seemed to be no right of way over surrounding land. Similarly, in *Hope v Walter*[200] it was thought unfair to a purchaser to order him to complete the sale of a house that, unknown to both parties, was being used as a brothel by the tenant. Again, in *Wroth v Tyler*[201] specific performance to order the defendant to convey title with non-vacant possession was refused because for the defendant's wife, but not the defendant, to have the right to continue to live in the house could encourage a split-up of the family.

A modern and particularly vivid example is *Patel v Ali*.[202] Here the defendant, a married Pakistani woman who could hardly speak English, had contracted to sell her home to the claimants. In the years after the contract was made, the defendant's husband was sent to prison, she bore two more children and had a leg amputated because of bone cancer. A number of friends and relatives brought her shopping and helped with household chores. However, if she was forced to move it was likely that she would lose this daily assistance. In such circumstances, Goulding J refused to order specific performance and left the claimants to their remedy of damages, even though the defendant's hardship did not exist at the time of the contract and was not in any way caused by the claimants.

On the other hand, specific performance will not be refused simply because the defendant is in financial difficulties[203] or because, on a rising market, the defendant vendor of a house is finding it difficult to acquire alternative accommodation.[204]

Again, it is interesting to see that in many situations of 'severe hardship', the defendant can escape from the contract and avoid all remedies for breach, by invoking doctrines such as common mistake or frustration. But that in this context a clear gap is left for the refusal

---

[195] *Ferguson v Wilson* (1866) 2 Ch App 77.   [196] [1974] Ch 30.   [197] [1973] QB 877.
[198] Or, sometimes, to third parties, eg *Thames Guaranty Ltd v Campbell* [1985] QB 210. See G Jones and W Goodhart, *Specific Performance* (2nd edn, Butterworths 1996) 121–122.
[199] (1857) 8 De GM & G 774. In addition to the cases cited below, see *Gravesham Borough Council v British Railways Board* [1978] Ch 379, at 405.
[200] [1900] 1 Ch 257.   [201] [1974] Ch 30.   [202] [1984] Ch 283.
[203] *Francis v Cowcliffe* (1976) 33 P & CR 368.   [204] *Mountford v Scott* [1975] Ch 258.

of specific performance alone is shown by *Patel v Ali*, and by Goulding J's comment that 'Equitable relief may ... be refused because of an unforeseen change of circumstances not amounting to legal frustration, just as it may on the ground of mistake insufficient to avoid a contract at law.'[205]

(10) The claimant's conduct[206]

(a) Serious breach

Specific performance will be refused if the claimant has committed a serious breach of contract. So, for example, in *Australian Hardwoods Pty Ltd v Railways Commissioner*[207] the Privy Council refused specific performance of a contractual obligation to take steps to ensure the transfer of a sawmill licence because, inter alia, of the claimant's own breach. Similarly, a claimant will not be awarded specific performance if the claimant is in breach of a time stipulation where time is of the essence.[208] But since the fusion of the common law and Chancery courts, the defendant rarely needs to rely on this defence, for a breach that is serious enough to justify refusing specific performance should and it seems does entitle the defendant to terminate the contract, rendering the defendant no longer liable to perform. Put another way, the sort of breach necessary to bar specific performance will never be less serious than a breach justifying discharge of the contract.[209]

(b) One who comes to equity must come with clean hands[210]

By this maxim specific performance will be denied to a claimant whose past conduct, as revealed by the facts of the dispute, has been highly improper. Indeed, one can regard the previous head of serious breach as incorporated within clean hands, although it is more usually treated separately. As such, clean hands plays a loose and residual role. An example is *Lamare v Dixon*,[211] where the owner of some cellars had orally promised the proposed lessee, prior to the signing of the contract for a lease, that he would make the cellars dry. This he had failed to do and as a result the court refused him specific performance. More recently in *Quadrant Visual Communications Ltd v Hutchison Telephone (UK) Ltd*[212] the defendant contracted to buy the claimant's car and portable telephone business. The price to be paid depended on the number of the claimant's customers prior to the completion date. Prior to completion, the claimant increased the number of its customers through two marketing deals that involved supplying free telephones. The claimant informed the defendant of the first but not the second deal. Following breach by the defendant, the Court of Appeal upheld the trial judge's decision not to award the claimant specific performance of the agreement because the claimant had tricked the defendant and had therefore not come to equity with clean hands.

---

[205] [1984] Ch 283 at 288. See, generally, E Sherwin, 'Law and Equity in Contract Enforcement' (1991) 50 Maryland LR 253.
[206] This refers to conduct other than in contract formation. For unfairness in formation see above, p 430.
[207] [1961] 1 WLR 425. In *Dyster v Randall & Sons* [1926] Ch 932, at 942–943, the breach was thought too trivial to be a bar.
[208] *Steedman v Drinkle* [1916] 1 AC 275.
[209] A Farnsworth, *Farnsworth on Contracts* (3rd edn, Aspen 2004) para 12.5.
[210] Generally, see Z Chafee, 'Coming into Equity with Clean Hands' (1948–9) 47 Mich LR 877, 1065.
[211] (1873) LR 6 HL 414. See also *Mason v Clarke* [1954] 1 QB 460, at 472.
[212] [1993] BCLC 442.

(c) One who seeks equity must do equity

This means that there will be no specific performance if the claimant is not willing and able to perform her own obligations from now on (or is otherwise not willing to do what is fair and right for the defendant). So, for example, in *Chappell v Times Newspapers Ltd*[213] employees were refused an injunction amounting to specific performance of a contract of employment because, inter alia, they could not show themselves ready and willing to perform their contracts without disruption as they were not prepared to renounce their union. Clearly this defence normally rests on similar grounds to that of want of mutuality but it differs in that the court is reacting to a clear indication of the claimant's unwillingness to counter-perform.

(d) Laches

By the Limitation Act 1980, s 36(1) the usual six-year limitation period does not apply to an action for specific performance whether directly or by analogy.[214] That the six-year limitation period applicable to damages for breach of contract does not apply by analogy was decided in the important decision of the Court of Appeal in *P & O Nedlloyd BV v Arab Metals Co*.[215] This was held to be because, first, one was a monetary remedy and the other was not; and, secondly, in contrast to common law damages, specific performance does not necessitate that there has been a breach of contract.

But under the equitable doctrine of laches specific performance may be denied for delay by the claimant in seeking it.[216] In general terms,[217] the doctrine of laches applies where the delay by the claimant in seeking an equitable remedy is such that it would be unjust to grant that remedy, especially where the delay has prejudiced the defendant or a third party although it would appear that prejudice is not a necessary element of the doctrine.

Traditionally, the classic authority on laches in the context of specific performance was *Milward v Earl of Thanet*,[218] where Sir Richard Arden MR said that a claimant wanting specific performance had to show himself to be 'ready, desirous, prompt and eager'; and although there were always exceptional situations (for example, delay, of whatever length, did not bar an action merely to transfer the legal estate)[219] delays of more than a few months were generally considered fatal to specific performance, particularly where there was prejudice to the defendant or the subject matter was property of fluctuating value.[220]

However, *Lazard Bros & Co Ltd v Fairfield Properties Co (Mayfair) Ltd*[221] indicates that in modern times the courts are more tolerant of a claimant's delay. There specific performance

---

[213] [1975] 1 WLR 482.
[214] See, generally, J Beatson, 'Limitation Periods and Specific Performance' in *Contemporary Issues in Commercial Law* (eds E Lomnicka and C Morse, Sweet & Maxwell 1997) 9–23. Under the Law Commission's proposals for reform, the standard limitation periods for breach of contract would apply to claims for specific performance, albeit that the doctrine of laches (and acquiescence) would also apply within those periods: see Law Commission, *Limitation of Actions* (2001) Report No 270, paras 4.268–4.278 and Draft Bill, cl 34.
[215] [2006] EWCA Civ 171, [2007] 1 WLR 2288.   [216] Limitation Act 1980, s 36(2).
[217] A classic formulation of the doctrine was given in *Lindsay Petroleum Co v Hurd* (1874) LR 5 PC 221, at 239–240 which was a rescission case.
[218] (1801) 5 Ves 720n.
[219] *Sharp v Milligan* (1856) 22 Beav 606 (18 years); *Williams v Greatrex* [1957] 1 WLR 31 (10 years); *Frawley v Neill*, The Times, 5 April 1999 (16 years). The rationale of this exception is that, applying the maxim 'equity treats as done that which ought to be done', a contract to transfer a legal interest in property is as good as a transfer of that interest when a party has taken possession of the property in reliance on that interest: see Law Commission, *Limitation of Actions* (2001) Report No 270, paras 4.268–4.273 and Draft Bill, cl 34(1).
[220] *Pollard v Clayton* (1855) 1 K & J 462 (11 months); *Huxham v Llewellyn* (1873) 28 LT 577 (five months); *Glasbrook v Richardson* (1874) 23 WR 51 (three and a half months).
[221] (1977) 121 Sol Jo 793.

of a contract for the sale of land was sought over two years after completion was due and was granted. Megarry V-C regarded *Milward v Earl of Thanet* and the idea that specific performance was a prize to be awarded to the zealous and to be denied to the indolent as the wrong approach today; and he went on to say, 'If between the plaintiff and the defendant it was just that the plaintiff should obtain the remedy, the court ought not to withhold it merely because the plaintiff has been guilty of delay.'[222] What exactly this means and hence how far the courts will grant specific performance despite lengthy delays by the claimant is left unclear; but it may be expected that in the absence of additional factors, such as prejudice to the defendant, a long delay—and certainly more than a few months—will be needed to bar specific performance.

(e) Acquiescence

While laches has often not been separated out from acquiescence, the essential difference is that acquiescence, unlike laches, requires a representation by the claimant, usually implied from its conduct, that it is giving up (ie waiving) its rights which the defendant then relies on. Acquiescence is therefore a form of estoppel. Although no case has been found, it has traditionally been assumed (and may be thought to have been accepted in s 36(2) of the Limitation Act 1980) that, as with injunctions, acquiescence is a bar to specific performance:[223] that is, that a claimant will be denied specific performance where it has encouraged the defendant to believe that it has no objection to the defendant doing what amounts to a breach of contract, and the defendant has (detrimentally) relied on that representation.

(f) Valid termination of the contract by the claimant

Where the claimant has validly terminated the contract for the defendant's breach, it can no longer claim specific performance. This was regarded as an 'incontrovertible' principle by Lord Wilberforce in dicta in *Johnson v Agnew*[224] and he later commented, '… it is easy to see that a party who has chosen to put an end to a contract by the other party's repudiation cannot afterwards seek specific performance. This is simply because the contract is dead—what is dead is dead.'[225] An alternative way of expressing this is to say that the claimant's election bars specific performance; but the terminology and supposed doctrine of election of remedy is likely to confuse rather than to clarify the law and, at least here, it is easier to manage without it.

Sharpe has criticised the present law on the ground that it should only be where the defendant has detrimentally relied on the claimant's termination that the claimant should be prevented from going back on it.[226] But such an approach would leave the issue too uncertain, hindering the parties' plans for future action. Under the present law the parties know for sure that once the claimant has made a clear decision to terminate they are each free to ignore the contract.

Finally, it should be stressed that merely claiming damages for breach does not bar specific performance, as specific performance and damages may be mutually consistent. Rather

---

[222] ibid.
[223] J Meagher, M Leeming, and P Turner, *Meagher, Gummow and Lehane's Equity, Doctrines and Remedies* (5th edn, LexisNexis 2015) para 21-170; E Fry, *Fry on Specific Performance* (6th edn, Stevens & Sons 1921) 516.
[224] [1980] AC 367, at 392.   [225] ibid, at 398.
[226] Ie the full requirements of estoppel by election are required, R Sharpe, *Injunctions and Specific Performance* (5th edn, Thomson Reuters 2017) paras 10.820–10.880.

specific performance is barred where the claim for damages shows that the claimant is terminating the contract, that is that the claimant is accepting the defendant's repudiation.[227]

(11) No partial specific performance?

The principle has sometimes been applied that there can be no specific performance of only some of the defendant's obligations under a contract; so if one or more of the obligations is not specifically enforceable, there can be no specific performance of the rest. For example, in *Ryan v Mutual Tontine Westminster Chambers Association*,[228] where the court refused to order specific performance of an obligation to provide a porter who would be constantly in attendance, an alternative claim that the defendants should merely be ordered to appoint a porter was also refused; '... when the court cannot grant a specific performance of the contract as a whole it will not interfere to compel specific performance of part of a contract.'[229]

There seems to be nothing in terms of policy to justify such a bar.[230] Damages (or equitable compensation) can be added to compensate the claimant for the unperformed part, as they are where performance will be late or where land being bought does not correspond to what was promised. In any event, as it is the claimant who is seeking the order, the claimant is clearly prepared to accept the disadvantage of part performance. Nor can the defendant validly complain if ordered to do part only of what the defendant agreed.

Fortunately, it is doubtful whether this principle has ever been generally accepted, since there are numerous decisions that conflict with it. In *Lytton v Great Northern Rly Co*,[231] for example, specific performance was ordered of the defendants' contractual obligation to build a railway siding while being refused of their obligation to keep it in repair; and in *Elmore v Pirrie*[232] the defendants' obligation to purchase patent rights was specifically enforced although there could be no specific performance of their obligation to form a company to work the patents and to pay royalties to the claimants. In Kay J's words:

'Why should not the plaintiffs have damages for that part of the agreement of which the court does not grant specific performance? The court has power to order specific performance of the whole of the agreement, or part of it, with damages for the rest.'[233]

Moreover in the more recent case of *Posner v Scott-Lewis*[234] Mervyn-Davies J ordered specific performance of a landlord's covenant to appoint a resident porter at a block of flats and, although there was no discussion of the 'no partial specific performance' idea, the decision does appear to be a direct contradiction of *Ryan*.

Finally, in *Rainbow Estates Ltd v Tokenhold Ltd*[235] Lawrence Collins QC, in ordering specific performance of a tenant's repairing obligation, said the following:

'[T]he court should not be constrained by the supposed rule that the court will not enforce the defendant's obligation in part ... it is by no means clear that there is such a principle, and in any event if there is such a principle, it applies where the contract is in part unenforceable ... it does

---

[227] See *Meng Leong Development Pte Ltd v Jip Hong Trading Co Pte Ltd* [1985] AC 511.
[228] [1893] 1 Ch 116. See also, eg, *Merchants' Trading Co v Banner* (1871) LR 12 Eq 18.
[229] [1893] 1 Ch 116, at 123 (per Lord Esher MR).
[230] *Ogden v Fossick* (1862) 4 De GF & J 426 may be justified, but if so this is because of want of mutuality and not because of the 'no partial specific performance' principle relied on.
[231] (1856) 2 K & J 394.
[232] (1887) 57 LT 333. See also, eg, *Peacock v Penson* (1848) 11 Beav 355; *Soames v Edge* (1860) John 669; *Wilkinson v Clements* (1872) 8 Ch App 96.
[233] (1887) 57 LT 333, at 336.   [234] [1987] Ch 25.   [235] [1999] Ch 64.

not mean that the court cannot in an appropriate case enforce compliance with a particular obligation such as a repairing covenant.'[236]

(12) Conclusion—the trend towards specific performance

Having completed an examination of the various bars to specific performance it is appropriate to take a brief overview of the present availability of the remedy.

In spite of some of the more radical proposals in some cases not finding favour in others, the general picture is one of a trend in favour of specific performance. Indeed in relation to no less than eight of the bars there have been developments favouring specific performance: adequacy of damages, constant supervision, personal service, want of mutuality, uncertainty, contracts not supported by valuable consideration, laches, and, in so far as it was ever a bar, no partial specific performance. So it appears that a claimant will now find it easier than ever before to obtain specific performance.

The one major case bucking this trend is *Co-operative Insurance Society Ltd v Argyll Stores (Holdings) Ltd*;[237] as has been explained above, while the decision in that case seems correct, their Lordships' support for the constant supervision objection was misplaced.[238]

Our examination of policy has further shown that, with the exception of the wide view of *Beswick v Beswick*, all such developments in favour of specific performance are either justified or at least unobjectionable. The verdict is therefore one of support for this trend.

Finally, it may be asked, why has this trend occurred in recent times? Several answers may be suggested; for example, there is now, arguably, a more flexible approach to precedent; damages are particularly problematical in times of high inflation and when insolvency is common: and the courts are more willing than ever before to intervene in individuals' lives.

3. Other issues

(1) Stipulated remedy

There are two issues here. The first, which no English case has explicitly dealt with, is whether a clause by which the parties indicate that specific performance should be the remedy for breach will be valid so as to ensure the granting of specific performance where it would otherwise not be available. Arguably such a clause, unlike a penalty clause, cannot be knocked down as unfair for it cannot be objectionable to insist, as at the time the contract is made, that the defendant performs as it promises. Rather such a clause, like a liquidated damages clause, has the merit of saving judicial time and expense, here in deciding between damages and specific performance. However, the courts are never keen to allow their jurisdiction to be ousted and, at the end of the day, it is likely that they would take the view that, if there are good grounds for otherwise refusing specific performance, an agreed remedy clause is not sufficient to undermine the validity of those grounds.[239]

The second issue is whether a liquidated damages clause ousts specific performance. It might be argued, for example, that the insertion of such a clause gives the defendant an option to perform or to pay agreed damages; or, more forceful still, that such a clause indicates

---

[236] ibid, at 73. [237] [1998] AC 1. [238] Above, pp 418–419.
[239] This is supported by obiter dicta in *Quadrant Visual Communications Ltd v Hutchison Telephone (UK) Ltd* [1993] BCLC 442, at 451 and 452. But see the views of R Sharpe, *Injunctions and Specific Performance* (5th edn, Thomson Reuters 2017) paras 7.710–7.810; S Rowan, 'For the Recognition of Remedial Terms Agreed Inter Partes' (2010) 126 LQR 448 (reprinted with light amendments in her *Remedies for Breach of Contract* (2012), ch 5). See also I Macneil, 'Power of Contract and Agreed Remedies' (1962) 47 Cornell LQ 495, 520–523.

that monetary remedies are adequate and that specific performance of the primary obligation is unwarranted. But the courts lean against a construction that would oust a judicial remedy and they have consistently taken the view that the money clause is added as security for performance and/or as clarifying the amount of damages the claimant will receive if suing for damages.[240] Specific performance is therefore not ousted.

(2) The flexibility of specific performance—additional damages or compensation and conditional enforcement

(a) Damages in addition to specific performance

The Senior Courts Act 1981, s 49 allows a claim for ordinary common law damages to be combined with an action for specific performance. In the same action, therefore, the claimant may be awarded specific performance and, where what is ordered is not identical with what was promised,[241] damages to overcome the deficiency. For example, since specific performance seldom results in performance at the time fixed by the contract, damages for delay may be awarded along with specific performance.[242]

Equitable damages may also be awarded in addition to specific performance under the Senior Courts Act 1981, s 50, the successor to Lord Cairns's Act.[243] But since *Johnson v Agnew*[244] has assimilated the principles of assessment, additional equitable damages are only more advantageous to a claimant in the situation where they are available and common law damages are not.[245]

(b) Specific performance with compensation or abatement of purchase price[246]

Prior to the Chancery Amendment Act 1858 (Lord Cairns's Act), s 2, the Court of Chancery had at most a very limited power to award damages in addition to specific performance. This was offset to an extent by the practice of awarding to a purchaser of land that is not as promised, the equitable remedy of compensation or abatement of price along with specific performance.[247] Yet purchasers and courts still respectively claim and award this additional remedy[248] despite the power the courts now have to award common law or equitable damages in addition to specific performance. The continuation of this habit is doubly surprising since, rather than offering advantages over damages, compensation seems less advantageous; for in *Rudd v Lascelles*,[249] several restrictions were placed on the power to award compensation in addition to specific performance and in, for example, *Grant v Dawkins*,[250] it was assumed that the amount of compensation, like abatement, could not exceed the

---

[240] *Howard v Hopkyns* (1742) 2 Atk 371; *Magrane v Archbold* (1813) 1 Dow 107; *Long v Bowring* (1864) 33 Beav 585. The same approach is taken with regard to injunctions, see below, p 462.
[241] But no order should be made for performance of something entirely different from what was promised: see analogously *Cedar Holdings Ltd v Green* [1981] Ch 129, esp at 141–143.
[242] *Jaques v Millar* (1877) 6 Ch D 153. See also *Seven Seas Properties Ltd v Al-Essa* [1988] 1 WLR 1272 (specific performance granted against a vendor of land along with an order for the holding back, and retention by the parties' solicitors, of so much of the purchase price as would cover the purchaser's damages claim against the vendor for loss of a sub-sale of the land).
[243] Eg *Grant v Dawkins* [1973] 1 WLR 1406.   [244] [1980] AC 367.
[245] As in example (i), above, p 317.
[246] C Harpum, 'Specific Performance with Compensation as a Purchaser's Remedy—a Study in Contract and Equity' [1981] CLJ 47.
[247] *Mortlock v Buller* (1804) 10 Ves 292.
[248] *Topfell Ltd v Galley Properties Ltd* [1979] 1 WLR 446 is a recent example.   [249] [1900] 1 Ch 815.
[250] [1973] 1 WLR 1406.

purchase price. Harpum thinks that the practice '… perhaps reflects no more than the conservatism of the legal profession who have preferred to stick with the devil they have known for so long'.[251] Seemingly no one would lose anything and unnecessary duplication and complexity would be avoided if the power to award compensation or abatement of price to a purchaser of land along with specific performance was simply abolished.

(c) Conditional specific performance

To protect the defendant, and to enable the remedy to be as widely applicable as possible, specific performance may be granted on terms. The most common example occurs where the vendor of land seeks specific performance against the purchaser and there is some non-substantial defect[252] in the property; specific performance will be ordered 'with compensation', that is, subject to the vendor paying compensation to the purchaser to cover the defect.[253]

Specific performance on terms has also been commonly adopted as a means of producing a just result for both parties in cases where the defendant is able to resist specific performance because of the defendant's mistake. The claimant may be granted specific performance if it agrees to conditions reflecting the defendant's understanding of the bargain. For example, in *Baskcomb v Beckwith*,[254] the defendant purchaser had contracted to buy an area of land, without realising—the plans not making it clear—that a small plot of land nearby was to be retained by the vendor, and was not covered by restrictive covenants preventing the building of a public house. The claimant vendor was given the choice: no specific performance or specific performance with the restrictive covenant extended to his own retained plot.

Langen and Wind Ltd v Bell[255] shows that where the courts want to protect the defendant against a subsequent failure by the claimant to perform they may make specific performance conditional, rather than denying specific performance altogether for want of mutuality. The defendant had there contracted to transfer shares to the claimants for a price that could only be fixed in the future. The defendant was ordered to transfer the shares but as security for future payment they were to be held by the claimants' solicitors until payment.

A more unusual illustration of conditional specific performance is provided by *Price v Strange*,[256] where simply to have ordered the defendant to grant the lease to the claimant would have given the claimant a windfall, since the claimant had promised in return to carry out the repairs which the defendant had had finished at her own expense. The claimant was therefore granted specific performance but subject to compensating the defendant for that expense.

Finally, in *Harvela Investments Ltd v Royal Trust Co of Canada Ltd*[257] the House of Lords granted specific performance to a purchaser of shares on condition that it paid the vendor interest from the date fixed for completion until payment.[258] Specific performance by itself would have put the claimant into a far better position than if there had been no breach because it would have had the use of the purchase money during the period of

---

[251] C Harpum, 'Specific Performance with Compensation as a Purchaser's Remedy – a Study in Contract and Equity' [1981] CLJ 47, 51.
[252] The leading case on the meaning of this is *Flight v Booth* (1834) 1 Bing NC 370, but it was actually dealing with rescission.
[253] *Re Fawcett and Holmes' Contract* (1889) 42 Ch D 150; *Shepherd v Croft* [1911] 1 Ch 521.
[254] (1869) LR 8 Eq 100. See also *Preston v Luck* (1884) 27 Ch D 497.   [255] [1972] Ch 685.
[256] [1978] Ch 337.   [257] [1986] AC 207.   [258] For rates of interest, see above, pp 305–306.

delay, plus taking the rise in value of the shares. Indeed irrespective of such a justification, ordinary equitable principles, generally rationalised in terms of equitable interests or constructive trusts, establish that a vendor is entitled to interest on the purchase price from the date of completion, while a purchaser is in return entitled to the interim profits from the property.[259]

(3) The effect of specific performance on termination and damages

In *Johnson v Agnew*,[260] the claimant vendor of land had obtained specific performance against the purchaser. The purchaser delayed in complying with the order, so that mortgagees of the land enforced their security by selling off the land. With specific enforcement no longer possible, the claimant now sought damages for the defendant's breach of contract. The defendant argued, first, that having obtained an order of specific performance the claimant had irrevocably forfeited his right to damages—all contractual rights had become merged in the specific performance decree;[261] and secondly, that having 'rescinded' the contract for breach, as the claimant had now done, there could in any event be no damages. The House of Lords rejected both arguments. The latter, which is beyond our immediate concern, was held to rest on an incorrect line of authority,[262] that had mistakenly regarded rescission for breach as meaning rescission *ab initio* rather than termination *in futuro*. The former was emphatically rejected, it being held that a contract remains in force after an order of specific performance so that the claimant can ask the court to dissolve the decree and revert to his rights to termination and damages.

However, the House of Lords did make one concession to the 'irrevocable election' view, namely that the claimant has no *right* to revert to termination and damages. In Lord Wilberforce's words:

'Once the matter has been placed in the hands of a court of equity ... the subsequent control of the matter will be examined according to equitable principles. The court would not make an order dissolving the decree of specific performance and terminating the contract (with recovery of damages) if to so do would be unjust, in the circumstances then existing to the other party, in this case to the purchaser.'[263]

This concession would appear to be designed to deal with the situation where it is because of the claimant's default that specific performance has not been complied with, so that had the contract been in force in the normal way, it would be the defendant rather than the claimant who would be entitled to damages.[264] Beyond this situation, there seems no justification for such a concession.[265]

---

[259] [1985] AC 207, at 236–237. See also *Re Hewitt's Contract* [1963] 1 WLR 1298; E Fry, *Fry on Specific Performance* (6th edn, Stevens & Sons 1921) 640–641; L Emmet et al, *Emmet on Title* (19th edn, Longman 1986) paras 7.021–7.033.
[260] [1980] AC 367.
[261] The terminology of election is often used; but, as in other instances, it is confusing and unnecessary.
[262] Eg *Horsler v Zorro* [1975] Ch 302.
[263] [1980] AC 367, at 399. See also *Singh v Nazeer* [1979] Ch 474, esp at 480–481; *GKN Distributors Ltd v Tyne Tees Fabrication Ltd* (1985) 50 P & CR 403.
[264] The extent of the concession is discussed by M Hetherington, 'Keeping the Plaintiff out of his Contractual Remedies: the Heresies that Survive *Johnson v Agnew*' (1980) 96 LQR 403, and D Jackson, 'Chimerical Heresies' (1981) 97 LQR 26.
[265] M Hetherington, 'Keeping the Plaintiff out of his Contractual Remedies: the Heresies that Survive *Johnson v Agnew*' (1980) 96 LQR 403, and J Heydon, M Leeming, and P Turner, *Meagher, Gummow and Lehane's Equity, Doctrines and Remedies* (5th edn, LexisNexis 2015) para 20-265 do not think the concession is ever justified.

23

Injunctions

1. Introduction	440
2. Final prohibitory injunctions	443
3. Final mandatory injunctions	462
4. Final *quia timet* injunctions	467
5. Interim injunctions	469
6. The claimant's conduct as a bar to an injunction	486
7. Appointment of a receiver	491

1. Introduction

An injunction is an equitable remedy available for torts and breach of contract (and equitable wrongs) as well as being available in other situations outside the scope of this book.[1] The approach adopted in this chapter will be to introduce briefly in this section the three important pairs of contrasting injunctions before going on in the next sections to examine in depth the principles governing the grant of each of the main types of injunction along with the function each performs as a remedy for torts and breach of contract. Although not an injunction, the final section of this chapter is considered the most appropriate place in this book to consider the remedy of the appointment of a receiver (and manager).

Six further points can be conveniently dealt with at this stage. First, a court will sometimes accept an undertaking from the defendant in substitution for, and in the same terms as, an injunction that it would otherwise have granted.[2] Since, contrary to its non-coercive appearance, such an undertaking plays exactly the same role as an injunction, being enforceable by contempt proceedings,[3] it is hard to see the justification for this judicial practice.

Secondly, by the Crown Proceedings Act 1947, s 21(1)(a) an injunction cannot be granted against the Crown.[4] But, as explained by the House of Lords in *M v Home Office*,[5] an injunction, including an interim injunction, can be granted against an officer of the Crown when sued in his or her personal capacity and, in judicial review proceedings (to which s 21 does not apply), when sued in an official capacity. Commonly a claimant will be equally

---

[1] The Senior Courts Act 1981, s 37(1) gives the High Court power to grant an injunction 'whenever just and convenient to do so'; and the County Courts Act 1984, s 38 gives county courts the same power to order injunctions as the High Court for cases within their jurisdiction (although by the County Court Remedies Regulations 2014, SI 2014/982 the county court generally has no jurisdiction to grant a search (*Anton Piller*) order). But while that power is, on the face of it, very wide-ranging generally the infringement of a legal or equitable right is required—J Glister and J Lee, *Hanbury and Martin Modern Equity* (21st edn, Sweet & Maxwell 2018) paras 28-012–28-015. For treatment of situations outside torts and breach of contract (and equitable wrongs) see R Sharpe, *Injunctions and Specific Performance* (5th edn, Thomson Reuters 2017) ch 3 and paras 5.190–5.540.
[2] *Evans Marshall & Co Ltd v Bertola SA* [1973] 1 WLR 349.
[3] *Camden London Borough Council v Alpenoak Ltd* [1985] NLJ Rep 1209; *Hussain v Hussain* [1986] Fam 134.
[4] However, an interim injunction can be granted against the Crown to protect the claimant's directly effective EU rights: *R v Secretary of State for Transport, ex p Factortame Ltd (No 2)* [1991] 1 AC 603.
[5] [1994] 1 AC 377.

satisfied with a declaration against the Crown and there is now power to award an interim declaration.[6]

Thirdly, an injunction can affect third parties: ie contempt proceedings can be brought against not only the tortfeasor or contract-breaker for failure to comply with the injunction but also against any person who frustrates the purpose of the injunction.[7]

Fourthly, it was held in *Bloomsbury Publishing Group plc v News Group Newspapers Ltd*[8] that an injunction (or an order for delivery up) can be granted against a person or persons who have not been named but merely described. There an interim injunction was granted to the claimant restraining, until the date of publication, 'the person or persons who have offered the publishers of [certain newspapers] a copy of the book Harry Potter and the Order of the Phoenix by JK Rowling' from disclosing to any person any part of the book.[9] There was no injustice to anyone in making such an order provided the description was sufficiently certain to identify those included and those who were not.

Fifthly, it was laid down by the Court of Appeal in *Wookey v Wookey*[10] that no injunction should be ordered against a person whose mental incapacity means that that person is incapable of understanding the order; nor, in the vast majority of cases, against a minor who has no earnings from which a fine for disobedience could be paid and is too young to be sent to prison.

Finally, where celebrities or others seek injunctions to prevent dissemination of private information, it is fairly commonplace, for obvious reasons, for the court to order that the claimant or the defendant or both must not be named.[11] In *PJS v News Group Newspapers*[12] the Supreme Court held that an interim injunction preventing publication of a story about the private life of the claimant, or the naming of the claimant, should continue—because the injunction still had some purpose—even though the story had been published, along with the name of the claimant, in the USA, Canada, and Scotland and on social media. In addition to anonymity, a court very exceptionally may go further and order—in what has been labelled a 'super-injunction'[13]—that the fact that the proceedings have taken place and that an injunction has been granted should themselves not be publicised.

---

[6] CPR 25.1(1)(b).
[7] *Z Ltd v A-Z and AA-LL* [1982] QB 558 (freezing injunction); *Attorney-General v Times Newspapers Ltd* [1992] 1 AC 191; *Attorney-General v Punch Ltd* [2002] UKHL 50, [2003] 1 AC 1046. But it has been held, rather surprisingly, that such contempt proceedings against third parties can be brought only in respect of interim, and not final, injunctions: *Jockey Club Ltd v Buffham* [2002] EWHC 1866 (QB), [2003] QB 462. This seems incorrect and compare the comments of Lord Neuberger MR in *Hutcheson v Popdog Ltd (News Group Newspapers Ltd, third party)* [2011] EWCA Civ 1580, [2012] 1 WLR 782, at [26]. See also ATH Smith, 'Third Parties and the Reach of Injunctions' [2003] CLJ 241.
[8] [2003] EWHC 1205 (Ch), [2003] 1 WLR 1633. See also *Secretary of State for Environment, Food and Rural Affairs v Meier* [2009] UKSC 11, [2009] 1 WLR 2780 (injunction against anonymous trespassers). There is no injustice to anyone in making such an order provided the description is sufficiently certain to identify those included and those who are not. See, generally, J Seymour, 'Injunctions Enjoining Non-Parties: Distinction without Difference' [2007] CLJ 605.
[9] Such a disclosure, prior to the publication date for the book, would constitute breach of copyright and/or breach of confidence and/or conversion.
[10] [1991] Fam 121.
[11] See, eg, *JIH v News Group Newspapers Ltd* [2011] EWCA Civ 42, [2011] 1 WLR 1645; *ETK v News Group Newspapers Ltd* [2011] EWCA Civ 439, [2011] 1 WLR 1827; *CTB v News Group Newspapers Ltd* [2011] EWHC 1232 (QB).
[12] [2016] UKSC 26, [2016] AC 1081.
[13] See, eg, *Donald v Ntuli* [2010] EWCA Civ 1276, [2011] 1 WLR 294. See, generally, the Report of the Committee on Super-Injunctions, *Super-Injunctions, Anonymised Injunctions and Open Justice* (chaired by Lord Neuberger MR, 2010). In that report there was awareness of only four such injunctions having been granted. Certainly, it seems numbers are now very much down: N Wilcox, 'Last Gasp of the Super-Injunction' (2014) 25 Ent LR 13 (summarising and commenting on the 2013 statistics supplied by the MoJ on the subject).

(1) Prohibitory and mandatory injunctions

A prohibitory injunction acts negatively, ie it orders the defendant not to do something. A mandatory injunction acts positively, ie it orders the defendant to do something. The distinction is one of substance and not one of form so that, for example, an injunction ordering the defendant not to allow a particular building to remain standing on its land is a mandatory injunction, since in substance the defendant is being ordered to knock the building down. Indeed, prior to *Jackson v Normanby Brick Co*[14] the courts tended to express mandatory injunctions in such a negative form but in that case it was laid down that form should reflect substance and that a mandatory injunction should be expressed in a positive form.

But so long as in substance breach of a negative obligation is being restrained the courts apply prohibitory injunction principles even though *in practice* it is most likely that compliance will necessitate particular positive steps. For example, an injunction restraining a factory-owner from continuing to pollute a river so as to cause a nuisance to the claimant is regarded as prohibitory and governed by prohibitory injunction, rather than mandatory injunction, principles. Only on the question of whether to suspend the injunction is any weight attached to the argument that compliance may in practice force the defendant to take particular positive steps, for example, replacing the factory's existing 'waste disposal' system with a new one. The justification for this is presumably that so long as the defendant *can* comply with the injunction without positive steps, for example by not continuing with that business, one cannot be sure that in complying it will take positive steps, and certainly one cannot predict with any accuracy which particular steps it might take. Traditionally the one judicially recognised exception is in the realm of breach of contract, where specific performance generally takes over the role of the mandatory injunction: it has long been recognised that an order which the defendant can comply with only by either not working (or not carrying on business) at all or carrying out particular positive contractual obligations is regarded as indirect specific performance, and is governed by specific performance, rather than prohibitory injunction, principles. The argument later advanced in regard to that area[15]—that, as indicated in some recent cases, the exception should be extended to wherever the order is in practice likely to force the defendant to take particular positive steps—is applicable also to the distinction between prohibitory and mandatory injunctions.

(2) *Quia timet*[16] injunctions and injunctions where a wrong has already been committed

In *Redland Bricks Ltd v Morris*[17] Lord Upjohn said that a '... *quia timet* action ... is an action for an injunction to prevent an apprehended legal wrong, though none has occurred at present', and Jolowicz has written that a *quia timet* injunction is granted where '... no actionable wrong has yet been committed by the defendant'.[18]

Most obviously, therefore, an injunction sought to prevent a continuing wrong is not *quia timet*. But the same can perhaps also be said of an injunction sought to prevent a *recurrence* of wrongful acts by the defendant, or a mandatory injunction sought to prevent the defendant's earlier acts causing a *further* wrong. In relation to the latter, Lord Upjohn in *Redland Bricks Ltd v Morris* treated as *quia timet* a mandatory injunction sought to compel the defendant to restore support to the claimant's land. As the land had slipped several times

---

[14] [1899] 1 Ch 438. [15] Below, pp 458–459, 461. [16] 'Since he fears.'
[17] [1970] AC 652, at 644.
[18] J Jolowicz, 'Damages in Equity—A Study of Lord Cairns' Act' (1975) 34 CLJ 224, 244.

before, so that the same sort of wrong as that now sought to be prevented had previously been committed by the defendant against the claimant, the injunction sought should perhaps not have been regarded as *quia timet*.[19]

(3) Final and interim injunctions

A final injunction, otherwise known as a perpetual injunction, is one that is granted at the trial of the action or other hearing in which final judgment is given.[20] In contrast, an interim injunction, as normally understood,[21] is one made at an earlier stage in the proceedings and is to last only until the trial at the latest. It may be expressed to continue in force 'until the trial of this action or further order'. Or it may be expressed to continue only until a specified pre-trial date: for example, 'until 10.30am on Wednesday 25th March (or so soon thereafter as counsel may be heard) or until further order'. For the claimant the great advantage of an interim injunction is that it can be gained quickly, without having to wait for the trial.

2. Final prohibitory injunctions[22]

(1) Torts[23]

(a) Prohibitory injunction as primary remedy

A prohibitory injunction is the appropriate remedy to prevent the continuation or repetition of a tort.[24] By it the defendant is ordered not to perform the acts that constitute the tort. While a prohibitory injunction can be granted in respect of any tort that can be continued or repeated—and has been granted, for example, to prevent trespass to the person,[25] harassment,[26] inducing breach of contract,[27] defamation,[28] infringement of copyright,[29] infringement of patent,[30] and passing off[31]—it has mainly been sought, particularly at the final rather than interlocutory stage, to restrain torts protecting the claimant's real property rights, namely the torts of nuisance and trespass to land. Moreover, it is in relation to the

---

[19] J Jolowicz, 'Damages in Equity—A Study of Lord Cairns' Act' (1975) 34 CLJ 224, 244–245.
[20] Eg summary judgment under CPR Pt 24.
[21] But freezing injunctions granted after final judgment have been treated as interim because they are ancillary to a final judgment. See *Orwell Steel v Asphalt and Tarmac (UK) Ltd* [1984] 1 WLR 1097; *Hill Samuel v Littauer* [1985] NLJ Rep 57. Also see *Distributori Automatici Italia SpA v Holford General Trading Co Ltd* [1985] 3 All ER 750 (search orders made after final judgment).
[22] *Quia timet* prohibitory injunctions are discussed below, pp 467–469.
[23] See, generally, J Murphy, 'Rethinking Injunctions in Tort Law' (2007) 27 OJLS 509.
[24] In *Weller v Associated Newspapers Ltd* [2015] EWCA Civ 1176, [2016] 1 WLR 1541, a prohibitory injunction preventing the publication of photographs was ordered in a situation where the defendant had said that they would not publish the photographs again but refused to give an undertaking to the court to that effect.
[25] *Egan v Egan* [1975] Ch 218 (interim).
[26] *Brand v Berki* [2014] EWHC 2979 (QB) (tort of harassment under the Protection from Harassment Act 1997).
[27] *Emerald Construction Co Ltd v Lowthian* [1966] 1 All ER 1013 (interim). The availability of the prohibitory injunction contrasts here with the reluctance to grant specific performance of positive obligations in the main contract.
[28] *Saxby v Easterbrook* (1878) 3 CPD 339; *Bonnard v Perryman* [1891] 2 Ch 269 (interim); *Grobbelaar v News Group Newspapers Ltd* [2002] UKHL 40, [2002] 1 WLR 3024.
[29] *Performing Right Society Ltd v Mitchell & Booker Ltd* [1924] 1 KB 762; *Phonographic Performance Ltd v Maitra* [1998] 1 WLR 870.
[30] *Coflexip SA v Stolt Comex Seaway MS Ltd* [2001] 1 All ER 952 (note).
[31] *Erven Warnink BV v J Townend & Sons (Hull) Ltd* [1979] AC 731; *British Telecommunications plc v One In A Million Ltd* [1999] 1 WLR 903; *Microsoft Corpn v Plato Technology Ltd*, The Times, 17 August 1999 (infringement of trade mark and passing off).

tort of private nuisance and some examples of the tort of trespass to land (in particular, involving trivial trespasses), that there has been long-standing case-law and debate about whether damages or an injunction should be the primary remedy. Our focus will therefore be on those torts.

It would appear that in relation to other torts, for example continuing torts causing personal injury or property damage, the prohibitory injunction is clearly the primary remedy as against damages. Moreover, not only is the injunction the primary remedy but it has strong primacy in the sense that it will be granted subject to there being exceptional circumstances. In other words, the courts rarely exercise their powers under the Senior Courts Act 1981, s 50, the successor to Lord Cairns's Act, to award damages in lieu of a prohibitory injunction sought to restrain the continuation or repetition of a tort (not involving a land conflict); and an award of ordinary common law damages is generally not in issue, since in this context such damages, in contrast to equitable damages, are almost inevitably 'inadequate', being available to compensate only for loss caused by past torts.

This is not to deny that, even in respect of torts other than private nuisance and trespass to land, damages may, exceptionally, be awarded in lieu of a prohibitory injunction, for example, because of the claimant's conduct[32] or because the injunction cannot be drawn up with sufficient certainty. As regards the latter, in *OPO v Rhodes*,[33] the Supreme Court overturned the grant of an interim[34] prohibitory injunction restraining the defendant from publishing a book about his life, including the sexual abuse he had suffered as a child, using 'graphic' language. The Supreme Court held that there was no arguable case that publication of the book would constitute the actionable tort of intentionally inflicting physical or psychological harm (ie the tort applied in *Wilkinson v Downton*).[35] But the Supreme Court also decided that the form of the injunction granted was objectionable because what is meant by 'graphic', even as amplified by the Court of Appeal, was too imprecise and uncertain. In the words of Lady Hale and Lord Toulson, giving the leading judgment, 'Any injunction must be framed in terms sufficiently specific to leave no uncertainty about what the affected person is or is not allowed to do.'[36]

The strong primacy afforded to a prohibitory injunction was also the traditional approach to the torts of private nuisance and trespass to land. But, as we shall see, that approach has been departed from in the most important recent case of *Coventry v Lawrence*.[37]

(b) The traditional approach to the tort of private nuisance (and trespass to land)

Prior to *Coventry v Lawrence*, the general approach of the courts in relation to injunctions restraining the continuation of a private nuisance or a trespass to land was that the prohibitory injunction was the primary remedy which would rarely be denied. The classic case indicating this was *Shelfer v City of London Electric Lighting Co.*[38] Here an electric housing station had been built next to a pub and the vibration and noise caused by the operation of the machines generating the electricity constituted an actionable nuisance to the lessee of the pub. The trial judge had awarded damages in lieu of the prohibitory injunction sought to restrain a further nuisance, but the Court of Appeal reversed this decision and granted

---

[32] See below, pp 486–491.
[33] [2015] UKSC 32, [2016] AC 219. See also *PA Thomas & Co v Mould* [1968] 2 QB 913, at 922–923 (breach of confidence).
[34] Although the injunction was interim not final that plainly had no bearing on the decision that the injunction was insufficiently certain.
[35] [1897] 2 QB 57.   [36] [2015] UKSC 32, [2016] AC 219, at [79].
[37] [2014] UKSC 13, [2014] AC 822.   [38] [1895] 1 Ch 287.

the injunction. Particularly important is A L Smith LJ's judgment where he said that damages should only be awarded in lieu of an injunction:

> 'If the injury to the plaintiff's legal rights is small. And is one which is capable of being estimated in money. And is one which can be adequately compensated by a small money payment. And the case is one in which it would be oppressive to the defendant to grant an injunction.'[39]

This statement was subsequently applied many times. Two excellent examples in the Court of Appeal are *Kennaway v Thompson*[40] and *Watson v Croft Promosport Ltd*[41] where prohibitory injunctions were granted to limit powerboat and car racing respectively, the noise from which was causing the claimants a nuisance.

The strong primacy of the prohibitory injunction was also stressed, without mentioning *Shelfer*, in the well-known case of *Pride of Derby and Derbyshire Angling Association Ltd v British Celanese Ltd*,[42] where a prohibitory injunction was granted to restrain the defendants from polluting a river with untreated sewage so as to constitute a nuisance to the claimant angling association which operated a fishery in the river. In Lord Evershed MR's words:

> 'It is, I think, well settled that if A proves that his proprietary rights are being wrongfully interfered with by B, and that B intends to continue his wrong, then A is prima facie entitled to an injunction, and he will be deprived of that remedy only if special circumstances exist, including the circumstance that damages are an adequate remedy for the wrong that he has suffered.'[43]

Similarly, in the early case of *Imperial Gas Light & Coke Co v Broadbent*,[44] where a prohibitory injunction was granted to restrain the defendants from operating their gas works so as to cause a nuisance to the claimant who carried on business as a market-gardener, Lord Kingsdown said:

> '... if a plaintiff applies for an injunction to restrain a violation of a common law right ... he must establish that right at law: but when he has established his right at law, I apprehend that unless there be something special in the case, he is entitled as of course to an injunction to prevent the recurrence of the violation.'[45]

Finally and more recently, Lord Upjohn in dicta in *Redland Bricks v Morris*,[46] the classic authority on mandatory injunctions, confirmed that a prohibitory injunction to prevent a person withdrawing support from his neighbour's land would be granted 'as of course'.[47]

Naturally the strong primacy of the prohibitory injunction has not meant that damages would never be awarded instead. The main traditional ground for refusing an injunction was where the claimant's conduct had been inequitable.[48]

Traditionally, a prohibitory injunction was also sometimes refused where the interference with the claimant's rights was trivial, although there was inconsistency in the authorities on this point. On the one hand, A L Smith LJ's principles in *Shelfer* indicated that, at least

---

[39] ibid, at 32.   [40] [1981] QB 88.
[41] [2009] EWCA Civ 15, [2009] 3 All ER 249. See also *Regan v Paul Properties Ltd* [2006] EWCA Civ 1391, [2007] Ch 135, in which Mummery LJ (giving the leading judgment) carefully summarised and applied *Shelfer* in granting an injunction to restrain continued infringement of the claimant's right to light. But as Mummery LJ recognised, at [1], the injunction there in question was mandatory (requiring part of a building being constructed to be pulled down) not prohibitory so that the decision not to award damages in lieu, and even the application of the *Shelfer* principles, was controversial. As we shall see, that approach has been disapproved (although without mentioning the mandatory injunction point) in *Coventry v Lawrence* [2014] UKSC 13, [2014] AC 822.
[42] [1953] Ch 149.   [43] ibid, at 181.   [44] (1859) 7 HL Cas 600.   [45] ibid, at 612.
[46] [1970] AC 652.
[47] ibid, at 664. See also *Cowper v Laidler* [1903] 2 Ch 337, at 341; *Wood v Conway Corpn* [1914] 2 Ch 47; *Attorney-General v PYA Quarries Ltd* [1957] 2 QB 169; *Armstrong v Sheppard and Short Ltd* [1959] 2 QB 384.
[48] Below, pp 486–491. Although rare, uncertainty was also a bar, ie it had to be possible to frame an order clearly specifying what the defendant was prohibited from doing: *PA Thomas & Co v Mould* [1968] 2 QB 913, at 922–923.

where the injunction was also oppressive to the defendant (and this requirement seemed to add next-to-nothing) damages in lieu should be awarded where the tortious interference was trivial. Several trespass cases also showed the application of a triviality restriction.[49] In *Llandudno Urban District Council v Woods*,[50] an injunction to restrain a clergyman from trespassing by holding services on the claimant local authority's seashore was refused, Cozens Hardy J saying that the injunction was '... a formidable legal weapon which ought to be reserved for less trivial occasions'.[51] Similarly, in *Behrens v Richards*,[52] having decided that the defendants, local inhabitants, were indeed trespassing on the claimant's land—an area of the Cornish coast—by crossing it to reach a beach, Buckley J refused a prohibitory injunction because the trespass was causing no real harm to the claimant. Nominal damages alone were considered sufficient. A further illustration was *Armstrong v Sheppard & Short Ltd*,[53] where the defendant was trespassing on a small strip of land at the rear of the claimant's premises by having a sewer discharging effluent there. An injunction to restrain this trespass was refused, inter alia, because the interference was trivial.

Again in *Jaggard v Sawyer*,[54] in refusing a prohibitory injunction restraining the defendants from trespassing over the claimant's road to reach their house (which also constituted a breach of covenant), the Court of Appeal considered it relevant that the harm to the claimant was minimal and that the claimant could have successfully sought an interim injunction but had not done so.

On the other hand, in granting a prohibitory injunction to restrain a trespass by the defendant's parking of vehicles on the claimant's land, the Court of Appeal in *Patel v W H Smith (Eziot) Ltd*[55] preferred the view that an injunction could be granted irrespective of the harm suffered and *Behrens v Richards* was put to one side as an exceptional case. And *Patel* was applied by Scott J in *Anchor Brewhouse Developments Ltd v Berkley House Docklands Developments Ltd*[56] in granting an injunction to restrain the defendants trespassing in the claimants' air space by their tower cranes.

It was also a very important feature of the traditional approach that, so long as any triviality threshold was crossed,[57] the courts were not prepared to deny a prohibitory injunction on the ground that the public interest was more important than the claimant's private interest. The *Shelfer* and *Pride of Derby* cases showed this.[58] In the former the public interest in having electricity generated was not allowed to override the claimant's private interest in living in and running a public house free from undue interference by noise and vibration. Similarly in the latter case the public interest in having the town's sewage cheaply and easily disposed of was not allowed to override the claimant club's private interest in being able to fish in the river. A particularly vivid illustration was provided by *Attorney-General v Birmingham Borough Council*,[59] where counsel for the defendant argued, in graphic detail, that if the injunction restraining the corporation from discharging sewage into the river were granted:

'... the evil that must ensue ... would be incalculable. If the drains are stopped ... the entire sewage of the town will overflow. Birmingham will be converted into one vast cesspool, which in

---

[49] See also *Lillywhite v Trimmer* (1867) 36 LJ Ch 525 (trivial nuisance).   [50] [1899] 2 Ch 705.
[51] ibid, at 710.   [52] [1905] 2 Ch 614.
[53] [1959] 2 QB 384. See also *Woollerton & Wilson Ltd v Richard Costain Ltd* [1970] 1 WLR 411; *League Against Cruel Sports Ltd v Scott* [1985] 2 All ER 489.
[54] [1995] 1 WLR 269.   [55] [1987] 1 WLR 853.   [56] [1987] 2 EGLR 173.
[57] *Llandudno Urban District Council v Woods* [1899] 2 Ch 705 and *Behrens v Richards* [1905] 2 Ch 614 are examples of the upholding of the public interest where interference was trivial.
[58] The public interest in the saving of jobs was also ignored in *Pennington v Brinsop Hall Coal Co* (1877) 5 Ch D 769.
[59] (1858) 4 K &J 528.

the course of nature, from the great elevation of the town (450 feet above sea-level) must empty itself into the Tame, only in a far more aggravated manner. The deluge of filth will cause a plague, which will not be confined to the 250,000 inhabitants of Birmingham, but will spread over the entire valley and become a national calamity ... In such cases private interests must bend to those of the country at large. The safety of the public is the highest law.'[60]

But to this Sir Page Wood V-C retorted, 'We cannot talk of that in this Court'[61] and in granting the interim prohibitory injunction sought he said, '... so far as this Court is concerned, it is a matter of almost absolute indifference whether the decision will affect a population of 250,000 or a single individual.'[62] In *Kennaway v Thompson*[63] the Court of Appeal, in granting the injunction sought, followed *Shelfer* and refused to allow the public interest in having facilities for powerboat racing to override the private interest of the claimant in living in her house without excessive interference by noise from the adjoining lake. A similar approach was taken by the Court of Appeal in *Watson v Croft Promosport Ltd*[64] in granting an injunction to restrict the use of the defendants' track for car racing. Prior to *Coventry v Lawrence*, *Dennis v Ministry of Defence*[65] was a rare case where the court did refuse a declaration (treated as being equivalent to an injunction) in respect of a nuisance because of the strong public interest involved. Buckley J held that the operations of RAF Wittering, where Harrier fighter pilots are trained, did constitute a private nuisance (because of the noise) to the claimant who lived nearby. But the declaration sought was refused because of the strong public interest (that is, the defence of the realm) in the continuation of training at RAF Wittering. Instead, damages of £950,000 (including £50,000 for 'loss of amenity') were awarded.

Similarly, and assuming that the interference with the claimant's rights was more than trivial, the hardship that compliance with the prohibitory injunction would cause to the defendant was traditionally not regarded as a reason to refuse it. For example, in *Pennington v Brinsop Hall Coal Co*[66] compliance with the injunction granted would have involved closure of the defendant's undertaking at a cost of £190,000, whereas the claimant's loss by the nuisance was at most £100 a year. This approach contrasted sharply with the balancing of benefit and burden applied to mandatory injunctions and the 'severe hardship' bar that is a defence to specific performance.

But while the courts rarely *refused* a prohibitory injunction to restrain a continuing nuisance or trespass, they did often suspend or restrict its operation, and it was through this power that some account was taken of the defendant's hardship or the public interest. In Tromans' words, the power '... can be seen as an uneasy compromise between the traditional fervour for the injunction as the appropriate remedy, and the realisation that an unlimited and immediate injunction may have undesirable effects'.[67]

So, for example, in *Pride of Derby v British Celanese*,[68] the injunction was suspended for two years; as it was by the Privy Council in *Stollmeyer v Petroleum Development Co Ltd*,[69] where the defendant's oil-drilling constituted a nuisance by polluting a stream flowing by the claimant's land, Lord Sumner saying, 'Their Lordships are of the opinion that it would not be right to enforce the injunction at once. The loss to the respondents would be out of all

---

[60] ibid, at 536. [61] ibid, at 536. [62] ibid, at 539–540. [63] [1981] QB 88.
[64] [2009] EWCA Civ 15, [2009] 3 All ER 249. [65] [2003] EWHC 793 (QB), [2003] NLJR 634.
[66] (1877) 5 Ch D 769. See also *Redland Bricks Ltd v Morris* [1970] AC 652, at 664 (defendant's financial difficulties irrelevant to prohibitory injunctions).
[67] S Tromans, 'Nuisance—Prevention or Payment?' [1982] CLJ 87, 95. [68] [1953] Ch 149.
[69] [1918] AC 498n.

proportion to the appellant's gain.'[70] Again in *Halsey v Esso Petroleum Co Ltd*,[71] an injunction restraining a nuisance constituted by the noise of tankers coming and going from an oil-depot at night was suspended for six weeks. In each of these cases the suspension gave the defendants ample opportunity to sort out how best to comply with the order. A particularly controversial use of the power to suspend was made in *Woollerton and Wilson Ltd v Richard Costain Ltd*.[72] There a crane being used to construct a building was trespassing into the claimant's airspace. The claimant was granted a prohibitory injunction to restrain this trespass but Stamp J suspended its operation until the date when the building was due to be completed, the crane then being no longer needed. By so doing, the injunction was prevented from having any effect: it might just as well have been refused. Not surprisingly therefore, in *John Trenberth Ltd v National Westminster Bank Ltd*,[73] where an injunction was granted to take immediate effect to prevent the defendant entering the claimant's land to erect scaffolding for work on his own property, Walton J considered that *Woollerton* was wrongly decided. If, as seems to be the case, the triviality of the damage was influencing Stamp J to suspend the injunction, it would indeed have been preferable if he had refused the injunction on that ground and awarded damages in lieu.

It should also be noted that, as one would expect, given the finding of liability, the defendant was generally held bound to pay damages for the claimant's loss during the period for which an injunction was suspended. Indeed, the suspension was likely to be made conditional on the defendant's undertaking to pay such damages.[74]

Cases on nuisance by noise have provided the main illustrations of the courts' imposition of restrictions on the operation of a prohibitory injunction. In *Vanderpant v Mayfair Hotel Co Ltd*,[75] for example, an injunction was granted to restrain noise from a hotel between 10.00 pm and 8.00 am; and in *Halsey v Esso Petroleum*[76] the injunction was to operate from 10.00 pm until 6.00 am. In *Dunton v Dover District Council*[77] an injunction was granted allowing a children's playground to be used by under-12s between 10.00 am and 6.30 pm. The injunction granted in *Kennaway v Thompson*[78] was notable for its particularly detailed specifications of what was and was not permitted. The injunction basically restrained 'motor boat racing, water skiing and the use of boats creating a noise of more than 75 decibels on the club's water', but this was made subject to the following restrictions:

> '... the club is allowed to have, each racing season, one international event extending over three days, the first day being given over to practice and the second and third to racing. In addition, there can be two national events, each of two days, but separated from the international event and from each other by at least four weeks. Finally there can be three club events, each of one day, separated from the international and national events and each other by three weeks. Any international or national event not held can be replaced by a club event of one day.'

Additionally the club was '... not to allow more than six motor boats to be used for water skiing at any one time'.

In applying the traditional approach of affording strong primacy to the prohibitory injunction, the courts often stated that one reason why the prohibitory injunction should

---

[70] ibid, at 500.   [71] [1961] 1 WLR 683.   [72] [1970] 1 WLR 411.
[73] (1980) 39 P & CR 104; H Street, '*John Trenberth Ltd v National Westminster Bank Ltd*' [1980] Conv 308 (note).
[74] *Stollmeyer v Trinidad Lake Petroleum Co* [1918] AC 485, at 497; A Ogus and G Richardson, 'Economics and the Environment: A Study of Private Nuisance' [1977] CLJ 284, 313–314.
[75] [1930] 1 Ch 138.   [76] [1961] 1 WLR 683.   [77] (1977) 76 LGR 87.
[78] [1981] QB 88, at 94–95. This was distinguished in *Tetley v Chitty* [1986] 1 All ER 663 where an unrestricted injunction was granted to restrain a nuisance by go-kart racing.

be the primary remedy was that otherwise the court would be enabling a defendant, who could afford to do so, to buy itself the right to commit wrongs. Typical was Lindley LJ's judgment in the *Shelfer* case in which he said, '... the Court has always protested against the notion that it ought to allow a wrong to continue simply because the wrongdoer is able and willing to pay for the injury he may inflict.'[79] In this respect, the courts showed themselves to be zealous to protect individual rights, by preventing defendants—and one thinks particularly of large-scale enterprises—riding roughshod over those rights by simply working into their calculations the costs of compensating for wrongs they might commit.

(c) The new approach in Coventry v Lawrence

While not disputing the strong primacy of the injunction in relation to other torts, in *Coventry v Lawrence*[80] the Supreme Court has weakened the primacy of the injunction, as against the award of equitable damages, at least in relation to private nuisance and probably in relation to some examples of trespass to land as well. In so doing, it may be regarded as having built upon cases which could not be reconciled with the traditional approach affording the prohibitory injunction strong primacy. In *Bracewell v Appleby*,[81] for example, Graham J refused a prohibitory injunction preventing the defendant trespassing on the claimants' private road because to grant it would in effect make the house the defendant had built 'uninhabitable and would put the claimants into an unassailable bargaining position'.[82] As we have seen, in *Dennis v Ministry of Defence*[83] a declaration (treated as equivalent to an injunction) was refused because of the public interest involved albeit that the public interest there involved was particularly strong because it concerned the defence of the realm. Most famously, in *Miller v Jackson*,[84] the majority of the Court of Appeal refused to grant an injunction restraining the defendant cricket club from playing cricket on a ground next to which the claimant's house had been built and into whose garden balls were quite often being hit. Cumming-Bruce LJ considered that, in granting the injunction, the trial judge had paid insufficient regard 'to the interest of the inhabitants of the village as a whole':[85] and Lord Denning, who would even have been prepared to decide that there was no actionable nuisance, was clear that the public interest dictated that no injunction should be granted. He said:

> 'The *public* interest lies in protecting the environment by preserving our playing fields in the face of mounting development, and by enabling our youth to enjoy all the benefits of outdoor games, such as cricket and football. The *private* interest lies in securing the privacy of his home and garden without intrusion or interference by anyone ... I am of opinion that that public interest should prevail over the private interest.'[86]

In *Coventry v Lawrence*,[87] the defendants were held to be committing a private nuisance by noise against the claimants, who lived in a bungalow 850 yards away from the defendants' speedway racing stadium. While much of the reasoning was concerned with the elements of the tort of private nuisance (for example, the relationship between that tort and the grant of planning permission), the Supreme Court went on to an important discussion of the law on remedies for the tort of private nuisance. Although the claimants

---

[79] [1895] 1 Ch 287, at 315–316.   [80] [2014] UKSC 13, [2014] AC 822.   [81] [1975] Ch 408.
[82] ibid, at 416.   [83] [2003] EWHC 793 (QB), [2003] NLJR 634. See above, p 447.
[84] [1977] QB 966.   [85] ibid, at 989.   [86] ibid, at 981–982.
[87] [2014] UKSC 13, [2014] AC 822.

had been awarded both damages and a prohibitory injunction—and there was no appeal against the grant of the injunction—the Supreme Court took the opportunity to restate the law. Lord Neuberger (with whom Lords Sumption, Mance, Clarke, and Carnwath agreed or essentially agreed) said that, while a prohibitory injunction should prima facie be ordered to stop a continuing nuisance, and the legal burden was on the defendant to show why an injunction should not be granted, the strong primacy traditionally afforded to the prohibitory injunction should no longer be applied. The approach put forward by AL Smith LJ in the *Shelfer* case, and recently applied in a case such as *Watson v Croft Promosport Ltd*,[88] was too rigid and inflexible. There should be no such fetter on the courts' discretion. The *Shelfer* principles should be treated as nothing more than a general guide. Particularly importantly, any public interest should always be a relevant consideration in deciding whether or not to grant an injunction. In the context of the tort of private nuisance, Lord Neuberger said the following:

> '[T]he approach to be adopted by a judge when being asked to award damages instead of an injunction should … be much more flexible than that suggested in the recent cases of *Regan* and *Watson*.[89] It seems to me that: (i) an almost mechanical application of AL Smith LJ's four tests; and (ii) an approach which involves damages being awarded only in 'very exceptional circumstances', are each simply wrong in principle … The court's power to award damages in lieu of an injunction involves a classic exercise of discretion, which should not, as a matter of principle, be fettered … I would accept that the prima facie position is that an injunction should be granted, so the legal burden is on the defendant to show why it should not.… However, it is right to emphasise that, when a judge is called on to decide whether to award damages in lieu of an injunction, I do not think there should be any inclination either way (subject to the legal burden …): the outcome should depend on all the evidence and arguments.… As for … public interest, I find it hard to see how there could be any circumstances in which it arose and could not, as a matter of law, be a relevant factor.'[90]

The Supreme Court did not go on to apply this restated approach to the facts because the dispute was as to whether or not the tort had been committed and was continuing and there was no appeal against the grant of the injunction (if the tort was continuing).

Lord Sumption indicated that the Supreme Court's rejection of *Shelfer* might not go far enough and that an even more radical rethink might be required which promoted damages at the expense of the injunction. He said this:[91]

> 'In my view, the decision in *Shelfer* is out of date, and it is unfortunate that it has been followed so recently and so slavishly. It was devised for a time in which England was much less crowded, when comparatively few people owned property, when conservation was only beginning to be a public issue, and when there was no general system of statutory development control. The whole jurisprudence in this area will need one day to be reviewed in this court. There is much to be said for the view that damages are ordinarily an adequate remedy for nuisance and that an injunction should not usually be granted in a case where it is likely that conflicting interests are engaged other than the parties' interests. In particular, it may well be that an injunction should as a matter of principle not be granted in a case where a use of land to which objection is taken requires and has received planning permission. However, at this stage, in the absence of argument on these points, I can do no more than identify them as calling for consideration in a case in which they arise.'

---

[88] [2009] EWCA Civ 15, [2009] 3 All ER 249. See above, pp 445, 447.
[89] For those cases, see above, pp 445, 445 n 41, 447.
[90] [2014] UKSC 13, [2014] AC 822, at [119]–[124].   [91] ibid, at [161].

This leads neatly on to the final section of this chapter which assesses whether the law, even as restated in *Coventry v Lawrence*, goes far enough in promoting damages at the expense of the prohibitory injunction.

Before moving on, however, we should note that there was a twist on the facts of *Coventry v Lawrence*. By the time of the trial of the action, the claimants were no longer living in the bungalow because there had been a fire which rendered it uninhabitable. As a minor issue in a second appeal to the Supreme Court (which was primarily concerned with the claim being brought against the landlord rather than the occupiers of the stadium),[92] it was decided that the injunction should be suspended until the bungalow was fit to be occupied residentially (each party having liberty to apply to vary or discharge the injunction).

(d) Is the present law satisfactory?

The traditional approach by which the claimant has nearly always been able to obtain a prohibitory injunction to restrain the continuance or repetition of a tort seems uncontroversial in respect of torts protecting the claimant against personal injury or property damage. But it has long been criticised in respect of the tort of nuisance,[93] and many of the arguments are equally applicable to some examples of the tort of trespass to land. Their central thrust is that damages for a continuing private nuisance, rather than a prohibitory injunction, should be awarded far more than they traditionally have been. The abandonment of that traditional approach signalled by the Supreme Court in *Coventry v Lawrence* is therefore to be welcomed but, as indicated by Lord Sumption in the passage set out above,[94] it may not have gone far enough. What then are the arguments for and against greater use of damages in preference to the prohibitory injunction?

(i) Arguments for greater use of damages

(i) As the courts weigh the defendant's hardship against the benefit to the claimant in deciding whether to grant a mandatory injunction, they should do the same for prohibitory injunctions. But it may be doubted whether this is a valid argument where one is dealing with a truly negative injunction. What is true, however, is that the courts sometimes regard as prohibitory, injunctions that are better viewed as mandatory, because in practice compliance will force the defendant to take particular positive steps.[95] If such injunctions were recognised as mandatory, traditional legal principle would rightly require the defendant's hardship to be considered. Beyond this, change seems unnecessary.

(ii) The courts should be prepared to refuse a prohibitory injunction where the public interest outweighs the claimant's private rights. Under the traditional approach, once any triviality threshold was crossed, the courts only took the public interest into account in suspending or restricting a prohibitory injunction. According to this argument, there is no reason why they should not go further and the reasoning in *Coventry v Lawrence* is absolutely correct to have finally recognised this.

(iii) The courts should be wary of awarding injunctions because, like all specific remedies, they allow the claimant too much of an advantage in pre- and post-judgment bargaining. So

---

[92] *Coventry v Lawrence (No 2)* [2014] UKSC 46, [2015] AC 106.
[93] A Ogus and G Richardson, 'Economics and the Environment: A Study of Private Nuisance' [1977] CLJ 284; S Tromans, 'Nuisance – Prevention or Payment?' [1982] CLJ 87; C Rotherham, 'The Allocation of Remedies in Private Nuisance: An Evaluation of the Judicial Approach to Awarding Damages in Lieu of an Injunction' (1989) 4 Canterbury LR 185; R Sharpe, *Injunctions and Specific Performance* (5th edn, Thomson Reuters 2017) paras 4.60–4.580.
[94] See above, p 450. [95] Above, p 442.

Tromans writes, 'The effect of an injunction may be certainty, but it is certainty achieved by tying one of the defendant's hands behind his back before negotiations begin. This is hardly likely to produce a fair or economic result.'[96]

(iv) The automatic granting of an injunction can be further criticised as absolving the claimant from any duty to mitigate its own loss. While, generally speaking, mitigation is less likely to be possible where one is dealing with negative tort obligations than positive contractual promises, there will be situations where a claimant could relatively easily take steps to avoid being harmed by the defendant's actions. Automatic injunctions remove the incentive to take such steps.

(v) The routine granting of an injunction may have an unfortunate effect on the substantive law, since the courts may steer clear of finding liability, knowing of the consequent drastic remedy. As Tromans writes in the context of nuisance, '... an unwillingness to give the plaintiff anything other than the best remedy can lead to his getting no remedy at all.'[97] As examples he instances the non-liability for temporary nuisances, and the wide construction courts give to the defence of statutory authority. The latter is shown by *Allen v Gulf Oil Refining Ltd*,[98] where the House of Lords' liberal construction of a private Act of Parliament enabled the defendants to construct and operate an oil refinery without incurring any liability in nuisance to the claimants who were affected by its noise, smell and vibration. No doubt the Lords were influenced by the fact that a finding of liability would inevitably lead to an injunction and hence the potential closure of the refinery. Lord Denning's solution in the Court of Appeal awarding 'damages to cover past or future injury in lieu of an injunction'[99] seems far preferable.

(vi) Calabresi and Melamed[100] have put forward a sophisticated economic analysis which would also seem to support a freer use of damages awards in relation to land use conflicts. According to their model, entitlements can be protected by either property or liability rules.[101] Where protection is by a property rule '... someone who wishes to remove the entitlement from its holder must buy it from him in a voluntary transaction in which the value of the entitlement is agreed upon by the seller'.[102] Protection is by a liability rule 'whenever someone may destroy the initial entitlement if he is willing to pay an objectively determined value for it'.[103]

It follows that there are four possible outcomes to a land use conflict. If D is polluting C's land, then first, C may have an entitlement to be free from pollution protected by a

---

[96] S Tromans, 'Nuisance—Prevention or Payment?' [1982] CLJ 87, 105. For detailed discussion of this, see B Thompson, 'Injunction Negotiations: An Economic, Moral, and Legal Analysis' (1975) 27 Stan LR 1563. Also see above, p 22. In *Phonographic Performance Ltd v Maitra* [1998] 1 WLR 870 the Court of Appeal did not think it a good reason for denying a final injunction of unlimited duration to restrain copyright infringement that the claimant would use that injunction as a lever to extract payment of licence fees for past (and future) 'infringements'.
[97] S Tromans, 'Nuisance—Prevention or Payment?' [1982] CLJ 87, at 107.   [98] [1981] AC 1001.
[99] [1980] QB 156, at 169.
[100] G Calabresi and D Melamed, 'Property Rules, Liability Rules and Inalienability: One View of the Cathedral' (1972) 85 Harv LR 1089. See also F Michelman, 'Pollution as a Tort: a Non-Accidental Perspective on Calabresi's Costs' (1971) 80 Yale LJ 647; R Ellickson, 'Alternatives to Zoning: Covenants, Nuisance Rules and Fines as Land Use Controls' (1972) 40 U Chi LR 681, esp 738–748; E Rabin, 'Nuisance Law: Rethinking Fundamental Assumptions' (1977) 63 Va LR 1299; J Krier and S Schwab, 'Property Rules and Liability Rules: The Cathedral in Another Light' (1995) 70 NYU LR 440; A Farnsworth, 'Do Parties to Nuisance Cases Bargain After Judgment? A Glimpse Inside the Cathedral' (1999) 66 U Chi LR 373; D Harris, D Campbell, and R Halson, *Remedies in Contract and Tort* (2nd edn, Butterworths 2002) 496–519.
[101] An entitlement can also be 'inalienable'.
[102] G Calabresi and D Melamed, 'Property Rules, Liability Rules and Inalienability: One View of the Cathedral' (1972) 85 Harv LR 1089, 1092.
[103] ibid, at 1092.

property rule; that is, C may be granted an injunction to restrain D's nuisance. Secondly, C may have an entitlement to be free from pollution protected by a liability rule; that is, C may be merely awarded damages for D's nuisance. Thirdly, D may have an entitlement to pollute protected by a property rule; that is, D may be held not liable for nuisance, so that C can only prevent the pollution by paying D to stop it. Finally D may have an entitlement to pollute protected by a liability rule; that is, D may be free to pollute unless C pays him a judicially determined price not to: this would most obviously be achieved by a 'compensated injunction', never yet used in England,[104] whereby C would be bound to pay D the costs of D's compliance with the injunction.

In deciding which of these four to choose, Calabresi and Melamed consider that economic efficiency dictates the following results. If transaction costs are low, so that it can be expected that parties will bargain round legal rights and remedies to correct any 'errors',[105] property rules should be chosen, thereby avoiding the costs of a judicial determination of values. Whether the first or third outcome is adopted depends on whether it is thought D or C is the cheaper cost-avoider. But where transaction costs are high, as they are likely to be in the pollution field, property rules should only be chosen if it is certain which party is the cheaper cost-avoider. No guessing should be undertaken, since the parties will not negotiate round to correct any error. If, as is likely in most pollution cases, it is uncertain who is the cheaper cost-avoider, a liability rule should be adopted; that is, the second or fourth outcome should be chosen. To decide between these two, the court should make a cost–benefit analysis, mimicking the transaction the parties would themselves have made.

So in a standard land use conflict, where transaction costs are high, and it is difficult to be certain who is the cheaper cost-avoider, this approach indicates that the claimant should be awarded damages or a compensated injunction.

(ii) **Arguments against greater use of damages**

(i) From the claimant's point of view an injunction is a better remedy than damages. Damages may be very difficult to assess either because one cannot know the extent of the claimant's future loss, or because his loss is non-pecuniary comprising, for example, interference with the enjoyment of land. Moreover the defendant may be unable to pay.

(ii) To allow a defendant to continue with the wrong by paying damages sacrifices to some degree the claimant's individual rights. On one view such rights merit absolute specific protection and should not be downgraded in this way.

(iii) An injunction prevents a ruthless defendant simply including the damages in a calculated decision to ride roughshod over the claimant's rights. But this objection could be countered to some extent by awarding an account of profits, or even punitive damages, rather than merely compensation.

(iv) The injunction is the best remedy for protecting the environment.[106] Hence the upholding of individual rights and the public interest in environmental control coincide in favouring the injunction as against damages.

---

[104] But see *Spur Industries Inc v Del E Webb Development Co* 494 P 2d 700 (Ariz, 1972).
[105] R Coase, 'The Problem of Social Cost' (1960) 3 J Law & Econ 1, above, p 16.
[106] J McLaren, 'The Common Law Nuisance Actions and the Environmental Battle—Well-Tempered Swords or Broken Reeds?' (1972) 10 Osgoode Hall LJ 505, esp 547–561.

(v) On one view it is not the function of the courts, nor are they properly equipped, to decide what the public interest demands.[107] Their role is and should be one of protecting individual rights which should not be sacrificed for social welfare goals. So, for example, the courts should never involve themselves in deciding whether it is in the public interest to keep open a nuclear power installation that is causing a nuisance by its occasional leaks of radiation. But examination of the common law shows that legal decision-making is best understood as a complex mix of principle and policy and that the courts do make decisions on where the public interest lies. So, for example, they judge the public interest in deciding whether to suspend an injunction, and sometimes even in deciding initially whether the defendant is liable. Moreover, this seems perfectly acceptable so long as the courts aim for consistency with the long-term policy goals enshrined in the common law.

(iii) Conclusion

Having weighed up the above arguments, it is submitted that, in relation to the tort of private nuisance and some examples of trespass to land (in particular, involving trivial trespasses), *Coventry v Lawrence* should be strongly supported and that, going beyond what was there decided, and in line with Lord Sumption's obiter dicta, there is a case for damages being awarded even more readily.[108] Where the defendant is pursuing what is in the long-term public interest, or where the claimant could easily take steps to remove the harm, equitable damages in lieu should be preferred to a prohibitory injunction. It is also true that the compensated injunction, whereby the claimant pays the defendant the costs of his compliance, would be a useful weapon for the English courts to add to their armoury. For while at first sight it is somewhat alarming to suggest that a claimant should pay the defendant for not infringing its rights, on closer inspection, it can be seen that this would add further remedial flexibility and would provide another sensible way of resolving the conflict between the public interest and private rights; and, after all, the claimant may well prefer a compensated injunction to no injunction at all.

(2) Breach of contract

(a) Prohibitory injunction as primary remedy

The prohibitory injunction is the appropriate remedy for restraining the breach[109] of a negative contractual promise—that is a promise not to do something: put another way, it enforces a negative contractual promise. It therefore belongs on the reverse side of the coin from specific performance, which enforces a positive contractual promise.

As in relation to torts, and in contrast to specific performance, the prohibitory injunction is the primary remedy as against damages for breach of a negative promise; and here, in contrast to torts, it is generally ordinary common law damages that are in issue as the alternative to the prohibitory injunction—for the breach of contract is not normally regarded as a prospective (rather than an accrued) wrong and hence common law damages are as advantageous as damages under the Senior Courts Act 1981, s 50.[110] Since common law damages must be shown to be inadequate before an injunction, being an equitable remedy, can be granted, the primacy afforded to the prohibitory injunction can be expressed by

---

[107] R Dworkin, *Taking Rights Seriously* (rev edn, Duckworth 1978).
[108] As in the US and Canada; see S Tromans, 'Nuisance—Prevention or Payment?' [1982] CLJ 87, 97–99.
[109] Including a threatened breach.
[110] But equitable damages may be the only alternative to a prohibitory injunction restraining breach of a restrictive covenant affecting land; see, eg, above, p 317.

saying that, in this context, adequacy is given a very narrow meaning, so that damages are hardly ever considered adequate.

The classic 'authority' on the primacy of the prohibitory injunction is the dictum of Lord Cairns LC in *Doherty v Allman*.[111] He said:

'... if there had been a negative covenant, I apprehend, according to well-settled practice, a Court of Equity would have no discretion to exercise. If parties, for valuable consideration, with their eyes open, contract that a particular thing shall not be done, all that a Court of Equity has to do is to say, by way of injunction that which the parties have already said by way of covenant, that the thing shall not be done; and in such case, the injunction does nothing more than give the sanction of the process of the Court to that which already is the contract between the parties. It is not then a question of the balance of convenience or inconvenience, or the amount of damage or of injury—it is the specific performance by the Court, of that negative bargain which the parties have made, with their eyes open, between themselves.'

To similar effect is Sir Page Wood V-C's statement in *Tipping v Eckersley*[112] that, '... if the construction of the instrument be clear and the breach clear, then it is not a question of damage but the mere circumstance of the breach of covenant affords sufficient ground for the Court to interfere by injunction'. He went on to grant an injunction whereby the defendant was not to increase the temperature of the water flowing down to the claimant's steam engine, such action constituting a breach of the defendant's covenant to allow the claimant the free use and enjoyment of the stream.

Lord Cairns's dictum in *Doherty v Allman* was applied recently, on beautifully simple facts, in *Araci v Fallon*.[113] On the morning of The Derby 2011, an interim prohibitory injunction was sought and granted against the jockey, Kieren Fallon, to prevent him breaking his express contractual obligation with the owner of the horse 'Native Khan' not to ride a rival horse. In Jackson LJ's words, 'Where the defendant is proposing to act in clear breach of a negative covenant, in other words to do something which he has promised not to do, there must be special circumstances ... before the court will exercise its discretion to refuse an injunction.'[114] Even if there were an adequacy of damages bar to a prohibitory injunction—and Elias LJ doubted this[115]—both judges agreed that damages were here inadequate.

Why is there this judicial readiness to order prohibitory injunctions to restrain the breach of a negative promise, contrasting as it does with the approach to specific performance, and given that both remedies more closely protect the claimant's expectation interest than damages? Perhaps the principal reasons are that prohibitory injunctions do not as commonly contradict a claimant's duty to mitigate, and nor do they infringe individual liberty to the same extent as positive orders. Additionally, damages are often less easy to assess for breach of a negative than a positive obligation. Nor do prohibitory injunctions fall foul of the constant supervision objection that has traditionally barred specific performance. But having said all this, the present automatic grant of a prohibitory injunction for breach of contract under *Doherty v Allman* probably goes too far. The arguments examined above in relation to torts suggest that sometimes damages should be awarded in preference to a prohibitory

---

[111] (1878) 3 App Cas 709, at 720. For examples of *Doherty* being applied see *Avon County Council v Millard* (1985) 274 Estates Gazette 1025; *Attorney-General v Barker* [1990] 3 All ER 257, at 261–262 (per Nourse LJ).
[112] (1855) 2 K & J 264, at 270.
[113] [2011] EWCA Civ 668. For other examples of *Doherty* being applied see *Avon County Council v Millard* (1985) 274 Estates Gazette 1025; *Attorney-General v Barker* [1990] 3 All ER 257, at 261–262 (per Nourse LJ); *AB v CD* [2014] EWCA Civ 229, [2015] 1 WLR 771.
[114] [2011] EWCA Civ 668, at [39]. [115] ibid, at [70].

injunction for breach of a negative promise.[116] This is particularly so where the claimant could take steps to mitigate its loss.

To say that the prohibitory injunction is the primary remedy does not of course mean that it will never be refused. Two main grounds for refusal[117] are that the claimant's conduct is a bar,[118] or that the harm suffered by the claimant is trivial.[119] But indisputably the most discussed ground for refusal is that to grant the prohibitory injunction would amount to indirect specific performance of a contractual promise for which specific performance would not be ordered. This will now be examined.

(b) Indirect specific performance

Strictly speaking this is not a ground for refusing a prohibitory injunction, but rather an argument that what appears to be a prohibitory injunction enforcing a negative obligation is in reality specific performance of a positive obligation, and should be governed by specific performance principles.

It should be emphasised straightaway that some cases provide no difficulty for it is pellucidly clear that, despite the prohibitory form in which the order is sought, in substance it amounts to specific performance. For example, an order to restrain the defendants breaking their positive contractual obligation is specific performance and not a prohibitory injunction. Again in *Sky Petroleum v VIP Petroleum Ltd*[120] and *Hill v Parsons*[121] the injunctions respectively sought—to restrain the defendants withholding supplies of petrol to the claimant and to restrain the defendants implementing their notice of dismissal terminating the claimant's employment—were negative in form, but clearly positive in substance.

The interesting and controversial cases are those where, although in substance breach of a negative obligation is being restrained, it is arguable that compliance with the negative obligation will *in practice* force the defendant to comply with his positive obligations. The essential question is to what extent do the courts accede to this argument? Sir George Jessel MR in *Fothergill v Rowland*[122] thought that it was difficult to find any consistent judicial approach:

'I cannot find any distinct line laid down … dividing … the class of cases in which the Court, feeling that it has not the power to compel specific performance, grants an injunction to restrain the breach by the contracting party of one or more of the stipulations of the contract, and the class of cases in which it refuses to interfere.'[123]

It is submitted, however, that a principle has traditionally been applied, namely that a prohibitory injunction will be regarded as indirect specific performance, and subject to specific performance principles, if compliance with the order will leave the defendant with the 'choice' of either performing positive obligations to the claimant or not being able to work or carry on any business at all. The issue has arisen with regard to two main types of contract—contracts for personal service and contracts for the sale of goods.

---

[116] A rare example of a case not following the traditional approach is *Baxter v Four Oaks Properties Ltd* [1965] Ch 816, where Cross J did not want to put the claimant into too strong a position in post-judgment bargaining.
[117] Although rare, uncertainty may also be a bar: *Hampstead and Suburban Properties v Diomedous* [1969] 1 Ch 248; *Bower v Bantam Investments Ltd* [1972] 1 WLR 1120.
[118] Below, pp 486–491.
[119] *Harrison v Good* (1871) LR 11 Eq 338, at 352. See also *Jaggard v Sawyer* [1995] 1 WLR 269, discussed above, at p 517, where a prohibitory injunction was refused which sought to prevent conduct which constituted a breach of covenant as well as a trespass.
[120] [1974] 1 WLR 576.
[121] [1972] Ch 305. See also *Davis v Foreman* [1894] 3 Ch 654.
[122] (1873) LR 17 Eq 132.
[123] ibid, at 141.

(i) Contracts for personal service

Lumley v Wagner[124] is the classic case. Here Mlle Wagner undertook that for three months she would sing at Mr Lumley's theatre in Drury Lane on two nights a week and not use her talents at any other theatre without Mr Lumley's written consent. She then agreed to sing for Mr Gye at Covent Garden for more money. Lord St Leonards LC granted an injunction restraining her from singing except for Mr Lumley, and considered that this did not amount to indirect specific performance of her obligation to sing for Mr Lumley, which he recognised could not be granted. He said:

> 'It was objected that the operation of the injunction in the present case was mischievous, excluding the defendant ... from performing at any other theatre while this Court had no power to compel her to perform at Her Majesty's Theatre. It is true, that I have not the means of compelling her to sing, but she has no cause of complaint, if I compel her to abstain from the commission of an act which she has bound herself not to do ... in continuing the injunction, I disclaim doing indirectly what I cannot do directly.'[125]

This approach was followed and explained further in *Warner Bros Pictures Inc v Nelson*,[126] where the film actress Bette Davis had agreed that she would render her exclusive services as an actress to the claimants for a certain period and would not during that time render any similar services to any other person. In breach of that contract she entered into an agreement to appear for another film company. The claimants were granted an injunction restraining her for three years from appearing for any other film company. Branson J reasoned that this did not amount to indirectly ordering specific performance of her contact with the claimants—for while the defendant was being ordered not to work as a film actress for anyone else, she was left free to work elsewhere in any other capacity. Branson J said:

> 'It was also urged that the difference between what the defendant can earn as a film artiste and what she might expect to earn by any other form of activity is so great that she will in effect be driven to perform her contract ... [but] no evidence was addressed to show that, if enjoined from doing the specified acts otherwise than for the plaintiffs, she will not be able to employ herself both usefully and remuneratively in other spheres of activity ... She will not be driven, although she may be tempted, to perform the contract, and the fact that she may be so tempted is no objection to the grant of an injunction.'[127]

In both these and other cases,[128] it was regarded as important that the negative promise in question was express. This is a red herring, and should not be allowed to cast confusion over the indirect specific performance discussion. As other authorities recognise,[129] so long as a clear negative promise can be made out, it should not matter whether that promise is express or implied.

---

[124] (1852) 21 LJ Ch 898. J Parks, 'Equitable Relief in Contracts Involving Personal Services' (1918) 66 U of Pa LR 251; R Stevens, 'Involuntary Servitude by Injunction: The Doctrine of *Lumley v Wagner* Considered' (1921) 6 Cornell LQ 235; D Tannenbaum, 'Enforcement of Personal Service Contracts in the Entertainment Industry' (1954) 42 Cal LR 18.
[125] (1852) 21 LJ Ch 898, at 902.
[126] [1937] 1 KB 209. See also *William Robinson & Co Ltd v Heuer* [1898] 2 Ch 451; *Marco Productions CLJ v Pagola* [1945] KB 111.
[127] [1937] 1 KB 209, at 219–220.
[128] Eg *Mutual Reserve Fund Life Assurance v New York Insurance Co* (1896) 75 LT 528; *Mortimer v Beckett* [1920] 1 Ch 571.
[129] *Wolverhampton & Walsall Rly Co v London & North Western Rly Co* (1873) LR 16 Eq 433; *Whitwood Chemicals Co v Hardman* [1891] 2 Ch 416, at 427.

458   Injunctions

Consistent with the emphasis on the freedom to take up other employment, albeit falling on the reverse side of the line, are *Whitwood Chemical Co v Hardman*,[130] *Ehrman v Bartholomew*,[131] and *Rely-a-Bell Burglar & Fire Alarm Co v Eisler*.[132] In each case the injunction sought was to restrain the breach of a promise not to accept any other employment at all. Therefore, if granted, the defendant would have had only the choice of working for the claimant or remaining idle. Since this was not a real choice, a prohibitory injunction would in practice amount to specific performance and, as specific performance would not be ordered of a contract for personal service, the injunction was refused.

However, there have been cases in which the courts have taken a different approach. In *Mortimer v Beckett*,[133] for example, the defendant agreed to employ the claimant as his boxing manager, to be solely in charge of arranging the defendant's boxing contracts. When the defendant agreed to box for someone else, the claimant sought an interim injunction to restrain him; that is, to enforce his implied promise not to box for anyone else. But even though the promise only related to boxing, the injunction was refused, inter alia,[134] because it was thought that it would amount to specific performance of the defendant's personal obligations. Russell J said, 'The effect will be to force the defendant to employ a particular person as his agent, so far as his boxing engagements are concerned, and to accept the agent's services.'[135] Similarly, in *Page One Records Ltd v Britton*[136] 'The Troggs' pop group employed the claimant as their sole agent and manager for five years, and agreed not to make records for anyone else during that time. In breach of that contract they then entered into an agreement to be managed by someone else. The claimant sought an interim injunction to restrain this breach. Stamp J refused to grant it because he thought that it would amount to indirect specific performance of the defendants' personal obligations:

> '... it was said in this case, that if an injunction is granted, The Troggs could without employing any other manager or agent ... seek other employment of a different nature ... I think that I can and should take judicial notice of the fact that these groups, if they are to have any great success, must have managers. As a practical matter ... I entertain no doubt that they would be compelled, if the injunction were granted, ... to continue to employ the plaintiff as their manager and agent ... I should if I granted the injunction, be enforcing a contract for personal services, in which personal services are to be performed by the plaintiff.'[137]

Clearly these cases differ factually from *Lumley* and *Warner Bros* in that it was the employee (the manager and agent) rather than the employer who was seeking the injunction. But that cannot account for the difference in result. The better view is that these cases go beyond the traditional principle in considering it insufficient that the defendant is left free to take up other employment or business. Rather it is the likelihood of the defendant doing so that is important. This is a preferable approach requiring, as it does, a closer examination of the practical realities of the injunction. Applying it to the facts of *Warner Bros v Nelson*, a different decision would be reached, for it was most unlikely that Bette Davis would take up another occupation and abandon making films for the three-year period. On the other hand, *Lumley v Wagner* might well be decided in the same way; for as Mlle Wagner was merely being restrained from singing elsewhere for three months, it was quite likely that she would choose to do something else, or nothing, for that short period, rather than singing for the claimant.

---

[130] [1891] 2 Ch 416.   [131] [1898] 1 Ch 671.
[132] [1926] Ch 609. See also *Kirchner & Co v Gruban* [1909] 1 Ch 413.   [133] [1920] 1 Ch 571.
[134] The other, and unsatisfactory, ground was the lack of an express negative covenant.
[135] [1920] 1 Ch 571, at 581.   [136] [1968] 1 WLR 157.   [137] ibid, at 166–167.

Final prohibitory injunctions

Authoritative support for that preferable approach has been provided by the Court of Appeal in the leading modern case of *Warren v Mendy*,[138] in which *Page One Records v Britton* was preferred to *Warner Bros v Nelson* on grounds of 'realism and practicality'.[139] The facts—which concerned a dispute over the management of the boxer, Nigel Benn—differed from the usual restrictive covenant case in that the injunction being sought by the claimant was not against Benn for breach of contract but against another manager in a tort action for inducing breach of Benn's contract with the claimant. But the Court of Appeal felt that, as the claimant would seek an injunction against anyone who arranged to manage Benn, the same principles should be applied as if the injunction had been sought against Benn for breach of contract. The injunction was refused on the ground that to grant it would constitute indirect specific performance of Benn's contract to be exclusively managed by the claimant for the three-year contract period. While disapproving the approach in *Warner Bros v Nelson*, the Court of Appeal did not doubt the correctness of the decision in *Lumley v Wagner* given the short contract period there in issue. Nourse LJ said:

> 'Although it is impossible to state in general terms where the line between short- and long-term engagements ought to be drawn it is obvious that an injunction lasting for two years or more (the period applicable in the present case) may practically compel performance of the contract.'[140]

In *Lauritzencool AB v Lady Navigation Inc*[141] the Court of Appeal, in upholding the grant of an injunction to restrain a shipowner from breaking a time charter by employing the ship with any other charterer, distinguished *Warren v Mendy* on the grounds that the personal service element involved in a time charter is far less significant than in a close working relationship between, for example, a boxing manager and a boxer. That is no doubt correct but it is far from clear that it justified the grant of the injunction in this case given that it was accepted that specific performance could not be ordered. A controversial distinction was drawn between a prohibitory injunction that juristically would amount to specific performance (eg an injunction restraining the defendant from taking any step which would prevent performance of the contract) and one that *as a practical matter* would amount to specific performance. Specific performance principles were thought applicable to the former but not the latter. But if one knows that as a practical matter the effect of the injunction is that the defendant will be compelled to perform, the decision to grant or refuse the injunction should surely be governed by specific performance principles as was recognised by the Court of Appeal in *Warren v Mendy*.

One might surmise that what was driving the decision was that, because the personal service element involved in a time charter is far less significant than in a close working relationship, the rule accepted by Lord Diplock in *The Scaptrade*[142]—that specific performance cannot be ordered of a time charter—is flawed. If that is so, that rule should have been attacked directly. It was unsatisfactory to attack it indirectly by pretending that what was here ordered did not, in substance, constitute specific performance.

Three final points should be made. First, there has traditionally been some doubt as to the application of the substantive restraint of trade doctrine to the sort of negative obligations in some of these cases, especially given that they apply during rather than after

---

[138] [1989] 1 WLR 853. See also, eg, *Vertex Data Science Ltd v Powergen Retail Ltd* [2006] EWHC 1340 (Comm), [2006] 2 Lloyd's Rep 591.
[139] [1989] 1 WLR 853, at 865 (per Nourse LJ).
[140] ibid, at 865–866.
[141] [2005] EWCA Civ 579, [2005] 1 WLR 3686.
[142] [1983] 2 AC 694.

the employment. The above discussion has assumed the substantive validity of the negative obligation but clearly if it is invalid there is no question of any remedy for breach. Secondly, it has further been assumed above that the claimant wants the defendant to perform her positive contractual obligations. Where this is not so, for example where there is a restrictive covenant to take effect after termination of the defendant's employment,[143] or where the claimant undertakes to pay the defendant and to give her other contractual benefits even though the defendant does no work for him,[144] there is no question of an injunction amounting to indirect specific performance. Finally, an approach adopted in the US is to grant an injunction to prevent the defendant working for a competitor of the claimant's but not otherwise.[145] So, for example, on the facts of *Lumley v Wagner* an injunction would be granted to prevent the defendant working for Mr Gye, a close rival of the claimant's, but would not be granted in respect of a theatre in, for example, northern England; the justification being that the claimant had a separate legitimate interest in preventing his audience being diverted to Gye's theatre. This has not found favour in England[146] and, while it will often arrive at the same decision as the preferred approach examined above, it fails to address sufficiently closely the problem of indirect specific performance; for to prevent the defendant working for any of the claimant's competitors may in practice leave no real choice but to work for the claimant.

(ii) Contracts for the sale of goods

The question of indirect specific performance has here arisen in relation to obligations not to buy one's requirements of particular goods other than from the claimant (requirements contracts), not to sell a particular output of goods other than to the claimant (output contracts), or not to distribute goods other than through the claimant (sole franchise/distributorship contracts).[147] Traditionally, specific performance of the positive obligations in such contracts would not be ordered because of the supposed adequacy of damages. The personal service or constant supervision bars are also sometimes in play. But the courts have generally been willing to grant injunctions restraining breach of the above 'negative' obligations, on the ground that this does not amount to indirect specific performance. Analogously to contracts of employment the unarticulated principle appears to be that so long as the defendant is left with more of a choice than either buying from/selling to the claimant or not carrying on any business at all the injunction does not amount to indirect specific performance.

As regards requirements contracts, there are several cases granting a prohibitory injunction restraining defendants from buying petrol for their service station[148] or beer for their pub[149] other than from the claimants. But the best-known authority is *Metropolitan Electric Supply Co Ltd v Ginder*.[150] An injunction was here granted restraining the defendant from breaking his promise not to take electricity from anyone but the claimant

---

[143] As in, eg, *General Billposting Co Ltd v Atkinson* [1909] AC 118; *Credit Suisse Asset Management Ltd v Armstrong* [1996] ICR 882; *Rock Refrigeration Ltd v Jones* [1997] ICR 938.
[144] *Evening Standard Co Ltd v Henderson* [1987] IRLR 64; *Provident Financial Group plc v Hayward* [1989] 3 All ER 298. The defendant under such an arrangement is described as being on 'garden leave'.
[145] Second Restatement of Contracts, para 367, illustration 4.
[146] See especially *Marco Productions v Pagola* [1945] KB 111.
[147] Again it is assumed that the obligation is not invalid under the restraint of trade doctrine.
[148] Eg *Texaco Ltd v Mulberry Filling Station Ltd* [1972] 1 WLR 814.
[149] Eg *Clegg v Hands* (1890) 44 Ch D 503.
[150] [1901] 2 Ch 799. This case also provides the classic example of terms being attached to an injunction to avoid any problems over want of mutuality, the condition attached being that the defendant could dissolve the injunction if the claimant failed to supply his requirements.

company. It was reasoned that this did not amount to forcing the defendant to take electricity from the claimants, since the defendant could, if he liked, use no energy at all or burn gas.

Donnell v Bennett[151] illustrates an injunction being granted in relation to what was in effect an output contract, being to sell to the claimant all the leftovers of fish not used by the defendant in his business. Fry J granted an injunction restraining the defendant from selling those leftovers to anyone else, albeit that he was clearly not totally convinced about the purported distinction between the injunction and specific performance.

Turning to sole distributorship/franchise contracts, in *Decro-Wall International SA v Practitioners in Marketing Ltd*[152] the claimants had contracted not to sell their goods in the UK to anyone other than the defendants. The Court of Appeal held that the defendants were entitled to an injunction to restrain breach of this negative promise, albeit that Salmon LJ recognised that '… the plaintiffs cannot be compelled to continue to supply the defendants until the termination of the contract'.[153] Similarly, in *Evans Marshall v Bertola SA*[154] the claimants had been appointed sole agents for the sale of the defendants' sherry in England under a long-term contract. They were granted an interim injunction restraining the defendants from breaking this contract by selling sherry other than through the claimants' agency. Sachs LJ applied *Warner Bros v Nelson* and the *Decro-Wall* case, and said, '… the specific performance of such an agreement will not be ordered, but it is no less plain that the courts will grant negative injunctions to encourage a party in breach to keep to his contract'.[155]

However, not all cases have adhered to the thin theoretical distinction being drawn between prohibitory injunctions and specific performance. The classic example is *Fothergill v Rowland*,[156] where the defendants had contracted to sell all of a particular seam of coal to the claimants. The claimants sought an injunction to prevent the defendants selling elsewhere, but this was refused on the ground that it amounted to indirect specific performance of a contract to sell non-unique goods, for which damages were adequate. This case can be regarded as equivalent to *Page One Records* and *Warren v Mendy* in the employment context, and as taking a more realistic view of the effect of the prohibitory injunction; for surely in almost all the above cases compliance with the prohibitory injunction would render it virtually certain that the defendant would perform his positive obligations to the claimant. In practical terms specific performance was being ordered.

But there is a final twist to the tale. It has been argued in chapter 22 that, whether because of commercial uniqueness or the difficulty of assessing damages, specific performance ought to be more readily granted than in the past in respect of long-term supply contracts such as these.[157] Therefore the actual decisions in these cases, now with the exception of *Fothergill v Rowland*, are to be welcomed, but on the basis that specific performance was in effect being ordered and was justified. Some commentators[158] have indeed used these cases as authorities on specific performance but, with the exception of *Fothergill v Rowland*, this would seem misleading, given that the reasoning took the opposite view.

---

[151] (1883) 22 Ch D 835.   [152] [1971] 1 WLR 361.
[153] ibid, at 372. Ultimately no injunction was necessary since the defendants gave an undertaking in the same terms.
[154] [1973] 1 WLR 349. See also *Thomas Borthwick v South Orago Freezing Co Ltd* [1978] 1 NZLR 538.
[155] [1973] 1 WLR 349, at 382.   [156] (1873) LR 17 Eq 132.   [157] Above, pp 405–409, 414–415.
[158] Eg E Peel, *Treitel on The Law of Contract* (14th edn, Sweet & Maxwell 2015) para 21-020.

(c) Stipulated remedy[159]

What effect will be given to a contractual term that the claimant should be entitled to an injunction for breach of a negative covenant? One of the few English cases dealing with this was *Warner Bros Pictures Inc v Nelson*.[160] In Branson J's words:

> '... parties cannot contract themselves out of the law; but it assists, in all events, on the question of evidence as to the applicability of an injunction in the present case, to find the parties formally recognising that in cases of this kind injunction is a more appropriate remedy than damages.'[161]

However, it is hard to see the courts attaching any real relevance to such a clause.[162] As has been indicated, true negative obligations are enforceable by prohibitory injunction as of course and hence irrespective of the parties agreeing on that remedy; and where the prohibitory injunction would in effect amount to specific performance of a contract that would not be directly specifically enforced it is hard to believe that the courts would allow such a clause to oust their refusal of the remedy.

A related but converse question is whether the existence of a liquidated damages clause will oust a prohibitory injunction that would otherwise be granted. Several cases show that the answer to this is in the negative,[163] and that the clause will rather be construed as indicating the amount of damages the claimant will recover if it sues for damages rather than an injunction. But in *General Accident Assurance Corpn v Noel*,[164] while this was agreed, it was held that the injunction and liquidated damages were exclusive remedies. While this must be correct as regards future loss, there seems no reason why liquidated damages for past loss and an injunction should not both be awarded, an approach adopted in the important Canadian case of *Elsley v J G Collins Insurance Agencies Ltd*.[165]

3. Final mandatory injunctions[166]

(1) Torts

The mandatory injunction—ordering the defendant to do something—is the appropriate remedy to remove the effects of a tort committed by the defendant; that is, it compels the defendant to undo the wrong. This function is conveniently and commonly emphasised by referring to the injunction as a mandatory restorative injunction. To give a couple of examples straightaway, in *Kelsen v Imperial Tobacco Co*,[167] the defendants were ordered to remove the advertising sign they had erected which was trespassing into the airspace above the claimant's shop; and in *Lawrence v Horton*,[168] the defendant was ordered to pull down buildings he had erected which obstructed the claimant's ancient lights. Conceivably a mandatory enforcing injunction could be granted to enforce a positive tort obligation. But given the rarity of such tort obligations, this injunction will be rare indeed, and there is no obvious example of its having been granted.

---

[159] See analogously above, pp 436–437.
[160] [1937] 1 KB 209. The best-known case in the US is *Stokes v Moore* 262 Ala 5977 (1955).
[161] [1937] 1 KB 209, at 221.
[162] But see the views of R Sharpe, *Injunctions and Specific Performance* (5th edn, Thomson Reuters 2017) paras 7.710–7.810; C Kyer, 'A Case Study in Party Stipulation of Remedy: the NHL Standard Player's Contract' (1981) 39 U of Tor Fac LR 1; S Rowan, 'For the Recognition of Remedial Terms Agreed Inter Partes' (2010) 126 LQR 448 (reprinted with light amendments in her *Remedies for Breach of Contract* (OUP 2012) ch 5).
[163] Eg *Jones v Heavens* (1877) 4 Ch D 636; *National Provincial Bank of England v Marshall* (1888) 40 Ch D 112.
[164] [1902] 1 KB 377.   [165] (1978) 83 DLR (3d) 1.
[166] *Quia timet* mandatory injunctions are discussed below, pp 467–469.   [167] [1957] 2 QB 334.
[168] (1890) 59 LJ Ch 440. See similarly *Allen v Greenwood* [1980] Ch 119.

The classic discussion of the general principles governing mandatory injunctions was Lord Upjohn's speech in *Redland Bricks v Morris*[169] though his controversial view that the injunction in issue was *quia timet*[170] meant that he included some principles that were relevant only to *quia timet* mandatory injunctions. The injunction being sought was for steps to be taken by the defendants to restore support to the claimant's land. The House of Lords discharged the mandatory injunction that had been granted—that the defendants '... do take all necessary steps to restore the support to the plaintiff's land within a period of six months'—because it left as too uncertain what the defendants were required to do. Lord Upjohn said, 'If ... it is a proper case to grant a mandatory injunction, then the court must be careful to see that the defendant knows exactly in fact what he has to do ...'[171] So uncertainty is a bar to mandatory injunctions as it is to specific performance and prohibitory injunctions. But in his espousal of the general principles, what is particularly important is that Lord Upjohn clearly accepted that a mandatory injunction is not granted as readily as a prohibitory injunction. He said, 'The grant of a mandatory injunction is, of course, entirely discretionary, and unlike a negative injunction can never be "as of course".'[172] The antipathy of the courts to positive orders is therefore shown in this area, as in relation to specific performance for breach of contract. Again, the desire not to undermine the claimant's duty to mitigate, and not to restrict unduly the defendant's freedom of action may be suggested as the root objections. There are also express indications in some cases that the argument that non-monetary remedies give the claimant too much of an advantage in pre- and post-judgment bargaining does here weigh with the courts. For example, in *Isenberg v East India House Estate Co Ltd*[173] Lord Westbury, in refusing an injunction to compel the defendant to pull down a building which interfered only slightly with the claimant's ancient lights, said that the court would not grant a mandatory injunction which would deliver 'the Defendants to the Plaintiff bound hand and foot, in order to be made subject to any extortionate demand that he may by possibility make'.[174]

So it is the case that, while the injunction may be the better remedy for the claimant, damages (in lieu) are generally regarded as sufficient and are the primary remedy. A fortiori, no mandatory injunction will generally be granted where the tortious interference is merely trivial.[175]

Furthermore, hardship to the defendant is here a bar. So, in dicta in *Pride of Derby v British Celanese*,[176] Lord Evershed commented '... the court will not impose ... an obligation to do something which is impossible, or which cannot be enforced, or which is unlawful.' The leading authority is again *Redland Bricks v Morris*, where Lord Upjohn indicated that hardship can here be a very wide restriction since, even in contrast to specific performance,

---

[169] [1970] AC 652. [170] Above, pp 442–443.
[171] [1970] AC 652, at 666. See also *Kennard v Cory Bros Co Ltd* [1922] 1 Ch 265, at 274 (per Sargant J), [1922] 2 Ch 1, at 13 (per Warrington LJ).
[172] [1970] AC 652, at 665. See also *Durell v Pritchard* (1865) 1 Ch App 244, at 250, and cases on breach of contract, below, pp 465–466. It is therefore misleading to say as some judges have—eg in *Smith v Smith* (1875) LR 20 Eq 500, and *Davies v Gas Light and Coke Co* [1909] 1 Ch 708—that the same principles govern mandatory as prohibitory injunctions.
[173] (1863) 3 De GJ & Sm 263. See also *Senior v Pawson* (1866) LR 3 Eq 330.
[174] (1863) 3 De GJ & Sm 263, at 273.
[175] *Isenberg v East India House Estate Co Ltd* (1863) 3 De GJ & Sm 263; *Colls v Home & Colonial Stores Ltd* [1904] AC 179; *Tollemache and Cobbold Breweries Ltd v Reynolds* (1983) 268 Estates Gazette 52; *Ketley v Gooden* (1997) 73 P & CR 305. Cf *Kelsen v Imperial Tobacco Co* [1957] 2 QB 334. In *London Borough of Harrow v Donohue* [1995] 1 EGLR 257, it was held that a different approach applies where the defendant has trespassed on a claimant's land by erecting a building: as a claimant in that situation is entitled to a possession order (see below, p 583), it was held that a claimant must, alternatively, have the right to choose a mandatory restorative injunction irrespective of the adequacy of damages.
[176] [1953] Ch 149, at 181.

the test can be a relative one; that is, so long as the defendant has acted reasonably, albeit wrongly, the courts can weigh the burden to him against the benefit to the claimant. In Lord Upjohn's words:

> '... the amount to be expended under a mandatory order by the defendant must be balanced ... against the anticipated possible damage to the plaintiff and if, on such balance, it seems unreasonable to inflict such expenditure ... then the court must exercise its jurisdiction accordingly.'[177]

Applying this to the facts, it was held that a mandatory injunction ordering the defendants to carry out the restoration work as described by the claimant's expert, while probably overcoming the uncertainty objection so long as set out in detail, would impose an excessive burden on the defendant who had acted reasonably and should not be granted; such work might cost £35,000, while the value of the claimant's land affected by the slip was only about £1,500.

On the other hand, Lord Upjohn made plain that no sympathy will be shown for a defendant who has tried 'to steal a march' on the claimant, or who has otherwise acted 'wantonly and quite unreasonably'.[178] Indeed in this situation, the courts appear to go to the opposite extreme, and to be only too willing to grant even an interim mandatory injunction against the defendant, revealing, seemingly, a punitive approach. For example, in *Daniel v Ferguson*,[179] on receiving notice of the claimant's complaint that the building being constructed would interfere with his ancient lights, the defendant doubled his efforts to have the building completed before any court order could be made. In view of this attempt 'to steal a march', the court granted an interim mandatory injunction ordering that that part of the building, which allegedly interfered with the claimant's rights, should be pulled down.

Consideration must finally be given to the constant supervision objection, which has traditionally been regarded as a bar to mandatory injunctions.[180] As with specific performance, however, the restriction has not always found favour. In this regard *Kennard v Cory Bros & Co Ltd*,[181] the 'moving mountain' case, is instructive, for while the Court of Appeal purported to accept the constant supervision objection, it indicated a lack of genuine support for it. The defendants argued that to order them to unblock a particular drain in the remedial works built to help prevent further landslides would in effect mean that they would be recognised as having a continuing obligation to repair and maintain those remedial works. As such the constant supervision objection would be infringed. While much of the judicial discussion focused on uncertainty, rather than constant supervision itself, the court rejected the above argument and stressed that the limited nature of the order being made meant that the constant supervision objection was inapplicable. But the judges were seemingly not enamoured of that objection. Lord Sterndale MR, after citing *Ryan v Mutual Tontine Westminster Chambers Association*,[182] the classic specific performance authority on

---

[177] [1970] AC 652, at 666. See also *Kelk v Pearson* (1871) 6 Ch App 809, at 812; *National Provincial Plate Glass Insurance Co v Prudential Assurance Co* (1877) 6 Ch D 757, at 761; *Rileys v Halifax Corpn* (1907) 97 LT 278; *Sharp v Harrison* [1922] 1 Ch 502 (breach of contract). In dicta in *Gravesham Borough Council v British Railways Board* [1978] Ch 379, at 405, the benefit to *the public of* the injunction was balanced against its hardship to the defendants.
[178] [1970] AC 652, at 666. See also *Colls v Home and Colonial Stores Ltd* [1904] AC 179; *Pugh v Howells* (1984) 48 P & CR 298; *Ottercroft Ltd v Scandia Care Ltd* [2016] EWCA Civ 867.
[179] [1891] 2 Ch 27. See also *Von Joel v Hornsey* [1895] 2 Ch 774; *Esso Petroleum Co Ltd v Kingswood Motors Ltd* [1974] QB 142.
[180] *Powell Duffryn Steam Coal Co v Taff Vale Rly Co* (1874) 9 Ch App 331; *Attorney-General v Staffordshire County Council* [1905] 1 Ch 336.
[181] [1922] 2 Ch 1.   [182] [1893] 1 Ch 116.

constant supervision, could not find '... any objection in principle to the imposition of such [a continuous] obligation upon a wrongdoer';[183] and in Scrutton LJ's words, '... the Court will in some cases make an order which involves future maintenance ... when and though that involves that applications from time to time may have to be made to the Court to supervise the carrying out of the order.'[184]

Moreover, even though constant supervision has traditionally been a bar to mandatory injunctions, one can strongly argue that, as some recent cases on specific performance suggest, it should no longer be so regarded. This indeed, was part of an argument considered in *Gravesham Borough Council v British Railways Board*,[185] where the cause of action was probably best viewed as tortious. One question was whether a mandatory enforcing injunction should be granted, assuming breach of a common law duty to maintain ferry crossings at reasonable times over the Thames. The objection put by the defendants was that this would necessitate a series of acts requiring the continuous employment of people over a number of years in a losing business.[186] Although this is not quite the same as just the constant supervision objection, counsel for the claimants argued that as some recent cases, such as *Tito v Waddell (No 2)*,[187] had suggested that there was no longer a constant supervision objection to specific performance, so, analogously, the court should be willing to grant a mandatory injunction even though this would require continuously employing people. Slade J's reaction to that argument was not entirely clear. On the one hand, in the light of the authorities, he accepted that '... it cannot be regarded, as an absolute and inflexible rule that the court will never grant an injunction requiring a person to do a series of acts requiring the continuous employment of people over a number of years'.[188] But he went on to say that he would still have refused the injunction if there had been a breach of duty inter alia because of the '... risk of potential practical difficulties in regard to enforcement arising from the grant of an injunction compelling British Rail to operate its ferry service to a particular timetable'.[189] This ultimately seems to represent an acceptance of the constant supervision objection. If so this is unfortunate; for, as discussed in relation to specific performance[190]—and despite the approval of the constant supervision objection to specific performance by the House of Lords in *Co-operative Insurance Society Ltd v Argyll Stores (Holdings) Ltd*[191]—the policy reasons for this objection are weak and calls for its removal should be supported. The better justification for the refusal of the mandatory injunction in the *Gravesham* case is that, whether as an aspect of hardship or as a separate bar, the courts will not order a defendant to carry on with a losing business.

(2) Breach of contract

At first sight, one might expect that the mandatory injunction would be the appropriate remedy to enforce a positive contractual promise—that is, a promise to do something. But other than at the interlocutory stage,[192] this role is entirely taken over by the remedy of specific performance.[193] This leaves the mandatory restorative

---

[183] [1922] 2 Ch 1, at 13.   [184] ibid, at 21.   [185] [1978] Ch 379.
[186] See also *Attorney-General v Colchester Corpn* [1955] 2 QB 207.   [187] [1977] Ch 106.
[188] [1978] Ch 379, at 405.   [189] ibid.   [190] Above, pp 418–419.
[191] [1998] AC 1. Above, pp 418–419.
[192] Below, pp 469, 482. Specific performance is a final remedy only.
[193] Viewed from this angle, it is perhaps surprising that specific performance developed as a separate remedy, since the mandatory injunction could have fulfilled its entire role.

injunction as the appropriate remedy for removing the effects of, that is for undoing, what the defendant has done in breach of a negative contractual promise, just as it is for undoing a tort.

The leading case in the contractual sphere is *Shepherd Homes Ltd v Sandham*,[194] even though what was there being sought was an *interim* mandatory injunction to remove a fence that the claimant alleged had been erected in breach of a restrictive covenant. Ultimately the injunction was refused, Megarry J stressing that the courts are particularly reluctant to grant interim mandatory injunctions and would not do so here, where it was unclear whether a mandatory injunction would be granted at trial, and where the claimant had delayed in bringing his application.

In discussing the relevant principles—which should be the same as those for torts (set out in the previous subsection)—Megarry J contrasted *Doherty v Allman*[195] and said that a mandatory injunction was not as easy to obtain as a prohibitory injunction.[196] Put another way, damages (in lieu) are generally regarded as sufficient and are the primary remedy. As regards specific bars Megarry J preferred not to try to particularise all the grounds upon which a mandatory injunction might be refused but he said that they at least included '... the triviality of the damage to the plaintiff and the existence of a disproportion between the detriment that the injunction would inflict on the defendant, and the benefit that it would confer on the plaintiff'.[197] The former is illustrated by *Sharp v Harrison*[198] where a mandatory injunction to remove a window overlooking the claimant's property and built in breach of a restrictive covenant was refused, since little or no interference was being caused. The latter is the important 'hardship' bar, which was also clearly recognised in *Sharp v Harrison* in a passage cited with approval by Megarry J. An example of its application, coupled with a desire to uphold the public interest, is *Wrotham Park Estate Co Ltd v Parkside Homes Ltd*.[199] There a mandatory injunction ordering the defendants to knock down a housing estate built in breach of a restrictive covenant (enforceable by the claimant in equity) was refused and damages awarded, because the court wished to avoid 'an unpardonable waste of much needed houses'.[200] By analogy to mandatory injunctions for torts and specific performance one would expect that of the bars not mentioned by Megarry J uncertainty would be the most important; it must be possible for a clear order to be made.

Of course all this does not mean that a mandatory injunction will never be granted to remove the effects of the breach of a negative promise. In *Charrington v Simons & Co Ltd*,[201] for example, the Court of Appeal granted a mandatory injunction ordering the defendant to remove a tarmac farm road the height of which contravened a restrictive covenant with the claimant; and in *Wakeham v Wood*[202] where, in flagrant disregard of a restrictive covenant (enforceable by the claimant in equity) and of the claimant's complaints, the defendant had erected a building that obscured the claimant's sea-view, the Court of Appeal distinguished *Wrotham Park*, albeit not very convincingly, and ordered the defendant to remove so much of the building as obscured the view.

---

[194] [1971] Ch 340. [195] (1878) 3 App Cas 709. [196] See also *Sharp v Harrison* [1922] 1 Ch 502.
[197] [1971] Ch 340. [198] [1922] 1 Ch 502.
[199] [1974] 1 WLR 798. See also *Gafford v Graham* [1999] 3 EGLR 75 (refusal to grant mandatory injunction to pull down riding school).
[200] [1974] 1 WLR 798, at 811. [201] [1971] 1 WLR 598.
[202] (1982) 43 P & CR 40. See also *Mortimer v Bailey* [2004] EWCA Civ 1514, [2005] 2 P & CR 9 (breach of restrictive covenant).

4. Final *quia timet* injunctions

(1) Torts

A *quia timet* injunction is granted where no wrong has yet been committed. The commonest type is a prohibitory injunction to restrain wrongful acts which the defendant has not before committed. Although there is no reason why such an injunction should not be ordered to restrain the commission of any tort, most cases concern nuisance. To give a couple of examples of such an injunction being ordered, in *Dicker v Popham Radford & Co*[203] a *quia timet* injunction was granted to restrain the defendant from continuing a building which when completed would infringe the claimant's right to light; and in *Goodhart v Hyatt*,[204] where the claimant had the right to have water pipes running through the defendant's land, a *quia timet* injunction was granted preventing the defendant from continuing with building work which would interfere with the claimant's access to the pipes.[205]

Far less common is a mandatory *quia timet* injunction, ordering positive steps to be taken to prevent earlier actions causing a wrong. The example that most obviously comes to mind is the removal of support from a neighbour's land where no subsidence of that land, and hence no tort of nuisance, has yet taken place.[206] So in *Hooper v Rogers*,[207] where the defendant's work in deepening a farm-track cut out of a slope threatened the foundations of the claimant's house standing at the top of the slope, the Court of Appeal held that a mandatory *quia timet* injunction to reinstate the natural angle of the slope could have been ordered and that the trial judge had therefore had jurisdiction to award damages in lieu.

The principles examined earlier dictating whether an ordinary injunction will be granted for tort apply in just the same way where the injunction is *quia timet*. This means, most importantly, that it will be easier to obtain a prohibitory than a mandatory *quia timet* injunction.

But the crucial importance of an injunction being classified as *quia timet* is that, as against ordinary injunctions where these requirements are presumed,[208] the claimant must show that the tort is highly probable to occur and to occur imminently. As Lord Dunedin said in *Attorney-General for Canada v Ritchie Contracting and Supply Co Ltd*,[209] 'it is not sufficient to say "timeo"'.

As regards the first requirement Chitty J in *Attorney-General v Manchester Corpn*[210] said, 'The principle which I think may be properly and safely extracted from the *quia timet* authorities is that the plaintiff must show a strong case of probability that the apprehended mischief will, in fact, arise';[211] and as the claimant could not so establish that a smallpox hospital when built would contravene statutory regulations, no *quia timet* injunction was granted. Again in *Pattisson v Gilford*[212] a *quia timet* injunction restraining the defendant from selling, for building, land over which the claimant had shooting rights was refused

---

[203] (1890) 63 LT 379.   [204] (1883) 25 Ch D 182.
[205] A more recent example is *Torquay Hotel & Co Ltd v Cousins* [1969] 2 Ch 106 (interim *quia timet* injunction to prevent tort of inducing breach of contract).
[206] See also *Express Newspapers plc v Mitchell* [1982] IRLR 465 (interim injunction ordering a trade union official to withdraw a strike notice that if acted on would constitute the tort of inducing breach of contract).
[207] [1975] Ch 43.
[208] The presumption can be rebutted: eg *Proctor v Bayley* (1889) 42 Ch D 390; *Race Relations Board v Applin* [1973] QB 815.
[209] [1919] AC 999, at 1005.
[210] [1893] 2 Ch 87. See also *Attorney-General v Kingston-on-Thames Corpn* (1865) 34 LJ Ch 481; *Attorney-General v Nottingham Corpn* [1904] 1 Ch 673.
[211] [1893] 2 Ch 87, at 92.   [212] (1874) LR 18 Eq 259.

because it had not been shown that building on the land would 'necessarily and inevitably'[213] interfere with those shooting rights; and in *Redland Bricks v Morris*[214] Lord Upjohn said that a mandatory *quia timet* injunction '... can only be granted where the plaintiff shows a very strong probability upon the facts that grave damage will accrue to him in the future.'[215] In *Hooper v Rogers*,[216] although it was found on the facts that future damage was a proven probability, Russell LJ criticised the need to show always that the tort is highly probable to occur when he said, 'In truth, it seems to me that the degree of probability of future injury is not an absolute standard: what is to be aimed at is justice between the parties, having regard to all the relevant circumstances.'[217] It can also be argued that a *quia timet* injunction does no harm to a law-abiding defendant. But granting such injunctions too readily may unduly hamper a defendant's freedom of action and may encourage excessive litigation and it is submitted that for such reasons the present high degree of probability should be retained as a requirement.

In other cases the stress has been on the tort being very likely to occur *imminently*. In *Fletcher v Bealey*,[218] for example, the claimant sought an injunction to prevent the dumping of 'vat-waste', his fear being that noxious liquid would flow from the waste into a river thereby causing him a nuisance. Pearson J refused the injunction and said that 'imminent danger'[219] must be proved. But his decision could equally be said to rest on the fact that the tort was not sufficiently likely to occur, for he stressed that it was quite possible for the defendants to prevent liquid flowing into the river, and in any case, they might find a means of rendering that liquid innocuous. Again in *Lemos v Kennedy Leigh Development Co*,[220] the claimant's application for a *quia timet* mandatory injunction ordering the removal of his neighbour's tree roots, which he alleged would cause damage to his land, was dismissed because the apprehended danger was not imminent. Finally, in the most recent and, it is submitted, sensible discussion of this requirement in *Hooper v Rogers*,[221] Russell LJ said that it meant that the action should not be premature, and that it would not be where, as in that case (and in contrast to *Fletcher v Bealey*) no other step could be taken to avoid the damage. So although subsidence of the claimant's house, following the defendant's removal of support, might not occur for many years, it was held that a mandatory *quia timet* injunction could have been granted and hence damages in lieu were justified.

(2) Breach of contract

The role of *quia timet* injunctions for breach of contract is unclear. This lack of clarity stems from the technicalities of the English doctrine of 'anticipatory breach'. According to that doctrine, an anticipatory breach does not constitute a breach unless and until it is accepted by the innocent party as terminating the contract. On that technical approach, an injunction to prevent a threatened breach of contract, where there has been no actual failure to perform, would class as a *quia timet* injunction.[222] But the better approach is to say that an anticipatory breach is automatically a breach of contract because it constitutes a breach of the implied promise to be ready, able, and willing to perform. On that better approach,

---

[213] ibid, at 264. [214] [1970] AC 652.
[215] ibid, at 665. Presumably 'grave' damage is stressed because a mandatory injunction was in issue.
[216] [1975] Ch 43. [217] ibid, at 50. [218] (1885) 28 Ch D 688. [219] ibid, at 698.
[220] (1961) 105 Sol Jo 178. See also *Lord Cowley v Byas* (1877) 5 Ch D 944; *Draper v British Optical Association* [1938] 1 All ER 115.
[221] [1975] Ch 43.
[222] See, eg, I Spry, *Equitable Remedies* (9th edn, Sweet & Maxwell 2014) 394–395 (and 80–81).

there are no *quia timet* injunctions for breach of contract because a threatened breach is itself a breach of contract.

5. Interim injunctions

Interim injunctions, which may be prohibitory or mandatory, *quia timet* or not *quia timet*, are injunctions given prior to trial or other hearing in which final judgment is given, and are intended to last until the trial at the latest. Although temporary in this sense their advantage, as against final injunctions, is that they can be obtained quickly: indeed in some situations, such as where the claimant seeks to prevent a particular threatened act, it would be too late for the claimant to wait until trial.

In contrast to, for example, a freezing injunction,[223] an ordinary interim injunction is within the scope of this book, since it is not best viewed as being concerned to aid the enforcement of other remedies, that is, as being concerned to enable a final injunction to be effective. Rather it is designed to protect, where justified, the claimant's alleged rights during the inevitable delay before trial, and this is so even where an injunction at trial can effectively protect those rights from then on without an interim injunction having been granted.

So as a remedy for torts and breach of contract an interim injunction fulfils analogous functions to a final injunction, but does so more quickly. For example, an interim prohibitory injunction is the appropriate remedy pre-trial to prevent an alleged continuing or recurring tort. In one respect, however, an interim injunction plays a wider role than a final injunction; for prior to trial, an interim mandatory injunction is the appropriate remedy to enforce a positive contractual obligation, whereas specific performance rather than a mandatory injunction would be granted at trial.

The fact that an interim injunction is granted at an earlier stage of proceedings means that different principles must be applied in deciding whether to grant this sort of injunction than a final injunction. In *American Cyanamid Co v Ethicon Ltd*[224] the House of Lords controversially reformulated the principles governing interim injunctions. However, in order to understand *American Cyanamid*, it is first necessary to consider briefly the law prior to it.

(1) The law prior to *American Cyanamid*

What should be stressed straightaway is that not all cases adopted the same approach to interim injunctions.[225] Nevertheless, as shown for example by the House of Lords in *Stratford & Son Ltd v Lindley*,[226] and at first instance and by the Court of Appeal in *American Cyanamid*[227] itself, a claimant generally needed to show: first, a prima facie case[228] both that the defendant was committing or was intending to commit a wrong against the claimant and (apparently) that the claimant would be entitled to a final injunction at trial for that wrong: and, secondly, that the balance of convenience favoured an interim injunction. Furthermore, given the uncertainty as to whether the granting of an injunction would turn out to have been unjustified, the court almost invariably insisted, as a condition of granting

---

[223] Below, p 485. [224] [1975] AC 396.
[225] See, eg, *Hubbard v Vosper* [1972] 2 QB 84. Interim injunctions pending appeals were also treated differently, as they still are: *Polini v Gray* (1879) 11 Ch D 741; *Orion Property Trust Ltd v Du Cane Court Ltd* [1962] 1 WLR 1085; *Erinford Properties Ltd v Cheshire County Council* [1974] Ch 261.
[226] [1965] AC 269. [227] [1974] FSR 312.
[228] Often a strong prima facie case was required: *Challender v Royal* (1887) 36 Ch D 425; *Smith v Grigg Ltd* [1924] 1 KB 655, at 659.

an interim injunction, that the claimant should give an undertaking to pay damages for any unjustifiable loss caused to the defendant in complying with the injunction.[229]

While the courts often talked of a prima facie case solely in relation to the defendant committing or intending to commit a wrong, it does appear to have been impliedly accepted that there must also be a prima facie case for a final injunction at trial. Certainly this is how Lord Diplock interpreted the approach of Graham J and of the Court of Appeal in *American Cyanamid*. He said that they had thought there was a rule:

> '... that the court is not entitled to take any account of the balance of convenience unless it has first been satisfied that if the case went to trial upon no other evidence than is before the court at the hearing of the application the plaintiff would be entitled to *judgment for a permanent injunction* in the same terms as the interlocutory injunction sought.'[230]

In essence then, the first requirement was that the courts undertook a 'mini-trial' of the dispute, according to the evidence and arguments then available to it.

Assessing the balance of convenience, on the other hand, required the court to do what was most just, on the assumption that it could not at the pre-trial stage decide on the merits whether an injunction was justified or not. The main factors taken into account in deciding this were whether damages would adequately compensate either party for any interim unjustifiable loss, and whether in general terms it would cause greater hardship to grant or refuse the injunction. It was also sometimes said that the courts would prefer to maintain the status quo: but this was ambiguous, since any one of several different positions could be regarded as the status quo, for example, the position at trial or the position prior to the issue of proceedings or the position prior to the alleged wrong. Moreover, there was no obvious justification for such a preference.[231]

What is perhaps particularly significant about the old law is that, at least in more recent times, it was the first mini-trial hurdle that parties regarded as the most important aspect of the interim application. In the words of Hammond, 'Counsel began to use the interlocutory injunction as a means of providing a rapid and relatively cheap method of arbitration of disputes.'[232] So even where it would not be too late to challenge the interim decision at trial, cases very rarely proceeded to trial (even as regards a claim for damages) because the parties accepted what was decided regarding the prima facie case as indicative of the trial outcome and settled accordingly. Indeed it has been said that 99% of cases in which the interim injunction was sought did not proceed to trial.[233] The parties' attitude was also reflected or, more arguably, inspired by the courts' refusal to treat the two requirements as rigidly sequential steps, and their consequent tendency to treat the balance of convenience as subsidiary to the strength of the claimant's case. So, for example, if the claimant had established a very strong prima facie case, the judges seemed happy to ignore the balance of

---

[229] The requirement of a cross-undertaking in damages remains applicable after *American Cyanamid*. The principles governing such damages are discussed in *Hoffmann-La Roche & Co AG v Secretary of State for Trade and Industry* [1975] AC 295, at 361. That case principally lays down that, where seeking to enforce the law, the Crown cannot be required to give such an undertaking. The same applies to other public authorities seeking interim injunctions to enforce the law: *Kirklees Metropolitan BC v Wickes Building Supplies Ltd* [1993] AC 227; *Financial Services Authority v Sinaloa Gold Plc* [2013] UKSC 11, [2013] 2 AC 28. For rejection of the argument that a defendant can recover, on a cross-undertaking in damages, not only for its own loss but also the loss of third parties, see *Smithkline Beecham Plc v Apotex Europe Ltd* [2006] EWCA Civ 658, [2007] Ch 71. See generally S Gee, 'The Undertaking in Damages' [2006] LMCLQ 181.
[230] [1975] AC 396, at 407 (author's italics).
[231] This remains a problem post-*Cyanamid*; below, pp 473–474. See R Sharpe, *Injunctions and Specific Performance* (5th edn, Thomson Reuters 2017) para 2.550.
[232] R Hammond, 'Interlocutory Injunctions: Time for a New Model?' (1980) 30 UTLJ 240, 251.
[233] *Fellowes & Son v Fisher* [1976] QB 122, at 133 (per Lord Denning).

convenience altogether. As Prescott wrote in 1975, '… in recent times the tendency has been to adopt a more robust attitude, and to be guided more and more by the apparent strength or otherwise of the plaintiff's case as revealed by the affidavits.'[234]

(2) *American Cyanamid v Ethicon*[235]

Lord Diplock, in a speech agreed with by the other Lords, here sought to put a stop to the approach of regarding the interim application as a mini-trial. The claimants were seeking an interim *quia timet* injunction to prevent the defendants marketing in Great Britain sterile sutures which they alleged infringed their patent. At first instance Graham J granted the injunction on the basis that the claimants had made out a prima facie case, and that the balance of convenience favoured them. But on appeal this was overturned, the Court of Appeal holding that the claimants had failed to make out a prima facie case. The House of Lords restored the first instance decision but on different reasoning, which was as follows.

First, the claimant must establish that there is a serious question to be tried; in other words, that its claim is not frivolous or vexatious. But it should *not* be required to establish a prima facie case.

Secondly, assuming that it establishes that there is a serious question, the claimant must go on to show that the balance of convenience favours granting the interim injunction. In assessing this, the following sequential approach should be adopted:

(i) The court should ask whether damages would adequately compensate the claimant for its interim loss and whether the defendant could pay them. If the answer is yes, the interim injunction should not be granted.

(ii) However, if the answer is no, the court should ask whether damages payable under the claimant's undertaking would adequately compensate the defendant for its interim loss and whether the claimant could pay them. If yes, there is a strong case for the interim injunction.

(iii) If, however, there is doubt as to the adequacy of the respective damages, the case turns on the balance of convenience generally. The main factor is whether it would cause greater hardship to grant or to refuse the injunction—or as Lord Diplock phrased it, 'the extent of the uncompensatable disadvantage to each party'.[236] Where this and other considerations are evenly balanced, two factors that can be taken into account as a last resort are, first, the desirability of maintaining the status quo and, secondly, the strength of one party's case being disproportionate to that of the other.

Applying this approach to the facts, an interim injunction was granted because, first, it was a serious question whether the defendants were infringing a patent of the claimants so as to entitle the claimants to a final injunction at trial; and, secondly, the balance of convenience favoured the grant of the interim injunction, particularly since the claimants' monopoly of the market would effectively be destroyed for ever if the interim injunction were refused.

Consideration of the parties' ability to pay damages, and the sequential structuring of the approach to the balance of convenience, with the adequacy of damages first having to be

---

[234] P Prescott, '*American Cyanamid v Ethicon Ltd*' (1975) 91 LQR 168, 169 (note).
[235] [1975] AC 396. W Baker, 'Interlocutory Injunctions – A Discussion of the New Rules' (1977) 42 Sask LR 53.
[236] [1975] AC 396, at 409.

looked at and in itself possibly resolving which way the balance lies, are two changes *American Cyanamid* made from the previous law. But the crucial change is that the claimant does not first have to establish a prima facie case. The much lower threshold of a serious question to be tried is all that needs to be satisfied, and the strength of the claimant's case is relevant only as a last resort within the balance of convenience. In Sharpe's words, '... the strength of case consideration of the traditional approach is stood on its head.'[237] The policy behind this is that the interim application should *not* serve as a mini-trial, in which the merits of the dispute are judged, since evidence is merely on affidavit, rather than being oral and subject to cross-examination. Nor are the legal arguments fully presented. The aim is to restore the interim injunction to its supposedly true function of protecting the claimant during the period of uncertainty before trial, where this is justified on the balance of convenience. In Lord Diplock's words:

> 'It is no part of the court's function at this stage of the litigation to try to resolve conflicts of evidence on affidavits as to facts on which the claim of either party may ultimately depend nor to decide difficult questions of law which call for detailed argument and mature consideration. These are matters to be dealt with at the trial.'[238]

Subsequent case law has further clarified the *American Cyanamid* principles.

So it was emphasised by Browne LJ in *Smith v Inner London Education Authority*[239] that the three phrases Lord Diplock used to describe the initial hurdle—'a serious question to be tried', 'not frivolous or vexatious', 'a real prospect of succeeding at the trial'[240]—are all ways of phrasing the same test; and although a relatively easy threshold to cross, there have been cases, *Smith* being one,[241] where a claimant has been denied an interim injunction for failure to overcome it.

In very few cases has the grant or refusal of the interim injunction been decided by the adequacy of damages for either the claimant or the defendant. Even where the courts have been willing to rest their decisions on this—as in *Foseco International v Fordath*,[242] where it was held that damages would adequately compensate the defendants and could be paid by the claimants, and *Roussel-Uclaf v GD Searle & Co*,[243] where damages were thought adequate for the claimant—they have gone on to justify their decision according to the general balance of convenience. This feature is hardly surprising. Adequacy is such an elusive concept that permissible reliance on other factors is almost always to be preferred.[244]

Only factors concerning the parties were traditionally thought to be relevant within the balance of convenience, an approach which was consistent with that for final prohibitory injunctions, where the public interest has not been allowed to override private rights. But in *Smith v ILEA* Browne LJ, in dicta, said that where the defendant was a local authority the court should take into account the interests of the public within the balance

---

[237] R Sharpe, *Injunctions and Specific Performance* (5th edn, Thomson Reuters 2017) para 2.140.
[238] [1975] AC 396, at 407.   [239] [1978] 1 All ER 411.
[240] [1975] AC 396, at 407–408. But it may be doubted whether 'a real prospect of success' sets as low a threshold as 'a serious question to be tried': see *Cream Holdings Ltd v Banerjee* [2003] EWCA Civ 103, [2003] Ch 650.
[241] Also, *Re Lord Cable* [1977] 1 WLR 7; *Morning Star Co-operative Society Ltd v Express Newspapers Ltd* [1979] FSR 113; *Associated British Ports v TGWU* [1989] 3 All ER 822.
[242] [1975] FSR 507; *Laws v Florinplace Ltd* [1981] 1 All ER 659.   [243] [1977] FSR 125.
[244] In *B v D* [2014] EWCA Civ 229, [2015] 1 WLR 771 the Court of Appeal held that a party could plead that damages were inadequate despite the fact that the reason they were inadequate was an agreement to limit their amount.

of convenience.[245] This has also been applied even where the defendant was not a public authority. In *Roussel-Uclaf v GD Searle & Co* the detriment to the public of being deprived of a life-saving drug was considered the major factor in deciding that the balance of convenience lay against the injunction; and in several industrial dispute cases,[246] the courts have regarded the detrimental impact of strike action on the public as a factor weighting the balance of convenience in favour of granting an interim injunction, thereby further curtailing the right to strike. It is also relevant here to mention *R v Secretary of State for Transport, ex p Factortame (No 2)*,[247] in which it was held by the House of Lords that, where an interim injunction is sought to restrain the enforcement by the Secretary of State of an English statute on the grounds that it is invalid under European Union law, the public interest in the enforcement of what, on the face of it, is the law of the land requires that no injunction should normally be granted unless the claimant establishes a strong prima facie case of invalidity. In contrast to Lord Jauncey, Lord Goff, giving the leading speech, saw this approach as not affecting the initial threshold to be crossed under *Cyanamid* but as going instead to the balance of convenience.[248]

Sir John Donaldson MR in *Francome v Mirror Group Newspapers Ltd*[249] expressed preference for the term 'balance of justice' as against 'balance of convenience'; and May LJ made a similar comment in *Cayne v Global Natural Resources plc*.[250] But it is hard to see what possible advantage there would be in such a change of terminology.

What is meant by the status quo has been discussed in several cases subsequent to *American Cyanamid*. In *Fellowes v Fisher*[251] Sir John Pennycuick regarded it as the position prior to the wrong, and this was supported by Geoffrey Lane LJ in *Budget Rent A Car International Inc v Mamos Slough Ltd*.[252] In *Alfred Dunhills v Sunoptic*[253] Megaw LJ took the rather vague view that '... the relevant point in time for the purposes of the "status quo" may well vary in different cases'. Lord Diplock attempted to clarify authoritatively what is meant in *Garden Cottage Foods Ltd v Milk Marketing Board*,[254] but his approach is far from simple:

> '... the relevant status quo to which reference was made in *American Cyanamid* is the state of affairs existing during the period immediately preceding the issue of the writ claiming the permanent injunction, or if there be unreasonable delay between the issue of writ and the motion for an interlocutory injunction the period immediately preceding the motion. The duration of that period since the state of affairs last changed must be more than minimal, having regard to the total length of the relationship between the parties in respect of which the injunction was granted; otherwise the state of affairs before the last change would be the relevant status quo.'[255]

---

[245] See also *R v Ministry of Agriculture, ex p Monsanto* [1999] QB 1161 where the main application was for judicial review of a public authority's approval of a rival company's product and interim relief, by way of a stay of the approval, was sought pending the decision of the European Court of Justice.
[246] *Star Sea Transport Corpn of Monrovia v Slater* [1978] IRLR 507; *Beaverbrook Newspapers Ltd v Keys* [1978] ICR 582; *NWL Ltd v Woods* [1979] 1 WLR 1294; *Duport Steel Ltd v Sirs* [1980] ICR 161.
[247] [1991] 1 AC 603.
[248] In *R v Secretary of State for Health, ex p Imperial Tobacco Ltd* [2001] 1 WLR 127, the House of Lords left unresolved the question whether domestic law or EU law applies to determine whether an interim injunction should be granted restraining the Secretary of State from making regulations to implement an allegedly invalid directive.
[249] [1984] 1 WLR 892. In *Attorney-General v Observer Newspapers Ltd* [1986] NLJ Rep 799 he preferred the term 'balance of inconvenience'.
[250] [1984] 1 All ER 225.   [251] [1976] QB 122.   [252] (1977) 121 Sol Jo 374.
[253] [1979] FSR 337.   [254] [1984] AC 130.
[255] ibid, at 140. Cf *Graham v Delderfield* [1992] FSR 313 where it was held to be the position at the date of the service, rather than at the date of the issue of the writ, that fixed the status quo.

These differences of judicial opinion serve to confirm the view that the preference expressed for maintaining the status quo lacks sound justification.

Finally, it has been argued by Gray that, irrespective of exceptions to *American Cyanamid*:

> 'A judge should be able to reach the same conclusion by applying the *Cyanamid* principles as he would have reached by the previous approach. So the difference between the pre-*Cyanamid* situation ... and the post-*Cyanamid* situation ... is superficial, a difference of appearance rather than substance, of approach rather than result.'[256]

But while it is true that the *American Cyanamid* principles do allow some flexibility, so that for example a judge eager to bring in his or her view of the merits of the case can do so by regarding the balance of convenience as equal, the principles *if applied* must affect results because, without a prima facie case hurdle to overcome, they must make it easier for a claimant to obtain an interim injunction. *Hubbard v Pitt*[257] is a good example, where the majority applying *American Cyanamid*, granted the interim injunction, whereas Lord Denning, applying the old law would have refused it. That many such examples are not forthcoming is best explained by the fact that important exceptions to *American Cyanamid* have been developed, and by the suspicion that, while purporting to apply Lord Diplock's principles, the judges have in fact been distorting them. But the submission is that, if applied, *American Cyanamid* does produce a change of result as well as approach. As Hammond has written:

> 'The classical model has been replaced by a balancing model. A cynic might contend that was merely window-dressing—that judges continued to do the same old things in the same old way—yet the reformulation of the remedy did in some cases affect the case-law results.'[258]

(3) Criticisms of *American Cyanamid*

(i) The mini-trial interim application was useful for parties, being a quick and relatively cheap means of achieving rough and ready justice. In Wallington's graphic phrase, 'The House of Lords has effectively closed down the economy-class option: we shall all have to travel in the Rolls—or not at all.'[259]

(ii) In many cases, the time factor and circumstances are such that the decision on the interim application ends the dispute, rendering a trial regarding a final injunction superfluous. In such cases, one cannot fairly decide the interim application on the basis of what is more convenient pending trial, and the merits of the claim must be regarded as decisive.

(iii) The basis of Lord Diplock's reasoning—that there is insufficient evidence and argument at the interim application to come to a sound conclusion on fact and law—appears not to be borne out by the reality for, as noted by one well-known barrister, in almost all cases that have proceeded to trial the decision has gone the same way as at the interim stage.[260]

---

[256] C Gray, 'Interim Injunctions since *Cyanamid*' (1980) 40 CLJ 307, 338–339.   [257] [1976] QB 142.
[258] R Hammond, 'Interim Injunctions: Time for a New Model?' (1980) 30 UTLJ 249, 259.
[259] P Wallington, 'Injunctions and the "Right to Demonstrate"' (1976) 35 CLJ 82, 87.
[260] P Prescott, '*American Cyanamid v Ethicon Ltd*' (1975) 91 LQR 168, 169 (note).

(iv) *American Cyanamid* is detrimental to civil liberties. This follows from the fact that in assessing the balance of convenience, the courts have traditionally regarded temporary interference with economic interests as more serious than temporary interference with non-tangible interests, such as the right to continue a strike or demonstration, or to speak freely. Where the primary emphasis was on the claimant's establishing a prima facie case this mattered less. But Lord Diplock's removal of that emphasis makes it too easy for a claimant to infringe the defendant's civil liberties. Wallington has been particularly critical of this aspect of *American Cyanamid*; '... failure to bring into account the intangibles is only tolerable where at least an arbitrary assessment of the legal merits has been made, so that the conduct prohibited is at least *probably* unlawful. If there is no determination of the legal issues, it is intolerable that such a vital factor as the defendant's liberties be left out of account in assessing the balance of convenience.'[261]

(v) Under *American Cyanamid*, the fact that the claimant appears to have a very strong case as opposed to a merely arguable one has no bearing except as a last resort. This seems unsatisfactory, for a very strong case is a factor that should outweigh whatever the balance of convenience would dictate.

(4) Exceptions to *American Cyanamid*

In view of the above criticisms, it is not surprising that the courts have recognised a number of exceptions to *American Cyanamid*, where the old law, or something similar to it, is applied.[262]

(a) Where no action for a final injunction will reach trial

This, the most important exception, is where the timing and circumstances are such that if the interim decision goes one way or, in some situations, either way it will resolve the dispute relating to injunctive relief without a trial.[263]

It would seem that this is what Lord Denning had in mind when in one of the first cases after *American Cyanamid*, *Fellowes v Fisher*,[264] in a judgment not agreed with by the majority, he said that *American Cyanamid* did not apply and the old law did, where '... it is urgent and imperative to come to a decision';[265] and he thought that this would be so in cases of industrial disputes, breach of confidence, covenants in restraint of trade, passing off, and in many commercial cases. Lord Denning applied the same approach in several subsequent cases.[266]

---

[261] P Wallington, 'Injunctions and the "Right to Demonstrate"' (1976) 35 CLJ 82, 92.
[262] See J Martin, 'Interlocutory Injunctions: *American Cyanamid* Comes of Age' (1993–4) 4 King's CLJ 52. For an additional exception, not discussed below, see *Re J (a minor)* [1993] Fam 15. See also *Deutsche Rückversicherung AG v Walbrook Insurance Co Ltd* [1995] 1 WLR 1017 on the courts' reluctance to grant an interim injunction restraining a bank, on the grounds of alleged fraud, from paying on a letter of credit. Interestingly in Australia there were initial doubts as to whether *Cyanamid* should be followed, given its contradiction of the old law embodied in *Beecham Group Ltd v Bristol Laboratories Pty Ltd* (1968) 118 CLR 618. But more recently *Cyanamid* has been followed in, eg, *Australian Coarse Grain Pty Ltd v Barley Marketing Board of Queensland* (1982) 57 ALJR 425; *Tableland Peanuts v Peanut Marketing Board* (1984) 58 ALJR 283; *Murphy v Lush* (1986) 60 ALJR 523. See J Heydon, M Leeming, and P Turner, *Meagher, Gummow and Lehane's Equity, Doctrines and Remedies* (5th edn, LexisNexis 2015) paras 21-350–21-375.
[263] But it is not sufficient simply that the parties are likely to settle out of court following the interim application, for this is always likely: D Newell, 'Trade Unions and Non-Striking Members' (1981) 97 LQR 214, 217.
[264] [1976] QB 122.   [265] ibid, at 133.
[266] *Hubbard v Pitt* [1976] QB 142; *Dunford and Elliot Ltd v Johnson & Firth Brown Ltd* [1977] 1 Lloyd's Rep 505, and as agreed with by the other CA judges in *Office Overload Ltd v Gunn* [1977] FSR 39, and *Newsweek Inc v BBC* [1979] RPC 441.

However, more recent cases have established that Lord Denning's approach of listing the sorts of case that would automatically fall within this exception was too wide-ranging. In *Lawrence David Ltd v Ashton*[267] and *County Sound plc v Ocean Sound Ltd*[268] the Court of Appeal clarified, without doubting the exception itself, that *American Cyanamid* principles apply in the normal way to covenants in restraint of trade and passing off cases respectively. Lord Denning's judgment in *Fellowes v Fisher* was expressly disapproved as was the approach of the Court of Appeal in *Office Overload Ltd v Gunn*[269] (covenant in restraint of trade) and *Newsweek Inc v BBC*[270] (passing off).

Authoritative support for at least a modification of *American Cyanamid* where no action for a final injunction will reach trial came from Lord Diplock himself; for in *NWL Ltd v Woods*,[271] faced with a legislative reaction embodied in what is now the Trade Union and Labour Relations (Consolidation) Act 1992, s 221(2),[272] Lord Diplock was forced to concede that *American Cyanamid* could not be straightforwardly applied in industrial dispute cases. He said that this was so because 'the grant or refusal of an interlocutory injunction generally disposes finally of the action: in practice actions of this type seldom if ever come to actual trial'.[273]

Further support for this exception was given by a strong Court of Appeal, even without Lord Denning, in *Cayne v Global Natural Resources*,[274] where the claimant shareholder sought an interim injunction to restrain the directors of Global from allegedly acting in breach of fiduciary duty by merging Global with another company. The claimant argued that the proposed merger was simply a means whereby the directors could resist the attempt by the claimant and other shareholders to remove them. In refusing the interim injunction, the Court of Appeal declined to apply *American Cyanamid* and referred to *NWL v Woods*, because in these circumstances the grant of the interim injunction would effectively decide the issue in the claimant's favour; for, if granted, the directors would be unlikely to resist removal by the claimant and, as the claimant and his supporters would then be directors, the proposed merger would be dropped.[275] As *American Cyanamid* was not being applied, the claimant needed to show an 'overwhelming'[276] case, that is a prima facie case, and this he had failed to do. Kerr LJ in characteristically clear terms stressed that *American Cyanamid* should be restricted to cases where:

> '... a trial is in fact likely to take place, in the sense that the plaintiffs' case shows that they are genuinely concerned to pursue their claim to trial, and that they are seeking the injunction as a means of a holding operation pending the trial.'[277]

Cayne should be followed and *American Cyanamid* ignored wherever the interim decision, one way or either way, will finally resolve the dispute relating to injunctive relief. This is supported by *Thomas v National Union of Mineworkers*:[278] Scott J, recognising that an action for a final injunction preventing the allegedly unlawful picketing of the claimants, who were working miners, would be unlikely ever to come to trial, followed *Cayne* and, in granting an interim injunction, in effect required the claimants to show a prima facie

---

[267] [1991] 1 All ER 385. Cf *Lansing Linde Ltd v Kerr* [1991] 1 WLR 251.　[268] [1991] FSR 367.
[269] [1977] FSR 39.　[270] [1979] RPC 441.　[271] [1979] 1 WLR 1294.
[272] Below, pp 477–479.
[273] [1979] 1 WLR 1294, at 1305. See also *Porter v National Union of Journalists* [1980] IRLR 404, at 406; D Newell, 'Trade Unions and Non-Striking Members' (1981) 97 LQR 214.
[274] [1984] 1 All ER 225. See also *Fulwell v Bragg* (1983) 127 Sol Jo 171.
[275] [1984] 1 All ER 225, at 232 per Eveleigh LJ, who thought also that a refusal of the injunction would decide the issue because the merger would then go ahead, the directors would successfully defeat the claimant and his supporters, and in practice this could not be reversed by a final injunction.
[276] [1984] 1 All ER 225, at 233, 236.　[277] ibid, at 234.　[278] [1986] Ch 20.

case that they would be entitled to a final injunction to restrain the picketing.[279] It is also supported by Kerr LJ in *Cambridge Nutrition Ltd v BBC*.[280] But the majority of the Court of Appeal in that case attempted to reconcile *Cayne* and *Cyanamid*[281] by elevating within the balance of convenience the importance of the claimant's prospects of success where a trial is unlikely. The Lords Justices were unanimous in discharging an interim injunction restraining the BBC from screening a programme (allegedly in breach of contract) about the claimant's low calorie diet.

(b) Trade dispute defence[282]

In reaction to *American Cyanamid*, the legislature added a new subsection (2) to the Trade Union and Labour Relations Act 1974, s 17, which is now contained in the Trade Union and Labour Relations (Consolidation) Act 1992, s 221(2). By this:

> 'Where (a) an application for an interlocutory injunction is made to a court pending the trial of an action; and (b) the party against whom the injunction is sought claims that he acted in contemplation or furtherance of a trade dispute, the court shall, in exercising its discretion, whether or not to grant the injunction, have regard to the likelihood of that party's succeeding at the trial of the action in establishing any matter which would afford a defence to the action under s 219 (protection from certain tort liabilities) or s 220 (peaceful picketing).'[283]

Although this subsection is based on the first exception already examined—that is, it recognises that *American Cyanamid* would make it too easy for an employer effectively to end lawful industrial action for ever, since once stopped industrial action is very difficult to reorganise—it has given rise to its own interesting jurisprudence on whether and how the subsection fits in with *American Cyanamid*; and this issue remains relevant despite the subsequent development of exceptions to the defence (eg where there has been no ballot) and the narrowing of what is meant by a trade dispute.[284]

In *Star Sea Transport Corpn of Monrovia v Slater*[285] Lord Denning thought that the effect of what is now the Trade Union and Labour Relations (Consolidation) Act 1992, s 221(2) was 'to restore the previous law'[286] in cases involving the defence of acts done in contemplation or furtherance of a trade dispute. This should have meant that the interim injunction would be refused because, taking this defence into account, the claimant could not establish a prima facie case. But Lord Denning considered that, as there was an arguable question of law, the balance of convenience should determine the issue in favour of granting the injunction—an approach which resembled *American Cyanamid*, rather than the previous law. The two other judges without clarifying the relationship between s 221(2) and *American Cyanamid* simply thought that there was insufficient likelihood of the defence succeeding to outweigh the balance of convenience, which was in favour of granting the injunction.

---

[279] ibid, at 68. [280] [1990] 3 All ER 523.
[281] See, analogously, the attempts to assimilate the Trade Union and Labour Relations (Consolidation) Act 1992, s 221(2) and *Cyanamid* in *Mercury Communications Ltd v Scott-Garner* [1984] Ch 37 and *Dimbleby & Sons Ltd v National Union of Journalists* [1984] 1 WLR 427: below, pp 478–479.
[282] P Davies and M Freedland, *Labour Law* (2nd edn, Weidenfeld & Nicolson 1984) 765–777.
[283] Where in contemplation or furtherance of a trade dispute, the Trade Union and Labour Relations (Consolidation) Act 1992, s 219 affords a defence to economic torts, and the Trade Union and Labour Relations (Consolidation) Act 1992, s 220 to peaceful primary picketing.
[284] The meaning of 'trade dispute' is now contained in the Trade Union and Labour Relations (Consolidation) Act 1992, s 244; see *Mercury Communications Ld v Scott-Garner* [1984] Ch 37.
[285] [1978] IRLR 507. [286] ibid, at 510.

Lord Scarman in *NWL v Woods*[287] considered that what is now the Trade Union and Labour Relations (Consolidation) Act 1992, s 221(2) could not fit within the *American Cyanamid* framework. But then, rather than simply reverting to the old law, he regarded the s 221(2) question as a third stage in the inquiry after the serious question to be tried and balance of convenience issues. This seems unnecessarily cumbersome, particularly since if the trade dispute defence is likely to succeed at trial, no interim injunction will be granted, irrespective of the answers to the first two stages. Nevertheless, Lord Scarman's approach is to be preferred to that adopted by Lords Diplock and Fraser. They considered that s 221(2) could be fitted within the *American Cyanamid* framework with the amendment that in these cases the claimant's likelihood of gaining an injunction at trial should be an important rather than a last resort factor within the balance of convenience. While, as we have seen, Lord Diplock's explanation of this modification was eminently sensible—the practical realities of industrial disputes mean that the grant or refusal of the interim injunction generally disposes finally of the claim—confining s 221(2) to a place within the balance of convenience potentially undermines the purpose of that provision: if there is a likelihood of the defence succeeding at trial, no interim injunction should be granted irrespective of other factors.

For a time, however, it looked as if even Lord Diplock was departing from his *American Cyanamid* framework in relation to what is now the Trade Union and Labour Relations (Consolidation) Act 1992, s 221(2). In *Hadmor Productions Ltd v Hamilton*,[288] in giving the sole judgment, he refused an interim injunction because of the very high likelihood of the trade dispute defence succeeding at trial and, although *American Cyanamid* and *NWL v Woods* were mentioned, his approach, with no reference to other factors in the balance of convenience, looked more like that of the old law. Furthermore in *Duport Steels Ltd v Sirs*,[289] the House of Lords, including Lord Diplock, did not even mention *American Cyanamid*.

But any hopes that *American Cyanamid* might be forgotten in the context of what is now the Trade Union and Labour Relations (Consolidation) Act 1992, s 221(2), particularly with the intervening decision in *Cayne v Global Natural Resources plc*,[290] proved shortlived for in *Mercury Communications Ltd v Scott-Garner*[291] and *Dimbleby & Sons Ltd v National Union of Journalists*[292] the Court of Appeal (under Sir John Donaldson) and the House of Lords respectively continued to grapple with the assimilation of *American Cyanamid* and s 221(2). The approach adopted in these cases, differing from *NWL v Woods*, was that s 221(2) applies at an initial stage, so that presumably, if the trade dispute defence is likely to succeed, no injunction should be granted. Otherwise *American Cyanamid* applies in the normal way. As respects all other issues raised by way of defence to the action the criterion to be applied in order to make recourse to the balance of convenience necessary is the ordinary criterion laid down in *American Cyanamid*—is there a serious question to be tried?[293] Curiously Lord Diplock thought that the practical realities that in *NWL v Woods* he had regarded as justifying modification of *American Cyanamid* no longer applied in an action against a trade union because now that a trade union could be sued an employer might well be interested in pursuing a claim for damages to trial. This is most misleading, for the important practical reality remains that to grant an interim injunction in an industrial

---

[287] [1979] 1 WLR 1294. [288] [1982] ICR 114. [289] [1980] ICR 161.
[290] [1984] 1 All ER 225. [291] [1984] Ch 37.
[292] [1984] 1 WLR 427. See also *Serco Ltd v National Union of Rail, Maritime & Transport Workers* [2011] EWCA Civ 226, [2011] ICR 848, at [10]–[14] (per Elias LJ). Cf *Govia Thameslink Railway Ltd v ASLEF* [2016] EWHC 985 (QB).
[293] [1984] 1 WLR 427, at 432 (per Lord Diplock).

dispute has the drastic effect of ending industrial action without the trial. Therefore, the justification for departure from *American Cyanamid* conceded in *NWL v Woods* remains as valid as ever. Furthermore, Lord Diplock was left without any coherent explanation as to why s 221(2) should have departed from *American Cyanamid*. But having said that, it is an ironic twist that the new approach adopted in these cases is far more acceptable than that adopted by Lord Diplock in *NWL v Woods*, and it seems to come very close to the old law. Indeed it merely serves to strengthen the view, indirectly supported by *Cayne v Global Natural Resources*, that it would have been preferable from the outset to have ignored *American Cyanamid* and to have regarded s 221(2) as restoring the old law in relation to cases involving the trade dispute defence.

(c) The need to protect free speech

Pre-*Cyanamid*, the principles governing interim injunctions in defamation (and injurious falsehood) cases were exceptional. The tradition that juries should hear such cases was one supposed reason for this. But the primary justification was the desire to protect free speech. As such, interim injunctions were to be refused wherever the defendant raised a defence, whether of justification, fair comment, or privilege unless the defence would obviously fail at trial.[294] It has now been established in a series of decisions[295] that these old principles survive *American Cyanamid*, for as Griffiths LJ said in *Herbage v Pressdram Ltd*,[296] *American Cyanamid* would represent 'a very considerable incursion into … [principles] based on freedom of speech'.[297] Indeed Martin has argued that interim injunctions for defamation are such an infringement of free speech that they should never be granted. 'If we are committed to the widest possible freedom of discourse on matters of public concern, the jurisdiction to make interlocutory injunctions, this undesirable judicial censorship, cannot on principle be accepted.'[298] Although put forward in respect of Canadian law, the argument is equally applicable here. But it seems to go too far, for the case against the defendant may be clear-cut and indisputable even at the interim stage. Nevertheless the argument does serve to highlight the importance of not weakening the test for interim injunctions in defamation cases, and thereby supports the courts' rejection of *American Cyanamid* in this context.

As regards freedom of expression protected under the Human Rights Act 1998, the position on interim injunctions has been specifically dealt with in s 12(3) of that Act. According to this, a court shall not grant an interim injunction restraining publication before trial, where this might affect the exercise of the Convention right to freedom of expression, 'unless the court is satisfied that the applicant is likely to establish that publication shall not be allowed'. This appears to be in line with the common law approach to defamation that has been set out above and constitutes a legislative departure from *American Cyanamid*. Indeed,

---

[294] *William Coulson & Sons v James Coulson & Co* (1887) 3 TLR 846; *Bonnard v Perryman* [1891] 2 Ch 269; *Fraser v Evans* [1969] 1 QB 349.

[295] *Bestobell Paints Ltd v Biggs* [1975] FSR 421; *Trevor and Sons v Solomon* (1978) 248 Estates Gazette 779; *Harakas v Baltic Mercantile and Shipping Exchange Ltd* [1982] 2 All ER 701; *Herbage v Pressdram Ltd* [1984] 1 WLR 1160; *Al-Fayed v The Observer Ltd*, The Times, 14 July 1986; *Khashoggi v IPC Magazines Ltd* [1986] 3 All ER 577; *Kaye v Robertson* [1991] FSR 62; *Holley v Smyth* [1998] QB 726. See also *Gulf Oil (GB) Ltd v Page* [1987] Ch 327 and esp *Femis-Bank (Anguilla) Ltd v Lazar* [1991] Ch 391 (similarly to defamation cases, the protection of free speech is an important factor in deciding whether to grant an interim injunction to restrain an alleged conspiracy to injure so that such an injunction should only be granted where the claimant has established a strong prima facie case). And the question of at least modifying *Cyanamid* to protect freedom of speech has also risen in respect of other causes of action such as, eg, breach of contract: *Cambridge Nutrition Ltd v BBC* [1990] 3 All ER 523; *Secretary of State for the Home Department v Central Broadcasting Ltd* [1993] EMLR 253.

[296] [1984] 1 WLR 1160.   [297] ibid, at 1163.

[298] R Martin, 'Interlocutory Injunctions in Libel Actions' (1982) 20 UWOLR 129, 140.

in *Greene v Associated Newspapers Ltd*[299] the Court of Appeal held that that common law approach in defamation cases had not been altered by s 12(3).

However, as regards breach of confidence, a somewhat different approach was taken to the application of s 12(3) of the Human Rights Act 1988 by the House of Lords in *Cream Holdings Ltd v Banerjee*.[300] This is discussed in chapter 26. Suffice it to say here that, in the *Greene* case, the Court of Appeal distinguished *Cream Holdings Ltd v Banerjee* on the basis that defamation and breach of confidence raise different issues: once confidentiality is lost, it is lost forever. However, in granting an anonymised interim injunction to restrain publication of information about the claimant's private life, the Supreme Court in *PJS v News Group Newspapers*[301] applied *Cream Holdings Ltd v Banerjee* while accepting that the tort of privacy, with which the case was concerned, differed from breach of confidence; and that privacy (one might say, like reputation in the context of defamation) should be accorded greater protection because it merits protection even where the information is known to some of the public, whereas confidential information, once known about, does not merit further protection.

(d) Little factual or legal dispute

Some judges, like Walton J in *Athletes Foot Marketing Associates Inc v Cobra Sports Ltd*[302] and Bridge LJ in *Office Overload Ltd v Gunn*,[303] have recognised a further wide-ranging exception, namely that *American Cyanamid* does not apply where there is little dispute on the facts and the law is not difficult.[304] This should be supported, for Lord Diplock's reasoning—that there should be no mini-trials on inadequate evidence and argument—is inapplicable to such a case. In similar vein, Sir John Pennycuick in *Fellowes v Fisher*[305] thought that it was particularly in cases 'depending in whole or in great part upon the construction of a written instrument'[306] that the prospect of success was within the competence of the judge hearing the interim application; and in *Official Custodian for Charities v Mackey*,[307] Scott J thought *American Cyanamid* inapplicable where there was no arguable defence to the claim. Particularly radical was the Court of Appeal's view in *Bradford City Metropolitan Council v Brown*[308] that *Cyanamid* was essentially concerned only with factual as opposed to legal disputes.

In *Series 5 Software v Clarke*[309] Laddie J built upon the idea, that the strength of the parties' cases on the facts or the law can usually be easily determined at the interim stage, to put forward a radical reinterpretation of *American Cyanamid*. According to this, the courts can always take into account any view that they can easily reach as to the relative strength of the parties' cases. The *Cyanamid* prohibition on examining the strength of the parties' cases therefore only applies where there are complex issues of disputed fact or law. In line with

---

[299] [2004] EWCA Civ 1462, [2005] QB 972. See too the privacy case of *LNS v Persons Unknown* [2010] EWHC 119 (QB), [2010] EMLR 16. For a straightforward example of the refusal of an interim injunction for the tort of privacy, see *McClaren v News Group Newspapers Ltd* [2012] EWHC 2466, [2012] EMLR 33.
[300] [2004] UKHL 44, [2005] 1 AC 253. [301] [2016] UKSC 26, [2016] AC 1081.
[302] [1980] RPC 343.
[303] [1977] FSR 39. Bridge LJ's approach was approved by the Court of Appeal in *Lawrence David Ltd v Ashton* [1991] 1 All ER 385, at 393, 396.
[304] The validity of this exception was left open in *Alfred Dunhill v Sunoptic* [1979] FSR 337.
[305] [1976] QB 122.   [306] ibid, at 141.
[307] [1985] Ch 168. See also *Attorney-General v Barker* [1990] 3 All ER 257, at 262 (per Nourse LJ).
[308] (1986) 19 HLR 16. This derives some support from the reasoning of Lords Jauncey and Bridge in *R v Secretary of State for Transport, ex p Factortame (No 2)* [1991] 1 AC 603.
[309] [1996] 1 All ER 853.

this, Laddie J controversially argued that *American Cyanamid* had not intended to change the traditional basis upon which courts had proceeded in relation to interim injunctions. He said:

> 'Lord Diplock did not intend ... to exclude consideration of the strength of the cases in most applications for interlocutory relief. It appears to me that what is intended is that the court should not attempt to resolve difficult issues of fact or law on an application for interlocutory relief. If, on the other hand, the court is able to come to a view as to the strength of the parties' cases on the credible evidence, then it can do so. In fact, as any lawyer who has experience of interlocutory proceedings will know, it is frequently the case that it is easy to determine who is most likely to win the trial on the basis of the affidavit evidence and any exhibited contemporaneous documents. If it is apparent from the material that one party's case is much stronger than the other's then that is a matter the court should not ignore. To suggest otherwise would be to exclude from consideration an important factor ...'[310]

Despite its merits, Laddie J's reinterpretation has not overtly found favour in subsequent decisions. Rather, as Laddie J himself commented in relation to the approach of the courts prior to his decision, the courts have continued to exercise their discretion in this area 'by paying lip-service to the guidance given in *American Cyanamid* while in practice applying different criteria'.[311]

(5) An alternative approach

The present law on interim injunctions can most helpfully be summed up by saying that, while the approach in *American Cyanamid* is, on the face of it, that generally followed, there are extensive exceptions where the old law, or something very similar, is applied.

While this is a workable compromise, it is submitted that the criticisms made of *American Cyanamid* are valid and that the old law was preferable. But having said that—and this is the positive aspect of *American Cyanamid*—the old law could produce injustice to a claimant who failed to satisfy the initial prima facie test. To overcome this, the ideal solution would be to revert to the old law, with its emphasis on the strength of the claimant's case, but with the qualification that, if the action for an injunction is likely to go to trial, a claimant who can merely show an arguable case, should still be granted an interim injunction if the balance of convenience is overwhelmingly in the claimant's favour.[312]

(6) Special types of interim injunction

(a) Interim mandatory injunction

It has been consistently stressed that the courts are particularly reluctant to grant an interim mandatory injunction, a reluctance which reflects the fact that, while a final mandatory injunction is more drastic than a prohibitory one, an interim mandatory injunction is doubly drastic, being granted where the court cannot be sure of the merits of the dispute. In *Gale v Abbott*,[313] for example, it was said that an application for an interim mandatory injunction was '... one of the rarest cases that occurs, for the court will not compel a man to do so serious a thing as to undo what he has done, except at the hearing'.[314] Cohen LJ in *Canadian*

---

[310] ibid, at 865.   [311] ibid, at 857.
[312] For other approaches, see R Sharpe, *Injunctions and Specific Performance* (5th edn, Thomson Reuters 2017) para 2.280; J Leubsdorf, 'The Standard for Preliminary Injunctions' (1978) 91 Harv LR 525.
[313] (1862) 6 LT 852.   [314] ibid, at 854.

*Pacific Rly v Gaud*³¹⁵ thought that an interim mandatory injunction was a 'very exceptional form of relief',³¹⁶ and this reluctance has again been stressed in more recent cases.³¹⁷

This is not to say that such an injunction is never granted.³¹⁸ In particular, and seemingly reflecting a punitive approach,³¹⁹ an interim mandatory injunction has been ordered to undo an alleged tort because the defendant had tried to 'steal a march' on the claimant by, for example, speeding up building work allegedly interfering with the claimant's light so as to have the building completed before a pending court hearing.³²⁰

Furthermore, there is perhaps not the same reluctance to grant an interim mandatory injunction enforcing a positive contractual obligation. In this context, the interim mandatory injunction performs the role which, at trial, is performed by specific performance rather than by a final mandatory injunction. It is therefore apt to view the interim mandatory injunction as temporary specific performance. It has fairly recently been confirmed by the Court of Appeal in *Astro Exito Navegacion SA v Southland Enterprise Co Ltd, The Messiniaki Tolmi*,³²¹ that there is indeed jurisdiction to grant an interim mandatory injunction amounting to temporary specific performance: and in that case, which concerned the sale of a ship, such an injunction was granted ordering the defendants to comply with their contractual obligations by instructing their bank to release the purchase price before their letters of credit expired. To support its view on jurisdiction, the Court of Appeal referred to *Smith v Peters*,³²² where an interim mandatory injunction had been granted ordering the vendor of a house, in accordance with the contract of sale, to allow a named third party to make a valuation of the fixtures and fittings. Not cited, but just as relevant, is the well-known case of *Sky Petroleum Ltd v VIP Petroleum Ltd*³²³ where an interim injunction was granted, restraining the defendants from withholding supplies of petrol to the claimants' filling stations. Although the form of the injunction was prohibitory, it was mandatory in substance, as Goulding J's judgment recognises, and amounted to temporary specific performance of the defendants' contract to supply all the petrol required by the claimants.

Prior to *American Cyanamid v Ethicon* the judicial reluctance to award interim mandatory injunctions was often reflected by insisting, as a first requirement, that the claimant should show a strong or very strong prima facie case.³²⁴ Lord Diplock in *American Cyanamid* can be taken to have disapproved of such a requirement because, although he did not expressly refer to mandatory injunctions, his reasoning criticising mini-trials at the interim stage appears

---

³¹⁵ [1949] 2 KB 239. ³¹⁶ ibid, at 249.
³¹⁷ *Shepherd Homes Ltd v Sandham* (1971) Ch 340; *Hounslow London Borough Council v Twickenham Garden Developments Ltd* [1971] Ch 233; *Shotton v Hammond* (1976) 120 Sol Jo 780; *John Trenberth Ltd v National Westminster Bank Ltd* (1980) 39 P & CR 104; *Taylor and Foulstone v NUM* [1984] IRLR 445; *Locabail International Finance Ltd v Agroexport* [1986] 1 WLR 657; *Leisure Data v Bell* [1988] FSR 367; *Jakeman v South West Thames RHA* [1990] IRLR 62; *Moran v University of Salford (No 2)* [1994] ELR 187.
³¹⁸ See, eg, the injunctions ordering withdrawals of strike notices, which gave rise to contempt proceedings in *Express Newspapers plc v Mitchell* [1982] IRLR 465; *Austin Rover Group Ltd v Amalgamated Union of Engineering Workers* [1985] IRLR 162.
³¹⁹ R Sharpe, *Injunctions and Specific Performance* (5th edn, Thomson Reuters 2017) paras 2.650–2.653.
³²⁰ *Daniel v Ferguson* [1891] 2 Ch 27; *Von Joel v Hornsey* [1895] 2 Ch 774. See also *Esso Petroleum Co Ltd v Kingswood Motors Ltd* [1974] QB 142.
³²¹ [1982] QB 1248. ³²² (1875) LR 20 Eq 511.
³²³ [1974] 1 WLR 576. Other examples are *Luganda v Service Hotels Ltd* [1969] 2 Ch 209; *Texaco Ltd v Mulberry Filling Station Ltd* [1972] 1 WLR 814; *Shotton v Hammond* (1976) 120 Sol Jo 780; *Peninsular Maritime Ltd v Padseal Ltd* (1981) 259 Estates Gazette 860; *Taylor v NUM* [1984] IRLR 445; *Parker v Camden London Borough Council* [1985] 2 All ER 141; *Land Rover Group Ltd v UPF (UK) Ltd* [2002] EWHC (QB) 3183, [2003] 2 BCLC 222.
³²⁴ *Hounslow London Borough Council v Twickenham Garden Developments Ltd* [1971] Ch 233; *Esso Petroleum Co Ltd v Kingswood Motors Ltd* [1974] QB 142. It should be remembered that when considering the availability of a final order in deciding whether to grant an interim mandatory injunction enforcing positive contractual obligations—ie in deciding whether there is a strong prima facie case (or, on *American Cyanamid*, a serious question to be tried)—the relevant principles are those of specific performance.

to have been directed to all interim injunctions. However, as the balance of convenience will almost always be against granting a mandatory injunction—since to order the defendant to take positive action, particularly where restorative, is usually more of a hardship to the defendant than the claimant's interim hardship—application of the *American Cyanamid* approach would be unlikely to lead to such injunctions being more readily granted.

The courts have sometimes said that the pre-*Cyanamid* approach to interim mandatory injunctions continues to apply on the ground that they are exceptional injunctions not covered by *American Cyanamid*.[325] That this should be so was expressly stated by the Court of Appeal in *Locabail International Finance Ltd v Agroexport*,[326] which was followed by Auld J in *Jakeman v South West Thames Regional Health Authority*.[327]

However, a slightly different approach was taken by Hoffmann J in *Films Rover International Ltd v Cannon Film Sales Ltd*[328] and repeated by him, as Lord Hoffmann, in obiter dicta, giving the opinion of the Privy Council, in *National Commercial Bank Jamaica Ltd v Olint Corp Ltd*.[329] In his view, the basic question is not so much whether the injunction sought is prohibitory or mandatory but whether the injustice to the defendant if the application were granted and the claimant subsequently failed at the trial would outweigh the injustice to the claimant if the application were refused and the claimant subsequently succeeded at the trial. *American Cyanamid* is applicable to mandatory, and not just prohibitory, injunctions albeit that one should recognise 'that mandatory injunctions, if granted at an interim stage, *generally* create greater risks of injustice to the defendant in the manner described than prohibitory injunctions. Applying that approach, Hoffmann J in *Films Rover* granted an interim mandatory injunction, enforcing a contractual obligation, even though the claimant could not establish a strong prima facie case. In *National Commercial Bank Jamaica Ltd v Olint Corp Ltd*, where an injunction was sought to prevent a bank closing a bank account, there was no serious question to be tried so that no interim injunction should have been granted (whether one described that injunction as prohibitory or mandatory). The lower Jamaican courts had disagreed as to whether the injunction sought was mandatory or prohibitory and Lord Hoffmann criticised their approach because 'arguments over whether the injunction should be classified as prohibitive or mandatory are barren… What matters is what the practical consequences of the actual injunction are likely to be.'[330]

Subsequent to *Films Rover*, in *Nottingham Building Society v Eurodynamics Systems*[331] Chadwick J clarified Hoffmann J's approach in a four-point formulation that was approved by the Court of Appeal in *Zockoll Group Ltd v Mercury Communications Ltd*[332] (although not mentioned in *National Commercial Bank Jamaica Ltd v Olint Corp Ltd*) 'as being all the citation that should in future be necessary'. Chadwick J's four-point formulation was as follows:

'First, the overriding consideration, as for all interim injunctions, is which course is likely to involve the least risk of injustice if it turns out to be "wrong". Secondly, in considering

---

[325] Indeed since granting the injunction will almost invariably finally resolve the claim without a trial, the exception discussed above, pp 475–477, is very likely to be applicable.
[326] [1986] 1 All ER 901. See also *De Falco v Crawley Borough Council* [1980] QB 460, at 481 (per Bridge LJ); *Leisure Data v Bell* [1988] FSR 367; *R v Kensington and Chelsea Royal London Borough Council, ex p Hammell* [1989] QB 518. Contra are *Meade v London Borough of Haringey* [1979] 1 WLR 637, at 657–658 (per Sir Stanley Rees); *Peninsular Maritime Ltd v Padseal Ltd* (1981) 259 Estates Gazette 860, at 868 (per Stephenson LJ).
[327] [1990] IRLR 62.
[328] [1986] 3 All ER 772. This is supported by J Heydon, M Leeming, and P Turner, *Meagher, Gummow and Lehane's Equity, Doctrines and Remedies* (5th edn, LexisNexis 2015) para 21-395.
[329] [2009] UKPC 16, [2009] 1 WLR 1405.   [330] ibid, at [20].   [331] [1993] FSR 468, at 474.
[332] [1998] FSR 354, at 366.

whether to grant a mandatory injunction, the court must keep in mind that an order which requires a party to take some positive step at an interlocutory stage, may well carry a greater risk of injustice if it turns out to have been wrongly made than an order which merely prohibits action, thereby preserving the status quo. Thirdly, it is legitimate, where a mandatory injunction is sought, to consider whether the court does feel a high degree of assurance that the plaintiff will be able to establish his right at a trial. That is because the greater the degree of assurance the plaintiff will ultimately establish his right, the less will be the risk of injustice if the injunction is granted. But, finally, even where the court is unable to feel any high degree of assurance that the plaintiff will establish his right, there may still be circumstances in which it is appropriate to grant a mandatory injunction at an interlocutory stage. Those circumstances will exist where the risk of injustice if this injunction is refused sufficiently outweigh the risk of injustice if it is granted.'

In the *Nottingham Building Society* case itself, the interim remedy sought, and granted, ordered the delivery up of computer software in a case where Chadwick J was satisfied, with a high degree of assurance, that the claimant would succeed at trial.[333] In the *Zockoll* case an interim mandatory injunction requiring performance of a contractual obligation was refused.

(b) 'Without notice' injunction[334]

An interim injunction can be granted without notice of the application having been given to the defendant so that it has had no opportunity to be heard. Normally a 'without notice' injunction lasts until a named day (ie it is an interim injunction) when an application on notice can be made. Nowadays the most common 'without notice' injunctions are freezing injunctions and search orders,[335] which are governed by their own special principles.

But to justify an ordinary 'without notice' injunction the claimant, in addition to satisfying the usual requirements for an interim injunction, will need to establish that there are good reasons (most obviously, that the matter is one of urgency) for not giving notice.[336] Indeed, in obiter dicta in *National Commercial Bank Jamaica Ltd v Olint Corp Ltd*,[337] Lord Hoffmann giving the opinion of the Privy Council said that, leaving aside where giving notice would enable the defendant to take steps to defeat the purpose of the injunction (as in the case of freezing injunctions and search orders), a 'without notice' injunction should not be granted unless there must have been 'literally no time to give notice before the injunction is required to prevent the threatened wrongful act'.[338] Cases within the latter category would be 'rare because even in cases in which there was no time to give the period of notice required by the rules, there will usually be no reason why the applicant should not have given shorter notice or even made a telephone call. Any notice is better than none.'[339]

It follows that delay, whereby an opportunity to apply on notice has been unjustifiably lost, will bar a 'without notice' injunction. In *Bates v Lord Hailsham*,[340] for example, the claimant applied, without notice, for an injunction at 2 pm to prevent a committee, due to meet at 4.30 pm, from making an order concerning the abolition of solicitors' scale fees. The injunction was refused because the claimant had known of the meeting for some weeks

---

[333] Although not mentioned, it would appear that the order fell within the Torts (Interference with Goods) Act 1977, s 4: see below, p 496.
[334] Formerly called an 'ex parte' injunction. [335] Below, pp 485–486. [336] CPR 25.3, 25 PD.4.
[337] [2009] UKPC 16, [2009] 1 WLR 1405. [338] ibid, at [13]. [339] ibid, at [13].
[340] [1972] 1 WLR 1373.

and had had ample opportunity to make an application on notice. A further requirement of a 'without notice' application is that the claimant should act in good faith by disclosing all relevant facts to the court, including those prejudicial to its case, and failure to do so will lead to the injunction being discharged.[341]

An important restriction is imposed by statute on the power to grant 'without notice' injunctions in industrial disputes. By the Trade Union and Labour Relations (Consolidation) Act 1992, s 221(1), no injunction shall be granted against a defendant who is absent and is likely to raise the defence that he was acting in contemplation or furtherance of a trade dispute unless all reasonable steps have been taken to give that person notice and an opportunity to be heard. In practice claimants appear to give, and courts accept as sufficient, about 24 hours' notice.

(c) Freezing injunction

A freezing injunction is what was previously known as a *Mareva* injunction.[342] This is an interim[343] prohibitory injunction, which is almost always granted without notice and usually restrains a person from removing assets from the jurisdiction or otherwise disposing of assets within the jurisdiction. It may also extend to restraining the defendant from dealing with its assets outside the jurisdiction (so-called 'world-wide freezing injunctions'). Regarded by Lord Denning as 'the greatest piece of judicial law reform in my time',[344] the freezing injunction has the purpose of preventing a defendant frustrating the satisfaction of a monetary judgment that the claimant may get against it. Typically it leads to the freezing of a person's bank accounts.[345] The injunction is governed by its own special principles, developed in the case law, and *American Cyanamid v Ethicon* does not apply. As it is designed to ensure that monetary remedies can be effective, rather than itself being a remedy for torts or breach of contract,[346] the freezing injunction lies outside the scope of this book, and no further consideration will be given to it.[347]

(d) Search order

A search order is what was previously known as an *Anton Piller* order.[348] The power of the High Court to grant such an order has been placed on a firm statutory footing by section 7 of the Civil Procedure Act 1997. It was described by Donaldson LJ as 'one of the law's two nuclear weapons',[349] the other being the freezing injunction. A search order is an interim mandatory injunction, which is almost invariably granted without notice and usually orders

---

[341] *R v Kensington Income Tax General Comrs* [1917] 1 KB 486; *Beese v Woodhouse* [1970] 1 WLR 586. Presumably there will usually also be a costs penalty.

[342] Named after *Mareva Cia Naviera SA v International Bulkcarriers SA* [1975] 2 Lloyd's Rep 509. The new terminology is that laid down in CPR 25.1(1)(f).

[343] This can include an injunction granted after final judgment, see above, p 443 n 21.

[344] A Denning, *The Due Process of Law* (Butterworths 1980) 134.

[345] A defendant may also be ordered to deliver up goods or to allow the claimant to enter his premises to seize goods in aid of a freezing injunction. See, eg, *CBS (UK) Ltd v Lambert* [1983] Ch 37.

[346] It may also be granted in other contexts, eg family law.

[347] Ie it assists enforcement. Hence it is best viewed alongside that large body of law dealing with the enforcement of monetary judgments. For detailed consideration of freezing injunctions, see S Gee, *Commercial Injunctions* (6th edn, Sweet & Maxwell 2016); *Clerk and Lindsell on Torts* (22nd edn, Sweet & Maxwell 2018) paras 29-45–29-56.

[348] Named after *Anton Piller KG v Manufacturing Processes Ltd* [1976] Ch 55. The new terminology is that laid down in CPR 25.1(1)(h).

[349] *Bank Mellat v Nikpour* [1982] Com LR 158, at 159.

the defendant to allow the claimant to enter its premises for the purposes of searching for, inspecting, and seizing property infringing the claimant's rights or documents relevant to the claim against the defendant. It is given where speed and secrecy are vital to prevent the destruction or disposal of such property or documents. While developed to deal with cases involving intellectual property, a search order has been granted in other contexts such as matrimonial[350] and ordinary commercial cases.[351] Special principles have been formulated to govern search orders and *Cyanamid* does not apply.

Like the freezing injunction, the search order is best regarded as outside this book's scope. Primarily it is a means of ensuring that essential evidence is not destroyed. In this role it most obviously belongs alongside orders of specific disclosure and inspection,[352] and is a means by which the claimant is enabled to prove its case.[353] A subsidiary function is to preserve goods[354] that are likely to be the subject matter of an action brought by the claimant and are endangered. In this, the search order is like a preservation order made under CPR 25.1(c)(i),[355] and is most sensibly viewed as seeking to ensure that subsequent remedies gained in relation to those goods can be effective.[356]

6. The claimant's conduct as a bar to an injunction

It has been considered convenient to discuss this as a separate head, since the six doctrines encompassed apply whether the injunction is final or interim, prohibitory or mandatory, *quia timet* or not *quia timet*.[357]

(1) Serious breach of contract

A good example here is *Telegraph Despatch and Intelligence Co v McLean*,[358] where a prohibitory injunction to restrain a defendant from transmitting news in breach of covenant was refused, because the claimants were themselves in serious[359] breach of their contract with the defendant by selling the news-agency business. However, it may be doubted whether a defendant now needs to rely on this equitable defence since it can simply terminate for breach and may thereby also escape liability for damages.[360]

---

[350] *Emanuel v Emanuel* [1982] 1 WLR 669.   [351] *Yousif v Salama* [1980] 1 WLR 1540.
[352] [1980] 1 WLR 1540, at 1543 (per Donaldson LJ); *Rank Film Distributors Ltd v Video Information Centre* [1982] AC 380.
[353] Above, p 5.
[354] Hence an undertaking has to be given that articles obtained will be retained by the claimant's solicitors in safe custody—*Universal City Studios Inc v Mukhtar & Sons Ltd* [1976] 1 WLR 568.
[355] Or an interim injunction to preserve property ordered under the courts' general jurisdiction to grant injunctions. See *Redler Grain Silos v BICC Ltd* [1982] 1 Lloyd's Rep 435; *Polly Peck International plc v Nadir (No 2)* [1992] 4 All ER 769; R Sharpe, *Injunctions and Specific Performance* (5th edn, Thomson Reuters 2017) paras 2.700–2.710.
[356] It therefore assists enforcement—above, p 485 n 347. Contrast interim delivery up *to the claimant*, below, ch 24. For general consideration of search orders, see S Gee, *Commercial Injunctions* (6th edn, Sweet & Maxwell 2016); *Clerk and Lindsell on Torts* (22nd edn, Sweet & Maxwell 2018) paras 29-34–29-44.
[357] A question relevant to the claimant's conduct, but not so far mentioned in this chapter, is whether it is a bar to a final injunction that the claimant has not sought an interim injunction (because it wished to avoid giving an undertaking in damages). See on this *Blue Town Investments Ltd v Higgs and Hill Plc* [1990] 1 WLR 696; *Oxy Electric Ltd v Zainuddin* [1991] 1 WLR 115; *Mortimer v Bailey* [2004] EWCA Civ 1514, [2005] 2 P & CR 9.
[358] (1873) 8 Ch App 658. See also *Goddard v Midland Rly Co* (1891) 8 TLR 126; *Litvinoff v Kent* (1918) 34 TLR 298.
[359] The breach was not serious enough to bar the injunction in *Western v MacDermott* (1866) 2 Ch App 72; *Chitty v Bray* (1883) 48 LT 860; *Meredith v Wilson* (1893) 69 LT 336; *Hooper v Bromet* (1903) 90 LT 234.
[360] Eg *General Billposting v Atkinson* [1909] AC 118.

(2) One who comes to equity must come with clean hands

This is a wide-ranging doctrine,[361] whereby the court may refuse an injunction, where it considers that the claimant's past conduct, as revealed by the facts of the dispute, has been so improper that the claimant does not deserve to be helped by the court's granting of an injunction. Clearly such conduct can take many forms. In *Hubbard v Vosper*[362] Megaw LJ considered that scientologists should be denied an interim injunction restraining publication of defamatory articles because of their own deplorable activities and beliefs; and in *Tollemache & Cobbold Breweries Ltd v Reynolds*,[363] no mandatory injunction ordering the removal of eaves trespassing into the claimant's air-space was granted because, inter alia, the claimant had acted pettily throughout.

On the other hand, in *Duchess of Argyll v Duke of Argyll*,[364] the claimant's own adultery and her own articles revealing some secrets of her former marriage did not prevent her from gaining an interim injunction on the basis of breach of confidence, to restrain her ex-husband publishing in a Sunday newspaper an account of her private life during their marriage. Although, strictly speaking, this case belongs in chapter 26 on equitable wrongs, it is usefully included here because the principle applied is obviously equally applicable to torts and breach of contract. In an important statement, Ungoed-Thomas J said, 'A person coming to Equity for relief ... must come with clean hands: but the cleanliness required is to be judged in relation to the relief that is sought.'[365] This emphasises that the 'clean hands' doctrine is a relative one, by which an injunction will still be granted to someone whose conduct has been improper, if the defendant's conduct was that much worse.

(3) One who seeks equity must do equity

This maxim is similar to that requiring 'clean hands', but looks to the claimant's future rather than past conduct so that, by it, a claimant will not be granted an injunction against the defendant, unless the claimant is prepared to do what is fair and right in relation to the defendant. With regard to breach of contract, for example, a claimant will be refused an injunction, unless ready and willing to perform its own obligations to the defendant. The classic authority is *Measures Bros Ltd v Measures*,[366] where it was held that employers, who had wrongfully repudiated an employee's contract,[367] could not enforce that employee's restrictive trading covenant because, inter alia, they were unwilling and unable to perform their side of the contract in the future.

(4) Acquiescence

In relation to equitable remedies for wrongs,[368] the defence of acquiescence requires that the claimant, actively or passively, has represented to the defendant that the claimant has

---

[361] For general discussion see Z Chafee, 'Coming into Equity with Clean Hands' (1948-9) 47 Mich LR 877, 1065.
[362] [1972] 2 QB 84. [363] (1983) 268 Estates Gazette 52.
[364] [1967] Ch 302. See also *Grobbelaar v News Group Newspapers Ltd* [2002] UKHL 40, [2002] 1 WLR 3024.
[365] [1967] Ch 302, at 332.
[366] [1910] 2 Ch 248. *Shell UK Ltd v Lostock Garage Ltd* [1976] 1 WLR 1187, at 1199 (per Lord Denning); *Agricultural Supplies Ltd v Rushmere* [1967] 3 KIR 55.
[367] Presumably, the employee could have terminated for breach, rather than relying on the equitable defence.
[368] There should be no difference in approach whether the wrong be legal or equitable—*Habib Bank Ltd v Habib Bank AG Zurich* [1981] 1 WLR 1265. Acquiescence, often alternatively referred to as equitable estoppel,

no objection to the defendant doing what amounts to a wrong against the claimant and that the defendant has acted to its detriment in that belief.[369] Before the claimant can be said to acquiesce, the claimant must be aware of the facts relevant to the remedy.[370]

In the leading case of *Shaw v Applegate*[371] the defendant had partly used his property for an amusement arcade in breach of a restrictive covenant with the claimant. The claimant had made no complaints about this for six years, although he knew about it, and in consequence the defendant had gone on to buy and install more amusement machinery. The Court of Appeal held that acquiescence barred the claim for a prohibitory and mandatory injunction. But damages in lieu were awarded, thereby showing that acquiescence can be a slightly wider defence for an injunction than for damages.[372]

In other cases, however, both an injunction and equitable damages have been barred. For example, in *Sayers v Collyer*,[373] where the defendant had broken a restrictive covenant not to use premises as a shop, but the claimant had turned a blind eye to this for three years, no damages, let alone an injunction, were awarded. Similarly, in *Habib Bank Ltd v Habib Bank AG Zurich*[374] the claimant bank sought an injunction to restrain the defendants from passing off their business as the claimant's. It was held that the tort had not been made out, since there had been no misrepresentation: but even if it had been, the injunction (and presumably, although not mentioned, equitable damages) would be barred by acquiescence, constituted by the claimant's predecessors having worked closely with the defendants and having helped them to set up their bank. As Oliver LJ said, 'One's initial reaction looking at the history of the matter is that there could hardly be a plainer case of acquiescence than this.'[375]

It should be realised that acquiescence may operate not merely to bar equitable remedies, but also to extinguish the defendant's liability, so that no common law remedies are available either. In a case such as *Shaw v Applegate*, it was indicated that a higher degree of acquiescence amounting to dishonesty or unconscionability[376] would be required to extinguish liability and hence common law remedies. But such a distinction lacks any sensible rationale.[377] The preferable approach is that a lesser degree of acquiescence may bar an injunction than will bar damages, whether they are equitable or common law.

Finally in *Johnson v Wyatt*,[378] it was said that the defence of acquiescence is more likely to apply as a bar to an interim than a final injunction. In particular, this follows because a shorter period of acquiescence will suffice.

---

may also bar the claimant's strict rights, and indeed create new rights, in situations where there is no question of wrongdoing by the defendant: eg *Willmott v Barber* (1880) 15 Ch D 96; *Crabb v Arun District Council* [1976] Ch 179; *Taylor Fashions Ltd v Liverpool Victoria Trustees Co Ltd* [1981] 1 All ER 897.

[369] *Bulmer Ltd and Showerings Ltd v Bollinger SA* [1977] 2 CMLR 625, at 682 (per Goff LJ). See also *Electrolux Ltd v Electrix Ltd* (1953) 71 RPC 23, at 34 (per Lord Evershed MR); *Habib Bank Ltd v Habib Bank AG Zurich* [1981] 1 WLR 1265, at 1284–1285 (per Oliver LJ); *Jones v Stones* [1999] 1 WLR 1739 (no acquiescence established).
[370] *Re Howlett* [1949] Ch 767, at 775.   [371] [1977] 1 WLR 970.
[372] *Sayers v Collyer* (1884) 28 Ch D 103, at 110 (Fry J).
[373] (1884) 28 Ch D 103. See similarly *Gafford v Graham* [1999] 3 EGLR 75.
[374] [1981] 1 WLR 1265.   [375] ibid, at 1283.
[376] [1977] 1 WLR 970, at 978 (per Buckley LJ); *Bulmer v Bollinger* [1977] 2 CMLR 625, at 681 (per Goff LJ).
[377] Arguably, *Habib* supports this criticism, although there it was the distinction between legal and equitable rights, that was regarded as 'archaic and arcane'. See, similarly, *Gafford v Graham* [1999] 3 EGLR 75.
[378] (1863) 2 De GJ & Sm 18.

(5) Laches

(a) Final injunction

By the Limitation Act 1980, s 36(1) the usual six-year limitation period for torts or breach of contract does not apply directly to injunctions; and, as is explained fully below, it would appear that it also does not apply 'by analogy' under the proviso to s 36(1).[379]

However, assuming that there is no statutory limitation period applicable by analogy, it is clear that the equitable doctrine of laches applies where an injunction is being sought. Indeed on one interpretation this may be what s 36(2) is declaring.[380] In general terms,[381] the doctrine of laches applies where the delay by the claimant in seeking an equitable remedy is such that it would be unjust to grant that remedy, especially where the delay has prejudiced the defendant or a third party although it would appear that prejudice is not a necessary element of the doctrine. While laches has often not been separated out from acquiescence, the essential difference is that acquiescence, unlike laches, requires a representation by the claimant, usually implied from its conduct, that it is giving up (ie waiving) its rights which the defendant then relies on. Acquiescence is therefore a form of estoppel. In contrast, laches can be established by a delay, without any representation. It is noteworthy that laches (as well as acquiescence) requires the claimant to have sufficient knowledge of the facts relevant to the remedy before the delay deprives the claimant of the remedy.[382] In other words, the equitable doctrine, without any statutory intervention and in contrast to the common law, has long been applying a discoverability approach so that the claimant cannot lose the remedy before reasonably knowing of it.

In the past it was sometimes suggested that laches is not a sufficient bar to an injunction, and that the additional requirements of acquiescence are necessary.[383] This, however, was departed from in cases such as *Cluett Peabody & Co Inc v McIntyre Hogg Marsh & Co Ltd*[384] and *HP Bulmer Ltd v J Bollinger SA*,[385] where 'inordinate delay'[386] was regarded as a bar in itself. In *Cluett Peabody* Upjohn J considered that a delay of 29 years from when the claimants first knew that the defendants were using their trade mark barred an injunction restraining the continued infringement of that trade mark. On the other hand, in the *Bollinger* case Goff LJ indicated that 16–17 years' delay in bringing an action in respect of a continuing passing off was not 'inordinate'.[387] One would expect that additional factors, such as consequential prejudice to the defendant, will lead to a lesser delay being a sufficient bar (especially where the injunction sought is mandatory).[388]

If all that is relatively clear, there are two difficult questions. First, we have so far been assuming that there is no statutory limitation period of six years that applies 'by analogy', under s 36(1) of the Limitation Act 1980, to a (final) injunction for a tort or breach of

---

[379] By s 36(1), the six-year time limits 'shall not apply to any claim for … an injunction or for other equitable relief, except in so far as any such time limit may be applied by the court by analogy in like manner as the corresponding time limit under any enactment repealed by the Limitation Act 1939 was applied before 1st July 1940'.

[380] By s 36(2), 'Nothing in this Act shall affect any equitable jurisdiction to refuse relief on the ground of acquiescence or otherwise'.

[381] A classic formulation of the doctrine was given in *Lindsay Petroleum Co v Hurd* (1874) LR 5 PC 221, at 239–240 which was a rescission case. See also *Fisher v Brooker* [2009] UKHL 41, [2009] 1 WLR 1764, at [64]. See further *Legends Live Ltd v Harrison* [2016] EWHC 1938 (QB), at [81]–[110] (injunction to restrain breach of restrictive covenant refused because of laches).

[382] *Lindsay Petroleum Co v Hurd* (1874) LR 5 PC 221. [383] *Fullwood v Fullwood* (1878) 9 Ch D 176.

[384] [1958] RPC 335. [385] [1977] 2 CMLR 625. [386] ibid, at 681.

[387] Also *Savile v Kilner* (1872) 26 LT 277 (20 years' delay no bar to injunction for continuing nuisance).

[388] In *Ketley v Gooden* (1997) 73 P & CR 305 a delay of some 18 months, coupled with the fact that the damage to the claimant was relatively minor, led the Court of Appeal to refuse a mandatory restorative injunction.

contract: but is that assumption correct? Secondly, if there is such a statutory limitation period, does that preclude the operation of laches during that period?

One might say that an injunction is analogous to damages because both are remedies for torts or breach of contract. This would especially be the case where the injunction is being sought to prevent the continuation of a tort of breach of contract rather than 'quia timet'. However, there appears to be no case in which that analogy has been drawn.[389] Although not concerning an injunction as such, the most detailed examination of the 'by analogy' argument in relation to a non-monetary remedy was in *P & O Nedlloyd BV v Arab Metals Co*.[390] The Court of Appeal there decided that the six-year limitation period applicable to damages for breach of contract did not apply by analogy to a claim for specific performance of a contract. This was because, first, one was a monetary remedy and the other was not; and, secondly, because, in contrast to common law damages, specific performance does not necessitate that there has been a breach of contract. The first of those reasons (although perhaps not the second) would indicate that the six-year period is most unlikely to be applied by analogy to an injunction for a tort or a breach of contract. If that is correct then laches alone—and not a statutory limitation period—applies to a claim for an injunction to prevent a tort or breach of contract.

Even if there were a statutory limitation period of six years, there would still be a question as to whether the courts could apply to laches within that period. It might be thought that s 36(2) means that the courts could still apply laches despite the statutory limitation period.[391] However, in so far as the laches is concerned purely with delay, the more persuasive interpretation—which avoids undermining the purpose of a statutory limitation period—is that laches should not operate during that period. As regards the general approach to statutory limitation periods and laches (although no case has dealt with injunctions), this appears to be the favoured view in the authorities;[392] and it was fully and clearly articulated in obiter dicta of the Court of Appeal in *P & O Nedlloyd BV v Arab Metals Co*. Moore-Bick LJ precisely reasoned that, if one is talking about mere delay and not delay plus prejudice, and a statutory limitation period is applicable allowing a claim for the remedy to be brought within six years, it would directly contradict the statute to bar the remedy within those six years. On that interpretation, it is only where laches involves delay plus prejudice that laches could operate to bar the remedy within a six-year limitation period.

(b) Interim injunction

What the court is here assessing is whether the claimant has delayed too long in seeking an *interim* injunction and hence much shorter periods of delay are a bar than would bar a final injunction. So in *Church of Scientology of California v Miller*[393] a delay of less than two months was held by the Court of Appeal to bar an interim injunction restraining an alleged

---

[389] The 'by analogy' argument has succeeded where a monetary remedy (eg equitable compensation) has been claimed for an equitable wrong, such as breach of fiduciary duty. See, eg, *Paragon Finance plc v DB Thakerar & Co* [1999] 1 All ER 400. See below, p 544.

[390] [2006] EWCA Civ 1717, [2007] 1 WLR 2288. See above, p 433.

[391] Under the Law Commission's proposals for reform, the standard limitation periods for breach of contract and torts (and equitable wrongs) would apply to claims for injunctions, albeit that the doctrine of laches (and acquiescence) would also apply within those periods: see Law Commission, *Limitation of Actions* (2001) Report No 270, paras 4.268–4.278 and Draft Bill, cl 34(2).

[392] Cases which have indicated that one cannot rely on laches within a statutory limitation period include *Re Pauling's Settlement Trusts* [1962] 1 WLR 86, at 115 (per Wilberforce J) approved [1964] Ch 303, at 353; *Re Loftus* [2006] EWCA Civ 1124, [2007] 1 WLR 1124, at [37]; *Cattley v Pollard* [2006] EWHC 3130 (Ch), [2007] Ch 353.

[393] *The Times*, 23 October 1987.

breach of confidence; in *Legg v ILEA*[394] Megarry J came close to declining interlocutory injunctions because the claimants had been guilty of 12 weeks' delay; and in *Morecambe and Heysham Borough v Mecca Ltd*,[395] in refusing an interim injunction to prevent the defendants holding a beauty competition, Wilberforce J appears to have been influenced by the finding that the claimants knew of the relevant facts by about mid-December, but did not give notice of motion until April. Again, at the interim stage in *Bracewell v Appleby*,[396] Pennycuick V-C had refused an injunction preventing the defendants trespassing over the claimant's road to build a house because of a few months' delay by the claimant. A four-month delay was also regarded as relevant by Megarry J in refusing an interim mandatory injunction in *Shepherd Homes Ltd v Sandham*.[397]

Even if the delay does not bar the interim injunction, one would expect it to be regarded as strong evidence that the interim harm to the claimant is not that serious, which is an important factor, particularly under *American Cyanamid*.

Where exactly delay (or acquiescence) fits within the *Cyanamid* principles is unclear. One might think that it would be applied separately, and would not be swallowed up in the balance of convenience. But this is not borne out in the cases.[398]

(6) Valid termination of the contract by the claimant

Where the claimant seeks an injunction to enforce negative or positive contractual obligations, that injunction is presumably barred where the claimant has chosen validly to terminate the contract. Although rarely discussed in relation to injunctions,[399] the law on this in relation to specific performance would seem to apply here also—once the contractual obligation has gone there is nothing to enforce.[400]

7. Appointment of a receiver

Although not an injunction, this seems the most appropriate place to consider the remedy of the appointment of a receiver (and manager) which goes beyond, but is analogous to, a mandatory enforcing injunction. That is, like a mandatory enforcing injunction the purpose behind appointing a receiver (and manager) as a remedy for a breach of contract or tort is to ensure that positive obligations are performed. This is achieved by the receiver performing the obligation or organising its performance.

In broad terms a receiver and manager is a person appointed to take in property (such as rents and profits), to recover property, and to carry on or superintend the business for which that property has been employed. There has long been an equitable jurisdiction to appoint a receiver and this power is now embodied in the Senior Courts Act 1981, s 37(1): 'The High Court may by order (whether interlocutory or final) … appoint a receiver in all cases in which it appears to the court to be just and convenient to do so.' Traditionally such a power was hardly ever used to remedy a tort or breach of contract.[401] But in *Hart v Emelkirk*

---

[394] [1972] 1 WLR 1245.   [395] [1962] RPC 145.
[396] Referred to at trial by Graham J [1975] Ch 408, at 415. Unfortunately Graham J seemed to regard this as also relevant to the final injunction: contra is *Wrotham Park Estate Co v Parkside Homes Ltd* [1974] 1 WLR 798.
[397] [1971] Ch 340.   [398] Eg *Roussel-Uclaf v GD Searle & Co Ltd* [1977] FSR 125.
[399] But this bar was implicitly accepted in *Thomas Marshall (Exports) Ltd v Guinle* [1979] Ch 227, at 239–243 (per Megarry V-C).
[400] Above, pp 434–435. But this may well not bar a mandatory restorative injunction, which arguably does not depend on the continuing rather than past existence of the obligation.
[401] Rare exceptions were *Riches v Owen* (1868) 3 Ch App 820; *Leney & Sons Ltd v Callingham and Thompson* [1908] 1 KB 79.

Ltd[402] and *Daiches v Bluelake Investments Ltd*[403] receivers were appointed in interlocutory actions to collect rents and to organise the repair of flats, which defendant landlords had allowed to fall into a serious state of disrepair in breach of their repairing covenants. In the former, Goulding J said:

> 'I know of no precedent for such relief, but I also know of no authority that forbids it under the provisions of … the Supreme Court Act 1981, s 37 … It clearly appears to me to be just to appoint a receiver in this case because it is done to support the enforcement by the court of covenants affecting property. It is also convenient because … the properties are in a condition that demands urgent action.'[404]

That there is an unfettered jurisdiction to appoint a receiver (and manager) was confirmed in *Parker v Camden London Borough Council*[405] which also concerned a breach of repairing covenants. But the Court of Appeal there refused to exercise its discretion to make an appointment because it thought that, as the flats were mainly sheltered homes provided by the local authority for the elderly and infirm, an appointment would contravene Parliament's intention, under what is now the Housing Act 1985, s 21, that only a local authority should have responsibility for the management of such homes.

The appointment of a receiver (and manager) is clearly a convenient remedy to 'enforce' many continuing positive obligations, and it is therefore surprising that greater use has not been made of this remedy for breach of contract. Perhaps any judicial reluctance is explicable as resting on similar ideas to those underpinning the controversial constant supervision objection to specific performance.

---

[402] [1983] 1 WLR 1289.   [403] (1985) 275 Estates Gazette 462.
[404] [1983] 1 WLR 1289, at 1291.
[405] [1986] Ch 162. See also *Evans v Clayhope Properties Ltd* [1988] 1 WLR 358, at 361 (although the actual decision was that the defendant could not be ordered at an interlocutory stage to meet the receiver and manager's expenses or remuneration).

24
Delivery up

1. Delivery up of goods	493
2. Delivery up for destruction or destruction on oath	497

1. Delivery up of goods

(1) Introduction

This is the appropriate remedy for the claimant to recover its goods where the defendant is tortiously 'interfering' with them under the Torts (Interference with Goods) Act 1977. By the remedy the defendant is ordered to deliver the goods to, or to allow them to be taken by, the claimant. Delivery up therefore belongs alongside the mandatory restorative injunction as a remedy concerned to compel the undoing of a wrong.

Prior to 1854 the common law courts could not make such an order; the most they could do was to order the defendant to return the goods or pay their value at his option. This contrasted with the position in equity, where the Court of Chancery had power to grant delivery up of the claimant's goods, which it exercised where there was no adequate remedy at common law. By the Common Law Procedure Act 1854, s 78, the common law courts too were given the power to order delivery up, in any action for the detention of any chattel, without giving the defendant the option of paying its value and this is now embodied in the Torts (Interference with Goods) Act 1977. By the Torts (Interference with Goods) Act 1977, s 3, the following remedies are available in proceedings for wrongful interference against a person in possession or in control of the goods:

> '(a) an order for delivery of the goods and for payment of any consequential damages; or (b) an order for delivery of the goods, but giving the defendant the option of paying damages by reference to the value of the goods, together in either alternative with payment of any consequential damages; or (c) damages.'[1]

As the Act abolished detinue, the actual torts for which delivery up can be ordered are conversion, as statutorily extended by the Torts (Interference with Goods) Act 1977, s 2(2), and trespass to goods.

(2) When will the courts order delivery up?

There is no reason to think that the Torts (Interference with Goods) Act 1977 has affected the principles governing when delivery up will be ordered. The primary principle, deriving from the remedy's roots in equity, is that delivery up will not be ordered if damages are adequate. At least if one puts the defendant's inability to pay (ie insolvency) to one side,[2] the

---

[1] For the assessment of damages, see above, pp 219–221.
[2] See below, p 495.

same approach to adequacy has traditionally been adopted as for specific performance of a contract for the sale of goods and specific performance and delivery up are regarded as directly analogous remedies. For example in *Cohen v Roche*[3] McCardie J said, 'In my view, the power of the Court in an action of detinue rests upon a footing which fully accords with s 52 of the Sale of Goods Act 1893 … The law is thus, I am glad to find, consistent in its several parts.' This also explains why cases dealing with delivery up for detinue are often used as authorities on specific performance.

In line with the approach to specific performance,[4] it can therefore be said that delivery up will not be ordered for most goods on the ground that damages will enable substitutes to be bought in the market. An extreme example is *Cohen v Roche* where delivery up was refused to a buyer of some Hepplewhite chairs (to whom property in the chairs had passed) because in McCardie J's view, citing Swinfen Eady MR's words in *William Whiteley Ltd v Hilt*,[5] '… the goods in question were ordinary articles of commerce and of no special value or interest.'[6] Again, therefore, the uniqueness of the goods is the most crucial concept in judging adequacy.

There are several excellent examples of the Court of Chancery ordering the delivery up of physically unique goods—that is, of goods possessing significant physical characteristics that very few, if any, other goods have. In *Pusey v Pusey*[7] it was the Pusey horn that was ordered to be delivered up; in *Somerset (Duke) v Cookson*[8] it was an antique altarpiece; in *Fells v Read*[9] some ceremonial ornaments; in *Lowther v Lowther*[10] a painting by Titian; and in *Earl of Macclesfield v Davies*[11] an order was made allowing the inspection of an iron chest on the assumption that if it contained certain heirlooms they must be delivered up.

Goods may also be ordered to be delivered up, if they are commercially unique—that is where, although the goods are not physically unique, buying substitutes would be so difficult or would cause such delay that the claimant's business would be seriously interrupted. So in *North v Great Northern Rly Co*[12] the commercial uniqueness of 54 coal waggons underlay the acceptance that they could be ordered to be delivered up. Sir John Stuart V-C said:

> 'There can be no doubt that … the coal waggons were of special value to him in order to carry on his business. The sudden sale of these waggons, without which the trade could not be conducted, must necessarily have inflicted serious injury by the interruption of his trade … It cannot be pretended that the plaintiff could have got on a sudden 54 other coal waggons fit for his business as readily and promptly as he could have purchased 54 tons of coal or 54 bushels of wheat.'[13]

Similarly, the even more drastic remedy of interim delivery up under the Torts (Interference with Goods) Act 1977, s 4 was ordered in respect of 500 tons of steel lying in railway depots in *Howard Perry & Co v British Rly Board*[14] because, in view of the steel strike then taking place, the claimants could not hope to acquire any other steel in the short term, and hence non-delivery up of their steel could cause substantial disruption to their business. Sir Robert Megarry V-C said:

> '… at present steel is obtainable on the market only with great difficulty, if at all. If the equivalent of what is detained is unobtainable, how can it be said that damages are an adequate remedy? They plainly are not … All that the plaintiffs are losing, said counsel for the defendants, is the

---

[3] [1927] 1 KB 169, at 180–181. [4] Above, ch 22. [5] [1918] 2 KB 808, at 819.
[6] [1927] 1 KB 169, at 181. [7] (1684) 1 Vern 273. [8] (1735) 3 P Wms 390.
[9] (1796) 3 Ves 70. [10] (1806) 13 Ves 95. [11] (1814) 3 Ves & B 16.
[12] (1860) 2 Giff 64. See also the Canadian case *Farwell v Walbridge* (1851) 2 Gr 332 (delivery up of sawlogs).
[13] (1860) 2 Giff 64, at 68–69. [14] [1980] 1 WLR 1375.

sale of some steel, and damages will adequately compensate them for that. I do not think that this is by any means the whole picture. Damages would be a poor consolation if the failure of supplies forces a trader to lay off staff and disappoint his customers ... and ultimately forces him towards insolvency.'[15]

Although there are no direct authorities clarifying this point, it appears to be the case that the analogy between delivery up and specific performance breaks down where the defendant is unable to pay (ie is insolvent). As we have seen, specific performance will not be ordered so as to overcome the defendant's insolvency (at least where other creditors would be prejudiced).[16] If an unsecured creditor could simply obtain specific performance where the defendant is insolvent, the distinction between secured and unsecured creditors would be eroded. In contrast, if property in goods is retained by a seller (where the purchaser has become insolvent)[17] or has passed to the purchaser (where the seller has become insolvent),[18] the 'owner' of the goods is able to avoid the insolvency. This is the most significant consequence of deciding whether property in goods has passed or not. The owner is assumed to be entitled 'to take his goods out' of the trustee in bankruptcy's or liquidator's possession so that they are removed from the assets that are available for distribution among the insolvent's creditors. This 'taking out of his goods' appears to mean[19] that, in a claim for wrongful interference where the tortfeasor is insolvent, the claimant is entitled to delivery up of his goods rather than being left to a (personal) remedy of damages for their value. In other words, in contrast to specific performance, it appears that delivery up will be ordered of non-unique goods because of the defendant's insolvency.

An interesting theoretical question is whether, even with the exception just explained, the analogy traditionally drawn with specific performance as regards adequacy is a sensible one. As is shown by the ease with which the adequacy hurdle is overcome in relation to prohibitory injunctions for the breach of a negative contractual promise, adequacy is an elastic concept and one might have thought that the wide view of adequacy adopted in relation to specific performance, which confines that remedy to a secondary role, would be inappropriate where the claim is for wrongful interference.[20] Certainly it seems surprising that if the defendant steals and keeps the claimant's (non-unique) goods the claimant has no prima facie civil right to recover them but must first overcome a substantial adequacy of damages hurdle.[21] Nor, contrary to the fears of McCardie J in *Cohen v Roche*, would the law be inconsistent if delivery up were to be easier to obtain than specific performance, for the basis of each is fundamentally different. The former rests on interference with an existing proprietary right whereas the latter is simply given for breach of promise.[22]

---

[15] ibid, at 1383.   [16] Above, pp 408–409.
[17] This was the issue in, eg, *Wait and James v Midland Bank* (1926) 31 Com Cas 523 and *Cheetham v Thornham Spinning Co* [1964] 2 Lloyd's Rep 17.
[18] This was the issue in, eg, *Re Wait* [1927] 1 Ch 606 and *Carlos Federspiel & Co SA v Charles Twigg & Co Ltd* [1957] 1 Lloyd's Rep 240.
[19] An alternative explanation, which has the merit of avoiding any 'inconsistency' between delivery up and specific performance but depends on an assumption as to how a trustee in bankruptcy or liquidator will act, is that, while the owner is merely entitled to damages, a trustee in bankruptcy or liquidator will in practice prefer to hand over the goods to the 'owner' rather than being held personally liable for wrongful interference with them.
[20] Arguably the Consumer Credit Act 1974, s 100(5) supports delivery up being easier to obtain; on termination of a regulated hire-purchase or conditional sale agreement, delivery up of goods wrongly detained by the debtor must be ordered unless 'it would not be just to do so'.
[21] See N Curwen, 'The Remedy in Conversion: Confusing Property and Obligation' (2006) 26 Legal Studies 570.
[22] Admittedly the maxim that 'equity treats as done that which ought to be done' blurs this line between obligation and ownership. A claimant who will be granted specific performance of the transfer of land (or goods) is treated, in equity, as being the owner from the time the contract was made.

Even where damages are inadequate, delivery up may still be refused.[23] For example, given its equitable roots, the courts may deny the remedy, while granting damages, because of the claimant's conduct, such as her acquiescence or 'unclean hands'. Whether the normal six-year limitation period for tort actions laid down in the Limitation Act 1980, s 2 applies to delivery up is not entirely clear. But, in so far as delivery up is treated as 'equitable relief', s 36(1) lays down that, as with specific performance and injunctions, the normal time bar does not apply directly although it might be applied 'by analogy'. But if there is no statutory limitation period, laches presumably does apply. Like specific performance and injunctions, delivery up may also be ordered on terms, for example, that the claimant compensates the defendant for improvements made to the goods.[24]

(3) Interim delivery up

So far (with the exception of the discussion on the *Howard Perry* case) it has been assumed that delivery up is sought at trial. But delivery up may also be granted pre-trial.

(a) Torts (Interference with Goods) Act 1977, s 4

By this, and by CPR 25.1(1)(e), the court is empowered to order the delivery up of goods which are or may become the subject matter of subsequent proceedings for tortious interference. The delivery is to be either to the claimant or to a person appointed by the court for the purpose. Where there are good reasons (for example, in cases of urgency) delivery up may be ordered on an application made without notice as with interim injunctions.

Delivery up to a person appointed by the court, like a preservation order under CPR 25.1(c)(i), is best viewed as outside the scope of this book, since it seeks to ensure that subsequent remedies in relation to those goods can be effective and therefore belongs alongside the law on the enforcement of remedies.[25] But interim delivery up to the claimant is a straightforward remedy for tortious interference. It is the equivalent of delivery up granted at trial under the Torts (Interference with Goods) Act 1977, s 3, and from the claimant's point of view has the advantage of being available quickly without waiting for trial. There has been little discussion of the principles governing such delivery up but one would expect them to be analogous to those governing interim mandatory injunctions: for example, the claimant should have to show a strong or very strong prima facie case and that the balance of convenience favours the remedy.[26] In *Howard Perry & Co v British Railways Board*,[27] which is the leading case on this remedy, Megarry V-C ordered interim delivery up of commercially unique steel kept in the defendant's yards, and stressed that there was no need to show a risk of the goods being disposed of, lost, or destroyed. He also explained that the order for delivery up could and in this case would require the defendant to permit the claimants to collect the goods.

---

[23] Delivery up cannot be ordered against the Crown—Crown Proceedings Act 1947, s 21(1)(b).
[24] As expressly laid down in the Torts (Interference with Goods) Act 1977, s 3(7).
[25] See analogously search orders, above, p 486.
[26] Above, pp 481–484. There is support for this in *Adventure Film Productions Ltd v Tully* [1993] EMLR 376; and *Nottingham Building Society v Eurodynamics Systems* [1993] FSR 468, above, pp 566–567 (although the remedy in this case was treated simply as an interim mandatory injunction without there being any mention of interim delivery up under the Torts (Interference with Goods) Act 1977, s 4).
[27] [1980] 1 WLR 1375. See also *Secretary of State for Defence v Guardian Newspapers Ltd* [1985] AC 339.

(b) Replevin

Replevin is an interlocutory procedure of ancient origin by which a defendant can be ordered to deliver up goods taken from the claimant. Theoretically replevin is available for any trespassory taking of the claimant's goods, but in practice it has been used only where the defendant has taken the goods by wrongful distress. The modern procedure is laid down in the County Courts Act 1984, Sch 1.[28] The claimant whose goods have been seized applies to the Registrar, who will order the goods to be 'replevied to that party' provided the claimant gives security to cover, for example, the probable costs of the action and the alleged rent or damage in respect of which the distress has been made, and with a condition of the security being that the claimant will prosecute the action without delay in a county court or the High Court.

Now that the Torts (Interference with Goods) Act 1977, s 4 provides for interim delivery up, it may be that delivery up in an action for replevin will wither away. Certainly the Law Reform Committee, upon whose report the Act was based, hoped that s 4 would 'pave the way for the abolition of replevin'.[29]

(4) The action for the recovery of land[30]—a contrast to delivery up of goods

This common law action enables a claimant to recover possession of its land by ordering the defendant to give up possession. But interestingly it is not a remedy for the tort of trespass to land as such. So, unlike a claim for that tort, the action for the recovery of land (formerly known as the action for ejectment) is necessarily available to an owner who is out of possession. Moreover, it is available to a claimant who was out of possession at the time of the unauthorised entry without any need to rely on the fiction of trespass by relation. Further differences from tortious trespass are that by the Limitation Act 1980, s 15(1) the limitation period is 12 years rather than six, and that the action rests to a greater extent than does trespass on the claimant establishing good title so that, for example, *ius tertii*[31] appears to be a good defence.

All this serves to emphasise the important theoretical point that in contrast (and in some commentators' views,[32] in enlightened contrast) to delivery up of goods, this remedy has retained its identity as a remedy within the law of property without becoming dependent on wrongdoing by the defendant. It also follows that recovery of land falls outside the true scope of this book.

2. Delivery up for destruction or destruction on oath

Where there has been a tortious infringement of intellectual property rights (whether by infringement of copyright,[33] patent,[34] trademark,[35] or design[36]) the courts have an inherent

---

[28] As amended by the Courts and Legal Services Act 1990.
[29] Law Reform Committee, *18th Report Conversion and Detinue* (1971) Cmnd 4774, para 97.
[30] FH Lawson, *Remedies of English Law* (2nd edn, Butterworths 1980) 203.
[31] 'The right to possession is in a third party.'
[32] See T Weir, *A Casebook on Tort* (10th edn, Sweet & Maxwell 2004) 483; N Curwen, 'The Remedy in Conversion: Confusing Property and Obligation' (2006) 26 Legal Studies 570.
[33] *Mergenthaler Linotype Co v Intertype Co Ltd* (1926) 43 RPC 381.
[34] *Paton Calvert & Co Ltd v Rosedale Associated Manufacturers Ltd* [1966] RPC 61.
[35] *Slazenger & Sons v Feltham & Co* (1889) 6 RPC 531.
[36] *Rosedale Associated Manufacturers Ltd v Airfix Products Ltd* [1956] RPC 360.

jurisdiction to order the defendant to deliver up to the claimant or the court for destruction, or itself to destroy, articles made in infringement of the claimant's rights or even in some cases[37] the means of making those articles. At first sight the function of these alternative equitable final remedies appears most closely allied to that of the mandatory restorative injunction since they generally compel the undoing of what has wrongfully been done. But as the claimant's principal concern is not with the mere continued existence of infringing material (that in itself causing her no harm) but is rather with the harmful *use* of that material, the primary function of the remedies is best viewed as being to prevent acts infringing the claimant's rights. As such the remedies go one step beyond, and protect the claimant even more effectively than, a prohibitory injunction. The classic judicial statement on the remedies' function is Russell J's in *Mergenthaler Linotype Co v Intertype Co Ltd*.[38] He said:

> '[The plaintiff] is protected as to further manufacture of infringing articles by the injunction which he obtains, but there remains this, that so long as there is still what I might call infringing stock in the possession of the infringer, he may be subject to too serious and grave a temptation and may therefore be tempted to commit a breach of the injunction which he would otherwise not commit. Accordingly, in order to assist the plaintiff and as a relief ancillary to the injunction he has obtained, the Court may in its discretion make an order for destruction or delivery up of infringing articles.'[39]

This passage also supports the view that there is no power to order destruction where a prohibitory injunction has not been granted. But of course just because such an injunction has been granted does not mean that the courts will exercise their power to order destruction. On the contrary there is always greater reluctance to grant positive than negative orders and the courts are also likely to be influenced by the hardship to the defendant and the waste of resources involved. Certainly if the claimant's rights can be effectively protected by ordering something less than full destruction, this will be preferred. For example, in *Slazenger & Sons v Feitham & Co*[40] the defendant was ordered merely to erase the claimant's trade mark from tennis racquets, rather than being ordered to destroy all racquets bearing the trade mark; and in *Rosedale Associated Manufacturers Ltd v Airfix Products Ltd*,[41] where buckets infringing the claimant's design and moulds and dies used for making those buckets were ordered to be destroyed, it was explained by Lloyd-Jacob J that, in respect of the moulds and dies, destruction meant '... a modification such as to render them inoperable to make an article of infringing shape'.[42]

When the courts will order delivery up for destruction as opposed to destruction on oath is unclear: but there is support for the view that the choice is essentially a matter for the defendant,[43] unless considered to be untrustworthy.[44]

It is important to emphasise that these remedies are granted even though the claimant does not own the articles ordered to be destroyed.[45] This is the key to avoiding confusion with the different remedy of delivery up of goods examined above. It follows that, while a claimant granted delivery up of goods belonging to her is entitled to do what she likes with that property, a claimant to whom delivery up for destruction is ordered ought to destroy that property. Unfortunately the distinction between these remedies is clouded by the tendency of judges, practitioners, and academics alike[46] to omit the words 'for destruction'

---

[37] ibid; *Wham-O Manufacturing Co v Lincoln Industries Ltd* [1982] RPC 281, at 318.
[38] (1926) 43 RPC 381.   [39] ibid, at 382.   [40] (1889) 6 RPC 531.   [41] [1956] RPC 360.
[42] ibid, at 368.   [43] *Paton Calvert & Co Ltd v Rosedale Associated Manufacturers Ltd* [1966] RPC 61.
[44] *Industrial Furnaces Ltd v Reaves* [1970] RPC 605.
[45] *Vivasseur v Krupp* (1878) 9 Ch D 351, at 360; *Chappell & Co Ltd v Columbia Gramophone Co* [1914] 2 Ch 745, at 756.
[46] A notable exception is G Forrai, 'Confidential Information—A General Survey' (1971) 6 Syd LR 382, 391.

after delivery up to a non-owner. Understanding of the true purpose of the destruction remedies would be further enhanced if delivery up for destruction was always ordered to be made to the court, rather than to the claimant.

Although these remedies are clearly ideally suited for the tortious infringement of intellectual property rights, there are other torts to which one would have thought they might be equally appropriate. The most obvious example is libel, for a claimant who has obtained an injunction would be even better protected by destruction (or erasing) of libellous material. The explanation for the present confinement of the remedies is presumably that the intellectual property torts had their roots in equity and these are equitable remedies. But this is clearly not a justification and it is suggested that, although they are drastic remedies, delivery up for destruction or destruction on oath could be usefully extended to other torts.

In relation to infringement of copyright and design right,[47] the Copyright, Designs and Patents Act 1988, ss 99 and 230 give the courts a specific statutory power (irrespective of the grant of an injunction) to order delivery up of infringing copies or articles, or anything designed or adapted for making infringing copies or articles.[48] Moreover, while the courts may require the material delivered up to be destroyed they can also simply order it to be forfeited to the copyright or design right owner.[49] That represents a difference from the remedies available under the inherent equitable jurisdiction: delivery up and forfeiture to the copyright or design owner (of material that is owned by the defendant) may be regarded as occupying a mid-position between delivery up of (one's) goods and delivery up for destruction.[50]

---

[47] Analogous provisions apply to infringement of a person's performer's or recording rights by illicit recording: Copyright, Designs and Patents Act 1988, ss 195 and 204.
[48] The courts' inherent jurisdiction is unaffected: see Copyright, Designs and Patents Act 1988, ss 99(4) and 230(7). By s 233(2) damages only can be awarded for innocent secondary infringement of a design right.
[49] Copyright, Designs and Patents Act 1988, s 114 (copyright); s 231 (design right). In effect the same remedy was previously available for infringement of copyright under the Copyright Act 1956, s 18 (now repealed): the copyright owner was treated as the owner of infringing copies and plates used to make infringing copies and could therefore seek delivery up of (his) goods for the tort of conversion.
[50] The primary function of delivery up and forfeiture is probably to compel the undoing of a wrong: cf above, p 498.

PART FIVE
DECLARING RIGHTS

25

Nominal and contemptuous damages and declarations

1. Nominal damages	503
2. Contemptuous damages	503
3. Declarations	504

1. Nominal damages[1]

Many torts are actionable only on proof of damage. But torts actionable per se, as well as breach of contract, are actionable without proof of damage. One consequence is that even though the court is satisfied that the claimant has not suffered any damage, it is still entitled to damages for the defendant's breach of contract or tort actionable per se. Such damages are termed nominal and they comprise a trivial sum of money, usually about £2–£10.[2] Nominal damages are therefore in no sense compensatory and must be distinguished from a small sum of compensatory damages.[3] Their function is merely to declare that the defendant has committed a wrong against the claimant and hence that the claimant's rights have been infringed. Given that the remedy of a declaration is specifically designed to serve this purpose, nominal damages are superfluous and could happily be abolished.[4] This is particularly so since what was previously an important practical consequence of an award of nominal damages has been removed by Devlin J's decision in *Anglo-Cyprian Trade Agencies v Paphos Wine Industries Ltd*[5] that a claimant awarded nominal damages should not necessarily be regarded as a successful claimant for the purposes of costs.

2. Contemptuous damages

Rarely awarded other than by a jury in a defamation case, these are damages of a very small amount—usually of the lowest coin of the realm (at present 1p)—whose function is to indicate that, while the defendant has committed the alleged wrong (including a tort actionable only on proof of damage) the claimant deserves no more than a technical acknowledgment

---

[1] Of the law on compensatory damages examined in Part Two, the form of damages (ch 9) and limitation periods (ch 16) are also relevant to nominal (and contemptuous) damages.

[2] For examples of nominal damages being awarded, see *C & P Haulage v Middleton* [1983] 1 WLR 1461 (£10) (above, p 78) and *R (on the application of Lumba) v Secretary of State for the Home Department* [2011] UKSC 12, [2012] 1 AC 245 (above, p 363).

[3] The term 'nominal damages' has very occasionally been used in the different sense of a sum of compensatory damages awarded where a loss has been proved but insufficient evidence of the loss has been provided to put an accurate figure on the loss: see J Edelman, *McGregor on Damages* (20th edn, Sweet & Maxwell 2018) paras 12-004–12-005. As is said in *McGregor on Damages*, at para 12-004, 'the fact of a loss is shown but the necessary evidence as to its amount is not given.' A very rare modern example of this usage is in *Greer v Alstons Engineering Sales and Services Ltd* [2003] UKPC 46, (2003) 147 SJLB 783.

[4] See Lord Millett's obiter dicta in *Cullen v Chief Constable of the Royal Ulster Constabulary* [2003] UKHL 39, [2003] 1 WLR 1763, at [81].

[5] [1951] 1 All ER 873.

of the infringement of his rights, because of his own conduct in the matter.[6] In other words the derisory award amounts to a declaration of the claimant's rights combined with an admonition of the claimant. As it is difficult to see how the grant of a declaration can achieve this 'double-edged sword' effect, contemptuous damages justify their continued, albeit very limited, existence.

3. Declarations

While all remedies impliedly declare what the parties' rights are, a declaration[7] is a remedy, generally regarded as statutory[8] albeit with equitable roots, by which a court simply pronounces on the rights or even the remedies of the parties. Available in relation to any sort of legal right, a declaration can quickly and easily, and without invoking any coercion, aid the resolution of a dispute or prevent one from arising. As Lawson wrote:

> 'If persons dispute among themselves as to their legal position, but are perfectly willing to respect and act upon it once they know what it is, there is no need to order them in any way. A mere declaration stating authoritatively their legal relations will suffice.'[9]

Prior to 1883, the Court of Chancery alone had the power to grant a declaration, and then this was exercised only where consequential relief was or could have been claimed. But by the Judicature Acts 1873–1875 and the accompanying Rules of the Supreme Court 1883, Ord 25, r 5, all divisions of the High Court were given power to make declarations 'whether or not consequential relief is or could be claimed'. It was this 'innovation of a very important kind'[10] that paved the way for the modern widespread use of declarations. The present procedural rule is CPR 40.20 which states, 'The court may make binding declarations whether or not any other remedy is claimed.'

Early this century it was said that the discretion to grant a declaration should be exercised 'with extreme caution',[11] but in Lord Radcliffe's words giving the Privy Council's judgment in *Ibeneweka v Egbuna*:[12]

> '... it is doubtful if there is more of principle involved than the undoubted truth that the power of granting a declaration should be exercised with a proper sense of responsibility and full realisation that judicial pronouncements ought not to be issued unless there are circumstances that call for their making. Beyond that there is no legal restriction on the award of a declaration.'

---

[6] A Ogus, *The Law of Damages* (Butterworths 1973) 26; S Waddams, *The Law of Damages* (6th edn, Thomson Reuters 2017) para 10.40. For examples see *Kelly v Sherlock* (1866) LR 1 QB 686; *Dering v Uris* [1964] 2 QB 669. Another possible example was the £1 awarded to the claimant in *Grobbelaar v News Group Newspapers Ltd* [2002] UKHL 40, [2002] 1 WLR 3024, albeit that their Lordships (with the exception of Lord Millett who described them as 'derisory damages') called them nominal damages. A claimant awarded merely contemptuous damages is even less likely to recover costs than one awarded nominal damages—*Martin v Benson* [1927] 1 KB 771.

[7] See, generally, H Woolf, J Woolf, and R Mackay, *The Declaratory Judgment* (4th edn, Sweet & Maxwell 2011); P Young, *Declaratory Orders* (Butterworths 1975); F Lawson, *Remedies of English Law* (2nd edn, Butterworths 1980) ch 16.

[8] *Chapman v Michaelson* [1908] 2 Ch 612 (affd [1909] 1 Ch 238); *Tito v Waddell (No 2)* [1977] Ch 106, at 259; *P & O Nedlloyd BV v Arab Metals Co* [2005] EWHC 1276 (Comm), [2005] 1 WLR 3733, at [21] (rvsd without casting doubt on this at [2006] EWCA Civ 1300, [2007] 1 WLR 2483); *Fisher v Brooker* [2009] UKHL 41, [2009] 1 WLR 1764. See below, p 505.

[9] F Lawson, *Remedies of English Law* (2nd edn, Butterworths 1980) 231.

[10] *Ellis v Duke of Bedford* [1899] 1 Ch 494, at 515 (per Lindley MR).

[11] *Faber v Gosworth Urban District Council* (1903) 88 LT 549, at 550.

[12] [1964] 1 WLR 219, at 225. See also *Guaranty Trust Co of New York v Hannay & Co* [1915] 2 KB 536, at 572 (per Bankes LJ); *Hanson v Radcliffe UDC* [1922] 2 Ch 490, at 507 (per Lord Sterndale MR); *Booker v Bell* [1989] 1 Lloyd's Rep 516; *Financial Services Authority v Rourke*, The Times, 12 November 2001.

Denning LJ earlier spoke in similar vein in *Pyx Granite Co Ltd v Ministry of Housing and Local Government*:[13] '... if a substantial question exists which one person has a real interest to raise and the other to oppose, then the court has a discretion to resolve it by a declaration, which it will exercise if there is good reason for so doing'. So in modern times a declaration is readily granted.

It has also now been accepted that, while an unusual remedy, negative declarations (that the claimant is under no liability) can also be granted where they would serve a useful purpose. In Lord Woolf MR's words in *Messier-Dowty Ltd v Sabena SA (No 2)*:[14]

'The deployment of negative declarations should be scrutinised and their use rejected where it would serve no useful purpose. However, where a negative declaration would help to ensure that the aims of justice are achieved the courts should not be reluctant to grant such declarations. They can and do assist in achieving justice ... [T]he development of the use of declaratory relief in relation to commercial disputes should not be contained by artificial limits wrongly related to jurisdiction. It should instead be kept within proper bounds by the exercise of the courts' discretion.'

Despite its equitable roots, a declaration is categorised as a statutory, not an equitable, remedy so that equitable defences relating to the claimant's conduct, such as laches and 'unclean hands', do not bar a declaration.[15] As was said at first instance by Colman J in *P & O Nedlloyd BV v Arab Metals Co*,[16] in the context of deciding whether delay barred a declaration as to contractual rights, 'a declaration, although a discretionary remedy, is not an equitable remedy but is a creation of the Judicature Acts 1873 and 1875'.

All this does not, of course, mean that a declaration will never be refused. The claimant must have a real interest in the matter and must not be merely an interfering busybody. Nor will it be granted where no dispute or infringement of legal rights has yet taken place and the chances of that occurring are regarded as too hypothetical.[17] Moreover, the dispute must normally be as between the parties.[18] In Lord Diplock's words in *Gouriet v Union of Post Office Workers*,[19] '... the jurisdiction is not to declare the law generally or to give advisory opinions; it is confined to declaring legal rights, subsisting or future, of the parties represented in the litigation before it and not those of anyone else.' And in *Meadows Indemnity Co Ltd v Insurance Corpn of Ireland Ltd*[20] a declaration sought by a reinsurer as to the invalidity of a claim made under the head insurance was refused by the Court of Appeal on the ground that there was no contested issue between the reinsurer and the head-assured.

As regards limitation periods, a declaration that there has been a breach of contract or a tort appears to fall within the normal limitation periods for breach of contract and torts; but there is no limitation period, because there is no accrual of a cause of action, where a claimant seeks a negative declaration that there has been no breach of contract or tort.[21]

---

[13] [1958] 1 QB 554, at 571.
[14] [2000] 1 WLR 2040, at 2050. See also, eg, *Greenwich Healthcare National Health Service Trust v London and Quadrant Housing Trust* [1998] 3 All ER 437 (claimant granted negative declaration that defendant would not be entitled to an injunction or damages if claimant went ahead with a development).
[15] *Fisher v Brooker* [2009] UKHL 41, [2009] 1 WLR 1764, at [78]–[79] (a delay of 38 years in asserting copyright in a piece of music could not, by reason of laches, bar a declaration as to the claimant's entitlement to the copyright because laches applies only to equitable relief and it was held that a declaration is not equitable relief).
[16] [2005] EWHC 1276 (Comm), [2005] 1 WLR 3733, at [21]; reversed without casting doubt on this at [2006] EWCA Civ 1300, [2007] 1 WLR 2483.
[17] *Mellstrom v Garner* [1970] 1 WLR 603.
[18] An exception is where a health authority or relative or next friend seeks a declaration in respect of a patient: see, eg, *Re S* [1995] 3 All ER 290.
[19] [1978] AC 435, at 501. See also Lord Wilberforce at 483.   [20] [1989] 2 Lloyd's Rep 298.
[21] *Aspect Contracts (Asbestos) Ltd v Higgins Construction plc* [2015] UKSC 38, [2015] 1 WLR 2961, at [21]–[22]. For discussion, in the context of personal injury, of the converse issue of a negative declaration potentially

As a remedy for a tort or breach of contract a declaration is generally concerned to pronounce authoritatively that the defendant's conduct did or does amount to a tort or breach of contract. So in *Harrison v Duke of Rutland*[22] the defendant, on a counterclaim, was granted a declaration that the claimant was trespassing when he rode his bicycle along the defendant's road as a means of interfering with the defendant's grouse-shooting; and in *Louis Dreyfus et Cie v Parnaso Cia Naviera SA*[23] the claimants were at first instance granted, but on appeal refused, a declaration that the defendant shipowners were in breach of a charterparty. A claimant may also seek a declaration of the defendant's duties to him, so as to counter a threatened tort or breach of contract. In *Rajbenbach v Mamon*,[24] for example, the claimant tenant was granted a declaration of the defendant landlord's contractual obligations to him following the defendant's anticipatory repudiation of a contract under which the defendant was to pay the claimant £300 for vacating premises by a certain date. It is especially where the claimant is seeking to enforce obligations in a continuing contractual relationship that the declaration shows its advantages, for as Borchard has written:

> 'The declaration rather than the more drastic and definitive coercive decree enables the parties to re-establish their questioned relations without irreparable injury. The declaration thus has a social advantage which should not be underestimated as an element in the administration of justice.'[25]

Two final points are noteworthy. First, in some cases the courts have found it useful to be able to grant a declaration, while refusing or suspending the more drastic remedy of an injunction.[26] Secondly, the courts now have power to award an interim declaration.[27]

---

undermining, by cutting short, the disability provision on limitation in s 28 of the Limitation Act 1980, see obiter dicta in *Toropdar v D* [2009] EWHC 567 (QB), [2010] Lloyd's R IR 358 (court could have granted negative declaration that a person was not liable to the injured party even though the limitation period had not run out—because the injured party was under 18—and might never run out if the injured party had suffered permanent brain damage). For criticism, see K Patten, 'When is a Limitation Period not a Limitation Period?' (2010) 29 CJQ 284.

[22] [1893] 1 QB 142.
[23] [1959] 1 QB 498; rvsd [1960] 2 QB 49. See also *Burdett-Coutts v Hertfordshire County Council* [1984] IRLR 91 (declaration that the defendant was in breach of contract of employment). For the grant of a declaration as to the correct interpretation of a contractual clause limiting damages for breach of contract see, eg, *Royal Devon and Exeter NHS Foundation Trust v ATOS IT Services UK Ltd* [2017] EWCA Civ 2196, [2018] 2 All ER (Comm) 535.
[24] [1955] 1 QB 283.
[25] E Borchard, *Declaratory Judgments* (2nd edn, Banks-Baldwin Law Publishing Co 1941) 554.
[26] *Llandudno Urban District Council v Woods* [1899] 2 Ch 705; *Stollmeyer v Trinidad Lake Petroleum Co* [1918] AC 485; *Race Relations Board v Applin* [1973] QB 815.
[27] CPR 25.1(1)(b). For discussion of the appropriateness of granting interim declarations in order to assist banks in relation to the criminal law on money laundering see, eg, *Bank of Scotland v A Ltd* [2001] EWCA Civ 52, [2001] 1 WLR 751; *Amalgamated Metal Trading Ltd v City of London Police Financial Investigation Unit* [2003] EWHC 703 (Comm), [2003] 1 WLR 2711. For the previous law, to the effect that the courts did not have power to grant interim declarations, see *Underhill v Ministry of Food* [1950] 1 All ER 591; *International General Electric Co of New York Ltd v Customs and Excise Comrs* [1962] Ch 784; *R v IRC, ex p Rossminster Ltd* [1980] AC 952; *Riverside Mental Health NHS Trust v Fox* [1994] 1 FLR 614; *Newport AFC Ltd v FA of Wales* [1995] 2 All ER 87.

PART SIX

REMEDIES FOR EQUITABLE WRONGS

26

Remedies for equitable wrongs

1. Introduction	509
2. Compensation for equitable wrongs	511
3. Restitution and punishment for equitable wrongs	525
4. Compelling performance or preventing (or compelling the undoing of) an equitable wrong	538
5. Declaring rights	541
6. Miscellaneous issues on remedies for equitable wrongs	542
7. Conclusion	544

1. Introduction

Torts and breach of contract are termed common law wrongs because they were historically developed in the common law courts. Equitable wrongs are civil wrongs that historically were developed in the Court of Chancery. Despite the fusion of the common law courts and the Court of Chancery by the Supreme Court of Judicature Acts 1873–1875, much of the substantive law has not been fused. One example is the continued distinction between common law and equitable wrongs. In a rational fused system, nothing should turn on whether a civil wrong is common law or equitable. But that is not the present law.

Three introductory points on equitable wrongs and remedies for equitable wrongs should be made.[1] First, at the present time, equitable civil wrongs comprise breach of fiduciary duty, breach of confidence (which is distinct from the tort of misuse of private information),[2] dishonestly procuring or assisting a breach of fiduciary duty,[3] and those forms of estoppel that constitute causes of action, in particular proprietary estoppel. In contrast to those equitable wrongs, it is not clear that 'intermeddling by knowing receipt and dealing', usually referred to as 'knowing receipt', is a wrong rather being an aspect of the law of (non-wrongful) unjust enrichment.[4] The liability in question traditionally covers where a third party, who is not a fiduciary, receives property, with the requisite knowledge, from a trustee (or other fiduciary) that is transferred in breach of trust. As knowing receipt is not clearly a wrong, it is not dealt with in this chapter (or book). If knowing receipt (or a sub-division of it, for example, dishonest receipt) were to be treated

---

[1] See also above, pp 11–13.   [2] See above, pp 12–13.
[3] *Royal Brunei Airlines v Tan* [1995] 2 AC 378; *Fyffes Group Ltd v Templeman* [2000] 2 Lloyd's Rep 643; *Grupo Torras SA v Al-Sabah (No 5)* [2001] Lloyd's Rep Bank 36; *Twinsectra v Yardley* [2002] UKHL 12, [2002] 2 AC 164; C Mitchell, 'Assistance' in *Breach of Trust* (eds P Birks and A Pretto, Hart Publishing 2002) 139–212; S Elliott and C Mitchell, 'Remedies for Dishonest Assistance' (2004) 67 MLR 16. It cannot yet be said that there is an accepted analogous equitable wrong of procuring or assisting a breach of confidence, although in principle there should be: for important obiter dicta supporting this, see *Vestergaard Frandsen A/S v Bestnet Europe Ltd* [2013] UKSC 31, [2013] 1 WLR 1556, at [26]; see also *Thomas v Pearce* [2000] FSR 718 (although it is not clear that the claim there was for assisting a breach of confidence as opposed to a breach of confidence by a 'third party' recipient of the information).
[4] See A Burrows, *The Law of Restitution* (OUP 2011) 424–431, 622–623 esp n 9.

as an equitable wrong, equitable compensation would be a standard remedy and what is otherwise said in this chapter about the remedies available for dishonest assistance would apply equally to knowing receipt.

Of the four types of equitable wrong, the most wide-ranging is breach of fiduciary duty which extends well beyond trustees.[5] In Australia, New Zealand, and Canada, claims for breach of fiduciary duty have for many years been commonplace. In England it is only relatively recently that the potential of breach of fiduciary duty has been fully realised: it has therefore been something of a new departure for claims for 'professional negligence' against, for example, solicitors to be pleaded not only in contract and tort but also for breach of fiduciary duty.

Secondly, while it would have been possible to examine remedies for equitable wrongs alongside torts and breach of contract throughout this book, it was thought that it would aid clear exposition, and make the book easier to use, to devote this final chapter to remedies for equitable wrongs. The aim is to enable the parallels—and contrasts—with remedies for the common law wrongs to be easily understood.

Thirdly, while it is still essentially true that only equitable remedies are available for equitable wrongs, it is also true that the same, or similar, functions are performed by the equitable remedies for equitable wrongs as by the (common law and equitable) remedies for torts and breach of contract that have been considered in chapters 1–25 of this book. An important purpose of this chapter is to enable the reader to see clearly the coherence of remedial function across the divide between common law and equitable wrongs. In understanding this, the reader may find helpful the following table of primary functions and remedies for equitable wrongs which can be compared with, and seen to be largely consistent with, the equivalent table for torts and breach of contract in chapter 1.[6]

Remedies for Equitable Wrongs	
Primary Function	*Remedies*
Compensation	Equitable compensation. (Equitable) compensatory damages.
Restitution	Account of profits. Award of money had and received. Constructive trust.
Punishment?	Punitive damages?
Compelling performance (of positive obligations)	Mandatory enforcing injunction. Appointment of a receiver.
Preventing a wrong	Prohibitory injunction. Delivery up for destruction or destruction on oath.
Compelling the undoing of a wrong	Mandatory restorative injunction. Delivery up of material containing confidential information.
Declaring rights	Declaration.

[5] There is a huge literature, which is outside the central focus of this book, on what constitutes a fiduciary duty and when it arises.

[6] See above, p 10. We do not consider in this chapter some specialised judicial remedies for breach of fiduciary duty: eg the removal by a court of a trustee (see J Glister and J Lee, *Hanbury and Martin on Modern Equity* (21st edn, Sweet & Maxwell 2018) para 18.040).

This chapter is structured according to the primary functions of the remedies for equitable wrongs. Its main sections therefore correspond with the four parts into which chapters 3–25 were divided, namely compensation, restitution (sometimes referred to as disgorgement) and punishment, compelling performance or preventing (or compelling the undoing of) an equitable wrong, and declaring rights. A final section deals with two miscellaneous issues on remedies for equitable wrongs, namely interest and limitation periods.

2. Compensation for equitable wrongs

Common law compensatory damages are, at present, available only for common law wrongs, that is, torts and breach of contract. They are not available for equitable wrongs. So one cannot be awarded common law compensatory damages for breach of fiduciary duty or (although there is on-going debate about this)[7] breach of confidence. This historical anachronism (although opponents of the fusion of common law and equity would, no doubt, disagree with that description) leaves no great lacuna in the law because there is an analogous equitable remedy performing the same function of compensation. This is the remedy of 'equitable compensation' (sometimes labelled 'accounting for loss') which, until relatively recently, had been little discussed or analysed.[8] We shall also see that equitable damages, awarded in substitution for, or in addition to, an injunction under the Senior Courts Act 1981, s 50 (the successor to Lord Cairns's Act) may sometimes be awarded to compensate the claimant for equitable wrongs just as they may be for common law wrongs.

(1) Equitable compensation

(a) Compensation for loss

That equitable compensation is a remedy available for breach of fiduciary duty has now been clearly established.[9] As we shall see below, the best view is that equitable compensation has absorbed, or been assimilated with, the remedy for breach of fiduciary duty of 'accounting (for loss)'. There are also proprietary estoppel cases where the monetary remedy awarded is best viewed as 'equitable compensation'.[10] The reasoning of the Privy Council in

---

[7] Below, pp 520–522.
[8] The catalyst for greater use being made of 'equitable compensation' may have been the path-breaking article by I Davidson, 'The Equitable Remedy of Compensation' (1982) 13 Melb Univ LR 349. For other examinations of equitable compensation see, eg, M Tilbury, *Civil Remedies* (Butterworths 1990) paras 3247–3254; W Gummow, 'Compensation for Breach of Fiduciary Duty' in *Equity, Fiduciaries and Trusts* (ed T Youdan, Carswell 1989) 57–92; J McCamus, 'Equitable Compensation and Restitutionary Remedies: Recent Developments' in *Law of Remedies: Principles and Proofs* (Special Lectures of the Law Society of Upper Canada, Carswell 1995) 295, 298–332; C Rickett, 'Compensating for Loss in Equity – Choosing the Right Horse for Each Course' in *Restitution and Equity* (eds P Birks and F Rose, Mansfield Press 2000) 173–191; J Getzler, 'Equitable Compensation and the Regulation of Fiduciary Relationships' in *Restitution and Equity* (eds P Birks and F Rose, Mansfield Press 2000) 235–237; M Conaglen, 'Equitable Compensation for Breach of Fiduciary Dealing Rules' (2003) 119 LQR 246. See also the essays by J Ward, J Edelman, J Penner, L Ho, J Hudson, P Turner, and S Degeling in *Equitable Compensation and Disgorgement of Profit* (eds S Degeling and J Varuhas, Hart Publishing 2017).
[9] *Fry v Fry* (1859) 27 Beav 144; *Nocton v Lord Ashburton* [1914] AC 932, *McKenzie v McDonald* [1927] VLR 134 (equitable compensation on terms); *Re Dawson* [1966] 2 NSWLR 211; *Wallersteiner v Moir (No 2)* [1975] QB 373; *Bartlett v Barclays Bank Trust Co (No 2)* [1980] Ch 515; *Re Bell's Indenture* [1980] 1 WLR 1217; *Target Holdings Ltd v Redfern* [1996] AC 421; *Bristol & West Building Society v Mothew* [1998] Ch 1; *Swindle v Harrison* [1997] 4 All ER 705; *AIB Group (UK) Ltd v Mark Redler & Co* [2014] UKSC 58, [2015] AC 1503.
[10] Eg *Dodsworth v Dodsworth* (1973) 228 Estates Gazette 1115; *Baker & Baker v Baker* (1993) 25 HLR 408; *Wayling v Jones* (1995) 69 P & CR 170; *Gillett v Holt* [2001] Ch 210; *Jennings v Rice* [2002] EWCA Civ 159, [2003] 1 P & CR 8. See also below, nn 98–99. For a detailed discussion of the courts' approach to proprietary estoppel remedies, see B McFarlane, *The Law of Proprietary Estoppel* (OUP 2014) ch 7.

Royal Brunei Airlines v Tan,[11] and cases subsequent to it,[12] also indicates that the primary monetary remedy for the equitable wrong of dishonestly procuring or assisting a breach of fiduciary duty is equitable compensation, albeit that the traditional language of 'accounting as a constructive trustee' has often tended to obscure this.[13]

Peculiarly, there has been no English case in which equitable compensation has been awarded for breach of confidence.[14] Instead, the courts have tended to think of equitable damages awarded in substitution for, or in addition to, an injunction under the Senior Courts Act 1981, s 50.[15] As the standard remedy for breach of fiduciary duty is equitable compensation, it is odd that the same is not also true of breach of confidence.

The basic aim of 'equitable compensation', as its name suggests, is to compensate a loss. In other words, it is concerned to put the claimant into as good a position as if no wrong had occurred. It therefore has exactly the same function as compensatory damages. This is why the House of Lords in *Target Holdings Ltd v Redfern*[16] and the Supreme Court in *AIB Group (UK) Ltd v Mark Redler & Co*[17] (the facts of which are examined below)[18] held that there could be no equitable compensation where the loss would have been suffered even if there had been no breach of duty; that is, where the breach of fiduciary duty had caused the claimant no loss. Of course, and just as at common law, what is a loss and hence what is required in order to compensate will vary according to the duty broken and fiduciary duties may be positive as well as negative. If the duty broken was a failure to invest on behalf of a trust fund the aim of the compensation will be to put the beneficiaries into as good a position as if there had been that investment. If the duty broken was in stealing money from the trust fund, the aim of the compensation will be to put the beneficiaries into as good a position as if that money had not been stolen (ie to restore the money).

In principle, in order to put the claimant into as good a position as if the equitable wrong had not occurred, the equitable compensation should cover non-pecuniary as well as pecuniary loss (albeit that, as a matter of policy, there may be particular restrictions on this). Although there has as yet been no English case awarding equitable compensation for non-pecuniary loss, there is support in Canada for this.[19]

An important question is whether the same limitations that apply to compensatory damages also apply to equitable compensation. In other words do limitations such as remoteness, intervening cause, and contributory negligence apply to equitable compensation? The practical importance of this is that where a claimant has a choice of causes of action, so that the claimant may choose to sue for breach of contract, tort, or an equitable wrong, it may be advantageous to found the claim on the equitable wrong if the limitations

---

[11] [1995] 2 AC 378. [12] See above, n 3.
[13] For criticism of this phrase in this context, see J Glister and J Lee, *Hanbury and Martin on Modern Equity* (21st edn, Sweet & Maxwell 2018) para 9.009; *Dubai Aluminium Co Ltd v Salaam* [2002] UKHL 48, [2003] 2 AC 366, at [142] (per Lord Millett).
[14] In Canada, 'equitable compensation' has been awarded by the Supreme Court for breach of confidence: see *Cadbury Schweppes v FBI Foods Ltd* (1999) 167 DLR (4th) 577. For the uncertainty in English law, see *Force India Formula One Team v 1 Malaysian Racing Team Sdn Bhd* [2012] EWHC 616 (Ch), [2012] RPC 29, at [392]–[393] (per Arnold J) (decision upheld on appeal at [2013] EWCA Civ 780, [2013] RPC 36).
[15] See, eg, *Attorney-General v Guardian Newspapers (No 2)* [1990] 1 AC 109 (per Lord Goff). In some cases, the courts have awarded damages for breach of confidence without discussing whether they were equitable or common law damages: see below, pp 520–522.
[16] [1996] AC 421. See also *Gwembe Valley Development Co Ltd v Koshy* [2003] EWCA Civ 1048, [2004] 1 BCLC 131, at [142]–[160] (no loss caused by breach of fiduciary duty by director and therefore no equitable compensation could be awarded).
[17] [2014] UKSC 58, [2015] AC 1503. [18] Below, pp 515–520.
[19] *M(H) v M(K)* (1992) 96 DLR (4th) 289, Supreme Court of Canada (equitable compensation for breach of fiduciary duty).

that would apply to compensatory damages do not apply (or apply in a less restrictive way) to equitable compensation.

Examination of the cases in the common law world on this central question reveals that there is a fundamental conflict of opinion. On the one hand, there are those judges who consider that the limitations on common law compensatory damages, such as remoteness, intervening cause, and contributory negligence, do not apply to equitable compensation. This was the opinion of Lord Browne-Wilkinson, giving the leading speech, in *Target Holdings v Redfern*. In emphasising that a trustee would be liable for breach of trust even if the immediate cause of the loss was a third party, his Lordship said, 'thus the common law rules of remoteness of damages and causation do not apply.'[20] This was also the approach of the minority, led by McLachlin J, in the influential Canadian case of *Canson Enterprises v Broughton*.[21] Here a claim for equitable compensation was brought against a solicitor for breach of fiduciary duty in relation to the claimant's purchase of land. While all the judges in the Supreme Court of Canada concurred in the result, namely that the solicitor was liable for the claimant's loss but only until the intervention of third parties which in effect broke the chain of causation, the minority and the majority disagreed in their reasoning. McLachlin J for the minority said:

> '[This case] raises the question of whether the plaintiff can hold the solicitor liable for loss suffered by the plaintiff due to the negligence of architects and engineers in subsequent construction on the land. I agree with La Forest J that the solicitor's liability does not extend this far ... I base this result, however, in equity. I cannot concur in the suggestion in my colleague's reasons that ... damages for breach of fiduciary duty should be measured by analogy to tort and contract ... The basis of the fiduciary obligation and the rationale for equitable compensation are distinct from the tort of negligence and contract. In negligence and contract the parties are taken to be independent and equal actors, concerned primarily with their own self-interest. Consequently the law seeks a balance between enforcing obligations by awarding compensation and preserving optimum freedom for those involved in the relationship in question, communal or otherwise. The essence of a fiduciary relationship, by contrast, is that one party pledges itself to act in the best interest of the other. The fiduciary relationship has trust, not self-interest, at its core, and when breach occurs, the balance favours the person wronged.'[22]

So the argument of the minority was that common law limitations were not directly applicable to equitable compensation and that no analogy should be drawn with contract and tort. In other words, common law and equity are here different and should remain so.

This is also the view in Australia. In *Pilmer v Duke Group Ltd*[23] the High Court, in obiter dicta, said that contributory negligence was inapplicable to equitable compensation for breach of fiduciary duty. In a joint judgment, McHugh, Gummow, Hayne, and Callinan JJ, said, '[I]n Australia, the measure of compensation in respect of losses sustained by reason of breach of fiduciary duty by a trustee or other fiduciary is determined by equitable principles and these do not necessarily reflect the rules for assessment of damages in tort or contract.'[24] Again in *Youyang Pty Ltd v Minter Ellison Morris Fletcher*[25] the High Court of

---

[20] [1996] AC 421, at 434.   [21] (1991) 85 DLR (4th) 129.   [22] ibid, at 154.
[23] (2001) 75 ALJR 1067. On the main point in the case, the majority of the High Court (Kirby J dissenting) held that a company that is induced by a negligent report on a 'target' company to issue shares in order to acquire that target company` suffers no loss. For criticism, see R Nolan and D Prentice, 'The Issue of Shares – Compensating the Company for Loss' (2002) 118 LQR 180. See also F Oditah, 'Takeovers, Share Exchanges and the Meaning of Loss' (1996) 112 LQR 424.
[24] (2001) 75 ALJR 1067, at [85].   [25] (2003) 196 ALR 482, at 492.

Australia (Gleeson CJ, McHugh, Gummow, Kirby, and Hayne JJ) cited with approval the second part of the passage from McLachlin J's judgment in the *Canson* case set out above.

Taking the opposing view—that common law restrictions on compensatory damages should apply also to equitable compensation—are, for example, the majority in the *Canson Enterprises* case, led by La Forest J; the New Zealand Court of Appeal in *Day v Mead*[26] and *Bank of New Zealand v New Zealand Guardian Trust Ltd*;[27] and, as regards equitable compensation for breach of fiduciary duty comprising a failure to use care and skill, Millett LJ in *Bristol & West Building Society v Mothew*.[28]

In *Day v Mead*, where contributory negligence was applied to equitable compensation for breach of fiduciary duty by a solicitor, Cooke P said:[29]

'As Lord Diplock put it (in *United Scientific Holdings Ltd v Burnley Borough Council*)[30] law and equity have mingled now; the [Judicature] Acts did not bring to a sudden halt the whole process of development of the common law of England that had been so notable a feature of the preceding decades; the legislation placed no ban upon further development of substantive rules by judicial decision ... Whether or not there are reported cases in which compensation for breach of fiduciary obligation has been assessed on the footing that the plaintiff should accept some share of the responsibility, there appears to be no solid reason for denying jurisdiction to follow that obviously just course, especially now that law and equity have mingled or are interacting. It is an opportunity for equity to show that it has not petrified and to live up to the spirit of its maxims.'

And Millett LJ in *Bristol & West Building Society v Mothew* said:[31]

'Although the remedy which equity makes available for breach of the equitable duty of skill and care is equitable compensation rather than damages, this is merely the product of history and in this context it is in my opinion a distinction without a difference. Equitable compensation for breach of the duty of skill and care resembles common law damages in that it is awarded by way of compensation to a plaintiff for his loss. There is no reason in principle why the common law rules of causation, remoteness of damage and measure of damages should not be applied by analogy in such a case.'

This 'opposing' view is to be preferred.[32] Given the discretion open at common law in applying limitations, and the different approach to limitations that has been taken in respect of, for example, the tort of deceit,[33] there is no good reason for equitable compensation going its own separate way from compensatory damages. On the contrary, compensatory damages and equitable compensation should be regarded as identical in function—compensation—and identical in relation to the application of limitations. This is not to say that identical compensation will always be awarded irrespective of whether the claimant sues for breach of fiduciary duty, breach of contract, or for the tort of negligence. But any differences should rationally turn on the different duties in question and not on the fact that the remedy is equitable compensation rather than common law damages.[34]

---

[26] [1987] 2 NZLR 443. [27] [1999] 1 NZLR 664. [28] [1998] Ch 1.
[29] [1987] 2 NZLR 443, at 451. [30] [1978] AC 904, at 924–925. [31] [1998] Ch 1, at 17.
[32] A Burrows, 'We Do This At Common Law But That In Equity' (2002) 22 OJLS 1, esp 9–12; A Burrows, 'Fusing Common Law and Equity: Remedies, Restitution and Reform' Hochelaga Lecture 2001 (Sweet & Maxwell 2002) esp 6–14.
[33] Above, ch 7. For a case denying the applicability of contributory negligence to dishonestly committed wrongs, whether common law or equitable, see *Corporacion Nacional del Cobre de Chile v Sogemin Metals Ltd* [1997] 1 WLR 1396: above, p 136 n 291.
[34] Sarah Worthington, in her review of A Burrows and E Peel, *Commercial Remedies* (OUP 2003), at (2005) MLR 497 suggests that, within fiduciary duties, the approach to compensation, including whether compensation is available at all, may differ depending on the type of fiduciary duty. For example, the approach to the duty of loyalty should differ from the approach to a duty of care. But types of duty can also differ as between contracts and as

(b) No separate non-compensatory 'account' remedy

It is also important to clarify that the remedy of equitable compensation has absorbed, or been assimilated with, the remedy of accounting (for loss).[35] The argument has been put that the latter remedy may operate differently as a remedy against a trustee than equitable compensation because it is concerned to restore a trust fund to where it was, prior to an unauthorised disposal of trust assets, rather than to compensate. The account remedy, so it is argued, is therefore analogous to an action in debt (or specific performance or a mandatory injunction) in contrast to equitable compensation which is analogous to an action for compensatory damages. Where there has been a breach of trust (eg by an unauthorised payment of money from the trust fund), it allows the beneficiaries to 'falsify' the account and therefore to require the trustee to restore the trust fund by the equivalent of a debt action (hence the traditional language of this as being an 'equitable debt' action).[36] Put another way, the account remedy, unlike equitable compensation, responds to a trustee's primary obligation rather than being a remedy for breach of a trustee's primary obligation. That there is this type of difference has been argued by, for example, Peter Birks,[37] Lord Millett,[38] Steven Elliott,[39] Charles Mitchell,[40] and James Edelman.[41]

But that argument is inconsistent with the central reasoning of the House of Lords in *Target Holdings Ltd v Redfern*[42] and was expressly considered and rejected by the Supreme Court in *AIB Group (UK) Ltd v Mark Redler & Co*.[43]

In the former case the defendants were solicitors who were acting for mortgagees (the claimants) in relation to the purchase of property by C Ltd. In breach of trust the defendants paid over the loaned money (£1,525,000) from the claimants to the vendors prior to the completion of the sale and charge. That was a breach of trust albeit that a few days

---

between contract and tort. There seems no reason to doubt that the flexibility within common law compensatory damages, depending on the type of duty, can be replicated within equitable compensation.

[35] Contrast the clearly different remedy of accounting for profits which is concerned to effect restitution and not compensation.

[36] In relation to damages for torts and breach of contract, we have explored the view, albeit to reject it, that so-called compensatory damages are sometimes not concerned to compensate a loss but to value the right infringed; and we have also explored the view that the courts are sometimes concerned to award as damages a non-compensatory cost of cure: see above, ch 3. There is some similarity between that debate and this one about the role of equitable compensation. Indeed, J Edelman, 'Money Awards of the Cost of Performance' (2010) 4 J Eq 122 argues that equitable compensation (in its substitutive sense) is the equivalent of the common law non-compensatory cost of cure: but, with respect, that may be misleading because, in contrast to the common law damages cases, there is surely no possible 'cure' in the relevant cases (it is too late for that) and, in any event, on the facts there is no question of the claimant seeking reimbursement for the cost of cure that it has itself undertaken. The better direct analogy would appear to be to the award of the agreed sum.

[37] P Birks, 'Equity in the Modern Law: an Exercise in Taxonomy' (1996) 26 Univ of Western Aus LR 1, 46–47.

[38] P Millett, 'Equity's Place in the Law of Commerce' (1998) 114 LQR 214, 225–227; and see Millett LJ's judgment in *Bristol & West Building Society v Mothew* [1998] Ch 1, at 18. See also *Bairstow v Queen's Moat Houses plc* [2001] EWCA Civ 712, [2001] 2 BCLC 531.

[39] In his Oxford D Phil thesis, S Elliott, *Compensation Claims Against Trustees* (2002). For the outline of his central argument, see S Elliott, 'Remoteness Criteria in Equity' (2002) 65 MLR 588, 590; S Elliott and C Mitchell, 'Remedies for Dishonest Assistance' (2004) 67 MLR 16, 23–36.

[40] C Mitchell, 'Stewardship of Property and Liability to Account' [2014] Conv 215. Mitchell contrasts 'substitutive performance claims' and 'reparative compensation claims'.

[41] J Edelman, 'Money Awards of the Cost of Performance' (2010) 4 J Eq 122; J Edelman, 'An English Misturning with Equitable Compensation' in *Equitable Compensation and Disgorgement of Profit* (eds S Degeling and J Varuhas, Hart Publishing 2017) 91. See also *Agricultural Land Management Ltd v Jackson (No 2)* [2014] WASC 102, where Edelman J uses Elliott's terminology by distinguishing, within equitable compensation, between 'substitutive compensation' and 'reparative compensation'.

[42] [1996] AC 421. *Target Holdings* was distinguished by the High Court of Australia in *Youyang Pty Ltd v Minter Ellison Morris Fletcher* (2003) 196 ALR 482, noted by S Elliott and J Edelman '*Target Holdings* Considered in Australia' (2003) 119 LQR 545.

[43] [2014] UKSC 58, [2015] AC 1503.

afterwards the completion of the sale and charge did take place. Subsequently C Ltd became insolvent and the claimants repossessed the property selling it for £500,000. The defendants argued that their breach of trust was technical only because the claimants had subsequently obtained the charge to which they were entitled. The breach of trust had not caused the claimants the loss they had suffered which was rather caused by the property having been overvalued so that the claimants' security was inadequate. The House of Lords agreed and held that there could be no equitable compensation and, although this was implied rather than expressly stated, *no account remedy* where, as on these facts, the loss would have been suffered even if there had been no breach of duty.[44]

However, applying the argument of Birks, Millett, Elliott, Mitchell, and Edelman, the House of Lords should have taken a different approach to the supposedly separate account remedy than to equitable compensation (even if ultimately the same result might have been reached on the facts) precisely because, like an action in debt (or specific performance), the account remedy does not require loss to have been caused by the breach of trust: the fact that the beneficiaries would have suffered the loss in question irrespective of the breach of trust should have been irrelevant.

While historically it may be that the account remedy was viewed in this way, it is hard to see why logically or as a matter of policy one would wish to retain a distinctive remedy of that type. Why should one regard a trustee, who has without authority paid money out of a trust fund, as having a continuing positive duty to restore the trust fund to where it was prior to the payment out even though the same loss would have been suffered even if the trustee had complied with its duty? A trustee does not (normally) undertake to pay a particular sum to the beneficiaries so there is no direct analogy to a contractual debt claim.[45] And it is misleading to separate out one part of the trustee's duties as if there is a continuing duty to maintain the trust fund irrespective of the trustee's other duties or what has subsequently happened. True it is that one is seeking to replicate, by a monetary remedy, the required performance of the trustee not to make an unauthorised payment from the trust fund (just as where one compensates loss for breach of contract). But the essential point is that, had the trustee properly performed its duties, the beneficiaries would still have suffered the loss to the trust fund. One ought not artificially to freeze the trustee's duty and performance at one point in the past thereby ignoring the trustees' other duties and the other facts relevant to working out what the claimant's loss has been.

Sarah Worthington makes the same point and illustrates its force by an example.[46] Say a trustee takes £1 million from the trust funds for its own use, and uses it non-traceably. Assume that what it should have done, according to the trust deed, was invest these particular funds in shares which would now be worth £½ million. According to Worthington, it is inappropriate to regard the beneficiaries as having a remedy which requires the trustee to restore the trust fund by paying £1 million. That is to concoct a duty to restore the fund whereas the correct analysis was that there was an ongoing duty to invest the funds in shares. It is to that ongoing duty that the remedy must respond and the equitable compensation remedy, responding to the loss to the trust fund, would correctly lead to an award of

---

[44] It would clearly have been preferable for their Lordships to have mentioned expressly the account remedy and to have dealt expressly with the view that that remedy is the equivalent of the common law debt claim.

[45] Note also that the equitable debt action, if it exists, is surely not confined just to payments out of the trust fund but extends to all incorrect disposals of trust assets, whether those assets comprise money or not. It is the monetary sum produced by the account not the nature of the asset that is relevant. So, for example, the same approach would apply if the trust fund had comprised shares, rather than money, which the trustee had transferred in breach of trust.

[46] S Worthington, 'Four Questions on Fiduciaries' (2016) 2 CJCCL 723, 762–763.

£½ million. As Worthington writes, 'The beneficiary could claim equitable compensation for breach of trust, requiring the trustee to restore the trust fund to the state it *would* have been in if proper performance had been delivered.'[47]

It is submitted, therefore, that *Target Holdings v Redfern*, which is most naturally interpreted as having impliedly laid down that loss must have been factually caused in respect of the remedy of accounting (for loss), should be applauded for (impliedly) rejecting older cases that may have supported the view that the accounting remedy can operate differently from the remedy of equitable compensation. It impliedly laid down that, at least where a trust is over, there is no duty on a trustee, who has paid out money in breach of trust, to restore the trust fund to the position as it was prior to the payment out and hence there is no equitable debt remedy in that situation.

The implied rejection in *Target Holdings v Redfern* of an account as being a separate remedy from equitable compensation, and as not concerned with the claimant's loss, has subsequently been explicitly and strongly endorsed by the Supreme Court in *AIB Group (UK) Ltd v Mark Redler and Co*.[48] The defendants were solicitors. They were acting for both the borrowers and the claimant bank who was lending money to the borrowers which was to be secured by a charge over the borrowers' property. There was already a first charge over the property in favour of another bank (Barclays) and the new borrowing was to be used to discharge that charge. In breach of trust to the claimant bank, in respect of the money paid to them by the claimant bank, the defendants failed to pay the correct amount of money to Barclays with the consequence that Barclays' first charge was not discharged as it should have been. In other words, the defendants, in breach of trust, had failed correctly to use, as the trust required of them, the £3.3 million paid to them by the claimant bank. The claimant bank claimed £3.3 million (subject to a deduction of £867,697 as is explained below) by means of the remedy of an account arguing that that was a remedy to reconstitute the trust fund as it had been prior to the incorrect payment out. The claimant bank had received from the defendants £867,697, from the subsequent sale of the property, so that their precise account remedy sought was for the difference between those two figures (ie some £2.5 million).

The Supreme Court held that the equitable compensation/account remedy was concerned to compensate for the claimant's loss; and that, had the defendants paid across the correct sum, so that Barclays' first charge had been discharged, the claimant would still have suffered most of the loss because they had entered into a bad bargain with the borrowers whereby they had insufficient security for the money they were lending. As it was, the claimant had negotiated a deal with Barclays so that Barclays' first charge priority was limited to £273,777. It followed that, as a result of the breach of trust, the claimant was overall worse off by £273,777 because its charge was worth less by that amount than it should have been. The Supreme Court therefore awarded £273,777 as equitable compensation.

It is very important to appreciate that there was no question here of the Supreme Court not being made aware of the argument that there is an account remedy that is analogous to a claim in debt and is different from compensating for loss. The claimant put that argument up front and drew to the Supreme Court's attention the judicial reasoning of Lord Millett sitting in Hong Kong[49] and Edelman J in Australia[50] and the academic writings (of, for

---

[47] ibid, at 763. If the shares would now have been worth £5 million, equitable compensation would require a payment of £4.5 million because that is the loss to the trust fund caused by the breach of trust.
[48] [2014] UKSC 58, [2015] AC 1503.
[49] In *Libertarian Investments Ltd v Hall* [2013] HKCFA 93, [2014] 1 HKC 368.
[50] In *Agricultural Land Management Ltd v Jackson (No 2)* [2014] WASC 102.

example, Charles Mitchell)[51] in which that argument had been forcefully put forward. The Supreme Court explicitly rejected that argument. There is no such separate remedy analogous to a claim in debt. *Target Holdings* was correctly decided and reasoned on this issue and did not require reinterpretation or rejection. In Lord Toulson's words, giving one of the two leading judgments:[52]

> '[The claimant's argument] involves effectively treating the unauthorised application of trust funds as creating an immediate debt between the trustee and the beneficiary, rather than conduct meriting equitable compensation for any loss thereby caused... it would not in my opinion be right to impose or maintain a rule that gives redress to a beneficiary for loss which would have been suffered if the trustee had properly performed its duties.'

And he later went on:

> 'To say that there has been a loss to the trust fund in the present case of £2.5M by reason of the solicitors' conduct, when most of that sum would have been lost if the solicitors had applied the trust fund in the way that the bank had instructed them to do, is to adopt an artificial and unrealistic view of the facts.'[53]

Even if it might perhaps be said that, while a trust is ongoing, it can be reconstituted by an account remedy which requires the trustee to pay money as required by its duty—although it may be thought more obvious for that to be accomplished by a mandatory injunction to that effect rather than an equitable monetary account remedy—plainly, once the trust is over, there is no such continuing duty. As was emphasised in Lord Toulson's judgment,[54] in both *Target Holdings* and *Redler* the trusts were over as a practical matter because the relevant transactions had been completed. So in neither case could it be said that the defendant solicitor should still be holding money paid by the claimant pending the sale and charge (in *Target Holdings*) or pending the discharge of the first charge (in *Redler*). Clearly the time for seeking a mandatory injunction had long since passed and no such injunction could now be granted.

A further point made in *Redler* was that the equitable compensation awarded would be of the same amount as an award of common law damages had the claimant bank sued the solicitors for breach of contract or the tort of negligence.[55] In that sense, there was welcome assimilation of the equitable and common law remedies. Similarly it should be noted that, had there been a claim brought in contract, specific performance could not have been granted because, in the light of what had subsequently happened, it was impossible for the trustees now to comply with their previous duties to reconstitute and continue the trust.

James Edelman has argued that the decision in *Redler* was plainly incorrect both at common law and in equity.[56] He presents the simple argument that, according to the express terms of the contract (and hence the terms of the trust), the loaned money was to be held on trust until 'completion'; and that, if completion were delayed, it was to be paid back. On his interpretation of those express terms, there never was a completion, so that the clause about delayed completion applied. There was therefore a common law debt claim (as

---

[51] See above, n 40.
[52] [2014] UKSC 58, [2015] AC 1503, at [61]–[62]. Lord Toulson's judgment was agreed with by Lord Neuberger, Lady Hale, and Lord Wilson. Lord Reed's judgment may also lay claim to be a leading judgment as it was also agreed with by Lord Neuberger, Lady Hale, and Lord Wilson.
[53] ibid, at [65].   [54] ibid, at [34]–[35], [40], [44], and esp [74].
[55] ibid, at [76]. This is not to deny the point made by Lord Reed that, where there are different obligations, the loss flowing from those different obligations may differ.
[56] J Edelman, 'An English Misturning with Equitable Compensation' in *Equitable Compensation and Disgorgement of Profit* (eds S Degeling and J Varuhas, Hart Publishing 2017) 91.

well as an equitable account debt claim although it was unnecessary to turn to that) for the repayment of the money. But it seems clear that the Supreme Court was taking a different interpretation of the contract and trust according to which there was no express provision for dealing with where the loaned money had been paid over but the charge of Barclays had not been fully discharged. In other words, the Supreme Court was taking the view that there had been completion for these purposes or, at least, that this situation was not covered by the provision on delayed completion.

Confusion has been caused by the Court of Appeal's subsequent decision in *Main v Giambrone & Law*.[57] The defendants were again solicitors and the claimants were prospective purchasers of holiday homes in Italy. The claimants had signed preliminary contracts and had paid deposits to the defendants on trust pending the issue of a bank loan guarantee issued by a financial institution listed in art 107 of an Italian decree. In breach of trust, the defendants had released the deposits on the issue of a bank loan guarantee issued by a financial institution listed in art 106. The institutions in art 106 were not as strong as those listed in art 107. As it transpired, it did not matter which guarantee was in place because the events that occurred, even though involving the loss of the deposits, did not constitute a 'crisis' situation so as to trigger either guarantee. In other words, it would appear that the breach of trust had not caused the claimants any loss. They would have lost their deposits even if the defendants had complied with their duty. The claimants had successfully rescinded the contracts of purchase but had not recovered their deposits. They were therefore claiming equitable compensation for breach of trust (as well as damages for breach of contract and for the tort of negligence). One would have thought that, applying *Target Holdings* and *Redler*, the claim for equitable compensation should have failed because the breach of trust had caused no loss.

But the Court of Appeal contrived to distinguish those cases and held that the claimants were entitled to recover the loss of the deposits as equitable compensation. The ground of distinction put forward was the solicitors' role in relation to the security. In both *Target Holdings* and *Redler* the defendant solicitors had had an obligation 'to take active steps'[58] to secure a charge or to remove a charge whereas here the defendant solicitors had an obligation 'to act as custodians of the deposit monies indefinitely'[59] and merely had to check that the guarantees were compliant. With respect, it is hard to see that these were valid grounds of distinction. In all three cases, the defendants had positive obligations to fulfil requiring active steps (checking the guarantee in *Giambrone* required an active step); and in all three cases one could say that the solicitors' obligation was to act as custodians of money indefinitely, ie until the required condition had been fulfilled (or had been overtaken by events).

Also controversial was the assertion by Jackson LJ that the same measure of damages would have applied had the claimants sought damages for breach of contract.[60] Surely if the solicitors had performed their contractual duty, the correct guarantee would have been put in place and the deposits would in any event have been lost. It is only if one assumes that no

---

[57] [2017] EWCA Civ 1193, [2018] PNLR 2. For an excellent case-note see P Davies, 'Equitable Compensation and the SAAMCO Principle' (2018) 134 LQR 165.
[58] [2017] EWCA Civ 1193, [2018] PNLR 2, at [61].   [59] ibid, at [62].
[60] ibid, at [63]. Jackson LJ also reasoned that, while the *SAAMCO* case (see above, p 125) should be applied to the claim for equitable compensation as it would to the claims for damages in contract and tort, it did not operate to limit the equitable compensation because this was a 'category two' case, above, p 125 n 220, where the whole loss was within the scope of the duty. With respect, that seems wrong. The solicitors were merely facilitating a decision to purchase property and the fact that that was a bad financial bargain for the claimants did not follow from any advice or information given by the solicitors.

correct guarantee would have followed on rejection of the incorrect guarantee, so that the whole deal would have been called off, that Jackson LJ's approach would hold good.

Also confusing is the Court of Appeal's decision in *Interactive Technology Corporation Ltd v Ferster*.[61] Here a director, in breach of fiduciary duty, had dishonestly induced a company to make an excessive remuneration payment to him. The Court of Appeal accepted that equitable compensation comprises two separate remedies: the restoration of the trust remedy and the compensation for loss remedy and that the claimant must elect between them. In so doing, the court explicitly endorsed the approach of Lord Millett and Charles Mitchell. The rejection of that approach in *Target Holdings* and *Redler* was ignored with the only mention of those leading cases being in the last sentence where it was simply said that the facts of those cases were different.

(2) Equitable (compensatory) damages

Equitable damages are damages awarded in addition to, or in substitution for, an injunction or specific performance under the Senior Courts Act 1981, s 50. We have seen in chapter 17 that they can be awarded, and can offer some advantages over common law damages, for a tort or breach of contract.

In respect of equitable wrongs, there appears to be no case illustrating the award of equitable damages other than for breach of confidence. But in principle there is no reason why, instead of equitable compensation, such damages should not be awarded for breach of fiduciary duty or dishonestly procuring or assisting a breach of fiduciary duty. Such damages would seem especially appropriate where the breach of fiduciary duty has not yet accrued and one is seeking damages for an anticipated breach. In that situation, it is unclear whether 'equitable compensation' as opposed to equitable damages could be awarded although, given that equitable compensation is an equitable remedy, it may be thought that there is not the same difficulty as where common law damages are sought.

Lest the point be lost, one should interject at this stage that all these technical distinctions between common law damages, equitable compensation, and equitable damages bring no credit to the legal system. They are the irrational historical residue of an unfused system that should be swept away.

As regards breach of confidence, damages, arguably best viewed as equitable damages, have been awarded in several cases. These will now be examined under two sub-headings. First, the jurisdiction to award damages for breach of confidence; and, secondly, the assessment of compensatory damages for breach of confidence.

(a) The jurisdiction to award damages for breach of confidence

There is an on-going debate as to the jurisdiction to award damages for breach of confidence. This directly links to general questions about the fusion of common law and equity and as to whether breach of confidence should be recognised as a tort rather than as an equitable wrong. In particular, if common law damages, rather than equitable damages (or equitable compensation) are being awarded for breach of confidence, this may be interpreted as showing either that breach of confidence is now a common law tort or that, contrary to the traditional 'anti-fusion' view, common law damages can be awarded for an equitable wrong.

---

[61] [2018] EWCA Civ 1594.

Whatever the attractions in principle, it is submitted that it cannot yet be said that breach of confidence (as a cause of action independent from breach of contract) is a tort. In so far as the judges have referred to, or discussed, this question, they have overwhelmingly viewed breach of confidence as an equitable wrong not a tort.[62] And in *Vidal-Hall v Google Inc*,[63] the tort of misuse of private information (ie the tort of privacy) was precisely distinguished from, and recognised as protecting different interests from, the equitable wrong of breach of confidence. Assuming then that breach of confidence (as opposed to the tort of privacy) is an equitable wrong, the 'jurisdictional' question is whether the damages awarded have always been equitable damages or whether, on the contrary, the best analysis is that common law damages have sometimes been awarded.

In some cases the damages are most naturally viewed as equitable. In *Saltman Engineering Co Ltd v Campbell Engineering Ltd*,[64] having established that the defendants were in breach of an equitable obligation of confidence in using drawings to make special tools, the Court of Appeal refused an injunction to restrain use or sale of the tools, but ordered an inquiry as to damages, Lord Greene MR saying that damages could be awarded under Lord Cairns's Act (now the Senior Courts Act 1981, s 50) '... to cover both past and future acts in lieu of an injunction'.[65] Again in *Seager v Copydex Ltd*[66] the Court of Appeal ordered damages to be awarded by the master for breach of confidence in manufacturing a carpet grip invented by the claimant. Although no explanation was offered as to the jurisdiction to award damages, the most natural interpretation, given the claimant's application for an injunction, was that they were granted in lieu of that injunction under Lord Cairns's Act.

Similarly, there are several cases in which the courts have accepted that damages in addition to an injunction can be awarded for breach of confidence. In *Peter Pan Manufacturing Corpn v Corsets Silhouette Ltd*,[67] for example, Pennycuick J said that, in addition to an injunction, the claimant had the option to claim damages or to take an account of profits (in fact the claimant chose the latter); and in *Ackroyds (London) Ltd v Islington Plastics Ltd*[68] Havers J, in addition to granting an injunction, ordered an inquiry into damages for breach of confidence. Although there was no explanation of the basis for the damages in these cases, it is natural to assume that they were additional to an injunction under Lord Cairns's Act.

However, in *Nichrotherm Electrical Co Ltd v Percy*[69] no application for an injunction had been made by the claimants and yet at first instance Harman J ordered an inquiry as to damages for breach of confidence. Unless one can make something of the fact that the claimants were also given leave to apply for an injunction it would seem that the damages

---

[62] See, eg, *Attorney-General v Guardian Newspapers (No 2)* [1990] 1 AC 109, at 286 (per Lord Goff): '[T]he remedy of damages ... in cases of breach of confidence is now available, despite the equitable nature of the wrong ...'; *Wainwright v Home Office* [2003] UKHL 53, [2003] 3 WLR 1137, at [18]. See also T Aplin et al, *Gurry on Breach of Confidence* (2nd edn, OUP 2012) paras 19.10–19.15. Cf *Aquaculture Corpn v New Zealand Mussel Co Ltd* [1990] 3 NZLR 299, at 301, where Cooke P said, 'Whether the obligation of confidence in a case of the present kind should be classified as purely an equitable one is debatable, but we do not think that the question matters for any purpose material to this appeal.' North has argued that breach of confidence is a tort: see P North, 'Breach of Confidence: Is There a New Tort?' (1972) 12 JSPTL 149. See also Law Commission, *Breach of Confidence* (1981) Report No 110.
[63] [2015] EWCA Civ 311, [2016] QB 1003. See above, p 13. This builds from Lord Nicholls' judgment in *Campbell v Mirror Group Newspapers Ltd* [2004] UKHL 22, [2004] AC 457, at [14]–[15], who reasoned that there is a tort of misuse of private information that has grown from the equitable cause of action of breach of confidence.
[64] [1948] 65 RPC 203.   [65] ibid, at 219.   [66] [1967] 1 WLR 923.
[67] [1963] RPC 45. See, similarly, the Australian case *Ansell Rubber Co Pty Ltd v Allied Rubber Industries Pty Ltd* [1972] RPC 811.
[68] [1962] RPC 97. See also the Australian cases *Interfirm Comparison (Australia) Pry Ltd v Law Society of New South Wales* [1977] RPC 137; *Talbot v General Television Corpn Pty Ltd* [1981] RPC 1.
[69] [1956] RPC 272.

cannot be regarded as equitable and that the decision is out of line with the other authorities. As Jones writes, 'Harman J's suggestion is mildly revolutionary in that, by implying that a damages claim can succeed independently of any prayer for equitable relief, it presupposes a fusion of law and equity.'[70] Significantly, the Court of Appeal[71] left open the question of whether there was jurisdiction to award damages in such a situation for breach of an equitable duty of confidence and instead upheld Harman J's decision on the ground that there had been a breach of a contractual duty of confidence where the jurisdiction to award damages was indisputable.

But the above interpretation of the cases is not the only one that can be offered. In particular it has been argued that, other than in respect of future acts, the damages in the above cases were ordinary common law, rather than equitable, damages.[72] Apart from the first instance decision in *Nichrotherm* the strongest point in support of this approach is that 'at first blush' one would expect damages in lieu of an injunction to cover only future and not past acts and, if so, the damages awarded for past acts, where no injunction was being granted, must have been given at common law. But Lord Greene MR in the *Saltman* case considered that damages in lieu of an injunction can cover past acts and ultimately this seems a preferable view.[73] For it avoids the anomaly of the courts being able to grant equitable damages to cover past acts in addition to an injunction, but only damages to cover future acts where no injunction is granted.

Meagher, Gummow, and Lehane have argued that even the award of equitable damages in these cases was incorrect because 'wrongful act' in Lord Cairns's Act referred only to legal and not equitable wrongs.[74] In their view, the remedy in question in these cases should therefore have been recognised as being not damages but 'equitable compensation'. But if there was ever any force in this narrow view, the re-enactment of the Lord Cairns's Act power in the Senior Courts Act 1981, s 50 has surely removed it; for that omits any reference to the detailed circumstances in which there is jurisdiction to entertain an application for an injunction or specific performance so that the term 'wrongful act' is no longer included.

More recent cases have continued to 'skirt' the issue as to whether the damages are equitable or common law. So while in obiter dicta in *Attorney-General v Guardian Newspapers (No 2)*[75] Lord Goff expressed the clear view that the damages were equitable, as being based on a generous interpretation of Lord Cairns's Act, the Court of Appeal in *Dawson & Mason Ltd v Potter*[76] awarded (compensatory) damages for breach of confidence without an injunction being granted or sought. A possible explanation for there being seen to be no problem with this was that, as in the *Nicrotherm* case, the breach of duty in question could have been viewed as purely contractual. In *Campbell v MGN Ltd*[77] the House of Lords upheld an award of £2,500 damages for mental distress plus £1,000 aggravated damages, in a claim framed as one for breach of confidence, without making any comment as to the jurisdictional basis of those damages: but that decision would now be viewed as awarding damages for the tort of privacy not the equitable wrong of breach of confidence.[78]

---

[70] G Jones, 'Restitution of Benefits Obtained in Breach Another's Confidence' (1970) 86 LQR 463, 491.
[71] [1957] RPC 207.
[72] P North, 'Breach of Confidence: Is There a New Tort?' (1972) 12 JSPTL 149. North's view that the damages were common law underpins his main argument that breach of confidence is recognised as a tort.
[73] This is supported by, eg, *Elsley v J G Collins Insurance Agencies Ltd* (1978) 83 DLR (3d) 1.
[74] J Heydon, M Leeming, and P Turner, *Meagher Gummow & Lehane's Equity – Doctrines and Remedies* (5th edn, LexisNexis 2015) paras 24-090–24-105, 42-191.
[75] [1990] 1 AC 109, at 286.   [76] [1986] 1 WLR 1419.   [77] [2004] UKHL 22, [2004] 2 AC 475.
[78] See above, p 285 n 73 and below, p 525.

(b) The assessment of compensatory damages for breach of confidence

Whether common law or equitable (and leaving aside a possible restitutionary analysis), damages for breach of confidence are compensatory with the aim being to put the claimant into as good a position as if no breach of confidence had occurred.

Where the breach has been of a commercial (rather than a personal) confidence, one would therefore expect the damages to be assessed in a directly analogous way to damages compensating pecuniary loss for wrongful infringement of intellectual property rights.[79] Confidential information is very similar to, and may even be regarded as, intellectual property. This is borne out by the approach to damages of the Court of Appeal in *Dowson & Mason Ltd v Potter*.[80] The claimants were manufacturers of a part for lorries. They would not have licensed the use of confidential information (obtained by the first defendant and used by the second defendant) relating to that part (which comprised the names and addresses of the suppliers to the claimants of the various components for the part and the price paid for them). The claimants were awarded as damages their lost sales profits consequent on the breach of confidence. This was to assess damages on the same basis as for (other) cases of intellectual property infringement.

The Court of Appeal distinguished *Seager v Copydex Ltd (No 2)*.[81] This dealt with a breach of confidence claim in respect of a carpet grip. The Court of Appeal put forward an approach that differs somewhat from the general approach to assessing damages for intellectual property infringement. Drawing an analogy with damages for conversion, Lord Denning viewed the issue in terms of the 'value' of the confidential information. He went on to say that the value depended on the nature of the confidential information. If there was nothing special about it, ie it was the sort of information which could be obtained by employing any competent consultant, the value was the fee which a consultant would charge for it because, by taking the information, the defendant has merely saved itself the time and trouble of employing a consultant. But if the information was special, for example, if it involved some inventive step, its value would be far higher: '... not merely a consultant's fee, but the price which a willing buyer—desirous of obtaining it—would pay for it. It is the value as between a willing buyer and a willing seller.'[82] It was suggested that this price might be calculated by a capitalisation of the royalties which the court thinks the defendant would have had to pay the claimant for the information.

This approach is controversial because Lord Denning's emphasis on the expense the defendant has saved makes it appear that he was more concerned to reverse the defendant's enrichment than to compensate the claimant's loss.[83] Although this has its attractions, and

---

[79] See above, pp 228–230.
[80] [1986] 2 All ER 418. See also *Talbot v General Television Corpn Pty Ltd* [1980] VR 224.
[81] [1969] 2 All ER 718. This case also indicates that the standard of liability for damages for breach of confidence may be strict: cf above, p 228 n 266.
[82] ibid, at 720.
[83] There is further tentative support for damages for breach of confidence sometimes being restitutionary in Sir Donald Nicholls V-C's judgment in *Universal Thermosensors Ltd v Hibben* [1992] 1 WLR 840. In assessing the defendants' damages on the claimant's cross-undertaking supporting an interim injunction restraining the defendants' breach of confidence, the Vice-Chancellor deducted the damages the claimant was entitled to 'for the benefits they derived from the wrongful use of its confidential information, in particular (but not exclusively) by saving themselves the time, trouble, and expense of compiling their own list of contacts without reference to the plaintiff's records' (at 858–859). He referred to *Seager v Copydex* and to the 'user principle' by which 'the plaintiff ought to be paid by the defendants for the use they made of the plaintiff's confidential information even if the plaintiff suffered no loss of profits in consequence' (at 856). Although he thereby used clear restitutionary reasoning, the strength of this is weakened by the fact that the Vice-Chancellor also described the damages as compensatory; and, despite the wrongdoing being intentional, he thought that the claimant was not entitled to an injunction (nor, by inference, to an account of profits) because that would put the claimant in a better position than if there had been no breach of confidence.

is supported by the reasoning in some other cases awarding 'negotiating damages' for torts and breach of contract,[84] it is difficult to reconcile with the Supreme Court's compensatory approach to 'negotiating damages' in *Morris-Garner v One Step (Support) Ltd*.[85]

Accepting, then, that the purpose of 'negotiating damages' is to compensate, there have been several other cases which support the view in *Seager v Copydex (No 2)* that 'negotiating damages'—aimed at awarding a reasonable licence or royalty fee—can be awarded for breach of confidence.[86]

For example, in obiter dicta in *Douglas v Hello! Ltd (No 6)*[87] the Court of Appeal indicated that, by analogy to intellectual property cases, licence fee damages could be awarded for breach of confidence in an appropriate case. Lord Phillips referred to such damages being awarded where there had been 'unauthorised use of, or unauthorised benefiting from, intellectual property *and similar rights* …'[88] On the facts, it was thought that such damages should not be awarded for various reasons, including that the claimants could not lawfully, and would not, have granted a licence to the defendants (Hello! Ltd) because they had already granted the exclusive licence to publish the wedding photographs to OK! Ltd.

Again, in *Vercoe v Rutland Fund Management Ltd*[89] the claimants had entered into a contract with the first defendant for them to purchase together a company. The first defendant in breach of contract had gone ahead and, along with other defendants, had purchased the company without involving the claimants. In so doing confidential information had also been used by the other defendants involved in the purchase. It was held that what are now called 'negotiating damages', assessed according to a reasonable price to buy a release from the claimants' rights, should be awarded against the first defendant for breach of contract and against the other defendants for breach of confidence. Sales J saw this award as compensatory. Particularly importantly and controversially he held that, even for the breach of confidence claim, the claimants were not entitled to elect for an account of profits rather than damages. The choice between damages and an account of profits was seen as being a matter for the court not the claimants. In his view, the extent of protection afforded by the law moves 'from lesser protection in relation to an ordinary commercial context to greater protection where there is a fiduciary relationship'.[90] Here one was in a commercial context and the remedy for breach of confidence should be analogous to that given for breach of contract. An account of profits was therefore inappropriate.

Finally, in *MVF 3 APS v Bestnet Europe Ltd*[91] damages were awarded for breach of confidence in respect of the defendants' manufacture and sale of mosquito nets. It was held that it was correct to have awarded damages on two bases. The first was the claimants' lost profits from the sales that, but for the breach of confidence, they would have made. This was referred to as the '*General Tire* measure' by analogy to the leading case on this approach to assessing damages for patent infringement.[92] The second, applicable to other sales made by the defendants in respect of which the claimants could not establish lost profits, was an award of a reasonably royalty fee (assessed at 4%) for the defendants' use of the confidential

---

[84] See above, ch 18.   [85] [2018] UKSC 20, [2018] 2 WLR 1353: see above, ch 18.
[86] In addition to the cases below, see, eg, *Force India Formula One Team Ltd v 1 Malaysian Racing Team Sdh Bhd* [2013] EWCA Civ 780, [2013] RPC 36; *Marathon Asset Management LLP v Seddon* [2017] EWHC 300 (in both cases, there were breach of contractual as well as equitable obligations of confidence).
[87] [2005] EWCA Civ 595, [2006] QB 125 (there was a further appeal on different matters by OK! magazine to the House of Lords: [2007] UKHL 21, [2008] 1 AC 1).
[88] [2005] EWCA Civ 595, [2006] QB 125, at [244] (author's emphasis).   [89] [2010] EWHC 424 (Ch).
[90] ibid, at [343].   [91] [2016] EWCA Civ 541, [2017] FSR 5.
[92] *General Tire Co v Firestone Tyre Co Ltd* [1975] 1 WLR 819: see above, p 229.

information. This was to apply the 'user principle' and is now referred to as an award of 'negotiating damages'.[93]

Where the breach is of a personal, rather than a commercial, confidence, damages can compensate for non-pecuniary, as well as pecuniary, loss. This is shown by *Campbell v MGN Ltd*[94] in which the House of Lords upheld an award of £2,500 damages for mental distress plus £1,000 aggravated damages[95] made to Naomi Campbell, the celebrity model, for breach of confidence by a newspaper. However, since the clarification of the law in *Vidal-Hall v Google Inc*,[96] the cause of action in the *Campbell* case (as is recognised in the judgment of Lord Nicholls) would now be viewed as one for the tort of misuse of private information (ie the tort of privacy) rather than the equitable wrong of breach of confidence.

3. Restitution and punishment for equitable wrongs

(1) Restitution for equitable wrongs

We have explained in chapter 19[97] that, in the context of restitution for wrongs, restitution is synonymous with disgorgement. In this book, the term restitution has been preferred but nothing does, or should, turn on whether one instead uses the term disgorgement.

As regards restitution for the four main types of equitable wrong (breach of fiduciary duty, breach of confidence, dishonestly procuring or assisting a breach of fiduciary duty, and proprietary estoppel), there is little to say in relation to the last wrong. This is because there appears to have been no English case in which restitution, rather than compensation, has been awarded for proprietary estoppel.

The monetary remedies for the wrong of proprietary estoppel have not been restitutionary but have been compensatory and concerned to protect the claimant's expectation[98] or, occasionally, reliance interests.[99] That is not surprising given that proprietary estoppel is closely

---

[93] See above, ch 18. A fee (referred to as a 'quasi-consultancy fee') was also awarded for the use of confidential information in accelerating the entry into the market of 'later formula' nets. This was viewed as compensating for a loss and appears to be a further example of 'negotiating damages'.

[94] [2004] UKHL 22, [2004] 2 AC 475. See also *Mosley v News Group Newspapers Ltd* [2008] EWHC 1777 (QB), [2008] EMLR 20 in which Eady J awarded £60,000 damages for mental distress, including aggravated damages, for breach of confidence/privacy (prior to the clear recognition that privacy is a tort). In *Douglas v Hello! Ltd (No 6)* [2005] EWCA Civ 595, [2006] QB 125, an award of £3,750 damages for mental distress to each of the Douglases for 'breach of confidence' was upheld by the Court of Appeal (there was a further appeal on different matters by OK! magazine to the House of Lords: [2007] UKHL 21, [2008] 1 AC 1).

[95] See above, pp 287–288. For the award of damages for mental distress (including aggravated damages) for the tort of privacy, see above, p 290.

[96] [2015] EWCA Civ 311, [2016] QB 1003. Above, p 13.   [97] Above, pp 336–337.

[98] See, eg, *Baker & Baker v Baker* (1993) 25 HLR 408; *Gillett v Holt* [2001] Ch 210. See also *Jennings v Rice* [2002] EWCA Civ 159, [2003] 1 P & CR 8 and *Suggitt v Suggitt* [2012] EWCA Civ 1140 (expectations protected unless it would be 'out of all proportion to the detriment which the claimant has suffered'). In *Davies v Davies* [2016] EWCA Civ 463, Lewison LJ, at [39], noted the 'lively controversy' about the aim of proprietary estoppel remedies, and that: 'One line of authority takes the view that the essential aim of the discretion is to give effect to the claimant's expectation unless it would be disproportionate to do so. The other takes the view that the essential aim of the discretion is to ensure that the claimant's reliance interest is protected, so that she is compensated for such detriment as she has suffered.' It was unnecessary on the facts of the case for the court to decide between those two views. See, generally, on the question of the extent to which expectations are protected by proprietary estoppel, S Moriarty, 'Licences and Land Law: Legal Principles and Public Policies' (1984) 100 LQR 376; E Cooke, 'Estoppel and the Protection of Expectations' (1997) 17 Legal Studies 258; S Gardner, 'The Remedial Discretion in Proprietary Estoppel' (1999) 115 LQR 438; and 'The Remedial Discretion in Proprietary Estoppel – Again' (2006) 122 LQR 492; A Robertson, 'The Reliance Basis of Proprietary Estoppel Remedies' [2008] Conv 295; J Mee, 'The Role of Expectation in the Determination of Proprietary Estoppel Remedies' in *Modern Studies in Property Law: vol 5* (ed M Dixon, Hart Publishing 2009).

[99] *Dodsworth v Dodsworth* (1973) 228 Estates Gazette 1115 (in effect protecting the reliance interest). For other awards of a sum lower than the value of the claimant's expectation see, eg, *Powell v Benney* [2007] EWCA Civ 1283; *Henry v Henry* [2010] UKPC 3, [2010] 1 All ER 988.

akin to breach of contract in resting on a breach of promise or conduct equivalent to a promise; and restitution has not traditionally been available for breach of contract. Whether, following *Attorney-General v Blake*,[100] it will be and *should* be more widely available turns on the issues concerning restitution for breach of contract considered in chapter 19.

In contrast to proprietary estoppel, restitution (as we shall see in the next two sections)[101] has been a common response to breach of fiduciary duty and breach of confidence through the remedy of accounting for profits. Indeed it has sometimes been assumed that restitution is so central to these wrongs that the claimant cannot alternatively claim compensation for them. That is incorrect. As we have seen,[102] compensation, through either the remedy of equitable compensation (sometimes referred to as accounting for loss) or equitable damages in substitution for, or in addition to, an injunction, is readily available as an alternative to restitution.[103]

As regards the equitable wrong of dishonestly procuring or assisting a breach of fiduciary duty, it has recently been recognised that, apart from equitable compensation, which is the usual remedy, an account of profits may be awarded. We look at this in the third section below.[104]

(a) Restitution for breach of fiduciary duty

It is helpful for the purposes of exposition to divide between secret or unauthorised profits made by a fiduciary and bribes or secret commissions taken by a fiduciary.

(i) Secret or unauthorised profit

There have been many cases of fiduciaries, usually trustees or company directors, being required by the remedy of an account of profits to disgorge unauthorised profits made out of their position as fiduciaries.[105] The duty is a strict one: no unauthorised profit can be made. Although the courts do have a discretion to give the fiduciary an allowance out of the profits made to remunerate the fiduciary for its skill and time, it is no defence for the fiduciary to establish that it was acting bona fide and in the best interests of the beneficiary. The leading cases are *Regal (Hastings) Ltd v Gulliver*[106] and *Boardman v Phipps*.[107]

In the former, the claimant company, Regal, owned a cinema and wanted to acquire two other cinemas. The directors found that Regal could not itself afford to buy the cinemas so they put up much of the money themselves by creating a subsidiary company in which they themselves took 2,000 £1 shares, the company's solicitor took 500 £1 shares, outside purchasers took 500 £1 shares, and Regal took 2,000 £1 shares. The two cinemas were bought and subsequently the shares in the subsidiary company were sold at a considerable profit (£2 16s 1d profit per share). Regal, now under new directors, sought to recover the profits

---

[100] [2001] 1 AC 268. [101] See below, pp 526–535. [102] See above, pp 511–525.
[103] The claimant must elect between compensation and restitution for the wrong: see above, pp 14–15 and 345–346.
[104] Below, pp 535–536.
[105] In addition to the two leading cases examined in the text, see *Keech v Sandford* (1726) Sel Cas Temp King 61; *Parker v McKenna* (1874) 10 Ch App 96; *Boston Deep Sea Fishing & Ice Co v Ansell* (1888) 39 Ch D 339; *Re North Australian Territory Co, Archer's Case* [1892] 1 Ch 322; *Cook v Deeks* [1916] 1 AC 554; *Williams v Barton* [1927] 2 Ch 9; *Industrial Development Consultants v Cooley* [1972] 1 WLR 443; *Canadian Aero Services v O'Malley* (1974) 40 DLR (3d) 371; *English v Dedham Vale Properties Ltd* [1978] 1 WLR 93; *Queensland Mines Ltd v Hudson* (1978) 52 ALJR 399; *Hospital Products Ltd v United States Surgical Corpn* (1985) 156 CLR 41; *Guinness plc v Saunders* [1990] 2 AC 663; *Warman International Ltd v Dwyer* (1995) 182 CLR 544; *Nottingham University v Fishel* [2000] ICR 1462; *CMS Dolphin Ltd v Simonet* [2001] 2 BCLC 704.
[106] [1967] 2 AC 134n. [107] [1967] 2 AC 46.

made by the former directors from the sale of the shares in the subsidiary company. The House of Lords held that the former directors were liable to account to Regal for the profits made. Although they had been acting bona fide, the fact remained that they had personally made unauthorised profits out of their fiduciary position as directors.

Viscount Sankey said:

'... the respondents were in a fiduciary position and their liability to account does not depend upon proof of mala fides. The general rule of equity is that no one who has duties of a fiduciary nature to perform is allowed to enter into engagements in which he has or can have a personal interest conflicting with the interests of those whom he is bound to protect.'[108]

In Lord Russell's words:

'The rule of equity which insists on those, who by use of a fiduciary position make a profit, being liable to account for that profit, in no way depends on fraud or absence of bona fides; or upon such questions or considerations as whether the profit would or should otherwise have gone to the plaintiff, or whether the profiteer was under a duty to obtain the source of the profit for the plaintiff or whether he took a risk or acted as he did for the benefit of the plaintiff, or whether the plaintiff had in fact been damaged or benefited by his actions. The liability arises from the mere fact of a profit having, in the stated circumstances, been made. The profiteer, however honest and well-intentioned, cannot escape the risk of being called upon to account.'[109]

And according to Lord Wright:

'... both in law and equity, it has been held that, if a person in a fiduciary relationship makes a secret profit out of the relationship, the court will not inquire whether the other person is damnified or has lost a profit which otherwise he would have got ... Nor can the court adequately investigate the matter in most cases. The facts are generally difficult to ascertain or are solely in the knowledge of the person who is being charged. They are ... hypothetical because the inquiry is as to what would have been the position ... or what he might have done if ... interest had not conflicted with duty.'[110]

In *Boardman v Phipps* the claimant was a beneficiary with a 5/18ths beneficial interest in the Phipps trust. The trust property, inter alia, comprised shares in a company. The defendants, who were another beneficiary and the solicitor to the trustees, sought to improve the value of the shares. Using information acquired while acting as agents for the trustees the defendants embarked on a skilful operation whereby they acquired for themselves the majority of shares in the company. The value of the shares in the company rose sharply so that the defendants' operations were profitable for themselves personally and for the trust holding. The claimant beneficiary nevertheless brought an action claiming a declaration that the defendants held 5/18ths of their shares on constructive trust for him and that they should account to him for 5/18ths of the profit they had personally made. The House of Lords by a three–two majority (Viscount Dilhorne and Lord Upjohn dissenting) granted the declaration sought and held the defendants liable to account as constructive trustees for the profit they had made. *Regal Hastings* was followed. Although the defendants had been acting bona fide, this did not alter the fact that they had made their gains out of their position as agents for the trustees and hence while acting as fiduciaries to the beneficiaries and the beneficiaries had not authorised their scheme. However, it was stressed that the defendants should be entitled to a liberal allowance for their work and skill.[111]

---

[108] [1942] 1 All ER 378, at 381. [109] ibid, at 386. [110] ibid, at 392.
[111] See also *Nottingham University v Fishel* [2000] ICR 1462. No such allowance was given, and *Boardman v Phipps* was distinguished, in *Guinness plc v Saunders* [1990] 2 AC 663.

The minority's reasoning was that to order a disgorging of profits was too harsh. The normal strict rule against unauthorised profits acquired by a fiduciary ought not to apply here where the fiduciaries had acted in good faith and the trustees, on behalf of the beneficiaries, had made it clear that they were not interested in any scheme to obtain majority shares in the company.

Four points should be made on those two leading cases. First, it is clear that the account of profits remedy awarded was restitutionary. It cannot realistically be reanalysed as compensatory. If the fiduciaries had not gone ahead with their schemes because unauthorised, the beneficiaries would not have otherwise made the gains that were required to be disgorged.

Secondly, in *Boardman v Phipps*, as is commonplace in this area of the law, a constructive trust was imposed. The personal liability to account was described as being a liability to account as a constructive trustee. The importance of imposing a constructive trust is that it gives the claimant equitable beneficial ownership of the unauthorised gains thereby affording priority if the fiduciary is insolvent. The imposition of a constructive trust also means that the claimant can trace the benefits acquired into further gains; and this means that the claimant is entitled to those further gains either by means of a personal remedy of an account of profits or by a proprietary constructive trust.

Thirdly, it is important to recognise that there is a judicial discretion—exercised in *Boardman v Phipps*—to afford a fiduciary an allowance for the time and skill expended in making the profit. It is submitted that this discretion to make an allowance affords the courts the necessary flexibility in deciding on the appropriate quantum of restitution. The application of an allowance, and its amount, may turn on a variety of factors such as the degree of skill and effort expended by the wrongdoer and whether the wrongdoer was acting honestly or not. Granting an allowance enables the courts to strip what they consider to be the appropriate proportion of the wrongdoer's profits.

Fourthly, the defendants were required to give up the profits made without consideration of whether, had they complied with their duty by informing the beneficiaries, some or all of those profits would have been made in any event because the beneficiaries would have consented. As we shall now see, this point—which goes to the causal link between the breach of duty and the profits made—was focused on in *Murad v Al-Saraj*.[112]

In this case, Mr Al-Saraj and the Murad sisters entered into a joint venture to purchase a hotel. They agreed how they would split the profits (from running or selling the hotel). The hotel was purchased but then the Murads discovered that Al-Saraj had deceived them because he had come to a deal with the vendor of the hotel whereby his supposed contribution of £500,000 cash to the purchase was largely illusory. It was clear that there had been a breach of fiduciary duty constituted by Al-Saraj's non-disclosure to the Murads of the true nature of his contribution. In the Murads' claim for an account of profits for that breach of fiduciary duty, the trial judge found that, even if there had been full disclosure, the Murads would have continued with the transaction albeit with an altered profit-sharing ratio. This was the basis for an argument by Al-Saraj that he should not be stripped of all his profits in the venture.[113]

The majority (Arden and Jonathan Parker LJJ) rejected that argument in relation to the facts of this case where the fiduciary was acting in bad faith. But it did accept that a

---

[112] [2005] EWCA Civ 959, noted by M McInnes, 'Account of Profits for Breach of Fiduciary Duty' (2006) 122 LQR 11. See, generally, M Conaglen, 'The Extent of Fiduciary Accounting and the Importance of Authorisation Mechanisms' [2011] CLJ 548.

[113] He relied on the Australian case of *Warman International Ltd v Dwyer* (1995) 182 CLR 544 in which the accounting of profits for dishonest assistance of a breach of fiduciary duty was limited to two years.

traditional strict inflexible approach to accountability might have to be reassessed in a future case. It also pointed out that the inflexibility was tempered to a degree by the discretion of the court to make an allowance for the skill and effort of the defaulting fiduciary. Clarke LJ, dissenting, thought that even in this case it was open to the court to be more flexible given that, had there been no breach of fiduciary duty, there would still have been a profit-sharing agreement between the parties.

In terms of causation, there appear to be two ways of understanding the traditional strict approach taken by the majority although neither is entirely convincing. One is to say that counter-factuals are ignored so that causation is satisfied where the profits flowed from the breach irrespective of whether some of the profits might have been gained even if there had been no breach. The alternative is to say that the courts require *the defendant* to prove the counter-factual that some of the profits would have been made even if there had been no breach and that usually defendants cannot satisfy that burden of proof. It is worth adding that peculiarities regarding causation are not confined to an account of profits in the context of breach of fiduciary duty. As we have seen in relation to an account of profits for patent infringement, it has similarly been held inappropriate to consider what profits the defendant would have made had it adopted the most likely non-infringing method of production.[114]

(ii) Bribes or secret commissions

The leading case is *FHR European Ventures LLP v Cedar Properties LLC*[115] in which the Supreme Court laid to rest, once and for all, the major controversy that has raged for more than a century in respect of bribes and secret commissions acquired in breach of fiduciary duty. The dispute has been whether there is merely a personal remedy to strip the bribe or secret commission from the fiduciary or whether the law imposes a proprietary constructive trust over the bribe or secret commission (thereby giving the principal priority on the fiduciary's insolvency and allowing the principal to trace to assets acquired with the bribe or secret commission). In order to put that decision in context, it is helpful first to examine three earlier leading cases[116] although the first does not concern the controversial issue that was resolved in *FHR*.

In the famous case of *Reading v Attorney-General*[117] Reading was a Sergeant in the British Army serving in Egypt and, in return for bribes totalling £20,000, he sat on several occasions in his military uniform on lorries illegally transporting alcohol thereby avoiding their inspection by the police. Ultimately he was found out, court-martialled, sent to prison, and £19,325 was seized by the Crown. He claimed recovery of that money. The House of Lords refused that claim. On the contrary, the Crown was held entitled to the money because in accepting bribes to sit in his military uniform Reading had been acting in breach of his fiduciary duty to the Crown as his employer. He was therefore liable to account for the bribe or to pay it over in an action for money had and received. The fact that the Crown had not

---

[114] *Celanese International Corpn v BP Chemicals Ltd* [1999] RPC 203. See above, p 344.
[115] [2014] UKSC 45, [2015] AC 250.
[116] Other cases on bribes include *Metropolitan Bank v Heiron* (1880) 5 Ex D 319; *Boston Deep Sea Fishing & Ice Co v Ansell* (1888) 39 Ch D 339; *Mahesan S/O Thambiah v Malaysian Government Officers' Cooperative Housing Society Ltd* [1979] AC 374; *Islamic Republic of Iran Shipping Lines v Denby* [1987] 1 Lloyd's Rep 367; *Logicrose Ltd v Southend United Football Club Ltd* [1988] 1 WLR 1256; *Petrotrade Inc v Smith* [2000] 1 Lloyd's Rep 486; *Fyffes Group Ltd v Templeman* [2000] 2 Lloyd's Rep 643. It is also well-established that the amount of the bribe or compensatory damages (for the tort of deceit or, more realistically, inducing a breach of contract or for the equitable wrong of dishonest assistance) can be recovered from the briber; see, eg, the *Mahesan*, *Logicrose*, and *Fyffes* cases. Recovery of the bribe from the briber probably cannot be justified on restitutionary principle. Cf P Birks, *An Introduction to the Law of Restitution* (rev edn, Clarendon Press 1989) 337–338.
[117] [1951] AC 507.

lost anything was irrelevant: the measure of relief, as in all bribe cases, was therefore indisputably restitutionary.

One peculiarity of some of the bribe cases, as illustrated by *Reading*, is that, as an alternative to the equitable remedy of accounting for the bribe, the claimant has been held to have an action for money had and received. The latter is a common law remedy and, on the face of it, flouts the conventional dogma that common law remedies cannot be given for equitable wrongs.[118] One radical explanation would be that the common law remedy is responding to a breach of contract: ie the breach of an implied term in the employment or agency contract. Support for this could be found in the vagueness of the fiduciary label. But this would then contradict the traditional view, prior to *Attorney-General v Blake*,[119] that there could be no restitution for breach of contract. As there is no logical, as opposed to historical, reason why common law remedies should not be given for equitable wrongs, probably the better view is that the bribe cases represent a long-accepted, but little appreciated, exception to the 'no fusion' dogma.

On the long-debated question of whether the bribe is held on constructive trust for the principal, the other two cases in our leading trio, *Lister v Stubbs*[120] and *Attorney-General of Hong Kong v Reid*, went in opposite directions.

In *Lister v Stubbs* it was decided that there was no constructive trust. The defendant was the foreman buyer for the claimants. He accepted a bribe of £5,541 from particular suppliers in return for showing them favouritism in orders. The defendant had invested some of that bribe in land and other securities. What the claimants sought in this action was not restitution of £5,541 (which they were clearly entitled to) but rather an order that the defendant should stop dealing with the investments and should hold them for the claimants. That order was refused.

In a very clear statement, exploring the implications of accepting the claimants' argument, Lindley LJ said:

'One consequence, of course, would be that, if Stubbs were to become bankrupt, this property acquired by him with the money ... would be withdrawn from the mass of his creditors and be handed over bodily to Lister. Can that be right? Another consequence would be that, if the appellants are right, Lister could compel Stubbs to account to them, not only for the money with interest, but for all the profits which he might have made by embarking in trade with it. Can that be right? It appears to me that those consequences show that there is some flaw in the argument ... the unsoundness consists in confounding ownership with obligation.'[121]

Lister v Stubbs meant that the bribe cases were treated differently from the unauthorised profit cases in that the fiduciary did not hold bribes on constructive trust.[122] There were some powerful supporters of that decision. For example, Birks[123] and Goode[124] long argued

---

[118] J Glister and J Lee, *Hanbury and Martin on Modern Equity* (21st edn, Sweet & Maxwell 2018) para 1.022.
[119] [2001] 1 AC 268.   [120] (1890) 45 Ch D 1.   [121] ibid, at 15.
[122] It was followed on this point in, eg, *Islamic Republic of Iran v Denby* [1987] 1 Lloyd's Rep 367; *Attorney-General's Reference (No 1 of 1985)* [1986] QB 491.
[123] P Birks, *An Introduction to the Law of Restitution* (rev edn, Clarendon Press 1989) 387–389, 473–474; P Birks, 'Personal Restitution in Equity' [1988] LMCLQ 128.
[124] R Goode, 'Ownership and Obligation in Commercial Transactions' (1987) 103 LQR 433, 441–445; R Goode, 'Property and Unjust Enrichment' in *Essays on the Law of Restitution* (ed A Burrows, Clarendon Press 1991) 215–246, esp 242; R Goode, 'Proprietary Restitutionary Claims' in *Restitution, Past, Present and Future* (eds W Cornish, R Nolan, J O'Sullivan, and G Virgo, Hart Publishing 1998) 63–77. V Finch and S Worthington, 'The Pari Passu Principle and Ranking Restitutionary Rights' in *Restitution and Insolvency* (ed F Rose, Mansfield Press 2000) 1–20 reach the similar conclusion, at 19–20, that 'unjust enrichment claimants merit proprietary status but disgorgement claimants do not'. See also D Crilley, 'A Case of Proprietary Overkill' [1994] RLR 57; C Rotherham, 'The Recovery of the Profits of Wrongdoing and Insolvency' [1997] CFILR 43. Note that Goode also argues that a form of proprietary remedy (he labels it a 'remedial constructive trust') which protects the interests of D's creditors

that the case was correct and that there was generally no justification for imposing proprietary, rather than personal, restitution to strip gains made by a wrongdoer. They principally argued that a proprietary restitutionary remedy is not justified other than where there has been a subtraction from the claimant's ownership. In Birks' terminology, the claimant must have a 'proprietary base'.[125] In contrast to where a trustee has misappropriated the beneficiary's equitable property, there is normally no such proprietary base here because a beneficiary does not own the bribe or the unauthorised gain before the (alleged) constructive trust takes effect.

But there were also critics. Typical of the latter were Goff and Jones who criticised the distinction in treatment between secret profits and bribes and suggested that *Lister v Stubbs* was wrongly decided. They wrote:

> 'This decision emphatically marks off the secret commission cases ... an honest fiduciary, such as Mr Boardman, who is deemed to have abused his position of trust, is a constructive trustee of his profits, even though he acted in the best interests of the trust and his beneficiary gained over £20,000 from his intervention. In contrast the corrupt agent, or Sergeant Reading, is simply obliged to account for the value of his bribe.'[126]

The Privy Council in *Attorney-General for Hong Kong v Reid*[127] refused to follow *Lister v Stubbs*. The defendant, a Crown Prosecutor and ultimately Director of Public Prosecutions in Hong Kong, had accepted bribes so as to obstruct the prosecution of certain criminals. He was convicted of criminal offences and imprisoned. The Hong Kong government successfully sought to establish that three properties in New Zealand, bought by the defendant using the bribe, were held on constructive trust for it so that its registration of caveats on the title of the three properties was valid. Lord Templeman contrasted the bribe cases with authorities on other unauthorised gains made by fiduciaries, such as *Keech v Sandford*,[128] and referred with approval to an article by Sir Peter Millett criticising *Lister v Stubbs*.[129] Lord Templeman said:

> 'The decision in *Lister & Co v Stubbs* is not consistent with the principles that a fiduciary must not be allowed to benefit from his own breach of duty, that the fiduciary should account for the bribe as soon as he receives it and that equity regards as done that which ought to be done. From these principles it would appear to follow that the bribe and the property from time to time representing the bribe are held on a constructive trust for the person injured. A fiduciary remains personally liable for the amount of the bribe if, in the event, the value of the property then recovered by the injured person proved to be less than that amount.'[130]

The Supreme Court in *FHR European Ventures LLP v Cedar Capital Partners LLP*[131] has emphatically endorsed the decision in *Attorney-General v Reid* and overruled *Lister v*

---

is justified where D makes a 'deemed agency gain' (ie a gain which D was bound in equity to make, if D made it at all, for C).

[125] P Birks, *An Introduction to the Law of Restitution* (rev edn, Clarendon Press 1989) 386–389.
[126] R Goff and G Jones, *The Law of Restitution* (4th edn, Sweet & Maxwell 1993) 668–669 (this passage did not appear in subsequent editions, having been overtaken by subsequent cases). See also, eg, C Needham, 'Recovering the Profits of Bribery' (1979) 95 LQR 536, 540–545; P Finn, *Fiduciary Obligations* (40th Anniversary Republication with Additional Essays, The Federation Press 2016) para 513.
[127] [1994] 1 AC 324. For a consideration of the consequences for criminal law, see J C Smith, '*Lister v Stubbs* and the Criminal Law' (1994) 110 LQR 180.
[128] (1726) Sel Cas temp King 61.
[129] P Millett, 'Bribes and Secret Commissions' [1993] RLR 7.
[130] [1994] 1 AC 324, at 336.
[131] [2014] UKSC 45, [2015] AC 250. See also *Daraydon Holdings Ltd v Solland International Ltd* [2004] EWHC 622 (Ch), [2015] Ch 119 in which Lawrence Collins J applied *Reid*, and distinguished *Lister v Stubbs*, in holding that a bribe acquired in breach of fiduciary duty was held on constructive trust.

Stubbs and other cases which confined the principal to a personal remedy only. The primary reasoning of the Supreme Court was that it was anomalous to distinguish between secret or unauthorised profits, where it was long accepted that a constructive trust should be imposed, and bribes or secret commissions. Although some had argued that that distinction was justified, as resting on the idea that the fiduciary was authorised to make profits for the principal whereas the fiduciary was not authorised to take bribes, the Supreme Court regarded that distinction, while having 'some force',[132] as unprincipled given that, in both situations, what the fiduciary had done was unauthorised.[133] Moreover, it was paradoxical that what might be regarded as a benefit obtained in 'far less opprobrious circumstances'[134] resulted in a more stringent remedy. There was also a strong policy in favour of deterring bribery and corruption;[135] and to assimilate the two areas would produce a law that was clear and simple to apply and did not require defining the exact boundary between a secret commission and secret profits.[136] Finally, it was noted that in other common law jurisdictions a constructive trust was imposed on a bribe and that, where possible, one should 'lean in favour of harmonising the development of the common law round the world'.[137]

Whatever one's views as to the correctness of the decision to impose a constructive trust in *FHR*, one must not lose sight of the uncontroverted starting point, namely that restitution can be, and commonly has been, granted for breach of fiduciary duty (including on a strict liability basis). Is this justified?

Jackman argues that it is, because trusts and other fiduciary relationships are facilitative institutions that merit special protection.[138] The imposition of restitution for breach of a strict fiduciary duty is therefore no more surprising than restitution for strict liability in the proprietary torts. On his view, the judicial discretion to make an allowance for the fiduciary's skill and time will primarily be exercised where the fiduciary aims bona fide to make the beneficiaries (perhaps as well as himself) better off and is successful in so doing and reflects the consistent idea that the moral quality of the wrongdoing is a discretionary factor going to the quantum of restitution not to whether it is justified in the first place. Birks also considered that restitution for breach of fiduciary duty is justified. The bribe cases fit his primary 'cynical wrongdoing' justification for giving restitution for a wrong.[139] Moreover, Birks went beyond his primary test to argue that a policy of 'prophylaxis' also justifies restitution on a strict liability basis for unauthorised gains made in breach of fiduciary duty.[140]

(b) Restitution for breach of confidence

It is clear that, as an alternative to compensatory damages, a claimant can be awarded an account of profits for breach of confidence at least if that breach was intentional.[141] Prior to *Morris-Garner v One Step (Support) Ltd*,[142] one could strongly argue that a restitutionary analysis of 'negotiating damages', which can be awarded for breach of confidence, was also

---

[132] [2014] UKSC 45, [2015] AC 250, at [34].   [133] ibid, at [37] and [40].   [134] ibid, at [41].
[135] ibid, at [42].   [136] ibid, at [35], [38]–[39].   [137] ibid, at [45].
[138] I Jackman, 'Restitution for Wrongs' [1989] CLJ 302, 311–314.
[139] P Birks, *An Introduction to the Law of Restitution* (rev edn, Clarendon Press 1989) 326–327. This was also supported by the Law Commission: see below, p 535 n 157.
[140] P Birks, *An Introduction to the Law of Restitution* (rev edn, Clarendon Press 1989) 332–333, 338–343.
[141] As the remedy of an account of profits is equitable, it is probably technically correct to say that there is no right to an account of profits which is a discretionary remedy: see *Walsh v Shanahan* [2013] EWCA Civ 411 (an account of profits for breach of confidence refused). But there has to be a principled reason for refusing an account of profits given that it is a very common remedy for equitable wrongs.
[142] [2018] UKSC 20, [2018] 2 WLR 1353. See above, ch 18.

attractive. But the Supreme Court in that case has taken the view that 'negotiating damages' are compensatory not restitutionary.

That an account of profits can be awarded is shown by, for example, *Peter Pan Manufacturing Corpn v Corsets Silhouette Ltd*[143] where the defendants had manufactured and sold brassieres knowingly using confidential information obtained from the claimants. And in *Attorney-General v Guardian Newspapers Ltd (No 2)*[144] the *Sunday Times* was held liable to account for profits made in publishing, in breach of confidence to the Crown, the first extract of Peter Wright's book, *Spycatcher*, that publication having taken place before the information had reached the public domain. Lord Keith said of an account of profits:

> 'The remedy is, in my opinion ... to be attributed to the principle that no one should be permitted to gain from his own wrongdoing. Its availability may also, in general, serve a useful purpose in lessening the temptation for recipients of confidential information to misuse it for financial gain.'[145]

And in Lord Brightman's words, 'the only remedy available to the Crown is the inadequate remedy of an account of profits, on the basis that the *Sunday Times* unjustly enriched itself and should therefore be stripped of the riches wrongfully acquired.'[146]

Although there is no case law on this, it would seem clear that, as with breach of fiduciary duty, in awarding an account of profits for breach of confidence the courts have a discretion to afford the defendant a liberal allowance for work and skill.

In *Seager v Copydex Ltd*,[147] which we have already examined under compensatory damages for breach of confidence, the Court of Appeal appeared to think that an account of profits was not an appropriate remedy on the facts. Although the reason for this was not given, the obvious explanation is that, in contrast to the *Peter Pan* and *Spycatcher* cases, the wrongdoing was not intentional in *Seager v Copydex*. In none of the English cases has it been held that the gains made in breach of confidence are held on constructive trust.[148] However, in the difficult Canadian case of *LAC Minerals Ltd v International Corona Resources Ltd*[149] a constructive trust was imposed for breach of confidence. In negotiations for a joint venture between them, the defendants acquired from the claimant information about the mineral potential of some land. The defendants subsequently outbid the claimant in buying that land and set up a successful gold-mine on it. The majority of the Supreme Court of Canada held that the claimant was entitled to a constructive trust of the land as a remedy for the defendants' breach of confidence, subject to an allowance to the defendants, secured by a lien, for expenses in developing the mine that the claimant itself would have necessarily had to incur.

---

[143] [1964] 1 WLR 96. See also *Ansell Rubber Co Ltd v Allied Rubber Industries Pty Ltd* [1972] RPC 811; *AB Consolidated v Europe Strength Food Co Pty Ltd* [1978] 2 NZLR 515.
[144] [1990] 1 AC 109.   [145] ibid, at 262.
[146] ibid, at 266. Lord Goff's general comments on restitution for wrongs at 286 are also of interest.
[147] [1967] 1 WLR 923, at 932.
[148] But in obiter dicta in *Attorney-General v Guardian Newspapers (No 2)* [1990] 1 AC 109, at 288 Lord Goff tentatively suggested that the copyright in *Spycatcher* might be held on constructive trust for the Crown. See also *Service Corpn International plc v Channel Four Television Corpn* [1999] EMLR 83, at 90–91; *United Pan-Europe Communications NV v Deutsche Bank AG* [2000] 2 BCLC 461.
[149] (1989) 61 DLR (4th) 14. In *Cadbury Schweppes Inc v FBI Foods Ltd* (1999) 167 DLR (4th) 577, the Supreme Court of Canada subsequently stressed that, in Canada, the imposition of a constructive trust is discretionary and dependent on the particular facts of a case. It was there held that compensation for breach of confidence, and not a proprietary remedy, was appropriate (the claimants not having sought an account of profits). See A Abdullah and T Hang, 'To Make The Remedy Fit the Wrong' (1999) 115 LQR 376.

La Forest J, giving the main majority judgment, rejected the argument that a proprietary restitutionary remedy is only justified where the claimant has a pre-existing right of property. He said:

> '... it is not the case that a constructive trust should be reserved for situations where a right of property is recognised. That would limit the constructive trust to its institutional function and deny it the status of a remedy, its more important role. Thus it is not in all cases that a pre-existing right of property will exist when a constructive trust is ordered ... it is not necessary, therefore, to determine whether confidential information is property...'[150]

As with a constructive trust imposed on unauthorised profits made, or bribes taken, in breach of fiduciary duty, some commentators have objected that the approach taken in the *Lac Minerals* case unjustifiably sacrificed the interests of the defendant's creditors.[151]

Why then did La Forest J consider that a constructive trust should be imposed? He suggested the following: 'Having specific regard to the uniqueness of the Williams property, to the fact that but for LAC's breaches of duty, Corona would have acquired it, and recognising the virtual impossibility of accurately valuing the property, I am of the view that it is appropriate to award Corona a constructive trust over the land.'[152]

It is hard to accept that difficulty of assessment is a valid reason for preferring a proprietary, as opposed to a personal, restitutionary remedy for a wrong. And even if a justification for a constructive trust could lie in there having been an unjust enrichment by interceptive subtraction,[153] that should surely have meant that the constructive trust existed from the date when LAC acquired the property.

Wilson J appeared to think that the constructive trust was being imposed as a compensatory remedy:

> '... the only sure way in which Corona can be fully compensated for the breach in this case is by the imposition of a constructive trust on LAC in favour of Corona with respect to the property. Full compensation may or may not have been achieved through an award of common law damages depending upon the accuracy of valuation techniques. It can most surely be achieved in this case through the award of an *in rem* remedy.'[154]

A merit of that approach is that the remedies of specific performance and delivery up suggest that, at least where the subject matter is unique, difficulty in assessing compensation for a wrong can constitute a valid ground for preferring a proprietary remedy. But, on the facts, to impose the constructive trust as a means of ensuring full compensation rested on the unrealistic assumption that, had there been no breach of confidence, not only would the claimant have developed the mine itself rather than jointly with the defendants but also would have developed it as profitably as the defendants had done.

The minority (Soprinka and McIntyre JJ) preferred to award compensatory damages. The remedy of an accounting of profits had not been in issue and they thought a constructive trust inappropriate because, on their view of the facts, the extent of the connection between the confidential information and the acquisition of the property was uncertain.

---

[150] (1989) 61 DLR (4th) 14, at 50.

[151] R Goode, 'Property and Unjust Enrichment' in *Essays on the Law of Restitution* (ed A Burrows, Clarendon Press 1991) 215, 239–240; W Gummow, 'Unjust Enrichment, Restitution and Proprietary Remedies' in *Essays on Restitution* (ed P Finn, Law Book Co 1990) 47, 78; P Birks, 'The Remedies for Abuse of Confidential Information' [1990] LMCLQ 460, 463.

[152] (1989) 61 DLR (4th) 14, at 52.

[153] For the controversial concept of 'interceptive subtraction', see P Birks, *An Introduction to the Law of Restitution* (rev edn, Clarendon Press 1989) 133–139.

[154] (1989) 61 DLR (4th) 14, at 17.

Leaving aside whether a constructive trust is justified or not, it is clear that a personal restitutionary remedy, in the form of an account of profits, may be granted for breach of confidence. Is that justified?

Certainly the leading cases are explicable on Birks' primary test of cynical wrongdoing.[155] Moreover, Jackman's 'facilitative institution' analysis[156] would suggest that an account of profits should be available even if there has been no conscious wrongdoing. A relationship of confidentiality (whether confidential information is property or not) is a facilitative institution which merits special protection by the courts. On this view, *Peter Pan* and the *Spycatcher* case are justifiably restitutionary but an account of profits might also have been awarded in *Seager v Copydex*.

(c) Restitution for dishonest assistance

It was decided in *Novoship (UK) Ltd v Mikhaylyuk*[157] that restitution, through an account of profits,[158] can be awarded for the equitable wrong of dishonestly procuring or assisting a breach of fiduciary duty ('dishonest assistance' for short). There were also obiter dicta to the effect that the same should apply to 'knowing receipt' although it is not yet clear how far knowing receipt is an equitable wrong rather than merely lying within the law of unjust enrichment[159] and there was no discussion of that issue by the Court of Appeal.

The decision is to be welcomed. Given that a breach of fiduciary duty triggers an account of profits, it follows naturally that the accessory liability of a dishonest assister should also trigger that remedy. Moreover, given the requirement of dishonesty for this wrong, the awarding of restitution is supported by Birks' view that it is the moral quality of the wrongdoing that is particularly important.[160]

In the *Novoship* case the Court of Appeal stressed that, for an account of profits to be awarded against a dishonest assister, there was no need for the breach of fiduciary duty being assisted to comprise a misapplication of trust property (on the facts, the breach of fiduciary duty primarily comprised the taking of bribes). But there did need to be a direct causal connection (beyond 'but for' causation) between the dishonest assistance and the profit for which the defendant was being required to account. It was therefore held, on the facts, that no account of profits should be awarded against the dishonest assisters because the direct cause of their profit was not the payment of the bribes but the increase in market

---

[155] P Birks, *An Introduction to the Law of Restitution* (rev edn, Clarendon Press 1989) 326–327. Cf Birks, at 345–346 which relies on his subsequently abandoned 'anti-enrichment wrong' test. See also Law Commission, *Aggravated, Exemplary and Restitutionary Damages* (1997) Report No 247, para 3.51 and Draft Bill, cl 12; below, n 157.

[156] See above, p 532.

[157] [2014] EWCA Civ 908, [2015] QB 499. For support for the availability of an account of profits for dishonest assistance, prior to this decision, see, eg, *Warman International v Dwyer* (1995) 182 CLR 544 (account of profits ordered for 'dishonest assistance' of Dwyer's breach of fiduciary duty). It was also accepted as regards 'dishonest assistance' (by a briber) in obiter dicta of Toulson J in *Fyffes Group Ltd v Templeman* [2000] 2 Lloyd's Rep 643. It was further supported by the Law Commission. In *Aggravated, Exemplary and Restitutionary Damages* (1997) Report No 247, para 3.51 and Draft Bill, cl 12, it recommended that, irrespective of any other power to award 'restitutionary damages', they may be awarded to a claimant for an equitable wrong (or tort) where the defendant's conduct shows a deliberate and outrageous disregard of the claimant's rights. An equitable wrong was defined as a breach of fiduciary duty, breach of confidence, or procuring or assisting a breach of fiduciary duty: paras 5.44, 5.54–5.55, and Draft Bill, cl 15(4).

[158] The claimant accepted that there was no proprietary claim, ie no constructive trust: see [2014] EWCA Civ 908, [2015] QB 499, at [66]. It is an open question whether a constructive trust can ever be imposed for the wrong of dishonest assistance.

[159] See above, p 509.

[160] P Birks, *An Introduction to the Law of Restitution* (rev edn, Clarendon Press 1989) 326–327.

value of the vessels that they had acquired at a commercial rate. In any event, an account of profits was regarded as a discretionary remedy and here to award it would be disproportionate to the wrongdoing.

In contrast, in the important High Court of Australia decision in *Ancient Order of Foresters in Victoria Friendly Society Ltd v Lifeplan Australia Friendly Society Ltd*[161] an account of profits was ordered for dishonest assistance. The value of the whole of a business acquired by assisting a breach of fiduciary duty was ordered to be disgorged. It was held to be sufficient that the claimant could show that that business would not have been acquired 'but for' the dishonest equitable wrong. No separate allowance was made for the defendants' skill, time, and cost incurred because this was already covered by the 'discounted cash flow' method of assessing the value of the business. It was stressed that because of the dishonesty involved, it was not open to the defendants to establish that some part of the profit would have been made had they acted honestly without committing a wrong. In contrast it was open to the defendants to prove that some of the profit was too indirectly related to the wrong—even though satisfying the 'but for' test—so as to fall outside its scope but they had failed to do that. The court's approach to causation, which might seem harsh on defendants, reflected the idea that the account of profits had a prophylactic or deterrent purpose. It was also made clear that the account could, and here should, cover anticipated wrongful profits as well as those already obtained.

It is worth noting that there is a close analogy between this equitable wrong of dishonest assistance and the economic torts. This supports the argument that restitution, through an account of profits, should be available for those torts even though, traditionally, it has not been.[162]

(2) Punishment for equitable wrongs

It is a controversial question whether punishment, most obviously through punitive damages, can be awarded for an equitable wrong. Those who argue against the fusion of common law and equity argue that punitive damages, being a common law remedy, simply cannot be awarded for an equitable wrong. And there is no indication that equitable damages or 'equitable compensation' have ever included a punitive element.

But leaving aside history, it is hard to see why as a matter of principle or policy punitive damages should be confined to torts. In *Kuddus v Chief Constable of Leicestershire Constabulary*[163] a cause of action limitation on punitive damages was rejected. And although the language of their Lordships was confined to torts, the majority's reasoning would suggest that there is no reason why punitive damages cannot be awarded for equitable wrongs.

The Law Commission recommended that punitive damages should be available for equitable wrongs. It argued that there was no reason of principle or practicality to exclude equitable wrongs from a rational expansion of punitive damages and said that it was 'unsatisfactory to perpetuate the historical divide between common law and equity, unless there is very good reason to do so'.[164] It argued that it would be wrong as a matter of policy to allow punitive damages for the tort of deceit and yet to deny them for dishonest breach of fiduciary duty or dishonest breach of confidence. Indeed one might argue that punitive damages are historically even more suitable for equitable wrongs than common law wrongs given that, as we have seen, restitution for equitable wrongs—stripping away gains—is a

---

[161] [2018] HCA 43.   [162] See above, p 351.
[163] [2001] UKHL 29, [2002] 2 AC 122. See above, ch 20.
[164] Law Commission, *Aggravated, Exemplary and Restitutionary Damages* (1997) Report No 247, para 5.55.

commonplace remedy, whereas it is still somewhat unusual for torts (and even rarer for breach of contract).

However, the contrary view was taken by Eady J in *Mosley v New Group Newspapers Ltd*.[165] At a time before the tort of privacy had been clearly distinguished from the equitable wrong of breach of confidence, Eady J rejected the possibility of awarded punitive damages for breach of confidence/privacy on the principal ground that this would be a novel development which would require a decision of an appellate court. The view that punitive damages cannot be awarded for the equitable wrong of breach of confidence has also been taken in Australia.[166] On the other hand, there is support from New Zealand and Canada for punitive damages being available for equitable wrongs. In the well-known decision of the New Zealand Court of Appeal in *Aquaculture Corpn v New Zealand Green Mussel Co Ltd*[167] a majority held that, in addition to compensation, punitive damages could be awarded for breach of confidence albeit that, on the facts, they were not merited. Cooke P, giving the majority's decision, said:

'Whether the obligation of confidence in a case of the present kind should be classified as purely an equitable one is debatable, but we do not think that the question matters for any purpose material to this appeal. For all purposes now material, equity and common law are mingled or merged. The practicality of the matter is that in the circumstances of the dealings between the parties the law imposes a duty of confidence. For its breach a full range of remedies should be available as appropriate, no matter whether they originated in common law, equity or statute ... [A]pplying the foregoing approach as to the available range of remedies, we see no reason in principle why exemplary damages should not be awarded for actionable breach of confidence in a case where a compensatory award would not adequately reflect the gravity of the defendant's conduct.'[168]

Following on from this, in *Cook v Evatt (No 2)*,[169] Fisher J in the New Zealand High Court added exemplary damages of NZ$5,000 to an account of profits of over NZ$20,000 for breach of fiduciary duty. Citing *Aquaculture*, he said, 'Exemplary damages may be awarded whether the cause of action is founded in law or in equity.'[170]

In Canada, in *Norberg v Wynrib*,[171] punitive damages were awarded for the tort of trespass to the person or, in the opinion of McLachlin J, for breach of fiduciary duty, where the claimant sued her defendant doctor for sexual assaults on her that she permitted in return for being prescribed drugs to which she was addicted.

It is submitted that, as in New Zealand and, it would seem, Canada, English law should allow the award of punitive damages for equitable wrongs as well as torts. Punitive damages can serve a useful function and it is irrational to rule them out on purely historical grounds.

---

[165] [2008] EWHC 1777 (QB), [2008] EMLR 20. Cf Lindsay J's judgment in *Douglas v Hello! Ltd (No 6)* [2003] EWHC 786, [2003] 3 All ER 996, at [273] (there were appeals to the CA and the HL but without any mention of this point): while refusing punitive damages for breach of confidence on the facts—because the defendants' wrongful conduct had not been sufficiently outrageous—he said, after considering *Kuddus*, 'I am content to assume, without deciding, that exemplary damages (or equity's equivalent) are available in respect of breach of confidence.'

[166] *Harris v Digital Pulse Pty Ltd* (2003) 197 ALR 626 (NSWCA). For criticism see J Edelman, 'A "Fusion Fallacy" Fallacy' (2003) 119 LQR 375. See also *Bailey v Namol Pty Ltd* (1994) 12 ALR 228, at 238 (Federal CA tentatively doubting, without deciding the point, whether punitive damages can be awarded for equitable wrongs). The position is also left open by P McDermott, 'Exemplary Damages in Equity' (1995) 69 ALJ 773–774.

[167] [1990] 3 NZLR 299.

[168] [1990] 3 NZLR 299, at 301–302. In contrast, Somers J dissented on this aspect of the reasoning saying, at 302, 'equity and penalty are strangers.'

[169] [1992] 1 NZLR 676.   [170] ibid, at 705.

[171] (1992) 92 DLR (4th) 440. See also, eg, *MacDonald Estate v Martin* [1995] CCL 1142 (Man CA); *Gerula v Flores* [1995] CCL 8583 (Ont CA).

4. Compelling performance or preventing (or compelling the undoing of) an equitable wrong

(1) Injunctions

In this section, we are concerned to clarify that injunctions, granted or refused according to similar principles as have been discussed in relation to torts and breach of contract,[172] are also available in respect of equitable wrongs. One technical difference is that, as common law compensatory damages are not available for equitable wrongs, there is no 'adequacy of damages' hurdle that a claimant seeking an injunction for an equitable wrong needs to overcome. However, at least in relation to prohibitory injunctions, this is unlikely to be a significant difference in practice because that hurdle is easily overcome in respect of prohibitory injunctions for torts and breach of contract. Moreover, while there may be no 'adequacy of damages' hurdle for injunctions for equitable wrongs, the courts, in the exercise of their general discretion to refuse an injunction, might do so on the basis that equitable compensation or equitable (compensatory) damages is a more appropriate remedy.

It is well established that a beneficiary may be granted an interim[173] or final prohibitory injunction to prevent the continuation or repetition of a breach of fiduciary duty or to prevent a threatened breach of fiduciary duty. So, for example, prohibitory injunctions have been granted to prevent a trustee, in breach of trust, from completing a detrimental contract for the sale of trust property;[174] or to restrain a proposed distribution of trust property contrary to the terms of the trust;[175] or to restrain a sale of trust property where the vendor was not complying with statutory requirements for the sale.[176] Mandatory enforcing injunctions have also been ordered against trustees ordering them to carry out their positive fiduciary duties.[177] Analogously, but going one step further, the court has jurisdiction to appoint a receiver to ensure that the duties owed by a fiduciary are performed.[178]

In respect of proprietary estoppel, orders to convey land—corresponding to specific performance of a contract to convey land—have been made;[179] and, in other cases, the courts 'treating as done that which ought to be done' have declared that, in equity, the expected right over another's land already exists.[180]

Interim or final prohibitory injunctions have also been commonly granted to prevent a breach of confidence.[181] As regards interim injunctions, an important question is whether

---

[172] See above, ch 23.

[173] Albeit that the injunction was refused, one of the most important decisions on the correct approach to interim injunctions, where a trial is unlikely to take place, concerned an alleged breach of fiduciary duty by company directors: see *Cayne v Global Natural Resources* [1984] 1 All ER 225, above, p 476.

[174] *Dance v Goldingham* (1873) 8 Ch App 902.   [175] *Fox v Fox* (1870) LR 11 Eq 142.

[176] *Wheelwright v Walker* (1883) 23 Ch D 752; *Waller v Waller* [1967] 1 All ER 305 (interim injunction).

[177] *Foley v Burnell* (1783) 1 Bro CC 274; *Fletcher v Fletcher* (1844) 4 Hare 67.

[178] Supreme Court Act 1981, s 37(1): see above, p 491. For a receiver appointed in respect of a fiduciary duty, see *Middleton v Dodswell* (1806) 13 Ves 266.

[179] *Dillwyn v Llewellyn* (1862) 4 De G F & J 517; *Pascoe v Turner* [1979] 1 WLR 431.

[180] *Inwards v Baker* [1965] 2 QB 29; *Crabb v Arun District Council* [1976] Ch 179; *Re Basham* [1986] 1 WLR 1498; *Gillett v Holt* [2001] Ch 210.

[181] *Peter Pan Manufacturing Corpn v Corsets Silhouette Ltd* [1964] 1 WLR 96; *Duchess of Argyll v Duke of Argyll* [1967] Ch 302 (interim injunction: see above, p 570); *Francombe v Mirror Group Newspapers Ltd* [1984] 1 WLR 892 (interim *quia timet* injunction); *X v Y* [1988] 2 All ER 648; *Imerman v Tchenguiz* [2010] EWCA Civ 908, [2011] WLR 592. See R Sharpe, *Injunctions and Specific Performance* (5th edn, Thomson Reuters 2017) paras 5.130–5.180. See also *Instil Group Inc v Zahoor* [2003] EWHC 165 (Ch), [2003] 2 All ER 252 (injunction to restrain a breach of confidence, in respect of legally privileged documents, refused on the facts). For the impact of interim injunctions, preventing a breach of confidence, on third parties, see *Attorney-General v Times Newspapers Ltd* [1992] 1 AC 191; *Attorney-General v Punch Ltd* [2002] UKHL 50, [2003] 1 AC 1046; *Jockey Club Ltd v Buffham* [2002] EWHC 1866 (QB), [2003] QB 462. The Law Commission in *Breach of Confidence* (1981) Report No 110, paras

the approach in *American Cyanamid v Ethicon*[182] applies given that, as we have seen,[183] that approach is not applied to the tort of defamation and similar free speech issues may be in play in restraining a breach of confidence.

In *Schering Chemicals Ltd v Falkman Ltd*,[184] concerning a television film, and *Francome v Mirror Group Newspapers Ltd*,[185] dealing with a newspaper article, interim injunctions were granted to restrain breach of confidence apparently on the application of *American Cyanamid*. Similarly, in *Attorney-General v Observer Newspapers Ltd*,[186] where an interim injunction was granted to restrain two newspapers publishing confidential information disclosed by a former member of the British secret service in his book *Spycatcher*, the Court of Appeal thought that in this context a proper approach was to grant the injunction unless the court was satisfied that there was a serious defence of public interest which was *very likely* to succeed at trial. Again in *Attorney-General v Guardian Newspapers Ltd*,[187] in a further round of the *Spycatcher* litigation, interim injunctions were upheld by the House of Lords apparently on the application of *American Cyanamid* principles.

In contrast, in *Woodward v Hutchins*[188] the Court of Appeal drew some analogy to libel cases in allowing a newspaper to publish articles about the private lives of the claimant pop singers, written by their former publicity agent, and this was also Lord Denning's approach dissenting in *Schering*. This latter view is further supported by *Lion Laboratories Ltd v Evans*.[189] The question here was whether an interim injunction should be granted to restrain publication in a newspaper of admittedly confidential information regarding the accuracy of the claimant's intoxication instrument being used by the police to test the breath of drivers. The Court of Appeal refused the injunction because the defendants had satisfied the court that at trial they would have a strong defence of public interest. *American Cyanamid* was not applied, and the approach adopted was somewhat analogous to that for defamation, although the court was anxious to stress that the public interest needed to be far more clearly made out than did the defence of justification for libel. 'To be allowed to publish confidential information the defendants must do more than raise the plea of public interest; they must show "a legitimate ground for supposing it is in the public interest for it to be disclosed".'[190] This seems sensible. For while breach of confidence should probably be easier to restrain by interim injunction than defamation—since once made public, confidentiality is destroyed for ever, whereas a lost reputation can be won back—where free speech is in issue, the courts should again be slow to grant an interim injunction, amounting as it does to prior censorship. Certainly *American Cyanamid* should not be applied.

This latter approach derives further support from the Human Rights Act 1998, s 12(3). According to this, a court shall not grant an interim injunction restraining publication before trial (where this 'might affect the exercise of the Convention right to freedom of expression') 'unless the court is satisfied that the applicant is likely to establish that publication shall not be allowed'. This constitutes a legislative departure from *American Cyanamid*. In *Cream Holdings Ltd v Banerjee*,[191] the House of Lords, Lord Nicholls giving the leading

---

6.110–6.112 recommended that the courts should be empowered (or, on the better view, should use their existing powers) to make conditional injunctions, whereby the claimant should pay fair compensation for wasted expenses incurred by the defendant before it knew, or ought to have known, that the information was confidential: cf the 'compensated injunction,' discussed above, p 453.

[182] [1975] AC 396.   [183] See above, pp 479–480.   [184] [1982] QB 1.
[185] [1984] 1 WLR 892.   [186] [1986] NLJ Rep 799.   [187] [1987] 1 WLR 1248.
[188] [1977] 1 WLR 760. Prior to *American Cyanamid*, see *Fraser v Evans* [1969] 1 QB 349; *Hubbard v Vosper* [1972] 2 QB 84.
[189] [1985] QB 526.
[190] ibid, at 528 (per Stephenson LJ citing Lord Denning in *Woodward v Hutchins* [1977] WLR 760, at 764).
[191] [2004] UKHL 44, [2005] 1 AC 253.

speech, held that s 12(3) of the Human Rights Act 1998 meant that, in general, the test for interim injunctions, in breach of confidence cases, was whether the applicant was 'more likely than not' to succeed at trial. But it accepted that there would be exceptional cases of breach of confidence where a lesser degree of likelihood would suffice in the particular circumstances, for example, where the potential adverse consequences of disclosure were particularly grave. So the underlying principle is that the court is not to make an interim restraint order in breach of confidence cases unless satisfied that the applicant's prospects of success at the trial are sufficiently favourable to justify such an order being made in the particular circumstances of the case.

In *Browne v Associated Newspapers Ltd*[192] the Court of Appeal, in applying the flexible approach laid down in *Banerjee*, upheld the grant of an interim injunction restraining publication by a newspaper of some (but not all) of what was allegedly confidential information relating to a relationship between the claimant and another man.[193] In the words of Sir Anthony Clarke MR, giving the judgment of the court:

> '[O]n the facts of this case it was for the claimant to persuade the judge, in respect of each category of information, that his prospects of success at the trial are sufficiently favourable to justify such an order being made in the particular circumstances of the case, the general approach being that the courts should be "exceedingly slow" to make interim restraint orders where the applicant has not satisfied the court that he will probably ("more likely than not") succeed at the trial. By "succeed at trial" we understand Lord Nicholls to mean that the claimant is likely to succeed after the court has carried out the relevant balance between the claimant's rights under article 8 and the newspaper's rights under article 10.'[194]

What the above examination of the case law has shown is that, as one would expect, prohibitory and mandatory injunctions (whether final or interim) are available for equitable wrongs on similar principles to those applying to injunctions for the common law wrongs.

(2) Accounting (for loss)?

As we have seen above in discussing equitable compensation,[195] it has been argued by some that the equitable remedy of accounting (for loss) available against a trustee is different from equitable compensation. According to that argument, accounting for loss is analogous to the award of an agreed sum or specific performance. It is a monetary remedy compelling performance of a trustee's positive obligations. But the House of Lords impliedly in *Target Holdings Ltd v Redfern*[196] and the Supreme Court explicitly in *AIB Group (UK) Ltd v Mark Redler & Co*[197] have rejected the view that the accounting (for loss) remedy can operate differently from equitable compensation. In other words, it appears that, whatever the historical position, there is no longer an equitable monetary remedy (as distinct from a mandatory injunction) compelling performance of a trustee's positive obligations.

---

[192] [2007] EWCA Civ 295, [2008] QB 103. *Banerjee* was also applied to the claim for breach of confidence in *Donald v Ntuli* [2010] EWCA Civ 1276, [2011] 1 WLR 294. It was also applied in *PJS v News Group Newspapers* [2016] UKSC 26, [2016] AC 1081 (but there it was made clear that the claim was for the tort of privacy which was distinguished from breach of confidence: see above, p 13). See also *ABC v Telegraph Media Group Ltd* [2018] EWCA Civ 2329 (where an interim injunction was ordered to restrain an alleged breach of confidence comprising breach of a non-disclosure settlement agreement).

[193] This would presumably now be classified as the tort of privacy.

[194] [2007] EWCA Civ 295, [2008] QB 103, at [42]. [195] See above, pp 515–520.

[196] [1996] AC 421. See above, pp 515–517.

[197] [2014] UKSC 58, [2015] AC 1503. See above, pp 517–519.

(3) Delivery up in relation to breach of confidence

(a) Delivery up of material containing confidential information

A claimant can be granted delivery up of material containing confidential information belonging to the claimant.[198] This is a remedy for the equitable wrong of breach of confidence[199] and is analogous to delivery up of goods for tortious interference with goods[200] although, a fortiori, no common law damages can be awarded and hence no usual adequacy hurdle needs to be overcome. Delivery up of material containing confidential information is a remedy concerned to compel the undoing of a wrong.

(b) Delivery up for destruction or destruction on oath

As with tortious infringement of intellectual property rights,[201] so with breach of confidence, the courts have an inherent jurisdiction to order, and have ordered, a defendant to deliver up to the claimant or the court for destruction, or itself to destroy, articles made in breach of the duty of confidence owed to the claimant.[202] This remedy is best viewed as being to prevent a breach of confidence and as going one step beyond a prohibitory injunction.[203]

It is important to realise that this remedy is granted even though the claimant does not own the articles ordered to be destroyed.[204] This is the key to avoiding confusion with the different remedy of delivery up of material containing confidential information. It follows that, while a claimant granted delivery up of confidential information belonging to the claimant is entitled to do what it likes with that property, a claimant to whom delivery up for destruction is ordered ought to destroy that property.

5. Declaring rights

Equity has no concept of nominal (or contemptuous) damages so that these cannot be awarded for an equitable wrong. This creates no difficulty or lacuna because the function of nominal damages is simply to declare rights and this can be done more straightforwardly and openly by a declaration. Declarations are available on the same principles in respect of equitable rights as they are for common law rights. All that has been said about declarations in chapter 25 therefore applies analogously here. As a remedy for an equitable wrong, a declaration will generally be concerned to pronounce authoritatively that the defendant's conduct did or does amount to an equitable wrong.[205]

---

[198] *Alperton Rubber Co v Manning* (1917) 86 LJ Ch 377; *Industrial Furnaces Ltd v Reaves* [1970] RPC 605.
[199] See, eg, *Industrial Furnaces Ltd v Reaves* [1970] RPC 605; T Aplin and others, *Gurry on Breach of Confidence* (2nd edn, OUP 2012) paras 21.01–21.02; Law Commission, *Breach of Confidence* (1981) Report No 110, paras 4.102–4.104.
[200] See above, ch 24.   [201] See above, pp 497–499.
[202] *Prince Albert v Strange* (1849) 2 De G & Sm 704; *Peter Pan Manufacturing Corpn v Corsets Silhouette Ltd* [1963] 3 All ER 402; *Ansell Rubber Co Pty Ltd v Allied Rubber Industries Pty Ltd* [1972] RPC 811; *Franklin v Giddins* [1978] Qd R 72.
[203] See above, p 498.
[204] *Ansell Rubber Co Pty v Allied Rubber Industries Pty Ltd* [1972] RPC 811.
[205] Note also that, in respect of proprietary estoppel, declarations of the claimant's equitable proprietary rights (that were promised by the defendant) have been made: see above, p 538 n 180.

6. Miscellaneous issues on remedies for equitable wrongs

In this section, we consider two issues not so far dealt with in this chapter: (pre-judgment) interest and limitation periods in respect of remedies for equitable wrongs.

(1) Interest

In so far as the equitable remedy is 'for the recovery of a debt or damages' a statutory power to add an award of simple pre-judgment interest is conferred by the Supreme Court Act 1981, s 35A. In *BP Exploration Co (Libya) Ltd v Hunt (No 2)*[206] Lord Brandon interpreted those words widely as covering any monetary remedy, whether common law or equitable. He said:

'In my opinion, the words "any debt or damages", in the context in which they occur, are very wide so that they cover any sum of money which is recoverable by one party from another, either at common law or in equity or under a statute of the kind here concerned.'[207]

There is also an inherent equitable jurisdiction empowering the courts to award pre-judgment interest. Under this inherent jurisdiction, in some cases in which equitable remedies have been granted (especially an account of profits), compound interest rather than merely simple interest has been awarded. But traditionally this power was confined to cases of fraud or breach of fiduciary duty.[208]

An opportunity to develop the law was first presented to the House of Lords in *Westdeutsche Landesbank Girozentrale v Islington London Borough Council*,[209] albeit that this case was concerned not with remedies for wrongs but restitution for the cause of action of unjust enrichment. The claim was a common law restitutionary claim for money paid under a void interest rate swap transaction. By a bare majority (Lords Goff and Woolf dissenting), their Lordships decided that compound interest could not be added to the restitutionary remedy. To develop the equitable jurisdiction to award compound interest beyond its two recognised categories (fraud or breach of fiduciary duty) was felt to be unacceptable as outflanking the Legislature's decision to allow simple interest only under the Supreme Court Act 1981, s 35A (and before that under the Law Reform (Miscellaneous Provisions) Act 1934, s 3(1)). Lord Lloyd also argued that to allow the award of compound interest might cause uncertainty and consequent litigation, for example as to the rate to be awarded.

In *Sempra Metals Ltd v IRC*[210] the law on interest was reformed both in relation to interest as damages for torts and breach of contract and, more directly, in relation to interest as restitution of an unjust enrichment. As regards interest as damages, we have explored this decision in detail in chapter 15 (where it was also pointed out that, as a decision on restitution of an unjust enrichment, as opposed to damages, *Sempra Metals* was overruled in *Prudential Assurance Co Ltd v HMRC*).[211] Suffice it to say here that, in the light of *Sempra Metals*, there is no need to rely on the limited equitable jurisdiction for the award of non-statutory

---

[206] [1983] 2 AC 352.
[207] ibid, at 373. The statute he was there referring to was the Law Reform (Frustrated Contracts) Act 1943.
[208] *Wallersteiner v Moir (No 2)* [1975] QB 373; *President of India v La Pintada Compania* [1985] AC 104; *Westdeutsche Landesbank Girozentrale v Islington London Borough Council* [1996] AC 669; *Kuwait Oil Tanker Co SAK v Al Bader* [2000] 2 All ER (Comm) 271, at 339–344.
[209] [1996] AC 669.   [210] [2007] UKHL 34, [2008] 1 AC 561.
[211] [2018] UKSC 39, [2018] 3 WLR 652.

interest. Although dealing only with common law remedies as such, what was said in that case about interest (including compound interest) as damages for torts and breach of contract must apply equally to allowing interest (including compound interest) as equitable compensation or as equitable (compensatory) damages or as part of an account of profits for the equitable wrongs. In other words, subject to a possible clash with the award of simple interest only under s 35A of the Senior Courts Act 1981 (this possible clash has not been explored or resolved in the cases), the best interpretation of the reasoning in *Sempra Metals* is that no special restrictive rules now apply as regards interest as equitable compensation or as equitable damages or as an account of profits for equitable wrongs: if normal principles would mean that interest would be recoverable as loss under equitable compensation or equitable damages, or as profits under an account of profits, interest should be awarded.

(2) Limitation periods[212]

As regards monetary remedies for the equitable wrongs of breach of trust, breach of fiduciary duty, and dishonest assistance, it is crucial to understand s 21 of the Limitation Act 1980. On any view, this is a tortuous and unclear provision. The correct interpretation of it emerges from two main cases. First, *Paragon Finance plc v DB Thakerar & Co*,[213] which concerned a claim for equitable compensation for breach of fiduciary duty brought by a client against negligent solicitors; and, secondly, the decision of the majority of the Supreme Court in *Williams v Central Bank of Nigeria*,[214] which concerned claims for dishonest assistance, knowing receipt, and the recovery of trust property that were brought against a bank which had received funds transferred in breach of an express trust under which the claimant was the beneficiary. What emerges from those leading (and other) cases is as follows.

(i) Section 21(1) of the Limitation Act is an exclusionary provision. It provides that no limitation period laid down by the Act shall apply in an action for breach of trust (or breach of fiduciary duty) against a trustee where there has been fraud or the beneficiary is seeking to recover trust property. The *Paragon* and *Williams* cases have established that this subsection is to be given a narrow interpretation so that the exclusion applies only where the claim is being brought against a true trustee (which includes a director holding the company's property).[215] As laid down in the *Williams* case, the subsection does not apply to claims for dishonest assistance (or knowing receipt) because the defendants to those claims are not trustees within this subsection even though they are sometimes loosely referred to as constructive trustees. There is a distinction between, on the one hand, a true trust and, on the other, a constructive trust imposed as a remedy or as a label for the sort of remedies that can be awarded against true trustees. Similarly as shown in the *Paragon* case, a solicitor who has acted negligently and hence in breach of fiduciary duty, but is not holding property for the claimant, is not a trustee within section 21(1).

---

[212] The Law Commission recommended that the same limitation regime should apply to remedies for equitable wrongs as for torts and breach of contract but that the discretion to refuse an equitable remedy under the doctrine of laches (or acquiescence) should still apply: see Law Commission, *Limitation of Actions* (2001) Report No 270, paras 4.101, 4.268–4.278, 4.293.
[213] [1999] 1 All ER 400. [214] [2014] UKSC 10, [2014] AC 1189.
[215] The application of s 21(1) to a company director has been the subject of several decisions. It is clear that s 21(1)(a) applies to directors (because they are trustees in relation to the company's property); but it appears that, while s 21(1)(b) applies to actions to recover the company's property or proceeds, it does not apply to a claim, for example, for secret profits made by the director: *First Subsea Ltd v Balltec Ltd* [2017] EWCA Civ 186, [2018] Ch 25; *Burnden Holdings (UK) Ltd v Fielding* [2018] UKSC 14, [2018] 2 WLR 885. Cf *Gwembe Valley Development Co Ltd v Koshy* [2003] EWCA Civ 1048, [2004] 1 BCLC 131.

(ii) Assuming the exclusion in s 21(1) does not apply, there is a six-year limitation period, running from the date when the right of action accrued,[216] for monetary remedies for breach of trust or for any other breach of fiduciary duty or for dishonest assistance (or for knowing receipt or to recover trust property). Although there was no discussion of the precise explanation for this by the Supreme Court in *Williams*, where it was common ground that there was a six-year limitation period unless the exclusion in s 21(1) applied, a six-year limitation period applies either directly by reason of s 21(3) (which is expressed as applying to actions by a beneficiary 'to recover trust property or in respect of any breach of trust') or by analogy (applying s 36(1) of the Limitation Act 1980) to either the six-year period for breach of trust in s 21(3) or for breach of contract in s 5 (the latter analogy applies, for example, where there is a breach of fiduciary duty in a contractual context).[217]

Where there is no statutory limitation period applicable to the equitable wrong—as is the case in respect of, for example, breach of confidence—the equitable doctrine of laches applies to equitable remedies for the equitable wrong.[218]

Finally it should be noted that, as with injunctions for torts and breach of contract,[219] so with injunctions for equitable wrongs, the doctrine of laches applies.[220]

7. Conclusion

The fact that both legal and equitable remedies are available for the common law wrongs (torts and breach of contract)[221] is one good reason for treating law/equity as a purely historical and not a rational division. This chapter indicates another. For while it is essentially true, as the non-fusionists stress, that only equitable remedies are available for equitable wrongs, it is also true—as this chapter has shown—that the same, or similar, functions are performed by the remedies awarded for equitable wrongs as by the remedies for torts and breach of contract. In other words, the functions that have been identified in this book as being performed by the remedies for torts and breach of contract—compensation, restitution and punishment, compelling performance, preventing (or compelling the undoing of) a wrong, and declaring rights—are also the functions (subject to there being some doubt about punishment) that lie behind the remedies for equitable wrongs. As was explained in

---

[216] For breach of trust, this is the date of the breach of trust: *Thorne v Heard and Marsh* [1894] 1 Ch 599.
[217] See *Paragon Finance plc v DB Thakerar & Co* [1999] 1 All ER 400; *Cia De Seguros Imperio v Heath* (*REBX*) *Ltd* [2001] 1 WLR 112; *Gwembe Valley Development Co Ltd v Koshy* [2003] EWCA Civ 1048, [2004] 1 BCLC 131; *Re Loftus* [2006] EWCA Civ 1124, [2007] 1 WLR 1124; *Cattley v Pollard* [2006] EWHC 3130 (Ch), [2007] Ch 353. It should be noted that, as far as limitation is concerned, it does not matter whether the monetary claim is for equitable compensation or an account of profits: although s 23 is a specific provision in the Limitation Act 1980 applying to actions for an account, it merely says that a limitation period that is 'applicable to the claim which is the basis of the duty to account' applies to an action for an account.
[218] Limitation Act 1980, s 36(2). As regards 'equitable damages', it appears that, because they are given in addition to or in lieu of an injunction or specific performance, they will be barred if the injunction or specific performance would be barred by laches: see above, p 314. It has been held, in the context of a monetary remedy for breach of trust that, where there is a statutory limitation period, laches does not apply: *Re Pauling's Settlement* [1962] 1 WLR 86, at 115 (per Wilberforce J) approved [1964] Ch 303, at 353; *Cattley v Pollard* [2006] EWHC 3130 (Ch), [2007] Ch 353. See, generally, on laches (if meaning mere delay) not ousting a limitation period, *P & O Nedlloyd BV v Arab Metals Co* [2006] EWCA Civ 1717, [2007] 1 WLR 2288. See above, pp 433, 490.
[219] See above, pp 489–491.
[220] For an example of laches barring an interim injunction for an alleged breach of confidence, see *Church of Scientology of California v Miller*, The Times, 23 October 1987: above, pp 490–491. In respect of injunctions for equitable wrongs, it appears that laches (if meaning mere delay) does not oust a limitation period: see above, n 218 and pp 433, 490.
[221] See above, pp 10–11.

chapter 1,[222] there is therefore a coherence in remedial function for civil wrongs that transcends the common law/equity divide. So, for example, to treat breach of fiduciary duty as a tort, giving rise to purely tortious remedies, or proprietary estoppel as a breach of contract, giving rise to solely contractual remedies, would produce no real change in the range of functions performed by the available remedies. All this illustrates that, in the context of remedies for civil wrongs, those who argue against the fusion of law and equity merely seek to perpetuate an historical and not a rational division.

---

[222] See above, p 12.

Index

For the benefit of digital users, indexed terms that span two pages (e.g., 52–53) may, on occasion, appear on only one of those pages.

abatement of purchase price 437–38
accelerated payments clause 389
accident insurance policy 158, 159
account of profits
   account of which profits? 343–44
   agreed sum, award of 392
   combining remedies 14
   confidence, breach of 521, 524, 532–33, 534–35
   and damages 345–46
   difficulty of 344–45
   dishonest assistance 535–36
   final prohibitory injunctions 453
   innocent wrongdoing 342–43
   interest 542–43
   legal and equitable remedies 11
   negotiating damages 326–27, 329–31
   punishment for equitable wrongs 537
   punitive damages 361
   restitution 336, 348, 350, 351–52, 356–59, 526
   secret or unauthorised profit 526, 528, 529
Achilleas, qualification of traditional contract test required by 98–105
   Achilleas, The 100–2
   assumption of responsibility 102–5
   rejection of test of acceptance of liability as term of contract 98–100
acquiescence 434, 487–88, 489, 491, 496
actio personalis rule 339, 340, 347–48
action in debt 381
actionability by injured person 257–58
actionable wrong 377–78
adaptation costs 220
additional sufficient events 52–55
adequacy of damages 436
   delivery up and breach of confidence 541
   delivery up of goods 493–94, 495
   indirect specific performance 460
   interim injunctions 471–72
   see also under specific performance
aggravated damages
   confidence, breach of 522, 525
   express authorisation by statute 367–68, 369
   mental distress or physical inconvenience 284–85, 287–88, 289–91
   punitive damages 361–62, 373, 376
agreed damages clause 396
agreed sum, award of 4, 5, 9, 11, 48–49, 381–400
   accelerated payments clause 389
   action in debt 381
   actual loss 389, 393, 394
   agreed price, award of 383–87
   conditional sale agreements 389, 398, 400
   depreciation compensation 389
   general points 382–83
   genuine pre-estimate of loss test 388, 389, 393–94, 396, 398
   interim payment pre-trial 382
   legally recoverable loss 393
   legitimate interest 390–91, 392, 393–94, 395
   liquidated damages 381, 388–97

   new law 390–91
   and penalties, distinction between 388–89, 398–400
   used to limit damages 393–94
   loss greater than penalty 394
   minimum payment clause 389
   payable on event other than breach 397–400
   penalties 394–95, 398, 400
   penalties, validity 395–97
   pre-estimate of claimant's loss 398–99
   price 381
   relief against forfeiture 394–95
   repudiation of contract 383, 384–85, 386
   underliquidated damages clause 393–94
   unliquidated damages 388, 394
Albazero exception 202, 203, 204
all-or-nothing approach 59–60, 80, 116
amends, offer of 273
amenity, loss of 36, 37
   mental distress or physical inconvenience 276, 278, 291–92
   pecuniary loss 198
   wrongful interference with land 221–22
   see also pain, suffering and loss of amenity
American Cyanamid 469–74, 491, 539
   criticisms 474–75
   exceptions to 475–81
      free speech, need to protect 479–80
      little factual or legal dispute 480–81
      trade dispute defence 477–79
      where no action for final injunction will reach trial 475–77
annoyance 277, 283–84, 291
annuity 166
anonymity 441
anti-restitution clauses 347–52
anticipatory breach 468–69, 520
Anton Piller orders *see* search orders
anxiety 28, 281
arbitration 174
arbitration clauses 202
arrest
   unconstitutional 363–64
   wrongful 289
   see also false imprisonment; malicious prosecution
artistic freedom, right of 423
assault and battery 28, 163
   mental distress or physical inconvenience 287–88, 290
   punitive damages 362–64, 367, 368–69, 372
assignment 203–4
assumption of responsibility
   exclusionary effect 102–3, 104
   inclusionary effect 102–3, 104
   negligence 231, 233
   remoteness 100, 102–5, 106
   SAAMCO principle 119–20
attachment of earnings order 5
Australia 510, 537

average earnings index for future care costs 166–67

balance of convenience 469–73, 474, 475, 477–79
  claimant's conduct as bar to injunction 491
  interim delivery up 496
  interim mandatory injunctions 482–83
balance of justice 473
balance of probabilities 28, 80
  factual causation 55, 56
  proof of loss and loss of a chance 58–60, 67–68, 72–73
bargain promises 40, 41
bargaining
  opportunity, loss of 324
  post-judgment 463
  pre-judgment 463
battery *see* assault and battery
benevolence 159–60, 208, 213–14
benefits
  incidental 155
  non-recoupable, loss of 157
  see also social security benefits
bereavement damages 37, 251, 252–53, 263–64
  compensatory damages, date for assessment of 171–72
  losses on death 256, 263–64, 267
  mental distress or physical inconvenience 276, 291
Beswick v Beswick—radical interpretation 410–11
betterment 217–18
binding promise, breach of 8
blameworthiness 85, 116, 134, 143, 373
blanket immunities 22
bodily integrity 29, 46
bonuses, lost 72
brain damage 237
breach by builder in carrying out work late 200
breach by builder refusing to carry out work or carrying it out defectively 197–200
breach by buyer refusing to accept goods 195–96
breach by owner refusing to allow work to proceed 200
breach by seller delivering defective goods wanted for use 194
breach by seller failing to deliver goods wanted for resale 191–92
breach by seller failing to deliver goods wanted for use 192–93
breach by seller making late delivery of goods wanted for resale 194–95
breach by seller making late delivery for goods wanted for use 195
breach of contract
  compensatory damages 39–42
  contributory negligence 138–44
  final mandatory injunctions 465–66
  final prohibitory injunctions 454–62
  final *quia timet* injunctions 468–69
  loss of reputation 268–71
  mental distress or physical inconvenience 277–83
  punitive damages 360–61
  remoteness 91–106
  restitutionary remedies 352–59
  to sell goods 403–7
  to sell land 403

  to sell shares or stocks 407
  see also basic pecuniary loss (breach of contract) *under* pecuniary loss
bribes or secret commissions 529–32, 535–36
business or contract, wrongful interference with 230–31
business, loss of 230, 269, 323
'but for' test 51, 52–53, 54, 55–56
  compensating advantages 147, 151
  contributory negligence 133
  dishonest assistance 535–36
  intervening cause 108–9
  losses on death 265

Canada 537
  equitable compensation 512
  free speech 479
  punitive damages 377–78
  reliance damages 78
  remedies 510
  taxation 183–84
cancellation clause 174
care, cost of 156–57
care, duty of 45, 65
  contributory negligence 138, 139, 141–42
  equitable compensation 514
  intervening cause 108–9, 110, 113
  mental distress or physical inconvenience 279–80, 281
  mitigate, duty to 131–32
  negligence 231, 232–33
  personal injury 249–50
  SAAMCO principle 121–22, 126
causation
  compensating advantages 147, 150, 153
  contributory negligence 142–43
  damages valuing right infringed 47
  equitable compensation 513, 514
  Human Rights Act 1998 26
  impecuniosity 144
  intervening cause 105–10, 111–16
  non-compensatory cost of cure 50
  proof of loss and loss of a chance 62
  punitive damages 371
  restitution 344
  SAAMCO principle 117–18, 119–20
  secret or unauthorised profit 529
  torts 43–44
  see also 'but for' test; factual causation
cause of action test 174
  abolition of 361, 362–63, 368–70, 374, 377
certainty, standard of 72–73
certificate of recoverable benefits 157
chance, loss of 57, 269
  see also proof of loss and loss of a chance
changes in value of property or services in internal value of money (inflation) 171–76
  non-pecuniary loss 171–72, 181
charging order 5
charitable payments 160–61
child (healthy but unwanted), cost of bringing up 250, 252
children 136, 247, 248, 249
  infancy 166
  minors 441
civil recourse theory 18–20

Coase theorem 16–17, 413–14
coercive remedies 5
collateral 153
  benefits (compensating advantages provided by third parties) 249
  warranty 202
commercial cases 302, 303, 305, 306, 475, 485–86
common sense or instinct 107
Commonwealth countries 22–23, 375
compelling performance or preventing equitable wrong 10, 538–41
  accounting for loss 540
  delivery up for destruction or destruction on oath 541
  delivery up of material containing confidential information 541
  injunctions 538–40
compensating advantages 147–62
  collateral 153
  direct 149
  indirect advantages are not deducted 148–52
  objective measure 152
  provision of by third parties 249
  provision of by third parties not deducted 148, 152–62
    general factors influencing courts 152–55
    non-state payments 158–62
    social security benefits 156–57
  res inter alios acta 153
  social security benefits 153–54
  subjective measure 152
compensation 9, 10, 11–12
  depreciation 389
  equitable 12
  full 14–15, 161, 175
  Human Rights Act 1998 25, 26, 27
  with specific performance 437–38
  see also equitable compensation; overcompensation; undercompensation
compensation for equitable wrongs 511–25
  confidence, breach of 532–35
    damages assessment 523–25
    jurisdiction to award damages 520–22
  dishonest assistance 535–36
  fiduciary duty, breach of 526–32
  no separate non-compensatory 'account' remedy 515–20
  restitution for equitable wrongs 525–36
  see also equitable compensation
'compensation neurosis' 164
Compensation Recovery Unit 153–54, 157
compensatory damages 14, 35–50, 83–146, 164–69
  assessment date *see* compensatory damages, date for assessment of
  compensatory aims 38–39
  consequential 46, 47–48
  contributory negligence 84, 85
  damages awarded unconditionally 168–69
  damages valuing right infringed 46–48
  express authorisation by statute 367–68
  Human Rights Act 1998 23–24
  impecuniosity, demise of as a limitation 144–46
  intervening cause 83, 84, 85
  limitation periods 309
  limiting 10–11
  mitigate, duty to 84–85

negotiating damages 322, 329
non-compensatory cost of cure 48–50
once-and-for-all assessment 163–68
  arguments for and against 163–64
  general rule 163
  interim payments 167–68
  provisional damages 165
  structured settlements 165–67
pecuniary loss, future 164, 166–67
periodical payments, reviewable 166
and punitive damages 370
remoteness 83, 84, 86–106
SAAMCO principle 83–84
theoretical underpinnings 39–46
  breach of contract 39–42
  torts 42–46
types of loss 35–38
see also contributory negligence; equitable damages; intervening cause; mitigate, duty to; remoteness; *SAAMCO* principle
compensatory damages, date for assessment of 169–81
  cause of action 174
  date of loss rule 176
  pecuniary loss 169
  time after which court assessing damages is barred from taking into account events that have already occurred 169–70
  value of money, property or services for damages assessment 170–81
    changes in external value of money—foreign money liabilities 177–81
    changes in value of property or services in internal value of money (inflation) 171–76
    date of accrual of cause of action 170, 176, 177, 179
    date of accrual of loss 170, 176, 177, 179
    non-pecuniary loss 171–72, 181
    pecuniary loss 172–76, 181
    pecuniary loss, future 171, 172
    pecuniary loss, past recurring 172
    sterling-breach-date rule 177, 179–80, 181
compound interest 295, 297, 298–300, 303–4, 542–43
concurrent events 53
concurrent liability 8
  between negligence and breach of contract 6–8
  contributory negligence 141–42, 144
  limitation periods 311
  mental distress or physical inconvenience 286–87
  remoteness 86, 105–6
  stricter test for 91
concurrent sufficient events 53
conditional fee agreement 236
conditional sale agreements 389, 398, 400
conduct 113–17, 371
  contributory negligence 116–17
  declarations 505
  delivery up of goods 496
  equitable damages 316
  final prohibitory injunctions 444
  has been calculated to make a profit 361–62, 364–67
  hypothetical 67–68
  hypothetical, minimum obligation principle 68–73

conduct (cont.)
  inequitable 445
  intentional or reckless 222
  merely unreasonable 385
  non-wrongful conduct 111, 112
  punishment for equitable wrongs 537
  punitive damages 376
  reasonable 113–14, 115–16
  showing deliberate and outrageous disregard of claimant's rights 377
  unreasonable 84–85, 108, 114–15, 142, 385
  wrongful 29
  see also conduct of claimant as bar to injunction; third party conduct; and under specific performance
conduct of claimant as bar to injunction 456, 486–91
  acquiescence 487–88
  laches 489–91
    final injunctions 489–90
    interim injunctions 490–91
  one who comes to equity must come with clean hands 487
  one who seeks equity must do equity 487
  serious breach of contract 486
  termination of contract, valid by claimant 491
confidence, breach of 12–13
  assessment of damages for 523–25
  claimant's conduct as bar to injunction 487, 490–91
  equitable compensation 512
  equitable damages 520
  free speech 480
  Human Rights Act 1998 22
  injunctions 539
  interim injunctions 475, 539–40
  jurisdiction to award damages for 520–22
  limitation periods 544
  negotiating damages 321–22, 329–30
  prohibitory injunctions 538–39
  punishment for equitable wrongs 537
  remedies 509–10, 511
  restitution 341–42, 343–44, 525, 531, 532–35
confidence, loss of 423
confidential information 541
confidentiality 12–13, 480
confidentiality clause, breach of 323, 324
confiscation orders 371
congenital abnormalities 249–50
consequential damages 493
  compensatory 46, 47–48
  restitutionary 46
consequential loss 103, 175–76, 211, 212–13, 214, 224
consequential relief 504
consideration
  failed 155
  inadequacy of 430
conspiracy 223–24, 230, 367
constant supervision objection 415–19
  final mandatory injunctions 464–65
  final prohibitory injunctions 455–56
  indirect specific performance 460
  specific performance 415–19, 428–29, 436
constitutional rights, infringement of 363–64
constructive knowledge 311, 313–14
constructive trust 438–39, 528, 529, 530, 531–32, 543

confidence, breach of 533, 534
consumer credit agreements 213–15
consumer surplus 16–18, 283
contempt of court 5, 413, 440–41
contingencies of life 244, 262
contingency fund 166
continuity principle between right and remedy 19
contract price 191–92, 193, 195–96, 200
  and market price, difference between 173, 174
contract as promise theory 40
contract unfairly obtained 430
contractual obligations, positive 11
contractual promise, negative, breach of 495
contractual warranty, breach of 39, 202, 227–28
contributory negligence 9, 132–44
  agreed sum, award of 393
  breach of contract 138–44
  category one case 139, 141, 143, 144
  category three case 139, 141, 142, 143
  category two case 139, 141–42, 143–44
  claimant's conduct 116–17
  compensatory damages 167–68
  equitable compensation 512–13
  factual causation 57
  losses on death 257–58
  punitive damages 371
  SAAMCO principle 124
  torts 133–38
    applicability 136–38
    damages reduction, extent of 134–36
    what defendant must establish 133–34
  wrongful interference with goods 219
conversion 46–47
  compensatory damages, date for assessment of 172, 176, 177–78, 179
  contributory negligence 138
  delivery up of goods 493
  mitigate, duty to 128–29
  multiple 55
  property damage including destruction 206
  remoteness 90
  restitution 340
  taxation 182
  wrongful interference with goods 219–21
copyright 342–43, 367–68, 497–98, 499
corporation tax 298
corrective justice 18–20, 43–44, 45, 337
Cory v Thames Ironworks Co principle 97
cost of cure 205–6, 219, 220
  basic pecuniary loss 189–90, 191, 193, 194, 197–200, 201, 203
  damage to property including destruction 206, 207–8, 209, 211
  interest 302
  non-compensatory cost of 48–50
  pecuniary loss 206
  restitution 353–54
cost-benefit analysis 453
counter-factual 328
counterclaim 167–68
court orders 4, 5
court pronouncement 4
Court of Protection 247
credit, damage to 93
Criminal Injuries Compensation Scheme 266
criminal punishment 371

custom, loss of 74, 221
cynical profit-making category 367–68
cynical wrongdoing test 355, 532

damage
  latent 8, 310, 313–14
  mere 209
  type of 94–97
damages 4, 5, 9
  and account of profits 345–46
  actionable 23–24
  additional 367–68, 437
  assessment, difficulty in 407–8
  assessment for Human Rights Act 1998 cause of action 26–29
  basic 287–88, 289
  calculation of 243–49
  compensatory 7–8, 9
  contemptuous 35, 503–4
  exemplary 366, 376, 537
    see also punitive damages
  expectation 355, 358
  general 93, 235, 296–97, 307
  Human Rights Act 1998 26, 27
  inability to pay 408–9
  incidental 205–6
  non-compensatory 46
  non-compensatory equitable 319–20
  non-recoverable 277
  ordinary 331, 354
  proportionate 66–67
  provisional 165, 167, 254, 258
  quantum of 168
  recoverable 277
  restitutionary 46, 221, 322
  special 93, 179–80, 235, 296–97
  and specific performance 439
  stigma 270
  substantial 202, 203–4, 321
  in substitution 317
  substitutive 46, 48–49
  threshold for recovery of 238
  unliquidated 388, 394
  vindicatory 25, 363–64
  see also adequacy of damages; aggravated damages; bereavement damages; compensatory damages; equitable damages; liquidated damages; negotiating damages; nominal damages; punitive damages; reliance damages
date of accrual of cause of action 170, 176, 177, 179
date of accrual of loss 170, 176, 177, 179
date of breach or date of tort rule 47
date of knowledge 311–12
date of loss rule 176
death
  compensatory damages 164, 165–68, 169
  contributory negligence 133, 137
  exceptions to normal time limits 312–13
  interest 301, 302, 304–5, 306, 307
  intervening cause 111, 112
  losses on 37
  proof of loss and loss of a chance 61, 63, 65–66
  pure economic loss 222
  remoteness 88–89
  torts 44–45
  wrong has caused 267
deceased's estate, claims by 253–55
deceit 6, 39
  compensatory damages, date for assessment of 175
  contributory negligence 136–37, 138, 139
  equitable compensation 514
  mental distress or physical inconvenience 283–84
  misrepresentation 223, 224, 225–26, 227–28
  punishment for equitable wrongs 536–37
  pure economic loss 222
  remoteness 86, 90
  restitution 336, 338–39, 349
  SAAMCO principle 122–23
declarations 4, 26, 504–6
declaring rights 9, 541
defamation 37
  free speech 479, 480
  injunctions 539
  mental distress or physical inconvenience 288–89
  proof of loss and loss of chance 73
  punitive damages 365, 368–69, 372
  reputation, loss of 271, 272, 274
defective delivery 195–96
delay 202, 203, 433–34, 491
delivery up
  confidence, breach of 534
  for destruction or destruction on oath 497–99, 541
  of goods 493–97, 498–99
    commercially unique 405
    courts ordering 493–96
    interim 494, 496–97
    recovery of land 497
    replevin 497
    Torts (Interference with Goods) Act 1977 496
  of material containing confidential information 541
  for wrongful detention 404
dependants and losses on death 256–57
dependency 88–89
depreciation compensation 389
depression 276
design rights 342–43, 367–68, 497–98, 499
destruction or destruction on oath and delivery up 497–99
deterrence 377–78
difference in value measures 189–90, 195, 213, 232, 353–54
diminution in value of capital 207
diminution in value of land 221–22, 321, 331
diminution in value of property 206–8, 209
direct effect 15, 369–70
directness principle 148
disability
  child's upkeep costs 249–52
  compensatory damages, form of 166
  disabled mother/healthy child and attributable costs 251
  payments (non-state) 159–60
  pension 154, 158–59, 160–61, 162
disappointment 277, 283–84
disclosure, specific 5, 486

discomfort 283–84, 291
discount
  average 136
  post-appeal 136
  rate 244, 245–46, 247, 260, 262
  rate, negative 242, 245
discretionary bonuses 71
discretionary defences 10–11
discretionary remedy 402
disgorgement 337–38, 356, 525
  terminology in preference to restitution 336–37
  see also restitution
dishonest assistance 344, 509–10, 535–36, 544
dishonesty 137, 270, 342, 488
dismissal
  necessitated by personal injury 148
  see also unfair dismissal; wrongful dismissal
distress 36–37, 237, 497
  emotional 376
  see also mental distress
distributive justice 44–45, 250
divorce
  between claimant widow and deceased 262–63
  resulting from claimant's injury 243
double recovery 14–15, 48–49, 214–15, 346
duress 335, 338–39, 430
duties, negative and positive 38–39
duty, breach of
  confidence, breach of 522
  contributory negligence 141
  final mandatory injunctions 465
  intervening cause 107–8, 111, 112, 115
  limitation periods 311
  SAAMCO principle 120
  see also fiduciary duty, breach of; statutory duty, breach of
duty of care deed 202

earnings, loss of 36, 69, 230–31, 269
  interest 297–98
  mitigate, duty to 128
  non-state payments 158, 160
  personal injury 170, 172, 182, 238, 241–43, 249–50, 253, 254
  pre-death 267
  pre-trial 306
  remoteness 88–89
  reputation, loss of 268, 270–71
  social security benefits 156–57
  see also future earnings, loss of
economic analysis 16–18
economic efficiency 42–43, 453
economic rights 331
economic support, loss of 247
Edelman's thesis 337–38
effectiveness principle 16
efficient breach theory 355–56, 396–97, 413, 414
employment, loss of 272
  see also dismissal; personal injury
employment and support allowance 156–57
employment tribunals 425
enforcement procedures 4, 5
equitable compensation 12, 83, 435, 509–10, 511–20
  accounting for loss 540
  compensation for loss 514
  equitable damages 520, 522
  equitable wrongs 526
  injunctions 538
  interest 542–43
  limitation periods 543
  no separate non-compensating account remedy 515–20
  punishment for equitable wrongs 536
equitable damages 315–20
  in addition to specific performance 437–38
  compensatory 35–36
  exceptions to normal time limits 314
  final prohibitory injunctions 444, 449, 454
  injunctions 315–17
  negotiating damages 328, 329
  non-compensatory 319–20
  power to award 315–16
  specific performance 315–17
  in substitution 526
  when more advantageous than common law damages 317–19
  wrongful interference with land 221–22
equitable wrongs 11–13, 22, 509
  punishment for 536–37
  see also compensation for equitable wrongs; equitable compensation; punishment for equitable wrongs; remedies for equitable wrongs; restitution for equitable wrongs
equity will not assist a volunteer 429
equivalence principle 16, 369–70
European Contract Code 143
European Union law, breach of 15–16
eurotorts 369–70
eviction 365, 366, 375
evidence collection, orders made to assist claimant with to establish case 5
evidence, fresh 169–70
exemplary damages 366, 376, 537
  see also punitive damages
expectation interest 14–15, 39–40, 41, 42
  adequacy of damages 413–14
  final prohibitory injunctions 455–56
  pecuniary loss 189–90
  and reliance damages 75, 76–77, 78–80, 81
  restitution 525–26
  SAAMCO principle 121–22
expectation of life, loss of 171, 237, 251
expectation measure 331
expectation principle 201
expenditure/expenses
  post-contractual 81
  pre-trial 36
  reasonable recoverable 130
  wasted 79
external value of money, changes in—foreign money liabilities 177–81

facilitative institution analysis 535
factual causation 6, 51–57
  additional sufficient events 52–55
  'but for' test 51, 52–53, 54, 55–56
  material increase of risk 55–57
fair comment (free speech) 479
fair trial 26–27, 310, 313
false imprisonment
  compensatory damages 37
  damages valuing right infringed 46
  Human Rights Act 1998 28

mental distress or physical inconvenience 283–84, 287–89, 290
punitive damages 362–63, 364, 367, 368–69, 372
reputation, loss of 272, 274–75
false representations 223, 224
Fatal Accidents Act 1976 265–67
fiduciary duty, breach of
and confidence, breach of 534
dishonestly procuring or assisting 525, 526
equitable compensation 511–12, 513–14, 520
equitable wrongs 12
interest 303, 542
interim injunctions 476
limitation periods 543–44
prohibitory injunctions 538
punishment for equitable wrongs 537
remedies 509–10, 511
restitution 337, 355, 356–58, 525, 526–32
restitution
bribes or secret commissions 529–32
secret or unauthorised profits 526–29
fieri facias writ 5
final injunctions 443, 469–70, 471, 475–77, 486, 489–90
see also final mandatory injunctions; final prohibitory injunctions; final *quia timet* injunctions
final mandatory injunctions 462–66, 540
breach of contract 465–66
torts 462–65
final prohibitory injunctions 443–62, 471, 538–39, 540
breach of contract 454–62
primary remedy, injunction as 454–56
specific performance, indirect 456–61
stipulated remedy 462
interim injunctions 472–73
torts 443–54
Coventry v Lawrence 449–51
final remedy, injunction as 443–44
greater use of damages, arguments for 451–53
greater use of damages, arguments against 453–54
private nuisance (and trespass to land) 444–49
final *quia timet* injunctions 467–69
breach of contract 468–69
torts 467–68
financial advantage, loss of 189–90, 206
financial dependence and losses on death 257
flooding, loss by 102–3
forbearance 141
foreign currency liabilities 177–81, 307–8
forfeiture 394–95, 417, 499
fraud
insurance 367
interest 300, 303, 542
intervening cause 109–10
limitation periods 543
punitive damages 372
reputation, loss of 274
whiplash claims, fraudulent 238
see also fraudulent misrepresentation
fraudulent inducement 90
fraudulent misrepresentation 223–26, 227–28
contributory negligence 137–38
restitution 349

free speech, need to protect 479–80
freedom of contract 399
freedom of expression 479–80, 539–40
freezing injunctions 484, 485–86
'world-wide' 485
frustration 28, 431–32
fund management charges 247
funeral expenses 252–53, 254–55, 264, 267
future earnings, loss of 66, 246, 247, 249
future pecuniary loss 171, 172
compensatory damages, form of 164, 166–67
interest 307
loss consequent on actional personal injury or death 65–66
personal injury losses 234–35, 242, 244, 246–47, 249
taxation 184

gain-based measures 336–37
genuine pre-estimate of loss test 388, 389, 393–94, 396, 398
good bargain 81
good faith, duty to act in 377–78
goods 209–17
destruction 209–11
interference with 541
loss of 220
mere damage 211–17
additional loss including loss of use 214–17
replacement or repair costs 211–14
property damage, including destruction 209–17
specific or ascertained 403–4
wrongful interference 219–21, 222
see also delivery up; trespass to goods
goodwill, loss of 269–70, 323, 330–31
Gourley principle 182–84
gratuitous carers/third parties 240–43
gratuitous nursing services 168–69
gratuitous payments 154, 159, 168–69
gratuitous services 265–67
grief and annoyance 272
group personal accident insurance policy 159–60

handicapped in the labour market (*Smith v Manchester Corp* damages) 239
happiness, loss of 36–37, 216–17, 237, 268, 276
harassment 90–91, 284–85, 365
hardship 10–11, 463–64
bar 466
severe 431–32
health insurance scheme (employer's) 158, 160
hire-purchase agreements and hire charges 70, 213, 214–15, 398, 400
horizontal effect 22
housekeeping capacity, loss of 242–43
Human Rights Act 1998 22–29
damages assessment for HRA cause of action 26–29
non-tortious public wrong 23–26
separate channels approach 25–26
human rights infringements 318–19, 364, 369, 370
humiliation 287–88

'if but only if' test 370
ill-health gratuity 159–60
ill-treatment in custody 28
see also false imprisonment; malicious prosecution

impecuniosity 144–46, 175, 296
implied terms 71, 386–87
impossibility 430–31
imprisonment 5, 28, 371
  see also false imprisonment
inaction, unreasonable 127–29
income, loss of *see* earnings, loss of
Index-Linked Government Stock (ILGS)
  personal injury losses 242, 244, 245–47
    interest 307
    losses on death 260, 262
industrial disputes 475, 476
industrial injuries scheme 44–45
infancy and disability 166
inflation 171–72
  compensatory damages, date for assessment of 176
  future 172
  and interest 306–7
  personal injury 245, 246–47
information and advice 124–25
information, failure to provide 117
injunctions 4, 5, 9, 10, 14, 17–18, 35, 440–92
  compelling performance or preventing equitable wrong 538–40
  compensated 452–53, 454
  delivery up of goods 496
  equitable damages 315–17
  Human Rights Act 1998 26
  limitation periods 314, 544
  ordinary 318
  preventing dissemination of private information (celebrities) 441
  prohibitory 355
  restitution 357, 526
  specific performance 422, 423, 424
  substitution for 321–22, 323–24, 329–30
  'without notice' 484–85
  see also conduct as bar to injunction; final injunctions; interim injunctions; mandatory injunctions; prohibitory injunctions; *quia timet* injunctions
injured person, claims by 234–53
  collateral benefits (compensating advantages provided by third parties) 249
  non-pecuniary loss 235–38
    pain, suffering and loss of amenity 235–37
    threshold for recovery of damages 238
  pecuniary loss 238–49
    damages, calculation of 243–49
    types of 238–43
  wrongful birth, damages for 249–53
injurious falsehood 73, 230, 479
injury
  intervening cause 107–8, 111–12, 114–15, 116
  physical 95, 273
  to feelings 90–91, 284–85, 287–88, 289–90, 291
  see also injured person, claims by; personal injury
innocent wrongdoing 342–43
insolvency 408–9, 493–94, 495, 515–16, 529
insurance
  contract 158
  fraud 367
  property damage including destruction 208
integrity, right to 48
intellectual property rights 14, 228–30, 523, 524
  delivery up and breach of confidence 541
  delivery up for destruction 497–98, 499
  pure economic loss 222
  reputation, loss of 272
  restitution 348, 356–57
  search orders 485–86
  wrongful infringement 228–30
  wrongful interference with 329–30
intention 198–200
intention justification theory 414
intentional wrongdoing 111, 112
interest 295–308
  actual interest losses 300
  awards of 35–36
  base rate 295–96
  charges 131
  charges, recoverability of 84
  commercial cases 302, 303, 305, 306
  compensatory damages, date for assessment of 176, 178
  compound 295, 297, 300, 303–4, 542–43
  conditional specific performance 438–39
  as damages 296–301
    no damages for failure to pay (old rule) 296–98
    Sempra Metals decision 298–301
  date of loss/date of cause of action 306
  death 301, 302, 304–5, 306, 307
  equitable 438–39
  future pecuniary loss 307
  inflation 306–7
  LIBOR rate 299
  loss of interest 298
  non-pecuniary loss 302–3, 304–5, 306, 307
  non-statutory 542–43
  pecuniary loss 189, 302, 303, 304
  performance 41–42, 189–90
  personal injury 171, 234–35, 301, 302, 304–5, 306, 307
  post-judgment 295
  pre-judgment 295, 301, 542
  pre-trial pecuniary loss 305, 306
  private 446, 447, 449
  property damage including destruction 216
  rates 180, 242
  relevant day 295–96
  remedies for equitable wrongs 542–43
  simple 295–96, 297, 299–300, 301, 305
  see also expectation interest; interest on damages; reliance interest; statutory interest
interest on damages 301–8
  Senior Courts Act 1981 301
  simple interest 303–4
  statutory interest 304
    compensatory purpose 302–3
    period payable 304–5
    rate 305–6
  statutory interest and assessment date of damages 306–8
    foreign currency liabilities 307–8
    liabilities other than foreign currency liabilities 306–7
interference
  by unlawful means 230, 366, 367, 368–69
  with contract 231
  with enjoyment of land 453
  with goods 541
  tortious 496

interim injunctions 440–41, 443, 469–86, 540
　alternative approach 481
　anonymised 480
　claimant's conduct as bar to 486
　confidence, breach of 539–40
　and freezing injunctions 485
　laches 490–91
　libel 539
　mandatory 401–2, 469, 481–84, 496, 540
　prohibitory 469, 471, 538–39, 540
　receiver, appointment of 491–92
　search orders 485–86
　specific performance 405, 406, 408, 417,
　　420–21, 422
　'without notice' injunctions 484–85
　see also American Cyanamid
interim payments 167–68, 382
interim restraint order 539–40
interlocutory judgment 360–61
intervening cause 6, 107–17
　claimant's conduct 113–17
　　contributory negligence 116–17
　　reasonable acts 115–16
　　unreasonable acts 114–15
　compensating advantages 148
　equitable compensation 512–13
　natural events 107–9
　SAAMCO principle 119–21
　specific performance 402
　third party conduct 109–13
　　duty was to guard against such third party
　　　intervention 109–11
　　third party intervention other than where
　　　there was a duty to guard against it 111–13
intimidation 230–31, 361, 362–63, 367
investment advice costs 247
irrevocable election view 439

jobseeker's allowance 156–57
joint defendants 373
judgment debt 301
judicial remedies 3–4, 9–10, 13
judicial review 20
'just satisfaction' 24, 364, 370
juries 274, 288–89, 372, 456
justification (free speech) 479

knowing receipt 509–10, 535, 544

laches 10–11, 489–91
　conduct of claimant 433–34
　declarations 505
　delivery up of goods 496
　final injunctions 489–90
　interim injunctions 490–91
　limitation periods 314, 544
land
　diminution in value 221–22, 321, 331
　interference with enjoyment of 453
　recovery of 497
　sale of 77, 81
　use conflict 452–53
　wrongful interference 221–22
　wrongful use 324–25, 329–30
　see also trespass to land
last-opportunity rule 116–17
lawful means conspiracy 272

legal compulsion 155
legal and equitable remedies 10–11
legitimate interest 390–91, 392, 393–94, 395
liability
　acceptance 99
　compensatory damages 84, 167–68
　for consequences 51–52
　disproportionate 102
　double 203
　foreign currency 177–81, 307–8
　insurance 43
　intervening cause 108–9
　negligence 231
　non-fault enterprise 43
　other than foreign currency liabilities 306–7
　promissory 8
　proof of loss and loss of a chance 61
　pure economic loss 222
　rule 452–53
　state 15
　statutory 225–26
　vicarious 44, 373
　see also concurrent liability; strict liability
libel 182
　delivery up for destruction 499
　injunctions 539
　interim injunctions 539
　intervening cause 110
　punitive damages 364–65, 373–74, 376
　reputation, loss of 268, 272
　restitution 351–52
liberty, loss of 28, 29, 283–84, 288–89
　see also imprisonment
LIBOR rate 299
licence fee damages 524
life assurance payments 265
life expectancy 244, 248
light, right to, infringement of 221–22, 350,
　467, 482
limitation periods 8, 9, 36, 309–14
　agreed sum, award of 382
　constructive knowledge 311, 313–14
　date of knowledge 311–12
　declarations 505
　deterioration of evidence over time 309
　exceptions to normal time limits 311–14
　　death 312–13
　　equitable damages 314
　　latent damage 310, 313–14
　　personal injury 311–13
　fifteen year long-stop bar 313–14
　interest 298
　normal time limits 310–11
　remedies for equitable wrongs 543–44
　six months 339, 340
　six years 310–11, 313–14, 339, 490, 544
　statutory 489–90
　three years 311–12
　twelve years 310, 497
liquidated damages 6
　agreed sum, award of 381, 388–97
　　new law 390–91
　　and penalties, distinction between 388–89,
　　　398–400
　　used to limit damages 393–94
　pecuniary loss 202
　stipulated remedy 436–37, 462

living expenses 248–49
loss
  accounting for 12, 540
  actual 119, 174, 389, 393, 394
  compensation for 511–14
  consequent on actionable personal injury or death 65–66
  constructive total 209
  contemplation of 83
  degree of likelihood of 95
  direct 119, 212–13, 214
  disproportionate, compared to contractual consideration: United States approach 97–98
  distribution 44
  economic 106, 119–20
  exceptional 98
  financial 96
  foreseeable 97
  future 163–64, 453
  future continuing 318
  greater than penalty 394
  indirect 119
  legally recoverable 393
  monetary 36
  net 158, 159–61
  non-recoverable 102–3
  non-remote 124
  out-of-pocket 189–90
  past 242
  past continuing 318
  post-trial 260, 261, 262
  potential future 212–13
  pre-trial 260, 261
  present 163
  property damage including destruction 206
  proprietary 36, 237
  recoverable 158
  reliance 124, 203, 331
  that would have been suffered even if claimant had complied with duty to mitigate 131–32
  trading 93, 115
  type of 94–97
  wrongful 340
  wrongful interference with goods 219
  see also consequential loss; genuine pre-estimate of loss test; losses on death; non-pecuniary loss; pecuniary loss; personal injury losses; pure economic loss
losses on death 256–67
  actionability by injured person 257–58
  benefits 265
  bereavement damages 256, 263–64, 267
  contingencies of life 262
  date of death 260
  death-after-retirement pension 261
  death-in-service pension 261
  dependants 256–57
  discount rate 260, 262
  divorce between claimant widow and deceased 262–63
  earnings from starting work after death of relative 265
  Fatal Accidents Act 1976 265–67
  financial dependence 257
  funeral expenses 264, 267
  gratuitous services 265–67
  Index Linked Government Stock (ILGS) 260, 262
  life assurance payments 265
  'lost years' earnings awards 267
  mother's or wife's services 258–59
  non-pecuniary loss 265, 267
  Ogden Tables 260
  pecuniary loss 258–63, 267
    business 259
    multiplier method 260–63
    post-trial 260
    pre-death 267
    proof of loss 259–60
  pensions 265
  post-trial loss 260, 261, 262
  pre-death loss of earnings 267
  pre-death personal injury losses 267
  pre-trial loss 260, 261
  re-marriage of widow(er) 263, 265
  social security benefits 265, 266–67
  trial date 260–61
  wrong has caused death 267
  wrongful act, neglect or default 256, 257–58
'lost years' 234–49, 254, 267
lump sum payments 164, 166, 415
  personal injury 235, 244, 249
  wrongful infringement of intellectual property rights 229
lying and breaking one's promise, difference between 223

malicious prosecution 37, 272, 274–75
  mental distress or physical inconvenience 287–89
  punitive damages 362–63, 368–69, 372
mandatory injunctions 442–43, 451, 538
  claimant's conduct as bar to 486
  equitable compensation 515, 518
  equitable damages 319
  quia timet 467–68
  receiver, appointment of 491
  restorative 493–98
  see also final mandatory injunctions
Mareva injunctions *see* freezing injunctions
market buying price 192, 219–20
market cost 206, 212
market deterrence theory 43
market fall losses 109
market, loss of 95
market price 191–92, 193, 194, 195, 196, 340
market selling price 219–20
  basic pecuniary loss 193, 194–95, 196, 197
  damage to property including destruction 206, 209–11, 212
market value 36, 199, 210
marriage prospects, loss of 247
material contribution 52
material gain 337
material increase of risk 55–57, 62–63
material non-disclosure 125–26
medical expenses 172
medical, nursing and hospital expenses 130, 239–41, 242–43, 253
mental benefits, expected, loss of 282–83
mental distress 7–8, 9, 35, 36–37
  adequacy of damages 414–15

compensatory damages, date for assessment of 171–72
confidence, breach of 522, 525
  losses on death 263
  negotiating damages 331
  pecuniary loss 198
  personal injury losses 251, 252
  property damage including destruction 216–17
  reputation, loss of 268, 271, 272
  restrictions on recovery for 6
  see also mental distress or physical inconvenience
mental distress or physical inconvenience 276–92
  amenity, loss of 276, 278, 291–92
  annoyance 277, 283–84, 291
  anxiety 281
  assessment of damages 288–92
  award of damages 277–88
    breach of contract 277–83
    torts 283–88
  disappointment 277, 283–84
  discomfort 283–84, 291
  distress 287–88
  happiness, loss of 276
  harassment 284–85
  humiliation 287–88
  inconvenience 283–84, 291
  injury to feelings 284–85, 287–88, 289–90, 291
  mental satisfaction 278–79
  mental suffering 280
  non-pecuniary loss 276, 283, 288–91
  non-recoverable damages 277
  peace of mind 278–79
  pecuniary loss 277, 281
  pleasure, loss of 278, 291–92
  recoverable damages 277
  reputation, loss of 276
  temper, loss of 277
  vexation 277, 280, 281
mental incapacity 441
mental satisfaction 278–79
mental suffering 280
mesne profits 221
'mini-trial' of dispute 470–71, 474, 482–83
minimum obligation principle 68–73
minimum payment clause 70, 389
minors and injunctions 441
misappropriation 206, 216, 219, 220
misrepresentation 7–8, 223–28
  aim of damages 223–26
  compensating advantages 150, 152
  compensatory damages, date for assessment of 174–75
  contract unfairly obtained 430
  contributory negligence 137–38
  expenses caused and gains forgone 226–28
  inducing contracts 39
  innocent 225–26, 338–39
  mental distress or physical inconvenience 283–84
  mitigate, duty to 131
  negligent 39
  non-fraudulent 338–39
  pure economic loss 222
  reliance damages 75, 76, 79–80
  remoteness 90
  restitution 336, 338–39

  SAAMCO principle 117, 121–23
  see also fraudulent misrepresentation
misstatement, negligent 225
mistake
  common 431–32
  compensating advantages 155
  contract unfairly obtained 430
  restitution 335, 338–39
  unilateral 430
mitigate, duty to 127–32
  adequacy of damages 413, 414–15
  agreed sum, award of 383, 387, 393
  anticipatory repudiation 132
  basic pecuniary loss 189, 190, 191–92, 193, 194, 195, 196, 197, 198–99
  compensating advantages 152
  compensatory damages, date for assessment of 174–75, 176
  contributory negligence 142
  damages valuing right infringed 46–47
  final mandatory injunctions 463
  final prohibitory injunctions 455–56
  impecuniosity 145, 146
  interest 299
  intervening cause 113
  loss that would have been suffered even if claimant had complied with 131–32
  pecuniary loss 205
  proof of loss and loss of chance 66
  property damage including destruction 209, 214
  specific performance 402
  unreasonable action 130–31
  unreasonable inaction 127–29
  wrongful interference with goods or land 219–20, 221
mitigation
  in contract 46–47
  of damages, compensating advantages 148
  Human Rights Act 1998 26
  of loss 169
  non-compensatory cost of cure 50
  personal injury 249–50
  see also mitigate, duty to
mobility allowance 156–57
mobility, loss of 156–57
money had and received 336, 338, 340–41
moral rights 16
morality, individualistic 43
Morris-Garner v One Step (Support) Ltd 321, 322, 323–24
mother's or wife's services 258–59
multiple claimants 373–74
multiplier method 244, 245, 246, 247–48, 249, 260–63
mutual confidence, trust and respect 270, 419, 420–21, 422, 425
mutuality, affirmative 403

National Health Service (NHS) 166–67, 239–40
natural events, intervening 107–9
natural justice, breach of 423, 424–25
negative mutuality *see* want of mutuality
neglect 127
negligence 6, 8
  acts or omissions under
    negligent interference with contract or business 231–32

negligence (*cont.*)
  pure economic loss 231–33
    services beneficial to claimant, negligent performance of 232–33
  causing injury 148
  compensating advantages 147, 149–50
  compensatory damages 84, 168, 175
  contributory negligence 136
  damages valuing right infringed 46
  equitable compensation 513, 514, 519
  factual causation 57
  Human Rights Act 1998 24
  intervening cause 107–8, 109, 110, 111–12, 113, 114–15
  limitation periods 311
  mental distress or physical inconvenience 277, 279–80, 281, 283–84, 286–88
  misrepresentation 223, 225
  mitigate, duty to 128–29
  non-state payments 160–61
  pecuniary loss 188, 202, 231–32
  personal injury 234, 249
  professional 12, 67–68, 510, 543
  proof of loss and loss of a chance 61, 62
  property damage including destruction 206, 207–10, 212–13, 217–18
  pure economic loss 222
  remoteness 86–88, 96, 105–6
  reputation, loss of 272
  restitution 342–43
  SAAMCO principle 117, 118, 119–20, 122–23, 124, 125–26
  torts 42–43, 45
  wrongful interference with goods 219
  see also contributory negligence
negotiating damages 35–36, 321–32
  account of profits 326–27, 329–31
  availability of 328–32
  confidence, breach of 523–25, 532–33
  damages valuing right infringed 48
  equitable damages 316, 319, 328, 329
  Morris-Garner v One Step (Support) Ltd 321, 322, 323–24
  non-competition covenant, breach of 323, 327, 330–31
  pecuniary loss 200
  profits, loss of 323
  property damage including destruction 216
  purpose of 324–28
  restitution 336, 337–38, 343–44, 348–49, 354
  restrictive covenant, breach of 321, 324, 327, 329–30
  substitution for an injunction 321–22, 323–24, 329–30
  trespass to land 324–26, 327
  wrongful interference with goods 220
  wrongful interference with land 221–22
  'Wrotham Park' damages 321, 323, 332
NESS test 51–52
New Zealand 510, 537
'no better off' principle 51–52
no claw-back rule 199
'no fusion' dogma 530
no legitimate interest 386–87
no partial specific performance 435–36
no separate non-compensatory 'account' remedy 515–20

no transaction approach 118
noise 221–22, 444–45, 446, 447–48, 449–50, 452
nominal damages 10–11, 35, 503
  compensating advantages 148–49
  compensatory damages, date for assessment of 174
  damages valuing right infringed 48
  declaring rights 541
  final prohibitory injunctions 445–46
  Human Rights Act 1998 23–24
  intervening cause 110
  pecuniary loss 196, 201, 202
  and privity 410
  restitution 354
  wrongful interference with goods 220–21
non-competition covenant, breach of 323, 327, 330–31
non-competition provision 390
non-delivery 195–96
non-disclosure 338–39
non-fault enterprise liability 43
non-monetary remedies, bargaining around 16–18
non-pecuniary loss 35, 36–37, 216–17
  claims by injured person 235–38
    pain, suffering and loss of amenity 235–37
    threshold for recovery of damages 238
  compensating advantages 153–54
  confidence, breach of 525
  equitable compensation 512
  final prohibitory injunctions 453
  Human Rights Act 1998 26, 27, 28–29
  interest 302–3, 304–5, 306, 307
  loss of reputation 268, 270–71, 272–73, 274–75
  losses on death 265, 267
  mental distress or physical inconvenience 276, 283, 288–91
  personal injury losses 234–35, 242–43, 247, 249–50, 251–53
  proof of loss and loss of chance 74
  social security benefits 157
  value of money, property or services for damages assessment 171–72, 181
non-performance 427
non-profit-earning ship cases 216–17
non-solicitation covenants 323
non-state payments 158–62
nuisance 6
  compensatory damages, date for assessment of 175
  factual causation 53, 56
  final prohibitory injunctions 443–44, 450, 451, 452–53, 454
  final *quia timet* injunctions 467, 468
  Human Rights Act 1998 24
  intervening cause 113
  limitation periods 311
  mental distress or physical inconvenience 283–84, 291
  private 444–50, 454
  property damage including destruction 206, 207
  punitive damages 361, 365, 366, 367, 368–69
  remoteness 89
  restitution 348–49, 350, 351
  temporary, non-liability for 452
  wrongful interference with land 221
nursing care costs 214–15

obligation 5–6
  negative 42, 45
  positive 9, 42, 45–46
office-holders (public employees) 423, 424–25
Ogden Tables 65–66, 244, 260
ombudsman 44–45
once-and-for-all assessment 235
  see also under compensatory damages
'one who comes to equity must come with clean hands' 10–11, 432, 487
'one who seeks equity must do equity' 433, 487
opportunity, loss of 150–51, 272
oppressive, arbitrary or unconstitutional actions by servants of the government 361–64, 375
ordinary lending loss 119
ordinary profits, recoverability of 96, 124
out-of-court settlements 37, 165–66
output contracts 460, 461
overcompensation
  agreed sum, award of 397
  compensatory damages, date for assessment of 177, 180
  pecuniary loss 190, 192, 203
  personal injury 245–46
  property damage including destruction 217–18

pain, suffering and loss of amenity 35, 36–37
  claims by injured person 235–37
  compensatory damages, date for assessment of 171, 181
  damages valuing right infringed 46
  interest 302
  mental distress or physical inconvenience 276, 288–89
  personal injury losses 249–50, 253
  proof of loss and loss of chance 74
partial defence 132–33
passing off
  interim injunctions 475–76
  restitution 342, 343, 351–52
  wrongful infringement of intellectual property rights 228
past fact and hypothetical or future events 59, 63
patents 342, 497–98
  confidence, breach of 524–25
  restitution 342–46
  secret or unauthorised profit 529
  wrongful infringement of intellectual property rights 229–30
peace of mind 216–17, 278–79
Pearson Commission 157, 238, 239–40, 265
pecuniary loss 35, 36, 37, 187–233
  additional (breach of contract) 187, 205–6
  Albazero exception 202, 203, 204
  amenity, loss of 198
  attributable to non-business relationship between deceased and dependant 258–63
    business pecuniary loss 259
    multiplier method 260–63
    proof of loss 259–60
  basic pecuniary loss (breach of contract) 187–204, 206
    breach by builder in carrying out work late 200
    breach by builder refusing to carry out work or carrying it out defectively 197–200
    breach by buyer refusing to accept goods 195–96
    breach by owner refusing to allow work to proceed 200
    breach by seller delivering defective goods wanted for use 194
    breach by seller failing to deliver goods wanted for resale 191–92
    breach by seller failing to deliver goods wanted for use 192–93
    breach by seller making late delivery of goods wanted for resale 194–95
    breach by seller making late delivery for goods wanted for use 195
    difference in value or cost of cure 189–90
    general formulae for assessment 190–91
    promise, content of 187–88
    third parties, contracts for benefit of 201–4
  business, loss of 230
  claims by injured person 238–49
    damages, calculation of 243–49
    types of 238–43
  compensatory damages, date for assessment of 169
  confidence, breach of 525
  consequential losses 211, 212–13, 214
  constructive total loss 209
  contract price 191–92, 193, 195–96, 200
  cost of cure 219, 220
    basic pecuniary loss 191, 193, 194, 197–200, 201, 203
    damage to property including destruction 205–6, 207–8, 209, 211
  delay 202, 203
  difference in value measures 195, 213, 232
  diminution in value 211, 212–13, 214, 219, 220
  diminution in value of capital 207
  diminution in value of property 206–8, 209
  direct loss 212–13, 214
  earnings, loss of 230–31
  equitable compensation 512
  goods, loss of 220
  happiness, loss of 216–17
  Human Rights Act 1998 26
  intellectual property rights, wrongful infringement of 523
  interest 189, 302, 303, 304
  loss of reputation 268, 269–73
  losses on death 258–63, 267
  market buying price 192, 219–20
  market cost 206
  market price 191–92, 193, 194, 195, 196
  market replacement cost 209–10, 212
  market resale price 192–93
  market selling price 219–20
    basic pecuniary loss 193, 194–95, 196, 197
    damage to property including destruction 206, 209–11, 212
  market value 199, 210
  mental distress or physical inconvenience 277, 281
  mitigate, duty to
    basic pecuniary loss 189, 190, 191–92, 193, 194, 195, 196, 197, 198–99
    damage to property including destruction 206, 210, 212, 214, 215
  past recurring 172

pecuniary loss (*cont.*)
  personal injury losses 234, 249–50, 251–53
  post-trial 260
  pre-death 267
  pre-trial 234–35, 243, 305, 306
  profit, loss of 194, 196, 209, 210–11, 212, 227–29, 230, 231
  property damage, including destruction 187, 206–18
    betterment 217–18
    goods 209–17
    real property 206–9
  punitive damages 360
  reinstatement costs 206, 207, 208
  remoteness 88–89
  repair costs 202, 206, 207, 208, 209, 217–18
  replacement costs 209, 210, 211, 217–18
  resale price 191–92, 193, 219–20
  substitute goods 192
  use, loss of 202, 203, 207–8, 213, 215–16, 221
    temporary 220, 221
  user profit, loss of 192, 194, 195, 205, 215, 220, 221
  value of money, property or services for damages assessment 172–76, 181
  wrongful interference (other than causing property damage) 187, 219–22
    goods 219–21
    land 221–22
  see also future pecuniary loss; pure economic loss
penalties
  agreed sum, award of 394–95, 398, 400
  and liquidated damages, distinction between 388–89, 398–400
  validity 395–97
pensions 265
  death-after-retirement 261
  death-in-service 261
  rights, loss of 239
performance
  actual 427
  alternative 131
  expenses 148
  interest 41–42, 189–90
  minimum reasonable 71
  pecuniary loss 189
  repeat 412
  skimped 353–54
  see also specific performance
periodic payments 164, 166
periodical payments order (PPO) 166–67, 235
perpetual injunctions *see* final injunctions
personal accident insurance policy 160–61
personal independence payment 156–57
personal injury 36–37
  award 46
  compensating advantages 148, 152–54
  compensatory damages 163, 164, 165–69
  compensatory damages, date for assessment of 169, 181
  contributory negligence 133, 134
  earnings, loss of 170, 172, 182
  exceptions to normal time limits 311–13
  factual causation 51
  final prohibitory injunctions 444, 451
  interest 171, 234–35, 301, 302, 304–5, 306, 307
  mental distress or physical inconvenience 276, 288–91
  misrepresentation 225
  mitigate, duty to 130
  non-state payments 158, 160–61, 162
  pecuniary loss 199
  proof of loss and loss of a chance 61–62, 63, 65–66
  property damage including destruction 208, 214–15
  pure economic loss 222
  remoteness 87, 88–89, 96–97
  reputation, loss of 274–75
  social security benefits 156
  torts 44–45
  see also personal injury losses
personal injury losses 234–54
  brain damage 237
  child (healthy but unwanted), cost of bringing up 250, 252
  children 247, 248, 249
  claims by deceased's estate 253–55
  congenital abnormalities 249–50
  contingencies of life 244
  deprivations 235–36, 237
  disabled child's upkeep costs 249–52
  disabled mother/healthy child and costs attributable to mother's disability 251
  discount rate 244, 245–46, 247
  discount rate, negative 242, 245
  disease 234
  distress 237
  divorce resulting from claimant's injury 243
  earnings, loss of 238, 241–43, 249–50, 253, 254
  economic support, loss of 247
  expectation of life, loss of 237, 251
  funeral expenses 252–53, 254–55
  future earnings, loss of 246, 247, 249
  future pecuniary loss 234–35, 242, 244, 246–47, 249
  gratuitous carers/third parties 240–43
  handicapped in the labour market (*Smith v Manchester Corp* damages) 239
  happiness, loss of 237
  housekeeping capacity, loss of 242–43
  Index-Linked Government Stock (ILGS) 242, 244, 245–47
  life expectancy 244, 248
  life expectancy prior to accident 248
  living expenses 248–49
  'lost years' 234–49, 254
  lump sum 244, 249
  medical, nursing and hospital expenses 239–41, 242–43, 253
  mental distress 251, 252
  multiplier method 244, 245, 246, 247–48, 249
  National Health Service (NHS) 239–40
  non-pecuniary loss 234–35, 242–43, 247, 249–50, 251–53
  pain, suffering and loss of amenity 249–50, 253
  past loss 242
  pecuniary loss 234, 249–50, 251–53
  pension rights, loss of 239
  physical illness 234
  physical inconvenience 237
  pre-death 267
  pre-trial pecuniary loss 234–35, 243

pregnancy and childbirth and initial workless
 years, loss of 252–53
psychiatric illnesses 234
pure economic loss 250
special accommodation, cost of buying, fitting
 out and moving to 242
tariff system 235–36
unconsciousness 237
visiting costs 241–42
whiplash claims, fraudulent 238
see also claims by injured person
personal non-proprietary tort 349
personal service bars 460
personal service contracts 419–26, 436
 private law 420–23
 public law 423–25
 specific performance, indirect 457–60
 unfair dismissal legislation 425–26
phone-hacking breach of privacy 290–91
physical damage 88–89, 96–97, 222
physical illness 234
physical inconvenience 36–37, 237
 see also mental distress or physical
  inconvenience
pleasure, loss of 278, 291–92
Polemis **rule/test** 86–87, 90
police misconduct 362–63, 375
 see also false imprisonment; malicious
  prosecution
post-traumatic stress disorder 276
potency of conduct 85, 134
practice, loss of 272
pregnancy and childbirth and initial workless
 years, loss of 252–53
preservation order 496
Press, outrageous infringement of rights
 by 367–68, 377
privacy 12–13, 522
 free speech 480
 Human Rights Act 1998 22
 phone-hacking breach 290–91
 punishment for equitable wrongs 537
 reputation, loss of 272
 restitution 341–42
 see also confidence, breach of; private
  information, misuse of
private information, misuse of 12–13, 521, 525
private international law 180
private law 18–20, 24, 420–23
private rights 454
privilege (free speech) 479
privity 201, 203–4, 317, 382–83
procedural autonomy 16, 298
procedural unfairness 425, 430
profit, loss of 192, 194, 195, 205, 215, 220, 221
 compensating advantages 147
 confidence, breach of 524–25
 in contract 63–64
 exceptional profit and irrecoverable loss 96
 negotiating damages 323
 property damage including
  destruction 210–11, 212
 pure economic loss 227–29, 230, 231
 real property damage 209
 reliance damages 77
 remoteness 91, 92, 94–95, 97, 98, 106
 reputation, loss of 269–70, 273

SAAMCO **principle** 124
 taxation 183
profit-stripping remedy 336
profits, unauthorised 534
prohibitory injunctions 442, 538
 claimant's conduct as bar to 486
 delivery up of goods 495
 and final mandatory injunctions 463
 interim 469, 471, 538–39, 540
 specific performance 401, 406–7, 408–9, 411
 to restrain wrongful acts 467
 see also final prohibitory injunctions
promise
 bargain 40, 41
 breach of 8, 9, 46, 496, 525–26
 content of 187–88
 gratuitous 429
promise-keeping 381, 401, 412
promissory estoppel 41
promissory notes 399
proof of loss and loss of a chance 58–74, 298–99
 difficulty of assessment is not a bar 73–74
 future or hypothetical events: assessment
  proportionate to chances 60–73
 claimant's hypothetical conduct 67–68
 loss of a chance 63–66
 loss consequent on actionable personal injury
  or death 65–66
 loss of profits in contract 63–64
 minimum obligation principle 68–73
 proportionate damages, scale of 66–67
 pure economic loss in negligence tort 64–65
 sometimes loss is presumed 73
 uncertainty about past fact: balance of
  probabilities 58–60
proof, standard of 299
property
 defective 204
 diminution in value 206–8, 209
 rights infringement 342–43, 367–68
 rights, real 443–44
 rule 452–53
 wrongful use 324–25, 329–30
 see also property damage
property damage 36
 compensatory damages 163
 factual causation 51
 final prohibitory injunctions 444, 451
 including destruction
  goods 206–18
  betterment 217–18
  goods 209–17
  pecuniary loss 205
  real property 206–9
 losses on death 267
 mitigate, duty to 128–29
 pecuniary loss 204, 205
 pure economic loss 222
 remoteness 88–89
proportionality 395
proprietary estoppel 12, 509–10, 511–12,
 525–26, 538
proprietary rights 329–31, 351, 355
proprietary torts 348–49, 351–52, 355, 356–57
psychiatric illness 90–91, 234, 270–71, 291
 distinguished from mental distress 276
public authorities 25–26, 27, 285

public interest 425
  final mandatory injunctions 466
  final prohibitory injunctions 446, 447, 449–50, 451, 453–54
  injunctions 539
  interim injunctions 472–73
  restitution 356
public law 22–23, 24, 363, 423–25
public outrage, sense of 363–64, 376
public wrong, non-tortious 23–26
punitive damages 7–8, 9, 10–11, 19–20, 35, 360–78
  agreed sum, award of 397
  breach of contract 360–61
  cause of action test, demise of 362–63, 368–70
  claimant's conduct 371
  compensating advantages 153
  compensatory damages adequate 370
  criminal punishment 371
  defendant's conduct calculated to make a profit for himself 361–62, 364–67
  express authorisation by statute 361–62, 367–68
  final prohibitory injunctions 453
  limitation periods 309
  punishment for equitable wrongs 536
  quantum 372–74
  reform of law on 374–78
    arguments for abolition of punitive damages 375
    arguments for extending punitive damages on principled basis 375–76
    Law Commission's recommendations 377–78
  and restitutionary remedies 346
  specific performance 402
  torts 361–71
  oppressive, arbitrary or unconstitutional actions by servants of the government 361–64
  see also exemplary damages
pure economic loss 8, 9, 46, 187, 222–33
  compensating advantages 155, 156–57
  limitation periods 311
  mental distress or physical inconvenience 286–87
  misrepresentation 223–28
  aim of damages 223–26
  expenses caused and gains forgone 226–28
  negligence, acts or omissions under 231–33
    contract or business, negligent interference with 231–32
    services beneficial to claimant, negligent performance of 232–33
  pecuniary loss 187
  personal injury losses 250
  proof of loss and loss of a chance 64–65
  remoteness 86, 91, 96–97
  wrongful infringement of intellectual property rights 228–30
  wrongful interference with business or contract 230–31

quantum meruit 338, 352–53
quantum reflecting cost of living in different jurisdictions 27
quasi-contractual remedies 338
quia timet injunctions 442–43
  claimant's conduct as bar to 486

equitable damages 318
and final mandatory injunctions 463
interim 469
mandatory 467–68
see also final *quia timet* injunctions
quiet enjoyment covenant, breach of 360–61

racial discrimination 90–91, 289–90, 291
rape 234
re-marriage of widow(er) 263, 265
reasonable care 45, 71–72, 188
reasonable certainty 66
reasonable contemplation contract test 98 , –99, 100, 102, 103–4
reasonable foreseeability
  compensatory damages 83
  impecuniosity 145
  intervening cause 111–12, 113
  remoteness 86, 92, 94–95
  as test for remoteness for all torts 89–91
  Wagon Mound 86–87
reasonable man 86–87
reasonableness 210, 213
reasonableness restriction 50
reasonableness test 190, 198–200
reasonably contemplated test 95
rebuttable presumption 80, 81
receiver, appointment of 491–92, 538
redundancy payments due to injury 160
reinstatement costs 206, 207, 208
reinstatement or reengagement order 425
release fee 331, 354
release from contract 141
reliance damages 75–82
  bad bargain 75, 78–81
  pre-contractual expenses 75–76, 81–82
  proof of loss and loss of a chance 60
  protection of when direct protection of expectation interest is not barred 77
  protection of where direct protection of expectation interest is barred 76–77
reliance interest 14–15, 39–40, 41, 42
  Human Rights Act 1998 26
  misrepresentation 223
  restitution 525–26
  SAAMCO principle 121–22, 124
remedies, combining 13–15
remedies for equitable wrongs 509–45
  declaring rights 541
  interest 542–43
  limitation periods 543–44
  punishment 536–37
  see also compelling performance or preventing equitable wrong
remedies, inconsistent 346
remoteness 6, 7–8, 9, 91, 105, 106
  agreed sum, award of 393
  Arpad test of 220–21
  breach of contract 91–106
    Achilleas, qualification of traditional contract test required by 98–105
    assimilation of contract and tort tests where there is contractual relationship 105–6
    Cory v Thames Ironworks Co principle 97
    disproportionate loss compared to contractual consideration: United States approach 97–98

loss or damage, type of 94–97
  traditional test 91–94
compensating advantages 148, 153
compensatory damages, date for assessment of 179
contributory negligence 134, 137
equitable compensation 512–13, 514
factual causation 51–52
impecuniosity 144, 145
interest 296–97, 298–99
mental distress or physical inconvenience 280–81, 282–83, 285–86
mitigate, duty to 131
negligence 231–32
pecuniary loss 192, 205
personal injury 249–50, 252–53
proof of loss and loss of chance 66
property damage including destruction 209, 214
SAAMCO principle 119–20, 124
specific performance 402
torts 86–91
  concurrent contractual liability, stricter test for 91
  reasonable foreseeability test 87–89
  reasonable foreseeability as test for remoteness for all torts 89–91
  Wagon Mound reasonable foreseeability test 86–87
wrongful interference with goods 219, 220–21
repair and/or replacement costs 48–49, 202, 206, 207, 208, 209–10, 211, 212, 217–18, 412
repairing covenant, breach of 492
repeat orders, loss of 269–70
repeat performance 412
replevin 497
representations, mere 223
repudiation of contract 73
agreed sum, award of 383, 384–85, 386
anticipatory 132, 506
compensating advantages 151
compensatory damages, date for assessment of 174
interest 297–98
reliance damages 78–79, 80
reputation, loss of 7–8, 9, 35, 36–37, 268–75
assessment of damages 273–75
award of damages 268–73
  breach of contract 268–71
  torts 271–73
mental distress or physical inconvenience 276
mitigate, duty to 129
non-pecuniary loss 268, 270–71, 272–73, 274–75
pecuniary loss 268, 269–73
personal injury losses 237
proof of loss and loss of chance 73
pure economic loss 222
remoteness 93
wrongful dismissal 268, 270–71
requirements contracts 460–61
res inter alios acta 153
resale price 191–93, 219–20
rescission of contract 137, 338–39, 439
restitutio integrum 206
restitution 9, 11
full 14–15
interest 295, 297, 298, 302, 542–43

for mistake of law 298
negotiating damages 325–26
pecuniary loss 200
punitive damages 361, 367–68
see also restitution for equitable wrongs; restitutionary remedies
restitution for equitable wrongs 525–36
confidence, breach of 532–35
dishonest assistance 535–36
fiduciary duty, breach of 526–32
  bribes or secret commissions 529–32
  secret or unauthorised profits 526–29
restitutionary remedies 335–59
alternative analysis 336
breach of contract 352–59
  Attorney-General v Blake and its aftermath 356–59
  law and analysis prior to *Attorney-General v Blake* 353–56
  and unjust enrichment 352–53
disgorgement terminology as alternative to restitution 336–37
Edelman's thesis 337–38
and punitive damages 375, 376, 377
restitution for wrongs 335–36
torts 338–52
  account of profits 341–46
  anti-restitution clauses 347–52
  Devenish Nutrition Ltd v Sanofi-Aventis SA 350–52
  Forsyth-Grant v Allen 350
  Halifax Building Society v Thomas 349
  money had and received 340–41
  Phillips v Homfray 347–48
  preference for tort over compensatory damages 339
  punitive damages, relationship with 346
  Stoke-on-Trent City Council v W & J Wass Ltd 348–49
see also restitution for equitable wrongs
restraint of trade covenants, breach of 475–76
restraint of trade doctrine 459–60
restrictive covenant, breach of 462
claimant's conduct as bar to injunction 487, 488
equitable damages 317
final mandatory injunctions 466
final prohibitory injunctions 446, 455
indirect specific performance 459–60
negotiating damages 321, 324, 327, 329–30
restitution 355, 357–58
retail prices index (RPI) 166–67, 171, 246–47, 290
reverse burden of proof 78–79
right to life, infringement of 264
rights 18–20
constitutional, infringement of 363–64
declaring 9, 541
individual 453–54
primary 4
proprietary 329–31, 351, 355
secondary 4
to sue 204
value of, loss of 324
rights of way 221–22
rights-based theory 18–20
risk, assumption of 99
risk, fair allocation of 104–5
royalty fees 229, 230, 524–25

SAAMCO principle 117–27, 188
  justification 120–22
  SAAMCO 'cap' 123
  scope of application and difficulties in applying 122–27
salary, loss of see earnings, loss of
sale of goods contracts 460–61, 493–94
sales, loss of 269
salvage value 209
scope of duty concept 119–20, 188
  SAAMCO principle 121, 122–23, 124, 126
Scottish law 253
search orders 484, 485–86
secret or unauthorised profits 526–29
self-help remedies 13
selling value 206
Sempra Metals decision 298–301
serious breach of contract 432, 486
service out of the jurisdiction 13
services beneficial to claimant, negligent performance of 232–33
settlement agreement, breach of 332
severe hardship bar as defence to specific performance 447
sex discrimination 289–90, 291
sexual assault 234, 362–63
Shelfer principles 445–46, 449–50
sick pay 154–55, 158, 160–61, 162
simple interest 123, 295–96, 542
  interest as damages 297, 299–300
  interest on damages 301, 303–4, 305
single causative agent restriction 62–63
skill, duty of 514
slander 268
social security benefits 156–57
  compensating advantages 153–54
  like for like deductions 156–57
  losses on death 265, 266–67
  relevant period 156–57
  small payments 157
sole franchise/distributorship contracts 460, 461
special accommodation, cost of buying, fitting out and moving to 242
specific performance 4, 5, 9, 10–11, 17–18, 19, 35, 401–39
  accounting for loss 540
  additional damages 437
  adequacy of damages 402–15, 436
    assessment of damages, difficulty in 407–8
    Beswick v Beswick—radical interpretation 410–11
    consumer's remedies 412
    contractual obligation to pay money 409
    inability to pay damages 408–9
    maintaining adequacy of damages hurdle 412–15
    nominal damages and privity 410
    termination of contract, immediate 409–10
    uniqueness—substitute availability 403–7
  agreed sum, award of 381, 384–85, 387
  breach of contract 41–42
  commercially unique goods 405–6
  with compensation or abatement of purchase price 437–38
  compensatory damages, date for assessment of 172, 173
  conditional specific performance 438–39
  conduct of claimant 432–35
    acquiescence 434
    as bar to injunction 490, 491
    improper past conduct 432
    laches 433–34
    one who comes to equity must come with clean hands 432
    one who seeks equity must do equity 433
    serious breach 432
    termination of contract, valid by claimant 434–35
  confidence, breach of 522, 534
  constant supervision objection 415–19, 428–29, 436
  contract unfairly obtained 430
  delivery up of goods 493–94, 495–96
  efficient breach theory 413, 414
  equitable compensation 515, 516
  equitable damages 315–17
  final mandatory injunctions 463–66
  final prohibitory injunctions 454, 455–56
  hardship, severe 431–32
  impossibility 430–31
  indirect 442, 456–61
    personal service contracts 457–60
    sale of goods contracts 460–61
  injunctions 422, 423, 424, 442, 538
  interim injunctions 405, 406, 408, 417, 420–21, 422, 469
  interim mandatory injunctions 401–2, 482
  laches 436
  limitation periods 314
  negotiating damages 323–24
  no partial specific performance 435–36
  no specific performance 438
  non-compensatory cost of cure 48–49
  pecuniary loss 201
  personal service contracts 419–26, 436
    private law 420–23
    public law 423–25
    unfair dismissal legislation 425–26
  physically unique goods 404–5
  prohibitory injunctions 401, 406–7, 408–9, 411
  restitution 355, 357, 358
  sentimental uniqueness 406
  and severe hardship bar 447
  stipulated remedy 436–37, 462
  temporary 405, 417, 420, 421–22, 482
  termination of contract 432
  termination and damages, effect on 439
  uncertainty 428–29, 436
  uniqueness 407
  valuable consideration, contracts not supported by 429, 436
  want of mutuality 426–28, 433, 436
state compensation scheme 44–45
state recoupment scheme 156
statutory compensation scheme for unfair dismissal 270–71
statutory duty, breach of 15
  contributory negligence 136, 139, 140
  factual causation 54, 55
  interest 298
  personal injury 234
  proof of loss and loss of a chance 62
  property damage including destruction 214

punitive damages 366
restitution 350
SAAMCO principle 122–23
torts 45
statutory interest 295, 296–97, 301, 304
   and assessment date of damages 306–8
      foreign currency liabilities 307–8
      liabilities other than foreign currency liabilities 306–7
   compensatory purpose 302–3
   period payable 304–5
   pre-judgment 301
   rate 305–6
sterling-breach-date rule 177, 179–80, 181
stipulated remedy 436–37, 462
Stoke-on-Trent City Council v W & J Wass Ltd 348–49
strict liability 9, 43–45
   contributory negligence 134, 142
   remoteness 89–90
   restitution 342–43
structured settlements 165–67
sub-buyer 191–92, 205–6
sub-contract 193
sub-sale 194
substantive law 4
substantive unfairness 430
substitute goods 192
substitution for an injunction 321–22, 323–24, 329–30
substitutive damages thesis 322
success fee 236
successive events 51–52, 53
super-injunctions 441
supervening event 107–8

tariff system 37
tariffs of value 35
taxation 182–84
   corporation tax 183
   Gourley principle 182–84
termination of contract 174
   agreed sum, award of 386–87
   immediate 409–10
   specific performance 432, 439
   valid by claimant 434–35, 491
'thin skull' principle 88
third parties 8
   agreed sum, award of 382–83
   compensating advantages 148, 152–62, 249
      general factors influencing courts 152–55
      non-state payments 158–62
      social security benefits 156–57
   compensatory damages, date for assessment of 169
   contracts for benefit of 201–4
   equitable compensation 513
   equitable damages 317
   injunctions 440–41
   knowing receipt 509–10
   losses on death 265
   nominal damages and privity 410
   pecuniary loss 190, 191–92
   property damage including destruction 208, 213–15
   wrongful interference 108
   see also third party conduct

third party conduct 109–13
   duty was to guard against such third party intervention 109–11
   third party intervention other than where there was a duty to guard against it 111–13
third party debt order 5
time limits *see* limitation periods
torts
   breach of contract 5–6, 8–9, 42–46
   contributory negligence 133–38
   final mandatory injunctions 462–65
   final prohibitory injunctions 443–54
   final *quia timet* injunctions 467–68
   loss of reputation 271–73
   mental distress or physical inconvenience 283–88
   punitive damages 361–71
   remoteness 86–91
   restitutionary remedies 338–52
trade dispute defence 477–79
trade marks 342, 343, 351–52, 497–98
transaction costs 16–17, 414, 453
trespass
   equitable damages 318
   future 327
   intentional 138
   punishment for equitable wrongs 537
   punitive damages 361, 362–63, 365
   taxation 182
   trivial 443–44, 454
   see also trespass to goods; trespass to land; trespass to the person
trespass to goods 38
   proof of loss and loss of chance 73
   property damage including destruction 206
   punitive damages 368–69
   restitution 340–41
   wrongful interference with goods 219
trespass to land
   final prohibitory injunctions 443–49, 451, 454
   mental distress or physical inconvenience 283–84
   negotiating damages 324–26, 327
   property damage including destruction 206
   punitive damages 368–69
   recovery of land 497
   restitution 341, 347, 348
   wrongful interference 221
trespass to the person
   contributory negligence 136–37
   Human Rights Act 1998 24
   punitive damages 371
   see also assault and battery
triviality restriction 445–46, 451, 456
trust, breach of
   equitable compensation 513, 515–16, 517, 519
   limitation periods 543–44
   prohibitory injunctions 538
   remedies 509–10
Tulk v Moxhay principle 317

ultra vires action 25–26
uncertainty 58–60, 428–29, 436
unclean hands 496, 505
unconscionability 488
unconsciousness 36–37, 237
undercompensation 177, 179, 246–47

underliquidated damages clause 393–94
undue influence 338–39, 430
undue pressure 430
unemployment benefits 157
unfair advantage 430
unfair dismissal
  mental distress or physical inconvenience 282
  personal service contracts 421, 424, 425–26
  reputation, loss of 270–71
uniformity 37, 273, 369–70
uniqueness 494
  commercial 405–6, 494
  physical 404–5, 494
  sentimental 406
  substitute availability 403–7
    breach of contract to sell goods 403–7
    breach of contract to sell land 403
    breach of contract to sell shares or stocks 407
United States 16
  Commercial Code 205–6
  disproportionate loss compared to contractual consideration 97–98
  indirect specific performance 459–60
  mitigate, duty to 132
  pecuniary loss 199
  proof of loss and loss of chance 66
  punitive damages 375
  reliance damages 78
  remoteness 101
  Second Restatement of Contracts 41
  sentimental uniqueness 406
universal credit 156
unjust enrichment 11–12, 19–20
  agreed sum, award of 394–95
  compensating advantages 155
  interest 295, 298, 302, 542–43
  punitive damages 365
  restitution 335, 336–39, 340, 347, 349
unlawful conduct, future 318
unlawful conspiracy 367
unreasonable action 84–85, 130–31
use, loss of 202, 203, 207–8, 211, 213, 215–16, 221
  temporary 220, 221
user principle 336, 524–25

valuable asset, loss of 330–31
valuable consideration, contracts not supported by 429, 436
valuation, negligent 83–84
value of money, property or services for damages assessment 172–76, 181
  see also under compensatory damages, date for assessment of

vertical effect 22–23
vexation 277, 280, 281
vicissitudes of life 54
visiting costs 241–42

Wagon Mound test 86–87, 89–90, 106, 220–21
want of mutuality 426–28, 433, 436
warrant of execution 5
warranty, breach of 188
  compensatory damages, date for assessment of 173, 174–75
  contractual 39, 202, 227–28
  misrepresentation 223, 225
  mitigate, duty to 131
  proof of loss and loss of chance 71–72
  SAAMCO principle 121
weakness, exploitation of 430
whiplash claims, fraudulent 238
will theory of contract 40
'without notice' injunctions 484–85
workplace accidents 159–60
wrong, compelling undoing of 9
wrong has caused death 267
wrong, preventing 9, 10
wrongful act, neglect or default 256, 257–58
wrongful arrest 289
wrongful dismissal
  compensating advantages 148, 149
  compensatory damages, date for assessment of 169
  interest 297–98
  loss of reputation 270–71
  mental distress or physical inconvenience 277, 282
  mitigate, duty to 127–28
  non-state payments 158–59
  personal service contracts 423
  proof of loss and loss of chance 64, 69, 71
  punitive damages 360
  social security benefits 157
  taxation 182–83
wrongful enrichment 220, 221–22
  see also restitutionary remedies
wrongful interference 219–22, 231–32
  with business or contract 222, 230–31
  by third party 108
  delivery up of goods 493, 495
  with goods 219–21, 222
  with intellectual property rights 329–30
  with land 221–22
wrongful occupation or use 221
wrongful use of property or land 324–25, 329–30
'Wrotham Park' damages 321, 323, 332